Building Java™ Enterprise Systems with J2EE

Paul J. Perrone

Venkata S. R. "Krishna" R. Chaganti

SAMS

201 West 103rd St., Indianapolis, Indiana, 46290 USA

International Standard Book Number: 0-672-31795-8

Library of Congress Catalog Card Number: 99-65339

Printed in the United States of America

First Printing: June 2000

02 01 4 3

Trademarks

All terms mentioned in this book that are known to be trademarks or service marks have been appropriately capitalized. Sams Publishing cannot attest to the accuracy of this information. Use of a term in this book should not be regarded as affecting the validity of any trademark or service mark.

Warning and Disclaimer

Every effort has been made to make this book as complete and as accurate as possible, but no warranty or fitness is implied. The information provided is on an "as is" basis. The authors and the publisher shall have neither liability nor responsibility to any person or entity with respect to any loss or damages arising from the information contained in this book or from the use of the CD or programs accompanying it.

EXECUTIVE EDITOR
Rosemarie Graham

ACQUISITIONS EDITOR
Steve Anglin

DEVELOPMENT EDITOR
Songlin Qiu

MANAGING EDITOR
Matt Purcell

PROJECT EDITOR
Elizabeth Roberts

COPY EDITOR
Cheri Clark

INDEXER
Heather McNeill

PROOFREADERS
Katherin Bidwell
Juli Cook
Kaylene Riemen
Matt Wynalda

TECHNICAL EDITOR
Charles Ashbacher

TEAM COORDINATOR
Pamalee Nelson

MEDIA DEVELOPER
Jason Haines

INTERIOR DESIGNER
Anne Jones

COVER DESIGNER
Anne Jones

COPYWRITER
Eric Borgert

LAYOUT TECHNICIANS
Ayanna Lacey
Heather Hiatt Miller
Stacey Richwine-DeRome
Mark Walchle

LINE ART
Steve Adams
Tammy Ludwig
Laura Robbins

Overview

Introduction **1**

PART I Enterprise Foundations

1 Enterprise Architectural Overview **11**

2 Object-Oriented Software Development for the Enterprise **19**

3 Component-Based Software Development for the Enterprise **39**

4 Java Foundations for Enterprise Development **53**

5 Java Enterprise System Architecture with the J2EE **105**

6 Enterprise User Interfacing **125**

7 Modeling Components with JavaBeans **141**

PART II Enterprise Data Enabling

8 Enterprise Data **173**

9 Basic JDBC **199**

10 Advanced JDBC **249**

PART III Distributed Enterprise Communications Enabling

11 Distributed Enterprise Communications **315**

12 Network Communications **325**

13 Web Communications **365**

14 Modeling Components with CORBA **385**

15 CORBA Communications **417**

16 RMI Communications **465**

17 Modeling Components with COM/DCOM **527**

18 DCOM Communications **541**

PART IV Common Services for Distributed Enterprise Communications

19 Naming Services **575**

20 Directory and Trading Services **633**

21 Activation Services **689**

22 Messaging Services **705**

23 Transaction Services **789**

Part V **Enterprise Systems Assurance**

24 High-Assurance Enterprise Applications **817**

25 Security Basics **837**

26 Basic Java Security **855**

27 Advanced Java Security **879**

28 CORBA Security **937**

Part VI **Enterprise Web Enabling**

29 Web Browsers and Servers in the Enterprise **967**

30 Traditional Web Programming and Java **985**

31 XML **1009**

32 Java Servlets **1067**

33 JavaServer Pages **1135**

Part VII **Enterprise Applications Enabling**

34 Enterprise Application Platforms **1191**

35 Application Servers and Enterprise JavaBeans **1207**

36 Modeling Components with Enterprise JavaBeans **1231**

37 Advanced Enterprise JavaBeans Serving **1315**

38 Enterprise Application Integration **1355**

Appendixes

A Software Configuration **1375**

B Additional Resources **1405**

Index **1415**

Contents

Introduction 1

Part I Enterprise Foundations

1 Enterprise Architectural Overview 11

The Enterprise 12
Enterprise Components 14
Information Technology in the Enterprise 16
Conclusions 17

2 Object-Oriented Software Development for the Enterprise 19

Enterprise Objects 20
Elements of Object-Oriented Software 21
Object-Oriented Software's Importance to the Enterprise 23
The Object-Oriented Development Process 24
Development Process Overview 25
Project Charter 26
Requirements Analysis 26
Preliminary System Design 27
Detailed Design 28
Implementation 28
Unit Test 29
Assembly 29
Thread Test 29
Configuration Specification 30
System Test 30
Deployment 30
Maintenance 30
Iteration and Phases of Development 30
Unified Modeling Language 31
Static Logical Structure Diagrams 32
Dynamic Behavior Diagrams 36
Conclusions 37

3 Component-Based Software Development for the Enterprise 39

Enterprise Components 40
Component Models 43
Generic Component Model 43
Component Model Interfaces 44
Component-Based Development 46

Standards....49
Standard Component Models 49
Design Patterns 50
Conclusions....52

4 Java Foundations for Enterprise Development 53
Java Features and Versions 54
Java's Attractive Enterprise Features....55
Java's Version History 56
Java Platform Architecture 57
Java Development and Runtime Environments....57
Java Runtime Platform Architecture 58
Java Runtime Optimizations 58
Java Files and Tools 59
Java File Types 60
Basic Java Source File Structure....60
Basic JAR and Manifest File Structure....62
Java Software Development Kit Tools 63
Java Language....64
Java Fundamental Types 64
Java Operators 64
Java Language Constructs....66
Core Java Language APIs....73
Base Language and System APIs 74
Errors and Exceptions 75
Type and Mathematical APIs 76
Reflection....77
Garbage Collection 79
Events 80
Collection APIs....81
Non-Keyed Collection Framework 82
Mapped Collection Framework....84
Input/Output and State Persistence APIs 87
Byte I/O Streams....87
Character I/O Readers and Writers 89
Archive File APIs 90
Properties Files 91
Threading APIs....93
Date and Time APIs 97
Java Applets 99
Conclusions....104

5 Java Enterprise System Architecture with the J2EE 105

The J2EE Model 106
J2EE Features 107
J2EE Component-Container Architecture 108
J2EE Restrictions 110
Enterprise Java and J2EE Architecture 111
Java Enterprise System Architecture Overview 111
Data Connectivity 114
Communication Mechanisms 115
Assurance Mechanisms 117
Client Connectivity 119
Web Connectivity 120
Application Connectivity 121
The J2EE Future 122
Conclusions 123

6 Enterprise User Interfacing 125

The Distributed Enterprise User Interface 126
Java AWT Components 130
AWT Components, Containers, and Layouts 130
AWT Events 131
Deployment Considerations 131
Java Swing Components 132
Swing Components, Containers, Layouts, and Events 132
Swing Models 132
Swing Look and Feel 133
Swing Component Helpers 133
Deployment Considerations 134
Utility and Accessibility Components 134
Data Transfer 134
Drag and Drop 134
Printing 135
Accessibility 135
JavaHelp 135
Graphics and Multimedia Components 135
AWT Images 136
2D Graphics 136
3D Graphics 136
Java Advanced Imaging 136
Java Media APIs 137
Input Method Framework 137

Web Page Interfaces 137
Web Interface Content 138
Web Interface Generators 139
Conclusions 140

7 **Modeling Components with JavaBeans** **141**
JavaBeans Overview 142
JavaBeans Containers 145
JavaBean Containers 145
JavaBean Components 147
JavaBean Context 148
JavaBeans Events 149
JavaBeans Properties 152
Simple Properties 153
Array and Indexed Properties 155
Bound Properties 155
Constrained Properties 157
JavaBeans Introspection 160
JavaBeans Persistence 163
JavaBeans Customization 164
Property Editors 164
Customizers 166
The InfoBus 167
Conclusions 169

PART II Enterprise Data Enabling

8 **Enterprise Data** **173**
Database Basics 174
Data Model Abstraction Levels 175
General DBMS Architecture 175
Transactions 177
Relational Databases 179
RDBMS Architecture 179
SQL 180
Data Model Diagram Conventions 185
Object Databases 186
ODBMS Architecture 186
RDBMSs Versus ODBMSs 188
Relational/Object Translations 190
CLIs 192
Embedded SQL 193

ODBC 195
JDBC....195
Conclusions....196

9 Basic JDBC 199

JDBC Architecture 200
JDBC Drivers and their Types 204
Driver Assessment 208
JDBC Driver Configuration 208
General Configuration Steps per Driver Type....211
Configuring the BeeShirts.com Example Data Model 212
JDBC Connections 213
Database URLs 214
Creating Connections 215
Example: Connecting to a Database 215
JDBC Statements 219
Using Regular Statements 219
Querying with Joins, Outer Joins, and LIKE Clauses 221
Example: Creating and Executing Statements 222
Using Prepared Statements 226
Example: Creating and Executing Prepared Statements....227
JDBC Result Sets 231
Manipulating Result Sets....231
Obtaining Information About Result Sets 233
Example: Manipulating Result Sets and Result Set MetaData....234
SQL and Java Mappings....239
JDBC MetaData 241
Obtaining Information about Databases and Drivers 241
Example: Simple Database Meta-Data Usage 243
Conclusions....247

10 Advanced JDBC 249

Scrollable Result Sets 250
Creating Scrollable Result Sets....251
Scrolling Around Result Sets 252
Driver Support for Scrollable Result Sets....254
Example: Scrollable Result Sets 255
Updateable Result Sets 262
Creating Updateable Result Sets....263
Updating Rows 263
Canceling Updates....264
Inserting Rows....264

Deleting Rows 264
Visibility into Database Changes 265
Driver Support for Updateable Result Sets 268
Example: Updateable Result Sets 269
Batch Updates 274
Creating Batch Updates 274
Executing a Batch Update 275
Example: Batch Updates 276
Advanced Data Types 278
Java Object Types 278
SQL3 Types 279
Custom Types 284
Extending the BeeShirts.com Example Data Model 286
Example: Using the Advanced SQL Types with JDBC 288
Row Sets 295
Row Set Architecture 295
Using Row Sets 297
Row Set Implementations 297
Managing Internal Row Set State and Behavior 297
Stored Procedures 298
Predefined Database Functions 298
Creating Stored Procedures 299
Executing Stored Procedures 301
Creating a Few BeeShirts.com Stored Procedures 301
Example: Calling Stored Procedures 302
Database Naming via JNDI 305
Connection Pools 307
Distributed Transactions 310
Conclusions 312

PART III Distributed Enterprise Communications Enabling

11 Distributed Enterprise Communications 315

Distributed Systems 316
Distribution Mechanisms 318
The Network Client 321
The Network Server 323
Conclusions 324

12 Network Communications 325

Network Computing 326
Protocols and Communication Layers 327
TCP/IP Protocol Suite....329
TCP/IP Roots....330
TCP/IP Communication Layers 330
TCP/IP Implementations and Tools 335
Socket Programming....336
Basic Socket Programming 337
UDP Datagrams....359
Custom Sockets and Factories....361
Communication Streams....363
Conclusions....364

13 Web Communications 365

The Internet and the World Wide Web 366
History of the Web....366
URLs 367
HTTP....370
Basic HTTP Behavior 370
MIME 372
HTTP Requests 373
HTTP Responses 375
Basic HTTP Handling in Java....377
Tracking Sessions outside of HTTP 379
HTTP-NG 380
CGI 380
Servlets 381
HTML Documents 382
Dynamic HTML Generation....383
Conclusions....384

14 Modeling Components with CORBA 385

CORBA Overview 386
The Object Management Architecture 388
CORBA 3.0 389
CORBA's Java Enterprise System Role 389
The ORB....390
The ORB Concept....390
Client Side ORB Components....391
ORB Protocols....392
Server-Side ORB Components 392

GIOP and IIOP 393
GIOP Overview 393
IIOP Overview 394
Interoperable Object References 395
Services, Facilities, and Business Objects 395
CORBAservices 396
CORBAfacilities 398
CORBA Domain Interfaces and Business Objects 399
IDL 400
Generic CORBA IDL File Format 400
CORBA IDL-to-Java Mappings 401
IDL Compilation 407
Java-to-IDL Mappings 409
Objects by Value 409
Value Types 409
Objects by Value Behavioral Sequence 410
Objects by Value Marshaling 411
Objects by Value Code Example 412
Conclusions 415

15 CORBA Communications 417

The Very Distributed CORBA 418
Designing for Scalability 419
CORBA Development Process 420
CORBA Vendors 421
Basic Tools and Configuration 421
Vendor Offerings 422
Java IDL 424
CORBA Interfaces 425
CORBA Servers and Skeletons 428
Compiling the IDLs and Generating Skeletons 428
Creating the CORBA Servers 430
Implementation Repository 443
Object Adapters 444
BOA-Based Server Registration 444
Java IDL Server Registration 446
POA-Based Server Registration 447
Interface Repository 448
CORBA Clients and Stubs 454
CORBA Clients and Static Stubs 454
DII-Based Clients 458
CORBA Naming 461
Conclusions 463

16 RMI Communications 465
RMI Basics 466
RMI Architecture 467
RMI Packages and Tools 469
RMI Infrastructure Configuration 470
RMI Development Process 471
JRMP 471
RMI and IIOP 473
Java-to-IDL Mapping 474
Objects by Value and RMI 476
RMI Interfaces 477
RMI Interface Definition Examples 479
RMI Servers and Skeletons 481
RMI/JRMP Servers 481
RMI/IIOP Servers 494
RMI Registration 497
Registration of RMI/JRMP Servers 498
Registration of RMI/IIOP Servers 503
RMI Clients and Stubs 506
RMI/JRMP Clients and Stubs 506
RMI/IIOP Clients and Stubs 511
RMI Lookup 514
RMI/JRMP Lookups 514
RMI/IIOP Lookups 515
RMI Object Activation 515
Creating an Activatable Server 517
Creating an Activatable Server Registrar 519
RMI Activatable Object Client 521
Compile and Run the Example 523
Custom Sockets 523
Conclusions 525

17 Modeling Components with COM/DCOM 527
COM and DCOM in a Nutshell 528
DCOM Architecture 529
Java-Based Development Tools 531
DCOM Interfaces 532
DCOM Identifiers 532
DCOM Monikers 532
Server Locality 533
Type Libraries and IDL 533
Dynamic Invocation 533

COM/DCOM Services 534
Interface Definition Language 535
Generic DCOM IDL File Format 536
DCOM IDL-to-Java Mappings 537
Conclusions....540

18 DCOM Communications 541

DCOM in the Machine 542
DCOM Development Process 543
DCOM Interfaces 544
DCOM Identifiers....547
DCOM Types 548
DCOM Servers and Skeletons 548
Generating Java Bindings 548
Generic DCOM Servers 549
Example DCOM Server Implementations 549
Compiling the DCOM Servers 563
DCOM Server Registration 564
Registration with `javareg` 564
Registration with a Registry File....564
Peering into DCOM Objects 565
DCOM Clients and Stubs 567
Generic DCOM Clients....567
Example DCOM Client Implementation....568
DCOM Client Registration and Spawning 570
DCOM Bridging....571
Conclusions....572

PART IV Common Services for Distributed Enterprise Communications

19 Naming Services 575

Naming Services in a Nutshell 576
Handles 577
Names 577
Naming Contexts and Systems 578
JNDI Naming Services 580
JNDI Architecture 580
Naming Objects....582
Referenceable Objects....588
Naming Events 591
JNDI Examples 593

Naming Files 605
File-System Interfaces 606
JNDI File SPI 606
CORBA Naming 609
CosNaming IDL 609
CosNaming Service Implementations 612
CORBA Naming Interfaces 613
JNDI CosNaming SPI 614
RMI Naming 618
RMI Naming System Interfaces 618
JNDI RMI SPI 618
DNS 626
The Domain Name System 626
Java-Based DNS Interfacing 628
DCOM Naming 629
DCOM Class Naming with CLSIDs and ProgIDs 629
DCOM Object Naming with Monikers 630
Conclusions 631

20 Directory and Trading Services 633

Directory and Trading Services in a Nutshell 634
JNDI Directory Services 636
Directory Contexts 636
NIS as a Directory Service 645
JNDI NIS SPI 645
NDS as a Directory Service 646
JNDI NDS SPI 646
LDAP as a Directory Service 648
LDAP Interfaces 649
JNDI LDAP SPI 651
JNDI LDAP V3 API Extensions 662
CORBA as a Trading Service 664
CORBA Trading Service Components 665
Service Exporting 666
Service Importing 668
CORBA Trading Example 671
Jini as a Trading Service 673
Jini Component Architecture 674
Jini Programming Model 676
Jini Infrastructure 676
Jini Tools and Configuration 677
Jini Class Architecture and Development Process 679
Jini Service Example 683

Microsoft Active Directory Services 686
Conclusions....687

21 Activation Services 689

Activation Services Overview 690
RMI Activation Framework 692
CORBA Activation Framework 694
CORBA Lifecycle Service 697
DCOM Activation Framework 699
JavaBeans Activation Framework....700
Web and Application Activation Frameworks 702
Conclusions....704

22 Messaging Services 705

Messaging Overview 706
- Message Service Locality 707
- Point-to-Point Messaging 708
- Publish-Subscribe Messaging 709
- Push and Pull Messaging Models 709
- Message Filtering, Synchronicity, and Quality....710
- Email Messaging....711

MOM....711
Java Message Service 714
- Core JMS Architecture 714
- Point-to-Point Message Queuing Model....727
- Extending the BeeShirts.com Example Data Model....729
- Point-to-Point Message Queuing Example 729
- Publish-Subscribe Model....738
- Publish-Subscribe Example....741

CORBA Messaging 747
- CORBA Event Service 748
- CORBA Notification Service 754
- CORBA Messaging Specification....755

JavaMail 757
- Email Messaging Systems....757
- JavaMail Architecture Overview 759
- JavaMail Generic Parts 760
- JavaMail Generic Messages 760
- JavaMail Multipart Messages 763
- JavaMail MIME Messages 764
- JavaMail Event Architecture 768
- Creating Mail Sessions 768
- Message Stores 772

Message Store Folders....773
Message Transports....777
JavaMail Example....778
Conclusions....787

23 **Transaction Services** **789**

Transactions....791
Transaction Services....795
Transaction Attributes....796
Transaction Isolation Levels....797
Transaction Models....798
X/Open Distributed Transaction Processing Standard....800
Two-Phase Commit Protocol....800
Object Transaction Service....801
Core OTS Types....801
OTS Interfaces....802
Java Transactions API....804
JTA Transaction Manager Interface....807
JTA Application Interface....809
JTA and X/Open XA....810
Java Transactions Service....812
Conclusions....813

PART V Enterprise Systems Assurance

24 **High-Assurance Enterprise Applications** **817**

What Is Assurance?....818
Who Should Provide Assurance?....819
Dilemma of Assurance and Delivery Costs....820
General Assurance Process....821
Identify the Assurance Problem....822
Assess Risk....823
Generate Risk-Reduction Plan....824
Assess Cost of Risk-Reduction Plan....825
Assess Residual Risk....825
To Be Assured or Not to Be Assured?....825
Failed Delivery Costs....826
Making Decisions....826
Security....827
Security Assurance Problem Models....827
Security Risk-Reduction Plans....828

Reliability 829
Reliability Assurance Problem Models 829
Reliability Risk-Reduction Plans 830
Availability 831
Availability Assurance Problem Models 831
Availability Risk-Reduction Plans 832
Maintainability 833
Maintainability Assurance Problem Models 833
Maintainability Risk-Reduction Plans....833
Safety 834
Safety Assurance Problem Models 834
Safety Risk-Reduction Plans....835
Conclusions....835

25 Security Basics 837

The Basic Security Model 838
Cryptography 839
Classes of Cryptography 839
Message Digests 842
Symmetric Keys 843
Asymmetric Keys 843
Authentication and Nonrepudiation 844
Authentication Types....845
Nonrepudiation 848
Secure Socket Layer (SSL)....848
Access Control 849
Discretionary Access Control 850
Role-Based Access Control....850
Mandatory Access Control 850
Firewall Access Control 851
Domains 851
Auditing 852
Policies and Administration 852
Conclusions....853

26 Basic Java Security 855

The History of Security in Java 856
Java Security Architecture 859
Core Java 2 Security Architecture....859
Java Cryptography Architecture 861
Java Cryptography Extension 861
Java Secure Socket Extension 862
Java Authentication and Authorization Service....862

Byte Code Verifier 862
Class Loader 864
Class Loader Architecture and Security 864
Class Loader Interfaces 865
Security Manager 868
Security Manager Interfaces 869
Custom Security Managers 871
Java Cryptography Architecture 873
The Architecture of JCA 873
Cryptographic Engines 875
Cryptographic Service Providers....876
Conclusions....878

27 Advanced Java Security 879

Permissions 880
Permissions Architecture....881
Permission Types....881
Custom Permission Types 890
Security Policies 891
Security Policy File Format....891
Referencing Properties in Policy Files 892
Using Security Policy Files....893
Security Policy Tool 894
Security Policy APIs 895
Java Access Control 896
Access Control Architecture 896
Guarded Objects 899
`SecurityManager` to Access Control Mapping 899
Fine-Grained and Configurable Access Control Example 903
Principal Identification 906
Keys 906
Certificates....908
Key and Certificate Storage....910
Using Keys and Certificates 911
Protecting Objects....916
Message Digests 916
Signatures 919
Signed Objects....922
Signing Code....924
The JAR Signer Tool 925
Code Signing Process 925
Code Signing Example 926

Java Security Extensions 929
Java Cryptography Extension 929
Java Secure Socket Extension 932
Java Authentication and Authorization Service....933
Conclusions....936

28 CORBA Security 937

CORBA Security Overview 939
CORBA Security Packages....940
CORBA Security Architecture 941
Core CORBA Security Interfacing 942
Authentication....946
Delegation....951
Authorization 952
Auditing 954
Nonrepudiation 956
Encryption....960
Security Policies 962
Security Administration 963
Conclusions....964

PART VI Enterprise Web Enabling

29 Web Browsers and Servers in the Enterprise 967

Web Browsers....968
Web Browser Architecture....969
Web Browser Implementations 970
Web Browser Security 971
Web Browser Security Problems....971
Web Browser Security Solutions....972
Java Plug-in....973
Installing the Java Plug-in into a Web Browser 973
Designating the Use of a Java Plug-in JRE....974
Web Servers 976
Web Server Architecture 976
Web Server Implementations 978
Web Server Security 979
Web Server Security Problems 979
Web Server Security Solutions 980
Web Server Availability 982
Conclusions....983

30 Traditional Web Programming and Java 985

HTML Programming 986
HTML in General 987
HTML Structure Control and Display Elements 988
HTML Forms....994
CGI Programming....995
Example CGI Program 996
Stateful CGI Applications 1000
CGI Pros and Cons 1000
Scripting Languages 1001
JavaScript....1002
VBScript 1004
Perl....1005
Active Server Pages 1006
Java-Based Web Programming 1007
Conclusions....1008

31 XML 1009

XML Overview....1010
XML Formatting....1012
Comments 1014
XML Declaration....1014
Elements 1014
Attributes 1015
Entity References....1016
Processing Instructions 1016
Unparsed Character Data....1017
Well-Formed XML Documents....1017
DTD Declaration....1018
Document Type Definition Header 1019
Element Declarations....1019
Notation Declarations 1021
Entity Declarations 1021
Attribute Declarations 1022
Valid XML Documents 1023
DTD Example 1023
Hyperlinking in XML....1025
XLinks 1026
XPointers 1029
XML Style Sheets....1029
Simple API for XML 1031

SAX Architecture 1032
Core SAX Objects 1032
SAX Application Handler Interfaces 1035
SAX Parser Interfaces 1043
Document Object Model 1047
DOM Architecture 1048
DOM Nodes 1050
DOM Node Types 1052
DOM Parsing 1058
Java and XML 1061
The Java Enterprise APIs and XML 1061
The J2EE and XML 1062
J2EE Application Deployment Descriptions in XML 1063
Conclusions 1066

32 Java Servlets 1067

Servlet Architecture 1068
Servlet Logical and Physical Architecture 1069
Servlet Lifecycle 1070
Servlet Interfaces 1071
Servlet Exception Abstractions 1071
Base Servlet Framework Abstractions 1072
Servlet Framework Examples 1076
Servlet HTTP Interfaces 1078
Base HTTP Servlet Framework Abstractions 1078
BeeShirts.com Java HTTP Servlet Examples 1081
Request Processing 1086
Request Handling Abstractions 1086
Servlet Request Dispatching Abstractions 1090
Request Handling Examples 1092
Response Generation 1095
Response Handling Abstractions 1096
Response Handling Examples 1099
Session Management 1103
Session Management Abstractions 1104
Session Management Examples 1107
Servlet Deployment 1110
Web Application Deployment Descriptor Format 1111
Web Application Deployment Procedures 1118
Web Application Directory Structure 1119
J2EE Reference Implementation Server Startup and Deployment 1120
BEA WebLogic Server Startup and Deployment 1122

Servlet Configuration 1122
Individual Servlet Configuration 1123
Servlet Context Configuration 1124
Servlet Application Configuration 1125
Servlet Service Management 1126
Servlet Thread and Activation Service Management 1127
EJB and Resource Naming Service Management 1128
Servlet Transaction Service Management 1128
Servlet Security Service Management 1130
Servlet Availability Service Management 1133
Conclusions 1134

33 JavaServer Pages 1135

JSP Overview 1136
JSP Architecture 1137
Phases of a JSP 1137
BeeShirts.com JSP Examples 1139
JSP Language Basics 1142
JSP Standard and XML-Based Elements 1143
Tags 1143
Comments 1144
Special Character Handling 1144
JSP Translation and Compilation Directives 1144
`include` Directive 1145
`page` Directive 1145
`taglib` Directive 1147
Directive Examples 1147
Java Scripting from JSP 1149
Declarations 1149
Expressions 1150
Scriptlets 1151
Java Abstractions of JSP 1152
Page Context 1152
Page Handles 1156
JSP Factories and Container Information 1157
Custom JSP Classes 1158
Standard Java Objects from JSP 1159
Implicit Objects 1159
Object Scope 1160
JSP Object Manipulation Examples 1160
Standard Java Actions from JSP 1164
`jsp:param` Action Sub-Elements 1165
`jsp:forward` Action 1165

`jsp:include` Action 1166
`jsp:useBean` Action 1167
`jsp:setProperty` Action 1169
`jsp:getProperty` Action 1170
`jsp:plugin` Action 1171
Standard Action Examples 1173
JSP Configuration and Deployment 1175
JSP Deployment Descriptor Considerations 1176
JSP Configuration 1177
Direct JSP Deployment Procedure Considerations 1179
Precompiled JSP Deployment Procedure Considerations 1180
Custom Java Actions and Tags from JSP 1181
JSP Custom Tag Extension Abstractions 1182
Tag Libraries 1183
Conclusions 1186

PART VII Enterprise Applications Enabling

34 Enterprise Application Platforms 1191
Enterprise Platforms Overview 1192
TP Monitor Platforms 1193
OTMs 1195
Generic Application Frameworks 1196
Standard Java-Based Generic Application Framework 1198
CORBAcomponents 1200
Microsoft's Generic Application Framework 1202
Application-Specific Platforms 1203
Enterprise Application Management 1205
Conclusions 1206

35 Application Servers and Enterprise JavaBeans 1207
Standalone Enterprise Applications 1208
Application Server–Based Enterprise Applications 1210
Application Server Architecture Provider Roles 1212
Application Server Components 1214
Application Server Client Interfaces 1218
Application Server Client Implementations 1220
Enterprise Application Configuration and Deployment 1225
Server Configuration and Deployment Example 1225
Client Configuration and Deployment Example 1226
Application Service Management 1228
Conclusions 1229

36 **Modeling Components with Enterprise JavaBeans** **1231**

EJB Overview 1232
EJB Architecture 1233
EJB Types 1235
EJB Exception Types....1236
EJB Development Considerations and Steps 1237
BeeShirts.com EJB Application 1239
EJB Configuration and Deployment Basics 1243
EJB Deployment Descriptor Top-Level Elements 1244
EJB JAR Files 1245
EJB Deployment Procedures....1246
J2EE Reference Implementation Server Startup and Deployment....1247
BEA WebLogic Server Startup and Deployment 1248
J2EE Test Client Startup 1249
Session Bean Server Components 1250
Stateless Session Beans....1250
Stateful Session Beans....1255
Session Bean Client Interfaces 1263
Session Bean Remote Interfaces 1263
Session Bean Home Interfaces 1267
Session Bean Configuration and Deployment 1273
EJB and JDBC 1277
Entity Bean Server Components....1279
Entity Bean Pooling....1280
Primary Keys 1280
Bean-Managed Persistence Entity Beans 1281
Container-Managed Persistence Entity Beans 1293
Entity Bean Client Interfaces 1299
Entity Bean Remote Interfaces 1299
Entity Bean Home Interfaces 1303
Entity Bean Configuration and Deployment 1307
Conclusions....1313

37 **Advanced Enterprise JavaBeans Serving** **1315**

EJB Transactions....1316
Bean-Managed Transaction Demarcation 1317
Container-Managed Transaction Demarcation 1321
EJB Security 1325
Standard Programmatic EJB Security Mechanisms 1326
Standard Declarative EJB Security Mechanisms 1327
Vendor-Specific Access Control Mapping 1329

Vendor-Specific Identity and Authentication 1330
Extending the BeeShirts.com Example Data Model....1332
BeeShirts.com Security 1332
EJB/Web Connectivity 1334
BeeShirts.com: An Integrated J2EE Web and EJB e-Commerce Application 1334
Web/EJB Connectivity Approach and Examples 1337
EJB/CORBA Connectivity 1341
EJBs as CORBA Clients 1342
EJBs as CORBA Servers....1342
EJB and XML....1343
EJB and JMS....1346
EJB as JMS Producer 1347
EJB as JMS Consumer 1348
EJB and JavaMail 1351
Conclusions....1354

38 Enterprise Application Integration 1355

Enterprise Application Integration Overview 1356
EAI with JNI....1357
EAI with Distributed Enterprise Communication Paradigms 1361
EAI with TCP/IP 1362
EAI with HTTP 1363
EAI with CORBA 1364
EAI with RMI 1364
EAI with DCOM 1365
EAI with Messaging Services and JMS 1365
EAI with XML 1367
EAI with J2EE Connectors....1368
Embedded Applications Integration 1370
Conclusions....1372

Appendixes

A Software Configuration 1375

Software on the CD 1376
Software Configuration per Chapter....1378
J2SE Configuration....1380
J2EE Configuration....1380
Java Environment Variable Configuration 1381
Microsoft Java Configuration 1381
BEA WebLogic Server Configuration 1381
Sample Software Configuration 1382

Database Configuration 1383
BeeShirts.com Data Model 1383
Cloudscape Database Configuration 1385
Oracle Database Configuration 1389
Web Configuration 1392
Web Configuration Properties for the J2EE Reference Implementation 1392
Web Configuration Properties for the BEA WebLogic Server 1393
Web Configuration Scripts for the J2EE Reference Implementation 1394
Web Configuration Scripts for the BEA WebLogic Server 1394
Application Server Configuration....................1395
Application Server Configuration Properties for the BEA WebLogic Server 1395
Application Server Configuration Scripts for the BEA WebLogic Server 1396
Application Server Configuration Scripts for J2EE Reference Implementation 1397
JavaBeans Configuration 1398
XML Configuration 1398
CORBA ORB Configuration 1398
CORBA Services Configuration....................1399
RMI/IIOP Configuration....................1399
JNDI Configuration 1400
LDAP Configuration....................1401
Jini Configuration 1402
JMS Configuration 1402
JavaMail Configuration....................1402

B Additional Resources 1405

Object-Oriented and Component-Based Software Development......1406
Java Basics 1406
J2EE Basics 1407
User Interfacing 1407
JavaBeans 1408
Database Development and JDBC 1408
General Distributed Communications and TCP/IP 1408
CORBA....................1409
RMI....................1409
COM/DCOM 1410
JNDI, Naming, Directory, Trading, and Jini Services 1410
MOM, JMS, and JavaMail 1411

Distributed Transactions, JTA, and JTS 1411
General Assurance and Security 1411
General Web, HTML, and Scripting 1412
XML 1413
Java Servlets and JSP 1413
Application Serving and EAI 1413
Enterprise JavaBeans 1414

Index 1415

About The Authors

Paul J. Perrone is the Founder, the President, and a Senior Software Consultant for Assured Technologies, Inc. Through Assured Technologies (http://www.assuredtech.com), Paul provides software consulting, training, products, and research for companies interested in economical, scalable, secure, and Internet-enabled distributed enterprise systems used for e-commerce, business-to-business (B2B) transactions, and general enterprise-wide application. Paul has enabled his specialized background in high-intelligence and high-assurance (for example, security) systems to be reflected in Assured Technologies's business practice and pursuits. Paul has been a key player in the architecture, design, and development of numerous large-scale n-tier distributed systems and products for both Fortune 500 and medium-sized organizations. Paul's key technology and training expertise areas are enterprise Java and the J2EE, Enterprise JavaBeans, embedded-enterprise system connectivity, CORBA, XML, UML, and object-oriented/component-based software. In addition to this book, Paul publishes his work in various trade journals. He has an MSEE from the University of Virginia and a BSEE from Rutgers University. He is a member of the IEEE and ACM and has served as chapter chair for the Northern Virginia IEEE Computer Society. Paul can be reached at pperrone@assuredtech.com or (703) 728-0115.

Venkata S. R. "Krishna" R. Chaganti is a senior software engineering consultant and has been developing distributed computing software for the past seven years using Java and C++ programming environments. Krishna has been working with Fortune 500 companies to develop EJB, CORBA, and DCE software for their distributed computing needs. He has also been teaching Java and related technologies for two years. He has an MSEE in Computer Engineering and an MSEE in Electrical Engineering from the University of Alabama in Huntsville. He also has a B.Tech in Electronics and Communications Engineering from Nagarjuna University, A.P., India. Krishna can be reached at chaganti@erols.com.

Dedication

Paul J. Perrone:
To my wife and parents.

Venkata S. R. "Krishna" R. Chaganti:
To my parents and wife.

Acknowledgments

This book has been a major undertaking that has consumed a considerable amount of time both to write and to develop supporting code examples. Paul Perrone has drawn upon both his communications and his software architect/designer/developer skills to write the book's material, develop the book's diagrams, help define the book's sample e-commerce application design, and develop a few snippets of code. Krishna Chaganti has drawn upon his software development skills to develop the supporting sample software, define the steps and scripts for building and executing the software, perform testing, and help verify technical accuracy of the manuscript.

The Sams Publishing staff have been absolutely fabulous and instrumental in making this a successful project. Steve Anglin deserves many thanks for managing the overall creation of this book and working with us on numerous issues. We would like to thank Songlin Qiu for enthusiastically managing the development side of this book with the utmost attention to detail and perfection. We'd also like to thank Tim Ryan for working with us early on to help promote this project and for having vision with its kickoff. The many other folks at Sams, including Elizabeth Roberts, Charles Ashbacher, Cheri Clark, Jason Haines, and Maggie Malloy (to name a few), have all also been instrumental in making this project a success.

In what follows, we would like to individually acknowledge those who have helped us make this project a reality in their own way.

Paul J. Perrone: Family and the culture they create have been the most influential factors that enabled me to make a book like this one a reality. To begin, I owe many thanks to Janie Perrone, my wife, for providing love, patience, understanding, and her unique ability to manage work, home, and both of our lives throughout this effort. I also thank my parents, Don S. Perrone and Judy Perrone, for fostering an independent, imaginative, and active thought process in the context of a close-knit family culture; my brother, Don A. Perrone, for helping me keep life in perspective and maintain a balance between realism and open-mindedness; my sister-in-law, Denise Perrone, and my nieces/goddaughters, Allison Perrone and Julia Perrone, for their love and perspective on life; my grandmother Catherine Stiles for love and prayers; my parents-in-law, Reid Vance and Margaret Vance; John and Joanne Heilmann and family; Frank and Caroline Izzo and family; and in general, my extremely large and extended family. Finally, I also owe much gratitude to my grandfather Anthony Perrone and my uncle Louis Perrone who helped me understand work, independence, courage, honor, loyalty, and family love. I know how proud they would have been and I miss them.

Many friends and colleagues also help make my life's work fun and possible, and contribute to its development. Of course, my friend and co-author, Krishna, deserves many thanks for being able to go the distance and work with me on a huge project such as this one. I also thank friends and colleagues including (to name a few) Caroline Russo, Dana Krochmal, Gary Miller, Dave Remkes, Mark Madalena, Karen Eglin, Dan Estepp, Tom Dickey, Peter Dahlstrom, Jeff Gilliatt, Jaime McKenzie, Mark Snyder, Dick Krol, Andy Stauffer, Jim Wamsley, Anup Ghosh, Paul Kirkitelos, Jeff Ebert, Charles Choi, Tom Schwenk, Doug Szajda, Geoff Hoekstra, Mike Woosley, Tom Hubbard, Frank Baglivio, Richard Hatch, Steve Wynne, Mike Carr, Catherine "McGill" Longo, Ben Collingsworth, Roy Tharpe, John Rollins, Malcolm McRoberts, Barry Clinger, Dave Castillo, Mark Thomas, Joe Hoff, Scott Lewand, Rami Zanoun, Kent Banks, Stefan Buchanan, Denise Taylor, Barry Johnson, Michael Bushnell, Richard Mammone, Julio Barros, Peter Thaggard, Fabrice Sarciaux, Eric Watson, Steven Sandler, Jim Moore, Jeff Oelschlagel, Anthony Guarino, Alan Polivka, Chris Roney, Christine Pepin, Jerome Pepin, and Vince Williams. Finally, thanks to "Cappy," who has kept me company while I was writing this book and has occasionally tried to stop me from writing by plunging his fangs and claws into my typing hands from time to time.

Venkata Chaganti: There are many people to thank who have helped me in some way to make this book possible, including family, friends, and co-workers. First and foremost, I would like to thank Geetha, my wife and friend, for all of her support, encouragement, and patience during the endless hours spent developing and testing the code used with this book. I would also like to thank my parents, Sitaravamma and Veera Reddy, who always encouraged and taught me the importance of education. I would like to thank Abhijit for his understanding and for not complaining about his dad being attached to the computer for the past six months.

I would like to thank Mr. Tommy Erskine and family for their help during my Huntsville stay and later. I would also like to thank Dr. Nagendra Singh, professor at the University of Alabama in Huntsville, who was a mentor during my graduate studies. For continually offering me challenging assignments, I thank Alok Nigam. I would also like to thank my friend Rajasekhar Ramireddy, who generously gave his time to verify our JavaMail code and write comments for a few code segments. I would like to thank my friend and co-author, Paul Perrone, for his encouragement and patience while I fixed code problems as they arose. I would also like to thank all of my friends and co-workers who have helped me along the way, including Dr. William S. Paciesas, Dr. Ray Emami, Dr. Narayan Reddy Ponaka, David Potter, Dan Parkins, Brian Mulrony, Julio Barros, Ram Sudireddy, Andy Wills, Jeff Phelps, Bhaskar Gudimetla, Srinivas Pasupuleti, Sankuratri V. Rao, Srinivas Mutyala, Caroline Russo, Dana Krochmal, Kartik Shyamsunder, Ted Kakavas, and many others. Finally, I would like to thank the Almighty God, who has been the true guide in my life.

Tell Us What You Think!

As the reader of this book, *you* are our most important critic and commentator. We value your opinion and want to know what we're doing right, what we could do better, what areas you'd like to see us publish in, and any other words of wisdom you're willing to pass our way.

As a Publisher for Sams Publishing, I welcome your comments. You can fax, email, or write me directly to let me know what you did or didn't like about this book—as well as what we can do to make our books stronger.

Please note that I cannot help you with technical problems related to the topic of this book, and that due to the high volume of mail I receive, I might not be able to reply to every message.

When you write, please be sure to include this book's title and author as well as your name and phone or fax number. I will carefully review your comments and share them with the author and editors who worked on the book.

Fax: 317-581-4770

Email: `feedback@samspublishing.com`

Mail: Michael Stephens
Publisher
Sams Publishing
201 West 103rd Street
Indianapolis, IN 46290 USA

Introduction

Before you delve into the contents of a huge tome such as this one, it is a good idea to first acquire an understanding of the problem you are trying to solve. In this way, you can best ensure that our book is addressing your needs. Furthermore, you should be aware of the topics to be presented that address such problems to ensure that our book's material is relevant to your technology interests. This introduction describes the problem being solved by this book, an overview of the topics discussed, the target audience addressed, and the approach for presenting the material.

This Is Your Enterprise on Caffeine!

Let's first acquire an overview of the scope and problems being addressed by this book. As software consultants who provide enterprise system solutions and who have used the technologies described in this book under the pressure of deadlines and schedules, we very much wish we had a book like this at our disposal a long time ago. Of course, such a book must also reflect the current technologies being used to build enterprise systems. We thus consider this book to be an extremely market-driven and technology-driven book directly addressing the needs of enterprise system developers. We begin this section by defining the mission statement and battle cry that have both initiated this book's effort and that have driven the course of its development along the way. We then specifically address the type of problems we are trying to solve, and describe how information technology and the Java enterprise solution can be infused throughout the veins of an enterprise.

Scope of the Book, Mission Statement, and Battle Cry

> *Building Java Enterprise Systems with J2EE* provides a comprehensive and practical guide for building scalable, secure, Web-enabled, and distributed enterprise systems with Java enterprise technologies and the Java 2 Platform, Enterprise Edition (J2EE). The technologies presented in this book can be used to rapidly build e-commerce (*aka* business-to-consumer or B2C) systems, business-to-business (B2B) systems, enterprise application integration (EAI) approaches, and general distributed and Internet-based enterprise wide systems with systems assurance for security, reliability, availability, maintainability, and scalability as a fundamental underlying consideration.

Problem to Be Solved

Enterprise systems encompass those distributed, scalable, multiuser, and business-critical systems that are intimately related to enhancing the productivity of a corporate or organizational enterprise via information technology. We are in the midst of an information and knowledge technology revolution that has catapulted economies and ways of life far beyond those that even the industrial revolution wrought. A primary engine of automation and productivity enhancement behind this revolution is the enterprise system. More and more, corporations and organizations are tying themselves into a complex informational network in an effort to further enhance the productivity of their operations for competitive and cost-reduction reasons. E-commerce, Internet/Web enabling, B2B connectivity, EAI, and data mining are just a few of the requirements that must be satisfied by enterprise system designs.

This is why effective means for building enterprise systems that address the unique problems and high demand for enterprise software development effectiveness are always being sought out by enterprise system development teams. Corporations and organizations more and more look for enterprise-class developers and engineers who can solve enterprise system problems. Java enterprise technologies and the J2EE in particular provide an approach for more rapidly and effectively building enterprise systems which address the needs for producing enterprise software that is reusable, scalable, distributable, maintainable, secure, reliable, and available.

This Is the Book to Address Your Needs!

This book is partitioned into seven major parts and a set of appendixes. The structure of the book is presented here so that you can better understand what to expect from each major part of the book. You can thus tailor how you'll approach reading the book and perhaps determine which chapters cover material with which you are already familiar. Finally, in this section, we also describe the notation conventions used within the chapter text.

Part I: Enterprise Foundations

The first part of the book explores the foundational concepts and solution paradigms on which the rest of the book depends. We begin with a description of the enterprise system development problem addressed by this book and a description of a generic framework for understanding solutions to this problem. The solution paradigms of object-oriented and component-based software development are then briefly highlighted in the context of how such paradigms are key to building enterprise systems. Descriptions of the foundational features of the Java programming and platform solution paradigm are then given, along with a brief coverage of those aspects of Java that make it a significant enabler for rapid enterprise system development. All of these fundamental features are tied together along with the Java 2 Platform, Enterprise Edition to define the generic architectural solution for building Java enterprise systems as advocated by this book. This part of the book closes with a discussion of user interfaces to the types of enterprise systems described herein and provides a more in-depth discussion of the JavaBeans component model on which a few core Java enterprise concepts depend. This part of the book thus serves as both an overview and a refresher to the primary audience of the book and as a rapid introduction to many basic concepts for an extended audience.

Part II: Enterprise Data Enabling

Access to warehouses of enterprise data is extremely important to building useful enterprise systems. There are various ways to connect enterprise Java applications with enterprise data stored in databases, but the Java Database Connectivity (JDBC) API is the most common and feature-rich Java-based enterprise data enabling framework. JDBC is a core part of the J2EE and has most often been used by organizations in its JDBC 1.0 flavor shipped with the JDK v1.1. JDBC 2.0 offers new core functionality in the Java 2 Platform, Standard Edition (J2SE) and a few important enterprise-specific extensions in the J2EE. The second part of the book covers the foundations of enterprise data enabling in general and then focuses on JDBC concepts and a practical step-by-step illustration of how to build JDBC API client applications. The gamut from basic to advanced JDBC topics is discussed. After reading this part of the book, you should be armed with the critical knowledge needed by enterprise systems developers for understanding enterprise data enabling issues, along with the primary mechanisms used to enable data in enterprise Java systems using the J2EE's JDBC underpinnings.

Part III: Distributed Enterprise Communications Enabling

The third part of the book covers the foundations of distributed enterprise communications enabling in general and then focuses on a few key solutions available to the enterprise Java engineer. Because all solutions depend in some way on the TCP/IP protocol suite, we describe the architecture of TCP/IP and any direct Java-based interfaces to TCP/IP. After giving an architectural description of Web-based HTTP communications, we focus on three key distributed object communication models. The CORBA distributed object model is incorporated into J2SE and J2EE environments via Java IDL and represents the most interoperable and standard model for distributed communications enabling. Also part of J2SE and J2EE environments, RMI provides a Java-based communications model that has more recently begun to merge with the CORBA communications model via RMI/IIOP. Finally, though not part of the J2EE, DCOM provides a means to interact with distributed components built on top of one very specific yet significant computing platform known as the Microsoft Windows platform.

Part IV: Common Services for Distributed Enterprise Communications

The fourth part of the book describes many of the services that are built on top of or augment the communication models described in the previous part of the book to make distributed enterprise communications more immediately useful in enterprise applications. Naming services are first described as a means for mapping between distributed object references and human-readable object names using technologies such as JNDI, the RMI registry, and the CORBA Naming Service. We then describe a means for locating and discovering distributed objects on a network both using descriptive attributes about such objects and via type information about those objects when we discuss directory and trading services using technologies such as JNDI, LDAP, Jini, and the CORBA Trading Service. The means by which objects are brought into active memory from dormant persistent storage are then described under the broad topic of activation services, including a discussion of the Java Activation Framework. We also discuss how asynchronous messages sent between message producers and consumers are encapsulated within one of various messaging service options available to the Java enterprise system developer, including JMS, JavaMail, and the CORBA Event Service. Finally, we describe the means for providing atomic, consistent, isolated, and durable transaction semantics to distributed operations across distributed resources using the CORBA Object Transaction Service, JTS, and the JTA. The services described here are thus common to many distributed enterprise communications-based applications and are also fundamental components of an integrated Java enterprise and J2EE solution.

Part V: Enterprise Systems Assurance

Assurance deals with providing for the security, reliability, availability, maintainability, and perhaps safety of your enterprise system. Although time-to-market demands may lead to a lack of assurance in these areas, the costs associated with not providing assurance can be particularly expensive with respect to an enterprise system. With a knowledge of how to practically trade off delayed deployment with a lack of assurance, you can make intelligent decisions when considering how far you should address your enterprise assurance needs. The fifth part of the book describes general assurance concepts and techniques and soon thereafter focuses on security assurance as one of the more involved facets of enterprise assurance. The basic security problem, concepts, and security models on which Java and CORBA security depend are first described. We then cover the basic Java security architecture and follow up that discussion with an in-depth look at how to use the Java security model in your enterprise applications. We also describe the CORBA security model for building secure CORBA-based systems.

Part VI: Enterprise Web Enabling

Putting an enterprise on the Internet for the sake of e-commerce has been a major objective for many organizations since the mid-1990s. Although selling products and services via the Web is a key focus of many enterprises, productivity enhancements to be achieved by providing seamless distributed access to applications from anywhere in the world also motivate enterprises to consider Web-enabled access to business applications for employees and business partners. In the sixth part of the book, we specifically address those technologies and approaches to Web-enabling an enterprise system using Java enterprise technologies and the J2EE. We describe how markup languages such as HTML and XML play key roles in representing enterprise data that traverses between Web server and Web client. HTML is most popularly used for creating Web-based presentation content, whereas XML is used in more general ways to represent J2EE component deployment information, as well as for representing messages passed between systems. Java Servlets and JavaServer Pages represent the two J2EE-based technologies that we explore in depth as the means by which enterprises are Web-enabled.

Part VII: Enterprise Applications Enabling

Many of the technologies and services described in this book can operate either as standalone enterprise applications or from within enterprise application framework environments. The seventh part of the book focuses on the use of component-based application server frameworks to make access to such technologies and services an easier proposition for developers than is the case when developing standalone applications. The J2EE Enterprise JavaBeans (EJBs) component model serves as the core way in which distributed Java enterprise applications can be rapidly built. We describe how to build and deploy J2EE-based EJBs, as well as how thick clients and Web clients can connect to EJBs. We also describe more advanced EJB topics, such as EJB-CORBA connectivity, EJB security, EJB transactions, and the relationship between EJB and the many other technologies described in this book. Finally, we close this part of the book with a discussion of how both EJBs and standalone Java enterprise applications can be used for B2B transactions and to integrate with auxiliary and legacy enterprise applications.

Appendixes

The final part of the book contains appendixes that support the content of this book. We describe how to configure the commercial and sample software used with this book, as well as provide additional references used to augment the book's material.

Notation Conventions

Throughout this book, we use certain notation conventions when presenting the material. The conventions used throughout the book can assume different meanings depending on the context in which they are used. For example, conventions used to describe artifacts of code or programming can differ from those used in textual descriptions. Although these conventions are often intuitive and easily understood when used in context, we list the conventions here for your reference:

- Three consecutive dots, ..., in text refers to additional text that naturally follows.
- Three consecutive dots, `...`, in code refers to code that has been left out of a code listing.
- Square brackets, `[ ]`, in directory names or filenames can serve as placeholders for information that should be replaced with an actual directory name or filename.
- Square brackets, `[ ]`, in text or code encapsulate information that is optional and can be replaced with some other data.
- Angle brackets, < >, used in text or code encapsulate information that is required and should be replaced with some other data.
- Italicized words in artifacts of code and programming also can be used to identify information that is required and should be replaced with some other data.
- Italicized words in plain text can be used to simply accentuate particular words to focus on.
- Boldface words in code and generic file formats accentuate key words or terms.
- Code that is inserted into a chapter from sample code on the CD is most often inserted as it was on the CD with any indentation left as is to preserve consistency between the manuscript and the CD as much as possible.

Other Conventions Used in This Book

This book uses different typefaces to differentiate between code and regular English, and also to help you identify important concepts.

Text that you type and text that should appear on your screen is presented in `monospace` type.

```
It will look like this to mimic the way text looks on your screen.
```

This arrow (➥) at the beginning of a line of code means that a single line of code is too long to fit on the printed page. Continue typing all characters after the ➥ as though they were part of the preceding line.

NOTE

A Note presents interesting pieces of information related to the surrounding discussion.

TIP

A Tip offers advice or teaches an easier way to do something.

CAUTION

A Caution advises you about potential problems and helps you steer clear of disaster.

This Is Your Brain After Reading This Book!

Now that you've seen the problems this book addresses and an outline of the topics discussed that help solve these problems, we want to describe the intended audience for this material and describe what you will have learned after reading the book. We also take the opportunity here to describe our specific approach to presenting the material.

Intended Audience

Building Java Enterprise Systems with J2EE will be of interest to professional software engineers fulfilling roles such as software developer, designer, and architect. The formally trained software developer, designer, and architect with a background in object-oriented software development and Java who has a demand for acquiring enterprise-level development skills using Java is the primary target audience for this book. However, enough background material is established early in the book to provide an overview and refresher of the core concepts and technologies on top of which enterprise-level Java technologies are built. As a side benefit of this overview and refresher material, formally trained and experienced software engineers who have little Java background but who have been thrust into an enterprise software development project using Java may also benefit from reading this book. Finally, managers and technically savvy business folk who aim to understand the basic concepts involved in building enterprise, e-commerce, and B2B systems can refer to this book's "front" material presented early in each chapter as well as in chapters specifically designed to be conceptual overviews for more technical chapters that follow.

Approach of the Book

Although many of the Java enterprise technologies that we use in this book have been around for some time, the J2EE platform integrates these technologies into one cohesive platform. Of course, the J2EE alone does not currently solve all Java enterprise problems. Consequently, we also describe other Java-based technologies that will be encountered during actual Java enterprise development efforts. We in fact are incorporating into this book a lot of practical and real-world experience with these technologies. Therefore, at times we stray from purist views in the interest of describing practical enterprise development solutions. Since this book's inception, our battle cry has been to provide a comprehensive and practical guide for building Java enterprise systems.

To this end we not only provide detailed coverage of Java enterprise architectural and design concepts, but also illustrate much of the material with practical examples and code. We focus on describing how to build Java enterprise applications via illustration of how to use core APIs and how to configure your Java enterprise system applications. We from time to time keep certain examples simple and deviate from pure object-oriented abstraction techniques and style in the interest of directly demonstrating how to use specific APIs for pedagogic reasons. Because the J2EE and auxiliary Java enterprise APIs are extremely rich with features, we focus on how to use the core and most commonly encountered APIs. Furthermore, because this book is meant to be a step-by-step guide for building applications and not an API reference, we also avoid defining and describing every possible API you might encounter. Instead we offer plenty of Web-based API references in Appendix B, "Additional Resources," to which you may refer. Because we are describing how to build Java enterprise systems in a practical manner, we also occasionally describe those APIs that are technically not part of the J2EE but have significant enterprise system relevance. Note that we often refer to the J2EE to collectively mean the J2SE in addition to those extensions to the J2SE that form the J2EE.

We focus on those aspects of a system that are utilized by middle-tier server-side applications. Thus, in a Model-View-Controller (MVC) approach to describing a system, you might say that we are primarily interested in the "C" aspect of a system. We are largely only interested in describing how to enable the "V" to be realized (user and Web interfaces) as well as encapsulate and enable access to the "M" (data enabling).

The End Result

In summary, after reading this book, you will walk away with a knowledge of how to apply and use Java enterprise technologies for enterprise distributed communications enabling, data enabling, assurance provisioning, Web enabling, and application enabling. Your knowledge will be comprehensive and practical by nature. Knowledge of the J2EE and other Java enterprise technologies will then serve as your primary toolkit for building enterprise systems.

So pour yourself a warm cup of joe, sit back, and enjoy the rest of the book as we describe for you how *Building Java Enterprise Systems with J2EE* can fully caffeinate your enterprise. We hope you enjoy, learn, and provide us with any feedback via `http://www.assuredtech.com/books/j2ee/feedback.html`.

Enterprise Foundations

PART I

IN THIS PART

1 Enterprise Architectural Overview 11

2 Object-Oriented Software Development for the Enterprise 19

3 Component-Based Software Development for the Enterprise 39

4 Java Foundations for Enterprise Development 53

5 Java Enterprise System Architecture with the J2EE 105

6 Enterprise User Interfacing 125

7 Modeling Components with JavaBeans 141

Enterprise Architectural Overview

CHAPTER

1

IN THIS CHAPTER

- The Enterprise 12
- Enterprise Components 14
- Information Technology in the Enterprise 16

This chapter provides an overview of the assumed boundaries of an enterprise as it is scoped by this book, its components, the relation between components, and the vision for how information technology can streamline the operations of an enterprise. In particular, we describe how the use of Java enterprise technology with the J2EE platform can help solve enterprise computing problems in a cohesive and comprehensive fashion.

In this chapter, you will learn:

- The definition of an enterprise as used in this book, the components of an enterprise, and how these components are related.
- The fundamental components of an enterprise system as they relate to needs driven by the goals and objectives of an enterprise.
- How information technology is utilized by and energizes the enterprise.
- How Java enterprise technologies provide a fully "caffeinated" enterprise, helping it to accomplish all its goals and objectives.

The Enterprise

In its most generic form, the term *enterprise* can simply refer to an organization that has set out to accomplish certain goals. The organization may be a small-, medium-, or large-scale commercial corporation; a nonprofit institution; or perhaps a government organization. In some contexts, including the context of this book, the term *enterprise* is typically used to refer to a large organization. It is usually assumed that enterprises have a desire to grow and expand their operations and human/inter-enterprise associations over time. It is also often assumed that pursuit of the enterprise's goals are essential both for survival of the enterprise and for the growth of the enterprise.

Figure 1.1 depicts the main components of an enterprise that are used to help the enterprise accomplish its goals. Physical resources and assets are one component of an enterprise utilized to accomplish enterprise goals. For example, computing equipment, manufacturing facilities, product supplies, and corporate accounts are all examples of resources and assets that are essential to the operations of an enterprise. People and users are another fundamental component of an enterprise, with customers, employees, contractors, and partners (with other enterprises) forming the core of those classes of people who help the enterprise accomplish its goals. Finally, enterprise information and enterprise knowledge are also key ingredients used to help further the goals of an enterprise.

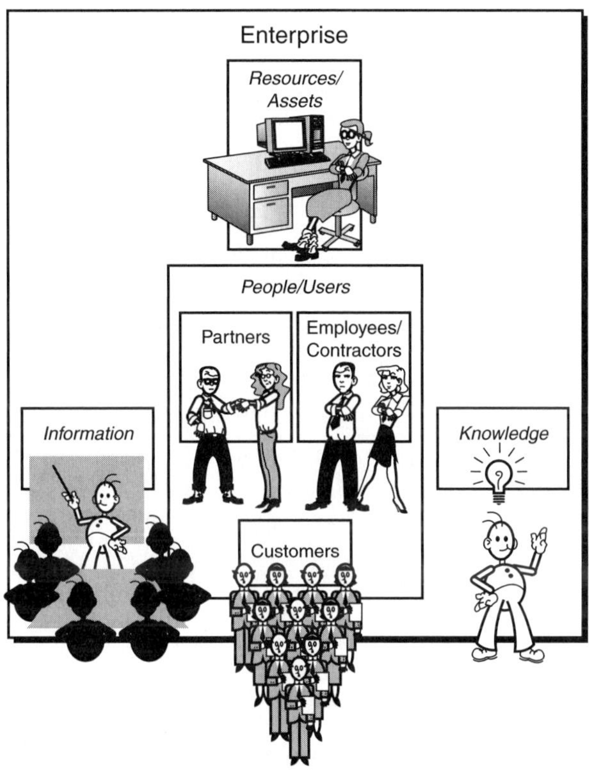

FIGURE 1.1
The components of an enterprise.

Because the various enterprise components help an enterprise accomplish its goals, they offer some value to the enterprise. It is in the best interest of an enterprise to preserve, protect, grow, make accessible, make efficient, and be sensitive to change in the value offered by the various enterprise components. These interests and primary objectives of an enterprise are to foster such desirable outcomes as these:

- Growth of a customer base
- Preservation of a customer base
- Sensitivity to a changing customer base
- Growth of an employee base
- Efficiency of an employee base
- Growth of a partnership base
- Growth of resources/assets

- Preservation of resources/assets
- Protection of resources/assets
- Accessibility of resources/assets
- Sensitivity to a change in resources/assets
- Growth of information and business knowledge
- Preservation of information and business knowledge
- Protection of information and business knowledge
- Accessibility of information and business knowledge
- Sensitivity to changes in information and knowledge

Enterprise Components

Given those components of an enterprise that have some value to the enterprise and the pursuit of an enterprise's interest in these valued components, Figure 1.2 presents the type of system a modern enterprise will strive to incorporate into its operations to maximize its goals. An enterprise generally attempts to develop the following example features shown in Figure 1.2 given the interests it has in striving to achieve its goals:

- Growth of a customer base can lead an enterprise to provide Internet/Web connectivity perhaps in the form of a Business-to-Commerce (B2C) or E-commerce application to open up the opportunity for more customers to patronize the enterprise. Furthermore, a growing customer base will also require the provision of a scalable Web and application connectivity solution.
- Preservation of a customer base may be accomplished by streamlining connectivity to legacy distribution supply chains so that customer satisfaction remains high due to the speed with which an enterprise can satisfy customers' orders.
- Sensitivity to a changing customer base can also be facilitated via a tailored presentation interface for different Web-based customers depending on customer profiles persisted in an enterprise database.
- Growth of an employee base can be managed by a streamlined and scalable human resources Enterprise Resource Planning (ERP) application.
- Efficiency of an employee base can be offered via direct connection to enterprise applications through a distributed enterprise client application over an intranet.
- Growth of a partnership base can be managed via the establishment of secure Business-to-Business (B2B) application logic and transaction handling.
- Growth and preservation of resources/assets can be managed and provided via Enterprise Application Integration (EAI) with legacy applications, distributed enterprise applications, and connectivity to embedded resources.

- Protection of resources/assets can be provided via the establishment of a security domain to protect valued resources distributed on an enterprise network.
- Accessibility of resources/assets can be provided via use of various distributed communications technologies to connect resources to the enterprise.
- Growth and preservation of information and knowledge can be efficiently managed in an enterprise Database Management System (DBMS).
- Protection of information and knowledge can also be managed in an enterprise database as well as by provision of assurance techniques to provide information and knowledge security and reliability.
- Accessibility of information and knowledge can also be provided via Web connectivity and various distributed communications paradigms.

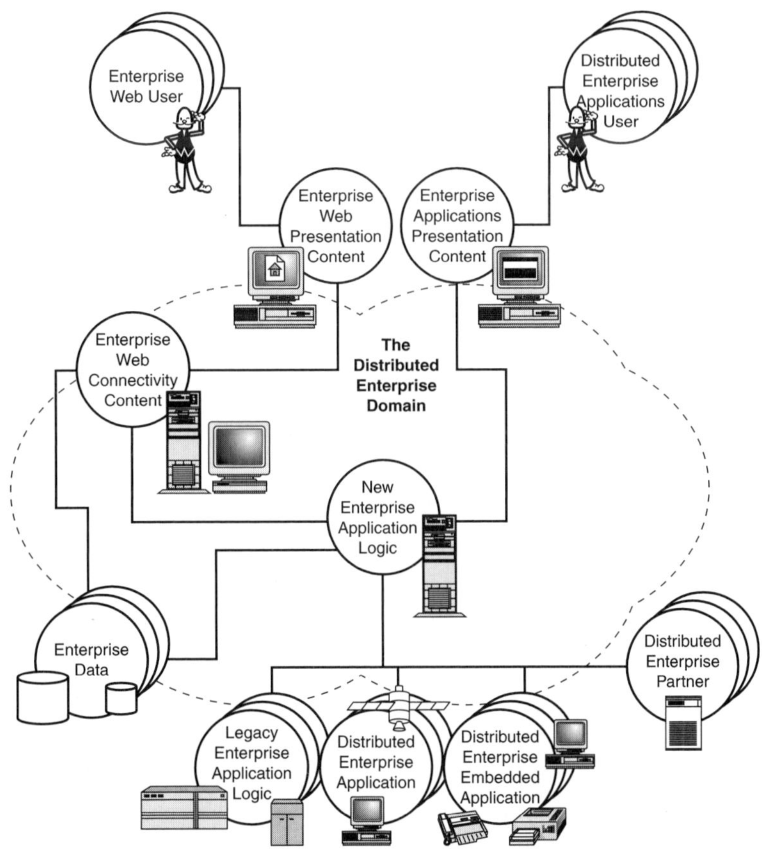

FIGURE 1.2
The components of an enterprise system.

Information Technology in the Enterprise

Information technology employed by an enterprise system can be broadly classified along the lines of the various enabling and service technologies depicted in Figure 1.3. These various enterprise enablers and services drive the very outline and approach taken by this book. The Java enterprise technologies described throughout the book can all be categorized according to the generic enterprise system architecture of Figure 1.3. These generic enterprise system architecture technology classifications are listed here:

- *Enterprise User Interfacing:* Provides a means to present content to both Web-based and standard applications-based users of an enterprise system. We highlight user-interface content development techniques in this book only via a brief discussion of Java-based AWT and Swing applications and applets, other Java-based user interface components, and Web-based presentation content via HTML and XML technologies.
- *Enterprise Data Enabling:* Provides a means to access, store, and manage enterprise information and knowledge via enterprise databases. Part II, "Enterprise Data Enabling," is dedicated to a discussion of data enabling using JDBC technology.
- *Distributed Enterprise Communications Enabling:* Provides a means to access information and applications throughout a distributed enterprise system. Such a service is considered a global service that permeates every aspect of a distributed enterprise system. Part III, "Distributed Enterprise Communications Enabling," is dedicated to a discussion of communications enabling via such technologies as TCP/IP, CORBA, RMI, and DCOM.
- *Common Services for Distributed Enterprise Communications:* Provides a set of common services used by distributed object communications paradigms. Such services are also considered global services that permeate every aspect of a distributed enterprise system. Part IV, "Common Services for Distributed Enterprise Communications," is dedicated to a discussion of higher-level communications services with a focus on Java-based naming and directory services via JNDI, CORBA trading services, Jini, activation services, messaging services via JMS and JavaMail, and transaction services using JTA and JTS.
- *Enterprise Systems Assurance:* Provides for the secure, reliable, available, maintainable, and safe qualities of an enterprise system. Such services are also considered global services that permeate every aspect of a particular enterprise system domain. Part V, "Enterprise Systems Assurance," is dedicated to a systems-assurance discussion with a focus on Java 2 platform security and CORBA security.
- *Enterprise Web Enabling:* Provides for the connectivity of the enterprise to the Internet/Web, as well as for generating Web-based presentation content. Part VI, "Enterprise Web Enabling," is dedicated to a Web-enabling discussion with a detailed discussion of Java Servlets, JSP, and XML.

- *Enterprise Applications Enabling:* Provides for the middle tier of application logic management with the connectivity to legacy enterprise application logic, the provision of new enterprise application logic, connectivity to distributed enterprise applications and embedded devices, and business-to-business connectivity with commerce partners. Part VII, "Enterprise Applications Enabling," is dedicated to an applications enabling discussion with a focus on Enterprise JavaBeans and Enterprise Application Integration.

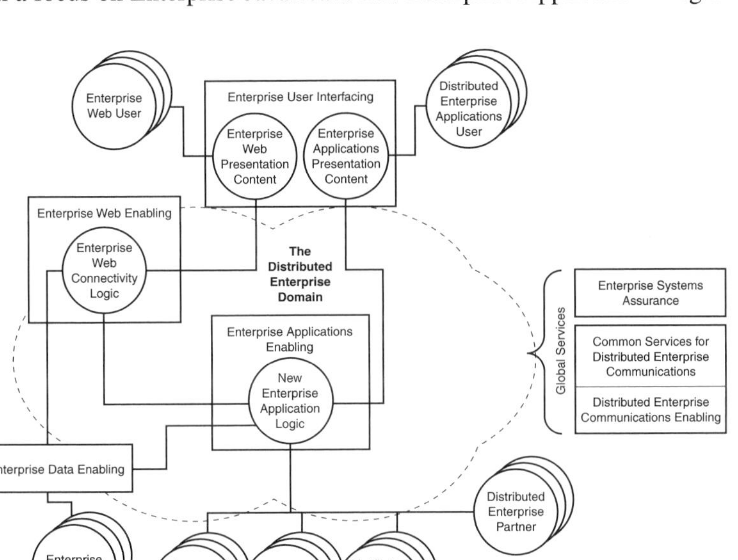

FIGURE 1.3
Information technology in an enterprise system.

Conclusions

Enterprises achieve their goals with the use of valued resources and assets, information, knowledge, and people. In an effort to preserve, protect, grow, make accessible, make efficient, and be sensitive to change of such enterprise components, modern enterprises pursue the use of information technology to build enterprise systems that help them effectively foster their goals and objectives. Information technology is used to build enterprise systems that provide user interfacing, data enabling, communications enabling, communications services, assurance services, Web enabling, and applications enabling. Java enterprise technologies with the J2EE provide standard means for covering all such bases of an enterprise system architecture's needs.

Object-Oriented Software Development for the Enterprise

CHAPTER

2

IN THIS CHAPTER

- Enterprise Objects 20
- The Object-Oriented Development Process 24
- Unified Modeling Language 31

This chapter presents an overview of the object-oriented concepts, software-development process, and modeling notation that serve as foundations for the practical construction of enterprise systems. Object-oriented software development represents a paradigm of development that offers many advantages when used to create enterprise software, including the facilitation of reusability, scalability, maintainability, and rapid development. Although this material may serve as simply a refresher for some readers, we encourage you to at least examine this chapter's section on the basic Unified Modeling Language (UML) notation that we use throughout the rest of the book.

In this chapter, you will learn:

- The basic concepts behind the object-oriented paradigm and how they enable practical enterprise software development.
- The concepts and methods behind employing a practical object-oriented software development process when building enterprise systems.
- A basic subset of the Unified Modeling Language notation used throughout this book to convey software analysis and design notions.

Enterprise Objects

The most common circumstances under which the earliest computer programs of the 1950s and early 1960s were created yielded programs that tended to be monolithic collections of computing instructions perhaps designed, developed, and maintained by an individual programmer or by fairly small groups of programmers. Such was the case even as assembly-language programming evolved into the use of higher-level language programming as depicted in Figure 2.1. Assembly-language programming (stage 1) was often necessarily monolithic in nature, with data being exposed for direct access by assembly-language instructions. Although higher-level programming languages (stage 2) permitted the construction of programs in a more natural and human-readable fashion, the structure and nature of programs in terms of monolithic behavior and exposed state still remained. Code could be modularized (stage 3) by partitioning software into separately compilable modules with the help of compiler and linkage technology, but the advent of more-advanced software engineering practices further helped encapsulate such modules into functional units (stage 4).

Functional programming fosters modularity but still exposes the state for manipulation by each module. Thus, separate functional modules aid in functional decomposition, but it wasn't until the birth of object-oriented programming (stage 5) that both modularity of behavior and encapsulation of state would become the new programming paradigm. By encapsulating state, clients of your object-oriented (OO) software module could not form undesirable dependencies on your code by directly interacting with exposed state. Thus, any undesired behavior of your software module stemming from a direct manipulation of state could be avoided by encapsulating that state to prohibit direct external access. The desired behavior of your module can thus be enforced by forcing any clients to interact with your module via a set of exposed interfaces.

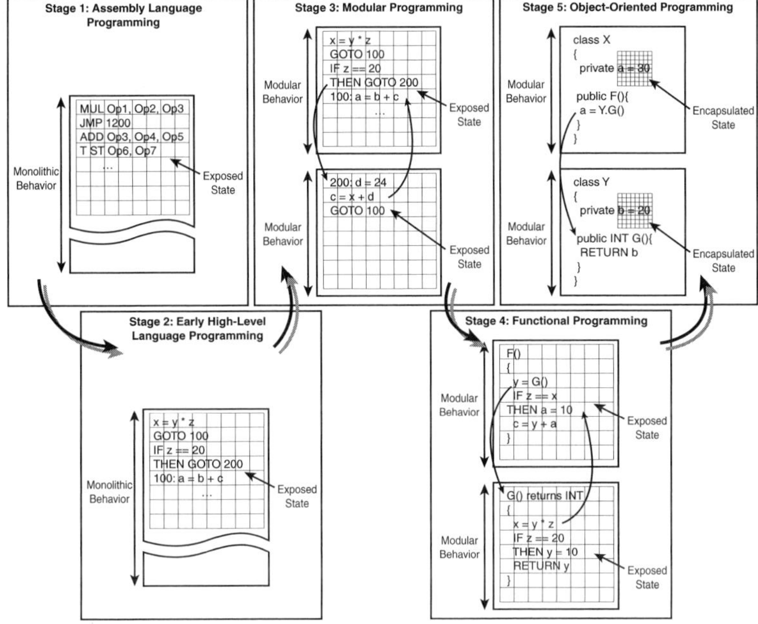

FIGURE 2.1
Evolving programming paradigms.

Elements of Object-Oriented Software

Central to the foundation of OO software is the concept of a "class." You can view the concept of a class from different OO lifecycle perspectives, but the most common view of a class in OO software development is that from an object-oriented programming (OOP) perspective. Programmatically speaking, a *class* is a discrete module of code that has a set of variables (*aka* fields) associated with it, as well as a set of function calls (*aka* methods). Methods define those interfaces to the class that take a set of zero or more input parameters and return a set of zero or more output parameters. During the process of a method call by a client of the class, the values of the class's fields may also change.

NOTE

The various elements of object-oriented software described in this section will be illustrated via a graphical notation in the "Unified Modeling Language" section later in this chapter.

An object represents an instance of a class in memory. The state of the object is defined by the values assumed by the class fields. The behavior of the object is a function of the method implementations, the return values from method calls, and the state change of the object. Objects can also be distributed such that while their instances sit in some process memory on one machine, an object in some process memory on another machine actually references the remote object. The reference to that distributed object (also known as *handle*) may be some value with embedded network address information and an object ID to refer to the distributed object.

Visibility levels associated with class fields and methods can define what level of access other classes have to those fields and methods. *Private visibility* refers to the fact that only the containing class and therefore object instances of that class can access such fields and methods. *Public visibility* means that other classes can access such fields and methods. *Protected visibility* refers to the concept of inheritance. *Inheritance* means that a class B, for example, can be defined such that it inherits the behavior of a class A from which it is inherited. Thus, a method defined on the base class A can be inherited by the subclass B. Protected visibility of fields and methods means that subclasses of a class can access the base class's protected fields and methods. Subclasses can also override methods of base classes by defining new methods with the same input and output types as the base class. Thus, instances of the subclass that have overridden base-class methods can have their method definitions called by clients versus their base class's method definitions.

Classes have class names that are scoped according to a class package. A *package* refers to a collection of one or more classes. Classes in a package have some cohesive logical relation and tend to offer a very specific service. Whenever classes are tightly coupled in some logical sense, they tend to be collected into a package. The fully qualified package name plus the class name represents a fully qualified class name.

Although such is the view of classes and objects from a strictly programmatic perspective, from an overall OO lifecycle and best-practices perspective, a class should be treated with more care. Otherwise, the strictly programmatic view that classes are just collections of fields and methods could lead to use of the OOP paradigm in a functional programming style. Rather, classes should also represent some concept or classification driven from the problem domain such as an entity (for example, `User`), a control process (for example, `UserLogManager`), or an interface of some sort (for example, `DatabaseLogInterface`). An object instance of the class should represent some unique identity of the concept or classification such as an identifier of an entity (for example, `joeUser`), the identification of a particular control process (for example, `theRemoteUserLogManager`), or the identity of a particular interface (for example, `theBackupDatabaseLogInterface`).

Object-Oriented Software's Importance to the Enterprise

OO as a software-development paradigm is one of most important foundations and enablers for building successful and expandable large-scale distributed enterprise systems. OO practices foster the development of modular programs with encapsulated state and implementation behavior, as well as facilitate the abstraction of problems. Modularity, encapsulation, abstraction, and reuse are rudimentary programming tenets that help in making large-scale distributed enterprise projects a reality.

Reuse of software can be achieved in other programming paradigms (for example, functional programming), but reuse in OO is inherently fostered by the paradigm. Modularity of classes enables one to discretely represent concepts that are used in defining a problem. Thus when the same problem occurs elsewhere on a project, those same concepts and therefore associated classes can be reused. Connecting objects together in OO via the realization of a sequence of method calls on objects actually represents a solution to a problem. That is, when object A calls a method on object B, which calls a method on object C, then that sequence corresponds to a functional solution to some problem using the associated concepts A, B, and C. In a functional programming paradigm, the functions themselves represent the specific solution to a problem. Therefore, unless the same solution to a problem exists, the code is difficult to reuse. OO, on the other hand, encapsulates concepts in classes and therefore facilitates use of the same concepts in different modular fashions to create different solutions. As the size of an enterprise project grows, the payback for reuse becomes more and more significant.

Solving a problem is usually most efficiently performed by first partitioning a problem and then addressing smaller pieces of the original problem. Modularity and abstraction in OO allow for the encapsulation of a problem domain into discrete classes and therefore facilitate more efficient problem solving. Efficient problem solving is of course particularly important for enterprise projects with time-to-market criticality.

Modularity of classes also leads to smaller and self-contained pieces of code. Smaller and self-contained pieces of code are easier to understand than large monolithic pieces of code. When code is easier to understand, it will be more easily maintained by other developers who may need to use or understand the code. The code will also be more easily maintained by the developer who originally wrote the code. Maintainability of code becomes very important if software bugs need to be resolved quickly, as well as if the code base needs to expand beyond its original functionality. Stumping the maintainability and expandability of enterprise code stumps the growth of your enterprise.

Modularity and the composition of one class that has another class as a field member also helps foster a component-based and reuse-oriented view of development. You may, for example, need to define a class `Customer` who "has" an `Address`. Odds are that you will be able to reuse another `Address` class that has been developed for another type of class. For example, someone may have created an `Employee` class which also utilized an `Address` class.

Of course, abstraction via inheritance can also enhance reuse. You may, for example, have a base class `User` who has an `Address`. Then both `Customer` and `Employee` as types of users can inherit the interfaces and access to an `Address` class from the base `User` class. Thus, a solution for the higher-level concept can be applied to a lower-level concept and enhance reuse.

Behavior is partially a function of state. That is, depending on the value of some object's state, it may behave differently when its methods are invoked. By encapsulating state, the implementation (that is, method definitions) of the class can be what dictates and enforces the class's behavior. Other modules thus cannot adversely affect behavior of an object by directly manipulating its state. Other modules are forced to affect the state of an object by using the exposed method interfaces for that object. In enterprise projects, the need for such state encapsulation grows as the number of other modules that can use your class grows.

Finally, dependencies between modules (that is, classes) are reduced by forcing dependencies to be created through interfaces as opposed to allowing dependencies to be created on state and functions that are to be encapsulated. Changes in a class's implementation can thus be made separate from changes to its interface. The tendency for dependencies being formed on your software will grow as the number of software modules that are added to your enterprise software project grows. Enforcing the fact that such dependencies are to be formed through interfaces as opposed to implementation will help enable you to change implementations without breaking dependencies created by other code. Thus you can separately recompile your implementation changes as opposed to requiring that a significant portion of your enterprise code base be recompiled.

The Object-Oriented Development Process

Much has been written about the OO process and how OO development should proceed on a project. We won't be expounding on the process topic much here since it is really outside the scope of this book, but we will present a basic process that can be followed with some specific consideration for certain enterprise software development issues. Many processes are defined with an ideal sequence of steps that should be followed by organizations to enable the creation of high-quality, reusable, maintainable, and extendable software. Many particular process recommendations are good, a few are bad, and a few more are completely infeasible.

Building enterprise systems can be a daunting task, especially when time-to-market criticality is involved. Furthermore, not everybody involved with a project behaves as nobly, reliably, or knowledgeably as many processes might assume. People, despite popular process belief, are not purely resources built to implement a process. Realistically, we are process participants who have a diverse array of goals, desires, and capabilities that all affect how a process is pursued. Group dynamics in particular becomes an issue when pursuing enterprise projects involving many people. What we will therefore describe here is an OO process that can be followed with enterprise project scale, time-to-market considerations, and human constraints in mind. We will no doubt leave out process details that may also be pursued, but you should leave this section with an understanding of the core and practical steps to be performed.

Development Process Overview

Most literature on OO development focuses on object-oriented analysis (OOA), object-oriented development (OOD), and object-oriented programming (OOP). These are, after all, the essential aspects of a development process that distinguish OO from other development paradigms. But the enterprise development process involves much more than just pure OO development. The creation of enterprise software by an enterprise software development team begins with an initial charter and only truly ends when the maintenance of such software is no longer needed. Although many iterations of such an end-to-end process may occur in an overall actual software-development process, the basic flow of OO software development from charter to maintenance can be given:

1. *Project Charter:* Establish a charter detailing goals and objectives for the effort to be undertaken.
2. *Requirements Analysis:* Perform analysis of expected system behavior and system interfaces.
3. *Preliminary System Design:* Perform a preliminary design of a system with consideration for Commercial Off the Shelf (COTS) software, custom software, and reuse. Partition design into smaller problems to solve.
4. *Detailed Design:* Perform detailed design of core classes and interfaces.
5. *Implementation:* Implement the software. May involve custom code writing, as well as integrating with COTS.
6. *Unit Test:* Unit test the implementation.
7. *Assembly:* Assemble individual elements into discrete elements of behavior.
8. *Thread Test:* Test threads of behavior on assembled elements.
9. *Configuration Specification:* Define the assumed COTS and custom software configuration and versions.
10. *System Test:* Test a fully assembled and configured system.
11. *Deployment:* Deploy the system per the configuration specification.
12. *Maintenance:* Maintain operational software for bug fixes and upgrades.

Project Charter

It is very important to either receive or create a project charter. A *project charter* is a written vision and mission statement for a project that summarizes the key goals and objectives to be accomplished for a particular development effort. The project charter should be brief and shared with the individuals involved with the project so that everybody has a cohesive and collective understanding of what is to be accomplished. Not only is it important to concisely convey what the primary goals and objectives are, but it also is important for people to have genuine belief in the charter's significance. It should become the battle cry for development.

Requirements Analysis

Requirements analysis involves creating an understanding and model of what the system to be developed should do. A well-understood scope and boundary for the software to be developed should also be formed at this stage. Requirements analysis can be partitioned into behavioral analysis and interface analysis. Architects or analysis gurus should perform an initial analysis of the system and collect analysis models into packages that can eventually be handed off to developers.

Although analysis is very important for getting architects and developers to understand what the system is supposed to do, analysis paralysis should be avoided. Analysis paralysis occurs when a system is being overly analyzed and the process is hampered from further progression. This usually occurs when too many or non-interoperable people are involved with the initial analysis phase. Because the products of analysis (that is, models or conceptual diagrams) are necessarily abstract and imperfect, there is a tendency to spend too much time perfecting models that only vaguely define what the system is to do. The focus of initial analysis should always be to create an understanding of the overall system and then group smaller analysis packages for eventual handoff to developers for more detailed understanding. It is very important that you convey the fact that conceptual-analysis models are imperfect and only serve the purpose of requirements understanding.

System Behavioral Analysis

Regardless of whether you are actually given well-written requirements describing what is to be produced from your project, some form of requirements-analysis effort must be pursued. If you are given requirements, you should read through each requirement and build a picture of what concepts are involved, how the concepts relate, and what actions are being performed by and to each concept. If written requirements have not been provided or have been very loosely defined, it is at least important to create a conceptual-analysis model based on any interactions you have had with a customer or perhaps based on any ideas that have been conceived. If possible, such models should be run by the prospective customer for feedback.

Use-case analysis represents one popular technique for performing behavioral analysis and generating conceptual-analysis models. Use-case analysis involves the identification of primarily user-driven behavioral scenarios (that is, a "use case") to analyze. Each use case is defined by describing a sequence of steps that are involved with each behavior. Actors in a use case are those entities involved with realizing the outcome of a use case. A *precondition* specifies the initial state of the system before beginning a use case, whereas *postconditions* specify the state of a system after the use case. We will also describe scenario diagrams in the next section as conceptual-analysis models that are closely related to use cases and are used to describe system behavior.

System Interface Analysis

Interfaces to your system and to software that lie outside of the system boundary should also be analyzed and modeled. Interfaces to external software tend to be one piece of information that is particularly important for development to proceed. An analysis model of your understanding of such interfaces should also be developed. Interfaces between your system and other entities include external system interfaces, legacy system interfaces, database models, and user interfaces.

Preliminary System Design

Preliminary system design involves taking your conceptual-analysis model and transforming it into something that can be realized using COTS or custom software. Many times during analysis and the creation of a conceptual-analysis model, you will start to inject actual design constructs into the model. Regardless, concepts created during an analysis transform into more concrete design constructs during preliminary system design and can be used to create conceptual design models. Conceptual design models may be high-level views of the system to be developed and refer only to core design entities, controller classes, or system interface classes of a design. The details of which helper classes are needed to support such core elements are usually not included in a conceptual design model.

Furthermore, only core interfaces (that is, operations) on the core classes themselves may be defined. Such interfaces scope the responsibility of a class and may not yet define each input and output parameter exactly. Input and output parameters can be defined to convey semantic meaning behind a particular interface, but no strict interface definition applies at this stage.

The purpose of preliminary system design is to capture those primary design components that are to be involved with a design. Decisions for use of particular COTS, development of custom software components, or identified reusable components should be defined here. COTS evaluation and custom software prototyping should be pursued here to help aid in the decision-making process.

The product of preliminary design should be packages of conceptual design models accompanied by any relevant conceptual-analysis models. These preliminary design packages can be given to individual designers and developers to flesh out more detailed designs and implementations. The preliminary system design team, though larger than an analysis team, should also be relatively small. Architects with design experience should lead such efforts and solicit assistance from lead developers with particular COTS or development experiences.

Conceptual design models that describe logical relations between concepts and design constructs can actually be defined in terms of what are traditionally viewed as class diagrams. We will describe class diagrams in the next section for modeling class relations in a system, as well as for modeling conceptual designs. Conceptual design models that describe the behavior of a proposed design can also utilize the scenario diagrams that are described in the next section.

Detailed Design

The model packages handed to the designer/developer should correspond to individual software packages. This enables designers and developers to focus on a cohesive component of the system to be developed. Once a package of conceptual design and analysis models is handed off to a software designer/developer, he or she may opt to provide models which define any helper classes that support the conceptual model and define detailed interfaces on the core design constructs that were identified during preliminary system design.

Detailed designs should, at the very least, define package names, class names, and the core public method names and input/output parameter types (that is, operation signatures) that need to be defined for the core design elements identified by the conceptual design model. Other classes and interfaces used to support the core classes and methods defined here should also be described. Detailed designs that attempt to define every single class, method, and attribute before proceeding to implementation may be overkill in many situations and will significantly slow the development process. Detailed designs can use the modeling approach described in the next section by using class diagrams to describe detailed logical structure, and scenario diagrams to describe detailed behavioral semantics.

Implementation

After the core classes and their operation signatures have been defined, the developer can begin implementation using an OOP technique and language. Of course, OOP in this book advocates the use of Java as an OO language to implement the desired interfaces and behavior required of each class.

Very often, time-to-market competition among developers may push them to begin implementation of code before a design has even been defined. Although the push for rapid development is actually a healthy desire, the need to understand what the code should do via analysis and design models is key for ensuring that the right functionality will be provided. Furthermore, the need to understand how code development should be approached via design models is key for ensuring that such code will interoperate with code developed by other developers on a project. This understanding will also ensure that such code is making use of the right COTS products already selected for use on the project.

Some developers may indeed understand exactly what should be done without analysis and design models. But it is particularly key on enterprise development projects involving multiple people that a cohesive and coordinated view of development be maintained. The analysis and design models are the key tools to ensure that implementation will yield interoperable code as well as the desired code. Furthermore, if reuse can indeed be defined in analysis and design models, implementation may proceed much faster if developers make use of such models to identify other components to use with their own implementation efforts.

Unit Test

Unit testing involves testing software at the class and package level. Many times such tests are performed during implementation of a particular class and collection of classes. Although a debugger is often used to unit test classes during development, it is also important to create standalone test utilities to help test your code. Such unit test software can then be used to quickly regression test code when bugs are fixed and when functionality is added.

Assembly

Assembly involves getting a small group of developers together and assembling individually developed software classes into groups of classes that perform some specific service. A subset of the entire system behavior needs to be identified, along with the code that has been targeted to implement that behavior. The responsible developers must then integrate their code preferably with a target platform and environment in mind.

Thread Test

Thread test involves demonstrating that any assembled classes can interoperate. Threads of behavior are then demonstrated during thread test. Such behavioral threads can provide incremental assurance that the total system will yield the desired behavior when fully assembled and integrated. Very often assembly and thread test can occur among developers and should be coordinated by a software lead who is aware of the schedule for integrating the total system.

Configuration Specification

Although sometimes overlooked, the means by which enterprise software is to be configured should be specified. This includes any assumed versions of COTS software used, software platforms used, and custom software configuration. Custom software configuration should include instructions for how to build as well as deploy the software that was developed.

System Test

System test involves the functional/behavioral test of a fully assembled set of software that is to be deployed. System test should be performed using the assumed configuration that will be deployed. Other types of testing orthogonal to functional testing, such as load testing, system security testing, and performance testing, should also be performed at this stage on the system that most closely mimics what will be fielded.

Deployment

Deployment involves packaging the system that was tested and deploying it onto the machines that will host it for actual enterprise operation. The configuration specification should resemble what the deployment environment can support. The deployment environment should therefore closely resemble the system test environment.

Maintenance

Maintenance involves repairing defects while the system is deployed and in operation. Maintenance also involves providing upgrades to a fielded and operational system. Time to repair defects should be minimized and the ease with which upgrades can be installed should be maximized to enhance the availability of an enterprise system to its enterprise user base.

Iteration and Phases of Development

Although the general development-process flow just described must occur for some unit of work to be completed, iteration within the process will very often also occur. For example, if requirements have not been fully established at the start of a project, a subset can be analyzed and perhaps some preliminary design may begin. It may be apparent from the subset of requirements that some general design approaches may be pursued that involve evaluation and purchase of a particular COTS product. Thus, evaluation of such a product could be pursued while more requirements are obtained and analyzed. The same case for iteration may be made for all the development-process steps listed above.

If a particular project is large enough, it is also usually wise to partition the project into phases of development. Each subsequent phase represents an incremental enhancement over the previous phase. Figure 2.2 depicts this process. Here we see an example of three phases of an actual development process. Each phase focuses on the development of some particular functionality, with phase 2, for example, building on the efforts of phase 1.

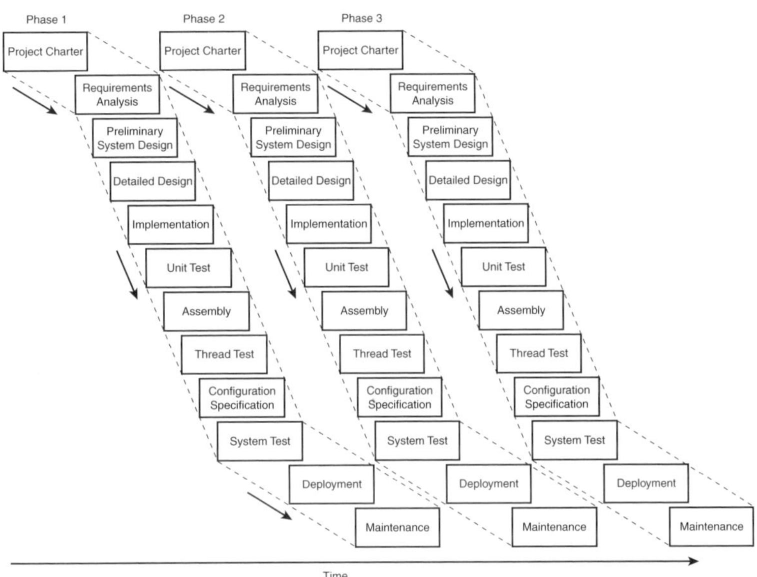

FIGURE 2.2
Phased project development.

Such a phased approach to development provides numerous benefits. The first key benefit is that after the first phase completes, the users of your enterprise system can begin to experience incremental upgrades in system features earlier, as opposed to waiting for the entire development process to complete for all functionality. The second key benefit is that engineering personnel who happen to have skills more catered to a specific set of steps in a development process can be gainfully employed throughout the software lifecycle. For example, developers who largely participate in detailed design, implementation, and unit test can begin work sooner rather than waiting for the entire analysis and preliminary design process to complete for a larger set of requirements. They can also work more consistently by moving on to subsequent phases rather than waiting for system test and deployment to complete and then waiting for the next large project to be analyzed and designed.

Unified Modeling Language

We talked a lot about generating models throughout an OO development process in the preceding section. Technically speaking, we use the term *model* here to mean an abstract and structured description of some system. A view of these system models is used to present such system descriptions to an end user in some form that they understand. Preferably, such views will have a graphical nature to facilitate ease of understanding. On large development teams, models and their views are essential to convey engineering analysis concepts and design ideas. A standard notation for such model views is also important so that people can better understand each other's analyses and designs. The Unified Modeling Language (UML) represents such a standard modeling notation.

UML represents a compromise and unification of primarily three major notation techniques. The Booch technique, Object Modeling Technique (OMT), and Object-Oriented Software Engineering technique (OOSE) represent the three techniques that have formed the core of UML. Other techniques have also been employed to model OO analyses and designs, such as Fusion and Coad/Yourdon. Nevertheless, we use UML throughout this book largely because of its currently large and growing industry-wide adoption.

Although UML has many features, we employ only a subset of UML in this book to keep our diagrams simple and focused on the topic at hand. Furthermore, UML is extensive, but it does have some drawbacks such as being overly complex in some regards and overly simplified in other regards. Thus we occasionally take some minor liberties in deviating from a purely standard notation. However, we point out such minor deviations when necessary.

Static Logical Structure Diagrams

A class diagram is primarily used as a design modeling view to depict classes, their relations, their attributes (*aka* fields), their operations (*aka* methods), and packages. Class diagrams can be used as both a preliminary design modeling tool and a detailed design modeling tool. When used as a detailed design modeling tool, the elements of a class diagram closely correspond to code. When used as a preliminary design modeling tool, the elements of a class diagram are less strictly defined and represent more of a conceptual design model to express ideas about a design. Class diagrams can also be used as a conceptual-analysis tool to model higher-level concepts and their relations. Thus class diagrams model some static logical structure that describes a conceptual analysis, conceptual design, or detailed design view.

Figure 2.3 presents, via example, the notation used in the various elements of a class diagram. The following bullet items describe each feature of this diagram and how such conventions will be used throughout the book for design models:

- *Classes:* Rectangular boxes represent classes.
- *Class Names:* Class names are indicated at the top of a class box, such as `ClassName`.
- *Class Packages:* Packages to which classes belong are optionally indicated beneath the class name, such as `(from PackageName)`.

- *Packages:* Packages are shown as a rectangle with a small box in the upper-left corner and have a package name displayed, such as PackageName.
- *Class Attributes:* One or more attributes may be optionally shown below the class name and package name. Some diagrams may choose to display only a select set of attributes.
- *Class Operations:* One or more operations may optionally be shown below the attributes in a class. Some diagrams may choose to display only a select set of operations.
- *Visibility:* Visibility of an attribute or operation is indicated as a solid rectangle (or plus symbol +) for public, a rectangle with a key (or pound symbol #) for protected, or a rectangle with a lock (or minus symbol -) for private. A rectangle with a hammer is also sometimes used to indicate implementation that simply corresponds to reverse-engineered or package private methods in our models. As a general practice in this book, if visibility is not shown, public visibility may be assumed.
- *Stereotypes:* A stereotype enclosed by << >> simply corresponds to a specialization of a class, attribute, or operation that it is associated with. We most often use <<static>> to designate a static attribute or method and <<Interface>> to indicate that a class is actually an interface.
- *Attribute Syntax:* Attribute descriptions follow a syntax whereby a visibility level may be optionally shown, followed by an optionally displayed stereotype, followed by an attribute name, followed by an attribute type, and followed by an optional initialization value. Attributes within a class tend to be listed in an order that represents a logical grouping of attributes.
- *Static Attributes:* Static attributes may be designated with a <<static>> stereotype label or a $ stereotype icon.
- *Operation Syntax:* Operation descriptions follow a syntax whereby a visibility level may be optionally shown, followed by an optionally displayed stereotype, followed by a method name, optionally followed by zero or more parameter name and type pairs, and followed by an optional return type. Operations are listed in an order within a class that represents a logical grouping of operations.
- *Pseudo-Operations:* Certain design diagrams, especially conceptual design diagrams, may display method names that are pseudonames displayed for informational purposes only. For example, we might use the name setXXX() to indicate that a method name has some pattern, such as setThis(), setThat(), setSomethingElse(), and so on.
- *Associations:* A class such as ClassName that has an association with another class such as NamedAssociationClass depicts the association as a straight line. An association can have a name, and each end of an association can have role names indicating what role the class closest to it plays in the association.

- *Navigability:* When one class such as `ClassName` can access another class such as `AssociatedClass` via a particular association, but not the other way around, an arrow displays navigability.
- *Multiplicity:* When a class such as `ClassName` has a relationship with another class such as `AssociatedClass`, multiplicity of such relations can be displayed. Multiplicity can have many forms, such as a one-to-zero-or-one relation, a one-to-zero-or-more (many) relation, and a one-to-one-or-more relation. If no multiplicity is shown, the default of one is generally assumed.
- *Qualified Association:* When a class such as `ClassName` has a special X-to-many relation with another class such as `KeyedClass` and that relation is "keyed," we designate this with a box displaying a key name and type at the end of the keyed relation. A keyed relation means that each element on the "many" end of a relation can be uniquely identified by a key name of a particular key type. Once a keyed relation is indicated, the multiplicity of the relation at the `KeyedClass` end goes to one.
- *Aggregation:* Aggregation is shown with a line and diamond on the end of the containing class when the one class such as `ClassName` contains another class such as `ContainedClass`. Aggregation implies that the lifetime of the relation to the `ContainedClass` is tied to the lifetime of the containing class `ClassName`.
- *Uses Relations:* When a class such as `ClassName` has a general dependency on another class such as `UsedClass`, a dashed-line arrow depicting the dependency is shown.
- *Inheritance:* When a `SubClass` inherits from a `BaseClass`, a solid line with a triangle at the end of the `BaseClass` is shown.
- *Inherited Operations:* Note that we often don't display certain methods on subclasses when the base class displays such a method. If the subclass overrides such a method, we may on occasion display that method on the subclass.
- *Abstract Classes:* An `AbstractClass` has an italicized class name.
- *Interfaces:* When an `InterfaceImplementation` implements a particular `InterfaceType`, a dashed line with a triangle at the end of the `InterfaceType` is shown.
- *Implemented Operations:* Note that we often don't display certain methods on interface implementations when the interface displays such a method.
- *Or-Association:* An or-association is indicated with the word `{or}` on a dashed line spanning two relations. Or-associations provide a means for indicating whether a particular `ClassA` has a relation to one class such as `ClassB` or another class such as `ClassC`, but not to both.
- *Notes:* Notes can also be displayed in a diagram and attached to various diagram elements.

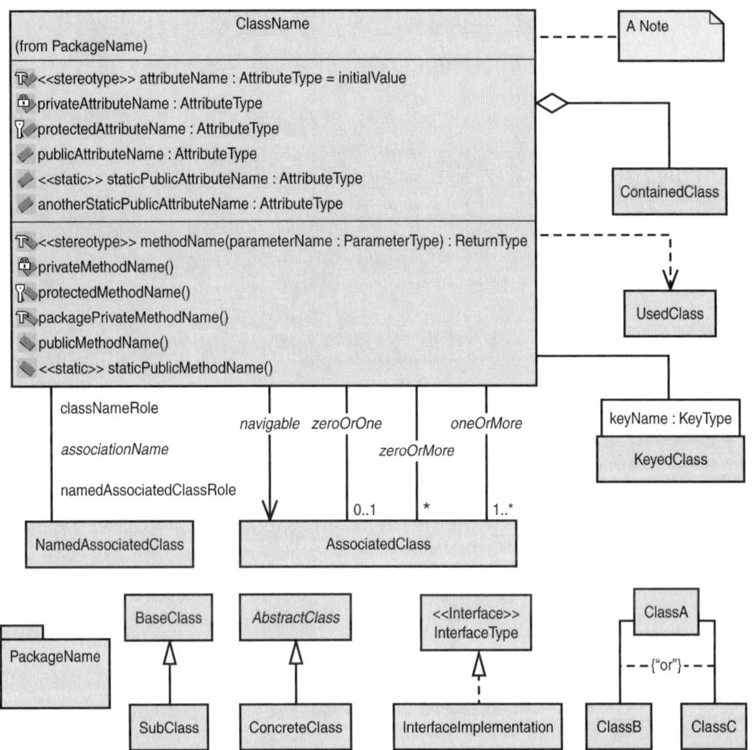

FIGURE 2.3
Class diagram notation.

Class diagrams can also be used with conceptual-analysis models. In such models, a concept correlates to a class, and relations between concepts are defined in the same way that they are defined for class diagrams. Attributes of a concept can also be displayed, but they will not have the rigid programmatic meaning that attributes on a design class will tend to convey. Operations can also be associated with a concept to convey what responsibilities and activities are to be associated with the concept. Operations of course also do not have the rigid programming semantics associated with operations on a design class. The loosely defined nature of conceptual-design model diagrams in fact may also adhere to the loosely interpreted semantic conventions of analysis models with the exception that concepts should correspond to elements of a design solution in conceptual design models.

Dynamic Behavior Diagrams

A scenario diagram is primarily used as a design modeling view to indicate dynamic behavior between object instances. Object instances of particular classes are the primary actors in scenario diagrams. Sequences of method calls between objects are also shown in scenario diagrams with parameter instances being passed between objects during calls. When used as a detailed design modeling tool, scenario diagrams actually correspond to an illustration of how object instances communicate with the use of actual method names and object parameters in the diagram. Conceptual design models have objects that may simply represent an instance of a design construct and may not necessarily correspond to real objects. Methods in the diagram may also simply correspond to a general type of behavior that can be performed on such design objects. Finally, objects in conceptual-analysis models represent some concept identity in the problem domain, and methods between such identities correspond to high-level responsibilities that are associated with concepts and messages passed between conceptual identities.

Figure 2.4 presents, via example, the notation used to represent the various elements of a particular type of scenario diagram that we use in this book called a *sequence diagram*. The following bullet items describe each feature of this diagram and how such conventions will be used throughout the book for analysis and design models:

- *Time:* Sequences in time proceed from top to bottom.
- *Objects:* Object instances are represented by boxes at the top of the diagram.
- *Object Names:* An object-instance name can be followed by a class name inside of an object box.
- *Methods:* Method calls are shown as arrows from the invoking object onto the invoked object. Method calls may also be made by an object onto itself.
- *Method Names:* Method names are displayed on method-call arrows, but may simply be more descriptive words designating an action to invoke on some concept or design entity in conceptual model diagrams.
- *Method Parameters:* Object parameters to such methods may also be optionally displayed in method calls. Although it's not standard UML, we also optionally show a return value from a method call.
- *Method Scope:* Scope of a method call is designated by a long rectangle on the dashed line under an object. Thus, a method call that calls an object which itself calls another object before it returns from the original call can be designated with scope.

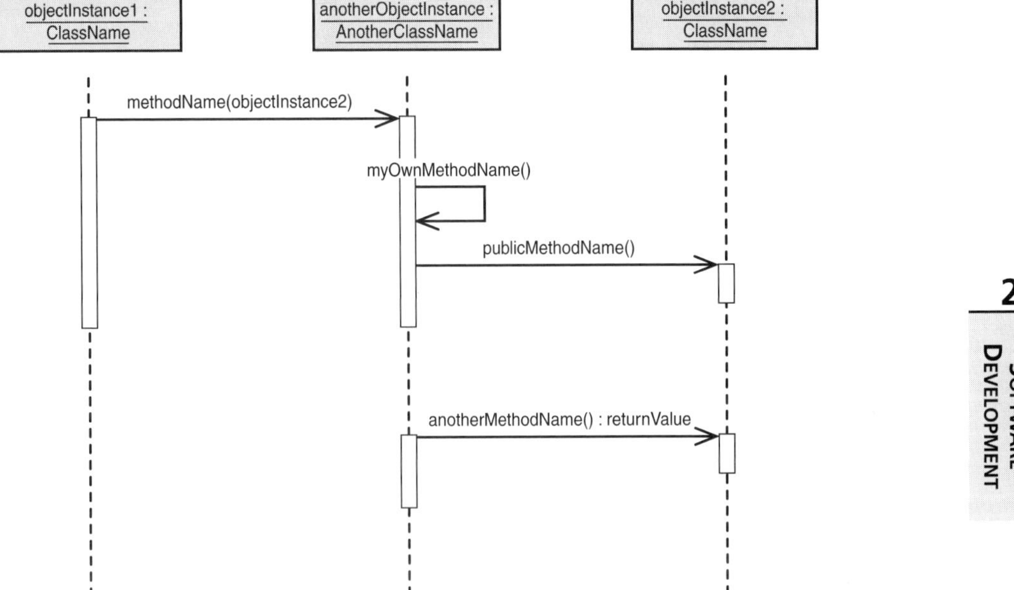

FIGURE 2.4
Scenario diagram notation.

Conclusions

The object-oriented software-development paradigm is an approach and a set of technologies that provide a foundation for enabling practical enterprise-system development. The principles of modularity, abstraction, and encapsulation inherent to OO enable reuse, scalability, maintainability, and rapid development, which serve as key enablers for enterprise-system development. Although OO is an enabler and makes enterprise software development practical, it is also a paradigm that must be used within the context of a practical development process. An iterative and phased process of analysis, design, implementation, assembly, deployment, and testing must complement the use of OO in the enterprise and follow a few important guidelines to account for practical issues of time-to-market and human dynamics. An OO process that generates conceptual-analysis models, design models, and detailed design models using standard modeling notations such as UML are also key ingredients for making an enterprise software-development effort a success. As we'll see in the next chapter, practical scalability of enterprise application development is further enabled by employing a component-based development paradigm that fundamentally builds on the object-oriented development paradigm.

Component-Based Software Development for the Enterprise

CHAPTER

3

IN THIS CHAPTER

- Enterprise Components 40
- Component Models 43
- Component-Based Development 46
- Standards 49

Component-based software development has blossomed in recent years due to its capability to enable enterprise software to be developed more rapidly and with a higher degree of reliability. Although component-based development builds on object-oriented development, components encapsulate a problem and solution domain at a higher level of abstraction than strict object-oriented methods provide. Because enterprise applications and the enterprise development approaches described in this book rely on component-based development concepts, we provide an overview of components, component models, component-based development processes, and component model standards in this chapter.

In this chapter, you will learn:

- The motivation behind the usage and creation of components to develop enterprise applications.
- The generic architecture and elements of a component model.
- The process used during a component-based development process.
- About the standard component models employed by this book.

Enterprise Components

The fundamental units of object-oriented (OO) software are classes and objects. Classes encapsulate fine-grained concepts of a problem and solution, whereas objects represent instances of classes created during the runtime operation of a system. The OO development process helps enable reuse at the class level, which is a level of encapsulation that is usually too low to be of immediate use on an enterprise project. Although it is possible to generate OO design models that closely map to classes, the jump from analysis to design on enterprise-scale development projects can often be a big one.

Components offer a coarser-grained means to encapsulate problems. As depicted in Figure 3.1, whereas a class having object state and a set of operations can encapsulate a singular concept, a component represents a particular service as a function of one or more such concepts. Components thus expose multiple interfaces as a service to component users. The interfaces encapsulate what the component offers as a service and shields any visibility into the implementation details. Because components represent a logical collection of one or more finer-grained classes and are defined at a higher and coarser-grained level, a component may directly encapsulate a partitioned problem that more directly can be produced from analyses and design models.

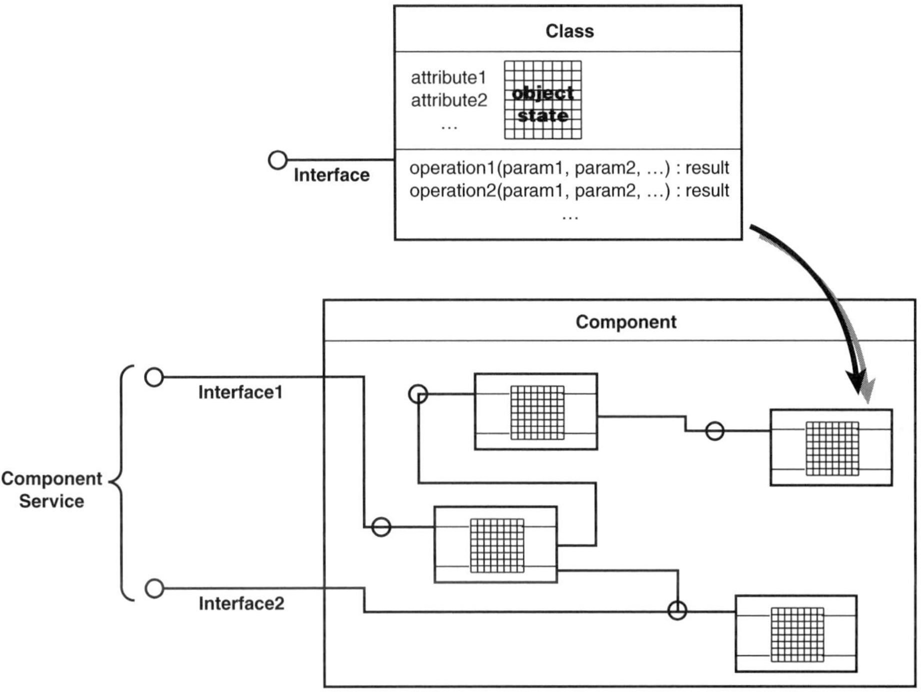

FIGURE 3.1
Classes/objects and components.

Thus, a problem, as shown in Figure 3.2, may be composed of a number of concepts that map to classes during design. If the problem is partitioned during analysis and preliminary design into higher-level services, also shown in Figure 3.2, then a more rapid enterprise development process can be enabled with the more direct mapping of services to coarse-grained components. Folks who are closer to the problem domain can also better understand the design of the system as it is described in terms of higher-level components.

Components thus offer many benefits to enterprise development. Components build on object-oriented software and development concepts to provide a higher-level model of development and enable the faster construction of enterprise applications. Furthermore, the quality of a system can be enhanced because it will most likely be in the interest of commercial component vendors to focus on enhancing the quality of a component and providing well-documented interfaces. The requirements for in-house personnel to have knowledge of a particular underlying implementation technology, as well as less service implementation–specific knowledge, will also be minimized.

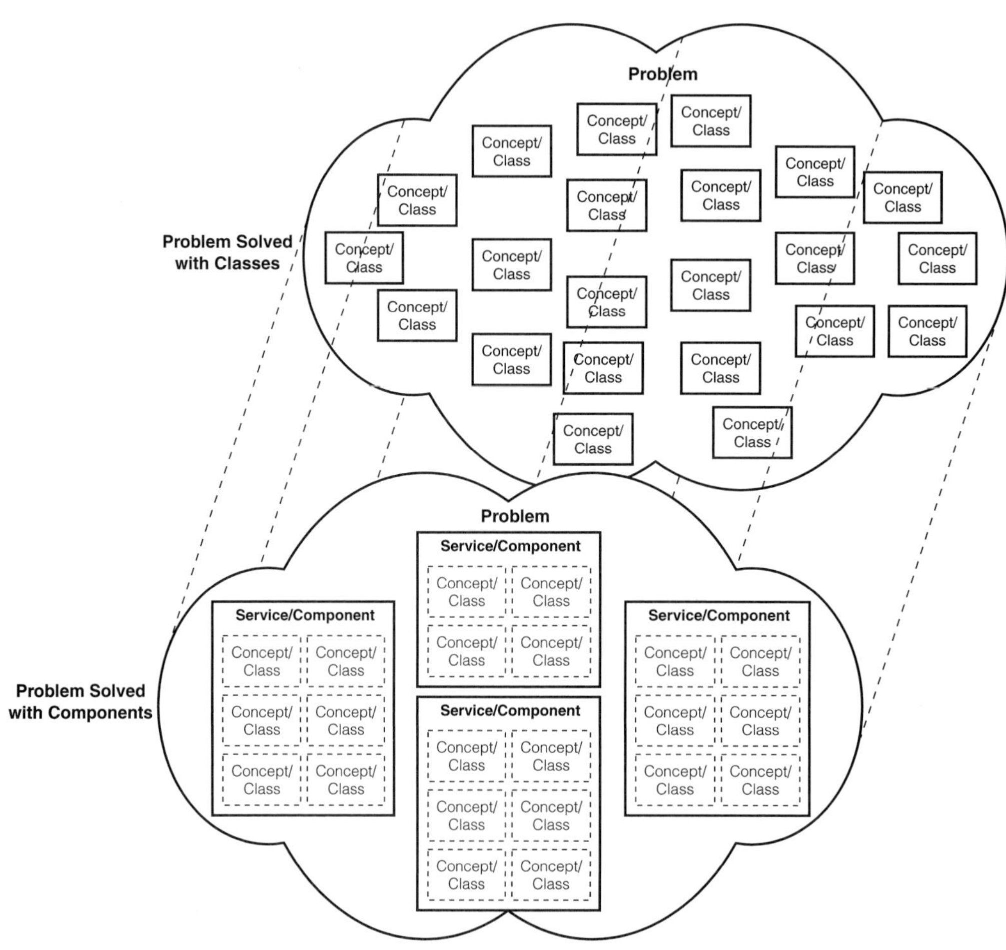

FIGURE 3.2
Problems, classes, and components.

As the availability of reusable components increases, the use of components in the enterprise will grow. Time-to-market factors have driven organizations to pursue use of components in enterprise systems. Furthermore, the growth and practicality of component models, development approaches, and standards have also enabled the popularity of component usage in the enterprise. As you'll see in this chapter, the shift in enterprise development has evolved to require that development staff spend less time on programming and dedicate more time to component assembly.

Component Models

A component model is a set of requirements to which components and their environments adhere. Component models are primarily concerned with constraining the nature of interfaces that a software component makes publicly available. By constraining a component's interface to adhere to some "knowable" nature, a component model can guarantee a certain level of interoperability between components, for application software using those components, and for application environments on top of which the components operate.

Many different views are held as to what exactly the term *component model* means. As you'll see, various criteria may be used to distinguish between different component models. To some people, *component models* are patterns of design to which software adheres. More generically, component models involve specifying interfaces on components, component environment assumptions, and inter-component contracts. We briefly explore these various facets of component models in this section.

Generic Component Model

Figure 3.3 depicts the basic elements of a component model. First and foremost in a component model is, of course, the component itself. The component is an encapsulation of the code utilized in an application. Although the component may itself be application-specific code, we separately diagram the fact that other application-specific code may rest on top of a component and utilize the services it provides. Finally, the container represents an environment in which a component operates. The container itself may offer a set of services that components from the same component model may tap in a standard fashion.

A component also has various facets to it. The most important facet is the set of interfaces that it exposes and assumes. In addition to interfaces to a component, the interfaces to a container utilized by a component may also be defined in a component model. Standard events that can be generated by a component, as well as events to which a component can subscribe, may also be defined in a component model. Component models may also specify a standard means by which a component exposes descriptive state attributes. Finally, many component models allow for a means to customize a component's behavior and attributes.

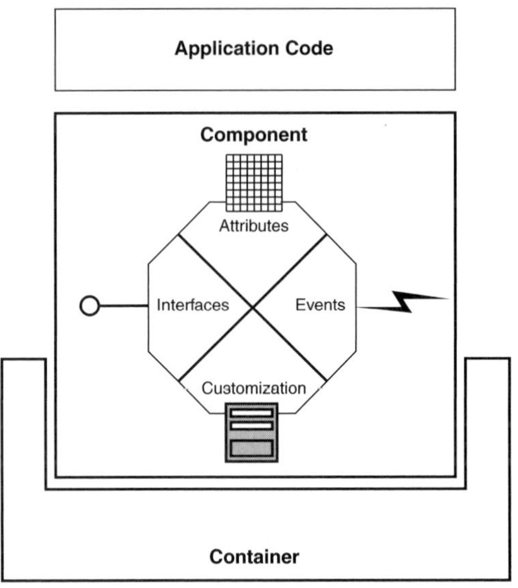

FIGURE 3.3
A generic component model.

Component Model Interfaces

Interfaces in a component model define the primary contract between other code entities and components. Other code entities may be containers, application code, other components, other component models, and providers of some proprietary service. Certain component models may attempt to rigidly define each type of interface, whereas others may be concerned only with the application interface to a component. Figure 3.4 depicts some of the more common interface styles that can be defined by a particular component model. These various interface classifications are defined here:

- *Component APIs*: A component Application Programming Interface (API) defines a set of standard interfaces that applications can use to tap the services of a component. We represent this type of direct interface usage in the figure by showing a generalized interface symbol depicting the component's exposed interface.
- *Design Patterns*: A design pattern is set of classes and interfaces and their relationships that provide a common design solution to a common problem classification. Application code specializes a design pattern by providing a more concrete and application-specific design behavior based on the design pattern. We represent this specialization nature in the figure with a UML inheritance arrowhead and solid line.

- *Component SPIs*: A component Service Provider Interface (SPI) defines a set of standard interfaces that the provider of some service adheres to and implements. Different underlying services can thus be plugged in and out without modification to the application or container code. We represent this exclusive interface implementation nature in the figure with a UML inheritance arrow and dashed line.
- *Component-to-Container Interfaces*: A component-to-container interface defines the interface to a container environment assumed by a component. We represent this type of direct interface usage in the figure by showing a generalized interface symbol depicting the container's exposed interface.
- *Container-to-Component Interfaces*: A container-to-component interface defines the interface to a component as assumed by a container. We represent this type of direct interface usage in the figure by showing a generalized interface symbol depicting the component's exposed interface.

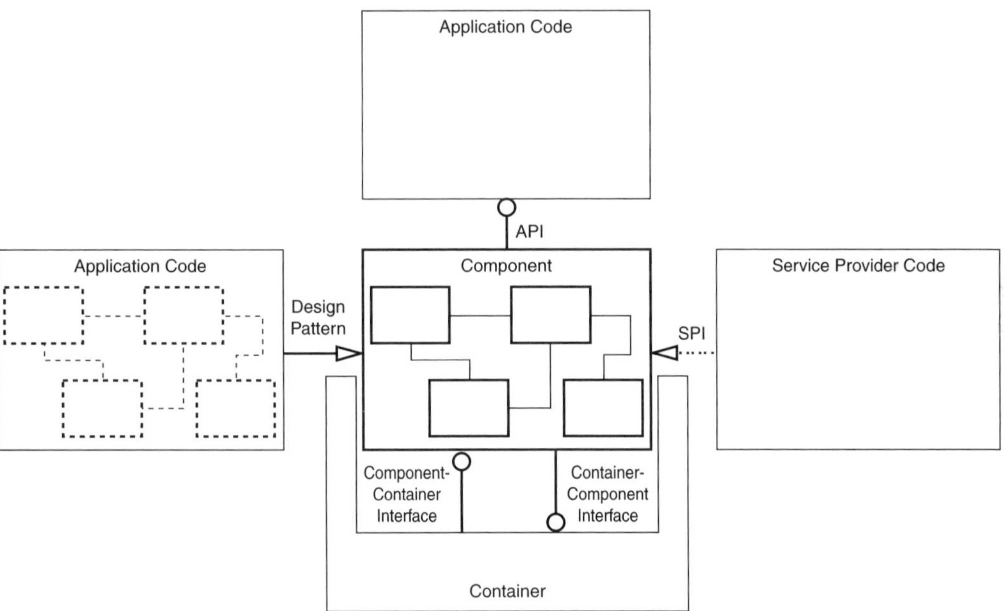

FIGURE 3.4
Component interface types.

Component model interfaces also may be defined in different manners. Some component model interfaces are defined in a language-independent fashion, whereas others are language-dependent. Language dependence, platform dependence, and communications protocol dependence are just a few examples of some of the component model interface specification styles. A few key ways in which component models can be defined are listed here:

- *Language Dependence*: Some component models define interfaces in a language-independent fashion. Other component models are defined in terms of a specific language. Language-independent component models use an interface definition language which serves as an intermediate language that can be mapped to a specific computing language.
- *Platform Dependence*: Some component models actually depend on a particular operating system or hardware platform, whereas most component models examined in this book are platform-independent.
- *Distributed Communications Protocol Dependence*: Component models may assume a particular underlying distributed communications protocol among components and applications. Other component models may be protocol-independent and defined at a higher level of abstraction.
- *Data Representation Dependence*: In addition to a communications protocol, some component model interfaces also define a standard data representation format for messages passed to and from component interfaces.
- *Communications Synchronicity*: Some component models may assume a synchronous model of component interfacing in which a caller of a component may block until it receives a result. Asynchronous communications may assume that a caller of a component passes a standard message/event to a component and allows an underlying message/event-handling service to deliver the message/event to the component.
- *Interface Definition Rigidity*: Some component models specify particular interface operation signatures. User-defined interface operation signatures will also typically be allowed. Some component models may instead permit and define a particular operation signature pattern that components should follow.
- *Behavior Customization*: Some components may expose their behavior completely by opening their implementation for access and modification by the component user (white box components). Other components may completely restrict the user to the defined interface with no behavior and implementation visibility (black box components). Still other components may enable modification of behavior via customization features (gray box components).

Component-Based Development

Along with the growth of component usage in the enterprise came the need for a new look at how enterprise software development should proceed using components. Component-Based Development (CBD) is the process by which organizations develop software using components. Components may be premade and purchased as commercial off the shelf (COTS) entities, they may be modified versions of COTS components, or they may be made from scratch by in-house staff. Although components are ideally purchased as COTS components, it will often be necessary to at least customize COTS components or perhaps create your own application-specific components. So how does one proceed with a development process assuming such a new model of software development?

A few approaches to CBD have been proposed by key OO and CBD players, such as the Rational Software Corporation and Sterling Software, Incorporated. Many approaches rely on UML as the notation from which components are described and related. We will not present a specific organization's CBD process here but will highlight some of the salient features involved in most CBD processes. Although the general process flow presented in Chapter 2, "Object-Oriented Software Development for the Enterprise," and illustrated in Figure 2.2 still applies to CBD, the process focus shifts for CBD, and the details behind a few steps are modified. With CBD the focus of the development process shifts away from time spent in implementation. More importance in CBD is ascribed to analysis, preliminary design, and assembly. A recommended CBD process that builds on the OO process recommended in Chapter 2 is described here:

- *Project Charter*: A CBD process benefits from a project charter as does an OO process.
- *Analysis Pattern Identification (During Requirements Analysis)*: Analysis patterns may be identified that are common problems described as system behaviors that can be used to map to design patterns. After an analysis pattern is identified, the specific system behavior requirements can be used to customize the analysis pattern.
- *External Component Interface Analysis (During Requirements Analysis)*: The component models, standard component interfaces, and specific component interfaces to external system components should also be identified at this stage.
- *System Component Interface Analysis (During Requirements Analysis)*: Any standard component model interfaces to the system under development should also be identified.
- *Component Model Technology Identification (During Preliminary System Design)*: The assumed component model interface to the system under development may indeed drive the technology and tools used to design the system.
- *Component Identification (During Preliminary System Design)*: Components of the system should be defined in terms of the interfaces and technology they must support.
- *Component Selection (During Preliminary System Design)*: COTS components should be evaluated for fitness and applicability of use. Components developed on other projects should also be evaluated for use. The component should be qualified in terms of functional support, quality, technology support, and degree of customization required and supported. The components should then be acquired for use.

- *Component Design Adaptation (During Detailed Design)*: A component's behavior will ideally be altered using an easy-to-use customization interface. This may involve specifying a component's behavior using a descriptor file or perhaps via a set of design-time attributes.
- *Component Implementation Specialization (During Implementation)*: A component may also need to be modified in code, perhaps extending the existing component code via subclassing. Design patterns in particular will need to have a concrete implementation.
- *Component Test (During Unit Test)*: After a component is selected, adapted, and perhaps specialized, it should be unit tested. The component test should proceed much quicker than the unit test of code created from scratch.
- *Component Assembly (During Assembly)*: Components should be assembled into individual modules that can be separately tested. Modules may also have their own customization descriptors.
- *Module Test (During Thread Test)*: The behavior of an individual module, serving as an assembly of components, should be tested and verified.
- *Component Configuration Specification (During Configuration Specification)*: The specification of a configuration is even more important with CBD. Because more COTS components will presumably be utilized, more component versioning needs to be tracked. Furthermore, any assumptions for custom components should be detailed, including their presumed deployment environment and constraints. Many CBD approaches even allow for the specification of a configuration using component descriptors themselves. The component modules are then configured into a cohesive application.
- *System Test*: System test with CBD involves testing a cohesive application per a particular component configuration.
- *Deployment*: Deployment of a component-based system should have a deployed configuration that matches a configuration in which it was validated. The flexibility with which a system can be deployed via customization of component, module, and application properties can actually be a pitfall of CBD. The particular configuration of a deployed system thus needs to have gone through some level of system test to qualify such a configuration.
- *Maintenance*: Lastly, the maintenance phase of a system will ideally be more efficient due to the component-based nature of the system. Components may ideally be swapped out for replacement with other component implementations with less time spent on repair. This, of course, enhances system availability for the user base.

With a CBD approach, less time needs to be spent on implementation, and more time can be dedicated to more careful analyses, design, planning, and integration. Tools for CBD have blossomed in the marketplace, including tools for the custom development of components, the operational management of components, and the assembly and deployment of components. This book and the J2EE, in fact, rely on the fundamental underlying principles of CBD.

Standards

Thus far in this chapter, we have discussed in detail the benefits of components, component models, and CBD. In all of this discussion, we have neglected to mention specific standards. Standard component models provide standard interface methodologies and technologies not only between applications and components, but also between components and their container environments. Standards define contracts between components and applications, other components, service providers, and container environments. In this section, we briefly define a few of the key standards that affect Java enterprise system development. We also describe a few common design patterns that can be utilized during Java enterprise system development.

Standard Component Models

Many standard component models exist in the market today. In this book, we aim to focus on those models that can be used to build Java enterprise systems. Although many independent Java-based components could be used in enterprise applications before the J2EE, the J2EE does offer an integrated and simplified means to access such components from applications, as well as to build new enterprise components. We define some of the pure Java-based component models here, as well as a few other key models, most of which can also be used in Java enterprise environments. The Object Management Group (OMG) and Microsoft Corporation have also defined enterprise component models. The OMG model has even been partially incorporated by the J2EE model. The various enterprise component models that are described or referenced throughout this book include the following:

- *Applets*: Java applets define simple container-to-component and component-to-container interfaces enabling Java code to run inside of an applet container that is embedded in a Web browser.
- *JavaBeans*: The JavaBeans component model defines a standard model for writing Java code that can be customized at design-time, and exposes its attributes, events, and interfaces to JavaBean containers. Containers are typically embedded into an integrated development environment such that JavaBean components can be customized during design-time using GUI-based tools. A standard JavaBeans container context interface and standard component-to-component interface model known as the InfoBus have also been defined for the JavaBeans component model.
- *CORBA*: The Common Object Request Broker Architecture (CORBA) defines a standard model for enabling distributed access to components implemented in any language. A standard communications container environment, known as the ORB, handles transforming calls from distributed clients into data sent via a standard communications protocol to server-side container code that invokes the distributed object method. In addition to a standard component communications and invocation infrastructure, a standard set of higher-level distributed component services and facilities is also defined within the CORBA model.

- *RMI*: The Remote Method Invocation (RMI) framework defines a Java-specific interface model for enabling distributed access to components. The RMI container environment is equipped with the Java platform and has been extended to support communication using the same underlying communications protocol as CORBA's standard protocol.
- *COM*: Microsoft's Component Object Model (COM) defines a standard model for interfacing with components implemented on Microsoft platforms. The Distributed Component Object Model (DCOM) is a distributed communications version of the COM model. ActiveX and OLE are also Microsoft-centric models that predate the COM and DCOM models.
- *Java APIs/SPIs*: Java is much more than just a language. Various Java APIs actually define a standard set of component services that can be used by applications to access services such as databases (JDBC), naming and directory services (JNDI), transaction services (JTA and JTS), messaging services (JMS), and trading/discovery services (Jini). Furthermore, many of these API models allow one to plug in different underlying service providers using an SPI.
- *J2EE Web Components*: Java Servlets and JavaServer Pages represent server-side components for handling Web requests and generating Web presentation content. Such Web components operate and run inside of J2EE-based Web container environments.
- *J2EE Enterprise JavaBeans*: Enterprise JavaBeans (EJBs) are server-side application components adhering to a standard model; they operate inside of EJB containers and servers. Such servers can provide a standard set of infrastructure services to EJBs, such as transactions, security, and scalability.
- *CORBAcomponents*: CORBAcomponents is a CORBA-based application serving model. CORBAcomponents was not a final standard at the time of this writing, but preliminary specification documentation indicates that the CORBAcomponent model will bear a close resemblance to the EJB model.
- *Microsoft DNA*: The Microsoft Distributed Network Architecture (DNA) is Microsoft's integrated distributed application serving architecture environment for Microsoft platforms. DNA incorporates many of Microsoft's standard components for enterprise applications running on the Microsoft platform.

Design Patterns

As a final note, we briefly describe a few common design patterns in this section. A design pattern is a set of classes, interfaces, and their relationships that provide a common design solution to a common problem classification. A design pattern is defined in terms of an intended use, the common problem that it attempts to solve, a design structure of classes/interfaces and their relationships, participant and collaborating objects, expected solution results, and implementation considerations. By identifying patterns that recur when solving problems, a developer can quickly recognize and select a solution to a problem given a suite of design pattern solutions. As we alluded to earlier, patterns of analysis can also be identified during requirements analysis. Analysis patterns can generate common analysis models, which can then be related to common design patterns. Some authors have even postulated the use of anti-patterns during development which identify those common design patterns that should be avoided when developing systems.

Identified design patterns are often expressed in terms of more abstract design models as opposed to concrete implementation solutions. Application designs can specialize a design pattern by providing the concrete and application-specific design features that make the design pattern useful. Nevertheless, many design patterns can be modeled in code and can provide a common component and interface framework that can be inherited and implemented by concrete application solutions. Following are some of the more common design patterns that we have found to be the most useful and to which we sometimes refer throughout the book:

- *Adapter Pattern*: An adapter is used to adapt the implementation of one class's interface to support a new underlying implementation. The client interface of the adapter remains constant. Java APIs can often be classified as satisfying the adapter pattern. APIs such as JDBC, JNDI, and JMS provide a standard interface to application clients while allowing for different underlying service providers.
- *Factory Pattern*: A factory is a general framework for creating new object instances. Some generic factory frameworks can create instances of objects of specific types given a type name and initialization parameters for the construction of that type. Factories can be used to create objects that are nondistributed or distributed.
- *Singleton Pattern*: A singleton provides a means to ensure that only one object instance of a class is created and referenced by clients accessing that class. Most often, singletons are defined for a particular process. However, means for defining singletons within a certain distributed processing domain can also be defined.
- *MVC Pattern*: The Model-View-Controller pattern defines a standard way to design systems such that the model, view, and control aspects are separately encapsulated. Model encapsulations represent system state and the relations between system states. View encapsulations represent means to present the same underlying model to different client views of that model. The controller encapsulation provides the means by which a model is manipulated by a client and stimulates updates to a client view.
- *Strategy Pattern*: Strategy patterns encapsulate interchangeable underlying algorithms and provide the same interface for accessing such algorithms. A strategy pattern is similar to an adapter pattern, but it is mainly used to provide pluggable policies and algorithmic processing modules in a design.

- *Command Pattern*: Command patterns encapsulate a command for performing some operation. Generic command handlers may also be defined to take a command and funnel it to a specific command handler that has been associated with the command.
- *Subject-Observer Pattern*: Subject-observer patterns encapsulate the subject of some event that should be observed. Subjects have many encapsulated observer objects that are interested in such events. Standard interfaces for registering, deregistering, and notifying observers can exist on subjects, whereas standard interfaces for being notified can exist on observers. Standard subject-observer event encapsulations may also be implemented.
- *Proxy Pattern*: Proxy patterns provide an intermediate object that is used to make a request to an endpoint object. Clients use the proxy, which, depending on certain configurable parameters, contacts the endpoint object.
- *Composite Pattern*: Composite patterns define entities which represent a component that can be contained by one or more composite objects. Composite objects themselves are components and can be contained by other composite objects.

Many other design patterns exist and can be used to create component frameworks within which you can define other application-specific components. We encourage you to explore Appendix B, "Additional Resources," to learn where you can find more design pattern information.

Conclusions

A component can help you encapsulate a collection of interfaces more directly useful to an enterprise as a particular service in a much broader sense than can classes and objects. Components have a coarse-grained nature that facilitates more rapid application development and reuse at a higher level. A component-based development process differs from a pure object-oriented development process in that the focus shifts to component identification, evaluation, and assembly and away from lower-level class identification and development. Component models define interface contracts between components and containers, between components and their applications, and among components themselves. Although software reuse has been somewhat of a pipe dream for many organizations, standard component models help stimulate more widespread reuse in the software industry by defining standard software interfaces. Standard software interface models facilitate exchange between software component producers and consumers. Enterprise systems development in particular has benefited from the use of components with components serving as one of the core underpinnings of Java enterprise development and the J2EE.

Java Foundations for Enterprise Development

CHAPTER

4

IN THIS CHAPTER

- **Java Features and Versions 54**
- **Java Platform Architecture 57**
- **Java Files and Tools 59**
- **Java Language 64**
- **Core Java Language APIs 73**
- **Collection APIs 81**
- **Input/Output and State Persistence APIs 87**
- **Threading APIs 93**
- **Date and Time APIs 97**
- **Java Applets 99**

The Java technologies to be described throughout this book can be directly applied to specific aspects of problems that plague an enterprise. All of these technologies rest on a bedrock of Java language, Java platform, and Java API features. This chapter provides a brief overview of these foundational Java concepts and technologies on which the technologies throughout the remainder of this book depend. This chapter may serve as a refresher for some readers, or some may decide to skip this chapter altogether if they are already familiar with such content. Only a subset of the total Java 2 Standard Edition platform features are discussed in this chapter. The remaining chapters in this book fill in the blanks and cover all other Java 2 Platform Standard Edition and Enterprise Edition packages and features.

In this chapter, you will learn:

- Some of Java's features that make it useful to the enterprise development process, as well as a brief history of Java's evolution from the research labs into the enterprise.
- The architecture of the standard Java development and runtime environments.
- The basic Java file types involved in development, the environment and tools used for building Java code, and the basic structure of common Java file types.
- The basic elements of the Java language.
- The basic elements of Java 2 that extend the Java language with encapsulated OO APIs.
- The basic elements of Java 2 collections for managing collections of objects.
- The basic elements of Java 2 input/output mechanisms for transferring data between the Java environment and an external environment.
- The concepts behind thread synchronization and basic Java 2 elements for creating threads.
- The basic Java 2 elements for manipulating dates and time.
- The basic Java 2 elements and steps for creating applets.

Java Features and Versions

Java is an object-oriented language with many APIs and standard frameworks enabling it to be used as an enterprise component model platform as well. Java has a lot of built-in features and a simplicity about it that has rendered it very popular with all types of developers. In particular, enterprise developers have gravitated to Java due to its features that enable the faster construction of more reliable enterprise applications. The applicability of Java to the enterprise didn't occur overnight, however. Java's initial conception, in fact, was spawned from embedded application research efforts. This section highlights some of Java's features that make it useful to the enterprise development process, as well as provides a brief history of Java's evolution from the research labs and into the enterprise.

Java's Attractive Enterprise Features

Java provides a simple and extremely rich set of programmatic features to facilitate rapid application development in an operating-system and hardware-platform–independent manner. Java also provides an object-oriented as well as a component-based platform for building sophisticated applications. Although Java was originally touted as the language for the Internet by enabling mobile Java code to be run inside of Web browsers, because of its features, it has fast become one of the most widely used languages and platforms for building enterprise systems. The reason for Java's growth as a tool to build enterprise systems lies within its features, including these:

- *Object-Oriented*: The Java language has a fairly pure and intuitive OO structure that provides all the benefits for using OO without the pitfalls present in other OO languages (for example, C++) that have more loosely defined OO structures.
- *Component-Based*: The Java platform has an enormous number of standard component APIs and a container-component model of programming that provides all the benefits for building enterprise applications using a CBD process.
- *Platform-Independent Architecture*: The architecture of the Java platform is operating-system and hardware-platform independent. The heterogeneous nature of enterprise environments can thus be accommodated by Java's support for "write once and run anywhere."
- *Rich Tool Suite*: Most of the development tools one needs to build applications come free with the Java development kits. Furthermore, the Java development kits also include tools for deploying component-based applications.
- *Many Language Features*: The Java language is a simple and easy language for developing applications faster. Garbage collection for automatic cleanup of resources and a pointer-free language also enable the programmer to worry less about language semantics and help in building more reliable applications faster.
- *Many Core APIs*: Most common programming tasks and abstractions are provided out of the box with a core set of standard APIs. No longer will a programmer spend time sweating over which vendor's collection classes to use.
- *Built-In I/O and Serialization*: Built-in facilities for streaming Java objects to and from a common underlying serialization format allow for a standard way to externalize Java objects and transfer Java object state between Java applications, thus enabling mobile code.
- *Threading*: A standard means for providing thread safety and building threaded applications is embedded into Java.
- *Dynamic Web-Based Applications*: Perhaps one of the most popular early aspects of Java was its capability to run as an application inside of Web browsers with Java applet code dynamically downloaded from a Web server.

Java's Version History

Java was born out of a 1991 research initiative at Sun when Patrick Naughton, Mike Sheridan, and James Gosling formed the "Green Project" to determine what would be the next new wave of computing. Their early conclusion was that consumer electronics devices and more sophisticated computing would converge. In the summer of 1992, the Green Project members (fully staffed at 13) unveiled their "*7" (pronounced "Star Seven") device, demonstrating a handheld home-entertainment controller having an animated touch-screen interface. Given the need for heterogeneity in device controllers, the team had created a platform-independent language called "Oak," which is now known to be the forerunner of Java. In 1994, the market focus for this new Java platform became the Internet when executable Java code was embedded inside of Web browsers in the form of Java applets.

In March of 1995, an alpha Java version 1.0a2 was released to the public. Within a few months, the Java platform was being downloaded by a growing number of developers, Netscape announced the integration of Java into its browser, and the official first release of Java was made public in May of 1995. The Java Development Kit (JDK) v1.0 was released in January 1996, and a final release of the JDK v1.1 was made public in February of 1997. With the release of the JDK v1.1 and a faster runtime environment, Java began to see a growth in applicability to enterprise environments.

Sun released the Java 2 platform in December of 1998. The Java 2 platform corresponds to the JDK v1.2. In June of 1999, Sun announced plans for a comprehensive reorganization of the means by which it released Java platforms. Although Sun previously encapsulated a collection of Java enterprise technologies and APIs under the marketing labels of "Java Technologies for the Enterprise" and the "Java Platform for the Enterprise," it wasn't until the June 1999 announcement that Sun would pursue a distinct and integrated Java enterprise platform. The major Java platform distinctions are partitioned along these lines:

- *J2ME*: The Java 2 Micro Edition (J2ME) is a Java platform catered for embedded and consumer-electronics platforms. It has a smaller footprint and embodies only those Java APIs needed for embedded applications.
- *J2SE*: The Java 2 Standard Edition (J2SE) is a Java platform catered for typical desktop and workstation environments. The J2SE is essentially what was once referred to as the Java 2 platform or JDK v1.2. The J2SE was distributed either as version 1.2 or as version 1.3 at the time of this writing.
- *J2EE*: The Java 2 Enterprise Edition (J2EE) is a Java platform catered for scalable enterprise applications. Web-enabling and application-enabling component-based environments and APIs are equipped with a J2EE platform. The J2EE is separate and dependent on the J2SE, but we often refer to the J2EE throughout this book as a platform to mean both the J2SE and the J2EE physical distributions combined.

Java Platform Architecture

Java specifications define standards that affect both the development of Java code and the runtime execution of Java code. All of these standards help provide a level of assurance that your Java applications written and developed for one Java platform implementation and operating system can also run on another Java platform implementation and operating system. Such standards decouple dependence of enterprise applications from specific operating-system platforms, hardware platforms, and Java platform implementations. This section provides an overview of the standard Java development and runtime environments.

Java Development and Runtime Environments

The Java architecture is standardized by a series of specifications defining both development and runtime environment standards as depicted in Figure 4.1. Java source code utilizes a standard Java development environment expressed in terms of a standard Java language syntax and semantics, standard Java APIs, and a compilation process that produces executable code adhering to a standard Java class file format. The Java runtime environment specifies standards that guarantee that the same executable Java application class files can execute on a standard Java runtime platform. This Java runtime platform presents the same execution environment to a Java application independent of an underlying operating environment.

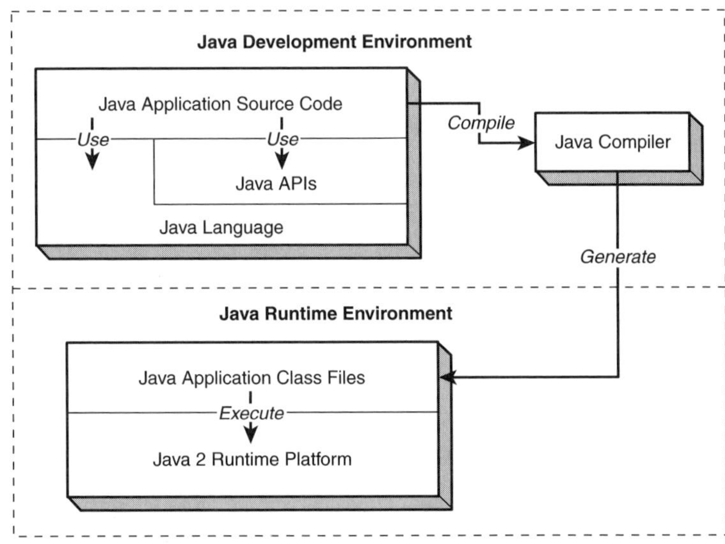

FIGURE 4.1
Java development and runtime environments.

Java Runtime Platform Architecture

The runtime environment architecture for the Java 2 platform is shown in Figure 4.2 in the context of both the executable Java application code and the underlying operating environment. The Java application class file format is actually expressed in terms of byte codes. Byte codes are similar to assembly-language instructions. As previously mentioned, one of the most attractive features of Java is its operating-system and hardware-platform independence. Byte code instructions are executed within the context of a virtual machine (that is, the Java Virtual Machine, or "JVM") that operates above an operating-system level. The main components illustrated in Figure 4.2 help provide such platform independence and are briefly described here:

- *Byte Code Verifier*: The byte code verifier analyzes a byte code stream corresponding to a Java class and verifies that this byte stream adheres to the Java language rules defined for classes. We discuss byte code verification in a bit more detail in the context of Java security in Chapter 26, "Basic Java Security."
- *Class Loader*: The class loader is responsible for loading Java class byte codes from an input stream (for example, file or network), inducing a byte code verifier to verify these byte codes, inducing security checks via the Java security interfaces, and then handing the classes off to the Java runtime execution engine. We have more to say about the class loader in the context of Java security in Chapter 26.
- *Java Runtime Execution Engine*: The runtime execution engine is the workhorse that actually executes the byte codes that have been loaded by the class loader and verified by the byte code verifier. The runtime engine maps abstract byte code instructions to platform-specific library calls and instructions. The runtime engine is the core of the Java Virtual Machine. The JVM also includes the class loader and byte code verifier.
- *Java API Class Files*: The Java API class files are the executable Java code implementing the standard Java platform APIs. Many of the standard Java APIs, such as networking and threading libraries, make native platform calls via a set of native platform interface libraries.
- *Native Platform Interface Libraries*: The native platform interface libraries make native calls to underlying platform libraries and resources on behalf of the Java APIs.

Java Runtime Optimizations

Optimizations for a Java runtime environment generally focus on optimizing the Java runtime execution engine. Some implementations simply interpret byte codes into platform-specific instructions and calls as they are encountered during the normal sequence of execution. Many optimizations come in the form of implementations that use certain platform-specific features (for example, IBM's JVM is optimized for Windows NT platforms). If an execution engine utilizes a just-in-time compiler, its byte codes are interpreted and compiled into native calls as they are encountered and subsequently cached. In this way, the native calls can be used without recompilation when the same byte codes are encountered later during processing. Sun's Java HotSpot VM optimizes native code execution for most recently used code. As a final note, in addition to runtime execution engine optimizations, some tools actually precompile any static packaging of Java code that you may have for a specific platform.

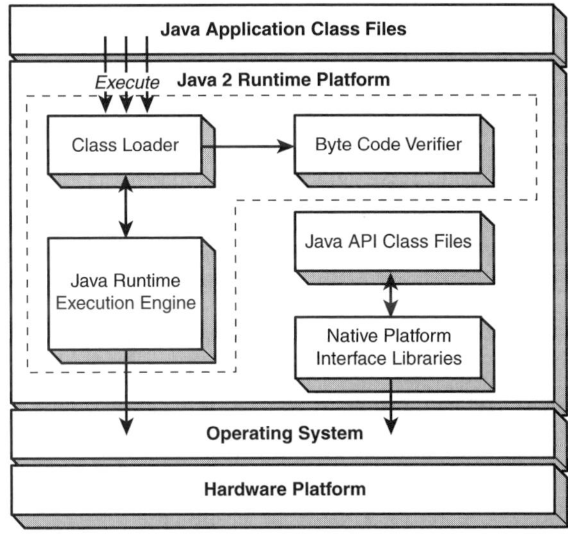

FIGURE 4.2
The Java 2 runtime platform architecture.

Java Files and Tools

The development of Java code involves the specification of Java source code and its compilation into executable Java class files. The Java class files then execute atop the JVM inside of a JVM runtime process. This section describes the basic types of files used to develop, deploy, and execute Java applications. The basic structure of Java source code developed using a standard Java coding and documentation convention is then briefly highlighted. Finally, we describe the basic set of development, deployment, and runtime tools that come freely equipped with the J2SE's Software Development Kit (SDK).

Java File Types

Various file types are utilized by the Java platform. Files exist to contain source code, executable code, object state, and archived code. The basic Java platform file types and any standard file naming extensions/conventions are listed here:

- *Source Code Files (.java)*: Contains Java source code. One file corresponds to one public class.
- *Class Files (.class)*: Contains the compiled Java source code and is described as a series of byte codes per standard Java specification. One class file corresponds to one Java class.
- *Java Serialization Files (.ser)*: Contains a serialized representation of a Java object's state and class description.
- *Java ARchive Files (.jar)*: Contains an optionally compressed collection of files according to the ZIP file archive format. A JAR file will typically hold files such as Java class files, serialization files, a manifest file, and multimedia files such as sound and image files. The Java 2 platform also enables Java code to be directly executed from the JAR file.
- *Java Manifest Files (MANIFEST.MF)*: Is used to describe the contents of an archive file.

Basic Java Source File Structure

The basic Java source file format consists of declaring the package of a class or interface, importing other classes and interfaces, declaring the class, declaring class and instance variables, and declaring/defining constructors and methods. Sun's Code Conventions for the Java Programming Language defines a simple standard for organizing and creating Java source code (`http://java.sun.com/docs/codeconv/index.html`). If code is documented in a particular format known as the JavaDoc convention, HTML documentation for that code can be automatically generated from the source code (`http://java.sun.com/products/jdk/javadoc/index.html`). The basic structure of a Java source code file that adheres to the standard JavaDoc and Java coding conventions is listed here with descriptive comments:

```
/*
 * Class/interface code documentation here
*/

// Package declaration
package ejava.foo;

// Import statements
import ejava.bar.*; // Import all elements of ejava.bar package
import ejava.bar.drinks.Martini; // Import a specific Martini class
```

```
/**
 * Class description here
 *
 * @version     Version Number and Date here
 * @author      Author Name here
 */

// Class declaration, optional single inheritance extension,
// and optional multiple interface implementations
public class ClassName extends BaseClass implements SomeInterface {

  // List static class variables first in order of decreasing
  // visibility: public, protected, package, private

  /** class variable documentation comment */
  public static VariableType publicClassVariableName;
  /** class variable documentation comment */
  private static VariableType privateClassVariableName = InitValue;

  // List instance variables in order of decreasing
  // visibility: public, protected, package, private

  /** instance variable documentation comment */
  public VariableType publicVariableName;
  /** instance variable documentation comment */
  protected VariableType protectedVariableName;
  /** instance variable documentation comment */
  VariableType packageVariableName;
  /** instance variable documentation comment */
  private VariableType privateVariableName;

  // List constructors before methods. Group constructors
  // and methods according to logical groupings. No preference
  // for ordering between class and object methods and visibility
  // such as public, protected, package, or private is assumed.

  /**
   * Constructor comment here
   */
  public ClassName() {
      // Implementation here
  }

  /**
   * Method comment here
   * @param aParameterName parameter description
```

```
    */
    public ReturnType methodCall(ParameterType aParameterName) {
        // Implementation here
    }
}

// List any non-public classes here
class NonPublicClassName { ... }
```

Basic JAR and Manifest File Structure

JAR files are optionally compressed collections of files that adhere to the ZIP file archive format. JAR files contain entries that include Java class files, serialization files, a manifest file, and multimedia files such as sound and image files. Manifest files can optionally be placed inside of a JAR file to describe special handling procedures for certain JAR file entries. Manifest files are placed in a JAR file with a path of `META-INF` and a filename of `MANIFEST.MF`. Files requiring associated security signatures are placed in a JAR file with a path of `META-INF` and have a file extension of `.SF`.

The manifest file contains a list of file entries that are placed in the JAR file. Only those files that have special handling instructions need to be designated in the manifest file. At the top of a manifest file, the manifest file standard version needs to be designated via this:

```
Manifest-Version: <version number>
```

A manifest file standard version that is required for use may optionally be specified this way:

```
Required-Version: <version number>
```

Each entry to be defined in a manifest file begins with a `Name:` header and is followed by a pathname and filename of the archived file. An entry description has one or more associated attribute values that can be used as special handling information for that entry. Each entry is defined using the following format, in which signature algorithm attributes and other attribute name/value pairs are optional:

```
Name: <directory path>/<filename>
<Signature Algorithm>-Digest: <Data representation of signature>
<Another Attribute Name>: <An Associated Attribute Value>
```

Executable JAR files can be built if a manifest file has a `Main-Class:` attribute name associated with a Java class that has a `main()` method to be called when executing the JAR file. For example:

```
Manifest-Version: 1.0
Main-Class: com.assuredtech.b2b.server.B2Bserver.class
```

Java Software Development Kit Tools

One of the nice features of Java that has made it very popular with developers is the fact that you can quickly begin programming in Java with a simple text editor and via use of the free Java SDK. The SDK distribution comes equipped with several tools for developing, deploying, and running Java applications (`http://www.javasoft.com/products/jdk/1.2/docs/tooldocs/tools.html`). Although the J2SE SDK is free for commercial use, it cannot be freely distributed with commercial applications. Rather, the runtime environment component of the J2SE SDK can be separately downloaded and is free for commercial distribution with your Java applications. These are the most commonly used basic command tools from the J2SE SDK:

- `javac`: Compiles Java source code into Java class files. The command `javac [options] [source files] [file list]` is used to compile a set of source files given a set of options and optionally using a separate file list to indicate the source files to be compiled. Although the `CLASSPATH` environment variable can define where to look when compiling Java files, the `-classpath classpath` option can also specify a class path. Other options exist as well, such as the `-d directory` option to specify an output directory for class files.
- `jar`: Creates and manipulates JAR files. The `jar [options] [manifest] destination [one or more input files]` command's behavior depends on the associated options. The `c` option creates a JAR file, the `x` option extracts the contents of a JAR file, and the `u` option updates an existing JAR file. The `f` option specifies a target destination JAR file. A directory or set of input files should be specified for JAR file creation. If the `m` option is used, a manifest file can be used to build the JAR file.
- `java`: Launches a JVM process using Java class files. The `java [options] ClassName [zero or more arguments]` form of the command initiates a JVM process using the `main()` method of the `ClassName` class and passing it a set of arguments. The `java [options] -jar JARfile.jar [zero or more arguments]` version of the command can initiate a JVM using the `main()` method of the executable class that is associated with the executable JAR file. If a `CLASSPATH` environment variable is not used to define the search location for Java classes, the `-classpath classpath` option may be used. Properties of the runtime system environment can be set using the `-DpropertyName=propertyValue` option. Various nonstandard options beginning with the prefix `-X` are also often used to specify such options as JVM process heap size and stack size. A `-jit` option can be used to execute the JVM with a just-in-time compilation optimization.

- `javadoc`: Creates a set of HTML files with documentation extracted from your Java source code if your code documentation adheres to the JavaDoc format.
- `jdb`: Is a Java debugger.
- `appletviewer`: Is a tool for running and debugging Java applets.

Java Language

The Java language has a fairly simple syntax that has helped it achieve popularity in the developer community. Simpler syntax means more rapid application development. If you're familiar with C/C++ syntax, you'll note the similarity to Java syntax. However, there are some subtle semantic differences. In this section, we briefly cover some of the most often-used Java types, operators, and language constructs.

Java Fundamental Types

Java has a set of fundamental types used to define basic data elements. Most of the fundamental Java types have a similarity in naming to C/C++ types but do not vary per platform as do C/C++ types. The fundamental Java types are listed and defined in Table 4.1.

TABLE 4.1 Fundamental Java Types

Type	*Size*	*Description*
`void`	N/A	Represents no type
`boolean`	1 bit	A Boolean `true` or `false` value
`char`	16 bits	A 2-byte uni-code character whose first byte is an ASCII character using an English locale
`byte`	8 bits	A 1-byte signed integer
`short`	16 bits	A 2-byte signed integer
`int`	32 bits	A 4-byte signed integer
`long`	64 bits	An 8-byte signed integer
`float`	32 bits	A 4-byte floating-point number
`double`	64 bits	An 8-byte floating-point number

Java Operators

Java also supports a set of standard operators used for operating on both fundamental Java types and Java objects. Table 4.2 lists some of these Java operations. The first column of the table lists the general classification of operator, and the second column indicates how many operands are involved per operator. Operators may be formulated in terms of two operands or one operand. Additionally, a special operator may also operate on three operands. The third column lists each operator and the fourth column describes the operator.

TABLE 4.2 Java Operators

<table>
<tr><th>Operator Type</th><th>Operands</th><th>Operator</th><th>Description</th></tr>
<tr><td>Arithmetic</td><td>Two</td><td>+</td><td>Addition</td></tr>
<tr><td></td><td></td><td>-</td><td>Subtraction</td></tr>
<tr><td></td><td></td><td>*</td><td>Multiplication</td></tr>
<tr><td></td><td></td><td>/</td><td>Division</td></tr>
<tr><td></td><td></td><td>%</td><td>Modulus</td></tr>
<tr><td></td><td>One</td><td>+</td><td>Plus</td></tr>
<tr><td></td><td></td><td>-</td><td>Negative</td></tr>
<tr><td></td><td></td><td>++</td><td>Increment</td></tr>
<tr><td></td><td></td><td>--</td><td>Decrement</td></tr>
<tr><td>Relational</td><td>Two</td><td>></td><td>Greater than</td></tr>
<tr><td></td><td></td><td>>=</td><td>Greater than or equal</td></tr>
<tr><td></td><td></td><td><</td><td>Less than</td></tr>
<tr><td></td><td></td><td><=</td><td>Less than or equal</td></tr>
<tr><td></td><td></td><td>==</td><td>Equal</td></tr>
<tr><td></td><td></td><td>!=</td><td>Not equal</td></tr>
<tr><td></td><td></td><td>&&</td><td>AND</td></tr>
<tr><td></td><td></td><td>||</td><td>OR</td></tr>
<tr><td>Bitwise</td><td>Two</td><td><<</td><td>Left shift</td></tr>
<tr><td></td><td></td><td>>></td><td>Right shift</td></tr>
<tr><td></td><td></td><td>>>></td><td>Right shift with zeroes shifted in from left</td></tr>
<tr><td></td><td></td><td>&</td><td>AND</td></tr>
<tr><td></td><td></td><td>|</td><td>OR</td></tr>
<tr><td></td><td></td><td>^</td><td>XOR</td></tr>
<tr><td></td><td>One</td><td>~</td><td>Complement</td></tr>
</table>

continues

TABLE 4.2 Continued

Operator Type	*Operands*	*Operator*	*Description*
Logical	Two	`&`	AND
		`|`	OR
		`^`	XOR
	One	`!`	Complement
Assignment	Two	`=`	Assignment
		op=	Perform *op* and then assign value (for example, += means add then assign)
Miscellaneous	Three	*exp?A:B*	If *exp* is true then do *A* else do *B*
	Two	`+`	Concatenate strings
		`instanceof`	Determines if an object is an instance of a particular type
	One	`(TYPE)A`	Cast object A to TYPE

Java Language Constructs

Java has a fairly simple syntax for defining classes, interfaces, objects, variables, and methods. Control structures are also fairly simplistic and have a familiar C/C++ structure. Although much of the syntax for Java bears a striking C/C++ resemblance, some key semantic differences, such as object passing by reference and lack of pointer semantics, make Java a significantly different and simpler language. The most commonly used Java language constructs are presented in Table 4.3. The table lists a construct, an example of use of the construct, and a brief description of the construct.

TABLE 4.3 Java Language Constructs

Construct	***Example***	***Description***

Comments	`// Comment here`
	
	`/* Comment here */`
		Used to add comments to code.

Construct	Example	Description

Identifiers	`myValue`
	`Howdy4`
	`_Egads`
	`$yikes`
		Identifiers are names for Java constructs such as variables, classes, and interfaces. Identifiers uniquely identify these Java constructs within a particular scope. Identifiers begin with letters, an underscore, or a dollar sign and can subsequently contain these characters and numbers.

Package Declaration	`package A.B;`	Declares that the class/interface in this file belongs to a package such as `A.B`.
`import` Statements	`import A.B.Foo;` `import A.B.C.*;`	This class/interface refers to a class named `Foo` in package `A.B` or refers to classes in package `A.B.C`.

Interface Declaration	`interface MyInterfaceName`
	` extends AnotherInterface {`
	`  public static final int a = 2;`
	`  public void bla();`
	`}`
	
	`// marker interface`
	`interface MyMarkerInterface{`
	`}`
		Declare an interface that can optionally extend zero or more other interfaces. Interfaces only define constants and declare methods with no implementations. Interfaces that define no methods ("marker interfaces") are created to enable classes that implement them to designate that they have some behavior not definable via methods.

continues

TABLE 4.3 Continued

Construct	*Example*	*Description*

Class Declaration	class MyClassName
	  extends BaseClass
	  implements Interface1,
	             Interface2 {
	}
		Declare a class named MyClassName. A class can optionally extend one other class (single inheritance) and implement zero or more interfaces.

Field Declaration	VariableType variableName = InitValue;	A variable of type VariableType with the name variableName and initialized to an InitValue.
Objects	Object obj = new Object(); MyClass myObj = new MyClass();	An object is an instantiation of a particular class type. Objects are passed around by reference.
Arrays	Object[]array1 = new Object[5]; int[]array2 = new int[20]; int[]array3 = {3, 5, 20};	Arrays of Java types can be declared for objects and fundamental types. Arrays can be constructed in a pre-initialized state using curly braces.
Visibility	public <Construct> protected <Construct> <Construct> private <Construct>	Some Construct can be accessed by other classes in public, subclasses if protected, classes in the same package if no visibility is defined, and only by the associated class if private.

Construct	*Example*	*Description*

Methods	`class MyClassName{`
	
	` public ReturnType`
	`  methName(Param paramName){`
	`    return someValue;`
	`  }`
	
	`  // getter`
	` public Type getData()`
	` {...}`
	
	`  // setter`
	` public void setData(Type data)`
	` {...}`
	`}`
		A method named `methName` returning a type `ReturnType` and accepting zero or more parameters of type `Param` and named `paramName`. A `return` statement is used within a method to return some value. Objects are passed by reference to and from method calls. The underlying references themselves are passed by value. Methods that simply retrieve attribute data from a class are called "getters," whereas data that simply sets attribute data are called "setters."

`static`	`static <Construct>`
	`static Object myObject;`
	`static void method(){...}`
		Some `Construct`, such as a method or variable, can be associated with a class. All objects of that class share the same `static` construct variable. A `static` method can be called on the class directly without an instance being created.

continues

TABLE 4.3 Continued

Construct	*Example*	*Description*

`final`	`final <Construct>`
	`final int val = 4;`
	`final void method(){...}`
		Some `Construct`, such as a method or variable, can be declared `final` such that it is not able to be overridden. Objects that are `final` are constant. Methods that are `final` cannot be overridden.

`main` Method	`class MyClassName{`
	`  public static void`
	`    main(String args[]){`
	`  }`
	`}`
		The `main` method is the method that is called from the command line with an array of command-line arguments.

Block	`{`
	`   // Code here`
	`   {`
	`     // More code here`
	`   }`
	`}`
		Can nest blocks of code within code using curly braces.

Throwing Exceptions	`public void myMethod()`
	`  throws SomeException`
	`{`
	`  // bla bla...`
	`  throw new SomeException();`
	`}`
		An exception is thrown when error or warning scenarios are encountered in code. A method declares that it throws an exception of some class type and throws the new exception in code.

<table>
<tr><th>Construct</th><th>Example</th><th>Description</th></tr>
<tr><td>Handling Exceptions</td><td><pre>
try{
  obj.myMethod();
}
catch(SomeException e){
  // handle exception
}
finally{ // optional
  // always execute this stuff
}

// Nested Exception Handling
try{
  obj.myMethod();
}
catch(SomeException e1){
  try{
    obj.close();
  }
  catch(AnotherException e2){
    // handle nested exception
  }
}
</pre></td><td>An exception is handled by code that uses a method that throws an exception using <code>try-catch-finally</code> blocks. The <code>try</code> block encapsulates the code that can throw the exception. The <code>catch</code> block is used to catch specific or base class exceptions that can be thrown by the <code>try</code> block. An optional <code>finally</code> block is used to always execute a block of code even if an exception is thrown or not thrown. Exception handling can be nested as well. Because exception-handling code can be lengthy and can clutter up a sample description, we sometimes leave out exception-handling snippets in the book where indicated. Of course, the code on the CD always contains the proper exception-handling code.</td></tr>
</table>

continues

TABLE 4.3 Continued

Construct	*Example*	*Description*

`if` Statement	`if(expression){`
	`  // Do this`
	`}`
	
	`if(expression){`
	`  // Do this`
	`}`
	`else if(bla){`
	`  // Else if bla, do this`
	`}`
	`else{`
	`  // Otherwise do this`
	`}`
		Create `if` statements and `if-then-else` statements.

`switch` Statement	`switch(value){`
	` case val1:`
	`   data = val1;`
	`   break;`
	` case val2:`
	`   data = val2*2;`
	`   break;`
	` default:`
	`  data = 300;`
	`}`
		A `switch` statement takes a value and executes a particular case statement based on that value; otherwise, any default statements are executed.

`for` Statement	`for(bla=val; bla < max; ++bla){`
	`  // do this loop`
	`}`
		Execute a loop given some initial value such as `bla=val` and executing a clause at the end of each loop such as `++bla`. Execute the loop for some `while` conditional such as `bla < max`.

Construct	Example	Description
while Statement	while(expression){ }	Execute a loop while some expression is true.
do/while Statement	do{ }while(expression);	Execute a loop while some expression is true, but execute the loop at least once first.

Core Java Language APIs

In addition to the language of Java, a set of OO types defined in terms of Java classes and interfaces serves to extend the Java language beyond its fundamental type and identifier support. Appropriately enough, most of these language extensions are contained in the packages beginning with java.lang. However, a few entities in the java.math package also serve as core Java language types. This section of the chapter provides an overview of these core language APIs. Although not strictly part of a Java language extension, the base means for handling events provided in the java.util package is also described in this section. The packages that define the core Java language extended API are shown here:

- java.lang: Contains constructs that extend the Java programming language with basic object encapsulations (http://java.sun.com/products/jdk/1.2/docs/api/java/lang/package-summary.html).
- java.lang.reflect: Contains constructs for tapping reflection capabilities of Java constructs (http://java.sun.com/products/jdk/1.2/docs/api/java/lang/reflect/package-summary.html).
- java.lang.ref: Contains constructs for reference-objects allowing for some visibility into garbage collection (http://java.sun.com/products/jdk/1.2/docs/api/java/lang/ref/package-summary.html).
- java.math: Contains constructs for performing arithmetic operations using decimal and integer operands of arbitrary precision (http://java.sun.com/products/jdk/1.2/docs/api/java/math/package-summary.html).
- java.util: Contains constructs for managing object collections, events, dates, time, locale-dependent data, and a few helper utilities (http://java.sun.com/products/jdk/1.2/docs/api/java/util/package-summary.html).

Base Language and System APIs

The `java.lang` package provides a set of classes that provide a few hooks into the internals of objects, classes, the JVM, processes, and the operating system. Figure 4.3 depicts some of these classes and their relationships. The various classes and interfaces shown in Figure 4.3 are described here:

- `Object`: Serves as the root class for all classes in Java. Basic operations on all objects are therefore supported by this class.
- `Class`: Encapsulates a description of a particular class. We discuss this class more when we describe reflection later in this section. Because every class inherits from `Object`, the `Object.getClass()` method can be used to return an instance of this object for a particular object.
- `Cloneable`: Utilized by classes that implement this marker interface to designate that the class provides an implementation of the `clone()` method inherited from `Object`. The class thus designates that it can return a copy of itself.
- `ClassLoader`: Encapsulates an interface to a JVM class loader used to load Java class files from a particular input stream. Methods such as `getResource()` return an object identifying a resource location given a resource name. Other methods like `loadClass()` can be used to return a `Class` instance from the class loader's input stream given the class name.
- `SecurityManager`: Encapsulates an interface to a security manager used to check for permissions to access system resources.
- `System`: Provides a hook for interfacing with the operating system on top of which a JVM runs. Operations are provided for accessing standard input, output, and error streams; mechanisms for loading libraries and files; and helper methods such as for computing system time and array copying.
- `Runtime`: Provides a hook for interfacing with the JVM process environment. Is also used to spawn a new process external to the JVM process.
- `Process`: Encapsulates an interface to a process spawned by the `Runtime.exec()` call.
- `Compiler`: Provides a hook for compiling Java source code into Java byte codes. JVM providers must implement this class, which is disabled by default.

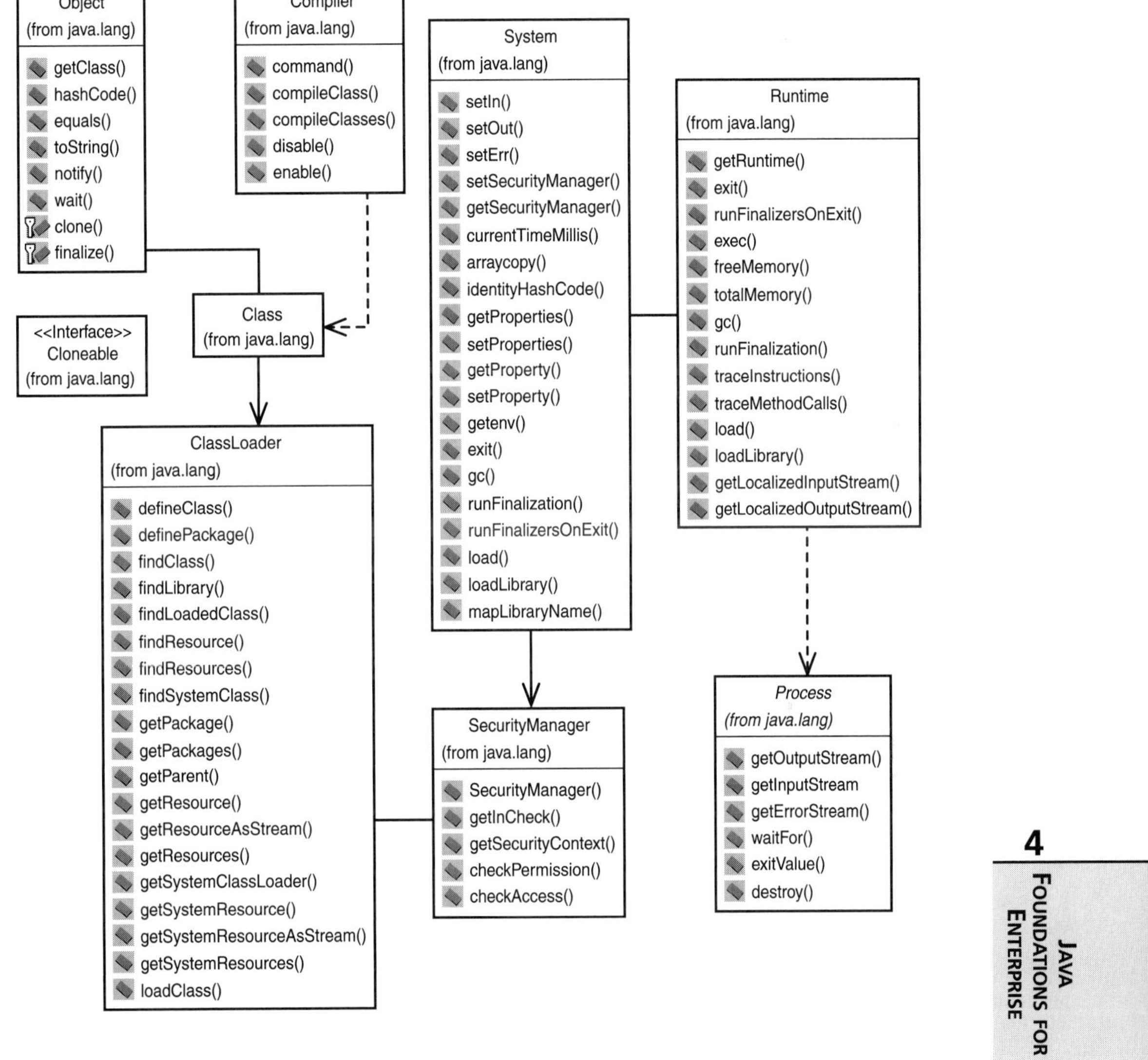

FIGURE 4.3
Core language and system classes.

Errors and Exceptions

Abnormal program execution conditions are thrown as exceptions or errors in Java code. Figure 4.4 depicts the base hierarchy for such throwable abnormal statuses. The entities of Figure 4.4 are defined here:

- `Throwable`: The base class for all errors and exceptions that can be thrown by Java code. Only this class and its subclasses can be thrown by a `throw` statement and can be caught in a `try-catch-finally` block.
- `Exception`: All exceptions that can be thrown inherit from this class. Exceptions should be caught by applications.
- `Error`: An error is thrown when a serious problem has occurred and should not be caught. Classes do not need to declare when they will throw an error.

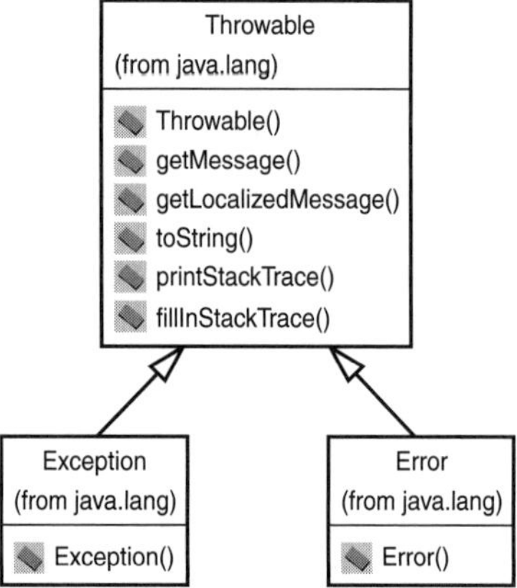

FIGURE 4.4
Base exception and error abstractions.

Type and Mathematical APIs

The `java.lang` and `java.math` packages provide a collection of object abstractions that can be used to encapsulate fundamental Java types and perform mathematical operations using method calls. Figure 4.5 depicts these fundamental type abstractions and mathematical operation classes. The various classes and interfaces depicted in Figure 4.5 are defined here:

- `Comparable`: Defines an interface for comparing the natural ordering of objects.
- `Math`: Defines a set of methods for performing mathematical operations such as exponential, logarithmic, and trigonometric operations.
- `Number`: Serves as an abstract base class for numbers that can convert between different fundamental data numeric types.
- `Byte`: Encapsulates an object wrapper for the Java `byte` type.
- `Short`: Encapsulates an object wrapper for the Java `short` type.

- `Integer`: Encapsulates an object wrapper for the Java `int` type.
- `BigDecimal`: Encapsulates an object representing an arbitrary precision integer.
- `BigInteger`: Encapsulates an object representing an arbitrary precision signed decimal number.
- `Long`: Encapsulates an object wrapper for the Java `long` type.
- `Float`: Encapsulates an object wrapper for the Java `float` type.
- `Double`: Encapsulates an object wrapper for the Java `double` type.
- `Void`: Encapsulates an object wrapper for the Java `void` type.
- `Boolean`: Encapsulates an object wrapper for the Java `boolean` type.
- `Character`: Encapsulates an object wrapper for the Java `char` type.
- `String`: Encapsulates a sequence of characters ending with a string terminator. String literals, such as `"HelloWorld"`, are implemented as `String` objects by the JVM. `String` objects cannot be changed after they are created.
- `StringBuffer`: Represents a modifiable `String` object.

Reflection

Java provides the capability to dynamically investigate the description of a class during runtime. A description of a class includes its members such as fields, constructors, and methods. Java reflection also provides a means for constructing new instances of objects and invoking methods on objects via generic reflection APIs. The `java.lang` package provides interfaces to `Class` and `Package` objects, but the `java.lang.reflect` package provides the framework for manipulating classes via the Java reflection capabilities. Here we describe each element in Figure 4.6 depicting the major classes and interfaces involved in reflection:

- `Class`: Provides a hook into the powerful features of Java's reflection support. After a `Class` object representing a description of a Java class is obtained, a series of getter methods can retrieve descriptive information about the construction of that class. The static `Class.forName()` methods can be used to obtain a handle to a `Class` object given a class name. An instance of a class having an empty constructor can even be created using the `newInstance()` call.
- `Package`: Encapsulates descriptive information about a package associated with a particular class.
- `Modifier`: Encapsulates a modifier and provides methods for decoding whether certain descriptive information obtained from class elements is a particular modifier type.
- `Member`: Defines an interface of common operations on a member of a class such as fields, constructors, and methods.

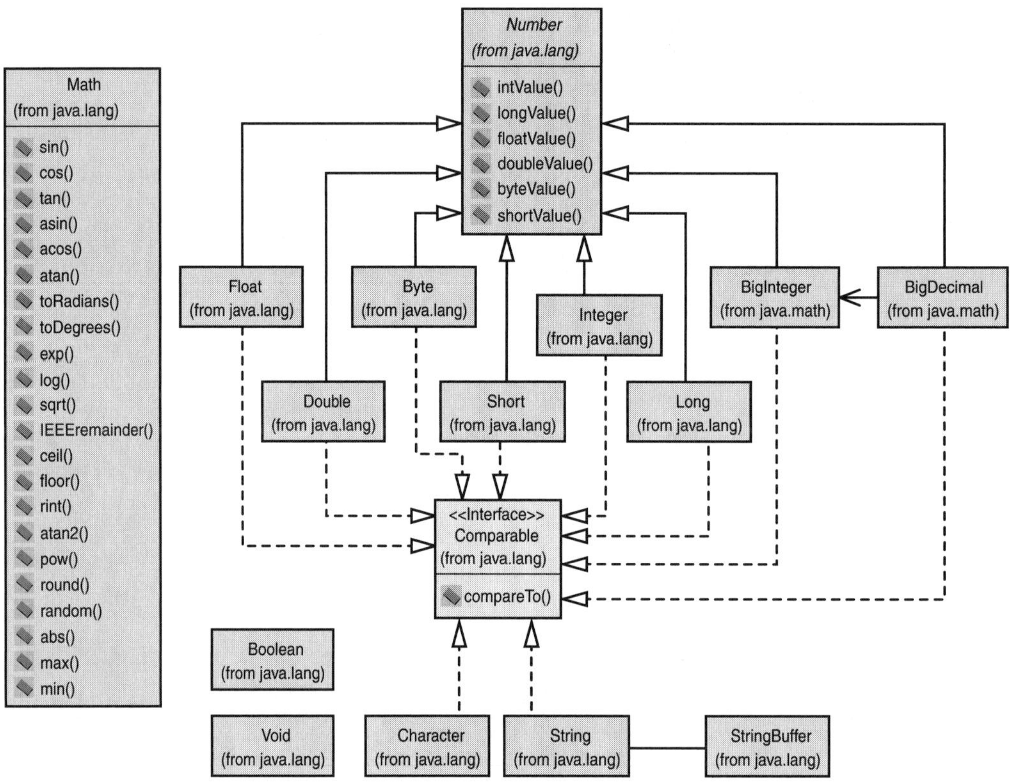

FIGURE 4.5
Fundamental type abstractions and mathematical operations.

- `AccessibleObject`: Serves as a base class for class members that can be used to control accessibility to perform reflective operations on certain classes.
- `Constructor`: Encapsulates a class constructor and access to its parameters and exceptions. A means to instantiate an object instance is also provided via `Constructor.newInstance()`.
- `Method`: Encapsulates a class method and access to its parameters, return type, and exceptions. A means to invoke the method is also provided via `Method.invoke()`.
- `Field`: Encapsulates a class field variable and access to its type and value.
- `Array`: Encapsulates a Java array with access to its elements, as well as the capability to create a new array.

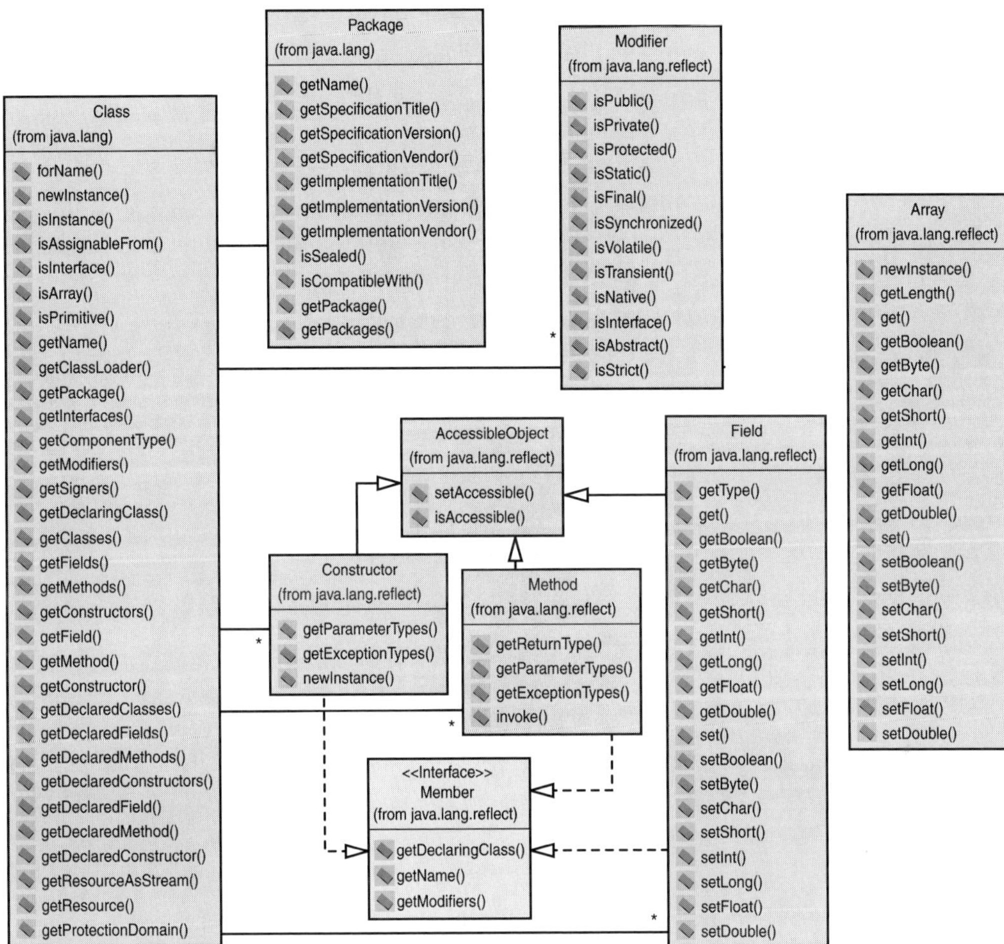

FIGURE 4.6
The Java reflection API.

Garbage Collection

One of the most attractive features of Java is its support for the automatic cleanup of objects that are no longer referenced. Such a feature is known as garbage collection. Programmers thus don't have to worry about memory leaks and deleting objects. The `java.lang.ref` package defines a set of classes that provides limited support for interfacing with the garbage collector. The classes that compose this Java garbage collector interaction are shown in Figure 4.7. We briefly describe the role of each class here:

- `Reference`: Serves as an abstract base class for all reference objects. The term *reference object* is used to mean an object that encapsulates a reference to an object. Thus, if object A has a reference to object B, a reference object would be created to represent the reference A has to B.
- `ReferenceQueue`: Encapsulates an interface to a queue where reference objects are appended by a garbage collector.
- `SoftReference`: Encapsulates a type of reference object that is cleared by the garbage collector when a demand for more memory is made.
- `WeakReference`: Encapsulates a type of reference object which does not allow objects that refer to them to be made finalized and subsequently reclaimed.
- `PhantomReference`: Encapsulates a type of reference object that is added to the reference queue when the garbage collector determines that the objects which refer to them can be reclaimed.

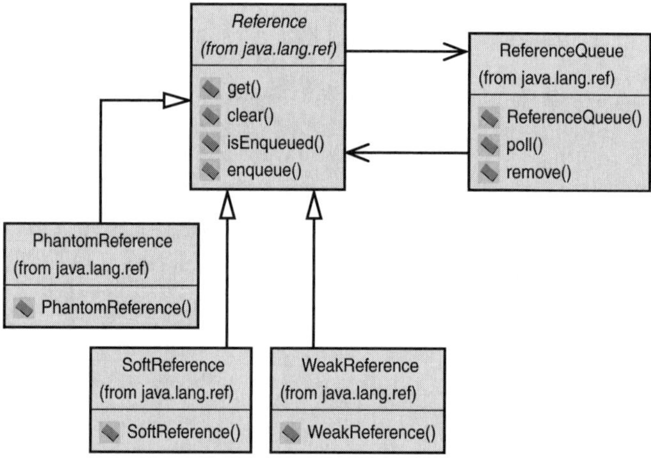

FIGURE 4.7
The Java garbage collection API.

Events

Java supports a simple standard event model for encapsulating events and their listeners. All other event-handling mechanisms in Java inherit from this base event model. Java also defines a standard subject-observer design pattern framework for notifying observers of changes in observable subject objects. Figure 4.8 depicts the simple and standard event model frameworks that we describe here:

- `EventObject`: An abstract base class for all event classes that adhere to the Java event model. The source of an event is associated with an event and can be obtained using `EventObject.getSource()`.
- `EventListener`: A marker interface that must be implemented by all classes that listen for events using the Java event model.
- `Observer`: A standard interface implemented by classes that want to be notified of changes made to observable objects using Java's standard subject-observer design pattern.
- `Observable`: A class for adding, deleting, and counting observers that want to be notified of changes in an observable class using the Java subject-observer design pattern. Also supports an interface for notifying observers of such changes.

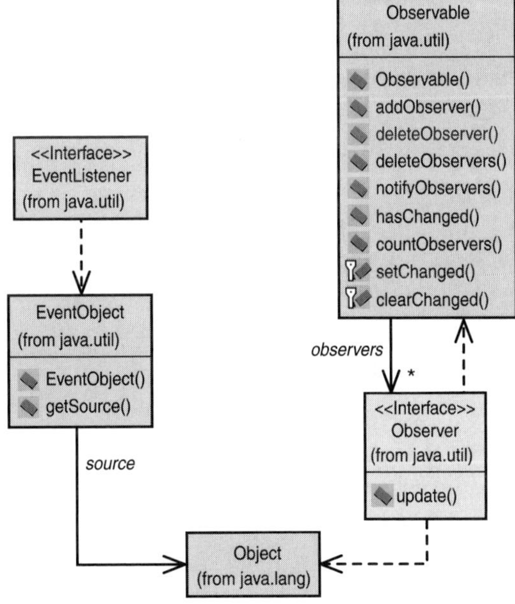

FIGURE 4.8
Java event models.

Collection APIs

Collections encapsulate a collection of one or more objects. Collections provide a useful means for grouping objects such that a single object reference can refer to the entire collection of objects. Collections have been a part of the Java platform since its inception, but the Java 2 platform introduced a much richer and more sophisticated suite of collection entities.

Figure 4.9 presents the top-level classifications of collection types and interfaces used to traverse such collections. A few interfaces and an abstract base class are used to distinguish between collections of objects that have an associated key name and those that do not have a key name. Two specialized classes for manipulating arrays and bits are also defined. A set of interfaces is defined for iterating over collections. The classes and interfaces illustrated in Figure 4.9 are described here:

- `Collection`: The root interface for collections of objects.
- `Map`: The root interface for collections that map key names to objects in the collection.
- `Dictionary`: An abstract base class for collections that map key names to objects in a collection. Is obsolete as of the J2SE in favor of objects that implement the `Map` interface.
- `Arrays`: A class used for manipulating collections of objects contained in arrays.
- `BitSet`: A class used for manipulating collections of bits in the form of a vector that can automatically grow in size.
- `Iterator`: An interface implemented by objects that enable the incremental traversal and removal of objects in a collection.
- `Enumeration`: An interface implemented by objects that enable the traversal of a collection of objects one at a time. Is obsolete as of the J2SE in favor of objects that implement the `Iterator` interface.
- `Comparator`: An interface implemented by objects that can compare two objects assuming some underlying order on a collection of objects.

Non-Keyed Collection Framework

Figure 4.10 presents the hierarchy of the non-keyed collections framework. Abstractions exist for generic lists, lists that require access in sequential order, sets without duplicate objects, and sorted sets of objects. Many new collection abstractions have been added in the J2SE with older JDK-style collections being integrated with this framework. The newer J2SE-style collections do not provide thread-safe access to collection elements and are consequently more efficient, whereas older JDK-style collections do provide thread synchronization. The various elements of Figure 4.10 are defined here:

- `Collection`: A top-level `Collection` interface that defines basic operations for manipulating collections of objects.
- `AbstractCollection`: An abstract class with a partial implementation of generic `Collection` interface functions.
- `List`: An interface with methods for manipulating an ordered collection of objects with next and previous elements in a sequence.
- `ListIterator`: A special type of iterator for traversing a collection in a reverse direction as well as forward direction.

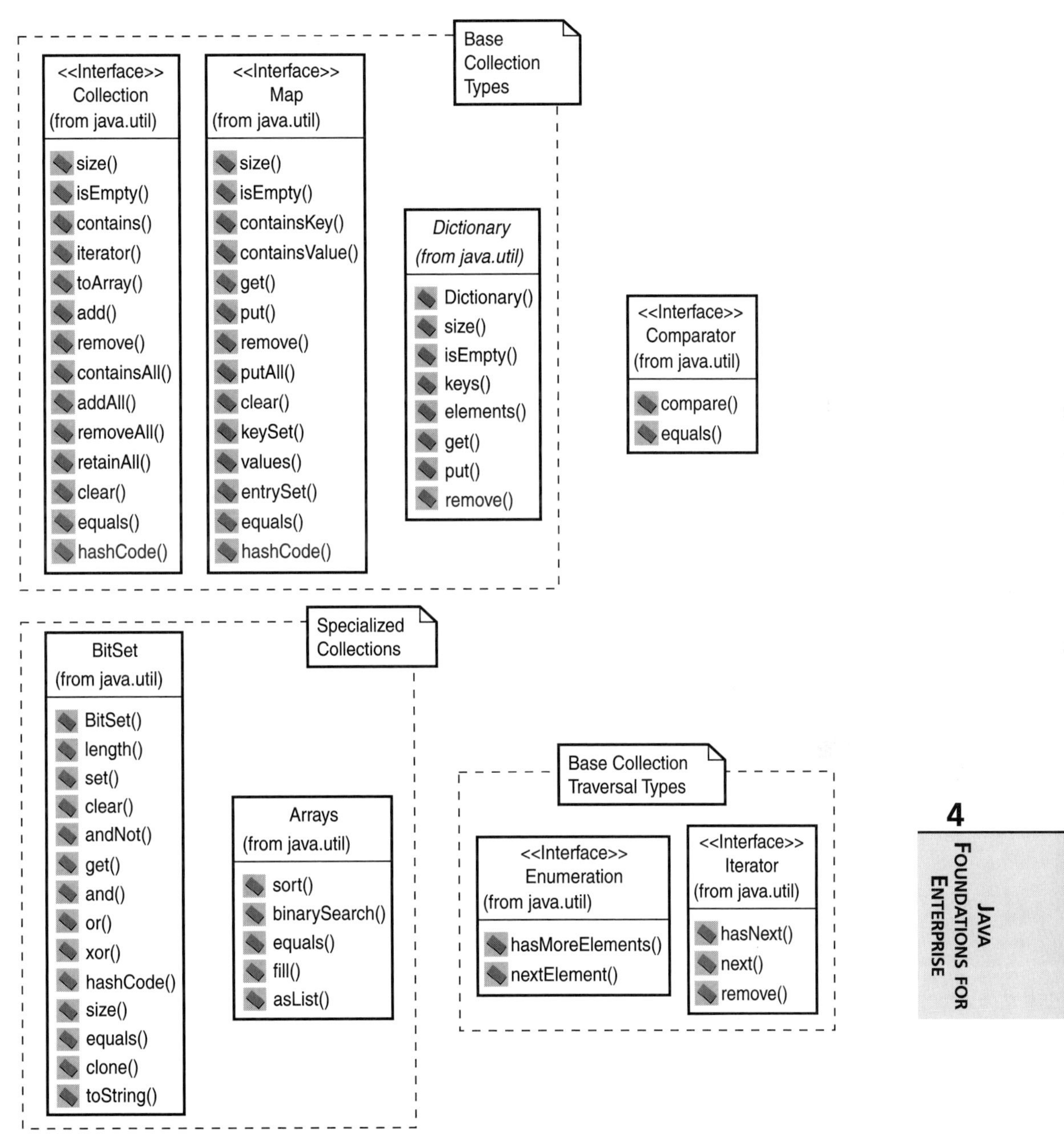

FIGURE 4.9
Top-level collection objects.

- `AbstractList`: An abstract class with a partial implementation of generic `List` interface functions. Can support random access of list elements.
- `AbstractSequentialList`: An abstract class that expands on the `AbstractList` implementation with a partial implementation that enforces sequential access of list elements.
- `LinkedList`: A concrete implementation of the `List` interface with support for sequential access to list elements.
- `Vector`: A concrete implementation of the `List` interface with support for sequential access to list elements and a growable vector of elements. The `Vector` class provides multiple thread synchronization support for its elements unlike its `LinkedList` counterpart.
- `Stack`: A type of vector that enforces last-in first-out (LIFO) behavior of elements in its collection. Also provides thread-safe synchronization of its elements.
- `Set`: An interface to a collection whose elements have no duplicates.
- `AbstractSet`: An abstract class with a partial implementation of generic `Set` interface functions.
- `HashSet`: A concrete implementation of a `Set` interface that enforces set-like behavior.
- `SortedSet`: An interface to a collection whose elements have no duplicates and are traversed in some natural order.
- `TreeSet`: A concrete implementation of a `SortedSet` interface that enforces sorted set-like behavior.

Mapped Collection Framework

Figure 4.11 presents the hierarchy of the keyed collections framework. Abstractions exist for generic mapping collections, mapped collections with a sortable order, and collections whose elements can be garbage collected when their keys are no longer referenced. Many new mapping abstractions have been added in the J2SE with older JDK-style mapping abstractions being integrated with this framework. J2SE-style map collections do not provide synchronized access to collection elements and are thus more efficient, whereas older JDK-style map collections do provide thread synchronization. The various elements of Figure 4.11 are defined here:

- `Map`: An interface that defines a set of operations that provide a means to access objects in a collection using a key name.
- `AbstractMap`: An abstract class with a partial implementation of generic `Map` interface functions.
- `HashMap`: A concrete implementation of a `Map` interface enforcing the behavior of mapping key names to objects in a collection.

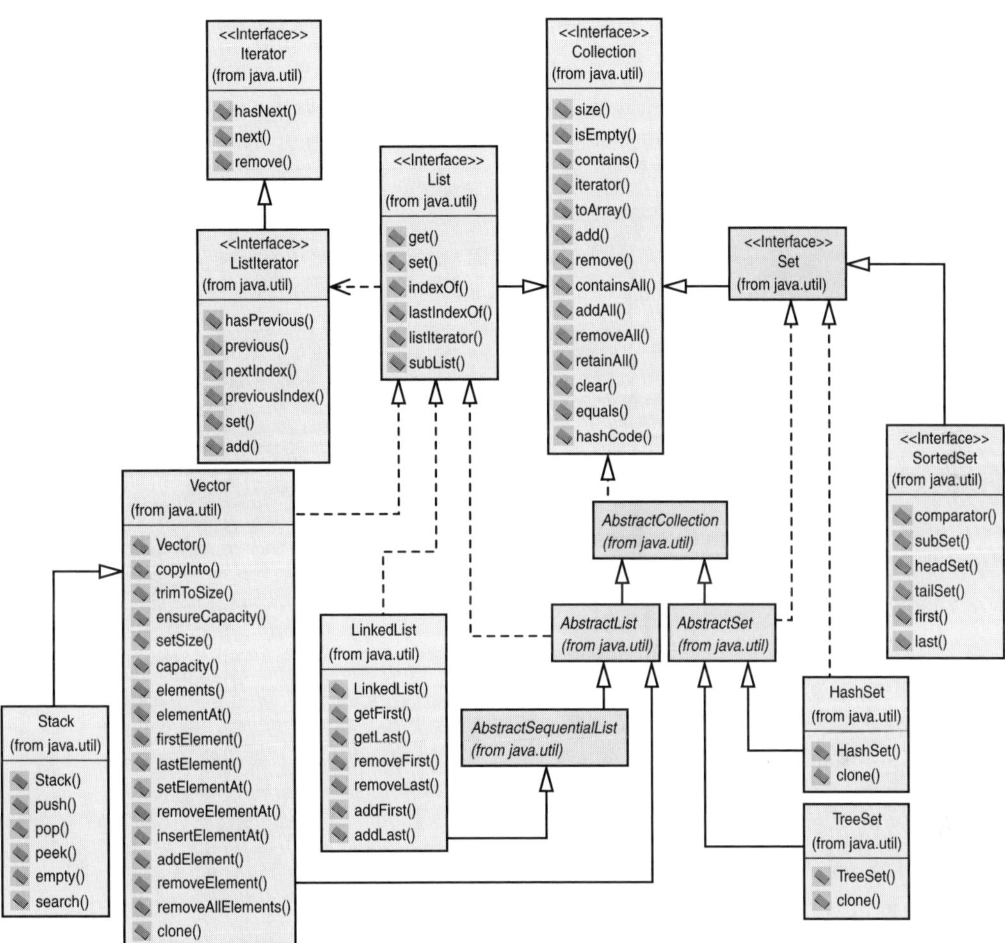

FIGURE 4.10

The non-keyed collection architecture.

- `SortedMap`: A type of `Map` interface that provides operations to enforce a natural ordering of elements in the map.
- `TreeMap`: A concrete implementation of a `SortedMap` interface enforcing the behavior of an ordered collection of mapped objects.
- `Dictionary`: An obsolete base class for providing map-like behavior.
- `Hashtable`: A concrete implementation of a `Map` interface enforcing the behavior of mapping key names to objects in a collection. The `Hashtable` class provides multiple thread synchronization support for its elements, unlike its `HashMap` counterpart.

- `Properties`: A type of `Hashtable` whose elements are properties of a system. That is, the element types are `String` objects that define some property of the system.
- `WeakHashMap`: A type of `Map` whose elements may be removed by the garbage collector when its keys are no longer referenced by other objects in the JVM process.

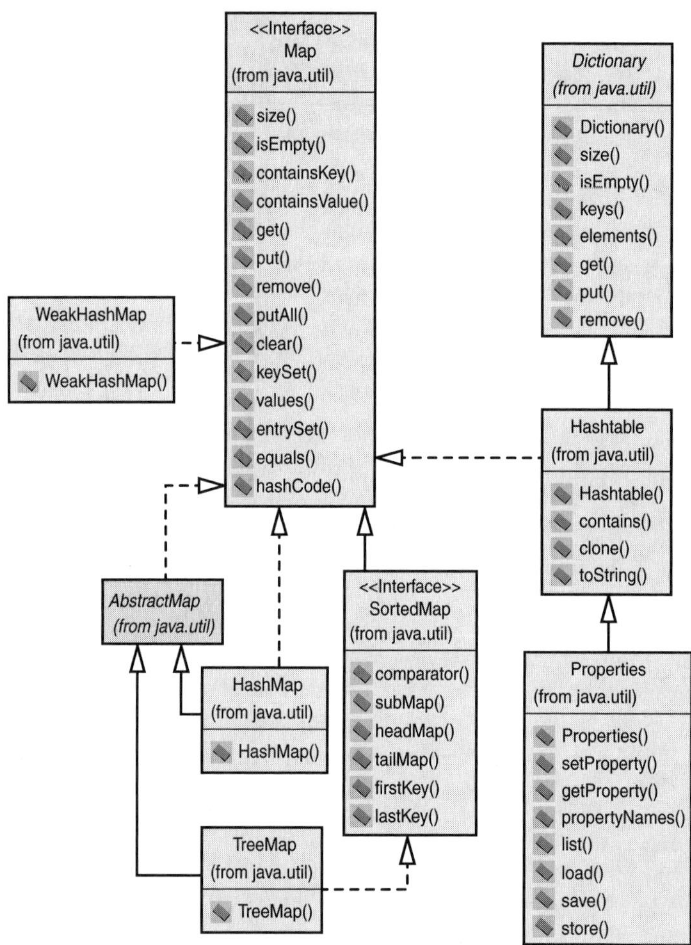

FIGURE 4.11
The map collection architecture.

Input/Output and State Persistence APIs

Input serialization is the process of reading data external to an application into data used within an application. Output serialization is the process of writing some data within an application to data external to the application. Input/Output (I/O) serialization is a common enough operation that the Java platform defines a framework and standard set of classes for serialization in the `java.io` package. The `java.io` package provides a basic set of abstractions for serializing objects, mapping bytes to and from I/O streams, mapping character data to and from I/O streams, and manipulating files. Figure 4.12 presents this base I/O architecture. A description of each entity in Figure 4.12 is provided here:

- `Serializable`: A marker interface implemented by classes whose state is serializable to an I/O stream.
- `Externalizable`: An interface implemented by classes that assume responsibility for writing and reading its context to and from an I/O stream.
- `InputStream`: A base abstract class for classes that read bytes from an input stream.
- `OutputStream`: A base abstract class for classes that write bytes to an input stream.
- `Reader`: A base abstract class for classes that read characters from an input stream.
- `Writer`: A base abstract class for classes that write characters to an output stream.
- `ObjectStreamClass`: A class which encapsulates a description of the object information contained in an I/O stream.
- `ObjectStreamField`: A class which encapsulates a description of a field within an object I/O stream.
- `ObjectInputValidation`: A callback interface permitting an object to be validated.
- `File`: A class which encapsulates a file and directory path.
- `FileDescriptor`: A class which encapsulates an interface to a system's file descriptor.
- `FileFilter`: An interface defining a filter for pathnames.
- `FilenameFilter`: An interface defining a filter for filenames.

Byte I/O Streams

Byte I/O streams represent those streams that inherit from the `InputStream` and `OutputStream` classes to support reading and writing bytes from and to an I/O stream. The byte I/O stream classes and interfaces provide mechanisms for converting data from I/O stream bytes into more manageable Java objects and data types, as well as providing a means for filtering and redirecting I/O data. Figure 4.13 depicts the entities involved in the byte I/O stream APIs. Each entity in Figure 4.13 is described here:

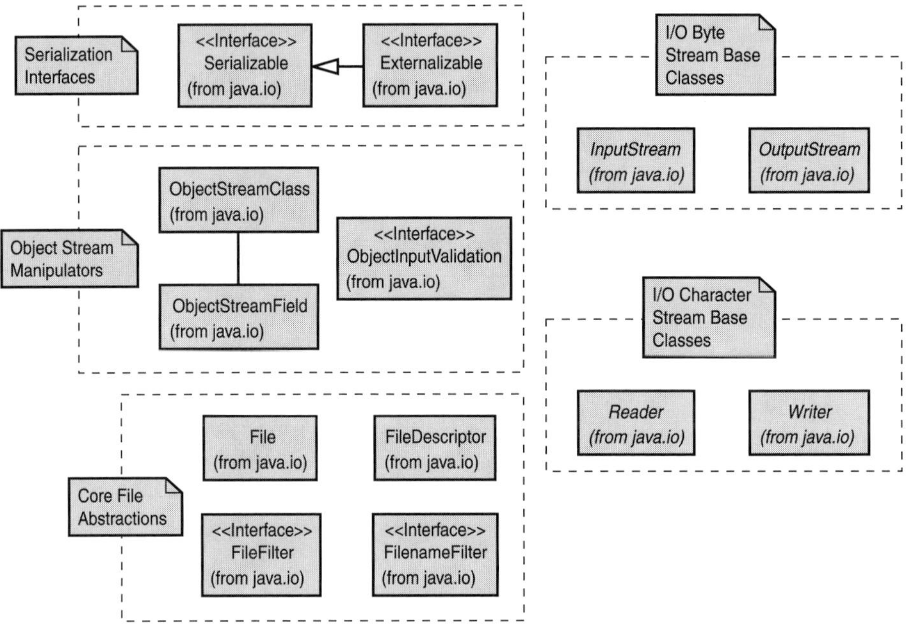

FIGURE 4.12
The base I/O architecture.

- `ByteArrayInputStream/ByteArrayOutputStream`: Used for reading/writing a sequence of bytes from/to an I/O stream.
- `FilterInputStream/FilterOutputStream`: Used for reading/writing data from/to an I/O stream by first passing the data through a filter that modifies the data in some way.
- `BufferedInputStream/BufferedOutputStream`: Used for reading/writing data from/to an I/O stream with a buffer in place to hold the data.
- `DataInput/DataOutput`: Defines interfaces for reading/writing bytes from/to an I/O stream with conversions to/from Java primitive types.
- `DataInputStream/DataOutputStream`: Encapsulates concrete implementations of the `DataInput/DataOutput` interfaces.
- `RandomAccessFile`: Provides interfaces to read and write from a file.
- `PushbackInputStream`: Used for reading data from an I/O stream with the capability to push data back to the input stream after it has been read.
- `FileInputStream/FileOutputStream`: Used for reading/writing data from/to a file I/O stream.

- `ObjectInput`/`ObjectOutput`: Defines interfaces for reading/writing Java objects from/to an I/O stream.
- `ObjectStreamConstants`: Defines constants used for writing objects to an I/O stream.
- `ObjectInputStream`/`ObjectOutputStream`: Encapsulates concrete implementations of `ObjectInput`/`ObjectOutput` interfaces.
- `PrintStream`: Provides a mechanism for printing formatted data to an I/O stream.
- `PipedInputStream`/`PipedOutputStream`: Enables one to create streams that are connected to one another such that data can be piped from a `PipedInputStream` directly into a `PipedOutputStream`.
- `SequenceInputStream`: Facilitates the concatenation of input streams.

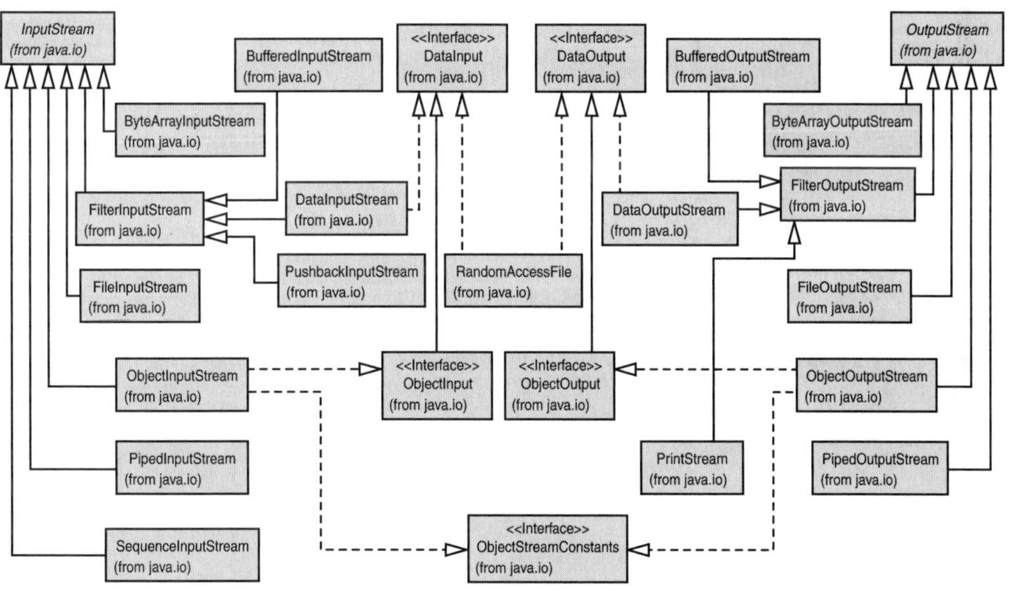

FIGURE 4.13
Byte I/O streams.

Character I/O Readers and Writers

Character I/O streams represent those streams that inherit from the `Reader` and `Writer` classes to support reading and writing characters from and to an I/O stream. The character I/O stream classes and interfaces provide a means for filtering and redirecting character I/O data. Figure 4.14 depicts the entities involved in the character I/O stream APIs. Each entity in Figure 4.14 is described here:

- InputStreamReader/OutputStreamWriter: Encapsulates concrete implementations of a Reader/Writer to support mapping bytes on an I/O stream from/to character data.
- FileReader/FileWriter: Used for reading/writing files of character data.
- BufferedReader/BufferedWriter: Used for reading/writing character data with an underlying buffer to manage data flow.
- LineNumberReader: Encapsulates a buffered character input stream that maintains a count of line numbers read.
- CharArrayReader/CharArrayWriter: Used to read/write data from/to a character array buffer.
- FilterReader/FilterWriter: Used for reading/writing character data by passing it through a filtering mechanism first.
- PushbackReader: Encapsulates a character stream reader enabling characters to be pushed back onto the character stream after they have been read.
- PipedReader/PipedWriter: Enables one to create character streams that are connected to one another such that character data can be piped from a PipedReader directly into a PipedWriter.
- StringReader/StringWriter: Used to read/write character data whose source is a String I/O stream.
- PrintWriter: Used to print formatted character data to a character stream.

Archive File APIs

The Java platform also contains APIs for programmatic manipulation of JAR, ZIP, and GZIP files. JAR file manipulation is accomplished via the java.util.jar package APIs. ZIP and GZIP file manipulation is accomplished via the java.util.zip package APIs. Because JAR files and their manifest files are the most common archive file format that we deal with throughout this book, we only briefly highlight the main features of JAR manipulation and manifest files in this section. The java.util.jar package is dependent on the java.util.zip package, and thus we necessarily describe some of the ZIP manipulation abstractions as well. Figure 14.15 presents the architecture of the APIs used to manipulate JAR files programmatically. Each class in Figure 14.15 is defined here:

- ZipEntry: Encapsulates a file entry in a ZIP file.
- JarEntry: Encapsulates a file entry, such as a Java class file, in a JAR file.
- ZipInputStream: Encapsulates an input stream from which ZIP files are read.
- JarInputStream: Encapsulates an input stream from which JAR files are read.
- Manifest: Encapsulates a manifest file and operations that can be performed to manipulate its attributes.

- `Attributes`: Encapsulates a mapping of `Manifest` file entry values.
- `ZipOutputStream`: Encapsulates an output stream to which ZIP files are written.
- `JarOutputStream`: Encapsulates an output stream to which JAR files can be written.

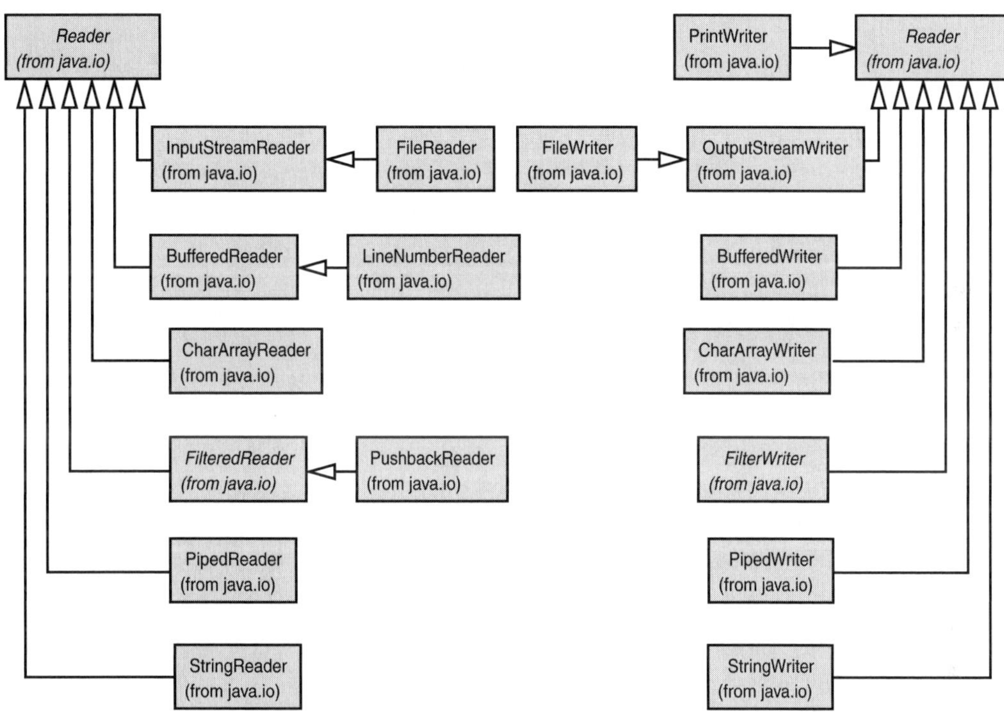

FIGURE 4.14
Character I/O readers and writers.

Properties Files

Throughout the book, we often utilize the inherent capability of the `java.util.Properties` class to initialize itself with properties read in from a file with support from the I/O serialization libraries. Although any type of `InputStream` can be passed into the `Properties.load(InputStream)` method to load in a set of properties from an input stream, we often create a `FileInputStream` associated with a properties file as input.

Each property is a name/value pair occupying one line of the properties file. Whitespace and lines beginning with `#` or `!` are ignored. A property on a line is defined with a key name, followed by `=` or `:`, and then followed by the `String` value for the property. A backslash (`\`) may be used to continue the definition of a property value throughout multiple lines.

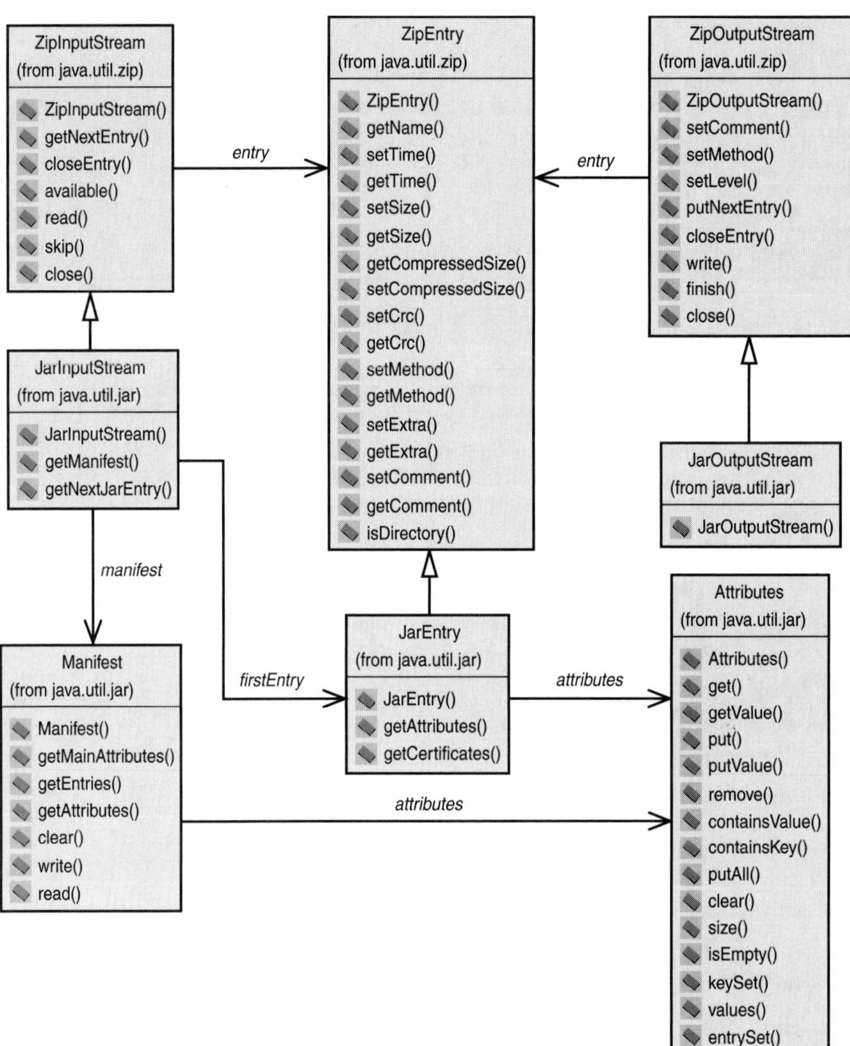

FIGURE 4.15
JAR I/O classes.

As an example, suppose we have a file named `Telecomm.properties` with the following contents:

```
# Server ID Name
ServerID = TelecommServerB2B
```

```
# B2C E-Commerce Web Site
B2Csite = http://www.assuredtech.com/demos/TelecommStore.html

# B2B Init Data
B2Bpartners = NetworksInc, PhonesGaloreCorp, EcommAdsInc, \
              SallysUsedPartsInc, MrAnnoyingTelemarketingCorp, \
              HappyTelcoContractorsLLC
```

We can then read in the three properties named `ServerID`, `B2Csite`, and `B2Bpartners` using this:

```
Properties properties = new Properties();
try{
  FileInputStream fin = new FileInputStream("Telecomm.properties");
  properties.load(fin); // Loads properties from file into object
  fin.close();
}
catch(IOException ioException){
  System.out.println("Error :"+ioException);
}
```

The `properties` object will then be loaded and can be accessed as `Properties` objects can normally be accessed. For example:

```
String serverID = properties.getProperty("ServerID");
String b2cSite = properties.getProperty("B2Csite");
String b2bPartners = properties.getProperty("B2Bpartners");
```

Threading APIs

Multiple threads of execution supported by an operating system generally provide a more efficient concurrent processing model than multiple processes of execution. Each thread has its own stack memory (for example, for parameters and method local variables pushed on the stack during method calls) but can share heap memory (for example, a class's instance variables) across all other threads. Multiple processes, on the other hand, must use interprocess communication mechanisms to share data. Although data sharing can provide advantages in terms of performance and reduced hand-coding, care must be taken to guarantee the "thread safety" of such shared data. If multiple threads attempt to access the same data at roughly equivalent times, concurrency issues can arise and induce unpredictable behavior for your application.

As an example, suppose a `Printer` object has an instance variable named `jobsCount` that is used by the `Printer` object to determine whether some maximum number of submitted print jobs has been exceeded before it submits a print job:

```
public class Printer{

  private static MAX_JOBS = 5;
  private int jobsCount = 0;

  public void printJob(PrintJob printJob) throws PrintException{
    if(jobsCount > MAX_JOBS){
      throw new PrintException("Max Jobs Exceeded");
    }
    else{
      // send printJob to printer device
      ++jobsCount;
    }
  }
  ...
}
```

Now suppose that multiple threads of execution can manipulate an instance of the same `Printer` object named `hallwayPrinter`. Then suppose that the following sequence occurs:

1. At one instant, the `hallwayPrinter` object's `jobsCount` value equals `5`.
2. Thread A calls `hallwayPrinter.submitJob(myJob)` at one instant. Thread A calls the `if(jobsCount > MAX_JOBS)` statement during the next instant, which evaluates to `false`, and Thread A enters the `else` block above.
3. Now suppose that Thread B's execution context is swapped in before Thread A can proceed.
4. Thread B calls `hallwayPrinter.submitJob(myJob)` at one instant. Thread B calls `if(jobsCount > MAX_JOBS)` the next instant, which evaluates to `false`, and Thread B also enters the `else` block above.
5. Both Thread A and Thread B complete their `else` block with `jobsCount` being incremented to `7`, which exceeds the maximum job count.
6. The printer now jams because it has six jobs in its queue, which exceeds the maximum load it may be capable of handling. Note that we're assuming a rather pitiful printer here for simplicity of describing our problem.

This issue can be avoided by making the `Printer` class thread-safe. One solution would be to use the `synchronized` Java keyword to declare that the `submitJob()` method must be executed completely before any other thread can access the `Printer` object. For example:

```
public synchronized void printJob(PrintJob printJob)
  throws PrintException{
  ...
}
```

The synchronized keyword can actually be used in Java in the following most common ways to provide thread safety:

- *Synchronized Instance Methods*: Adding synchronized in front of an instance method definition requires that the invoking thread obtain a "lock" on the object associated with that object instance before it can execute the method. If another thread already has the object's lock, the invoking thread will block. For example:

```
public synchronized void printJob(PrintJob printJob)
 throws PrintException {...}
```

- *Synchronized Class Methods*: Adding synchronized in front of a static class method definition requires that the invoking thread obtain a "lock" on the associated class before it can execute the method. If another thread already has the class's lock, the invoking thread will block. For example:

```
public static synchronized void printJob(PrintJob printJob)
 throws PrintException {...}
```

- *Synchronized Objects in Methods*: Finer-grained synchronization can be provided by adding the synchronized keyword with parentheses encapsulating an object that needs to be protected before the block of code within a method that needs to be guarded. For example:

```
public void printJob(PrintJob printJob)
 throws PrintException{
  synchronized(jobsCount){
    if(jobsCount > MAX_JOBS){
      // Bla bla bla
    }
    else{
      // Bla bla bla
      ++jobsCount;
    }
  }
  // Execute other code here
}
```

- *Synchronized Object Blocking and Notification*: The Object.wait() method can be used in one synchronized block of code to cause the invoking thread to release its lock and block. The Object.notifyAll() or Object.notify() method can then be used elsewhere within a synchronized block of code to notify blocking objects that they should go ahead and try to obtain the lock and proceed with processing. For example:

```
// This method call obtains lock on object
// Assume application code to use printer calls this method
public synchronized void printJob(PrintJob printJob){
  // This while loop will loop until jobsCount <= MAX_JOBS
```

```
    while(jobsCount > MAX_JOBS){
      wait(); // if jobsCount > MAX_JOBS, then release lock and block
    }
    // Only gets to this point in code if jobsCount <= MAX_JOBS
    ++jobsCount;
  }

  // This method also obtains lock on object
  // Assume a printer callback device calls this method when job done
  public synchronized void jobComplete(String jobID){
    // When a job is complete, the jobsCount gets reduced
    --jobsCount;
    // All blocked threads are notified that can obtain lock again
    notifyAll();
  }
```

As demonstrated, Java provides many simple ways to synchronize threads and make objects thread-safe. Creating the actual threads in Java is even easier. Figure 14.16 depicts the primary interfaces to the Java thread API. Whenever you create a thread, you can choose to have a class that serves as your thread of execution (for example, `MyExecutionClass`) either implement the `Runnable` interface or extend the `Thread` class. The entities in Figure 14.16 are defined here:

- `Thread`: Encapsulates a thread in Java and operations that can be performed on a thread. An execution class that wants to operate as a thread may extend this class and implement the `run()` method. A thread is then started by simply calling `start()` on the execution class. For example:

```
public MyExecutionClass extends Thread{

  public void run(){
     // Implement thread of execution code here
  }

  // example of creating a thread
  public static void main(String args[]){
    MyExecutionClass threadClass = new MyExecutionClass();
    threadClass.start();  // starts thread
  }
}
```

- `Runnable`: Defines an interface implemented by those execution classes that want to operate as a thread. An execution class that wants to operate as a thread then implements the `run()` method. Objects of the execution class are passed in as an argument to a `Thread` object constructor, and the `start()` method is called on that `Thread` object instance. For example:

```
public MyExecutionClass implements Runnable{
```

```
    public void run(){
       // Implement thread of execution code here
    }

    // example of creating a thread
    public static void main(String args[]){
      MyExecutionClass threadClass = new MyExecutionClass();
      Thread myThread = new Thread(threadClass);
      myThread.start();  // starts thread
    }
  }
```

- `ThreadGroup`: Encapsulates a group of threads and operations that can be applied to the entire thread grouping. A thread group may have a parent group and zero or more children thread groups.
- `ThreadLocal`: Encapsulates a thread's local variables which represent variables visible only to the current thread's execution context.
- `InheritableThreadLocal`: Encapsulates a type of thread local variable that can be inherited by the children of a thread.

Date and Time APIs

Manipulating dates and times is a very common programming task with plenty of inherent Java support. Java provides support for encapsulating a generic time instant down to the millisecond, as well as in the form of a calendar date. Dates can even be manipulated to account for changes in daylight savings time and time zones using Java APIs. The particular region in which an application is running can also dynamically adjust for locale-specific expressions of dates and times.

Java accomplishes these various date and time expressions and manipulations using a few core classes in the `java.util` and `java.text` packages. Figure 14.17 lists a few of the most important date and time Java APIs. The various classes shown in Figure 14.17 are described here:

- `Locale`: Encapsulates a geographical, political, or cultural region.
- `Date`: Encapsulates an instant in time with the precision of milliseconds.
- `DateFormat`: Serves as an abstract class for formatting dates and times.
- `DateFormatSymbols`: Encapsulates locale-specific symbols used for formatting dates and times (for example, names of months and days).
- `SimpleDateFormat`: Serves as a concrete class for formatting dates and times in a locale-aware fashion.

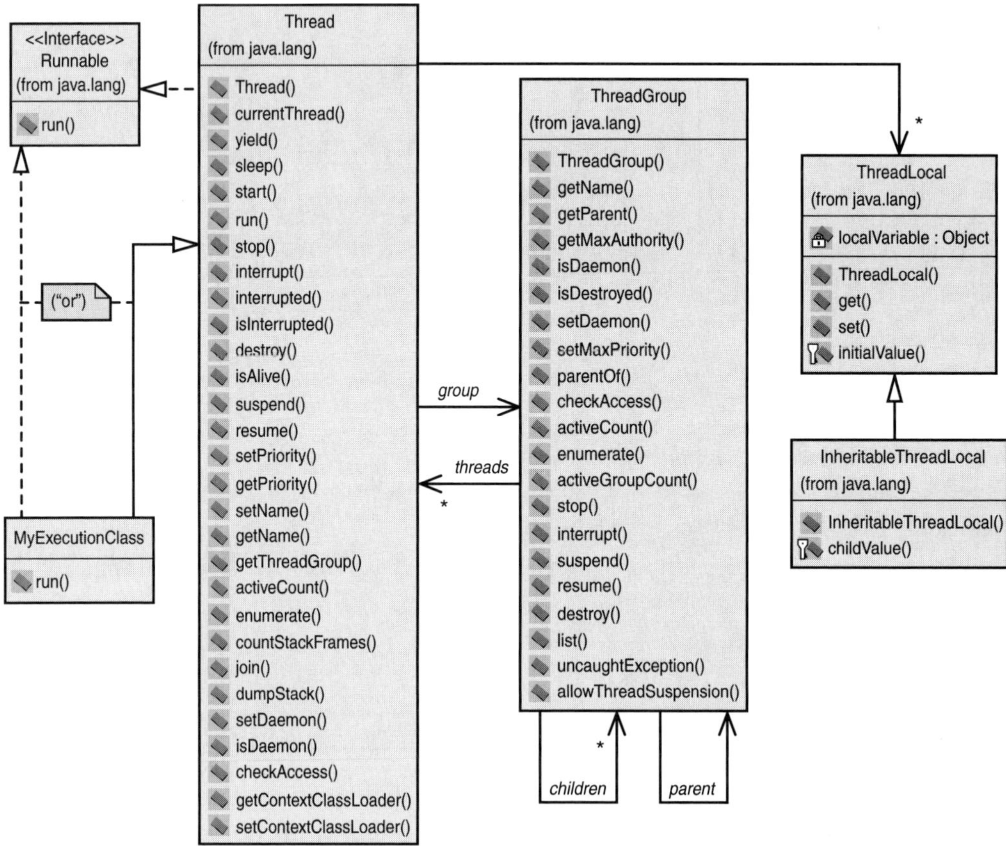

FIGURE 4.16

Java threads.

- `Calendar`: Serves as an abstract class encapsulating a particular conversion between a `Date` object and a numeric element of a calendar date such as a year, month, day, or hour.
- `GregorianCalendar`: Serves as a concrete implementation of a `Calendar` for converting to the Gregorian calendar format.
- `TimeZone`: Serves as an abstract class encapsulating a time-zone offset accounting for daylight savings time.
- `SimpleTimeZone`: Serves as a concrete implementation of a `TimeZone` used with a Gregorian calendar.

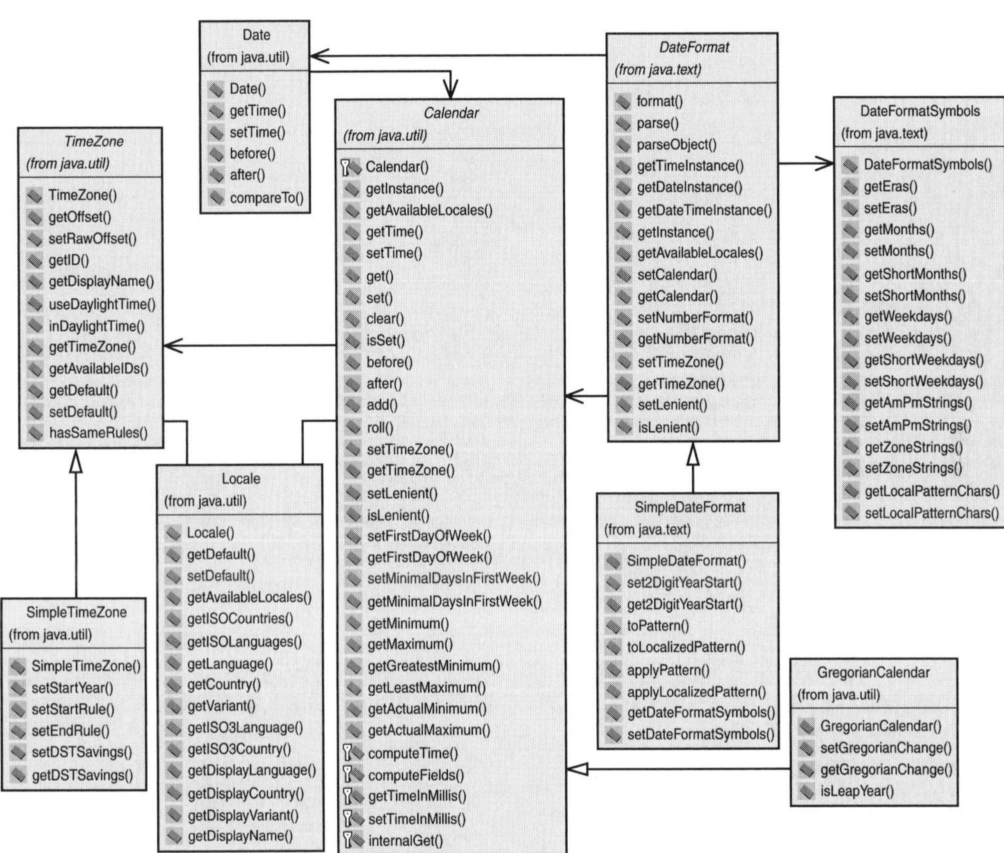

FIGURE 4.17
Date and time APIs.

Java Applets

Java applets were one of the original reasons why Java was so well received early in its history. The birth of the World Wide Web and widespread Internet access, coupled with the capability to download executable Java code to Web browsers in the form of Java applets, was cause for much excitement on the part of developers. Furthermore, the ease with which all of this could be accomplished was one of the key factors that helped spawn Java's initial popularity.

A Java applet that can execute inside of a Web browser is created by making a class (for example, `MyApplet`) that extends the `java.applet.Applet` class as depicted in Figure 4.18. The `AppletStub` interface is implemented by browsers to return a handle to the context environment in which the applet runs. The `AppletStub` returns various environment information about an applet to the `Applet` on request. A subset of information about the context is returned via an `AppletContext` object. An `AppletContext` may have a handle to one or more `Applet` objects that were embedded in a particular Web page document.

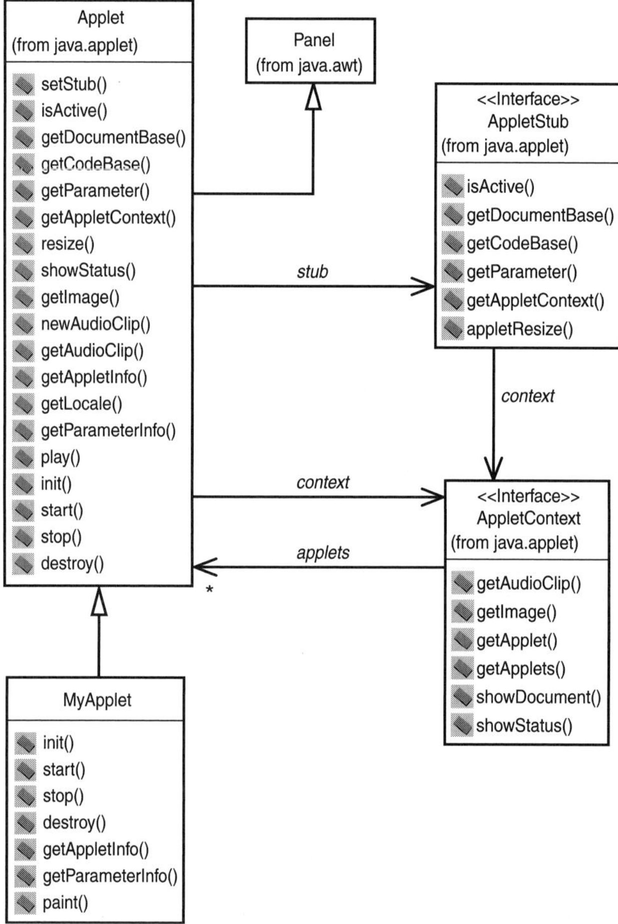

FIGURE 4.18
Java applets.

The `Applet` class extends a graphical interface `Panel` that displays as a blank slate inside of a browser window. A custom applet, such as `MyApplet`, is responsible for "painting" the blank slate with user-interface components that a user can interact with via the Web browser window. As an example, we may initially define our `MyApplet` class to display a few simple applet parameters as shown here:

```
package ejava.applet;

import java.awt.*;
import java.awt.event.*;
import java.applet.Applet;

public class MyApplet extends Applet {
  private boolean isStandalone = false;
  private int sampleValue1;
  private String sampleValue2;

  public void paint(Graphics g)
  {
    System.out.println("Paint");
    g.setColor(Color.blue); // Set working color to blue

    Dimension dimension = getSize(); // Get Panel.size()
    g.drawRect(0, 0, dimension.width-1,dimension.height-1); // Draw box

    g.setColor(Color.red); // Set working color to red

    // Get a parameter and print String
    String parameterOneInfo = "SAMPLE_VALUE_1 : " +
      this.getParameter("SAMPLE_VALUE_1");
    g.drawString(parameterOneInfo, 15, 25);

    // Get a parameter and print String
    String parameterTwoInfo = "SAMPLE_VALUE_2 :"+
      this.getParameter("SAMPLE_VALUE_2");
    g.drawString(parameterTwoInfo, 15, 75);
  }

  // Get a parameter value
  public String getParameter(String key, String def) {
    // If standalone boolean set true, return system property
    // Else return Java Applet.getParameter()
    return isStandalone
           ? System.getProperty(key, def)
           : (getParameter(key) != null ? getParameter(key) : def);
  }
}
```

The lifecycle operations of an `Applet` may also be implemented by `MyApplet`. Lifecycle operations include `init()` for initial applet loading, `start()` for whenever an applet is viewed on a Web page, `stop()` for whenever the applet becomes nonvisible, and `destroy()` for whenever the applet is unloaded from a Web browser. The `getAppletInfo()` and `getParameterInfo()`

methods can also be implemented by an applet to return a custom information `String` about an applet and an array of `String` information about applet parameters, respectively. For example, the following methods may be added to `MyApplet`:

```
//Initialize the applet
public void init() {
  try {
    sampleValue1 = Integer.parseInt(
      getParameter("SAMPLE_VALUE_1", "-1"));
  }
  catch (Exception exception) {
    exception.printStackTrace();
  }
  try {
    sampleValue2 = getParameter("SAMPLE_VALUE_2", "");
  }
  catch (Exception exception) {
    exception.printStackTrace();
  }
}

//Start the applet
public void start() {
  System.out.println(" Applet is starting ...");
}

//Stop the applet
public void stop() {
  System.out.println("Applet is stopping ...");
}

//Destroy the applet
public void destroy() {
  System.out.println("Preparing to remove the applet from browser...");
}

//Get Applet information
public String getAppletInfo() {
  return "Sample Applet";
}

//Get parameter info
public String[][] getParameterInfo()
{
  String[][] parametersInformation =
  {
```

```
      {"SAMPLE_VALUE_1", "int", "Sample Value 1"},
      {"SAMPLE_VALUE_2", "String", "Sample Value 2"},
    };
    return parametersInformation;
  }
```

The Java class files for an applet are most often stored as a cohesive application inside of a JAR file on a Web server. A Web page may reference such code to be automatically downloaded to the user's Web browser when that user visits the Web page. Here's the basic structure of an applet reference embedded inside of a Web page with self-explanatory field descriptions:

```
<APPLET
  CODEBASE = optional_URL_from_where_applet_is_downloaded
  ARCHIVE = optional_comma_separated_list_of_JARs_containing_applet_code
  CODE = required_class_name_of_Applet_subtype
  ALT = optional_text_to_be_displayed_if_applet_can't_load
  NAME = optional_name_of_applet_instance
  WIDTH = required_width_of_applet_in_pixels
  HEIGHT = required_height_of_applet_in_pixels
  ALIGN = optional_alignment_of_applet_on_web_page
  VSPACE = optional_space_in_pixels_above_and_below_applet
  HSPACE = optional_space_in_pixels_left_and_right_of_applet
>
<PARAM NAME = some_attribute_name VALUE = some_attribute_value>
<PARAM NAME = another_attribute_name VALUE = another_attribute_value>
 . . .
some_alternate_HTML_to_display_if_applet_can't_load
</APPLET>
```

Thus, using our earlier `MyApplet` example, we might define an HTML Web page to reference our applet stored in a `MyApplet.jar` file and pass it two applet parameters as shown here:

```
<HTML>
<HEAD>
<TITLE>
HTML Applet Test Page
</TITLE>
</HEAD>
<BODY>
SampleApplet will appear below in a Java enabled browser.<BR>
<APPLET
  CODEBASE = "."
  CODE     = " ejava.applet.MyApplet.class"
  NAME     = "MyApplet"
  ARCHIVE = "MyApplet.jar"
  WIDTH    = 400
  HEIGHT   = 300
```

```
  HSPACE   = 0
  VSPACE   = 0
>
<PARAM NAME = "SAMPLE_VALUE_1" VALUE = "123">
<PARAM NAME = "SAMPLE_VALUE_2" VALUE = "Hi There!">
</APPLET>
</BODY>
</HTML>
```

Conclusions

Java provides a simple and very rich suite of platform features, tools, language features, and common APIs that have enabled developers to rapidly develop and deploy more reliable applications. Such features of Java made it particularly attractive for use in building enterprise applications. We have provided a quick overview and refresher here for the reader to understand those foundations of the Java language and platform that have been so fundamental to enabling Java to be used in the enterprise.

Java enterprise systems and the remainder of this book build on these core features of Java to make the rapid development of enterprise systems a practical proposition. We not only describe the specific Java enterprise packages and features of the J2EE throughout this book, but also cover many of the packages and features of the J2SE that have a common enterprise application. Thus, although this chapter provided only a summary of J2SE features such as those provided in the `java.lang`, `java.util`, `java.io`, and `java.text` packages, future chapters delve deeper into the J2SE features heavily utilized by enterprise applications, including a discussion of the `java.net`, `java.rmi`, `java.security`, and `java.sql` packages. Of course, throughout the remainder of the book, we also describe all of the Java packages used for standard Java enterprise development and with the J2EE. The next chapter provides an overview of such technologies.

Java Enterprise System Architecture with the J2EE

CHAPTER

5

IN THIS CHAPTER

- The J2EE Model 106
- Enterprise Java and J2EE Architecture 111
- Data Connectivity 114
- Communication Mechanisms 115
- Assurance Mechanisms 117
- Client Connectivity 119
- Web Connectivity 120
- Application Connectivity 121
- The J2EE Future 122

This chapter describes the J2EE in the context of an overall enterprise systems environment. We discussed the needs of an enterprise system in Chapter 1, "Enterprise Architectural Overview." Chapter 2, "Object-Oriented Software Development for the Enterprise," and Chapter 3, "Component-Based Software Development for the Enterprise," presented arguments for the use of object-oriented technologies and component-based technologies in building such systems. Chapter 4, "Java Foundations for Enterprise Development," presented the basic features of Java that make it such an excellent language and platform for use in building enterprise systems. This chapter describes those object-oriented and component-based technologies that can be used to build enterprise systems using Java enterprise technologies and the J2EE.

The J2EE model and Java enterprise technologies, means for data connectivity, client and user interfacing, communications enabling, systems assurance, Web enabling, and application enabling are considered part of an overall enterprise architecture. In addition to describing what the J2EE currently provides for developing Java enterprise systems, we highlight those key components used for building Java enterprise systems that fall outside the realm of J2EE environments.

In this chapter, you will learn:

- The model for developing enterprise applications using the J2EE.
- The top-level architecture for building Java enterprise applications with the J2EE as advocated by this book.
- The Java enterprise technology solutions for database connectivity, client and user interfacing, distributed communications and communication services, systems assurance, enterprise Web enabling, and enterprise application enabling.
- The future extensions targeted for J2EE-based development.

The J2EE Model

Before there was a formal Java enterprise model of development, the Java Development Kit (JDK) versions 1.0 and 1.1 were the original standard platforms defined by Sun to create standalone Java-based applications and Web-based Java applets. The JDK did indeed offer many advantages for use in enterprise development projects by providing an easy-to-use and platform-independent approach to rapidly building enterprise systems. In addition to the core JDK platform support, a collection of enterprise APIs emerged, some of which were part of the JDK and others of which were offered as standard extensions to the Java platform. Java APIs useful to enterprise applications such as those for database connectivity and distributed communications were all employed by developers wanting to rapidly build enterprise applications with Java.

The use of Java to build enterprise systems was catching on. In addition to the standard Java platform and standard Java extension APIs, many third-party Java-based APIs began to enter the market. In particular, Java-based COTS implementations of the CORBA distributed computing platform further stimulated interest in developing enterprise applications with Java. While Sun was originally touting Java as the platform for the World Wide Web and focusing on Java applets, the explosion in back-end server-side enterprise usage of Java by industry soon aligned Sun's marketing efforts to consider the enterprise application of Java more formally and seriously.

Marketers originally coined the terms *Java Technologies for the Enterprise (JTE)* and *Java Platform for the Enterprise (JPE)* to refer to a collection of APIs that were extensions to the Java platform and had direct relevance to enterprise applications. However, the APIs were often developed by different groups and at times grew apart from one another. Furthermore, it was not always clear to developers just how these APIs could relate to one another and how they could be used to keep their systems open for use with different underlying vendor implementations of the various enterprise services. This is where the Java 2 Platform, Enterprise Edition (J2EE) entered the picture and attempted to address these needs. The J2EE was introduced by Sun Microsystems in June 1999 as a standard platform and environment for building enterprise systems using Java.

J2EE Features

The J2EE is defined as an umbrella platform and programming model for building Java enterprise systems for use with different underlying vendor implementations of an enterprise system infrastructure. The J2EE (`http://www.java.sun.com/j2ee`) is most accurately defined and scoped according to five standard documents and software libraries:

- *Specification:* The J2EE specification defines the requirements that a J2EE vendor product implementation must satisfy.
- *Programming Model:* The programming model is cast in the form of a developer's guide explaining how application developers might use various aspects of the J2EE. The guide is primarily described at a conceptual and very high level with a sample application at the end of the guide.
- *Platform:* The J2EE platform is the set of integrated enterprise API library software and development tools. The J2EE platform depends on installation of the J2SE v1.2 platform.
- *Reference Implementation:* The J2EE reference implementation is a sample implementation of the underlying services utilized by the J2EE platform APIs. It is primarily meant to be used in early development and prototyping environments.
- *Compatibility Test Suite:* The compatibility test suite is used by vendors to determine whether their implementation of the J2EE services satisfies the J2EE specification requirements.

J2EE Component-Container Architecture

The J2EE model for enterprise application development involves a component-container approach to development as discussed in Chapter 3. A J2EE container environment essentially offers the following:

- *J2SE Platform:* The standard J2SE v1.2 Java runtime environment atop of which the J2EE operates.
- *Java Enterprise APIs:* A collection of standard Java enterprise API versions.
- *Java Enterprise Implementations:* Any Java enterprise service provider implementations of the Java enterprise APIs.
- *Deployment Services:* An environment for configurably deploying J2EE components.
- *Management Services:* Management services offered by the container for providing an efficient, scalable, and dependable computing environment.

J2SE v1.2 versus J2SE v1.3

It is important to highlight the fact that the J2EE v1.2 based architecture assumed by this book depends upon the J2SE v1.2 and not the J2SE v1.3. Indeed this choice of versioning by Sun may be confusing. That is, many folks wonder why "v1.1" still refers to the Java 1.1 platform, and "v1.2" applies to the Java 2 or J2SE platform, but "v1.3" also refers to the Java 2 or J2SE platform. In terms of what this all means to enterprise developers, the J2SE v1.3 platform is essentially the J2SE v1.2 platform with JNDI and RMI/IIOP included with the platform, whereas JNDI and RMI/IIOP are considered standard extensions to J2SE v1.2 platform users. The J2SE v1.3 also provides numerous performance, security, and GUI enhancements as well as bug fixes.

Specifically, four major classes of components and their containers are defined within the J2EE specification. These four component-container classifications, depicted in Figure 5.1, can be classified according to whether they are client-oriented or server-oriented and whether they are Web-oriented or purely application-oriented. The four J2EE component-container models are described here:

- *EJB Application Servers:* Enterprise JavaBean components represent application-specific components built by a developer or third party to operate inside of an EJB application container environment. EJB container environments are implemented by third-party vendors to offer scalable application services to EJB component developers.
- *Web Application Servers:* Web components come in two flavors: Java Servlets and JavaServer Pages (JSPs). Web components represent application-specific handling of requests received by a Web server and generate Web responses.

- *Applet Clients:* Applets are Java applications that can run inside of a Web browser and offer a GUI inside of a Web browser. The J2EE specification outlines a methodology for hosting applets inside of a standardized applet container environment with added support for acting as J2EE-based clients to J2EE-based servers.
- *Application Clients:* Application clients are Java-based clients that typically run on a user desktop or workstation and offer a GUI. The J2EE specification outlines a methodology for hosting application clients inside of a standardized application client container environment with added API support for acting as J2EE-based clients to J2EE-based servers.

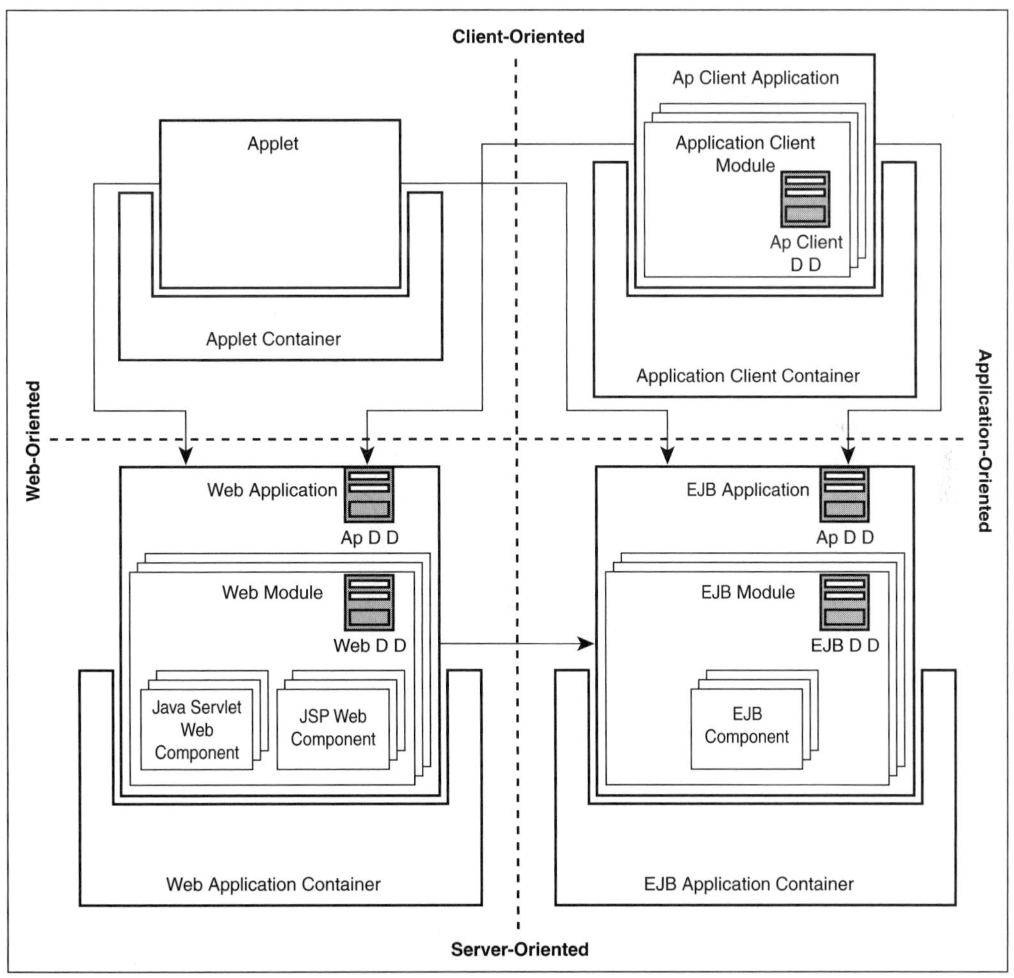

FIGURE 5.1
J2EE components and containers.

In addition to the four classes of components and containers, Figure 5.1 also illustrates the basic component assembly model assumed by the J2EE. At the finest level of granularity, both Web and EJB components can be grouped into a module that has its own component-level deployment descriptor (DD). A deployment descriptor describes configurable properties of container services and components utilized by a particular deployed instance of its associated components (for example, security levels, transactions semantics, initialization parameters). Modules and an application DD are assembled into concrete applications that run inside of a particular container environment. Application DDs are actually defined in such a way that multiple types of modules can be assembled into a cohesive application if a J2EE provider so chooses (for example, combining a Web module with one or more EJB modules to create an integrated Web-enabled enterprise application).

Modules, applications, and their associated DDs are also deployed in their own type of JAR files. A Web module is deployed in a Web application archive (WAR) file with a `.war` extension. An EJB module is deployed in an EJB JAR file with a `.jar` extension. Enterprise applications composed of one or more J2EE modules are deployed in an enterprise archive (EAR) file with a `.ear` extension.

J2EE Restrictions

Because J2EE container environments include an underlying J2SE platform and Java enterprise APIs, without further restrictions, J2EE components could simply perform all the operations that an application in a standalone J2SE environment could perform. However, this would violate the fundamental component-container model of the J2EE and affect a container's capability to provide management services for its components. This is why the J2EE specification defines a minimum set of permissions that scope which operations a J2EE-based component can invoke on its underlying J2SE and Java enterprise API environment. Although certain J2EE product service providers may allow for a wider set of permissions, J2EE-based component application developers are at a minimum restricted to the following set of permissions:

- *EJB Application Servers:* EJB application components can queue print jobs, create socket connections as a client (but not server connections), and read system properties.
- *Web Application Servers:* Web components can also queue print jobs, create socket connections as a client, and read system properties. Additionally, Web components can load external libraries and can read and write files.
- *Applet Clients:* Applet components can only connect to the server defined within its `CODEBASE` and can read a limited set of properties.
- *Application Clients:* Application client components have the most freedom out of all J2EE-component types. Application clients can create socket connections as a client and accept and listen for socket connections as a server on a local machine's ports above and

including port 1024. Application clients can also read system properties, queue print jobs, exit a JVM process, and load external libraries. Application clients can also perform various security-sensitive GUI operations such as accessing a clipboard, accessing an event queue, and displaying a window without a warning banner.

Enterprise Java and J2EE Architecture

Although the J2EE is a centerpiece of Java enterprise development and a fundamental aspect of this book, this book focuses on more than just the development of components that operate inside of J2EE-based environments. We also describe many of the Java enterprise APIs that are part of the J2EE in general such that they can also be used in standalone Java environments and not necessarily used from within the context of a J2EE container. In addition to the standard Java enterprise APIs that are incorporated by the J2EE, we describe a host of other Java-based technologies that can be used to facilitate the practical construction of enterprise systems. Although such auxiliary technologies are currently outside of the J2EE scope, we suspect, and in certain cases are already aware of the fact, that in due time such technologies will become integrated with the J2EE platform. We comment on the future of the J2EE at the end of this chapter.

There are many advantages to the approach taken by this book. For one, immediate widespread vendor availability of fully integrated J2EE-based container environments will be limited for some time as opposed to the availability of individually mature Java enterprise component API implementations on the market. Furthermore, many real-world enterprise system applications still have widely distributed and disparate legacy system and application needs that make it difficult to invest in J2EE-based environments for all distributed enterprise server scenarios. Rather, a standalone Java enterprise application may be just fine for certain enterprise system deployment scenarios. It will certainly be the case for many near-term legacy enterprise application integration (EAI) solutions to consider use of standalone Java application environments until EAI connector technologies can be integrated with the J2EE. For all of these reasons, we describe many of the Java enterprise APIs that can be used in standalone Java applications in a largely J2EE-independent and unrestricted fashion early in the book. We then focus on Web-enabling and application-enabling technologies later in the book in the context of using J2EE containers. Furthermore, we also describe how use of such J2EE environments can simplify usage of the Java enterprise APIs that were described in earlier chapters. After all, the aim of this book is to turn you into a well-rounded and well-informed enterprise systems engineer.

Java Enterprise System Architecture Overview

Figure 1.3 of Chapter 1 presented a broad classification of the various enabling and service technologies used to create enterprise systems. Figure 5.2 shows the more concrete architecture solution components advocated by this book for building enterprise systems using Java enterprise technologies. The diagram in Figure 5.2 is primarily logical by nature and is not meant to depict a physical architecture for enterprise systems. Rather, the diagram depicts the various logical needs for construction of an enterprise system and the various Java enterprise technologies that are used to support such needs. The logical architecture defined within Figure 5.2 actually has many physical architecture permutations.

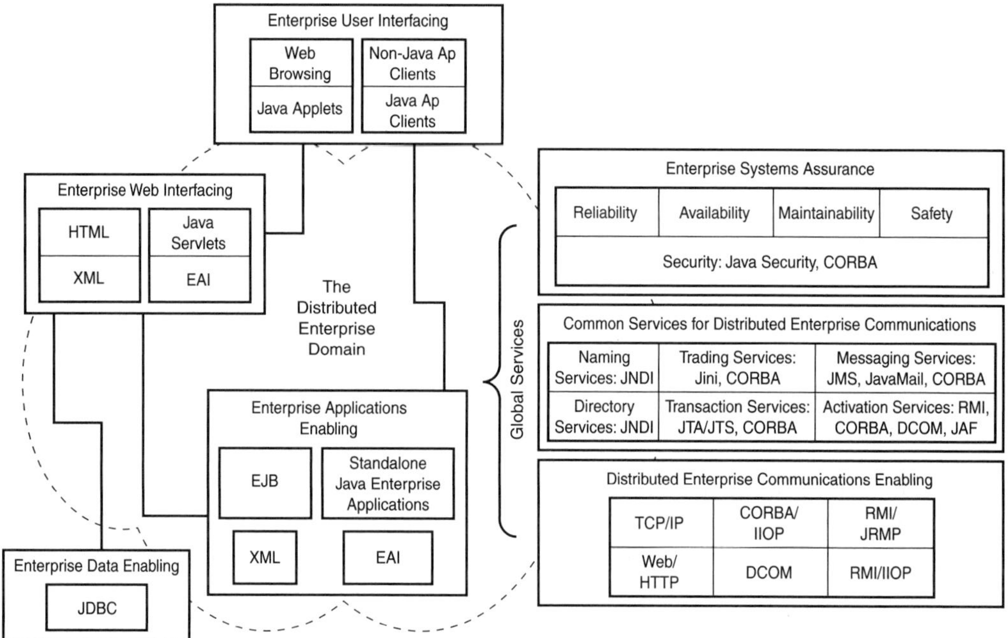

FIGURE 5.2
The Java enterprise system logical architecture.

As you'll see in subsequent sections of this chapter, all the enterprise APIs specified within the J2EE are represented in Figure 5.2. Figure 5.2 also identifies a few technologies that we describe in this book that currently fall outside of the J2EE scope. Each logical enterprise component depicted in Figure 5.2 has a corresponding enterprise technology solution provided in the following fashion:

- *Enterprise User Interfacing:* Web-based Java applets and desktop Java application clients can be built using Java-based GUI techniques and can be hosted in standalone J2SE environments or inside J2EE container environments. Traditional non-Java–oriented Web browsing applications can also be used with J2EE-based Web servers. Additionally, non-Java–based clients can also interface with server-side components using distributed communication technologies such as CORBA, DCOM, and TCP/IP.

- *Enterprise Data Enabling:* The Java Database Connectivity (JDBC) solution is used to communicate with databases. J2EE Web, EJB application, and application client containers all utilize the JDBC API. Standalone Java enterprise applications running outside of a J2EE environment can also be used with JDBC.
- *Distributed Enterprise Communications Enabling:* Technologies for distributed communications such as CORBA, RMI, DCOM, TCP/IP, and Web-based HTTP are all possible within Java enterprise environments, whether they're embedded in Web servers, application servers, standalone Java applications, or enterprise user interface clients.
- *Common Services for Distributed Enterprise Communications:* A host of communication services are possible within Java enterprise environments. Naming services enable the lookup of named objects across a network. Directory services allow for more sophisticated searching of objects via attribute descriptions of those network objects. Trading services offer a more dynamic means to connect with services on a network. Messaging services allow for the asynchronous communication of messages. Activation services are underlying services that activate objects based on client requests. Transaction services allow for the management of atomic and dependable operations across distributed resources and clients.
- *Enterprise Systems Assurance:* Various properties of systems assurance such as reliability, availability, maintainability, safety, and security are more inherent properties of a system as opposed to a distinct service. However, Java-based enterprise environments encapsulate many security services with distinct APIs. CORBA has also defined security services within a CORBA Security Service Specification and is primarily useful for security interoperability across application environments.
- *Enterprise Web Enabling:* Although HTML has been the most traditional format for creating Web pages, XML is a more flexible and extensible mechanism for describing data and controls such as those needed within Web pages. Java Servlets and Java Server Pages are the standard J2EE-based mechanisms for receiving Web-based requests and for generating HTML- or XML-based responses. Web-enabled applications can also take advantage of the various global services for distributed communications, communication services, and assurance services.
- *Enterprise Applications Enabling:* XML can also be used to enable enterprise applications to communicate with other applications within and outside of a particular enterprise. EJBs are the primary means defined within the J2EE to create server-side application business logic. Various enterprise application integration technologies are also a part of application enabling. Enterprise-enabled applications can also take advantage of the various global services for distributed communications, communication services, and assurance services. Finally, when J2EE-based application enabling is not possible, a standalone Java enterprise application environment composed of a Java 2 platform and standard Java enterprise API extensions can be used.

Data Connectivity

Enterprise information and knowledge are most often managed inside of a database management system (DBMS). Such data is often accumulated over many years and also is often heavily depended on by legacy applications. It should come as no surprise that such data is thus highly valued by an enterprise. Enterprises also end up creating strong dependencies and ties to particular vendor DBMS implementations. For all of these reasons, it is important to have a DBMS-independent solution for accessing enterprise data in a fashion that enables enterprise applications to remain stable despite changes in DBMS vendor product selections.

The Java Database Connectivity API is an enterprise API that provides a means for accessing and managing enterprise data stored in a DBMS. The JDBC API is defined in a fashion that permits DBMS-independent construction of commands to access the database using a DBMS command language known as the Structured Query Language (SQL). As with most Java enterprise APIs, an underlying Service Provider Interface (SPI) allows a particular DBMS vendor interface to be adapted for use with the JDBC libraries and permit enterprise applications to use the same JDBC API.

The JDBC API can be divided into three categories:

- *JDBC 1.0 Core API:* Defines most of the basic JDBC functionality.
- *JDBC 2.0 Core API:* Includes all the functionality contained in the JDBC 1.0 version plus a host of new features for managing query results and manipulating new data types. The JDBC 2.0 core API is included with the J2SE, and with the J2EE by virtue of its inclusion with the J2SE.
- *JDBC 2.0 Standard Extension API:* Offers a range of more sophisticated enterprise features useful in middle-tier servers for managing scalable database access.

There are two primary scenarios in which Java enterprise applications can utilize JDBC to access a DBMS. In a standalone J2SE application environment scenario, an enterprise application has unrestricted access to the JDBC API. In a J2EE application environment scenario, a J2EE container provides a set of management services that manage JDBC-based resources. The J2EE environment restricts some of the JDBC API operations allowed to be performed by J2EE components.

J2EE application client, Web, and EJB container environments must support the JDBC 2.0 core API. Inclusion of JDBC with J2EE applet containers is optional. Inclusion of the JDBC 2.0 standard extension API is required for J2EE containers, but an underlying implementation is optional (although it is recommended for J2EE EJB container environments).

Communication Mechanisms

Enabling applications for distributed communications is a fundamental necessity when building an enterprise system. An enterprise application may need to offer its services in a distributed server mode, or it may need to tap the services of a distributed server and act as a distributed client. Both modes of operation require an interface to some distributed communications code for enabling an application to communicate over a network.

This book describes two main approaches for enabling an enterprise application to utilize distributed communications. One approach advocates use of a standalone Java enterprise environment that uses an underlying distributed communications API and implementation. Another approach advocates use of an underlying communications infrastructure embedded into a J2EE container environment that offers distributed communication services transparently to J2EE components.

Regardless of the approach, a particular methodology of communications and underlying protocol must be selected to enable clients and servers to communicate with one another. These are the primary approaches adopted in this book:

- *TCP/IP:* The Transmission Control Protocol/Internet Protocol (TCP/IP), a standard protocol suite used on the Internet, serves as the underlying protocol for all distributed computing paradigms discussed in this book. Java provides a set of libraries that allow an application to communicate directly via TCP/IP and is thus equipped with the J2EE by virtue of its inclusion with the J2SE.
- *Web/HTTP:* The Hypertext Transfer Protocol (HTTP) v1.0 is the protocol over TCP/IP used for communicating between Web browsers and servers. APIs for communicating directly via HTTP are provided by the J2SE. Furthermore, HTTP requests and responses are encapsulated by higher-level abstractions for use by programmers in J2EE Web-container environments. The use of a Secure Socket Layer (SSL) v3.0 protocol must also be available for use with HTTP to enable secure Web communications.
- *CORBA/IIOP:* The Common Object Request Broker Architecture (CORBA) is an industry-standard and language-independent distributed object communications paradigm that transparently handles the mapping of object method calls to and from an underlying communications message data representation. The Internet Inter-ORB Protocol (IIOP), which is the underlying communications protocol used by CORBA, operates above TCP/IP. Although the term *IIOP* is frequently used, a higher-level protocol known as the General Inter-Orb Protocol (GIOP) is actually used above IIOP. Java IDL is a Java-based API and implementation of the CORBA communications paradigm, and it is equipped

with the J2EE by virtue of its inclusion with the J2SE. However, although creating CORBA clients in a J2EE environment is possible for EJB, Web, and application client containers, only application client components can create their own CORBA server instances. There is no requirement for J2EE EJB containers to offer their services as CORBA servers transparent to the component developer, either.

- *RMI/JRMP:* Remote Method Invocation (RMI) is the distributed object communications paradigm that was developed for use with Java. Java Remote Method Protocol (JRMP) is the original protocol used by RMI for communications under the RMI interface and also operates above TCP/IP. RMI/JRMP is equipped with the J2EE by virtue of its inclusion with the J2SE.
- *RMI/IIOP:* RMI has also been adapted to operate over IIOP. With RMI/IIOP, Java-based applications that use the RMI distributed object communications interface can communicate with CORBA-based applications. RMI/IIOP v1.0 adds a few API features to RMI that must be included by J2EE EJB, Web, and application client environment vendors. However, the actual implementation of RMI/IIOP to enable RMI/IIOP-based clients and servers using the IIOP protocol is not a current requirement for the J2EE. Standalone J2SE v1.2 environments can use RMI/IIOP as a standard Java extension, whereas JDK v1.3 environments include RMI/IIOP.
- *DCOM:* The Distributed Component Object Model (DCOM) is a Microsoft platform–specific distributed object communications paradigm. Java applications can also act as DCOM clients and DCOM servers. However, a Microsoft platform–specific Java environment is needed.

Use of the distributed communications paradigms alone enables one to build distributed application clients and servers. However, a set of common services hosted atop a distributed communications paradigm makes creating distributed enterprise applications an easier task. The core common services for distributed enterprise communications discussed in this book are listed here:

- *Naming Services:* Naming services are used to reference and look up distributed objects on a network in terms of a human-readable name. The Java Naming and Directory Interface (JNDI) is used to provide a common Java API to various underlying naming service implementations and types. A file system, an RMI registry, and a CORBA Naming Service are all examples of specific naming services accessible via JNDI. Additionally, naming services without current JNDI SPI mappings such as DNS and a means for mapping DCOM names to objects are also important to the Java enterprise developer. J2EE EJB, Web, and application client environment vendors must include the JNDI v1.2 API with their products. Standalone J2SE v1.2 environments must use JNDI as a standard Java extension, whereas JDK v1.3 environments include the JNDI API.

- *Directory Services:* Directory services are a type of naming service that adds the capability to reference and search for distributed objects on a network in terms of descriptive attributes about the object. JNDI is also used to provide a common Java API to various underlying directory service implementations and types. NIS, NDS, and LDAP are all examples of directory services with JNDI-based interfaces. Additionally, the Microsoft Active Directory Service is also important for DCOM-based directory service lookups.
- *Trading Services:* Trading services are a type of directory service that adds support for a more dynamic means to locate objects on a network and join communities of distributed services on a network. Trading services can also look up objects based on descriptive attributes, as well as based on object type. The CORBA Trading Service and Jini are both examples of trading services discussed in this book.
- *Activation Services:* Activation services provide an important underlying mechanism for distributed communication paradigms to transparently bring a persisted object into active memory based on a client request. RMI, CORBA, and DCOM all have an underlying activation service framework. Additionally, the CORBA LifeCycle Service provides a means to create, copy, and move active objects in a distributed network. The Java Activation Framework (JAF) v1.0 provides a means to activate an object handler proxy based on received data and is used by J2EE EJB and Web environments to support the use of JavaMail.
- *Messaging Services:* Messaging services provide an asynchronous means for sending and receiving messages on a network. The Java Message Service (JMS) v1.0 API is part of J2EE EJB, Web, and application client environments, but no underlying implementation is mandatory. The JavaMail v1.1 API for sending and receiving email messages is also part of J2EE EJB and Web environments, but only requires email sending implementation support. The CORBA Event Service, CORBA Notification Service, and CORBA Messaging specification are also types of messaging services important to Java enterprise applications and are discussed in this book.
- *Transaction Services:* A transaction service provides a mechanism for encapsulating inseparable operations performed over a distributed network into an atomic operation. The CORBA Object Transaction Service (OTS) is mapped to Java by virtue of the Java Transaction Service (JTS). The Java Transaction API (JTA) is a higher-level framework for managing transactions and resources from Java enterprise applications. JTA v1.0 is required by J2EE EJB and Web environments with implementation support only required for API client demarcation of transactions.

Assurance Mechanisms

Needless to say, there is not much demand in industry for enterprise applications that fail, are not available, cannot be maintained for upgrades and bugs, have security holes, or perhaps cause safety hazards. Assurance involves providing software that can be depended on. Assurance may be defined according to one or more of the following qualities:

- *Security:* The likelihood that your system will operate in a secure and security breach–free fashion.
- *Reliability:* The likelihood that your system will operate correctly and as intended.
- *Availability:* The likelihood that your system will actually be operational and offering service. Scalability of your system to support growth in usage is one aspect of availability.
- *Maintainability:* The likelihood that your system will be capable of being maintained, upgraded, and extended for future growth.
- *Safety:* The likelihood that your system will operate in a safe and accident-free manner.

Many such qualities of assurance are more inherent properties of software rather than discretely definable components of software. In fact, process and techniques, such as the object-oriented and component-based software development techniques employed throughout this book, are very important to enable the creation of higher assurance software. Nevertheless, because security is a sensitive and important aspect of enterprise assurance, certain discrete aspects of security have been independently encapsulated in terms of software components. The CORBA Security Service Specification defines a set of specifications used in distributed CORBA environments to provide security. Security is also built into the Java 2 platform.

Security in J2EE-based environments is inherited from the underlying J2SE platform's security features. Java security features can be tapped programmatically in standalone J2SE-based applications by use of the various Java security APIs. J2EE-based applications can take advantage of declarative security in addition to programmatic security. Declarative security refers to the specification of security features in the deployment descriptor associated with a J2EE-based component. The J2EE container environment then handles the management of security on behalf of the component.

Java-based security helps provide identity and authentication, as well as authorization for your enterprise application environments. Identity and authentication involves the secure identification of a user associated with an object that is making a request of the system on behalf of that user (for example, a password-based login). Authorization involves the association of an authenticated user's identity with permission to access or use a particular system resource. Enterprise Java environments also have the capability to provide for the integrity and confidentiality of data exchanged and stored via a security-critical medium. Standard facilities for auditing security-critical events and providing nonrepudiation evidence of data transmissions and receptions are currently not inherent APIs of the J2SE or its standard extensions.

Client Connectivity

Various types of clients can talk to Java enterprise server environments. As mentioned earlier, we can generally classify Java clients according to the categories of Java applet clients, Java application clients, general Web browser–based clients, and non-Java clients. Clients implemented in Java, such as Java applets and Java application clients, can take advantage of the numerous Java-based GUI components, such as from the AWT and Swing libraries, to rapidly build user interfaces. However, use of Java-based clients will not always be possible in all situations for enterprise user interfacing. J2EE-based client containers will also not always be possible or practical. This is why we assume a much broader range of client interfacing techniques using open and standard distributed communication paradigms.

Java applets are essentially Java applications embedded into Web browsers. Java applets can run inside of J2EE-based applet containers as well. J2EE applet containers assume a J2SE platform and thus may require the Java Plug-in product for Web browsers that do not come equipped with the J2SE and need to automatically download Java platform upgrades. Applets can use distributed communication paradigms such as RMI/JRMP, Web/HTTP, and CORBA/IIOP.

A standard Web browser can also be used with J2EE-based Web-enabling applications. J2EE Web components can generate HTML and XML documents viewable inside of Web browsers. The J2EE container environment handles translating HTTP requests and responses to and from standard Java object abstractions.

Java-based application clients can talk to Java-based servers using the various distributed computing paradigms described earlier. Whereas DCOM clients need to run inside of a Microsoft Java environment, all other Java application client types can operate inside of a standard J2SE-based environment. The J2EE also defines an application client container that has many of the standard Java extension APIs needed to communicate with J2EE-based servers.

Various non-Java clients can communicate with Java enterprise servers. TCP/IP, CORBA/IIOP, and DCOM-based clients are the most significant examples of distributed computing paradigms usable by various non-Java clients. The type of client you can connect to your server will, of course, be dependent on the protocol supported by your particular Java enterprise application. J2EE-based EJB environments are currently required to support only RMI/JRMP implementations and thus are required to support only Java-based clients by consequence. Future versions of the specification open up J2EE-based EJB applications to support RMI/IIOP and CORBA/IIOP implementations.

Web Connectivity

Enterprise Web connectivity involves providing a solution for handling Web requests and generating Web responses via a Web server. A Web server tier is often best thought of as a middle-tier layer whose responsibility is to handle Web-based client interface requests and to generate a new Web presentation interface for the Web client. Web server tiers often delegate to an enterprise application serving tier for any significant business logic processing that must be performed.

The most popular need in Web browser data generation support requires Web presentation pages to be generated in the form of HTML documents. HTML is used to display content within a Web browser and also present user-interface controls that can be used to capture data and actions from a user. The eXtensible Markup Language (XML) is a more flexible and extendible type of language being integrated into Web environments as an extension to HTML. XML documents can represent data in a hierarchical form and can be accompanied by Document Type Definitions (DTDs), which describe the structure and semantics of a particular class of documents.

Although XML has grown out of the World Wide Web, it also has a much broader application to the generic representation of data in general. Thus, data exchanged or stored via a particular medium can be described using the standard syntax of XML. In fact, J2EE deployment descriptors are described and stored in a standard XML format. This is why XML document parsing libraries are currently shipped with J2EE-based products. A standard XML API will be required of J2EE-based products in the future for general data exchange usage by J2EE applications. The Java API for XML Parsing (JAXP) is a standard Java extension that can be used in the meantime.

Java Servlets is a Java API that encapsulates HTTP requests, HTTP responses, and HTTP session management interfaces. The J2EE allows Java Servlet components to operate inside of a J2EE Java Servlet Web container. The Web container handles the mapping of requests to specific servlet instances and handles transforming request and response objects to and from the underlying HTTP I/O stream. The approach to Web connectivity advocated by this book recommends use of J2EE Java Servlet Web container environments as a key approach for enterprise Web enabling.

JavaServer Pages are documents written in a scripting-based language. JSPs can interact with Java code and actually are described using a syntax considered to be familiar and easily comprehended by Web developers. JSPs are constructed to manage Web requests and responses as are servlets. JSPs are actually converted into Java Servlets by a J2EE JSP Web container environment when the JSP is first loaded or referenced. The approach to Web connectivity advocated by this book recommends use of J2EE JSP Web container environments as another key approach for enterprise Web enabling.

Application Connectivity

Writing server-side enterprise applications can be significantly more difficult than writing client-side applications. Enterprise applications must be scalable, be secure, handle a large number of client requests, manage server-side resources, and manage external resources, among many other multiple client/application/resource management duties. This book describes two main approaches to accomplishing this task: standalone Java enterprise applications and J2EE-based EJB applications.

Standalone Java enterprise applications are applications written on top of the Java platform that take advantage of standard Java enterprise API extensions. Standalone Java applications offer maximum flexibility in terms of choices for COTS and the capability to support many types of client connectivity paradigms. J2EE-based EJB container environments are also used to build enterprise applications. The container environment offers a vendor-independent interface to a host of enterprise services for building scalable enterprise applications. J2EE EJB container services reduce the amount of infrastructure hand-coding required of the developer and allow developers to concentrate on the development of business logic embedded within EJB components.

However, the direct instantiation of distributed communication server instances (for example, RMI and CORBA) by application components in J2EE EJB application servers is not permitted by the container environment. You thus have to rely on those distributed communications server types that can be created by the J2EE container environment. J2EE EJB container environments are required only to support RMI/JRMP-based implementations. RMI/IIOP and full CORBA/IIOP mappings will be required in a future specification release. Some vendors do provide IIOP-based connectivity, however.

Thus, enabling your J2EE-based servers to support connectivity from different distributed communication paradigm clients is currently a function of your particular J2EE vendor's offering. Standalone Java enterprise applications can, of course, support many types of client connectivity. Although creating and managing distributed server instances in standalone environments can require more hand-coding, it may be your only choice for certain client connectivity solutions in some cases. Furthermore, the scalability requirements and complexity of a particular enterprise application may not warrant the investment in a J2EE-based COTS EJB application server. For many other large-scale and complex enterprise application cases, however, use of a J2EE-based EJB application server may be your only option given your time-to-market needs, cost limitations, and human-resource availability.

In addition to building J2EE-based EJBs or standalone Java enterprise applications, the enabling of legacy and embedded applications for access by the enterprise will also be a key consideration in enterprise application enabling. Enterprise application integration techniques require the provision of a means to integrate a legacy or embedded application into your Java enterprise application environment. Technologies such as CORBA, JMS, XML, the Java Native Interface (JNI), and J2EE Connectors are all examples of technologies used for EAI in some fashion. JMS, XML, and CORBA are particularly important for enterprise applications to interoperate with other enterprise applications in business-to-business (B2B) integration scenarios. B2B integration may occur between separately managed business units within an enterprise or with partner businesses external to an enterprise.

The J2EE Future

The J2EE v1.2 specification defines a minimal set of requirements to be provided by service providers of J2EE-based containers in order to satisfy the J2EE compatibility test. Such minimal requirements more rapidly enable vendors to provide J2EE-compliant products. However, many enhancements above and beyond the J2EE v1.2 specification requirements are expected in the future. We can only hope that future versions of the J2EE specification will be defined in terms of compliance levels and packages such that more vendor implementation options may enter the marketplace. Nevertheless, Sun has made it clear that these are some potential future J2EE specification requirements:

- *Application Client Service Enhancements:* A future specification may define more deployment service and management service support for J2EE application clients.
- *Service Provider Interfaces:* A future specification may define standard interfaces to be implemented by J2EE vendor service providers.
- *JDBC 2.0 Extension Implementation:* A future specification may require J2EE EJB containers to implement the JDBC 2.0 Extension API.
- *RMI/IIOP Implementation:* A future specification may require the implementation of the RMI/IIOP API.
- *IIOP Communication:* A future specification may define a requirement for J2EE EJB containers to support IIOP-based communication with an EJB.
- *JMS Implementations:* A future specification may define a requirement to provide implementation of the JMS messaging APIs.
- *Asynchronous EJB Messages:* A future specification may define a means for JMS to direct asynchronous messages to EJBs.
- *JTA Implementations:* A future specification may require the implementation of many APIs in the JTA.
- *Security Authentication and Authorization:* A future specification may define a standard authentication and authorization interface to a J2EE environment via the Java Authentication and Authorization Service (JAAS) API standard Java extension.

- *Security Auditing:* A future specification may define standard interfaces to audit security-critical–related events.
- *Security Permission Extensions:* A future specification may define a means for applications to specify their own types of security permissions that fall outside of the standard types provided by Java security.
- *Security Interoperability:* A future specification may define standards for EJB environments operating in different domains to share security identification context information. This security interoperability will be based on CORBA/IIOP.
- *Transaction Interoperability:* A future specification may define standards for EJB environments to share transaction context information. This security interoperability will be based on CORBA/IIOP.
- *EAI Connectors:* A future specification may define standards for extending J2EE services to external non-J2EE applications.
- *XML APIs:* A future specification may require XML APIs to be provided by J2EE containers. This API will most likely be the JAXP.
- *Administration Tools:* A future specification may define standard interfaces for deployment, management, and system monitoring tools.

Conclusions

This chapter presented an overview of the J2EE model for building enterprise systems using Java in the context of a more general Java enterprise system architecture. Given the set of enterprise-system needs outlined in Chapter 1, this chapter demonstrated how Java enterprise technologies can satisfy those needs. You learned that although J2EE container environments provide many advantages for Web and application enabling, certain application scenarios and needs may not warrant use of a J2EE container environment. In such cases, many of the Java enterprise APIs that form the core of J2EE will indeed still be of use. They may, however, be useful only in certain standalone Java application configurations. Additionally, many other non-J2EE but Java-based enterprise APIs are also useful in building enterprise systems.

Nevertheless, the J2EE is a centerpiece of current and future Java enterprise development. This chapter presented a Java enterprise system architecture useful in many different enterprise system scenarios. Solutions for enterprise database connectivity, client and user interfacing, distributed communications, communication services, systems assurance, Web enabling, and application enabling were all discussed in this chapter. Lo and behold…all enterprise system problems have solutions that can use Java enterprise technologies.

Enterprise User Interfacing

CHAPTER

6

IN THIS CHAPTER

- The Distributed Enterprise User Interface 126
- Java AWT Components 130
- Java Swing Components 132
- Utility and Accessibility Components 134
- Graphics and Multimedia Components 135
- Web Page Interfaces 137

The user interface provides the presentation of your enterprise system to the enterprise user base. Although this book largely revolves around server-side and middle-tier enterprise systems development, it is important to possess a basic knowledge of which frontline user-interface methodologies will be available to connect to the enterprise systems you build. A knowledge of which user-interface techniques will be used to communicate with your enterprise system and their constraints will enable you to make more informed enterprise interface-enabling design decisions.

This chapter provides an overview of the mechanisms available for presenting enterprise system information to users of an enterprise system. We provide only an overview of the various Web-based and Java-based GUI components and APIs that will typically be used to interface with a server-side and middle-tier enterprise system in this chapter. Because user-interface design is an extensive topic in and of itself, we do not cover the details of user-interface design here. Rather, we outline the technologies that can be used, as well as the specific technologies that should ideally be used, to interface with your enterprise system.

In this chapter, we present:

- An overview of the various technologies used for enterprise user-interface development that will need to interface with server-side and middle-tier enterprise systems.
- An overview of the Java Abstract Windowing Toolkit (AWT) GUI components, AWT architecture features, and deployment considerations.
- An overview of the Java Swing GUI components, Swing architecture features, and deployment considerations.
- An overview of extended and standard Java GUI components for providing drag-and-drop, printing, online JavaHelp documentation, and accessibility support.
- An overview of the extended and standard Java-based support available for providing graphics and multimedia to Java applications.
- An overview of the techniques available for providing Web-based user interfaces.

The Distributed Enterprise User Interface

A user interface (UI) provides a means by which people interact with a system. Computer-based UIs are, of course, key for making computers useful to people. Graphical user interfaces (GUIs) are the most popular types of computer UIs. They present a graphical interface for people to interact with a system in a more user-friendly fashion. UIs connected to an enterprise system are very often distributed across many types of users and thus offer varied levels of access to the enterprise system and different styles of presentation.

Figure 6.1 illustrates various enterprise users and the networks from which they access an enterprise system. The user type and network from which they interface with the system drives the style of interface offered to a particular user. For example, you may develop an enterprise user interface for prospective customers to shop via a Web-based enterprise store front. You may also provide a special interface to access certain enterprise information to be used exclusively by a business partner. Access to enterprise information via a corporate intranet or local area network (LAN) may also be provided to employees and contractors. Such networks may be used to conduct actual business for the enterprise or perhaps access information pertinent to a user's personal relation with the enterprise.

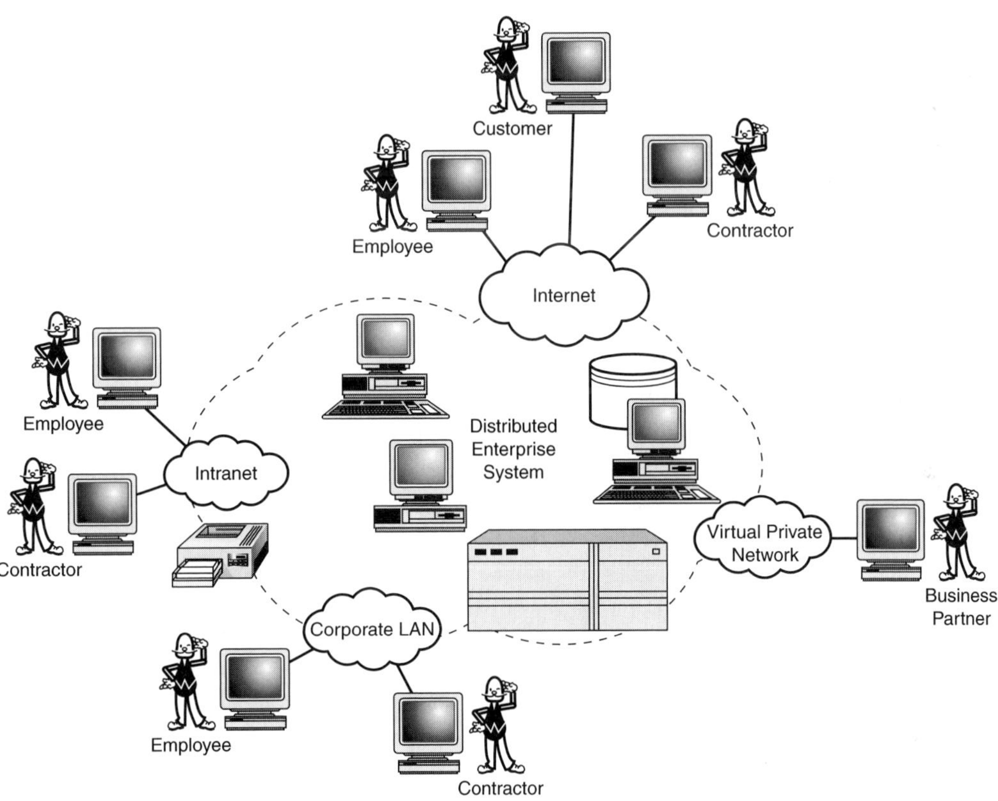

FIGURE 6.1

Enterprise users and networks.

Although enterprise user interfaces are extremely important additions to an enterprise system, the topic of interface design does lay outside of the scope of this book. This book focuses on how an enterprise system can be built, whereas the design of endpoint UIs is a broad topic in and of itself with a large variety of techniques existing to realize interface designs. Thus, in a Model-View-Controller (MVC) approach to describing a system, you might say that our interest in describing the "View" component of a system is in describing how an enterprise system can be designed to best enable such views, as well as describing what techniques exist to connect your enterprise from system infrastructure to end user.

Thus, in this chapter we cover only the basic techniques that can be employed by you and your enterprise development team to provide a user interface for your enterprise Java applications. As an enterprise systems developer, you'll find that an understanding of enterprise user-interface design needs will help you develop a system that can most effectively enable it to be connected with various enterprise user interfaces. Figure 6.2 depicts the major enterprise user-interface classes that will be supported by the enterprise system development techniques employed by this book.

NOTE

We only describe the basic techniques and technologies that are used to build enterprise user interfaces in this chapter. Be sure to check out Appendix B, "Additional Resources," for more information. In Appendix B we provide references and Web links for many of the technologies discussed in this chapter.

CORBA-based client applications utilize a technology described in Chapter 14, "Modeling Components with CORBA," and Chapter 15, "CORBA Communications," which enables a client written in any language to communicate with an enterprise using a standard protocol and interface technology. Thus any UI technique supported by the client language and platform can be used. Similarly, Chapter 12, "Network Communications," describes a technique that uses lower-level standard communications protocol connectivity for bridging clients and servers via a protocol known as TCP/IP. Thus, clients that can communicate with an enterprise using this standard protocol can also be implemented in any language and can utilize any UI technique.

Client applications that are written for the Windows platform can talk with enterprise Java applications using a Windows-specific technology known as DCOM. We describe DCOM in Chapter 17, "Modeling Components with COM/DCOM," and Chapter 18, "DCOM Communications." Thus, Windows-based UIs may be easily customized to access your enterprise by exposing some of your enterprise's services using DCOM interfacing technology.

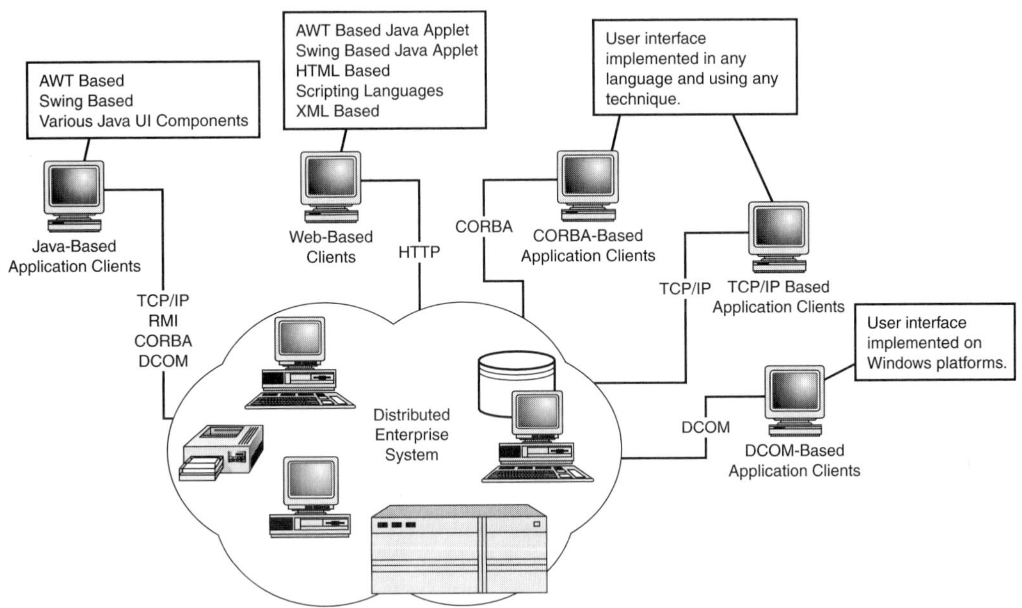

FIGURE 6.2
Enterprise user interfaces.

Web-based clients can utilize interface technologies communicated over a Web-based protocol known as HTTP. Java applets embedded into Web browsers can be implemented using Java-based UI technologies known as AWT and Swing. HTML-based, scripting language–based, and XML-based Web interfaces may also be utilized. We describe some of these techniques in more detail throughout this chapter. Specific details behind server-side Web enabling are discussed in Part VI, "Enterprise Web Enabling."

Java-based application clients represent those desktop applications built using Java technology such as that offered by the J2SE or via J2EE application clients. Java UI technologies such as AWT and Swing can be effectively utilized by Java applications. Other Java UI technologies have also been developed to enable the creation of more sophisticated Java user interfaces. We present some of these UI technologies in this chapter. As you'll see in Part III, "Distributed Enterprise Communications Enabling," Java clients can also act as TCP/IP, CORBA, and DCOM clients. Java also uses a distributed communications technology known as RMI that's described in Chapter 16, "RMI Communications."

Enabling your applications to speak HTTP, CORBA, TCP/IP, or DCOM may open your client base to a wider variety of legacy and newly created user interfaces. However, Java-based interface applications and applets themselves offer the capability to interface with enterprise systems using these and other enterprise connectivity solutions. Use of Java on the client also enables reuse of common development tools, processes, and application code shared between your enterprise user-interface and enterprise system design teams.

Part VI of this book describes how to Web-enable an enterprise system such that Web interface design techniques, including HTML, XML, and scripting languages, can be used in addition to Java applets. Web enabling an enterprise system represents one of the more important technical challenges for an enterprise systems developer to consider. The Web-enabling solutions pursued by this book offer the most flexibility in enterprise user-interface design. Thus your solutions as an enterprise systems developer will not preclude certain enterprise user-interface solutions.

In summary, the enterprise system design practices of this book enable the use of a wide range of enterprise user-interface design approaches such as those depicted in Figure 6.2.

Java AWT Components

The Abstract Windowing Toolkit is a set of Java packages that are used to create graphical user interfaces. The AWT has been equipped with the Java platform since Java 1.0. The AWT API follows a component-container model for GUI development in which GUI components are displayed inside of GUI containers according to particular layout policies. GUI-related events and interfaces for receiving these events are also defined by the AWT API. We describe the core support for GUI-based components, containers, and event handling by the AWT in this section. Indeed, many other classes and interfaces are strewn throughout various `java.awt.XXX` packages, and those also are covered in subsequent sections throughout this chapter.

AWT Components, Containers, and Layouts

An AWT componentis a GUI-based component that will have some graphical presentation display presence and perhaps be capable of receiving events input from a user. AWT components may be, for example, buttons, check boxes, drop-down lists, scrollbars, and text fields. The `java.awt` package contains many of the core interfaces and classes used to create AWT-based user interfaces and graphics and images. The `java.awt.Component` abstract class is the superclass for most of the AWT GUI components. Such components in the AWT package actually use native platform UI libraries and are thus considered heavyweight components. AWT components can also extend directly from the `Component` class to support lightweight interfaces not bound to native-platform UI libraries. Finally, AWT components may also be menu-related, such as menu bars and menu items. The `java.awt.MenuComponent` abstract class is a superclass for such GUI-related menu components.

An AWT container is itself a GUI-based component that contains one or more other GUI components. A window frame, a pop-up dialog window, a panel embedded in a window, and a scroll panel are all examples of containers that contain various GUI components. Because containers are components, they can contain instances of one another. For example, a window frame may contain one panel to display a set of button components and another panel to display a canvas component that responds to button events by displaying information in some graphical fashion. The `java.awt.Container` class encapsulates a container of components.

Containers are associated with layout managers that describe a policy for the placement of components within a container. The `java.awt.LayoutManager` interface defines a base set of container layout operations. The `java.awt.LayoutManager2` sub-interface of `LayoutManager` adds the capability to specify constraints to be considered during the layout of components in a container. Various implementations of these interfaces are provided out of the box in the `java.awt` package to support various types of layout policies.

AWT Events

A `java.awt.AWTEvent` abstract class encapsulates events that can be generated by GUI-related events. Various types of AWT events that extend `AWTEvent` are defined in the `java.awt.event` package to deal with events such as actions on components, mouse-generated events, and keyboard-generated events. Events that are generated are received by registered listeners such as classes that implement one of the `java.awt.event.XXXListener` interfaces. A collection of `java.awt.event.XXXAdapter` abstract helper classes implement `XXXListener` interfaces with empty methods as a way to allow for classes to subclass these `XXXAdapter` classes and implement only relevant methods instead of every method defined on an `XXXListener`.

Deployment Considerations

Because the AWT libraries have been a part of Java for some time now, many Web browsers that support the dynamic execution of Java programs as Java applets will be able to execute purely AWT-based Java programs without a need to download any extra GUI libraries. That is, the AWT libraries equipped with the Web browser software can be used without the overhead of downloading these libraries to a Web browser. Although newer browsers can support use of the Java Plug-in product for updating your Web browser with more current Java runtime libraries, requiring your enterprise user base to make use of browsers that support the Java Plug-in may not be feasible. Furthermore, those browsers that do support the Java Plug-in will still have to download updated large JVM libraries to handle code that supports Java GUI library updates. Chapter 29, "Web Browsers and Servers in the Enterprise," describes the Java Plug-in in more detail.

Many extensions to the AWT libraries also exist and are made available as third-party products. However, these libraries will impose additional overhead needed to download such libraries when used in Java applets. If your application needs to implement such functionality offered by the third-party product, it may make more sense to use the third-party product. Of course, Java applications installed on a client machine don't have application download time concerns, nor do they have GUI library compatibility concerns because updated GUI libraries can be installed along with the Java application.

Java Swing Components

The Java Swing libraries offer an alternative means for developing Java based GUIs. Swing was introduced to remedy many of the shortcomings of AWT. Swing's implementation is a lightweight GUI framework without the native platform dependence that is present in the AWT implementation. That is, Swing GUI elements don't depend on platform-specific GUI components as do AWT components, and thus they can offer the same look and feel when run on different platforms. Furthermore, Swing even encapsulates look and feel by providing a framework that allows one to plug in different look-and-feel styles to be used when displaying Swing GUI components. Aside from being part of the Java 2 platform, Swing is part of the JFC v1.1 that can be used with Java 1.1.

Swing Components, Containers, Layouts, and Events

The `javax.swing` library contains the core set of Swing elements used to implement GUIs using pure Java classes and interfaces. A new set of classes in this package beginning with the letter *J* represents lightweight components and containers without the level of native platform dependence required by AWT components and containers. The `javax.swing.JComponent` class is the base class for all Swing components. Various Swing components and containers extend from this base class. Most top-level containers use the `JFrame`, `JDialog`, or `JApplet` containers. Intermediate containers such as a `JPanel`, `JScrollPane`, and `JTabbedPane` are typically used inside top-level containers to hold Swing GUI components.

Finally, although Swing containers can use the same layout mechanisms available with the AWT packages, a different suite of events and event handlers can be used by the Swing components. The `javax.swing.event` package encapsulates Swing-specific events that can be generated by Swing components. Event types and listeners particular to the Swing components are contained in this package.

Swing Models

Many of the Swing components that are not containers can be associated with underlying models. Models encapsulate underlying representations of data and state. Such distinguishing encapsulation of models stems from Swing's goal of adhering to a Model-View-Controller architecture. Models expose data and state used by GUI components as a separate entity that can be managed apart from the GUI component. As an example of a model, the `JList` component represents a GUI list whose contents are contained in a `ListModel` object and whose current selection is contained in a `ListSelectionModel` object.

Swing Look and Feel

The `javax.swing.plaf` package provides an interface and a host of abstract classes used to define a pluggable look-and-feel framework. Different look-and-feel styles subclass the abstract classes in this `javax.swing.plaf` package. A default look and feel is implemented by classes in the `javax.swing.plaf.basic` package. A slightly more stylish look and feel known as the "metal" look and feel is implemented in the `javax.swing.plaf.metal` package. Finally, different look and feels can be combined with the default look and feel using entities in the `javax.swing.plaf.multi` package.

Swing Component Helpers

In addition to the core Java Swing libraries, various packages are implemented in Swing to support the core Swing components. These helper libraries are listed here:

- The `javax.swing.border` package contains classes and interfaces used to draw borders around Swing components.
- A `javax.swing.JColorChooser` GUI Swing component offers a set of controls used to select colors to be used for various GUI operations and uses additional helper classes from the `javax.swing.colorchooser` package.
- A `javax.swing.JFileChooser` GUI Swing component provides a set of controls for selecting a file and uses additional helper classes from the `javax.swing.filechooser` package.
- A `javax.swing.JTable` GUI Swing component is used to display and manipulate data in a visual grid and makes use of additional helper classes from the `javax.swing.table` package.
- A `javax.swing.JTree` GUI Swing component enables the hierarchical display of data with additional helper classes implemented in the `javax.swing.tree` package.
- The `javax.swing.text` package contains classes for managing GUI components such as `javax.swing.JTextField` and `javax.swing.JTextArea` that manipulate text on the screen. Such helper classes for text manipulation include text selection, highlighting, editing, and key map behaviors.
- The `javax.swing.text.html` and `javax.swing.text.html.parser` packages contain classes for allowing GUI-based editing of HTML text.

- A `javax.swing.text.rtf.RTFEditorKit` package offers minimal support for enabling Rich Text Format (RTF) editing capabilities.
- The `javax.swing.undo` package provides classes for implementing undo and redo capabilities in editors such as text editors.

Deployment Considerations

Swing offers many advantages over AWT in terms of lighter-weight components, a consistent look and feel, and a richer set of APIs. Swing is thus a better solution for GUI-based Java applications than AWT. However, using Swing for Java applets that get downloaded to Web browsers is a bit more problematic. Older browser versions do not support Swing. Although newer browsers can support Swing via the Java Plug-in, the upgrade to a browser with new JVM libraries may still be an undesirable solution for some deployment scenarios. Furthermore, requiring your entire enterprise user base to utilize the latest browser upgrade to support Java Plug-ins may also be unfeasible. Chapter 29 describes the Java Plug-in in more detail.

Utility and Accessibility Components

Building enterprise user interfaces is not all about designing standalone and self-contained Java UI applications and applets. UIs often must interact with other UIs. Furthermore, common utilities such as printing and providing online help are embedded in almost every commercial-ready UI application. The Java platform, JFC, and standard Java extensions provide such utilities and accessibility packages for you to use in building commercial-ready enterprise UIs. We'll briefly describe some of the core utility and accessibility packages here, including data transfer between and within applications, drag-and-drop support, printing support, assistive technology interfacing, and online help support.

Data Transfer

The `java.awt.datatransfer` package contains classes and interfaces for transferring data between applications, as well as within an application. A `Transferable` interface is implemented by those classes that support being transferred between and within applications. A `Clipboard` class encapsulates a means for transferring data to a Clipboard via copy, cut, and paste operations.

Drag and Drop

The `java.awt.dnd` package contains classes and interfaces for more sophisticated drag-and-drop capability between applications. A `DragSource` object encapsulates a source from which information is to be dragged. A `DropTarget` object encapsulates a sink into which information is to be dropped from a dragged source. `DropTarget` objects are associated with GUI components when they want to receive objects dropped onto them. Support is also provided by the Drag-and-Drop package to display visual cues from source to target during drag-and-drop operations.

Printing

Built-in support for printing in Java was very minimal before Java 2. The `java.awt.print` package added in Java 2 contains a set of classes and interfaces to support general-purpose printing. A `PrinterJob` class in this package serves as the primary class for configuring print jobs, spawning print dialogs, and actually submitting the job to a printer. Classes also exist to specify paper type and page formats.

Accessibility

The JFC also has support for interacting with assistive UI technologies such as screen magnifiers, screen readers, Braille terminals, and speech-recognition systems. Such UI technologies open access to your enterprise system for users with physical disabilities. Classes and interfaces in the `javax.accessibility` package define an interface to which Java-based GUI applications adhere in order to enable connectivity to assistive UI technologies. GUI components must implement an `Accessible` interface, which returns an `AccessibleContext` object. The `AccessibleContext` object contains information useful for assistive technologies to interact with a Java-based GUI.

JavaHelp

JavaHelp is a standard extension to the Java platform used for creating online documentation as a standalone window or a window that is embedded inside of another Java application or applet. JavaHelp comes with a default help viewer window offering toolbar controls, a navigation pane, and a document-content display window. The navigation pane includes built-in support for displaying a hierarchical table of contents, a document index, and a full-text document search interface. Although HTML-based documents are the default standard used for content viewing, JavaHelp can be extended to view various other types of help document formats.

Graphics and Multimedia Components

Enterprise information can be conveyed and input in many forms other than those forms encapsulated by the GUI components of AWT and Swing. Images, sophisticated 2D graphics, and 3D graphics provide ways in which enterprise information can be conveyed in a more easily understood and digestible fashion. Furthermore, sound, video, and speech also offer important techniques for conveying enterprise information, as well as perhaps inputting information (for example, speech recognition). Finally, enabling input from various types of devices is also important for international acceptance of Java, as well as for providing efficient means to input data from devices such as pens and drawing pads. This section briefly highlights some of the built-in and extended standard graphical and multimedia APIs available for use with your enterprise Java UI applications.

AWT Images

The Java 2 platform's built-in `java.awt.Image` class and `java.awt.image` package can be used for creating and manipulating images. Images can be rendered even while they are being read from an underlying stream. Image producers that implement the `ImageProducer` interface are responsible for creating a particular image. Image consumers that implement the `ImageConsumer` interface are endpoints interested in receiving a produced image. Various image filters that subclass the `ImageFilter` class can filter image data according to some algorithm as it passes from producer to consumer.

2D Graphics

Java 2D is an API that enables a more sophisticated two-dimensional rendering of objects and images. For example, to create images (perhaps even animated images) that display the distribution of sales for a product over the years via a graph using gradients of colors along each graph, you might consider utilizing the 2D graphics APIs. APIs that have been created for Java 2D support are actually strewn throughout the Java AWT packages. The `java.awt` package contains some of the base classes used to create 2D graphics and images. The `java.awt.color` package contains classes used to add various colors to 2D images. The 2D classes that relate to creating and transforming 2D geometrical shapes are contained in the `java.awt.geom` package. Image-rendering operations are contained in both the `java.awt.image` and the `java.awt.image.renderable` packages.

3D Graphics

The Java 3D API is a collection of classes and interfaces used to create and manipulate three-dimensional graphics. Java 3D provides interfaces for creating and manipulating 3D shapes, as well as adding animation, texture, lighting, and shading to these objects. 3D charts, graphs, and displays can be useful to convey depth to information not readily apparent by examining 2D images. For example, a graphical depiction of a stock portfolio may choose an x-axis to depict time, a y-axis to depict value, and a z-axis to convey price/earning ratio.

Java Advanced Imaging

The Java Advanced Imaging API is used for creating and rendering images according to sophisticated and perhaps application-specific algorithms. The Advanced Imaging API is extensible in that different algorithms and imaging techniques can be used with the framework.

Advanced imaging is primarily useful for those applications that have either very specific or very advanced types of imaging requirements such as geological, astrophysical, and photographic applications.

Java Media APIs

In addition to some of the packages described already, a Java Media API collection provides a Java Media Framework API for building applications whose media varies over time. Media in this case may include audio and video. For example, manipulation of audio WAV files falls under the auspices of the Java Media Framework API, as do MPEG and Quicktime video data. The Java Media Framework can be used as a building block for other time-based Java Media APIs.

The Java Sound, Speech, Shared Data Toolkit, and Telephony APIs are all part of the Java Media API collection with a few of the APIs having or expected to have dependence on the Java Media Framework. The Java Sound API provides support for audio data manipulation, including the mixing and capture of MIDI-formatted data. The Java Speech API provides support for speech recognition, speech-based command control, and speech synthesis. The Java Shared Data Toolkit provides support for collaborative media-based interactions among users over a network, including collaborative whiteboards and chat rooms. The Java Telephony API is provided to enable telephone-based communications over a network.

Input Method Framework

The Input Method Framework is part of the Java 2 platform and enables Java GUI text components to receive information from alternative input methods. Alternative input methods include different keyboard types, speech input devices, and pen-based input devices. International character sets input through different keyboard types can thus can be used to input text into Java-based GUI components. The `java.awt.im` package contains the core classes and interfaces used to support the Input Method Framework.

Web Page Interfaces

Given the growth of the Internet and World Wide Web (WWW), many enterprises realize the importance of having a Web-based interface to their enterprise systems. Web pages displayed in a Web browser represent an important marketing brochure or perhaps employee work-flow interface for the enterprise. The exact type of interface depends on the end enterprise user. Customers, for example, may have an Internet Web interface to an enterprise that allows them to purchase products from the company's "e-store." Employees may have an intranet Web interface that enables them to access and perhaps modify their benefits options, or even to interactively participate in conducting the very business of the enterprise.

A key facet of this book, in fact, is to describe how enterprises can Web-enable their enterprise information systems such that prospective clients, customers, employees, contractors, and business partners can access these enterprise systems via a Web interface. Part VI describes how to connect an enterprise system to the Web in a rapid development fashion such that a scalable Web user base can be supported. Although we do focus on the engineering tasks involved with creating that connectivity in Part VI, we do not focus on the art of Web user-interface design. Such user-interface design topics are outside the scope of this book. However, in this section we briefly highlight those technologies involved with building Web interfaces using Java technology. After such a discussion, you will hopefully walk away from this chapter with a more cohesive view of the options available to you in providing a user interface for your enterprise system.

Web Interface Content

Most of us are familiar with the use of a Web browser as the tool by which we access information over the WWW. Web browsers display Web pages, which display information to users in the form of text, hyperlinks, images, audio, and video. The Web user interacts with such Web pages using various GUI input techniques that depend on the Web interface technology being used. User input from a Web page is sent as a request to a Web server, which is then responsible for handling the request. Regardless of the technique for handling the request by the Web server, the result received from the Web server is one or more Web pages with which the user can continue to interact. Following are the primary techniques by which users interface with an enterprise via the Web and to which we refer throughout this book:

- *HTML-Based Interfaces*: HTML stands for Hypertext Markup Language. HTML is a text-based data format used by Web browsers to interpret how embedded text, hyperlinks, images, audio, and video should be displayed. HTML also contains GUI elements that can be used for input from the user. Chapter 30, "Traditional Web Programming and Java," discusses HTML in more detail.
- *Client-Side Script-Based Interfaces*: Client-side scripting languages are embedded into HTML documents and interpreted by a Web browser that can support such a language. Scripting languages offer more control and programmatic flexibility than do HTML pages for implementing dynamic behavior inside of a Web browser. We talk about scripting languages in Chapter 30 in more detail.
- *Applet-Based Interfaces*: Java applets are executable Java programs that can run inside of a Web browser. The power of Java's programmatic flexibility, richness of API, and GUI-based support make applets an attractive Web interface solution. Applets are downloaded to a Web browser by inserting specific tags into an HTML document. Running Java applets inside of Web browsers, however, has seen widespread application only for smaller programs due to a perceived performance issue in both code download and browser execution times.

- *XML-Based Interfaces*: XML stands for the eXtensible Markup Language. XML is an extension of HTML that supports a more flexible framework for describing information contained within a data stream. XML information is self-describing and is becoming the de facto standard for data interchange, including Web-based data interchange. Chapter 31, "XML," is dedicated to our XML discussion.

Web Interface Generators

Although Web browsers represent the end consumer of Web-based information such as HTML, client-side scripts, applets, and XML, this information must be generated in some fashion by the server side of an enterprise. Web servers are the frontline platforms responsible for performing or inducing the generation of such Web-based information. The techniques for performing such tasks are the focus of Part VI. Some common techniques used to generate Web-based information and the techniques we refer to and discuss throughout this book are listed here:

- *File-Based Interface Generators*: Web servers most commonly store HTML files on disk and serve them to Web browsers requesting such information. Other data referenced by such HTML files including images, scripting files, and audio files will also be retrieved from a server-side disk and served to the Web browser. We discuss Web servers more generically in Chapter 29.
- *CGI-Based Interface Generators*: The Common Gateway Interface (CGI) represents one of the oldest techniques for dynamically generating content for the Web browser. CGI applications are spawned as separate processes by a Web server and return information to the Web server that can be packaged up as a response to the Web browser. We provide an overview of CGI-based generation in Chapter 30.
- *Script-Based Interface Generators*: Scripting languages can also be executed on the server side inside of a Web server to dynamically generate Web page content. Server-side scripting requires that a server-side runtime engine process Web requests and generate responses to be sent to a Web browser. We provide an overview of Web server scripting approaches in Chapter 30.
- *Servlet-Based Interface Generators*: Java Servlets are Java-based code that executes inside of a Web server process to handle Web requests. Servlets can also dynamically generate and handle Web content and are one of two Web-enabling techniques that form the core of this book. Chapter 32, "Java Servlets," is dedicated to our servlet discussion.
- *JSP-Based Interface Generators*: JavaServer Pages (JSPs) represent another approach for dynamically generating and handling Web content. JSPs are scripting language like elements having a Java syntax. Chapter 33, "JavaServer Pages," is dedicated to our JSP discussion.

Conclusions

Enterprise user interfaces built in other languages can be connected to your server-side enterprise Java system using distributed communications technologies such as TCP/IP, CORBA, and DCOM. Enterprise user interfaces can also be built using a large suite of standard Java-based libraries. User interfaces built as Java applications or applets can make use of two GUI component technologies built into the Java platform known as AWT and Swing. Whereas Swing is a lighter-weight GUI component model, AWT offers some Web browser deployment advantages when used inside of Java applets.

Various extended Java-based UI utilities and accessibility APIs also make Java-based UIs more feature rich by supporting connectivity to printers, drag and drop between applications, online help, and connectivity to assistive technologies. A suite of extended Java-based graphics APIs for 2D, 3D, and high-resolution graphics as well as multimedia APIs for sound, speech, and video also enhance the capabilities of Java-based UIs. Web-based interfaces employ various technologies, including HTML, scripting languages, Java applets, and XML. Generators of Web-based content include file-based, CGI, scripting-language, Java Servlet, and JavaServer Page Web-enabling techniques.

Modeling Components with JavaBeans

CHAPTER

7

IN THIS CHAPTER

- JavaBeans Overview 142
- JavaBeans Containers 145
- JavaBeans Events 149
- JavaBeans Properties 152
- JavaBeans Introspection 160
- JavaBeans Persistence 163
- JavaBeans Customization 164
- The InfoBus 167

JavaBeans provide a way to define methods, events, and properties for Java classes such that they can allow external manipulation and customization during design-time. Component event registration and delivery, recognition and utilization of properties, customization, and state persistence are all built into this model. This chapter describes usage of the JavaBeans component model in the context of how a user may create components for enterprise applications.

This chapter provides a simple introduction to the JavaBean component model and is not meant to serve as an in-depth coverage of JavaBeans. It is simply meant to introduce the basic elements of one of the original Java-based component models and serve as a premise for understanding the other more enterprise-relevant component models described throughout the rest of the book. We particularly want the reader to be able to distinguish between the JavaBeans component model discussed here and the Enterprise JavaBeans component model discussed later in the book. JavaBeans and Enterprise JavaBeans are often mistakenly thought to be similar, and this chapter should help make clear the precise nature and application of regular JavaBeans. Furthermore, the JavaBeans component model is also relevant to understanding how JavaServer Pages can interact with server-side JavaBean objects as described in Chapter 33, "JavaServer Pages."

In this chapter, you will learn:

- The basic architecture and concepts behind the JavaBeans component model.
- The means by which JavaBeans are embedded in applications for design-time manipulation and the basic requirements of a JavaBeans component.
- The JavaBeans event model.
- The means by which JavaBeans expose controllability and visibility of their internal nature and structure.
- The means by which JavaBeans allow the persistence of their state.
- The means by which JavaBeans enhance their design-time customizability via GUI property editors and arbitrary GUI customizers.
- The mechanisms by which JavaBeans can better communicate with one another via the InfoBus architecture.

JavaBeans Overview

The JavaBeans architecture was one of the first comprehensive standard component-based models to grace the Java platform. JavaBean components are Java classes that adhere to an interface format such that method names, underlying behavior, and inherited or implemented behavior are structured in such a way that the class can be treated as a standard JavaBean component. Containers of these components can then interact with the JavaBean in a standard fashion. This facilitates the JavaBean's capability for being deployed in various design tools and runtime environments where the JavaBean's standard design-time and runtime interface behavior can be relied on.

So how is all of this accomplished? Figure 7.1 depicts a top-level architecture of the JavaBeans component model. At the top of this diagram is shown a JavaBean container, which provides the context and environment in which a JavaBean operates. The Java 2 platform has begun to more rigidly standardize this container environment for JavaBeans. The JavaBean component represents the JavaBean that you as an applications developer create or that you perhaps use.

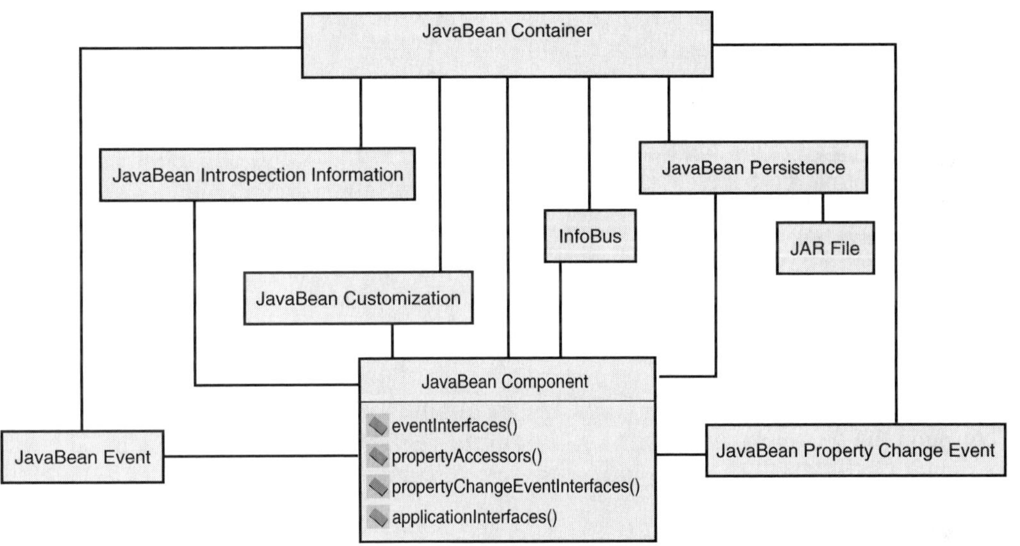

FIGURE 7.1
The JavaBeans architecture.

JavaBeans can generate events in a standard way according to the JavaBean event model and expose standard event interfaces. JavaBeans can also expose standard accessor methods for getting and setting properties of a JavaBean in a standard fashion. Property manipulation also includes standard interfaces for changes in property values, as well as the generation of property change events by JavaBeans in a standard fashion. Beans may also be analyzed by a container using JavaBean introspection facilities. Furthermore, if the generic means by which manipulating a JavaBean as provided by a container implementation is not sufficient, then interfaces for JavaBean customization may also be utilized. The persistence of a JavaBean component's state may also come in handy with particular consideration for deployment in a JAR file. Finally, a standard extension to the JavaBean's platform known as the InfoBus provides a standard mechanism for JavaBean components to pass information among themselves.

Integrated Development Environments (IDEs) such as Symantec's Visual Café and Inprise/Borland's JBuilder tools provide container implementations within which your JavaBean can be manipulated during design-time. Design-time manipulation of a JavaBean's events, properties, and customization features is a key feature of the JavaBean component model. The JavaBeans Development Kit (BDK), downloadable from the Sun Web site at `http://java.sun.com/beans/software/bdk_download.html`, provides a minimalist environment for creating JavaBean components and includes a reference JavaBean container known as the "BeanBox."

The basic JavaBean component APIs are contained in the `java.beans` package equipped with the Java 1.1 and 1.2/2.0 platforms. The newer `java.beans.beancontext` package provides standard interfaces to JavaBean container environments and is equipped with the Java 1.2/2.0 platform. The InfoBus standard extension to Java can be retrieved from `http://java.sun.com/beans/infobus/` and used with the Java 1.2/2.0 platform.

Throughout the chapter, we introduce the basic elements of the JavaBean component architecture with a few examples. We first describe a very basic container/component infrastructure and incrementally build on a core example with additional JavaBean capabilities throughout the rest of the chapter. Because an in-depth discussion of JavaBeans development is beyond the scope of this book, we have omitted some sample code from the chapter and instead refer you to the sample code on the CD.

NOTE

All the sample code that we incrementally build on and to which we refer throughout this chapter can be found on the CD in the `examples\src\ejava\beansch7` directory. Furthermore, in the interest of keeping this chapter short and simple, we often exclude exception handling and other code elements from the snippets that we incorporate throughout the chapter. The complete collection of source code can be found on the CD in the `examples\src\ejava\beansch7` directory.

Note that a `run.bat` file is also included with this code as a sample Windows script file for building the code example. This `run.bat` file compiles the sample code and creates a JAR file that can be loaded by a JavaBeans container environment. Refer to Appendix A, "Software Configuration," for general build and execution instructions for all sample code on the CD.

Although many JavaBeans examples found in literature are created with an illustration of a GUI-based JavaBean, our sample code demonstrates a more enterprise business logic–oriented example of a JavaBean. A basic auditing bean is created that can be used in a nonvisual fashion to implement a basic service for auditing events that can occur in an enterprise system.

JavaBeans Containers

JavaBean components operate inside of a JavaBean container environment. In the Java 1.1 model for JavaBeans, the container environments were loosely defined environments provided by IDEs or other environment implementations to host JavaBean components. It was the JavaBean component model that was standard and well-defined. The Java 2 platform extends the container model to support more standard JavaBean container interfaces. We explore the JavaBean container model in this section, along with the most basic JavaBean component requirements needed for a JavaBean to operate inside of a JavaBean container. Subsequent sections build on the basic JavaBean component model. Finally, we briefly explore the more standard JavaBean container model provided in the Java 2 platform.

Figure 7.2 depicts the basic architecture and relationship between JavaBean components and their containers. JavaBean containers instantiate one or more JavaBean component instances using one of the `java.beans.Beans.instantiate()` methods. JavaBean components can then be manipulated via the JavaBean container according to the standard component model rules to which the JavaBean components adhere. JavaBean containers are most often implemented inside of an IDE or another JavaBean environment. JavaBean components are implemented by applications developers.

JavaBean Containers

When creating JavaBeans, you will most likely not need to create a JavaBean container because you, as an applications developer, will often use an IDE or another JavaBean container environment into which you'll plug your standard JavaBean components. Nevertheless, we will talk about JavaBean containers here and even develop a simple sample container to enhance our capability to manipulate the JavaBean component that we create in this chapter. A basic JavaBean container must inherit from the `java.awt.Container` class or one of its subclasses. Both AWT- and Swing-based components have containers that extend this class or one of its subclasses, but purely Swing-based JavaBean components may also have containers that directly extend the `javax.swing.JComponent` class or one of its `Swing` container subclasses.

As an example of a JavaBean container, the `ejava.beansch7.AuditBeanContainer` extends the `javax.swing.JPanel` class (which extends the `javax.swing.JComponent`). The `AuditBeanContainer` holds a reference to an `ejava.beancsh7.AuditBean` JavaBean instance, which we will discuss shortly. The `AuditBeanContainer`'s constructor instantiates an instance of an `AuditBean` by calling the static `instantiate()` method on the `java.beans.Beans` class with a null `ClassLoader` and fully qualified `AuditBean` classname as parameters. The null `ClassLoader` designates the fact that the system class loader is to be used. Additionally, getter and setter methods for the `AuditBean` have also been added to the `AuditBeanContainer` as convenience methods. Only a portion of the `AuditBeanContainer` code on the CD is shown here, with exception handling and other features excluded for simplicity:

```
public class AuditBeanContainer extends JPanel
{
  private AuditBean auditBean;

  public AuditBeanContainer()
  {
    ClassLoader  useClassLoader = null;
    auditBean = (AuditBean)Beans.instantiate(useClassLoader,
      "ejava.beansch7.AuditBean");

    // Exception handling and other code excluded here...
  }

  public AuditBean getBean(){ return auditBean; }

  public void setBean(AuditBean newBean) { auditBean = newBean; }

  // More code to show later in the chapter...
}
```

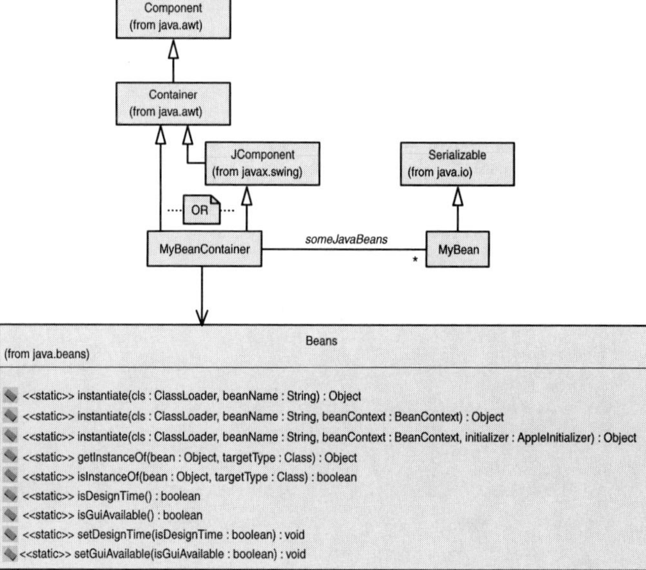

FIGURE 7.2

JavaBeans containers and components.

JavaBean Components

JavaBean components must adhere to a few simple rules to satisfy the JavaBean component model and be callable from a JavaBean container. We'll introduce only the most basic rules in this section and discuss additional rules of JavaBean component modeling in subsequent sections on JavaBean component events, properties, methods and introspection, persistence, and customizers. The most basic rules of JavaBean component standard modeling are that the JavaBean be a public class, have a default public constructor with no parameters, and implement the `java.io.Serializable` interface. If the JavaBean component is to be a visual bean, it should also extend the `javax.swing.JComponent` class if it is a purely Swing-based bean, and the `java.awt.Component` class if it is AWT-based.

As an example of a JavaBean component, the public `ejava.beansch7.AuditBean` class implements an empty default constructor. The `AuditBean` class also implements an `auditMessage(String)` method that logs a message `String` and current date to a log file via a `PrintStream`. Although a default log filename is assumed for now, a subsequent section demonstrates how such a file can be configured via JavaBean properties. Only a portion of the `AuditBean` code on the CD is shown here, with exception handling and other features excluded for simplicity:

```
public class AuditBean implements Serializable
{
   private transient PrintStream streamToWrite;
   private final String DEFAULT_FILE_NAME  =  "default.txt";
   private File file = new File(DEFAULT_FILE_NAME);
   // More variable definitions to show later in the chapter...

   public AuditBean()
   {
       // default constructor, it should be implemented for a bean
   }

   public void auditMessage(String message)
   {
      Date nonCreditAuditDate = null;

      if(streamToWrite == null ){
          FileOutputStream foutStream = new FileOutputStream(file);
          boolean flushOut = true;
          streamToWrite = new PrintStream(foutStream,flushOut);
         // Exception handling excluded...
      }
      Date currentTime = new Date();
      String auditMessage = message + " : " + currentTime;
      streamToWrite.println(auditMessage);
   }
```

```
  // More method definitions to show later in the chapter...
}
```

JavaBean Context

In addition to the loosely defined Java 1.1 means for providing a JavaBean container environment, the `java.beans.beancontext` package now equipped with the Java 2 platform provides a more standard means for implementing an environment for JavaBean components. JavaBean contexts define an environment in which a bean's lifecycle can be managed in a standard fashion in addition to providing a standard interface for beans to interrogate their environment, access standard container services, and receive container environment information. Figure 7.3 depicts this newer JavaBean context architecture.

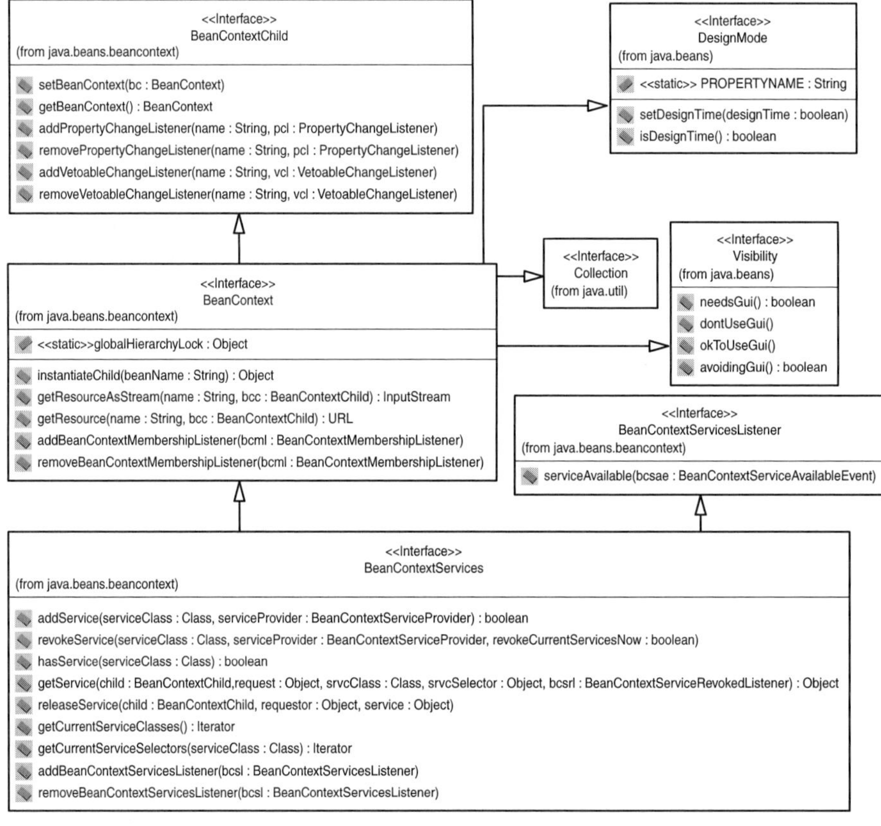

FIGURE 7.3
JavaBean context.

The BeanContext interface is the root of all JavaBean container environments using this newer JavaBean context model. The BeanContext extends the java.util.Collection interface and thus defines add, remove, and other operations for manipulating collections of objects. In the case of a BeanContext, it can contain JavaBean components and other BeanContext objects. The BeanContext interface also extends the BeanContextChild interface, which adds the capability for a BeanContext to obtain a handle to its containing BeanContext environment if it has one. JavaBean components also wanting access to their BeanContext environment can implement the BeanContextChild interface.

JavaBean containers that want to provide services to their JavaBean components can implement the BeanContextServices interface. Services are added to the container environment using the BeanContextServices.add() method. Those services may then be retrieved by the JavaBean component after it obtains a handle to its JavaBean container environment and then via a call to getService() on the container implementing the BeanContextServices interface.

Although we do not expand on the use of the BeanContext in our sample JavaBean here, you can think of our AuditBeanContainer as a JavaBean container that could implement the BeanContext or BeanContextServices interface. The AuditBeanContainer could then create an AuditBean JavaBean component instance using the Beans.instantiate(ClassLoader, String, BeanContext) interface in which the AuditBean instance could be created with a reference to the AuditBeanContainer object itself. The AuditBean operating inside of the AuditBeanContainer could then utilize the standard interfaces defined by the BeanContext or BeanContextServices interface to interact with its JavaBean container environment.

JavaBeans Events

JavaBean container environments can receive notification of JavaBean component events and allow for the design-time selection of which events a JavaBean component will respond to if the JavaBean component adheres to a few simple rules. Public add and remove methods on a JavaBean component must be defined in a standard fashion to add and remove event listeners, respectively. JavaBean containers can then add and remove references to event listeners with the JavaBean components that allow for the container to interact with a component's events. Events on JavaBean components can be registered with a bean if it implements a method of the form add*XXX*Listener(*XXX*Listener), where *XXX* is the name of some event type. Similarly, events can be unregistered if the bean implements a method of the form remove*XXX*Listener(*XXX*Listener). As a final note, if your JavaBean component allows only one listener to be registered for events at a time, the add*XXX*Listener(*XXX*Listener) method should declare that it throws a java.util.TooManyListenersException.

These rules for a JavaBean component and the relationship between it and a listener (for example, *XXX*Listener) and an event type (for example, *XXX*) are shown in Figure 7.4. The *XXX*Listener extends the java.util.EventListener class or one of its subclasses.

A JavaBean container may utilize one of the standard Java listeners or an application-specific listener. The JavaBean container may simply hold references to a listener or implement a listener interface itself. Events generated from a JavaBean component extend the `java.util.EventObject` class or one of its subclasses.

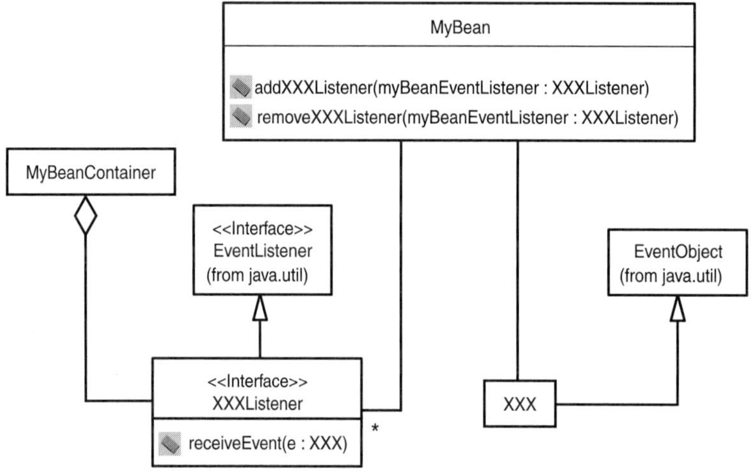

FIGURE 7.4
JavaBean events.

As an example of a simple audit event that can be generated from our `AuditBean` class, we create an `ejava.beansch7.AuditEvent` class. It has two constructors, one of which can receive an `AuditBean` instance and another of which can receive an `AuditBean` instance and audit message `String`. A `getMessage()` method returns a handle to the associated audit message `String`. The `AuditEvent` class is rather simple and is shown in its entirety here:

```
package ejava.beansch7;
import java.util.EventObject;

public class AuditEvent extends EventObject
{
   private String auditMessage;

   public AuditEvent(AuditBean source){ super(source); }

   public AuditEvent(AuditBean source, String message)
   {
      this(source);
      auditMessage = message;
   }
```

```
   public String getMessage(){ return auditMessage; }
}
```

An `ejava.beanch7.AuditListener` interface is implemented by objects that want to obtain notification of generated `AuditEvent` objects from a JavaBean component. The `AuditListener` is defined as follows in its entirety:

```
package ejava.beansch7;
import java.util.EventListener;

public interface AuditListener extends EventListener
{
   public void auditEvent(AuditEvent e);
}
```


Our `AuditBean` component can then be made to work with events in a standard fashion for use by containers. We extend our `AuditBean` class defined previously to first include a `Vector` collection of audit listeners. A `notifyAuditEvent()` method has also been added to the `AuditBean` class to notify each listener in the `Vector` of listeners of a generated `AuditEvent` containing both the `AuditBean` source reference and an audit event message `String`. This `notifyAuditEvent()` method is called at the very end of the `auditMessage()` method. Finally, we also implement `addAuditListener()` and `removeAuditListener()` methods so that our `AuditBean` can satisfy the requirements of the JavaBean component model for enabling events to be received by JavaBean containers. Only the addition of code for our JavaBean component to support events is illustrated here:

```
public class AuditBean implements Serializable
{
   // List of Listeners to be notified of an event
   private Vector  auditListeners = new Vector();

   // Other member variables defined not shown...

   public void auditMessage(String message)
   {
      Date nonCreditAuditDate = null;

      if(streamToWrite == null ){
          FileOutputStream foutStream = new FileOutputStream(file);
          boolean flushOut = true;
          streamToWrite = new PrintStream(foutStream,flushOut);
          // Exception handling excluded...
      }
      Date currentTime = new Date();
      String auditMessage = message + " : " + currentTime;
      streamToWrite.println(auditMessage);
      notifyAuditEvent(auditMessage);
   }
```

```
    protected void notifyAuditEvent(String auditMessage)
    {
       Vector listeners = null;
       AuditEvent auditEvent = new AuditEvent(this, auditMessage);
       synchronized(this) {
         listeners = (Vector) auditListeners.clone();
       }

       for (int i = 0; i < listeners.size(); i++) {
         AuditListener auditListener =
           (AuditListener)listeners.elementAt(i);
         auditListener.auditEvent(auditEvent);
       }
    }

   public synchronized void addAuditListener(AuditListener auditListener)
   {
     auditListeners.add(auditListener);
   }

   public synchronized
       void removeAuditListener(AuditListener auditListener)
   {
     auditListeners.remove(auditListener);
   }

   // Additional methods not shown...
}
```

JavaBeans Properties

Properties defined on a JavaBean are those attributes of the component defined in a standard way such that the values can be set during design-time. Thus, for example, a property on some generic `Printer` JavaBean component may define whether a printer supports color printing. JavaBean properties must have public getter and setter methods defined on the JavaBean component according to a particular standard pattern in order for JavaBean container environments to recognize JavaBean properties.

JavaBean properties come in various flavors, as illustrated in Figure 7.5. Simple properties and Boolean properties simply rely on a standard naming convention for getter and setter methods on a JavaBean. Array properties allow for the getting and setting of entire arrays, whereas indexed properties allow for the individual getting and setting of array elements by using an array index number. Bound properties are those properties whose changes in value must be broadcast to property change listeners. Vetoable properties are those properties whose changes in value must be validated by vetoable property change listeners before the changes are effected. We expand on these various property types below.

Simple Properties

As illustrated in Figure 7.5, simple properties adhere to a few simple rules for general properties and Boolean properties. Objects defined as properties must be `Serializable` as a first rule. Getters for simple properties are defined according to `getSimplePropertyName()`, returning the property type in which the `SimplePropertyName` in the getter name is the name of the simple property and must be preceded by the word `get`. Setters for simple properties are defined according to `setSimplePropertyName()`, taking a property type as an input parameter and requiring that `SimplePropertyName` in the setter name correspond to the simple property name and be preceded by the word `set`. The exception to this rule is for `boolean` values where the getter differs in that instead of `get`, the word `is` precedes the property name.

As an example, our `AuditBean` may now be extended to support two simple properties. A `getFile()` getter and a `setFile(File)` setter are first added for our `Serializable File` object. Additionally, a `setFile(String)` method is also added as a helper to first create a `File` object from a filename `String` and then call `setFile(File)`. As an example of a calculated simple property with no underlying attribute for the property, we also define the `getFileName()` and `setFileName(String)` methods, which are recognized as simple `fileName` properties. For example:

```
public class AuditBean implements Serializable
{
   private final String DEFAULT_FILE_NAME  =  "default.txt";
   private File file = new File(DEFAULT_FILE_NAME);

   // Other member variables defined not shown...

   public File getFile(){ return file; }

   public void setFile(File newFile){file = newFile;}

   public void setFile(String newFileName)
   {
      File file = new File(newFileName);
      setFile(file);
   }

   public String getFileName(){ return file.getName(); }

   public void setFileName(String fileName){ setFile(fileName); }

  // Other method definitions not shown...
}
```

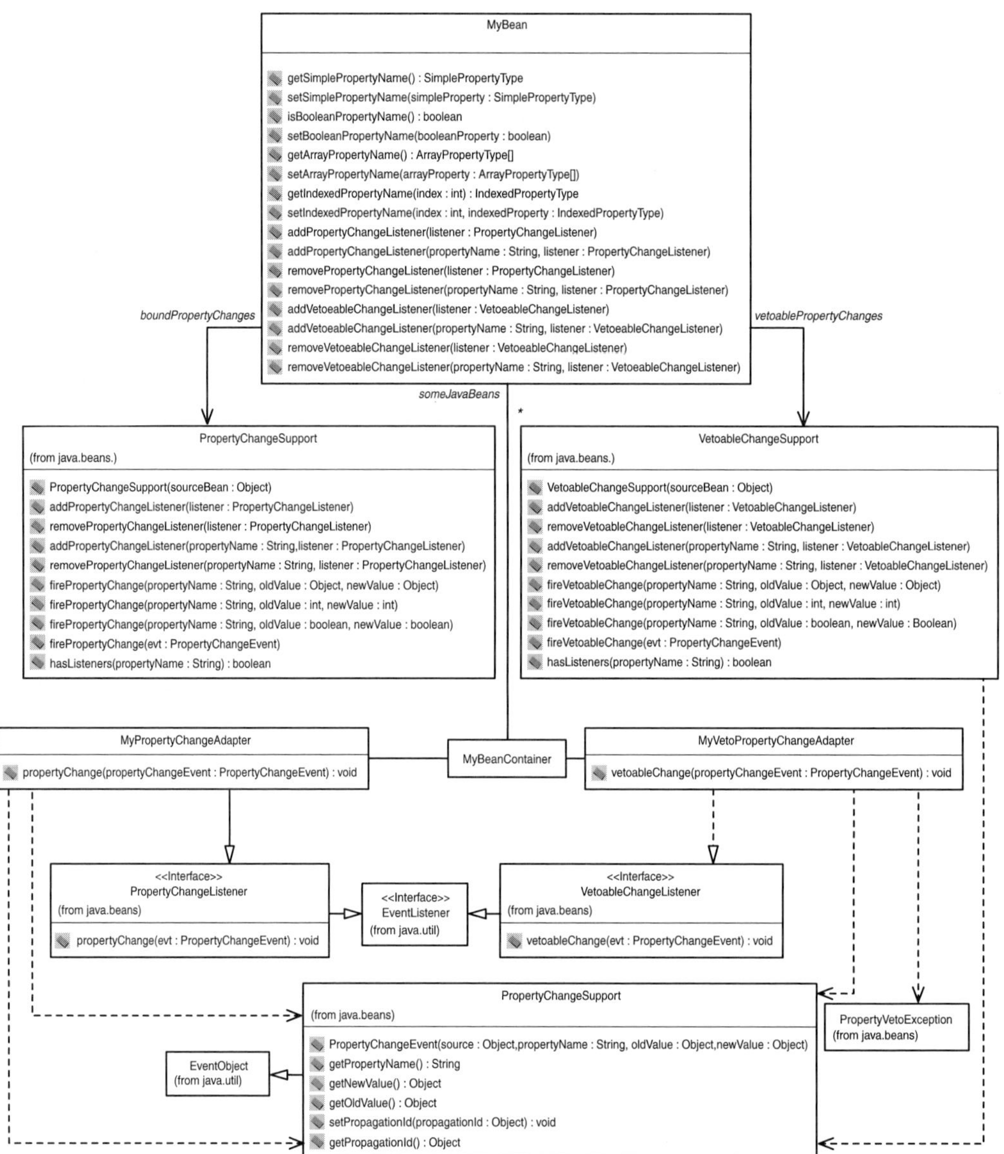

FIGURE 7.5

JavaBean properties.

Array and Indexed Properties

Arrays of properties are treated similarly to the way in which simple properties are treated. Figure 7.5 illustrates the convention for array properties. A `getArrayPropertyName()` method returns an array of property types with `ArrayPropertyName` corresponding to the name of the array property. A `setArrayPropertyName()` takes an array property as a parameter with `ArrayPropertyName` also corresponding to the name of the array property. For example, an underlying array of user group names may be retrieved and set using this:

```
private String[] userGroups = new String[100];

public String[] getUserGroups(){
  return userGroups;
}

public void setUserGroups(String[] groups){
  userGroups = groups;
}
```


You can also set and get indexed properties as shown in Figure 7.5. A `getIndexedPropertyName(int)` method returns an element of a property collection given an index number into that collection with `IndexedPropertyName` corresponding to the name of the indexed property. A `setIndexedPropertyName(int, IndexedPropertyType)` takes an index and a property element as parameters with `IndexedPropertyName` also corresponding to the name of the indexed property. For example, underlying indexed user group names may be retrieved and set using this:

```
private String[] userGroups = new String[100];

public String getUserGroup(int idx){
  return userGroups[idx];
}

public void setUserGroup(int idx, String group){
  userGroups[idx] = group;
}
```

Bound Properties

Bound properties provide a mechanism for notifying listeners of changes in a JavaBean component's property value. As shown in Figure 7.5, listeners implement the `PropertyChangeListener` interface and receive `PropertyChangeEvent` objects that have been generated by JavaBean components. `PropertyChangeEvent` objects contain a property name, an old property value, and a new property value to which the listener may want access.

The JavaBean component can use the `PropertyChangeSupport` helper class to fire the actual event to be received by the listeners. A `PropertyChangeSupport` object is constructed with a reference to the JavaBean component instance, and it relies on the fact that the JavaBean implements `addPropertyChangeListener()` and `removePropertyChangeListener()` methods to add and remove property change listeners, respectively. One of the `PropertyChangeSupport.firePropertyChange()` methods can be used, passing in such information as the property name, old value, and new value. As an example, our `AuditBean` may be extended to support bound properties indicating when an audit file changes as shown here:

```
public class AuditBean
{
  private PropertyChangeSupport propertyChange   =
        new PropertyChangeSupport(this);
  // Not all variable definitions shown here...

  public void setFile(File newFile)
  {
      File oldFile = file;
      file = newFile;
      propertyChanage.firePropertyChange("file",
        oldFile, newFile);
      fileChanged(file);
  }

   public void fileChanged()
   {
        FileOutputStream foutStream = new FileOutputStream(file);
        boolean flushOut = true;
        streamToWrite = new PrintStream(foutStream,flushOut);
       // Exception handling excluded...
   }

   public void addPropertyChangeListener(
      PropertyChangeListener propertyChangeListener)
   {
      propertyChange.addPropertyChangeListener(propertyChangeListener);
   }

   public void removePropertyChangeListener(
      PropertyChangeListener propertyChangeListener)
   {
      propertyChange.removePropertyChangeListener(
                                         propertyChangeListener);
   }
```

```
   // Not all methods shown here...
}
```

An AuditPropertyChangeAdapter class acts as a simple PropertyChangeListener implementation:

```
public class AuditPropertyChangeAdapter
  implements  PropertyChangeListener
{
  public void propertyChange(PropertyChangeEvent propertyChangeEvent)
  {
    System.out.println("Property Name :"+
      propertyChangeEvent.getPropertyName());
    System.out.println("Old Value :"
                        + propertyChangeEvent.getOldValue());
    System.out.println("New  Value :"
                        + propertyChangeEvent.getNewValue());
  }
}
```


A JavaBean container can then create an instance of our custom AuditPropertyChangeAdapter property change listener and register it with the AuditBean for bound property change events, as we do here in the constructor of our AuditBeanContainer:

```
public class AuditBeanContainer extends JPanel
{
   private AuditBean auditBean;
   public AuditBeanContainer()
   {
      auditBean = // instantiate bean

      AuditPropertyChangeAdapter auditPropertyChangeAdapter =
        new AuditPropertyChangeAdapter();
      auditBean.addPropertyChangeListener(
        auditPropertyChangeAdapter);
     // Exception handling excluded here...
   }
}
```

Constrained Properties

Constrained properties are similar to bound properties, but the change in value of a property must first be validated by all listeners before the value change can be effected by the JavaBean component. Any listener may veto the property change, and the JavaBean component then agrees to not effect the change.

As shown in Figure 7.5, listeners implement the `VetoableChangeListener` interface and receive `PropertyChangeEvent` objects that have been generated by JavaBean components. The JavaBean component can use the `VetoableChangeSupport` helper class to fire the actual event to be received by the listeners. A `VetoableChangeSupport` object is constructed with a reference to the JavaBean component instance and relies on the fact that the JavaBean implements `addVetoableChangeListener()` and `removeVetoableChangeListener()` methods to add and remove vetoable property change listeners, respectively. One of the `VetoableChangeSupport.fireVetoableChange()` methods can be used by passing in such information as the property name, old value, and new value. If any of the listeners veto the change from being made, a `PropertyVetoException` will be thrown. As an example, our `AuditBean` may be extended to support vetoable properties indicating when an audit file changes as shown here:

```
public class AuditBean
{
  private   VetoableChangeSupport vetoableChange =
    new  VetoableChangeSupport(this);
  // Not all variables shown here...

  public void setFile(File newFile)
  {
      File oldFile = file;
      try {
        vetoableChange.fireVetoableChange("file",
          oldFile, newFile);
        file = newFile;
        fileChanged();
      }
      catch(PropertyVetoException propertyVetoException) {
         // Some of the listeners does not like to change the file
         file = oldFile;
      }
   }

  public void addVetoableChangeListener(VetoableChangeListener
    vetoableChangeListener)
  {
    vetoableChange.addVetoableChangeListener(vetoableChangeListener);
  }

  public void removeVetoableChangeListener( VetoableChangeListener
      vetoableChangeListener)
  {
    vetoableChange.removeVetoableChangeListener(vetoableChangeListener);
```

```
  }

  // Not all methods shown here...
}
```

A simple `AuditVetoPropertyChangeAdapter` serving as a `VetoableChangeListener` vetoes a change if the audit filenames are the same:

```
public class AuditVetoPropertyChangeAdapter
                             implements VetoableChangeListener
{

   public void vetoableChange(PropertyChangeEvent propertyChangeEvent)
                                          throws PropertyVetoException
   {
       String propertyName =  propertyChangeEvent.getPropertyName();
       Object oldValue = propertyChangeEvent.getOldValue();
       Object newValue = propertyChangeEvent.getNewValue();
       String newFileName = newValue.toString();
       String oldFileName = oldValue.toString();
       if(oldFileName.equalsIgnoreCase(newFileName)){
        throw new PropertyVetoException("NotReady to change",
                                               propertyChangeEvent);
       }
   }
}
```

A JavaBean container can then create an instance of our custom `AuditVetoPropertyChangeAdapter` vetoable property change listener and register it with the `AuditBean` for bound property change events, as we do here in the constructor of our `AuditBeanContainer`:

```
public class AuditBeanContainer extends JPanel
{
   private AuditBean auditBean;
   public AuditBeanContainer()
   {
      auditBean = // instantiate bean

      AuditVetoPropertyChangeAdapter auditVetoPropertyChangeAdapter
        = new AuditVetoPropertyChangeAdapter();
      auditBean.addVetoableChangeListener(
        auditVetoPropertyChangeAdapter);
      // Exception handling excluded here...
   }
}
```

JavaBeans Introspection

Introspection involves the analysis of a JavaBean component at runtime. JavaBean containers and JavaBean-capable IDEs can discover properties and behavior of a JavaBean by using introspection. The Java reflection API supported by the `java.lang.Class` method and the `java.lang.reflect` package provides a low-level means for analyzing Java code that is utilized by JavaBeans introspection. Figure 7.6 depicts some of the core interfaces and classes used for JavaBeans introspection. A container and an IDE use these classes to dynamically discover information about JavaBean components that adhere to the JavaBean component model.

The `Introspector` class is the frontline interface to JavaBeans introspection. In particular, the `Introspector.getBeanInfo()` methods are used to return a `BeanInfo` object that is used to describe the methods, properties, events, and other features of a JavaBean component. Features of a JavaBean are described via subclasses of the `FeatureDescriptor` class. These subclasses and the information that they convey about a JavaBean component are listed here:

- `BeanDescriptor`: Describes general information about a JavaBean.
- `EventSetDescriptor`: Describes the type of events that can be generated by a JavaBean.
- `MethodDescriptor`: Describes the methods that are supported by the JavaBean.
- `ParameterDescriptor`: Describes the parameters of a JavaBean method.
- `PropertyDescriptor`: Describes the properties exported by a JavaBean.
- `IndexedPropertyDescriptor`: Describes the indexed properties exported by a JavaBean.

The `SimpleBeanInfo` class is a default helper class implementation of the `BeanInfo` interface. "No-op" values are returned from the various interface implementations. JavaBean components that want to present more information about themselves can then subclass the `SimpleBeanInfo` class without implementing every method in the `BeanInfo` interface.

As an example, we provide an `AuditBeanBeanInfo` class on the CD in the `ejava.beansch7` sample package that extends the `SimpleBeanInfo` class. We also provide a `BeanIntrospectorExample` class on the CD that demonstrates how the introspection APIs can be used by a container and an IDE to dynamically use the information provided by the `AuditBeanBeanInfo` class. We show `BeanInfo` method implementations here by the `AuditBeanBeanInfo` class for `getBeanDescriptor()`, `getPropertyDescriptors()`, `getMethodDescriptors()`, and `getEventDescriptors()` with exceptions and other extraneous code excluded for simplicity (the complete implementations can be found on the CD):

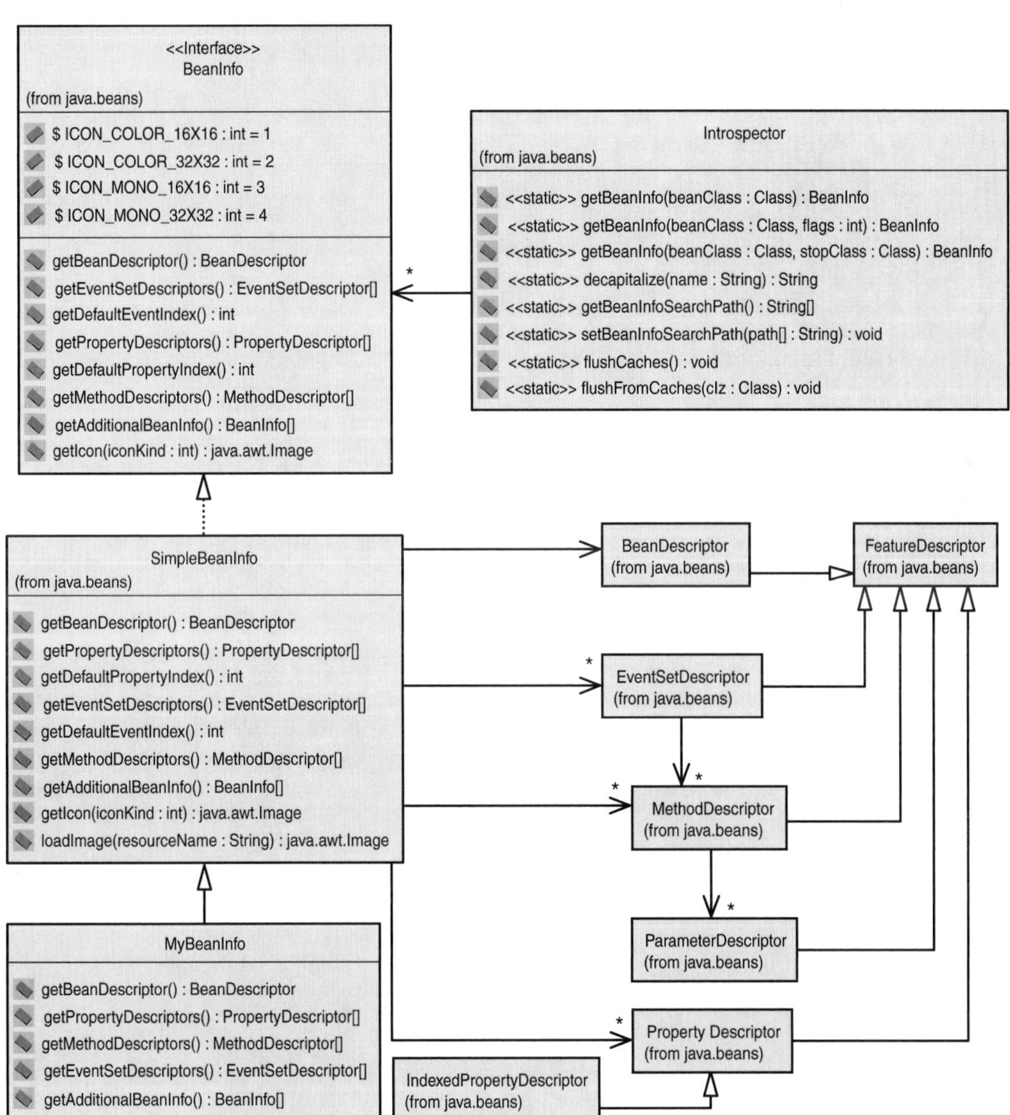

FIGURE 7.6

JavaBean introspection.

```
public BeanDescriptor getBeanDescriptor()
{
 BeanDescriptor beanDescriptor =
   new BeanDescriptor(ejava.beansch7.AuditBean.class);
```

```
    beanDescriptor.setDisplayName("AuditBean");
    return beanDescriptor;
   }

   public PropertyDescriptor[] getPropertyDescriptors ()
   {
    PropertyDescriptor fileP =
      new PropertyDescriptor("file", AuditBean.class,
                                            "getFile", "setFile");

    PropertyDescriptor fileNameP =
      new PropertyDescriptor("fileName", AuditBean.class,
                                     "getFileName", "setFileName");
    fileNameP.setDisplayName("File Name");
    fileNameP.setBound(true);

    PropertyDescriptor auditTypeP = new
       PropertyDescriptor("AuditType", AuditBean.class);
    auditTypeP.setPropertyEditorClass(AuditPropertyEditor.class);

    PropertyDescriptor[] descriptors =
       new PropertyDescriptor[] {fileP, fileNameP, auditTypeP};

    return descriptors;
   }

   public MethodDescriptor[] getMethodDescriptors ()
   {
    MethodDescriptor[] descriptors = {
      new MethodDescriptor (
      AuditBean.class.getMethod ("auditMessage", new Class[0]))};

    return descriptors;
   }

   public EventSetDescriptor[]  getEventSetDescriptors ()
   {
    EventSetDescriptor[] events = {
       new EventSetDescriptor (AuditBean.class,
          "audit", AuditListener.class, "notifyAuditEvent")};
     return events;
   }
```

As a final note, you'll notice that the `BeanInfo` interface has a `getIcon(int)` method and four static `ICON_XXX` values. When a container calls your `getIcon()` on your JavaBean component's `BeanInfo` class using one of the `ICON_XXX` values, your `BeanInfo` class may optionally return a java.awt.Image object that encapsulates a reference to a JavaBean's icon image. Color and monochrome images at sizes of 16×16 or 32×32 pixels can be returned from this getIcon() call.

JavaBeans Persistence

Persistence of JavaBean components allows for a JavaBean component to save its state to be retrieved later. The most basic form of JavaBean persistence uses the Java serialization interfaces to transform a bean to and from a JavaBean object's instance values and a serializable stream (for example, file stream). JavaBean containers and IDEs may invoke the actual serialization and deserialization process, but you may also want to serialize your JavaBean for deployment inside of a JAR file.

The first thing that must be accomplished to permit serialization is to make a JavaBean component implement the Serializable interface. A JavaBean component must then follow any necessary semantics for persisting or not persisting fields of your component based on the rules for object serialization, such as designating transient fields if necessary. Our AuditBean, for example, follows these simple rules and is thus a persistable JavaBean component.

A JavaBean container and IDE must persist and restore the state of a JavaBean to and from its serialized representation. However, you may also want to deploy your JavaBean inside of a JAR file with some initial serialized state. Serialization of a JavaBean involves the creation of a serialization file with a .ser extension, as shown here:

```
String serializedFileName = "AuditBean.ser";

FileOutputStream fileOutputStream
  = new FileOutputStream(serializedFileName);
ObjectOutputStream  objectOutputStream
  = new ObjectOutputStream(fileOutputStream);

AuditBean beanToBeSerialized = // get handle to bean

objectOutputStream.writeObject(beanToBeSerialized);
objectOutputStream.flush();
objectOutputStream.close();
```

To package your JavaBean inside of a JAR file, you must create a manifest file indicating those Java classes inside of the JAR file that correspond to JavaBeans. This is accomplished by adding the property Java-Bean: True to a manifest entry for a JavaBean class. Those classes that are not JavaBeans but are used for design-time introspection of JavaBeans add a Design-Time-Only: True property to the manifest. As an example for our audit bean code, we have this:

```
Name: ejava/beansch7/AuditBean.class
Java-Bean: True

Name: ejava/beansch7/AuditBeanBeanInfo.class
Java-Bean: False
Design-Time-Only: True
```

Although incorporation of serialized JavaBean state and JavaBean icon images is optional, the JavaBean class itself is, of course, necessary. You may then create a JAR file with the `jar` utility using the `-m` option to specify a manifest file to use. You should, of course, create your JAR file with all of your JavaBean's class files, serialization files, and any images in the directory corresponding to your JavaBean's package. For example, if you want to create an audit bean JAR file with a manifest file named `manifest.mf` and a set of icons that are to be read from the `ejava\beansch7` directory, you might use this command:

```
jar -cmf manifest.mf audit.jar
➥ ejava\beansch7\AuditBean.class
➥ ejava\beansch7\AuditBean.ser
➥ ejava\beansch7\AuditBean_color16.gif
➥ ejava\beansch7\AuditBean_color32.gif
➥ ejava\beansch7\AuditBean_mono16.gif
➥ ejava\beansch7\AuditBean_mono32.gif
```

JavaBeans Customization

When you adhere to the JavaBean component model standards for defining events, properties, introspective beans, and persistable beans, your JavaBean will be manipulable by most JavaBean containers and IDEs using their built-in property sheet editors and other bean manipulation features. However, you may also want to extend the standard property sheet editing capabilities provided by your IDE using custom property editors. Furthermore, more advanced GUI-based tools for customizing a JavaBean may also be provided using JavaBean customizers. We only briefly describe what is involved here with JavaBean property sheet editors and JavaBean customizers.

Property Editors

Figure 7.7 presents the basic architecture involved in using JavaBean property editors to create custom property sheets. The `PropertyEditor` interface is a base interface that must be implemented to provide a custom property editor. The `PropertyEditorSupport` class provides a default implementation of the `PropertyEditor` interface that may be inherited by or directly referenced by custom property editors. For example, a custom property editor such as the `MyPropertyEditor` class in Figure 7.7 extends the `PropertyEditorSupport` class. A `PropertyEditorManager` class is used to register and retrieve custom `PropertyEditor` classes. A property can also be associated with a custom `PropertyEditor` using the `PropertyDescriptor.setPropertyEditorClass()` method from within a `BeanInfo` implementation.

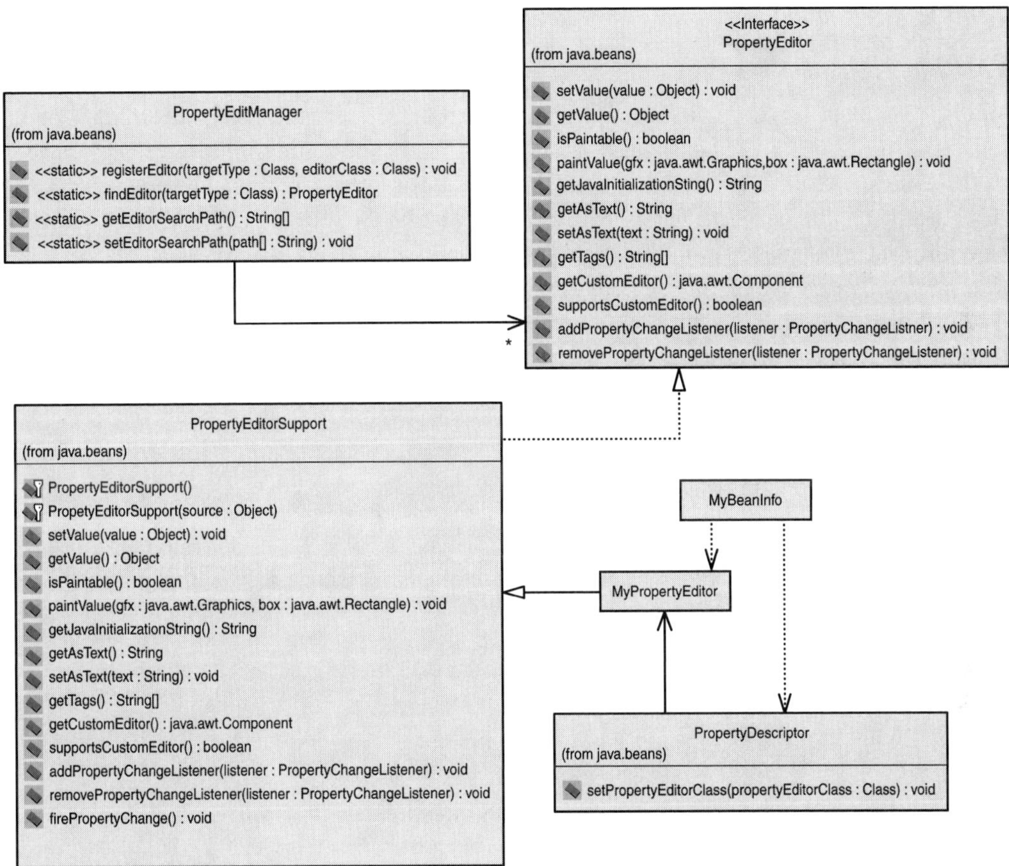

FIGURE 7.7
JavaBean property editors.

We include a simple example of a custom property editor on the CD in the `AuditPropertyEditor.java` file for our `AuditBean` that can work inside of the BDK's BeanBox. The `AuditBean` is extended to support a new `int` property called `auditType`. An interface defining `static` constants for audit type `int` values and corresponding displayable `String` values is defined in an `AuditTypes` interface. Finally, the `AuditPropertyEditor` class extends `PropertyEditorSupport` to implement a custom property editor mapping audit type values to displayable `String` values. The custom `AuditPropertyEditor` is then associated with the `auditType` property owned by the `AuditBean` from within the `AuditBean` class's `getPropertyDescriptor()` method as shown here:

```
PropertyDescriptor auditTypeP
  = new PropertyDescriptor("AuditType", AuditBean.class);

auditTypeP.setPropertyEditorClass(AuditPropertyEditor.class);
```

Customizers

Figure 7.8 presents the basic architecture behind JavaBean customizers. A JavaBean customizer (for example, `MyBeanCustomer`) must implement the `Customizer` interface and provide a GUI to solicit input from a user that can be used to manipulate a JavaBean component. Although no requirements are imposed on the nature of the GUI, it will either be AWT-based requiring inheritance from a subclass of `Component`, or Swing-based requiring inheritance from a subclass of `JComponent`. The `Customizer.setObject()` method is implemented to associate the JavaBean component instance with the customizer. The `addPropertyChangeListener()` and `removePropertyChangeListener()` methods on the `Customizer` interface signify the fact that a `Customizer` implementation must generate `PropertyChangeEvent` objects when it updates a JavaBean's properties.

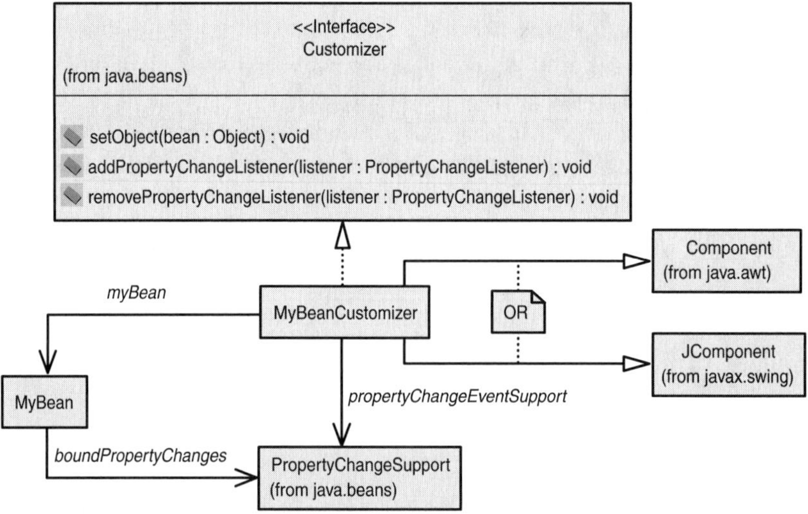

FIGURE 7.8
JavaBean customizers.

We also include a simple example of a JavaBean customizer on the CD in the `AuditBeanCustomizer.java` file for our `AuditBean`. The `AuditBeanCustomizer` class extends the Swing `JPanel` class and implements a `Customizer` interface. A drop-down box displays and allows the selection of audit type property values, and a text field displays and allows the user to enter filename values. Whenever the audit type or filename values are changed, the `AuditBeanCustomizer` generates property change events. The JavaBean container is notified of these events by a `PropertyChangeListener` interface that it registered with the customizer by calling `addPropertyChangeListener()` defined by the `Customizer` interface. The `AuditBeanCustomizer` is registered with the JavaBean container environment by modifying the `AuditBeanBeanInfo` class's `getBeanDescriptor()` method to return a `BeanDescriptor` constructed with the customizer's class, as shown here:

```
public BeanDescriptor getBeanDescriptor()
{
   BeanDescriptor beanDescriptor =
     new BeanDescriptor(ejava.beansch7.AuditBean.class,
                        ejava.beansch7.AuditBeanCustomizer.class);
   beanDescriptor.setDisplayName("AuditBean");

   return beanDescriptor;
}
```


The InfoBus

The InfoBus is an extension to the Java platform for JavaBean components to exchange information in a dynamic and standard fashion. JavaBean components that want to receive data from other JavaBean components implement standard InfoBus consumer interfaces. JavaBean components that want to make data available to other JavaBean components implement InfoBus producer interfaces. Both consumers and producers implement standard InfoBus interfaces to become a member of the InfoBus community. Data that is exchanged between members of the InfoBus is also encapsulated in a standard way by JavaBean component producers such that JavaBean component consumers can receive this data in standard form.

The basic InfoBus architecture is shown in Figure 7.9. The classes and interfaces from the `javax.infobus` package that compose this architecture are listed here:

- `InfoBus`: InfoBus is a standard JavaBeans service class that can be retrieved from a bean context's `getService()` method. An InfoBus holds a list of `InfoBusMember` objects representing components that have joined the InfoBus for communication. The InfoBus is used by members to request, make available, and revoke data items of interest to other members on the InfoBus.
- `InfoBusMember`: The `InfoBusMember` interface must be implemented by all producers and consumers on the InfoBus.
- `InfoBusDataProducer`: The `InfoBusDataProducer` interface is implemented by those components that provide data to the InfoBus. Data is made available and revoked by implementers of this interface. Implementers of this interface also register with the InfoBus to receive requests for data.
- `InfoBusDataConsumer`: The `InfoBusDataConsumer` interface is implemented by those components that receive data from the InfoBus. Data is requested by implementers of this interface. Implementers of this interface are also notified of data availability and revocation by producers.

- `InfoBusEvent`: The `InfoBusEvent` class and its subclasses encapsulate events on the InfoBus such as data requests, availability announcements, and revocations.
- `DataItem`: The `DataItem` interface is implemented by classes that encapsulate data passed via the InfoBus in events. `DataItem` objects may also implement a `DataItemChangeManager` interface for consumers implementing a `DataItemChangeListener` interface to subscribe for changes in the state of some `DataItem`.

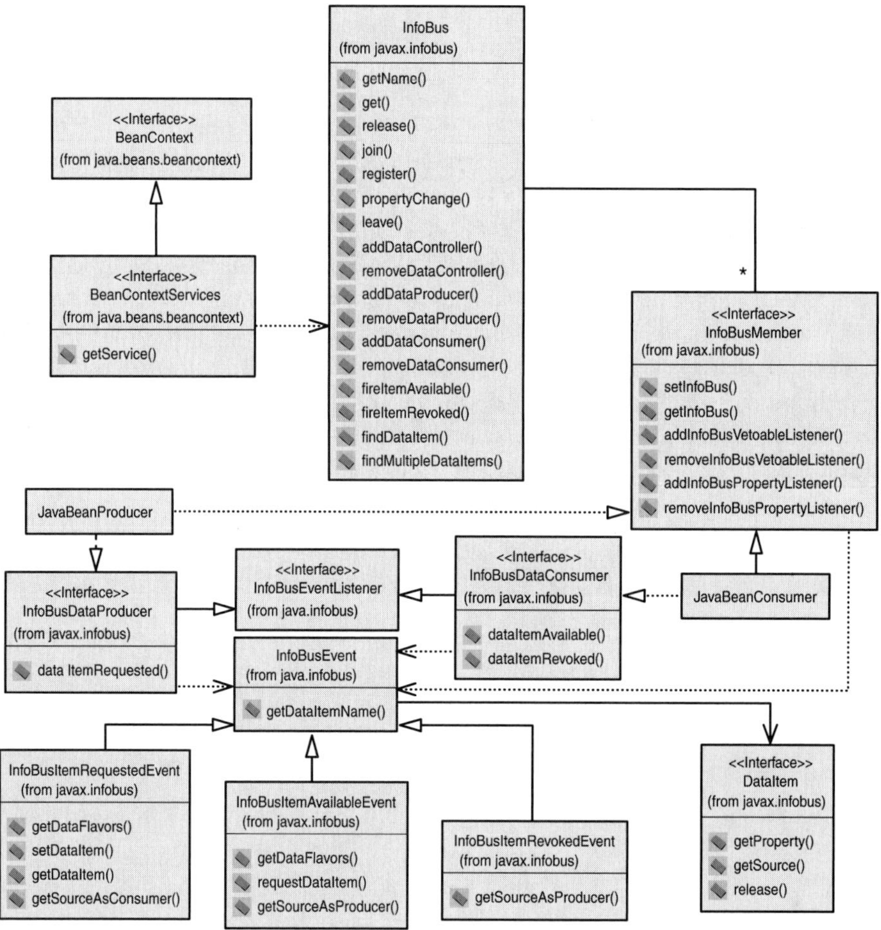

FIGURE 7.9

The JavaBean InfoBus architecture.

Conclusions

The JavaBeans component model provides a standard way for developers to define Java classes such that their components can operate inside of JavaBean container environments. JavaBean components expose their attribute properties according to various property definition models, expose their events, expose introspective information about themselves, and allow for the customization of design tools that allow the beans themselves to be customized at design-time. By developing classes that adhere to the JavaBeans component model, you help foster the reusability of your components by virtue of the advanced level of design-time customization that you permit for your component. Aside from design-time customization, the persistence of your component's state can also be used when deploying and initializing a component's state for runtime usage.

Use of the JavaBean component model has gained particular popularity among GUI-based development efforts. Developers often customize JavaBean components that implement GUI components using an IDE that understands the JavaBean component model. JavaBean components can, however, also have a nonvisual nature, but the utility of such components is often limited in scope. The primary services offered by JavaBean containers are the design-time customization of properties and events as well as a GUI-based means for easily interconnecting JavaBean components. Enterprise class features needed by the container, such as middle-tier security, transaction, and database connectivity services, are provided by a server-side cousin to the JavaBean component model known as the Enterprise JavaBean component model. We discuss the Enterprise JavaBean component model in Chapter 36, "Modeling Components with Enterprise JavaBeans," and Chapter 37, "Advanced Enterprise JavaBeans Serving."

Enterprise Data Enabling

IN THIS PART

8 Enterprise Data 173

9 Basic JDBC 199

10 Advanced JDBC 249

Enterprise Data

CHAPTER

8

IN THIS CHAPTER

- Database Basics 174
- Relational Databases 179
- Object Databases 186
- RDBMSs Versus ODBMSs 188
- Relational/Object Translations 190
- CLIs 192
- Embedded SQL 193
- ODBC 195
- JDBC 195

Interfacing with enterprise data is one of the most important steps involved in building an enterprise system. General database concepts and issues, as well as concepts and issues specific to relational and object database management systems, are very important for the enterprise systems developer to understand. Knowing basic architectural constructs for such database systems helps one more easily grasp how to interface with enterprise data. Most significant to this book, understanding how to interface with enterprise data from Java is important. The options available to the enterprise Java developer and having knowledge of which of these options is most important help one to focus on more rapidly assembling an enterprise data-enabling solution.

This chapter describes the basic concepts involved in enterprise databases and the options for interfacing to databases from within the enterprise Java programming paradigm. In this chapter, you will learn:

- The concepts and architecture of most database management systems.
- The concepts and architecture of relational database management systems.
- The basics of SQL as the standard language interface to RDBMSs.
- The concepts and architecture of object database management systems.
- The pros and cons of object versus relational database management systems.
- The basic steps behind using object/relational mapping products.
- A description of CLIs, Embedded SQL, ODBC, and JDBC.

Database Basics

Information is one of the most significant assets of any enterprise. Information must flow in and out of an enterprise, flow through an enterprise, and be manipulated by an enterprise. Information must be easily disseminated to the right people at the right time. Information also has security constraints that mandate access control based on the type and content of the information. Information is plentiful and tends to grow exponentially in time and with the growth of an enterprise. Many different people in an enterprise often must concurrently access the same information at a given time. Clearly, information is extremely important to an enterprise; it must be persisted in such a way that it is not lost and must be efficiently and easily retrieved and updated. A database management system (DBMS) is precisely the information-technology component used by enterprises to efficiently retrieve, update, and generally solve the problem of managing enterprise data. The collection of data managed by a DBMS is often referred to as a database. However, the term *database* also is often used to refer to the DBMS itself.

Data Model Abstraction Levels

When one is referring to databases, it is important to understand the different levels of abstraction at which people think about databases. Database designers sometimes think of databases at the lowest level of abstraction in terms of a physical data model used to represent storage of data on physical media, including how the data is structurally related. A higher level of abstraction describes a logical data model (*aka* a conceptual data model) wherein logical-data-model entities correspond to one or more underlying physical-data-model entities and their relationships. Logical data models describe data in terms of what is stored in the database, such as "customer information" or "order information." The logical data model typically relates to an object model and is largely used to describe specific database designs to an enterprise programmer. The logical data model is thus the level of modeling employed by this book. The highest level of data abstraction is referred to as a *view* and corresponds to a specific customization of a logical data model for use by a particular enterprise user class. Data from the logical model is eliminated from the view level, and new information is derived from the logical level for the view level. Many different views can exist above the logical-data-model level.

A different way to describe the database generally exists at all three levels of database abstraction. The description of the database structure at each abstraction level is called the *database scheme*. At the physical level of abstraction, the database is described in terms of an internal scheme. At the logical level, a database is described in terms of a conceptual scheme. Views of the database are described in terms of an external scheme or subscheme. Although a database scheme at each level describes the structure of the database, the term *database instance* is typically used to describe a particular instantiation of a database scheme. Thus database A on a host machine X and database B on a host machine Y may adhere to the same database scheme but represent two separate database instances.

General DBMS Architecture

The diagram in Figure 8.1 depicts a generic architecture for DBMSs and databases. The DBMS is broken out separately from the database in this diagram. The database represents the physical storage of actual allocated file space for all data and structures being managed by the DBMS. While we have made a distinction between the database and DBMS, we should note that the terms DBMS and database are sometimes individually used to mean both the DBMS and database.

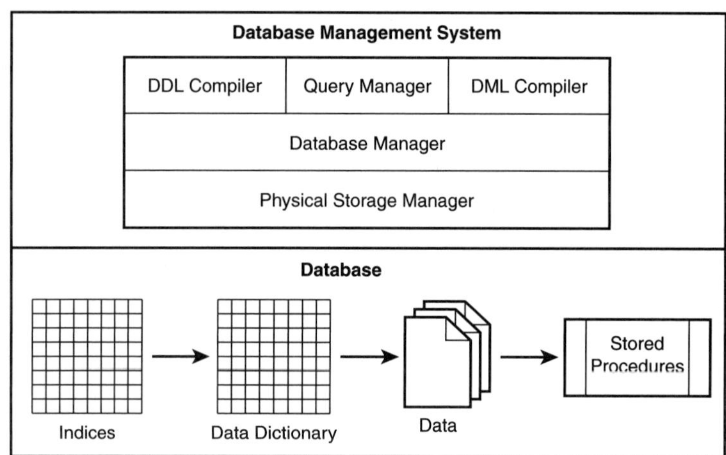

FIGURE 8.1
Generic DBMS and database architectural diagram.

The database itself contains the physical manifestation of all data files, data dictionaries, indices, and stored procedures. Data files are used for storing the actual enterprise information values (for example, credit-card numbers, employee names, and so on). A data dictionary stores all meta-data about the enterprise data, including data attribute names, relationships between data, and data value constraints. Indices are used to provide indexing of information stored in the data dictionary for faster access of the associated data. Stored procedures are predefined and user-defined functional code stored in the database to operate directly on the data stored in the database.

Technically speaking, the term *DBMS* encompasses all the software that rests atop the physical database layer. A DBMS will make use of a physical storage manager to allocate and deallocate physical file space for data, meta-data, indices, and procedures to be stored. The higher-level database manager provides a layer of abstraction for manipulating data, meta-data, and stored procedures related to a way that higher-level DBMS components desire to view the database. DDL compilers map database schemes described in a database definition language (DDL) into lower-level calls that create and delete new structures and data types in the database. A query manager maps high-level statements described in some query language into lower-level calls that can retrieve data from the database. DML compilers use a data manipulation language (DML) to map high-level database access and update calls into lower-level calls according to a particular data model. Although a query language technically corresponds to a subset of DML pertaining to data retrieval, the term *query language* is very often used to refer to functionality provided by a DML as well.

Transactions

The inherent distributed nature of DBMSs and databases is not apparent from the generic logical architecture of DBMSs and databases depicted in Figure 8.1. Not only are databases and DBMSs often physically distributed, but client applications to these DBMS are typically plentiful, especially in enterprise environments. These inherent distribution facets of DBMSs and databases raise a set of concurrent access issues around which a whole science has developed, known as *transaction management*.

Whenever a sequence of processing steps that either must all take place or must have no individual step takes place at all, we say that such a sequence of steps represents a transaction. When all steps occur as an inseparable operation, we say that the transaction may be committed. When no steps are allowed to occur because one or more steps failed, we say that the transaction must be rolled back (to the original system state). The classic example illustrating a transaction is the example involving a withdrawal from one bank account that must be followed by a deposit to another account. If both steps occur, the transaction can be committed. If one step fails, neither must be allowed to occur and the transaction is rolled back (aborted).

Transactions must be managed such that they are governed by what the ISO/IEC calls ACID principles. ACID is an acronym standing for atomicity, consistency, isolation, and durability. Atomicity of a transaction means that any failure occurring during a transaction will result in an undoing of all changes made during the transaction. Consistency means that all data affected by a transaction is restored to its original state before the transaction in the event of a failure during the transaction. Isolation means that any data changes made during a transaction are not visible to other transactions until the transaction is complete. Durability means that all committed data is saved such that, in the event of a failure, the state of the data will be correct.

A distributed transaction is a transaction that involves operations being performed by multiple distributed applications, as well as perhaps involving multiple distributed databases. Guaranteeing that transactions can adhere to the ACID principles in a distributed transaction processing environment can be difficult, by and large due to the heterogeneous nature of both distributed applications invoking the transactions and the distributed databases involved with the transactions. Such complexity affecting heterogeneous environments has led to some key standards that have been developed to handle distributed transaction processing (DTP). One such DTP standard has been developed by the Open Group (*aka* X/Open). The X/Open DTP standard defines the DTP model utilized by the J2EE.

Figure 8.2 depicts the most basic view of the X/Open DTP model. The X/Open DTP model is composed of transaction managers (TM), resource managers (RM), communication resource managers (CRM), and application programs (AP). The DTP standard specifies standard roles for these components and standard interfaces between the components. In addition to these components, we depict a resource adapter between APs and RMs to be described shortly.

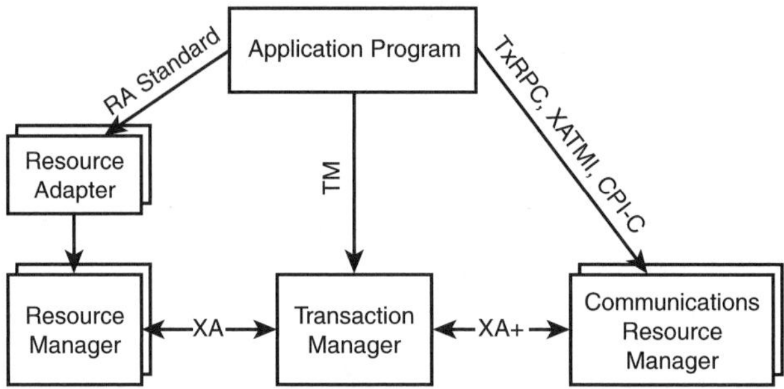

FIGURE 8.2
X/Open distributed transaction processing model.

The X/Open term *resource manager* is used to describe a management process for any shared resource, but it is most often used to mean a DBMS. Although the interface between application programs and resource managers is RM-specific under the X/Open DTP model, a resource adapter can be used as an interface to provide a common means for communicating with various resource manager types. Thus, as we'll see, database interfaces such as ODBC and JDBC can be thought of as resource adapters following the "Adapter Pattern" mentioned in Chapter 3, "Component-Based Software Development for the Enterprise."

Transaction managers represent the heart of the X/Open DTP model and are the modules responsible for coordinating transactions among the various distributed entities. Resource managers participate in distributed transactions by implementing a transaction resource interface (XA) to communicate information needed by transaction managers for coordinating transactions. Using information from the distributed resource managers, the transaction manager can ensure that all steps in a transaction are atomically completed. A commit protocol (that is, two-phase commit) implemented by transaction managers helps guarantee ACID principles by ensuring that all resource managers commit to transaction completion or rollback to an original state in the event of a failure. The TX interface between application programs and transaction managers enables applications to initiate the begin, commit, and rollback of transactions, as well as to obtain the status of transactions. As we'll see in Chapter 34, "Enterprise Application Platforms," a middle-tier server, sometimes referred to as a transaction monitor, can help provide support for communicating with transaction managers, as well as resource managers. Use of transaction monitors can help reduce the amount of knowledge needed by applications programmers for managing transactions.

Transaction managers are often configured to manage a particular domain of distributed resource managers and applications. Communication resource managers provide a standard means for connecting distributed transaction managers to propagate transaction information between different transaction domains for more widely distributed transactions. The standard interface between transaction managers and communication resource managers is defined by an XA+ interface, while communication-resource-manager to application-program interfaces are defined by three different interfaces known as TxRPC, XATMI, and CPI-C.

Relational Databases

R&D and commercial developments have produced a few general architectural approaches for DBMSs over the years. Nevertheless, the relational database management system (RDBMS) architecture has clearly been the most successful architecture used in the most popular of DBMS products on the commercial market today. As a result, much of today's legacy enterprise data is hosted inside of RDBMSs. This fact alone makes a basic understanding of RDBMS principles key for any serious enterprise systems developer. The fact that RDBMSs are also the assumed underlying DBMS model for J2EE data connectivity makes understanding RDBMSs even more critical for the Java enterprise systems developer.

RDBMS Architecture

Figure 8.3 depicts the general architecture for an RDBMS in terms of its primary logical components. A table in an RDBMS serves to group a collection of attribute values for a type of logical entity. A table actually contains the collection of element attributes in what are called rows of a database. Each row corresponds to one instance of a particular entity. The columns of a table correspond to particular attributes of the entity that the table represents. Thus, for example, Figure 8.4 shows a database table called Customer that has one row per customer instance in the table. Each column of the table corresponds to an attribute of a particular customer.

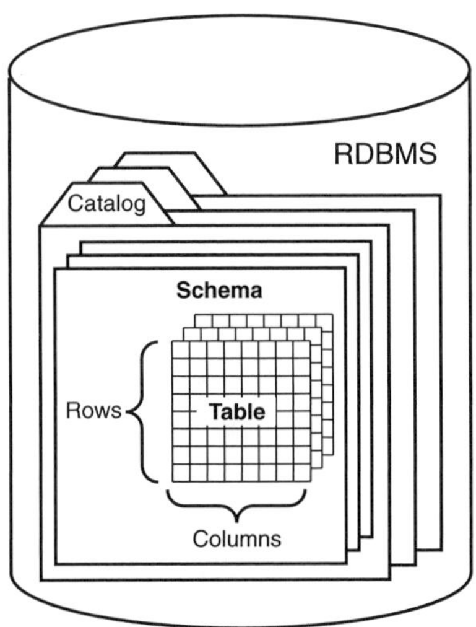

FIGURE 8.3
RDBMS architecture.

Customer Table

Last Name	First Name	Account Number	
Shorr	Pauly	149-6423-00	
Dooley	Stax	149-6425-00	
⋮	⋮	⋮	
Ziemba	Jack	111-2763-00	

FIGURE 8.4
Table entries in an RDBMS.

One or more columns per table can be used to uniquely identify a row entry in a table. These one or more columns taken together form what is called the table's primary key. No two rows in a table can have the same primary key value. Some tables can also have columns containing foreign keys, which are primary key values from other tables. Foreign keys are used to explicitly relate one table to another. For example, if a Customer table uses the Account Number as a primary key, then an Order table used to capture the details for a particular customer order may have a foreign key containing the Account Number column value for the customer associated with a particular order.

Tables are organized into schemas, whereby a schema encapsulates a collection of tables. Catalogs can also be used to group schemas. Catalogs and schemas help organize tables as well as other entities such as views into groups such that access control and maintenance policies can be defined at the group level. With catalogs and schemas, data can also be scoped by referring to data such as in the format `<Catalog>.<Schema>.<Table>.<Column>`. Not all RDBMSs support grouping of tables into catalogs and schemas, and the separator used to delimit the scope of data can also vary between DBMS vendors.

SQL

Structured Query Language (SQL) is the most widely used query language for RDBMSs. Even though it is called a *query language*, SQL is used for much more than just data retrieval. SQL is also used to create and define database structures like a DDL and to update data like a DML. SQL was created by IBM in the 1970s and became standardized in the 1980s. Although a few standard versions of SQL exist, the version of SQL used by the J2EE database connectivity solution is the American National Standards Institute's (ANSI) SQL-92, as well as some extensions to SQL via the SQL3 standard. Within such standards, different levels of compliance are defined.

Although we will discuss mappings between SQL data types and Java types in subsequent chapters, we present brief descriptions of some of the more core SQL types here in Table 8.1 to better explain how SQL statements are created.

TABLE 8.1 Core SQL Types

SQL Type	*Description*
CHAR	Fixed-length string
VARCHAR	Variable-length string
LONGVARCHAR	Large variable-length string
BIT	Binary digit
BINARY	Fixed-length binary array
VARBINARY	Variable-length binary array
LONGVARBINARY	Large variable-length binary array
TINYINT	8-bit integer
SMALLINT	16-bit integer
INTEGER	32-bit integer
BIGINT	64-bit integer
REAL	Small floating-point number
FLOAT	Regular floating-point number
DOUBLE	Large floating-point number
NUMERIC	Variable base fixed-point number
DECIMAL	Base 10 fixed-point number
DATE	The date
TIME	The time
TIMESTAMP	A date and time instant

Creating and Deleting Tables

Databases, catalogs, and schemas can be created using statements such as `CREATE DATABASE`, `CREATE CATALOG`, and `CREATE SCHEMA`. However, the precise command syntax often varies from vendor to vendor. Creating tables is a more common operation and fortunately is fairly standard across SQL-compliant DBMSs. This is the syntax for creating a table:

```
CREATE TABLE <table_name> ( <comma-separated column definition list> );
```

Each column definition is sometimes expressed in one of various forms:

```
<column_name>   <data_type>
<column_name>   <data_type> <column_constraint>
<column_name>  <data_type> NOT NULL <unique specification>
```

For example, to create a table to store customer information including two-character state codes, we might have this:

```
CREATE TABLE state
(
  state_code          CHAR(2) NOT NULL,
  state_name          VARCHAR(50)
);
CREATE TABLE customer
(
  customer_id         INTEGER NOT NULL PRIMARY KEY,
  first_name          VARCHAR(32) NOT NULL,
  last_namc           VARCHAR(32) NOT NULL,
  middle_initial     VARCHAR(10),
  address_1               VARCHAR(32) ,
  address_2            VARCHAR(32),
  city                    VARCHAR(50),
  state                    CHAR(2),
  zip                    CHAR(5),
  phone                CHAR(10)
);
```

You can also delete tables from a database using the DROP TABLE <table_name> command, as in this example:

```
DROP TABLE customer;
```

Modifying Tables

The standard syntax for modifying a table is

```
ALTER TABLE <table_name> <alter_table_action>;
```

in which *alter_table_action* may be one of following:

```
<ADD column_name  data_type column_constraints>
<DROP column_name>
<MODIFY column_name data_type column_constraints>
\
```

For example, if you want to add a new column called Email to the Customer table, you can do so as shown here:

```
ALTER TABLE customer ADD email VARCHAR(70);
```

If you were to modify the column definition of a previously defined column Email in the Customer table, you might have this:

```
ALTER TABLE customer MODIFY email VARCHAR(100);
```

You can also remove the Email column from the Customer table as shown here:

```
ALTER TABLE customer DROP email;
```

Inserting and Deleting Rows from a Table

Rows are inserted into a table according to the general syntax

```
INSERT INTO <table_name> VALUES (<column_value_1>, ..., <column_value_n>);
```

if all columns are being newly inserted, or

```
INSERT INTO <table_name> (<column_name_1>, ..., <column_name_n>)
➥ VALUES (<column_value_1>, ..., <column_value_n>);
```

if only a select number of columns are being inserted. For example, to insert data into a selected set of columns, use this:

```
INSERT INTO customer(customer_id, first_name, last_name,
➥address_1, city, state, zip, phone)
➥VALUES(1,'Sam','Sung','Oracle Rd.','Reston','VA','20191','7035551212');
```

To insert data into all the columns, you might have the following:

```
INSERT INTO customer VALUES
➥('2', 'Sam', 'Mellone', 'R','123 Drive.', 'Suite 5', 'Fairfax', 'VA',
➥ '22222', '7034567899');
```

You can delete a row from a table via the following general syntax:

```
DELETE FROM <table_name>;
DELETE FROM <table_name>  WHERE  <search condition>;
```

The WHERE clause may be added if a set of search criteria is to be added to limit the criteria by which a row is to be deleted. Otherwise, all rows from the table are deleted. For example:

```
DELETE FROM customer WHERE customer_id=1;
```

Modifying Rows in a Table

The UPDATE statement is used to modify rows already present in a table according to the syntax

```
UPDATE <table_name> SET <set_clause_list> ;
UPDATE <table_name> SET <set_clause_list> WHERE <search condition>;
```

in which <set_clause_list> is of the following form:

```
<column_name_1>=<column_value_1>, ..., <column_name_n>=<column_value_n>
```

When a WHERE clause is not used, all rows of the table are updated. As an example of an UPDATE, we have this:

```
UPDATE customer SET address_1 = '1901 Bay Dr.' WHERE customer_id = '1';
```

Queries

Queries are the most common form of SQL statement submitted to a database. SQL queries typically adhere to the following general form:

```
SELECT <*|DISTINCT|column_list> FROM <table_names>
➥[WHERE <condition>] [ORDER BY <column_list>];
```

The `SELECT` portion of a SQL query can take a `*` value to indicate that all column values are to be returned, a `DISTINCT` value indicating only those column values that are unique, or a comma-separated column list of column names identifying those column values to return. The `FROM` portion of a SQL query indicates which tables to query given a comma-separated list of table names. The optional `ORDER BY` clause takes a comma-separated list of columns specifying the order in which column values are returned from a query. The optional `WHERE` clause in a SQL query is expressed in terms of column names, column values, and various operators that define a search criteria. Aside from a fairly intuitive set of logical operators that may be used in a `WHERE` clause, the `IS` qualifier can be used to test whether a column adheres to a particular criterion (for example, `myColumn IS NULL`). The `IN` qualifier in a `WHERE` can be used to check whether a value is in a set of values defined after the `IN` qualifier (for example, `myColumn IN ('VA', 'MD')`). All the following statements are valid SQL queries (with embedded comments preceded by #):

```
#select all individual states to which customers belong
SELECT DISTINCT state FROM customer;

#select all columns and rows in the customer tables
SELECT * FROM customer;

#get all customer_id, first_name, last_name, and state from customer table
SELECT customer_id, first_name, last_name, state FROM customer;

#select distinct states of the customers whose phone is not null
SELECT DISTINCT state FROM customer WHERE phone IS NOT NULL;

#select first_name and last_name of customers whose phone number value is null
SELECT first_name, last_name FROM customer WHERE phone IS NULL;

# select first_name, last_name of customers in state of VA, MD, or DC
SELECT first_name, last_name FROM customer
➥WHERE state IN('VA','MD','DC');

#select the customers' first_name and last_name who live in VA, MD or DC
SELECT first_name, last_name FROM customer
➥WHERE ( state = 'VA' OR state = 'MD' OR state ='DC');
```

```
#select the customers' first_name, last_name who don't live in VA, MD or DC
SELECT first_name , last_name FROM customer
➥WHERE STATE NOT IN('VA','MD','DC');

#select customer state, first_name, and last_name in order of state
SELECT state,first_name, last_name FROM customer ORDER BY state;

# This query selects all customers whose first_name has FR in it.
SELECT first_name, last_name FROM customer
➥WHERE phone is not null AND first_name LIKE '%FR%';

# This query selects all customers whose first_name starts with FR.
SELECT first_name, last_name FROM customer
➥WHERE phone is not null AND first_name LIKE 'FR%';
```

If a query fruitfully proves to yield data, one or more results will be returned in the form of a result set. Each result set is composed of one or more "rows." Because queries return only selected column data from one or more tables, these rows don't necessarily correspond to regular table rows. One scrolls through result set rows to pluck data results from each row for use. A result set cursor maintains a pointer to the current result set row being accessed. Because result sets may be distributed, cursors may be pointing to result set row data that could exist somewhere on a remote server. Of course, result set data may also be cached locally.

Data Model Diagram Conventions

Because the data model abstraction pursued here is at a logical/conceptual level, the data model diagramming convention used in this book closely resembles the object-oriented model diagramming convention described in Chapter 2, "Object-Oriented Software Development for the Enterprise." The modeling convention also employs some features that closely follow typical data modeling conventions. The data model used here can actually be thought of as a subset of a general object model. Nonetheless, we take a few liberties in describing data models in this book to bridge the gap between traditional data modeling and object modeling without resorting to explaining a completely new modeling paradigm. The simple set of conventions used for data model diagrams in this book and their UML object model diagram analogues are described here:

- Tables are represented by squares much like classes are represented in object diagrams.
- Columns are represented as elements of the table much like attributes in classes are represented in object diagrams.
- Columns are defined according to the following general form:

  ```
  [<<optional_key_stereotype>>] column_name : column_type //
  column_description
  ```

- Primary keys and foreign keys appear as stereotypes for a particular column.
- Column types are defined in terms of SQL types.
- Two forward slashes are used after a `column_type` to delineate the beginning of a column description.
- Table relations are represented by lines much like lines are used to represent relationships in object diagrams.
- The same multiplicity notation at the end of a relationship is used for data models here as is used for object models.
- Directionality of a relationship indicates how one table explicitly references another table via a foreign key (this is different from object modeling conventions).
- Roles are used at each end of a directional relation to indicate which primary or foreign keys are involved in the explicit relationship.
- No directionality of a relationship indicates how one table implicitly relates to another table.

Object Databases

Relational data models are used to describe an RDBMS design for storing and relating data. Because storing and relating data is precisely the problem that RDBMSs attempt to solve, relational data models are well suited for their intended purpose. However, the types of systems that evolve from using relational data models are much more limited than the types of systems that evolve from object-oriented and component-based models. Wouldn't it be nice if we could continue to model our scalable enterprise systems using the object-oriented and component-based models that we've grown to love and then simply be able to indicate what elements of state in those models should be persisted? Enter the object database management system (ODBMS).

Object database management systems are DBMSs that allow one to directly store and retrieve objects to and from a database. An ODBMS stores class attributes and relations in such a way that database operations can be accomplished in a manner that is most natural to the object-oriented programmer. Thus, in the case of Java, Java objects can be saved to an ODBMS by one JVM and later retrieved by another JVM.

ODBMS Architecture

ODBMS architectures for Java typically include a tool to map Java class references to database calls. This mapping tool is usually either baked into a modified JVM or external to a JVM and used as a post-compiler. Although using a modified JVM is undesirable for some applications, post-compilation tools can normally be used only on user-defined classes. User-defined persistable Java objects can automatically store and retrieve any persistable Java objects they reference during database operations.

The Object Data Management Group (ODMG) is a standards body that has defined a standard model for ODBMSs. The basic model consists of an Object Definition Language (ODL) for defining object databases and an Object Query Language (OQL) for ODBMS querying. Language-specific APIs are used for manipulating objects. An Object Interchange Format (OIF) is used for importing and exporting objects between different ODBMSs.

The basic class architecture for the ODMG's ODBMS Java language binding is shown in Figure 8.5. Note that none of the standard classes defined by the ODMG belong to a standard package because package naming is up to the vendor. A `Database` class is used to open and close database connections, bind objects to names, and look up objects' given names. The Java 2.0 collection types are extended by the standard's `DCollection`, `DList`, `DArray`, `DSet`, and `DBag` interfaces to allow persistable versions of a collection of objects. The classes `ListOfObject`, `SetOfObject`, and `BagOfObject` implement these extended persistable interfaces. One typically must bind a collection to a name so that it can be used to query, update, insert, and delete objects from such collections using a name. The creation of a `Transaction` object creates a transaction that the current thread joins. You can also call `join()` on a `Transaction` object passed in from another thread to join the current thread to that transaction. Standard transaction `begin()`, `commit()`, and `abort()` methods also exist on a `Transaction` object. Finally, a few exception types not shown in the diagram are also defined by the ODMG.

The OQL is to ODBMSs as SQL is to RDBMSs. Calls to `select()`, `selectElement()`, and `query()` on `DCollection` objects can be used to issue queries in a manner much like `SQL SELECT` clauses are formulated. An `Iterator.next()` call can then be used to obtain query results in the form of objects by executing such OQL calls. For example:

```
Database d = Database.open("MyDataBase");
Transaction t = new Transaction();

DList customerList = (DList) d.lookup("Customers");
Iterator i = customerList.query("ZIP = 11111");

while(i.hasNext()){
  Customer c = (Customer) i.next();
  c.setZip("20177");
}
t.commit();
```

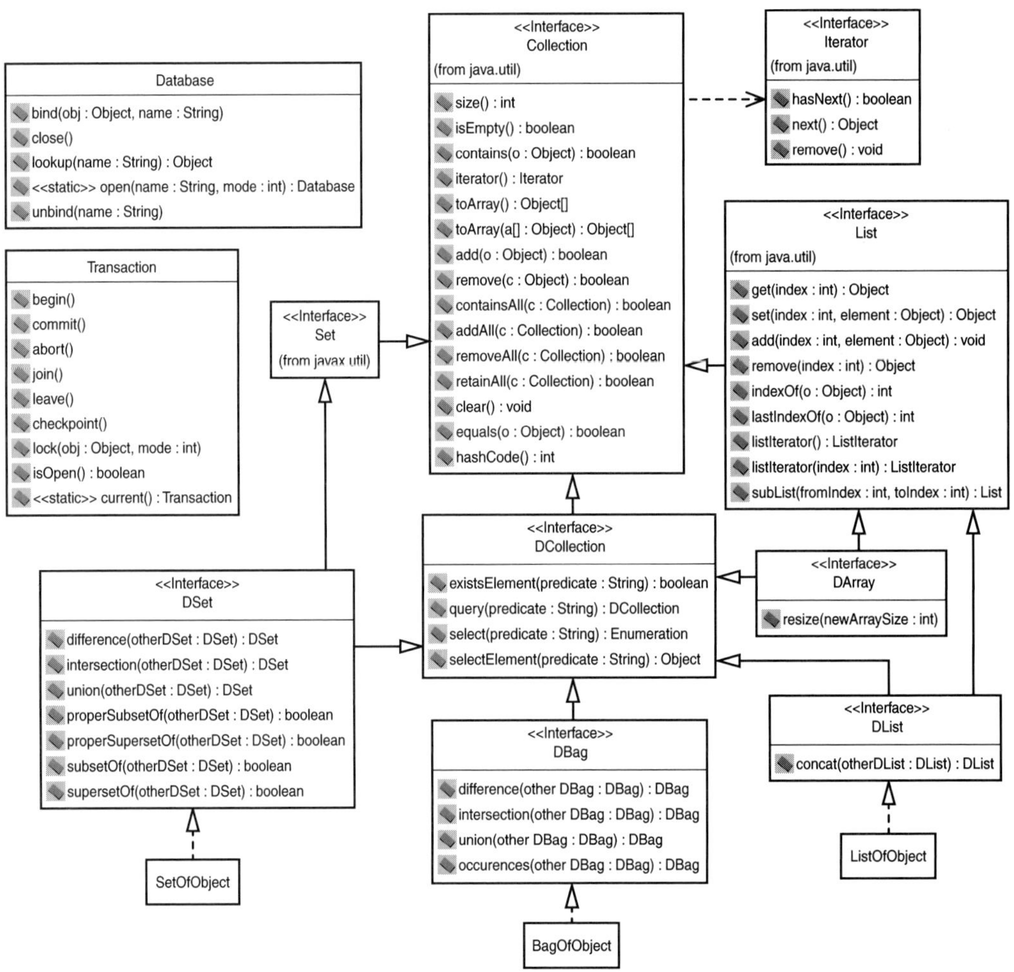

FIGURE 8.5
ODMG's ODBMS architecture.

RDBMSs Versus ODBMSs

For most enterprise development situations, the question of whether you should use an ODBMS or a RDBMS is usually moot. For one, the database to which you must provide connectivity may be a legacy database for which exists many configuration scripts or perhaps much in-house knowledge, or most certainly the product has already been purchased and you have a maintenance/upgrade contract established with the vendor. If a legacy database is not already in place, the question of purchasing a new database may still be skewed by political or business factors such as pre-established vendor relationships, previous engineering staff and management product familiarity, or flat-out blind dislike of "new" ODBMS technologies or "old" RDBMS technologies. Regardless of such business, political, or personal realities, it is important to compare and contrast RDBMS and ODBMS technologies from a pure and unbiased technical and economical perspective. In what follows, we offer some pros and cons of RDBMSs and ODBMSs.

RDBMS pros:

- More mainstream solution means that more support and experience will be available.
- More mainstream nature also means that more tools will be available for use.
- More mainstream nature also means more comfort and assurance in security, scalability, and overall enterprise-class nature of the product.

RDBMS cons:

- Developers must hand-code the mapping of data retrieved from or stored to an RDBMS from a relational model to attributes and objects in a Java object-oriented model.
- Developers must understand the SQL language above and beyond understanding Java, which can be a significant investment in time.
- Performance degrades as object model complexity increases when creating, traversing, and querying for objects that are mapped to an RDBMS.

ODBMS pros:

- Object-oriented software solutions more easily map to and from ODBMS persistence solutions without as much hand-coding.
- Performance does not degrade significantly when object model complexity increases for object creation, traversal, and queries.

ODBMS cons:

- Developers using the ODMG model still must understand OQL.
- ODMG standards don't specify packages for standard classes and leave out other specifics like constructors on collection classes. Thus, portability of ODBMS-based Java code is an issue.
- A lack of certain key features in the ODMG standard also leads to vendor tie-in because vendors will often supply these features.
- Because ODBMSs tend to be newer than many RDBMSs, product maturity for enterprise-class applications is a risk item. Integrated solutions to enterprise-class issues dealing with remote access, concurrency, scalability, and security are always questionable in newer products.

ODBMSs indeed do provide a database platform that more closely maps to the types of object models the Java developer uses. However, replacement of long-lived RDBMSs can be a futile endeavor. Enterprise data is typically plentiful, and converting legacy RDBMS data into a form exportable by ODBMSs can be time-consuming and can possibly require more effort than would be required by developers' RDBMS-to-OO hand-coding. Furthermore, the enterprise-class capabilities of certain ODBMSs over RDBMSs are still questionable for certain application demands. Projects defining new databases may be in a position to consider ODBMSs but should evaluate vendor offerings very carefully to ensure enterprise-class applicability. Given the relative youth of the current ODBMS standards, such standards will need to be evolved to help ensure vendor portability.

We believe that ODBMSs will be the DBMS of choice in the future when vendor offerings become more suitable to handle the full gamut of enterprise-class applications, as well as when the standards mature enough to the point of helping ensure true cross-platform portability. Most RDBMS vendors have seen this as a potential direction of industry as well and thus have been evolving their back-end architectures appropriately toward supporting the needs of object-oriented (and in particular Java) programming paradigms. A new breed of object/relational hybrid databases and data-mapping products now on the market clearly highlights the trend from relational to object-oriented data modeling.

Relational/Object Translations

Because many enterprises already make use of RDBMSs hosting legacy enterprise data, object-oriented developers are usually stuck with more programming overhead than they care to have. Mapping object-oriented classes and relationships to RDBMS tables and relations can be a tedious and complex task. However, tools now exist to facilitate relational/object translations.

Many RDBMS vendors are now providing hybrid object/relational back-end database architecture solutions. Additionally, a host of object/relational mapping solutions is now on the market to provide an OO layer above an RDBMS. Object/relational mapping products usually either generate object models from relational schemas or create relational models for you from pre-existing object models. Object/relational mapping products can be purchased separately or are sometimes found integrated with other enterprise products. Data-aware GUI JavaBeans, for example, implicitly map GUI components to RDBMS database calls according to GUI-based customizers used by the developer to define such mappings. More sophisticated and general-purpose object/relational mapping products are also now being integrated into middle-tier products with particular applicability in Enterprise JavaBeans, as we'll see in later chapters.

Mapping Java objects to RDBMS tables involves an object/relational mapping tool analyzing Java class relationships and then generating an associated relational model. Each class will often map to a table. Class attributes that correspond to fundamental SQL types map to table columns. Classes having references to other class objects map to a table with a foreign key to another table that represents the referenced class.

However, given the prevalence of legacy RDBMSs in the world, the most common object/relational mapping scenario encountered by the enterprise developer is to map an existing RDBMS schema into an object model. An example process for mapping an RDBMS schema into an object model is as shown here:

- *Step 1:* Open your object/relational mapping tool.
- *Step 2:* Provide your tool with the schema name for which the object-relational mapping must be performed.
- *Step 3:* The tool will display all the tables contained by that schema.
- *Step 4:* Now select the tables from which you want to create Java classes.
- *Step 5:* Select each table name and provide a class name to which you want it to be mapped. Many tools will use the table name as the default name for the class but in a Java language format. For example, the Customer table will by default map to a public class named `Customer` in a `Customer.java` source file.
- *Step 6:* Depending on the particular mapping tool, the generated Java class might be extended from some sort of persistable class or perhaps implement some persistable interface. For example, a mapped object may be produced in this way:

```
public class Customer extends Persistable
{
  int customerId;
  String firstName;
  String lastName;
  String middleInitial;
  String address1;
  String address2;
  String city;
  State  state;
  String zip;
  String phone;
     ..
     ..
// Generated getter/setter methods for the columns
public void setXXX()
{
}
public XXX getXX()
{
}
// For one to one relationship with other tables, we have...
```

```
public XXX getXXX()
{
}
// For one to many relationship with other tables, we have...
public Enumeration getXXX()
{
}
// To select a particular Customer from the database, we might have...
public static Customer selectElement(String predicate)
{
}
// To select one or more Customers from the database, we might have...
public static Enumeration select(String predicate)
{
}
```

- *Step 7:* Use the generated classes as regular Java objects by your Java application code. The underlying RDBMS queries, inserts, deletes, and updates are transparent to the Java application programmer. For example:

```
Customer c = Customer.selectElement("customerID=1");
String firstName = c.getFirstName();
String lastName = c.getLastName();
State  state = c.getState();
String stateCode = c.getStateCode();
String stateName = c.getStateName();
    ...
c.setState("VA");
c.updateCustomer(); // Updates the state of customer to VA
    ...
Enumeration customers = Customer.select("state = VA");
```

- *Step 8:* Compile code and run your application.

CLIs

A Call Level Interface (CLI) represents a functional call API to a database. CLIs provided for the various RDBMS vendor solutions are often proprietary and have a native SQL API implementation. Typically, C language–based APIs are provided, but bindings for Cobol and FORTRAN are also common. CLI calls can be made directly to an underlying database driver or can be remotely invoked over a network.

The Open Group has specified the X/Open SQL CLI standard for interfacing to databases via a CLI. The X/Open SQL CLI interfaces define function calls at the level of allocating and deallocating system resources, controlling database connections, obtaining database status information, executing dynamic SQL statements, and controlling transactions. The X/Open SQL CLI specification was published as an addendum to the SQL-92 standard and is now also part of the ISO standard. X/Open SQL CLI support for SQL3 features is also being considered.

Embedded SQL

We have talked about the prevalence of RDBMSs and SQL a lot so far. So how does one use SQL to talk with an RDBMS from Java? SQLJ offers one standard created by key DBMS industry players such as Oracle, Sybase, and IBM for embedding SQL directly into Java applications. Java source code containing embedded SQL commands is run through a SQLJ preprocessor to generate new Java source code with the appropriate database calls (mainly JDBC calls). During the precompilation process, the SQLJ runtime engine can access the database to determine whether all the tables, columns, and SQL statements are syntactically correct with respect to the database. Certain security restrictions can also be checked at this time. The main utility of SQLJ is that a significant set of SQL errors can be caught at compile-time rather than during runtime as with other Java database connectivity solutions such as JDBC.

By embedding SQL directly into a Java program, SQLJ extends the Java API with a whole new set of programming interfaces. Each embedded SQL command in the Java code begins with a `#sql` token. A colon in an embedded SQL statement is placed before a Java variable used as either input or output in a SQL command. A database connection can be created using the expression `#sql context` *`ContextName`*`;`. The context is compiled into a Java class having a set of constructors with arguments used to create database connections. Some vendor solutions also read Java properties files to obtain connection-related information.

Iterators are used to map SQL results from queries into Java objects. Iterators can be defined using the command `#sql [`*`modifiers`*`] iterator` *`IteratorType`* `(`*`colType1`*`, ...,` *`colTypeN`*`);`. Such a form is used to retrieve query result values by an index number in the result set and subsequently map these result values to an associated Java object. Optional Java modifiers such as `static` and `public` can be used to modify the visibility and semantics of the iterator. An iterator of the preceding type is declared using the regular Java variable declaration syntax *`IteratorType myIterator`*. The command `#sql` *`myIterator`* `= {` *`SQL_Command`* `};` is used to populate `myIterator` with the result of a query. The mapping of iterator results to a Java object is then accomplished using `#sql {FETCH :` *`myIterator`* `INTO :`*`JavaVar1`*`, ... , :`*`JavaVarN`*`};`. Here, the `JavaVarX` values refer to regular Java attributes in a Java class. Iterators can also be defined to retrieve database values by name such as this: `#sql [`*`modifiers`*`] iterator` *`IteratorType`* `(`*`colType1 JavaVar1`*`, ...,` *`colTypeN JavaVarN`*`);`. After declaring your iterator instance and querying the database as before, you can then use regular Java calls such as `myIterator.JavaVarX()` to obtain values from the query result by name.

As an example of using SQLJ with an Oracle database, we first make the proper imports, declare a SQL context, and declare a Java class as shown here:

8

ENTERPRISE DATA

```
import java.sql.*;
import sqlj.runtime.ref.DefaultContext;
import oracle.sqlj.runtime.Oracle;

#sql context ExampleContext;

public class Customer{...}
```

A `Customer` class and set of connection properties are used by Oracle to configure a database connection. A SQL context can then be instantiated using the connection created by Oracle:

```
Oracle.connect(Customer.class, "connect.properties");
Connection conn = DefaultContext.getDefaultContext().getConnection();
ExampleContext context = new ExampleContext(conn);
```

An iterator can then be defined inside the `Customer` class like this:

```
#sql public static iterator Customers (String first_name, String last_name) ;
```

A customer retrieval can be achieved by embedding a SQL `SELECT` statement into a Java method as shown here:

```
public static Customers selectCustomers(String whereClause,
  ExampleContext ctx) throws SQLException
{
  Customers myCustomers;

  #sql [ctx] myCustomers =
     {SELECT first_name, last_name FROM customer WHERE :whereClause};

  return myCustomers;
}
```

The returned set of customer values might be accessed like this:

```
while (myCustomers.next()) {
  System.out.println(  myCustomers.firstName() + " : "
                     + myCustomers.lastName());
}
```

A customer update may be achieved by simply embedding a SQL `UPDATE` statement into a method that uses a customer's attributes and SQL context:

```
public static void updateCustomer(String fname,String  lname,
  int id, ExampleContext ctx) throws SQLException
{
  #sql [ctx] {
    UPDATE CUSTOMER
    SET first_name = :fname , last_name = :lname
```

```
    WHERE customer_id = :id };
}
```

Similarly, a customer insert may be achieved by embedding a SQL `INSERT` statement into a method taking a customer's attributes and SQL context:

```
public static void insertIntoCustomer(String fname, String  lname,
  int id, ExampleContext ctx) throws SQLException
{
  #sql [ctx] {
    INSERT INTO
    CUSTOMER(first_name, last_name, customer_id)
    VALUES(:fname, :lname, :id };
}
```

ODBC

In addition to embedding SQL directly into programs, a more common solution for standard database connectivity involves use of a standard API for making database calls. In an effort to alleviate developers from database vendor dependence and use of vendor-specific database protocols to communicate with databases, Microsoft defined the open database connectivity (ODBC) solution. ODBC is based on SQL/CLI standards and has been widely supported since its introduction.

ODBC applications depend only on the ODBC API and the SQL standard. SQL statements are submitted to ODBC API calls, and results are retrieved using standard ODBC API constructs. The ODBC API is defined in terms of the C programming language. Given the C language dependence, ODBC requires that API libraries be pre-installed on client machines.

The ODBC API communicates with an underlying ODBC driver manager that loads an appropriate ODBC driver as specified by the ODBC API client application. ODBC drivers are code libraries that adhere to a standard ODBC service-provider interface. The ODBC service-provider interface is implemented by ODBC driver vendors to map standard ODBC calls to database-vendor–specific calls. ODBC drivers may call the database directly via a CLI or via some networking protocol.

JDBC

Providing a Java binding for the ODBC API would have required some modifications to the ODBC API because not all C-based constructs (for example, pointers) have decent corresponding Java analogues. Thus, Sun has created the Java Database Connectivity (JDBC) solution as Java's answer to database-vendor interface independence. JDBC provides a database connectivity solution for Java applications just as ODBC provides for C and Microsoft applications.

As we'll see in Chapter 9, "Basic JDBC," JDBC has a basic architecture philosophy similar to the ODBC architecture. That is, JDBC has a standard JDBC API which communicates with a JDBC driver manager that loads JDBC drivers. JDBC drivers implement a JDBC service-provider interface and map standard JDBC calls into database-vendor–specific calls.

To better understand why Sun created a Java-specific database connectivity solution, consider the fact that client-side installs of ODBC API libraries would have made it difficult to run Java anywhere (that is, such as within Web-based applets). Regardless, ODBC was still an attractive database-connectivity solution when JDBC was created, largely due to widespread ODBC driver implementations. To make JDBC a viable Java-based database connectivity solution, Sun created a JDBC-ODBC bridge to solve the temporary problem of JDBC driver unavailability while enabling Java applications to capitalize on use of ODBC driver availability.

Of all methods for data-enabling your enterprise using Java technologies, JDBC is the preferred solution utilized by the J2EE. For one, in light of the widespread RDBMS database vendor solutions available, JDBC's gearing for RDBMSs makes it a commercial-ready solution. ODBMS databases and Java binding standards are still in their relative enterprise-class infancy. Furthermore, some of the ODMG ODBMS mappings may require modified JVMs and package naming, which affects portability. Because ODBC cannot map directly to Java, Java bindings for ODBC are not possible. Because embedded SQL for Java requires a post-compiler and clutters Java code, it is also not as desirable a solution for database connectivity.

Object/relational mapping tools are a very good idea and can off-load much of the model mapping hand-coding work for you. Nevertheless, some object/relational mapping tools are not yet suitable for use in many enterprise-class applications. Thus, knowledge of JDBC as a solution for interacting with databases is key for any serious enterprise developer and architect. JDBC is by far the most common way to interact with databases, and JDBC drivers now exist for most database vendor solutions. Finally, if you are still wondering why understanding JDBC is important, consider the fact that JDBC provides a very rich set of database connectivity features available to Java enterprise applications and is an integral part of the J2EE.

Conclusions

Clearly, the development of an enterprise system will involve connecting to enterprise data from within your enterprise applications. RDBMSs currently have the most significant market presence of any database architecture. Even though ODBMSs have less presence now, RDBMS vendors are evolving their architectures toward the more object-oriented interfacing needs of enterprise developers. Capitalizing on this shortcoming, object/relational mapping products bridge the gap from relational data models of RDBMS demand to object-oriented models of enterprise applications development demand.

Many database connectivity solutions for RDBMSs have been around for some time. SQL CLIs and ODBC represent two approaches and standards for interfacing with RDBMSs from non-Java applications. SQLJ offers one means to interface with RDBMSs from Java programs, but it requires more overhead in terms of development. The Java Database Connectivity solution is the J2EE-recommended means for enterprise Java data connectivity. Just about every object/relational mapping tool available for Java maps Java objects to JDBC calls. Whether you are using JDBC directly, using an object/relational mapping tool, or creating object/relational mappings yourself, an understanding of JDBC is key for the enterprise Java architect and developer. The next two chapters cover JDBC from the basics to fairly advanced topics to arm you with the knowledge you need to successfully connect your enterprise data to your enterprise Java applications.

Basic JDBC

CHAPTER

9

IN THIS CHAPTER

- JDBC Architecture 200
- JDBC Drivers and their Types 204
- JDBC Driver Configuration 208
- JDBC Connections 213
- JDBC Statements 219
- JDBC Result Sets 231
- SQL and Java Mappings 239
- JDBC MetaData 241

This chapter presents the architecture of JDBC, JDBC driver configuration, and the most commonly used API features of JDBC. A detailed example supports the material throughout this chapter and introduces an example e-commerce enterprise application's data model for use throughout the remainder of the book.

Database connectivity represents one of the most fundamental problems for which any enterprise system must have a solution. Because enterprise data is often plentiful, must be archived, and must be shared among many distributed users, it is key for distributed enterprise systems to provide a scalable, reliable, and highly available means for accessing and updating data. Furthermore, the complexity inherent with communicating to a wide variety of DBMS vendor solutions and legacy data models presents a time-to-market impediment that also often hampers the enterprise system solutions provider. The creators of the Java platform have realized these problems and have provided the Java Database Connectivity (JDBC) solution now incorporated as part of both the J2SE and the J2EE platforms. JDBC represents the standard means for connecting to DBMSs from Java applications in a fashion that is largely DBMS-independent and enables connectivity to both legacy and newly defined enterprise data.

In this chapter, you will learn:

- The architecture of JDBC as the standard means for connecting to databases from Java applications
- A classification of JDBC driver types and their pros and cons for usage
- The steps involved in configuring various JDBC driver types
- The mechanisms for establishing database connections via JDBC
- The creation and execution of regular and prepared SQL statements in JDBC
- The handling of query results and obtaining information about query results in JDBC
- The mappings between SQL data types and Java types
- Obtaining information about databases and database drivers via JDBC

JDBC Architecture

The Java Database Connectivity architecture represents the de facto standard means for connecting to databases from Java applications. JDBC is both an API for Java programmers and an interface model for service providers who implement connectivity to databases. As an API, JDBC provides a standard interface for Java applications to interact with multiple types of databases. As an interface model for service providers, JDBC provides a standard way for database vendors and third-party middleware vendors to implement connectivity to databases. JDBC leverages off of existing SQL standards and provides support for bridging to other database connectivity standards such as ODBC. JDBC accomplishes all of these standards-oriented goals with an interface that is simple, strongly typed, and capable of high-performance implementation.

JDBC version 1.0 was initially offered separately from the JDK 1.0 platform but was integrated with the JDK 1.1 platform in the `java.sql` package. The JDBC 1.0 version contains most of the core and commonly used features of JDBC. The material in this chapter almost exclusively focuses on JDBC 1.0 version functionality.

Sun has also introduced the JDBC 2.0 version, which is partitioned into two separate categories: the JDBC 2.0 Core API and the JDBC 2.0 Standard Extension API. The JDBC 2.0 Core API includes all the functionality contained in the JDBC 1.0 version plus a host of new features that includes query result enhancements, enhancements for updating batches of data, persistence of Java objects, and support for a whole slew of new SQL types. The JDBC 2.0 Core API is contained in the J2SE/J2EE `java.sql` packages. The JDBC 2.0 Standard Extension API offers a range of more sophisticated enterprise features such as a new and simpler paradigm for connecting to databases in a three-tier architecture, support for connection pooling, distributed transactions, and enhanced management of query result sets. The JDBC 2.0 Standard Extension API is incorporated into the J2EE in the `javax.sql` package. The next chapter focuses on some of the more sophisticated aspects of the JDBC 1.0 API, as well as the JDBC 2.0 APIs.

Because the JDBC 1.0 API specification has been around longer, support for this API by driver vendors is more prevalent than support for the JDBC 2.0 API. Sun maintains a fairly thorough list of JDBC driver-compliant vendors for all JDBC versions on its Web site at `http://java.sun.com/products/jdbc/drivers.html`.

The conceptual diagram in Figure 9.1 depicts a high-level view of the JDBC architecture. Here we see a Java application using the JDBC API via usage of the `java.sql` package. The interfaces in the `java.sql` package are implemented by a JDBC driver vendor. JDBC driver implementations provide Java-based wrappers to one or more DBMS interfaces. We will go into the various types of DBMS interfaces shortly, but suffice it to say that a DBMS interface represents an existing method for connecting to a database provided either in a vendor-specific way or via some vendor-independent means for interfacing with the database. Many JDBC driver implementations will connect only to a single type of database, but some middleware vendor driver implementations actually allow for connectivity to various database types.

A Java application must first load a JDBC driver into memory. JDBC API database commands from the Java application are then delegated to the loaded JDBC driver implementation. The JDBC driver implementation talks to the vendor-specific or vendor-independent DBMS interface, and calls to this DBMS interface are then routed to the specific DBMS in use.

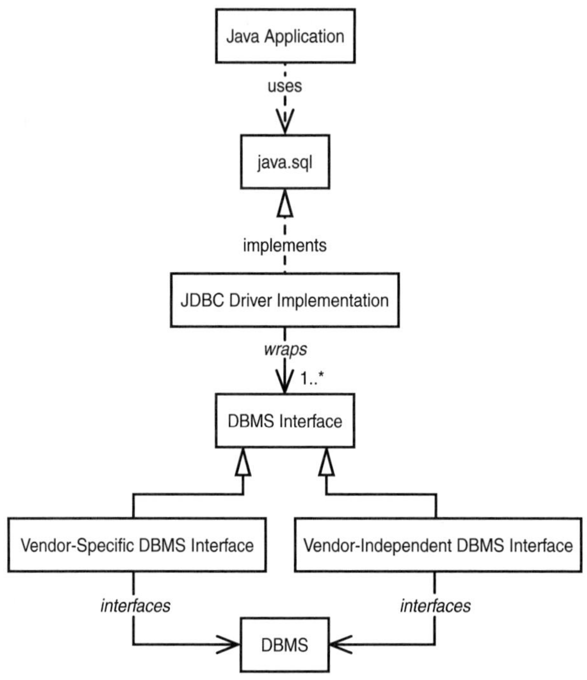

FIGURE 9.1
A JDBC architecture conceptual diagram.

The class diagram in Figure 9.2 depicts a set of classes, interfaces, exceptions, and key relations for the most basic subset of the `java.sql` package. The diagram is partitioned into three groupings showing the core JDBC 1.0 classes and interfaces, the basic exceptions, and a set of key helper classes used to wrap and identify SQL types. The additional classes, interfaces, and exceptions added to the JDBC 2.0 API are not shown in this diagram because the next chapter more completely presents the advanced functionality inherent in the JDBC 2.0 API.

You can see from the diagram that the `DriverManager` is at the top of the JDBC API composition serving as the basic class for managing zero or more JDBC drivers. Such JDBC drivers must implement the `Driver` interface, which is obligated to return a `DriverPropertyInfo` instance to allow an IDE or application to discover information about the driver. The `DriverManager` is also used to manage and return `Connection` objects to the Java application that represent connection sessions with the database. The `Connection` object may then be consulted to obtain meta-data information about the particular database via the `DatabaseMetaData` interface. The `Connection` object's main usage involves creating statements to execute commands against the associated database. Static SQL statements (`Statement` interface), precompiled SQL statements (`PreparedStatement` interface), and stored SQL procedures

(`CallableStatement` interface) may all be created and used to execute database commands. Database queries issued against such statements will return a `ResultSet` object reference that corresponds to zero or more query results from the database query. The `ResultSet` is used to obtain the desired query results and may also be used to obtain `ResultSetMetaData` to find out information about the properties of the returned result set.

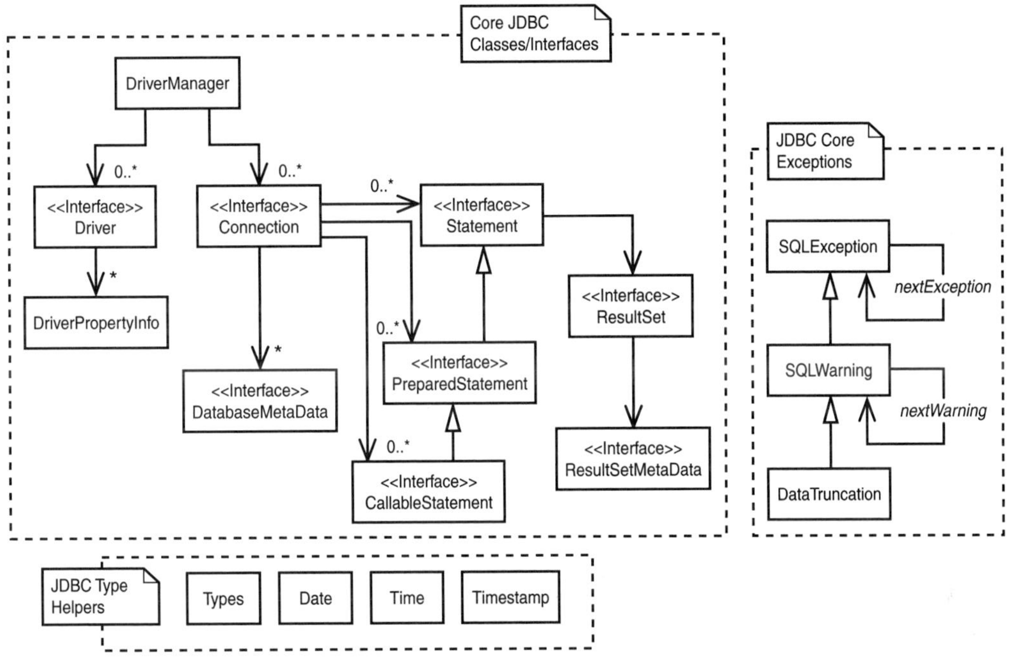

FIGURE 9.2
A basic JDBC class diagram.

A hierarchy of exceptions may be thrown during usage of the various JDBC API calls. `SQLExceptions` are the basic types of exceptions that return information regarding database access errors. Because more than one exception may be thrown by the database during certain calls, a chain of `SQLException` objects is returned and the `SQLException` class enables traversal of such exceptions. `SQLException` thus has a `setNextException()` method to chain exceptions and a `getNextException()` method to traverse chained exceptions. `SQLExceptions` can also return error-code information via a `getErrorCode()` call and SQL state information via a `getSQLState()` call. The `SQLWarning` exception is a special type of `SQLException` returning information regarding a database access warning. `SQLWarnings` also have `setNextWarning()` and `getNextWarning()` calls for chaining and traversing `SQLWarnings`. Finally, the `DataTruncation` exception returns information regarding a database read or write warning when the JDBC driver truncates a value returned from or sent to the database.

The JDBC type helpers of Figure 9.2 will be used throughout this chapter and represent the basic type helpers in JDBC 1.0 for identifying and managing data types submitted to and returned from the database through JDBC. A major enhancement in JDBC 2.0 is its provision of a much richer set of data types. The `java.sql.Types` class is simply a container of constants used to identify SQL types. The values used by the `Types` class are taken from the X/Open standard and are used to uniquely identify SQL standard types (for example, `VARCHAR`, `INTEGER`, `FLOAT`, `DATE`). A mapping between these types and Java types is presented later in this chapter.

JDBC Drivers and their Types

The basic JDBC architecture presented in the preceding section described two broad categories of DBMS interfaces with which JDBC driver implementations may interact. These interfaces were classified according to interface openness as vendor-specific and vendor-independent DBMS interfaces. Sun has in fact come up with a classification scheme for JDBC drivers that is even more specific. Although the distinction by Sun is still made between JDBC drivers that speak to vendor-specific interfaces and those that speak to vendor-independent interfaces, an additional discriminator is employed to offer four distinct types of drivers. This discriminator indicates whether the JDBC driver talks with an interface that has a native platform implementation or with an interface that has a remote network listener with which the JDBC driver communicates. We refer to this additional classification discriminator as interface locality. Table 9.1 shows each JDBC driver type number and name in the context of how they are classified according to interface openness and interface locality. It should be noted that this classification of the four driver types according to interface openness and interface locality is not a formally defined classification scheme but one presented here for you to more rapidly grasp the fundamental and most common distinctions among the four driver types.

TABLE 9.1 JDBC Driver Types

		Interface Openness	
		Vendor-Independent	*Vendor-Specific*
Interface Locality	*Client-Side Native*	`Type 1`: JDBC -ODBC Bridge	`Type 2`: Native-API Partly Java Technology-Enabled
	Remote Network Listener	`Type 3`: Net-Protocol Fully Java Technology-Enabled	`Type 4`: Native-Protocol Fully Java Technology-Enabled

> ### The J2EE and JDBC Driver Type Selection
> Selection of JDBC drivers per the instructions of this section are only relevant to standalone Java enterprise applications. As we'll see in Part VI, "Enterprise Web Enabling," and Part VII, "Enterprise Applications Enabling," J2EE container environments shift JDBC driver type selection from the application developer's concern to the concern of J2EE container providers.

Figure 9.3 illustrates a typical configuration for type 1 JDBC drivers. Type 1 JDBC-ODBC Bridge drivers provide a means for Java applications to make JDBC calls that in turn are mapped to ODBC calls. An ODBC driver thus must be installed on the client side typically as a set of native libraries. Because ODBC is a popular DBMS interface standard for which there exists many ODBC drivers already available to talk with a wide variety of databases, and because JDBC is designed with ODBC in mind, Sun provides a JDBC/ODBC driver implementation with the JDK 1.1 and the J2SE. Sun's implementation of the `java.sql.Driver` interface for the JDBC-ODBC bridge driver is encapsulated by the `sun.jdbc.odbc.JdbcOdbcDriver` class. Use of this bridge is typically not recommended in production environments but is useful as a way to perhaps bootstrap your enterprise development efforts.

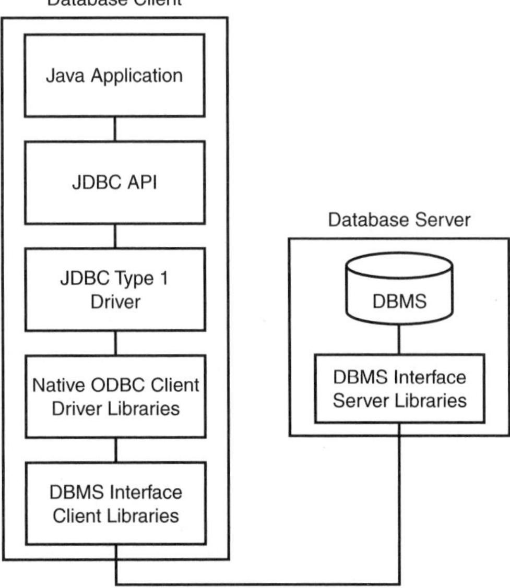

FIGURE 9.3
Typical Type 1 JDBC driver configuration.

Figure 9.4 illustrates a typical configuration for type 2 JDBC drivers. Type 2 Native-API Partly Java Technology-Enabled drivers provide a mechanism for Java applications to make JDBC calls that are directly mapped to vendor-specific DBMS native library interface calls. Thus the JDBC driver is specifically designed to call native client libraries provided for DBMSs such as Oracle, Sybase, or Informix. Most database vendors now ship JDBC type 2 drivers with their databases. Such type 2 drivers will most typically offer better performance than using a JDBC/ODBC bridge because they bypass the ODBC intermediate layer.

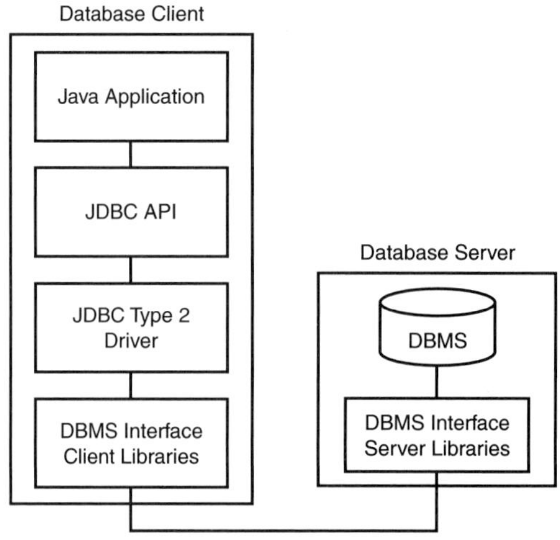

FIGURE 9.4
Typical Type 2 JDBC driver configuration.

Figure 9.5 illustrates a typical configuration for type 3 JDBC drivers. Type 3 Net-Protocol Fully Java Technology-Enabled drivers provide a mechanism for Java applications to make JDBC calls that are mapped to calls embodied in some DBMS vendor-independent network protocol. These over-the-wire calls are then mapped to a specific DBMS vendor's interface calls. This vendor-independent remote listener is typically implemented by a middleware vendor offering support for connecting to various back-end database types. Thus the Java client application is freed from any dependence on having a set of native libraries installed on the client and has a very flexible means for communicating with various database types. The configuration of vendor-specific DBMS interfaces is thus localized to the middleware database server. Although the choice of network protocol for communicating to the middleware listener is left up to the middleware listener vendor, many vendors have been implementing fairly open solutions that are usable in Internet and intranet environments.

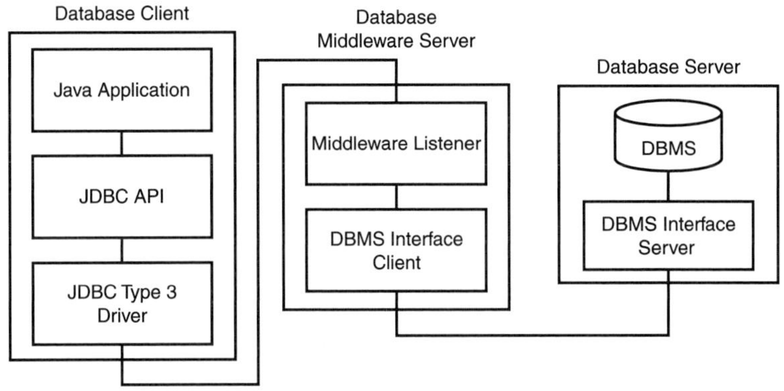

FIGURE 9.5
Typical Type 3 JDBC driver configuration.

Figure 9.6 illustrates a typical configuration for type 4 JDBC drivers. Type 4 Native-Protocol Fully Java Technology-Enabled drivers provide a mechanism for Java applications to make JDBC calls that are mapped to calls embodied in a DBMS vendor's specific remote network listener protocol, which in turn are used to directly access that vendor's database. As with the type 3 drivers, type 4 drivers also enable a Java client application to be freed from dependence on the loading of a set of native client-side libraries. However, because these drivers are vendor specific, this driver type solution does make for a less-flexible configuration on the client side because clients can now talk only with that vendor's DBMS.

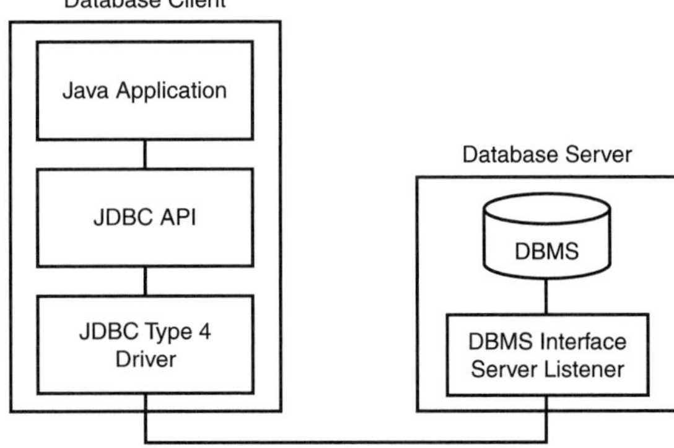

FIGURE 9.6
Typical type 4 JDBC driver configuration.

Driver Assessment

Choosing a driver for your enterprise application is an important step that affects performance, reliability, flexibility, and maintainability. Different drivers will have different performance characteristics, but some general assumptions and trade-offs are typically made when considering the various driver classes:

- Client-side native drivers are usually more appropriate in networks in which client-side native libraries can be easily installed and configured or in situations in which a middle tier is assumed to provide intermediate database access on behalf of the client tier.
- Client-side native drivers are difficult to configure for Web clients and usually involve trusted applets and client-side library installs.
- Remote network listener-based drivers result in thinner, pure Java clients.
- Type 1 drivers offer more database vendor independence at the price of lower performance as compared with type 2 drivers.
- Type 2 drivers offer higher performance at the price of database vendor-dependence as compared with type 1 drivers.
- Type 3 drivers offer more database vendor-independence at the potential price of lower performance as compared with type 4 drivers.
- Type 4 drivers offer potentially higher performance at the price of database vendor-dependence as compared with type 3 drivers.

Such driver comparisons based on type are indeed gross comparisons. Evaluations of drivers should be performed on an individual basis because drivers will vary in performance according to specific features, databases in use, and other system environment factors. System environment factors such as client usage, client-side platforms, network bandwidth and usage, and server-side platforms all affect the performance of an application. Because driver implementation details are often not known a priori, information about the performance in a particular environment is not always obvious until it's evaluated in a simulated or actual system environment. Other issues such as security and level of JDBC compliance are also worthwhile attributes of a particular JDBC driver vendor to take into consideration. Of course, as we'll see in Parts VI and VII of this book, the application developer typically does not worry about such issues in J2EE container-based enterprise applications.

JDBC Driver Configuration

Now that you know what a JDBC driver is and the various types available, it is important to know how to configure a JDBC driver for use in your enterprise application. Figure 9.7 depicts a class diagram of the key entities involved in configuration of a JDBC driver. Note that although Figure 9.7 shows many of the core JDBC 1.0–style operations, a few newly introduced JDBC 2.0–style operations are also shown.

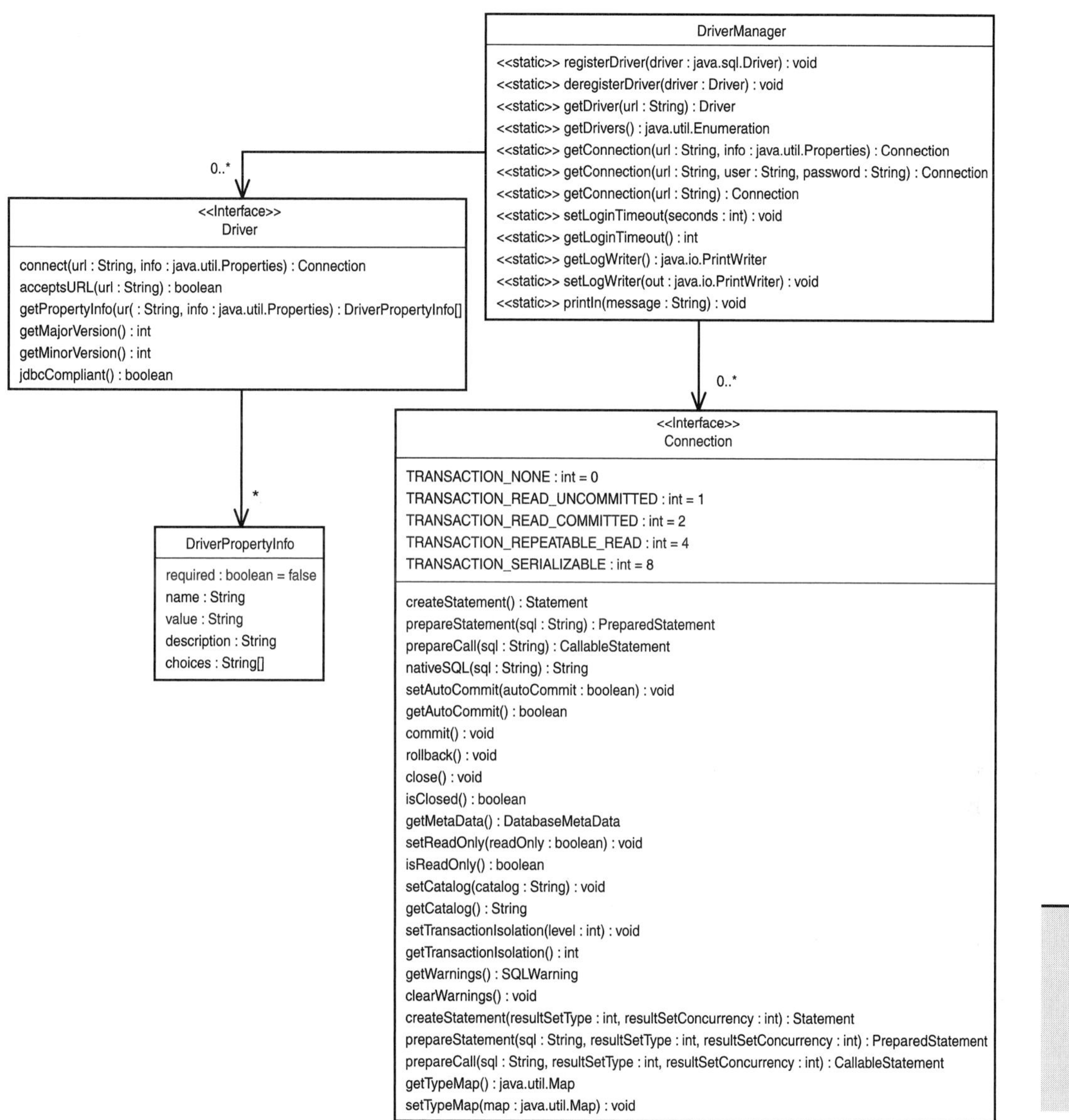

FIGURE 9.7
Driver management class diagram.

The `java.sql.DriverManager` class represents the primary interface to the JDBC API user for loading and managing JDBC drivers. The `DriverManager` can either load the driver classes implicitly by setting the system property `jdbc.drivers` or load them explicitly with calls to `Class.forName()`. The `DriverManager` is also used when creating new connections associated with the pool of loaded drivers.

The J2EE and JDBC Driver Configuration

Configuration of JDBC drivers per the instructions of this section are only relevant to standalone Java enterprise applications. As we'll see in Part VI and Part VII, J2EE container environments shift JDBC driver configuration from the application developer's concern to the concern of J2EE application assemblers and deployers as well as J2EE container providers.

To implicitly load a set of drivers, simply specify the driver class names separated by a colon (`:`) in the `jdbc.drivers` system property. Note that the driver class name specified must, of course, be in your `CLASSPATH`. For example:

```
java -Djdbc.drivers=sun.jdbc.odbc.JdbcOdbcDriver:
➥com.assuredtech.jdbc.JdbcDriver MyProgram
```

To explicitly load a driver, use the `Class.forName()` method in your Java program as shown here:

```
Class.forName("com.assuredtech.jdbc.JdbcDriver");
Class.forName("sun.jdbc.odbc.JdbcOdbcDriver");
```

A flexible scheme for configuring a set of drivers for your application may be to provide a set of JDBC driver names in a file adhering to a format readable by a `java.util.Properties` object and then to load these driver names and call `Class.forName()` for each driver. The example presented in the next section demonstrates how to accomplish this.

As a final note on driver configuration, the constructors of some drivers are occasionally used for driver registration. Although this scheme lacks flexibility because you are now rendered with a hard-wired driver name in your code, it is exemplified here for completeness:

```
com.assuredtech.jdbc.JdbcDriver driver
    = new com.assuredtech.jdbc.JdbcDriver();
// Note: com.assuredtech.jdbc.JdbcDriver() calls
//          DriverManager.registerDriver(Driver);
```

Note that the `com.assuredtech.jdbc.JdbcDriver` shown here would have to implement the `java.sql.Driver` interface as all JDBC drivers must. The `Driver` interface specifies the need to return a `DriverPropertyInfo` object that may be used to get and set properties for a connection associated with the driver. The JDBC API user rarely needs to interact with the `Driver` interface and the `java.sql.DriverPropertyInfo` class. Rather, the JDBC API user usually has the `DriverManager` class as the point of contact with the loaded JDBC drivers.

General Configuration Steps per Driver Type

The general steps for configuring type 1 JDBC-ODBC bridge drivers are detailed here:

- Install the native DBMS interface client libraries and ODBC client driver for the DBMS to which you want to connect according to your DBMS vendor's instructions. It should be noted that Microsoft Windows often comes pre-installed with many Microsoft-related ODBC drivers ready to connect to Microsoft databases such as MSAccess and SQL Server.
- Start the Control Panel from your Windows 95/98/NT platform. You can get to the Control Panel by first clicking the Start button, then selecting the Settings menu item, and finally selecting the Control Panel menu item (and the Control Panel window pops up).
- Find and double-click on the ODBC icon (the Data Source Administrator window pops up).
- Select the System DSN tab.
- Click the Add button (the Create New Data Source window pops up).
- Select the driver for the database with which you want to communicate.
- Click the Finish button (an ODBC window specific to the selected driver pops up).
- Type the data source name, fill in a description, and select or type the information regarding the database instance to which you want to connect.
- Load the type 1 JDBC driver class (in your `CLASSPATH`) from your Java client application according to the instructions described previously in this section.

The general steps for configuring type 2 Native-API Partly Java Technology-Enabled drivers are detailed here:

- Install the native DBMS interface client libraries for the DBMS to which you want to connect according to your DBMS vendor's instructions.
- Load the type 2 JDBC driver class (in your `CLASSPATH`) from your Java client application according to the instructions described previously in this section.

The general steps for configuring type 3 Net-Protocol Fully Java Technology-Enabled drivers are detailed here:

- You may first have to install the native DBMS interface client libraries for the DBMS to which you want to connect according to your DBMS vendor's instructions on your middleware server.
- Install the middleware component libraries for your middleware remote network listener according to your middleware vendor's instructions.

- Configure the middleware vendor's remote network listener to use one or more natively installed DBMS interfaces with a JDBC type 1 or JDBC type 2 driver or perhaps a JDBC type 4 driver for connection to a database vendor's remote network listener.
- Load the middleware vendor's type 3 JDBC driver class (in your `CLASSPATH`) from your Java client application according to the instructions described previously in this section.

The general step for configuring type 4 Native-Protocol Fully Java Technology-Enabled drivers is detailed here:

- Load the type 4 JDBC driver class (in your `CLASSPATH`) from your Java client application according to the instructions described previously in this section.

Configuring the BeeShirts.com Example Data Model

Of course, configuring a JDBC driver and data enabling an enterprise Java application with JDBC would be pointless without a database hosting useful data. To demonstrate how to data-enable an enterprise application with JDBC, we use an actual database and some sample data. The sample data and associated data model define a commercial retail T-shirt business model that we will continue to communications-enable, Web-enable, application-enable, and infuse with assurance throughout the remainder of this book. After reading this book, you will have gone through all the key enterprise-enabling steps to be considered in building a distributed Java-based e-commerce enterprise system known as BeeShirts.com.

If you don't already have a database available, you can follow the steps outlined in Appendix A, "Software Configuration," for installing the underlying database that we have used to create these examples. Appendix A also demonstrates how to configure the database with the BeeShirts.com data model and data used throughout this book. You of course can configure and populate your own database with the BeeShirts.com data. The next section demonstrates how you can connect to this database.

Throughout the book, we incrementally introduce parts of the BeeShirts.com data model as its elements become relevant to understanding the example code that utilizes the model. We take this approach so that you are not plagued with attempting to understand a complete data model before parts of it are even utilized or relevant. Appendix A describes the full-blown example data model used in the example BeeShirts.com application for the reader interested in understanding the data model now before proceeding.

As described in Chapter 8, "Enterprise Data," we use a UML-like type notation and SQL type names from the `java.sql.Types` class for describing the data models throughout the book. Figure 9.8 depicts the most basic subset of the BeeShirts.com data model relevant to the examples of this chapter. The item table includes the information related to a particular item (that is, a T-shirt) that may be purchased. The item table is related to an actual order via an order number. The orders table contains the order information for a particular set of items. The orders table is related to a customer table via a customer number. The customer table includes all information related to a potential or existing BeeShirts.com customer. An auxiliary state table contains the mapping from a two-character state code to a complete state name.

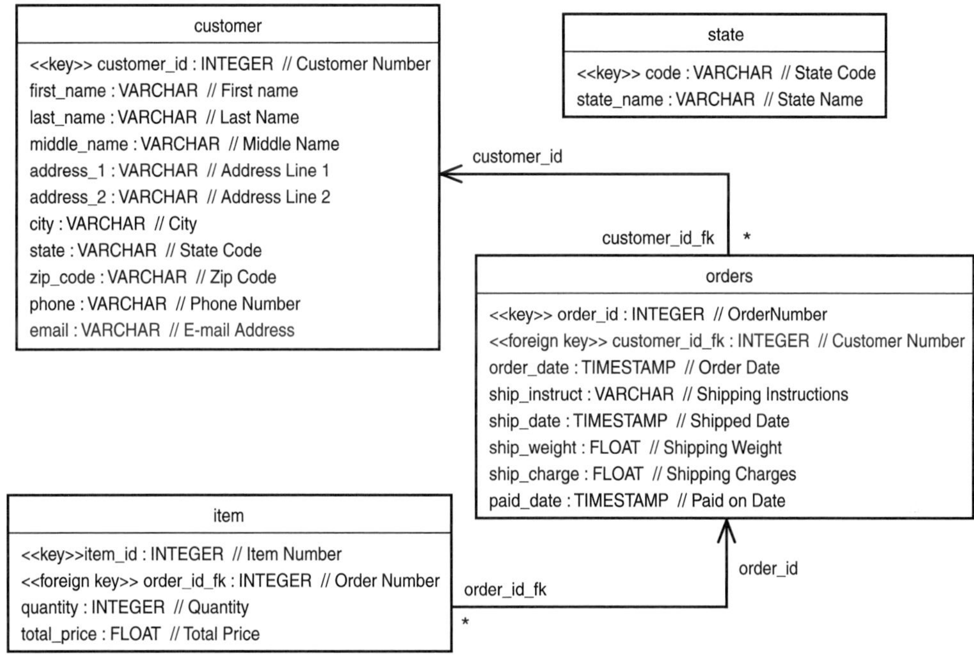

FIGURE 9.8

BeeShirts.com customer, orders, and items basic data model.

JDBC Connections

A database connection represents a communications session in which a communications channel is opened and SQL commands are executed between a database client and the database server. The `java.sql.Connection` interface represents this database connection. A database connection is closed when the database session between the database client and the database is terminated (that is, via `Connection.close()`).

The J2EE and JDBC Connections

Configuration and creation of JDBC connections per the instructions of this section are only relevant to standalone Java enterprise applications. As we'll see in Part VI and Part VII, J2EE container environments shift JDBC connection creation from the application developer's concern to the concern of J2EE container providers. Connections are yielded from a connection pool for application code in J2EE container environments. J2EE assembly and deployment providers configure any specific connection information on behalf of the application code.

Database URLs

A database Uniform Resource Locator (URL) represents a fully qualified database connection name identifying the database and database driver to which you are connecting. To fully describe a connection name, one needs to know information such as the type of database driver, the type of database, the type of database connection, and some connection-instance information like the username, password, and IP address of the database instance. The database URL is represented as a `String` in the form

```
jdbc:subprotocol:subname
```

in which

- `jdbc` is a database driver type keyword used in the URL for all JDBC database URLs.
- *`subprotocol`* represents the type of database to which one desires connectivity.
- *`subname`* provides additional information needed by the database type for establishing connectivity.

The *`subprotocol`* and *`subname`* to use for a particular database instance should be described in your JDBC driver vendor's documentation, but some examples are listed here for different driver types:

- Type 1: JDBC-ODBC Bridge Driver URLs

  ```
  jdbc:odbc:customer;UID:dba;pwd:dba
  jdbc:odbc:customer;CacheSize=100
  jdbc:odbc:<datasource name>;param=value;param=value;....
  ```

- Type 2: Native-API Partly Java Technology-Enabled Driver URL

  ```
  jdbc:oracle:oci7:@SQLNETinstance Name
  ```

- Type 3: Net-Protocol Fully Java Technology-Enabled Driver URLs

  ```
  jdbc:dbAnywhere:1529
  ```

- Type 4: Native-Protocol Fully Java Technology-Enabled Driver URLs

  ```
  jdbc:oracle:thin:@<machine name>:<port Number>:<DBMS instance name>
  ```

Creating Connections

To create a connection object instance, one of the `DriverManager`'s `getConnection()` methods must be invoked with the database URL as a parameter. When invoking this method, `DriverManager` first finds a driver from its pool of loaded drivers that can accept the database URL and then asks the driver to connect to the database with the associated database URL. A `Connection` object is then returned to the object that invoked `DriverManager.getConnection()`. Three forms of `getConnection()` exist on the `DriverManager` class:

- `getConnection(String url)` simply attempts to connect given the database URL.
- `getConnection(String url, String user, String password)` attempts to connect given the database URL, a database username, and the database user's password.
- `getConnection(String url, java.util.Properties info)` attempts to connect given the database URL and a set of properties used as connection arguments. Sometimes, a `user` and `password` property are passed in via the `Properties` object.

As an option, the `DriverManager.setLoginTimeout()` method may be invoked to specify the timeout in seconds for a driver to wait while attempting to connect to a database.

Example: Connecting to a Database

This next example demonstrates how to establish a connection to the database. The example code is contained in the `ejava.jdbcch09.ConnectToDatabase` class and has the following definition:

```
public class ConnectToDatabase{ ... }
```

NOTE

The following complete code example can be found on the CD in the `examples\src\ejava\jdbcch09` directory using the `ConnectToDatabase.java` and the `JDBCCH09Properties.txt` files. Some exception handling and other handling mechanisms have been left out of the book here for simplicity but can be found in the examples on the CD. A description of the database-relevant properties used in `JDBCCH09Properties.txt` can be found in Appendix A and a tad later in this chapter.

continues

A runconnecttodb.bat example script file (for Microsoft Windows) is also included in the examples\src\ejava\jdbcch09 directory to demonstrate how to compile and execute the example code. We provide such example scripts throughout the book and describe our general build and execution procedures in Appendix A. Such scripts can be extended to operate on Unix and other platforms utilizing the same core Java commands.

The main() method of ConnectToDatabase is invoked like

```
java ejava.jdbcch09.ConnectToDatabase <propertiesFileName>
```

where the <propertiesFileName> is the location of a properties filename with the set of properties set as in the JDBCCH09Properties.txt file. The main() method then instantiates a new ConnectToDatabase object and calls setProperties() with a filename and then getConnection() to return the Connection object. A series of exceptions are handled and the status of the connection attempt is returned. The key elements of the main() function are shown here:

```
public static void main(String[] args)
{
    if(args.length == 0){
      System.out.println("Error: Run the program as:"
      + " java ejava.jdbcch09.ConnectToDatabase <propertiesFileName>");
      System.exit(0);
    }

    String fileName = args[0];
    ConnectToDatabase connectionToDatabase = new ConnectToDatabase();
    . . .
    connectionToDatabase.setProperties(fileName);
    Connection connection = connectionToDatabase.getConnection();
    . . .
    // Catch exceptions here.
    . . .
    // Else print results of successful connection attempt.
    . . .
}
```

The following member variables of the ConnectToDatabase class are used to maintain the relevant variables used in this example:

```
private String driverClass; // Driver class name
private String dbURL; // Database URL
private Properties dbProperties; // Properties read from properties file
private Connection connection; // A database connection object
```

The ConnectToDatabase.setProperties() method creates a new java.util.Properties object reference (dbProperties), creates a new FileInputStream object with the propertiesFileName, and calls load() on the Properties object with the newly created FileInputStream object. Any exceptions that may be thrown are simply passed back to the invoking object. The setProperties() method is defined as shown here:

```
public void setProperties(String fileName)
    throws FileNotFoundException, IOException
{
    dbProperties = new Properties();
    FileInputStream propertiesFileStream= new FileInputStream(fileName);
    dbProperties.load(propertiesFileStream);
}
```

As described in Chapter 4, “Java Foundations for Enterprise Development,” we generally use property files throughout the book for most of our examples to enable you to experiment with the examples via setting properties with different values. In this example, we read properties such as the driver class and database URL, which you will probably have and want to change to run with your particular configuration and database. We will also usually provide you with some variations that may be set for each property that you may comment or uncomment according to your desired experiment. The relevant properties for this example are shown here:

```
# Refer to Appendix A for more info on configuring the JDBC
# driver via setting of the DRIVER_CLASS and DATABASE_URL properties

#JDBC Driver Class
# for ODBC Driver:
#DRIVER_CLASS=sun.jdbc.odbc.JdbcOdbcDriver
# for Oracle Driver
#DRIVER_CLASS=jdbc.oracle.driver.OracleDriver
# for CloudScape Driver equipped with J2EE reference implementation
#DRIVER_CLASS=RmiJdbc.RJDriver
# for CloudScape Driver equipped with BEA Weblogic Server
DRIVER_CLASS=COM.cloudscape.core.JDBCDriver

#Database URL
# for ODBC URL
#DATABASE_URL=jdbc:odbc:tShirts
# for Oracle URL
#DATABASE_URL=jdbc:oracle:thin:@localhost:1521:ORCL
# for URL with CloudScape equipped with J2EE reference implementation
#DATABASE_URL=jdbc:rmi:jdbc:cloudscape:beeshirtsdb
# for URL with CloudScape equipped with BEA Weblogic Server
DATABASE_URL=jdbc:cloudscape:D:\\weblogic\\eval\\cloudscape\\beeshirts

#UserName to connect to database
```

```
UserName=TSHIRTS
#Password to connect to database
Password=TSHIRTS
#otherParameters
SUB_PROPERTIES=
```

The `ConnectToDatabase.getConnection()` method called from `main()` first extracts the driver class name (`driverClass`), database URL (`dbURL`), username (`userName`), and password (`password`) from the `dbProperties` object. The driver class name is then used to call `Class.forName()` to load the driver. Finally, the database URL, username, and password are used to create a connection via `DriverManager.getConnection()`. The `ConnectToDatabase` class also demonstrates use of the `DriverManager.getConnection()` call using two of its other overloaded `getConnection()` methods. Depending on whether or not you include a `UserName`, `Password`, or a `SUB_PROPERTIES` set of values in the `JDBCCH09Properties.txt` file, you can induce the example code to demonstrate use of the other two `DriverManager.getConnection()` methods. A convenience method called `convertStringToProperties()` is used to convert a comma-separated set of `NAME=VALUE` pairs from the `SUB_PROPERTIES` string into a `Properties` object if it is supplied (for example, `SUB_PROPERTIES=User=Scott, Password=tiger`). The key elements of the `getConnection()` method are shown here:

```
public Connection getConnection()
    throws ClassNotFoundException, SQLException, Exception
{
    if(connection != null){
     return this.connection;
    }
    // Get connection properties from properties file
    driverClass = (String)dbProperties.get("DRIVER_CLASS");
    dbURL    = (String)dbProperties.get("DATABASE_URL");
    String userName = ((String)dbProperties.get("UserName")).trim();
    String password = ((String)dbProperties.get("Password")).trim();
    String otherProperties = (String)dbProperties.get("SUB_PROPERTIES");

    if(driverClass == null || dbURL == null){
      throw new Exception("Driver Class or
➥Driver URL should not be null");
    }
    // Load driver
    Class.forName(driverClass);
    // Create connection in one of three ways depending on whether
    // a user name, password, or sub-properties were in properties file
    if( (userName.length() == 0) && (password.length() == 0)
➥&& (otherProperties.length() == 0) ){
```

```
      connection = DriverManager.getConnection(dbURL);
    }
    else if(otherProperties.length() == 0){
      connection = DriverManager.getConnection(dbURL, userName,
➥password);
    }
    else if(otherProperties.length() != 0){
      Properties subProperties
        = convertStringToProperties(otherProperties);
      connection = DriverManager.getConnection(dbURL, subProperties);
    }
    return connection;
}
```

JDBC Statements

After a connection to a database is opened, a Java application typically makes actual use of the connection via the creation and execution of a series of SQL commands. These SQL commands are executed as database statements that perform such operations as querying for data, updating data, inserting data, and deleting data. The `java.sql.Statement`, `java.sql.PreparedStatement`, and `java.sql.CallableStatement` interfaces shown in Figure 9.9 encapsulate various forms of database statements that are created by a `Connection` object and that can be issued to the database. We will not cover use of all the methods on the statement interfaces in this section, but throughout the rest of this chapter and the next chapter, most of the functionality that demonstrates use of these methods will be presented.

The `Statement` interface represents a basic SQL statement that can be executed. The `PreparedStatement` represents a type of Statement that can be precompiled with query information as a performance enhancement. The `CallableStatement` is a type of `PreparedStatement` that serves to encapsulate execution of stored procedures in the database. Because stored procedures are a more advanced database processing topic, the discussion on `CallableStatement` objects is deferred until the next chapter.

Using Regular Statements

SQL commands are contained in Java `String` objects passed to JDBC calls. These `String` objects simply contain SQL commands as described in Chapter 8. A regular `Statement` object can be created by invoking `createStatement()` on a `Connection` object. Such nonprepared types of statements will be useful for infrequent queries because they are not precompiled for efficiency, as are `PreparedStatement` objects. You can create a `Statement` object as shown here:

```
Statement statement = connection.createStatement();
```

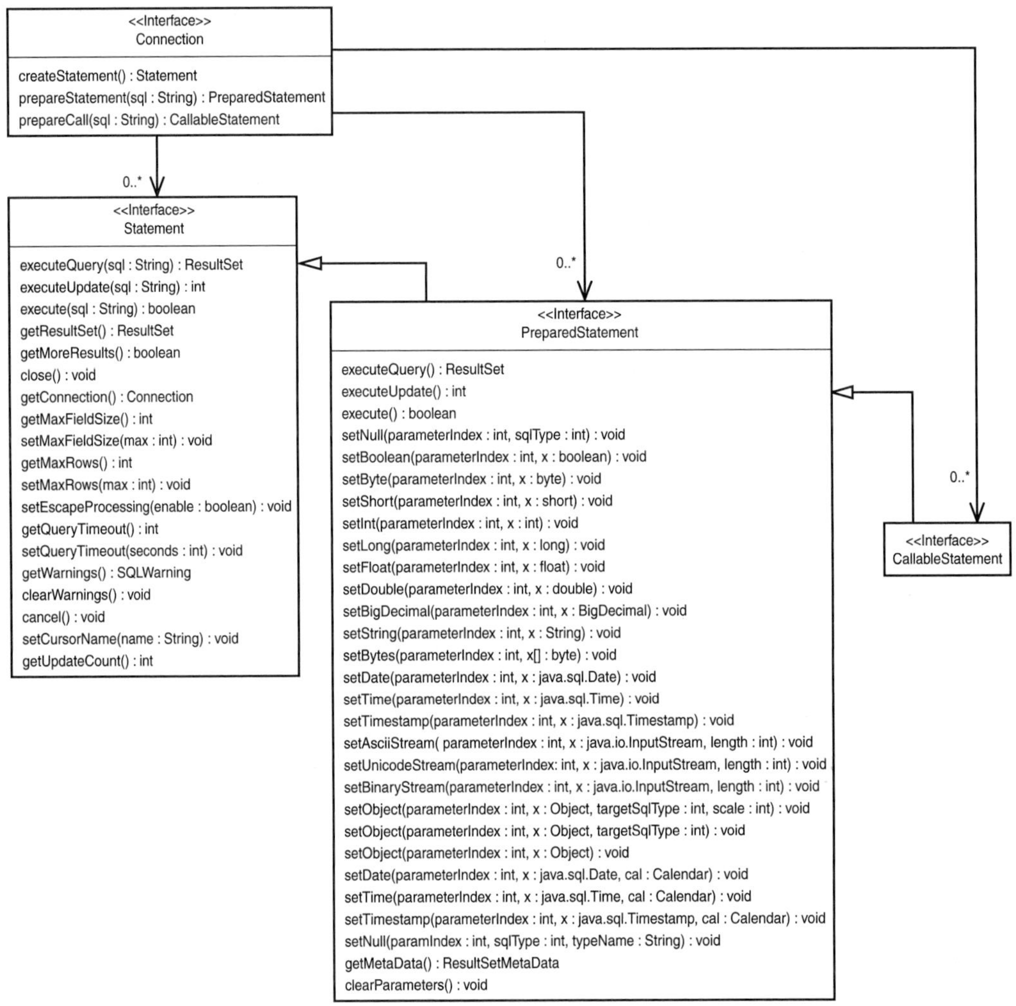

FIGURE 9.9
Statements class diagram.

The `Statement` object is then called upon to execute an actual SQL command using one of three basic methods:

- `ResultSet executeQuery(String sql)` allows one to execute SQL queries and obtain a `ResultSet` object. For example

```
ResultSet rs = statement.executeQuery("SELECT * FROM CUSTOMER");
```

- `int executeUpdate(String sql)` allows one to execute SQL inserts, deletes, and updates and then obtain a count of updated rows. For example

```
int nValues = statement.executeUpdate("INSERT INTO CUSTOMER VALUES"
  + " ('129','Sam','Cheng','s','123 Sam St.', '12','Baltimore','MD',"
  + "'20222', '(410)444-4444' ,'sc@scheng.com') ");
```

- `boolean execute(String sql)` is the most generic type of execute call allowing one to execute SQL DDL commands and then obtain a `boolean` value indicating whether a `ResultSet` was returned. For example

```
boolean returnValue = statement.execute("SELECT * FROM CUSTOMER" );
```

Querying with Joins, Outer Joins, and LIKE Clauses

Aside from queries, inserts, deletes, updates, and DDL commands that operate on a single table as in the code snippets shown previously, joins in queries are used when data from more than a single table needs to be returned with a value in one table equaling a value in another table. As an example join that may be issued on the example database, we have this:

```
String joinStatement = "SELECT CUSTOMER.*, ORDERS.* FROM "
   + "CUSTOMER, ORDERS WHERE CUSTOMER.CUSTOMER_ID = ORDERS.CUSTOMER_ID_FK";
Statement statement = connection.createStatement();
ResultSet rs = statement.executeQuery(joinStatement);
```

Outer joins are used when we are trying to join tables that have data in one table that has no cross-reference in the other table yet we still want to return its value from the resultant query. Joins are executed in JDBC statements like any other SQL command, but outer joins may take a different syntax. One database vendor's syntax for outer joins may differ from another vendor's syntax. For example, an outer join `String` in MS Access may be formulated this way:

```
String joinStatement= "SELECT C.* , S.* FROM CUSTOMER C OUTER JOIN"
                      + "STATE S on C.STATE = S.CODE";
```

The same outer join in Oracle may be formulated like this:

```
String joinStatement = "SELECT C.*, S.* FROM CUSTOMER C, STATE S "
    + "WHERE C.STATE(+) = S.CODE(+)";
```

There are also differences for issuing SQL statements with an embedded `LIKE` clause. For example, an MS Access SQL `String` with a `LIKE` clause it in may be formulated like this:

```
String sqlString = " SELECT * FROM CUSTOMER
➥WHERE FIRST_NAME like '*R*' ";
```

The same `LIKE` clause for Oracle is formulated this way:

```
String sqlString = " SELECT * FROM CUSTOMER
➥WHERE FIRST_NAME like '%R%' ";
```

There does exist a standard JDBC escape syntax for handling such outer join and `LIKE` clause anomalies, but the level of particular support for such features from many driver implementations remains minimal.

Example: Creating and Executing Statements

This next example demonstrates how to create and execute a series of simple statements. The example code is contained in the `ejava.jdbcch09.SimpleStatementExample` class. This example builds off of the previous database-connection example. In fact, the `SimpleStatementExample` class extends the `ConnectToDatabase` class:

```
public class SimpleStatementExample extends ConnectToDatabase{...}
```

> **NOTE**
>
> The following complete code example can be found on the CD in `examples\src\ejava\jdbcch09` directory using the `SimpleStatementExample.java`, `ConnectToDatabase.java`, and `JDBCCH09Properties.txt` files. Some exception handling and other handling mechanisms have been left out of the book here for simplicity but can be found in the examples on the CD. Additionally, a `runsimplestatement.bat` example Windows script file is included in the `examples\src\ejava\jdbcch09` directory to demonstrate how to build and execute this example. See Appendix A for more information on general database and example code configuration procedures.

The `main()` method of `SimpleStatementExample` is invoked as

```
java ejava.jdbcch09.SimpleStatementExample <propertiesFileName>
```

where the *`propertiesFileName`* is the location of a properties filename with the properties set as in the `JDBCCH09Properties.txt` file. The `main()` method then calls `setProperties()` and `getConnection()` on the example class as it did in the `ConnectToDatabase` example to load the properties file and establish the database connection. However, now we also create a `Statement` object and attempt to execute two regular queries, an update, a join query, an outer join query, and a query with a `LIKE` clause. We also close the associated `Statement` object after all the example statements are executed. A series of exceptions are handled and the status of each command executed is reported but left out of the following listing:

```
public static void main(String[] args)
  {
    if(args.length == 0){
      System.out.println("Error: Run the program as:"
        + " java ejava.jdbcch09.SimpleStatementExample "
```

```
 + " <propertiesFileName> ");
      System.exit(0);
    }

    String fileName = args[0];
    SimpleStatementExample simpleStatementExample
      = new SimpleStatementExample();
     . . .
      // Establish properties from properties file and get connection
      simpleStatementExample.setProperties(fileName);
      Connection connection = simpleStatementExample.getConnection();

      // Get SQL statements from properties file and execute them...

      String sqlString =
        (String)(simpleStatementExample.getProperties()).
➥get("SQL_QUERY_STATEMENT");
      boolean executionStatus = simpleStatementExample.
➥execute(sqlString);
. . .
      ResultSet resultSet = simpleStatementExample.
➥executeQuery(sqlString);
    . . .
      sqlString =
        (String)(simpleStatementExample.getProperties()).
➥get("SQL_UPDATE_STATEMENT");
      int count = simpleStatementExample.executeUpdate(sqlString);
    . . .
      String joinStatement =
        (String)(simpleStatementExample.getProperties()).
➥get("SQL_QUERY_STATEMENT_JOIN");
      resultSet = simpleStatementExample.executeQuery(joinStatement);
    . . .
      String outerJoinStatement =
        (String)(simpleStatementExample.getProperties()).
➥get("SQL_QUERY_STATEMENT_OUTER_JOIN");
      resultSet = simpleStatementExample.
➥executeQuery(outerJoinStatement);
    . . .
      String likeStatement =
        (String)(simpleStatementExample.getProperties()).
➥get("SQL_QUERY_STATEMENT_WITH_LIKE");
      resultSet = simpleStatementExample.executeQuery(likeStatement);
    . . .
      simpleStatementExample.closeStatement();
    . . .
}
```

In addition to the state implicitly inherited from `ConnectToDatabase`, we have added another attribute to this class for containing a reference to the `Statement` object:

```
private Statement  statement; // Statement object
```

Each query or update `String` issued is read from the properties file. You of course can modify this properties file to demonstrate different types of queries. These are the newly introduced properties that are relevant to the preceding example and beyond those properties used in the `ConnectToDatabase` example:

```
#SQL Query
SQL_QUERY_STATEMENT = SELECT * FROM TSHIRTS.CUSTOMER

#SQL Update

SQL_UPDATE_STATEMENT = INSERT INTO TSHIRTS.CUSTOMER
➥ VALUES ('129','Sam','Cheng','S','123 Sam St.', 'C3',
➥'Baltimore','MD','20222','4104444444' ,'sc@scheng.com')

#Join STATEMENT

SQL_QUERY_STATEMENT_JOIN = SELECT TSHIRTS.CUSTOMER.*, TSHIRTS.ORDERS.*
➥ FROM TSHIRTS.CUSTOMER, TSHIRTS.ORDERS
➥ WHERE CUSTOMER.CUSTOMER_ID = ORDERS.CUSTOMER_ID_FK

#OUTER JOIN for ORACLE
#SQL_QUERY_STATEMENT_OUTER_JOIN = SELECT CUSTOMER.*
➥ FROM TSHIRTS.CUSTOMER,STATE
➥ WHERE CUSTOMER.STATE(+) = STATE.CODE(+)
#OUTER JOIN for MSACCESS
#SQL_QUERY_STATEMENT_OUTER_JOIN = SELECT C.* , S.*
➥ FROM  CUSTOMER C  OUTER JOIN STATE S on C.STATE = S.CODE
#OUTER JOIN for MSACCESS and Cloudscape
SQL_QUERY_STATEMENT_OUTER_JOIN = SELECT C.* , S.*
➥ FROM  TSHIRTS.CUSTOMER C
➥ LEFT OUTER JOIN TSHIRTS.STATE S on C.STATE = S.CODE

#SQL Statement with Like for MSACCESS
#SQL_QUERY_STATEMENT_WITH_LIKE = SELECT CUSTOMER.* FROM CUSTOMER
➥ WHERE CUSTOMER.FIRST_NAME LIKE  \'*R*\'
#SQL Statement with Like for ORACLE  and Cloudscape
SQL_QUERY_STATEMENT_WITH_LIKE = SELECT *
➥ FROM TSHIRTS.CUSTOMER WHERE FIRST_NAME LIKE  '%R%'
```

When each type of example execute statement is invoked on the `SimpleStatementExample` object, each method attempts to retrieve the `Statement` object. Each method does this by calling a `createStatement()` method that retrieves the connection object from the base class and creates the `Statement` if it does not already exist. The `createStatement()` method is defined as shown here:

```
protected void createStatement()
  throws SQLException, Exception
{
    if(statement == null){
      Connection connection = super.getConnection();
      statement = connection.createStatement();
    }

}
```

Each type of execute command on a `Statement` object is demonstrated from the `SimpleStatementExample`'s `main()` method by calling one of the following three methods on the `SimpleStatementExample` object:

```
public boolean execute(String sqlString)
    throws SQLException, Exception
  {
    if(statement == null){
      createStatement();
    }

    boolean returnValue = statement.execute(sqlString);
    return returnValue;
  }

public ResultSet executeQuery(String sqlString)
    throws SQLException, Exception
  {
    if(statement == null){
      createStatement();
    }

    ResultSet rs = statement.executeQuery(sqlString);
    return rs;
  }

public int executeUpdate(String sqlString)
    throws SQLException, Exception
  {
    if(statement == null){
      createStatement();
    }

    int returnValue = statement.executeUpdate(sqlString);
    return returnValue;
  }
```

We finally close the statement with this:

```
public void closeStatement()
    throws SQLException
  {
    if(statement != null){
      statement.close();
      statement = null;
    }
  }
```

Using Prepared Statements

Although each `Statement` object used in the preceding set of examples represents a SQL statement that must be compiled each time it is executed, a prepared statement represents a precompiled SQL statement and is identified by the `java.sql.PreparedStatement` interface. A `PreparedStatement` has advantages over a regular `Statement` in that it is created with a parameterized SQL statement. Each `PreparedStatement`'s SQL command parameter is indicated by a question mark (`?`) in the SQL `String` and represents an input (`IN`) variable that can be dynamically set before the statement is executed. Because only the values of each parameter need to be set after the statement is created, the statement itself can be compiled when the statement is created (assuming that the database or driver or both fully support this feature). This provides an obvious benefit when sending SQL commands to the database that have the same basic command structure but differ only in the `IN` values used by each submitted command. A `PreparedStatement` is created with the `prepareStatement()` method on the `Connection` object as shown here:

```
PreparedStatement statement = connection.
➥prepareStatement("SELECT * FROM CUSTOMER WHERE CUSTOMER_ID= ?");
```

After the prepared statement is created, the `IN` values must be set. This is accomplished via use of the various `setXXX()` methods that exist on the `PreparedStatement` object. The basic format for each `setXXX()` method is

```
void setXXX(int parameterIndex, XXX value);
```

where *`XXX`* is the type of object being inserted into the parameterized prepared statement at the index specified by `parameterIndex`. The various `setXXX()` methods available to a `PreparedStatement` are shown in Figure 9.9. For example, one way to set the parameter for the select clause created in the preceding `PreparedStatement` object would be as follows:

```
statement.setInt(1, new Integer(129));
```

After each `setXXX()` method is called for each `IN` parameter in the `PreparedStatement`, the statement may be executed. This is accomplished via a call to one of three parameterless execute methods on the `PreparedStatement` object as defined here:

- `ResultSet executeQuery();` to execute SQL queries and obtain a `ResultSet` object
- `int executeUpdate();` to execute SQL updates and obtain a count of updated rows
- `boolean execute();` to execute SQL DDL commands and obtain a `boolean` value indicating whether a `ResultSet` was created

Example: Creating and Executing Prepared Statements

This next example demonstrates how to create and execute a series of `PreparedStatement` objects. The example code is contained in the `ejava.jdbcch09.SimplePreparedStatementExample` class. This example also builds off of the database connection example with the `SimplePreparedStatementExample` class extending the `ConnectToDatabase` class:

```
public class SimplePreparedStatementExample extends ConnectToDatabase{...}
```

NOTE

The following complete code example can be found on the CD in the `examples\src\ejava\jdbcch09` directory using the `SimplePreparedStatementExample.java`, `ConnectToDatabase.java`, and `JDBCCH09Properties.txt` files. Some exception handling and other handling mechanisms have been left out of the book here for simplicity in describing the example. Additionally, we have included an example `runsimplepreparedstatement.bat` script in the `examples\src\ejava\jdbcch09` directory to demonstrate how to build and execute the example code. Appendix A describes general database and example code configuration procedures used by the book.

The `main()` method of `SimplePreparedStatementExample` is invoked like

```
java ejava.jdbcch09.SimplePreparedStatementExample <propertiesFileName>
```

where the `<propertiesFileName>` is the location of a properties filename with the properties set as in the `JDBCCH09Properties.txt` file. The `main()` method calls `setProperties()` and `getConnection()` on the example class as it did in the `ConnectToDatabase` example to load the properties file and establish the database connection. Here we also create `PreparedStatement` objects to execute queries and an update. For each type of execute command, a parameterized prepared SQL `String` and a `Vector` of `IN` parameter values are read from the properties file and submitted to the execution method. A special helper method for converting the `IN` parameters read from the property files as a `String` into a `Vector` object is also provided. A series of exceptions are handled and the status of each attempt is reported but left out of the following code snippet:

```
public static void main(String[] args)
  {
    if(args.length == 0){
      System.out.println("Error: Run the program as:"
        + " java ejava.jdbcch09.SimplePreparedStatementExample"
        + " <propertiesFileName> ");
      System.exit(0);
    }

    String fileName = args[0];
    SimplePreparedStatementExample simplePreparedStatementExample =
➥new SimplePreparedStatementExample();
    . . .
      // Establish properties from properties file and get connection
      simplePreparedStatementExample.setProperties(fileName);
      Connection connection = simplePreparedStatementExample.
➥getConnection();
    . . .
      // Get SQL statements from properties file and execute them...

      String sqlString  = (String)
         (simplePreparedStatementExample.getProperties()).
➥get("PREPARED_SQL_QUERY_STATEMENT");
      String parameters  = (String)
         (simplePreparedStatementExample.getProperties()).
➥get("PREPARED_SQL_QUERY_STATEMENT_VALUES");
      Vector values = simplePreparedStatementExample.
➥parseStringToVector(parameters);

      boolean executionStatus = simplePreparedStatementExample.
➥execute(sqlString,values);
    . . .
      String insertString = (String)
        (simplePreparedStatementExample.getProperties()).
➥get("PREPARED_SQL_INSERT_STATEMENT");
      String insertValuesString = (String)
        (simplePreparedStatementExample.getProperties()).
➥get("PREPARED_SQL_INSERT_STATEMENT_VALUES");
      values = simplePreparedStatementExample.
➥parseStringToVector(insertValuesString);

      int nResults = simplePreparedStatementExample.
➥executeUpdate(insertString, values);
    . . .
      String updateString = (String)
         (simplePreparedStatementExample.getProperties()).
➥get("PREPARED_SQL_UPDATE_STATEMENT");
```

```
      String updateValuesString = (String)
       (simplePreparedStatementExample.getProperties()).
➥get("PREPARED_SQL_UPDATE_STATEMENT_VALUES");
      values =  simplePreparedStatementExample.
➥parseStringToVector(updateValuesString);

       nResults =  simplePreparedStatementExample.
➥executeUpdate(updateString, values);
    . . .
      String sqlString  = (String)
        (simplePreparedStatementExample.getProperties()).
➥get("PREPARED_SQL_QUERY_STATEMENT");
      String parameters = (String)
        (simplePreparedStatementExample.getProperties()).
➥get("PREPARED_SQL_QUERY_STATEMENT_VALUES");
      Vector values = simplePreparedStatementExample.
➥parseStringToVector(parameters);

      ResultSet rs = simplePreparedStatementExample.
➥executeQuery(sqlString,values);

      simplePreparedStatementExample.closeStatement();
}
```

In addition to the state inherited from `ConnectToDatabase`, another private variable is used to store a `PreparedStatement` object:

```
private PreparedStatement statement; // PreparedStatement object
```

In addition to the properties contained in the `JDBCCH09Properties.txt` property file used for the `ConnectToDatabase` example, the following properties from the `JDBCCH09Properties.txt` property file are now used for this example:

```
#Prepared QUERY Statement
PREPARED_SQL_QUERY_STATEMENT = SELECT * FROM TSHIRTS.CUSTOMER
➥WHERE FIRST_NAME = ?
PREPARED_SQL_QUERY_STATEMENT_VALUES = Roy

#Prepared Insert

PREPARED_SQL_INSERT_STATEMENT = INSERT
➥ INTO TSHIRTS.CUSTOMER VALUES(?,?,?,?,?,?,?,?,?,?,?)
PREPARED_SQL_INSERT_STATEMENT_VALUES =130,John,Hiller,Miller,
➥ 125 S St.,C6,Baltimore,MD,20100,4104444444,jh@jhiller.com

#Prepared Update
PREPARED_SQL_UPDATE_STATEMENT = UPDATE TSHIRTS.STATE SET STATE_NAME =
➥'California' WHERE CODE = ?
PREPARED_SQL_UPDATE_STATEMENT_VALUES =CA
```

When each prepared statement is executed, a new `PreparedStatement` object is created and stored locally in this example using the `createStatement()` method as shown here:

```
protected void createStatement(String sqlString)
    throws SQLException, Exception
  {
 Connection connection = super.getConnection();
      statement = connection.prepareStatement(sqlString);

  }
```

Three types of SQL command executions are performed in the `execute()`, `executeQuery()`, and `executeUpdate()` methods. For each method, a `PreparedStatement` is created and the SQL `String` and `Vector` of `IN` values passed into the method are used to call `setObject()` for each prepared statement value. Finally, the appropriate command execution method on the `PreparedStatement` object is called. These three execute method variations are shown here:

```
public boolean execute(String sqlString, Vector values)
    throws SQLException, Exception
  {

    createStatement(sqlString);
for(int i = 1; i <= values.size(); i++){
      statement.setObject(i,values.elementAt(i-1));
    }
    boolean returnValue = statement.execute();
    return returnValue;
  }
  public ResultSet executeQuery(String sqlString, Vector values)
    throws SQLException, Exception
  {

    createStatement(sqlString);

    for(int i = 1; i <= values.size(); i++){
      statement.setObject(i,values.elementAt(i-1));
    }
    ResultSet rs = statement.executeQuery();
    return rs;
  }


  public int executeUpdate(String sqlString, Vector values)
    throws SQLException, Exception
  {

    createStatement(sqlString);
```

```
    for(int i = 1; i <= values.size(); i++){
      statement.setObject(i,values.elementAt(i-1));
    }
    int returnValue = statement.executeUpdate();
    return returnValue;
}
```

JDBC Result Sets

Creating statements and executing SQL queries would be of little value if there were not a way to actually retrieve the results of your database query. The `java.sql.ResultSet` interface encapsulates an object that represents zero or more results from a database query. Each result in a `ResultSet` represents a database row that can span one or more tables (which could be the result of a join). Figure 9.10 presents a class diagram depicting the class interfaces and classes involved with `ResultSet` usage. Because the `ResultSet` class has an absolutely enormous number of methods, we do not show them all here. Although most of the methods are simply type-safe `getXXX()` and `updateXXX()` methods, the total number of methods on the JDBC 2.0 `ResultSet` interface amounts to 129 methods! The `java.sql.ResultSetMetaData` interface simply provides information about the `ResultSet` itself such as the types and properties of the columns returned from the query.

Manipulating Result Sets

A `ResultSet` object is returned from the `executeQuery()` method call on the `Statement` interface or one of its sub-interfaces. A `ResultSet` object may also be returned to the `Statement` object when `execute()` is called on the `Statement` object, but it is not directly returned from the method call. Rather, the `Statement` method `getResultSet()` may be called to obtain a handle on the returned `ResultSet` object. A null value is returned from `getResultSet()` if there is no result set object or if an update count was returned instead due to a SQL update command. Because a SQL statement executed with the `execute()` statement may sometimes produce more than one `ResultSet` object, the `getMoreResults()` method on the `Statement` interface may be called to move to the next `ResultSet` and return a true `boolean` value indicating that a `ResultSet` was returned. Any existing result sets that were returned from `getResultSet()` are closed when the `getMoreResults()` method is called. The `execute()` command may also produce multiple updates and the method `getMoreResults()` will return `false` if the current result was an update. Thus, if `getResultSet()` returns a null and `getMoreResults()` returns `false`, the method `getUpdateCount()` may be used to return the number of updates present for the current result.

FIGURE 9.10

A result set class diagram.

Only one ResultSet instance (which maps to an underlying cursor) can be open at a time for a particular statement. Whenever a new query is issued on a Statement, or a new ResultSet is obtained via the getResultSet() method on the Statement object, the existing ResultSet instance and associated cursor are closed. Of course, multiple statements may be created so that more than one cursor can be open at a time. However, different database configurations will limit the number of cursors that can be open associated with a single connection.

It should also be noted that different ResultSet driver implementations embody different design decisions for populating the ResultSet with data. Implementations may perhaps dynamically consult the database for data as the ResultSet is scrolled forward, may perhaps build up an entire set of data at once and contain this on the client-side ResultSet buffer, or may implement some hybrid of these two extremes.

After a handle to a ResultSet object is obtained, you will typically want to retrieve the column data from each row, scroll forward to the next row, retrieve its data, and then continue this sequence until there is no more data to retrieve from the ResultSet. The methods used to accomplish this task are the get*XXX*() series of methods and the next() method on the ResultSet object. When a ResultSet is returned, the cursor is initially positioned before the first row. When the next() method is called, a boolean value is returned indicating whether there is a next row and then positions itself on that row. Thus, if at least one row is returned in a ResultSet, the first call to next() will return true and be positioned on the first row. Calls to one of the get*XXX*() methods are then to be made to retrieve data from the current row. There are additional methods with JDBC 2.0 that allow for bidirectional and positional scrolling through result sets, but this topic is deferred until Chapter 10, "Advanced JDBC."

Two general forms of get*XXX*() exist. One form takes a column index int, and the other form takes a column name String as an input parameter. Each form of get*XXX*() returns a type corresponding to the actual *XXX* type asked for in the get*XXX*() call. The next section lists the various Java types that are mapped from SQL types via the get*XXX*() methods available to the API programmer. As an example, to obtain the FIRST_NAME in the second column from the CUSTOMER query SELECT * FROM CUSTOMER, you can use either call on a ResultSet object named resultSet:

```
String firstName = resultSet.getString(2);
        // or
String firstName = resultSet.getString("FIRST_NAME");
```

9

BASIC JDBC

Obtaining Information About Result Sets

If you call getMetaData() on a ResultSet object, you can obtain a handle to a java.sql.ResultSetMetaData object that can be used to provide dynamic information about the returned ResultSet object. With the ResultSetMetaData object, the following key types of calls can be made:

- `int getColumnCount()` returns the number of columns associated with this `ResultSet` object.
- `String getColumnName(int column)` returns the name of a column.
- `String getColumnClassName(int column)` returns the class name of a column (JDBC 2.0 only).
- `String getColumnLabel(int column)` returns the column label recommended for display purposes.
- `int getColumnDisplaySize(int column)` returns the column's maximum character width.
- `int getColumnType(int column)` returns the `java.sql.Types` constant value of a particular column.
- `String getColumnTypeName(int column)` returns a column's type name specific to the database.
- `String getSchemaName(int column)` returns the table's schema name associated with a column.
- `String getCatalogName(int column)` returns a column's table catalog name given a column number.
- `String getTableName(int column)` returns the table name associated with a column.
- `boolean isCaseSensitive(int column)` indicates if the column is case-sensitive.
- `boolean isReadOnly(int column)` indicates if the column is read-only.
- `boolean isWritable(int column)` indicates if it is possible for this column to be writable.
- `boolean isDefinitelyWritable(int column)` indicates if a write will absolutely succeed on this column.
- `int isNullable(int column)` indicates if the column is able to be null.
- `boolean isSearchable(int column)` indicates if the column can be used in a `where` clause.

Example: Manipulating Result Sets and Result Set MetaData

This next example demonstrates how to use `ResultSet` and `ResultSetMetaData` objects. The example code is contained in the `ejava.jdbcch09.ResultSetExample` class. This example actually builds off of the simple statement example with the `ResultSetExample` class extending the `SimpleStatementExample` class:

```
public class ResultSetExample extends SimpleStatementExample{...}
```

NOTE

The following complete code example can be found on the CD in the `examples\src\ejava\jdbcch09` directory using the `ResultSetExample`, `SimpleStatementExample.java`, `ConnectToDatabase.java`, and `JDBCCH09Properties.txt` files. Some exception handling and other handling mechanisms have been left out of the book here for simplicity in describing the example. A runresultset.bat example script file is also contained in the `examples\src\ejava\jdbcch09` directory to demonstrate how to build and execute this example software. Appendix A provides more general database and example software configuration procedures.

The `main()` method of `ResultSetExample` is invoked as

```
java ejava.jdbcch09.ResultSetExample <propertiesFileName>
```

where the `<propertiesFileName>` is the location of a properties filename with the properties set as in the `JDBCCH09Properties.txt` file. The `main()` method calls `setProperties()` and `getConnection()` on the example object as it did in the `ConnectToDatabase` example to load the property file and establish the database connection. A simple SQL query `String` is read from the loaded `Properties` object and then used to execute a simple SQL statement on the `ResultSetExample` object's inherited `executeQuery()` method. The returned `ResultSet` is then used to analyze the meta-data of the `ResultSet` and then parse and display the entire `ResultSet` structure. The key elements of the `main()` function are shown here:

```
public static void main(String[] args)
 {
    if(args.length == 0){
      System.out.println("Error: Run the program as:"
       + " java ejava.jdbcch09.ResultSetExample <propertiesFileName> ");
      System.exit(0);
    }

    String fileName = args[0];
    ResultSetExample resultSetExample = new ResultSetExample();
    . . .
      // Establish properties from properties file and get connection
      resultSetExample.setProperties(fileName);
      Connection connection = resultSetExample.getConnection();

      // Get SQL from properties, execute, get and view results...
```

```
      String sqlString = (String)(resultSetExample.getProperties())
➥.get("SQL_QUERY_STATEMENT");
      ResultSet resultSet = resultSetExample.executeQuery(sqlString);

      ResultSetExample.analyzeMetaData(resultSet);

      ResultSetExample.parseResultData(resultSet);

      resultSetExample.closeStatement();
    . . .
}
```

The ResultSetExample class also has one additional member variable to store the ResultSet object in addition to the state its base class maintains:

```
private ResultSet resultSet; // ResultSet Object
```

The analyzeMetaData() call on ResultSetExample obtains a handle to the ResultSet object's ResultSetMetaData and displays some key information about the result set columns such as the column name, column label, and column type name. A special helper function called getColumnClass() is also provided here to demonstrate how you might deduce the column class in JDBC 1.0 with the column java.sql.Types information. In JDBC 2.0, one might choose to use the new method getColumnClassName() to assist with obtaining some column class information. The analyzeMetaData() and getColumnClass() methods are shown here:

```
public static void analyzeMetaData(ResultSet resultSet)
    throws SQLException
  {
    ResultSetMetaData rMetaData = resultSet.getMetaData();

    for(int i = 1; i<= rMetaData.getColumnCount(); i++){
      System.out.println("Column Name : "+rMetaData.getColumnName(i));
      System.out.println("Column Label :  "+rMetaData.getColumnLabel(i));
      System.out.println("Column Display Size : "+
      ➥rMetaData.getColumnDisplaySize(i));
      int type = rMetaData.getColumnType(i);
      System.out.println("Column Java Type :  " + getColumnClass(type));
      System.out.println("Column Type Name :  "
      ➥+rMetaData.getColumnTypeName(i));
      System.out.println("Null Value Allowed :  " +rMetaData.isNullable(i));
      System.out.println("Is Read Only :  " +rMetaData.isReadOnly(i));
    }
  }

public static Class getColumnClass(int type)
  {
```

```
        switch(type) {
          case Types.CHAR:
          case Types.VARCHAR:
          case Types.LONGVARCHAR:
              return String.class;

          case Types.BIT:
              return Boolean.class;

          case Types.TINYINT:
          case Types.SMALLINT:
          case Types.INTEGER:
              return Integer.class;

          case Types.BIGINT:
              return Long.class;

          case Types.FLOAT:
          case Types.DOUBLE:
              return Double.class;

          case Types.DATE:
              return java.sql.Date.class;

          default:
              return Object.class;
        }
    }
```

Finally, the rather long `parseResultData()` call on `ResultSetExample` demonstrates how to scroll through a `ResultSet` object and use the `getXXX()` methods to obtain the values from the column of interest. The `parseResultData()` method is generalized such that for each column index in the row, we obtain the `java.sql.Types` information about the column, output the mapping from `java.sql.Types` value to the Java type, and then print the column value. The `parseResultData()` method is shown here:

```
public static void parseResultData(ResultSet resultSet)
    throws SQLException
  {
    ResultSetMetaData rMetaData = resultSet.getMetaData();
    int nColumns = rMetaData.getColumnCount();

    while(resultSet.next()){
      for(int i = 1; i <= nColumns; i++ ){
         int type =  rMetaData.getColumnType(i);
         switch(type) {
```

```
            case Types.CHAR:
                System.out.print("(CHAR->String "+
➥resultSet.getString(i) + "):");
                break;
            case Types.VARCHAR:
                System.out.print("(VARCHAR->String " +
➥resultSet.getString(i) + "):");
                break;
            case Types.LONGVARCHAR:
                System.out.print("(LONGVARCHAR->String " +
➥resultSet.getString(i) + "):");
                break;
            case Types.BIT:
                System.out.print("(BIT->byte " +
➥resultSet.getByte(i)+ "):");
                break;
            case Types.TINYINT:
                System.out.print("(TINYINT->int " +
➥resultSet.getInt(i)+ "):");
                break;
            case Types.SMALLINT:
                System.out.print("(SMALLINT->int " +
➥resultSet.getInt(i)+ "):");
                break;
            case Types.INTEGER:
                System.out.print("(INTEGER->int " +
➥resultSet.getInt(i)+ "):");
                break;
            case Types.BIGINT:
                System.out.print("(BIGINT->long " +
➥resultSet.getLong(i)+ "):");
                break;
            case Types.FLOAT:
                System.out.print("(FLOAT->float " +
➥resultSet.getFloat(i)+ "):");
                break;
            case Types.DOUBLE:
                System.out.print("(DOUBLE->double " +
➥resultSet.getDouble(i)+ "):");
                break;
            case Types.DATE:
                System.out.print("(DATE->Date " +
➥resultSet.getDate(i)+ "):");
                break;
            case Types.TIME:
                System.out.print("(TIME->Time " +
➥resultSet.getTime(i)+ "):");
```

```
                break;
        case Types.TIMESTAMP:
                System.out.print("(TIMESTAP->Timestamp " +
➥resultSet.getTimestamp(i)+ "):");
                break;
         default:
                System.out.print("(<other type>->Object " +
➥resultSet.getObject(i)+ "):");
                break;
        }
      }
      System.out.println();
    }
  }
```

SQL and Java Mappings

We have seen some examples by now demonstrating how to obtain column data from a `ResultSet` as Java types. Database vendors may instruct you to use their type names when coding your applications, but a much more portable means for manipulating data is possible when you stick with the JDBC standard SQL and Java mappings. Table 9.2 shows the standard mappings for SQL types to Java types, and Table 9.3 show the standard mappings for Java types to SQL types.

TABLE 9.2 SQL Type to Java Type Mapping

From SQL Type	*To Java Language Type*
CHAR	java.lang.String
VARCHAR	java.lang.String
LONGVARCHAR	java.lang.String
BIT	boolean
BINARY	byte[ ]
VARBINARY	byte[ ]
LONGVARBINARY	byte[ ]
TINYINT	byte
SMALLINT	short
INTEGER	int
BIGINT	long
REAL	float

continues

TABLE 9.2 Continued

From SQL Type	*To Java Language Type*
FLOAT	double
DOUBLE	double
NUMERIC	java.lang.math.BigDecimal
DECIMAL	java.lang.math.BigDecimal
DATE	java.sql.Date
TIME	java.sql.Time
TIMESTAMP	java.sql.Timestamp

TABLE 9.3 Java Type to SQL Type Mapping

From Java Language Type	*To SQL Type*
String	VARCHAR or LONGVARCHAR
boolean	BIT
byte [ ]	VARBINARY or LONGVARBINARY
byte	TINYINT
short	SMALLINT
int	INTEGER
long	BIGINT
float	REAL
double	DOUBLE
java.math.BigDecimal	NUMERIC
java.sql.Date	DATE
java.sql.Date	TIME
java.sql.Date	TIMESTAMP

When a `String` is mapped to a SQL type, it typically maps to a `VARCHAR`. However, a `String` can also map to a `LONGVARCHAR` if the `String`'s size exceeds some driver-specific `VARCHAR` length limit. Similarly, `byte` arrays map to either a `VARBINARY` or a `LONGVARBINARY` depending on the driver's length limit for `VARBINARY`. Fixed-length SQL strings read from the database are usually read in as a `String` of the same length but with some padded spaces at the end. `LONGVARCHAR`s that are excessively long may be retrieved from the database using an input stream `get`*`XXX`*`()` function such as `getAsciiStream()` or `getUnicodeStream()` on the `ResultSet` object. Similarly, the `LONGVARBINARY` value can also be retrieved as an input stream.

The DECIMAL and NUMERIC types are used when absolute precision is needed. Thus, database values for currency are typically returned as either DECIMAL or NUMERIC types. These types can also be retrieved as Strings using getString() on the ResultSet object.

The java.util.Date class does not provide enough granularity for certain database timestamp values and also includes both date and time information that is not suitable for how the SQL types delineate date and time as separate entities. To this end, three classes that extend java.util.Date are employed as basic JDBC type helpers. These are the java.sql.Date, java.sql.Time, and java.sql.Timestamp types:

- java.sql.Date stores hour, second, and millisecond fields of java.util.Date as zero.
- java.sql.Time stores the year, month, and day of java.util.Date as the "zero date" of January 1, 1970.
- java.sql.Timestamp adds nanosecond precision to the time provided by java.util.Date.

JDBC MetaData

It is sometimes necessary to obtain information about the database to which you are connected. Information such as the table descriptions, level of SQL support, and stored procedure listings is sometimes useful in creating your Java applications. Sometimes certain databases and database drivers are able to support certain JDBC calls but others are not. This becomes problematic when attempting to offer seamless portability across databases and database drivers. Although you can log exceptions thrown when such support is not offered, it may make more sense to determine a priori what support is provided before a call is even made. The java.sql.DatabaseMetaData class can provide such database, table schema, and driver support information. However, some drivers will not even support certain DatabaseMetaData calls. Such calls typically result in a SQLException being thrown.

Obtaining Information about Databases and Drivers

A DatabaseMetaData object handle is obtained by calling a Connection object's getMetaData() method. Some DatabaseMetaData calls return information in the form of ResultSet objects. Thus, the getXXX() methods can be used to obtain information from the ResultSet as you would with a regular SQL query. With the DatabaseMetaData object, the following key types of calls can be made:

- ResultSet getSchemas() returns a set of schema names available in the database.
- ResultSet getCatalogs() returns the catalog names used in the database.
- ResultSet getTables(String catalog, String schemaPattern, String tableNamePattern, String[] types) returns a set of tables available in a particular catalog.

- `ResultSet getTableTypes()` returns the set of table types available in the database.
- `String getCatalogSeparator()` returns the separator value between catalog and table names.
- `ResultSet getTablePrivileges(String catalog, String schemaPattern, String tableNamePattern)` returns a set of access permissions for each table in this database.
- `ResultSet getColumnPrivileges(String catalog, String schema, String table, String columnNamePattern)` returns the access permissions for a table's columns.
- `ResultSet getColumns(String catalog, String schemaPattern, String tableNamePattern, String columnNamePattern)` returns a description of the table's columns.
- `ResultSet getPrimaryKeys(String catalog, String schema, String table)` retrieves information describing this table's primary keys.
- `ResultSet getExportedKeys(String catalog, String schema, String table)` retrieves information describing which foreign keys reference this table's primary keys.
- `ResultSet getImportedKeys(String catalog, String schema, String table)` retrieves information describing which primary keys are referenced by this table's foreign keys.
- `String getDatabaseProductName()` returns the database product name.
- `String getDatabaseProductVersion()` returns the database product version.
- `String getDriverName()` returns the JDBC driver's name.
- `String getDriverVersion()` returns the JDBC driver's version.
- `String getURL()` returns the database URL.
- `String getUserName()` returns the username associated with this connection.
- `Connection getConnection()` returns the connection object associated with this metadata (JDBC 2.0).
- `int getMaxConnections()` returns the maximum number of connections allowed.
- `int getMaxStatements()` returns the maximum number of statements allowed to be open at one time.
- `ResultSet getTypeInfo()` returns a list of standard SQL types supported by the database.
- `boolean supportsANSI92EntryLevelSQL()` indicates if it is ANSI92 entry level SQL compliant.
- `boolean supportsANSI92IntermediateSQL()` indicates if it is ANSI92 intermediate level SQL compliant.

- `boolean supportsANSI92FullSQL()` indicates if it is fully ANSI92 SQL compliant.
- `boolean supportsMinimumSQLGrammar()` indicates if it is ODBC minimum SQL compliant.
- `boolean supportsCoreSQLGrammar()` indicates if it is ODBC core SQL compliant.
- `boolean supportsExtendedSQLGrammar()` indicates if it is ODBC extended SQL compliant.
- `boolean supportsOuterJoins()` indicates if it has some outer join support.
- `boolean supportsLimitedOuterJoins()` indicates if it has limited outer join support.
- `boolean supportsFullOuterJoins()` indicates if full nested outer joins are supported.
- `boolean supportsLikeEscapeClause()` indicates if it supports `LIKE` clauses.

Example: Simple Database Meta-Data Usage

This next example demonstrates a few uses of the `DatabaseMetaData` object. The example code is contained in the `ejava.jdbcch09.DatabaseMetaDataExample` class. This `DatabaseMetaDataExample` class extends the `ConnectToDatabase` example class:

```
public class DatabaseMetaDataExample extends ConnectToDatabase{...}
```

NOTE

The following complete code example can be found on the CD in `examples\src\ejava\jdbcch09` directory using the `DatabaseMetaDataExample.java`, `ResultSetExample.java`, `ConnectToDatabase.java`, and `JDBCCH09Properties.txt` files. Some exception handling and other handling mechanisms have been left out of the book here for simplicity in describing the example. A `runmetadata.bat` example script file is also included in the examples\src\ejava\jdbcch09 directory for building and executing this example software. General database and example software configuration steps are described in Appendix A.

The `main()` method of `DatabaseMetaDataExample` is invoked as

```
java ejava.jdbcch09.DatabaseMetaDataExample <propertiesFileName>
```

where the `<propertiesFileName>` is the location of a properties filename with the properties set as in the `JDBCCH09Properties.txt` file. The `main()` method calls `setProperties()` and `getConnection()` on the example class as it did in the `ConnectToDatabase` example to load the property file and establish the database connection. The schemas, tables, columns, and keys in the database are then retrieved and listed. The key elements of the `main()` method are defined here:

```
public static void main(String[] args)
  {
    if(args.length == 0){
      System.out.println("Error: Run the program as:"
        + " java ejava.jdbcch09.DatabaseMetaDataExample "
 +   " <propertiesFileName> ");
      System.exit(0);
    }

    String fileName = args[0];
    DatabaseMetaDataExample databaseMetaDataExample
      = new DatabaseMetaDataExample();
. . .
      // Establish properties from properties file and get connection
      databaseMetaDataExample.setProperties(fileName);
      Connection connection = databaseMetaDataExample.getConnection();
      // Induce analysis of meta data in various ways...
      databaseMetaDataExample.printAvailableSchemas();
      databaseMetaDataExample.printTablesInAllSchemas();
      String schemaName = (String)(databaseMetaDataExample.
➥getProperties()).get("SCHEMA_NAME");
      databaseMetaDataExample.printTablesInASchema(schemaName);
      databaseMetaDataExample.printColumnsInATable(schemaName,
➥"CUSTOMER");
      databaseMetaDataExample.printPrimaryKeysInATable(schemaName,
➥"CUSTOMER");
    . . .
  }
```

The `DatabaseMetaDataExample` also maintains one `DatabaseMetaData` object:

```
private DatabaseMetaData dbMetaData; // Database MetaData Object
```

This example also makes use of one additional property in the property file:

```
#Database schema name
SCHEMA_NAME =TSHIRTS
```

All the example methods called from `main()` need first to create the `DatabaseMetaData` handle from `getDatabaseMetaData()`:

```
public void getDatabaseMetaData()
    throws SQLException, Exception
  {
     if(dbMetaData == null){
```

```
      Connection connection = super.getConnection();
      dbMetaData = connection.getMetaData();
     }

  }
```

The printAvailableSchemas() method on the DatabaseMetaDataExample illustrates obtaining and displaying the database schema information. This example uses ResultSetExample to parse and display the returned ResultSet. The printAvailableSchemas() method is defined as shown here:

```
public void printAvailableSchemas()
    throws SQLException, Exception
  {
    if(dbMetaData == null){
      getDatabaseMetaData();
    }

    ResultSet resultSet = dbMetaData.getSchemas();
    ResultSetExample.parseResultData(resultSet);
    resultSet.close();
  }
```

The printTablesInAllSchemas() method on the DatabaseMetaDataExample retrieves and displays all the tables and views available in the database. After obtaining the schemas available as a ResultSet object using the DatabaseMetaData.getSchemas() call, we retrieve the schema name from each ResultSet element. The schema name in addition to a catalog, table name pattern, schema pattern, and table type specification are used to retrieve a list of all the tables and views in the database using DatabaseMetaData.getTables(). A null is used to indicate no catalog preference, and a null is also used for the table name pattern to indicate that all tables in the current schema should be retrieved. Finally, we use the TABLE and VIEW types to indicate that database table and database view descriptions should be retrieved. The printTablesInAllSchemas() method is described here:

```
public  void printTablesInAllSchemas()
    throws SQLException, Exception
  {
    if(dbMetaData == null){
getDatabaseMetaData();
    }

    ResultSet resultSet = dbMetaData.getSchemas();

    while(resultSet.next()){
      String schemaName = resultSet.getString(1);
```

```
        String catalog = null;
        String schemaPattern = schemaName;
        String tableNamePattern = null;
        String types[]  = {"TABLE", "VIEW"};

        ResultSet tableInformation = dbMetaData.getTables(catalog,
➥schemaPattern,tableNamePattern, types);
        ResultSetExample.parseResultData(tableInformation);
      }
    }
```

The `printTablesInASchema()` method on the `DatabaseMetaDataExample` illustrates how to obtain information about a particular schema in the database. The schema name is passed in from a value read from the property file. The `printTablesInASchema()` method is shown here:

```
public  void printTablesInASchema(String schemaName)
    throws SQLException, Exception
  {
    if(dbMetaData == null){
getDatabaseMetaData();
    }

    String catalog = null;
    String schemaPattern = schemaName;
        String tableNamePattern = null;
    String types[]  = {"TABLE", "VIEW"};

    ResultSet tableInformation = dbMetaData.getTables(catalog,
➥schemaPattern,tableNamePattern, types);
    ResultSetExample.parseResultData(tableInformation);
  }
```

The `printColumnsInATable()` method on `DatabaseMetaDataExample` illustrates how to obtain a description of the columns in a database for a particular table. The `printColumnsInATable()` method is defined here:

```
public void printColumnsInATable(String schemaName, String tableName)
    throws SQLException , Exception
  {

    if(dbMetaData == null){
 getDatabaseMetaData();
    }

    String catalogName = null;
    String columnPattern = null;
```

```
    ResultSet resultSet = dbMetaData.getColumns(catalogName,
➥schemaName,tableName, columnPattern);
    ResultSetExample.parseResultData(resultSet);
  }
```

Finally, the `printPrimaryKeysInATable()` method demonstrates how to obtain information regarding the primary keys associated with a particular schema name and table name. Here, we read the schema name from a file and pass in the value `CUSTOMER` for the table name. The `printPrimaryKeysInATable()` method is defined as shown here:

```
public  void printPrimaryKeysInATable(String schemaName, String tableName)
    throws SQLException, Exception
  {
    if(dbMetaData == null){
 getDatabaseMetaData();
    }

    String catalog = null;
    String schemaPattern = schemaName;

    ResultSet tableInformation = dbMetaData.getPrimaryKeys(catalog,
➥schemaPattern,tableName);
    ResultSetExample.parseResultData(tableInformation);
  }
```

Conclusions

JDBC offers a database-independent means for performing some of the most important types of operations needed in enterprise systems to enable enterprise data for use in Java applications. JDBC offers a simple means for configuring different types of drivers, establishing database connections, executing SQL statements, manipulating query result data, and obtaining meta-data about the database itself. Most of the core features of JDBC have been presented in this chapter. The next chapter describes more advanced features of JDBC that can be used in building your enterprise applications.

Advanced JDBC

CHAPTER

10

IN THIS CHAPTER

- Scrollable Result Sets 250
- Updateable Result Sets 262
- Batch Updates 274
- Advanced Data Types 278
- Row Sets 295
- Stored Procedures 298
- Database Naming via JNDI 305
- Connection Pools 307
- Distributed Transactions 310

In the preceding chapter, you learned the basic steps for configuring and using JDBC to enable your enterprise data for use within enterprise applications. This chapter builds on the preceding one with advanced material describing some of the more sophisticated and newer features of JDBC. The JDBC 2.0 features in particular are plentiful and are covered from the perspective of how you, the enterprise developer, will be able to utilize these features in your enterprise applications.

In this chapter, you will learn:

- The definition and use of scrollable result sets with JDBC 2.0.
- The definition and use of updateable result sets with JDBC 2.0.
- The submission of a batch of SQL update statements with JDBC 2.0.
- The use of custom and more advanced SQL types with JDBC 2.0.
- The concepts behind JDBC 2.0 row sets and how they can be used in enterprise applications.
- Calling database functions and user-defined stored procedures from JDBC.
- The connection of JDBC clients to a database through a middle tier via JDBC 2.0 data sources and JNDI.
- The concepts and architecture behind middle-tier JDBC 2.0 connection pooling.
- The concepts and architecture behind distributed transaction handling in the middle tier with JDBC 2.0.

Scrollable Result Sets

The preceding chapter demonstrated how to view the data returned from a query result via use of a `java.sql.ResultSet` object instance. After reading a row from the `ResultSet` object, you were shown how to make a call to `ResultSet.next()` to advance to the next row and retrieve any of that row's data. This model of scrolling forward in a `ResultSet` to retrieve its data via calls to `next()` was the only scroll model possible in JDBC 1.0. The JDBC 2.0 Core API extends the scrolling model for `ResultSet` objects by adding the capability to scroll backward as well as forward in a `ResultSet`. Furthermore, the capability to indicate which row you want to point to in the `ResultSet` can now be indicated in terms of an absolute position as well as a position relative to the current row you are pointing to.

In light of this expanded model for result set scrollability, the JDBC 2.0 Core API specification classifies result sets according to three types:

- Forward-only
- Scroll-insensitive
- Scroll-sensitive

Forward-only result sets allow one to advance forward only using `ResultSet.next()`. This was the only scroll model allowed in JDBC 1.0. A `static public final int` identifier is defined in the `ResultSet` class to identify forward-only result set types:

```
ResultSet.TYPE_FORWARD_ONLY
```

Scroll-insensitive result sets allow one to scroll forward and backward and also allow for absolute and relative positioning. However, the state of the query result values returned from a query remains the same throughout the lifetime of the returned `ResultSet` object instance. Thus it can be said that this `ResultSet` type is insensitive to any database update operations performed because the result set no longer interacts with the database after it is created. This is the `ResultSet static public final int` field to identify scroll-insensitive result set types:

```
ResultSet.TYPE_SCROLL_INSENSITIVE
```

Scroll-sensitive result sets also allow one to scroll forward and backward and allow for absolute and relative positioning. However, these result set types permit one to dynamically view changes that are made to the underlying data. Thus it can be said that this `ResultSet` type is sensitive to any database operations performed because the result set interacts with the database even after it is created. This is the `static public final int` in `ResultSet` for identifying scroll-sensitive result set types:

```
ResultSet.TYPE_SCROLL_SENSITIVE
```

Creating Scrollable Result Sets

When calling `createStatement()` or `prepareStatement()` on a `Connection` object, the default scroll model assumed for a `ResultSet` that might be returned by such a `Statement` or `PreparedStatement` is forward-only. JDBC 2.0 now allows for a `Statement` and `PreparedStatement` to be created specifying a preferred `ResultSet` type identifier as a parameter to the `createStatement()` and `prepareStatement()` methods. These methods also take a parameter for specifying concurrency type used when working with updateable result sets. Updateable result sets will be covered in the next section, but for now we will always assume a non-updateable result set type with a `ResultSet.CONCUR_READ_ONLY` parameter value. After creating a statement with a specified result set type, the `executeQuery()` and `execute()` methods may be called as usual to generate `ResultSet` objects. The significance of using the `ResultSet.CONCUR_READ_ONLY` type for the examples in this section simply indicates that the result set objects returned from executed statements are read-only and cannot be used to update the database, as will be demonstrated in the next section describing updateable result sets. However, the returned `ResultSet` is now specialized according to whether it is a forward-only, scroll-insensitive, or scroll-sensitive result set type.

The signatures for creating `Statement` objects and `PreparedStatement` objects from a `Connection` object with a preferred result set type are defined here:

```
public Statement createStatement(int resultSetType,
➥int resultSetConcurrency) throws SQLException;
public PreparedStatement prepareStatement(String sql,
➥int resultSetType, int resultSetConcurrency) throws SQLException;
```

The following code snippets illustrate a few options now available to the JDBC API programmer for creating statements that can return different result set types:

```
Connection connection = ...// Get a connection as usual.
String sql = "SELECT * FROM TSHIRTS.CUSTOMER";

// Return forward-only result sets
Statement s1 = connection.createStatement();
ResultSet r1= s1.executeQuery(sql);

// Also returns forward-only result sets
Statement s2 =
    connection.createStatement(ResultSet.TYPE_FORWARD_ONLY,
                               ResultSet.CONCUR_READ_ONLY);
ResultSet r2= s2.executeQuery(sql);

// Return scroll insensitive result sets
Statement s3 =
    connection.createStatement(ResultSet.TYPE_SCROLL_INSENSITIVE,
                                 ResultSet.CONCUR_READ_ONLY);
ResultSet r3= s3.executeQuery(sql);

// Returns scroll sensitive result sets
PreparedStatement ps1 =
       connection.prepareStatement(sql, ResultSet.TYPE_SCROLL_SENSITIVE,
                                 ResultSet.CONCUR_READ_ONLY);
ResultSet r4 = ps1.executeQuery();
```

Scrolling Around Result Sets

After creating a `Statement` or `PreparedStatement` object sensitized to returning a scrollable result set (that is, either scroll-insensitive or scroll-sensitive), you will have to call `executeQuery()` or `execute()` with a SQL query command on the `Statement` or `PreparedStatement` object so that you can obtain a handle to a `ResultSet`. After you have this `ResultSet` object, you can use the JDBC 2.0 API calls for scrolling through the result set. The API calls for supporting scrollable result sets are indicated in the following list. Note that, though not shown here, each call can throw a `SQLException`. For all calls, except for `next()`, that attempt to move the cursor, a `SQLException` may be thrown if the `ResultSet` is a forward-only type. These are the key method calls on the `ResultSet` class that can be used for scrolling around result sets:

- `boolean next()` moves the cursor to the next row from the current position.
- `boolean previous()` moves the cursor to the previous row from the current position.
- `boolean first()` positions the cursor on the first row.
- `boolean isFirst()` returns `true` if the cursor is positioned on the first row.
- `void beforeFirst()` positions the cursor before the first row.
- `boolean isBeforeFirst()` returns `true` if the cursor is positioned before the first row.
- `boolean last()` positions the cursor on the last row.
- `boolean isLast()` returns `true` if the cursor is positioned on the last row.
- `void afterLast()` positions the cursor after the last row.
- `boolean isAfterLast()` returns `true` if the cursor is positioned after the last row.
- `boolean absolute(int rowNumber)` positions the cursor on the row identified by `rowNumber`. Positive `rowNumbers` position the cursor relative to the beginning of the result set. Negative `rowNumbers` position the cursor relative to the end of the result set. Position numbers can result in a cursor being placed before the first row or after the last row, but they return a `false` value to indicate that the cursor is not on the result set.
- `boolean relative(int rowNumber)` positions the cursor on the row identified by `rowNumber` relative to the current cursor position. Positive `rowNumbers` position the cursor forward relative to the current cursor position. Negative `rowNumbers` position the cursor backward relative to the current cursor position. Position numbers can result in a cursor being placed before the first row or after the last row, but they return a `false` value to indicate that the cursor is not on the result set.
- `int getRow()` returns the row number where the cursor is currently positioned.

As an example, the following call sequence (exception handling not shown) can be used on a scrollable result set to freely move around a result set in a fashion that was previously not supported in JDBC 1.0. You may recall from Chapter 9, "Basic JDBC," that an `executeQuery()` invocation on a `Statement` object returns a `ResultSet` object whose cursor is positioned before the first row. A call to `next()` on the `ResultSet` object then positions the cursor on the first row, and scrolling around the result set can proceed via some of the new scrollable result set calls, as shown here:

```
Connection connection = ... // Get connection as usual
Statement statement =
connection.createStatement(ResultSet.TYPE_SCROLL_INSENSITIVE,
                           ResultSet.CONCUR_READ_ONLY);
```

```
ResultSet rs = statement.executeQuery("SELECT * FROM CUSTOMER");
rs.next(); // Cursor is on first row
rs.absolute(10); // Cursor is on 10th row
rs.previous(); // Cursor is on 9th row
rs.relative(-3); // Cursor is on 6th row
rs.relative(4); // Cursor is on 10th row again
rs.relative(3); // Cursor is on 13th row
rs.absolute(-2); // Cursor is on 2nd to last row
rs.first(); // Cursor is on first row again.
```

Driver Support for Scrollable Result Sets

Although scrollable result sets represent a powerful and convenient new feature in JDBC 2.0, the JDBC 2.0 Core API specification currently makes scrollable result set support optional. However, the JDBC 2.0 Standard Extension API used by the J2EE does require scrollable result set support from driver vendors. Support for result set scrollability may be dynamically determined by passing in the result set type identifier to a `supportsResultSetType()` call on `DatabaseMetaData` as exemplified here:

```
DatabaseMetaData databaseMetaData
                        = ... // Obtain database meta data handle
boolean supportsFwdOnly = databaseMetaData.supportsResultSetType(
➥ResultSet.TYPE_FORWARD_ONLY);
boolean supportsScrollIns = databaseMetaData.supportsResultSetType(
➥ResultSet.TYPE_SCROLL_INSENSITIVE);
boolean supportsScrollSens = databaseMetaData.supportsResultSetType(
➥ResultSet.TYPE_SCROLL_SENSITIVE);
```

Applications may still attempt to make calls that pertain only to scrollable result sets even if the driver does not support this feature. In the event that an application attempts to create a scrollable result set not supported by an underlying driver, the driver is expected to throw a `SQLWarning` when the `Connection` object attempts to create a statement that is supposed to return result sets of the specified scrollable type. The driver is then expected to create a statement capable of returning a supported result. If an application requests use of a scrollable result set type not supported by the driver, the driver should first attempt to use some other scrollable result type that it does support; otherwise, it should use a forward-only result set type.

Even if a driver does support scrollable result sets and can create statements with a scrollable result set type, certain SQL queries may be executed on that statement object that cannot return a scrollable result set. In these cases, a `SQLWarning` should be thrown by the call and the driver should select a result set type it can support for that specific SQL query. The returned result set type may then be dynamically determined by calling `getType()` on the `ResultSet` object itself to return the result set type identifier (that is, `ResultSet.TYPE_`*`XXX`*).

You may also attempt to give your driver hints about how your application will use the result set returned. This allows the driver vendor implementation to dynamically optimize decisions that affect cache sizes and communications with the database. One such hint is the `setFetchDirection()` call on the `ResultSet` object. After a `ResultSet` object is returned, `setFetchDirection()` with a result set type identifier (that is, `ResultSet.Type_XXX`) may be used to tell the driver in which direction your application will attempt to access the result set rows. The method `getFetchDirection()` on the `ResultSet` object will return a result set type identifier defining in which direction the result set is currently optimized to return rows.

The `setFetchSize()` call on `ResultSet` may also be made to set the number of rows the driver should attempt to fetch from the database when it needs to retrieve more rows. The `getFetchSize()` call can be used to return the result set's current fetch size.

Example: Scrollable Result Sets

This next example demonstrates how to use the JDBC 2.0 scrollable result set features. The example code is contained in the `ejava.jdbcch10.ScrollableResultSetExample` class, which extends the `ejava.jdbcch09.ConnectToDatabase` class from Chapter 9:

```
public class ScrollableResultSetExample extends ConnectToDatabase { ... }
```

NOTE

The complete set of code examples for the `ScrollableResultSetExample` can be found on the CD in the `examples\src\ejava\jdbcch10` directory. Some exception handling and other handling mechanisms have been left out of the book here for simplicity but can be found in the examples on the CD. The `runscrollableresultset.bat` example Windows script can be used to build and execute this example. Appendix A, "Software Configuration," describes the general build procedures for all examples in the book and specifies those common environment variables that must be set to execute our example scripts.

Note that at the time of this writing, support for scrollable results sets was not fully adopted by all database and JDBC driver vendors. Consult Appendix A for more information on support and the vendor product with which you can test the `ScrollableResultSetExample`.

The `main()` method of `ScrollableResultSetExample` is invoked as:

```
java ejava.jdbcch10.ScrollableResultSetExample <propertiesFileName>
```

where the <propertiesFileName> is the location of a properties filename with properties set as in the JDBCCH10Properties.txt file. The main method then instantiates a new ScrollableResultSetExample object and calls setProperties() with a filename. The remaining code in main() then demonstrates the three types of ResultSet scroll models available in JDBC 2.0. The method executeQueryScrollSensitiveReadOnly() will demonstrate the creation of a scroll-sensitive result set, the method executeQueryScrollInsensitiveReadOnly() will demonstrate the creation of a scroll-insensitive result set, and the executeQueryScrollForwardOnly() will demonstrate forward-only result sets for completeness. We will also call two versions of the executeQueryScrollInsensitiveReadOnly() method to demonstrate how both a Statement and a PreparedStatement can be used to create different ResultSet types. Each result set type returned is then traversed in various ways according to a set of static print*XXX*() methods defined on the ScrollableResultSetExample class. The ScrollableResultSetExample.main() method is shown here:

```
public static void main(String[] args) {
  if (args.length == 0) {
    System.out.println("Error: run the program as "
       + " java ejava.jdbcch10.ScrollableResultSetExample
➥ <fileFileName> ");
    System.exit(0);
  }

  String fileName = args[0];
  ScrollableResultSetExample scrollableResultSetExample =
    new ScrollableResultSetExample();
...
    scrollableResultSetExample.setProperties(fileName);

    String sqlString =
      (String) (scrollableResultSetExample.getProperties())
        .get("SCROLLABLE_SQL_STATEMENT");


    System.out.println(" Scrollable Result Set Example ");

    ResultSet rs =
      scrollableResultSetExample
        .executeQueryScrollInsensitiveReadOnly(sqlString);

    scrollableResultSetExample
      .printResultSetRowsInForwardDirection(rs);
    scrollableResultSetExample
      .printResultSetRowsInReverseDirection(rs);
```

```
    scrollableResultSetExample.printResultSetNthRow(rs, 3);
    scrollableResultSetExample.printNthMinusIthRow(rs, 4, 2);
  ...
    String sqlString =
      (String) (scrollableResultSetExample.getProperties())
        .get("SCROLLABLE_SQL_STATEMENT");
    ResultSet rs =
      scrollableResultSetExample
        .executeQueryScrollSensitiveReadOnly(sqlString);

    scrollableResultSetExample
      .printResultSetRowsInForwardDirection(rs);
    scrollableResultSetExample.printResultSetNthRow(rs, 3);
...
    String sqlString =
      (String) (scrollableResultSetExample.getProperties())
        .get("SCROLLABLE_SQL_PREPARED_STATEMENT");
    Vector v = new Vector();

    v.addElement((String) (scrollableResultSetExample.getProperties())
        .get("SCROLLABLE_SQL_PREPARED_STATEMENT_VALUES"));
    System.out
      .println("Scroll Insensitve ResultSet using a PreparedStatement ");

    ResultSet rs =
      scrollableResultSetExample
        .executeQueryScrollInsensitiveReadOnly(sqlString, v);

    scrollableResultSetExample
      .printResultSetRowsInForwardDirection(rs);
    scrollableResultSetExample
      .printResultSetRowsInReverseDirection(rs);
    scrollableResultSetExample.printResultSetNthRow(rs, 3);
...
    System.out
      .println("Result Example for Scroll Forward Only using Statement");

    String sqlString =
      (String) (scrollableResultSetExample.getProperties())
        .get("SCROLLABLE_SQL_STATEMENT");
    ResultSet rs =
      scrollableResultSetExample
        .executeQueryScrollForwardOnly(sqlString);

    scrollableResultSetExample
      .printResultSetRowsInForwardDirection(rs);
  }
```

In addition to the DRIVER_CLASS and DATABASE_URL properties read in from the property file as in Chapter 9, this class also reads in a SQL statement used in regular Statement queries, as well as a parameterized statement and input values for use in a PreparedStatement. These SQL statements defined in the JDBCCH10Properties.txt file are shown here:

```
#Simple SQL Statement
SCROLLABLE_SQL_STATEMENT = SELECT * FROM TSHIRTS.CUSTOMER

#SQL Statement for Prepared Statement
SCROLLABLE_SQL_PREPARED_STATEMENT = SELECT * FROM TSHIRTS.CUSTOMER
➥ WHERE TSHIRTS.CUSTOMER.FIRST_NAME LIKE  ?
SCROLLABLE_SQL_PREPARED_STATEMENT_VALUES = %R%
```

The three types of result set scrolling used in this example first call one of two methods on the example object instance to create either a Statement or a PreparedStatement object. Each statement-creation method first creates a connection object. One getStatement() method returns a regular Statement given a result set type identifier and a concurrency type identifier. Note that the concurrency type is described in the next section. A second getStatement() method returns a PreparedStatement given a prepared statement SQL string, a result set type identifier, and a concurrency type identifier. Both getStatement() methods are defined here:

```
protected Statement getStatement(int scrollType, int updateType)
        throws SQLException, Exception {
  Connection connection = super.getConnection();
  connection.setAutoCommit(false);
  Statement statement = connection.createStatement(scrollType,
          updateType);

  return statement;
}

protected PreparedStatement getStatement(String sqlString,
                                         int scrollType,
                                         int updateType) throws SQLException,
                                         Exception {
  Connection connection = super.getConnection();
  connection.setAutoCommit(false);
  PreparedStatement preparedStatement =
    connection.prepareStatement(sqlString, scrollType, updateType);

  return preparedStatement;
}
```

The four forms of execute*XXX*() called on the ScrollableResultSetExample object by main() simply demonstrate how to create an appropriate statement, execute a query on the statement, and return the result set object:

```
public ResultSet executeQueryScrollForwardOnly(String sqlString)
        throws SQLException, Exception {
  Statement statement = getStatement(ResultSet.TYPE_FORWARD_ONLY,
                                     ResultSet.CONCUR_READ_ONLY);
  ResultSet rs = statement.executeQuery(sqlString);

  return rs;
}

public ResultSet executeQueryScrollSensitiveReadOnly(String sqlString)
        throws SQLException, Exception {
  Statement statement = getStatement(ResultSet.TYPE_SCROLL_SENSITIVE,
                                     ResultSet.CONCUR_READ_ONLY);
  ResultSet rs = statement.executeQuery(sqlString);

  return rs;
}

public ResultSet executeQueryScrollInsensitiveReadOnly(String sqlString)
        throws SQLException, Exception {
  Statement statement = getStatement(ResultSet.TYPE_SCROLL_INSENSITIVE,
                                     ResultSet.CONCUR_READ_ONLY);
  ResultSet rs = statement.executeQuery(sqlString);

  return rs;
}

public ResultSet executeQueryScrollInsensitiveReadOnly(String sqlString,
        Vector values) throws SQLException, Exception {
  PreparedStatement preparedStatement = getStatement(sqlString,
          ResultSet.TYPE_SCROLL_INSENSITIVE,
          ResultSet.CONCUR_READ_ONLY);

  for (int i = 1; i <= values.size(); i++) {
    preparedStatement.setObject(i, values.elementAt(i - 1));
  }
  ResultSet rs = preparedStatement.executeQuery();

  return rs;
}
```

The `printResultSetRowsInForwardDirection()` method is called from `main()` after each `execute`*`XXX`*`()` method is called in order to simply demonstrate how one can scroll forward in a result set as shown here:

```
public void printResultSetRowsInForwardDirection(ResultSet rs)
        throws SQLException {
```

```
    ResultSetMetaData rMetaData = rs.getMetaData();
    int nColumns = rMetaData.getColumnCount();

    for (int i = 1; i <nColumns; i++) {
      System.out.print(rMetaData.getColumnName(i) + " : ");
    }
    System.out.println(rs.getString(nColumns));

    while (rs.next()) {
      for (int i = 1; i <nColumns; i++) {
        System.out.print(rs.getString(i) + " : ");
      }
      System.out.println(rs.getString(nColumns));

    }
  }
```

The `printResultSetRowsInReverseDirection()` is called from `main()` after the `executeXXX()` methods that return scrollable result sets are called. The `printResultSetRowsInReverseDirection()` method then demonstrates how to obtain information about the type of result set returned, positions the cursor after the last row in the result set, and then scrolls backward in the result set from there using the `previous()` method on `ResultSet`. The `printResultSetRowsInReverseDirection()` method is shown here:

```
  public void printResultSetRowsInReverseDirection(ResultSet rs)
          throws SQLException {
    int rsType = rs.getType();

    if (rsType == ResultSet.TYPE_FORWARD_ONLY
            || rsType == ResultSet.TYPE_SCROLL_SENSITIVE) {
      System.out
        .println("Error : ResultSet is not TYPE_SCROLL_INSENSITIVE");

      return;
    }

    ResultSetMetaData rMetaData = rs.getMetaData();
    int nColumns = rMetaData.getColumnCount();

    for (int i = 1; i < nColumns; i++) {
      System.out.print(rMetaData.getColumnName(i) + " : ");
    }
    System.out.println(rMetaData.getColumnName(nColumns));

    int fetchDirection = rs.getFetchDirection();
```

```
    if (fetchDirection == ResultSet.FETCH_FORWARD) {
      System.out
        .println("Result Set is  set to Fetch Forward Direction ");
    }

    rs.afterLast();

    while (rs.previous()) {
      for (int i = 1; i <nColumns; i++) {
        System.out.print(rs.getObject(i) + " : ");
      }
     System.out.println(rs.getObject(nColumns));

    }
  }
```

The `printResultSetNthRow()` method is also called from `main()` after `executeXXX()` methods that return scrollable result sets are called. This method positions the cursor at the row position passed to the method as a parameter, verifies that the row is located at the correct position via a call to `getRow()`, and then reports a true or false status resulting from indications of the cursor's position in the result set. The `printResultSetNthRow()` method is shown here:

```
  public void printResultSetNthRow(ResultSet rs,
                                       int nthRow) throws SQLException {
    int rsType = rs.getType();

    if (rsType == ResultSet.TYPE_FORWARD_ONLY
            || rsType == ResultSet.TYPE_SCROLL_SENSITIVE) {
      System.out
        .println("Error : ResultSet is not TYPE_SCROLL_INSENSITIVE");

      return;
    }

    int fetchDirection = rs.getFetchDirection();

    if (fetchDirection != ResultSet.FETCH_FORWARD) {
      System.out
        .println("Result Set is not set to Fetch Forward Direction ");

      return;
    }

    ResultSetMetaData rMetaData = rs.getMetaData();
    int nColumns = rMetaData.getColumnCount();
```

```
        rs.absolute(nthRow);

        int rowNumber = rs.getRow();

        System.out.println(" it is " + nthRow + "th Row in Result Set");

        if (rs.isAfterLast()) {
          System.out.println(" the Present Row is after last Row");
        }

        if (rs.isBeforeFirst()) {
          System.out.println(" The present Row is before first Row");
        }

        if (rs.isFirst()) {
          System.out.println("The present Row is Ist row");
        }

        if (rs.isLast()) {
          System.out.print(" The present Row is last Row");
        }

        for (int i = 1; i <nColumns; i++) {
          System.out.print(rMetaData.getColumnName(i) + " : ");
        }
        System.out.println(rMetaData.getColumnName(i));

        for (int i = 1; i < nColumns; i++) {
          System.out.print(rs.getObject(i) + " : ");
        }
        System.out.println(rs.getObject(i));

      }
```

Updateable Result Sets

In addition to scrollable result sets, the JDBC 2.0 specification introduces a new feature for manipulating result sets not previously possible with JDBC 1.0. Updateable result sets in JDBC 2.0 now allow for the update of rows, insertion of rows, and deletion of rows in a result set all through the `ResultSet` interface itself, whereas JDBC 1.0 previously returned only result sets that were read-only.

Result sets may thus now be further classified according to two new types:

- Read-only
- Updateable

This new additional result set discriminator is referred to as the *concurrency type* of the result set. Read-only result sets are the result sets you were used to using in JDBC 1.0 that offered you only a view of the data returned from the database. Updates, inserts, and deletes were exclusively accomplished via execution of SQL update, insert, or delete commands using the `executeUpdate()` or `execute()` methods on a statement object. In JDBC 2.0, this work can now be done conveniently from the `ResultSet` handle that you obtained after a query if that `ResultSet` object is updateable. Read-only result sets are identified by the `java.sql.ResultSet.CONCUR_READ_ONLY static public final int` value. Updateable result sets are identified by the `java.sql.ResultSet.CONCUR_UPDATABLE static public final int` value.

Creating Updateable Result Sets

The `Statement` and `PreparedStatement` objects may be created to use read-only result set types using the `Connection.createStatement()` and `Connection.prepareStatement(String sqlCommand)` methods as usual. As you've seen in the preceding section, a new form for each method has now been added to the `Connection` interface to support passing in result set type identifiers and result set concurrency type identifiers as well. Although you can use these two methods to create read-only result sets using the `ResultSet.CONCUR_READ_ONLY` identifier, you can also request usage of the new updateable types as shown here:

```
Connection connection = ... // Get connection as usual
String sqlString = "SELECT * FROM CUSTOMER";
Statement statement =
     connection.createStatement(ResultSet.TYPE_SCROLL_SENSITIVE,
                                ResultSet.CONCUR_UPDATABLE);
ResultSet rs1 = statement.executeQuery(sqlString);
PreparedStatement preparedStatement =
    connection.preparedStatement(sqlString, ResultSet.TYPE_FORWARD_ONLY,
                                  ResultSet.CONCUR_UPDATABLE);
ResultSet rs2 = preparedStatement.executeQuery();
```

After calling `executeQuery()` or `execute()` with a SQL query command on a statement object created to return updateable result sets, an updateable `ResultSet` object may then be returned. A new series of `updateXXX()` methods added to the `ResultSet` interface are then called to update individual columns associated with the current cursor row.

Updating Rows

Two general forms of `updateXXX()` exist. One form takes a column index `int`, and the other form takes a column name `String` as an input parameter as with the `getXXX()` methods described in Chapter 9. However, each `updateXXX()` method also takes a second parameter corresponding to the actual *XXX* type you intend to update in the associated column. For example:

```
int columnIndexFirstName = resultSet.findColumn ("FIRST_NAME");
resultSet.updateString(columnIndexFirstName ,"Tony");
        or
resultSet.updateString("FIRST_NAME","Tony");
```

These `updateXXX()` calls don't actually update the database row when called. Rather a call to `ResultSet.updateRow()` must be made to induce the actual change. You of course can then use `getXXX()` on the result set to see the change:

```
resultSet.updateRow();
```

Canceling Updates

If youdon't call `updateRow()` before you move the cursor to another row, the updates made using the `updateXXX()` calls will be cancelled. You can also explicitly cancel a row update before calling `updateRow()` using the `cancelRowUpdates()` method call:

```
resultSet.cancelRowUpdates();
```

Inserting Rows

Inserting a row into the database may now be done directly from a `ResultSet` handle. First call `moveToInsertRow()` to position the cursor on a special insert row location. This creates a temporary buffer that will contain the contents of all new column information to place in the new row. The `updateXXX()` method must then be called for each column in the new row that does not allow null values. The values for each column will remain undefined until they are set with an `updateXXX()` call. Finally, a call to `insertRow()` is made to commit the insert to the database. If a non-null column value was left undefined by not calling `updateXXX()` for that column, the `insertRow()` call will throw a `SQLException`. By calling `moveToCurrentRow()` after calling `moveToInsertRow()` and inserting the row, you can move back to the row that was current just before you inserted the new row. The basic sequence for inserting a row is illustrated here:

```
resultSet.moveToInsertRow();
resultSet.updateInt("CUSTOMER_ID_FK", 101);
resultSet.updateString("SHIP_INSTRUCT", " Deliver to offc if not home");
    ...
// Call other updateXXX() methods
    ...
resultSet.insertRow();
```

Deleting Rows

Deleting a row from the database is also fairly straightforward after you have a `ResultSet` handle. With a call to `deleteRow()` on the `ResultSet`, the current row pointed to by the cursor will be deleted from the ResultSet as well as from the database. A call to this method will throw a SQLException if you are positioned on the insert row buffer (that is, after a call to moveToInsertRow()):

```
resultSet.deleteRow();
```

Visibility into Database Changes

When you're updating the database, it is important to understand how these updates are propagated to other views of the system, as well as understand when you can view updates made by others. Understanding update visibility issues such as these requires an understanding of database transactions. Transaction concepts are briefly described in Chapter 8, "Enterprise Data," and Java-based transaction services are discussed in depth in Chapter 23, "Transaction Services." Nevertheless, the JDBC API offers some support for interfacing with transaction services, and we briefly cover these features in this section and in the section on distributed transactions later in this chapter.

As mentioned in Chapter 8, it is sometimes important to ensure that with a set of changes to the database, either all occur or none occurs. For example, it would be bad for BeeShirts.com business if we charged a customer before actually taking the order for delivery to his home. We can avoid this problem in our enterprise data-enabling efforts by encapsulating any database operations that change customer charge-related data and those that change customer order-related data into a single database transaction.

The most simplistic view of a transaction from a JDBC programmer's point of view is to understand the significance of beginning, committing, and rolling back a transaction. The Connection object is the point of contact for database transaction interfacing in JDBC. Referring to Figure 9.7, we see that the Connection class has a setAutoCommit() method. This method takes a boolean value indicating whether you want that particular database connection to automatically commit transactions after each update-related SQL statement is submitted to the database. By default, a Connection object is created in auto commit mode. However, you can also turn auto commit mode off by calling setAutoCommit(false) on the Connection object.

If you turn auto commit off, you are obligated to either call commit() on the Connection object if the group of update operations sent to the database was successful or call rollback() on the Connection object if one of the desired database operations failed. For example:

```
Connection connection = ... // Get connection as usual.
String chargeCustomerSQLString = ... ;
String placeCustomerOrderSQLString = ...;
try{
  connection.setAutoCommit(false);
```

```
    Statement s1 = connection.createStatement();
    Statement s2 = connection.createStatement();
    s1.executeUpdate( chargeCustomerSQLString );
    s2.executeUpdate( placeCustomerOrderSQLString );
    connection.commit();
    s1.close();
    s2.close();
}
catch( SQLException e){
    try{
      connection.rollback();
    }
    catch(SQLException e){
      // bla
    }
}
```

All updates within a transaction are visible to objects associated with the transaction itself. Because the `Connection` object represents where a transaction is managed from a JDBC programmer's point of view and because a `Connection` object can create more than one statement, a transaction can thus be associated with multiple statements. Thus a transaction can also be associated with multiple result sets, because each statement can potentially have a result set open.

You can view changes made by other transactions in accordance with a transaction's isolation level. You can think of the term *isolation level* to mean the degree to which a viewpoint of the data is isolated from changes in the data. A transaction isolation level can be set by calling `setTransactionIsolation()` on the `Connection` object with one of the `Connection` class's `static public final` identifiers for isolation levels. The transaction levels are described here in order from least-restrictive isolation levels to most-restrictive isolation levels:

- `TRANSACTION_NONE`: Transactions are not supported at all when identified by this isolation level.
- `TRANSACTION_READ_UNCOMMITTED`: This level allows other transactions to see row updates made by this transaction before a commit has been issued.
- `TRANSACTION_READ_COMMITTED`: This level does not allow other transactions to see row updates made by this transaction until a commit has been issued (that is, it does not allow "dirty reads").
- `TRANSACTION_REPEATABLE_READ`: In addition to `TRANSACTION_READ_COMMITTED` level support, this level also does not allow a transaction to read a row more than once and observe different data values because some other transaction made data updates to that row in the meantime (that is, it does not allow "nonrepeatable reads" or "dirty reads").

- TRANSACTION_SERIALIZABLE: In addition to TRANSACTION_REPEATABLE_READ level support, this level does not allow a transaction to read a collection of rows more than once, satisfying a particular WHERE clause. Furthermore, this level does not allow a transaction to observe a newly inserted row because some other transaction inserted a row satisfying that WHERE clause in the meantime (that is, it does not allow "phantom reads," "nonrepeatable reads," or "dirty reads").

For updateable result sets, the type of result set, in addition to the isolation level, is important to consider when you're trying to understand update visibility. After a scroll-insensitive updateable result set is opened, no changes from other transactions or even result sets in the same transaction are visible to the holder of the scroll-insensitive result set. Although updates to scroll-sensitive updateable result sets made by other transactions or result sets in the same transaction are visible to the holder of the scroll-sensitive result set, inserts and deletes may not be visible. Despite these general rules for visibility according to result set type, actual support is ultimately a function of what your database and driver vendor supports. You can find out the level of visibility of changes from within a ResultSet object made either by other result sets or by your own result set by calling one of the others*XXX*Visible() or own*XXX*Visible() calls on the DatabaseMetaData object:

- boolean othersUpdatesAreVisible(int type) returns true if updates made by other result sets for the ResultSet.TYPE_*XXX* identifier are visible.
- boolean othersInsertsAreVisible(int type) returns true if inserts made by other result sets for the ResultSet.TYPE_*XXX* identifier are visible.
- boolean othersDeletesAreVisible(int type) returns true if deletes made by other result sets for the ResultSet.TYPE_*XXX* identifier are visible.
- boolean ownUpdatesAreVisible(int type) returns true if updates made by your own result set for the ResultSet.TYPE_*XXX* identifier are visible.
- boolean ownInsertsAreVisible(int type) returns true if inserts made by your own result set for the ResultSet.TYPE_*XXX* identifier are visible.
- boolean ownDeletesAreVisible(int type) returns true if deletes made by your own result set for the ResultSet.TYPE_*XXX* identifier are visible.

After you've determined whether you can even view updates, inserts, and deletes for ResultSet objects, before using a ResultSet, you can also determine whether a specific ResultSet row was updated, inserted, or deleted by calling one of the row*XXX*() methods on the ResultSet object as defined here:

- boolean rowUpdated() returns true if the current row has been updated.
- boolean rowInserted() returns true if the current row has experienced a database insert.
- boolean rowDeleted() returns true if the current row has been deleted.

To complicate matters, the indications returned by the `ResultSet.rowXXX()` methods may not even be possible to determine by your driver. A set of `XXXAreDetected()` methods have been added to the `DatabaseMetaData` interface to support your attempt to determine whether the `ResultSet.rowXXX()` methods are supported:

- `boolean updatesAreDetected(int type)` returns `true` if updates for the `ResultSet.TYPE_XXX` type identifier can be determined when calling `ResultSet.rowUpdated()`.
- `boolean insertsAreDetected(int type)` returns `true` if inserts for the `ResultSet.TYPE_XXX` type identifier can be determined when calling `ResultSet.rowInserted()`.
- `boolean deletesAreDetected(int type)` returns `true` if deletes for the `ResultSet.TYPE_XXX` type identifier can be determined when calling `ResultSet.rowDeleted()`.

When all else fails, simply call `refreshRow()` on the `ResultSet` object to refresh the current row with the most up-to-the-minute updates in the database. Of course, calling this method will hamper performance because the database is accessed for each call. Some caveats also exist for calling `refreshRow()` during updates or inserts. Calling `refreshRow()` when in the midst of updating a row before calling `updateRow()` will cause you to lose all updates made. Furthermore, a `SQLException` will be thrown when you call `refreshRow()` while on the insert row.

Driver Support for Updateable Result Sets

Driver support requirements for updateable result sets are not precisely defined in the JDBC 2.0 specification. You can call `supportsResultSetConcurrency()` on the `DatabaseMetaData` interface with the `ResultSet.CONCUR_XXX` identifier to determine whether your driver will support that type of concurrency model. However, if an application attempts to create a statement with the `ResultSet.CONCUR_UPDATABLE` concurrency model and the driver cannot support this model, then the driver should throw a `SQLWarning` when attempting to create such a statement. The driver should then fall back to using the read-only concurrency model.

As with the dynamic determination of a result set type for certain calls even when a particular result set type is supported, the concurrency type may also have to be determined dynamically. In such a case, if a statement was created to use updateable result sets, when the `ResultSet` object is generated during an `execute()` or `executeQuery()` call on that statement, a `SQLWarning` should be thrown and a read-only result set should be generated instead. You can now call `getConcurrency()` on the `ResultSet` object in JDBC 2.0 to determine its concurrency type. Selection of a result set type has precedence over selection of a concurrency type if neither the result set type nor the concurrency type is supported.

Example: Updateable Result Sets

This next example demonstrates how to use some of the JDBC 2.0 updateable result set features. The example code is contained in the `ejava.jdbcch10.UpdateableResultSetExample` class, which extends the `ejava.jdbcch09.ConnectToDatabase` class from Chapter 9:

```
public class UpdateableResultSetExample extends ConnectToDatabase { ... }
```

NOTE

The complete set of code examples for the `UpdateableResultSetExample` can be found on the CD in the `examples\src\ejava\jdbcch10` directory. Some exception handling and other handling mechanisms have been left out of the book here for simplicity but can be found in the examples on the CD. The `runupdateableresultset.bat` example Windows script can be used to build and execute this example. Appendix A describes the general build procedures for all examples in the book and specifies those common environment variables that must be set to execute our example scripts. However, note that at the time of this writing, most database and JDBC driver vendors did not support updateable results sets.

The `main()` method of `UpdateableResultSetExample` is invoked like

```
java ejava.jdbcch10.UpdateableResultSetExample <propertiesFileName>
```

where the *`propertiesFileName`* is the location of a properties filename with properties set as in the `JDBCCH10Properties.txt` file. The main method then instantiates a new `UpdateableResultSetExample` object and calls `setProperties()` with a filename as with the other examples.

The `main()` method demonstrates the update of result sets using forward-only, scroll-sensitive, and scroll-insensitive concurrency types. Three `executeXXX()` methods are called on an `UpdateableResultSetExample` instance to return a `ResultSet` of a particular concurrency type. This `ResultSet` is then manipulated in various ways using a host of methods that demonstrate the nature of updateable result sets. The `main()` method is defined here:

```
public static void main(String[]  args)
{
 if(args.length == 0){
   System.out.println("Error: run the program as "+
     "java ejava.jdbcch10.UpdateableResultSet <propertiesFileName>");
    System.exit(0);
  }
  String fileName = args[0];
```

```
    UpdateableResultSetExample updateableResultSetExample =
      new UpdateableResultSetExample();
  ...
      updateableResultSetExample.setProperties(fileName);
      System.out.println("Forward Only Updateable ResultSet ");
      String sqlString = (String)(updateableResultSetExample.
        getProperties()).get("UPDATEABLE_SQL_STATEMENT");
ResultSet rs = updateableResultSetExample.
        executeQueryScrollForwardOnlyUpdateable(sqlString);
      updateableResultSetExample.
        printResultSetRowsInForwardDirection(rs);
      updateableResultSetExample.
        insertNewRowIntoOrdersTableUsingColumnNames(rs);
      updateableResultSetExample.
        insertNewRowIntoOrdersTableUsingColumnIndexes(rs);
      updateableResultSetExample.
        updateNthRowIthColumnValue(rs,1,4,"Deliver at Office " );

      System.out.println("ScrollInsensitive Updateable ResultSet ");
      rs = updateableResultSetExample.
        executeQueryScrollInsensitiveUpdateable(sqlString);
      updateableResultSetExample.
       printResultSetRowsInForwardDirection(rs);
      updateableResultSetExample.
       printResultSetRowsInReverseDirection(rs);
      updateableResultSetExample.printResultSetNthRow(rs,3);
      updateableResultSetExample.printNthMinusIthRow(rs,4, 2);

      System.out.println(" Scroll Sensitive Updateable ResultSet ");
      rs = updateableResultSetExample.
        executeQueryScrollSensitiveUpdateable(sqlString);
      updateableResultSetExample.
        printResultSetRowsInForwardDirection(rs);
      updateableResultSetExample.
        printResultSetRowsInReverseDirection(rs);
      updateableResultSetExample.
        printResultSetNthRow(rs,3);
      updateableResultSetExample.
        printNthMinusIthRow(rs,4, 2);
 ...
  }
```

A SQL statement used to generate an updateable result set is read from the properties file:

```
UPDATEABLE_SQL_STATEMENT = SELECT * FROM TSHIRTS.ORDERS
```

A `getStatement()` method is used here as with the `ScrollableResultSetExample` to create a SQL statement with the associated scroll type and concurrency type:

```
protected Statement getStatement( int scrollType,
  int updateType) throws SQLException, Exception
{
  Connection connection = super.getConnection();
  connection.setAutoCommit(false);
  Statement  statement = connection.createStatement(scrollType,
    updateType);
  return statement;
}
```

The `executeXXX()` method called from `main()` actually calls the `getStatement()` method to return a `Statement` of the appropriate concurrency type and then executes the `sqlString` query passed in as a parameter. An `executeXXX()` demonstration method exists for returning scroll-insensitive result sets, scroll forward-only result sets, and scroll-sensitive result sets:

```
public ResultSet executeQueryScrollInsensitiveUpdateable(String
  sqlString)
  throws SQLException, Exception
{
  Statement statement = getStatement(
    ResultSet.TYPE_SCROLL_INSENSITIVE,
    ResultSet.CONCUR_UPDATABLE);
   // Execute a SQL statement that returns a single ResultSet.
  ResultSet rs = statement.executeQuery(sqlString);
  return rs;
}

public ResultSet executeQueryScrollForwardOnlyUpdateable(String
  sqlString)
  throws SQLException, Exception
{
   Statement statement = getStatement(ResultSet.TYPE_FORWARD_ONLY,
    ResultSet.CONCUR_UPDATABLE);
   // Execute a SQL statement that returns a single ResultSet.
   ResultSet rs = statement.executeQuery(sqlString);
   return rs;
}

public ResultSet executeQueryScrollSensitiveUpdateable(String
  sqlString)
  throws SQLException, Exception
{
  Statement statement = getStatement(ResultSet.TYPE_SCROLL_SENSITIVE,
    ResultSet.CONCUR_UPDATABLE);
```

```
    // Execute a SQL statement that returns a single ResultSet.
   ResultSet rs = statement.executeQuery(sqlString);
   return rs;
 }
```

Two methods for inserting a row into an updateable result set exist in this example and are called from `main()`. One method inserts a row into our BeeShirts.com `ORDERS` table using the column names in `ResultSet.updateXXX()` calls. Another method inserts a row into the `ORDERS` table using column indices instead of column names. These methods are defined here:

```
public void insertNewRowIntoOrdersTableUsingColumnNames(ResultSet rs)
          throws SQLException {

    // this method works only if the table is Orders Table in the Demo
    // database.
    // if the table is different you should change most of this code
    // for that purpose.
    rs.moveToInsertRow();
    rs.updateInt("CUSTOMER_ID_FK", 101);
    rs.updateInt("ORDER_ID", 1001);
    rs.updateDate("ORDER_DATE",  new Date(System.currentTimeMillis()) );
    rs.updateString("SHIP_INSTRUCT",
                    " deliver at Apt. office" + " if no one at home");
    rs.updateString("BACKLOG", "N");
    rs.updateString("PO_NUM", "BSD100");
    rs.updateDate("SHIP_DATE", new Date(System.currentTimeMillis()));
    rs.updateFloat("SHIP_WEIGHT", 22.0f);
    rs.updateFloat("SHIP_CHARGE", 44.56f);
    rs.updateDate("PAID_DATE", new Date(System.currentTimeMillis()));
    rs.insertRow();
  }

public void insertNewRowIntoOrdersTableUsingColumnIndexes(ResultSet rs)
          throws SQLException {
    rs.moveToInsertRow();
    rs.updateInt(1, 101);
    rs.updateInt(2, 1001);
    rs.updateDate(3, new Date(System.currentTimeMillis()));
    rs.updateString(4, " deliver at Apt. office if no one at home");
    rs.updateString(5, "N");
    rs.updateString(5, "BSD100");
    rs.updateDate(6, new Date(System.currentTimeMillis()));
    rs.updateFloat(7, 22.0f);
    rs.updateFloat(8, 44.56f);
    rs.updateDate(9, new Date(System.currentTimeMillis()) );
    rs.insertRow();
  }
```

Finally, an update method is also called from `main()` to demonstrate how a particular column in a specified row of an updateable result set can be updated with a new value:

```
public void updateNthRowIthColumnValue(ResultSet rs,
  int nThRow, int iThColumn, Object value) throws SQLException
{
  ResultSetMetaData rMetaData = rs.getMetaData();
  int type    =  rMetaData.getColumnType(iThColumn);
  String colName = rMetaData.getColumnName(iThColumn);
  rs.absolute(nThRow);
  switch(type) {
    case Types.CHAR:
    case Types.VARCHAR:
    case Types.LONGVARCHAR:
      rs.updateString(colName, value.toString());
      break;
    case Types.BIT:
      rs.updateByte(colName,
        Byte.valueOf(value.toString()).byteValue());
      break;
    case Types.TINYINT:
    case Types.SMALLINT:
    case Types.INTEGER:
      rs.updateInt(colName,
        Integer.valueOf(value.toString()).intValue());
      break;
    case Types.BIGINT:
      rs.updateLong(colName,
        Long.valueOf(value.toString()).longValue());
      break;
    case Types.FLOAT:
      rs.updateFloat(colName,
        Float.valueOf(value.toString()).floatValue());
      break;
    case Types.DOUBLE:
      rs.updateDouble(colName,
        Double.valueOf(value.toString()).doubleValue());
      break;
    case Types.DATE:
      rs.updateDate(colName,
        Date.valueOf(value.toString()));
      break;
    case Types.TIME:
      rs.updateTime(colName,
        Time.valueOf(value.toString()));
      break;
```

```
        case Types.TIMESTAMP:
          rs.updateTimestamp(colName,
            Timestamp.valueOf(value.toString()));
          break;
        default:
          rs.updateObject(colName, value);
          break;
      }
      rs.updateRow();
    }
```

Batch Updates

When submitting updates to the database using JDBC 1.0, you could submit only one update at a time using either the `executeUpdate()` or the `execute()` method calls on a `Statement` interface or one of its sub-interfaces. The JDBC 2.0 Core API has introduced a new feature that enables you to create a batch of update commands associated with a statement and subsequently submit the entire batch of commands to the database in a single call. The database can then process all the updates at once, offering a significant performance enhancement over submitting the same set of updates individually. Whether or not such batch updates are supported is a function of both the database and the driver vendor implementation. You can determine whether batch updates are supported in your database and driver configuration by calling `supportsBatchUpdates()` on a `DatabaseMetaData` object that returns a boolean `true` or `false` indication.

Creating Batch Updates

Before creating a batch update, you must first turn off auto commit on the `Connection` object by calling `Connection.setAutoCommit(false)`. Your code, as the JDBC API client, now determines when to commit a transaction during the submission of multiple updates. You then must create a `Statement` object or one of its sub-interface instances as usual. Each SQL update command is then added to a `Statement` using the new `addBatch(String command)` method on the `Statement` interface. If you have created a `PreparedStatement`, you should call the `setXXX()` methods on the `PreparedStatement` to set each parameterized value and then call `addBatch()` on the `PreparedStatement` object. For example:

```
Connection connection = ... // Create connection as usual
connection.setAutoCommit(false);

Statement statement = this.getStatement();
statement.addBatch("INSERT INTO STATE VALUES(\'VA\', \'VIRGINIA')");
statement.addBatch("INSERT INTO STATE VALUES(\'MD\', \'MARYLAND')");
```

```
PreparedStatement preparedStatement =
        connection.prepareStatement("INSERT INTO STATE VALUES (?,?)");
preparedStatement.setString(1,"CA");
preparedStatement.setString(2,"California");
preparedStatement.addBatch();
preparedStatement.setString(1,"OH");
preparedStatement.setString(2,"Ohio");
preparedStatement.addBatch();
```

Executing a Batch Update

Executing a batch after it has been created is a simple matter of calling `executeBatch()` on the `Statement` interface or a sub-interface. The `executeBatch()` method takes no parameters and returns an `int[]` array of update counts in the order in which updates were added to the batch. A `SQLException` is thrown if any one of the SQL commands added to the batch attempts to generate a `ResultSet`. A `BatchUpdateException` is thrown if any of the update commands fails. After one command fails, no more update attempts are made. The `BatchUpdateException` added in JDBC 2.0 has a `getUpdateCounts()` method to return the number of updates that were executed. You can use the `clearBatch()` call on the `Statement` interface to clear any commands added to a batch. For example:

```
Connection connection = ... // Create connection as usual
connection.setAutoCommit(false);
Statement statement = this.getStatement();
try{
  statement.addBatch("INSERT INTO STATE VALUES(\'VA\', \'VIRGINIA')");
  statement.addBatch("INSERT INTO STATE VALUES(\'MD\', \'MARYLAND')");
  int[] nResults = statement.executeBatch();
  connection.commit();
}
catch(BatchUpdateException bupdateException){
  System.out.println("SQL STATE:" + bupdateException.getSQLState());
  System.out.println("Message:" + bupdateException.getMessage());
  System.out.println("Vendor Code:" + bupdateException.getErrorCode());
  System.out.println(" Update Counts :" );
  int[] nRowsResult = bupdateException.getUpdateCounts();
  for(int i = 0; i < nRowsResult.length; i++){
    System.out.println("Result "+ i +":" + nRowsResult[i]);
  }
  statement.clearBatch();
}
catch(Exception e){
  // Handle other exceptions here
}
```

Example: Batch Updates

This next example demonstrates how to use a few JDBC 2.0 batch update features. The example code is contained in the `ejava.jdbcch10.BatchUpdatesExample` class, which extends the `ejava.jdbcch09.ConnectToDatabase` class from Chapter 9:

```
public class BatchUpdatesExample extends ConnectToDatabase { ... }
```

> **NOTE**
>
> The complete set of code examples for the `BatchUpdatesExample` can be found on the CD in the `examples\src\ejava\jdbcch10` directory. Some exception handling and other handling mechanisms have been left out of the book here for simplicity but can be found in the examples on the CD. The `runbatchupdates.bat` example Windows script can be used to build and execute this example. Appendix A describes the general build procedures for all examples in the book and specifies those common environment variables that must be set to execute our example scripts. Consult Appendix A for more information on support and the vendor product with which you can test the `BatchUpdatesExample`.

The `main()` method of `BatchUpdatesExample` is invoked as

```
java ejava.jdbcch10.BatchUpdatesExample <propertiesFileName>
```

where the *`propertiesFileName`* is the location of a properties filename with properties set as in the `JDBCCH10Properties.txt` file. The `main()` method then instantiates a new `BatchUpdatesExample` object and calls `setProperties()` with a filename as with the other examples.

The `main()` method for the `BatchUpdatesExample` calls two methods on a `BatchUpdatesExample` instance to demonstrate how a batch of rows can be inserted into the database for both regular statements and prepared statements as shown here:

```
public static void main(String[]  args){
...
  BatchUpdatesExample batchUpdatesExample = new BatchUpdatesExample();
...
  batchUpdatesExample.insertBatchofRowsUsingStatement();
  batchUpdatesExample.insertBatchofRowsUsingPreparedStatement();
...
}
```

The `insertBatchofRowsUsingStatement()` method calls `getStatement()` to obtain a reference to a regular `Statement` object. After checking to see whether batch updates are supported, two regular SQL statements are added to the batch and then executed. Likewise, the `insertBatchofRowsUsingPreparedStatement()` goes through a similar sequence using a `PreparedStatement`. Both methods are shown here:

```
public void insertBatchofRowsUsingStatement()
  throws SQLException, BatchUpdateException, Exception
{
  Connection connection = super.getConnection();
  DatabaseMetaData dbMetaData  = connection.getMetaData();
  if(dbMetaData.supportsBatchUpdates()){
...
      connection.setAutoCommit(false);
      Statement statement = this.getStatement();
      statement.addBatch("INSERT INTO STATE VALUES(\'VA\', "+
        "\'VIRGINIA')");
      statement.addBatch("INSERT INTO STATE VALUES(\'MD\',"
                         + " \'MARYLAND')");

      int[] nResults = statement.executeBatch();
      connection.commit();
      for(int i = 0; i< nResults.length; i++){
          System.out.println(i + " th statement executed with " +
            nResults[i] + " results");
      }
    }
...
}

public void insertBatchofRowsUsingPreparedStatement()
  throws SQLException,  Exception
{
  Connection connection = super.getConnection();
  DatabaseMetaData dbMetaData  = connection.getMetaData();
  if(dbMetaData.supportsBatchUpdates()){
...
      connection.setAutoCommit(false);
      PreparedStatement preparedStatement =
        this.getStatement("INSERT INTO STATE VALUES (?,?)");
      preparedStatement.setString(1,"CA");
      preparedStatement.setString(2,"California");
      preparedStatement.addBatch();
      preparedStatement.setString(1,"OH");
```

```
            preparedStatement.setString(2,"Ohio");
            preparedStatement.addBatch();
            int[] nResults = preparedStatement.executeBatch();
            connection.commit();
            for(int i = 0; i< nResults.length; i++){
              System.out.println(i + " th statement executed with " +
                nResults[i] + " results");
            }
      ...
        }
      }
```

Advanced Data Types

The JDBC 2.0 Core API introduces a whole new rich set of advanced data types that may be used to map complex database structures to and from Java objects. Persistable Java object types now enable a means for storing and retrieving entire Java objects to and from the database, as well as defining meta-data about these objects. Java mappings for SQL3 types such as BLOBs, CLOBs, Arrays, Distincts, Structs, and Refs are also now possible. Along these lines, custom user-defined database type to Java type mappings are now also a possibility with JDBC 2.0. Although the JDBC 2.0 specification standardizes on this support, driver support for these advanced typing features is optional.

Java Object Types

The JDBC 2.0 Core API introduces a new standard for storing and retrieving Java objects to and from the database. Such persistable Java object support results in databases that become a sort of Java-relational database. The Java object may be serialized to the database or stored in some vendor-dependent fashion. There is no special JDBC-defined storage format as of yet.

Storing a persistable Java object can be straightforward. A regular Java object type is simply first referenced in a SQL update or insert statement and subsequently supplied to the database by calling `setObject()` on that statement. It should be noted that although the JDBC API has not changed to support this new notion, the SQL statement syntax is not yet standardized for this functionality and will thus be vendor-dependent. For example, if we attempt to insert some new customer into the database, we might have this:

```
Customer cust = new Customer();
cust.setName("Sam", "Cheng");
  ...
  // Set other customer values
  ...
PreparedStatement statement =
  connection.preparedStatement("INSERT CUSTOMER SET Customer = ?");
```

```
statement.setObject(1, cust);
statement.executeUpdate();
```

Retrieving the Java object is equally straightforward. A regular Java type is referenced in the SQL query statement and then retrieved from the database by a call to `getObject()` on the `ResultSet`. For example:

```
ResultSet resultSet = statement.executeQuery(
            "SELECT Customer FROM CUSTOMER WHERE LAST_NAME = Cheng");
resultSet.next();
Customer cust = (Customer) resultSet.getObject(1);
```

The `java.sql.Types` class now defines `JAVA_OBJECT` as a new type identifier for persistable Java objects. If you are uncertain whether your database and driver support persistable Java objects, a call to `DatabaseMetaData.getTypeInfo()` will return a `ResultSet` that can be used to determine whether `JAVA_OBJECT` types are supported.

You can then call `DatabaseMetaData.getUDTs()` to obtain a `ResultSet` object that describes those user-defined types defined in a particular schema of interest. A catalog `String`, a schema pattern `String`, a type name pattern `String`, and an `int` array with `java.sql.Types.JAVA_OBJECT` as an element are all taken as parameters for the `getUDTs()` method. The `ResultSet` of user-defined types known to the database contains a row per supported type, each with the following column of `Strings`:

- `TYPE_CAT` identifying the catalog.
- `TYPE_SCHEM` identifying the schema.
- `TYPE_NAME` identifying the type name.
- `CLASS_NAME` identifying the associated Java class name.
- `DATA_TYPE` identifying the `java.sql.Types` (for example, `JAVA_OBJECT`).
- `REMARKS` containing optional comments about the type.

SQL3 Types

The SQL3 standard introduces a set of new data types usable in Java environments incorporated by the JDBC 2.0 Core API specification. For each new type, an identifier was added to the `java.sql.Types` class. Support for each new SQL3 type by your database and driver vendors can be determined by calling `DatabaseMetaData.getTypeInfo()` and looking for the type of interest as identified by a `java.sql.Types` identifier in the returned `ResultSet`. These were the new SQL3 types targeted by the JDBC specification:

- BLOBs (binary large objects) represent a very large set of binary data (`java.sql.Types.BLOB` identifier).
- CLOBs (character large objects) represent a very large set of character data (`java.sql.Types.CLOB` identifier).

- Reference types represent references to persisted data (`java.sql.Types.REF` identifier).
- Arrays represent simple arrays of data (`java.sql.Types.ARRAY` identifier).
- Structured types represent simple collections of attributes (`java.sql.Types.STRUCT` identifier).
- Distinct types represent new type name aliases for existing type names (`java.sql.Types.DISTINCT` identifier).

The `ResultSet` interface has also been embellished to now be more Java SQL3 type-aware by supporting a host of new `getXXX()` methods that serve to return objects from the result set in a type-safe fashion. Recall that `getXXX()` type methods such as `getString()` for `String` types and `getDouble()` for `double` types already exist on the `ResultSet` interface. The `getXXX(int)` method style retrieves objects from a `ResultSet` by column number, and the `getXXX(String)` method style retrieves objects from a `ResultSet` by column name. Thus, as we'll soon see, `getXXX()` methods for a few SQL3 types can be used to retrieve SQL3 types from the `ResultSet` object by column number using `getXXX(int)` type methods or by column name using `getXXX(String)` type methods.

The `PreparedStatement` interface's `setXXX()` type methods have also been extended to set some of the new SQL3 types in a type safe fashion into indexed parameters of a prepared statement (see the Chapter 9 discussion on the `PreparedStatement` interface). Thus, much like a method `setBoolean(int, boolean)` exists to set a `boolean` value into a prepared statement parameter indexed by the associated `int` parameter to `setBoolean()`, a set of `setXXX()` methods is also now available for a few core SQL3 types, as you'll soon see.

SQL BLOBs and CLOBs

Manipulating database data as a BLOB or CLOB type is useful when you want to defer the actual transfer of large binary (BLOB) or large character (CLOB) data between a Java application and the database until it is needed. Thus you might see a BLOB type in a returned `ResultSet`, but the actual data for this BLOB is not downloaded to your Java application from the database until you explicitly ask for it.

JDBC 2.0 has introduced two new `Blob` and `Clob` Java interfaces to the `java.sql` package. Instances of these types are valid only for the lifetime of the transaction in which they were created. These are the `java.sql.Blob` interface methods:

- `long length()`: Returns the number of bytes in the BLOB.
- `byte[] getBytes(long startPosition, int byteLength)`: Returns `byteLength` number of bytes of the BLOB data as a byte array starting at `startPosition` in the BLOB.
- `InputStream getBinaryStream()`: Returns a binary `InputStream` reference of this BLOB.

- `long position(Blob blobPattern, long startPosition)`: Starting at the `startPosition` location in this BLOB, the position in the BLOB is returned where the associated `blobPattern` begins.
- `long position(byte[] bytePattern, long startPosition)`: Starting at the `startPosition` location in this BLOB, the position in the BLOB is returned where the associated `bytePattern` begins.

An analogous set of `Clob` methods exists in `java.sql.Clob`:

- `long length()`: Returns the number of characters in the `Clob`.
- `String getSubString(long startPosition, int charLength)`: Returns a `charLength` string of CLOB data as a `String` starting at `startPosition` in the CLOB.
- `InputStream getAsciiStream()`: Returns an ASCII `InputStream` referencc of this CLOB.
- `Reader getCharacterStream()`: Returns a Unicode Reader stream reference of this CLOB.
- `long position(Clob clobPattern, long startPosition)`: Starting at the `startPosition` location in this CLOB, the position in the CLOB is returned where the associated `clobPattern` begins.
- `long position(String stringPattern, long startPosition`: Starting at the `startPosition` location in this CLOB, the position in the CLOB is returned where the associated `stringPattern` begins.

Retrieving `Blob` or `Clob` data from the database is a simple matter of calling the `getBlob(int)`, `getBlob(String)`, `getClob(int)`, or `getClob(String)` methods on a `ResultSet` object when a particular set of `Blob` or `Clob` data is returned from the database. These methods are new JDBC 2.0 additions to the `ResultSet` class. For example:

```
Blob myBlob = resultSet.getBlob(1);
Blob myOtherBlob = resultSet.getBlob("BIG_PICTURE_FILE");
Clob myClob = resultSet.getClob(3);
Clob myOtherClob = resultSet.getClob("BIG_TEXT_FILE");
```

Storing `Blob` or `Clob` data is also a simple matter. By calling the JDBC 2.0 `setBlob()` or `setClob()` methods on a `PreparedStatement`, you can submit a `Blob` or `Clob` update to the database. You can also use the `setBinaryStream()` or `setObject()` methods to set `Blobs` and the `setAsciiStream()`, `setUnicodeStream()`, or `setObject()` methods to set `Clobs` on a `PreparedStatement` object. Here's an example for setting `Blobs` and `Clobs` on some `PreparedStatement` object that was created to take four input parameters:

```
preparedStatement.setBlob(1, myBlob);
```

```
preparedStatement.setBinaryStream(2, myOtherBlob.getBinaryStream(),
➥myOtherBlob.length());
preparedStatement.setClob(3, myClob);
preparedStatement.setAsciiStream(4, myOtherClob.getAsciiStream(),
➥myOtherClob.length());
```

SQL References

SQL3 references to persistent data are encapsulated by the `Ref` interface new to the `java.sql` package in JDBC 2.0. The `Ref` interface has one method called `getBaseTypeName()`, which returns a `String` that identifies the SQL type it references. `Ref` objects can be retrieved from a `ResultSet` object using the `getRef()` method. The data associated with this reference is not retrieved until the reference is de-referenced. Reference objects are valid for the lifetime of the connection in which they were created. A `Ref` object may also be persisted to the database using the `setRef()` method on a `PreparedStatement`. As an example use of `Ref`, we have this:

```
Ref myRef = resultSet.getRef(1);
    ...
preparedStatement.setRef(1, myRef);
```

SQL Arrays

SQL arrays can also now be manipulated in JDBC 2.0. SQL arrays are simply arrays of data, the lifetime of which is also bound to the enclosing transaction. An `Array` interface has been added to the `java.sql` package to encapsulate the SQL array type. Type information about the SQL array elements can be obtained from the `getBaseType()` and `getBaseTypeName()` methods on the `Array` interface:

- `int getBaseType()` returns the `java.sql.Types` identifier identifying the elements of this SQL array.
- `String getBaseTypeName()` returns the SQL type name associated with the elements of this SQL array.

The `Array` interface can also be used to map the SQL array into a form usable by Java programs. The array may thus be retrieved as an `Object` referencing a regular Java array or as a `ResultSet` object in which each row in the `ResultSet` corresponds to an element in the SQL array. Either the entire array contents can be retrieved for each of these Java types or a subset of the SQL array can be retrieved with a given start index of the array and a desired array length. The `Object` and `ResultSet` types of arrays can be retrieved completely or as a subset of the SQL array also by passing in a `java.util.Map` object, which specifies how each SQL type name maps to a Java class. When no `java.util.Map` object is provided, a default SQL type to Java mapping is assumed. These methods are defined here:

- `Object getArray()` returns the Java `Object` form of array.
- `ResultSet getResultSet()` returns the Java `ResultSet` form of array.

- `Object getArray(long startElement, int arraySize)` returns a subset of the Java `Object` form of array beginning at the `startElement` index and for an `arraySize` number of elements.
- `ResultSet getResultSet(long startElement, int arraySize)` returns a subset of the Java `ResultSet` form of the array beginning at the `startElement` index and for an `arraySize` number of elements.
- `Object getArray(Map map)` returns the Java `Object` form of the array according to the `Map` object.
- `ResultSet getResultSet(Map map)` returns the Java `ResultSet` form of the array according to the `Map` object.
- `Object getArray(long startElement, int arraySize, Map map)` returns a subset of the Java `Object` form of array beginning at the `startElement` index, for an `arraySize` number of elements, and according to the `Map` object translating between SQL type names and Java classes to which they map.
- `ResultSet getResultSet(long index, int count, Map map)` returns a subset of the Java `ResultSet` form of the array beginning at the `startElement` index, for an `arraySize` number of elements, and according to the `Map` object translating between SQL type names and Java classes to which they map.

You can obtain a reference to a SQL array retrieved from a database query from the `ResultSet` class's JDBC 2.0 `getArray()` methods. For example, to obtain `Array` objects from columns 1 and 2 in a `ResultSet`, you would use this:

```
Array myArray = resultSet.getArray(1);
Array myOtherArray = resultSet.getArray(2);
```

You can store such arrays using the `setArray()` method added to `PreparedStatement` in JDBC 2.0 or the `setObject()` method. For example:

```
PreparedStatement.setArray(1, myArray);
```

SQL Structures

SQL structured types provide a C++ or IDL-like means for encapsulating a collection of data types into a unified structure. Such a structure becomes a new type in and of itself. In Javaland, we can think of a structured type as a Java class with only public member variables. SQL structured types are encapsulated by a `java.sql.Struct` interface in JDBC 2.0. The methods on the `Struct` interface are quite simple:

- `String getSQLTypeName()` returns the name of the SQL type represented by this `Struct` object.
- `Object[] getAttributes()` returns an `Object` array of attribute values from this `Struct` object. This method assumes a default mapping of SQL types to Java types for each element returned in the `Object` array.

- `Object[] getAttributes(Map map)` returns an `Object` array with each array element containing a Java class instance that is mapped according to the `java.util.Map` object specifying how each SQL type maps to a Java class.

Structured types are retrieved from `ResultSet` objects using `getObject()` and are persisted to the database using `setObject()` on `PreparedStatement` objects. For example:

```
Struct ipHostStruct = (Struct) resultSet.getObject("IP_HOST_STRUCTURE");
    ...
preparedStatement.setObject(1, ipHostStruct);
```

The `DatabaseMetaData.getUDTs()` method can be used to obtain a description of the `Struct` types that are currently defined in the database given a catalog name, a schema name pattern, a type name pattern, and an `int` array with the `java.sql.Types.STRUCT` identifier as an element.

SQL Distinct Types

As mentioned previously, Distinct types are useful when you want to alias SQL types with another type name. There is no specific `Distinct` interface added to the JDBC 2.0 interface. Distinct types may be created in the database using a SQL statement of the form `CREATE TYPE <DISTINCT_ALIAS_NAME> AS <EXISTING_SQL_NAME>`. For example:

```
statement.execute("CREATE TYPE CITY AS VARCHAR(25)");
```

A `Distinct` type can be retrieved from a database query `ResultSet` via the `getXXX()` method for whatever type the `Distinct` type aliases. Likewise, a `Distinct` type can be used in a database update statement making the appropriate `setXXX()` calls on a `PreparedStatement`. For example:

```
String myCity = resultSet.getString("CITY");
    ...
preparedStatement.setString("CITY", myCity);
```

The `DatabaseMetaData.getUDTs()` method can be used to obtain a description of the `Distinct` types that are currently defined in the database given a catalog name, a schema name pattern, a type name pattern, and an `int` array with the `java.sql.Types.DISTINCT` identifier as an element.

Custom Types

The new SQL3 types supported by JDBC 2.0 offer a means for mapping user-defined SQL types that are stored to and retrieved from a relational database to types that can be used by your Java applications.

When describing custom types to the database via JDBC, the `java.util.Map` class is used to map user-defined SQL types to Java classes. Each SQL type name is mapped to a `java.lang.Class` instance. If you want to override the standard type mappings from SQL type to Java type, you can do this at the connection level by calling `setTypeMap()` on the connection object with the desired type mapping. The map for that connection may be retrieved by calling `getTypeMap()`. Various statement and result set calls associated with the connection may override the connection's mapping.

When creating a new Java class that is mapped to the database in this new custom fashion, that class must implement the `java.sql.SQLData` interface. The `SQLData` interface requires that a `getSQLTypeName()` method, `readSQL()` method, and `writeSQL()` method be implemented. The `getSQLTypeName()` method must simply return a user-defined SQL type name represented by the Java class.

Third-party vendors will ideally provide the automated mapping of SQL types to Java classes given a user-defined mapping. Such tools would use a design-time set of properties to create the actual `java.util.Map` object and automatically generate the user-defined Java classes that implement the `SQLData` interface. As JDBC 2.0 compliance becomes more widespread and as IDE vendors provide greater levels of support for the Java 2 platform, such automated processes will become more prevalent. In lieu of that level of support, we briefly describe and subsequently demonstrate how to implement the `SQLData` interface for a user-defined class.

The `writeSQL()` method of the `SQLData` interface takes a `SQLOutput` stream object as a parameter. This method is called when the custom class is being dumped to a SQL data stream (that is, during persistence of the Java object to the database). The Java class-specific `writeSQL()` method must make a series of `writeXXX()` calls on the `SQLOutput` stream to write each fundamental element of the class to the stream. A different `writeXXX()` method exists on the `SQLOutput` interface for all the most fundamental Java to SQL type mappings that exist in JDBC 2.0 (for example, `writeString()` and `writeBlob()`). For Java classes that contain Java class field members whose SQL type mappings represent a nonfundamental SQL type, it too must implement the `SQLData` interface, and `writeSQL()` must be called on it when writing the parent class to the stream. This all must be done in the order in which the types are defined in the SQL type structure.

The `readSQL()` method on the `SQLData` interface takes a `SQLInput` object and `String` object as input parameters. This method is used to stream the database data into the user-defined Java object implementing this method. The `String` object passed into this method simply identifies the SQL type for which the associated `SQLInput` stream is containing. The actual streaming of data from `SQLInput` into the Java object is accomplished by calling a series of `readXXX()` methods on the `SQLInput` object according to the order in which each SQL type is defined in the SQL structure. In addition to the `readXXX()` methods defined on the `SQLInput` interface, a `wasNull()` method is defined that can be used to return a `boolean` value indicating whether the last value read from the stream was null. A class implementing `readSQL()` calls `readXXX()` on the `SQLInput` object for all fundamental JDBC 2.0 SQL types or `readSQL()` on a member object that is not a fundamental JDBC 2.0 type.

Extending the BeeShirts.com Example Data Model

To demonstrate some of the neat new features of the JDBC 2.0 data types, we've extended the BeeShirts.com data model. Figure 10.1 depicts this new model. Here we see that three new entities have been added to the model. First we see a `TSHIRT` table added, which provides extra information specific to T-shirts above and beyond the `ITEM` table. The `TSHIRT` table references the `ITEM` table that it extends with extra data. The `TSHIRT` table contains two SQL `BLOB` types that refer to pictures to be contained on the front and back of a T-shirt. The `CREDIT` table represents credit information related to a customer's particular order. This `CREDIT` table contains a `CHARGE_CARD_TYPE` to be defined as a new SQL type in the database. The `CHARGE_CARD_TYPE` contains information related to a charge card used in a purchase.

Appendix A, "Software Configuration," provides the details behind configuring a database to handle these tables and types. However, as an example to illustrate here, the `CHARGE_CARD_TYPE` might be configured in your database with the following command:

```
CREATE TYPE CHARGE_CARD_TYPE AS OBJECT
(
   CARD_TYPE          CHAR(10)      ,
   CARD_NAME          VARCHAR(20) ,
   CARD_NUMBER        CHAR(16)      ,
   EXPIRE_DATE        DATE       ,
   CARD_CONFIRMATION_NUMBER VARCHAR(20)
)
```

The `CREDIT` table may then use this new type via the following SQL command:

```
CREATE TABLE CREDIT
(
  CUSTOMER_ID_FK           INTEGER      NOT NULL,
  ORDER_ID_FK              INTEGER     NOT NULL,
  PAYMENT_INFORMATION      CHARGE_CARD_TYPE      NOT NULL
)
```

NOTE

Figure 10.1 depicts the BeeShirts.com data model used to illustrate a few of the advanced data types described in this chapter. Appendix A provides instructions for configuring a database to utilize such a model. However, because of limited JDBC driver support for such features at the time of this writing, the actual data model assumed for use by the remaining chapters in this book differs slightly from the one presented in Figure 10.1. Appendix A's Figure A.2 provides an overview of the complete data model assumed by the BeeShirts.com examples used in the last chapter and throughout the remaining chapters of this book.

One key difference is that the `CHARGE_CARD_TYPE` structure used for this chapter's example is configured as a regular database table for use in other chapters. The `CREDIT` table thus maintains a foreign key to the `CHARGE_CARD_TYPE` table. Another key difference is this chapter's assumption that the `TSHIRT` table defines `BLOB` types for the `PICTURE_FRONT` and `PICTURE_BACK` columns. Other chapters assume that these two columns are of the `VARCHAR` type defining file names of binary image data rather than contain the binary image data itself in the form of a `BLOB` type. Appendix A describes how to configure the Oracle 8i database to specifically work with this chapter's advanced JDBC examples and also describes how to configure both the Cloudscape and Oracle databases to work with the all other chapters in this book.

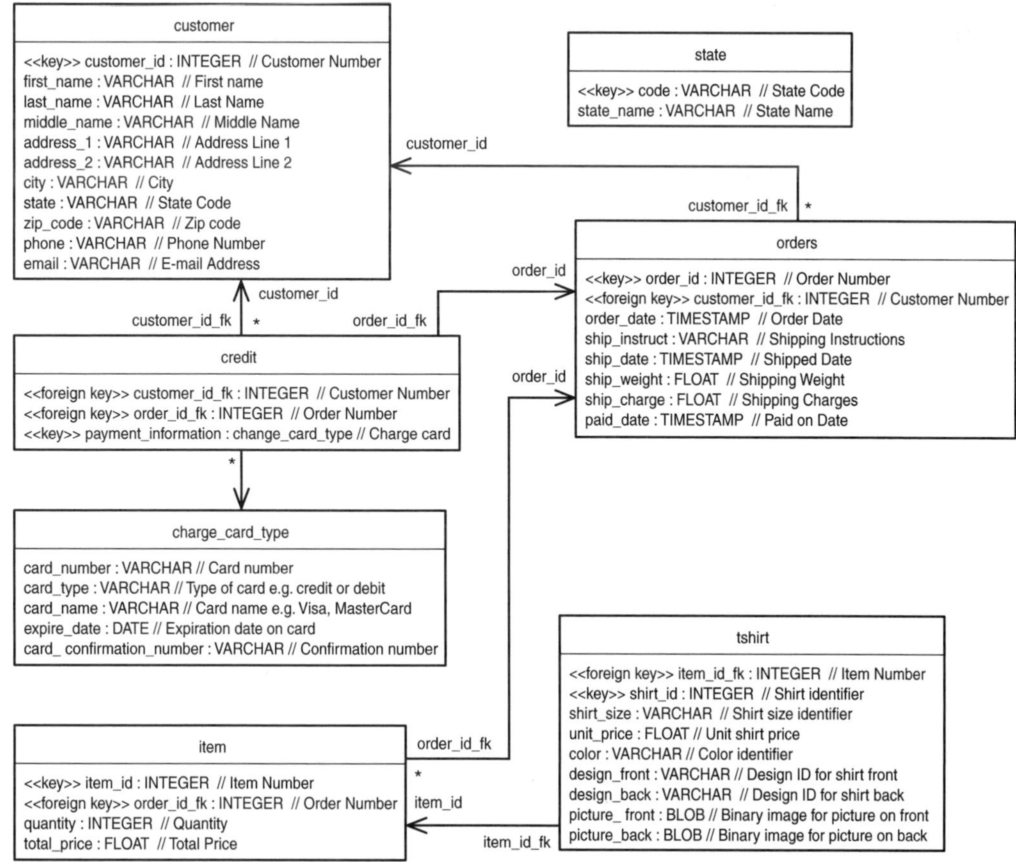

FIGURE 10.1

The BeeShirts.com customer, orders, items, T-shirt, credit, and charge-card data model.

Example: Using the Advanced SQL Types with JDBC

This next example demonstrates how to use a few JDBC 2.0 advanced data type features. The example code is contained in the `ejava.jdbcch10.NewSQLTypeExample` class, which extends the `ejava.jdbcch09.ConnectToDatabase` class from Chapter 9 and the `ejava.jdbcch10.ChargeCard.java` class:

```
public class NewSQLTypeExample extends ConnectToDatabase { ... }
```

NOTE

The complete set of code examples for the `NewSQLTypeExample` and `ChargeCard` can be found on the CD in the `examples\src\ejava\jdbcch10` directory. Some exception handling and other handling mechanisms have been left out of the book here for simplicity but can be found in the examples on the CD. The `runnewsqltypes.bat` example Windows script can be used to build and execute this example. Appendix A describes the general build procedures for all examples in the book and specifies those common environment variables that must be set to execute our example scripts.

Note that at the time of this writing, support for advanced SQL types was not fully adopted by all database and JDBC driver vendors. Consult Appendix A for more information on support and the vendor product with which you can test the `NewSQLTypeExample`.

The `main()` method of `NewSQLTypeExample` is invoked like

```
java ejava.jdbcch10.NewSQLTypeExample <propertiesFileName>
```

where the *`propertiesFileName`* is the location of a properties filename with properties set as in the `JDBCCH10Properties.txt` file. The `main()` method then instantiates a new `NewSQLTypeExample` object and calls `setProperties()` with a filename as with the other examples.

The `main()` method calls `NewSQLTypeExample` instance methods that demonstrate how to insert and retrieve a BLOB, how to insert and retrieve a structured type, and the mapping of a custom type that handles `SQLData`:

```
public static void main(String[]  args)
   {
     if(args.length == 0){
      System.out.println("Error: run the program as java "+
        "ejava.jdbcch10.NewSqlTypeExample <propertiesFileName> ");
      System.exit(0);
    }
```

```
    String fileName = args[0];
    NewSQLTypeExample newSqlTypeExample = new NewSQLTypeExample();
  ...
      newSqlTypeExample.setProperties(fileName);
...
      String blobTypeInsert =
        (String)(newSqlTypeExample.getProperties()).
        get("INSERT_A_BLOB_TYPE_STATEMENT");
      System.out.println(" Blob Type Insert Example ");
      newSqlTypeExample.insertABLOBtype(blobTypeInsert);
      System.out.println( " Blob Type retrieval ");
      String blobTypeRetrieve =
        (String)(newSqlTypeExample.getProperties()).
        get("RETRIEVE_A_BLOB_TYPE_STATEMENT");
      newSqlTypeExample.retrieveBLOBType(blobTypeRetrieve);

      System.out.println( " Struct  Type Insert Example ");
      String structTypeInsert = (String)
        (newSqlTypeExample.getProperties()).
        get("INSERT_STRUCT_TYPE_STATEMENT");
      newSqlTypeExample.insertAStructTypeData(structTypeInsert);
      System.out.println( " Struct  Type Retrieve Example ");
      String structTypeRetrieve = (String)
        (newSqlTypeExample.getProperties()).
        get("RETRIEVE_STRUCT_TYPE_STATEMENT");
      newSqlTypeExample.retrieveAStructTypeData(structTypeRetrieve);

      System.out.println( " ChargeCard Type mapping ");
      newSqlTypeExample.mapCardClassToSQLTypes();
      System.out.println( " ChargeCard Type insertion example ");
      newSqlTypeExample.insertCardTypeData();
      System.out.println( " ChargeCard Type retrieval example ");
      newSqlTypeExample.retrieveCardTypeData();
  ...
}
```

The properties file has properties used by the `NewSQLTypeExample` for BLOB and structured type insert and retrieval SQL statements:

```
#Insert A BLOB Type
INSERT_A_BLOB_TYPE_STATEMENT = UPDATE TSHIRTS.TSHIRT
➥ SET FRONT_PICTURE = ? WHERE TSHIRTS.SHIRT_ID = 10;

#Retrieve a BLOB Type
RETRIEVE_A_BLOB_TYPE_STATEMENT = SELECT FRONT_PICTURE
➥ FROM TSHIRT WHERE SHIRT_ID = 10;
```

```
#Insert a STRUCT Type
INSERT_STRUCT_TYPE_STATEMENT = INSERT INTO CREDIT (101, 1001,
➥ CHARGE_CARD_TYPE ('CREDIT','VISA','1234567890123456',
➥ '31-JUNE-2000', '1234567890123456') )

#Retrieve a STRUCT Type
RETRIEVE_STRUCT_TYPE_STATEMENT = SELECT * FROM CREDIT
➥ WHERE CUSTOMER_ID_FK =101 AND ORDER_ID_FK = 1001
```

The `insertABLOBType()` method takes an update `String` that was read from the properties file and sets a large binary image onto a prepared statement. The prepared statement is then executed. Later, when the `retrieveBLOBType()` method is called, the BLOB is gotten from the result set and restored to a file. BLOB inserts and retrievals are shown here:

```
public void insertABLOBtype(String updateString)
  throws SQLException, Exception
{
  PreparedStatement preparedStatement = getStatement(updateString);
  String fileToReadBlob = "blobExample.gif";
  File f = new File(fileToReadBlob);
  int lengthofFile = (int) f.length();
  FileInputStream fileInputStream = new FileInputStream(f);
  preparedStatement.setBinaryStream(1, fileInputStream,lengthofFile);
  preparedStatement.execute();
}

public void retrieveBLOBType(String queryString)
  throws SQLException, Exception
{
  Statement statement = getStatement();
  ResultSet rs = statement.executeQuery(queryString);
  ResultSetMetaData rsMetaData = rs.getMetaData();
  boolean blobTypeInResult = false;
  int indexOfBlobTypeColumn = -1;
  for(int i = 1; i<= rsMetaData.getColumnCount(); i++){
    int type = rsMetaData.getColumnType(i);
    if(type == java.sql.Types.BLOB){
       blobTypeInResult = true;
       indexOfBlobTypeColumn = i;
    }
  }
  if(blobTypeInResult == false){
    System.out.println(" There is no Blob in the ResultSet,"+
        " this method is written to demonstrate the Blob Data");
    return;
  }
```

```
    while(rs.next()){
     Blob b = rs.getBlob(indexOfBlobTypeColumn);
      InputStream inputStream = b.getBinaryStream();
      // open the stream to read data from Blob reference
      long length = b.length();
      byte[] x = new byte[BLOB_DATA_BUFFER_SIZE];

     int lengthRead = 0;
     String fileToWriteBlob = "blobExample.gif";
     FileOutputStream outputStream
        = new FileOutputStream(fileToWriteBlob);
     while( (lengthRead = inputStream.read(x)) != -1){
       outputStream.write(x);
     }
     inputStream.close();
     outputStream.close();
    }
  }
```

Inserting structured types is demonstrated via a call to the `insertAStructTypeData()` method from `main()`. The subsequent retrieval of a structured type from `retrieveAStructTypeData()` illustrates how to reconstruct the restored `Struct` from the database. Both insert and retrieval are shown here:

```
  public void insertAStructTypeData(String insertString)
    throws SQLException, Exception
  {
    Statement statement = getStatement();
    int nRows = statement.executeUpdate(insertString);
  }

  public void retrieveAStructTypeData(String queryString)
    throws SQLException, Exception
  {
    Statement statement = getStatement();
    ResultSet rs = statement.executeQuery(queryString);
    ResultSetMetaData rsMetaData = rs.getMetaData();
    while(rs.next()){
      for(int i = 1; i<= rsMetaData.getColumnCount(); i++){
        int type = rsMetaData.getColumnType(i);
        switch(type){
          case Types.STRUCT:
                System.out.println("Struct Type Value is :");
                Struct s = (Struct)rs.getObject(i);
                String structTypeName = s.getSQLTypeName();
                Object[]  contents    = s.getAttributes();
```

```
                    for(int j = 0; j< contents.length; j++){
                      System.out.println(contents[j]);
                    }
                    break;
              default :
                    System.out.println("Non Struct Type value is
:"+rs.getObject(i));
                    break;
             }
           }
         }
       }
           }
         }
       }
```

To illustrate the use of a custom type with the database, we have introduced the `ChargeCard` type defined next. `ChargeCard` defines methods for returning its SQL type name, reading SQLData streams, and writing SQLData streams. The `ChargeCard` class is shown here:

```
import java.sql.Date;
import java.sql.SQLData;
import java.sql.SQLInput;
import java.sql.SQLOutput;
import java.sql.SQLException;

public class ChargeCard implements SQLData
{
  public String cardType;
  public String cardName;
  public String cardNumber;
  public Date   expireDate;
  public String cardConfirmationNumber;
  public String sqlType;

  public ChargeCard()
  {
  }

  public ChargeCard(String sqlType, String cardType,
              String cardName, String cardNumber,
              Date expireDate , String cardConfirmationNumber )
  {
    this.cardType = cardType;
    this.cardName = cardName;
    this.cardNumber = cardNumber;
```

```
    this.expireDate = expireDate;
    this.cardConfirmationNumber = cardConfirmationNumber;
    this.sqlType = sqlType;
  }
  public String getSQLTypeName()
  {
    return sqlType;
  }

  public void readSQL(SQLInput stream, String type)
    throws SQLException
  {
    cardType = stream.readString();
    cardName = stream.readString();
    cardNumber = stream.readString();
    expireDate = stream.readDate();
    cardConfirmationNumber = stream.readString();
    sqlType = type;
  }

  public void writeSQL(SQLOutput stream)
    throws SQLException
  {
    stream.writeString(cardType);
    stream.writeString(cardName);
    stream.writeString(cardNumber);
    stream.writeDate(expireDate);
    stream.writeString(cardConfirmationNumber);
  }

  public String toString()
  {
    String rString = "cardType :" + cardType + "cardName :"+ cardName+
      "cardNumber"+ cardNumber + "expireDate :"+ expireDate +
      "cardConfirmationNumber :" + cardConfirmationNumber ;
    return rString;
  }
}
```

Such a custom `ChargeCard` type is registered with the connection from within the `NewSQLTypeExample` `mapCardClassToSQLTypes()` method. A `ChargeCard` instance is inserted into the database from the `insertCardTypeData()` method. Finally, `ChargeCard` data is retrieved from the database from within the `retrieveCardTypeData()` method. Each custom type demonstration method is shown here:

```
public void mapCardClassToSQLTypes()
    throws SQLException, Exception
  {
    Connection connection = super.getConnection();
    Map map = connection.getTypeMap();
    map.put("CHARGE_CARD_TYPE",
        Class.forName("ejava.jdbcch10.ChargeCard"));
  }

  public void insertCardTypeData()
    throws SQLException , Exception
  {
    String insertString = "INSERT INTO CREDIT VALUES( 100, 1001 , ?) ";
    Date expirationDate = Date.valueOf("2001-10-10");

    ChargeCard c = new ChargeCard("TSHIRTS.CHARGE_CARD_TYPE","CREDIT","VISA",
      "1234567890123456", expirationDate, "1234567890123456");
    PreparedStatement preparedStatement = getStatement(insertString);
    // In real case it should work with Types.JAVA_OBJECT
    // but with oracle driver 8i(8.1.5), it throws exception
    // It works for OracleTypes.STRUCT;
    //preparedStatement.setObject(1, c, Types.JAVA_OBJECT);
    preparedStatement.setObject(1, c, OracleTypes.STRUCT);

    preparedStatement.execute();
  }

  public void retrieveCardTypeData()
    throws SQLException, Exception
  {
    String retrieveData =
      "SELECT * FROM CREDIT WHERE"
      + " CUSTOMER_ID_FK =101 AND ORDER_ID_FK = 1001 ";
    Statement statement = getStatement();
    ResultSet rs = statement.executeQuery(retrieveData);

    while(rs.next()){
     ChargeCard c = (ChargeCard)rs.getObject(3);
     System.out.println(c);
    }
  }
```

Row Sets

The JDBC 2.0 Standard Extension specification has introduced the `javax.sql.RowSet` interface. The `RowSet` interface encapsulates a set of rows retrieved from a relational database akin to a `ResultSet`. The `RowSet` interface actually extends the `ResultSet` interface and adds the capability to be used as a JavaBean in an IDE environment. Arguably, this capability to be manipulated as a JavaBean is the sole distinction between a `RowSet` and a `ResultSet`. However, Sun's vision for the `RowSet` interface seems to revolve around the use of `RowSet` objects as the primary interface to encapsulate any direct interaction with the JDBC API in enterprise development environments.

Row Set Architecture

The diagram in Figure 10.2 depicts the main relations and methods involved with `RowSet` interfaces in the `javax.sql` package. As you can see from the diagram, `RowSet` interfaces extend the `ResultSet` interface and can return or be initialized with meta-data about its contents via a `RowSetMetaData` interface that extends the `ResultSetMetaData` interface. `RowSetMetaData` is used to initialize the state of a `RowSet` if it offers a `RowSetInternal` handle on its interior state. Readers and writers of row sets from and to data sources implement the `RowSetReader` and `RowSetWriter` interfaces respectively and use the `RowSetInternal` interface to accomplish their task. Finally, `RowSet` objects can have zero or more `RowSetListener` objects associated with them to listen for row set events encapsulated by `RowSetEvent` objects.

When using `RowSet` objects in an IDE environment, you can associate a series of design-time Bean properties with a `RowSet`. Properties such as SQL to Java type maps, data sources, database URLs, and transaction isolation levels can all be set and associated with a `RowSet` Bean during design-time. For such properties, JavaBeans-compliant getter and setter methods must be present on the `RowSet`. `RowSetListener` objects can be added to a `RowSet` using the `RowSet.addRowSetListener()` method. Three types of `RowSetEvent` objects are of interest to objects implementing the `RowSetListener` interface. Row set change events signify that an entire `RowSet` has changed, whereas row change events signify a change in only one row of the row set. Cursor movement events signify that the cursor in a row set has moved to another row in the row set.

`RowSet` objects may also be used during runtime as a key point of interface for JDBC API clients. The `RowSet` may be used in such a way that `Statement` objects and `ResultSet` objects become irrelevant to the JDBC programmer. SQL commands may be set on the `RowSet`, executed via the `RowSet`, retrieve any command execution results to populate the `RowSet`, and subsequently provide an interface to traverse the data in a `RowSet`.

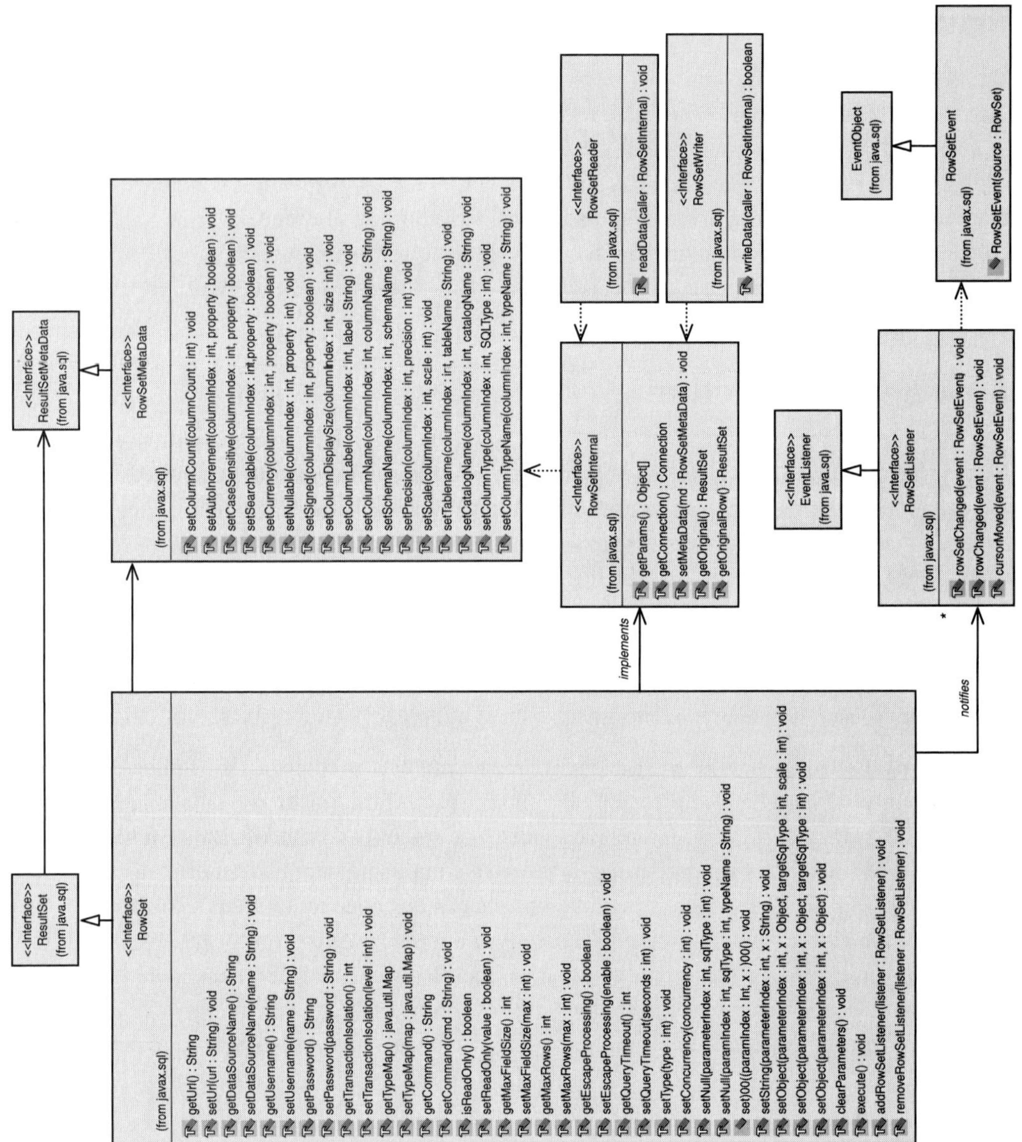

FIGURE 10.2

A `RowSet` *and* `RowSetMetaData` *class diagram.*

Using Row Sets

The `setCommand()` method on a `RowSet` can be set with a SQL `String` parameterized with question mark (`?`) input parameters. A series of `setXXX()` calls on the `RowSet` interface can then be used to set the value for each parameter according to the parameter position in the command `String` akin to the way `PreparedStatement` objects are set. For example:

```
rowSet.setCommand("SELECT * FROM CUSTOMER WHERE FIRST_NAME = ?");
rowSet.setString(1, "Roy");
rowSet.execute();
```

Scrolling forward and backward through `RowSet` objects and obtaining data from `RowSet` objects is accomplished the same way as for `ResultSet` objects. Again, the big bonus for using `RowSet` objects is that they can be used as a JavaBean. Different `RowSet` implementations may require or relax requirements for certain properties to be set. Because this will be implementation dependent, you should consult your `RowSet` vendor's documentation for the `RowSet`'s precise requirements.

Row Set Implementations

`RowSet` implementations may be provided by IDE vendors, JDBC driver vendors, or middleware vendors, or you may indeed decide to implement your own `RowSet` interface. Sun has delineated three potential classes of `RowSet` implementations in their JDBC 2.0 Standard Extension API Specification that they've hinted may become part of a future JDBC standard:

- One such `RowSet` is the `CachedRowSet`, for providing a `RowSet` that can be serialized and cached inside a JDBC client sans any cursor connectivity back to the database. In fact, at the time of this book's writing, an early access release from Sun of a `CachedRowSet` was available from its Web site.
- Another `RowSet` type described by Sun is the `JDBCRowSet`, which maintains a connection back to the database and simply serves as a JavaBeans-compliant wrapper of a `ResultSet`.
- Finally, a third `RowSet` described by Sun is a `WebRowSet`, which provides a thin interface for Web-based clients whereby the `WebRowSet` communicates via HTTP to a back-end Web server for providing database access.

Managing Internal Row Set State and Behavior

The `RowSetInternal` interface may be implemented by a `RowSet` to expose some of its internal field members to another object for viewing or updating those values. Values such as the `RowSet` connection, the original state of the `RowSet`, and an array of parameters set on the `RowSet` may all be retrieved. Additionally, a `RowSetMetaData` object may also be set onto the `RowSet` if it implements the `RowSetInternal` interface.

By setting RowSetMetaData onto a RowSet, key meta-data values can be set onto the RowSet object to instruct the RowSet how to behave when retrieving and updating data. Such information as automatic column numbering, case sensitivity, column counts, column names, column types, searchability, and associated schema, catalog, and table names may all be set onto a RowSetMetaData object.

A RowSet object can call an object that implements a RowSetReader interface. The RowSetReader has one method called readData(), which takes a RowSetInternal object and uses it to populate the contents of a RowSet with new data or a data update. Similarly, a RowSet may call a RowSetWriter object's writedata() method with a RowSetInternal object in order to have the RowSetWriter write the RowSet contents to a data source. Such de-coupling of data source reader/writer capabilities can offer flexibility in delegating how data is retrieved or persisted to an underlying reader/writer mechanism.

Stored Procedures

Most databases provide a set of helper functions that database programmers can use to operate on data while it is in the database versus retrieving it, computing some result, and possibly updating the database with the new value. The main benefits of such database functions are the performance enhancements involved with avoiding data retrieval and storage. This is particularly apparent when many small functions need to be performed.

Most databases also allow for the definition of user-defined functions that can also be used to operate on data without a remote retrieval or storage call. Such user-defined database functions are called stored procedures because they are functions that are actually stored in the database. Although there may be performance enhancements associated with changing the state of data due to some function call directly within the database, there are many disadvantages as well. Maintainability and code portability are often the two key problem areas associated with using stored procedures. Stored procedures become a maintenance issue when it comes time to provide enhanced or altered functionality. Portability is an issue when you try to relocate stored procedures to another database. The trend in enterprise development has been to move as much of the business logic as possible out of a database and into the middle tier. Nevertheless, at times use of stored procedures is justified, and there will certainly be cases when enterprise systems developers must interface with legacy databases containing stored procedures. Because of these reasons, JDBC has provided support for interfacing with stored procedures since version 1.0 of the specification.

Predefined Database Functions

Four types of function calls are identified by JDBC for potential (although not required) support by your JDBC driver. These are numeric functions, string manipulation functions, time and date functions, and a few system functions. It is the driver's responsibility to make sure that any supported functions can be mapped from the JDBC syntax for accessing such functions to the underlying database calls for executing the functions. The basic syntax for calling a function from within a JDBC `Statement` is of this general form:

```
"{ fn FCN_NAME( ARGS ) }"
```

For example:

```
ResultSet resultSet = statement.executeQuery("{fn RAND("+ num + ")}");
```

To determine which functions are supported by your database and driver, a series of calls can be made on the `DatabaseMetaData` object:

- `String getNumericFunctions()` returns the list of names identifying supported mathematical functions separated by commas.
- `String getStringFunctions()` returns the list of names identifying supported string manipulation functions separated by commas.
- `String getSystemFunctions()` returns the list of names identifying supported system functions separated by commas.
- `String getTimeDateFunctions()` returns the list of names identifying supported time and date functions separated by commas.

Creating Stored Procedures

Manipulating database stored procedures is accomplished via the `java.sql.CallableStatement` interface. The `CallableStatement` interface and a few of its key call signatures are shown in Figure 10.3. The `CallableStatement` interface extends the `PreparedStatement` interface, which in turn extends the `Statement` interface. `CallableStatement` objects are created by calling `prepareCall()` on a `Connection` object. `Connection.prepareCall()` is invoked with a stored procedure call `String` of the following general form:

```
"{ call PROCEDURE_NAME (?,?,...,?) }"
```

Given a stored procedure name, you can create a stored procedure `String` with a set of input parameters (`IN`), output parameters (`OUT`), or input/output parameters (`INOUT`) by using the question mark (`?`) for each parameter in the `String`. Stored procedures that return values may also potentially be called with the following syntax:

```
"{ ? = call PROCEDURE_NAME (?,?,...,?) }"
```

Stored procedure syntax is by no means always standard across JDBC driver and database vendors. For example, a stored procedure in Oracle may be created as in this example:

```
String sqlStatement = "begin ? := getTotalPriceForOrder(1001);end;";
CallableStatement callableStatement
      = getCallableStatement(sqlStatement);
callableStatement.registerOutParameter(1, Types.INTEGER);
```

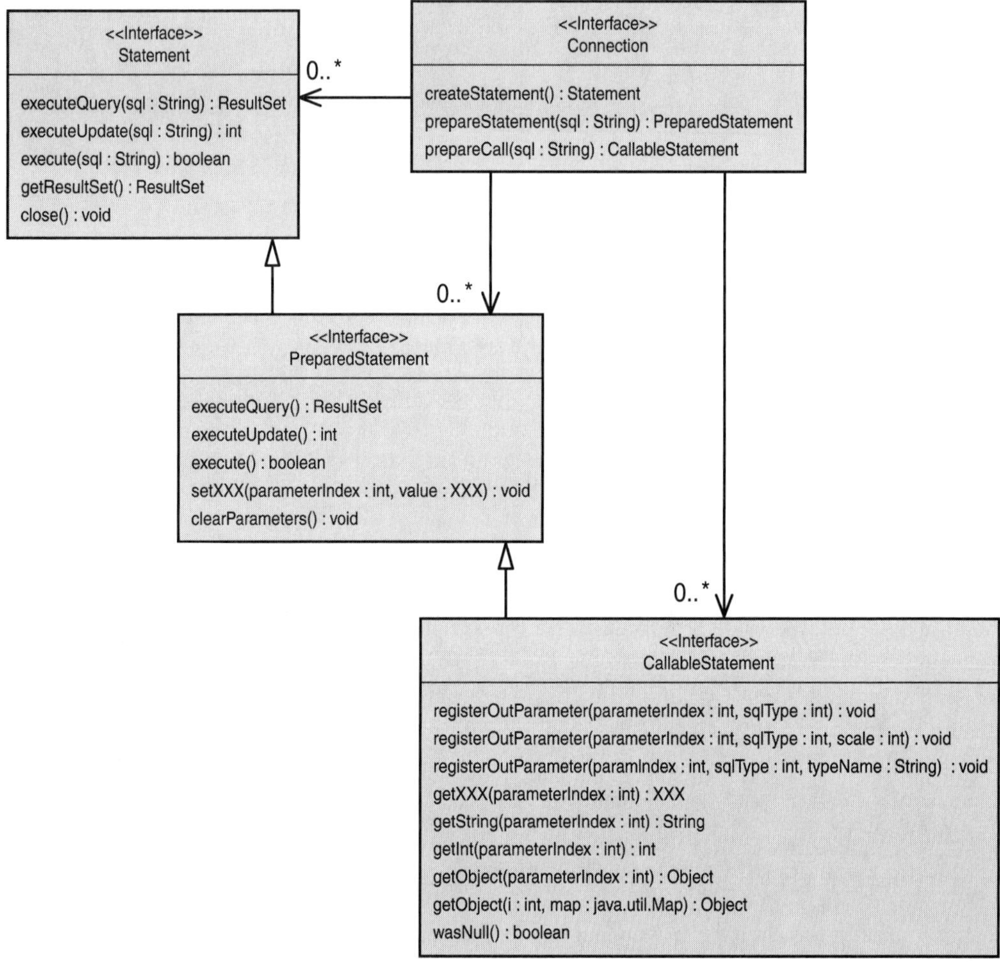

FIGURE 10.3
A `CallableStatement` *class diagram.*

The `IN` and `INOUT` parameters used in a `CallableStatement` are set in the same fashion as input parameters are set on the extended `PreparedStatement` interface. Thus, a call to `setXXX()` (inherited from the `PreparedStatement` interface) given the parameter index and the actual value of the *XXX* type must be called for each IN and INOUT parameter. Return parameters, OUT, and INOUT parameters must have their SQL type defined by calling one of the three following methods on the CallableStatement object:

- void registerOutParameter(int index, int type) registers the parameter in the index position to be of the java.sql.Types type specified. The java.sql.Types.OTHER type should be used if this type is specific to the database.
- void registerOutParameter(int index, int type, int scale) registers the parameter in the index position to be of the java.sql.Types type specified. This method form should be used if the type is a Numeric or Decimal type. The scale value defines the number of digits on the right side of the decimal point.
- void registerOutParameter(int index, int type, String typeName) registers the parameter in the index position to be of the java.sql.Types type specified. This JDBC 2.0 method form is used for REF types or user-defined types such as named arrays, JAVA_OBJECTs, STRUCTs, and DISTINCTs. The typeName is the complete SQL type name being registered.

If a return value is generated from a stored procedure of the form { ? = call *PROCEDURE_NAME* (?,?,...,?) }, the parameter index for this value should be registered as position number 1.

Executing Stored Procedures

Executing a stored procedure is accomplished by calling one of the execute methods on the CallableStatement object. Because a stored procedure may return more than one ResultSet, you'll have to scroll through the entire result set before you can obtain any values returned to the statement's OUT and INOUT parameters. On scrolling through the entire result set, a series of get*XXX*() calls on the CallableStatement must be made to obtain the OUT and INOUT values returned from the stored procedure. Calls for get*XXX*() exist for various types with just a few shown in Figure 10.3.

Creating a Few BeeShirts.com Stored Procedures

The BeeShirts.com database has a few stored procedures in it to compute the total price for a particular order, retrieve a customer's phone number, and obtain the total sum for a set of orders. The SQL statements used to create these functions in the database are as shown here:

```
-- Create procedure for getting total price for the order

CREATE OR REPLACE
FUNCTION getTotalPriceForOrder (vorder_id IN NUMBER )
RETURN NUMBER
```

```
IS
    vtotal_value NUMBER;
BEGIN
    SELECT I.total_price INTO vtotal_value
    FROM orders O,item I
    WHERE O.order_id =vorder_id AND O.order_id = I.order_id_fk;
  RETURN vtotal_value;
END;

/

-- Create getCustomerPhoneNumber function

 CREATE OR REPLACE FUNCTION getCustomerPhoneNumber(
    vcustomer_id IN NUMBER)
   RETURN VARCHAR
 IS
   vphone VARCHAR(12);
 BEGIN
    SELECT phone
     INTO  vphone
    FROM customer
    WHERE customer_id = vcustomer_id;
    return vphone;
 END getCustomerPhoneNumber;
/

--  Create procedure for getTotalOrders
CREATE OR REPLACE PROCEDURE getTotalOrders(
    vcustomer_id_fk IN ORDERS.CUSTOMER_ID_FK%TYPE,
    vtotal_items OUT NUMBER)
  IS
  BEGIN
    SELECT sum(I.quantity) INTO vtotal_items
    FROM item I, orders O
    WHERE O.order_id = I.order_id_fk AND
          O.customer_id_fk = vcustomer_id_fk;
  END getTotalOrders;
/
```

Example: Calling Stored Procedures

This next example demonstrates how to call stored procedures in the database. The example code is contained in the `ejava.jdbcch10.CallableStatementExample` class, which extends the `ejava.jdbcch09.ConnectToDatabase` class from Chapter 9:

```
public class CallableStatementExample extends ConnectToDatabase { ... }
```

NOTE

The complete set of code examples for the `CallableStatementExample` can be found on the CD in the `examples\src\ejava\jdbcch10` directory. Some exception handling and other handling mechanisms have been left out of the book here for simplicity but can be found in the examples on the CD. The `runcallablestatement.bat` example Windows script can be used to build and execute this example. Appendix A describes the general build procedures for all examples in the book and specifies those common environment variables that must be set to execute our example scripts. This `CallableStatementExample` was specifically used and tested with the Oracle 8i database. Refer to Appendix A for database configuration instructions.

The `main()` method of `CallableStatementExample` is invoked as

```
java ejava.jdbcch10.CallableStatementExample <propertiesFileName>
```

where the *`propertiesFileName`* is the location of a properties filename with properties set as in the `JDBCCH10Properties.txt` file. The `main()` method then instantiates a new `CallableStatementExample` object and calls `setProperties()` with a filename as with the other examples. Subsequently, the `main()` method then calls all three stored procedures in the BeeShirts.com database:

```
public static void main(String[]  args)
{
 if(args.length == 0){
    System.out.println("Error: run the program as "+
      "java ejava.jdbcch10.CallableStatement <propertiesFileName> ");
    System.exit(0);
  }
  String fileName = args[0];
  CallableStatementExample callStExample =
    new CallableStatementExample();
...
    callStExample.setProperties(fileName);
    callStExample.executeGetCustomerPhoneNumberFunction();
    callStExample.executeGetTotalPriceFunction();
    callStExample.executeTotalOrdersFortheCustomer();
}
```

A new `getCallableStatement()` method is defined here for the various `execute`*`XXX`*`()` methods for creating a `CallableStatement` given a SQL `String`:

```
protected CallableStatement getCallableStatement(String sqlStatement)
  throws SQLException, Exception
{
```

```
    Connection connection = super.getConnection();
    CallableStatement statement =
      connection.prepareCall(sqlStatement);
    return statement;
  }
```

These are the three `executeXXX()` methods used for executing queries against the stored procedures from BeeShirts.com using an Oracle stored procedure call syntax:

```
  public void executeGetTotalPriceFunction()
    throws SQLException, Exception
  {
    String sqlStatement
      = "begin ? := getTotalPriceForOrder( 1001);end;";

    CallableStatement callableStatement =
      getCallableStatement(sqlStatement);
    callableStatement.registerOutParameter(1, Types.FLOAT);
    callableStatement.execute();
    System.out.println("Total price :" + callableStatement.getFloat(1));
  }

  public void executeGetCustomerPhoneNumberFunction()
    throws SQLException,Exception
  {
    String sqlStatement = "begin ? := getCustomerPhoneNumber(101); end;";
    CallableStatement callableStatement =
      getCallableStatement(sqlStatement);
    callableStatement.registerOutParameter(1, Types.VARCHAR);
    callableStatement.execute();

    System.out.println("Phone #  :" + callableStatement.getString(1) +
        " for Customer_id 101");
  }


   public void executeTotalOrdersFortheCustomer()
    throws SQLException,Exception
  {
    String sqlStatement = "begin  getTotalOrders(104, ?); end;";
    CallableStatement callableStatement =
      getCallableStatement(sqlStatement);
    callableStatement.registerOutParameter(1, Types.INTEGER);
    callableStatement.execute();

    System.out.println("Total Orders #  :" +
      callableStatement.getInt(1) + " for Customer_id 104");
  }
```

Database Naming via JNDI

The Java Naming and Directory Interface (JNDI) is a Java extension and set of APIs that are part of the J2EE used to provide a standard interface to naming and directory services. Naming services provide a mechanism for binding human-readable names to objects and resolving objects to names. Directory services are similar to naming services with the exception that more sophisticated object searching is provided. Basically, you can think of things like file systems that map filenames to and from file objects as naming services. Chapter 19, "Naming Services," discusses naming services, and Chapter 20, "Directory and Trading Services," discusses directory services in detail. Suffice it to say, though, that JNDI provides a standard interface to various naming and directory services that can be adapted for use with a JNDI mapping much like database services are mapped to the standard JDBC interface via a JDBC driver (that is, mapping).

JNDI clients obtain a handle to a naming or directory service by creating an initial context using the `javax.naming.InitialContext` class. The `InitialContext` class implements the `javax.naming.Context` interface and has methods on it to bind an object to the naming service with a name and to look up an object in the naming service given a name. The JDBC 2.0 standard extension specification defines a new standard for being able to bind database references to a name presumably from a server-side middle-tier entity or by some JavaBean provider. A database client can then obtain a handle to the database by using a simple name. This in essence replaces the need for using a `DriverManager` to register drivers and using database URLs to obtain a `Connection`.

The `javax.sql.DataSource` interface introduced in the JDBC 2.0 standard extension will typically be implemented by driver vendors to serve as a factory for JDBC connections. Such `DataSource` objects are the database resource that will be registered with a naming service by a middle-tier server via JNDI. After a handle to a `DataSource` object is retrieved from JNDI using a name that always begins with a root context name of `jdbc`, a `DataSource.getConnection()` method is called to obtain a database connection.

The J2EE and JDBC 2.0

Use of JNDI is the primary means by which J2EE components obtain handles to JDBC `DataSource` objects and subsequently obtain JDBC `Connection` handles. Such a mechanism will be demonstrated throughout Part VI, "Enterprise Web Enabling," and Part VII, "Enterprise Applications Enabling," when we describe how Java Servlets, JavaServer Pages, and Enterprise JavaBeans obtain JDBC 2.0 `DataSource` handles from their middle-tier container/server environments. Use of such features also best enables a middle-tier J2EE server environment to manage database connection resource pools.

There are two main differences between obtaining a connection from a `DataSource` via JNDI and using the `DriverManager`. For one, the `DataSource` is registered with JNDI by the middle tier, and therefore any retrieved connections can be managed remotely for distributed clients versus locally, as is the case with clients that use a local `DriverManager` object. For another, names used to obtain `DataSource` objects from JNDI are registered by the middle tier, and therefore the client code is unaffected by database URL changes, as is the case with using URLs to obtain connections from a local `DriverManager` interface.

`DataSource` implementations have a set of properties that are set at design-time when implemented as a JavaBean. Getters and setters for these properties should be implemented following the JavaBeans standard naming convention. Only a description property is mandatory for implementation by a `DataSource` JavaBean. Nevertheless, a set of standard property names is specified here, and `DataSource` vendors must adhere to this convention if implementation of such a property is provided by the JavaBean:

- `String serverName`: A database server name.
- `String databaseName`: The name of a database.
- `String dataSourceName`: The name of a data source used when pooling database connections.
- `String description`: A description of the data source.
- `int portNumber`: A port number for database requests.
- `String networkProtocol`: The protocol used by the database server.
- `String user`: A database username.
- `String password`: A database password.
- `String roleName`: A SQL role name.

`DataSource` registration is typically performed by a middle-tier or JavaBean implementation. `DataSource` instances are created by such middle-tier or Bean deployers, and calls to methods such as `setServerName()`, `setDatabaseName()`, and `setDataSourceName()` are made as such:

```
SimpleDataSource sds = new SimpleDataSource();
sds.setServerName("EASTERN_SERVER");
sds.setDatabaseName("EASTERN_US_TSHIRTS_REPOSITORY");
sds.setDescription("Eastern U.S. Data Server for TShirts Database ");
sds.setPort(1521);
sds.setNetworkProtocol("TCP/IP");
```

These instances are then bound to a name server using names such as `jdbc/TSHIRTS/EASTERN`:

```
Context initialContext = new InitialContext();
initialContext.bind("jdbc/TSHIRTS/EASTERN", sds);
```

A client application will then look up DataSource object handles using such names, will call getConnection() on the DataSource to obtain a Connection handle, and subsequently should call close() on the Connection when finished.

```
Context initialContext = new InitialContext();
SimpleDataSource sds = initialContext.lookup("jdbc/TSHIRTS/EASTERN");
Connection connection = sds.getConnection("SCOTT", "TIGER");
  ...
connection.close();
```

Connection Pools

Pooling of resources in general is a key feature that enterprise development projects must consider carefully. Because enterprise systems are typically designed for scalability and must often cope with many concurrent users, pools of resources that are used by user sessions are frequently implemented by middle tiers. The basic concept of a resource pool is to maintain a collection of "hot" resources ready to be doled out to a client upon request or need for that resource. Database connection pools are one type of important resource that can be cached in memory in the middle tier such that upon request from a client, a connection will be immediately available for use by the client (versus spending time creating and initializing a connection). When the client is done using the connection, it is returned to the pool to await allocation to another request. Connection pooling is a new feature introduced in the JDBC 2.0 Standard Extension specification for middle-tier management of database connection pools.

The diagram in Figure 10.4 depicts the key entities and relationships involved with connection pooling. JDBC 2.0 driver vendors that implement connection pooling provide an implementation of the javax.sql.ConnectionPoolDataSource interface. ConnectionPoolDataSource has two getPooledConnection() methods used to return PooledConnection objects. PooledConnection objects encapsulate pooled connections to data sources. Middle-tier vendors implement DataSource objects that talk with ConnectionPoolDataSource interfaces implemented by JDBC driver vendors in order to provide handles to data sources offering pooled connection features. Middle-tier vendors maintain a pool of PooledConnection objects returned from ConnectionPoolDataSource objects. Middle-tier vendor implementations can also register a ConnectionEventListener with the PooledConnection object to be notified of connection events such as connection closing and errors encapsulated by ConnectionEvent objects. As you can see from Figure 10.4, connection pooling is completely transparent to middle-tier client Java applications.

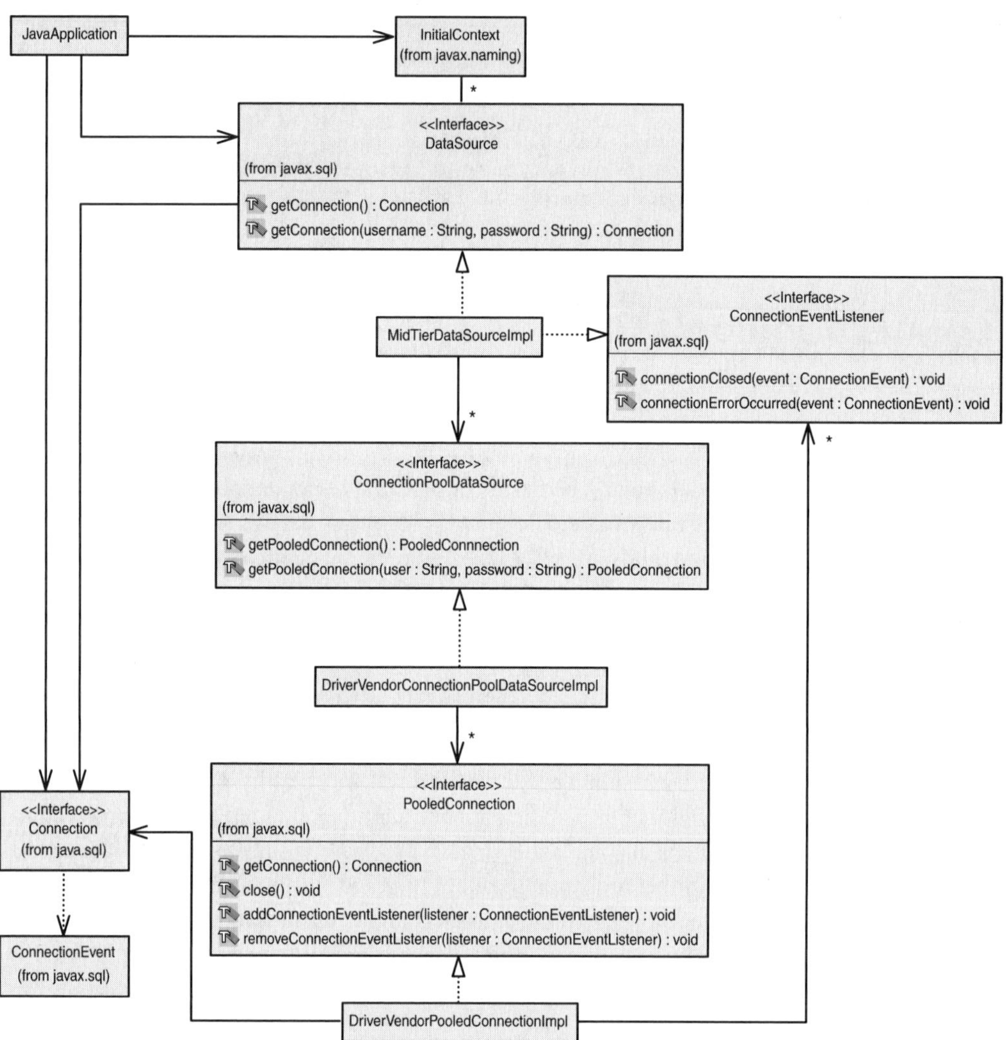

FIGURE 10.4

A connection pooling class diagram.

Figure 10.5 shows the basic flow behind the scenes of connection pooling in the middle tier. Here we see the Java Application client looking up a `DataSource` object via JNDI and requesting a connection from the `DataSource`. The middle-tier remote `DataSource` implementation will first look within its connection pool to see whether a pooled connection is ready to hand off to the client. In this scenario we depict what occurs when a connection is not available and the data source implementation must request a new `PooledConnection` from a driver vendor's

`ConnectionPoolDataSource` interface object. The middle-tier data source implementation then registers a `ConnectionEventListener` with the `PooledConnection` and subsequently obtains a reference to a new `Connection` object. The `Connection` object gets returned to the Java Application client, who then uses the connection and calls `close()` when it is finished. Such a call generates a `ConnectionEvent` instance, which gets returned to the middle-tier data source implementation registering interest in such events. On notification of the connection closing, the middle tier can place the connection object back into a pool of connections.

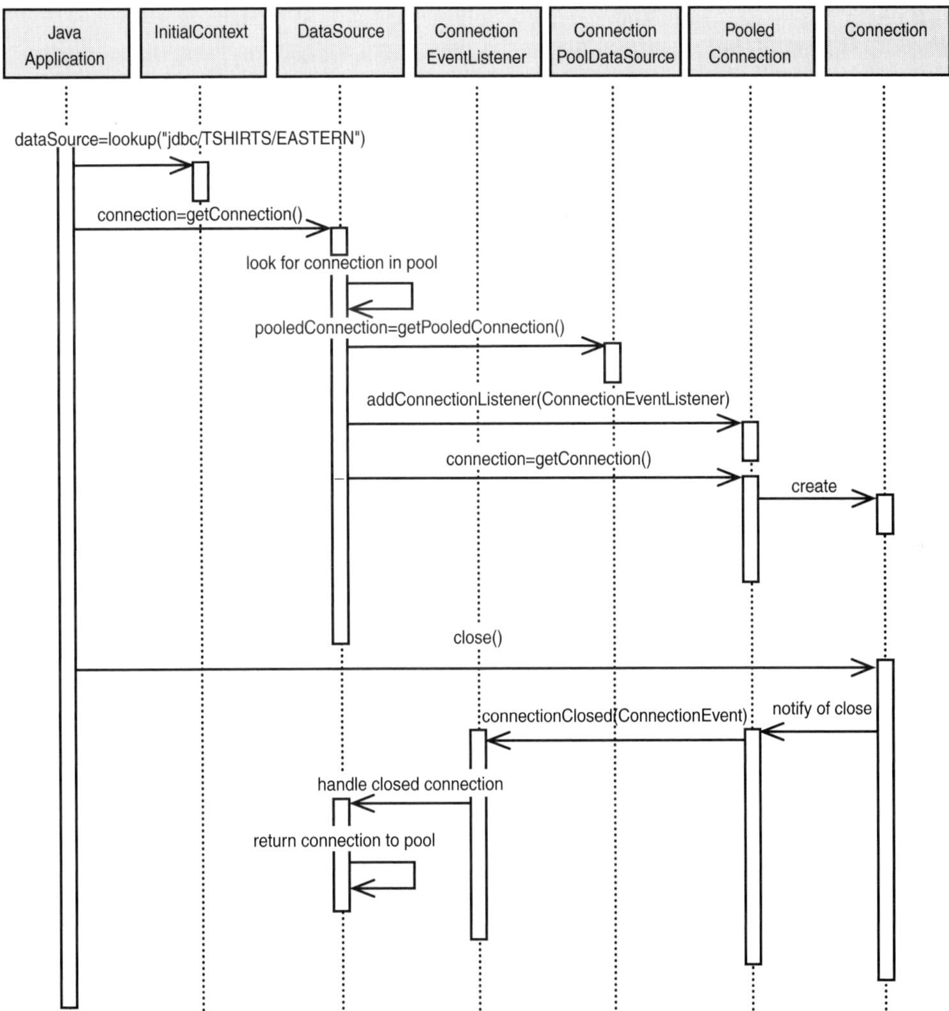

FIGURE 10.5
A connection pooling scenario diagram.

Distributed Transactions

Chapter 8 presented a general architecture for database transaction management. We saw how a transaction manager manages atomic transactions that can potentially span multiple resource managers (that is, DBMS servers). Such distributed transactions that can span multiple data sources and need to be treated as one atomic transaction inevitably require the need for a centralized transaction manager to coordinate distributed commits and rollbacks. Transaction managers must also contend with issues such as concurrency and deadlock, in addition to the fact that X/Open XA standards-compliant transaction managers must guarantee that different resource managers will be assigned different branches of a transaction that compose a distributed transaction. To facilitate a transaction manager's ease of interfacing with a heterogeneous network of resource managers, a resource adapter is often provided to present a common interface to various resource managers. The JDBC interface provides just such a resource adapter interface to DBMSs that can be used by transaction managers. The hooks needed to offer distributed transaction support have been added to JDBC in the JDBC 2.0 Standard Extension API specification.

Figure 10.6 shows some of the key entities involved in providing distributed transactions support using JDBC 2.0. This figure is very similar to Figure 10.4, which depicts the entities involved with connection pooling. The middle-tier vendor implements the `DataSource` interface, which now must interact with JDBC vendor-supplied `XADataSource` interfaces instead of `ConnectionPoolDataSource` interfaces. The data source implementation will also interact with an XA-compliant transaction manager via a transactions service interface to be described in Chapter 23. `XADataSource` objects return `XAConnection` objects that extend the `PooledConnection` interface and can participate in a distributed transaction. The middle-tier data source implementation calls `getXAResource()` on the `XAConnection` object to obtain a handle to a `javax.transaction.XAResource` object that is passed to the transaction manager. The transaction manager uses the `XAResource` object to manage distributed transactions using resources (that is, connections) managed by the associated XA-compliant resource manager.

Even though the middle-tier Java client can remain unaware of the underlying distributed transaction support provided by the middle tier, a few things not to do must be taken into consideration. For one, the Java client application must not call `commit()` or `rollback()` on the `Connection` object. Setting auto-commit to `true` on the `Connection` object using `setAutoCommit(true)` is also forbidden. Nevertheless, `SQLExceptions` will be thrown if the Java application does make such transaction-related calls from the client side.

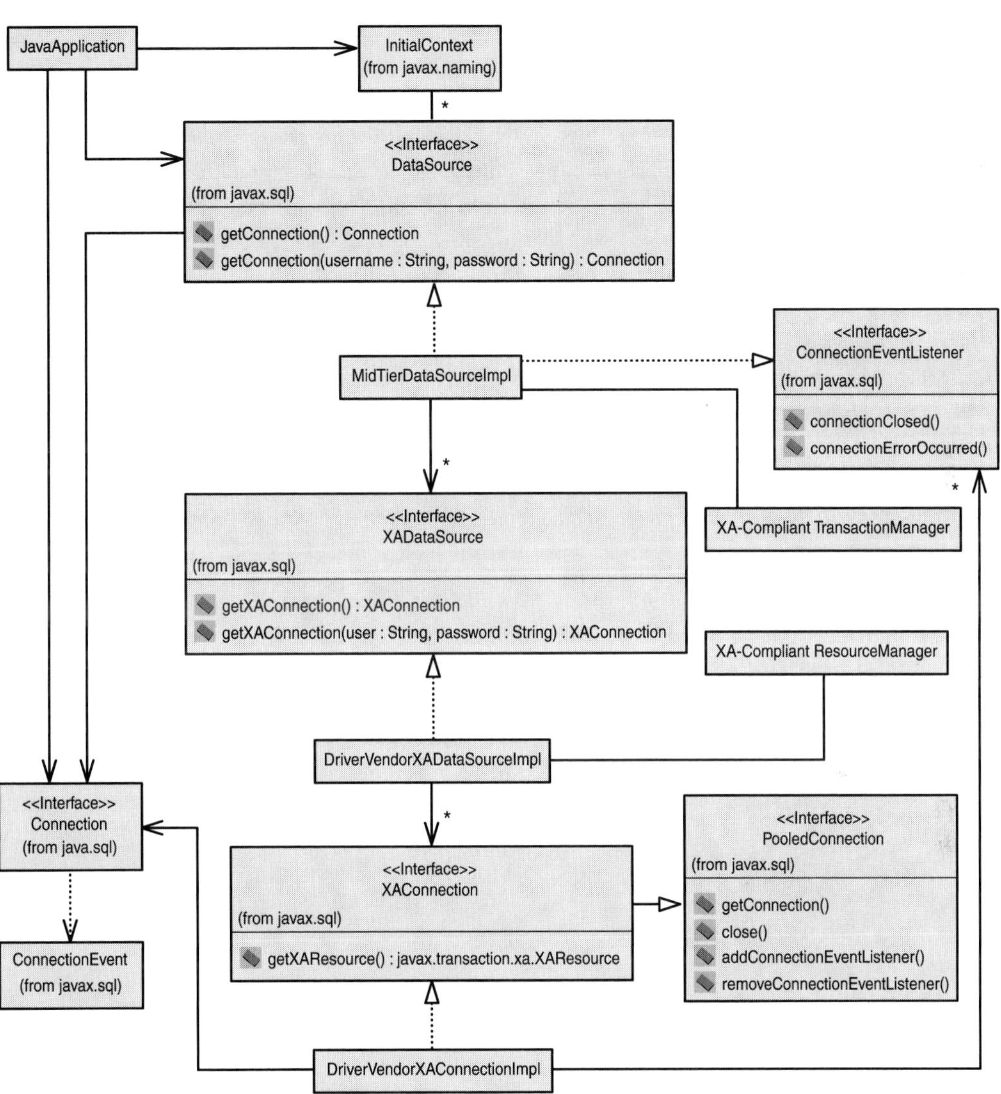

FIGURE 10.6

A distributed transactions class diagram.

Conclusions

JDBC 2.0 has introduced a wide range of specifications outlining new standard APIs for both the JDBC client applications programmer and the middle-tier programmer. For the JDBC 1.0 and above client application, calling database functions and stored procedures is provided via the JDBC API. For the JDBC 2.0 client application, we now also have the capability to scroll around JDBC result sets and make updates to the database directly from a result set for both a singular database row and a batch of database rows. JDBC applications can also now capitalize on the use of new SQL types such as BLOBs and CLOBs and map custom-defined SQL types to and from Java classes. The use of row sets now allows one to interface with JDBC result sets during design-time as a JavaBean, as well as provide a new way to interact with the JDBC API. JDBC clients can also connect to the database using JDBC data sources and the JNDI interface for resolving database names to database connection handles. Finally, JDBC 2.0 client applications can now transparently reap the benefits of standard connection pooling and distributed transaction handling with JDBC's new API extensions for the middle tier.

Although many standards offer only the lowest common denominator of functionality for vendor offerings, JDBC 2.0 is clearly pushing the envelope by providing extended standards for Java database connectivity. The pros of standardized database access being cross-vendor platform portable can thus be taken advantage of while being less afflicted with the cons of limited functionality often inherent in many standards. Enterprise Java applications are thus now more able to grow and scale in more sophisticated directions.

Distributed Enterprise Communications Enabling

PART

IN THIS PART

11 Distributed Enterprise Communications 315

12 Network Communications 325

13 Web Communications 365

14 Modeling Components with CORBA 385

15 CORBA Communications 417

16 RMI Communications 465

17 Modeling Components with COM/DCOM 527

18 DCOM Communications 541

Distributed Enterprise Communications

CHAPTER

11

IN THIS CHAPTER

- Distributed Systems 316
- Distribution Mechanisms 318
- The Network Client 321
- The Network Server 323

The distributed enterprise systems problem can involve issues such as scalability, wide-area geographical distribution, and heterogeneous platform interfacing. A better understanding of the problems you'll face in providing solutions will help you more effectively be able to partition the problem space into more discrete and solvable chunks. Having a general model against which all potential solution paradigms can be cast further enables you to more rapidly and deeply understand the pros and cons of each communications paradigm.

In this chapter, you will learn:

- About the problems that affect distributed systems in general.
- About the generic logical and physical models of distributed enterprise communication solutions.
- About a general model and various kinds of network client paradigms to be examined in subsequent chapters.
- About a general model and various kinds of network server paradigms to be examined in subsequent chapters.

Distributed Systems

A distributed system in the context of information technology is a system composed of many physically independent computing mechanisms. Whenever the need arises to make two such independently operating mechanisms talk to one another, technically speaking, you have a distributed systems problem. If you truly have only two such devices that need to talk to one another, your solution may be the quickest and dirtiest solution you can find, or perhaps it will be something somewhat proprietary in the interest of being cost-effective. However, the term *distributed system* used in the context of an enterprise system usually means connecting many more than just two independently operating devices. Thus, your solution to such a problem takes on a much different face. Your solutions will most likely have to consider economies of scale, vastly diverse computing environments, wide-area geographical distribution of computing mechanisms, and vastly diverse communications mediums (see Figure 11.1).

Let's compare computing to hamburgers for a moment. Mom and Pop hamburger shops typically have to serve only a small customer base, and the decisions they make in the exchange of hamburgers for revenue may result in small inefficiencies such as using certain high-quality ingredients or perhaps using certain spices or cooking techniques to cater to the cultural region in which they run their business. For large-scale hamburger businesses, however, small inefficiencies multiplied by the thousands of businesses they may operate, translate into a huge cost. Furthermore, catering a cooking style to each particular geographical region could be devastating to a large-scale hamburger business. Thus, the vastly distributed mega-hamburger businesses must agree on conventions of cooking, consider economies of scale, deal with vastly diverse customer bases, and conduct all of this business over a wide-area geographical distribution chain. Needless to say, a whole host of problems can arise.

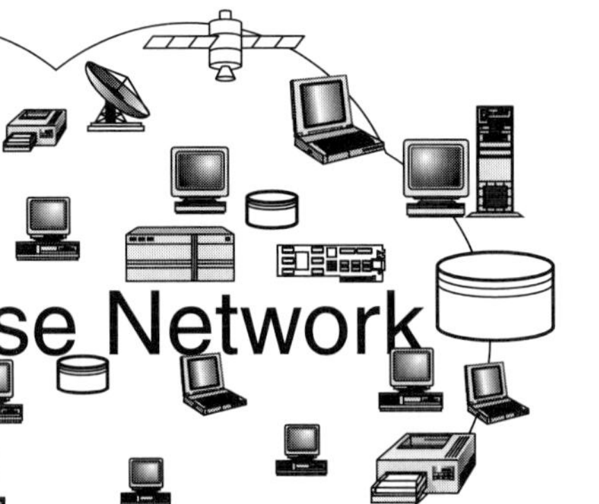

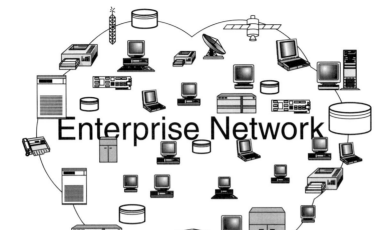

FIGURE 11.1
The distributed systems quagmire.

Okay, comparing computing to hamburgers is a bit of a stretch, but the point remains valid that building a distributed system for an enterprise requires a whole different thought process than might be used to solve smaller-area distribution issues. Luckily, given that we will pursue building distributed systems using object-oriented and component-based techniques in this book, solving distributed system problems can be cast in terms that are easier to understand and that can be more modularly described. Modularity of problem description results in modularity of solution. Table 11.1 summarizes some of these distributed object system issues.

TABLE 11.1 Distributed System Issues

Distributed System Issue	*Description*
Reliable Transport Communications	Reliable means of communication between client and server objects.
Language Dependencies	Dependencies on legacy language client and server implementations.
Platform Dependencies	Dependencies on operating system and processor platforms.
Client/Server Interfacing	Provide client/server interfaces for mapping requests and responses between the applications and communications layers.

continues

TABLE 11.1 Continued

Distributed System Issue	*Description*
Object Activation	Activation of server objects upon receipt of client requests.
Object Name Binding and	Binding names to objects and Lookupresolving objects to names.
Service Trading	Discovery, advertisement, and searching for object services using meta-data about such services.
Creation and Deletion	Creation and deletion of distributed objects.
Copying and Moving	Copying and moving distributed objects around a distributed system.
Event Handling	Generation and notification of distributed events.
Transactions	Managing a set of distributed operations as an atomic operation such that either all occur or none occurs.
Concurrency	Acquiring and releasing locks to distributed resources.
Persistence	Storage and retrieval of distributed objects.
Security	Distributed authentication, encryption, authorization, and auditing.
Usage Licensing	Acquisition, renewal, and cancellation of licenses for object usage.

Distribution Mechanisms

The first step involved with attempting to solve any problem is to attempt to partition the problem into modular and individually solvable components. At the coarsest granularity of distributed enterprise communications problem partitioning, we distinguish between the application and the communications layers. In no way do we want our communications architecture to be dependent on our application code, and we would ideally prefer to have a way to keep our application code clean and free from any explicit calls to send or receive data over any communications protocol software libraries (that is, a protocol stack). Figure 11.2 depicts a layer of application/communications interface code that would ideally exist between your application code and communications code to provide just such insulation.

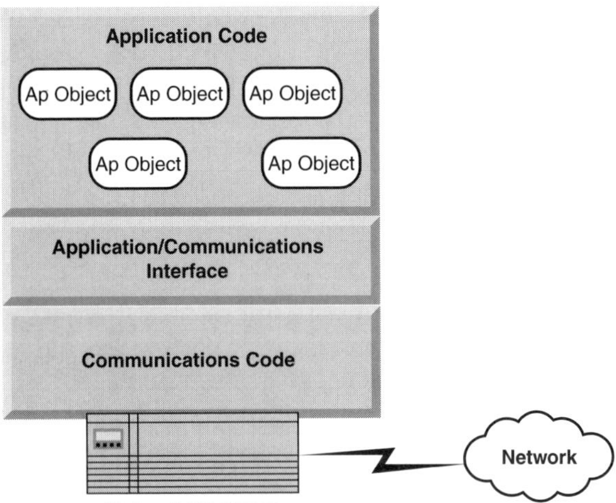

FIGURE 11.2
Basic distributed system layers.

Aside from the logical partitioning between application layer and communications layer as shown in Figure 11.2, the distributed systems problem can also be physically partitioned. That is, different distributed systems solutions will vary in how they physically distribute the processing load and type of processing to be performed across different distributed network elements. Figure 11.3 roughly depicts how distributed-system architectures have evolved over time. Each evolutionary stage of Figure 11.3 not only depicts a step in time of the evolutionary process, but also depicts a physical distribution architectural option that may still be employed today. The following text describes each stage in detail:

- *Dumb Terminal and Mainframe Computing*: Stage 1 depicts the basic dumb-terminal–to–mainframe relationship popular during the earliest stages of computing. A database of some sort may also be involved that maintains the corporate enterprise data.
- *Desktop Computing*: Stage 2 represents the next stage in development, in which the desktop environment becomes more powerful and computing resources can be shifted away from the mainframe to the individual workstations. Desktop platforms may now even access the database directly.
- *LAN Computing*: The birth of the LAN is depicted in Stage 3, in which standard local networking protocols begin to emerge and products that can support those protocols enter the network environment.
- *Internet Computing*: Stage 4 depicts the birth of internetworking, in which wide area networking becomes possible due to the standard interoperability offered by internetworking protocols. Now disparate networking communities can be connected to share resources and exchange data.

- *World Wide Web Computing*: Stage 5 depicts the birth of the World Wide Web, in which Web servers assist with enabling remote Web clients to more securely interact with back-end legacy systems and databases. Clients behind the firewall and on the LAN may still communicate with such back-end systems with less restrictions and perhaps even communicate with an intranet Web server.
- *N-Tier Enterprise Computing*: Finally, Stage 6 depicts the N-tier architecture that has emerged today, with a middle-tier server helping to further isolate Web access from the back end to offer greater levels of security, scalability, transaction support, and a host of other centrally maintained distributed-systems management services for the enterprise.

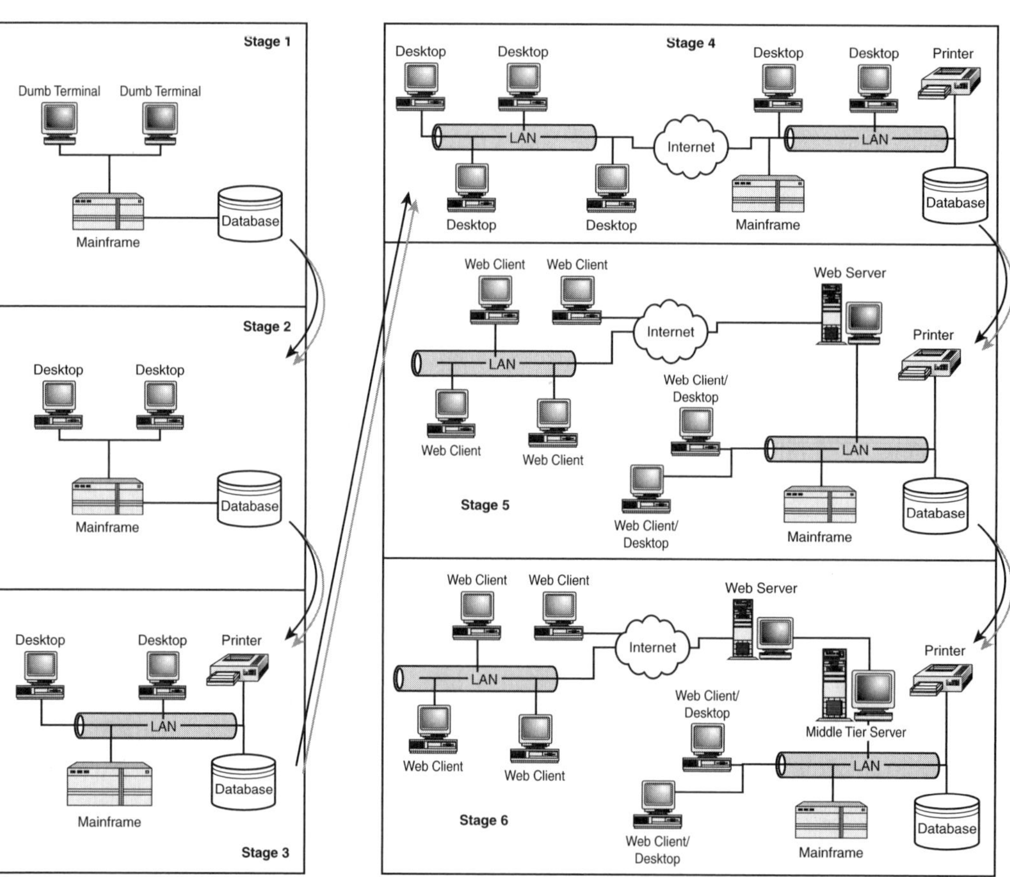

FIGURE 11.3
Distributed systems evolution and architectures.

Despite all the physical architecture options that can exist in a distributed system, there is still always the concept of a network client and network server (that is, there is always one client entity that desires some service from another server entity). Although it is true that such a distinction may blur in cases in which some application software may act as both network client and network server, the roles themselves still apply. The next two sections further decompose the distributed-systems problem in terms of the distributed system roles of a network client and network server. Different communications paradigms result in different architectures for both network client and server. We explore these architectures generally in this chapter and then in much more detail in Chapters 12 through 18 for five key communications paradigms utilized by enterprise Java applications.

The Network Client

Figure 11.4 depicts a generic network-client reference architecture that we will be casting most other enterprise Java communication paradigms against throughout the rest of this book. The network client is thus composed of the network-client application code and communications code as usual. However, we will also be examining architectures that have application/communications interface layers that fit the basic structure depicted in Figure 11.4.

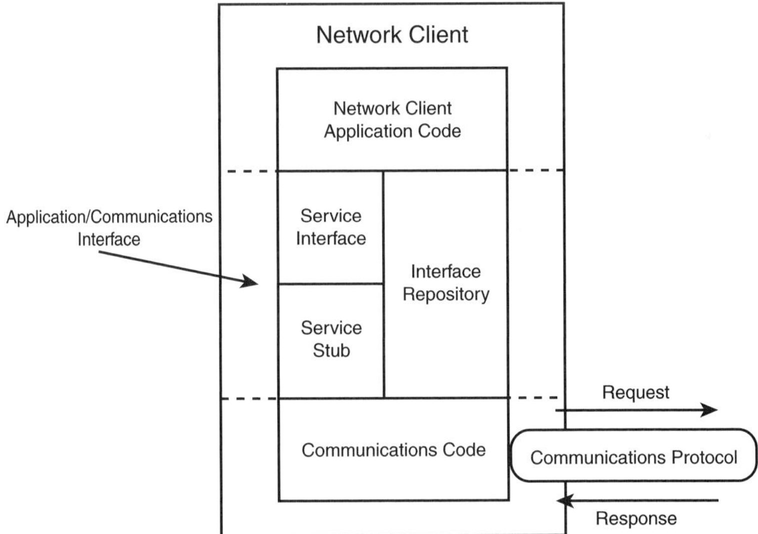

FIGURE 11.4
A general network client architecture.

A service interface can provide the network client with a view of a distributed network service, perhaps as it might interact with that service even if it were in the same local process (that is, location transparency). This interface is actually implemented by an underlying service stub that takes care of mapping regular Java calls into whatever message types and formats are used by the underlying distributed communications protocol code. The mapping of the language calls and parameters to the communication protocol message formats is called *marshaling*. The reverse process of transforming responses from messages to language types is called *unmarshaling*. Note that all the communications protocols we will examine for enterprise Java-based development are hosted in some way over the popular TCP/IP protocol suite.

An interface repository may be employed to help store meta-data about whatever service interfaces can be accessed by the network client. Note that some paradigms may not use or need an interface repository. Rather, the stub and interface may be available at compile-time for the network client to use directly.

Also note that the architecture of Figure 11.4 usually assumes a distributed object communications paradigm that can provide the necessary encapsulation and modularity of the application/communications interface. We will examine the following types of network client models throughout the remainder of Part III of this book:

- *TCP/IP clients*: TCP/IP-based clients either communicate directly over the TCP/IP communications protocol code or talk to a higher-level TCP/IP-based application client such as Telnet client or FTP client code. Application/communication interfaces in these paradigms are virtually non-existent or must be hand-coded.
- *HTTP clients*: HTTP clients create HTTP requests and process HTTP responses from HTTP servers. Such a protocol is used in Web-based communications and operates over TCP/IP. The HTTP client application here also may lack a decent application/communications interface layer. Some support for abstracting the HTTP client layer may be offered by third-party products.
- *CORBA clients*: CORBA is a standard distributed object computing paradigm specified by the Object Management Group that can be used to create CORBA clients in any language. The CORBA client model has CORBA service interfaces, stubs, interface repositories, and a protocol over TCP/IP. CORBA service interfaces have a definite object-oriented flavor to them.
- *RMI clients*: RMI is Java's built-in distributed object computing paradigm. RMI clients use an interface and stub to communicate over TCP/IP in either a proprietary protocol or a protocol that is compatible with the CORBA communications protocol.
- *DCOM clients*: DCOM is Microsoft's Windows-centric distributed object computing paradigm. DCOM is based on a specification by the Open Group known as the Distributed Computing Environment (DCE). DCOM clients have interfaces and stubs (although they refer to stubs as proxies). DCOM uses the DCE Remote Procedure Call (RPC) mechanism built on top of TCP/IP.

The Network Server

Figure 11.5 depicts a generic network server reference architecture that we will be casting most other enterprise Java communication paradigms against throughout the rest of this book. The network server application code uses whichever communications code implements the particular communications protocol being used. Different implementations of the application/communications interface layer exist (or may not exist at all) for different communication paradigms.

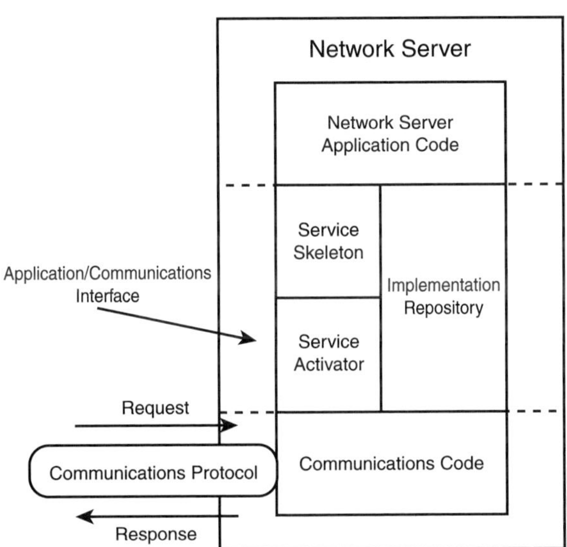

FIGURE 11.5
A general network server architecture.

A service activator may be used to handle requests made from network clients by bringing the requested network server into memory if it is not already active. This may involve pulling the implementation of the server from some form of implementation repository or perhaps pulling the state of the object from some sort of persistent storage. The activator then hands the request data to a service skeleton. The service skeleton acts as an intermediary on the server end to unmarshal requests from the protocol stream to actual network server application code calls. Responses from the network server are marshaled into messages that can be sent back over the wire to the network client.

Note that the architecture of Figure 11.5 also assumes a distributed object communications paradigm that can provide the necessary encapsulation and modularity of the application/communications interface, as was the case with the network client architecture. We will examine the following types of network server models throughout the remainder of Part III of this book:

- *TCP/IP servers*: TCP/IP-based servers listen on a TCP/IP socket for incoming client requests. Application/communication interfaces in this paradigm are virtually non-existent or must be hand-coded.
- *HTTP servers*: HTTP servers receive HTTP requests and generate HTTP responses. HTTP servers communicating directly with the HTTP protocol will not be offered the application insulation that an application/communications interface layer would offer. However, Java libraries such as Servlets help insulate your HTTP server applications from the HTTP protocol to a certain extent.
- *CORBA servers*: CORBA servers use an object adapter (activator) and skeletons to insulate your application from the CORBA communications protocol layer. Furthermore, CORBA servers can use an implementation repository.
- *RMI servers*: RMI servers are insulated from the RMI protocol using RMI skeletons. Activator functionality has recently been added to RMI, allowing for more sophisticated activation services.
- *DCOM servers*: DCOM servers use skeletons (referred to as stubs in DCOM lingo) and Microsoft Windows specific implementation registration and activation. DCOM comes prewired with all modern Windows-based platforms.

Conclusions

The distributed enterprise systems problem can involve issues such as scalability, wide-area geographical distribution, and heterogeneous platform interfacing. An application/communications interface layer between your application code and communications code can help make providing solutions to such problems transparent to application code. Furthermore, different physical architectures exist to support different physical distribution system needs.

All distributed communication paradigms that we examine throughout Part III of this book operate over TCP/IP and include pure TCP/IP-based applications, HTTP-based applications, CORBA-based applications, RMI-based applications, and DCOM-based applications. Each paradigm's network client and server that we will examine will be referenced against a generic application/communications interface layer and distributed systems architecture model outlined in this chapter. To make it easy for you to compare and contrast such paradigms, we will also implement examples using the same basic BeeShirts.com functionality, but in the context of the different distributed communication paradigms. However, we do defer practical example illustrations of the HTTP-based communications paradigm to Part VI's "Enterprise Web Enabling" chapters.

Network Communications

CHAPTER

12

IN THIS CHAPTER

- Network Computing 326
- TCP/IP Protocol Suite 329
- Socket Programming 336
- Communication Streams 363

Network communications in enterprise systems *is* TCP/IP (Transmission Control Protocol/Internet Protocol). TCP/IP represents the fundamental communications protocol utilized by all other enterprise Java communications paradigms that you encounter in this book. Socket programming offers an API to the TCP/IP protocol stacks. The J2SE comes with a set of Java-based standard socket programming APIs in the `java.net` package.

In this chapter, you will learn:

- The basic concepts behind network and client/server computing.
- The architecture of TCP/IP on top of which many other communication mechanisms are built.
- The concepts and techniques for building client/server applications with sockets in Java.
- The basic approach for connecting various input and output stream types to a socket.

Network Computing

All the modern distributed enterprise communications paradigms described in this book and used in enterprise Java systems have evolved from the basic principles of network computing. Network computing itself is the result of an evolutionary process in data communications, as depicted in Figure 12.1. Toward the early end of the network computing evolutionary timeline, we have the foundations of data communications dealing with issues of basic data transmission, data encoding and decoding, and the low-level management of communicating data over a communications medium. Enhancements in the science and engineering of data communications was of course a natural first step in being able to provide such things as telephone, radio, television, and satellite communications. Practical application of data communications networks gave rise to the need for providing more and more sophisticated *data* communications networking science and engineering solutions to enable complex connectivity scenarios between many devices on a network.

Pure data communications and networking issues are concerned with the transmission and routing of data and not with the content of the data itself. When the devices on a network are computing devices, however, the content of the data does become important. Moreover, as the number of intelligent computing devices attached to a network proliferates, a whole host of new problems emerge far beyond those taken into consideration by the earlier data communications network precursors such as our telephone, radio, and television networks. The term for such content-aware networks is *computer communications networking*. Given that computers are intelligent devices that can perform useful functions over such a computer communications network, the term *network computing* can be used to describe how computing devices not only communicate over the network, but also make functional use of such information in producing results. These results may also be shared by one or more other computing devices connected to the network.

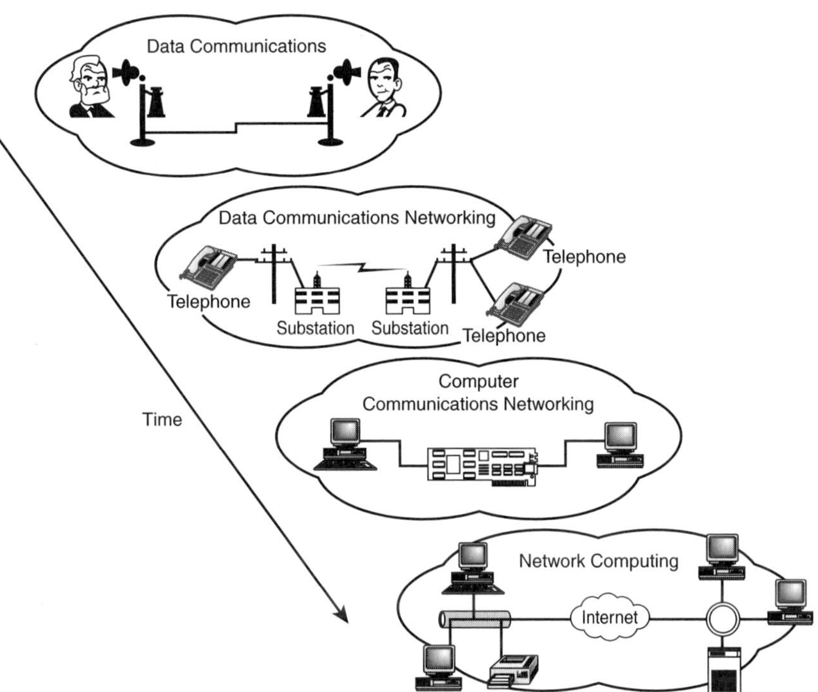

FIGURE 12.1
The evolution of network computing.

Protocols and Communication Layers

Given the fact that computer A wants to send data to computer B and computer B wants to receive that data and use it in some way, a set of fundamental communications issues must first be addressed. For one, the data in computer A needs to be formatted such that computer B will be able to understand it. There thus must exist a set of rules by which the data is formatted. Furthermore, in the event of an error during transmission of the data, computer A may want to resubmit a portion of the data that experienced the corruption. Computer B needs to be aware of such error control and retransmission rules if it is to be capable of repackaging the data into the correct format on the receiving end. These and other conventions for exchanging data between computing devices are referred to as a *protocol*.

Protocols can exist at many layers of abstraction. For example, the set of rules to describe how data is to be transferred across a particular physical medium can be distinctly defined apart from the higher-level set of rules defining how connections between two endpoints are created, destroyed, and managed. Although many different communications protocols exist, an organization known as the International Standards Organization (ISO) developed the Open Systems

Interconnection (OSI) model as a standard way to layer computer communications architectures. Each OSI layer described in Table 12.1 defines the scope of a particular protocol in terms of the functionality it performs. Although the OSI layers help partition how protocols are defined into more discrete layers, there are still instances of protocols existing in industry today that perform functions spanning multiple layers of the OSI model.

TABLE 12.1 The OSI Computer Communications Layer Model

Layer	*Layer's Mission and Description*
Physical Layer (Layer 1)	*The physical communications medium.* Deals with transmission of data over physical medium and electrical and mechanical specifications.
Data Link Layer (Layer 2)	*From blocks of data to physical medium access.* Given a block of data, it handles pushing this data onto the physical medium for you and retrieving data from the physical medium. Deals with how data is broken up to reliably send over the Physical Layer, media access control specification, error and flow control of data blocks (frames).
Network Layer (Layer 3)	*From packets of data to reliable data block transfer.* Maps packets of data to and from blocks of data to reliably communicate over a network. Also deals with the creation, management, and destruction of connection resources.
Transport Layer (Layer 4)	*From higher-level messages to reliable packet transfer.* Transforms higher-level messages to and from discrete packets. Deals with flow control of packets over a network. Also deals with internetworking issues.
Session Layer (Layer 5)	*Your virtual communications session.* Provides a virtual session between endpoints. Manages sessions and potentially monitors a session for billing purposes.
Presentation Layer (Layer 6)	*The transformation of messages from one dialect to another.* Performs conversion, compression, and encryption of messages from one format to another to deal with syntactic differences in data representation.
Application Layer (Layer 7)	*Piping messages to and from your applications.* Provides access to the communications infrastructure for applications.

Despite many violations in practice of the OSI model, the general concept of layered communications architectures still prevails whereby higher-level layers create and use header information that gets passed to lower layers as data. The general relation between layers above and below another layer in the protocol stack on the communications sending side is defined here:

- Layer I creates a block of header data.
- Layer I then passes its header plus any Layer I+1 (layer above it) data it received to Layer I-1 (layer below it).
- Layer I-1 (lower layer) then creates a block of header data that it prepends to the data given to it by Layer I.

NOTE

Of course at the highest level of a protocol stack, this relation will not have any Layer I+1 data to utilize aside from application data. Likewise, at the lowest level of the protocol stack, no Layer I-1 will be involved. These steps are simply meant to illustrate a general relation between layers and do not define a precise algorithm that is followed.

On the receiving side, we also have the following general relation between layers above and below another layer in the protocol stack:

- Layer I receives a block of data from Layer I-1 (lower layer).
- Layer I strips off the Layer I header data and behaves according to whatever protocol is defined at this layer as controlled by the data in its header.
- Layer I then gives the data with the Layer I header removed to Layer I+1.

NOTE

These steps do not apply if we are talking about Layer I as the lowest layer in the protocol stack. It just receives data from the physical medium itself. Similarly, these steps do not apply if we are talking about Layer I as the highest layer in the protocol stack. It just gives data to the application.

TCP/IP Protocol Suite

The TCP/IP (Transmission Control Protocol/Internet Protocol) protocol suite is a set of standards defining how diversely distributed computing entities can interact over the Internet. All distributed computing paradigms you will encounter in this book rely on TCP/IP in some shape or form. Indeed, as consultants, we authors have both spent many hours struggling with an enterprise's TCP/IP network configuration just to get our distributed enterprise computing applications up and running. Pure academic belief in a hard separation between network infrastructure and application may claim otherwise, but the fact remains that understanding TCP/IP and the basics of an enterprise's particular configuration may save you countless hours or perhaps many embarrassing moments when an enterprise application fails due to a TCP/IP infrastructure issue. Such issues usually become most apparent when the time comes to deploy an application to a particular site far removed from the safe haven of your development environment. Hopefully, the material in this section will help you understand and appreciate the complexity of TCP/IP-based networks and help you prepare for potential enterprise design and deployment issues over a TCP/IP-based network.

TCP/IP Roots

In the 1960s, computing equipment was far more expensive than it is today. After World War II, the United States Department of Defense (DOD) was beginning to build a computing infrastructure that only it could afford to finance. With the proliferation of a diverse array of DOD computing devices and protocols for communicating between such devices, the DOD became the first organization that would experience the problems which plague wide-area and diversely distributed computing environments. To alleviate such problems, a DOD initiative pursued by the Advanced Research Project Agency (ARPA) dating back to the 1960s spawned the development of the ARPAnet to support diversely distributed and decentralized network computing. The TCP/IP protocol suite was the standard collection of protocols for supporting this ARPAnet infrastructure. The United States National Science Foundation (NSF) later began to extend the ARPAnet infrastructure to create what we now regard as "the Internet." The underlying TCP/IP protocol suite of ARPAnet was thus destined to become today's most widely used set of standard protocols.

TCP/IP Communication Layers

TCP/IP was born before the OSI model was defined, but the TCP/IP protocol suite can be roughly classified according to the seven-layer OSI model. Although some technical documents describe the TCP/IP protocol suite in terms of a three-layer or five-layer protocol, the most commonly used model describes TCP/IP in terms of a four-layer protocol stack. Table 12.2 defines these layers and shows how they roughly stack up against the OSI layers. Subsequent sections that follow describe each TCP/IP layer in more detail.

TABLE 12.2 The TCP/IP Four-Layer Model

TCP/IP Layer	*TCP/IP Layer's Description*	*Sister OSI Layer(s)*
Network Access Layer	Provides physical medium access and defines the physical medium interface.	**Physical and Data Link Layers**
Internet Layer	Defines how data is routed among interconnected networks and maps between physical and logical addresses.	**Network Layer**
Transport Layer	Error and flow control services as well as the primary interface to the network by applications.	**Transport Layer**
Application Layer	Provides common network application services for file transfer, mail, and network maintenance.	**Session, Presentation, and Application Layers**

TCP/IP Network Access Layer

At the lowest level of abstraction, the Network Access Layer receives packets from the Internet Layer and interfaces with the underlying network hardware. The network hardware then interfaces with the physical communications medium. Packets are formatted by the Network Access Layer into frames of data that are then converted to a bit stream transmitted to the physical medium. Although the interface to the Network Access Layer remains the same from the Internet Layer's point of view, various Network Access Layer implementations can exist.

The Ethernet standard is a common low-cost Network Access Layer implementation in which each Ethernet network card has a 48-bit physical address and connects to other computers over a local area network (LAN). Different Ethernet conventions vary according to operating speed, maximum connectivity distance, and physical medium:

- Ethernet 10BASE-2 or 10BASE-5 operating at 10Mbps over 185 meters maximum distance or 500 meters maximum distance, respectively, using coaxial cables.
- Ethernet 10BASE-T or 100BASE-TX operating at 10Mbps or 100Mbps, respectively, over 100 meters maximum distance using twisted-pair cables.
- Ethernet 10BASE-F or 100BASE-FX operating at 10Mbps or 100Mbps, respectively, over 2,000 meters maximum distance using fiber-optic cables.

Other LAN technologies are more expensive, but they offer other advantages in terms of robustness, connectivity distance, and speed. For example, the Fiber Distributed Data Interface (FDDI) configuration can operate at a 100Mbps data rate over 100 kilometers using dual-redundant fault-tolerant fiber-optic cables.

What is even more commonplace for a Network Access Layer implementation is the use of a modem to physically connect to a network. Your desktop or laptop, for example, most likely contains a modem you use to dial up an Internet service provider (ISP). Your ISP hosts dial-up servers that connect to the telephone network using a dial-up TCP/IP Network Access Layer protocol. Likewise, your desktop or laptop must contain dial-up TCP/IP Network Access Layer software to enable your machine's higher-level TCP/IP interfacing and therefore connectivity to the Internet. The Serial Line Internet Protocol (SLIP) was a popular dial-up protocol in the early 1990s for connecting to dial-up servers via TCP/IP. SLIP's incapability to support dynamic IP address assignment has helped the Point-to-Point Protocol (PPP) become the dial-up TCP/IP Network Access Layer of choice.

TCP/IP Internet Access Layer

The Internet Access Layer takes data from the Transport Layer called segments and converts them into the packets needed by the Network Access Layer. The Internet Access Layer is also responsible for routing messages between distinct networks on the Internet. The Internet Access Layer is defined by three key protocol components: the IP Protocol, the ICMP protocol, and the ARP protocol.

The Internet Protocol (IP) relies on the use of IP addresses, which provide the standard way to logically identify computing machines on the Internet. At the lower-level Network Access Layer, different physical addressing schemes can be used on local network segments as long as higher-level IP addresses are used as the standard way to identify machines on the more widely geographically defined Internet.

IP addresses are 32 bits of data that can be partitioned into network ID and host ID fields. Network IDs form the first portion of an IP address and are assigned by the Internet Assigned Numbers Authority (IANA) to uniquely identify a network on the Internet to which IP data should be routed. Host IDs representing the second portion of an IP address uniquely identify a machine within a particular network ID's domain. For example, when dialing into your ISP, you are often dynamically assigned an IP address, meaning that your machine dynamically becomes a member of a particular network domain for the lifetime of your dial-up session.

IP address are usually textually defined in the form "X.X.X.X" in which each X identifies an 8-bit value in a 32-bit IP address. The IANA determines how organizations in need of network IDs are to be classified. Class A networks have network IDs defined only by the first 8 bits of an IP address, with the most significant bit always set to `0` and seven bits remaining for a network ID. The remaining 24 bits can be used by the organization to uniquely identify hosts on their network. Class B networks have uniquely defined network IDs consuming the first 2 bytes of an IP address, with the most significant bits set to `10` and 14 bits remaining for a network ID. Class C networks have network IDs consuming the first 3 bytes of an IP address, with the most significant bits set to `110` and 21 bits remaining for a network ID. Additionally,

Class D network IP addresses with the most significant bits set to `1110` and Class E network IP addresses with the most significant bits set to `11110` also exist, but such networks are of far less significance to everyday life than are Class A, B, and C networks. After an organization is assigned a network ID, it can further partition its network into subnetworks (aka subnets) according to its own internal organization requirements.

Subnets in an organization often become LANs in which each machine has a compatible Network Access Layer. IP software on a machine that is part of a LAN needs to be configured itself with an IP address or can be assigned to the machine by a another host machine on that subnet. A default gateway IP address configured with a machine's IP software also defines a computer on its LAN to consult if a destination IP address is different from one on its local network. A subnet mask configured with the IP software is used to determine which part of an IP address is used to distinguish between addresses on its local subnet and those external to its subnet.

The Address Resolution Protocol (ARP) is used to map between IP addresses and physical addresses. ARP software caches up mappings between IP addresses and local physical network addresses and is used by IP software to determine which network card on its subnet should be the recipient of an IP message if it receives such a message. If the ARP software does not have such a mapping cached, it broadcasts an ARP request message to which the machine on the subnet belonging to the desired IP address responds with its IP address and network address pair. The machine on the subnet originally receiving the IP message then can submit the IP message to the desired destination network card on its subnet.

The Internet Control Message Protocol (ICMP) defines a set of messages utilized by routers and computing elements to generate and handle a set of Internet Layer messages used to control the flow of IP messaging, as well as to provide status at the Internet Layer level. For example, Echo Request and Reply ICMP messages are used by the well-known `ping` command to send a status message to a remote IP address and expect the remote host's ICMP software to respond with an echoed reply. Such messages can be used to check connectivity between computers on the Internet.

TCP/IP Transport Layer

The Transport Layer of TCP/IP can implement one of two protocols. The Transmission Control Protocol (TCP) and the User Datagram Protocol (UDP) are the two protocol options available at the Transport Layer. The Transport Layer maps messages from the Application Layer into either segments (TCP lingo) or datagrams (UDP lingo) for use by the Internet Layer. The Transport Layer provides an interface for network applications to the core part of the TCP/IP stacks. Additionally, the Transport Layer protocols support multiplexing of multiple connections from multiple network clients as well as error and flow control of data over the Internet Layer.

Both TCP and UDP are end-node protocols, meaning that such layers are implemented by only the computers participating in a TCP/IP network computing environment. Such computers must implement the Transport Layer, Internet Layer, and Network Access Layer in order to network-compute over TCP/IP. Routers on the network, however, need implement only the Internet and Network Access Layers because they only need to route IP messages throughout a network, as well as handle and generate ICMP- and ARP-related messages.

A Transport Layer segment or datagram is directed to a network application acting as a network computing server from another network application acting as a network computing client. Although the Internet Layer defines source and destination addresses of machines using IP addresses, the identification of source and destination applications on such machines needs to be further resolved. The concept of a *port* is thus used to uniquely identify such applications (that is, processes) running on network clients and servers. Ports are a Transport Layer concept. The combination of an IP address defined at the Internet Layer and a port defined at the Transport Layer form what is termed a *socket*. Both TCP and UDP protocols transmit 16-bit source and 16-bit destination ports in their Transport Layer packets of data. Many applications will listen for TCP/IP connection requests on a well-known port and allocate a new port to the requesting client for subsequent communications handling.

TCP is a connection-oriented protocol in which a connection between network client and server is established and maintained over the lifetime of a server and client communications session. TCP provides a standard for opening and closing connections. Data communicated between client and server over TCP can vary in length between different segments of data, but the sequence of such segments is carefully managed by the protocol. The receiving machine must acknowledge each segment received and can slow the rate of data sent by the sender in accordance to how fast the receiver can handle such data.

UDP is a simpler, connectionless, and less reliable Transport Layer protocol. UDP does not retransmit dropped packets as does TCP and also does not guarantee sequencing of data or provide flow control. UDP is a protocol that simply sends data from the client side to a server and makes no assumption or guarantee of delivery. UDP is not completely unreliable, however. Both UDP and TCP provide minimal data-corruption checking on received data by use of checksum error checking on the sent data.

TCP/IP Application Layer

The Application Layer of the TCP/IP protocol suite implements useful network services between network clients and servers via a TCP or UDP Transport Layer. Depending on the type of network application, a particular Application Layer protocol is assumed. File servers, print servers, and mail servers are all examples of useful network services. Table 12.3 list some of the more common TCP/IP-based applications and the set of well-known ports that have been allocated to them by the IANA.

TABLE 12.3 Some Common Network Services and Their Ports

Service	*Port**	*Description*
FTP	20/21	File transfer protocol data (20) and control (21) ports for TCP.
TFTP	69	Trivial file transfer protocol for UDP.
SMTP	25	Simple mail transport protocol for TCP.
ECHO	7	Echo for retransmitting received packets for TCP and UDP.
Telnet	23	Terminal network connection for remote login via TCP.
Gopher	70	Menu-based Internet access service for TCP.
HTTP	80	Web browser–based Internet access service for TCP.
Finger	79	Display user information via TCP.
Time	37	Time of day server for both TCP and UDP.
qotd	17	Quote of the day server for both TCP and UDP.

**Note that the Port numbers given are in base-10 form.*

The domain name service (DNS) is a network service that provides for the translation between human-readable machine *hostnames* (for example, `www.assuredtech.com`) and harder-to-remember IP addresses (for example, `209.207.135.133`). Chapter 19, "Naming Services," discusses DNS in more detail in the context of other naming systems.

TCP/IP Implementations and Tools

No matter what modern operating system you are using, you can be certain that software implementing the TCP/IP protocol suite either is already installed or can be easily installed. Many modern operating systems ship these days with TCP/IP installed as the default networking software. Even if it is not pre-installed as the default, it can typically be configured or installed right from your OS vendor's installation disks. You will, of course, also need to have some network-access hardware connected to your machine, such as an Ethernet network card. As previously mentioned, a phone modem can also be used to obtain access to the Internet by dialing into an ISP.

Configuring the TCP/IP software on your machine will depend on your particular platform. Typically, assigning an IP address, a default gateway, and a subnet mask are three primary configuration variables that need to be set. Your software may even allow you to be dynamically assigned an IP address from a Dynamic Host Configuration Protocol (DHCP) server. Regardless, configuring your TCP/IP these days is most often performed through GUI-based software, depending on your particular platform. For example, on Windows 95, 98, and NT, you use the Control Panel's Network icon to bring up a Network configuration window, select the Protocols tab, and then choose the TCP/IP Protocol properties to configure your TCP/IP

Protocol Suite. On UNIX, the `hosts`, `protocols`, and `services` files (among others) in your `/etc` directory can be used to configure your networking environment. Note that your UNIX system admin may redirect access to these files to a centrally located and protected server.

Additionally, a set of TCP/IP tools can come in handy when debugging enterprise applications to determine network connectivity, security issues, and so on. Table 12.4 lists some of these tools. Note that many of these tools are available on UNIX and Windows platforms, and there is some availability for Mac OSs.

TABLE 12.4 Some TCP/IP Networking Tools

Tool Name	*Tool Description*
`ping`	Is used to determine connectivity to specific hosts and IP addresses.
`ipconfig` and `winipcfg`	Are used to determine and configure current TCP/IP network configuration. Can use `winipcfg` on Windows 95/98 for GUI version of `ipconfig`.
`netstat`	Displays statistics for TCP/IP protocol usage.
`traceroute` and `tracert`	Track the routing path from your machine to a destination. Use `tracert` on Windows platforms.
`route`	Is used to configure network routing tables.
`hostname`	Returns your machine's hostname.
`arp`	Is used to display and configure any IP to physical network address mappings used by ARP.
`net`	Allows you to view and configure various network-related information on Windows platforms. Use `net help` for more info.
Network sniffers	Allow you to view the network traffic on your local network. Various network sniffers exist for different platforms.

Socket Programming

As discussed in the preceding section, sockets are endpoints in a TCP/IP-based network through which network applications communicate. From a conceptual standpoint, you can think of a socket as simply an IP address and port pair. Each IP address and port combination represents a unique entry and exit point on the Internet for a network computing application. Network clients connect to network servers via sockets to exchange network packets. Socket programming is simply the practice of writing network computing applications to communicate using such TCP/IP sockets.

Socket programming is an important thing for any enterprise developer to understand. You will inevitably at some time encounter a situation in which the best, most efficient, or least time-consuming way to interact with a legacy application offering TCP/IP connectivity is to communicate with it using the TCP/IP connectivity it supports. Furthermore, many standard network services to which you may want to connect (see Table 12.3 for examples) already offer interconnectivity from TCP/IP. You may also want to make your Java program interact with an application written in another language without incurring the expense of using some COTS package for providing connectivity. The efficiency and availability of using TCP/IP software libraries may thus be your best option at times. Of course, Java's `java.net` libraries packaged with every Java runtime environment offer you just the socket programming support you'll need.

UNIX socket libraries and Windows socket libraries (WinSock) provide one with a platform-dependent socket programming API. The `java.net` libraries provide a Java-based API for platform-independent socket programming. Calls to the `java.net` libraries are mapped to native socket API calls on the platform to which the JVM has been ported. Aside from basic TCP socket programming using classes like `InetAddress`, `Socket`, and `ServerSocket`, UDP-style programming can be performed using classes like `DatagramSocket` and `DatagramPacket`. The Java socket libraries can even be customized to modularly implement protocols above TCP and UDP using classes and interfaces such as `SocketImplFactory`, `SocketImpl`, and `DatagramSocketImpl`. A host of socket-oriented exceptions such as `SocketException`, `BindException`, `ConnectException`, and `NoRouteToHostException` further encapsulates common socket-based error scenarios.

Basic Socket Programming

The diagram in Figure 12.2 depicts the core classes involved in doing basic socket programming in Java. The `InetAddress` class encapsulates an IP address, as well as provides some minimal helper function support for mapping hostnames to IP addresses. The `ServerSocket` class is used to create a server socket by a network server. Given a port, the IP address of the machine on which the `ServerSocket` is created is used when instantiating a `ServerSocket` instance. A network server can then listen on that port for incoming socket requests via the `ServerSocket.accept()` call (which blocks). A `Socket` instance created by a network client given the IP address and port of that server makes the actual socket connection. On the server side, a `Socket` object will be returned from the `accept()` call representing the connection made from that client.

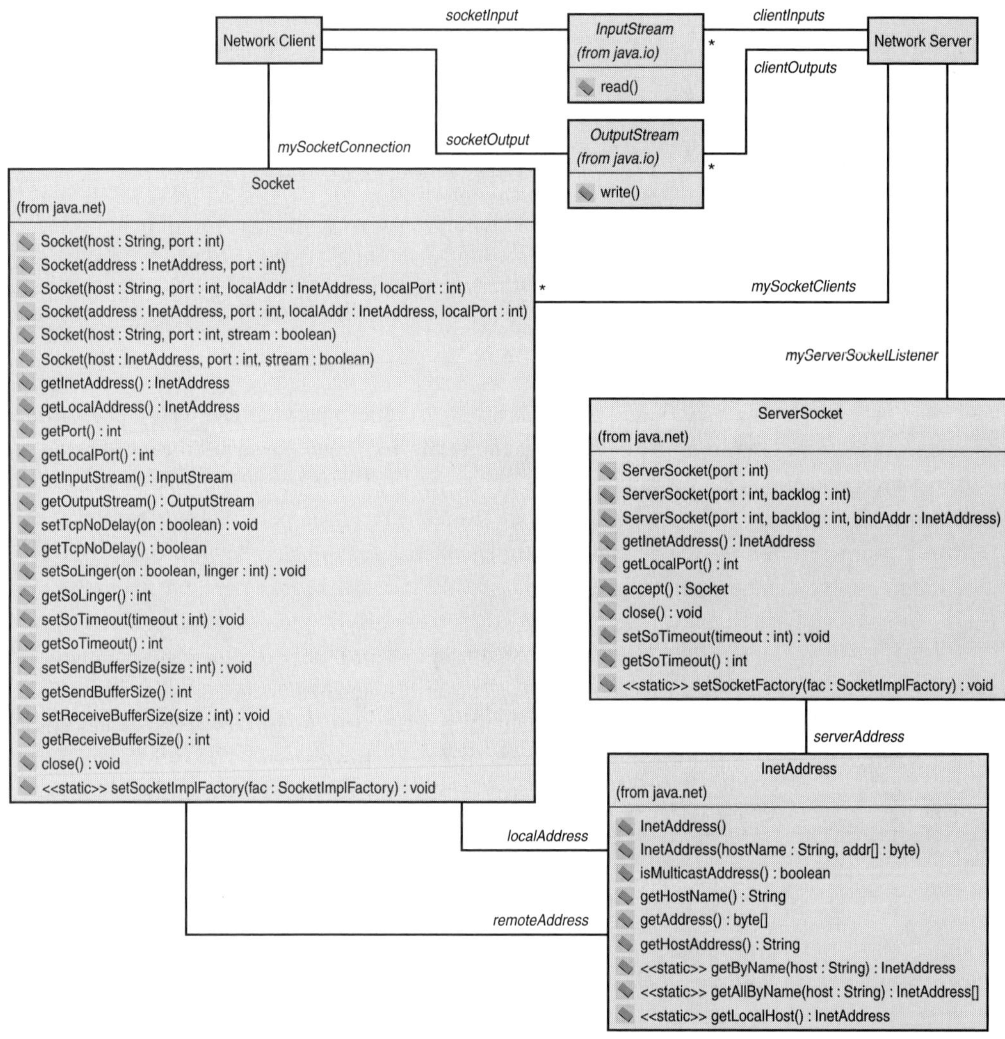

FIGURE 12.2
Basic socket entities.

Java Socket Programming and the J2EE

In standalone Java enterprise application environments, developers can create both client sockets and server sockets. As we'll see in Part VI, "Enterprise Web Enabling," and Part VII, "Enterprise Applications Enabling," J2EE Web and EJB container environments impose some restrictions on how sockets can be created. Java Servlets, JSPs, and EJBs cannot create server sockets due to J2EE container restrictions. However, the creation of socket clients is permitted. In more general practice and for certain enterprise application integration needs, server socket programming via use of standalone Java applications will be a necessity for some time to come.

As an example of basic socket programming in Java, Listings 12.1 through 12.8 demonstrate how to create a TCP/IP-based server providing some specific sample BeeShirts.com query service results to a TCP/IP-based client. The TCP/IP-based server allows TCP/IP clients to make a specific sample query request for BeeShirts.com `Customer` information. A server-side TCP/IP socket listener hands off such requests to a separate thread, which interfaces with the database to obtain the desired query results. The client can also register a client-side listener with the TCP/IP query server so that the server can make a callback to the client with results from a specific sample BeeShirts.com Order information request.

NOTE

All example code used in this chapter is contained on the CD in the `examples\src\ejava\tcpipch12` directory. An example `runtcpip.bat` Windows script file in that directory can be configured and used to build and run the examples to be described. As described in Appendix A, "Software Configurations," you must set your `DRIVER_CLASS` and `DATABASE_URL` properties as appropriate in the properties file (`TCPIPCH12.Properties`) equipped with this chapter. Refer to Appendix A for general database configuration instructions.

The `Server` class in Listing 12.1 is the main entry point into the sample network TCP/IP server. This class will be called from the `runtcpip.bat` file to start your TCP/IP server and pass it the name of a configurable properties file (`TCPIPCH12.Properties`). Given a configurable `SERVER_PORT` property read from the properties file, an instance of `Server` is created. The server is then started by calling `startServer()` on the server instance with the set of properties read in from the properties file.

The `Server.startServer()` method is where the remainder of processing occurs inside the server. The `startServer()` method first creates a `ServerSocket` instance with a port number and a configurable maximum number of client connections (the default is 10) that may be queued up on the underlying server socket listening port. The `Server` then creates an instance of a `DatabaseHelper` object used to interface with the database for BeeShirts.com data (see Listing 12.4 describing the `DatabaseHelper` class). The `Server` then initiates a connection to a database on the `DatabaseHelper` instance. The `Server` then blocks on its socket using the `ServerSocket.accept()` method. When a client connects to this server, the server creates an instance of a `ServerHelper` object, passing it the `Socket` instance returned from the `accept()` method and the `DatabaseHelper` instance. The `ServerHelper` object is actually a separate thread created to handle client requests while the `Server` object continues to listen for incoming socket connections.

LISTING 12.1 TCP/IP Server Socket Listener (`Server.java`)

```
package ejava.tcpipch12;
import java.net.InetAddress;
import java.net.ServerSocket;
import java.net.Socket;
import java.io.IOException;
import java.util.Properties;
import java.io.FileInputStream;
import java.io.ObjectOutputStream;

public class Server
{
  private int defaultPort = 5555;
  private ServerSocket serverSocket;
  private Socket newConnection;
  private DatabaseHelper dbHelper;
  private Properties properties;
  private int numberOfClients = 10;
  private int connectedClientsCounts = 0;


  public Server(int serverPort )
  {
    if(serverPort > -1){
     this.defaultPort = serverPort;
    }
  }

  public void startServer(Properties properties)
    throws IOException, Exception
  {
    this.properties = properties;

    // Get number of clients and set this number in server
    String nClientsString = (String)properties.get("NUMBER_OF_CLIENTS");
    if(nClientsString != null && nClientsString.length() != 0){
      int nClients = Integer.parseInt(nClientsString);
```

```
    if(nClients > 0){
      this.numberOfClients = nClients;
    }
  }
  serverSocket = new ServerSocket(this.defaultPort, numberOfClients);

  // Lazy instantiation of database helper and create connection
  if(dbHelper == null ){
    dbHelper = new DatabaseHelper(this.properties);
    dbHelper.makeDbConnection();
  }
  /**
    * until user exists from the server using keyboard, CTRL-C
    * or by shutting down from the server, it waits for
    * clients to connect
    */    while(true){
      this.newConnection = serverSocket.accept();
      ServerHelper sHelper =
        new ServerHelper(this.newConnection,dbHelper);
      sHelper.start();
  }
}

public void cleanResources()
  throws IOException
{
  serverSocket.close();
}

public void finalize()
  throws Throwable
{
  try{
    this.cleanResources();
  }
  catch(IOException e){
  }
  super.finalize();
}

public static void main(String[] args)
{
  if(args.length == 0){
    System.out.println(" you need to provide the configuration info");
    System.out.println(" java ejava.tcpipch12.Server "+
```

continues

LISTING 12.1 Continued

```
        "<tcpipch.Properties> ");
      System.exit(0);
    }

    try{
      // Create file input stream and read properties
      FileInputStream fin = new FileInputStream(args[0]);
      Properties p = new Properties();
      p.load(fin);
      fin.close();
      // Get and parse server port
      String serverPortString = (String)p.get("SERVER_PORT");
      int serverPort = -1;
      if(serverPortString != null &&
         serverPortString.length() != 0){
        serverPort = Integer.parseInt(serverPortString);
      }
      // Create new instance of this server and start it
      Server s = new Server( serverPort);
      s.startServer(p);

    }
    catch(IOException ioe){
      System.out.println(" Error :"+ioe);
      ioe.printStackTrace();
      System.exit(0);
    }
    catch(Exception e){
      System.out.println(e);
      e.printStackTrace();
      System.exit(0);
    }
  }
}
```

The `ServerHelper` class of Listing 12.2 is the handler thread that does all the work in our example. It implements a simple protocol over TCP/IP that we call the `QueryServiceProtocol` (see the `QueryServiceProtocol` marker interface in Listing 12.3). When it is created, the `ServerHelper` calls `getOutputStream()` and `getInputStream()` on the `Socket` object representing a connection with the client. The output stream is used to push data to the network client, and the input stream receives data from the network client. Within the `run()` method of this thread, we see the main functionality of the simple protocol at work. An integer read from the input stream identifies the type of request made by the client. Depending on this request, the `ServerHelper` will perform one of the following actions:

- For a CUSTOMERS_QUERY type, read a minimum orders value number from the client input stream and use the DatabaseHelper object to find a Vector of Customer objects whose orders exceed that amount. The Vector of Serializable Customer objects is then written to the TCP/IP output stream sent to the client. Listing 12.5 presents the Serializable Customer object composed of a series of simple getter and setter methods.
- For a REGISTER_RECEIVER type, read a client-side hostname and port number from the client input stream and use this information to register a clientReceiverServerHost and clientReceiverPort value to be used as a callback to the client.
- For an ORDERS_QUERY type, read a state code from the client input stream and use the DatabaseHelper object to find a Vector of Order objects associated with that state. A Socket connection is then made to the network client using the previously registered client-side host and port, and an output stream to that socket is obtained. The Vector of Serializable Order objects is then written to that output stream. Listing 12.6 presents the Serializable Order object composed of a series of simple getter and setter methods.

LISTING 12.2 TCP/IP Server Socket Handler (ServerHelper.java)

```
package ejava.tcpipch12;
import java.net.Socket;
import java.io.IOException;
import java.io.ObjectInputStream;
import java.io.ObjectOutputStream;
import java.util.Vector;
import java.net.ServerSocket;
import java.net.Socket;
import java.net.InetAddress;

public class ServerHelper extends Thread
  implements QueryServiceProtocol
{
  private Socket socket;
  private ObjectInputStream remoteInStream;
  private ObjectOutputStream remoteOutStream;
  private String clientReceiverServerHost;
  private int    clientReceiverPort;
  private DatabaseHelper databaseHelper;

  public ServerHelper(Socket socket, DatabaseHelper dbHelper)
    throws IOException
  {
    this.socket = socket;
```

continues

LISTING 12.2 Continued

```
    this.displayClientInformation();
    this.databaseHelper = dbHelper;
    this.remoteOutStream =
        new ObjectOutputStream(socket.getOutputStream());
    this.remoteInStream =
      new ObjectInputStream(socket.getInputStream());
  }

  private void displayClientInformation()
  {
    System.out.println(" I am serving Client :");
    InetAddress address = socket.getInetAddress();
    System.out.println(" at Host "+address.getHostName());
    System.out.println(" IP address :"+address.getHostAddress());
  }


  public synchronized void run()
  {
    boolean listening = true;
   /**
    * Until finalize method of this class is invoked by Garbage
    * Collector, it waits for client requests
    */
    while(listening){
    try{
      int requested = (int)this.remoteInStream.readInt();
      switch(requested){
        case CUSTOMERS_QUERY:
          {
            float queryValue = this.remoteInStream.readFloat();
            Vector customers  = this.getCustomers(queryValue);
            this.remoteOutStream.writeObject(customers);
            break;
          }
        case ORDERS_QUERY:
          {
            String state = (String)this.remoteInStream.readObject();
            this.findOrdersWhichAreFrom(state);
            break;
          }
        case REGISTER_RECEIVER:
          {
            String hostName = (String)this.remoteInStream.readObject();
            int portNumber  = this.remoteInStream.readInt();
```

```
          this.registerReceiver(hostName, portNumber);
          break;
        }

      }
    }
    catch(IOException ioException){
      System.out.println("Error :"+ioException);
      ioException.printStackTrace();
      try{
        System.in.read();
        clean();
      }
      catch(Exception ex){
        ex.printStackTrace();
      }
    }
    catch(Exception exception){
      System.out.println("Exception :"+exception);
      exception.printStackTrace();
      try{
        System.in.read();
        clean();
      }
      catch(Exception ex){
        ex.printStackTrace();
      }
    }
    }
  }

  private Vector getCustomers(float chargeValue)
    throws Exception
  {
    return this.databaseHelper.
      findCustomersWhoOrderedForMoreThan(chargeValue);
  }

  private void findOrdersWhichAreFrom(String state)
    throws Exception
  {
    // Get Vector of orders, get Inet Address, create callback socket,
    //   and write orders to client callback
    Vector orders = this.databaseHelper.findOrdersWhichAreFrom(state);
➡   if(this.clientReceiverServerHost != null &&
```

continues

LISTING 12.2 Continued

```
         this.clientReceiverServerHost.indexOf("local") != -1){
          this.clientReceiverServerHost = null;
    }
    InetAddress serverAddress = InetAddress.
      getByName(this.clientReceiverServerHost);

    Socket socket = new Socket(serverAddress
      this.clientReceiverPort);
    ObjectOutputStream clientOutStream =
      new ObjectOutputStream(socket.getOutputStream());
    clientOutStream.writeObject(orders);
    clientOutStream.flush();

  }

  private void registerReceiver(String hostName, int port)
  {
    this.clientReceiverServerHost = hostName;
    this.clientReceiverPort = port;
  }

  protected void finalize()
    throws Throwable
  {
    try{
      if(remoteOutStream != null){
        this.remoteOutStream.close();
      }
      if(this.remoteInStream != null) {
        this.remoteInStream.close();
      }

    }
    catch(IOException ex){
    }
    super.finalize();
  }
}
```

Thus, the `ServerHelper` acts as the main protocol handler and workhorse for processing client requests on the server side. Depending on the request type, it will take one of the following actions: perform a customer query and return results, register a client-side callback handle, or perform an orders query and make a callback to the client with results. As you'll see in later chapters covering more object-oriented distributed computing techniques, much less hand-coding will be involved due to the infrastructure layers that exist between the TCP/IP protocol layer and the Application Layer code that you as a developer must write.

LISTING 12.3 TCP/IP Query Service Protocol Marker Interface (QueryServiceProtocol.java)

```
package ejava.tcpipch12;
public interface QueryServiceProtocol
{
  public final int CUSTOMERS_QUERY    = 100;
  public final int ORDERS_QUERY       = 101;
  public final int REGISTER_RECEIVER  = 102;
}
```


LISTING 12.4 Query Service Specific Database Interface (DatabaseHelper.java)

```
package ejava.tcpipch12;

import java.util.Vector;
import java.util.Hashtable;
import java.util.Properties;
import java.sql.Connection;
import java.sql.Statement;
import java.sql.ResultSet;
import java.sql.ResultSetMetaData;
import java.sql.PreparedStatement;
import java.sql.SQLException;
import java.sql.DriverManager;
import java.util.Date;
import java.util.Properties;

public class DatabaseHelper
{
  private Connection connection;
  private Statement  statement;
  private Properties properties;
  private String receiverHostName;
  private int receiverPort;

  public DatabaseHelper(Properties properties)
  {
    this.properties = properties;
  }
```

continues

LISTING 12.4 Continued

```
public void makeDbConnection()
  throws Exception
{
  // Get driver class, database URL, username, and password,
  // and then create DB Connection with this info
  String driverClass = (String)properties.get("DRIVER_CLASS");
  Class.forName(driverClass);
  String dbUrl = (String)properties.get("DATABASE_URL");
  String userName = (String)properties.get("UserName");
  String password = (String)properties.get("Password");
  if(userName == null || userName.length() == 0){
    connection = DriverManager.getConnection(dbUrl);
  }
  else{
    connection = DriverManager.getConnection(dbUrl,userName,password);
  }
}

public void setConnection(Connection connection)
{
  this.connection = connection;
}

public synchronized ResultSet getResultSet(String sqlQuery,
  Object whereValue) throws SQLException
{
  // Create prepared statement, set where value, execute query
  PreparedStatement preparedStatement =
    connection.prepareStatement(sqlQuery);
  preparedStatement.setObject(1, whereValue);
  ResultSet rs = preparedStatement.executeQuery();

  return rs;
}

public synchronized Vector findCustomersWhoOrderedForMoreThan
  (float value)
  throws SQLException, Exception
{
  // Get query from properties file
  String customerQueryString =
    (String) properties.get("CUSTOMER_QUERY");
  if (customerQueryString == null) {
    throw new Exception("CUSTOMER_QUERY  is null");
  }
```

```
    // Get result set, meta data, and column count
    ResultSet rs = this.getResultSet(customerQueryString,
      new Float(value));
    ResultSetMetaData rsMetaData = rs.getMetaData();
    int nColumns = rsMetaData.getColumnCount();
    Vector customers = null;
    // For each result, populate customer object with data
    while (rs.next()) {
      if(customers == null){
        customers = new Vector();
      }
      String customerID = rs.getString("CUSTOMER_ID");
      String firstName = rs.getString("FIRST_NAME");
      String lastName = rs.getString("LAST_NAME");
      String address1 = rs.getString("ADDRESS_1");
      String address2 = rs.getString("ADDRESS_2");
      String city = rs.getString("CITY");
      String state = rs.getString("STATE");
      String phoneNumber = rs.getString("PHONE");
      String eMail = rs.getString("EMAIL");
      String zip = rs.getString("ZIP_CODE");
      Customer customer = new Customer();
      customer.setFirstName(firstName);
      customer.setLastName(lastName);
      customer.setAddress1(address1);
      customer.setAddress2(address2);
      customer.setCity(city);
      customer.setState(state);
      customer.setZip(zip);
      customer.setEmailAddress(eMail);
      customer.setPhoneNumber(phoneNumber);
      customers.addElement(customer);
    }

    return customers;
  }

  public synchronized Vector findOrdersWhichAreFrom(String state)
    throws SQLException, Exception
  {
    // Get orders query from properties file
    String orderQueryString = (String) properties.get("ORDER_QUERY");
➥     if (orderQueryString == null) {
      throw new Exception("ORDER_QUERY in  file is null");
    }
```

continues

LISTING 12.4 Continued

```
    // Get result set from query, and column count
    ResultSet rs = this.getResultSet(orderQueryString, state);
    ResultSetMetaData rsMetaData = rs.getMetaData();
    int nColumns = rsMetaData.getColumnCount();
    Vector orders = null;
    // For each result, populate and Order object
    while (rs.next()) {
     if(orders == null){
      orders = new Vector();
     }
     int orderID = rs.getInt("ORDER_ID");
     Date orderDate = rs.getDate("ORDER_DATE");
     double orderValue = rs.getDouble("TOTAL_PRICE");
     Order order = new Order(orderID, orderDate.toString(),
                             orderValue);

     orders.addElement(order);
    }
    return orders;
}

  public synchronized void register(String hostName, int port )
  {
    this.receiverHostName = hostName;
    this.receiverPort = port;
  }
}
```

The `DatabaseHelper` class is the workhorse for interfacing with the database to handle all JDBC-related calls. The `DatabaseHelper` translates between application-specific interfaces and JDBC-specific calls that satisfy the customer- and order-related queries issued by the `ServerHelper`. The `DatabaseHelper` also handles creating and managing the database connection. As you'll see in later chapters covering application enabling, such hand-coding can also be alleviated by using Enterprise JavaBeans.

LISTING 12.5 Customer Object (`Customer.java`)

```
package ejava.tcpipch12;
import java.io.Serializable;

public class Customer implements Serializable
{
  private String firstName;
  private String lastName;
  private String address1;
```

```
    private String address2;
    private String city;
    private String state;
    private String zip;
    private String phoneNumber;
    private String emailAddress;

    public Customer(){ super(); }

    public String getFirstName(){ return this.firstName; }

    public String getLastName(){ return this.lastName; }

    public String getAddress1(){ return this.address1; }

    public String getAddress2(){ return this.address2; }

    public String getState(){ return this.state; }

    public String getPhoneNumber(){ return this.phoneNumber; }

    public String getEmailAddress(){ return this.emailAddress; }

    public String getZip(){ return this.zip; }

    public void setZip(String zip){ this.zip = zip; }

    public String getCity(){ return this.city; }

    public void setCity(String city){ this.city = city; }

    public void setFirstName(String firstName)
      { this.firstName = firstName; }

    public void setLastName(String lastName){ this.lastName = lastName; }

    public void setAddress1(String address1){this.address1 = address1; }

    public void setAddress2(String address2){ this.address2 = address2; }

    public void setState(String state){ this.state = state; }

    public void setPhoneNumber(String phoneNumber)
      { this.phoneNumber = phoneNumber; }

    public void setEmailAddress(String emailAddress)
      { this.emailAddress = emailAddress; }
}
```

Because the `Customer` object represents a simple encapsulation of customer-related information directly mapped from database table information, it too should be an easy class to automatically generate. However, we use the `Customer` class here as a container of such information that can be serialized for wire transport. The automatic generation of such information from database descriptions can also be aided by the use of Enterprise JavaBeans technology.

LISTING 12.6 Order Object (`Order.java`)

```
package ejava.tcpipch12;
import java.io.Serializable;

public class Order implements Serializable
{
  private int orderID;
  private String orderDate;
  private double orderValue;

  public Order()
  {
    super();
  }

  public Order(int orderID, String orderDate, double orderValue)
  {
    this();
    this.orderID = orderID;
    this.orderDate = orderDate;
    this.orderValue = orderValue;
  }

  public void setOrderID(int orderID){ this.orderID = orderID; }

  public void setOrderDate(String orderDate)
    { this.orderDate = orderDate; }

  public void setOrderValue(double orderValue)
    { this.orderValue = orderValue; }

  public int getOrderID(){ return this.orderID; }

  public String getOrderDate(){ return this.orderDate; }

  public double getOrderValue(){ return this.orderValue; }
```

```
  public String toString()
  {
    return "OrderID :" + orderID + " order Date :" + orderDate
           + "orderValue :" + orderValue;
  }
}
```

On the client side, the `Client` class of Listing 12.7 first reads the same set of properties into memory from the properties file sent to it from the command line. The properties `SERVER_HOST` and `SERVER_PORT` are passed to a new `Client` object constructor and are used in the `makeConnection()` call on that object to create a new `Socket` object connection to the TCP/IP server and obtain a handle to the socket's output stream.

LISTING 12.7 TCP/IP Client Object (`Client.java`)

```
package ejava.tcpipch12;
import java.io.FileInputStream;
import java.io.IOException;
import java.util.Properties;
import java.net.Socket;
import java.net.InetAddress;
import java.io.ObjectInputStream;
import java.io.ObjectOutputStream;
import java.util.Vector;

public class Client  implements QueryServiceProtocol
{
  private Properties properties;
  private String serverHost = "localhost";
  private int    serverPort = 5555;
  private Socket socket;
  private ObjectInputStream remoteInputStream;
  private ObjectOutputStream outputStream;
  private ClientReceiverServer clientReceiver;

  public Client(String serverHost, int port, Properties p)
  {
    if(serverHost != null &&
      serverHost.length() != 0){
      this.serverHost = serverHost;
    }
    if(port > -1){
      this.serverPort = port;
    }
```

continues

LISTING 12.7 Continued

```
    this.properties =p;
  }

  public void makeConnection()
    throws IOException
  {
    if(this.serverHost.indexOf("local") != -1){
      serverHost = null;
    }
   InetAddress serverAddress =
    InetAddress.getByName(this.serverHost);

   socket = new Socket(serverAddress,
    this.serverPort);
   this.outputStream =
        new ObjectOutputStream(socket.getOutputStream());

  }

  public void queryForCustomersWhoSpendGreaterThan(float value)
    throws IOException, Exception
  {
    // Write customer query to server socket
    this.outputStream.writeInt(this.CUSTOMERS_QUERY);
    this.outputStream.writeFloat(value);
    this.outputStream.flush();

    if(remoteInputStream == null){
      remoteInputStream =
        new ObjectInputStream(socket.getInputStream());
    }
    // While still getting results from server
    boolean received = false;
    while(!received){
      Vector vector = (Vector)this.remoteInputStream.readObject();
      for(int i = 0; i< vector.size(); i++){
        // For each Vector element result, create a Customer object
        Customer customer = (Customer)vector.elementAt(i);
        System.out.println("First Name :"+customer.getFirstName());
        System.out.println("Last Name :"+customer.getLastName());
        System.out.println("Address1 Name :"+customer.getAddress1());
        System.out.println("Address2 Name :"+customer.getAddress2());
        System.out.println("City :"+customer.getCity());
        System.out.println("State :"+customer.getState());
        System.out.println("Zip :"+customer.getZip());
```

```
      System.out.println("Email Address :"+customer.getEmailAddress());
      System.out.println("Phone :"+customer.getPhoneNumber());
    }
   received = true;
  }
}

public void registerReceiverHostAndPort()
  throws IOException
{
  // Read client socket info from properties file
  String receiverHost = (String)this.
    properties.get("CLIENT_RECEIVER_HOST");
  String receiverPortString = (String)this.
    properties.get("CLIENT_RECEIVER_PORT");
  int receiverPort = Integer.parseInt(receiverPortString);
  if(receiverHost == null){
     receiverHost = "localhost";
  }
   // Create and start client callback socket
  if(this.clientReceiver == null){
    this.clientReceiver = new ClientReceiverServer(receiverPort);
    this.clientReceiver.start();
  }
  // Write client callback info to server
  this.outputStream.writeInt(this.REGISTER_RECEIVER);
  this.outputStream.writeObject(receiverHost);
  this.outputStream.writeInt(receiverPort);
  this.outputStream.flush();
}

public void queryForOrderFromState(String state)
  throws IOException
{
  this.outputStream.writeInt(this.ORDERS_QUERY);
  this.outputStream.writeObject(state);
  this.outputStream.flush();
}

public void clean()
  throws IOException
{
  this.remoteInputStream.close();
  this.outputStream.close();
  this.socket.close();
}
```

continues

LISTING 12.7 Continued

```
public static void main(String[] args)
{
  if(args.length == 0){
    System.out.println(" you need to provide the configuration info");
    System.out.println(" java ejava.tcpipch12.Client "+
      "<tcpipch12.Properties> ");
    System.exit(0);
  }
  Client c = null;
  try{
    // Read info from properties file
    FileInputStream fin = new FileInputStream(args[0]);
    Properties p = new Properties();
    p.load(fin);
    fin.close();
    String serverHost = (String)p.get("SERVER_HOST");
    String serverPortString = (String)p.get("SERVER_PORT");
    int serverPort = -1;
    if(serverPortString != null &&
       serverPortString.length() != 0){
      serverPort = Integer.parseInt(serverPortString);
    }
    // Create client, make server connection, issue customer query,
    //    register callback, issue order query to receive callback
    c = new Client( serverHost, serverPort, p);
    c.makeConnection();
    c.queryForCustomersWhoSpendGreaterThan(100.00f);
    c.registerReceiverHostAndPort();
    c.queryForOrderFromState("VA");
    c.clean();
  }
  catch(IOException ioe){
    System.out.println(" Error :"+ioe);
    ioe.printStackTrace();
    try{
      if(c != null){
        c.clean();
      }
    }
    catch(Exception ex){
    }
    System.exit(0);
  }
  catch(Exception e){
    System.out.println(e);
```

```
            e.printStackTrace();
            try{
              c.clean();
            }
            catch(Exception ex){
            }
            System.exit(0);
          }
      }
}
```


The rather long-winded name of a `queryForCustomersWhoSpendGreaterThan()` method writes the `QueryServiceProtocol` marker interface's `CUSTOMERS_QUERY` value and the desired minimum spending value to the TCP/IP output stream. The resultant `Vector` of `Serializable` `Customer` objects is then read from the stream and displayed.

A call to `registerReceiverHostAndPort()` on the `Client` object then induces the `Client` to create and start a new instance of the `ClientReceiverServer` thread class shown in Listing 12.8. The `ClientReceiverServer` thread simply creates a `ServerSocket` and listens on it to receive a `Vector` of `Serializable` `Orders` sent from the `ServerHelper` in our example. The `Client` object then registers the `ClientReceiverHelper` host and port with the `ServerHelper` object using the `QueryServiceProtocol`'s `REGISTER_RECEIVER` type message.

Finally, the Client object's `queryForOrderFromState()` call is made to create an `ORDERS_QUERY` message to send to the `ServerHelper`. The `ServerHelper` object then makes the callback onto the `ClientReceiverHelper` object with the `Order` results.

LISTING 12.8 TCP/IP Client Callback Handler (`ClientReceiverServer.java`)

```
package ejava.tcpipch12;
import java.io.IOException;
import java.util.Vector;
import java.util.Hashtable;
import java.io.ObjectInputStream;
import java.io.ObjectOutputStream;
import java.net.Socket;
import java.net.ServerSocket;

public class ClientReceiverServer extends Thread
  implements QueryServiceProtocol
{
  private Socket socket;
  private ObjectInputStream remoteInStream;
```

continues

LISTING 12.8 Continued

```
  private ObjectOutputStream remoteOutStream;
  private int portNumber = 5556;
  ServerSocket serverSocket = null;

  public ClientReceiverServer(int portNumber)
    throws IOException
  {
    if(portNumber > -1)
      this.portNumber = portNumber;
    serverSocket =
      new ServerSocket(this.portNumber, 1);
  }
  public synchronized void run()
  {
    boolean listening = true;
    /**
      * Until finalize method of this class is called by GC
      * it waits for the server to write.
      */
    while(listening){
      try{
        // Block on socket and read data when connection made
        Socket socket = serverSocket.accept();
        this.remoteInStream = new ObjectInputStream(
          socket.getInputStream());
        Vector receivedOrders  =
          (Vector)this.remoteInStream.readObject();
         // For each vector received, create an Order object
        for(int i = 0; i< receivedOrders.size(); i++){
          Order order = (Order)receivedOrders.elementAt(i);
          System.out.println("Received the Orders :");
          System.out.println("Order Data :"+ order.getOrderDate());
          System.out.println("Order ID :"+order.getOrderID());
          System.out.println("Value :"+ order.getOrderValue());
        }
      }
      catch(IOException ioe){
        System.out.println("Error :"+ioe);
        ioe.printStackTrace();
      }
      catch(Exception e){
        System.out.println("Exception :"+e);
        e.printStackTrace();
      }
    }
  }
}
```

Running the `runtcpip.bat` file will compile all TCP/IP classes and interfaces described in this section, as well as start your TCP/IP server and TCP/IP client demonstration programs. Aside from the database-specific properties defined in the `TCPIPCH12.Properties` file equipped with the book, the following key TCP/IP-oriented properties will be of interest and need to be set for your environment:

```
# TCP-IP Server Name
SERVER_HOST=localhost
# TCP-IP Server Port
SERVER_PORT=9000

# TCP-IP Client Callback Name
CLIENT_RECEIVER_HOST=localhost
# TCP-IP Client Callback Port
CLIENT_RECEIVER_PORTS=9001
```


The `SERVER_HOST` and `SERVER_PORT` properties need to be set to the hostname (or IP address) and port number for wherever you want to run the TCP/IP server in this example. The `CLIENT_RECEIVER_HOST` and `CLIENT_RECEIVER_PORTS` properties need to be set to the hostname (or IP address) and port number for wherever you want to run the TCP/IP client in this example. Note that the predefined properties equipped with the `TCPIPCH12.Properties` file should be fine to run on your `localhost` machine if the ports 9000 and 9001 are available.

UDP Datagrams

The preceding section demonstrated how to use the basic `java.net` socket programming libraries with TCP as the Transport Layer protocol. Java also provides support for using UDP as the Transport Layer protocol for socket programming. Figure 12.3 shows the key UDP-related classes part of the `java.net` package. The `DatagramSocket` class is used to receive and send `DatagramPacket` objects via UDP. `Datagram` packets can arrive in any order when sent between endpoints, and the routing of packets always differs between successive transmissions because no TCP-like connection is involved. The `MulticastSocket` class is a type of UDP `DatagramSocket` used for receiving and sending multicast datagram packets in which a group of subscribing UDP endpoints can receive packets sent to the entire group.

`DatagramSocket` objects can be created on a particular port for a particular IP address as shown here:

```
DatagramSocket datagramSocketRemote =
  new DatagramSocket(2020, InetAddress.getByName("206.26.48.100"));
```

Or you can create a `DatagramSocket` on your local host in this way:

```
DatagramSocket datagramSocket =  new DatagramSocket(2020);
```

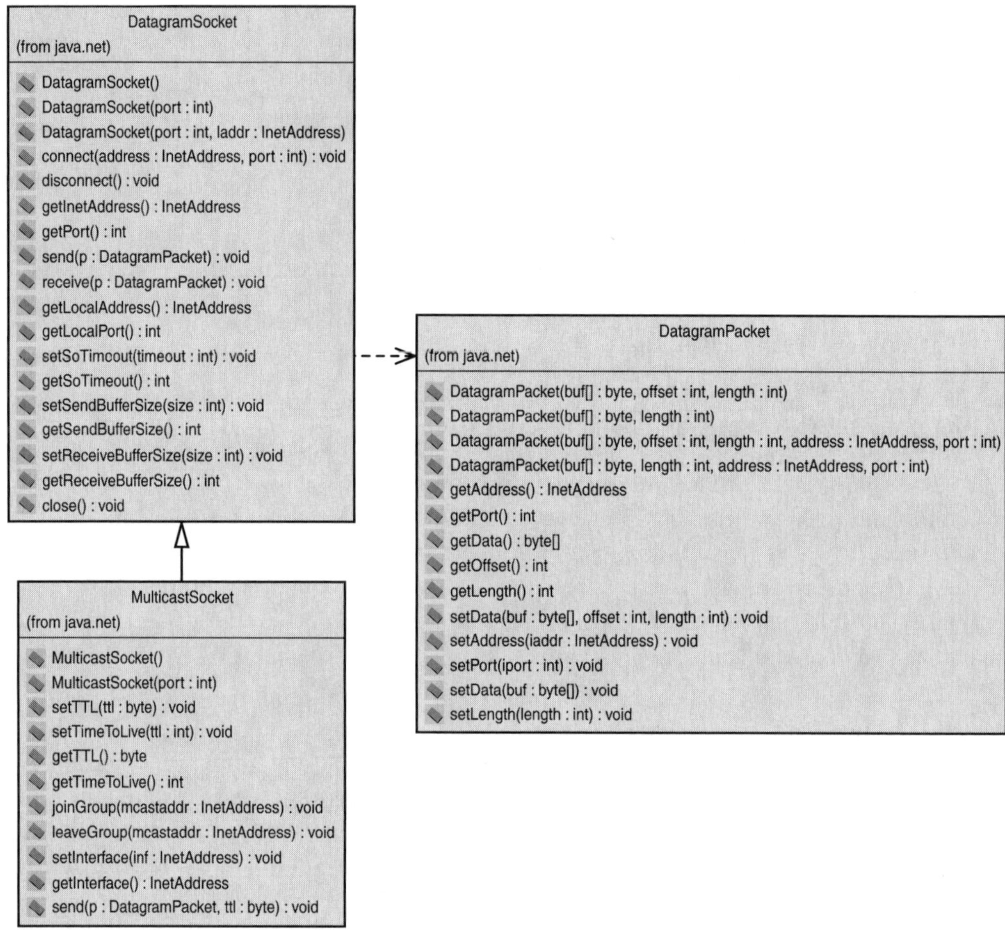

FIGURE 12.3
UDP datagram entities.

`DatagramPacket` objects can then be created to receive packets on a specified UDP socket and perhaps convert it to an object more directly useful, such as a `String`:

```
byte[] bufferToReceive = new byte[16];
DatagramPacket receivedPacket =
  new DatagramPacket(bufferToReceive, bufferToReceive.length);

datagramSocket.receive(receivedPacket);
String stringReceived = new String(receivedPacket.getData());
```

You can then extract the IP address and UDP port from which the datagram was sent and perhaps send the client a datagram using their IP address and UDP port during the construction of a new DatagramPacket as shown here:

```
String stringToSend = "Hello";
byte [] bufferToSend = stringToSend.getBytes();
InetAddress clientAddress = receivedPacket.getAddress();
int clientPort = receivedPacket.getPort();
DatagramPacket packetToSend = new DatagramPacket(bufferToSend,
                    bufferToSend.length, clientAddress, clientPort);
datagramSocket.send(packetToSend);
```


As for multicast sockets, it is a rather straightforward process to join a multicast UDP group using the MulticastSocket class. After that, you can send and receive packets as usual; now, however, sent packets are broadcast to the group listening on this multicast channel, and you can also receive packets broadcast over this channel. For example:

```
MulticastSocket dgsocket = new MulticastSocket();
dgsocket.joinGroup(InetAddress.getByName("166.0.0.1"));
  ...
// Datagram business as usual
  ...
dgsocket.leaveGroup(InetAddress.getByName("166.0.0.1"));
```

Custom Sockets and Factories

The diagram in Figure 12.4 shows some of the remaining entities you can use to customize your TCP/IP-based applications. The SocketImpl class and SocketImplFactory interface can be used to create custom socket implementations that can then be associated with the Socket and ServerSocket classes. The implementation of Berkeley Software Design (BSD) style socket options and use of default TCP and UDP transport implementations are all also provided by the java.net package.

The SocketImpl abstract class represents the base class for implementing TCP-based sockets. The PlainSocketImpl class extending the SocketImpl class is not a public API class, but it is the underlying default TCP-based socket implementation used by both the ServerSocket and the Socket classes. By extending the SocketImpl class with your own socket implementation, you can provide your own custom transport layer. By creating your own SocketImplFactory that returns an instance of your custom SocketImpl, you can call the static methods Socket.setSocketImplFactory() and ServerSocket.setSocketFactory() to register your custom socket factory from both the client and the server side of a TCP/IP connection.

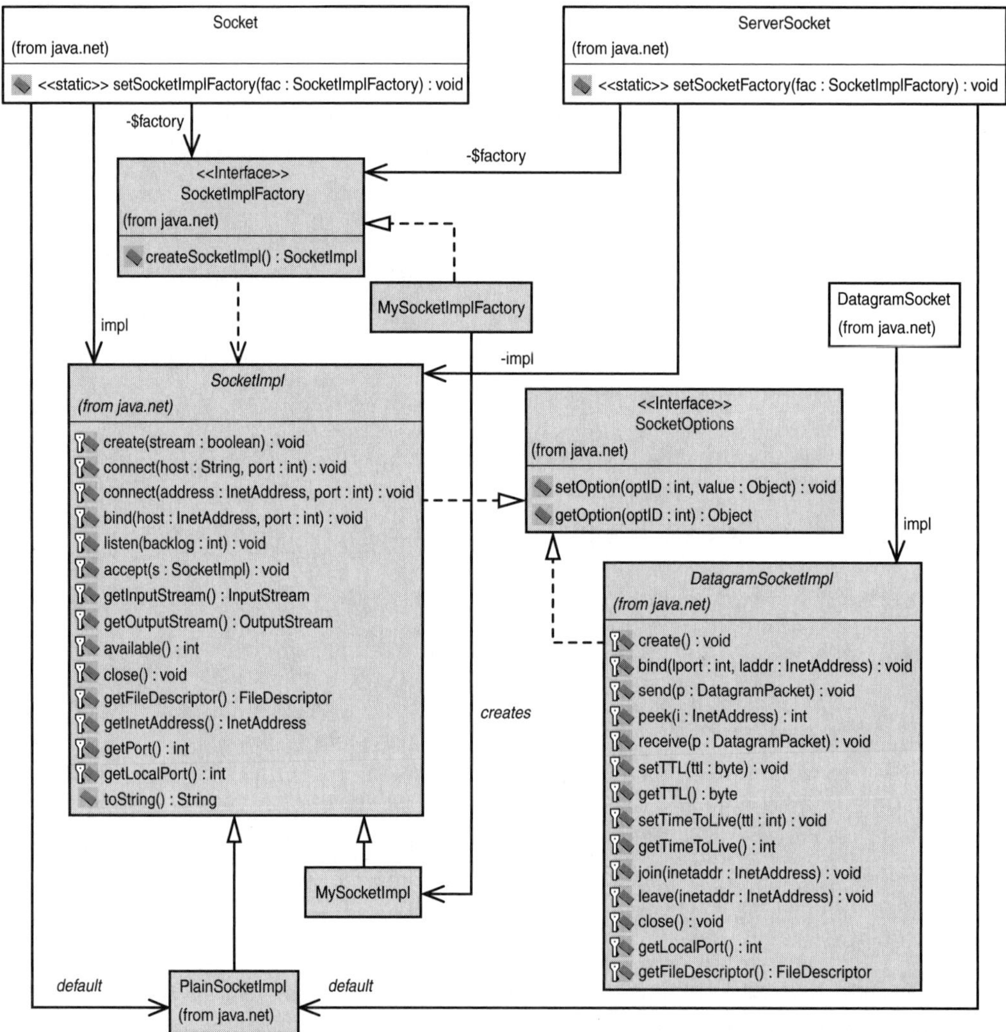

FIGURE 12.4
Customizing sockets and factories.

Both the `SocketImpl` and the `DatagramSocketImpl` classes implement the `SocketOptions` interface. `SocketOptions` allow you to get and set BSD-style socket options for your socket connection. Options such as `TCP_NODELAY` (Nagle's algorithm enabling/disabling), `SO_LINGER` (time for connection to linger on a close), and `SO_TIMEOUT` (read calls block for this timeout duration) all have type-safe getter and setter methods on the `Socket` class itself. The `ServerSocket` has the capability to get and set to the `SO_TIMEOUT` option.

Communication Streams

As you've seen from the TCP/IP examples of the preceding section, I/O streams from the `java.io` library are used in conjunction with the socket classes from the `java.net` library to exchange data between TCP/IP clients and servers. On a particular `java.net.Socket` connection object, one can obtain handles to the `java.io.InputStream` and `java.io.OutputStream` over which you can receive or send data, respectively. Many subclasses of `InputStream` and `OutputStream` can be constructed with a handle to such stream objects in order to chain I/O streams together. Given many of the built-in `java.io` stream classes, this gives Java socket programmers the added advantage of implementing a set of fairly clean interfaces to TCP/IP connection streams.

For example, as with the example in the preceding section, object streams can offer a fairly type-safe interface to TCP/IP connections, as demonstrated here:

```
outStream = new ObjectOutputStream(socket.getOutputStream());
outStream.writeObject("CustomerAddressQuery");
outStream.writeObject("Heilmann");

inStream = new InputOutputStream(socket.getInputStream());
String lastName = (String) inStream.readObject();
int id = inStream.readInt();
Address addr = (Address) inStream.readObject();
```

Or perhaps use a `BufferedReader` to read buffered text from an input stream or send text over an output stream with a `BufferedWriter`. For example:

```
InputStream inStream = socket.getInputStream();
InputStreamReader isReader = new InputStreamReader(inStream);
BufferedReader bufferedReader = new BufferedReader(isReader);
String theTime = bufferedReader.readLine();
```

Aside from these and other `java.io` streams, you can also implement object-oriented type-safe protocols over TCP/IP of your own ilk by creating your own `InputStream` and `OutputStream` types. That is, you might consider encapsulating any proprietary protocol that needs to operate over TCP/IP inside one or more classes which can be constructed with the `InputStream` or `OutputStream` objects associated with a `Socket`. Type-safe calls on such custom protocol classes can then be made and can allow you to handle any socket protocol transparent to users of the custom streaming classes.

Conclusions

TCP/IP is an extremely important communications protocol underlying all other higher-level distributed communications schemes examined in this book. TCP/IP is a reliable and connection-oriented protocol acting as the backbone of the Internet. A basic understanding of TCP/IP is of tremendous importance for the serious enterprise Java developer.

Socket programming is a term used to describe how to interface with the TCP/IP protocol suite from your applications. The `java.net` packages offer a simple and standard means to interact with a platform's underlying socket resources from Java. Socket programming can yield very efficient applications and is sometimes the only choice for solving a particular problem. However, the lack of any application/communications interface layer over TCP/IP causes one to perform a lot of hand-coding. As you could see from the examples in this chapter, a lot of programming effort was expended in just building an interface between the example application and the TCP/IP stacks. Future chapters on communications paradigms like CORBA, RMI, and DCOM help illustrate how such work can be handled for you by auxiliary distributed communications libraries and utilities.

Web Communications

CHAPTER

13

IN THIS CHAPTER

- The Internet and the World Wide Web 366
- HTTP 370
- CGI 380
- Servlets 381
- HTML Documents 382
- Dynamic HTML Generation 383

The Hypertext Transfer Protocol (HTTP) over TCP/IP is the protocol used between Web-browser– and Web-server–based communications. Common Gateway Interface (CGI) programs have long been the traditional means by which Web servers allowed a programmatic interface to HTTP requests and responses. Servlets offer a simple and more efficient Java-based mechanism for interfacing with HTTP requests and responses from within a Web server process. This chapter is mostly conceptual in nature and describes the Web-based communications model for you in the context of your reading about the other communications models utilized by enterprise Java applications in this part of the book. Part VI of this book, "Enterprise Web Enabling," describes how to practically Web-enable your enterprise in much more detail.

In this chapter, you will learn:

- A brief history of the Internet and the World Wide Web.
- The architecture of the HTTP protocol used for Web-based communications.
- The basics behind the CGI for handling HTTP requests and responses.
- The basics behind the Java Servlet framework for handling HTTP requests and responses.
- The basic concept of how HTML documents affect HTTP request and response streams.
- The concept of Dynamic HTML.

The Internet and the World Wide Web

We briefly described the foundations of the Internet's TCP/IP protocol suite in Chapter 12, "Network Communications." The ARPAnet began using TCP/IP in 1969 where it grew from just four hosts to approximately 200 hosts in 1981, 1,000 hosts in 1984, 300,000 hosts in 1990, and more than 35 million hosts at present. Clearly, the Internet has exploded as a medium to share and exchange information among people. But what is behind this explosion? Most people realize that without the user-friendly face of the World Wide Web (WWW), the market demand for Internet-based information delivery would never have grown so quickly, nor would it have changed our lives so much.

History of the Web

In 1980, Tim Berners-Lee wrote a simple program at the European Laboratory for Particle Physics (CERN) that allowed for arbitrary traversal between nodes using hyperlinks. Almost 10 years later, in 1989, Berners-Lee wrote a proposal describing a means for organizing the vast amounts of information shared by many people on many machines at CERN using hypertextual links between such information. Although the concept of hypertextual linking was not new, Berners-Lee put together a very feasible and simple proposal for building a distributed hypertextual document-linking system that was pursued later in 1990. Eventually, the term

"World Wide Web" was coined to describe the GUI-based browsing community that tapped into the prototype infrastructure.

Over the next few years and with the help of a few co-workers, Berners-Lee and crew deployed working versions of the WWW browsers for CERN and took a demonstration of their WWW on the road to a few key conferences. By that time, various servers of hypertext pages usable by a WWW browser were established around the globe (approximately 50 WWW servers were available by January 1993). Later that year, Marc Andreessen, working at the National Center for Supercomputing Applications (NCSA) at the University of Illinois at Urbana-Champaign, created the Mosaic WWW browser capable of running on various operating-system platforms and enabling true multimedia content delivery via the WWW. CERN announced that the WWW technology would be available free for commercial use, and by the end of 1993 there would be approximately 200 WWW servers. Early in 1994, Marc Andreessen and a few NCSA co-workers left NCSA to form the Mosaic Communications Corporation, which became the Netscape Communications Corporation. Eventually, the W3 Organization was formed by MIT and CERN to help push standardization of the WWW, which has explosively grown to levels supporting more than 4 million WWW servers, more than 35 million Internet hosts, and more than 40 million Internet users.

Thus, in just about 10 years of time, the World Wide Web grew from a laboratory concept to the economical, sociological, and political force that it is today. In 1990, most people still had to either physically transplant themselves to a library or bookstore to obtain certain information they were looking for or wait for such information to make its way into their home or business via newspaper or television. The overhead involved with pursuing information usually resulted in never even obtaining such information. Now, you can simply turn on your computer from work or home and locate just about any information you want on any topic in a matter of minutes.

This economical and ease-of-information access has penetrated the enterprise and has thus become one of the key ways organizations present information to their employees, customers, and business partners. Enterprise development is thus inextricably intertwined with pushing and pulling information through this WWW-based communications medium. In this chapter, we will pursue understanding the basic concepts and approaches for communications-enabling such information via the Web so that you can put it in context with other distributed computing paradigms described in this part of the book. Part VI describes in much more detail how to Web-enable your enterprise applications using Java.

URLs

Before you can retrieve a Web page via the WWW, or for that matter access any resource on the Internet (an email address, an executable program, and so on), you'll need a way to identify where that resource is. Uniform Resource Identifiers (URIs) represent standard identifiers for any resource accessible via the Internet. A Uniform Resource Name (URN) is a type of URI that identifies a resource via some alias name. A Uniform Resource Locator (URL) is a type of URI that identifies a resource by specifying the exact location of such a resource on the Internet.

Because URNs identify where to obtain resources on the Internet via a logical name, the actual location of the resource can change and the URN will still be valid. However, URLs are much more widely employed by Web-based software used on the Internet today. In fact, because URLs were first used by most people when referring to Web sites, some might think that URLs refer exclusively to Web-based resources, but they do not.

URLs assume this general form:

```
scheme://user:password@host:port/path/resource#section?parameters
```

The *scheme* represents the protocol operating over TCP/IP through which the referenced Web resource can be accessed (for example, `http`, `ftp`, `telnet`, `file`). The optional *user* and *password* fields represent part of a standard way to transfer credential information via a URL for authentication that may be required for access to the requested resource. A hostname or IP address must be used in the *host* portion of the URL to identify the TCP/IP host location of the resource. The *port* may also be optionally supplied, depending on whether the requested resource has a socket listener on the default port for that *scheme* (that is, there's no need to add `80` for the scheme `http` if the WWW server is running on this default port for the Web).

After the protocol, the client identity, and a socket have identified a unique machine and process running somewhere on the Internet, the process resource and set of parameters used by that resource need to be specified. The *path* identifies the path to that resource on the particular host (that is, a subdirectory from some root context). The *resource* identifies the actual resource of interest (for example, HTML file), and the *section* can optionally be used to specify a sublocation within the resource location. Finally, the *parameters* field is also optionally used to pass a set of parameters that may be used by the resource if it is some sort of executable program requiring such values. Parameters are an ampersand-separated (`&`) set of name/value pairs of the following form: *name1*=*value1*&*name2*=*value2*&....

Finally, because URLs have parameters that can contain an arbitrary selection of characters in them, a mechanism for encoding such characters must exist to prevent certain control and nonprintable characters from corrupting processing along their path of delivery. The basic rule is that a control or nonprintable character that is embedded into a URL must be represented in its two-byte hexadecimal ASCII form prepended with a percent sign (`%`). Space characters, however, are encoded with a plus (+) sign. Generally speaking, any characters used in a URL that are not meant to be interpreted by any Web or network hardware/software and that are not letters, numbers, periods, underscores, or hyphens should be URL-encoded. Thus, to reference an HTML file named `Buy Me!.html` at `www.beeshirts.com`, your encoded URL might look as follows: `http://www.beeshirts.com/Buy+Me%21.html`.

As shown in Figure 13.1, an encapsulation for a URL is provided by the `java.net.URL` class. In addition to getting and setting the various elements of a URL, a `URL` object can also be used to obtain a reference to a `java.net.URLConnection` object. The abstract `URLConnection` class is a base class encapsulating a connection between a client application and the resource location identified by the URL. Information can be read from and written to the URL via a `URLConnection` instance. A concrete instance of the abstract `java.net.URLStreamHandler` class is also associated with a `URL` to encapsulate a protocol handler for a particular URL protocol connection scheme. The `java.net.URLStreamHandlerFactory` is used to create a `URLStreamHandler` object given a particular URL protocol scheme name.

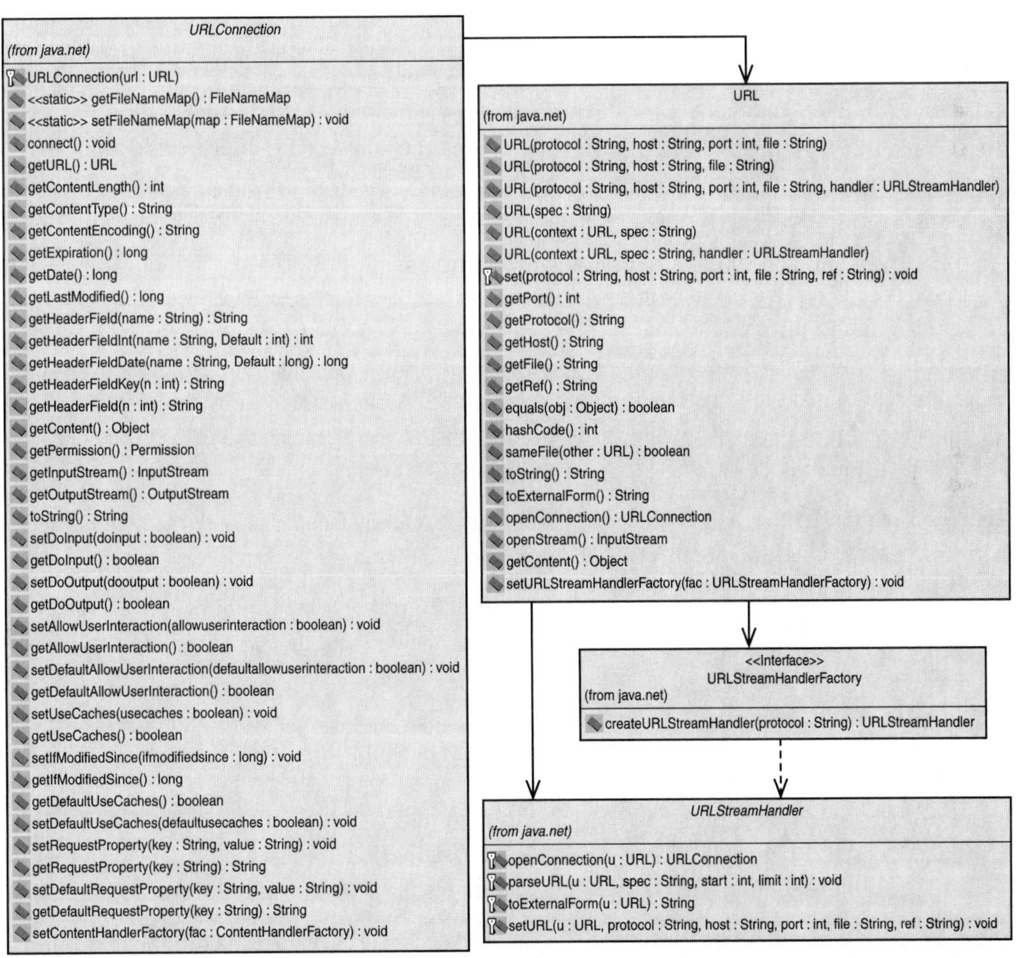

FIGURE 13.1
Basic Java URL abstractions.

HTTP

The Hypertext Transfer Protocol (HTTP) is a protocol built atop the TCP/IP protocol. HTTP began as a connectionless and stateless protocol whereby an HTTP client opened a socket connection to an HTTP server, issued an HTTP request stream of data, received an HTTP response stream of data back from the server, and closed the connection. That was it. Since the early days of HTTP, it has evolved only mildly into a protocol that can keep connections open for multiple response and request transactions. Furthermore, common techniques now exist outside of the protocol to provide a stateful nature to HTTP.

HTTP/0.9 was first used during the early development stages of the WWW in 1990 as the protocol over which the hypertextual document-linking system created by Berners-Lee would operate. HTTP/1.0, introduced thereafter, made HTTP commercially viable and is currently the most widely implemented version of HTTP. The latest version, HTTP/1.1, improves on HTTP/1.0 by providing more functionality and support for allowing multiple transactions to occur between an HTTP client and server over the same connection.

Basic HTTP Behavior

Figure 13.2 depicts a basic collaboration diagram for HTTP client/server behavior. In this figure, we see the HTTP client side on the left and the HTTP server side on the right. The HTTP client software represents the software implementing the HTTP protocol above the client-side TCP/IP stacks. An HTTP client making use of such HTTP client software will typically be a Web browser, for example. The HTTP server software also implements the HTTP protocol above a set of server-side TCP/IP stacks. A typical HTTP server example is a Web server.

The basic sequence of steps illustrated in Figure 13.2 are described here, with the step numbers in the diagram enclosed in parentheses:

- *Server listens for requests (step 1):* First, an HTTP server must listen for requests on a particular socket. For Web servers, port 80 is a standard and default port on which to listen for Web requests.
- *Client creates HTTP URL (step 2):* The HTTP client software then submits a URL designating the protocol, hostname, optional port number, and path of the desired Internet resource to retrieve.
- *Client creates socket connection (step 3):* The HTTP client software creates a TCP/IP socket connection given the desired hostname (or IP address) and a port number (default port 80).
- *Server accepts socket request (step 4):* The HTTP server software listening for a request on that port accepts the client socket connection request.

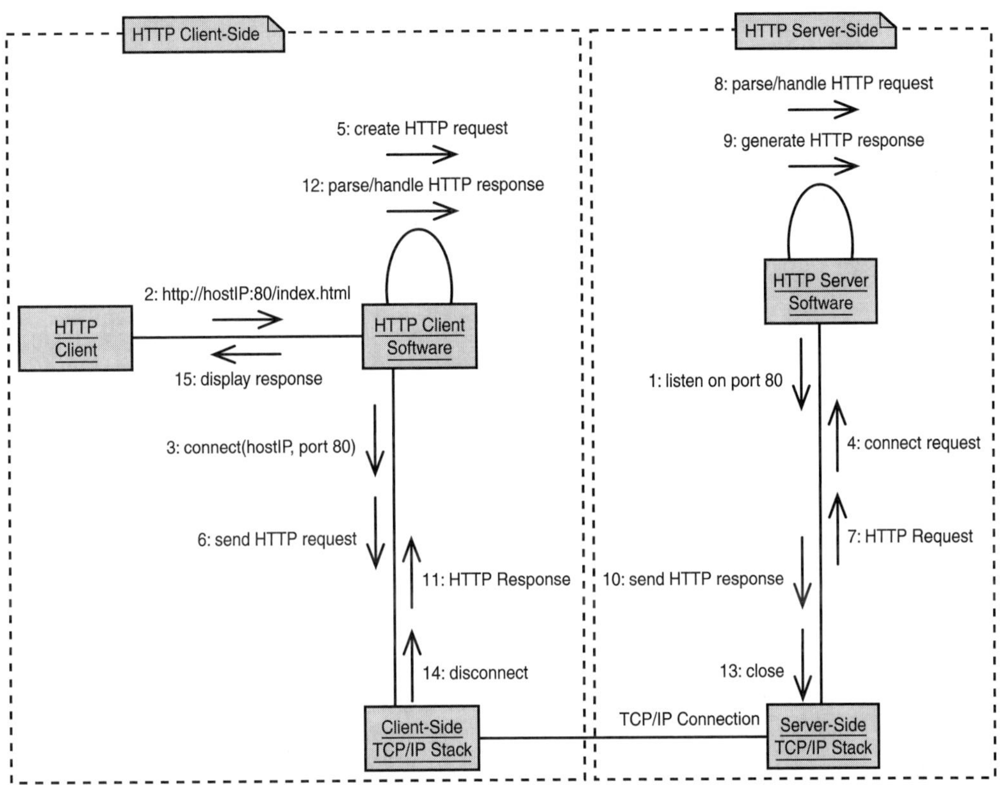

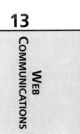

FIGURE 13.2
A basic HTTP behavioral diagram.

- *Client creates HTTP request (step 5):* Back on the client side, the HTTP client software creates an HTTP request out of the URL. The HTTP client software may also formulate an HTTP request given additional data to send to the HTTP server from the HTTP client.
- *The HTTP request is sent (steps 6 and 7):* The HTTP request is then pushed through the open TCP/IP socket connection and received on the server side.
- *Server parses/handles request (step 8):* The HTTP server software then parses the HTTP request and takes whatever action is specified in the request.
- *Server generates HTTP response (steps 9, 10, and 11):* The HTTP server software then generates an HTTP response message, which is sent back over the TCP/IP socket connection.
- *Client parses/handles HTTP response (step 12):* The HTTP client software parses and handles the HTTP response from the server.

- *Socket connection is closed (steps 13 and 14):* The underlying socket connection is closed.
- *Relay result (step 15):* The result from all of this processing is then returned to the HTTP client that triggered this whole sequence of events.

As can be seen from Figure 13.2, a connection is created, a single request is handled with a response being generated, and then the connection is closed. Thus, server-side scalability becomes very practical because an HTTP server won't have to deal with as many open connections at a single time as would be the case if such connections remained open for the life of an HTTP client and server session. Of course, the concept of a "session" from the perspective of the HTTP protocol is meaningless because no such information is baked into the protocol.

MIME

The Multipurpose Internet Mail Extensions (MIME) specifications define a standard for encoding binary data into ASCII, as well as a standard for indicating the type of data contained inside a message. Although MIME was originally used by email client software to describe how to interpret mail sent with multiple forms of media types (for example, pictures, text, and audio), MIME is now also used by HTTP to facilitate the exchange of multiple media types between Web servers and Web browsers. Web browsers use MIME types to tell Web servers what types of data they can support, and Web servers use MIME types to indicate the type of data they are sending.

MIME types are identified in the following general format: `type/subtype`. The `type` classifies the general type of data being sent, such as application, audio, image, text, or video. The `subtype` defines the specific type of format used within the general class of types, such as `gif` or `jpeg` for `image` types. Thus, for example, the designation of a GIF-format image sent via the Web is formatted as `image/gif`. Nonstandard subtypes are designated with an `x-` in front of the subtype, such as `image/x-bitmap` for Microsoft bitmap images. Table 13.1 defines some typical MIME types and subtypes, along with typical file extensions.

TABLE 13.1 A Few Key MIME Types

MIME Type	*MIME Subtype*	*Description*
`text`	`html`	HTML files (`*.htm`, `*.html`)
	`plain`	Regular ASCII files (`*.txt`)
`image`	`gif`	GIF image (`*.gif`)
	`jpeg`	JPEG image (`*.jpg`)
	`x-bitmap`	Microsoft bitmap (`*.bmp`)

MIME Type	*MIME Subtype*	*Description*
audio	basic	Basic audio files (*.au)
	x-wav	Microsoft sound wave files (*.wav)
video	mpeg	Moving Pictures Experts Group videos (*.mpg)
	quicktime	Apple QuickTime videos (*.mov)
	x-msvideo	Microsoft Audio Video Interleave (*.avi)
application	java	Java Class file (*.class)
	pdf	Adobe Acrobat file (*.pdf)
	postscript	Postscript file (*.ps)
	msword	Microsoft Word file (*.doc)
	zip	Compressed ZIP file (*.zip)

As shown in Figure 13.3, `java.net.ContentHandlerFactory` objects can be used to create a special content handler instance that is associated with a particular MIME type. The abstract `java.net.ContentHandler` class is extended to represent a concrete content handler object associated with a particular MIME type. The `ContentHandler` returns an object of a particular MIME type read from a `URLConnection`. The `java.net.FileNameMap` interface is used to define a mapping between a file name and a MIME type `String`. Finally, a `java.net.URLEncoder` utility class encodes a string into a URL encoded MIME type format and the `java.net.URLDecoder` utility class decodes a MIME type URL encoded string.

HTTP Requests

An HTTP request needs to indicate the nature of the request, indicate the resource desired, supply any other information to control the request nature, and supply any other data that may be of use in satisfying the request. HTTP requests tend to be human-readable and of the following general form:

- *Request Method:* An identifier for the type of HTTP request being made.
- *Resource ID:* An identifier of the particular resource being requested (on same line as request method). The resource is usually the result of a concatenation of the path, resource, and parameters submitted in a URL.
- *HTTP Version:* Specifies the HTTP protocol version to use (on the same line as request method and resource ID). The version is followed by a carriage return and line feed.
- *Header Name and Value Pairs:* Optional sequence of standard header names and associated values are used to control the request-handling behavior. Each header is followed by a carriage return and line feed.

- *Blank Line:* Blank line is followed by a carriage return and line feed.
- *Request Body:* Optional data that can be used as part of a particular request.

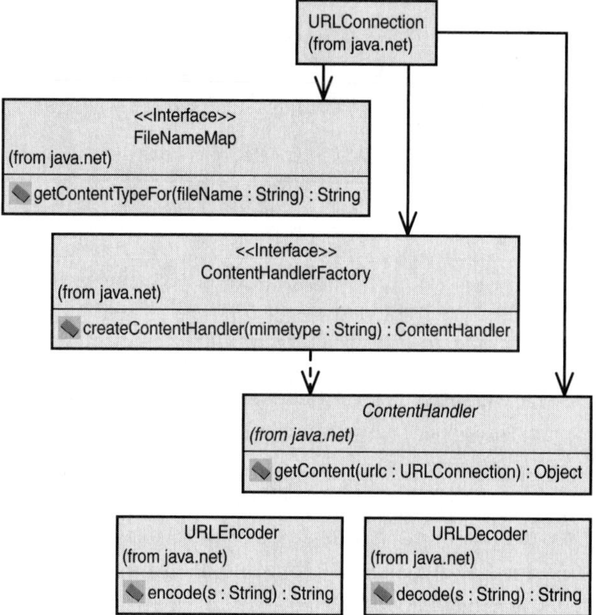

FIGURE 13.3
Basic Java MIME type handling utilities.

HTTP request methods come in the core flavors:

- `GET`: The `GET` request type is the most common type of request and is used to obtain a resource from the HTTP server. A `GET` request specifies the resource solely in the resource ID portion of the HTTP request and does not include any data in the request body. Because Web servers typically store `GET` information in environment variables, there is a limit to the amount of data that can be sent in a `GET` method.
- `POST`: Post request types don't have the request data limit that `GET` requests have. They store auxiliary request data in the request body typically in the form of name value pairs.
- `HEAD`: These requests fulfill the same function as `GET` requests but force the Web server to return only an HTTP header as opposed to any HTTP entity response data.
- `PUT`: This HTTP/1.1 type uploads a resource to the HTTP server.
- `DELETE`: This HTTP/1.1 type deletes a resource from the HTTP server.
- `OPTIONS`: This HTTP/1.1 type requests that the HTTP client be sent a set of HTTP server configuration options.

The complete set of request header types can be found in RFC 1945, but we list a collection of the most common request header types here:

- `Accept`: Specifies the type of MIME types supported by the HTTP client.
- `Accept-<Behavior>`: Specifies other types of data or behavior supported by the client (for example, `Accept-Language: en`).
- `Content-Length`: Specifies the length of data in the request body.
- `Authorization`: Authorization information.
- `User-Agent`: Specifies browser information.
- `Host`: The hostname and port requested.
- `Connection`: Client indicates the desire to keep the connection alive (`Keep-Alive`) for multiple requests.

As an illustration of what an HTTP request looks like, consider the following example of a `GET` HTTP request generated from a Netscape Web browser when you enter the URL `http://www.assuredtech.com`:

```
GET /index.html HTTP/1.0
Connection: Keep-Alive
User-Agent: Mozilla/4.5 - (WinNT; U)
Host: www.assuredtech.com
Accept: image/gif, image/x-xbitmap, image/jpeg, image/pjpeg, image/png, */*
Accept-Encoding: gzip
Accept-Language: en
Accept-Charset: iso-8859-1,*,utf-8
```


Here we see that the first line contains the `GET` request method and the resource `/index.html`, and uses HTTP version `HTTP/1.0`. This is followed by a series of header name and value pairs.

HTTP Responses

An HTTP response must return the status of the response and information to control the response behavior, as well as perhaps the requested data itself. HTTP responses also tend to be human-readable and of this general form:

- *HTTP Version:* Identifies the HTTP version used.
- *HTTP Status Code:* A numeric identifier of the status for the response (on the same line as HTTP version).
- *HTTP Status Description:* An optional short description of the HTTP status code (on the same line as HTTP version and status code). It is followed by carriage return and line feed.

- *Header Name and Value Pairs:* Optional sequence of standard header names and associated values are used to control the response-handling behavior. Each header is followed by a carriage return and line feed.
- *Blank Line:* Blank line is followed by a carriage return and line feed.
- *Response Body:* Optional data that can be used as part of a particular response.

There are many response codes, but the general classes of codes are as shown here (the complete specification is in RFC 1945):

- *100-199:* Response is informational in nature only.
- *200-299:* Response was successful.
- *300-399:* Response is a redirection to another location.
- *400-499:* Response designates a client request error.
- *500-599:* Response designates a server-side error.

Furthermore, some common response headers are shown here (the complete specification is in RFC 1945):

- *Date:* Date and time response was created.
- *Server:* Identifies the server.
- *Content-Type:* Identifies the MIME type of the response body.
- *Content-Encoding:* Indicates MIME encoding scheme.
- *Connection:* Although keeping connections open for multiple client-side requests over a small timeout period is the default for HTTP/1.1, a server may issue a `close` value response to indicate that it has closed the connection.

As an illustration of what an HTTP response looks like, consider the response to the HTTP request sent earlier:

```
HTTP/1.1 200 OK
Date: Sat, 30 Oct 1999 15:36:30 GMT
Server: Apache/1.2.5 FrontPage/3.0.4
Connection: close
Content-Type: text/html

<!DOCTYPE HTML PUBLIC "-//W3C//DTD HTML 3.2//EN">
<HTML>
<HEAD>
  <META HTTP-EQUIV="Content-Type" CONTENT="text/html;CHARSET=iso-8859-1">
  <META NAME="description" CONTENT="Assured Technologies is a unique
➥corporation dedicated to relentlessly pursuing the application
```

```
➥ and progress of high-intelligence, high-assurance, diversely-
➥distributed, practical, and economical enterprise information
➥and knowledge systems.">
  <META NAME="keywords" CONTENT="software,consulting,java,corba,internet,
➥web,database,intelligence,agents,reliability,assurance,security">
  <META NAME="GENERATOR" Content="Visual Page 1.1a for Windows">
  <TITLE>Assured Technologies, Inc.</TITLE>
</HEAD>
<FRAMESET   COLS = "100% "   >
  <FRAMESET  ROWS = "145,100% "    BORDER="0" FRAMESPACING="0"
➥FRAMEBORDER="NO">
    <FRAME SRC="fronttop.html" NAME="frametop" SCROLLING="NO"
➥MARGINWIDTH="17" MARGINHEIGHT="10" NORESIZE>
    <FRAMESET   COLS = "190,100% "    BORDER="0" FRAMESPACING="0"
➥FRAMEBORDER="NO">
      <FRAME SRC="frontleft.html" NAME="frameleft"
➥SCROLLING="NO" NORESIZE>
    <FRAME SRC="frontmain.html" NAME="framemain" NORESIZE>
    </FRAMESET>
  </FRAMESET>
</FRAMESET>
<NOFRAMES>
<BODY>
<P>
</BODY>
</NOFRAMES>
</HTML>
```


Here we see that the first line contains the HTTP version used, `HTTP/1.1`, the success status code `200`, and the success status description `OK`, followed by a series of header name and value pairs, a blank line, and then the actual response entity data (that is, the HTML page).

Basic HTTP Handling in Java

Figure 13.4 shows an extension of the `URLConnection` class built into Java by way of the `java.net.HttpURLConnection` abstract class. `HttpURLConnection` represents a type of `URLConnection` with support for the HTTP protocol. The `HttpURLConnection` defines a collection of static HTTP response codes. A request method `String` and a flag indicating whether or not redirects should be followed can be get or set as part of the `HttpURLConnection` interface. Furthermore, response messages as well as various error and status information about the connection can be obtained from the `HttpURLConnection` object. The `HttpURLConnection` class can thus be used as the basis for building basic web client functionality into your Java applications.

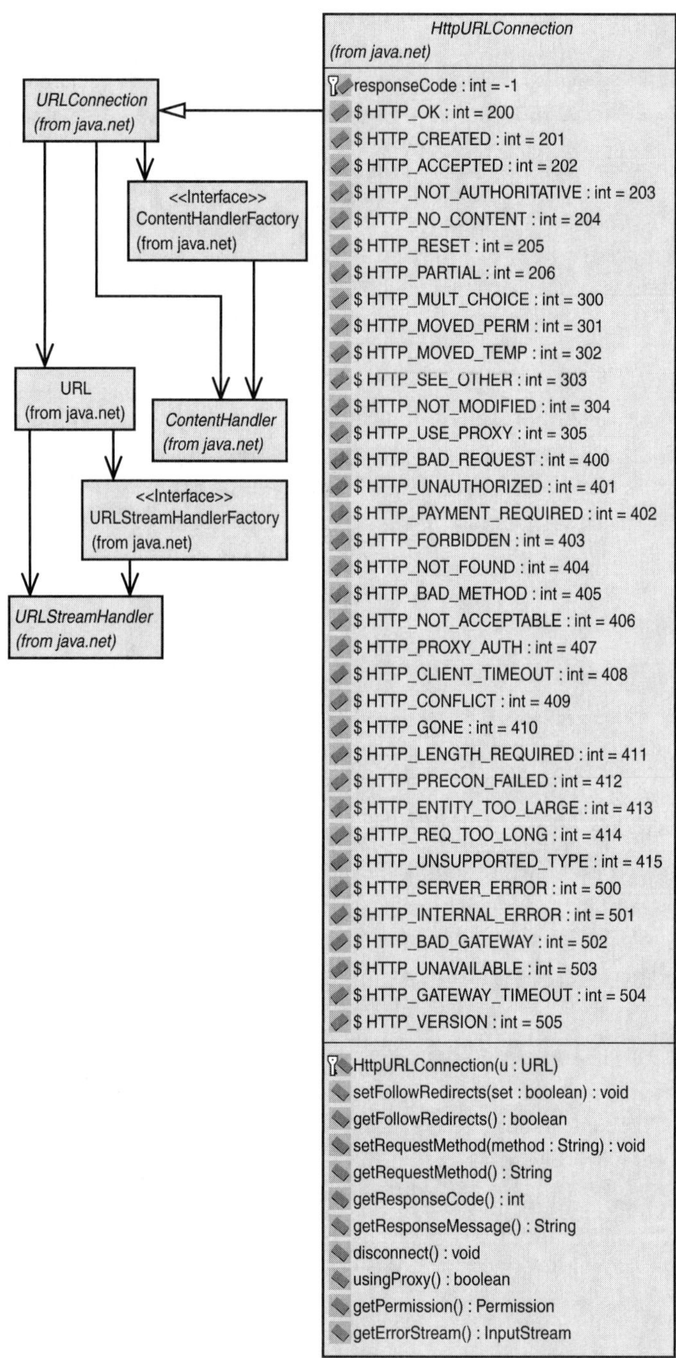

FIGURE 13.4
Basic Java HTTP URL connections.

Tracking Sessions outside of HTTP

Given that HTTP is a stateless protocol, how do Web sites such as `Amazon.com` know that the HTTP request sending your credit-card information at one instant is to be associated with another HTTP request for your book order the next instant? The answer is that the Web servers at Amazon.com somehow force your subsequent HTTP requests to contain some identifying information that the server side can associate with your user session. But how you ask?

Baking Session IDs into the URL and Request Body

One way to accomplish the tracking of sessions outside of HTTP is to force your subsequent URL requests to contain some sort of session ID information. On the server side, the server can then relate all HTTP requests that are received with such a session ID. The server can force your URL requests to be formulated in such a way because the servers are what generate the embedded URL links that you click on after you first enter their Web site. Thus, you may be clicking on a hyperlink that should vector you to some `sales.html` page, but in actuality, the hyperlink in the Web page might refer to `http://bla.com/sales/ID5656/sales.html`. Of course, the parameter portion of the URL may also embed session ID information. Another technique is to generate HTML pages on the server side which will cause session identifying information to be embedded into the request body portion of an HTTP request unbeknownst to you.

Cookies

Cookies are simple additions to the HTTP protocol first used by Netscape to maintain the state of a particular user's session on the Web. Cookies are values that are initially generated by a Web server and contained in one or more HTTP response headers. A cookie-capable Web browser maintains the cookie information so that future requests to a URL that match the information contained in a cookie can be sent back to the server via the HTTP request. The server can then relate such information with the cookie information that it saved in order to make the association that these two requests come from the same user session.

The header on the server side that is packed into an HTTP response follows this form:

```
Set-Cookie: name=value; expires=date; domain=domainName; path=pathName;
➥ secure
```

If the Web browser is sending an HTTP request to a URL whose domain and path match one or more of the cookies stored, it will send each cookie name and value pair back to the Web server in an HTTP request header of the following form:

```
Cookie: name1=value1; name2=value2; ...
```

HTTP-NG

The "Next Generation" HTTP architecture currently being developed is HTTP-NG. HTTP-NG is a protocol architecture being pursued that not only will be connection oriented, but also will offer the capability to build stateful HTTP-NG–based servers. HTTP-NG will not only be downward-compatible with the existing HTTP protocols, but it will also support an extended application and messaging layer, allowing for the marshaling of types and the capability to group HTTP request methods into objects. HTTP-NG will thus offer the capability for applications built using CORBA, RMI, and DCOM to directly map to the type system supplied by HTTP-NG. Because such other computing paradigms as CORBA, RMI, and DCOM traditionally must "tunnel" through HTTP with a lot of extra overhead, this will further the cause for building truly object-oriented Web-based applications.

CGI

The Common Gateway Interface (CGI) provides for a standard way to allow Web servers to pass off HTTP requests to external processes by spawning such processes, passing them the request data, and receiving response data. CGI determines the interface for Web servers to identify the fact that an HTTP request is indeed supposed to result in a CGI call. CGI also defines the way in which Web servers pull data from the HTTP request and set appropriate environment variables for the CGI process, as well as for how the Web server spawns the process passing it the HTTP request's resource parameters. CGI also puts constraints on the CGI programs themselves for determining how to return data to the Web servers (that is, as HTML pages perhaps with HTTP response headers).

The basic flow of a CGI request via a Web server works as shown here:

- A Web browser sends an HTTP request formulated from some URL. For example, the URL `http://www.bla.com/cgi-bin/customerQuery.cgi?customer=heilmann` may get transformed into an HTTP request with the HTTP request header line `POST /cgi-bin/customerQuery.cgi?customer=heilmann HTTP/1.0`.
- A Web server receives an HTTP request with a resource ID specifying the path to a resource, the resource name, and possibly a set of parameters to pass to this resource.
- If the Web server supports CGI, either it should have been configured to recognize the fact that the path refers to a directory where CGI programs are stored (for example, `cgi-bin`) or it will be configured to recognize the fact that the resource name ends with an appropriate extension (for example, `cgi`).
- The Web server will set certain environment variables derived from the HTTP request used by the CGI program. It will then spawn the CGI program identified by the pathname and resource name as a separate process, passing it the parameters also sent over to the Web server via the HTTP request.

- The spawned CGI program uses the environment variables and parameters passed to it to do whatever job it is supposed to do (for example, database query or remote printing).
- By virtue of being a CGI program, the program either must format the results in the form of an HTML page for the response body or must return the response headers and alleviate the Web server from this duty (that is, is a nonparsed CGI program).
- The CGI program then returns the results to the Web server via a standard output stream.
- The Web server then returns the results to the Web client by either first prepending the header values or sending the results back without further modification (if the CGI program is of the nonparsed persuasion).

To infuse state into your CGI programs, they too can implement one of the techniques mentioned earlier for providing state across HTTP session requests. That is, the CGI program could implement a technique forcing the client to send its session ID information via a URL or the request data body, or by using cookies. Of course, a lot of hand coding is required on the part of the CGI programmer to persist such session information so that it can be obtained and used during successive requests.

CGI is one of the oldest and still very popular techniques for handling HTTP requests and generating HTTP responses. Part VI comments more on the scalability and actual usage of such techniques in much more depth, but we wanted to highlight here how CGI can really be viewed as one way to create applications that interface with the HTTP protocol.

Servlets

The Java Servlet standard provides a way to allow Web servers to pass off HTTP requests to Java-based code by starting such code as a separate thread, passing request data to the servlet, and receiving back response data. Servlets are a sort of Java equivalent to CGI programs, with the major difference being that servlets run inside a thread as opposed to running as a separate process like CGI programs. Servlets are built by adhering to a standard interface defined by the `javax.servlet` packages. A servlet engine can then be installed inside a Web server to provide a mechanism by which Web servers can map HTTP requests to servlet requests and HTTP responses from servlet responses.

The basic flow of a servlet request via a Web server works as shown here:

- A Web browser sends an HTTP request formulated from some URL. For example, the URL `http://www.bla.com/servlets/CustomerQuery?customer=heilmann` may get transformed into an HTTP request with the HTTP request header line `POST /servlets/CustomerQuery?customer=heilmann HTTP/1.0`.
- A Web server receives an HTTP request with a resource ID specifying the path to a resource, the resource name, and possibly a set of parameters to pass to this resource.

- If the Web server supports servlets (that is, has a servlet engine), it should have been configured to recognize the fact that the path refers to a directory where servlet programs are stored (for example, `servlets`).
- If the requested servlet has not been loaded, it will be loaded.
- The servlet engine then creates an instance of the servlet and calls a standard initialization method on the servlet.
- The servlet engine then funnels the HTTP request to the servlet.
- The specific servlet program services the request and creates an HTTP response passed back from its standard interface.
- The servlet engine transforms the Java-based HTTP response into an HTTP response packet for the Web server.
- The Web server then returns the results to the Web client.

Servlets also make creating state-based HTTP applications much simpler. This is achieved by offering a simple API to a session object that can be used to store information from a request from a particular HTTP client. The session object can then be retrieved later during a subsequent request from the same HTTP client. The underlying servlet engine handles the details of how such state is maintained for you. As a default, cookies are used. If the particular browser being used by the HTTP client does not support cookies, URL rewriting can be used instead.

Servlets are one of the core ways Java-based applications can efficiently handle HTTP requests and generate HTTP responses. Part VI dedicates Chapter 32, "Java Servlets," to Java Servlet programming, but we wanted to highlight here how servlets can be viewed as yet another way to create applications that interface with the HTTP protocol.

HTML Documents

The Hypertext Markup Language (HTML) provides the primary data format used to describe how a document is displayed inside a Web browser, as well as the controls provided by this document. HTML pages are sent in the response body of an HTTP response from the Web server to the Web browser. When inside your Web browser, HTML pages display familiar GUI widgets such as hyperlinks, text boxes, and submit buttons. When a user interfaces with the displayed widgets and submits a request, the Web browser transforms such events into HTTP requests that are sent back to the Web server.

HTML has gone through several version upgrades and is now at HTML 4.0 in its versioning lifeline. HTML pages are by and large static constructs that are typically either read locally from a disk on the Web server or generated by some server-side application in a more dynamic fashion. Nonetheless, when the HTML documents leave the Web server in the form of an HTTP response, they end up at the browser and rest there in a fairly static state whereby statically defined text, images, audio, and a whole slew of HTML GUI widgets create the Web-based interface with which we are all familiar. Client-side scripting such as client-side JavaScript can help produce some behavior on the Web browser, but most pages you see today still remain constrained by the nature of their HTML elements identified by the HTML standard's set of tags.

An HTML form (that is, `<FORM>...</FORM>`) is one type of HTML element used to describe a type of HTTP request and an action to take. Some event, of course, must induce this action to occur. An HTML input element (that is, `<INPUT ...>`) defined within a set of HTML form tags is used to designate a GUI element to display, as well as to either capture request data or induce the submission event of the actual HTTP request. HTML input elements can have different types such as text boxes, submission buttons, reset buttons, and check boxes. Of course, it is the submission type of input that is key for inducing the Web browser to collect all the data in between the form tags, create an HTTP request, and send it over to the Web server.

Another type of HTML input element is known as a hidden input element. The hidden input element does not result in the display of any actual GUI element. Rather, the hidden element defines a name and value pair that can be set with some data which will then be mapped into the request body of an HTTP request. By sending such data to and from the HTTP server and the HTTP client, we then have the means by which session information can be baked into the HTTP request such that the HTTP server can keep track of which requests are from the same HTTP client.

Dynamic HTML Generation

Dynamic HTML generation is a term that some people use to designate the creation of HTML pages dynamically on the server side. Servlets and CGI programs alike are often created to do just this. That is, based on some input from the HTTP request and perhaps any maintained session information, the servlet or CGI program can generate an HTML page with the appropriate tags, controls, and data embedded into the document. Different request data or session data may produce different HTML output for different users. Such Dynamic HTML generation can be expensive because it means a trip back to the Web server from the Web browser every time new HTML content needs to be brought down to the client.

Dynamic HTML generation can also occur on the client side using some newly defined features in HTML 4.0. With Dynamic HTML being performed on the client side, trips back to the Web server can be alleviated and thus your Web server environments won't be taxed as much. Of course, the con is that more processing power is required on the client side than for static client-side HTML processing, but most modern desktop environments can handle the load. Of course, your browser version must support such Dynamic HTML extensions, but Netscape Communicator 4.0 and Microsoft Internet Explorer 4.0 both offer such support. However, as is to be expected, there exists a host of nonstandard Dynamic HTML features that one browser supports which the other does not. With Dynamic HTML's object-oriented interface, features now permit the Web browser to perform such activities as dragging and dropping from within the HTML page, moving objects around the page, displaying dynamic fonts, and layering content.

So what does Dynamic HTML have to do with the Web communications focus of this chapter? It means that your interface to the HTTP response stream may have gotten a lot more difficult. Although generating simple static HTML pages from the server side may be fairly straightforward, going beyond the simple can become a tedious chore. As you'll see in Part VI, and in Chapter 33, "JavaServer Pages," in particular, JavaServer Pages can make creating HTML content a lot easier than was the case with using Java Servlets. The programming paradigm for interfacing with the HTTP response stream will thus become a lot more palatable because the Web-enabling framework provided by the J2EE will prove to make your life a lot simpler.

Conclusions

Web-based communications focus around the HTTP protocol built atop TCP/IP. The HTTP protocol is an inherently connectionless and stateless protocol. Furthermore, the interface to the HTTP protocol is currently very functionally oriented rather than object-oriented. Although there exists no real application/communications interface layer above HTTP in its current form, HTTP-NG provides a glimmer of hope for providing such an interface in the future. In the meantime, frameworks such as Java servlets can help simplify the interface to the HTTP request and response communications paradigm. Requests from the same user over multiple HTTP transactions can be related as a unique user session via a few hand-coding–based tricks outside of the HTTP protocol. However, the Java Servlet framework can also be used to handle some of the details for managing HTTP sessions for you.

Modeling Components with CORBA

CHAPTER

14

IN THIS CHAPTER

- CORBA Overview 386
- The ORB 390
- GIOP and IIOP 393
- Services, Facilities, and Business Objects 395
- IDL 400
- Objects by Value 409

The Common Object Request Broker Architecture (CORBA) is a language- and platform-neutral body of specifications for building distributed object applications. CORBA applications are built in such a way that they are largely isolated from the details of communications code. In fact, CORBA applications are so defined that, from a CORBA client perspective, the distributed nature of a CORBA server can be completely transparent. The Common Object Services Specification (CORBAservices), the Common Facilities Architecture (CORBAfacilities), and CORBA business objects are all standards built atop CORBA to provide an even richer suite of distributed communication services and frameworks. The CORBA Interface Definition Language (IDL) offers up a language-neutral mechanism for defining distributed object interfaces with standards that exist for mapping IDL to Java, as well as for mapping Java to IDL. Finally, CORBA objects now have the capability of being passed either by reference or by value.

In this chapter, you will learn:

- The concept and architecture of the OMG's Common Object Request Broker Architecture (CORBA)
- The basic structure of the Object Request Broker (ORB)
- The architecture of the General Inter-Orb Protocol (GIOP) and Internet Inter-Orb Protocol (IIOP) protocols over which CORBA clients and servers communicate
- The basic subcomponents of CORBAservices, CORBAfacilities, and CORBA Business Objects
- The basic structure of the CORBA Interface Definition Language (IDL), as well as the basic transformation rules for mapping IDL elements to Java elements
- The behavior and means by which CORBA objects can now be passed around by value

CORBA Overview

As depicted in Figure 14.1, the Common Object Request Broker Architecture represents a standard model for creating objects and components whose services are to be distributable to remote clients. CORBA uses a standard communications model over which clients and servers implemented in a heterogeneous mix of languages and running on a heterogeneous mix of hardware and operating-system platforms can interact. CORBA is described via a collection of standards created by an organization known as the Object Management Group (OMG).

NOTE

You'll find the OMG's Web site at `http://www.omg.org`. All CORBA specifications, proposals for specifications, and the latest news on CORBA can be found there.

The OMG was founded in 1989 by a collection of largely hardware-oriented companies (including Sun Microsystems) with the mission of making standard and interoperable component-based software a reality. Since then, the OMG has grown to include more than 800 member organizations. The membership of the OMG ranges from large companies like Sun, IBM, Oracle, and even Microsoft to smaller companies and university groups. Aside from CORBA and platform interoperability, now the OMG also oversees standards established for UML. CORBA has become one of the most widely adopted standard architectures since the CORBA 1.1 specification was published in 1991. Since that time, the CORBA 2.X series of specifications has been the standard that has enabled CORBA to become more viable for the marketplace. CORBA 2.3.1 (`http://www.omg.org/library/c2indx.html`) was the latest specification finalized at the time of writing this book and is the standard in which we present most of our material. CORBA 3.0 is scheduled to be released in final form sometime in mid to late 2000 (`http://www.omg.org/news/pr98/compnent.html`). Nevertheless, we will comment on enhancements to expect in CORBA 3.0–based products throughout this book as well.

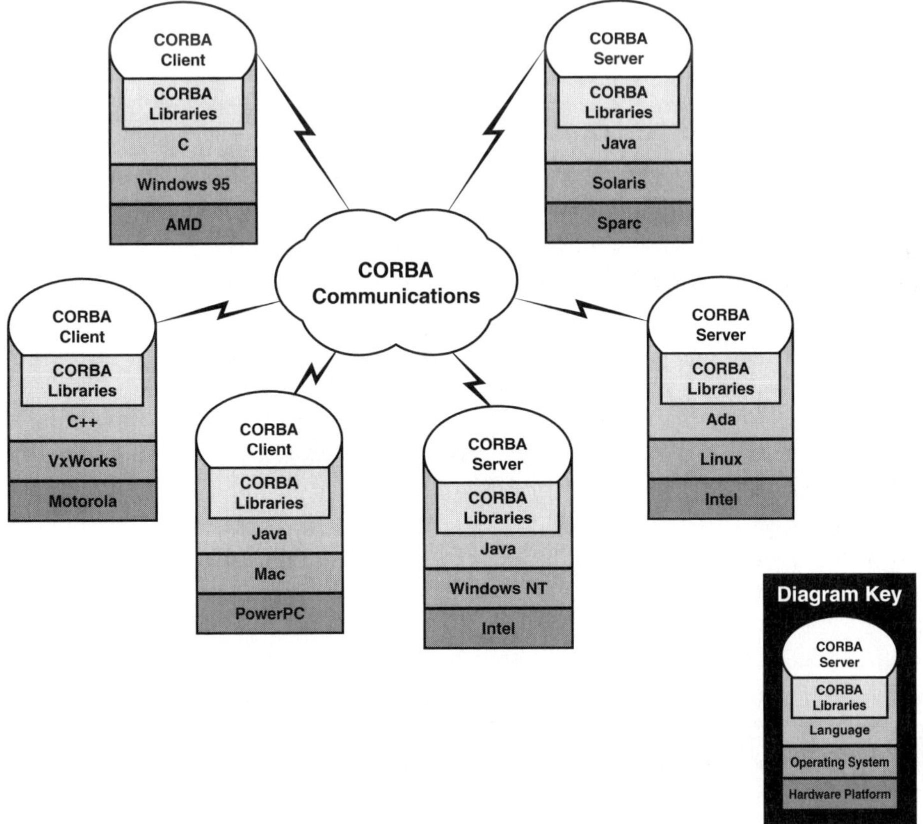

FIGURE 14.1
Heterogeneous CORBA communications.

The Object Management Architecture

Figure 14.2 depicts the Object Management Architecture (OMA). This high-level diagram provides scope and context for the CORBA specifications. At the highest level, we have application objects—perhaps created by you or purchased off the shelf—to offer business-specific services in a distributed fashion via CORBA. Application objects are specific to an application and are not governed by any CORBA specification standard. However, the application-level CORBA Domain Interfaces *are* defined in actual OMG specifications to deal with application-specific services for a particular domain such as the Telecommunications, Manufacturing, and Finance application domains. At the lowest level, specifications that deal with the Object Request Broker (ORB) define exactly how distributed clients can remotely utilize the services of distributed servers in a language- and platform-independent fashion, as well as describing the underlying communications protocol in which such service utilization occurs. Interfacing with an ORB is by far the most commonly accessed layer by CORBA application developers. Above the layer of the ORB, we have CORBAservices (*aka* Common Object Services) specifications to define those distributable CORBA services that CORBA-based applications commonly rely upon, such as providing human-readable object names to object reference mappings and querying for objects using some search criteria. At a higher level than CORBAservices, we have CORBAfacilities to provide frameworks for building directly useful distributed services such as printing, email, and document-management facilities. Distributable application objects may use one or more of the services provided by any one of these OMA levels.

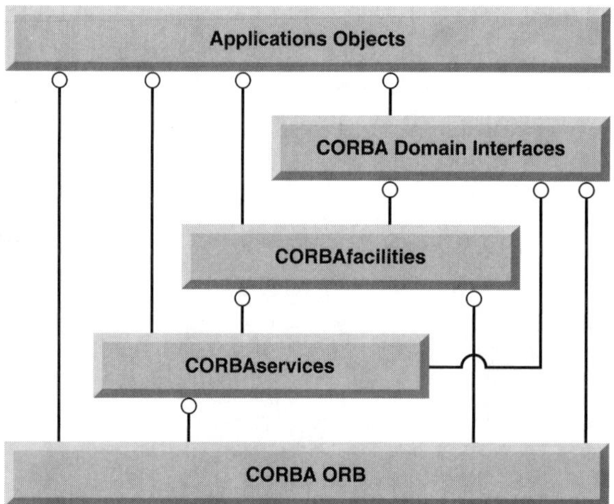

FIGURE 14.2
The Object Management Architecture (OMA).

CORBA 3.0

CORBA 3.0 will enhance the basic OMA with two fundamental additions: minimumCORBA and CORBAcomponents. The ORB layer of CORBA most suited for enterprise applications will now also come in an embedded flavor known as minimumCORBA. Thus minimumCORBA will result in a new ORB profile with features removed from the typical enterprise-style ORB to better enable usage of CORBA from within embedded applications. Of more relevance to the enterprise developer, the CORBAcomponents specification will define a standard set of interfaces to which CORBA components can be programmed to automatically inherit the services offered by a component container environment. The CORBAscripting specification will define how CORBAcomponents can be assembled in a standard way using whatever scripting language is defined for such component assembly. As we'll see in later chapters, the CORBAcomponents specification closely relates to the Enterprise JavaBeans specification. Because CORBA 3 was still under development at the time of this book's writing, Figure 14.3 is a sort of speculative view of what the new OMA model may look like when CORBA 3.0 comes to fruition in mid to late 2000.

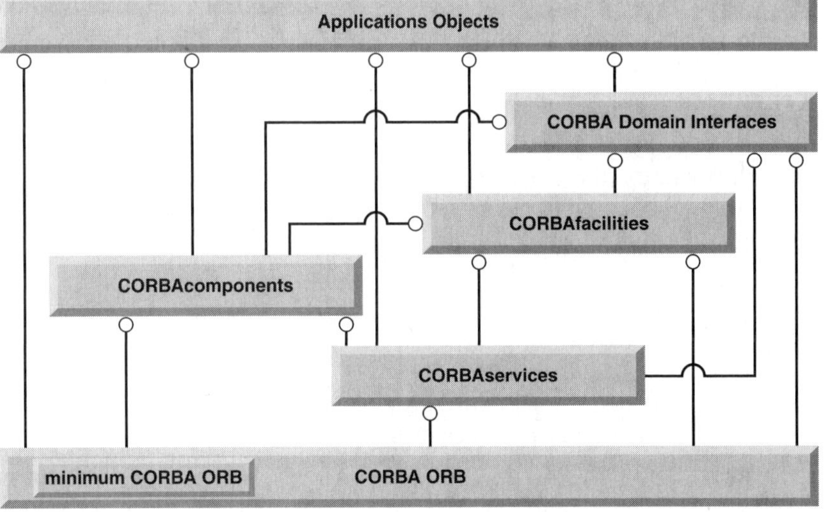

FIGURE 14.3
The OMA after CORBA 3.0?

CORBA's Java Enterprise System Role

Based on this short blurb of CORBA, you can see that the OMA offers much more than distributed object communications enabling capabilities. Rather, although the ORB will help communications-enable your distributed objects, the CORBAservices, CORBAfacilities, CORBA Domain Interfaces, and CORBA 3.0's CORBAcomponents all provide higher-level services and frameworks that help build entire enterprise applications. This chapter continues to describe the CORBA computing model in general, but the next chapter focuses on communications-enabling your enterprise applications with the CORBA ORB. Part IV, "Common Services for Distributed Enterprise Communications," and Part V, "Enterprise Systems Assurance," discuss some of the CORBAservices in the context of distributed object security services. Part VII, "Enterprise Applications Enabling," describes applications-enabling technologies that have relevance to CORBAfacilities and CORBA Domain Interfaces, as well as the new CORBAcomponents specifications.

The ORB

The CORBA ORB is the key component of the OMA with which most CORBA developers and architects will come into contact. The reasons for this are fairly straightforward. For any technology to be useful in the practical world, it must be built from the ground up. That is, you might as well forget about building a CORBAservice unless you have an ORB to use it with. Furthermore, the robustness of any architecture greatly depends on the robustness of its lower layers. If the lower layers are unreliable, the higher-level layers will topple down or simply will not be very evolvable. At this stage of CORBA's evolution, CORBA developers are at a point where most will purchase relatively robust and interoperable ORB software off the shelf and spend their time interfacing with such products. As time goes on, implementations of higher-level OMA specifications will become more and more dependable, and more developers will have time to become familiar with use of such products. Interfacing with the ORB itself will be as low-level a consideration as directly interfacing with the Ethernet is now.

The ORB Concept

The ORB is really just a set of CORBA specifications. The ORB specifications are implemented by CORBA vendors to produce what we also sometimes refer to as "an ORB." In such context, the term *ORB* actually refers to a collection of software libraries used either by CORBA clients to access distributed services or by CORBA servers to make their services distributed. The architecture of an ORB and the types of components involved in its use are shown in Figure 14.4.

The two most important players in distributed object communications via an ORB are the CORBA client and the CORBA server. The CORBA server is simply a distributed object offering up some of its method calls for remote access. CORBA clients are those objects that make remote method calls on CORBA servers.

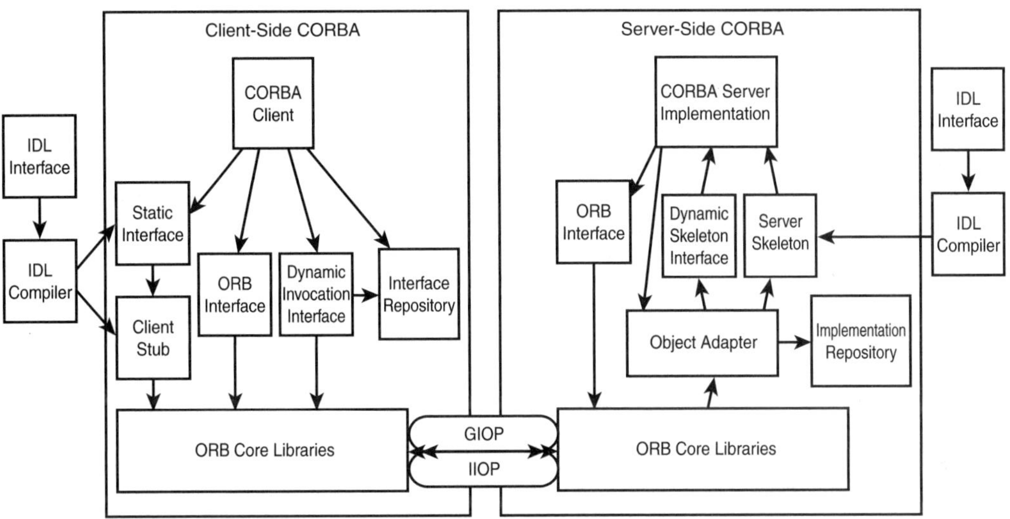

FIGURE 14.4
The ORB architecture.

Client Side ORB Components

Interface Definition Language (IDL) interfaces are language-independent descriptions of interfaces to CORBA server objects. Think of IDL as a language used for describing the methods you want to make distributed on your CORBA server classes. Most ORB vendors or other third-party vendors provide IDL compilers that map IDL interface specifications (typically stored in IDL files) into CORBA static interfaces and CORBA client stubs. CORBA static interfaces are the language-specific analogues of the IDL interfaces from which they were mapped. The CORBA client stubs handle the transformation of calls made on the CORBA static interfaces into calls that can be made over the wire on a distributed CORBA server. Client stubs handle packing (that is, *marshaling*) method-call parameters and unpacking (that is, *unmarshaling*) method-call return values to and from CORBA communications protocol message formats. Stubs also handle identifying which method on a particular CORBA server is being invoked by packing such identifying information into the marshaled data stream to be sent to the server.

In addition to the static interfaces that can be generated from IDL, CORBA provides support for CORBA clients being able to invoke a remote method by dynamically providing information identifying the remote object and method to call, as well as providing the parameters to be used in the remote method to be invoked. This Dynamic Invocation Interface (DII) technique essentially bypasses use of any static interface definitions to directly talk with an ORB's remote method invocation mechanisms. Conceptually, you can think of DII being to CORBA programming as the Java reflection API is to Java programming.

Interface Repositories are small databases used in some ORB implementations to hold the metadata descriptions of CORBA server interfaces in a machine-readable version of the CORBA Interface Definition Language. Interface Repositories have a standard API callable by CORBA clients and are also used by DII implementations.

ORB Protocols

The ORB interface provides programmatic interfaces to the actual underlying ORB core. The ORB core libraries are those libraries needed on the client side for implementing the CORBA communications protocol. The higher-level CORBA communications protocol is the General Inter-ORB Protocol (GIOP), which maps messages created by stubs into message-transport formats capable of being communicated between ORB implementations. The lower-level protocol used by CORBA is called the Internet Inter-ORB Protocol (IIOP); it is a transport layer for handling how GIOP messages are communicated over TCP/IP. Although other transports besides IIOP can be used, IIOP is by far the most popular protocol used in CORBA applications today.

Server-Side ORB Components

On the server side, we have CORBA server skeletons, which are also generated by IDL compilers. Server skeletons are the server-side analogue of client stubs in that they unmarshal method parameter data into language-dependent types from the marshaled data sent over from the client. When a server skeleton method is invoked, it will unpack the marshaled data and call the appropriate server-side method with the expected parameter types. Likewise, any return data from the CORBA server implementation will be marshaled by the GIOP message data that can be sent back over the wire to the CORBA client.

The Dynamic Skeleton Interface (DSI) is basically an API your CORBA implementations can utilize, allowing your servers to avoid generating any static skeletons and instead supporting a generic interface that your server implementation object must implement. This generic interface implementation must handle determining the type of call being made and extract the parameters passed over from the client. DSI essentially requires your server implementation to handle many of the steps that a server static skeleton would provide you, but it allows your server implementation to be implemented in a flexible fashion and handle calls dynamically.

The Implementation Repository is a small database on the server side containing a runtime description of available object implementations, as well as information on how such objects should be activated upon client request. Such activation information in the Implementation

Repository is used by the Object Adapter. The Object Adapter takes requests from the ORB core communications libraries and determines how to activate (that is, bring into memory) server implementations and funnel such requests to their static or dynamic skeletons. Both the Object Adapter and the core ORB libraries have interface APIs that CORBA servers can use.

GIOP and IIOP

The General Inter-Orb Protocol (GIOP) and Internet Inter-Orb Protocol (IIOP) represent the communications layer above TCP/IP for CORBA-based applications. Both protocols are fairly simple in nature and offer the capability to build scalable CORBA servers. GIOP defines a means for mapping marshaled IDL data into a common way to represent data over the wire and a set of message formats encapsulating the request and reply semantics of distributed calls. IIOP maps GIOP message data into TCP/IP connection behavior.

GIOP Overview

GIOP maps marshaled IDL data types into binary data streams to be sent over the wire. GIOP accomplishes this using a Common Data Representation (CDR) syntax for efficiently mapping between IDL data types and binary data streams. The binary data streams are formatted in one of eight simple inter-ORB message formats. Although not discussed here, certain Environment Specific Inter-Orb Protocols (ESIOPs) serve to replace GIOP for particular communications environments and tend to use their own transport layers as well (that is, not IIOP).

NOTE

GIOP versions are defined according to the format *major.minor*. GIOP version 1.0 specified only seven message types, whereas GIOP versions 1.1 and 1.2 use an eighth message type.

GIOP messages also allow for object instance representations to dynamically relocate among ORBs. GIOP messages support all of CORBA's necessary functionality, as well as some fundamental CORBAservice-specific features. GIOP v1.0 and v1.1 permit only client-to-server connection establishment whereby only clients can initiate connections and send requests. GIOP v1.2 relaxes this restriction. Finally, in GIOP, multiple clients may share a connection via multiplexing.

GIOP messages sent between CORBA clients and servers contain a message header and message data. The header format simply consists of these elements:

- Four bytes of characters always of the form: `GIOP`.
- Two GIOP protocol version numbers.

- A Boolean value indicating the byte order of the message (used in GIOP v1.0 messages only).
- A byte of bit flags used to indicate things like byte ordering, as well as whether this message is fragmented into multiple subsequent messages (used in GIOP v1.1 and v1.2 messages).
- A single byte message type identifier.
- The size of the message following the header.

These are the eight GIOP message types:

- `Request` *(type 0)*: Encapsulate CORBA server object invocations from a client to a server.
- `Reply` *(type 1)*: Encapsulate replies sent from CORBA server objects based on CORBA client requests. Exception data may be included in such messages.
- `CancelRequest` *(type 2)*: Encapsulate notifications from clients to servers that it is no longer interested in receiving a reply from a previous request.
- `LocateRequest` *(type 3)*: Encapsulate requests from a client to a server that attempt to resolve whether a server reference is valid and determine the address to which requests should be sent.
- `LocateReply` *(type 4)*: Encapsulate responses from servers to clients from `LocateRequest` messages.
- `CloseConnection` *(type 5)*: Encapsulate notifications from servers to clients about an impending connection closing.
- `MessageError` *(type 6)*: Encapsulate notifications from either server or client in the event of an erroneously received message.
- `Fragment` *(type 7)*: This message type was introduced in GIOP v1.1 and is sent following a previous message that has more fragments (that is, more messages) to send.

IIOP Overview

IIOP maps GIOP message data into TCP/IP connection behavior and input/output stream reading/writing. When a CORBA server object is to be distributed, the ORB will make information uniquely identifying that object on the network available via an Interoperable Object Reference (IOR). IORs contain the IP address and TCP port of the CORBA server object's process. CORBA servers listen on those sockets for incoming client connection requests. CORBA clients obtain IOR handles and open connections to the associated socket.

Depending on the ORB policy, the server will either accept or reject the connection requested by the client. Clients and servers then communicate GIOP messages over this connection. After a `CloseConnection` message is received, the ORB must close the TCP/IP connection.

NOTE

IIOP versions are also defined according to the format *major.minor*. IIOP v1.0 is used with GIOP v1.0, whereas IIOP v1.1 can be used with GIOP v1.0 or v1.1, and IIOP v1.2 can be used with GIOP v1.0, v1.1, or v1.2.

Interoperable Object References

An Interoperable Object Reference (IOR) is an address identifying a particular CORBA server object on a particular machine. Different transport protocols of CORBA have different IOR profiles. The standard part of an IOR and the profile of an IIOP-IOR contains such key information as this:

- Identifier of byte ordering (standard part of IOR).
- A repository ID identifying the object type (standard part of IOR).
- Two bytes designating the major and minor versions of IIOP supported (IIOP-IOR profile).
- A host or IP address string identifying where the CORBA server object resides (IIOP-IOR profile).
- A TCP port number on which the CORBA server object listens (IIOP-IOR profile).
- A sequence of bytes representing the object key to which requests are directed. This value is proprietary to an ORB implementation but is not interpreted in any way by the client (IIOP-IOR profile).
- As of GIOP v1.1, a sequence of tagged components is also included in an IOR. Tagged components contain additional information used during object invocations (IIOP-IOR profile).

Services, Facilities, and Business Objects

CORBA provides a number of specifications for defining standard interfaces to higher-level enterprise services. Above the ORB level, a set of common services utilized by most distributed enterprise objects are defined within the CORBAservices. Above the CORBAservices level, a set of common application interfaces and standard set of interfaces for specific application markets are defined within the CORBAfacilities. Finally, CORBA also has specifications particular to certain market domains as well as a more generic business object framework. This section will briefly explore these various higher level CORBA specifications that rest above the ORB infrastructure.

CORBAservices

The specification of the set of common CORBA object services is referred to as CORBAservices. CORBAservices are a collection of component specifications, each of which provides a service that can be used by distributed objects in general. That is, there is no application- or domain-specific nature to a CORBAservice. They represent truly modular components designed to solve one discrete and particular problem. We discuss a few of the key CORBAservices in more detail in the context of general distributed enterprise services in later chapters, but the following list of CORBAservices at least summarizes the distributed-system issues that each CORBAservice attempts to address:

- *Naming Service (aka* `CosNaming`*):* Naming is the principal mechanism for locating objects (primarily in a distributed paradigm) via a human-readable name. The Naming Service maps these human-readable names to object references. Resolving a name means obtaining an object reference associated with the name. Binding a name means to create a name-to-object relation. A name binding is always defined in terms of some naming context.
- *Trading Object Service (aka* `CosTrading`*):* The role of a Trader Service is to let your applications discover and obtain object references based on the services they provide. Exporters advertise services with the Trader, whereas importers discover services. An exporter gives the trader its object reference, a service type name, and a collection of service properties. Traders from various domains can pool their services into a federation. One can search for services via policies, constraints, and preferences. You can also use a policy to identify the set of service offers to examine, constraints to specify the search criteria, and preferences to order the results.
- *Relationship Service:* The Relationship Service allows for the dynamic creation of relationships between objects. Relationships have roles, cardinality, and attributes. The Relationship Service also lets you link roles to relationships, create relationships, create roles, destroy relationships and roles, identify identical objects, navigate relationships, and iterate through relationships. Two base relationships exist for containment and reference.
- *Life Cycle Service:* The Life Cycle Service provides services for creating, deleting, copying, and moving objects. Life Cycle Services provide mechanisms for locating factories that can be used to create objects, and also provide basic interfaces for copying, moving, and removing the object. Compound Life Cycle interfaces provide support for deep copies, moves, and deletes. Compound Life Cycle Services can collaborate with the Relationship Service in maintaining associations.
- *Externalization Service:* Externalization Services provide a mechanism for transforming an object into and out of a stream. A stream factory can create a stream object. The client

tells the stream object to externalize the object reference needing to be externalized. The Stream object then notifies the Streamable object to externalize itself. The object then writes its contents to the stream. A client telling the Stream object to internalize itself will go through a reverse process (that is, the Streamable object is told to internalize and the I/O stream is read). Externalization can make use of Relationship and Life Cycle Services.

- *Persistent Object Service:* The Persistent Object Service (POS) provides interfaces for managing persistent objects. The POS is defined to be independent of an underlying storage medium (that is, ODBMS versus RDBMS versus flat files). Persistent Objects (POs) are objects whose state can be persisted. A Persistent Object Manager (POM) provides an interface for persistence operations and is called by POs for storage-independent interfaces to an underlying storage medium. Specific storage medium interfaces are provided with Persistent Data Services (PDSs). PDSs perform the actual work of moving data between storage and memory. Persistence may use Externalization, Life Cycle, and Naming to accomplish its duties.
- *Query Service:* The Query Service is a service for finding objects whose attributes adhere to a set of search criteria. Queries are created using SQL or OQL. Query Service operations include search, selection, insertion, and deletion on collections of objects. A query can be either directly executed or delegated to a query evaluator (for example, native RDBMS query facilities). Querying also involves creating collections and iterating over collections. A query evaluator evaluates a query. A query manager allows you to create query objects that encapsulate the preparation, execution, and status retrieval of query results.
- *Object Collection Service:* The Object Collection Service enables one to manipulate objects in a group (that is, queues, stacks, lists, arrays, sets, trees, and bags). Collections can be ordered or unordered, and key based or non–key based. Ordered collections can be sorted or sequential. Restricted access on collections is possible for collections such as queues and stacks.
- *Property Service:* The Property Service is used for dynamic association of named attributes with components. Properties have a name (a string), a value (any), and a mode of operation (for example, read-only). Properties can be manipulated as a set.
- *Events Service:* The Events Service provides a framework for objects to dynamically register and unregister for specific events. Event suppliers produce event data, and event consumers process event data. Suppliers can push events to consumers. Consumers can also pull event data from suppliers. Multiple suppliers and consumers communicate asynchronously over an event channel.
- *Licensing Service:* Licensing provides services for starting, stopping, and monitoring object service usage, as well as for locating license managers. Licensing can also be used for recording time spent utilizing a particular service, as well as for limiting use.

- *Time Service:* Time Services can be used to perform certain date- and time-related functions such as to obtain a commonly synchronized current time common across distributed systems, determine an ordering for events, and generate timer-based events. The Time Service is thus basically an interface to universal time and timers.
- *Transaction Service:* An Object Transaction Service (OTS) lets multiple distributed objects participate in atomic transactions. Here, transactions involve agreeing on when use of a shared resource begins, when it ends, and the appropriate unit of rollback mechanism after a failure. Nested transactions could also be supported.
- *Concurrency Control Service:* The Concurrency Control Service manages concurrent access to a shared resource by multiple objects. Concurrency prevents multiple users from simultaneously owning locks on objects.
- *Security Service:* The rather-lengthy Security Service specification provides a set of services for minimizing the probability of a malicious attack on the system to be secured. Authentication of trusted objects, object privileges, access control, audit trails, object accountability and certification, encryption, federated security domains, and security administration are all part of the CORBA security service model.

CORBAfacilities

CORBAfacilities represent higher-level and more application-specific services and frameworks used in building distributed systems than is the case with CORBAservices. CORBAfacilities can provide component services such as email, printing, and global-positioning information. CORBAfacilities are further broken down into two categories: *Horizontal Common Facilities* and *Vertical Market Facilities*.

Horizontal Common Facilities

Horizontal Common Facilities are those component service frameworks that are used by many distributed systems such as the following working specifications:

- *User Interface Common Facility*: Provide frameworks for building user interfaces with interfaces for user-interface styles, user-interface hardware, application enablers, user working-environment management, and user task management
- *Information Management Common Facility*: Provide frameworks for building general information management systems with interfaces for modeling information, information storage and retrieval, information interchange, and information encoding and representation
- *System Management Common Facility*: Provide frameworks for building system-administration functionality with interfaces such as policy management, quality-of-service management, instrumentation, data collection, security, and event management

- *Task Management Common Facility*: Provide frameworks for building user task-management functionality with interfaces such as workflow management, static and mobile agents, rule management, and automation

Vertical Market Facilities

Vertical Market Facilities are those component service frameworks that are used to achieve interoperability in specialty distributed-system markets such as the following working specifications:

- *Imagery Facility*: Provide interfaces for the exchange and access of imagery data retrieved from sensors or artificially generated
- *International Information Superhighway (IIS) Facility*: Provide interfaces for the management of wide-area networks
- *Manufacturing Facility*: Provide interfaces to systems used in the manufacturing of products
- *Distributed Simulation Facility*: Provide interfaces to distributed system components used for computer simulation
- *Oil and Gas Industry Exploration and Production Facility*: Provide interfaces to systems used in the production and exploration of natural resources such as oil and gas
- *Accounting Facility*: Provide interfaces for accounting software used in an enterprise
- *Application Development Facility*: Provide interfaces for systems used in the development of software applications
- *Mapping Facility*: Provide interfaces for systems used to create geospatial maps

CORBA Domain Interfaces and Business Objects

CORBA Domain Interfaces represent collaboration between vendors and customers of systems being used in a particular industry to create CORBA standard interfaces to such systems, allowing for interoperability between the various system implementations. CORBA Domain Interfaces have been defined already for four key industries:

- Manufacturing System Domain Interfaces
- Telecommunication System Domain Interfaces
- Financial System Domain Interfaces
- Healthcare/Medical System Domain Interfaces

Regardless of the domain-specific nature of such specifications, the OMG has created a Business Object Task Force in order to create a generic framework for creating such domain-specific objects based on a common Business Object Facility (BOF). The BOF specifies a generic business-object component from which all domain-specific business objects inherit. The BOF also specifies ways to assemble such business objects and how to mix-in use of particular CORBAservices. At the time of this book's writing, the BOF specification was still under development.

IDL

The Interface Definition Language (IDL) in CORBA provides a way to describe interfaces to distributed CORBA servers in a language-independent fashion. An IDL description in an IDL file may be run through an IDL compiler to generate the language-specific stubs and skeletons to be used in a distributed CORBA application. CORBA clients use the generated stubs, whereas CORBA servers make use of the CORBA skeletons. Actually, CORBA skeletons call your CORBA server implementations. Thus, in situations whereby you already have a class implemented in which you want to make its methods callable as a CORBA server object, you may then have to generate the IDL definition from the class definition manually or perhaps by using a tool if it is available.

Various specifications describing mappings from IDL to particular languages exist, including mappings for Java, C++, C, Ada, Smalltalk, and COBOL. Additionally, a Java-to-IDL specification mapping also exists (to be described later).

Generic CORBA IDL File Format

IDL is not terribly foreign looking. In fact, many syntax conventions may look familiar to you. A rough general format of an IDL file is defined as shown here:

```
[#include ReferencedIDLFileName]

module ModuleName
{
   /* An IDL Comment */

   Module's Type Declarations here:
     e.g. typedef type name;
     e.g. struct StructName {StructDeclaration};
     e.g. enum EnumType {EnumValues};

   Module's Constant Declarations here:

   Module's Exception Declarations here:
     e.g. exception ExceptionName {[AttributeType name,…]};

   Module's Interface Declarations here:
     e.g. interface InterfaceName [:InheritedInterfaceName]
```

```
        {
              Interface's Type Declarations here

              Interface's Constant Declarations here

              Interface's Exception Declarations here

              Interface's Attribute Declarations here
                e.g. [readonly] attribute AttributeType name;

              Interface's Method Declarations here
                e.g. [ReturnType] MethodName
➥                          ([in|out|inout ParamType ParamName, …])
➥                               [raises (ExceptionName, …)];
        };
};
```

CORBA IDL-to-Java Mappings

Table 14.1 defines many of the key IDL entities referred to in the basic IDL file previously outlined and provides examples for how IDL maps to Java code. On the left-hand side of the table, we present example snippets from an IDL file for the most significant types of IDL entities. On the right-hand side of the table, we present the main elements of Java code that are generated from the example IDL. Note that the mappings in the right-hand column reflect the most recent IDL-to-Java mappings assumed by the J2SE v1.3.

TABLE 14.1 OMG IDL to Java Mappings

OMG IDL Entity	*Java Mapping*
Core Constructs	

Module
module ejava
{
  module corbach14
  {
    …
  };
};
	Java package
	package ejava.corbach14;

continues

OMG IDL Entity	*Java Mapping*
Core Constructs	

`interface`
`module ejava`
`{`
`  module corbach14`
`  {`
`    interface Customer`
`    {`
`      …`
`    };`
`  };`
`};`
	Operations interface containing all defined methods of `interface`:
	`public interface CustomerOperations`
	`{…}`
	
	and a signature interface implemented by stub and skeleton:
	`public interface Customer`
	`  extends CustomerOperations,`
	`  org.omg.CORBA.Object,`
	`  org.omg.CORBA.portable.IDLEntity {}`
	
	and helper class:
	`abstract public class CustomerHelper`
	` {…}`
	
	and holder class:
	`public final class CustomerHolder`
	`  implements`
	`  org.omg.CORBA.portable.Streamable`
	`  {…}`
	
	and stub class:
	`public class _CustomerStub extends`
	`  org.omg.CORBA.portable.ObjectImpl`
	`  implements`
	`  ejava.corbach14.Customer {…}`
	
	and skeleton class (see “Other Constructs”). See note below for differences between this J2SE v1.3 style of Java generation from IDL versus the J2SE v1.2 style.

`exception`
`exception FailedToGetCustomerInfo`
`{`
`      string reason;`
`      long    reasonCode;`
`};`
	Java Exception:
	`public final class`
	`FailedToGetCustomerInfo`
	`extends org.omg.CORBA.UserException`
	`implements`
	`org.omg.CORBA.portable.IDLEntity`
	`{`

OMG IDL Entity	*Java Mapping*
Core Constructs	

	public String reason = null;
	  public int reasonCode = (int) 0;
	 ...
	}

attribute
 	
attribute boolean hasEmail;
	Get and set methods on the associated interfaces and classes:
	boolean hasEmail();
	void hasEmail(boolean newHasEmail);

read-only attribute readonly attribute boolean hasEmail;	Get method on associated interfaces and classes: boolean hasEmail();

methods with in parameters
void login(in string userName,
            in string password)
      raises (failedToLogin);
	Java methods:
	void login(String userName,
	            String password)
	  throws <Package>.failedToLogin;

methods with out and inout parameters Void getLatestOrderByCustomer(in string customerID, out Order o); void addNewOrder(inout Order o);	Holder class for out and inout parameters and methods: void getLatestOrderByCustomer(String customerID, <Package>.OrderHolder o); void addNewOrder(<Package>.OrderHolder o);
Primitive Types	
void	void
boolean	boolean
char, wchar	char
octet	byte
short, unsigned short	short
long, unsigned long	int

continues

<table>
<tr><th>OMG IDL Entity</th><th>Java Mapping</th></tr>
<tr><td colspan="2">Primitive Types</td></tr>
<tr><td>long long, unsigned long long</td><td>long</td></tr>
<tr><td>float</td><td>float</td></tr>
<tr><td>double</td><td>double</td></tr>
<tr><td>fixed</td><td>java.math.BigDecimal</td></tr>
<tr><td>string, wstring</td><td>java.lang.String</td></tr>
<tr><td>FALSE</td><td>false</td></tr>
<tr><td>TRUE</td><td>true</td></tr>
<tr><td colspan="2">Extended Constructs</td></tr>
<tr><td>const</td><td>public static final</td></tr>
<tr><td>any</td><td>org.omg.CORBA.Any</td></tr>
<tr><td>enum
enum ShirtColor {RED, GREEN};</td><td>Java class version of enum:
public class ShirtColor implements
org.omg.CORBA.portable.IDLEntity
{
public static final int RED = 0;
public static final int GREEN = 1;
public static <Package>.ShirtColor
from_int(int value) {…}
…
}</td></tr>
<tr><td>struct
struct Order{
long orderID;
long customerID;
string orderDescription;
};</td><td>Java class with public members:
public final class Order implements
org.omg.CORBA.portable.IDLEntity {
public int orderID = (int) 0;
public int customerID = (int) 0;
public String orderDescription =
null;
…
}</td></tr>
</table>

OMG IDL Entity	*Java Mapping*
Extended Constructs	

An array:
`typedef Order listOfOrders[30];`
	Array helper:
	`abstract public class`
	`  listOfOrdersHelper{…}`
	
	and Array holder:
	`public final class listOfOrdersHolder`
	` implements`
	`  org.omg.CORBA.portable.Streamable`
	`  {…}`

Unbounded or Bounded sequence:
`typedef sequence<Order>`
`        Orders;`
 	
`typedef sequence<Order, 32>`
`        Orders;`
	Sequence helper:
	`abstract public class OrdersHelper{…}`
	
	Sequence holder:
	`public final class OrdersHolder`
	`  implements`
	`   org.omg.CORBA.portable.Streamable`
	`  {…}`

`union`
`union DataStoreUnion`
` switch(DataStore){`
` case ORACLE: string oracleValue;`
` case SYBASE: string sybaseValue;`
` default : long defaultValue;`
`};`
	Java class:
	`public final class DataStoreUnion`
	`  implements`
	`  org.omg.CORBA.portable.IDLEntity {`
	
	` public String oracleValue()`
	`  {…}`
	` public void oracleValue(String value)`
	`  {…}`
	` public String sybaseValue()`
	`  {…}`
	` public void sybaseValue(String value)`
	`  {…}`
	` public int defaultValue()`
	`  {…}`
	` public void defaultValue(int value)`
	`  {…}`
	`  …`
	`}`

continues

OMG IDL Entity	*Java Mapping*
Extended Constructs	
	and helper: abstract public class DataStoreUnionHelper{…} and holder: public final class DataStoreUnionHolder implements org.omg.CORBA.portable.Streamable {…}
Other Constructs	
CORBA::ORB	org.omg.CORBA.ORB
CORBA::Object	org.omg.CORBA.Object
CORBA::<Type> pseudo-objects in general	Pseudo-object definition in CORBA IDL maps to a particular type in Java such as: org.omg.CORBA.<Type>
Server implementation using inheritance (sometimes confusingly referred to as the "BOA approach").	Java CORBA server implementation must extend the IDL-generated _<InterfaceName>ImplBase skeleton class.
Server implementation using delegation ("TIE approach").	The IDL-generated _tie_<InterfaceName> skeleton class will delegate calls to your Java CORBA server implementation. Your Java server must implement the IDL-Generated <InterfaceName>Operations interface.

NOTE

Note that the Java mappings presented in Table 14.1 are with respect to the most recent standard mappings for IDL to Java (http://www.omg.org/corba/clchpter.html#ijlm) and integration of RMI/IIOP with CORBA. The J2SE v1.3 IDL-to-Java compiler utilities assume such a mapping standard. The J2SE v1.2 IDL-to-Java compiler utilities differ slightly and do not assume as complete of an integration between RMI/IIOP and CORBA. In particular, IDL interface entities using J2SE v1.2 style mappings do not generate Java operations interfaces by default and such interfaces are therefore not extended by the signature interfaces. Furthermore, helper classes are not declared abstract when generated using the J2SE v1.2 compiler utilities.

IDL Compilation

Compiling IDL into Java code requires use of an IDL-to-Java compiler. An IDL-to-Java compiler utility is used with the Java IDL CORBA component that comes equipped with the J2SE. The Java IDL IDL-to-Java compiler is a command line utility that is used to generate Java stubs and skeletons given an IDL file. The Java IDL component IDL-to-Java tool comes packaged with the J2SE v1.3 distribution and is referred to as `idlj`. A special Java IDL IDL-to-Java tool must be separately downloaded if you are using the J2SE v1.2 (the version used with the J2EE) and is referred to as `idltojava`.

NOTE

The J2SE v1.3 `idlj` compiler utility is located beneath the `bin` directory of your root J2SE v1.3 installation. The J2SE v1.2 compatible `idltojava` compiler utility can be downloaded from `http://developer.java.sun.com/developer/earlyAccess/jdk12/idltojava.html`. Note that you will need to use the `-fno-cpp` flag when using `idltojava` to tell the compiler not to attempt any C/C++ preprocessing before compiling the IDL.

To generate Java code from an `Example.idl` file, simply type the following for `idlj`:

```
idlj Example.idl
```

...and similarly for `idltojava` we have the following:

```
idltojava -fno-cpp Example.idl
```

Note that we use the `-fno-cpp` flag to tell the compiler not to attempt any C/C++ preprocessing before compiling the IDL. To generate client-side Java bindings from an `Example.idl` file, simply type the following for `idlj`:

```
idlj -fclient Example.idl
```

...and similarly for `idltojava` we have the following:

```
idltojava -fno-cpp -fclient Example.idl
```

To generate server-side Java bindings from an `Example.idl` file, simply type the following for `idlj`:

```
idlj -fserver Example.idl
```

...and similarly for `idltojava` we have the following:

```
idltojava -fno-cpp -fserver Example.idl
```

By default, the IDL-to-Java compiler will generate server-side skeletons which will require you to implement a CORBA server that inherits from a base class in order to be CORBA-enabled (to be discussed in more detail in the next chapter). You can flag the compiler to generate skeletons that will enable your server implementation to use delegation (the "TIE" approach) versus inheritance if you so desire, by using the following for `idlj`:

```
idlj -fserverTIE Example.idl
```

...and similarly for `idltojava` we have the following:

```
idltojava -fno-cpp -ftie Example.idl
```

IDL files can include other IDL files for definitions of types. When compiling an IDL file that includes another IDL file as reference, you may want to generate Java code for every included IDL file as follows for `idlj`:

```
idlj -emitAll Example.idl
```

...and similarly for `idltojava` we have the following:

```
idltojava -fno-cpp -fmap-included-files Example.idl
```

Although you can nest modules inside of modules to produce a desired package naming for your Java classes, it may be desirable to keep your IDL files fairly clean by eliminating any unnecessary outer-level modules such as this:

```
module com
{
  module BeeShirts
  {
    module Example
    {
      …
    };
  };
};
```

You may rather prepend the package prefixes that would be generated from such module definitions and avoid adding these definitions to your IDL file by using this command for `idlj`:

```
idlj -pkgPrefix Example com.BeeShirts Example.idl
```

This will prepend the `com.BeeShirts` package prefix to a module named `Example` in your `Example.idl` file. Similarly for `idltojava`, a package may be directly prepended to the modules defined in an IDL file as in the following case:

```
idltojava -fno-cpp -p com.BeeShirts Example.idl
```

Java-to-IDL Mappings

In addition to mapping IDL to Java, you can map your Java code to IDL. Tools such as Inprise's Caffeine perform just such a task. Caffeine provides the `Java2IIOP` utility for generating CORBA stubs and skeletons and `Java2idl` for generating actual IDL according to a set of rules thought up by the folks at Inprise. However, more recently, with the help of Inprise, the CORBA 2.3 specification has outlined a standard way to map Java classes to IDL. We will discuss this procedure in more detail in Chapter 16, "RMI Communications."

Caffeine and the OMG standard Java-to-IDL mappings allow you to take servers defined in Java using Java's built-in distributed object communications paradigm known as RMI and convert them into CORBA-enabled servers. This paves the way for enabling your Java-based servers to be accessed by non-Java clients via the CORBA communications paradigm. This provides the benefit to Java developers of being able to create Java programs using the programming language that they are already familiar with and alleviate their having to know and understand the semantics and syntax of IDL.

Objects by Value

Most of the distributed computing performed by CORBA-based programs involves a CORBA client invoking methods on a CORBA server sitting somewhere on the network. As discussed previously, the CORBA client by and large accomplishes this by communicating with a client-side stub that packs up the request and ships it over the wire. A server-side skeleton takes the request and calls the CORBA server, retrieves the results, and ships them back over the wire. The client-side stub then unpacks the results for the CORBA client. The client thus only communicates with a reference to the server. The actual work is performed somewhere else on the network.

Inprise's Caffeine extension was one of the first products to introduce the idea of passing around CORBA objects by value instead of exclusively by reference. With objects by value, a CORBA object is passed by value as a method parameter. The OMG later came up with a standard CORBA objects-by-value specification that happens to be part of the CORBA 2.3 specification. However, the standard as it exists right now is somewhat overly complicated and even has a few holes. CORBA product vendors have been thus somewhat slow to implement the specification as it currently stands. Some of the objects-by-value specification's current shortcomings may be addressed in CORBA 3.0.

Value Types

The `valuetype` keyword is a new core construct in CORBA identifying an object that is to be passed by value. The `valuetype` keyword is used inside of a module to tag such objects much in the same way that the `interface` keyword tags objects to be passed by reference. For example

```
module ejava
{
  module corbach15
  {
    valuetype Order
    {
     …
    };
  };
};
```

The identified `valuetype` can then be used as a parameter inside of a method call on a regular CORBA interface:

```
module ejava
{
  module corbach15
  {
    interface Customer
    {
     void setOrder(in Order myOrder);
     …
    };
  };
};
```

Objects by Value Behavioral Sequence

As an example behavioral sequence involving passing objects by value, the following general sequence of events occurs between an object (`SEND`) that sends a value type (VT) to a receiving object (`RECEIVE`):

- `SEND` *makes a call on* `RECEIVE`: An object named `SEND` calls a distributed method on an object named `RECEIVE`, which takes a `valuetype` object `VT` as a parameter.
- `VT` *is marshaled on the sending side*: The ORB being used by `SEND` marshals the state of `VT` and packs this information and a Repository ID associated with the `VT` type into the GIOP message sent to the ORB used by `RECEIVE`.
- `VT` *is unmarshaled on the receiving side*: The ORB being used by `RECEIVE` unmarshals the state description sent by `SEND`'s ORB.
- *Attempt reconstitution of* `VT` *with local implementation*: The ORB being used by `RECEIVE` then uses the Repository ID associated with this type and attempts to map this ID to a

locally available implementation. This step is language dependent, but a factory is generally used for this step and reconstitutes a new instance of the VT object on the receiving side.

- *Else, attempt reconstitution of* VT *with downloadable (*CODEBASE*) implementation*: If the implementation could not be found locally, the ORB for RECEIVE will attempt to load the object from a location defined in a CODEBASE parameter sent along in the GIOP message with the VT object by SEND's ORB. This CODEBASE may refer to a downloadable implementation. This step is also language dependent.
- *Else, attempt reconstitution of* VT *with base class implementation*: If the implementation could not be downloaded, a base type of the VT object will be used if the keyword truncatable was used in the IDL specification for any base type used by the VT valuetype.
- *Else, throw exception*: If VT could not be reconstituted, the exception NO_IMPLEMENT is raised.
- *If* VT *is available, use it*: If an implementation of VT was available locally or was downloadable, the RECEIVE object can make calls onto the VT instance. Such calls will not be delegated to a remote server instance as is the case with passing objects by reference, but rather will be made on the local copy of the VT object.

Objects by Value Marshaling

Objects being passed by value can opt either to use the built-in ORB marshaling features for packing and unpacking the state of an object being passed by value or to customize how the state of an object being passed by value is packed and unpacked for over-the-wire transmission. If you want to use the built-in state marshaling, you simply use the valuetype keyword to identify the CORBA type as usual. Otherwise, you must prepend the keyword custom in front of the valuetype keyword to designate the desire to customize the marshaling of the state. For example

```
module ejava
{
  module corbach15
  {
    custom valuetype Order
    {
      …
    };
  };
};
```

The org.omg.CORBA.portable.ValueBase Java interface is mapped from the CORBA::ValueBase pseudo-object used to identify a CORBA value type. Two types of sub-interfaces to `ValueBase` exist: `StreamableValue` and `CustomValue`. If a value type is to use the ORB's underlying state marshaling mechanisms, the mapped Java value type will generate a class that extends the `org.omg.CORBA.portable.StreamableValue` Java interface. If you desire to customize state marshaling for your object, the `org.omg.CORBA.portable.CustomValue` Java interface is used.

On the receiving side in Java, when the ORB attempts to reconstitute an object instance with a particular implementation class, it attempts to strip off leading data in the `RepositoryID` field passed over the wire in the IIOP message and append `DefaultFactory` to the data retrieved. If the data in the middle was a valid Java class name, a factory can be reconstituted (if that factory class name is in the `CLASSPATH`). Otherwise, an exception is thrown. By declaring a method as returning a `factory` type, you can explicitly generate a factory interface to be used by the ORB on the receiving side to reconstitute an instance of the passed-by-value object implementation.

Objects by Value Code Example

As an example, let's define a type `Order` as a `valuetype` in IDL as follows:

```
module ejava
{
  module corbach15
  {
    valuetype Order
    {
      private long orderID;
      private string orderDate;
      private double orderValue;

      void setCustomerID(in string customerID);
      string getCustomerID();

      factory createOrder(in long id, in string date, in double value);
    };
  };
};
```

This IDL will generate a collection of interfaces and classes that can be used to implement pass-by-value semantics in your Java programs. For example, the `abstract class Order` implementing the `StreamableValue` interface will handle all basic state marshaling and unmarshaling functionality:

```
public abstract class Order implements
org.omg.CORBA.portable.StreamableValue
{
```

```
  protected int orderID = (int)0;
  protected String orderDate = null;
  protected double orderValue = (double)0;

  private static String[] _truncatable_ids = {
    ejava.corbach15.OrderHelper.id ()
  };

  public String[] _truncatable_ids() {
    return _truncatable_ids;
  }

  public abstract void setCustomerID (String customerID);

  public abstract String getCustomerID ();

  public void _read (org.omg.CORBA.portable.InputStream istream)
  {
    this.orderID = istream.read_long ();
    this.orderDate = istream.read_string ();
    this.orderValue = istream.read_double ();
  }

  public void _write (org.omg.CORBA.portable.OutputStream ostream)
  {
    ostream.write_long (this.orderID);
    ostream.write_string (this.orderDate);
    ostream.write_double (this.orderValue);
  }

  public org.omg.CORBA.TypeCode _type ()
  {
    return ejava.corbach15.OrderHelper.type ();
  }
}
```

An `OrderHelper` and an `OrderHolder` are also generated as usual with most Java mappings:

```
public final class OrderHolder implements
           org.omg.CORBA.portable.Streamable
{
  public ejava.corbach15.Order value = null;
  public OrderHolder (){}
  public OrderHolder (ejava.corbach15.Order initialValue){…}
  public void _read (org.omg.CORBA.portable.InputStream i){…}
  public void _write (org.omg.CORBA.portable.OutputStream o){…}
  public org.omg.CORBA.TypeCode _type (){…}
}
```

```
abstract public class OrderHelper
{
  public static void insert (org.omg.CORBA.Any a,
                             ejava.corbach15.Order that){…}
  public static ejava.corbach15.Order extract (org.omg.CORBA.Any a){…}
  synchronized public static org.omg.CORBA.TypeCode type (){…}
  public static String id (){…}
  public static ejava.corbach15.Order read(
      org.omg.CORBA.portable.InputStream istream){…}
  public static void write (org.omg.CORBA.portable.OutputStream ostream,
                            ejava.corbach15.Order value){…}
  public static ejava.corbach15.Order createOrder(org.omg.CORBA.ORB orb,
                                   int id, String date, double value){…}
}
```

The `valuetype factory` defined within the `Order valuetype` and associated with the `createOrder()` method is used to generate and define factory objects for the `Order`. An `OrderValueFactory` interface extends the `ValueFactory` with the specific creation method defined in the interface and returning the `Order` value object:

```
public interface OrderValueFactory extends
    org.omg.CORBA.portable.ValueFactory
{
  Order createOrder (int id, String date, double value);
}
```

Finally, an `OrderDefaultFactory` class can provide a default implementation of the value type `factory`:

```
public class OrderDefaultFactory implements OrderValueFactory {

  public Order createOrder (int id, String date, double value)
  {
    return new OrderImpl (id, date, value);
  }

  public java.io.Serializable read_value
    (org.omg.CORBA_2_3.portable.InputStream is)
  {
    return is.read_value(new OrderImpl ());
  }
}
```

Conclusions

CORBA represents a standard model for creating objects and components whose services are to be distributable to remote clients. CORBA uses a standard communications model over which clients and servers implemented in a heterogeneous mix of languages and running on a heterogeneous mix of hardware and operating-system platforms can interact. The CORBA ORB provides a standard framework for communications via GIOP and IIOP, as well as for implementing an application/communication interface layer to insulate your CORBA clients and servers from communications-specific logic. Thus, CORBA clients and servers are offered a completely transparent interface to the underlying CORBA distributed computing platform.

CORBAservices, CORBAfacilities, and CORBA domain and business objects offer higher-level suites of distributed object communication services and frameworks with which you can more rapidly build distributed applications that also adhere to a common standard. IDL offers you a means to describe your CORBA-based distributed objects in a language-neutral fashion. Standard IDL-to-Java and Java-to-IDL bindings exist that fully enable Java-based CORBA programming. Finally, CORBA now allows one to pass objects around by value as well as by reference.

CORBA is perhaps the most comprehensive and standard component model for building distributed applications. CORBA's ORB infrastructure offers a true separation of application code from communications code. The next chapter will provide code snippets and develop a simple client-server example application demonstrating all the concepts discussed in this chapter.

CORBA Communications

CHAPTER

15

IN THIS CHAPTER

- The Very Distributed CORBA 418
- CORBA Vendors 421
- Java IDL 424
- CORBA Interfaces 425
- CORBA Servers and Skeletons 428
- Implementation Repository 443
- Object Adapters 444
- Interface Repository 448
- CORBA Clients and Stubs 454
- CORBA Naming 461

Building a CORBA-enabled application involves several considerations and steps that may be new to you. Design for scalability and choosing the right ORB products are key considerations and decisions to be made up front. Beyond ORB product selection and scalable design considerations, you'll need to be cognizant of a few core CORBA server implementation issues. Creating CORBA clients is much easier, but some design options still do exist. Because CORBA represents the collective catchall distributed communications standard from many organizational inputs, a lot of flexibility in design has been introduced into the CORBA-application enabling process, as you'll see in this chapter. Flexibility in design, of course, means some overhead added to the very process of design, development, and infrastructure configuration.

In this chapter, you will learn:

- How CORBA's distributed architecture can be used and how it can scale in the enterprise.
- About the key product vendors in providing CORBA-compliant ORBs and services.
- About the Java IDL package equipped with the J2SE/J2EE and its limitations.
- How to create and compile CORBA IDL files.
- How to create CORBA servers that use static or dynamic invocations and are implemented using either inheritance- or delegation-based approaches.
- How the implementation repository and object adapters are used by CORBA servers.
- How the interface repository is used by CORBA clients.
- How to create CORBA clients that use static or dynamic invocations.
- How CORBA clients can obtain initial references to CORBA servers.

The Very Distributed CORBA

Inherent in the specification of CORBA is its presumed application in distributed enterprise environments. Such environments mean potentially large network client bases, which means that an individual CORBA server may be required to support a large number of CORBA client requests. Designing your CORBA servers to be scalable is thus paramount to good CORBA enterprise development practices. The actual development process you follow also affects how distributable your CORBA servers will be. Development of scalable distributed object-based applications requires a different mindset than is the case with other development paradigms, such as the development of desktop applications or simple client/server interactions. This section describes which design issues affect the scalability of your CORBA servers and how the development process for building CORBA server applications generally may proceed.

Designing for Scalability

From the outset, CORBA has mainly been applied in enterprise computing environments. This is a logical expectation because building enterprise-scale applications often involves connecting heterogeneous platforms, and organizations are very sensitive to the need for building systems that can interoperate. However, the very generic nature involved with creating a CORBA server allows one to essentially make any object distributable. If you were to follow this paradigm to the extreme and indeed make every object distributed, you would also be plagued with an extremely inefficient system due to all the communications and marshaling overhead that would be involved. That is, although you may enhance the parallel processing nature of your distributed application by creating many fine-grained CORBA servers, the effects of increased communications overhead and resource utilization (for example, process and socket creation) will rapidly begin to far outweigh the benefits of parallel processing.

It thus behooves you, the enterprise developer, to follow a few simple guidelines when creating standalone CORBA applications for the enterprise:

- Create CORBA servers that act as service points that CORBA clients communicate with on a more coarse-grained basis.
- Create CORBA servers with methods that can process a large batch of similar operations and return a batch of results versus only providing finer-grained methods that must be called successively.
- Create CORBA servers that avoid offering direct getter and setter methods at the attribute layer on a distributed object.
- Create CORBA servers that act as service points to communicate with more fine-grained objects on the server side behind the wall of its service interface to the client.
- Where possible, employ a smart proxying design on the CORBA client side. Smart proxying involves a design in which your client can make getter type calls on CORBA proxy objects that retrieve data from a local cache. The proxy defers making a distributed call until cache data is updated via a setter method call. You may be able to utilize an ORB vendor's support for such smart proxying features, or perhaps you can create the smart proxy framework for your CORBA clients if you happen to have a priori knowledge of the client-side implementation language.
- Become cognizant of the connection allocation policies of your ORB vendor implementation. ORBs that create a new connection for each CORBA client to CORBA server association will not scale very well. ORBs that can intelligently pool connections or use more efficient transports will offer a scalability advantage.
- Become cognizant of the thread allocation policies of your ORB vendor implementation. Many commercial ORBs will offer you options in terms of how threads are assigned to incoming requests. You might also consider creating your own thread pooling and request handling framework on the back end to support a scalable number of clients.

The J2EE and CORBA

CORBA application design for scalability is of particular concern when creating standalone CORBA applications. As we'll see in Part VII, "Enterprise Applications Enabling," use of J2EE containers and Enterprise JavaBeans (EJB) does not require as much developer cognizance of scalable application development techniques and principles. Chapter 37, "Advanced Enterprise JavaBeans Serving," in particular directly addresses how EJB and CORBA relate. Hosting EJBs as CORBA servers is primarily accomplished by the J2EE EJB container. EJB developers do however utilize CORBA APIs when the EJBs act as CORBA clients. Regardless, as we have stated throughout this book, there will indeed be many instances when implementation of standalone CORBA applications is still needed to solve particular enterprise application problems.

CORBA Development Process

The steps to take in building a CORBA client and server can seem tedious at first, but at least Java-based CORBA development is easier than CORBA development in other languages. When CORBA-enabling a server, you either may have a predefined application for which you want to provide a distributed interface or may be creating a distributed server from scratch. Regardless, the same basic steps can be followed:

- *Define your IDL interface*: You must first create an IDL file with a description of the distributed CORBA server methods to be exposed via a CORBA interface. You may also choose to define types to be passed by value between CORBA clients and servers.
- *Compile your IDL file*: With an IDL file in hand, you can run such a file through an IDL-to-Java compiler to generate all necessary Java bindings for interfaces, stubs, skeletons, helpers, and holders. Depending on the desired server implementation method, you can generate server skeletons requiring that your server either inherit from or be delegated calls from the generated server skeletons.
- *Implement the CORBA server*: You can then implement a CORBA server either by inheriting from a generated skeleton or by being delegated calls from a generated skeleton. If using a static skeleton is not to your liking, you can also use the Dynamic Skeleton Interface (DSI) to implement your server. After selecting how calls are mapped from either a static skeleton interface or DSI, you can implement the functionality behind your calls if they were not already implemented, and compile your server.
- *Implement a CORBA server registrar*: You should then typically implement a separate class that registers a CORBA server implementation with an object adapter's implementation repository. The registrar will also typically register any "frontline" server object instances with an object adapter. You may also use the CORBA Naming Service to

register human-readable names to any newly created object references. Note that only initial references to certain frontline server objects need be registered with a naming service and object adapter from a server registrar. After any initial CORBA server object handles are obtained by CORBA clients, other CORBA server objects will most typically be instantiated and registered by the CORBA servers that were initially or subsequently created.

- *Possibly register interfaces with an Interface Repository*: You may optionally register a description of the CORBA server interfaces with an Interface Repository on the client side. However, for Java-based CORBA clients, access to a CORBA stub is usually available or perhaps remotely downloadable. If the Dynamic Invocation Interface (DII) is used, use of an Interface Repository will be needed.
- *Implement the CORBA client*: A CORBA client can now be created using either the CORBA stubs created in a previous step or DII to make distributed calls on a CORBA server. A CORBA client must obtain a reference (IOR) to the CORBA server. It can do this by using a CORBA Naming Service, by converting an IOR in string form to a concrete IOR, or perhaps by using a vendor-specific approach. The client code can then be compiled and you are ready to begin client/server computing CORBA style.

CORBA Vendors

Selecting the right CORBA products to use for your enterprise application can make or break acceptance and the success of CORBA in your projects. Knowing which components of a CORBA standard you need to purchase and which ones you might pursue implementing yourself is also important. In what follows, we first describe the set of tools you'll need in order to build a CORBA-based application. We then describe which major CORBA product vendors do exist and what they offer in the way of CORBA implementations.

Basic Tools and Configuration

Before you dive into developing a CORBA-based application, you'll want to pick up a few tools. Unless you're in the ORB-making business, you'll want to pick up a set of ORB libraries from a third-party vendor. You'll need to identify the target language in which you want to implement your CORBA server or from which you want to make a CORBA client. You should indeed evaluate your ORB vendor's implementation before deploying it into an enterprise application, especially in consideration of the scalability issues highlighted previously. And although you as a reader of this book will presumably be developing your CORBA-based applications in Java, you should still investigate the operating-system platform dependency of your ORB, because many commercial vendors will equip platform-specific utilities with their products. The good news for us enterprise Java developers, however, is that we already know our target language and we already have the J2SE/J2EE's Java IDL ORB reference implementation to use during development while we take time to evaluate an actual commercial ORB implementation to plug into a deployed enterprise environment. We will examine some ORB vendor implementations and Java IDL later in this chapter. In addition to the ORB libraries, you'll need an IDL-to-Java compiler, which usually comes packaged with a development environment from the vendor whose ORB libraries you have selected.

Although use of a CORBAservice is not necessary, your particular application's demands may warrant use of one of the services described in Chapter 14, "Modeling Components with CORBA." At the very least, use of a CORBA Naming Service will help you keep your CORBA applications more portable because without such a service, you will inevitably get locked into using a vendor-specific CORBA Naming Service analogue. CORBA Naming Services are often sold separately, however.

With the proper tools in hand, configuring the infrastructure for running CORBA applications may depend largely on the ORB implementation you've selected. In the purest scenario, you will only need to install the ORB libraries on your server and client platforms and then start a CORBA Naming Service process somewhere on your network. The remaining steps to take depend on your particular CORBA application. Particular ORB vendor implementations may also require that you kick off other processes on your network.

Although ORBs and CORBAservices have traditionally been key COTS products to purchase when building CORBA-based applications, more and more we are seeing a trend for such products to be integrated with other products. Server-side products such as Web servers, application servers, and even database servers are deploying their products with ORBs and a few CORBAservices built in. Even client-side Web browsers like the Netscape Communicator offer baked-in CORBA libraries that facilitate the capability to create Java applets with CORBA connectivity (aka Orblets). As more and more applications employ CORBA technology under the hood, your need for knowing the details behind creating CORBA-based applications may diminish. Rather, application servers and CORBAcomponents-based frameworks will increasingly make writing distributed CORBA-based applications more transparent.

Vendor Offerings

Vendor offerings of products enabling CORBA connectivity currently tend to come in three basic flavors: (1) standalone ORB and CORBAservice products, (2) ORB and CORBAservice product suites, and (3) ORB and CORBAservice products integrated into another framework. Although some products are free, they typically are useful only in prototype and early development environments while you select a more commercial-ready product. Of course, most commercial vendors allow you to download free evaluation copies of their software from their Web site. The vendors in the following list offer ORB and CORBAservice products for Java largely in standalone or product-suite form (with a few exceptions noted):

- *Sun Microsystems's JavaSoft Organization* (`http://www.javasoft.com`): Perhaps you've heard of Sun Microsystems…they have defined this neat new enterprise framework called the J2EE. The Java IDL product equipped with the J2SE (and therefore used with the J2EE) is a reference implementation of a set of Java-based ORB libraries and a naming service.
- *Iona Technologies, Inc.* (`http://www.iona.com`): OrbixWeb is its Java-based package of ORB libraries and development tools with COM integration (OrbixCOMet) and a CORBA Naming Service (OrbixNames). CORBAservices are also offered by Iona, such as a Trading Service (OrbixTrader), Security Service (OrbixSecurity), and the Events Service (OrbixEvents). CORBA-based application frameworks offer more integrated support such as the OrbixOTM and the Iona iPortal Suite.
- *Inprise Corporation* (`http://www.inprise.com`): The Inprise Corporation is the result of a merger between Borland and Visigenic. This merged Inprise Corporation and the Corel Corporation were also about to merge at the time of this writing. Visigenic created the Visibroker for Java Orb product. CORBAservices are offered by Inprise such as a Naming Service, an Event Service, and a Transactions Service. CORBA-based application frameworks also offer integrated support such as the VisiBroker Integrated Transaction Service (ITS) and Inprise Application Server.
- *PrismTech* (`http://www.prismtechnologies.com`): PrismTech offers many kinds of CORBAservices, such as the Naming Service, Event Service, Trading Service, LifeCycle Service, Property Service, Collection Service, Concurrency Service, Time Service, and Relationship Service. A suite of these services can be purchased via the OpenFusion package.
- *PeerLogic* (`http://www.peerlogic.com`): PeerLogic makes a Java-based ORB called DAIS J^2. They also make C++–based CORBAservices such as Naming, Event, Transaction, Trader, LifeCycle, and Security Services.
- *Object Oriented Concepts, Inc.* (`http://www.ooc.com`): OOC makes the ORBacus for Java ORB product and a set of CORBAservices such as a Naming Service (ORBacus Names) and a Trading Service (ORBacus Trader).
- *Expersoft* (`http://www.expersoft.com`): Expersoft makes its CORBAplus ORB product for Java. It also makes a C++ implementation of the Naming and Event Services, as well as a Trading Service.
- *JacORB* (`http://www.inf.fu-berlin.de/~brose/jacorb`): The JacORB is a free Java-based ORB, as well as a free Naming, Event, and Trading Service.

- *Jorba* (`http://jorba.castle.net.au`): Jorba is another Java-based shareware ORB currently in prototype form.

Additionally, as a few key examples, the following vendors offer COTS products and server frameworks that make use of an ORB and CORBAservices:

- *Oracle* (`http://www.oracle.com`): Although Oracle uses Java and CORBA in a variety of its products, its Oracle8i Database Server's architecture completely revolves around a baked-in Java Virtual Machine and an older version of the Visigenics ORB.
- *Netscape* (`http://www.netscape.com`): Netscape's Web server (the Netscape Enterprise Server) and Web browser (Netscape Communicator) both come equipped with an older version of the Visigenics ORB.
- *BEA WebLogic* (`http://www.beasys.com`): Aside from the J2EE-based WebLogic Server that we discuss in Part VII, BEA WebLogic Enterprise integrates the J2EE with a CORBA ORB.

Thus, as you can see, there are many vendors out there who have either created the building blocks for building CORBA-based systems or have already begun to integrate CORBA into their server frameworks as the distributed communications enabler of choice. Apart from CORBA vendor solutions, many other more proprietary and application-specific uses of CORBA have been permeating our marketplace. Visit the OMG Web site (`http://www.omg.org`) to keep abreast of where CORBA is being used today.

Java IDL

Java IDL is a Java-based set of CORBA 2.0–compliant libraries for Java, including an IDL-to-Java compiler and a CORBA Naming Service implementation (`tnameserv`). Java IDL currently does not implement an Interface Repository, however, and as a result, Java IDL-based CORBA clients cannot use DII. CORBA servers built atop the Java IDL ORB are also limited to being transient by nature, meaning that dormant CORBA objects cannot be stored for activation upon client request given a persistent reference to that object. Other commercial ORBs do support such activation of dormant CORBA objects, however.

Java IDL also does not support many of the usual BOA calls in light of the fact that the BOA is deprecated in favor of the POA. However, Java IDL also did not implement the POA at the time of this writing. Instead, a few calls on the `org.omg.CORBA.ORB` class exist to connect and disconnect servers from the ORB, and run as a transient CORBA server. Similarly, `tnameserv` also runs only as a transient service, meaning that all registered object information will be lost when it is shut down.

Java IDL was first available as a separately downloadable package of Java libraries that could be used with your JRE. The J2EE (by virtue of requiring the J2SE physical distribution) comes equipped with Java IDL for building Java-based CORBA clients and servers. Because Java IDL is packaged with the J2SE, any J2SE-based application can act as a CORBA server or client.

NOTE

As mentioned in the last chapter, the J2SE v1.3 comes with an `idlj` compiler for IDL-to-Java compilation. A separate `idltojava` IDL-to-Java compiler can also be separately downloaded for use with the J2SE v1.2. Additionally, a special IDL-to-Java compiler used with RMI/IIOP can be downloaded and used with the examples in this chapter. We describe how to obtain and use such a compiler in a subsequent section.

CORBA Interfaces

You should now be armed with the conceptual framework and knowledge of which tools you'll need to build CORBA-based applications. Now you can begin the first step in creating an actual CORBA application. Such a first step requires that you define a distributed interface to each CORBA server class via CORBA IDL. The IDL interfaces used in our example application that we will create here are shown in Listing 15.1 (`Order.idl`), Listing 15.2 (`ClientReceiver.idl`), Listing 15.3 (`Customer.idl`), and Listing 15.4 (`QueryServer.idl`).

NOTE

The CORBA IDL interfaces and all code examples used in this chapter are contained on the CD in or under the `examples\src\ejava\corbach15` directory. Four subdirectories also exist under the Chapter 15 directory, including `examples\src\ejava\corbach15\regular`, which contains the basic CORBA example code used here. The `examples\src\ejava\corbach15\delegation` directory contains example code almost identical in nature to the basic example code with the exception that the CORBA servers use the CORBA delegation (that is, "TIE") implementation technique instead of the inheritance used by the core examples. The directory `examples\src\ejava\corbach15\dynamic` contains example code for DII and DSI, and the `examples\src\ejava\corbach15\irquery` directory is used to illustrate what gets inserted into an Interface Repository.

Listing 15.1 depicts an `Order` IDL `struct` and `typedef` for a sequence of `Orders` to encapsulate the minimum information needed to satisfy a simple BeeShirts.com order. Note that the `Order` object here could also have been appropriately defined as a `valuetype` if the Orbs you are using support Objects By Value. Chapter 14 illustrated just such a concept.

LISTING 15.1 CORBA IDL Order (`Order.idl`)

```
module ejava
{
  module corbach15
  {
    struct Order
    {
      long orderID;
      string orderDate;
      double orderValue;
    };

    typedef sequence<Order> OrdersSeq;
  };
};
```

The `ClientReceiver` interface shown in Listing 15.2 will be used to implement a CORBA server on the client side of our application that the server side will call (that is, a callback). Thus the client side's `ClientReceiver` object will simply take a sequence of `Order` objects from the server side.

LISTING 15.2 CORBA IDL Client Callback (`ClientReceiver.idl`)

```
#include "Order.idl"

module ejava
{
  module corbach15
  {
    interface ClientReceiver
    {
      void setResultOrders(in OrdersSeq orders);
    };
  };
};
```

The `Customer` interface of Listing 15.3 is used to distribute an interface encapsulating a BeeShirts.com customer. Note that in an actual application, you would typically want to avoid defining an interface at this low level of granularity in order to be used in scalable enterprise environments. That is, defining IDL interfaces at the attribute level in particular will mean that a distributed call will result for each client attempt to get or set an attribute value. However, for the sake of simplifying our example and seeing utility in demonstrating a CORBA anti-pattern, we will refrain from the best practices for the time being.

LISTING 15.3 CORBA IDL for a Customer (`Customer.idl`)

```
module ejava
{
  module corbach15
  {
    interface Customer
    {
       attribute string firstName;
       attribute string lastName;
       attribute string address1;
       attribute string address2;
       attribute string city;
       attribute string state;
       attribute string zip;
       attribute string phoneNumber;
       attribute string emailAddress;
    };

    typedef sequence<string> RegisterdCustomerNames;
  };
};
```

The `QueryServer` interface of Listing 15.4 describes the primary server-side CORBA interface for our application. It is CORBAservices that operate at this level of granularity that are of the kind most appropriate for building scalable applications. The `QueryServer` offers a very specialized set of interfaces to illustrate the CORBA-enabling concepts at work. A call to `findCustomersWhoOrderdForMoreThan()` finds customers who spend more than a certain amount of money, binds them to a lookup service, and returns a sequence of customer IDs. A method `register()` takes a `ClientReceiver` callback interface and client receiver name to register CORBA client callbacks. A method `findOrdersWhichAreFrom()` finds the orders for a given state and passes the set of associated orders to the registered `ClientReceiver` objects.

LISTING 15.4 CORBA IDL for a Query Server (`QueryServer.idl`)

```
#include "Customer.idl"
#include "ClientReceiver.idl"

module ejava
{
  module corbach15
  {
    interface QueryServer
    {
      RegisterdCustomerNames
        findCustomersWhoOrdcrdForMoreThan(in float value);
      void findOrdersWhichAreFrom(in string state);
      void register(in string name, in ClientReceiver clientReceiver);
    };
  };
};
```

CORBA Servers and Skeletons

Whereas IDL defines the distributed interfaces available to a distributed service, a CORBA server and skeleton represent the implementation of that interface. Most of the complex design and implementation decisions associated with building a CORBA-based application are associated with server-side development. Compilation of IDL can generate CORBA skeletons that are then linked to your CORBA server implementations. The remaining discussion in this section describes how to implement CORBA servers using the CORBA skeletons generated by IDL compilation.

Compiling the IDLs and Generating Skeletons

After defining your IDL, you'll want to run the IDL through an IDL-to-Java compiler to generate the CORBA skeletons used by your CORBA server implementations. The IDL-to-Java compiler used with Java IDL and RMI/IIOP is called `idlj`. Before you use `idlj`, however, you'll want to determine what type of servers you'll want to create. That is, do you want to implement your CORBA server using skeleton inheritance or delegation (*aka* the TIE approach)? After this decision is made, the appropriate option can be added to the command line of your `idlj` invocation to generate the appropriate skeleton types.

NOTE

At the time of this writing, the separately downloadable IDL-to-Java compiler (that worked with Java IDL in the J2SE v1.2) required a separate C++ preprocessor for compiling our IDL files. Even though C++ preprocessing could be turned off with a simple flag, the compiler was then not able to interpret our IDL `#include` directives. You can use the J2SE v1.3 Java IDL IDL-to-Java compiler with our examples, but we wanted to explain how to use our examples with the J2SE v1.2, since that is the Java runtime used with J2EE v1.2.

Therefore, as an IDL-to-Java compiler choice for use with our examples, we use the compiler that can also be used with RMI/IIOP. You must first download and install the RMI/IIOP standard extension for use with the J2SE v1.2 platform. The RMI/IIOP download package and instructions can be found at `http://java.sun.com/products/rmi-iiop/index.html`. You also must set a `RMI_IIOP_HOME` environment variable to the root directory for your RMI/IIOP installation when running any examples. Note that it is very important to make sure the `orb.properties` file generated during this installation is copied properly to your `[JAVA_HOME]\jre\lib` directory. The installation program may attempt to copy this file to another directory that it perceives as the JRE library directory, so step through the installation process carefully.

The IDL-to-Java compiler used with RMI/IIOP can then be downloaded and installed. The RMI/IIOP IDL-to-Java compiler can be downloaded from `http://developer.java.sun.com/developer/earlyAccess/idlc/index.html`. A single `idlc1_0_1ea.zip` file is downloaded which contains a single `idlj.jar` file that must be copied into the `[RMI_IIOP_HOME]\lib` directory.

The `run.bat` file in the `examples\src\ejava\corbach15\regular` directory generates stubs and skeletons for regular inheritance-based implementations using something akin to this:

```
idlj -fall Order.idl
idlj -fall Customer.idl
idlj -fall QueryServer.idl
idlj -fall ClientReceiver.idl
```

The `run.bat` file in the `examples\src\ejava\corbach15\delegation` directory generates stubs and skeletons for regular inheritance-based implementations using something akin to this:

```
idlj -fallTie Order.idl
idlj -fallTie Customer.idl
idlj -fallTie QueryServer.idl
idlj -fallTie ClientReceiver.idl
```

The inheritance technique involves generating a skeleton from which your CORBA server implementation will inherit. The delegation technique involves generating a skeleton that will call your CORBA server, which implements a generated Java interface. The con, of course, with the inheritance approach is that your server will be unable to inherit from any other class due to Java's single-inheritance limitation.

Creating the CORBA Servers

If you are using the inheritance approach, you should take note that it may be a good general idea to separate your business logic implementation from any CORBA-specific library dependencies by hand-coding the delegation of calls from your CORBA server implementation to a business logic class. This is why we illustrate such an adapter in Figure 15.1's depiction of a CORBA server built using inheritance. Note the similarity to Figure 15.2's illustration of a CORBA server built using delegation.

In both cases of building a `MyServer` implementation from the `MyServer.idl` file, a `MyServerOperations` interface and a `MyServer` interface are generated. However, in the case of Figure 15.1, the `_MyServerImplBase` abstract class needs to be inherited from your `MyServerImpl` object, which can also delegate to your business logic code. Delegation to your business logic code helps keep your logic separate from your distribution paradigm (CORBA here). Of course, in using the delegation model (that is, the TIE approach) of Figure 15.2, the `_MyServer_TIE` delegation class will be generated for you and will delegate calls to your `MyServerImpl` implementation, which now must implement the `MyServerOperations` interface.

Listings 15.5, 15.6, and 15.7 show the implementations for our `CustomerImplementation`, `ClientReceiverImplementation`, and `QueryServerImplementation` CORBA servers, respectively.

NOTE

The complete set of code examples for the regular CORBA servers implemented using inheritance can be found on the CD-ROM in the `examples\src\ejava\corbach15\regular` directory. We have also included a set of code examples on the CD not shown here that implement the same servers using delegation; this can be found in the `examples\src\ejava\corbach15\delegation` directory. The `run.bat` files in both directories will compile your server implementations. These `run.bat` files actually build and execute all files associated with the example. Pause statements are inserted into these scripts before each process that is spawned. You should wait for each process to start and initialize before allowing the next process to start.

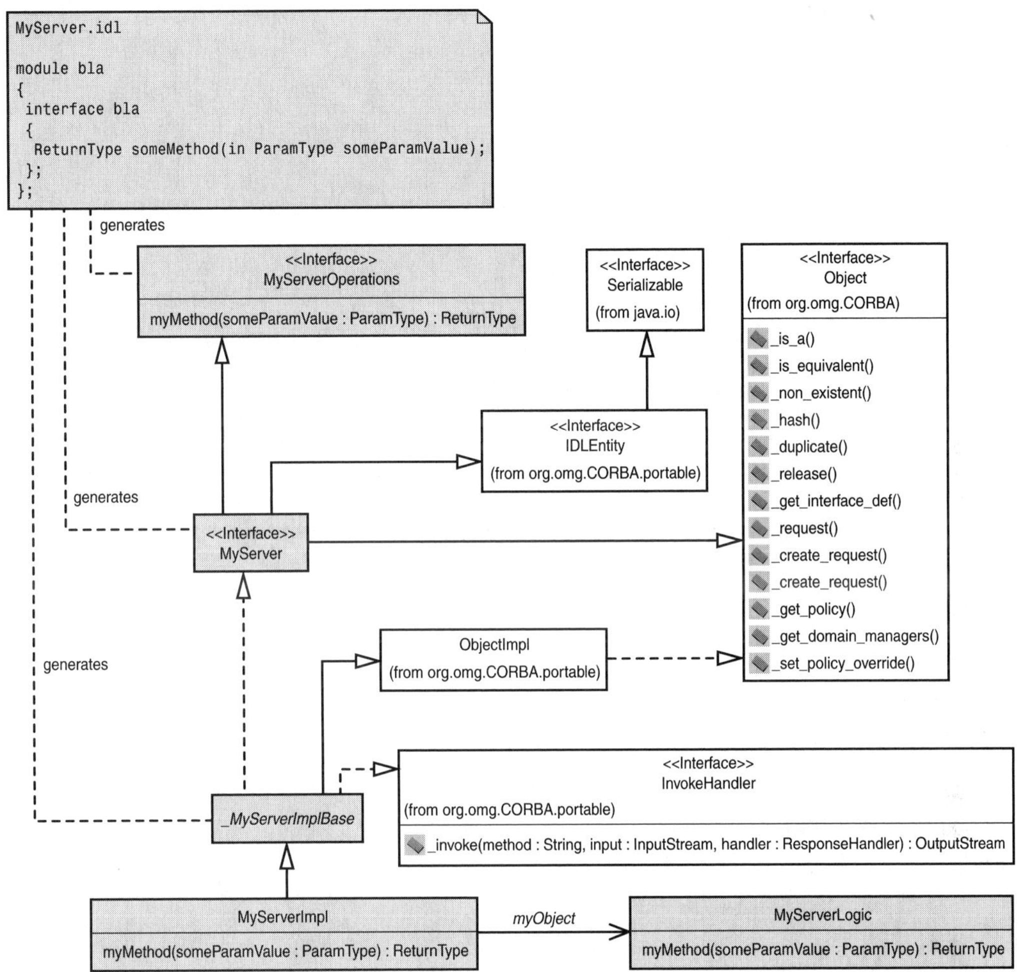

FIGURE 15.1

A CORBA server built using inheritance.

You can ignore the `bind()` method implemented by the `CustomerImplementation` class defined in Listing 15.5 for now. But note that all getters and setters needing implementation based on the attributes defined in the IDL Listing 15.3 have been implemented by this class for a distributable `Customer` object instance.

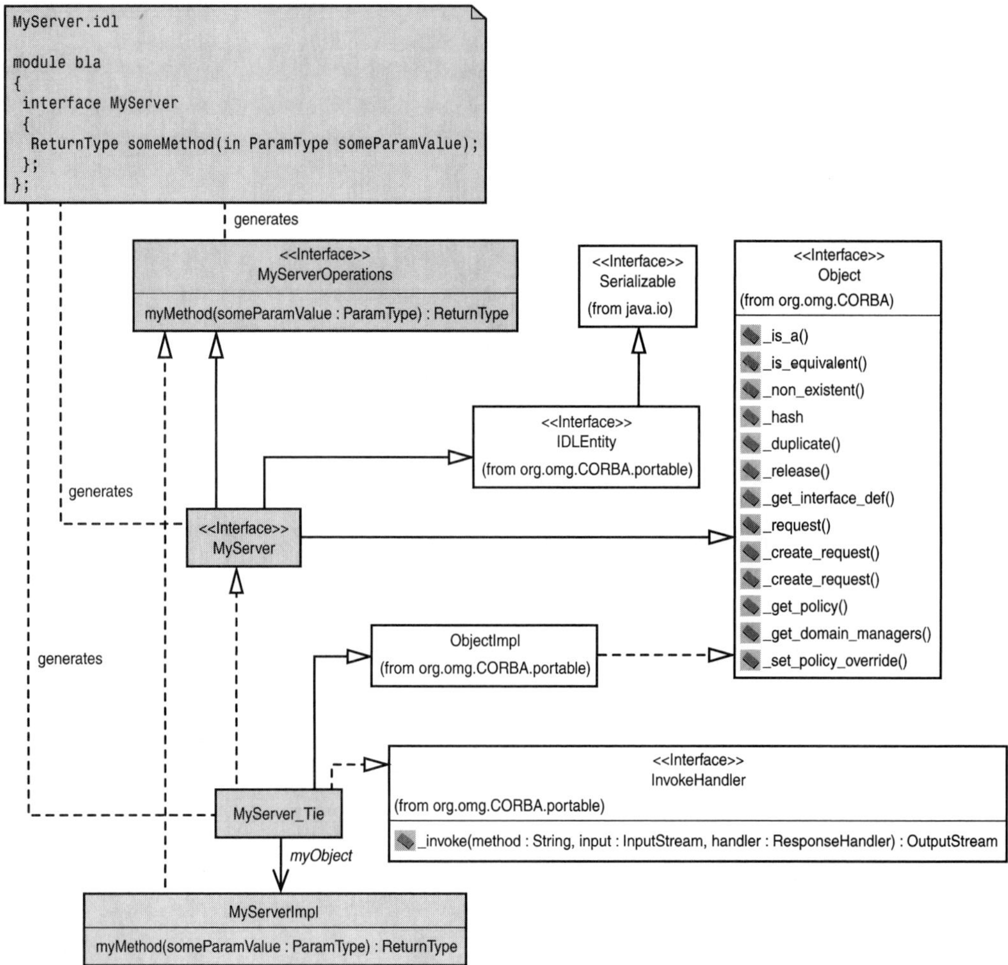

FIGURE 15.2

A CORBA server built using delegation.

LISTING 15.5 CORBA Customer Implementation (`CustomerImplementation.java`)

```
package ejava.corbach15.regular;
import org.omg.CosNaming.NamingContextPackage.*;
import org.omg.CosNaming.*;
import ejava.corbach15.*;

public class CustomerImplementation extends _CustomerImplBase
{
```

```
private String firstName;
private String lastName;
private String address1;
private String address2;
private String city;
private String state;
private String zip;
private String phoneNumber;
private String emailAddress;


public void bind(String name)
{
  try{
    NamingContext namingContext =
      NamingContextUtility.getNamingContext();
     // bind the Object Reference in Naming
    NameComponent namingComponent =
      new NameComponent(name, "");
    NameComponent nameComponent[] = {namingComponent};
    namingContext.rebind(nameComponent, this);
  }
  catch(Exception e){
    System.err.println("Error:"+e);
    e.printStackTrace();
  }
}
public String firstName ()
{
  return firstName;
}
public void firstName (String newFirstName)
{
  firstName = newFirstName;
}
public String lastName ()
{
  return lastName;
}
public void lastName (String newLastName)
{
  lastName = newLastName;
}
public String address1 ()
{
```

continues

LISTING 15.5 Continued

```
    return address1;
  }
  public void address1 (String newAddress1)
  {
    address1 = newAddress1;
  }
  public String address2 ()
  {
    return address2;
  }
  public void address2 (String newAddress2)
  {
    address2 = newAddress2;
  }
  public String city ()
  {
    return city;
  }
  public void city (String newCity)
  {
    city = newCity;
  }
  public String state ()
  {
    return state;
  }
  public void state (String newState)
  {
    state = newState;
  }
  public String zip ()
  {
    return zip;
  }
  public void zip (String newZip)
  {
    zip = newZip;
  }
  public String phoneNumber ()
  {
    return phoneNumber;
  }
  public void phoneNumber (String newPhoneNumber)
  {
    phoneNumber =  newPhoneNumber;
```

```
  }
  public String emailAddress ()
  {
    return emailAddress;
  }
  public void emailAddress (String newEmailAddress)
  {
    emailAddress = newEmailAddress;
  }}
```

The `ClientReceiverImplementation` class of Listing 15.6 implements the one remote method declared in the IDL Listing 15.2. The `setResultOrders()` method simply prints the list of orders received.

LISTING 15.6 CORBA Client Receiver Implementation (`ClientReceiverImplementation.java`)

```
package ejava.corbach15.regular;
import ejava.corbach15.*;

public class ClientReceiverImplementation
  extends _ClientReceiverImplBase
{

public void setResultOrders (ejava.corbach15.Order[] orders)
  {
    System.out.println("Received :"+orders.length);
    for(int i =0; i<orders.length; i++){
      System.out.println("Received Order :"+orders[i]);
      System.out.println("Order ID:" +orders[i].orderID);
      System.out.println("Order Date:" +orders[i].orderDate);
      System.out.println("Order Value:" +orders[i].orderValue);
    }
  }
}
```

The `QueryServerImplementation` of Listing 15.7 implements the `QueryServer` IDL interface declared in Listing 15.4. The `QueryServer` object represents the frontline interface for CORBA clients and contains most of the business logic for our example. The `QueryServerImplementation` constructor requires that a properties object be supplied with properties for a database driver class, URL, username, and password. This information is used to establish a connection with the BeeShirts.com database via JDBC. The `getResultSet()` method takes an SQL query for creating a prepared statement and subsequently for returning a result set. The `findCustomersWhoOrderedForMoreThan()` method retrieves the customer query from the properties object and issues the query using `getResultSet()`. The results of this query are then used to create a new distributed `CustomerImplementation` object reference. We will discuss how this reference is made available to the CORBA client shortly. The `register()` method is used to register a `ClientReceiver` with the `QueryServer`. The `findOrdersWhichAreFrom()` method retrieves an order query from the properties object and then issues this query for obtaining a set of related orders.

LISTING 15.7 CORBA Query Server Implementation (`QueryServerImplementation.java`)

```
package ejava.corbach15.regular;
import org.omg.CosNaming.*;
import org.omg.CosNaming.NamingContextPackage.*;
import org.omg.CORBA.*;
import java.util.Properties;
import java.sql.DriverManager;
import java.sql.Connection;
import java.sql.Statement;
import java.sql.SQLException;
import java.sql.PreparedStatement;
import java.sql.ResultSet;
import java.sql.ResultSetMetaData;
import java.util.Vector;
import java.sql.Date;
import ejava.corbach15.*;

public class QueryServerImplementation  extends _QueryServerImplBase
{
  private ClientReceiver clientReceiver;
  private String clientReceiverName;
  private Properties properties;
  private Connection connection;

  public QueryServerImplementation(Properties properties)
  {
    // Get properties from properties file data
    this.properties = properties;
    String dbDriverClassName = (String) properties.get("DRIVER_CLASS");
    String dbURL = (String) properties.get("DATABASE_URL");
    String userName = (String) properties.get("UserName");
    String password = (String) properties.get("Password");
    // Load JDBC driver and create connection
    try {
      Class.forName(dbDriverClassName);
```

```
    if (userName == null || password == null || userName.length() == 0
            || password.length() == 0) {
      connection = DriverManager.getConnection(dbURL);
    } else {
      connection = DriverManager.getConnection(dbURL, userName,
                                                password);
    }
  } catch (ClassNotFoundException cnfEx) {
    System.out.println("Driver Class Not found " + cnfEx);
  } catch (SQLException sqlEx) {
    System.out.println("SQL Exception :" + sqlEx);
  }
}

public String[]
  findCustomersWhoOrderdForMoreThan (float value)
{
  // Get customer query info
  String customerQueryString =
    (String) properties.get("CUSTOMER_QUERY");
  if (customerQueryString == null) {
    System.out.println("CUSTOMER_QUERY in  file is null");
  }

  try {
    // Get results from query
    ResultSet rs = this.getResultSet(customerQueryString,
                                     new Float(value));
    ResultSetMetaData rsMetaData = rs.getMetaData();
    int nColumns = rsMetaData.getColumnCount();
    Vector customerIDs = new Vector();
    // Create and bind CustomerImplementation per result
    //    and also set IDs into customerIDs Vector
    while (rs.next()) {
      String customerID = rs.getString("CUSTOMER_ID");
      String firstName = rs.getString("FIRST_NAME");
      String lastName = rs.getString("LAST_NAME");
      String address1 = rs.getString("ADDRESS_1");
      String address2 = rs.getString("ADDRESS_2");
      String city = rs.getString("CITY");
      String state = rs.getString("STATE");
      String phoneNumber = rs.getString("PHONE");
      String eMail = rs.getString("EMAIL");
      String zip = rs.getString("ZIP_CODE");
      CustomerImplementation custImpl =
        new CustomerImplementation();
```

continues

LISTING 15.7 Continued

```
        custImpl.firstName(firstName);
        custImpl.lastName(lastName);
        custImpl.address1(address1);
        custImpl.address2(address2);
        custImpl.city(city);
        custImpl.state(state);
        custImpl.zip(zip);
        custImpl.emailAddress(eMail);
        custImpl.phoneNumber(phoneNumber);
        String name =  customerID;
        custImpl.bind(name);
        customerIDs.addElement(customerID);
      }
      // Create and return String array of Customer IDs
      String[] registeredNames = new String[customerIDs.size()];
      for(int i = 0; i<registeredNames.length; i++){
        registeredNames[i] = (String)customerIDs.elementAt(i);
      }
      return registeredNames;

    } catch (SQLException sqlEx) {
      System.out.println(sqlEx);
      sqlEx.printStackTrace();
    }
    return new String[0];
  }

  public void findOrdersWhichAreFrom (String state)
  {
    // Get order query information from properties data
    String orderQueryString = (String) properties.get("ORDER_QUERY");
    if (orderQueryString == null) {
      System.out.println("ORDER_QUERY in  file is null");
    }
    try {
      // Get results from query
      ResultSet rs = this.getResultSet(orderQueryString, state);
      ResultSetMetaData rsMetaData = rs.getMetaData();
      int nColumns = rsMetaData.getColumnCount();
      Vector orders = new Vector();
      // Create an Order for each result and add to Vector
      while (rs.next()) {
        int orderID = rs.getInt("ORDER_ID");
        Date orderDate = rs.getDate("ORDER_DATE");
        double orderValue = rs.getDouble("TOTAL_PRICE");
        Order order = new Order(orderID, orderDate.toString(),
```

```
                                  orderValue);
        orders.addElement(order);
      }
      // Create array of orders
      Order[] returnOrders = new Order[orders.size()];
      for(int i =0;i<orders.size(); i++){
        returnOrders[i] = (Order)orders.elementAt(i);
      }
      // Add array of orders to client callback
      if (this.clientReceiver != null) {
        clientReceiver.setResultOrders(returnOrders);
      }
    } catch (SQLException sqlEx) {
      System.out.println(sqlEx);
      sqlEx.printStackTrace();
    }
  }

  public void register (String name,
    ejava.corbach15.ClientReceiver clientReceiver)
  {
    System.out.println("registered Client :" + clientReceiver);
    this.clientReceiver = clientReceiver;
    this.clientReceiverName = name;
  }

  private ResultSet getResultSet(String sqlQuery,
    java.lang.Object whereValue) throws SQLException
  {
    PreparedStatement preparedStatement =
      connection.prepareStatement(sqlQuery);
    preparedStatement.setObject(1, whereValue);
    ResultSet rs = preparedStatement.executeQuery();
    return rs;
  }
}
```

These orders are used to create a sequence of serializable `Order` objects and then for making a callback on the distributed CORBA client `ClientReceiver` references that were registered using the `register()` method. The `Order` object generated by the IDL-to-Java compilation of Listing 15.1 is shown in Listing 15.8 and simply defines the data to be serialized as public field variables. Note that because the `Order` class implements the `org.omg.CORBA.portable.IDLEntity` interface, it is declared a `Serializable` object because `IDLEntity` extends the `Serializable` interface.

LISTING 15.8 Generated Serializable IDLEntity Order Class (Order.java)

```
package ejava.corbach15;

public final class Order implements org.omg.CORBA.portable.IDLEntity
{
  public int orderID = (int)0;
  public String orderDate = null;
  public double orderValue = (double)0;

  public Order ()
  {
  } // ctor

  public Order (int _orderID, String _orderDate, double _orderValue)
  {
    orderID = _orderID;
    orderDate = _orderDate;
    orderValue = _orderValue;
  } // ctor
} // class Order
```

DSI-Based Servers

The CORBA servers just implemented make use of IDL to generate skeletons to which your CORBA implementations statically relate. The Dynamic Skeleton Interface can be implemented by your servers in order to avoid such dynamic bindings. Figure 15.3 shows how to create a DSI-based server. Your server must thus extend the `org.omg.CORBA.DynamicImplementation` abstract class and implement the `invoke()` method. The example in Listing 15.9 demonstrates implementation of such a DSI-based server.

NOTE

The example in Listing 15.9 is a simple example and is also contained on the CD in the `examples\src\ejava\corbach15\dynamic` directory. Note that this example would not work with Java IDL at the time of this book's writing. We have thus used the Visibroker for Java ORB found on the CD. Please refer to Appendix A, "Software Configuration," for where to find this product on the CD and how to configure it (setting `VISIGENIC_HOME`) with our examples. A `run.bat` file in the `examples\src\ejava\corbach15\dynamic` directory also provides an example script for building and executing this example. Note that the Visibroker for Java ORB is an enterprise class ORB that can also be used with all of the examples in this chapter.

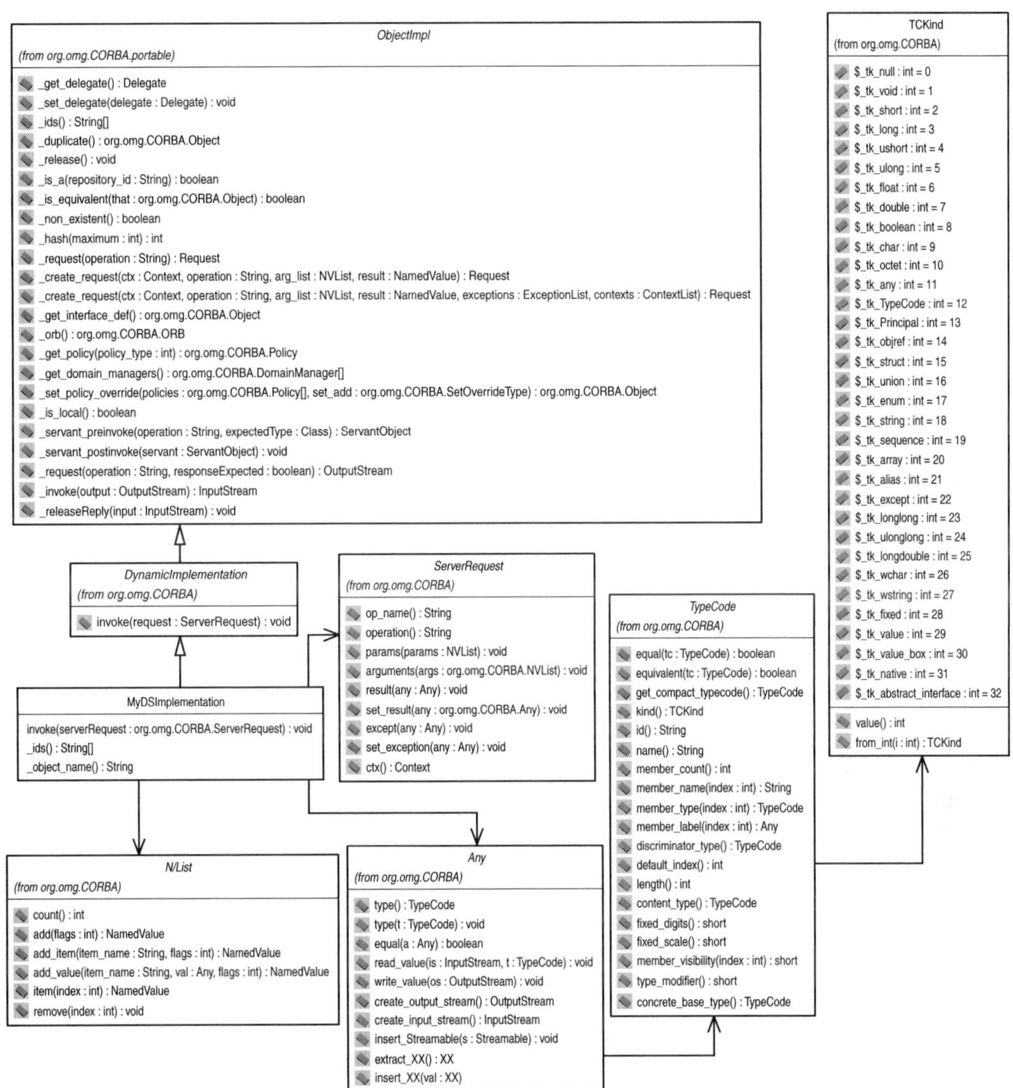

FIGURE 15.3

A CORBA server built using DSI.

Inside of the `invoke()` method, your server takes a `org.omg.CORBA.ServerRequest` object as a parameter, and you use this object to retrieve the request parameters and store the result. An `org.omg.CORBA.NVList` is used to build up a list of parameters. Here we use the `org.omg.CORBA.Any` object to create a parameter identified by an `org.omg.CORBA.TCKind` type and add it to the parameter list. After the parameter values are retrieved from the request object, the actual result can be generated and set onto the request object.

LISTING 15.9 Sample DSI Server (SampleDynamic.java)

```
package ejava.corbach15.dynamic;
import java.util.*;

public class SampleDynamic
  extends org.omg.CORBA.DynamicImplementation
{
  private String returnValue;
  private String[] ids;
  private org.omg.CORBA.BOA boa;
  private String objectName;
  private final String OPERATION_NAME = "sayHello";
  private final String IN_PARAMETER_NAME = "hello";

public SampleDynamic(String name, org.omg.CORBA.BOA boaRef)
  {
    objectName = name;
    boa = boaRef;
    ids =  new String[] { "IDL:SampleDynamic:1.0" };
  }

  public void invoke(org.omg.CORBA.ServerRequest serverRequest)
  {
    // Check if operation names are valid
    if(!serverRequest.op_name().equals(OPERATION_NAME)){
      throw new org.omg.CORBA.BAD_OPERATION();
    }

    // Create a parameter list
    org.omg.CORBA.NVList parameters = _orb().create_list(0);



    // Create a parameter and set its type
    org.omg.CORBA.Any nameOfParameter = _orb().create_any();
    nameOfParameter.type(_
             orb().get_primitive_tc(org.omg.CORBA.TCKind.tk_string));

    // Add the parameter to the parameter list
parameters.add_value(IN_PARAMETER_NAME, nameOfParameter,
      org.omg.CORBA.ARG_IN.value);

    // Induce the parameters to be populated with values from the request
    serverRequest.params(parameters);

    // Extract the parameter value and use it to invoke a method
```

```
    String receivedValue = nameOfParameter.extract_string();
    String returnValue = this.sayHello(receivedValue);

     // Create a result and add it to the request
    org.omg.CORBA.Any stringAny = _orb().create_any();
    stringAny.insert_string(returnValue);
    serverRequest.result(stringAny);
  }

  String sayHello(String receivedValue)
  {
    return "You send me :"+ receivedValue;
  }

  public String[] _ids()
  {
    return ids;
  }

  public String _object_name()
  {
    return this.objectName;
  }
}
```

Implementation Repository

After you have created a CORBA server, your server implementation must typically be registered with an implementation repository. Let's take some time here to discuss what is happening under the hood when this occurs.

The implementation repository is a runtime repository of information describing the classes supported on the server side of a particular ORB. Implementation repositories are used to register and unregister object implementations on the server side as well as provide meta-data about the implementation. Other information like current instances and object identifiers can be stored in an implementation repository. The implementation repository is mainly an idea described by CORBA specifications, and it lacked standardization in early specification versions. It is simply an assumed part of any server-side ORB needing to store object implementation information.

The implementation repository is utilized and managed by the ORB's object adapter implementation. The actual underlying storage methodology in an implementation repository is vendor specific because it depends on a vendor's object adapter implementation. Because early versions of the specification lacked sufficient definition of ORB object adapters, both object adapter and implementation repository implementations tended to contain many vendor-specific features.

The Visibroker for Java ORB's implementation of the implementation repository is called the Object Activation Daemon (OAD). Technically speaking, the OAD takes on some more object-adapter–specific roles as well. The Visibroker implementation repository is stored in a file rooted relative to your Visibroker install in the absolute filename `<Visibroker_Root>\adm\impl_rep`. The Visibroker OAD can be accessed via the command line or programmatically. From the command line, the utility named `oadutil` can be used to register, unregister, and list implementations in the implementation repository. Programmatically, the class `com.visigenic.vbroker.Activation.OAD` can also be used for implementation repository registration, unregistration, and listing.

Java IDL uses the `org.omg.CORBA.ORB.connect()` method call to perform object registration. Java IDL seemed to be holding out for a final release of the Portable Object Adapter specification, in order to avoid creating proprietary interfaces to an underlying implementation repository. The next section discusses this topic in a little more detail and continues with the creation of our CORBA-based application.

Object Adapters

Your CORBA server objects need to be brought into memory (activated) upon a client request on those objects. The client request indeed must somehow map to a call onto the specific skeleton used by your CORBA server. Furthermore, the decision must be made as to whether a new process is to be created, a new thread is to be created, or perhaps an existing thread is to be reused for your CORBA server. The ORB's object adapter is responsible for this type of ORB functionality.

The Basic Object Adapter (BOA) was required for implementation by all CORBA 2.0–compliant ORBs, but it soon became apparent that the BOA had gaping holes in the specification. Thus, various vendor-specific features emerged. The BOA has since been deprecated, and the Portable Object Adapter (POA) specification now helps ensure that object implementations can be portable across ORBs. Chapter 21, "Activation Services," describes activation models, such as the CORBA activation models, in more detail, but for now it is important to at least understand how your CORBA servers need to communicate in a basic fashion with an underlying object adapter.

BOA-Based Server Registration

As an example using BOA, the `DynamicServer` class of Listing 15.10 was used with the Visibroker ORB to register the CORBA server of Listing 15.9. Here, we see that a call to the Visibroker-specific `org.omg.CORBA.ORB.BOA_init()` method is made to obtain a handle to an `org.omg.CORBA.BOA` reference using the default activation policy (can use overloaded `BOA_init()` calls for different activation behavior). Subsequently, each CORBA object is registered with the BOA to receive calls from CORBA clients on the network using the `BOA.obj_is_ready()` call. Finally, calling `BOA.impl_is_ready()` causes the CORBA server to enter into a loop so that the CORBA server can remain active in memory while calls to any CORBA objects registered with `obj_is_ready()` can be handled by the ORB.

NOTE

The dynamic server registration example in Listing 15.10 is also contained on the CD in the `examples\src\ejava\corbach15\dynamic` directory.

LISTING 15.10 Server Registration Example Using the BOA (`DynamicServer.java`)

```
package ejava.corbach15.dynamic;
import org.omg.CORBA.*;
import ejava.corbach15.*;
import org.omg.CosNaming.*;
import org.omg.CosNaming.NamingContextPackage.*;
import org.omg.CORBA.*;

public class DynamicServer
{


  public static void main(String[] args)
  {
    // Obtain ORB reference
    org.omg.CORBA.ORB orb = org.omg.CORBA.ORB.init(args,null);

    // Obtain BOA reference
    org.omg.CORBA.BOA boa = orb.BOA_init();

    // Create a distributable CORBA object reference
    SampleDynamic sampleDynamic =
      new SampleDynamic("SampleDynamic",boa);

    // Make object instance available to network
    boa.obj_is_ready(sampleDynamic);
    System.out.println(sampleDynamic + " is ready.");

    // Enter into loop to remain active in memory while handling requests
    boa.impl_is_ready();
  }
}
```

Java IDL Server Registration

In the static server example, we have created a separate server registrar to register our frontline `QueryServer` object with the Java IDL ORB. This `ServerRegistrar` implementation is shown in Listing 15.11. Because the BOA is deprecated, Java IDL uses the `org.omg.CORBA.ORB.connect()` call to register the server object with the Java IDL ORB replacing the `BOA.obj_is_ready()` call. Also take note from this listing that we use the CORBA Naming Service to bind the object to a name in the CosNaming service that we demonstrate toward the end of this chapter. As you'll see, the CosNaming service will allow our CORBA clients to obtain a handle to our CORBA server object in a portable fashion using the name with which it was registered on the server side into the CosNaming service. Finally, the `org.omg.CORBA.ORB.run()` call can serve to replace the `BOA.impl_is_ready()` call and wait for client requests until the particular server is shut down.

LISTING 15.11 Server Registration Example Using Java IDL (`ServerRegistrar.java`)

```
package ejava.corbach15.regular;
import org.omg.CosNaming.*;
import org.omg.CosNaming.NamingContextPackage.*;
import org.omg.CORBA.*;
import java.io.IOException;
import java.io.FileInputStream;
import java.util.Properties;
import ejava.corbach15.*;

public class ServerRegistrar
{

-

  public static void main(String[] args)
  {
    if (args.length == 0) {
      System.out
        .println("You should provide properties file :"
          + "java ejava.corbach15.ServerRegistrar corbach15.txt");
      System.exit(0);
    }
    String propertiesFileName = args[0];
    try{
      Properties properties = new Properties();
      FileInputStream fin = new FileInputStream(propertiesFileName);
      properties.load(fin);
```

```
      String name = (String) properties.get("QUERY_SERVER_NAME");
      ORB orb = NamingContextUtility.getORB();
      NamingContextUtility.initializeOrb(args);

      // createQueryServerImplementation
      QueryServerImplementation queryServer =
        new QueryServerImplementation(properties);

      orb.connect(queryServer);
      NamingContext namingContext =
        NamingContextUtility.getNamingContext();

      // bind the Object Reference in Naming
      NameComponent namingComponent =
        new NameComponent(name, "");
      NameComponent nameComponent[] = {namingComponent};

      namingContext.rebind(nameComponent, queryServer);

      // wait for the clients
      orb.run();
      }
    }
    catch(IOException ioe){
      System.out.println(ioe);
      ioe.printStackTrace();
      System.exit(0);
    }
    catch(Exception e){
      System.out.println(e);
      e.printStackTrace();
      System.exit(0);
    }
  }
}
```

POA-Based Server Registration

Assuming that your ORB supports POA and you wanted to use the new POA-based techniques for registering your server-side implementations, you would have first had to generate your static skeletons appropriately. For example, the JacORB IDL-to-Java compiler (`idl`) uses the `-p` option on the `idl` command line as shown here:

```
idl -p QueryServer.idl
```

Such a command would generate POA-compliant files such as QueryServer.java, QueryServerPOA.java, QueryServerPOATie.java, and QueryServerOperations.java. You would then implement your QueryServerImplementation by extending the generated QueryServerPOA class as such:

```
public class QueryServerImplementation
  extends ejava.corbach15.QueryServerPOA {...}
```

The server registration process would then need to be changed by first obtaining a handle to the POA, creating your specific CORBA object to register, and then registering the object with the POA. Your server program can enter into a loop to keep the server process active by calling org.omg.CORBA.ORB.run(). For example, you might change the ServerRegistrar code described earlier to look like this:

```
// Create ORB reference as usual
ORB orb = ORB.init(args,null);

// Now create POA reference
org.omg.CORBA.PortableServer.POA poa =
            org.omg.CORBA.PortableServer.POAHelper.narrow(
                           orb.resolve_initial_references("RootPOA"));

// Create your specific distributed object reference
QueryServerImplementation queryServer =
     new QueryServerImplementation(initArgs);

// Now register object with the POA
org.omg.CORBA.Object objID =
    poa.activate_object(queryServer);

// Waits until the ORB process stops
orb.run();
```

Interface Repository

An Interface Repository (IR) is an online database of object interface definitions used under the hood of the client-side ORB to know how to package calls to distributed servers. The IR is thus essentially a container of runtime IDL information that describes how to interface with remote objects.

Java IDL in fact does not implement an IR and instead relies on the fact that CORBA clients will be able to generate or obtain the CORBA stubs needed to communicate with the remote server. However, IRs do come in handy when you're desiring to use things such as DII to dynamically interact with a CORBA server whose interface is unknown at compile-time. DII uses the IR to understand the server's interface. Also, by providing a distributed interface to the IR itself, remote servers can actually dynamically publish their interfaces to the IR.

We have placed the discussion of IRs at this point in the chapter, because if you did not for some reason have the stubs you needed to build your CORBA clients, then you would need to be sure and register the remote interfaces with the IR to which your CORBA client desired access.

An IR can be accessed via the command line, from a GUI interface, or programmatically. The Visibroker for Java ORB's IR can be accessed from the command line and via a GUI interface using the `irep` command. Updates to the Visibroker IR can be made with the `idl2ir` command.

To programmatically access the IR, you'll need to use the various `org.omg.CORBA.<IDL_Entity_Name>Def` interfaces. Such an interface exists for each type of IDL entity that can exist in an IR (most of the entities listed in Table 14.1), such as `ModuleDef`, `InterfaceDef`, `StructDef`, `TypeDef`, `OperationDef`, `AttributeDef`, `ParameterDef`, `ConstantDef`, and `ExceptionDef`. Each IDL entity can inherit from a `Container` interface designating that such an IDL entity can contain other entities and from a `Contained` interface designating that such an IDL entity can be contained by other entities. Both `Container` and `Contained` types inherit from the base `IRObject` interface designating a generic IDL entity sitting inside of an Interface Repository. The IR, encapsulated by the `Repository` interface, can contain one or more `IRObjects` and itself extends the `Container` interface.

Each `IRObject` type is identifiable by a constant in the `org.omg.CORBA.DefinitionKind` class. This can be contrasted with the `TCKind` class identifying all the possible type codes that can exist but don't necessarily belong in an IR (for example, fundamental types such as `long`).

Listing 15.12 demonstrates how to view the contents of an IR using the Visibroker for Java ORB. The `main()` method takes in the name of an IDL module from the command line, creates an instance of a `ModuleDef` interface representing that module in the IR, and passes this `ModuleDef` into the `printAModule()` call. The `printAModule()` call will first retrieve an array of the elements contained in the particular module. Depending on the type of element, some informative information will be printed. We do this only for a few key element types.

NOTE

The Interface Repository viewing example in Listing 15.12 is also contained on the CD in the `examples\src\ejava\corbach15\irquery` directory. We have used the Visibroker for Java ORB found on the CD with this example. Please refer to Appendix A for where to find this product on the CD and how to configure it (setting `VISIGENIC_HOME`) with our examples. A `run.bat` file in the `examples\src\ejava\corbach15\irquery` directory also provides an example script for building and executing this example.

LISTING 15.12 Viewing the Contents of an IR (`ListContentsAModule.java`)

```
package ejava.corbach15.irquery;

public class ListContentsAModule
{

  public static String getIDLName(org.omg.CORBA.IDLType idlType)
  {
    org.omg.CORBA.Contained contained =
      org.omg.CORBA.ContainedHelper.narrow(idlType);
    if(contained == null){
      return idlType.type().toString();
    }else{
      return  contained.absolute_name();
    }

  }

  public static void printAModule(org.omg.CORBA.Container container)
  {
    // get content of a module
    org.omg.CORBA.Contained[] contained =
      container.contents(org.omg.CORBA.DefinitionKind.dk_all, true);
    // For each element, run through case statement to print info
    for(int i = 0; i < contained.length; i++) {
    {
      switch(contained[i].def_kind().value())
      {
        case org.omg.CORBA.DefinitionKind._dk_Attribute:
        {
          org.omg.CORBA.AttributeDef attributeDef =
            org.omg.CORBA.AttributeDefHelper.narrow(contained[i]);
          String readonly = "";
          if( attributeDef.mode() ==
            org.omg.CORBA.AttributeMode.ATTR_READONLY ){
            readonly = "readonly \" : \"";
          }
          System.out.println(readonly + "attribute " +
            getIDLName(attributeDef.type_def()) + " " +
            attributeDef.name() + ";");
        }
          break;
        case org.omg.CORBA.DefinitionKind._dk_Constant:
        {
          org.omg.CORBA.ConstantDef constantDef =
```

```
    org.omg.CORBA.ConstantDefHelper.narrow(contained[i]);
  System.out.println("const " +
    getIDLName(constantDef.type_def()) +
    " " + constantDef.name() + " = " + constantDef.value() +
   ";");
}
  break;
case org.omg.CORBA.DefinitionKind._dk_Exception:
{
  org.omg.CORBA.ExceptionDef exceptionDef =
    org.omg.CORBA.ExceptionDefHelper.narrow(contained[i]);
  System.out.println("exception " + exceptionDef.name() + " {");
  org.omg.CORBA.StructMember[] members = exceptionDef.members();
  for(int j = 0; j < members.length; j++) {
    System.out.println(getIDLName(members[j].type_def) + " " +
       members[j].name + ";");
  }
}
  break;
case org.omg.CORBA.DefinitionKind._dk_Interface:
{
  org.omg.CORBA.InterfaceDef interfaceDef =
    org.omg.CORBA.InterfaceDefHelper.narrow(contained[i]);
  org.omg.CORBA.InterfaceDefPackage.FullInterfaceDescription
    interfaceDescription  =
      interfaceDef.describe_interface();
  System.out.println("Operations in :"+interfaceDef.name());
  for(int i1 = 0; i1 < interfaceDescription.operations.length;
    i1++){
    System.out.println("  " +
      interfaceDescription.operations[i1].name +";");
  }

  for(int i2 = 0; i2 < interfaceDescription.attributes.length;
    i2++){
    System.out.println("  " +
      interfaceDescription.attributes[i2].name +";");
  }
}
  break;
case org.omg.CORBA.DefinitionKind._dk_Operation:
{
  System.out.println("Error : not implemented operation");
}
```

continues

LISTING 15.12 Continued

```
          break;
        case org.omg.CORBA.DefinitionKind._dk_Module:
        {
          org.omg.CORBA.ModuleDef module =
             org.omg.CORBA.ModuleDefHelper.narrow(contained[i]);

          System.out.println("Module name :" + module.name());

         printAModule(org.omg.CORBA.ModuleDefHelper.narrow(contained[i]));
        }
        break;
        case org.omg.CORBA.DefinitionKind._dk_Alias:
        {
          System.out.println("Error :not implemented alias");
        }
          break;
        case org.omg.CORBA.DefinitionKind._dk_Struct:
        {
          org.omg.CORBA.StructDef structDef =
            org.omg.CORBA.StructDefHelper.narrow(contained[i]);
          System.out.println("struct " + structDef.name() + " {");
          org.omg.CORBA.StructMember[] structMemembers = structDef.members();
          for(int j = 0; j < structMemembers.length; j++)
          {
              String printValue = structMemembers[j].name;
              System.out.println(printValue);
          }
          System.out.println("};");
         }
         break;
        case org.omg.CORBA.DefinitionKind._dk_Union:
        {
          System.out.println("Error : not implemented Union");
        }
          break;
        case org.omg.CORBA.DefinitionKind._dk_Enum:
        {
          System.out.println("Error : not implemented Enum");
        }
          break;
        case org.omg.CORBA.DefinitionKind._dk_none:
        {
          System.out.println("Error : not implemented none");
        }
        break;
```

```
        case org.omg.CORBA.DefinitionKind._dk_all:
        {
          System.out.println("Error : not implemented All");
        }
        break;
        case org.omg.CORBA.DefinitionKind._dk_Typedef:
        {
          System.out.println("Error : not implemented Typedef");
        }
        break;
        case org.omg.CORBA.DefinitionKind._dk_Primitive:
        {
          System.out.println("Error :not implemented Primitive");
        }
        break;
        case org.omg.CORBA.DefinitionKind._dk_String:
        {
          System.out.println("Error :not implemented String");
        }
        break;
        case org.omg.CORBA.DefinitionKind._dk_Sequence:
        {
          System.out.println("Error :not implemented Sequence");
        }
        break;
        case org.omg.CORBA.DefinitionKind._dk_Array:
        {
          System.out.println("Error :not implemented Array");
        }
        break;
        default:
        break;
      }
    }
  }
  }

  public static void main(String[] args)
  {
    if ( args.length == 0 ) {
      System.out.println("Error: java ejava.corbach15.irquery "+
        " ListContentsAModule IdlName");
      System.exit(1);
    }
    String queryingFor = args[0];
```

continues

LISTING 15.12 Continued

```
    org.omg.CORBA.ORB orb = org.omg.CORBA.ORB.init(args,null);

    org.omg.CORBA.Repository repository =
      org.omg.CORBA.RepositoryHelper.bind(orb);

    org.omg.CORBA.ModuleDef moduleDefinition =
    org.omg.CORBA.ModuleDefHelper.narrow(repository.lookup(queryingFor));

    printAModule(moduleDefinition);
  }
}
```

CORBA Clients and Stubs

After your CORBA servers have been registered with their server-side ORBs and perhaps registered with a CosNaming-compliant naming service, your CORBA clients can then tap their services. For your CORBA clients to use such services, you will need to obtain a CORBA stub class acting as a proxy to the remote server. This stub can be generated by the IDL description of the server. Optionally, you may be able to use DII if your ORB implementation supports an Interface Repository and a DII.

CORBA Clients and Static Stubs

The `idlj` compiler command that was used earlier with the `-fall` option also created client-side stubs. As shown by the general client-side CORBA diagram in Figure 15.4, a stub named `_MyServerStub` is generated from an IDL file with an interface named `MyServer`. The CORBA client code makes calls on the generated `MyServer` interface, which is implemented by the `_MyServerStub` class. CORBA stubs extend the `ObjectImpl` class, which in turn extends the `org.omg.CORBA.Object` class. Additionally, the IDL compiler generates a `MyServerHolder` class for passing around `inout` and `out` IDL types, as well as a `MyServerHelper` class used by the client for narrowing object references and other helper methods.

The `Client` class in Listing 15.13 not only demonstrates how a CORBA client in our example can make distributed calls on a CORBA server, but also demonstrates how a CORBA client can register a distributed callback with a CORBA server.

TIP

Because in communications paradigms as flexible as CORBA the boundary between what is truly a server and what is truly a client becomes blurred, the term *servant* is often used to designate the merging of the traditionally distinct roles.

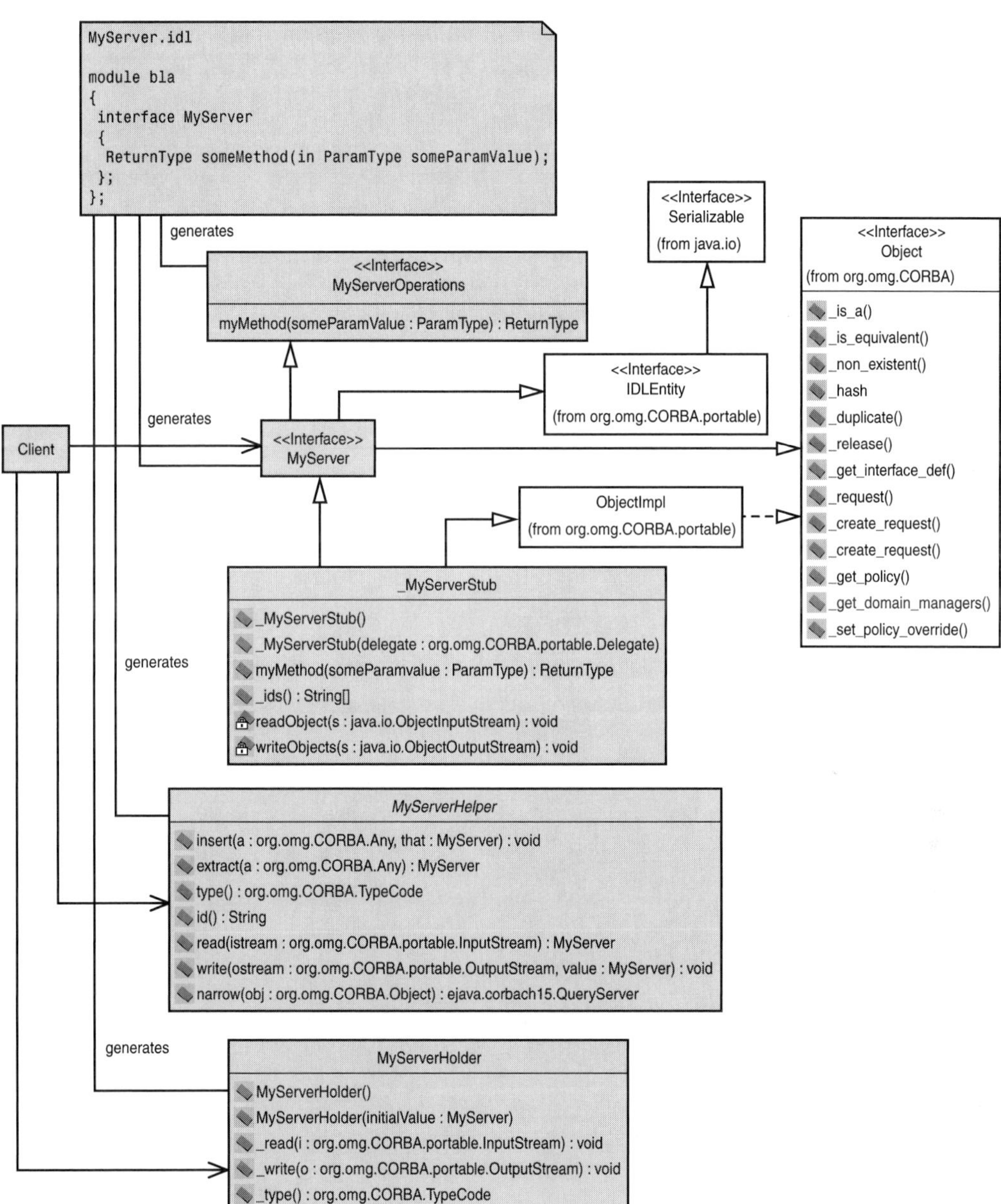

FIGURE 15.4
A CORBA client using static stubs.

The `Client.main()` method first reads in a set of properties describing a few configurable variables read in from the `corbach15.txt` properties file (assuming you have not forgotten to set your `DATABASE_URL` and `DRIVER_CLASS` environment variables as described in Appendix A). After obtaining a reference to a `QueryServer` (the mechanism for which is described in the next section), our `Client` creates an instance of a distributed `ClientReceiverImplementation` object and registers it with the `QueryServer` using the `register()` distributed call. The `Client` then makes the `findCustomersWhoOrderdForMoreThan()` distributed call on the `QueryServer` and displays some basic information about each returned `Customer`. When the `Client` calls `findOrdersWhichAreFrom()` on the `QueryServer`, the `QueryServerImplementation` makes a callback on the CORBA client's `ClientReceiver` object with a `ClientReceiver.setResultOrders()` call.

LISTING 15.13 CORBA Query Client (`Client.java`)

```
package ejava.corbach15.regular;
import java.util.Properties;
import java.io.IOException;
import java.io.FileInputStream;
import org.omg.CosNaming.*;
import org.omg.CosNaming.NamingContextPackage.*;
import org.omg.CORBA.*;
import ejava.corbach15.*;

public class Client
{


  public static void main(String[] args) {
    if (args.length == 0) {
      System.out
        .println("You should provide properties file :"
          + "java ejava.corbach15.Client corbach15.txt");
      System.exit(0);
    }
    String propertiesFileName = args[0];
    try{
      Properties properties = new Properties();
      FileInputStream fin = new FileInputStream(propertiesFileName);
      properties.load(fin);
      String name = (String) properties.get("QUERY_SERVER_NAME");
```

```
    // Initialize Orb and get a naming context
    NamingContextUtility.initializeOrb(args);
    NamingContext namingContext =
      NamingContextUtility.getNamingContext();
    // Bind the Object Reference in Naming
    NameComponent namingComponent =
      new NameComponent(name, "");
    NameComponent nameComponent[] = {namingComponent};
    System.out.println("Looking for name :"+name);
    // Obtain QueryServer reference
    QueryServer queryServer =
      QueryServerHelper.narrow(namingContext.resolve(nameComponent));

     // Create client callback reference
    ClientReceiverImplementation clientReceiver =
      new ClientReceiverImplementation();
    // Register callback with the QueryServer
    queryServer.register("ClientReceiver", clientReceiver);

    // Call QueryServer
    String[] customersNames =
      queryServer.findCustomersWhoOrderdForMoreThan(100.0f);
    // For each customer, obtain Customer ref and display info
    for( int i = 0; i < customersNames.length; i++){
      System.out.println("CustomersNames :"+customersNames[i]);
      namingComponent =
        new NameComponent(customersNames[i], "");
      NameComponent custNameComponent[] = {namingComponent};
      System.out.println("Looking for name :"+name);
      Customer customer =
       CustomerHelper.narrow(namingContext.resolve(custNameComponent));
      System.out.println(customer.firstName());
      System.out.println(customer.lastName());
    }

    // Induce client callback
    queryServer.findOrdersWhichAreFrom("VA");

    System.out.println("Waiting to Quit:");
    System.in.read();
  }
  catch(IOException ioe){
    System.out.println(ioe);
    ioe.printStackTrace();
```

continues

LISTING 15.13 Continued

```
      System.exit(0);
    }
    catch(Exception e){
      System.out.println(e);
      e.printStackTrace();
      System.exit(0);
    }
  }
}
```

DII-Based Clients

As illustrated in Figure 15.5 and demonstrated in Listing 15.14, your CORBA client can also use DII to communicate with a remote server. As it turns out, the DII client in Listing 15.14 talks to the DSI server in Listing 15.10 just to demonstrate both server-side and client-side dynamic communication without any IDL. Of course, there are no limitations requiring that DII clients talk with DSI servers. DII can talk just as easily with static skeleton-based servers, and DSI servers can talk just as easily with IDL-based clients.

A DII client thus must first create a new `Request` object from a bound `org.omg.CORBA.Object` instance. We talk about such bindings in the next section. In DII it's key to consider the fact that after such a `Request` object is made with the name of the method to call (for example, `METHOD_NAME = "sayHello"`), a request needs to be built up in the `Request` object instance. This is accomplished by setting the return type, creating any parameter types, and setting each parameter's value directly onto the `Request` object. The request can then be invoked using `Request.invoke()`. Subsequently, the return value can be retrieved from the request stream using `Request.return_value()`.

NOTE

The example in Listing 15.14 is a simple DII example and is also contained on the CD in the `examples\src\ejava\corbach15\dynamic` directory. Note that this example would not work with Java IDL at the time of this book's writing. We have thus used the Visibroker for Java ORB equipped with the CD and described in Appendix A.

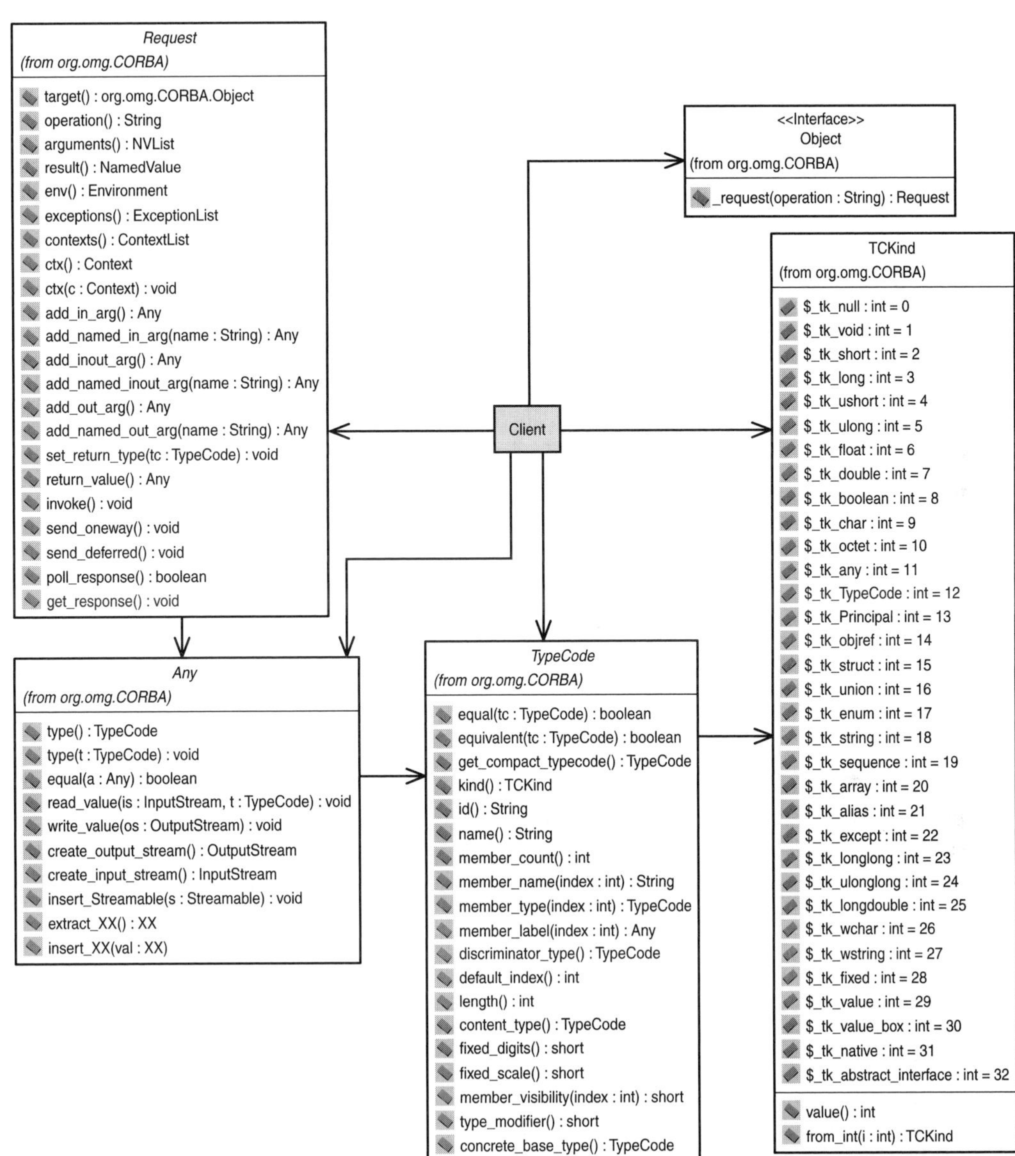

FIGURE 15.5
CORBA Client using DII.

LISTING 15.14 CORBA DII-Based Example Client (`DynamicClient.java`)

```
package ejava.corbach15.dynamic;
import org.omg.CORBA.*;
import ejava.corbach15.*;
import org.omg.CosNaming.*;
import org.omg.CosNaming.NamingContextPackage.*;
import org.omg.CORBA.*;

public class DynamicClient
{
  private static final String METHOD_NAME = "sayHello";
  public static void main(String[] args)
  {
    try{
      org.omg.CORBA.Object sampleDynamic;
      // create ORB reference as usual
      org.omg.CORBA.ORB orb = org.omg.CORBA.ORB.init(args,null);

      String name = "SampleDynamic";
      // Bind using Visibroker call
      sampleDynamic =
       ((com.visigenic.vbroker.orb.ORB)orb).bind("IDL:SampleDynamic:1.0",
                                              name, null, null);

      // Create a request object with the method name to call
      Request request = sampleDynamic._request(METHOD_NAME);
      // Set the return type to expect on the request object
      request.

set_return_type(orb.get_primitive_tc(org.omg.CORBA.TCKind.tk_string));
       // Create a parameter to send as part of call
      org.omg.CORBA.Any sendValue = request.add_in_arg();
      // Set parameter value
      sendValue.insert_string("Hi There");
      // Now invoke the call
      request.invoke();
      // Retrieve the result
      String resultValue = request.return_value().extract_string();

      System.out.println(" Received :"+resultValue);
    }
    catch(Exception e){
      e.printStackTrace();
    }
  }
}
```

CORBA Naming

In all of our discussions thus far in this chapter, we have glossed over exactly how our clients and servers make the initial connection with one another. We've covered how to build a CORBA server, how to build a CORBA client, how to register or associate implementations on the server-side ORB, and how to register or associate interfaces on the client-side ORB. But how does a CORBA client obtain an object reference (IOR) and establish a connection with the CORBA server?

The most portable and the recommended way is to start up and use a CORBA Naming Service. The CORBA Naming Service is used on the server side by associating a human-readable name to an IOR with the CosNaming server. The CORBA Naming Service is used on the client side by using a human-readable name to obtain a handle to the CORBA server object via the IOR associated inside of the CosNaming server.

We describe the CosNaming service and naming services in general in Chapter 19, "Naming Services," but recall that we've used a helper class throughout our examples that we created called `NamingContextUtility`, as in Listing 15.15. The `NamingContextUtility.getNamingContext()` call simply resolves an initial reference to a CosNaming service to which your ORB can connect and narrows this reference to an `org.omg.CosNaming.NamingContext` object. The `NamingContextUtility` class also was used to obtain a reference to an `org.omg.CORBA.ORB` object as well.

A handle to a CosNaming service will be obtained if you first have activated a CosNaming server on your network. In Java IDL, the `tnameserv` command can be used to start the J2EE reference implementation of a transient name server. We have included such a step in the `run.bat` files equipped with each of the Chapter 15 examples on the CD.

> **NOTE**
>
> The example in Listing 15.15 is a simple CORBA Naming Service interface example and is also contained on the CD in the `examples\src\ejava\corbach15` directory.

LISTING 15.15 CORBA Naming Service Interfacing (`NamingContextUtility.java`)

```
package ejava.corbach15;
import org.omg.CosNaming.*;
import org.omg.CosNaming.NamingContextPackage.*;
import org.omg.CORBA.*;
```

continues

LISTING 15.15 Continued

```
public class NamingContextUtility
{
  static ORB orb;


  public static void initializeOrb(String[] args)
  {
    if(orb == null){
      orb = ORB.init(args,null);
    }
  }

  public static  NamingContext getNamingContext()
    throws Exception
  {
    //get the namingContextReference and namingContext
    org.omg.CORBA.Object namingServiceReference =
      orb.resolve_initial_references("NameService");
    NamingContext namingContext =
      NamingContextHelper.narrow(namingServiceReference);
    return namingContext;
  }

  public static ORB getORB()
  {
   if(orb == null){
      String[] args = new String[0];
      initializeOrb(args);
    }

    }
    return orb;
  }
}
```

After a handle to the CosNaming server is obtained, recall that the server-side `ServerRegistrar` of Listing 15.11 created an `org.omg.CosNaming.NameComponent` instance with a particular name `String`. A `NameComponent` array is then used as an argument to a `NamingContext.rebind()` call along with the CORBA server to which to register the name. This same technique was used inside of the `CustomerImplementation` object in Listing 15.5 to bind an instance of itself using a customer ID as a CORBA name `String` component.

On the client side, the `Client` class of Listing 15.13 obtains a handle to a `NamingContext` instance via the `NamingContextUtility` helper class. The client then constructs a name for referring to the `QueryServer` in the same fashion as the `ServerRegistrar` created a name. A `NamingContext.lookup()` call made by the client using the constructed `NameComponent` array is then narrowed to a reference for the `QueryServer` object.

Because the CosNaming service is not strictly part of the ORB and is considered an add-on CORBAservice, vendors that have shipped their ORB products without such a service have tended to produce non-interoperable means for binding names to objects and looking up objects with names.

For example, the Visibroker for Java ORB generates a server-side skeleton which takes a `String` argument in its constructor that subclassed server implementations can use to pass a name for that object. When using the `BOA.obj_is_ready()` call, this name is bound to a process known as `osagent` supplied by Visigenics along with the object's IOR. The `osagent` essentially fulfills the role of a non-interoperable naming service because clients can then obtain handles to the distributed objects using a `bind()` call on the `Helper` object generated by the Visibroker `idl2java` utility. The `bind()` call takes the name of the object as an argument, consults the `osagent`, and returns a reference to the distributed object.

Iona's OrbixWeb also has a non-interoperable means for naming service binds and lookups using just its core Orb products. Of course, both vendors also offer a CosNaming service–compliant product for an added cost.

The bottom line from our perspective is that you should never construct your code in such a way that it depends on a vendor's specific naming-service mechanisms. Rather you should seek the purchase or development of a CosNaming-compliant naming service. If money or time makes such a proposition problematic, you should at least pursue creating an adapter or wrapper class (perhaps similar to the `NamingContextUtility` class used in our examples) that can isolate your code from change associated with switching between ORB vendors.

Conclusions

Creating a CORBA-based application involves defining an IDL interface, compiling the IDL interface to generate Java bindings, implementing a CORBA server, implementing a CORBA client, and determining how servers will register their services such that clients can obtain initial handles to them. A host of server-side implementation considerations abound, such as these: Do I use inheritance or delegation for my implementation? Do I use dynamic or static skeletons? How do I register my object implementation? How can I create scalable server designs? What scalable Orb product do I use? Did I start a name server yet? On the client side, the decision-making process can be much simpler if your client is purely a client and not a servant.

Nevertheless, creating CORBA-based applications can seem daunting at first introduction, but the amount of hand-coding required is significantly reduced as compared to creating a similar TCP/IP-based application. The built-in support offered by CORBA for the application/communications interface layer relieves you from the need to create such ugly pieces of code as activators, stubs, and skeletons. Rather, the CORBA framework and utilities do it for you. Of course, in the interest of providing an extremely flexible way to build such applications, CORBA also introduces overhead in decision making and configuration that you otherwise would not have. But after you've created your first couple of CORBA-based applications, such thought processes and configuration tasks will become second nature to you.

RMI Communications

CHAPTER

16

IN THIS CHAPTER

- RMI Baics 466
- JRMP 471
- RMI and IIOP 473
- Java-to-IDL Mapping 474
- Objects by Value and RMI 476
- RMI Interfaces 477
- RMI Servers and Skeletons 481
- RMI Registration 497
- RMI Clients and Stubs 506
- RMI Lookup 514
- RMI Object Activation 515
- Custom Sockets 523

The Java Remote Method Invocation (RMI) framework has been Java's distributed object communications framework since Java was born. RMI was originally distributed separately from the JDK 1.0 and later was integrated with the JDK 1.1. RMI now has grown in feature richness and yet remains elegantly simple for Java developers to rapidly create distributed client/server applications. The RMI and CORBA paradigms are also now merging as the RMI/IIOP APIs and framework evolves.

In this chapter, you'll learn:

- The basic concepts behind and architecture of Java's Remote Method Invocation interface.
- The architecture of the Java Remote Method Protocol (JRMP) as a protocol developed specifically for Java's remote object capabilities.
- The architecture of RMI/IIOP including Java to IDL mapping and the relevance of passing objects by value in RMI/IIOP.
- The definition of RMI interfaces for RMI/JRMP and RMI/IIOP.
- The implementation and compilation of RMI servers for RMI/JRMP and RMI/IIOP.
- The registration of server objects for client lookup for both RMI/JRMP and RMI/IIOP.
- The creation of RMI/JRMP and RMI/IIOP clients including their means for looking up RMI server references.
- The procedure for creating RMI objects that can be activated and brought into memory from disk upon client request.
- The basics behind customizing the underlying socket transport protocol used by RMI.

RMI Basics

The Remote Method Invocation platform is a Java-centric distributed object communications model in Java. By using the RMI packages and infrastructure, RMI-based Java clients can remotely invoke methods on RMI-based Java server objects. RMI is a purely distributed object communications model. Java object methods are invoked remotely versus any remote invocation of functional procedures as is the case with RMI's conceptual forerunner: Remote Procedure Calling (RPC). RMI clients transparently communicate with distributed servers by invoking methods on a client-side proxy object. The proxy serializes the method parameters passed to it and streams them to a distributed server representative. The distributed server representative then deserializes the parameters and passes them on to the appropriate distributed server object instance. Method return values go through a similar marshaling process.

RMI offers a rich set of features for the distributed enterprise communications programmer. RMI allows for client and server passing of objects as method parameters and return values either by value or by reference. If a class type used in a method parameter or return type is unknown to either the client or the server, it can be dynamically loaded using RMI codebases. Although server objects can be explicitly constructed and bound on the server side to a lookup service, server objects can also be automatically activated upon client request without any prior server-side object instantiation. RMI also provides a means for distributed garbage collection to clean up any distributed server objects that are no longer referenced by any distributed clients. In cases in which firewalls limit port connections, RMI can tunnel through firewalls via HTTP. RMI also now allows for the complete customization of the type of underlying socket connection made between clients and servers.

Conceptually, the RMI platform provides many of the same roles that a CORBA Orb and CORBA Naming Service provides. However, RMI also has the capability to pass Java objects by value and download new Java classes between clients and servers. Although the CORBA v2.3 standard has defined an Objects by Value specification for CORBA objects, it remains a rather complex and in some cases loosely defined specification. In fact, the drive to reconcile RMI and CORBA seems to have largely driven the CORBA Objects by Value specification to make CORBA interoperability possible via RMI/IIOP.

Nevertheless, transferring mobile Java objects via RMI between Java clients and Java servers is still and always will be considerably easier to implement than passing around objects by value in CORBA. RMI is also a much lighter-weight solution for Java applications. Of course, although CORBA still has language interoperability in its favor, this fact will become less important as more applications are built using Java. RMI and Java are Sun-owned platforms, whereas CORBA standard interfaces do allow for truly open distributed computing platform vendor implementations. Distributed services can be freely built atop RMI now, but use of Sun's new Jini distributed communications service technology built atop RMI is not "as free" for commercial use, as we'll see in Chapter 20, "Directory and Trading Services."

RMI Architecture

The core RMI infrastructure was first shipped with the JDK 1.1 platform and is embodied by the `java.rmi.*` packages (although a beta version was available for use with the JDK 1.0). The Java 2.0 platform incorporated the RMI v1.2 distributed computing platform. RMI v1.2 added support for dynamically activatable objects, customizable sockets, distributed garbage-collection improvements, and a host of API additions. RMI v1.2 also provides a set of standard Java abstractions for supporting RMI over IIOP in the `javax.rmi.*` packages. While RMI over IIOP is incorporated within the J2SE v1.3 platform, the J2SE v1.2 platform can only make use of RMI over IIOP as a separately installed standard extension.

The J2EE and RMI

As we'll see in Part VII, "Enterprise Applications Enabling," use of J2EE containers and Enterprise JavaBeans (EJB) does not require as much detailed knowledge about how to create RMI servers as this chapter describes. J2EE EJB developers simply must be aware of a few RMI interfaces and exceptions when creating EJB components. J2EE EJB containers and deployment tools take care of creating the necessary stubs, skeletons, and resource management logic. However, creating standalone RMI servers will still be warranted in other situations you encounter in the course of enterprise development. EJB developers also utilize RMI APIs when their EJBs must act as RMI clients.

The basic RMI architecture is depicted in Figure 16.1. RMI clients talk to an object implementing a Java interface that corresponds to those remote interfaces being exposed by a particular RMI server. The interface is actually implemented by an RMI stub that takes calls from the RMI client and marshals them into serialized packets of information that can be sent over the wire. Similarly, the stubs unmarshal serialized response information from the RMI servers into Java objects that can be utilized by the RMI client. On the server side, an RMI v1.1 server is called by a server-specific RMI skeleton. RMI v1.2 uses a more generic RMI server calling mechanism, and thus no server-specific skeleton is used to call the RMI server. Regardless, an RMI skeleton of some sort unmarshals requests from the client into Java objects passed as parameters to the server's methods and marshals responses from the server into the serialized form suitable for transmission over the wire.

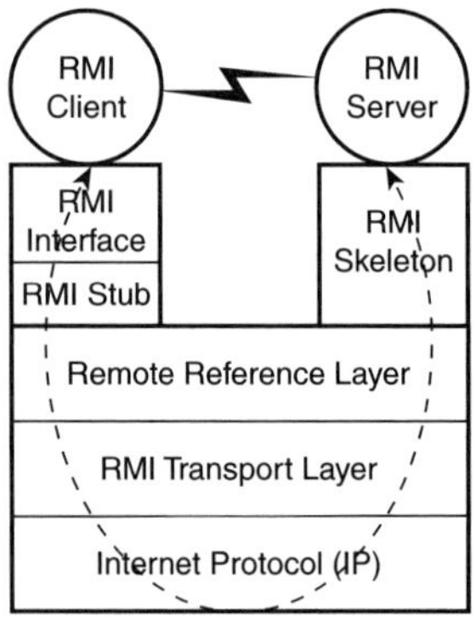

FIGURE 16.1
The RMI architecture.

The RMI remote reference layer takes serialized data from RMI stubs and handles the RMI-specific communications protocol built atop a transport protocol. Duties of the remote reference layer include resolving RMI server locations, initiating connections, and activating remote servers. RMI currently supports two general reference-layer messaging protocols. JRMP is the standard RMI communications messaging protocol that has been used by RMI since its inception. CORBA's IIOP messaging protocol is now also possible with the RMI/IIOP standard extension.

The RMI transport layer is responsible for connection management and for the provision of reliable data transfer between endpoints. The most widely used type of RMI transport layer is TCP. Both JRMP and IIOP operate over TCP. However, RMI v1.2 has introduced the capability for customizing which type of underlying transport protocol to use, with IP still being the networking protocol.

RMI Packages and Tools

The RMI logical architecture is partitioned into several packages. We will describe the classes, interfaces, and exceptions contained in these packages as we describe how to build actual RMI applications. These are the RMI packages:

- `java.rmi` is the core package for RMI containing the Remote interface, a few key classes, and many standard exceptions.
- `java.rmi.server` is the core package for server-side RMI interfaces, classes, and interfaces.
- `java.rmi.registry` provides an interface and a class for interfacing with the RMI lookup service.
- `java.rmi.activation` provides the interfaces and classes needed to implement server objects that can be activated upon client request.
- `java.rmi.dgc` provides an interface and classes for performing distributed garbage collection.
- `javax.rmi` currently contains a class for implementing portable RMI/IIOP objects.
- `javax.rmi.CORBA` contains all CORBA-specific classes and interfaces for implementing and using RMI/IIOP objects.

In addition to the API and SPI packages that come with RMI, a set of tools is used to implement RMI applications and provide an RMI runtime infrastructure. These are the tools:

- *RMI Compiler* (`rmic`): This command-line utility is used to generate stub and skeleton Java class files based on a compiled RMI server implementation. This tool comes equipped with RMI in the J2SE/J2EE. Previously, the version of this tool that permitted RMI/IIOP stub and skeleton generation was equipped with a separately distributed RMI/IIOP download, but it is now integrated with the J2SE/J2EE.

- *IDL-to-Java Compiler* (`idlj`): This tool is used to generate RMI/IIOP-suitable Java stubs and skeletons from an IDL definition.
- *RMI Registry* (`rmiregistry`): This command is used to start a process that allows one to register RMI server object references to names that can be looked up by distributed RMI clients. This tool comes equipped with RMI in the J2SE/J2EE.
- *RMI/IIOP Naming Service* (`tnameserv`): This command is used to start a process that allows one to register RMI/IIOP server object references to names that can be looked up by distributed CORBA clients. This tool is equipped with the J2SE/J2EE.
- *RMI Activation Daemon* (`rmid`): This command is used to start a process that allows one to register RMI server objects that can be activated (that is, started and brought into memory) upon client request. This tool comes equipped with RMI in the J2SE/J2EE.
- *HTTP Server*: RMI can use an HTTP server for dynamically downloading Java classes to clients or servers needing to load such classes into their environments. Although any HTTP server can be used, RMI requires only minimal HTTP `GET` functionality. The BEA Weblogic server on the CD provides Web-serving functionality, and you can also download a minimalist Web server from Sun as described later in this chapter.

RMI Infrastructure Configuration

Before an RMI server can make its services available to RMI clients, a runtime infrastructure must be configured and brought online. We describe the details behind configuration of such infrastructures later in this chapter, but be aware that you'll need to follow the following general steps:

- *Configure and start HTTP servers*: You must configure and start simple HTTP servers on hosts that will serve downloadable Java code. Code that may need downloading includes any code on one side of the distributed fence (client or server) that needs to be dynamically loaded by the other side of the fence.
- *Configure and start an RMI registry*: You must configure and start an RMI registry service to which active RMI server object references are bound and from which RMI clients can look up distributed object references.
- *Configure and start an RMI/IIOP naming service*: You must configure and start an RMI/IIOP naming service (CORBA Naming) to which RMI/IIOP server object references are bound and from which IIOP clients can look up distributed object references.
- *Configure and start RMI activation daemons*: You must configure and start an RMI activation daemon on hosts that will serve activatable Java code. This step is necessary only for those RMI servers that are activatable.

RMI Development Process

Developing an RMI-based client server application is a fairly straightforward process. Either you may already have an existing service for which you want to provide a distributed interface or you may be creating a distributed interface and a newly defined server process from scratch. Regardless, we can follow the same basic general steps for making an RMI application:

- *Define the remote interface*: You must first define a Java interface extending the `java.rmi.Remote` interface with all the methods defined that you want to make distributed.
- *Implement the RMI server*: You must then implement the remote interface and extend one of RMI's remote server object classes. Different remote server objects can be extended to provide either pre-activated, dormant but activatable, or RMI/IIOP server object behavior. You must then compile your RMI servers for use by the next step.
- *Generate the RMI skeletons and stubs*: By using the `rmic` tool, you can generate RMI server skeletons for your compiled RMI server classes. Generation of RMI skeletons is not necessary for RMI v1.2–based applications. The `rmic` tool also generates the appropriate RMI client stubs. RMI v1.2 stubs are created by passing in `-v1.2` as a parameter to `rmic`.
- *Implement an RMI server registrar*: You will then typically implement a separate class that either registers an RMI server with the RMI registry, registers an activatable RMI server with the RMI activation daemon, or registers an RMI/IIOP server with the RMI/IIOP naming service. Note that only initial references to certain "frontline" server objects need be registered with a registry or naming service from a server registrar. After any initial RMI server objects are looked up by RMI clients, other RMI server objects will most typically be instantiated and registered by the RMI servers that were initially or subsequently created.
- *Implement the RMI client*: An RMI client can now be created using the RMI stubs created in a previous step. An RMI client must first look up any initial references to an RMI server object using the RMI registry or RMI/IIOP naming service. The RMI stubs that correspond to these initial RMI server references and any stubs needed for subsequently referenced RMI servers are used transparently by the client, because they make calls only on an object that happens to implement the particular RMI server interface.

JRMP

RMI is one of the more important distributed object communications paradigms employed by enterprise Java architectures. RMI and CORBA are slowly reconciling as interoperable communications paradigms, but there was a time very recently when the only underlying communications messaging model available to RMI was the Java Remote Method Protocol (JRMP).

JRMP is a fairly simplistic Sun-proprietary wire transport protocol that operates over TCP/IP. JRMP was exclusively used by RMI in RMI v1.1 and is still used by RMI v1.2. However, RMI is now capable of operating over either JRMP or IIOP. Nevertheless, understanding a tiny bit of the internals of JRMP helps shed light on RMI for the enterprise developer desiring to understand RMI/JRMP's true enterprise-class communications limits and capabilities.

JRMP packets sent between communications endpoints contain a message header and one or more messages. The header format is simply

- Four bytes of ASCII characters: `JRMI`.
- The two-byte protocol version number.
- A single-byte subprotocol identifier.

Three subprotocol identifiers are defined to indicate the type of message data stream that follows the message header:

- `SingleOpProtocol`: Indicates that one message data packet follows.
- `StreamProtocol`: Indicates that one or more message data packets follow. The RMI client and RMI server both offer a server socket listener for incoming calls and a socket client endpoint for outgoing calls.
- `MultiplexStreamProtocol`: Indicates that one or more message data packets follow. The RMI client and RMI server multiplex incoming and outgoing messages over a single socket connection. This subprotocol is typically used when the RMI client is restricted from creating server socket listeners to handle incoming calls (for example, due to applet security restrictions).

To facilitate RMI's capability to tunnel through HTTP servers, JRMP allows for the prepending of an `HTTPPostHeader` identifier to sent messages and an `HTTPResponseHeader` identifier to received messages. Aside from these identifiers, six key message types are supported by JRMP. Three of the six JRMP message types pertain to messages that are output to an RMI protocol stream from the client's perspective:

- `Call CallData`: This form of message is used for remote method invocation calls. Call data has an object identifier used to indicate the target object of the call. An operation number is used in RMI v1.1 to identify the target operation to invoke. A hash number is used as a version identifier to verify that the stub and skeleton being used are compatible. Finally, zero or more argument values serialized according to the object serialization protocol are contained by the call data. To facilitate dynamic class loading, certain class information is embedded into the message streams.

- `Ping`: Tests to see whether a remote virtual machine is still alive.
- `DgcAck UniqueID`: This message is sent from a client to a server's distributed garbage collection to indicate that remote object references returned from a server were obtained.

The other three JRMP message types pertain to messages received by a client that are input from an RMI protocol stream:

- `ReturnData ReturnValue`: This form of message is used for returning results of remote method invocation calls. The return value has a return byte indicating whether the returned value is normal or the result of an exception. A unique ID is also sent to identify the return object used by the client when notifying the distributed garbage collector. Finally, an object serialization of the returned value or exception is sent in the return value. To facilitate dynamic class loading, certain class information is embedded into the message streams.
- `HttpReturn`: This message is sent as a result from an invocation in an HTTP call.
- `PingAck`: This message acknowledges a Ping message.

Multiplexing over a single socket connection using the `MultiplexStreamProtocol` subprotocol requires some extra JRMP logic. Five multiplexing operations are defined to accomplish multiplexing. `OPEN`, `CLOSE`, and `CLOSEACK` operations handle connection opening, closing, and close acknowledgement, respectively. `REQUEST` and `TRANSMIT` operations are used to signal when messages are being exchanged. Furthermore, because up to 65,536 virtual connections can be opened over a single concrete connection, a four-byte identifier accompanies each multiplexing operation to identify the virtual connection on which it operates. One side of the RMI client/server session can host 32,768 virtual server socket connections with identifiers in the range of 0x0000 to 0x7FFF, and the other side can host 32,768 virtual server socket connections with identifiers in the range of 0x8000 to 0xFFFF.

RMI and IIOP

RMI/IIOP is a standard Java extension incorporated as part of the J2SE and J2EE and developed jointly by both Sun and IBM. As described in Chapter 14, "Modeling Components with CORBA," and Chapter 15, "CORBA Communications," CORBA represents the most significant advancement our industry has seen for enabling the development of a standard communications framework in building enterprise software systems. With CORBA's IIOP as the standard transport wire protocol for distributed object communications, RMI's capability to communicate over IIOP enables RMI applications to interoperate with CORBA-based systems. JRMP, on the other hand, was a nonstandard protocol and could not enable communication with cross-language CORBA objects. Although RMI/IIOP still depends on some JRMP features, RMI/IIOP now provides Java RMI-based communications interoperability with objects implemented in other languages. Java programmers can still make use of the simplicity of building RMI applications and then generate IDL using the new Java-to-IDL compiler also provided with RMI/IIOP.

RMI/IIOP Versus Java IDL

Because Java IDL and RMI/IIOP both may be utilized with the J2SE/J2EE, you may be wondering what packages to use for CORBA-enabling your Java applications. The main way to think of Java IDL is to use it as a way for your Java programs to communicate with any CORBA-compliant clients and servers. Java IDL and traditional CORBA programming will mainly be useful when you're creating Java-based CORBA clients using a predefined IDL interface or creating Java-based CORBA servers that must map to a predefined CORBA service. RMI/IIOP can be used when you want to capitalize on the relative programming simplicity of RMI to create Java-based RMI servers wanting to expose their services to CORBA clients under some minimal programming constraints. In summary, think of Java IDL when you have IDL that needs to map to distributed clients and servers (that is, from interface to code), and think of RMI/IIOP when you have Java RMI servers that need to be exposed in terms of IDL interfaces (that is, from code to interface). Also be aware of the fact that when RMI/IIOP is installed as a standard extension to the J2SE v1.2 platform, it will extend your Java IDL Orb libraries to work with RMI/IIOP.

Java-to-IDL Mapping

Alongside RMI's capability to operate over IIOP, the RMI compiler can now map RMI directly into well-formed IDL. By providing a Java RMI-to-IDL mapping, Java developers can create RMI applications as usual and then automatically generate IDL and CORBA stubs and skeletons from Java code. To accomplish this task, some compromises have been made. The Java-to-IDL mapping allows for method overloading and for most of the Java naming conventions to be preserved in the mapping (aside from case), but not all IDL entities are supported. For example, IDL structs, unions, and inout parameters are never generated from the Java-to-IDL mapping. Furthermore, the mapping from Java to IDL does not inversely map from IDL to Java. Such compromises were made in order to make RMI/IIOP a possibility.

The various Java RMI-to-OMG IDL mappings are detailed in the CORBA v2.3 specification's Java language-to-IDL mapping (accessible from the `http://www.omg.org` Web site under `ptc/99-03-09`). A summary of some of the more common Java-to-IDL mappings is presented in Table 16.1.

TABLE 16.1 Java RMI-to-OMG IDL Mappings

Java RMI Entity	*OMG IDL Mapping*
Special Cases	
`java.lang.Object`	`::java::lang::_Object`
`java.lang.String`	`::CORBA::WStringValue`
`java.lang.Class`	`::javax::rmi::CORBA::ClassDesc`
`java.io.Serializable`	`::java::io::Serializable`
`java.io.Externalizable`	`::java::io::Externalizable`
`java.rmi.Remote`	`::java::rmi::Remote`
`org.omg.CORBA.Object`	`Object`
Primitive Types	
`void`	`void`
`sboolean`	`boolean`
`char`	`wchar`
`byte`	`octet`
`short`	`short`
`int`	`long`
`long`	`long long`
`float`	`float`
`double`	`double`
Java Names	
Java packages, such as `x.y.z`	IDL modules, such as `::x::y::z`
Java names colliding with IDL keywords, such as `oneway`	Underscore added to name, such as `_oneway`
Java names having leading underscores, such as `_MyClass`	`J` added before name, such as `J_MyClass`
Java inner class names, such as `Bar` inside `Foo`	*`OuterClass_InnerClass`*, such as `Foo_Bar`
Overloaded Java methods, such as `foo()` and `foo (x.y.z param)`	Method name followed by __ and fully qualified parameter types also separated by __, such as `foo__()` and `foo__x_y_z()`
Method names colliding with variable names	Variable names get trailing underscores

continues

Java RMI Entity	*OMG IDL Mapping*
RMI/IDL Interface	
Methods with setXXX() and getXXX() or isXXX()	IDL read/write attribute named XXX with lowercase first letter and of type in setXXX()
Methods with getXXX() and no setXXX()	IDL read attribute named XXX with lowercase first letter and of type returned by getXXX()
Method parameters	IDL method in parameters
java.rmi.RMIException and subclasses	CORBA system exceptions
Other exceptions	IDL exceptions named appropriately
RMI/IDL Arrays	
Arrays of primitive types, such as boolean[]	Placed in boxedRMI module with valuetype of primitive sequence type named seq<arraySize>_<primitiveType>, such as ::org::omg::boxedRMI module with valuetype seq1_boolean sequence<boolean>
Arrays of Java objects in package, such as x.y.Z[]	Placed in boxedRMI ::x::y module with valuetype of primitive sequence type named seq<arraySize>_<primitiveType>, such as ::org::omg::boxedRMI::x::y module with valuetype seq1_Z sequence<x::y::Z>
RMI/IDL Exceptions	
Exception subclasses	Mapped to valuetypes with subclassed exceptions
Exception names in throws clauses with or without Exception on the end, such as java.io.IOException	IDL raise clauses use any Exception name removed add Ex to the end of the name, such as ::java::io::IOEx

Objects by Value and RMI

Chapter 14 describes the CORBA Objects by Value specification for providing a standardized mechanism to pass CORBA objects around by value. Although the CORBA Objects by Value specification is language independent, types passed by value between clients and servers implemented in different languages need re-implementation in those other languages. Java

RMI's capability to dynamically download code between Java clients and Java servers is unaffected by this fact. However, the Objects by Value specification in the CORBA v2.3 specification is somewhat overly complicated and still not completely defined in some respects. Irrespective of this fact, it is important to understand why RMI/IIOP depends on Objects by Value.

Java RMI allows for serializable objects to be passed as parameters to remote methods and returned from remote methods. Furthermore, Java RMI also allows for automatic downloading of Java classes between RMI clients and servers. To create RMI/IIOP, IIOP and CORBA were extended to incorporate the capability to support these features that were available in RMI applications but were not yet available for pure CORBA applications. The Objects by Value specification in CORBA has thus helped make RMI/IIOP a reality. Thus, regardless of whether Orb vendors can easily support Objects by Value in the general sense, the specification still plays an important albeit impractical role for reconciling the RMI and CORBA worlds. Hopefully, future versions of the CORBA standards will simplify the Objects by Value and Java-to-IDL specifications.

RMI Interfaces

With much of the conceptual framework for RMI out of the way, let's focus on building an actual RMI application now. Throughout the next few sections, we will create both an RMI/JRMP and an RMI/IIOP application side-by-side, not only to illustrate how RMI applications are built, but also to enable you to compare and contrast RMI/JRMP versus RMI/IIOP firsthand. Both examples are created with an RMI server registrar binding active objects for remote RMI clients to look up.

The first step in creating any RMI application (RMI/JRMP or RMI/IIOP) is to define an RMI interface. Figure 16.2 provides an overview of all RMI and application-specific entities that are involved with defining an RMI interface. We will use diagrams such as these throughout the chapter to visually summarize all the rules involved with creating RMI applications. That is, by visually examining the relations and classes in the diagram, you should be able to quickly see all the rules involved with implementing a development step to which the diagram corresponds.

Figure 16.2 summarizes the rules for defining your application-specific interface named `MyRemoteInterface`. The first thing to note is that `MyRemoteInterface` must extend the `java.rmi.Remote` interface. You can think of the `Remote` interface as a marker interface for referring to objects by reference analogous to the `Serializable` interface being a market interface for referring to objects by value.

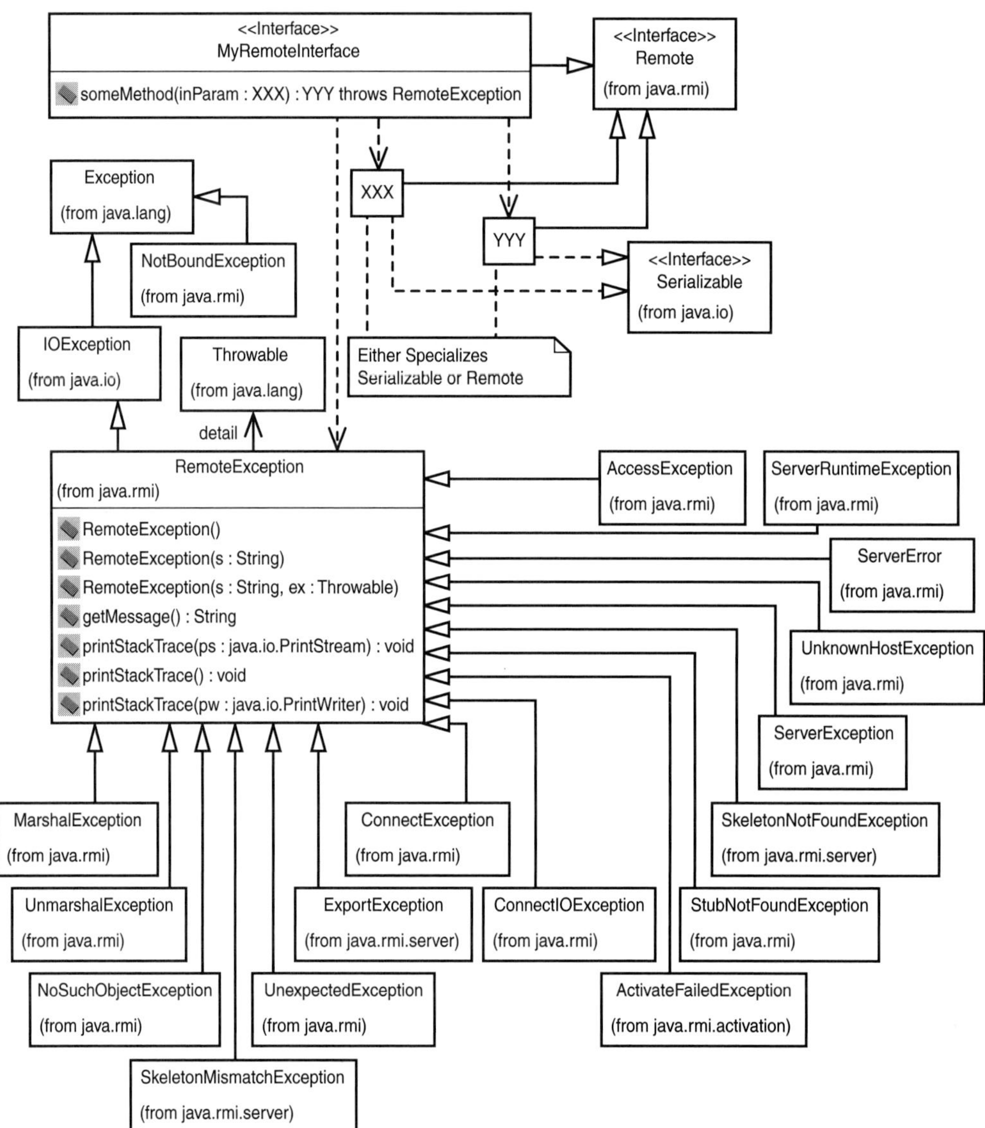

FIGURE 16.2
RMI interfaces.

Methods you want to distribute should be defined on your RMI interface. For example, the `someMethod()` on `MyRemoteInterface` is a remote method. Remote methods like `someMethod()` can take one or more input parameters like `XXX` and return an output parameter like YYY. XXX and YYY must be either serializable or remote objects. Furthermore, all remote methods must also throw the `java.rmi.RemoteException`. `RemoteException` can be constructed with a nested detail exception and is the base class for just about every other RMI-related exception.

RMI Interface Definition Examples

Three RMI interfaces are defined to illustrate how to build an RMI-based application. These interfaces are the `ClientReceiver`, `Customer`, and `QueryServer` interfaces. The same interfaces are used for both the RMI/JRMP and the RMI/IIOP examples developed throughout this chapter.

NOTE

Both RMI/JRMP and RMI/IIOP interfaces are contained on the CD in the `examples\src\ejava\rmich16` directory. All RMI/JRMP implementation classes are contained on the CD under the `examples\src\ejava\rmich16\queryservicejrmp` directory. All RMI/IIOP implementation classes are contained on the CD under the `examples\src\ejava\rmich16\queryserviceiiop` directory. Most RMI applications are created with the interface and implementations in the same package. We separate them into different packages here only for ease of explaining both the RMI/JRMP and the RMI/IIOP examples.

The `ejava.rmich16.ClientReceiver` interface for both RMI/JRMP and RMI/IIOP is used by an RMI server to make RMI callbacks on the RMI clients. It has one simple method, `setResultOrders()`, to obtain a vector of BeeShirts.com client orders. The `ClientReceiver` interface is defined in Listing 16.1.

LISTING 16.1 The RMI Interface for RMI Client Callbacks from an RMI Server (`ClientReceiver.java`)

```
package ejava.rmich16;

import java.rmi.Remote;
import java.rmi.RemoteException;
import java.util.Vector;

public interface ClientReceiver extends Remote
{
  void setResultOrders(Vector orders) throws RemoteException;
}
```

The `ejava.rmich16.Customer` interface for both RMI/JRMP and RMI/IIOP is returned by an RMI server to conceptualize a distributed handle to a BeeShirts.com `Customer` object. It has a series of getter methods to obtain BeeShirts.com customer information. The `Customer` interface is defined in Listing 16.2.

LISTING 16.2 RMI Interface BeeShirts.com Customer Information (`Customer.java`)

```
package ejava.rmich16;

import java.rmi.Remote;
import java.rmi.RemoteException;

public interface Customer  extends Remote
{
  public String getFirstName() throws RemoteException;
  public String getLastName() throws RemoteException;
  public String getAddress1() throws RemoteException;
  public String getAddress2() throws RemoteException;
  public String getCity() throws RemoteException;
  public String getState() throws RemoteException;
  public String getZip() throws RemoteException;
  public String getPhoneNumber() throws RemoteException;
  public String getEmailAddress() throws RemoteException;
}
```

The `ejava.rmich16.QueryServer` interface for both the RMI/JRMP and the RMI/IIOP examples is the main frontline interface for RMI clients to communicate with a back-end RMI server application. The `QueryServer` offers a very specific set of interfaces to illustrate some of the concepts revolving around RMI discussed thus far. The method `findCustomersWhoOrderedForMoreThan()` finds customers who spend more than a certain amount of money, binds them to a lookup service, and returns a `Vector` of customer IDs. A method `register()` takes a `ClientReceiver` callback interface and client receiver name to register RMI client callbacks. A method `findOrdersWhichAreFrom()` finds the orders for a given state and passes the set of associated orders to the registered `ClientReceiver` objects. The `QueryServer` interface is defined in Listing 16.3.

LISTING 16.3 The RMI Interface Querying the RMI Server Application (`QueryServer.java`)

```
package ejava.rmich16;

import java.rmi.Remote;
import java.rmi.RemoteException;
```

```
import java.util.Vector;

public interface QueryServer extends Remote
{
  Vector findCustomersWhoOrderedForMoreThan(float value)
    throws RemoteException;
  void findOrdersWhichAreFrom(String state)
    throws RemoteException;
  void register(String name, ClientReceiver clientReceiver)
    throws RemoteException;
}
```

RMI Servers and Skeletons

With an interface properly defined, you can now create an RMI server. It is entirely possible and a common situation to already have some code you would like to turn into a distributed object. In such a case, you might create an RMI server that delegates calls to the existing code and then define those methods that should be distributed in the form of an RMI interface. Regardless of the ordering of your steps, you need to create an RMI server that implements an RMI interface. We demonstrate how to create an RMI server in this section for both regular RMI/JRMP and RMI/IIOP servers.

RMI/JRMP Servers

We are now in a position to discuss more details behind what is involved with building an RMI/JRMP server. After a description of what APIs RMI/JRMP server implementations utilize, we will demonstrate via example the construction of an actual server. We will then follow up that discussion with a description of how to compile such servers.

Creating the RMI/JRMP Servers

Figure 16.3 depicts some of the key classes, interfaces, and exceptions involved in building an RMI/JRMP server. The key class to focus on in this diagram is the `MyRemoteImpl` class. `MyRemoteImpl` corresponds to your application-specific RMI server. Your RMI server must implement the RMI interface such as the `MyRemoteInterface` shown in the diagram and defined in the preceding section. It must also throw the appropriate exceptions as defined by the implemented interface. As you'll see, the RMI skeletons actually create and throw `RemoteExceptions`. Any application-specific exceptions defined for the interface of course must be thrown by the application-specific server implementation. Beyond these rules, you should also ensure that your RMI server is thread-safe.

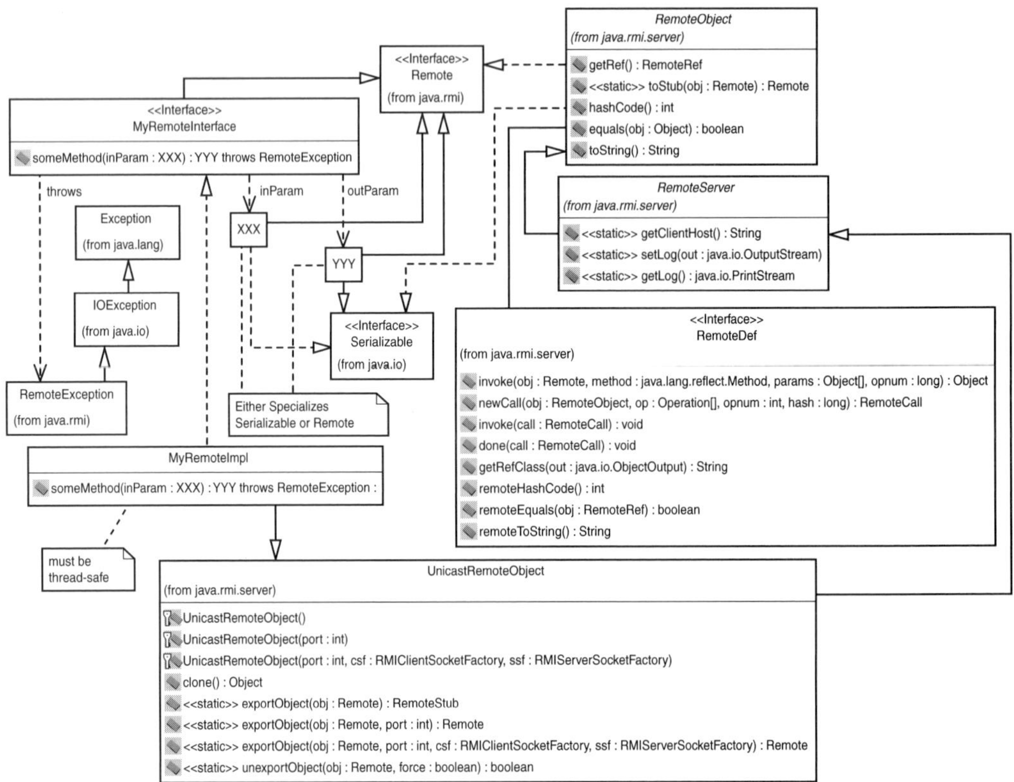

FIGURE 16.3
RMI/JRMP servers.

In addition to the implementation of the particular `MyRemoteInterface`, `MyRemoteImpl` needs to extend the `java.rmi.server.UnicastRemoteObject` class. The RMI/IIOP and activatable servers created later in this section and chapter extend different types of remote objects, but the `UnicastRemoteObject` class is used for RMI servers that must be pre-activated by a server process. The `UnicastRemoteObject` supports remote references of servers by clients in a point-to-point access fashion. The `UnicastRemoteObject` class itself extends from the `java.rmi.server.RemoteServer`, which in turn extends the `java.rmi.server.RemoteObject` class. RMI/JRMP servers may also export themselves as remote servers using one of the static `exportObject()` calls on the `UnicastRemoteObject` class and avoid subclassing from `UnicastRemoteObject`.

The `RemoteObject` class implements both the `Remote` and the `Serializable` interfaces and overrides most of the `java.lang.Object` methods for the purpose of making regular Java `Objects` capable of remote distribution. For example, `hashCode()`, `equals()`, and `toString()`

are all overloaded. Additionally, `RemoteObject` returns a remote reference to the remote object with `getRef()`. The `java.rmi.server.RemoteRef` object returned by `getRef()` represents a direct handle on the remote object. The `RemoteRef` object contains many method calls that are deprecated in RMI v1.2 for manipulating RMI skeletons and calls directly. The `RemoteServer` class extends `RemoteObject` to provide a few server-side remote-object–specific calls such as obtaining the RMI client hostname, as well as getting and setting server-side logging streams.

RMI/JRMP Server Implementation Examples

Listings 16.4 through 16.6 show the implementations for our `Customer`, `ClientReceiver`, and `QueryServer` RMI servers, respectively.

> **NOTE**
>
> The complete set of code examples for RMI/JRMP can be found on the CD-ROM in the `examples\src\ejava\rmich16\queryservicejrmp` directory with some commonly used files under `examples\src\ejava\rmich16`. The `rmi.policy` and `RMICH16Properties.txt` file placed beneath the `examples\src\ejava\rmich16` directory contain both RMI security policy information and general application configuration information, respectively. An example `run.bat` Windows script file in the `examples\src\ejava\rmich16\queryservicejrmp` directory can be used to build and execute the example server and client. Note that the Cloudscape database must be running and configured in your `RMICH16Properties.txt` file per instructions in Appendix A.

You can ignore the `bind()` method implemented by the `CustomerImplementation` class defined in Listing 16.4 for now. But note that all getters and setters as defined in Listing 16.1 have been implemented by this class for a distributable `Customer` object instance.

LISTING 16.4 The RMI Customer Implementation (`CustomerImplementation.java`)

```
package ejava.rmich16.queryservicejrmp;
import java.rmi.server.UnicastRemoteObject;
import java.rmi.Naming;
import java.rmi.RemoteException;
import ejava.rmich16.*;
public class CustomerImplementation extends UnicastRemoteObject
  implements Customer {
  private String firstName;
  private String lastName;
  private String address1;
```

continues

LISTING 16.4 Continued

```
private String address2;
private String city;
private String state;
private String zip;
private String phoneNumber;
private String emailAddress;

public CustomerImplementation() throws RemoteException
{
  super();
}
public void bind(String customerID)
{
  try {
    Naming.rebind(customerID, this);
  } catch (Exception e) {
    System.out.println("Error in binding the customer :" + e
                       + "customerID :" + customerID);
  }
}


public String getFirstName() throws RemoteException
{
  return firstName;
}

public String getLastName() throws RemoteException
{
  return lastName;
}

public String getAddress1() throws RemoteException
{
  return address1;
}

public String getAddress2() throws RemoteException
{
  return address2;
}
```

```
public String getState() throws RemoteException
{
  return state;
}

public String getPhoneNumber() throws RemoteException
{
  return phoneNumber;
}

public String getEmailAddress() throws RemoteException
{
  return emailAddress;
}

public String getZip() throws RemoteException
{
  return zip;
}

public void setZip(String newZip)
{
  zip = newZip;
}

public String getCity() throws RemoteException
{
  return city;
}

public void setCity(String newCity)
{
  city = newCity;
}

public void setFirstName(String newFirstName)
{
  firstName = newFirstName;
}


public void setLastName(String newLastName)
{
  lastName = newLastName;
}
```

continues

LISTING 16.4 Continued

```
  public void setAddress1(String newAddress1)
 {
    address1 = newAddress1;
  }

  public void setAddress2(String newAddress2)
 {
    address2 = newAddress2;
  }

  public void setState(String newState)
 {
    state = newState;
  }

  public void setPhoneNumber(String newPhoneNumber)
  {
    phoneNumber = newPhoneNumber;
  }

  public void setEmailAddress(String newEmailAddress)
  {
    emailAddress = newEmailAddress;
  }

}
```

The `ClientReceiverImplementation` class implements the one remote method declared in Listing 16.1. The `setResultOrders()` method simply prints the list of orders received.

LISTING 16.5 The RMI Client Receiver Implementation (`ClientReceiverImplementation.java`)

```
package ejava.rmich16.queryservicejrmp;
import java.rmi.server.UnicastRemoteObject;
import java.rmi.RemoteException;
import java.util.Vector;
import ejava.rmich16.*;

public class ClientReceiverImplementation extends UnicastRemoteObject
  implements ClientReceiver
```

```
{
  public ClientReceiverImplementation()
    throws RemoteException
  {
    super();
  }

  public void setResultOrders(Vector orders)
    throws RemoteException
  {
    if(orders != null){
      System.out.println("Number of Received Orders :"+orders.size());
      for(int i=0; i<orders.size(); i++){
        System.out.println(" Values for Order :" +i);
        System.out.println((Order)orders.elementAt(i));
      }
    }
    else{
      System.out.println("Received Orders : null Results ");
    }
  }
}
```

The `QueryServerImplementation` of Listing 16.6 implements the `QueryServer` interface declared in Listing 16.3. The `QueryServer` represents the frontline interface for RMI clients and contains most of the business logic for our example. The `QueryServerImplementation` constructor requires that a `Properties` object be supplied with properties for a database driver class, URL, username, and password. This information is used to establish a connection with the BeeShirts.com database via JDBC. The `getResultSet()` method takes a SQL query for creating a prepared statement and subsequently for returning a result set. The `findCustomersWhoOrderedForMoreThan()` method retrieves the customer query from the `Properties` object and issues the query using `getResultSet()`. The results of this query are then used to create a new distributed `Customer` object reference. We will discuss how this reference is made available to the RMI client shortly. The `register()` method is used to register a `ClientReceiver` with `QueryServer`. The `findOrdersWhichAreFrom()` method retrieves an order query from the `Properties` object and then issues this query for obtaining a set of related orders. These orders are used to create a serializable `Orders` object and then for making a callback on the distributed RMI client `ClientReceiver` references that were registered using the `register()` method. The `Order` object, shown in Listing 16.7, simply defines a set of getters and setters.

LISTING 16.6 The RMI Query Server Implementation (`QueryServerImplementation.java`)

```
package ejava.rmich16.queryservicejrmp;
import ejava.rmich16.*;
import java.util.Vector;
import java.util.Properties;
import java.rmi.RemoteException;
import java.rmi.server.UnicastRemoteObject;
import java.rmi.Remote;
import java.rmi.Naming;
import java.rmi.RMISecurityManager;
import java.sql.Connection;
import java.sql.SQLException;
import java.lang.ClassCastException;
import java.sql.Statement;
import java.sql.PreparedStatement;
import java.sql.ResultSet;
import java.sql.ResultSetMetaData;
import java.sql.DriverManager;
import java.sql.Date;
import java.io.FileInputStream;
import java.io.IOException;


public class QueryServerImplementation extends UnicastRemoteObject
  implements QueryServer
{
  ClientReceiver clientReceiver;
  String clientReceiverName;
  Connection connection;
  Properties properties;

  public QueryServerImplementation(Properties properties)
    throws RemoteException
  {
    super();
    // Establish DBMS info from properties file info
    String dbDriverClassName =
      (String)properties.get("DRIVER_CLASS");
    String dbURL = (String)properties.get("DATABASE_URL");
    String userName = (String)properties.get("UserName");
    String password = (String)properties.get("Password");
    this.properties = properties;
    // Get Connection based on properties info
    try{
```

```
      Class.forName(dbDriverClassName);
      if(userName == null || password == null
        || userName.length() == 0 || password.length() == 0 ){
        connection = DriverManager.getConnection(dbURL);
      }
      else{
        connection = DriverManager.getConnection(dbURL,
          userName,password);
      }
    }
    catch(ClassNotFoundException cnfEx){
      System.out.println("Driver Class Not found "+cnfEx);
    }
    catch(SQLException sqlEx){
      System.out.println("SQL Exception :" +sqlEx);
    }
  }

private ResultSet getResultSet(String sqlQuery,
    java.lang.Object whereValue) throws SQLException
  {
    PreparedStatement preparedStatement =
      connection.prepareStatement(sqlQuery);
    preparedStatement.setObject(1, whereValue);
    ResultSet rs = preparedStatement.executeQuery();
    return rs;
  }

  public Vector findCustomersWhoOrderedForMoreThan(float value)
    throws RemoteException
  {
    // Get customer query
    String customerQueryString =
      (String)properties.get("CUSTOMER_QUERY");
    if(customerQueryString == null){
       throw new RemoteException("CUSTOMER_QUERY in  file is null");
    }
    // Issue query and create/bind Customer server for each result
    //  ...also return Vector of customer IDs
    try{
      ResultSet rs = this.getResultSet(customerQueryString,
        new Float(value));
      ResultSetMetaData rsMetaData = rs.getMetaData();
      int nColumns = rsMetaData.getColumnCount();
```

continues

LISTING 16.6 Continued

```
      Vector customerIDs = new Vector();
      while(rs.next()){
        String customerID = rs.getString("CUSTOMER_ID");
        String firstName  = rs.getString("FIRST_NAME");
        String lastName   = rs.getString("LAST_NAME");
        String address1   = rs.getString("ADDRESS_1");
        String address2   = rs.getString("ADDRESS_2");
        String city       = rs.getString("CITY");
        String state      = rs.getString("STATE");
        String phoneNumber= rs.getString("PHONE");
        String eMail      = rs.getString("EMAIL");
        String zip        = rs.getString("ZIP_CODE");
        CustomerImplementation custImpl = new CustomerImplementation();
        custImpl.setFirstName(firstName);
        custImpl.setLastName(lastName);
        custImpl.setAddress1(address1);
        custImpl.setAddress2(address2);
        custImpl.setCity(city);
        custImpl.setState(state);
        custImpl.setZip(zip);
        custImpl.setEmailAddress(eMail);
        custImpl.setPhoneNumber(phoneNumber);
        String registryURL =
            (String)properties.get("REGISTRY_SERVER_URL");
        String name = registryURL+customerID;
        custImpl.bind(name);
        customerIDs.addElement(customerID);
      }
      return customerIDs;
    }
    catch(SQLException sqlEx){
      throw new RemoteException("failed to getCustomers",sqlEx);
    }
  }

  public void register(String name, ClientReceiver clientReceiver)
    throws RemoteException
  {
     this.clientReceiver = clientReceiver;
     this.clientReceiverName = name;
  }

  public  void findOrdersWhichAreFrom(String state)
```

```
    throws RemoteException
  {
    // Get orders query
    String orderQueryString =
      (String)properties.get("ORDER_QUERY");
    if(orderQueryString == null){
       throw new RemoteException("ORDER_QUERY in  file is null");
    }
    // Issue orders query and callback client with each Order object
    try{
      ResultSet rs = this.getResultSet(orderQueryString,state);
      ResultSetMetaData rsMetaData = rs.getMetaData();
      int nColumns = rsMetaData.getColumnCount();
      Vector orders = new Vector();
      while(rs.next()){
        int orderID = rs.getInt("ORDER_ID");
        Date   orderDate  = rs.getDate("ORDER_DATE");
        double orderValue   = rs.getDouble("TOTAL_PRICE");
        Order order = new Order(orderID,orderDate,orderValue);
        orders.addElement(order);
      }
      if(this.clientReceiver != null){
        clientReceiver.setResultOrders(orders);
      }
    }
    catch(SQLException sqlEx){
      throw new RemoteException("failed to getCustomers",sqlEx);
    }
  }

  public static void main(String[] args)
  {
    if(args.length == 0){
      System.out.println("You should provide properties file :"+
        "java ejava.rmich16.queryservicejrmp.QueryServerImplementation
➥ RMICH16Properties.txt");
      System.exit(0);
    }
    String propertiesFileName = args[0];

    try{
      // Load properties from file
      Properties properties = new Properties();
      FileInputStream fin = new FileInputStream(propertiesFileName);
```

continues

LISTING 16.6 Continued

```
      properties.load(fin);
      // Get Query server name and create query server impl
      String name = (String)properties.get("QUERY_SERVER_NAME");
      QueryServerImplementation queryServerImpl =
        new QueryServerImplementation(properties);
      // Set security manager
      System.setSecurityManager(new RMISecurityManager());
      System.out.println("Set system properties :");
      // Get registry URL and bind query server to registry
      String registryURL =
        (String)properties.get("REGISTRY_SERVER_URL");
      System.out.println("Binding :");
      Naming.rebind(registryURL+name, queryServerImpl);
      System.out.println("Bound:");
    }
    catch(IOException ioe){
      System.out.println("Error in Reading properties File :"+ioe);
    }
  }
}
```

LISTING 16.7 The Serializable Order Class (`Order.java`)

```
package ejava.rmich16;

import java.io.Serializable;
import java.sql.Date;

public class Order implements Serializable {
  private int orderID;
  private Date orderDate;
  private double orderValue;

  public Order() {
    super();
  }
  public Order(int orderID, Date orderDate, double orderValue) {
    this.orderID = orderID;
    this.orderDate = orderDate;
    this.orderValue = orderValue;
  }
  public void setOrderID(int orderID) {
    this.orderID = orderID;
```

```
  }
  public void setOrderDate(Date orderDate) {
    this.orderDate = orderDate;
  }
  public void setOrderValue(double orderValue) {
    this.orderValue = orderValue;
  }
  public int getOrderID() {
    return this.orderID;
  }
  public Date getOrderDate() {
    return this.orderDate;
  }
  public double getOrderValue() {
    return this.orderValue;
  }
  public String toString() {
    return "OrderID :" + orderID + " order Date :" + orderDate
           + "orderValue :" + orderValue;
  }
}
```

Compiling the RMI/JRMP Servers

After you have your RMI servers implemented, you must first compile the Java source files into Java class files. The `rmic` compiler is then used to generate the application-specific RMI stubs and skeletons. The `rmic` compiler takes one or more compiled RMI server class files and generates an associated set of stubs and possibly skeletons for those RMI servers; it can take a `-d <directory>` option indicating which directory to output generated stubs and skeletons to. If you're using the RMI v1.1 `rmic` compiler, stubs and skeletons will automatically be generated. The RMI v1.2 `rmic` compiler will also generate stubs and skeletons accessible from RMI `UnicastRemoteObject`-based v1.1 clients and all RMI v1.2 clients. When you use the `-v1.2` option, `rmic` will generate stubs for use with RMI v1.2 clients. Because application-specific skeletons are not necessary with RMI v1.2, none will be generated when the `-v1.2` option is used. Stubs and skeletons are generated with the same package as your RMI server. A server implementation named `MyRemoteImpl` generates stubs with the name `MyRemoteImpl_Stub` and skeletons with the name `MyRemoteImpl_Skel`.

The `run.bat` file in the `examples\src\ejava\rmich16\queryservicejrmp` directory compiles stubs and skeletons for all three RMI server class files into the same directory using this:

```
rmic -d . ejava.rmich16.queryservicejrmp.QueryServerImplementation
rmic -d . ejava.rmich16.queryservicejrmp.CustomerImplementation
rmic -d . ejava.rmich16.queryservicejrmp.ClientReceiverImplementation
```

RMI/IIOP Servers

RMI/IIOP servers are created in a fashion that is very similar to the creation of RMI/JRMP servers. After a description of the APIs that RMI/IIOP server implementations utilize, we will demonstrate via example the construction and compilation of an actual RMI/IIOP server.

Creating the RMI/IIOP Servers

Figure 16.4 depicts the key relations and entities involved in defining an RMI/IIOP server. As can be seen, the only difference between declaring an RMI/IIOP server and declaring an RMI/JRMP server is that you extend the `javax.rmi.PortableRemoteObject` class instead of the `UnicastRemoteObject` class. Thus, the `MyRemoteImpl` for RMI/IIOP can have the same method signatures (including exception throwing) and the same method implementations. RMI/IIOP servers can also export themselves as a remote server object using the `exportObject()` method on `PortableRemoteObject` instead of subclassing `PortableRemoteObject`. In fact, using such a method can make your servers more portable between RMI/JRMP and RMI/IIOP applications.

Other `PortableRemoteObject` methods also assist with the management of RMI/IIOP objects. An `unexportObject()` method is useful for making registered objects available for distributed garbage collection. The method `connect()` can be used to explicitly connect currently unconnected objects to the Orb given an object that has already been connected to the Orb. The `narrow()` method can be used to convert a general RMI/IIOP reference into a specific `java.lang.Class` type to be returned from `narrow()`. If no exceptions are thrown, the returned object can be converted into the desired type. Finally, `toStub()` returns an RMI/IIOP stub that can be used by RMI clients to talk with the RMI server. Under the hood, the `PortableRemoteObject` actually delegates calls to an object that implements the `javax.rmi.CORBA.PortableRemoteObjectDelegate` interface.

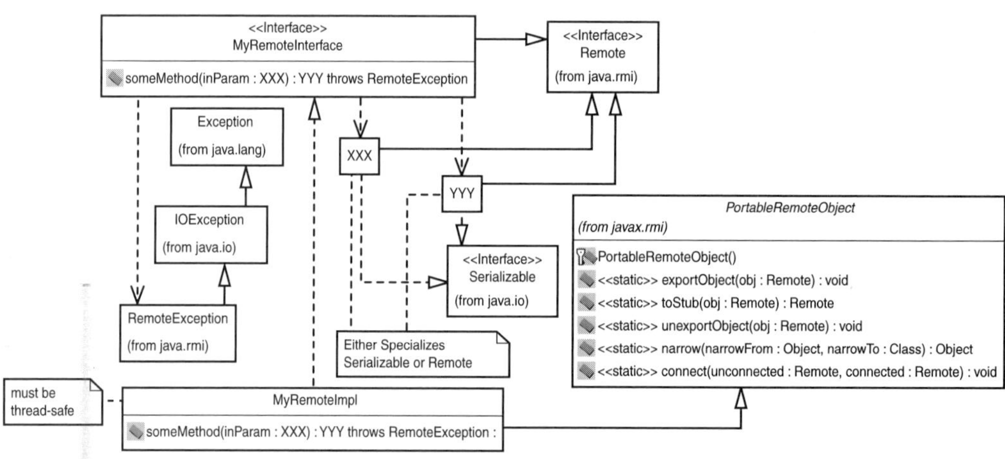

FIGURE 16.4
RMI/IIOP servers.

RMI/IIOP Server Implementation Examples

The RMI/IIOP server implementations for `ClientReceiver`, `Customer`, and `QueryServer` are nearly identical to the RMI/JRMP implementations. In what follows, we present only those aspects of the RMI/IIOP that differ from the RMI/JRMP servers presented in Listings 16.4 through 16.6. The complete source-code listings for the RMI/IIOP class server implementations can be found on the CD.

NOTE

The complete set of code examples for RMI/IIOP can be found on the CD-ROM in the `examples\src\ejava\rmich16\queryserviceiiop` directory with some commonly used files under `examples\src\ejava\rmich16`. The `rmi.policy` and `RMICH16Properties.txt` file placed beneath the `examples\src\ejava\rmich16` directory contain both RMI security policy information and general application configuration information, respectively. An example `run.bat` Windows script file in the `examples\src\ejava\rmich16\queryserviceiiop` directory can be used to build and execute the example server and client. Note that the Cloudscape database must be running and configured in your `RMICH16Properties.txt` file per instructions in Appendix A.

You must also download and install the RMI/IIOP standard extension for use with the J2SE v1.2 platform. The RMI/IIOP download package and instructions can be found at `http://java.sun.com/products/rmi-iiop/index.html`. You also must set a `RMI_IIOP_HOME` environment variable to the root directory for your RMI/IIOP installation when running any examples. Note that it is very important to make sure the `orb.properties` file generated during this installation is copied properly to your `[JAVA_HOME]\jre\lib` directory. The installation program may attempt to copy this file to another directory that it perceives as the JRE library directory, so step through the installation process carefully. The RMI/IIOP IDL-to-Java compiler can be downloaded from `http://developer.java.sun.com/developer/earlyAccess/idlc/index.html`. A single `idlc1_0_1ea.zip` file is downloaded that contains a single `idlj.jar` file that must be copied into the `[RMI_IIOP_HOME]\lib` directory.

The `ejava.rmich16.queryserviceiiop.ClientReceiverImplementation` class differs from its RMI/JRMP analogue only in extending the `PortableRemoteObject` as shown here:

```
package ejava.rmich16.queryserviceiiop;

import java.rmi.RemoteException;
import javax.rmi.PortableRemoteObject;
import java.util.Vector;
import ejava.rmich16.*;
```

```
public class ClientReceiverImplementation
    extends PortableRemoteObject
    implements ClientReceiver
{
    ...
}
```

Similarly, the `ejava.rmich16.queryserviceiiop.CustomerImplementation` differs only slightly from its RMI/JRMP counterpart. It does differ more significantly in the `bind()` method implementation, however, as you'll soon see in a subsequent section. The `CustomerImplementation` imports and class declaration are shown here:

```
package ejava.rmich16.queryserviceiiop;

import java.rmi.RemoteException;
import javax.rmi.PortableRemoteObject;
import javax.naming.InitialContext;
import ejava.rmich16.*;

public class CustomerImplementation
    extends PortableRemoteObject
    implements Customer
{
    ...
}
```

The `ejava.rmich16.queryserviceiiop.QueryServerImplementation` class also differs in its base class from the RMI/JRMP class, as well as in the means for binding the server to a lookup service, as you'll see. A few key imports and class declaration for `QueryServerImplementation` are shown here:

```
package ejava.rmich16.queryserviceiiop;

import java.rmi.RemoteException;
import javax.rmi.PortableRemoteObject;
import javax.naming.InitialContext;
import javax.naming.NamingException;
import ejava.rmich16.*;
  ...

public class QueryServerImplementation
    extends PortableRemoteObject
    implements QueryServer
{
    ...
}
```

Compiling the RMI/IIOP Servers

As with RMI/JRMP, you must also compile your RMI/IIOP classes. The same `rmic` compiler is then used to generate the RMI/IIOP stubs and skeletons as was done with RMI/JRMP. However, we now simply must pass the `-iiop` option to `rmic` when generating the stubs and skeletons.

The `run.bat` file in the `examples\src\ejava\rmich16\queryserviceiiop` directory is now set up to compile IIOP stubs and skeletons for all three RMI/IIOP server class files into the same directory using this:

```
rmic -iiop -d . ejava.rmich16.queryserviceiiop.QueryServerImplementation
rmic -iiop -d . ejava.rmich16.queryserviceiiop.CustomerImplementation
rmic -iiop -d .
➥ ejava.rmich16.queryserviceiiop.ClientReceiverImplementation
```

IIOP skeletons (ties) are generated according to the CORBA TIE methodology for providing CORBA connectivity to your distributed objects. Thus, given some class named `MyRemoteObjectImpl`, a skeleton class will be generated with the name `MyRemoteObjectImpl_Tie` that extends `javax.rmi.CORBA.Stub` and that implements the `javax.rmi.CORBA.Tie` interface, as well as the application-specific `MyRemoteInterface`. The `Tie` interface implemented by the skeleton class extends `org.omg.CORBA.portable.InvokeHandler` and unmarshals remote calls into regular Java calls on the `MyRemoteObjectImpl`, and marshals responses as well. The `rmic` compiler will also generate the RMI/JRMP or RMI/IIOP stubs that are utilized by the RMI client. We describe how the client uses such stubs in a subsequent section.

RMI Registration

After you make a distributable server object, it is only natural that you would want to "distribute it." That is, you now need to make your RMI server accessible to distributed clients. Making your servers distributed involves registering remote references to your servers with a naming service. Naming services then allow clients to look up these distributed references given some name string. After a remote reference is obtained, a client may either consult the naming service again for additional remote references or perhaps be handed one directly from a server that has produced a remote reference to a new object. We discuss naming services in more detail in Chapter 19, "Naming Services," but we step through the configuration of two different name servers in this chapter. RMI/JRMP servers use the "RMI Registry," and RMI/IIOP servers use a "CosNaming Service." In addition to a naming service, RMI requires that you provide a means for enabling distributed JVMs to be capable of downloading new Java classes that they currently do not have loaded into memory or on their local `CLASSPATH`. We also discuss the use of codebases in this section for addressing dynamic and distributed class loading issues.

Registration of RMI/JRMP Servers

The diagram in Figure 16.5 contains a few important classes and interfaces for you to consider when registering an RMI/JRMP server with the RMI registry. Here we see a Server registrar named `MyServerRegistrar` that has a handle to the `MyRemoteImpl` server implementation. The duty of the Server registrar is to create an active instance of `MyRemoteImpl` and register it with the naming service. Server registrars are simple classes that take care of creating one or more server instances and registering them with a naming service. Many examples you'll see in this book as well as in other publications implement the functionality of a server registrar inside of a `main()` method or other function inside the server implementation class itself. However, in production systems, you will almost always want to have one or more separate server registrar classes to register an initial set of servers to be distributed for the sake of modularity and maintainability.

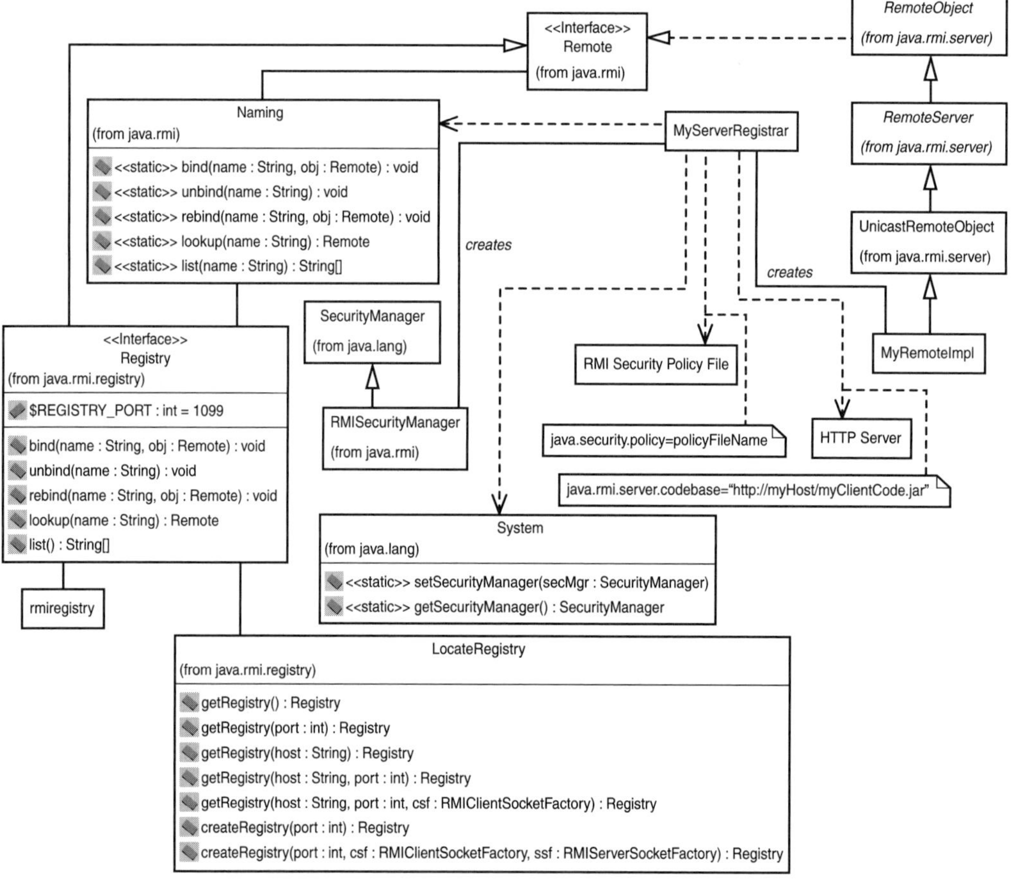

FIGURE 16.5
RMI/JRMP object registration.

Starting an RMI Registry

Before your Server registrar can register RMI servers, you first need to start an RMI registry process somewhere in your distributed network. The RMI registry equipped with the J2SE/J2EE can be simply invoked from the command line with this:

```
rmiregistry
```

This will cause the RMI registry to listen for incoming requests on port 1099. The RMI registry can also run on a port number specified by you on the `rmiregistry` command line as we do in our RMI/JRMP example `run.bat` script as shown here:

```
rmiregistry  5000
```

Configuring RMI/JRMP Security

The RMI server registrar (`MyServerRegistrar` in Figure 16.5) needs to install a security manager for the servers it will register. A default `java.rmi.RMISecurityManager` instance is created and passed into the `System.setSecurityManager()` call. We discuss Java-based security in more depth in Chapter 26, "Basic Java Security," and Chapter 27, "Advanced Java Security."

Additionally, the Java 2.0 security model allows for specification of security permissions in a separate properties file. Our example here uses a properties file with no restrictions for simplicity. We expand on setting Java security policy files in Chapters 26 and 27. Figure 16.5 shows the registrar's dependence on an RMI security policy file and the fact that a server registrar is made aware of which security policy file to use with the default `RMISecurityManager`. The security policy file is designated via setting of a `java.security.policy` system property, such as in passing `-Djava.security.policy=rmi.policy` as the command-line argument when starting the RMI server registrar.

Interfacing with RMI Registries

RMI server registrars use the `java.rmi.Naming` class to interface with an RMI registry for binding remote server objects to names for distributed client access. RMI names used by `Naming` are of this general form:

```
rmi://optionalHost:optionalPort/serverName
```

The *`optionalHost`* is the name of the host where you have started the RMI registry. This can be a remote host or perhaps `localhost (127.0.0.1)` if you've run the RMI registry on your local machine. If no hostname is provided, the default `localhost` is used. The *`optionalPort`* is used to indicate the port number on which you've run the RMI registry. If no port is provided, the default port of 1099 is assumed. The *`serverName`* is the name you want to give for your RMI server object implementation instance.

The server registrar can use the static `Naming.bind()` or `Naming.rebind()` method to register an instantiated server object implementation with a name in the RMI registry. The difference between `bind()` and `rebind()` is that `bind()` throws an `AlreadyBoundException` if an object of that name is registered with the RMI registry, whereas `rebind()` replaces any objects already bound with that name. The `Naming` class actually uses a `java.rmi.registry.Registry` interface to an object that talks with the associated `rmiregistry` instance running. For example

```
MyRemoteImpl myRemote = new MyRemoteImpl();
Naming.bind("rmi://localhost/MyRemoteImplInstance", myRemote);
Naming.rebind("rmi://localhost/MyRemoteImplInstance", myRemote);
```

The `java.rmi.registry.LocateRegistry` can be also used to obtain a direct reference to an RMI registry on the local or a remote host. The `LocateRegistry.getRegistry()` methods take parameters such as a hostname and port number to identify the particular RMI registry of interest. Additionally, the `LocateRegistry.createRegistry()` methods can also be used to create an RMI registry instance on the `localhost` directly from within a Java application if desired.

Dynamic RMI/JRMP Class Downloading

As most Java developers are aware, Java objects can be serialized across a network using Java's object serialization format. A standard Java network client can manipulate a serializable Java class if the Java class is already associated with the serialized object loaded into the JVM or is loadable from the client's local `CLASSPATH`.

Java applets also enable Java binary classes to be automatically downloaded from a Web server to a Web browser. The distributed client in this case is the Web browser making calls on a subclass of the `java.applet.Applet` class. From the Web browser's perspective, it is using the application-specific `Applet` without having any explicit reference to the application-specific class. A class loader such as an `Applet` class loader is then used to load classes from a "codebase." The codebase simply specifies those locations from which the class loader can download Java binary classes. Depending on the specific class-loader implementation, such locations may be specified in terms of HTTP URLs, file locations, or some other naming scheme. Of course, in the case of an `Applet` class loader, such codebase values specified inside of an `Applet` tag are typically HTTP URLs specified relative to the download location of the associated Web page.

RMI also uses such features for dynamic code downloading. RMI stubs can be dynamically downloaded to RMI clients using the same codebase infrastructure used for applet downloading. Such dynamic stub downloading alleviates the need for manually installing the proper RMI stubs inside of the RMI client. Also, any classes used by the RMI stubs can be downloaded dynamically and avoid client-side installs. Classes can be downloaded to the RMI client using a URL specified in terms of a file system (`file:///`), via an FTP server (`ftp://`), or via a Web server (`http://`).

Although classes can be downloaded from a file system and FTP, the most common method for downloading RMI code to clients is using an HTTP server. The HTTP server for RMI class downloading needs only to implement basic HTTP `GET` functionality. Although any Web server will do, we utilize a very small (under 10KB above and beyond the Java 2.0 libraries) HTTP server provided by Sun called `ClassFileServer`. `ClassFileServer` can be run using the following command:

```
java examples.classServer.ClassFileServer <port> <classpath>
```

NOTE

The small footprint HTTP server provided by Sun called `ClassFileServer` can be downloaded from `http://java.sun.com/products/jdk/rmi/class-server.zip`. You should extract this zip file to a directory of your choice.

The *<port>* specifies the port on which the HTTP server will listen for incoming requests. A default port of 2001 is assumed if no port is specified. The *<classpath>* is a `CLASSPATH` that tells the HTTP server where to locate Java files requested during HTTP `GET` requests. Such HTTP servers must be initiated to run on each machine that has RMI code to download to RMI clients.

To make code downloadable to RMI clients, the `java.rmi.server.codebase` system property for the JVM running the server registrar should be set equal to the base location from which all RMI client code can be downloaded to RMI clients. For example, if you have an HTTP server running on `myHost.com` and port 2001 with all downloadable code sitting in the `myClientCode` directory relative to that HTTP server, then the server codebase property might look like this:

```
-Djava.rmi.server.codebase="http://myHost.com:2001/myClientCode/" "
```

Such a property can be set for your server JVM via the command line when your server registrar is being run. When an RMI server is bound to the RMI registry, this codebase value is automatically associated with the remote server object reference. When an RMI client retrieves a reference to the remote server object, the RMI client's `CLASSPATH` will first be searched for the associated RMI stub. If the RMI stub is not found locally, the `CODEBASE` is then searched for the stub. If it's found via the `CODEBASE`, the RMI stubs and any other classes needed by the RMI client will be downloaded according to whatever protocol is specified in the `CODEBASE` (HTTP, FTP, or file) and relative to the location specified in the server `CODEBASE` property value.

TIP

The classes to download to the RMI client should not be in the RMI registry's `CLASSPATH`. When they are absent from the RMI registry's `CLASSPATH`, the RMI registry will properly consult the `CODEBASE` property associated with the registered RMI server.

CAUTION

Be careful to properly define the `java.rmi.server.codebase` property. Absence of trailing forward slashes (/) in a URL (`http://host/myDir/`) or misspelled URLs can lead to hard-to-resolve `ClassNotFoundExceptions` being thrown.

When an RMI client makes a call on an RMI server method, there may be cases in which the RMI client passes a parameter to the remote method, which either implements some interface type or extends some base class specified in the remote method signature. In such a case, the RMI server itself can download the binary Java class used by the RMI client if the RMI client itself has specified a `java.rmi.server.codebase` property for its JVM process.

Example RMI/JRMP Server Registration

The `main()` method of the `QueryServerImplementation` in Listing 16.6 implements the RMI server registrar functionality for registration of a `QueryServerImplementation` instance. A properties file is used to load all properties relevant to the particular example. Included in the properties utilized by the `QueryServerImplementation` constructor are an RMI registry URL (`REGISTRY_SERVER_URL`) and a name for the server implementation instance (`QUERY_SERVER_NAME`). After setting the `RMISecurityManager`, the server object instance is bound to the RMI registry using `Naming.rebind()`.

The `run.bat` file in the `examples\src\ejava\rmich16\queryservicejrmp` directory can be used not only to build the example and generate client stubs and server skeletons, but also to start your HTTP class download server and RMI registry with `EJAVA_HOME` and `JAVA_HOME` environment variables appropriately. You must set a `CLASSSERVER_HOME` environment variable to the root directory into which the contents of the `class-server.zip` file have been extracted in order to use our example build and execute scripts. The example `run.bat` script compiles the `ClassFileServer` code and spawns the `ClassFileServer` as follows:

```
java examples.classServer.ClassFileServer 2001
➥ %EJAVA_HOME%\examples\classes
```

The RMI server registrar for the `QueryServerImplementation` is invoked with a system security policy file and `CODEBASE` set from `run.bat` with the following command:

```
java -Djava.security.policy=rmi.policy
➥-Djava.rmi.server.codebase="http://localhost:2001/"
➥ejava.rmich16.queryservicejrmp.QueryServerImplementation
➥RMICH16Properties.txt
```

Notice also from Listing 16.6 that `Customer` objects are also dynamically bound to the RMI registry when the `findCustomersWhoOrderedForMoreThan()` method is called by the

RMI client. The `Customer.bind()` method defined in `CustomerImplementation` calls `Naming.rebind()` with the name being passed in from the `QueryServerImplementation findCustomersWhoOrderedForMoreThan()` call.

Registration of RMI/IIOP Servers

As with the registration of RMI/JRMP-based servers, RMI/IIOP servers can be registered using an RMI server registrar, as shown in Figure 16.6. The difference between RMI/JRMP and RMI/IIOP registration involves registration of RMI/IIOP servers with a CosNaming service versus an RMI registry. As was the case with CORBA servers created in the preceding chapter, an `Orb`, CosNaming `NamingContext`, and CosNaming `NameComponent` are all used to register an object with a CosNaming service.

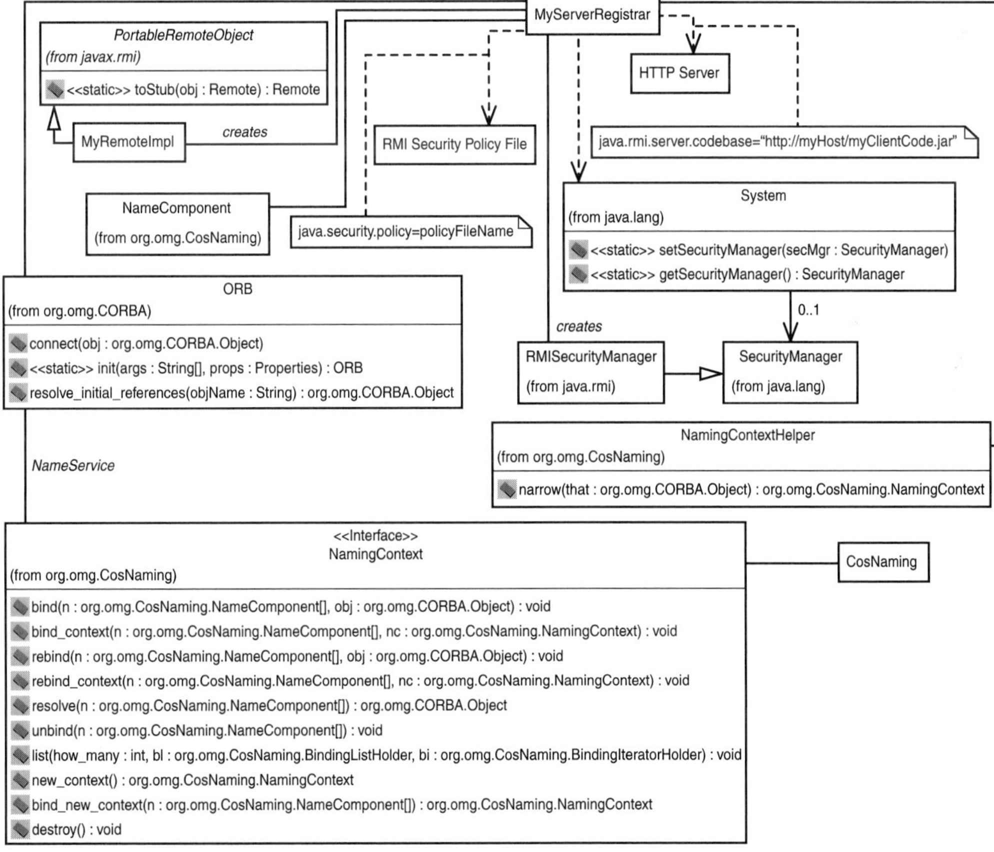

FIGURE 16.6
RMI/IIOP object registration.

Starting an RMI/IIOP Naming Service

The CosNaming server to use with RMI/IIOP is equipped with the separately downloadable RMI/IIOP standard extension for use with J2SE v1.2 environments. RMI/IIOP is integrated with the J2SE v1.3 and thus you may use the CosNaming server equipped as a standard part of the J2SE v1.3, platform. The CosNaming server is simply started using this:

```
tnameserv
```

The `tnameserv` command starts a CosNaming service on the default port 900. To override this default port, use this:

```
tnameserv -ORBInitialPort <PortNum>
```

Interfacing with RMI/IIOP Naming Services

Registering a server with CosNaming requires a few more steps than doing so using the RMI registry. Recall that the RMI registration simply involved a single call to `Naming.bind()` or `Naming.rebind()`. CosNaming registration with RMI/IIOP requires the following six general steps:

- Obtaining an Orb reference:

  ```
  ORB orb = ORB.init(args, null);
  ```

- Obtaining an initial reference to a naming service:

  ```
  org.omg.CORBA.Object namingReference =
  ➥ orb.resolve_initial_references("NameService");
  ```

- Narrowing the naming reference:

  ```
  cosNaming = NamingContextHelper.narrow(namingReference);
  ```

- Obtaining a remote stub reference:

  ```
  java.rmi.Remote myStub = PortableRemoteObject.toStub(myImpl);
  ```

- Creating a `name` component array:

  ```
  NameComponent path[] = {new NameComponent(name, "")};
  ```

- Binding the name to the remote stub reference:

  ```
  cosNaming.rebind(path, (org.omg.CORBA.Object) myStub);
  ```

Dynamic RMI/IIOP Class Downloading

Dynamic downloading of RMI stubs under RMI/IIOP is set up in the same fashion it was for RMI/JRMP. The extensions to CORBA via the Objects by Value specification include support for codebases and automatic code downloading. Thus, by running an HTTP server such as the `ClassFileServer` used for RMI/JRMP and by setting the `java.rmi.server.codebase` system property in the RMI/IIOP server process, we can dynamically download RMI/IIOP code to RMI clients on demand as was the case with RMI/JRMP.

Example RMI/IIOP Server Registration

RMI/IIOP server registration is one of the areas where RMI/JRMP and RMI/IIOP differ. The `main()` method of the `QueryServerImplementation` for RMI/IIOP implements the server registrar functionality of a `QueryServerImplementation` object:

```
public static void main(String[] args) {
  if (args.length == 0) {
    System.out.println("You should provide properties file :"
    + "java ejava.rmich16.queryserviceiiop.QueryServerImplementation"
    + "RMICH16Properties.txt");
    System.exit(0);
  }

  String propertiesFileName = args[0];

  try {
    // Load properties from file
    Properties properties = new Properties();
    FileInputStream fin = new FileInputStream(propertiesFileName);
    properties.load(fin);
    // Get Query server name and create query server impl
    String name = (String) properties.get("QUERY_SERVER_NAME");
    QueryServerImplementation queryServerImpl =
      new QueryServerImplementation(properties);
    // Set security manager
    System.setSecurityManager(new RMISecurityManager());
    System.out.println("Set system properties :");

     // Get Name Service reference and bind server to name service
    org.omg.CORBA.ORB orb = ORB.init(args, System.getProperties());

    System.out.println("Getting Naming Reference");
    org.omg.CORBA.Object namingReference =
      orb.resolve_initial_references("NameService");

    System.out.println("Getting Context Reference");
    queryServerImpl.context =
      NamingContextHelper.narrow(namingReference);



    java.rmi.Remote stub =
      PortableRemoteObject.toStub(queryServerImpl);
    NameComponent nc = new NameComponent(name, "");
    NameComponent path[] = {nc};
```

```
        queryServerImpl.context
          .rebind(path, (org.omg.CORBA.Object) stub);
        System.out.println("Bound:");
      } catch (IOException ioe) {
        System.out.println("Error in Reading properties File :" + ioe);
      } catch (Exception ne) {
        System.out.println("Error   :" + ne);
      }
    }
```

Within the `findCustomersWhoOrderedForMoreThan()` method of `QueryServerImplementation`, a `Customer` reference (`custImpl`) is bound using this:

```
custImpl.setContext(this.context);
custImpl.bind(name);
```

Here, `Customer` reference has its context set to a CosNaming service reference before the RMI/IIOP registration inside the `bind()` method on the `CustomerImplementation` instance is triggered:

```
  public void bind(String customerID) {
    try {
      java.rmi.Remote stub = PortableRemoteObject.toStub(this);
      NameComponent nc = new NameComponent(customerID, "");
      NameComponent path[] = {nc};
      this.context.rebind(path, (org.omg.CORBA.Object) stub);
    } catch (Exception e) {
      System.out.println("Error in binding the customer :" + e
                         + "customerID :" + customerID);
    }
  }
```

RMI Clients and Stubs

After active RMI servers have been registered with an RMI registry or CosNaming service, RMI clients can utilize the services provided by such servers. In this section, we cover the creation of both RMI/JRMP clients and RMI/IIOP clients. Both types of clients use a stub that delegates calls to the appropriate distributed server process. To this end, we also demonstrate how stubs can be generated and downloaded to the clients on demand.

RMI/JRMP Clients and Stubs

The `rmic` compiler command used to generate server-side skeletons also creates client-side stubs. As shown in Figure 16.7, a stub named `MyRemoteImpl_Stub` is generated from a server named `MyRemoteImpl`. The RMI client code makes calls on the `MyRemoteInterface`, which is implemented by the `MyRemoteImpl_Stub` class. RMI stubs extend the `RemoteStub` class, which in turn implements the `RemoteObject` class offering distributed semantics to remote object calls.

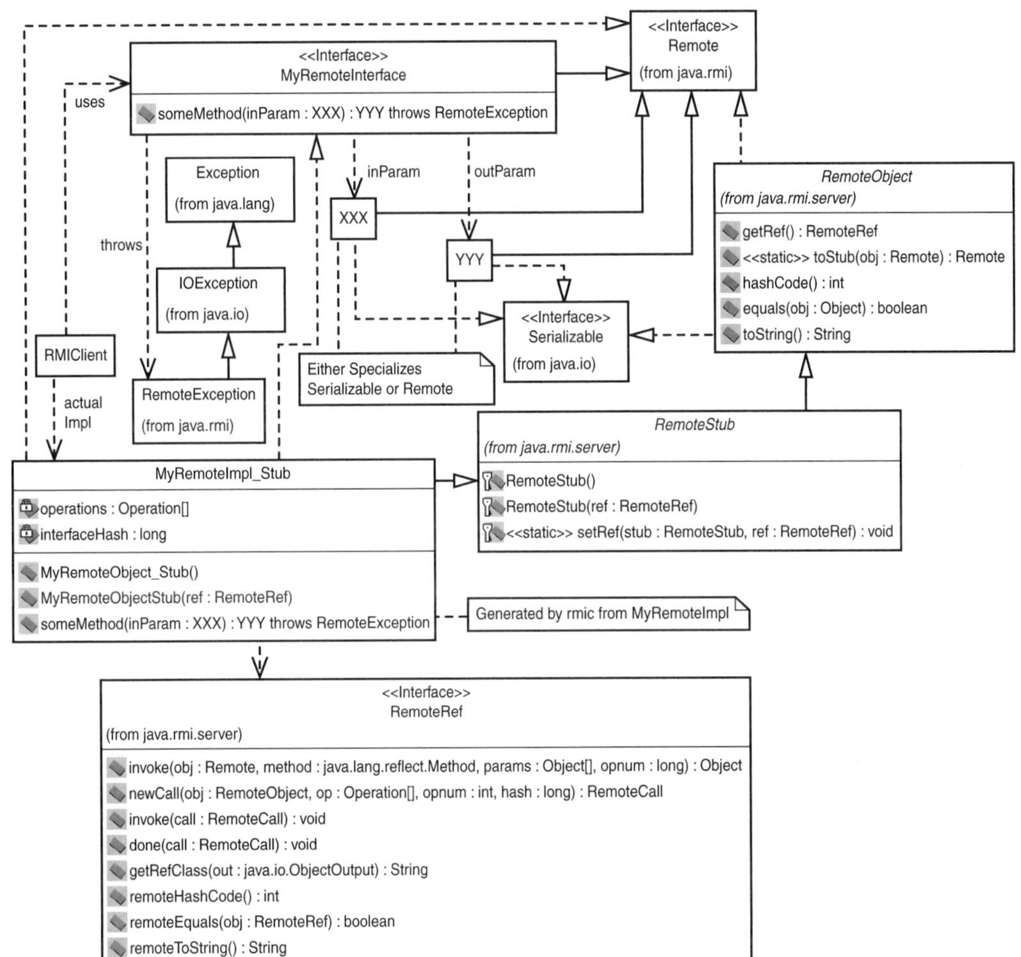

FIGURE 16.7
RMI/JRMP clients.

The RMI client thus is a lightweight client needing only the stub and interface for a server, as well as the Java/RMI platform. Whereas regular `java.lang.Objects` compare objects based on reference equality, the `RemoteStub` class extended by the application-specific stub translates such types of calls into appropriate distributed object reference equality semantics transparent to the RMI client. The application-specific RMI v1.1 stub uses `java.rmi.server.RemoteRef`, `java.rmi.server.RemoteCall`, and `java.rmi.server.Operation` to marshal and unmarshal calls to and from the remote object implementation. `RemoteRef` serves as a handle on the remote object. The `Operation` and `RemoteCall` constructs are not needed for RMI v1.2–style stubs and are thus deprecated. In RMI v1.1, these constructs encapsulated remote operations and calls.

The `QueryClient` in Listing 16.8 not only demonstrates how an RMI client makes distributed calls on an RMI server but also demonstrates how an RMI client can register a distributed callback with an RMI server. The `QueryClient.main()` method first instantiates an `RMISecurityManager` to set as the system security manager using `System.setSecurityManager (new RMISecurityManager())`.

After obtaining a reference to a `QueryServer` (the mechanism for which is described in the next section), our `QueryClient` makes the `findCustomersWhoOrderedForMoreThan()` distributed call on the `QueryServer`. The `QueryClient` subsequently creates an instance of a distributed `ClientReceiverImplementation` object and registers it with the `QueryServer` using the `register()` distributed call. When the `QueryClient` calls `findOrdersWhichAreFrom()` on the `QueryServer`, the `QueryServerImplementation` makes a callback on the RMI client's `ClientReceiver` object with a `ClientReceiver.setResultOrders()` call.

LISTING 16.8 The RMI/JRMP Query Client (`QueryClient.java`)

```
package ejava.rmich16.queryservicejrmp;
import java.rmi.RemoteException;
import java.rmi.RMISecurityManager;
import java.rmi.Naming;
import java.net.MalformedURLException;
import java.rmi.NotBoundException;
import java.util.Vector;
import java.io.IOException;
import ejava.rmich16.*;

public class QueryClient
{


  public void list()
  {
    try{
      String[] names = Naming.list("");
      for(int i=0; i<names.length; i++){
        System.out.println("Registered objects :"+names[i]);
      }
    }
```

```
  catch(Exception e){
    System.out.println("Failed to lookup :"+e);
  }
}

public static void main(String[] args) {
  if (args.length == 0) {
    System.out
      .println("You should provide properties file :"
                + "java rmich16.queryservicejrmp.QueryClient
                ➥RMICH16Properties.txt");
    System.exit(0);
  }

  String propertiesFileName = args[0];

  try {
    // Load properties from properties file
    Properties properties = new Properties();
    FileInputStream fin = new FileInputStream(propertiesFileName);
    properties.load(fin);
    // Get query server name
    String queryServerName = (String) properties.get("QUERY_SERVER_NAME");

    System.out.println("Set system properties :");
    // Get registry name
    String registryURL =
      (String) properties.get("REGISTRY_SERVER_URL");
    System.out.println("QueryServerName :" +
      registryURL + queryServerName);
    String name =  registryURL + queryServerName;
    // Set security manager
    if (System.getSecurityManager() == null) {
      System.setSecurityManager(new RMISecurityManager());
    }
    System.out.println("Client Looking for Server :" + name);
    System.out.println("Type Enter Key");
    System.in.read();    // to hold the screen
    // Lookup QueryServer reference
    QueryServer qserver = (QueryServer) Naming.lookup(name);
    System.out.println("Client querying for customers :");
    System.out.println("Type Enter Key");
    System.in.read();
```

continues

LISTING 16.8 Continued

```
      // Query for customers and traverse results
      Vector v = qserver.findCustomersWhoOrderedForMoreThan(10.0f);
      System.out.println("Result Customers :"+v);
      for(int i = 0; i<v.size(); i++){
        String cid = (String)v.elementAt(i);
        Customer c = (Customer)Naming.lookup(cid);
        System.out.println(i +" : is " +c);
        System.out.println("FirstName :" +c.getFirstName());
        System.out.println("LastName:"+c.getLastName());
      }

      System.out.println("Server Writing Orders ");
      System.out.println("Type Enter Key");
      // Register client callback with query server
      ClientReceiverImplementation cr =
        new ClientReceiverImplementation();
      qserver.register("ClientReceiver",cr);
      // Induce callbacks to be made by requesting order info
      qserver.findOrdersWhichAreFrom("VA");
      QueryClient qc = new QueryClient();
      System.out.println("list all registered objects :");
      System.out.println("Type Enter Key");
      qc.list();
    }
    catch(RemoteException remoteEx) {
      System.out.println("RemoteException: " + remoteEx.getMessage());
      remoteEx.printStackTrace();
    }
    catch(MalformedURLException  malformedURLException){
      System.out.println("RemoteException: " + malformedURLException);
      malformedURLException.printStackTrace();
    }
    catch(NotBoundException  notBoundEx){
      System.out.println("NotBoundException: " + notBoundEx);
      notBoundEx.printStackTrace();
    }
    catch(IOException e){
      System.out.println("IO Exception :"+e);
    }
  }
}
```

RMI/IIOP Clients and Stubs

When the parameter `-iiop` was passed to the `rmic` compiler, a set of client-side RMI/IIOP stubs was created. Figure 16.8 depicts the constructs involved with client-side RMI/IIOP. The `MyRemoteImpl_Stub` class generated by the `rmic` compiler implements the `MyRemoteInterface` and extends the `javax.rmi.CORBA.Stub` class. The `Stub` class extends the OMG `ObjectImpl` class, which implements the standard CORBA `Object` interface. The `Stub` class provides all the necessary semantics for remote object operations involved with RMI/IIOP, such as distributed versions of `equals()` and `toString()`. RMI/IIOP clients thus also remain lightweight like their RMI/JRMP counterparts.

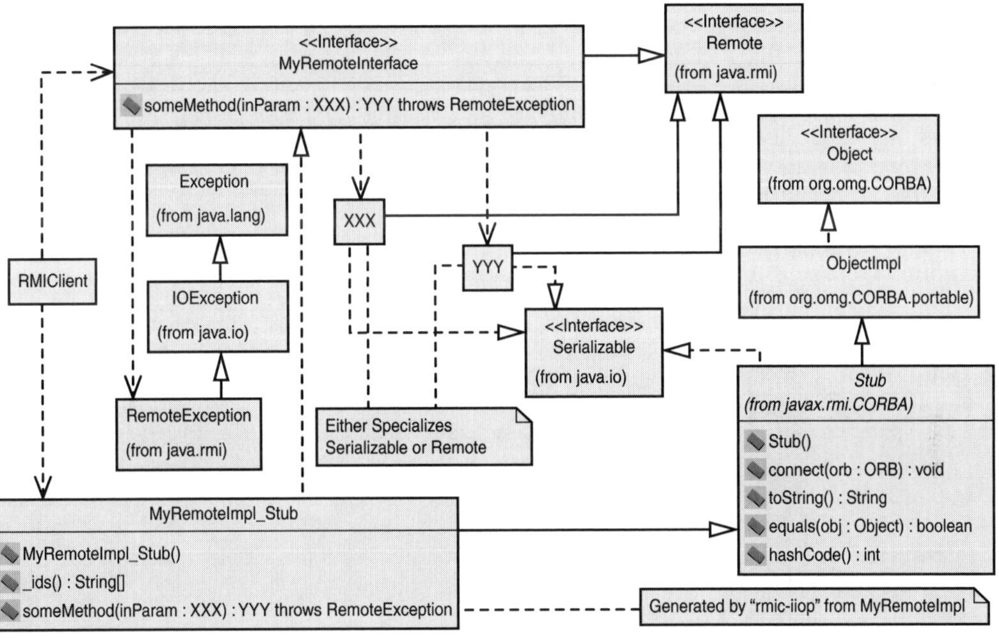

FIGURE 16.8
RMI/IIOP clients.

The RMI/IIOP Query Client in Listing 16.9 performs the same tasks as the RMI/JRMP Query Client. The `QueryServer` is queried and a RMI client-side callback is registered with the RMI query server. The `QueryServer` then invokes a callback on the RMI client. The only difference between the RMI/IIOP client and the RMI/JRMP client, as you'll see in the next section, is how the client interacts with the registration and lookup processes.

LISTING 16.9 The RMI/IIOP Query Client (`QueryClient.java`)

```
package ejava.rmich16.queryserviceiiop;

import java.rmi.RemoteException;
import java.rmi.RMISecurityManager;
import java.net.MalformedURLException;
import java.rmi.NotBoundException;
import java.util.Vector;
import java.io.IOException;
import javax.naming.InitialContext;
import javax.naming.Context;
import java.util.Properties;
import javax.naming.NamingException;
import java.io.FileInputStream;
import javax.rmi.PortableRemoteObject;
import org.omg.CORBA.*;
import org.omg.CosNaming.*;
import org.omg.CosNaming.NamingContextPackage.*;
import ejava.rmich16.*;

public class QueryClient {



  public static void main(String[] args) {
     if (args.length == 0) {
        System.out.println("You should provide properties file :"
                 + "java rmich16.queryserviceiiop.QueryClient
                 ➥RMICH16Properties.txt");
     System.exit(0);
    }
    try {
      // Set security manager
      if (System.getSecurityManager() == null) {
        System.setSecurityManager(new RMISecurityManager());
      }
      // Load properties from properties file
      String fileName = args[0];
      Properties properties = new Properties();
      FileInputStream fin = new FileInputStream(fileName);
      properties.load(fin);
      // Get orb reference
      System.out.println("Getting initial Context");
      ORB orb = ORB.init(args, System.getProperties());
```

```
// Get the root naming context
org.omg.CORBA.Object objRef =
  orb.resolve_initial_references("NameService");
NamingContext context = NamingContextHelper.narrow(objRef);
String name = (String) properties.getProperty("QUERY_SERVER_NAME");

System.out.println("Got Query Server reference :");

// Resolve the object reference in naming
NameComponent nc = new NameComponent(name, "");
NameComponent path[] = {
  nc
};

System.out.println("Client Looking for Server :" + name);
System.out.println("Type Enter Key");
System.in.read();    // to hold the screen

// Lookup QueryServer reference
org.omg.CORBA.Object object = context.resolve(path);
QueryServer qserver =
  (QueryServer) PortableRemoteObject.narrow(object,
                                 QueryServer.class);

System.out.println("Client querying for customers :");
System.out.println("Type Enter Key");
System.in.read(); // to hold the screen
// Query for customers and traverse results
Vector vector = qserver.findCustomersWhoOrderedForMoreThan(10.0f);

System.out.println("Result Customers :" + vector);

for (int i = 0; i < vector.size(); i++) {
  String cid = (String) vector.elementAt(i);

  nc = new NameComponent(cid, "");

  NameComponent path1[] = {
    nc
  };

  object = context.resolve(path1);

  Customer customer =
     (Customer) PortableRemoteObject.narrow(object,
                                  Customer.class);
```

continues

LISTING 16.9 Continued

```
          System.out.println(i + " : is " + c);
          System.out.println("FirstName :" + customer.getFirstName());
          System.out.println("LastName:" + customer.getLastName());
        }

        System.out.println("Server Writing Orders ");
        System.out.println("Type Enter Key");
           System.in.read(); // to hold the screen
        // Register client callback with query server
        ClientReceiverImplementation cr =
          new ClientReceiverImplementation();
        NameComponent nc1 = new NameComponent("ClientReceiver", "");
        NameComponent path2[] = {
          nc1
        };
        java.rmi.Remote stub = PortableRemoteObject.toStub(cr);

        context.rebind(path2, (org.omg.CORBA.Object) stub);
        qserver.register("ClientReceiver", cr);
        // Induce callbacks to be made by requesting order info
        qserver.findOrdersWhichAreFrom("VA");
      } catch (Exception ex) {
        System.out.println("Error: " + ex);
        ex.printStackTrace();
        System.exit(0);
      }
    }
}
```

RMI Lookup

Distributed RMI server objects that have been registered with a naming service are "looked up" by RMI clients. RMI/JRMP and RMI/IIOP clients look up server objects in different manners. In this section, we describe how client-side RMI lookups are performed by both types of clients.

RMI/JRMP Lookups

Figure 16.5 presented the core classes and interfaces involved in RMI registration on the server side. The same constructs are used for RMI lookup on the client side. The Naming classes' static `lookup()` method is used by RMI clients to obtain a remote server object reference, given a name `String` corresponding to the name with which the server object was registered. The `list()` method can also be used to retrieve an array of distributed object name `Strings`, given a URL name `String` of a particular RMI registry.

The RMI/JRMP `QueryClient` shown in Listing 16.8 demonstrates RMI/JRMP lookup. The name `rmi://localhost/BeeShirtsRmiServer` is passed as a parameter to `Naming.lookup()`. The returned `Remote` object instance is then cast to the `QueryServer` type. Similarly, `Customer` object names returned from the `QueryServer findCustomersWhoOrderedForMoreThan()` call are used to look up registered `Customer` object references later in the code. Such a simple means for looking up RMI objects has been one of the features of RMI that makes it attractively easy to use. Finally, one of the last steps performed by the `QueryClient` in Listing 16.8 is to look up and print a list of distributed objects registered in the default RMI registry.

RMI/IIOP Lookups

Figure 16.6 depicted the key entities involved in both distributed CosNaming object registration and lookup in RMI/IIOP. Our RMI/IIOP `QueryClient` shown in Listing 16.9 goes through the same steps for obtaining an initial handle on a CosNaming service object as did the RMI/IIOP `QueryServerImplementation`. However, instead of calling `rebind()` on the CosNaming reference, the `QueryClient` calls `resolve()`, given the name of the desired server object reference. The CORBA object returned must then be narrowed via a call to `narrow()` on the `PortableRemoteObject` class. These two steps are shown here:

```
org.omg.CORBA.Object object = context.resolve(cosNaming);
MyRemoteInterface myServer = (MyRemoteInterface)
    PortableRemoteObject.narrow(object, MyRemoteInterface.class);
```

RMI Object Activation

RMI v1.2 introduced automatic server object activation. Thus, instead of activating and registering an RMI server object instance ahead of time, RMI server objects can now be activated upon RMI client request. When you make your server objects activatable, an activation daemon can activate your objects in a separate JVM process upon demand of clients.

Figure 16.9 illustrates some of the new classes involved in creating and registering activatable objects. Two of the application-specific classes to focus on are `MyRemoteImpl` and `MyServerRegistrar`. `MyRemoteImpl` implements your application-specific `MyRemoteInterface` as usual, but it now extends `java.rmi.activation.Activatable` instead of `UnicastRemoteObject` or `PortableRemoteObject`. Instead of registering active objects, `MyServerRegistrar` is now responsible for creating all the information necessary to register the activatable server with the RMI activation daemon.

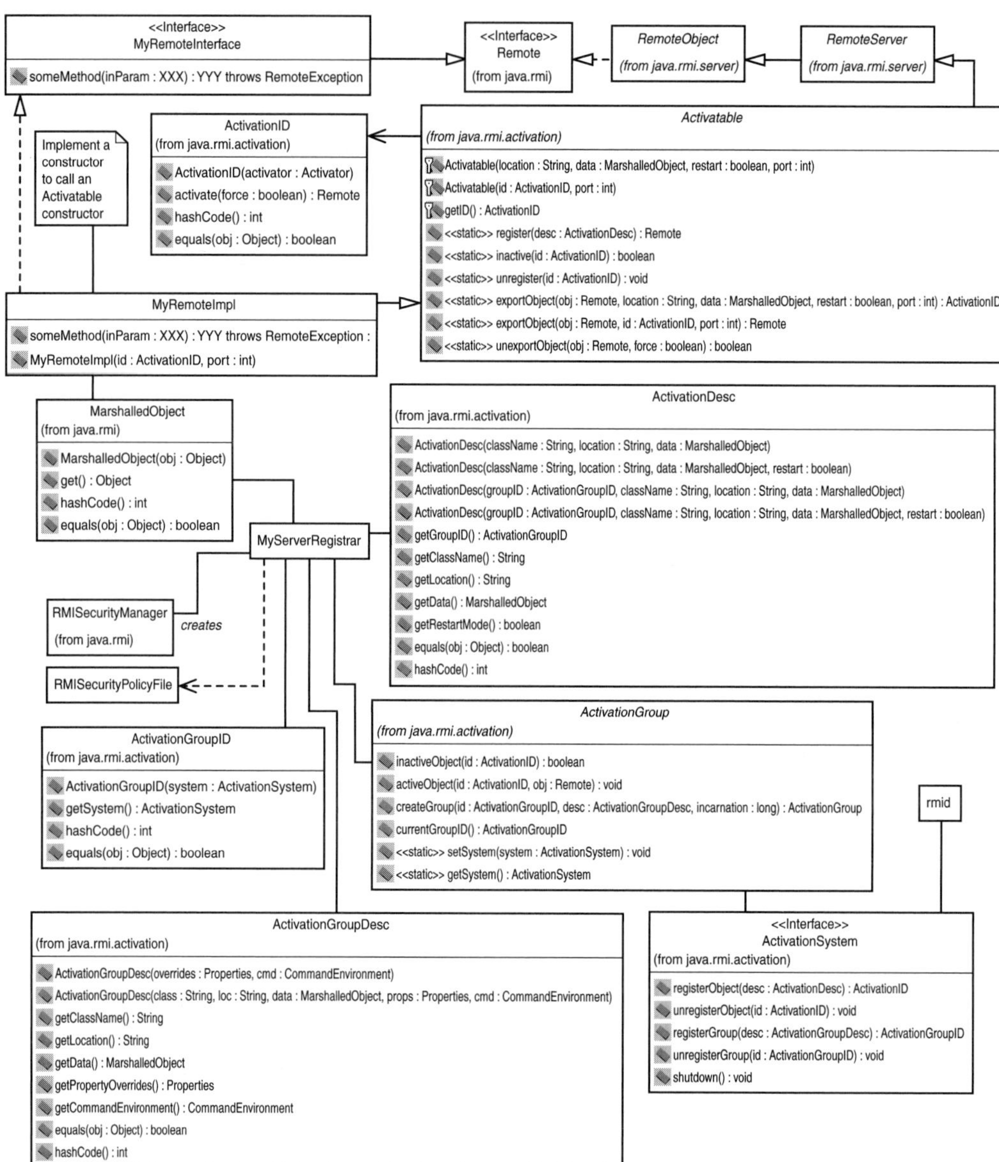

FIGURE 16.9

Activatable objects.

In addition to the RMI registry and potentially an HTTP server for dynamic class downloading, the RMI activation daemon must be started to support use of activatable objects. You can start the RMI activation daemon simply by typing **rmid** on the command line. The RMI activation daemon will satisfy registration requests to register activatable objects on the server side and satisfy client-side requests to activate a particular RMI server object.

Creating an Activatable Server

There is nothing special to note about the `MyRemoteInterface` interface shown in Figure 16.9 and the `SampleServer` interface in Listing 16.10 that we'll be using to illustrate a simple activatable object example. The same rules for defining RMI interfaces apply for activatable as they do for the other non-activatable types of remote objects. However, `MyRemoteImpl` of Figure 16.9 and `SampleServerImplementation` of Listing 16.11 differ in two important regards. First, the servers now extend the `Activatable` class. Second, an activatable server implementation should implement a constructor that can be used to call a constructor on the base `Activatable` object class. Classes may also opt to not extend `Activatable` and instead call one of the static `exportObject()` calls on `Activatable` with a reference to itself.

NOTE

The complete set of code examples for activatable RMI objects can be found on the CD-ROM in the `examples\src\ejava\rmich16\sampleactivatable` directory. The `RMICH16Properties.txt` file in this directory is used to configure the example. In particular, the `LOCATION` property should be modified to reference the class files in your `[EJAVA_HOME]` directory. Finally, a `run.bat` example script file in the `sampleactivatable` directory is used to build and execute the example. Note that the Cloudscape database should not be running for this example to work.

LISTING 16.10 The Sample Activatable Object Interface (`SampleServer.java`)

```
package ejava.rmich16.sampleactivatable;

import java.rmi.Remote;
import java.rmi.RemoteException;
import java.util.Vector;

public interface SampleServer extends Remote {
  Object[] givemeArrayOfObjects() throws RemoteException;
}
```

LISTING 16.11 The Sample Activatable Object Implementation (`SampleServerImplementation.java`)

```
package ejava.rmich16.sampleactivatable;

import java.rmi.RemoteException;
import java.rmi.activation.Activatable;
import java.rmi.activation.ActivationID;
import java.rmi.MarshalledObject;
import java.rmi.Remote;
import java.rmi.Naming;
import java.rmi.RMISecurityManager;

public class SampleServerImplementation extends Activatable
  implements SampleServer {
  private final int OBJECTS_TO_SEND = 10;

  public SampleServerImplementation(ActivationID activationID,
    MarshalledObject data) throws RemoteException {
    super(activationID, 0);
  }

 public Object[] givemeArrayOfObjects() throws RemoteException {
    // create simple test set of objects to return
    Object[] someObjects = new Object[OBJECTS_TO_SEND];

    for (int i = 0; i < someObjects.length; i++) {
      someObjects[i] = new Integer(i);
    }

    return someObjects;
  }

}
```

Two primary constructor forms are available to the `Activatable` object. One constructor form takes an `ActivationID` and a port on which the object takes requests (uses an anonymous port if the port number is 0). Another constructor form takes an `Activatable` class file location, a `java.rmi.MarshalledObject` instance, a `true/false` flag indicating whether the object is started with the activator daemon or on demand, and a port number. `MarshalledObject` object instances contain a marshaled byte stream of the object passed into its constructor. When `get()` is called on a `MarshalledObject`, a copy of the underlying stream is unmarshaled and returned. Constructors on your `Activatable` object are actually called by the activation system when your object is activated by the activation daemon due to a client request.

Creating an Activatable Server Registrar

`MyServerRegistrar` in Figure 16.9 represents the activatable server registrar. The server registrar for our simple example is defined in Listing 16.12. First an `RMISecurityManager` is instantiated and registered with the JVM as was done with the non-activatable RMI registration process. After that, an activation group and activation object description is created and registered with the activation daemon.

LISTING 16.12 The Sample Activatable Server Registrar (`SampleServerConfigure.java`)

```
package ejava.rmich16.sampleactivatable;

import java.io.IOException;
import java.util.Properties;
import java.io.FileInputStream;
import java.rmi.MarshalledObject;
import java.rmi.activation.ActivationGroupDesc;
import java.rmi.activation.ActivationGroupID;
import java.rmi.activation.ActivationGroup;
import java.rmi.activation.ActivationException;
import java.rmi.activation.ActivationDesc;
import java.rmi.RMISecurityManager;
import java.rmi.activation.Activatable;
import java.rmi.Naming;

public class SampleServerConfigure {



  public static void main(String[] args) {
    if (args.length == 0) {
      System.out
        .println("Error : start using java "
             + "ejava.rmich16.queryserviceactivatable.QueryServerMain "
             + "RMICH16ActivatableProperties.txt");
      System.exit(0);
    }

    System.setSecurityManager(new RMISecurityManager());

    try {
      String fileName = args[0];
      Properties p = new Properties();
      FileInputStream fin = new FileInputStream(fileName);
```

continues

LISTING 16.12 Continued

```
      p.load(fin);

      SampleServer server;
      String serverClassName =
        (String) p.getProperty("SERVER_CLASS_NAME");
      String location = (String) p.getProperty("LOCATION");
     // initialized data to set in object is null
     MarshalledObject dataToTheObject = null;

      // for our case we will use same jvm as rmid's
      ActivationGroupDesc.CommandEnvironment ace = null;
      ActivationGroupID activationID =
        ActivationGroup.getSystem()
          .registerGroup(new ActivationGroupDesc(p, ace));

      ActivationDesc acdesc = new ActivationDesc(activationID,
         serverClassName,   location, dataToTheObject);

      server = (SampleServer) Activatable.register(acdesc);

      System.out.println("Registered and got the Stub :");

      String serverRegistryName = (String) p.get("SERVER_BOUND_NAME");

      Naming.rebind(serverRegistryName, server);
      System.out.println("Exported Server:");

      System.exit(0);
    } catch (IOException ioe) {
      System.out.println("Io ecception :" + ioe);
    } catch (ActivationException ae) {
      System.out.println("Activation Exception :" + ae);
      ae.printStackTrace();
    }
  }
}
```

Activation groups collect groups of activatable objects and are used to notify an `ActivationMonitor` of the status of its activatable objects. As shown in Listing 16.12, an `ActivationGroupDesc` is instantiated with the properties object read in from the file but only uses the `java.security.policy` property value in this example. An `ActivationGroupDesc` object contains all the information needed for activating an object belonging to a particular group. The ActivationGroupDesc is registered with the ActivationSystem returned from the static getSystem() call on ActivationGroup using the ActivationSystem's registerGroup() method.

After obtaining an ActivationGroupID object from the ActivationSystem.registerGroup() method, the ActivationGroupID is used along with a fully qualified server class name, a class file location, and any marshaled initialization data for the Activatable object to create an ActivationDesc object. The server class name for the SampleServerImplementation and location are read from the properties file associated with the example. The ActivationDesc object contains all the information the activation daemon needs to automatically activate a particular object. This object is passed into the static register() method of the Activatable class and returns the stub for the activatable object. Finally, the stub returned from the activation daemon registration is bound to the RMI registry.

RMI Activatable Object Client

Listing 16.13 shows the RMI client used for this activatable object example. As shown in the code listing, no special considerations need to be made on the client side. From the client's perspective, the fact that the RMI server needs to be activated is transparent to the client.

LISTING 16.13 The Sample Activatable Object Client (SampleServerClient.java)

```
package ejava.rmich16.sampleactivatable;

import java.rmi.RemoteException;
import java.rmi.RMISecurityManager;
import java.rmi.Naming;
import java.net.MalformedURLException;
import java.rmi.NotBoundException;
import java.util.Vector;
import java.io.IOException;
import java.io.FileInputStream;
import java.util.Properties;

public class SampleServerClient {



  public static void main(String[] args) {
    try {
      if (System.getSecurityManager() == null) {
        System.setSecurityManager(new RMISecurityManager());
      }
```

continues

LISTING 16.13 Continued

```
        String fileName = args[0];
        Properties p = new Properties();
        FileInputStream fin = new FileInputStream(fileName);

        p.load(fin);

        String name = (String) p.get("SERVER_BOUND_NAME");
        String registryURL = (String) p.get("REGISTRY_SERVER_URL");

        System.out.println("Client Looking for Server :" + name);
        System.out.println("Type Enter Key");
        System.in.read();    // to hold the screen

        SampleServer server = (SampleServer) Naming.lookup(registryURL
                + name);

        System.out.println("Client querying for Objects :");
        System.out.println("Type Enter Key");
        System.in.read(); // to hold the screen
        Object[] receivedObjects = server.givemeArrayOfObjects();

        System.out.println("Resulting Objects");

        for (int i = 0; i < receivedObjects.length-2; i++) {
          System.out.print(((Integer) receivedObjects[i]).intValue()
                           + ":");
        }
        System.out.print(((Integer)
          receivedObjects[receivedObjects.length-1]).intValue() + "");

      } catch (RemoteException remoteEx) {
        System.out.println("RemoteException: " + remoteEx.getMessage());
        remoteEx.printStackTrace();
      } catch (MalformedURLException malformedURLException) {
        System.out.println("RemoteException: " + malformedURLException);
        malformedURLException.printStackTrace();
      } catch (NotBoundException notBoundEx) {
        System.out.println("NotBoundException: " + notBoundEx);
        notBoundEx.printStackTrace();
      } catch (IOException ioEx) {
        System.out.println("IO Exception :" + ioeEx);
      }

  }
}
```

Compile and Run the Example

As usual, the RMI stubs and skeletons must be generated from the RMI compiler. The `run.bat` file equipped with the activatable object examples generates the stubs and skeletons with this:

```
rmic -d . ejava.rmich16.sampleactivatable.SampleServerImplementation
```

After starting the simple HTTP server and RMI registry, the RMI activation daemon is started with this:

```
/min %JAVA_HOME%\bin\rmid
```

The RMI activatable `SampleServerImplementation` is then registered with the RMI activation daemon by starting the RMI server registrar with this:

```
java -Djava.security.policy=rmi.policy
➥ejava.rmich16.sampleactivatable.SampleServerConfigure
➥RMICH16Properties.txt
```

Finally, the RMI client is started with the following command:

```
java -Djava.security.policy=rmi.policy
➥ejava.rmich16.sampleactivatable.SampleServerClient
➥RMICH16Properties.txt
```

Custom Sockets

RMI provides the capability to replace the underlying transport protocol used by the RMI framework. Custom sockets are useful for distributed object communications using protocols that encrypt data or that must communicate via some application-specific standard. Customization of sockets in RMI is accomplished by configuring an RMI socket factory to use a non-TCP transport protocol over IP. Not only can such sockets be customized on an object-by-object basis, but the socket factories can be downloaded to RMI clients on demand. Figure 16.10 shows the main classes and interfaces involved in customizing the underlying socket transport for RMI clients and servers.

An object that implements the `java.rmi.server.RMIClientSocketFactory` interface can be associated with RMI server objects and downloaded to RMI clients when the RMI client obtains a reference to the distributed RMI server. The `RMIClientSocketFactory` is then used to create socket connections to the RMI server for RMI calls. Thus, your custom client socket factory must simply implement the `RMIClientSocketFactory` interface and return a specialized socket from the `createSocket()` call. For example

```
public class CustomClientSocketFactory implements
  RMIClientSocketFactory, Serializable
{
```

```
  public Socket createSocket(String host, int port)
    throws IOException
  {
    return new CustomSocket(host, port);
  }
}
```

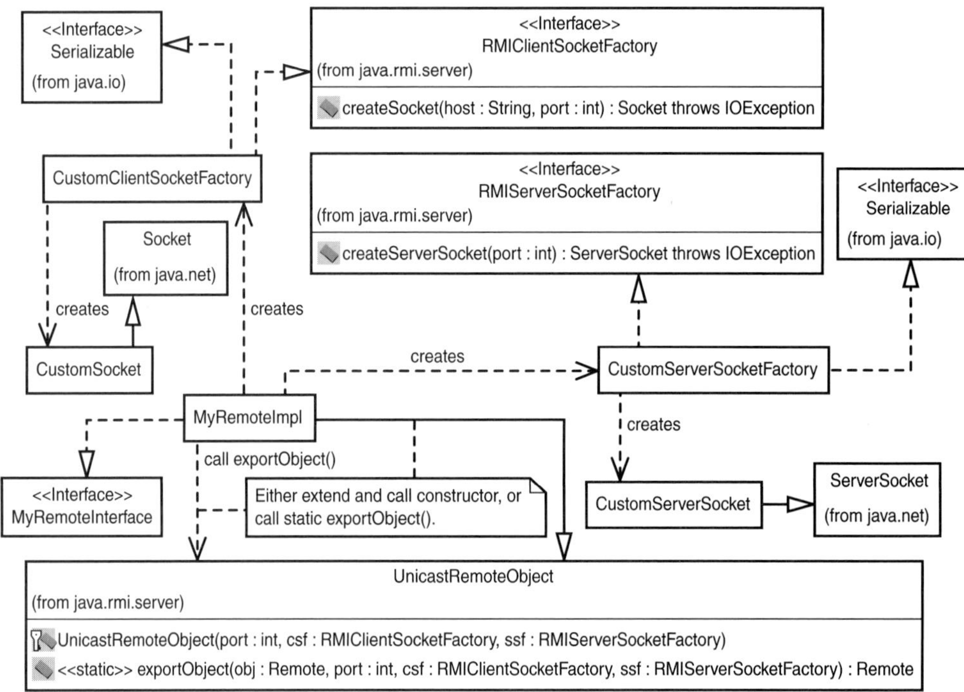

FIGURE 16.10
Custom sockets.

Similarly, an object that implements the `java.rmi.server.RMIServerSocketFactory` interface can be associated with RMI server objects to ensure that the correct server-side socket connection for RMI calls will be created. For example

```
public class CustomServerSocketFactory implements
  RMIServerSocketFactory, Serializable
{
  public ServerSocket createServerSocket(int portNumber)
    throws IOException
  {
    return new CustomServerSocket(portNumber);
  }
}
```

An RMI server object is configured to utilize a specific `RMIClientSocketFactory` and `RMIServerSocketFactory` pair by passing the factories into the RMI server object's constructor or into the `exportObject()` method calls for both `UnicastRemoteObject` and `Activatable` object types. For the constructor case, we have this:

```
public class CustomSocketImpl
  extends UnicastRemoteObject
  implements CustomSocketInterface
{
  public CustomSocketImpl() throws RemoteException
  {
    // port 0 means that anonymous port is chosen
    super(0, new CustomClientSocketFactory(),
             new CustomServerSocketFactory());
  }
...
}
```

For the case in which a `UnicastRemoteObject` or an `Activatable` object is exported directly, we have this:

```
public class CustomSocketImpl
  implements CustomSocketInterface
{
  public CustomSocketImpl() throws RemoteException
  {
    UnicastRemoteObject.exportObject(this, 0,
             new CustomClientSocketFactory(),
             new CustomServerSocketFactory());
  }
...
}
```

Finally, a `java.security.policy` file must be created and set as a system property for your JVM to allow the program to create sockets.

Conclusions

RMI is a feature-rich and simple framework for providing a distributed object communications infrastructure in enterprise environments. RMI is simpler to use than CORBA but has traditionally been frowned on due to its Java-centric nature. All of this changed when RMI/IIOP started to become a reality. RMI servers can now export their interfaces via IDL and offer their services to CORBA clients implemented in any language over IIOP. Furthermore, the transition between RMI/JRMP servers and RMI/IIOP servers is straightforward and differs only from a programming interface perspective in RMI/IIOP's use of the `PortableRemoteObject` and the underlying naming service.

Given RMI's direction to reconcile with CORBA and the associated language interoperability issues, RMI also offers some advantages over CORBA. Not the least of these advantages involves how practical and simple it is to exchange objects by value and entire Java classes between RMI clients and servers. In stark contrast, CORBA's Objects by Value specification is still very complicated and impractical. Although CORBA will remain important as an industry standard to define interoperable services and a communications framework, as more systems are built using Java, future evolutions of RMI will always have an advantage over CORBA.

Modeling Components with COM/DCOM

CHAPTER

17

IN THIS CHAPTER

- COM and DCOM in a Nutshell 528
- COM/DCOM Services 534
- Interface Definition Language 535

The Microsoft Component Object Model (COM) and Distributed Component Object Model (DCOM) offer a Microsoft Windows platform-dependent way to build nondistributed and distributed components, respectively. Java-based DCOM clients and servers can be built and hosted inside of the Microsoft Java Virtual Machine (MSJVM). The MSJVM offers a link to the COM and DCOM library dependence on binary interfacing with the Windows platform. This chapter provides an overview of the COM and DCOM component models and how Java-based applications can interface with such models.

In this chapter, you will learn:

- The basic architecture and concepts behind Microsoft's COM and DCOM architecture.
- What basic component services are available to COM- and DCOM-based applications.
- The basic IDL language for describing component interfaces in COM and DCOM.

COM and DCOM in a Nutshell

The roots of DCOM stem from object linking and embedding (OLE), which was a Microsoft Windows–centric compound document solution for embedding documents within documents (for example, Excel spreadsheet into a Word document). The beginning of a Windows-based Component Object Model, technology was first put to use with the release of OLE2. COM provided an underlying general framework for allowing software components to expose its services to other software. Although *OLE* used to mean any software that made use of COM, OLE took on a more focused marketing role, and the term *ActiveX* eventually came to mean any software that made use of COM.

Despite all the marketing-induced confusion, the term *COM* can still be most broadly and accurately defined as a component interface model for Windows-based applications. COM clients can make use of such components by interfacing with COM libraries to obtain component handles and then making calls to such interfaces, which in turn map to local procedure calls. Such local calls map to a call on the actual COM component service. Although COM interfaces were defined at a binary level in the past, COM now has evolved to enable the definition of components using higher-level language interfaces.

Furthermore, although COM is indeed a component model, the terminology used in COM-land is sometimes completely different from similar terms used by object-oriented and other component-based technologies. For example, COM objects are by and large stateless collections of function calls. We will nonetheless use the term *COM interface* to mean a collection of functions and use the term *COM class* to mean an entity that implements one or more interfaces. We will use *COM object* to mean the instantiation of a COM class.

Distributed COM (DCOM) is often referred to as "COM with a longer wire." DCOM ships with the Windows 98 and NT platforms and can be installed on Windows 95 platforms. DCOM clients can use DCOM libraries to obtain handles to interfaces that map calls to Remote Procedure Calls (RPC) over TCP/IP. At the distributed receiving end, these remote calls map to calls on the actual DCOM component. At the receiving end, we'll use the term *DCOM server* to mean a server that offers one or more DCOM objects for remote access. However, much like COM objects, DCOM objects are by and large stateless entities and thus do not by default persist object state between calls. As we'll later see, monikers can be used to help simulate stateful COM and DCOM objects by providing interfaces that serve as handles to persisted COM and DCOM objects.

As an enterprise Java developer, you may be asking yourself why you would ever want to learn about COM and DCOM technology, because it is a platform-dependent and Microsoft-centric technology, and we all know that practical enterprise development involves interfacing with a heterogeneous plethora of platforms. The simple answer is that the Microsoft Windows platform happens to be one of the most significant platforms with which you must interact, and there are COM- and DCOM-based applications on such platforms with which you will want your Java-based applications to interface effectively. COM and DCOM components enable access to important applications like Excel, Word, and a vast array of other Windows-based applications, as well as access to Windows-based resources like Windows print drivers. Thus, creating Java applications that act as COM or DCOM components can offer you access to the Windows platform in a way that may be otherwise very inefficient or impossible. In summary, you can build Java applications that can connect to COM and DCOM components as a client, serve as Java wrappers around existing COM server implementations, or act as a Java-based DCOM server implementation. Such capabilities offer many advantages in your enterprise application construction efforts.

DCOM Architecture

Figure 17.1 depicts a high-level view of the DCOM architecture. On the client side of DCOM, a DCOM client talks with the DCOM libraries to create an instance of a DCOM object interface. The DCOM libraries then consult the Windows Registry to extract information on how to create and find such an object. Note that this presumes that such activation information was preregistered with the Windows Registry. Information extracted from the Registry identifies a remote DCOM component location. This information can point the DCOM libraries to interact with the Service Control Manager. The DCOM libraries consult a Service Control Manager to induce the activation of a remote DCOM object instance. The Service Control Manager on the server side then uses the DCOM libraries to create an instance of the requested object.

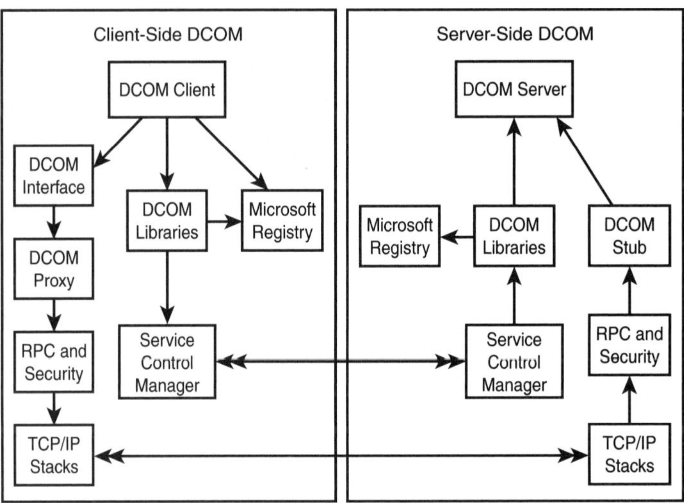

FIGURE 17.1
The DCOM architecture.

A DCOM interface is returned from the DCOM client's request to create a DCOM object instance. The DCOM interface is actually an interface to a DCOM proxy object. In DCOM lingo, the term *proxy* is akin to the stub in both RMI and CORBA lingo. Calls on a proxy object are marshaled using RPC into requests that are sent over the wire via TCP/IP. On the server end, such requests are handled by RPC and delegated to a stub that first unmarshals the request and then calls the DCOM server component itself. Note that we use the term *stub*, following the convention that most literature on DCOM follows. That is, a DCOM stub is equivalent in role to an RMI or CORBA skeleton.

As previously mentioned, COM and DCOM interfaces are nothing more than a collection of functions. Such interfaces are realized as pointers to what is called a Vtable (Virtual Table). The Vtable is simply an array of function pointers. Vtable function pointers point to the actual block of code that implements the particular COM/DCOM functionality. Thus, a Java Virtual Machine that is rigged to make DCOM calls must be altered to map Java-based interface calls to Vtable pointers. This allows other languages to use the same underlying COM and DCOM objects in their pre-existing binary form. A language-specific binding would thus need to be specified at the binary level. What JVM vendor would create such a platform dependence for their JVM implementation? Enter the Microsoft Java Virtual Machine and the controversy that has surrounded such developments.

Java-Based Development Tools

As we just mentioned, the Microsoft Java Virtual Machine will be a key component to facilitate your writing of Java-based COM/DCOM applications. The MSJVM is also referred to as jview and comes with the Microsoft Java SDK version 3.2 or higher. You can download the latest Microsoft Java SDK from `http://www.microsoft.com/java`. The MSJVM also provides an API called J/Direct that allows you to talk to native Windows-based DLLs in a more efficient fashion than by hand-coding an interface yourself with the Java Native Interface (JNI). Furthermore, the MSJVM also provides a collection of Java-based interfaces to the Windows Foundations Classes, further facilitating direct linkage to the Windows platform from Java.

Of course, all of this comes at the cost of creating Java applications that are not portable across different platforms. But if your development demands require the need to tap into some Windows-based functionality, using the MSJVM still may be a good solution for you. From a general enterprise development perspective, however, we would recommend that you make such interfacing as modular as possible and localize any MSJVM-specific interfacing to a few interface or adapter classes that can be swapped out for something more platform-independent when the need arises. This will help you reuse the application code built around such Windows-specific features.

To help you develop DCOM applications, it will be wise for you to pick up a copy of Microsoft Visual J++ version 6.0 or higher. Microsoft Visual J++ makes your life much easier when creating COM- and DCOM-based applications using Java as the language. The Microsoft Visual J++ tool of most use to you will be the Professional Edition, with better support for building COM and DCOM applications than with other editions. Evaluation copies and more information on Visual J++ can be retrieved from `http://msdn.microsoft.com/visualj`.

NOTE

An evaluation copy of the Microsoft Visual J++ development environment is also on the accompanying CD-ROM for your convenience.

Some of the specific utilities we'll use from the previously mentioned suite of tools are the `jvc`, `midl`, `jactivex`, and `javareg` utilities. The `jvc` utility is the MSJVM compiler. The `midl` utility compiles IDL into a set of language-independent type libraries. These type libraries are then compiled into Java classes using `jactivex`. The `javareg` utility will be used to register your DCOM components with the Windows Registry. Finally, much of the Java-based DCOM API documentation that will be very useful to your development efforts is available on the Microsoft Developer's Network CDs that come packaged with the Microsoft Visual J++/C++ development suite of tools or via the MSDN Web site at `http://msdn.microsoft.com`.

DCOM Interfaces

Under the hood of DCOM, DCOM interface pointers reference a Vtable that points to a collection of Windows-based functions. Because Java does not explicitly support the notion of pointers, the MSJVM maps these DCOM interface pointers to client-side DCOM proxies that implement a Java interface.

One very important DCOM interface is the `IUnknown` interface. The fully qualified name of the Java interface equivalent for this interface is `com.ms.com.IUnknown`. `IUnknown` is the root type of interface from which all DCOM-based interfaces inherit. `IUnknown` thus serves as a marker designating that a particular object is of the DCOM persuasion.

As another example, the `com.ms.com.IClassFactory` interface must be implemented by any class that will be registered with the Windows Registry. The Registry will call this interface on a class when creating a new instance of an object.

DCOM Identifiers

In DCOM, Globally Unique Identifiers (GUIDs) are 128-bit values used to identify various DCOM elements. Such identifiers are guaranteed to be globally unique across all realistic spatial boundaries for a significantly long time according to a fairly sophisticated algorithm (`http://www.microsoft.com/asf/spec3/c.htm`). Java access to a GUID is encapsulated by the `com.ms.com._Guid` class. Instances of `_Guid` objects can be created via a native call to the OLE32 DLL's `CoCreateGuid()` call.

Different types of GUIDs exist for different DCOM element types. Interface Identifiers (IIDs) are GUIDs that uniquely identify DCOM interfaces. Class Identifiers (CLSIDs) are GUIDs that uniquely identify a DCOM class (that is, a collection of interfaces).

DCOM Monikers

Typical usage of DCOM objects occurs in a fairly stateless fashion. The `com.ms.com.IMoniker` interface can help you interact with DCOM objects such that they will persist their state over a series of calls. Monikers in DCOM can thus be used to obtain a handle to an object previously instantiated. If a client has a handle to an `IMoniker` interface, the client can refer to an existing server. If the underlying DCOM libraries cannot find a reference to the actual running DCOM server to which the `IMoniker` refers, then a handle to a new one will be created. The `BindToObject()` call on an `IMoniker` object executes the bind to a stateful DCOM object. A number of predefined `IMoniker` objects are equipped with the DCOM libraries. Of course, the semantics of the `BindToObject()` call are specific to the object implementing the `IMoniker` interface.

Server Locality

Three types of COM servers can be created based on where they sit relative to the COM clients. These server locality types are referred to as *in-process*, *local*, or *remote*. Depending on the type of server locality desired, you will register the server differently with the Windows Registry. We of course will be interested in remote types of servers throughout this distributed communications part of the book.

In-process servers run inside of the same process as the COM client. Thus, in this mode, a COM client talks to a COM server that may be in another DLL but still runs inside of the same process.

Local servers run in different processes from the client but on the same machine. Thus, a different executable COM-based server application can receive calls from your separately compiled and running COM-based client application.

Remote servers are of the most interest to us here because they represent the distributed communications paradigm embodied by DCOM. Remote servers run on different machines across a network.

Type Libraries and IDL

A type library structure is a binary description of a COM/DCOM interface. A type library structure contains binary information about DCOM method signatures and certain properties about DCOM classes. After a type library is generated for a DCOM class, it must be registered with the Windows Registry so that it can be used by DCOM clients. Thus, a type library is sort of equivalent to the CORBA concept of an entry in the interface repository, and the Windows Registry essentially acts as a sort of interface repository.

A DCOM-specific interface definition language can be used to describe type libraries in a higher-level and language-independent fashion. Microsoft refers to this as an Interface Definition Language (IDL). Of course, DCOM IDL is different from the OMG's CORBA IDL.

Dynamic Invocation

Automation is DCOM's version of dynamic invocation. It allows you to dynamically invoke calls on interfaces without requiring explicit compile-time knowledge of the interface. During the creation of a DCOM object, a type library will be created that describes the interfaces of a DCOM object. A DCOM server wanting to expose itself as an Automation server must implement the `IDispatch` interface. `IDispatch` allows your DCOM server to expose its interfaces for dynamic invocation. Each method that can be called on an Automation component is identified by a dispatch identifier.

The Java-based `com.ms.com.Dispatch` class can be used to access DCOM Automation components that implement the `IDispatch` interface. Clients use the `com.ms.com.Dispatch` class to identify which method on the Automation component to invoke, based on a dispatch identifier. A `com.ms.com.Variant` object instance is returned from calls to the `Dispatch` interface that allow your client to get and set information from and onto the Automation component.

COM/DCOM Services

As might be evident from our discussions thus far, DCOM has been a component model that has truly grown from the bottom up. That is, DCOM has grown from COM, which has grown from OLE—all of which have grown from the current Windows platform architecture. If you've ever spent some time trying to understand the Windows platform architecture or using the Windows APIs, you've probably spent some time learning about some relatively low-level concepts and have been stuck in the mud of a very functional (as opposed to object-oriented) architecture. This is largely due to the fact that the whole Microsoft operating-system platform product line has been evolving for a time that is relatively long for our industry. Although it may be easy for modern developers and architects to discount the Windows architecture, the fact remains that it has been a part of our lives for some time now. Thus, it seems only natural that the DCOM architecture inherit some of these "old-fashioned" traits. And indeed it does. However, it is also difficult to believe that what was once a desktop-based architecture will ever truly evolve into a scalable enterprise architecture.

The point of all this is that although the DCOM architecture is indeed a hodgepodge of ill-defined Windows-based constructs pieced together to provide you with a working component framework for Windows-based systems, it does offer the services you need to build a distributed application. Indeed, if you come from an object-oriented or truly component-based background, COM and DCOM will be difficult to understand at first. And although modularity is lacking, the distributed service functionality is there. You just have to look for it. It is true that there isn't the concept of an official suite of services built atop DCOM as there is in CORBA, but there is indeed equivalent functionality baked into DCOM and the Windows platform somewhere. We highlight some of those services here:

- *Naming Service:* DCOM monikers provide a way to refer to objects using human-readable names. Monikers can even be associated with a context. Monikers, in conjunction with a Running Object Table that keeps track of currently running and named objects, provide a sort of Naming Service API and functionality for DCOM objects.
- *Trading Service:* Windows 2000 will come wired with the Microsoft Active Directory Service. The Active Directory Service will be capable of maintaining DCOM component information such as server names, activation information, and component properties. Thus, the Active Directory Service may serve as a Trading Service.

- *Persistence Service:* A simple persistence interface (`IPersist`) mechanism exists to perform simple loads from and saves to a particular persistent medium. This framework in conjunction with monikers helps to build different mechanisms to persist objects. DCOM comes with a file persistence medium out of the box. More recently, the Microsoft Transaction Service (MTS) can be used to persist object state.
- *Concurrency/Transactions Service:* The Microsoft Transaction Service provides most of the support for concurrency and transactions needed for building scalable stateful DCOM objects.
- *Security Service:* Security is built into the Microsoft platform. Furthermore, both COM and DCOM have added security features into the mix in consideration of security issues involved with both component sharing and distributed procedure calling.
- *Events/Messaging Service:* Although the CORBA services do not have a direct analogue for Microsoft Message Queuing, we mention it here because DCOM can benefit from use of this service to provide asynchronous message delivery. The CORBA Events service may be most similar in role to messaging.

Interface Definition Language

Microsoft's IDL was based on a DCE standard for generating RPC interfaces. DCOM IDL is defined in a C-like manner and thus does not support certain OO language notions such as inheritance. However, Microsoft later merged its DCOM Object Definition Language (ODL) with IDL to become what we refer to in this book as DCOM IDL. ODL is a much better language for generically describing objects and thus is now a key aspect of DCOM IDL.

The 3.0 version of the `midl` compiler supports the older style IDL as well as the newer style IDL incorporating ODL syntax. As mentioned previously, the `midl` compiler can be used to generate type libraries for your DCOM components. However, tools such as Visual J++ can generate type libraries for you directly from your code without writing any DCOM IDL. Nevertheless, it is important to understand the IDL-to-Java mapping process, because you will inevitably run across either examining or using DCOM IDL during any commercial DCOM for the enterprise development engagement.

The basic steps to follow in generating DCOM Java bindings from DCOM IDL are as listed here:

- Create your DCOM IDL file (for example, named `<fileName>.idl`).
- Compile the DCOM IDL file with the `midl` utility. This step will generate a type library structure in a file named `<fileName>.tlb`. Optionally, you can use a `/tlb` flag to specify your own type library filename to generate.
- Use the `jactivex` utility to generate DCOM Java bindings from the type library file.

Generic DCOM IDL File Format

DCOM IDL is a tad more difficult to understand than CORBA IDL. A rough general format of a DCOM IDL file is defined as shown here:

```
[import "referenceIDLFileName.idl"]

// A DCOM Comment

[
   uuid(7361a240-3e51-11d0-b4c1-333553541111), // A long GUID
   version(versionNumber),
   // Other attributes here
]

library LibraryName
{
  typedef struct StructName
  {
    typeName variableName;
    ...
  } StructAlias;

  [ version(versionNumber), object,  uuid(GUID), otherAttributes ]
  interface AnInterface : IUnknown
  {
   [someAttributes] anMethod([in|out|returnValue] type variable);
  };

  [ version(versionNumber), object,  uuid(GUID), otherAttributes ]
  interface ChildOfOtherInterface : AnInterface
  {
    HRESULT someOtherMethod([in] long l);
  };

  [ version(versionNumber), object,  uuid(GUID), otherAttributes ]
  dispinterface InterfaceName
  {
    HRESULT someOtherMethod([in]long l);
  };

  [ version(versionNumber), object,  uuid(GUID), otherAttributes ]
  coclass Name
  {
      [attribute values] interface InterfaceName;
      [attribute values] dispinterface InterfaceName;
  };
};
```

DCOM IDL-to-Java Mappings

Table 17.1 defines many of the key DCOM IDL entities referred to in the basic IDL file previously outlined and how they map to Java code.

TABLE 17.1 DCOM IDL to Java Mappings

DCOM IDL Entity	*Java Mapping*
Primitive Types	
`void`	`void`
`boolean`	`boolean`
`char`	`char`
`unsigned char`	`byte`
`short`	`short`
`int, long`	`int`
`float`	`float`
`int64`	`long`
`BSTR, LPCOLESTR, LPWSTR, LPSTR`	`java.lang.String`
`VARIANT`	`com.ms.com.Variant`
`SAFEARRAY`	`com.ms.com.SafeArray`
Extended Constructs	
`struct`	`public final class`

`typedef struct ShirtDefinition{`
`long shirtColor;`
`BSTR shirtSize;`
`} ShirtDefinition;`
	`public final class ShirtDefinition{`
	`public int shirtColor;`
	`public String shirtSize;`
	`}`

`enum`	`public interface`

continues

DCOM IDL Entity	*Java Mapping*
Extended Constructs	

enum
{ RED, LARGE, SMALL, MEDIUM,
GREEN, WHITE } SimpleEnum;
	public interface SimpleEnum
	{
	  public static final int RED = 0;
	  public static final int LARGE = 1;
	  public static final int SMALL = 2;
	  public static final int MEDIUM = 3;
	  public static final int GREEN = 4;
	  public static final int WHITE = 5;
	}

Method Calls	
HRESULT sayOne([in] int y);	void sayOne(int y);
HRESULT sayOne([in, out] int* y);	void sayOne(int[] y);
HRESULT sayOne([in, retval] int* y);	int sayOne(int y);
HRESULT sayHello([in] BSTR value);	void sayHello (java.lang.String value);
HRESULT sayHello ([in, out] BSTR* value)	void sayHello (java.lang.String[] value);
HRESULT sayHello ([out, retval] BSTR* value);	java.lang.String sayHello(java.lang.String value);
HRESULT useAny([in] VARIANT anyValue);	void sayHello (com.ms.com.Variant anyValue);
HRESULT useAny([in, out] VARIANT* anyValue);	void sayHello (com.ms.com.Variant anyValue);
HRESULT useAny([out, retval] VARIANT* anyValue);	com.ms.com.Variant anyValue();
HRESULT useAny([in, out] VARIANT** anyValue);	void sayHello (com.ms.com.Variant[] anyValue);

<table>
<tr><th colspan="2">Interface</th></tr>
<tr><td><code>interface</code></td><td><code>public interface</code></td></tr>
<tr><td><pre>
importlib("stdole32.tlb");
   [
      uuid(AB4C0BC0-5A45-22d2-
      88C5-00B02414C666),
      dual
   ]

interface IInOutReturn : IUnknown
  {
    HRESULT setACharValue([in]
      char aValue);
    HRESULT getACharValue([out]
      char* aValue);
    HRESULT aCharValue([in, out]
      char* aValue);
  }
</pre></td><td><pre>
public interface IInOutReturn
  extends IUnknown
{
 public static final
  com.ms.com._Guid iid =
 new com.ms.com._Guid(
    (int)0xab4c0bc0, (short)0x5a45,
    (short)0x22d2, (byte)0x88,
    (byte)0xc5, (byte)0x0,
    (byte)0xb0, (byte)0x24,
    (byte)0x14, (byte)0xc6,
    (byte)0x66);

  public void setACharValue(char
              aValue);
  public void setACharValue(char[]
              aValue);
  public void aCharValue(char[]
               aValue);
}
</pre></td></tr>
<tr><th colspan="2">CoClass</th></tr>
<tr><td><code>coclass</code></td><td><code>public class</code></td></tr>
<tr><td><pre>
[
  uuid(AB4C0BC1-5A45-22d2-
      88C5-00B02414C666)
]

coclass InOutReturnx
  {
      interface IInOutReturn;
  };
</pre></td><td><pre>
public class InOutReturnx implements
IUnknown,com.ms.com.NoAutoScripting,
IInOutReturn
{
public static final com.ms.com._Guid
 clsid = new com.ms.com._Guid(
  (int)0xab4c0bc1,
  (short)0x5a45,
  (short)0x22d2,
  (byte)0x88,
  (byte)0xc5,
  (byte)0x0,
  (byte)0xb0,
  (byte)0x24,
</pre></td></tr>
</table>

continues

<table>
<tr><th>DCOM IDL Entity</th><th>Java Mapping</th></tr>
<tr><td colspan="2">CoClass</td></tr>
<tr><td></td><td><pre>
    (byte)0x14,
    (byte)0x6c,
    (byte)0x66);

    public native void
➥ setACharValue(
      char aValue);
    public native void
➥ setACharValue(
      char[] aValue);
    public native void aCharValue(
      char[] aValue);
}
</pre></td></tr>
<tr><td colspan="2">IDispatch</td></tr>
<tr><td><code>IDispatch</code></td><td><code>java.lang.Object</code></td></tr>
<tr><td><pre>
interface RegisterReceiver:IUnknown
{
  HRESULT register([in]
         IDispatch receiver);
};
</pre></td><td><pre>
public interface RegisterReceiver
   {
 void register(Object receiver);
}
</pre></td></tr>
<tr><td colspan="2">HRESULT</td></tr>
<tr><td><code>HRESULT</code></td><td><pre>
com.ms.com.ComException
      (A RuntimeException)
</pre></td></tr>
</table>

Conclusions

COM provides a component model with which you can build Microsoft Windows platform-dependent services. DCOM allows you to build distributed Microsoft Windows platform-dependent services. DCOM clients and servers thus have a binary dependency on the Windows platform. Java can be used as both a DCOM client and a DCOM server with the use of the Microsoft Java Virtual Machine. Although it is not a desirable option to create platform-dependent enterprise applications, it indeed will be useful to tap into the power and application base of the Windows platform from time to time. We will demonstrate how to build such DCOM clients and servers in the next chapter. Toward the end of the next chapter, we will also discuss how you can bridge between DCOM and other frameworks so that your entire enterprise does not get locked into a Windows platform dependence.

DCOM Communications

CHAPTER

18

IN THIS CHAPTER

- DCOM in the Machine 542
- DCOM Interfaces 544
- DCOM Identifiers 547
- DCOM Types 548
- DCOM Servers and Skeletons 548
- DCOM Server Registration 564
- DCOM Clients and Stubs 567
- DCOM Client Registration and Spawning 570
- DCOM Bridging 571

This chapter describes how to enable your distributed applications using Microsoft's Distributed Component Object Model (DCOM). You may one day encounter the need to build either a DCOM client or a DCOM server in the course of your enterprise development endeavors. Using Java to build such DCOM clients and servers is now a possibility with a suite of tools created by Microsoft. Of course, all of this DCOM-enabling is at the expense of binding you to the Microsoft platform and to Microsoft-based development products. Certain auxiliary tools and techniques, however, can help you bridge the gap between the proprietary DCOM world and the pure enterprise Java world.

In this chapter, you will learn:

- The basic approaches and process for developing DCOM clients and servers using Java.
- The creation of DCOM IDL files.
- The generation of unique IDs for DCOM components and interfaces.
- The creation of binary type libraries for DCOM components and interfaces.
- The creation of DCOM Java language bindings and the implementation of DCOM servers in Java.
- The registration of DCOM servers with the Windows Registry.
- The implementation of DCOM clients in Java.
- The means by which DCOM clients register remote DCOM server access information with the Windows Registry.
- The basic approaches available for bridging between Microsoft platform–dependent DCOM-based applications and more pure Java-based applications.

DCOM in the Machine

The preceding chapter described the basic COM and DCOM component models. This chapter describes how to build a distributed application using DCOM. Specifically, we describe and demonstrate how your enterprise Java applications can hook into the DCOM component model world. This is accomplished from the point of view of two basic scenarios in which you may encounter the need for DCOM-enabling your Java applications.

The first point of view is from the server side in which you may need to build a DCOM server. We describe and demonstrate all the steps you might take to build a basic DCOM server application using Java as the target language. The second point of view is from the client side in which we describe and demonstrate how to build a basic DCOM client, also using Java as the target language. Toward the end of the chapter, we also describe another approach to interfacing with the DCOM world via a brief discussion of some techniques for bridging DCOM with models such as RMI, CORBA, TCP-IP, and JavaBeans.

DCOM Development Process

This chapter is primarily meant to show you how to create basic DCOM-based applications using DCOM IDL. Other DCOM-enabling techniques using OLE automation to enable connectivity from Windows-based applications are not covered here, but the interested reader is encouraged to examine some of our DCOM references in Appendix B, "Additional Resources." Nevertheless, the approach taken here for using DCOM IDL to build DCOM clients and servers should be the most common scenario you as an enterprise developer will encounter. Using IDL as a basis from which to develop a DCOM application, the basic DCOM development process requiring use of a Microsoft-specific suite of Java tools can be pursued as detailed here:

- *Define your IDL interface:* You must first create an IDL file with a description of the distributed DCOM interfaces and components to be accessible by DCOM clients.
- *Generate your GUIDs:* The `guidgen` utility is used to generate the GUIDs needed by your IDL files to uniquely identify each interface and component.
- *Generate a type library:* Using the `midl` utility, you compile your IDL file to generate a type library file defining each interface and component at the binary level.
- *Generate Java bindings:* Using the `jactivex` utility, you generate the Java bindings for all interfaces and components using the type libraries as input.
- *Implement the DCOM server interfaces:* You can then implement a DCOM server by implementing each of the generated Java binding interfaces. Each implementation must then be compiled using the Microsoft Java `jvc` compiler.
- *Register the DCOM server:* The compiled server class files are copied to a location accessible by the Windows Registry on the server machine. The `javareg` utility can then be used to register DCOM server activation and type information with the Windows Registry on the server machine.
- *Implement the DCOM client:* A DCOM client can now be created using the generated Java binding interfaces and components as an API to the remote server implementation. The client must also be compiled using the Microsoft Java `jvc` compiler.
- *Register the DCOM client-side interfaces:* The `javareg` utility can then be used to register remote DCOM server access information with the Windows Registry on the client machine.
- *Run the Client:* The client code must then be run using the Microsoft Java `jview` runtime environment to access remote DCOM servers.

DCOM Interfaces

As a first step, we define our DCOM IDL here using interfaces to the same basic example application demonstrated for the TCP/IP, CORBA, and RMI communications paradigm examples of previous chapters. We use DCOM IDL in this chapter to generate a type library and then a set of Java bindings for these interfaces. Using a tool like Visual J++, you may not even have the need to define such IDL, because you can simply define your Java classes and have Visual J++ handle most of the other work for you. Nevertheless, we show you how to create a DCOM-based application here from the ground up and following the same basic development process used for the other distributed object communications paradigms.

The DCOM IDL interfaces that describe our example application are shown in Listing 18.1 for an `Order` structure, `IClientReceiver` interface, `ICustomer` interface, and `IQueryServer` interface. Each interface derives from the `IUnknown` interface which is defined in the `unknwn.idl` file that comes equipped with the standard DCOM libraries.

NOTE

The DCOM IDL interfaces and all example code used in this chapter are contained on the CD in the `examples\src\ejava\dcomch18` directory. Note that although we place our source code in this directory, the compiled package names generated from this DCOM example do not follow the standard Java packaging scheme of other examples. That is, our DCOM code does not get placed into the `ejava.dcomch18` Java package. Note also that the Cloudscape database must be running and configured in the `examples\src\ejava\dcomch18\dcomch18.txt` file per instructions in Appendix A, "Software Configuration."

In order to use our example scripts equipped on the CD for this chapter, the `MSDK_JAVA` environment variable must be set to the root directory of a Microsoft SDK installation (we have used the Microsoft SDK for Java v3.2). Additionally, we require that you set a `VSTUDIO_HOME` environment variable to the root directory of a Microsoft Visual Studio 6.0 installation in order to use our `compile.bat` script on the CD. As we describe in a subsequent section in this chapter, Visual Studio is only needed to use the `midl` utility. You can also modify the `compile.bat` script to not depend on `midl` if you use Visual J++ to generate a DCOM type library for you.

The `Order` IDL `struct` encapsulates the minimum information needed to fill out a simple BeeShirts.com order. The `IClientReceiver` interface is used on the client side of our application and will be called by the server-side (that is, a callback) with an array of `Order` structures inside of the `VARIANT` type. The `ICustomer` interface is used to define an interface encapsulating a BeeShirts.com customer with calls to get and set various Basic String (BSTR) based DCOM types used to represent customer attributes.

The IQueryServer interface describes the frontline server-side DCOM service interface for our example. A call findCustomersWhoOrderedForMoreThan() finds customers who spend more than a certain amount of money, binds them to a lookup service, and returns a VARIANT pointer to an array of customer references. A method register() takes a ClientReceiver callback interface reference and client receiver name to register DCOM client callbacks. A method findOrdersWhichAreFrom() finds the orders for a given state and passes the set of associated orders to the registered ClientReceiver objects. Note that we also define a coclass to declare our CoQueryServer DCOM component class's support of the frontline IQueryServer interface. The CoQueryServer class will represent our client-side interface to our DCOM component. The CoQueryServer and interfaces are defined within a dcomch18 type library, which also imports the base type COM library stdole32.tlb. The base type COM library needs to be imported by every COM/DCOM type library definition.

LISTING 18.1 The DCOM IDL Example (QueryServer.idl)

```
import "unknwn.idl" ;
// each interface should be derived from IUnknown interface,
➥ the IUnknown is defined in unknwn.idl


typedef struct  Order
{
  long orderID;
  LPSTR orderDate;
  double orderValue;
}Order;


[
  object,
  uuid(CDACDBC7-5A65-22d2-8875-00B02414C777),
    pointer_default(unique)
]

interface IClientReceiver : IUnknown
{
  HRESULT setResultOrders([in]  VARIANT values);
};


[
  object,
```

continues

LISTING 18.1 Continued

```
  uuid(CDACDBC4-5A65-22d2-8875-00B02414C777)
]

interface ICustomer : IUnknown
{
  //BSTR is  Basic String to send across DCOM
  HRESULT setFirstName([in] BSTR value);
  HRESULT setLastName([in] BSTR value);
  HRESULT setAddress1([in] BSTR value);
  HRESULT setAddress2([in] BSTR value);
  HRESULT setCity([in] BSTR value);
  HRESULT setState([in] BSTR value);
  HRESULT setZip([in] BSTR value);
  HRESULT setPhoneNumber([in] BSTR value);
  HRESULT setEmailAddress([in] BSTR value);
  HRESULT firstName([out,retval] BSTR* value);
  HRESULT lastName([out,retval] BSTR* value);
  HRESULT address1([out,retval] BSTR* value);
  HRESULT address2([out,retval] BSTR* value);
  HRESULT city([out,retval] BSTR* value);
  HRESULT state([out,retval] BSTR* value);
  HRESULT zip([out,retval] BSTR* value);
  HRESULT phoneNumber([out,retval] BSTR* value);
  HRESULT emailAddress([out,retval] BSTR* value);
};


[
  object,
  uuid(CDACDBC1-5A65-22d2-8875-00B02414C777)
]
interface IQueryServer : IUnknown
{
  HRESULT  findCustomersWhoOrderedForMoreThan([in] float value,
    [out, retval] VARIANT* customerReferences );
  HRESULT  findOrdersWhichAreFrom([in] BSTR state);
  HRESULT  registerReceiver([in] BSTR name,
                            [in] IDispatch* clientReceiver);
};

[
 uuid(CDACDBC0-5A65-22d2-8875-00B02414C777)
]
library dcomch18
```

```
{
  // standard OLE type library
  importlib("stdole32.tlb");
  [
    uuid(CDACDBC9-5A65-22d2-8875-00B02414C777)
  ]
  coclass CoQueryServer
  {
    [default] interface IQueryServer ;
  };
  interface ICustomer;
  interface IClientReceiver;
};
```

DCOM Identifiers

You've inevitably noticed the GUIDs (that is, `uuid` values) that are part of the `QueryServer.idl` file in Listing 18.1. Although you can specify the main elements of the DCOM IDL file, you might be wondering how to determine which 128-bit ID value to insert into your files. The easiest way to generate such values is to use the `guidgen` utility that comes with both the MSJVM SDK and the Visual J++ installations. Figure 18.1 shows what the `guidgen` utility looks like when generating a GUID (uses the standard `CoCreateGuid` COM API call) in the Windows Registry format used by our IDL file. Using this tool, you simply copy the generated GUID to the Clipboard and then paste it into your IDL file.

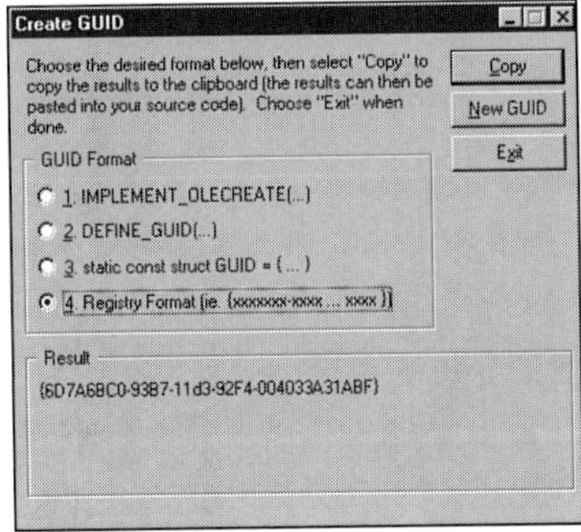

FIGURE 18.1
Generating GUIDs with the `guidgen` *utility.*

DCOM Types

After creating your IDL file, you can use the midl utility to generate a DCOM type library file. Note, however, that at the time of this writing, the midl utility was still not being shipped with either the MSJVM SDK or the Visual J++ Version 6.0 tool. The midl utility ships with Visual Studio 6.0, but at the time of this writing a copy of midl could be obtained only by specifically installing the Visual C++ component of Visual Studio. You can also download midl as part of the Microsoft Platform SDK Build environment from http://msdn.microsoft.com/developer/sdk.

We use the midl utility in our compile.bat compilation script equipped in the examples\src\ejava\dcomch18 directory. The midl utility is called with the QueryServer.idl file as a command-line argument. The midl utility is also passed a set of flags that turn off the generation of C-file proxies and headers, as well as defining the target Win32 environment. For example:

```
midl /proxy nul /header nul /iid nul /dlldata nul /win32
➥ -I [VSTUDIO_HOME]\vc98\include QueryServer.idl
```

Such a command then generates the type library filename QueryServer.tlb in the same directory in which you issued the midl command. As we mentioned in the preceding chapter, type library files contain binary descriptions of your COM/DCOM interfaces.

DCOM Servers and Skeletons

Creating DCOM servers and skeletons involves the generation of Java bindings from binary type libraries, as well as the implementation and compilation of your servers. Creating DCOM servers can seem a bit more obscure than creating other types of distributed servers. Nevertheless, the basic concepts involved in distributing a DCOM server are similar to those involved in distributing other types of servers. This section describes the generation of DCOM Java bindings, the implementation of a DCOM server, and the compilation of a DCOM server.

Generating Java Bindings

After a type library is generated, you'll want to generate the Java bindings for your application. That is, you'll want to generate the Java classes and interfaces your DCOM server implementations will utilize to expose their services for DCOM-based access. The jactivex utility that comes equipped with both the MSJVM SDK and Visual J++ can be used to generate the Java bindings you'll need. The command-line call for jactivex is also contained in the compile.bat file and is passed the type library filename and a directory for output as command-line parameters:

```
jactivex -d [EJAVA_HOME]\examples\src\ejava\dcomch18 QueryServer.tlb
```

This command will generate an Order.java final class, an IClientReceiver.java interface, an ICustomer.java interface, an IQueryServer.java interface, and a CoQueryServer.java class corresponding to the struct, interfaces, and coclass defined in our IDL file of Listing 18.1. Technically speaking, the type library generated previously can be viewed as our DCOM equivalent of interface skeletons that call our DCOM servers upon client request. The interfaces generated from using jactivex with the type library file serve as our communications interfaces called by such skeletons and implemented by our DCOM servers.

Generic DCOM Servers

Figure 18.2 shows a typical arrangement of DCOM interfaces and implementations used to create a DCOM server. Hanging off of each interface or class are COM directives (represented here as UML notes) generated by the jactivex utility for use by the MSJVM in recognizing such Java code as first-class DCOM citizens. The IMyServer Java interface is generated from an interface in the IDL file with any specified method signatures appropriately mapped to a Java method signature. You create the MyServerImpl class, which implements the IMyServer interface called by the MSJVM.

The CoMyServer Java class is generated from a coclass in the IDL file defining any method signatures associated with the DCOM interfaces that the DCOM component class implements. The defined methods of CoMyServer happen to bind to native calls that the MSJVM will map to calls onto the particular interface that this class implements (for example, IMyServer). In a remote DCOM server scenario, it is the CoMyServer class that will interact with your client-side DCOM libraries to initiate a remote call on your MyServerImpl implementation.

Example DCOM Server Implementations

Listings 18.2 through 18.4 show the implementations for our CustomerImplementation, ClientReceiverImplementation, and QueryServerImplementation DCOM interfaces, respectively. Note that in each listing, a public static final com.ms.com._Guid object is inserted into each implementation file. This object declaration must be copied and pasted from the implementation's corresponding generated Java interface definition.

Note from Listing 18.2 that in DCOM you don't have to implement any sort of bind functionality in your CustomerImplementation as was needed for the CORBA and RMI examples. You of course will have to implement all getters and setters based on the ICustomer IDL description of Listing 18.1. As described previously, the com.ms.com._Guid object that has been pasted into the CustomerImplementation file was copied from the generated ICustomer interface file.

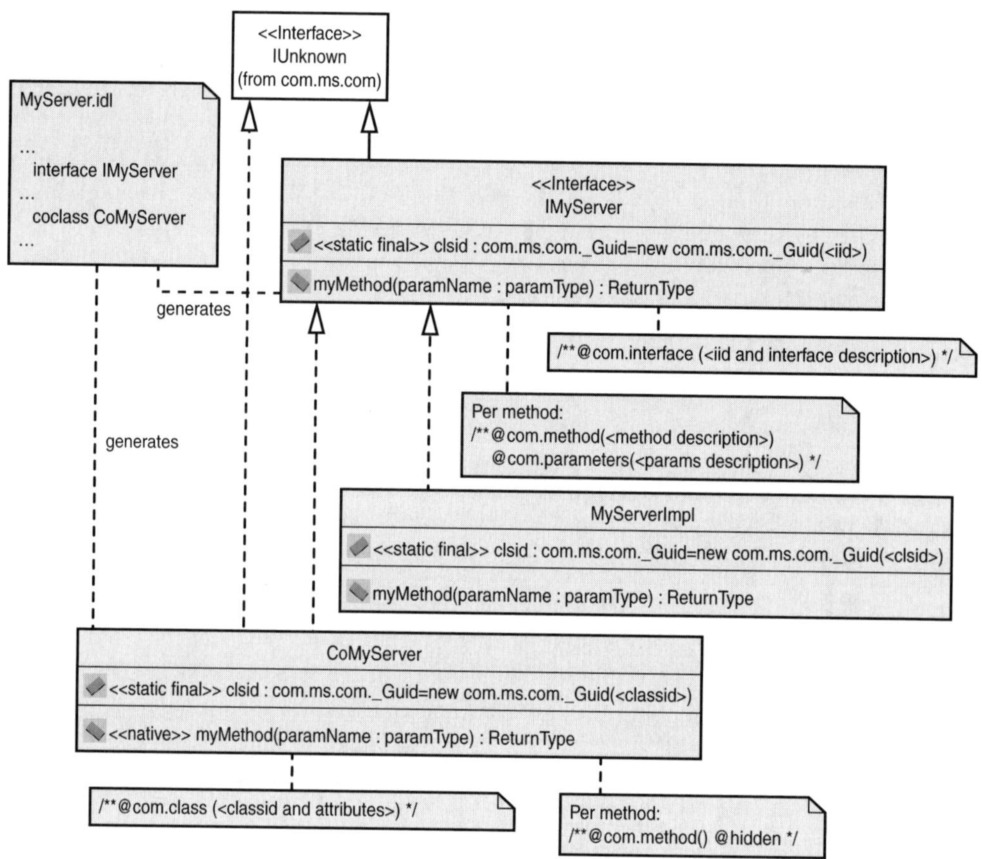

FIGURE 18.2
A DCOM server.

LISTING 18.2 The DCOM Customer Implementation (`CustomerImplementation.java`)

```
package queryserver;

import com.ms.com.*;


public class CustomerImplementation implements ICustomer {
  private String firstName;
  private String lastName;
  private String address1;
  private String address2;
```

```
private String city;
private String state;
private String zip;
private String phoneNumber;
private String emailAddress;



public String firstName() {
  return this.firstName;
}

public String lastName() {
  return this.lastName;
}

public String address1() {
  return this.address1;
}

public String address2() {
  return this.address2;
}

public String city() {
  return this.city;
}

public String state() {
  return this.state;
}

public String zip() {
  return this.zip;
}

public String phoneNumber() {
  return this.phoneNumber;
}

public String emailAddress() {
  return this.emailAddress;
}
```

continues

LISTING 18.2 Continued

```
  public void setFirstName(String value) {
    this.firstName = value;
  }

  public void setLastName(String value) {
    this.lastName = value;
  }

  public void setAddress1(String value) {
    this.address1 = value;
  }

  public void setAddress2(String value) {
    this.address2 = value;
  }

  public void setCity(String value) {
    this.city = value;
  }

  public void setState(String value) {
    this.state = value;
  }

  public void setZip(String value) {
    this.zip = value;
  }

  public void setPhoneNumber(String value) {
    this.phoneNumber = value;
  }

  public void setEmailAddress(String value) {
    this.emailAddress = value;
  }

// This is a generated GUID for ICustomer Interface uuid
// in the idl definition
  public static final com.ms.com._Guid iid =
    new com.ms.com._Guid((int) 0xcdacdbc4, (short) 0x5a65,
                         (short) 0x22d2, (byte) 0x88, (byte) 0x75,
                         (byte) 0x0, (byte) 0xb0, (byte) 0x24,
                         (byte) 0x14, (byte) 0xc7, (byte) 0x77);
}
```

The `ClientReceiverImplementation` class of Listing 18.3 implements the one remote method declared in the IDL Listing 18.1 for the `IClientReceiver` interface. The `setResultOrders()` method simply prints the list of orders received. Note that it takes a `com.ms.com.Variant` object instance as a parameter and converts its contents into an array of `Variant` types. Each `Variant` type is then used to extract and cast a particular `Order` object (described in Listing 18.5). As described earlier, the `com.ms.com._Guid` object that has been pasted into the `ClientReceiver` file was copied from the generated `IClientReceiver` interface file.

LISTING 18.3 The DCOM Client Receiver Implementation (`ClientReceiverImplementation.java`)

```
package queryserver;

import com.ms.com.*;

/**
 *  Client Receiver implementation.
 */
public class ClientReceiverImplementation implements IClientReceiver {
  public void setResultOrders(Variant values) {
    Variant[] variantArray = values.toVariantArray();

    System.out.println("Client Received :"
                         + variantArray.length + " Orders ");

    for (int i = 0; i < variantArray.length; i++) {
      Variant variant = variantArray[i];
      Order order = (Order) variant.getObject();

      System.out.println("ID :" + order.orderID);
      System.out.println("Date :" + order.orderDate);
      System.out.println("Value :" + order.orderValue);
    }
  }

 // Generated Guid for the IClientReceiver Interface uuid in the idl
  public static final com.ms.com._Guid iid =
    new com.ms.com._Guid((int) 0xcdacdbc7, (short) 0x5a65,
                         (short) 0x22d2, (byte) 0x88, (byte) 0x75,
                         (byte) 0x0, (byte) 0xb0, (byte) 0x24,
                         (byte) 0x14, (byte) 0xc7, (byte) 0x77);

}
```

The QueryServerImplementation of Listing 18.4 implements the IQueryServer IDL interface declared in Listing 18.1. Note that our QueryServerImplementation does not have a main() method as does our frontline server implementation from other examples. Such main() methods are not needed here because this IQueryServer implementation is called by the MSJVM whenever calls to the DCOM CoQueryServer component (Listing 18.7) are made. As described earlier, the com.ms.com._Guid object that has been pasted into the QueryServerImplementation file was copied from the generated IQueryServer interface file.

NOTE

To simplify the example, we have bound the location of the properties file used by this class to the fixed location of C:\temp\dcomch18.txt instead of reading in such a value from the command line as was done for previous examples. This properties file is read in the QueryServerImplementation constructor and is used to establish a connection with the BeeShirts.com database via JDBC. The dcomch18.txt contained in the examples\src\ejava\dcomch18 directory can be modified and moved to whatever directory you want to reference in the QueryServerImplementation constructor.

The QueryServerImplementation's findCustomersWhoOrderedForMoreThan() method retrieves the customer query from the properties object and issues the query using getResultSet(). The results of this query are then used to create a new distributed CustomerImplementation DCOM reference. What is different about this example is that the Vector of created CustomerImplementation objects is then used to populate a com.ms.com.SafeArray object of Variant objects created with the object reference of each CustomerImplementation object. This SafeArray object is then returned in the form of a Variant object itself.

The register() method is used to register a ClientReceiver with the QueryServerImplementation. The findOrdersWhichAreFrom() method issues an order query retrieved from the properties object and then creates a Vector to store the resultant orders. The Vector of created Order objects is then used to populate a com.ms.com.SafeArray object of Variant objects created with the actual object value of each Order object. This SafeArray object is then set into a Variant form and used for making a callback on the distributed DCOM client ClientReceiver references that were registered using the register() method.

LISTING 18.4 The CORBA Query Server Implementation (QueryServerImplementation.java)

```
package queryserver;

import com.ms.com.*;
import java.util.*;
```

```
import java.sql.*;
import java.io.*;


public class QueryServerImplementation implements IQueryServer {
  private IClientReceiver clientReceiver;
  private String clientReceiverName;
  private Properties properties;
  private Connection connection;

// This is Generated GUID for IQueryServer Interface uuid
// in the idl definition
    public static final com.ms.com._Guid clsid =
      new com.ms.com._Guid((int)0xcdacdbc9,
        (short)0x5a65, (short)0x22d2,
        (byte)0x88, (byte)0x75,
        (byte)0x0, (byte)0xb0,
        (byte)0x24, (byte)0x14,
        (byte)0xc7, (byte)0x77);

  public QueryServerImplementation() {

    // The QueryServer is instantiated by the
    // DCOM activation framework, to send the initialization data
    // to the Object.
    // Thus, we need to make sure the dcomch18.txt file is copied
    // to the C:\\temp directory before running this application.
    String propertiesFileName = "C:\\temp\\dcomch18.txt";


    // Read properties info
    readProperties(propertiesFileName);
    String dbDriverClassName = (String) properties.get("DRIVER_CLASS");
    String dbURL = (String) properties.get("DATABASE_URL");
    String userName = (String) properties.get("UserName");
    String password = (String) properties.get("Password");
    // Configure database driver and connection
    try {
      Class.forName(dbDriverClassName);

      if (userName == null || password == null || userName.length() == 0
              || password.length() == 0) {
        connection = DriverManager.getConnection(dbURL);
      } else {
```

continues

LISTING 18.4 Continued

```
        connection = DriverManager.getConnection(dbURL, userName,
                                                 password);
      }
    }

     catch (ClassNotFoundException cnfEx) {

       System.out.println("Driver Class Not found " + cnfEx);
    }
    catch (SQLException sqlEx) {

      System.out.println("SQL Exception :" + sqlEx);
    }
  }
  // Get ResultSet for the given queryString
  private ResultSet getResultSet(String sqlQuery,
          java.lang.Object whereValue) throws SQLException {
    PreparedStatement preparedStatement =
      connection.prepareStatement(sqlQuery);

    preparedStatement.setObject(1, whereValue);
    ResultSet rs = preparedStatement.executeQuery();

    return rs;
  }
  public void readProperties(String fineName) {
    try {
      properties = new Properties();

      FileInputStream fin = new FileInputStream(fineName);

      properties.load(fin);
      fin.close();
    } catch (IOException e) {
      System.out.println("Error :" + e);
    }
  }

  public Variant findCustomersWhoOrderedForMoreThan(float value) {
    String customerQueryString =
      (String) properties.get("CUSTOMER_QUERY");

    Variant returnValues = null;
```

```
// If the QueryString is null, it displays
// that information on the Server Screen.
if (customerQueryString == null) {
  System.out.println("CUSTOMER_QUERY in file is null");
  returnValues = new Variant();
  return returnValues;
}
```

```
try {
  // Read Customer results from database query
  ResultSet rs = this.getResultSet(customerQueryString,
                                   new Float(value));
  ResultSetMetaData rsMetaData = rs.getMetaData();
  int nColumns = rsMetaData.getColumnCount();
  Vector vector = new Vector();
  // Create a Customer object for each result and add to vector
  while (rs.next()) {
    String customerID = rs.getString("CUSTOMER_ID");
    String firstName = rs.getString("FIRST_NAME");
    String lastName = rs.getString("LAST_NAME");
    String address1 = rs.getString("ADDRESS_1");
    String address2 = rs.getString("ADDRESS_2");
    String city = rs.getString("CITY");
    String state = rs.getString("STATE");
    String phoneNumber = rs.getString("PHONE");
    String eMail = rs.getString("EMAIL");
    String zip = rs.getString("ZIP_CODE");
    CustomerImplementation custImpl = new CustomerImplementation();

    custImpl.setFirstName(firstName);
    custImpl.setLastName(lastName);
    custImpl.setAddress1(address1);
    custImpl.setAddress2(address2);
    custImpl.setCity(city);
    custImpl.setState(state);
    custImpl.setZip(zip);
    custImpl.setEmailAddress(eMail);
    custImpl.setPhoneNumber(phoneNumber);

    String name = customerID;
```

continues

LISTING 18.4 Continued

```
vector.addElement(custImpl);
     }
     // SafeArray to hold ICustomer References, to send Across DCOM wire.
     SafeArray varray = new SafeArray(Variant.VariantVariant, vector.size());

     for (int i = 0; i < vector.size(); i++) {
       Variant rcustomer = new Variant();
       // Get the ICustomer reference from the Vector and set in a Variant

       rcustomer.putObjectRef((ICustomer) vector.elementAt(i));
      // Add the variant to safe Array
       varray.setVariant(i, rcustomer);
     }

     returnValues = new Variant(varray, true);

     return returnValues;
   } catch (SQLException sqlEx) {
     System.out.println(sqlEx);
     sqlEx.printStackTrace();

     return returnValues;
   }
 }

 public void findOrdersWhichAreFrom(String state) {
   // Get Order query and set null orders if no query available
   String orderQueryString = (String) properties.get("ORDER_QUERY");
   if (orderQueryString == null) {
     System.out.println("ORDER_QUERY in file is null");
     returnOrders = new Variant();
     if (this.clientReceiver != null) {
       clientReceiver.setResultOrders(returnOrders);
     }
     return ;
   }


   try {
     // Issue query for Order results
     ResultSet rs = this.getResultSet(orderQueryString, state);
     ResultSetMetaData rsMetaData = rs.getMetaData();
     int nColumns = rsMetaData.getColumnCount();

     Vector orders = new Vector();
```

```
    // For each result, create an Order object and add to vector
    while (rs.next()) {
      int orderID = rs.getInt("ORDER_ID");
      java.sql.Date orderDate = rs.getDate("ORDER_DATE");
      double orderValue = rs.getDouble("TOTAL_PRICE");
      Order order = new Order();

      order.orderID = orderID;
      order.orderDate = orderDate.toString();
      order.orderValue = orderValue;

      orders.addElement(order);
    }
    // create SafeArray to hold orders and send across DCOM Wire.
    SafeArray ordArray = new SafeArray(Variant.VariantVariant,
                                       orders.size());


    for (int i = 0; i < orders.size(); i++) {
      Variant variant= new Variant();
      // extract order object from the Vector and add
      // element as Variant

      variant.putObject((Order) orders.elementAt(i));
     // add the variant to SafeArray
      ordArray.setVariant(i, variant);
    }

    returnOrders = new Variant(ordArray, true);

    if (this.clientReceiver != null) {
      clientReceiver.setResultOrders(returnOrders);
    }
  } catch (SQLException sqlEx) {
    System.out.println(sqlEx);
    sqlEx.printStackTrace();
  }
 }
/*
 * Register receiver, call back object
 */
 public void registerReceiver(String name, Object clientReceiver) {
   this.clientReceiverName = name;
   this.clientReceiver = (IClientReceiver) clientReceiver;
 }
}
```

The Order object generated by the DCOM of Listing 18.1 is shown in Listing 18.5. It simply defines as public the data associated with an order.

LISTING 18.5 The Generated Order Class (Order.java)

```
//
// Auto-generated using JActiveX.EXE 5.00.2918
// (C:\PROGRA~1\MICROS~4\VJ98\JACTIVEX.EXE -d C:\temp QueryServer.tlb)
//
// WARNING: Do not remove the comments that include "@com" directives.
// This source file must be compiled by a @com-aware compiler.
// If you are using the Microsoft Visual J++ compiler, you must use
// version 1.02.3920 or later. Previous versions will not issue an error
// but will not generate COM-enabled class files.
//
package queryserver;

import com.ms.com.*;
import com.ms.com.IUnknown;
import com.ms.com.Variant;

/**
 * @com.struct(noAutoOffset)
 */
public final class Order {

  /**
   * @com.structmap([offset=0,type=I4] orderID)
   */
  public int orderID;

  /**
   * @com.structmap([offset=4,
                    customMarshal="com.ms.com.AnsiStringMarshaller",
                    type=CUSTOM] orderDate)
   */
  public String orderDate;

  /**
   * @com.structmap([offset=8,type=R8] orderValue)
   */
  public double orderValue;
}
```

Finally, to give you a better sense of what a `jactivex` generated `interface` and `coclass` look like, we have included the generated `IQueryServer` interface in Listing 18.6 and the generated `CoQueryServer` class in Listing 18.7. Note that the DCOM `interface` is a Java interface with all exposed methods defined and associated with DCOM method and parameter descriptors. The `coclass` is a Java class also with all exposed methods defined and designated as `native` method definitions. Thus, your `coclass` is tightly coupled with native Windows platform libraries.

LISTING 18.6 The Generated `IQueryServer` interface (`IQueryServer.java`)

```
//
// Auto-generated using JActiveX.EXE 5.00.2918
// (C:\PROGRA~1\MICROS~4\VJ98\JACTIVEX.EXE -d C:\temp QueryServer.tlb)
//
// WARNING: Do not remove the comments that include "@com" directives.
// This source file must be compiled by a @com-aware compiler.
// If you are using the Microsoft Visual J++ compiler, you must use
// version 1.02.3920 or later. Previous versions will not issue an error
// but will not generate COM-enabled class files.
//
package queryserver;

import com.ms.com.*;
import com.ms.com.IUnknown;
import com.ms.com.Variant;

// VTable-only interface IQueryServer

/**
 * @com.interface(iid=CDACDBC1-5A65-22D2-8875-00B02414C777, thread=AUTO)
 */
public interface IQueryServer extends IUnknown {

   /**
    * @com.method(vtoffset=0, addFlagsVtable=4)
    * @com.parameters([in,type=R4] value, [type=VARIANT] return)
    */
   public Variant findCustomersWhoOrderedForMoreThan(float value);

   /**
    * @com.method(vtoffset=1, addFlagsVtable=4)
    * @com.parameters([in,type=STRING] state)
    */
   public void findOrdersWhichAreFrom(String state);
```

continues

LISTING 18.6 Continued

```
  /**
   * @com.method(vtoffset=2, addFlagsVtable=4)
   * @com.parameters([in,type=STRING] name, [in,
       iid=00020400-0000-0000-C000-000000000046,
       thread=AUTO,type=DISPATCH] clientReceiver)
   */
  public void registerReceiver(String name, Object clientReceiver);

  public static final com.ms.com._Guid iid =
    new com.ms.com._Guid((int) 0xcdacdbc1, (short) 0x5a65,
                        (short) 0x22d2, (byte) 0x88, (byte) 0x75,
                        (byte) 0x0, (byte) 0xb0, (byte) 0x24,
                        (byte) 0x14, (byte) 0xc7, (byte) 0x77);
}
```

LISTING 18.7 The Generated `CoQueryServer` class (`CoQueryServer.java`)

```
//
// Auto-generated using JActiveX.EXE 5.00.2918
// (C:\PROGRA~1\MICROS~4\VJ98\JACTIVEX.EXE -d C:\temp QueryServer.tlb)
//
// WARNING: Do not remove the comments that include "@com" directives.
// This source file must be compiled by a @com-aware compiler.
// If you are using the Microsoft Visual J++ compiler, you must use
// version 1.02.3920 or later. Previous versions will not issue an error
// but will not generate COM-enabled class files.
//
package queryserver;

import com.ms.com.*;
import com.ms.com.IUnknown;
import com.ms.com.Variant;

/**
 * @com.class(classid=CDACDBC9-5A65-22D2-8875-00B02414C777,DynamicCasts)
 */
public class CoQueryServer implements IUnknown,
                                      com.ms.com.NoAutoScripting,
                                      queryserver.IQueryServer {
```

```
    /**
     * @com.method()
     * @hidden
     */
    public native Variant findCustomersWhoOrderedForMoreThan(float value);

    /**
     * @com.method()
     * @hidden
     */
    public native void findOrdersWhichAreFrom(String state);

    /**
     * @com.method()
     * @hidden
     */
    public native void registerReceiver(String name,
                                        Object clientReceiver);

    public static final com.ms.com._Guid clsid =
      new com.ms.com._Guid((int) 0xcdacdbc9, (short) 0x5a65,
                           (short) 0x22d2, (byte) 0x88, (byte) 0x75,
                           (byte) 0x0, (byte) 0xb0, (byte) 0x24,
                           (byte) 0x14, (byte) 0xc7, (byte) 0x77);
}
```


Compiling the DCOM Servers

The `compile.bat` compilation script can then be used to compile the generated Java files and your server implementations. You'll need to use the `jvc` Java compiler that comes equipped with either the MSJVM SDK or Visual J++ because your Java code has a few nonstandard COM and DCOM that only `jvc` can understand (and needs). Note that the command used in `compile.bat` will also attempt to compile the client code in that directory, so you may also choose to compile each piece of DCOM server-side code separately for now. As an example, to compile all files in the `[EJAVA_HOME]examples\src\ejava\dcomch18` directory and its newly created `queryserver` subdirectory, the compilation commands are simply typed as:

```
jvc -d [EJAVA_HOME]\examples\classes *.java
jvc -d [EJAVA_HOME]\examples\classes queryserver\*.java
```

The `compile.bat` script also copies the `dcomch18.txt` properties file to the location required by your `QueryServerImplementation`, as well as copying the compiled Java class files to a location where the Windows registry can find them. Your Windows platform is configured to search for COM/DCOM-enabled Java class files in a particular directory. On our Windows NT platform, this directory is `C:\winnt\java\classes`. Thus, after creating a `queryserver` subdirectory beneath the `C:\winnt\java\classes` directory, our `compile.bat` file copies the `.class` files to that directory as shown here:

```
mkdir C:\winnt\java\classes\queryserver

copy  "%EJAVA_HOME%"\examples\classes\queryserver\*.class
➥ C:\winnt\java\classes\queryserver
```

DCOM Server Registration

After you create, compile, and copy your DCOM server implementations to the Windows DCOM java class directory, you will need to register the classes with the Windows Registry. You can do this in various ways, but two free ways are by using the `javareg` utility equipped with the MSJVM SDK or via the creation of a registry file you can directly load into the Windows Registry. You might also choose to use Visual J++'s built-in mechanisms for interacting with the Windows Registry in a more user-friendly fashion.

Registration with `javareg`

The `javareg` utility can be used to register and unregister DCOM Java classes to and from the Windows Registry. Class name, path, CLSID, and human-readable program IDs can all be associated with the registered Java class. Furthermore, COM classes can be tagged as `surrogate` to indicate that the class will run in a surrogate process, and they can also be tagged as `remote` to indicate that the activation of the class occurs on a remote machine (used by clients). The basic structure of the `javareg` utility is as follows:

```
javareg </register | /unregister>
        /class:<Java class file name> /codebase:<Path to Java class>
        /clsid:<CLSID> [/progid:<human-readable ID>]
        [/surrogate] [/remote:<Server name for remote activation>]
```

We have equipped a file named `serverregistration.bat` with our example code that registers our `QueryServerImplementation` interface using this command:

```
javareg /register
➥ /class:queryserver.QueryServerImplementation /codebase:.
➥ /clsid:{CDACDBC9-5A65-22d2-8875-00B02414C777} /surrogate
```

Registration with a Registry File

If you are so inclined and want to deal with the Windows Registry one-on-one, you can also create an ASCII file with a `.reg` extension containing Windows Registry information, spawn the `Regedit.exe` program (in your `\winnt` or `\windows` directory), and then import the registry file into the Windows Registry directly. For example, you may have a `serverregistration.reg` file like this:

```
REGEDIT4
[HKEY_CLASSES_ROOT\CLSID\{CDACDBC9-5A65-22d2-8875-00B02414C777}]
@="Java Class: QueryServerImplementations"
"AppID"="{CDACDBC9-5A65-22d2-8875-00B02414C777}"

[HKEY_CLASSES_ROOT\CLSID\{CDACDBC9-5A65-22d2-8875-00B02414C777}
➥\InprocServer32]
@="MSJAVA.DLL"
"ThreadingModel"="Both"
"JavaClass"="QueryServerImplementations"

[HKEY_CLASSES_ROOT\CLSID\{CDACDBC9-5A65-22d2-8875-00B02414C777}
➥\LocalServer32]
@="javareg /clsid:{CDACDBC9-5A65-22d2-8875-00B02414C777} " /surrogate

[HKEY_CLASSES_ROOT\CLSID\{CDACDBC9-5A65-22d2-8875-00B02414C777}
➥\Implemented Categories]

[HKEY_CLASSES_ROOT\CLSID\{CDACDBC9-5A65-22d2-8875-00B02414C777}
➥\Implemented Categories\{CEACDBC1-5A65-22d2-8875-00B02414C777}]

[HKEY_CLASSES_ROOT\AppID\{CDACDBC9-5A65-22d2-8875-00B02414C777}]
@="Java Class: QueryServerImplementations"
```

Then you can execute the `regedit.exe` program, which displays a user interface to the Windows registry; select Registry from the pull-down menus; and then select Import Registry File to read in the contents of this file.

Peering into DCOM Objects

The OLEview tool that comes with Visual J++ is a GUI-based tool allowing you to view and manipulate the contents of the Windows Registry's COM/DCOM object registrations. For example, after registering your `QueryServerImplementation` object, you can open OLEView and view its entry under the Object Classes folder, Grouped By Component Category, Java Classes folder as exemplified in Figure 18.3 for our `QueryServerImplementation`.

If you have installed Visual J++, experimenting with the OLEView tool will be worth your time. It provides a very insightful GUI-based interface to the repository of all COM and DCOM components registered on your machine. Not only can you view traits about such components, but you also can modify how they will be activated in a simple GUI-based manner.

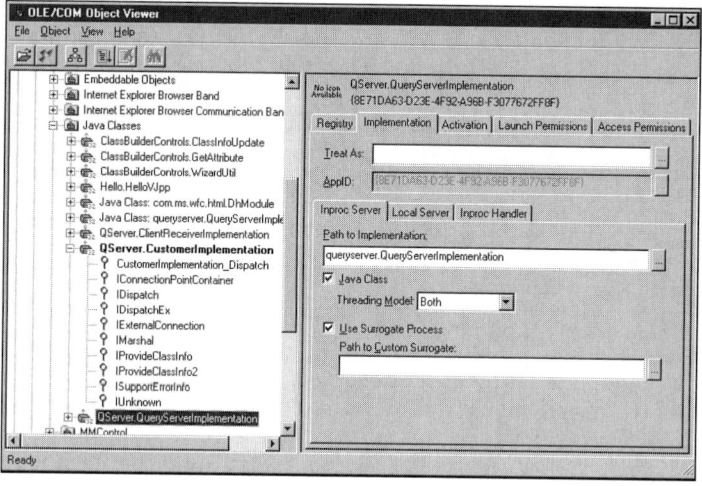

FIGURE 18.3
An OLEView DCOM server registration entry.

There is also a tool called `dcomcnfg` (the DCOM Configuration Tool) that comes pre-installed on most Windows 98 and Windows NT platforms (for example, under the `\winnt\system32` directory). The DCOM configuration tool can be used to configure COM and DCOM components, as well as view certain component properties. Component security and server locality are two of the main properties that can be examined and configured for your COM and DCOM objects. Figure 18.4 shows the main `dcomcnfg` entry dialog for selecting components to view, and Figure 18.5 shows a few properties set for a particular component. You will at least need to enable DCOM access for your DCOM server's machine, as shown in Figure 18.5.

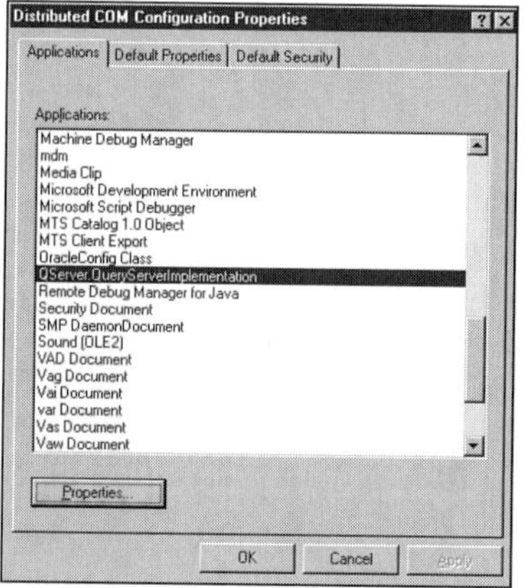

FIGURE 18.4
DCOM configuration tool component selection.

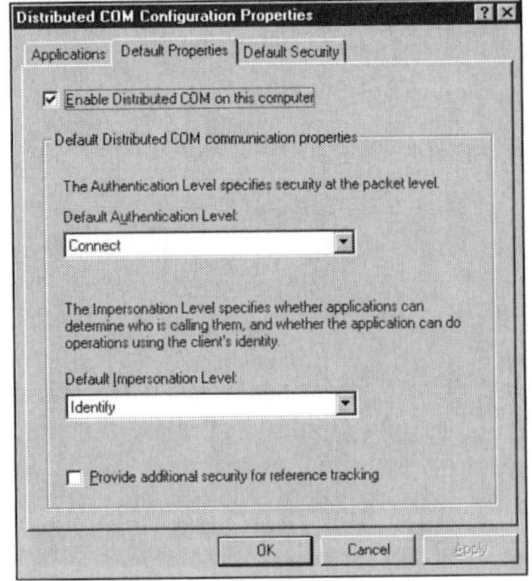

FIGURE 18.5
DCOM configuration tool component properties.

DCOM Clients and Stubs

After you've created and registered your server-side DCOM objects, you can tap the services they provide via a DCOM client. If you've created your server using some of the dynamic invocation and OLE automation techniques briefly touched on in Chapter 17, "Modeling Components with COM/DCOM," you may even be able to easily tap into its services via a standard Windows application. However, we will only show you how to talk to such a DCOM server as a Java-based DCOM client here in order to (1) illustrate how to create Java-based DCOM clients and (2) best allow you to compare our example DCOM application with the other similarly developed distributed applications presented in our previous chapters on TCP/IP, CORBA, and RMI.

Generic DCOM Clients

Figure 18.6 depicts the general dependence a DCOM client (for example, `MyClient`) will have on the DCOM server interfaces and classes. The DCOM client generally must create an instance of a DCOM object using the `CoMyServer` class. The client may then cast this object reference to a particular interface (for example, `IMyServer`) implemented by the `CoMyServer` class.

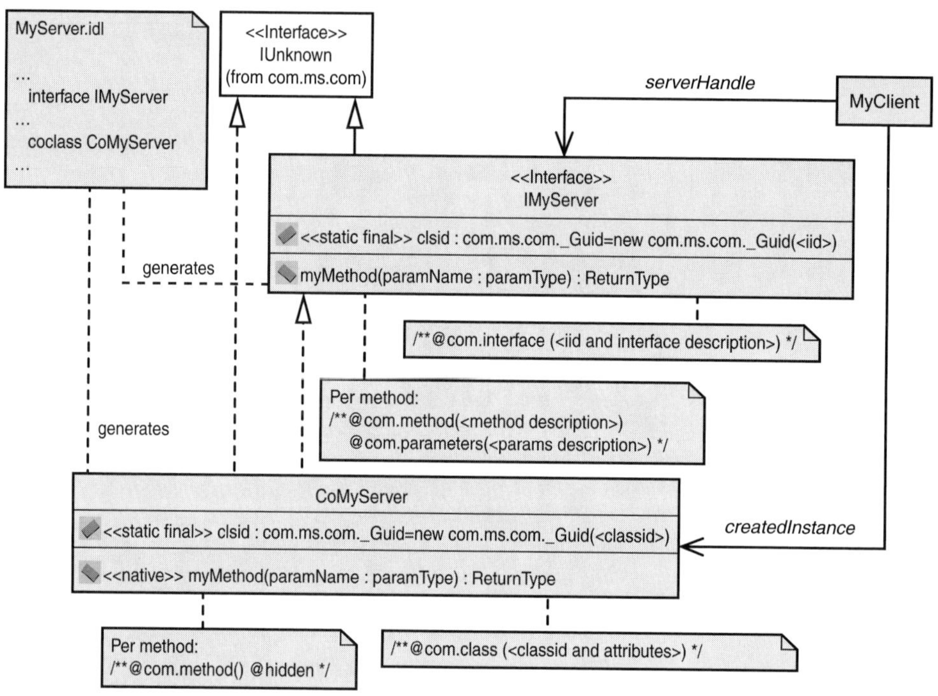

FIGURE 18.6
A DCOM client.

Example DCOM Client Implementation

The `Client` class in Listing 18.8 demonstrates how a DCOM client can make distributed calls on a DCOM component server, as well as demonstrates how a DCOM client can register a distributed callback with a DCOM server. The `Client.main()` method first obtains a handle to an `IQueryServer` interface by constructing an instance of the `CoQueryServer` class. It is at this moment that the native calls implemented by the `CoQueryServer` class talk with the locally registered type libraries (to be described in the next section) and the DCOM libraries to coordinate the activation of a remote DCOM server instance.

After obtaining a reference to an `IQueryServer`, the `Client` makes a `findCustomersWhoOrderedForMoreThan()` distributed call on the `IQueryServer` and displays some basic information about each returned customer via use of the `ICustomer` references retrieved from a `Variant` array. The `Client` creates an instance of a distributed `ClientReceiverImplementation` object and registers a reference to this object with the `IQueryServer` using the `register()` distributed call. When the `Client` calls `findOrdersWhichAreFrom()` on the `IQueryServer`, the `QueryServerImplementation` makes a callback on the DCOM client's `IClientReceiver` reference with an `IClientReceiver.setResultOrders()` call.

LISTING 18.8 The DCOM Query Client (`Client.java`)

```
package queryserver;

import com.ms.com.*;

public class Client {

  public static void main(String[] args) {
  try {
       // QueryServer
      IQueryServer queryServer = (IQueryServer) new CoQueryServer();
      // ClientReceiver
      ClientReceiverImplementation clientReceiver =
        new ClientReceiverImplementation();
      // Get Customers
      Variant variant =
        queryServer.findCustomersWhoOrderedForMoreThan(100.0f);
      // Extract array of Variants from the variant object
      Variant[] variantArray = variant.toVariantArray();

      System.out.println("Client Received :" + variantArray.length
                         + " Customers ");

      for (int i = 0; i < variantArray.length; i++) {
        // Get Variant at the given index
        Variant presentVariant = variantArray[i];
        // Extract customer reference object in the variant
        Object object = presentVariant.getObjectRef();
        ICustomer customer = (ICustomer) object;

       ICustomer customer = (ICustomer) object;
        System.out.println("FirstName :" + customer.firstName());
        System.out.println("LastName :" + customer.lastName());
        System.out.println("State :" + customer.state());
      }
      // register receiver
      queryServer.registerReceiver("ClientReceiver", clientReceiver);
      // induce query server to sent orders to the client receiver
      queryServer.findOrdersWhichAreFrom("VA");
    } catch (com.ms.com.ComFailException comFailException) {
```

continues

LISTING 18.8 Continued

```
        System.out.println("COM Exception:");
        System.out.println(comFailException.getHResult());
        System.out.println(comFailException.getMessage());
      } catch (com.ms.com.ComError comError) {

        System.out.println("COM Error:" + comError);
      } catch (Exception exception) {

        System.out.println(" Exception:" + exception);
      }
    }
}
```

DCOM Client Registration and Spawning

The implementation of the `Client` code in Listing 18.8 makes the following call:

```
IQueryServer queryServer = (IQueryServer) new CoQueryServer();
```

You may be wondering how such a call obtains a handle to the remote `QueryServerImplementation`. Well, the instantiated `CoQueryServer` object must first make native calls to the DCOM libraries to obtain a handle to the remote object. The DCOM libraries consult the Windows Registry for such information. We explicitly register this information with the Windows Registry using a process nearly identical to the registration process that took place on the server side. That is, we use `javareg` with a `/remote` parameter to indicate the hostname of our remote server implementation as exemplified in our `clientregistration.bat` script file:

```
javareg /register
➥ /class:queryserver.QueryServerImplementation /codebase:.
➥ /clsid:{CDACDBC9-5A65-22d2-8875-00B02414C777}
➥ /remote:dcom.bshirts.com
```

Note that we can also create a file such as `clientregistration.reg` to load into our Windows Registry directly:

```
REGEDIT4
[HKEY_CLASSES_ROOT\CLSID\{CDACDBC9-5A65-22d2-8875-00B02414C777}]
@="Java Class: QueryServerImplementations"
"AppID"="{CDACDBC9-5A65-22d2-8875-00B02414C777}"
```

```
[HKEY_CLASSES_ROOT\CLSID\{CDACDBC9-5A65-22d2-8875-00B02414C777}
➥\LocalServer32]
@="javareg /clsid:{BC4C0AB9-5A45-11d2-99C5-00A02414C655} "
➥/remoteserver:dcom.beeshirts.com
```

Finally, spawning our particular DCOM application is a trivial matter. Although the `runclient.bat` equipped with the examples can be used, you simply must copy the generated `interface` and `coclass *.class` files to your `C:\winnt\java\classes` directory, and then use the MSJVM runtime (`jview`) to run the client as shown here:

```
jview queryserver.Client
```

DCOM Bridging

You have seen how to create DCOM clients and servers using Java as an implementation language. The DCOM servers can be communicated with by clients implemented in any DCOM-capable language, and the DCOM clients can talk to DCOM servers implemented in any language. However, the DCOM clients and servers you implement in Java must use the Microsoft JVM due to the way in which Microsoft has chosen to provide such COM/DCOM access from Java. Of course, most commercial enterprise environments make such platform dependence undesirable if not completely impractical.

Two main issues thus arise:

- *Building Pure Java COM/DCOM Clients:* This issue involves providing a solution in which your Java-based client code could run in a standard JVM and somehow tap the services of a COM/DCOM server.
- *Building Pure Java COM/DCOM Servers:* This issue involves providing a solution in which your Java-based server code could run in a standard JVM and offer its services to COM/DCOM clients.

As far as solutions are concerned, static CORBA bridges are one option, such as Iona's Orbix ActiveX integration product, which are products COM-based clients use to bridge to statically defined CORBA stubs, which in turn delegate calls to a pure CORBA server (perhaps your Java-based CORBA server). Dynamic CORBA bridges, such as Iona's OrbixCOMet product, enable COM-based clients to talk with a CORBA Interface Repository to make CORBA DII calls onto a pure CORBA server. Sun has also provided an ActixeX-to-JavaBeans bridge (now part of the Java Plug-in) for enabling any pure JavaBeans-based component to be hosted in an ActiveX type container.

Another strictly server-side solution may be to simply wrap your pure Java component with a home-grown DCOM interface wrapper. Thus, your Java code would still run inside the MSJVM, but now there would exist a layer of interfacing between your code and the DCOM-specific code such that your pure Java business logic could be swapped out and reused with another communications paradigm if needed. Of course, this solution will require more hand-coding and you will need to keep an eye out for what standard Java language syntax and semantics cannot be fully utilized by the MSJVM.

As an added degree of separation, but still requiring more hand-coding, you can create a DCOM server to run inside the MSJVM as usual, but now simply implement a client/server TCP-IP, CORBA, or RMI bridge yourself between the DCOM server and a pure Java server. Similarly, if you are looking to create pure Java COM/DCOM clients, your pure Java client could be hand-coded to talk with a proxy server of your own creation via TCP-IP, CORBA, or RMI. The proxy server would then run inside of the MSJVM as the TCP-IP, CORBA, or RMI server and delegate all calls as a COM/DCOM client to the COM/DCOM server of interest.

Conclusions

Creating DCOM-based clients and servers with Java as an implementation language can be a bit more tedious and confusing than is the case with developing applications using other distributed paradigms. Although tools like Visual J++ can aid the development process, the model for creating distributed applications with DCOM can be starkly contrasted with the development process employed to build other Java-based distributed communications-enabled applications. First, the whole process of registering objects with the Windows Registry on both the client and the server side can yield a certain degree of inflexibility. Although programmatic interfaces to the Windows Registry can alleviate some of this inflexibility, the dependence on the Windows Registry means dependence on the Windows platform, which is problematic for most enterprise development solutions. Second, dependence on the use of Microsoft-based Java development tools and on the Microsoft JVM also presents a problem for enterprise development in a heterogeneous environment. Compromises such as bridging technologies and techniques can enable a more heterogeneous platform environment, but they are employed at the cost of adding extra COTS product expenses or extra development expenses.

Common Services for Distributed Enterprise Communications

PART

IV

IN THIS PART

19 Naming Services 575

20 Directory and Trading Services 633

21 Activation Services 689

22 Messaging Services 705

23 Transaction Services 789

Naming Services

CHAPTER

19

IN THIS CHAPTER

- Naming Services in a Nutshell 576
- JNDI Naming Services 580
- Naming Files 605
- CORBA Naming 609
- RMI Naming 618
- DNS 626
- DCOM Naming 629

A naming service is the principal mechanism used in distributed and nondistributed systems for referring to objects from within your applications via a name identifying that object. The term *name* used here typically means a name that is human readable or at least easily converted into a human-readable `String` format. A file system uses filenames when doling out references associated with file media to programs requesting access to those files. Similarly, CORBA clients can use object names to obtain handles to CORBA objects, which reference objects that may be sitting in some remote system process. These name-to-object associations are referred to as *name bindings*. A name binding is always defined relative to a naming context. Here, a naming context encapsulates a domain of names in which each name binding in that naming context is unique.

This chapter describes the basic concepts and programmatic interfaces available for accessing naming services in Java-based enterprise systems. The distributed computing paradigms described in Part III, "Distributed Enterprise Communications Enabling," all use a naming service to either explicitly or implicitly bind object references to names and resolve names to objects. This chapter explores naming services in more detail from a general perspective, as well as specific and common implementations of naming services. The Java Naming and Directory Interface (JNDI) component of the J2EE is described and exemplified as the primary means for hooking into naming systems from enterprise Java applications.

In this chapter, you will learn:

- Naming service–related concepts such as compound and composite names, name bindings, naming contexts, and the common roles of a name service.
- The architecture, API components, and use of Java's framework for commonly accessing various naming services via the Java Naming and Directory Interface.
- Why a file system is a naming service and how to use JNDI to access your file system.
- The architecture of a CORBA Naming Service (CosNaming) and the access of a CosNaming Service via JNDI.
- How to access the RMI Registry via JNDI.
- How to use JNDI with RMI/IIOP.
- The architecture of the Internet's domain name system (DNS) and how to look up an IP address given a DNS name.
- The DCOM equivalent for implementing the role of a naming service.

Naming Services in a Nutshell

Naming services provide a way for you to write code that refers to objects in a system using human-readable names. Names very often have a string form enabling you to write code that is more readable, as well as providing you with a simple way to obtain an initial handle to an object. Handles, names, and the context in which names are scoped are all fundamental concepts relevant to an understanding of naming systems. Before we explore the different types of naming systems and a standard way to interface with such systems, we'll first explore the general concepts involved in naming systems in this section. When you're armed with this knowledge, understanding each naming system will most often simply be a matter of translating service-specific terminology into the terms of our basic naming service concepts. Such conceptual framework will also aid in understanding the standard naming service interfaces provided by the Java Naming and Directory Interface service infrastructure.

Handles

An object in a system corresponds to an instance in memory or some range of addresses relating to some discrete collection of functions or data. "Handles" to such objects are often referred to as *references* or *pointers*. Such handles can be associated with objects residing in a process local to your current execution environment or with distributed objects on an entirely different machine. However, these handles are often not human readable, frequently are numeric by nature, perhaps have some embedded communications protocol-specific information, sometimes are platform-dependent, and usually are dependent on the current execution environment. That is, a handle to an object instance `hallwayPrinter` of some class `NetworkPrinter` may have some 32-bit reference value at time t_1 on machine A and an entirely different value at time t_2 on some machine B.

Names

Object handles referring to some logical entity can take on different values over time and across different process spaces but still refer to the same logical entity from your program's perspective. Variable or object instance names in traditional nondistributed programs are one way to refer to the same logical entity even though the underlying object reference may perhaps vary in value over time and in different execution scenarios of the code. Variable and object instance names are meaningful only to the compiled code in your current execution environment, however. For example, given the object instance name `hallwayPrinter` from

```
NetworkPrinter hallwayPrinter = new NetworkPrinter();
```

the `hallwayPrinter` name is meaningful only to your current execution environment's compiled program and is completely meaningless to a process running somewhere else on the network. Given the need to access such an object from distributed processes, wouldn't it be nice to simply refer to such handles to a hallway printer as "hallwayPrinter" in code? That is precisely what is in a name!

A name is simply a logical and generally human-readable value for referring to an object in both distributed and nondistributed systems. Here are some examples of what a name can be:

- A filename string referring to a file object reference.
- An Internet hostname string referring to a machine on the Internet.
- An object service name referring to a CORBA server object on a remote machine.

Each name is expressed in a syntax understandable by the naming system for which it is relevant (for example, the file system, the Internet, a CORBA Naming Service). Each naming system has its own naming convention syntax for which valid names are expressed. Thus, for example, a Windows file-naming system requires absolute filenames to be expressed in terms of a root drive and semicolon with directory names separated by backslashes (\) and ending with a filename and extension (for example, `C:\MyDir\myFile.txt`). Each name-to-object association is typically referred to as a name binding.

Naming Contexts and Systems

Names always have some meaning in a specific context. For example, the name "Leesburg" designates a U.S. city in the states of Virginia, New Jersey, Florida, Georgia, Alabama, Indiana, and Ohio. The fully qualified name of "Leesburg, Virginia, USA" pinpoints the name "Leesburg" to the context of "Virginia, USA."

The same need for referring to names within some context also applies to computer systems. Thus, as illustrated in Figure 19.1, whereas the name `index.html` on your computer hosting a Web server refers to a specific file you have created in the directory `C:\public_html`, this same filename in your Web server's directory `C:\public_html\sales` refers to an entirely different file object. The name `index.html` has to be put in context to determine what specific file object is being referenced. Any files that are to be uniquely referenced relative to your local file system's root context have names like `C:\public_html\index.html` and `C:\public_html\sales\index.html`. Such filename-to-file-object mapping is provided by your machine's file-naming system.

Other computers wanting to read such HTML files served up by your Web server via the Internet need an entirely new naming system and a different context. For example, suppose your company has reserved the name `assuredtech.com` as your corporate domain name, and you establish a machine within your corporate domain named www to be your Web server. Let us further assume that you've configured your Web server such that the root context for all incoming HTTP requests is your machine's `C:\public_html` directory. Remote systems connected to the Internet use the Internet's domain name system to first retrieve access to your machine's Web server with the first part of a name like `www.assuredtech.com`. Such requests are directed to the root context for your Web server (that is, `C:\public_html` from your local file system's point of view). Thus, a request for a page named `http://www.assuredtech.com/`

`sales/index.html` will be used by the domain name system and your Web server to retrieve the appropriate file object relative to your Web server's root context. Your Web server's root context is actually a subcontext of the Internet domain name system's root context.

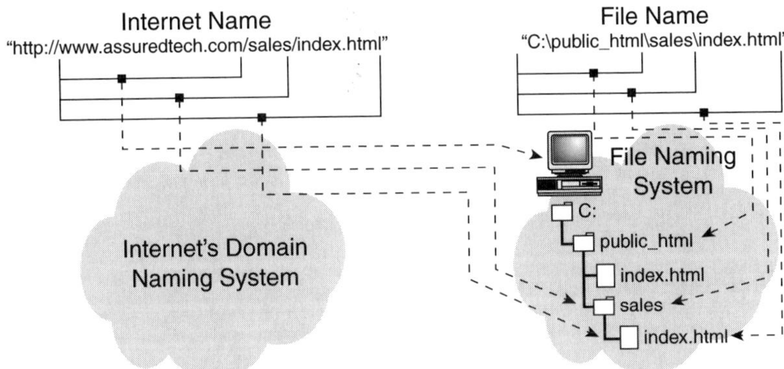

FIGURE 19.1
Naming systems.

Each context thus holds a set of name-to-object bindings in which the object may be an actual system resource (for example, file object) or perhaps another context (that is, a subcontext). Each context will have its own standard for naming the objects and subcontexts to which it binds names. A naming system serves to provide a standard for managing a set of contexts with the same naming convention and with similar means for binding names to objects and resolving objects to names.

Although many systems such as the Lightweight Directory Access Protocol (LDAP), the Network Information System (NIS), and the Novell Directory Service (NDS) provide the name binding and resolving functionality of naming services, we defer discussion of such services until the next chapter in the context of directory and trading services. As you'll see, such services go beyond providing pure naming-service functionality and provide support for more sophisticated retrieval of object handles via complex lookups using characteristics and properties of such objects. In this book, we stick with the pure OMG approach for classifying naming services as those services providing pure name-to-object associations akin to a telephone White Pages. Services such as LDAP, NIS, and NDS may indeed provide such services, but their sophisticated services for retrieval and advertisement by object characteristics render them more like a telephone Yellow Pages service. The OMG has distinguished between these two service types via specification of a CORBA Naming Service and CORBA Trading Service.

JNDI Naming Services

The Java Naming and Directory Interface (JNDI) provides a standard Java interface-to-naming system that can be used with various types of underlying naming systems. JNDI can also be used to name and reference objects that lie outside of a particular naming system. Furthermore, JNDI also provides interfaces for encapsulating and handling events that can be generated from a naming service. This section first describes the architecture of JNDI and then follows that discussion with a description of the interfaces used to name objects and resolve object references from names in a naming system. The means for referencing objects outside of the naming system and for handling naming-system events are also described. Finally, we describe a generic sample program that can be used with various actual underlying naming services.

JNDI Architecture

As depicted in Figure 19.2, JNDI is a Java extension and a fundamental component of the J2EE, providing a standard way to interface with many naming services and directory services. JNDI provides a Java API for commonly interfacing with any naming or directory service for which there exists an adapter to map JNDI API calls to the specific calls provided by the particular naming or directory service provider. After a few simple initialization parameters are set that tell the JNDI API to which service to delegate calls, all calls to the JNDI API are properly delegated to the particular service via the adapter. This adapter is referred to as a *Service Provider Interface* (SPI). SPIs are provided by Sun Microsystems for some of the more popular services, by the vendors of those services wanting to provide their users a JNDI interface, or by third parties that have implemented an SPI.

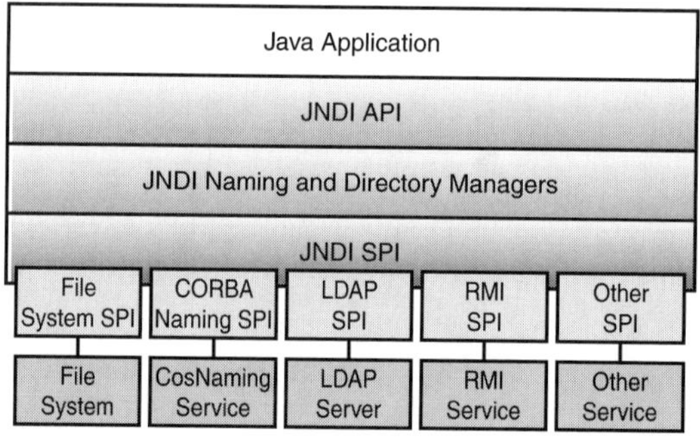

FIGURE 19.2
A JNDI architectural overview.

The JNDI class libraries are included as a core component of the J2EE and the J2SE v1.3. The JNDI libraries can also be separately downloaded from the JavaSoft Web site at `http://www.javasoft.com/products/jndi` for use with standalone J2SE v1.2 applications. As of the writing of this book, the latest version of JNDI available is version 1.2. You will also need an SPI for the naming system used in your Java application. The JavaSoft Web site also offers a collection of SPIs for some of the more popular naming systems at `http://www.javasoft.com/products/jndi/serviceproviders.html`. Vendor-specific SPI implementations will also typically be shipped with the vendor's product and may even include the specific JNDI class library version for which it has been certified for use. Of course, the availability of the underlying naming service is specific to each type of naming system. The file-naming system, for example, is a given for most environments, but a naming service for CORBA will typically be purchased off the shelf or packaged as part of an overall vendor-specific product offering.

NOTE

Note that our sample scripts provided on the CD for this chapter assume use of the J2SE v1.2 platform with JNDI v1.2 installed as a standard extension. Further note that a `JNDI_HOME` environment variable must be set to the root directory of the downloaded and installed JNDI standard extension in order to use our sample scripts. The scripts, of course, can be modified for use with the JNDI libraries that come equipped with a J2EE environment as well.

The JNDI class libraries are partitioned into the following packages:

- `javax.naming`: Contains all the core JNDI API classes and interfaces used by Java applications needing access to various naming services.
- `javax.naming.directory`: Contains the JNDI API classes for performing more sophisticated directory-service functionality extending the basic naming-service functionality.
- `javax.naming.event`: Contains the JNDI API classes and interfaces (new as of JNDI v1.2) for providing event notification services for naming and directory systems.
- `javax.naming.ldap`: Contains the JNDI API classes and interfaces (new as of JNDI v1.2) for specific support of the more advanced management features of the LDAPv3 standard when using the LDAP SPI.
- `javax.naming.spi`: Contains the JNDI SPI classes and interfaces for implementers of SPIs to map standard JNDI API calls to a particular naming or directory service.

This chapter on naming services and the next chapter on directory and trading services make use of the JNDI APIs for naming services and directory services. The JNDI SPI classes and interfaces are transparent to the API programmer and are of specific interest to those programmers creating SPIs for specific naming or directory services. Thus, the JNDI SPI package is not covered in this book because the needs for the enterprise applications programmer are of primary concern.

The goal of describing the JNDI APIs for naming services in this chapter is met by first describing JNDI with general API usage examples that can be flexibly configured to work with different JNDI SPIs. We then use this general JNDI API sample framework in the specialized context of a few of the more significant types of naming services. Specifically, the file-naming system, RMI naming system, and CORBA naming system are all described in this chapter with illustrations and use of the JNDI APIs where appropriate. An auxiliary means for interfacing with each associated naming system is also mentioned. Finally, the domain name system and a means by which DCOM applications name and look up objects are covered in more detail.

Naming Objects

Before a naming service can be utilized, JNDI clients need to obtain handles to an initial JNDI context. Names can then be bound to objects, and objects can be looked up relative to such a context using standard JNDI interfaces. Names have a syntax that can be described using regular Java `String` objects or using some of the interfaces provided by JNDI to encapsulate names. Various other JNDI operations such as listing the contents of a particular naming context can also be performed using JNDI. This subsection describes JNDI contexts, name binding and lookup, name formatting and encapsulation, and context listing using JNDI.

JNDI Contexts

The JNDI client API user will first be required to create a reference to an initial context of the naming service of interest. This initial context creation process establishes a connection with the service when constructed with a set of properties describing the specific naming or directory service provider library to use, the URL of the naming or directory service process, and perhaps a username and user credentials. Other properties may also be set whose names are defined as static public attributes in the `javax.naming.Context` interface, as shown in Figure 19.3. A `javax.naming.InitialContext` class implementing the `Context` interface can be used to create an actual handle to a particular naming service. By passing a `Properties` object set with elements using the `java.naming.XXX` key names defined in the `Context` interface to the constructor of `InitialContext`, any necessary `Context.XXX` static public properties will be set and used during initialization of the `InitialContext`. The valid static public properties are defined in Table 19.1.

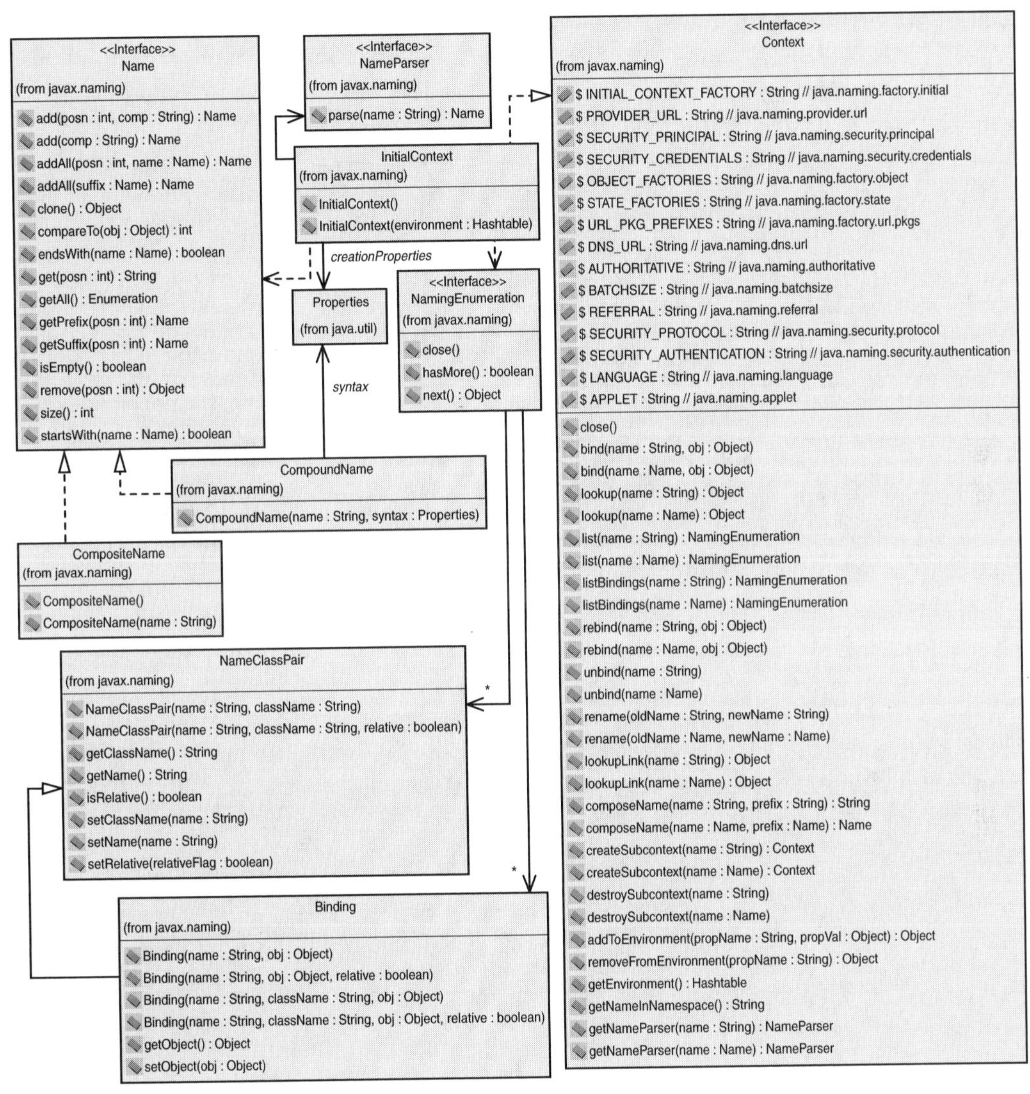

FIGURE 19.3
Core JNDI naming entities.

TABLE 19.1 Context Properties

Context Property	*Description*
`INITIAL_CONTEXT_FACTORY`	Fully qualified package and classname of class used to create a JNDI context.
`PROVIDER_URL`	URL specifying the protocol, host, and port on which the naming or directory service is running, that is, *<protocol>://<host>:<port>*.
`SECURITY_PRINCIPAL`	Principal name (for example, username) to be checked by the naming or directory service if authentication for use is required.
`SECURITY_CREDENTIALS`	Principal's credentials (for example, a password) to be checked by the naming or directory service if authentication for use is required.
`OBJECT_FACTORIES`	Colon-separated list of object context factories to use during invocation of naming and directory service operations.
`STATE_FACTORIES`	Colon-separated list of state factories used to get an object's state given a reference to the object.
`URL_PKG_PREFIXES`	Colon-separated list of package prefixes to use when loading context factories.
`DNS_URL`	URL defining the DNS host to use for looking up addresses associated with JNDI URLs.
`AUTHORITATIVE`	Value of `true` indicates that service access offers the most authoritative source.
`BATCHSIZE`	Specifies batch size of data returned from service protocol.
`REFERRAL`	Value of `follow` causes naming service to follow a service referral, `ignore` causes service referrals to be ignored, and `throw` causes a `javax.naming.ReferralException` to be thrown.
`SECURITY_PROTOCOL`	Specifies security protocol to use (for example, `SSL`).
`SECURITY_AUTHENTICATION`	Specifies security level to use such as `none`, `simple`, or `strong`.
`LANGUAGE`	Colon-separated list of human languages to use for this naming service scheme using tags as defined by RFC 1766.
`APPLET`	Specifies applet to use by initial context for finding additional properties.

The J2EE and JNDI

The JNDI v1.2 API is required to be equipped with a J2EE v1.2–compliant application client, Enterprise JavaBeans, and Web environments. The means by which J2EE components obtain handles to J2EE-managed `InitialContext` objects is simplified in J2EE environments, as compared with the approach described in this section. J2EE components can then use this `InitialContext` object to access configurable environment information, obtain references to Enterprise JavaBeans, and obtain references to resource connection factories (for example, factories for JDBC, URL, and messaging service connections). Initial context creation and use of the JNDI API in the more generalized sense described within this chapter, however, will still apply in many different Java enterprise application scenarios.

Out of all properties defined in Table 19.1, the first two properties (`INITIAL_CONTEXT_FACTORY` and `PROVIDER_URL`) will probably be the most commonly used properties in your programs. The `SECURITY_PRINCIPAL` and `SECURITY_CREDENTIALS` properties are also sometimes used. If any property is left undefined, a default value is usually assumed, which is typically fine for many situations encountered. The creation of an `InitialContext` is therefore typically straightforward:

```
Properties properties = new Properties();
properties.setProperty(Context.INITIAL_CONTEXT_FACTORY,
      "com.sun.jndi.fscontext.RefFSContextFactory");
properties.setProperty("PROVIDER_URL", "file:C:\\public_html");
Context  context = new InitialContext(properties);
```

In general, it is a good idea to close a context when you are done using it to ensure graceful resource cleanup. When attempting to close a context from within a block that can throw an exception, you may want to surround the context closing within a `finally` block to ensure that it is called:

```
try{
  ...
}
catch(...){
  ...
}
finally{
  try{
    context.close();
  }
  catch(NamingException ex){
    ...
  }
}
```

Subcontexts can be created and removed using the `InitialContext` `createSubcontext()` and `destroySubcontext()` methods, respectively. Subcontexts can be looked up by using the `lookup()` method, with the subcontext name defined according to whatever naming convention is employed to separate components of the name, such as this:

```
Context salesBrochureContext = context.lookup("sales\\brochures");
```

JNDI Binding and Lookup

After a context reference is obtained, an object from the server side can be bound to the context in a standard fashion using the `bind()` and `rebind()` methods. The difference between `bind()` and `rebind()` is simply that `rebind()` overwrites any existing bindings, whereas `bind()` throws an exception. As an example of a rebind call, we have this:

```
String eProducts = "eProducts.html";
Brochure eProductBrochure = new Brochure();
 ...
salesBrochureContext.rebind(eProducts, eProductBrochure);
```

From the client side, a lookup of a particular object yields a reference to that object which is simply cast to the object of the appropriate type:

```
String eProductsName = "sales\\brochures\\eProducts.html";
Brochure brochure = (Brochure) context.lookup(eProductsName);
```

JNDI Names

Binding objects to names and looking up objects given a name can be accomplished using a `String` form of a name, as well as using a class implementing the `javax.naming.Name` interface. A `Name` is composed of a sequence of name components. `Name` objects provide a more type-safe means to manipulate names according to the syntax convention of the particular naming system with which the name is associated. One can add and remove name components as well as accomplish other helper operations on names given a `Name` interface implementation.

The `CompoundName` class implements the `Name` interface for names that are confined within a single hierarchical naming system. Thus, the `CompoundName` can be viewed as a more type-safe way to manipulate regular names in a particular naming system. The syntax convention of the particular naming system for a compound name is established via a set of properties that can be passed into the `CompoundName` constructor. These are the valid properties that can be passed into the `CompoundName` constructor:

- `jndi.syntax.direction`: Parsing direction such as `left_to_right`, `right_to_left`, or `flat`.
- `jndi.syntax.separator`: Separator to use between name components (for example, / or .).

- `jndi.syntax.ignorecase`: Name components are case-insensitive if `true`.
- `jndi.syntax.escape`: Escape string for overriding separators (for example, /).
- `jndi.syntax.beginquote`: Beginning of quote delimiter.
- `jndi.syntax.endquote`: Ending of quote delimiter.
- `jndi.syntax.beginquote2`: Alternative begin quote.
- `jndi.syntax.endquote2`: Alternative end quote.
- `jndi.syntax.separator.typeval`: Name-value separators (for example, = as in `mfg=Dodge`).
- `jndi.syntax.separator.ava`: Name-value pair separator (for example, , as in `mfg=Dodge,make=Raider,color=red`).
- `jndi.syntax.trimblanks`: Leading and trailing whitespace of a name is trimmed if `true`.

For example, the following `String` may be parsed into a compound name using the `CompoundName` class:

```
String name = "PrinterPublicGroup.Printer19";
CompoundName cName = new CompoundName(name, rmiNamingProperties);
```

The `javax.naming.CompositeName` class also implements the `Name` interface and is a sequence of name components that span one or more naming systems. Each name component of a `CompositeName` belonging to a particular naming system may itself be parsed into a hierarchical name for that naming system using the `CompoundName` class. `CompositeName` objects represented as `Strings` are parsed from left to right and with name components separated by forward slashes (`/`). Escapes characters (`\`), single quotes (`'`), and double quotes (`"`) can also be used in `CompositeNames`.

JNDI Context Listings

The contents of a JNDI naming service may also be listed using the `list()` and `listBinding()` methods defined by the `Context` interface and implemented by `InitialContext`. The `list()` method requires a name parameter identifying the particular context level at which to search for name service bindings. The `list()` method returns a `javax.naming.NamingEnumeration` of `javax.naming.NameClassPair` objects in which each `NameClassPair` represents an object name and its classname of an object bound at the desired context level. For example (exception handling excluded)

```
NamingEnumeration namesList = context.list(someContextName);
 ...
while(namesList.hasMore()){
  NameClassPair pair = (NameClassPair) namesList.next();
```

```
  String objectName = pair.getName();
  String className = pair.getClassName();
  ...
}
```

In addition to returning the object name and its associated classname, the `listBindings()` method call on a context returns the actual bound object as well. Given the particular context level to list, the `listBindings()` method returns a `NamingEnumeration` of `javax.naming.Binding` objects that extend `NameClassPair` objects with the capability to store and retrieve the object bound at the listed context level. For example, to retrieve each name, classname, and bound object from a `NamingEnumeration` returned from a `listBindings()` call, we would use this:

```
NamingEnumeration namesList = context.listBindings(someContextName);
 ...
while(namesList.hasMore()){
  Binding binding = (Binding) namesList.next();
  String objectName = binding.getName();
  String className = binding.getClassName();
  MyObject obj = (MyObject) binding.getObject();
  ...
}
```

Referenceable Objects

Aside from binding and looking up object references in a naming system using names via JNDI, JNDI also provides support for binding and looking up references to objects that sit somewhere outside of the naming system (that is, referenceable objects). A *referenceable object*, in JNDI lingo, is an object with a reference that can be stored in a JNDI service with information telling JNDI how to associate lookups for that object to the object itself. Referenceable objects can be useful when an object not belonging to any particular naming system needs to be bound to a naming service for ease of lookup. Referenceable objects are also useful when an object from one naming system needs to be bound to an entirely different naming system. The set of classes and interfaces provided by JNDI to support such an infrastructure is shown in Figure 19.4.

A referenceable object is first created by implementing the `javax.naming.Referenceable` interface. The `Referenceable` interface has one method called `getReference()`, which returns a handle to a `javax.naming.Reference` object. The `Reference` object corresponds to a reference to an object located somewhere outside of the naming system (that is, not bound to the naming service).

<<Interface>>
Referenceable
(from javax.naming)
getReference() : Reference

<<Interface>>
ObjectFactory
(from javax.naming.spi)
getObjectInstance(obj : Object, name : Name, ctx : Context, env : Hashtable) : Object

MyReferenceableObject
getReference() : Reference

MyReferenceableObjectFactory
getObjectInstance(obj : Object, name : Name, ctx : Context, env : Hashtable) : Object

Reference
(from javax.naming)
Reference(className : String)
Reference(className : String, factory : String, factoryLocation : String)
Reference(className : String, addr : RefAddr)
Reference(className : String, addr : RefAddr, factory : String, factoryLocation : String)
add(posn : int, addr : RefAddr)
add(addr : RefAddr)
clean()
clone() : Object
equals(obj : Object) : boolean
get(posn : int) : RefAddr
get(addrType : String) : RefAddr
getAll() : Enumeration
getClassName() : String
getFactoryClassLocation() : String
getFactoryClassName() : String
hashCode() : int
remove(posn : int) : Object
size() : int
toString() : String

*

RefAddr
(from javax.naming)
RefAddr(addrType : String)
equals(obj : Object) : boolean
getContent() : Object
getType() : String
hashCode() : int
toString() : String

StringRefAddr
(from javax.naming)
StringRefAddr(addrType : String, addr : String)
getContent() : Object

LinkRef
(from javax.naming)
LinkRef(linkName : String)
LinkRef(linkName : Name)
getLinkName() : String

BinaryRefAddr
(from javax.naming)
BinaryRefAddr(addrType : String, src : byte[])
BinaryRefAddr(addrType : String, src : byte[], offset : int, count : int)
equals(obj : Object) : boolean
getContent() : Object
hashCode() : int
toString() : String

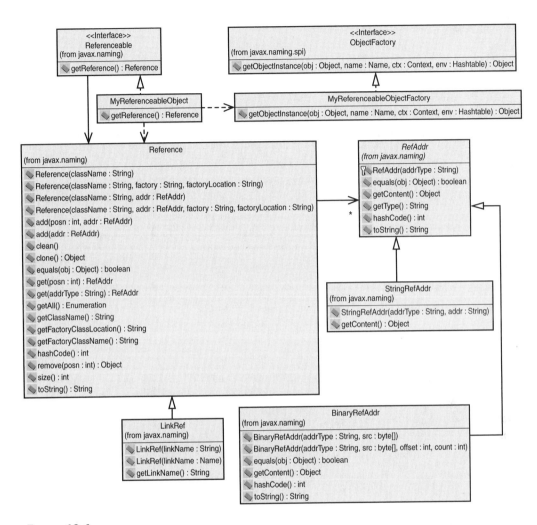

FIGURE 19.4
Referenceable objects.

`Reference` objects contain sequences of `javax.naming.RefAddr` objects. `RefAddr` objects represent communications addresses each having both a type and a value. The type of address is retrieved from the `RefAddr.getType()` method. The particular address value can be retrieved via the `getContent()` abstract method that is defined specifically by each subclass of the abstract `RefAddr` class. The `javax.naming.BinaryRefAddr` class is a specific type of `RefAddr` encapsulating binary communications addresses expressible in terms of byte arrays such as a serialized object handle or network card address. The `javax.naming.StringRefAddr` subclass of `RefAddr` can be used to encapsulate communications address strings such as URLs and hostnames.

As a special type of `Reference`, a `javax.naming.LinkRef` provides a reference corresponding to a link that can be followed to a particular object. The content of the `LinkRef` object is a link name that can be resolved to other links. The `Context.lookupLink()` methods can be used to look up an object following any links to get to that object.

`Reference` objects also contain information useful to JNDI object factories for creating instances of referenced objects such as the referenced object classname, as well as the classname and the URL of the object's specific class factory. Your application-specific referenceable object (such as `MyReferenceableObject` in Figure 19.4) implements the `Referenceable` interface with an implementation of the `getReference()` method. `getReference()` creates a `Reference` object using such objects as an application-specific object factory (for example, `MyReferenceableObjectFactory` in Figure 19.4), the type of object, and the content of the object. The `MyReferenceableObjectFactory` can then be used by the JNDI service to reconstruct the state of a `MyReferenceableObject` after calling `getContent()` on the `Reference` object.

For example, some `com.beeshirts.customer.Customer` class that you've defined may implement the `getReference()` method as shown here:

```
public javax.naming.Reference getReference()
      throws NamingException
{
  String className = "com.beeshirts.customer.Customer";
  String factoryName = "com.beeshirts.customer.CustomerFactory";
  String contents = this.getAsString(); // Get state as a String

  javax.naming.StringRefAddr refAddr
      = new javax.naming.StringRefAddr("Customer", contents);

  return new javax.naming.Reference(className, refAddr,
                                    factoryName, null);
}
```

After binding the `Customer` referenceable object, the naming service can reconstruct the object during a lookup by consulting the `com.beeshirts.customer.CustomerFactory` object factory implementing the `getObjectInstance()` method like this (excluding error handling):

```
public Object getObjectInstance(Object obj, Name objName,
                                Context objContext, Hashtable objEnv)
                                throws Exception
{
  javax.naming.Reference reference = (javax.naming.Reference) obj;
```

```
  javax.naming.StringRefAddr refAddr
        = (javax.naming.StringRefAddr) reference.get("Customer");

  String contents = (String) refAddr.getContent();

  Customer customer= new Customer();
  customer.setAsString(contents); // Reconstructs state from a String

  return customer;
}
```

Naming Events

JNDI also now provides (as of JNDI v1.2) an infrastructure for encapsulating and handling naming and directory service events. Naming and directory services can generate naming-related events such as the renaming of an object, the removal or addition of an object from or to the naming service, and the state change of an object registered with the naming service. Distributed naming and directory service clients may be interested in such events, and the JNDI infrastructure now provides a standard means for interfacing with such features. Of course, support for such features is completely dependent on the underlying SPI implementation. Figure 19.5 depicts the core entities defined for the event-handling infrastructure for naming services.

The `javax.naming.event.NamingEvent` class represents an event that can be generated from a naming service when one of its registered objects changes. `NamingEvent` objects extend the standard `java.util.EventObject`; they have a type and contain an event source, SPI-specific change information, and a reference to binding information both before and after the event. The source of an event is a context implementing the `javax.naming.event.EventContext` interface. An `EventContext` is simply a type of `Context` that allows for the addition and removal of listeners interested in naming events. A special `javax.naming.event.NamingExceptionEvent` event object can also be generated in the event of a failure during the generation of a normal naming event for notifying naming listeners. When objects of an identified target and scope generate a naming event, any `javax.naming.event.NamingListener` that has registered to receive such an event will be contacted:

```
EventContext eventContext = // Construct an event context
NamespaceChangeListener customerManager = // Construct a listener
eventContext.addNamingListener("AllisonPerrone",
                              EventContext.OBJECT_SCOPE, customerManager);
```

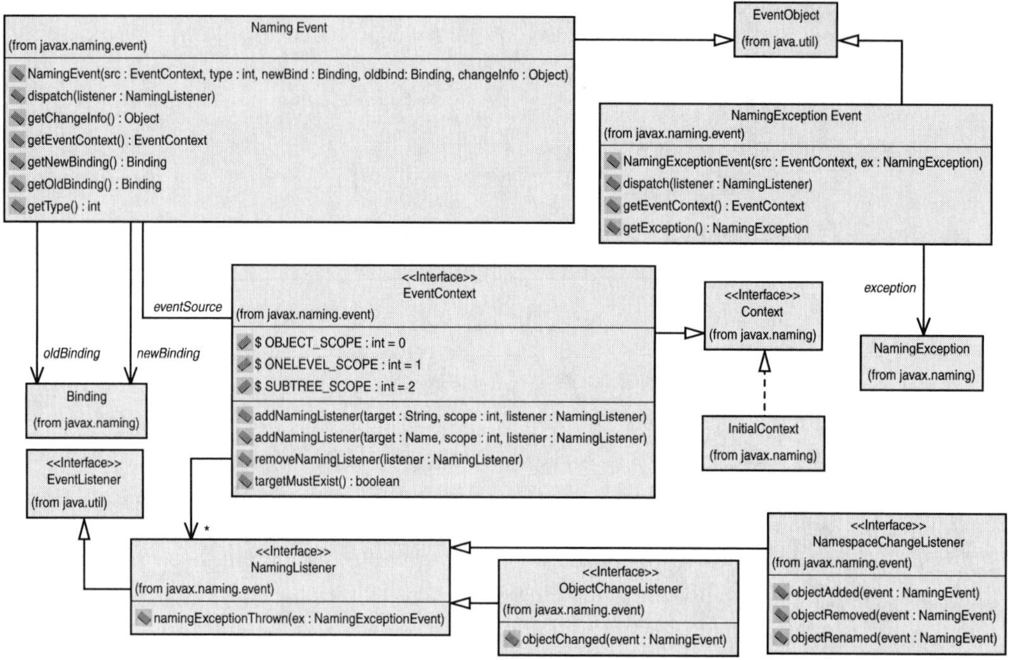

FIGURE 19.5
JNDI naming service events.

Either the `javax.naming.event.ObjectChangeListener` or the `javax.naming.event.NamespaceChangeListener` sub-interfaces of `NamingListener` typically is implemented to handle generated naming events. The `ObjectChangeListener` interface is implemented to handle events associated with an object's state change (`NamingEvent.OBJECT_CHANGED`), such as attribute addition, deletion, or modification, as well as the replacement of an object in the naming system. The old and new bindings of an object may be examined to determine the specific type of change. The `NamespaceChangeListener` interface is implemented by those objects wanting to handle the addition (`NamingEvent.OBJECT_ADDED`), removal (`NamingEvent.OBJECT_REMOVED`), or renaming (`NamingEvent.OBJECT_RENAMED`) of objects registered with the naming service. As an example of a naming event listener, the following skeleton structure implements methods for handling both object change and namespace change naming events:

```
import javax.naming.event.NamespaceChangeListener;
import javax.naming.event.ObjectChangeListener;
import javax.naming.event.NamingEvent;
import javax.naming.event.NamingExceptionEvent;
```

```
public class SampleNamingListener
  implements NamespaceChangeListener, ObjectChangeListener
{
  public void objectAdded(NamingEvent namingEvent)
  {
      // Handle object addition
  }

  public void objectRemoved(NamingEvent namingEvent)
  {
     // Handle object removal
  }

  public void objectRenamed(NamingEvent namingEvent)
  {
    // Handle object renaming
  }

  public void objectChanged(NamingEvent namingEvent)
  {
    // Handle object attribute changing
  }

  public void namingExceptionThrown(NamingExceptionEvent
                                         namingExceptionEvent)
  {
    // Handle naming exception
  }
}
```

JNDI Examples

This section introduces how to use JNDI in your enterprise applications as a generic naming service interface. To highlight the generic nature of JNDI, we develop a set of base examples whose code does not change at all between use with a few important SPIs introduced in later sections. In fact, the only thing that will differ from one example to another is a set of properties stored in a properties file and the underlying SPI and naming service to use.

NOTE

The complete set of code examples for all code listed in this chapter can be found on the CD-ROM in the `examples\src\ejava\jndich19` directory. General software build and configuration instructions are presented in Appendix A, "Software Configuration."

The SampleLookupExample class in Listing 19.1 demonstrates how JNDI clients can generically look up distributed object references given a prebound object name. By passing in an object name to the example from the command line, the main() method will serve as the main driver to illustrate a lookup. After some initial error checking, the main() method uses a set of properties read in from a jndi.properties file to construct a SampleLookupExample instance. After the construction of a SampleLookupExample object, the lookupBoundObject() method is called to perform the actual lookup given the object name passed in from the command line.

The lookupBoundObject() method first calls getInitialContext() to retrieve a handle to an InitialContext object constructed using the properties read in during the SampleLookupExample constructor call. As you'll see in subsequent sections, these properties will vary per SPI example. The String name passed into the lookupBoundObject() method call is then used as a parameter to a Context.lookup() call, and the associated object reference is returned.

NOTE

You will be able to experiment with the generic JNDI examples given in Listings 19.1 through 19.3 only when you run these examples with a specific SPI to be described in subsequent sections.

LISTING 19.1 A Generic JNDI Lookup Example (SampleLookupExample.java)

```
package ejava.jndich19;

import javax.naming.Context;
import javax.naming.InitialContext;
import javax.naming.NamingException;
import java.util.Properties;
import java.io.FileInputStream;
import java.io.IOException;
import org.omg.CORBA.*;
import org.omg.CosNaming.*;
import java.util.Hashtable;

/**
 * This example looks up an object for a given name.
 */
public class SampleLookupExample
{
  private Context context ;
  private Properties contextProperties = new Properties();
```

```
// Default Naming Client Example

/**
 * Constructor

 */
public SampleLookupExample()
{
  super();
}

//

/**
 * Constructor
 * Naming Client which is initialized with a jndi.properties file.
*/
public SampleLookupExample(String propertiesFileName)
  throws IOException
{
  // Open a file input stream for the associated properties
  // fileName.
  FileInputStream propertiesFileStream =
    new FileInputStream(propertiesFileName);
  // Now load the file input stream into the JNDI environment
  // properties.
  // This of course assumes that the file input stream is in a valid
  // Properties format.
  contextProperties.load(propertiesFileStream);
}

/**
 * Constructor with assigned properties
*/
public SampleLookupExample(Properties systemProperties)
{
  contextProperties = systemProperties;
}

/**
* returns ContextInstance.
*/
public Context getInitialContext()
```


continues

LISTING 19.1 Continued

```
    throws NamingException
  {
    // Create initial context if it is not already created
    if (context == null) {
        // Read in a set of default parameters.
      context = new InitialContext(contextProperties);
    }
    return context;
  }

  /**
* Look up the object associated with The Name
*/
  public java.lang.Object lookupBoundObject(String name)
  {
    Context context ;
    java.lang.Object boundObject = null;

    // Retrieve initial context
    try {
      context = this.getInitialContext();
    }
    catch (NamingException namingException) {
      System.out.println("Error :" + namingException);
      namingException.printStackTrace();
      return null;
    }

    // Now lookup the bound object with this name
    try {
      boundObject = context.lookup(name);
    }
    catch (NamingException namingException) {
      System.out.println("Error :" + namingException);
      namingException.printStackTrace();
      return null;
    }

    System.out.println(" Name is : " + name + "    Bound Object is : "
                       + boundObject);

    return boundObject;
  }
```

```
  /**
   * Return the context properties
   */
  public Properties getContextProperties()
  {
    return contextProperties;
  }


  /**
  * Main Test Driver:
  *       java ejava.jndich19.SimpleLookupExample <ObjectNameToLook>
*/
  public static void main(String[] args)
  {

    // Ensure that a filename to look up is passed as a parameter.
    if (args.length != 1) {
      System.out .println("Run example as: java "
          + "ejava.jndich19.SampleLookupExample <ObjectNameToLookup>");

      System.exit(0);
    }

    // Set name of properties file to use in initializing the simple
    // lookup.
    String propertiesFileName = "jndi.properties";

    // Instantiate an instance of this NamingClient
    SampleLookupExample sampleLookupExample = null;

    try {
      sampleLookupExample =
          new SampleLookupExample(propertiesFileName);
    }
    catch (IOException ioException) {
      System.out.println("Error :" + ioException);
      System.exit(0);
    }

    // Demonstrate lookup of a bound object name
    String name = args[0];

    System.out.println("Going to Lookup " + name);
    sampleLookupExample.lookupBoundObject(name);
  }
}
```

The SampleListAndSearchExample class of Listing 19.2 extends the SampleLookupExample class by demonstrating how one can generically list the names and the bindings of a naming context. The main() example driver method also assumes that a name is passed in from the command line as with the SampleLookupExample. This target name will be used as the context name whose contents should be listed. The jndi.properties file is used to load a set of properties from within a SampleListAndSearchExample constructor. The listNames() and listNamesAndBindings() methods are then called to demonstrate listing of a context and the listing of a context's bound objects, respectively. By constructing a CompoundName using a set of syntax properties read from the properties file, the listNames() and listNamesAndBindings() calls that take a Name object are also demonstrated.

LISTING 19.2 A Generic JNDI List and Search Example (SampleListAndSearchExample.java)

```
package ejava.jndich19;

import javax.naming.Context;
import javax.naming.InitialContext;
import javax.naming.NamingException;
import javax.naming.NamingEnumeration;
import javax.naming.CompoundName;
import javax.naming.CompositeName;
import javax.naming.Binding;
import javax.naming.Name;
import javax.naming.InvalidNameException;
import java.util.Properties;
import java.io.FileInputStream;
import java.io.IOException;
import java.util.StringTokenizer;

/**
    This class lists and searches the given object in a naming or
    directory service
*/
public class SampleListAndSearchExample extends SampleLookupExample
{
  public SampleListAndSearchExample(String propertiesFile)
    throws IOException
  {
      super(propertiesFile);
  }

  /** list Names in a given target
  */
  public void listNames(String target)
```

```
{
   Context context ;

  try{

    context = super.getInitialContext();

    NamingEnumeration namesList = context.list(target);

    if(namesList == null){
      System.out.println(target + " contains empty names ");
    }
    else{
      while(namesList.hasMore()){
        System.out.println(namesList.next());
      }
    }
  }
  catch(NamingException namingException){
      System.out.println("Error :"+namingException);
  }
}

/** list Names in a given target Name
*/
public void listNames(Name target)
{
  Context context ;

  try{
    context = super.getInitialContext();
    NamingEnumeration namesList = context.list(target);
    if(namesList == null){
      System.out.println(target + " contains empty names ");
    }
    else{
      while(namesList.hasMore()){
        System.out.println(namesList.next());
      }
    }
  }
  catch(NamingException namingException){
      System.out.println("Error :"+namingException);
  }
}
```


continues

LISTING 19.2 Continued

```
/** list Bindings for the given target Name
*/
public void listNamesAndBindings(Name target)
{
  Context context ;

  try{
    context = super.getInitialContext();
    NamingEnumeration namesList = context.listBindings(target);
    if(namesList == null){
      System.out.println(target + " contains empty names ");
    }
    else{
      while(namesList.hasMore()){
        Binding binding = (Binding)namesList.next();
          System.out.println("Name is : " + binding.getName()
                      + " Binding is : " + binding.getObject() + " ");
      }
    }
  }
  catch(NamingException namingException){
      System.out.println("Error :"+namingException);
  }
}

/** list Bindings for the given target
*/
public void listNamesAndBindings(String target)
{
  Context context ;

  try{
    context = super.getInitialContext();
    NamingEnumeration namesList = context.listBindings(target);
    if(namesList == null){
      System.out.println(target + " contains empty names ");
    }
    else{
      while(namesList.hasMore()){
        Binding binding = (Binding)namesList.next();
          System.out.println("Name is : " + binding.getName()
          + " Binding is : " + binding.getObject() + " ");
      }
    }
  }
```

```
    catch(NamingException namingException){
        System.out.println("Error :"+namingException);
    }
  }

  public static void main(String[] args)
  {
    // Ensure that a name to look up is passed as a parameter.
    if(args.length != 1){
      System.out.println("Run example as: java "
                      + "ejava.jndich19.SimpleListAndSearchExample"
                      + " <TargetObjectName>");


      System.exit(0);
    }

    // Set name of properties file to use in initializing the lookup.
    String propertiesFileName = "jndi.properties";

    // Instantiate an instance of this naming client
    SampleListAndSearchExample sampleListAndSearchExample = null;
    try{
      sampleListAndSearchExample =
        new SampleListAndSearchExample(propertiesFileName);
    }
    catch(IOException ioException){
      System.out.println("Error :"+ioException);
      System.exit(0);
    }
    String target = args[0];

    System.out.println(
        "Listing Names using listNames(String target) method");
    sampleListAndSearchExample.listNames(target);
    System.out.println(
         "Listing Names and Bindings using listNamesAndBindings " +
         " (String target) method");

    sampleListAndSearchExample.listNamesAndBindings(target);
    try{
        String n = target;
        Properties properties
```

continues

LISTING 19.2 Continued

```
            = sampleListAndSearchExample.getContextProperties();
        // construct a Compound Name using the Compound Name
        // properties in the properties file.
        CompoundName compoundName = new CompoundName(n, properties);
        // Search the Name Repository using the CompoundName
        System.out.println("Listing Names using "+
          "listNames(Name target) method: Here target is CompoundName");
        sampleListAndSearchExample.listNames(compoundName);
        // Search the Name Repository Names and
        //     Binding Object using CompoundName
        System.out.println("Listing Names and Bindings"+
          " using listNamesAndBindings(Name target) method: Here"+
          " target is CompoundName");
        sampleListAndSearchExample.listNamesAndBindings(compoundName);
    }catch(InvalidNameException invalidNameException){
         System.out.println("Error :"+invalidNameException);
          System.exit(0);
    }
  }
}
```

The `SampleBindingExample` of Listing 19.3 extends the `SampleListAndSearchExample` class and demonstrates how JNDI objects can be bound, renamed, and deleted within a context. The `main()` method uses a set of properties read in from a `jndi.properties` file to construct a `SampleBindingExample` instance. The target object name passed in from the command line is then used to call `lookupBoundObject()` on the `SampleBindingExample`'s base `SampleLookupExample` class. After renaming the target name to a new object name via a call to `renameAnObject()` on the `SampleBindingExample` object, the object is bound to its original target name with a call to `bindNewObject()`. At this point the object is bound to both the `target` name and the `newObjectName`. A call to `deleteAnObject()` with the `newObjectName` then deletes that particular named object instance.

LISTING 19.3 A Generic JNDI Binding Example (`SampleBindingExample.java`)

```
package ejava.jndich19;

import javax.naming.Context;
import javax.naming.InitialContext;
import javax.naming.NamingException;
import javax.naming.NamingEnumeration;
import javax.naming.CompoundName;
import javax.naming.CompositeName;
```

```
import javax.naming.Binding;
import javax.naming.Name;
import java.util.Properties;
import java.io.FileInputStream;
import java.io.IOException;
import java.io.File;

public class SampleBindingExample extends SampleListAndSearchExample
{
  public SampleBindingExample(String propertiesFile)
    throws IOException
  {
    super(propertiesFile);
  }

  /**
     fsContext provider will not delete directory.
     Some of the providers may not support delete method at all.
     LADP provider deletes corresponding name and object from directory
  */
  public void deleteAnObject(String target)
    throws NamingException
  {
     Context context ;
     context = super.getInitialContext();
     context.unbind(target);
     // This method is called to check that it removed the name.
     super.listNames("");
    //unbinds the named object from the given namespace.
  }

  public void deleteAnObject(Name target)
    throws NamingException
  {
     Context context ;
     context = super.getInitialContext();
     context.unbind(target);
     // This method is called to check that it removed the name.
     super.listNames("");
    //unbinds the named object from the given namespace.
  }
  /**
      rename any target ObjectName
  */
```

continues

LISTING 19.3 Continued

```
public void renameAnObject(String target, String newName)
  throws NamingException
{
   Context context ;
   context = super.getInitialContext();
   context.rename(target,newName);
   // This method is called to check that it removed the name.
   super.listNames("");
}
/**
     rename any target ObjectName.
*/
public void renameAnObject(Name target, Name newName)
  throws NamingException
{
     Context context ;
     context = super.getInitialContext();
     context.rename(target,newName);
}
/**
      bind a new Object for the existing Name
*/
public void bindNewObject(String target, Object newObject)
  throws NamingException
{
     Context context ;
     context = super.getInitialContext();
     context.rebind(target,newObject);

}
/**
      bind a new Object for the existing Name
*/
public void bindNewObject(Name target, Object newObject)
  throws NamingException
{
    Context context ;
    context = super.getInitialContext();
    context.rebind(target,newObject);
}

public static void main(String args[])
{
  // Ensure that a name to look up is passed as a parameter.
```

```
    if(args.length != 1){
      System.out.println("Run example as: "
                         + "java ejava.jndich19.SampleBindingExample "
                         + "<targetObject>");
      System.exit(0);
    }

    // Set name of properties file to use in initializing the lookup.
    String propertiesFileName = "jndi.properties";

    String target = args[0];
    try{
      SampleBindingExample simpleBindingExample =
                           new SampleBindingExample(propertiesFileName);

      String newObjectName = "newObject1";
      Object o = simpleBindingExample.lookupBoundObject(target);
     //   Renaming can be done only for the object not the subcontext.
      simpleBindingExample.renameAnObject(target,newObjectName);

      simpleBindingExample.bindNewObject(target,o);

      // To delete an object always give a complete
      //      Name or Composite Name
      simpleBindingExample.deleteAnObject(newObjectName);
    }
    catch(IOException ioException){

      System.out.println("Error opening jndi.properties file :"
                         +ioException);
      System.exit(0);
    }
    catch(NamingException namingException){

      System.out.println("Error  :"+namingException);
      System.exit(0);
    }
  }
}
```


Naming Files

The file-naming system is the most basic and common naming system that computer users encounter. In a file-naming system, filenames correspond to the names of the naming service, file-system directories correspond to the contexts that make up names, and the file objects and descriptors correspond to the handles of the system resource of interest. Different file systems will have different naming syntax conventions. Thus, whereas Windows-based file systems use the backslash (\) to separate context-space (that is, directories) and components of a name, UNIX-based systems use the forward slash (/). Similarly, Windows-based systems ignore differences between upper- and lowercase, whereas UNIX-based systems are case-sensitive.

File-System Interfaces

Before JNDI, the most common and obvious way to interact with a file system was to use the classes available in the `java.io` package, as shown in Figure 19.6. The Java 2.0 platform has provided many enhancements to the `java.io` package, including a host of new methods added to the `java.io.File` class. The `File` class encapsulates an interface to a file system's files and directory paths. Operations such as file renaming and deleting, as well as directory listing, can be achieved via the `File` class. The `FileInputStream` and `FileOutputStream` classes can be used to create new files, as well as populate such files with data or reading files. The `FileReader` and `FileWriter` classes can also be used to read and write character files.

JNDI File SPI

A file-system SPI exists for use with the JNDI API and is freely downloadable from the Sun Web site. Many developers may still elect to use the core Java support for file manipulation via use of the file streaming and reader/writer APIs provided in the `java.io` package. In fact, the JNDI file SPI provided by Sun actually heavily depends on the `java.io.File` class. However, use of a JNDI file-system SPI has its advantages by providing classes and interfaces for making file management more flexibly independent across different file-system types (depending on your underlying SPI implementation), as well as providing a standard interface to the file system that can be used even in a composite naming scheme.

NOTE

A file-system JNDI SPI provided by Sun is available for download from `http://java.sun.com/products/jndi/serviceproviders.html`.

Depending on the set of properties passed into the constructor of an `InitialContext` class or on those set via the system properties, a file-system SPI can be configured to function with your particular file system. Because the Sun file SPI uses the `java.io.File` object, it can be used with whatever platform to which your JRE has been ported. The Sun file SPI can be used with a local file system, as well as a networked file system. The Novell corporation also ships a Novell Developer's Kit that has a file SPI for the NetWare file system.

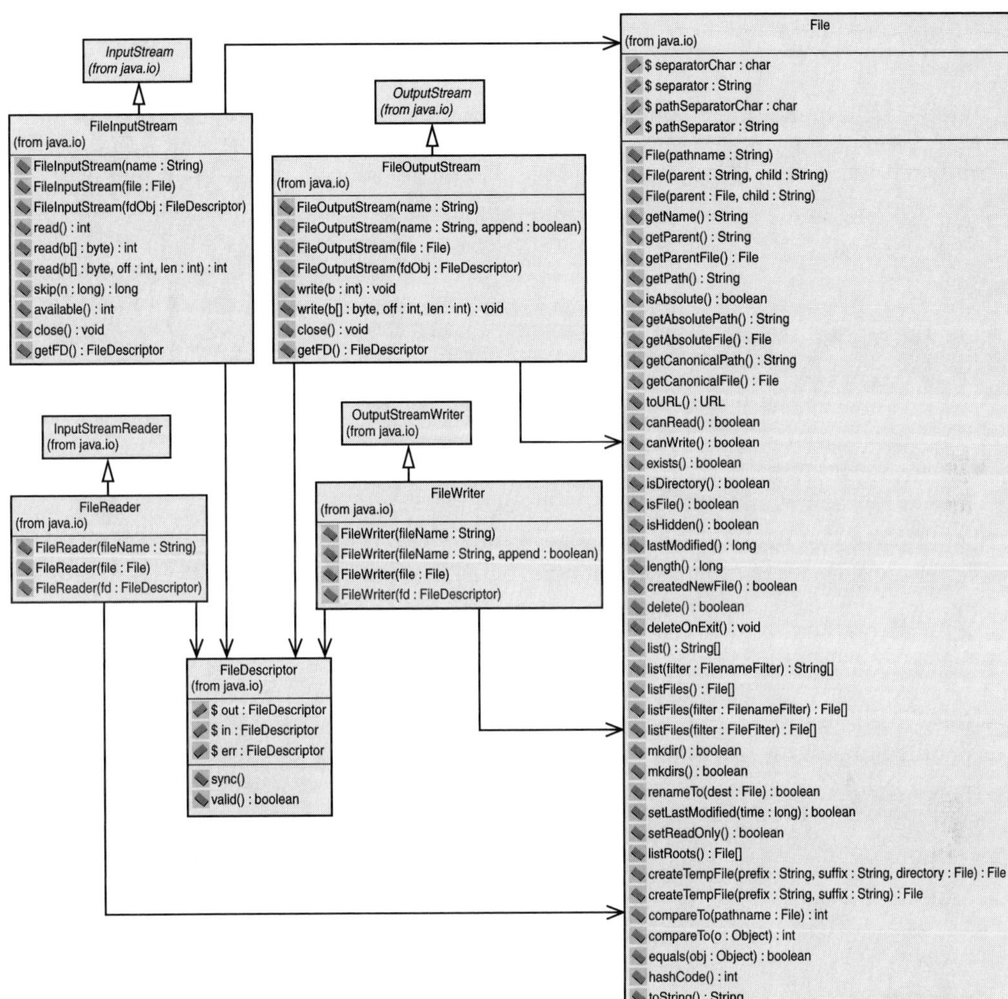

FIGURE 19.6

Traditional Java file-system interfaces.

NOTE

Under the `examples\src\ejava\jndich19` directory, an example `runfscontext.bat` script can be run on a Windows platform to demonstrate use of the file-system JNDI SPI. Note that an `FSCONTEXT_HOME` environment variable must be set to the root directory of your file-system JNDI SPI installation in order to run the example `runfscontext.bat` script. The `jndich19fsContext.properties` file is also used and can be further configured to establish a set of particular file-SPI–specific properties. The `java.naming.provider.url` property of the `jndich19fsContext.properties` file should be set to the root file directory context for which you wish to test the example code (we used the `EJAVA_HOME` directory).

The `runfscontext.bat` file copies the file-SPI–specific `jndich19fsContext.properties` file to the `jndi.properties` filename read by the generic examples in Listings 19.1 through 19.3. After that, the `SampleLookupExample`, `SampleListAndSearchExample`, and `SampleBindingExample` programs are all run to illustrate use of the generic JNDI API with a file system. Feel free to experiment with establishing your own JNDI properties (shown in Figure 19.3 and described in Table 19.1). These are the properties of interest in the `jndich19fsContext.properties` file:

```
# Sun file system SPI context factory
java.naming.factory.initial=com.sun.jndi.fscontext.RefFSContextFactory

# File system root context used with the example
java.naming.provider.url=file:D:\\bookp

# File system naming syntax properties
jndi.syntax.direction=left_to_right
jndi.syntax.separator="\"
```

NOTE

The `SampleLookupExample` should be executed with a command line parameter value of a filename or directory name defined relative to the context specified in the `java.naming.provider.url` property. The `SampleListAndSearchExample` should be executed with a command-line parameter value of a directory name defined relative to the context specified in the `java.naming.provider.url` property. The `SampleBindingExample` should be executed with a command-line parameter value of a filename defined relative to the context specified in the `java.naming.provider.url` property. You will want to edit the `runfscontext.bat` example script to define the associated command-line parameters to these example applications.

CORBA Naming

The OMG's CORBA Naming Service (also called Object Naming Service and CosNaming) presents the primary and standard way for mapping between names and objects on a CORBA ORB. The Object Naming Service was proposed by the OMG as a means to provide a standard interface to various underlying naming services. The idea was that the Object Naming Service standard would serve as the language-independent and standard way to wrap existing name servers for connectivity from various clients. As you are now aware, this goal for providing a standard way to interface with naming services is also the goal of JNDI but only in the context of Java clients. Although the JNDI API has some similarities to the Java mapping of the CORBA Naming Service API, it is not identical. It is conceivable that you could encounter a situation in which your Java client will use JNDI with a CORBA SPI that maps calls to a CORBA name server. The server in turn actually maps CORBA Naming calls to a naming service that could have been directly communicated with from your Java application or at least via another Java SPI. Alas, these multiple layers of interface mapping are the price that must be paid for flexibility and maintainability.

CosNaming IDL

Names in CORBA are sequences of name components. A name with a single component is referred to as a *simple name*, whereas a name with more components is called a *compound name*. Name components are defined by an ID and a kind. The "kind" attribute of a name simply serves to classify names for use by application software. Each ID is unique within a particular naming context. Naming contexts in CORBA contain a list of names that are all unique to that context in which each binding has a binding type indicating whether the name is bound to either a CORBA object or another naming context. Even though a logical name can be bound to a naming context, naming contexts do not need to be associated with logical names. Operations on naming contexts include binding and rebinding names to objects, resolving objects given a name, unbinding objects, creating subcontexts, and listing names associated with the context. The CosNaming module shown in Listing 19.4 defines the CORBA Naming Service IDL interfaces.

LISTING 19.4 The CosNaming IDL

```
module CosNaming
{
  typedef string Istring;

  struct NameComponent {
    Istring id;
```

continues

LISTING 19.4 Continued

```
  Istring kind;
};

typedef sequence <NameComponent> Name;

enum BindingType {nobject, ncontext};

struct Binding {
  Name binding_name;
  BindingType binding_type;
};

typedef sequence <Binding> BindingList;

interface BindingIterator;

interface NamingContext {
  enum NotFoundReason { missing_node, not_context, not_object};

  exception NotFound {
    NotFoundReason why;
    Name rest_of_name;
  };
  exception CannotProceed {
    NamingContext cxt;
    Name rest_of_name;
  };
  exception InvalidName{};
  exception AlreadyBound {};
  exception NotEmpty{};

  void bind(in Name n, in Object obj)
    raises(NotFound, CannotProceed, InvalidName, AlreadyBound);
  void rebind(in Name n, in Object obj)
    raises(NotFound, CannotProceed, InvalidName);
  void bind_context(in Name n, in NamingContext nc)
    raises(NotFound, CannotProceed, InvalidName, AlreadyBound);
  void rebind_context(in Name n, in NamingContext nc)
    raises(NotFound, CannotProceed, InvalidName);
  Object resolve (in Name n)
    raises(NotFound, CannotProceed, InvalidName);
  void unbind(in Name n)
    raises(NotFound, CannotProceed, InvalidName);
  NamingContext new_context();
```

```
    NamingContext bind_new_context(in Name n)
      raises(NotFound, AlreadyBound, CannotProceed, InvalidName);
    void destroy( )
      raises(NotEmpty);
    void list (in unsigned long how_many,
               out BindingList bl, out BindingIterator bi);
  };

  interface BindingIterator {
    boolean next_one(out Binding b);
    boolean next_n(in unsigned long how_many, out BindingList bl);
    void destroy();
  };
};
```

Because naming is such a fundamental part of manipulating objects, the CORBA Naming Service specification also provides for the efficient representation of names with a names library pseudo-IDL (PIDL) specification as shown in Listing 19.5. The names library is implemented in the CORBA client's native language. These client-side libraries provide the client with a lightweight means for manipulating names in which the names actually refer to CORBA pseudo-objects. Although these pseudo-object references cannot be passed between CORBA entities, the names library does provide a means for converting between library names and values usable by the CosNaming module's naming context.

LISTING 19.5 A CORBA Names Library PIDL

```
// PIDL
interface LNameComponent {
  exception NotSet{};
  string get_id() raises(NotSet);
  void set_id(in string i);
  string get_kind() raises(NotSet);
  void set_kind(in string k);
  void destroy();
};

// PIDL
interface LName {
  exception NoComponent{};
  exception OverFlow{};
  exception InvalidName{};
  LName insert_component(in unsigned long i, in LNameComponent n)
```

continues

LISTING 19.5 Continued

```
        raises(NoComponent, OverFlow);
    LNameComponent get_component(in unsigned long i)
        raises(NoComponent);
    LNameComponent delete_component(in unsigned long i)
        raises(NoComponent);
    unsigned long num_components();
    boolean equal(in LName ln);
    boolean less_than(in LName ln);
    Name to_idl_form() raises(InvalidName);
    void from_idl_form(in Name n);
    void destroy();
};

// C and C++
LName create_lname();
LNameComponent create_lname_component();
```

CosNaming Service Implementations

The CORBA name service used in Chapter 15, "CORBA Communications," and Chapter 16, "RMI Communications," was the transient name service that comes equipped with Java IDL and RMI/IIOP. The command `tnameserv` is used to start the CosNaming-compliant name service on a particular machine on the default port 900. The command-line flag `-ORBInitialPort <PortNum>` may also be used to run the name service on a different port number. From within your CORBA client and server applications, a handle to the name service can be retrieved using the `org.omg.CORBA.ORB.resolve_initial_references()` method. If the name service is run on a new port number other than the default, naming-service clients must set the `org.omg.CORBA.InitialPort` property associated with the ORB object.

The term *transient* is used in referring to the `tnameserv` naming service to highlight the fact that all name/object binding information is lost whenever the naming service terminates. Other naming-service options do exist, however. Most commercial CORBA vendors provide Java-based, CosNaming-compliant naming services such as these:

- IONA Technologies' OrbixWeb Orbix Names (`http://www.iona.com/products/orbix/names.html`)
- Inprise's VisiBroker Naming Service (`http://www.borland.com/visibroker/cosservices/`)
- Prism Technologies' OpenFusion Naming Service (`http://www.prismtechnologies.com/products/openfusion/products/naming-service.html`)

CORBA Naming Interfaces

Figure 19.7 presents the key programmatic interfaces to a CosNaming service. Only key components are shown; the helpers and holders associated with the various interfaces are not shown to simplify the diagram.

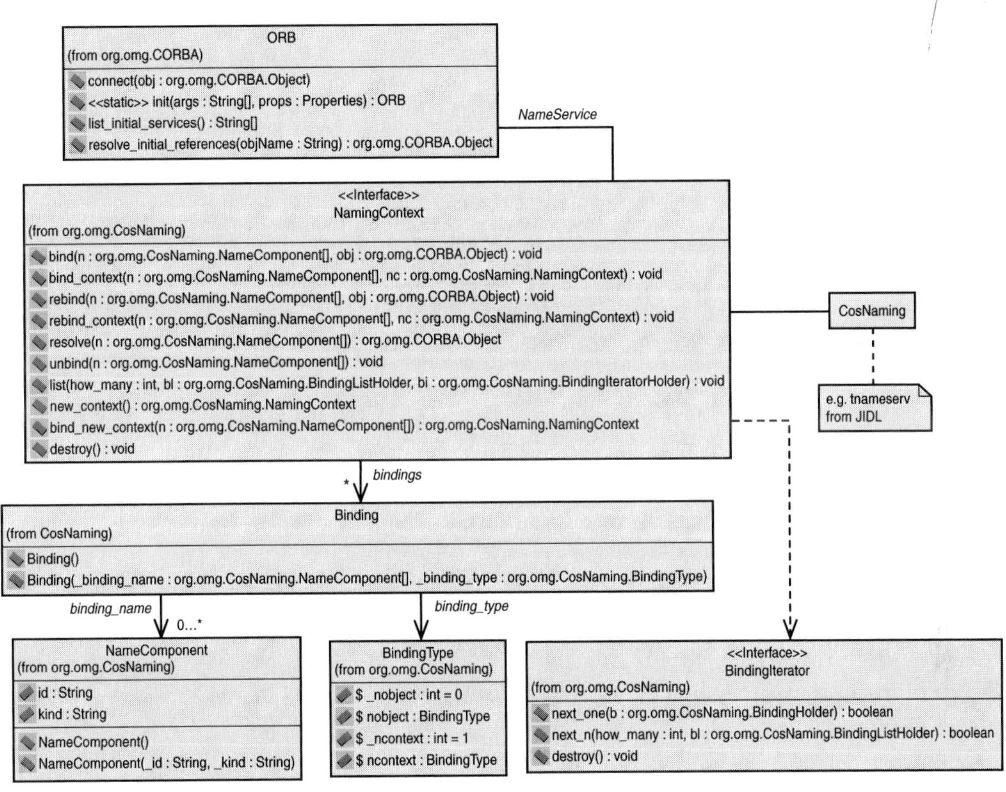

FIGURE 19.7
Traditional CosNaming service interfaces.

By narrowing an initial reference to the `NameService` returned from the ORB, we can obtain a handle to a `NamingContext` interface like this:

```
ORB orb = ORB.init(args,null);
org.omg.CORBA.Object namingRef =
    orb.resolve_initial_references("NameService");
NamingContext namingContext = NamingContextHelper.narrow(namingRef);
```

A CORBA server can then be registered from the server side by first creating a `NameComponent` array (that is, a CORBA name) and calling `bind()` or `rebind()` on the `NamingContext` reference as such:

```
MyMessageImpl server = new MyMessageImpl();
NameComponent nameComponent = new NameComponent("SampleServer", "");
NameComponent nameComponent1 = new NameComponent("SampleServer2", "");
NameComponent path[] = { nameComponent , nameComponent1 };
namingContext.rebind(path, server);
```

A CORBA client obtains an initial reference to a naming service in the same fashion as a CORBA server. The CORBA client can then use the naming context to look up (that is, "resolve" in CORBA lingo) the object reference given the CORBA name as shown here:

```
NameComponent nameComponent = new NameComponent("SampleServer", "");
NameComponent nameComponent1 = new NameComponent("SampleServer2", "");
NameComponent path[] = { nameComponent , nameComponent1 };
MyMessage obj = MyMessageHelper.narrow(namingContext.resolve(path));
```

JNDI CosNaming SPI

A CosNaming JNDI SPI exists as part of the J2EE v1.2 and can also be downloaded separately for use with the J2SE v1.2. When you interface with the CosNaming service directly, you need to understand a host of CosNaming-specific APIs. By using JNDI with a CosNaming SPI, you are provided with a standard way (as a Java developer) to interact with a host of naming-service interfaces, and thus it is not necessary to learn all the semantics specific to CosNaming. However, as mentioned, JNDI with a CosNaming SPI adds an extra layer of processing into the mix. Furthermore, by using an SPI, there exists additional risk associated with requiring proper JNDI SPI-to-CosNaming mapping by your vendor above and beyond that already required of the CosNaming vendor's mapping from the CORBA interface standard to the actual underlying naming service implementation.

NOTE

A CosNaming JNDI SPI provided by Sun is available for download from `http://java.sun.com/products/jndi/serviceproviders.html` and can be used with the J2SE v1.2 platform using the JNDI v1.2 standard extension.

NOTE

Under the `examples\src\ejava\jndich19` directory, a `runcosnamingcontext.bat` file can be run on a Windows OS to demonstrate use of the CosNaming JNDI SPI. Note that a `COSCONTEXT_HOME` environment variable must be set to the root directory of your CosNaming JNDI SPI installation in order to run the sample `runcosnamingcontext.bat` script. Additionally, the `RMI_IIOP_HOME` environment variable will need to be set to the root directory of your RMI/IIOP installation (installed in Chapters 15 and 16). The `jndich19CosNamingContext.properties` file is used to establish a set of CosNaming SPI–specific properties. `Sample.idl` and `SampleCosNamingServer` classes are also used to illustrate JNDI CosNaming SPI usage.

The `Sample.idl` file in Listing 19.6 exports a simple "Hello-World" sample method embedded inside of a `Message` interface. The `SampleCosNamingServer` of Listing 19.7 implements this interface and also registers the server with a CosNaming server via JNDI. The `runcosnamingcontext.bat` file included on the CD copies the `jndich19CosNamingContext.properties` file over to the `jndi.properties` filename used by both the `SampleCosNamingServer` of Listing 19.7 and the generic JNDI examples of Listings 19.1 through 19.3.

After a `Message` server is bound to two different names from within the `SampleCosNamingServer.bindWithDifferentNames()` method, the `SampleLookupExample`, `SampleListAndSearchExample`, and `SampleBindingExample` programs are all run to illustrate usage of the generic JNDI API with a CosNaming system. These are the properties of interest in the `jndich19CosNamingContext.properties` file that comes with the book:

```
# Sun CosNaming system SPI context factory
java.naming.factory.initial=com.sun.jndi.cosnaming.CNCtxFactory

# CosNaming system root context
java.naming.provider.url=iiop://localhost/

# CompoundName properties
jndi.syntax.separator="."
jndi.syntax.escape = "\"
jndi.syntax.beginquote ="""," '"
jndi.syntax.endquote=""","'"
jndi.syntax.reservednames: ".:", "..."
jndi.syntax.codeset= ISOLatin1
jndi.syntax.locale = US_EN

# These properties are used by the SampleCosNamingServer
SIMPLE_NAME1=SampleServer
```

```
SIMPLE_NAME2=SampleServer2
COMPOUND_NAME1=Samples.SampleServer6
COMPOUND_NAME2=Samples.Servers.SampleServer5
```

LISTING 19.6 A Sample Message IDL (`Sample.idl`)

```
module ejava
{
  module jndich19
  {
    module Sample
    {
      interface Message
      {
        string sayHi(in string value);
      };
    };
  };
};
```

LISTING 19.7 A Sample CosNaming Server (`SampleCosNamingServer.java`)

```
package ejava.jndich19;
import ejava.jndich19.Sample.*;
import java.util.Properties;
import java.io.FileInputStream;
import java.io.IOException;
import javax.naming.NamingException;
import javax.naming.Context;
import javax.naming.InitialContext;

public class SampleCosNamingServer  extends _MessageImplBase
{
  public SampleCosNamingServer()
  {
    super();
  }

  public String sayHi(String s)
  {
   return "You Send :"+s;
  }

  public void bindWithDifferentNames(Context context)
    throws NamingException
```

```
{
  Properties properties = (Properties)context.getEnvironment();

  String namingServerURL =
    (String)properties.get("java.naming.provider.url");
  String simpleName  = (String) properties.get("SIMPLE_NAME1");
  String simpleName1 = (String) properties.get("SIMPLE_NAME2");;

  // binding this object with different Names
  context.bind(namingServerURL+simpleName, this);
  System.out.println("Bound As :"+namingServerURL+simpleName);
  context.bind(namingServerURL+simpleName1, this);
  System.out.println("Bound As :"+ namingServerURL+simpleName1);
}

public static void main(String[] args)
{

  if(args.length  == 0){
    System.out.println(" You should provide properties file :"+
      "java ejava.jndich19.SampleCosNamingServer jndi.properties");
    System.exit(0);

  }
  String propertiesFileName = args[0];
  try{
    FileInputStream fin = new FileInputStream(propertiesFileName);
    Properties properties = new Properties();
    properties.load(fin);
    Context context = new InitialContext(properties);
    SampleCosNamingServer serverObject = new SampleCosNamingServer();
    serverObject.bindWithDifferentNames(context);
    System.out.println("Bound : Waiting for clients...");
    // wait for invocations from clients
    java.lang.Object sync = new java.lang.Object();
    synchronized (sync) {
      sync.wait();
    }
  }
  catch (NamingException namingException) {
    System.out.println(" Failed to Bind :" + namingException);
    namingException.printStackTrace();
    System.exit(0);
  }
```


continues

LISTING 19.7 Continued

```
    catch (IOException ioException) {
      System.out.println(" Failed to open properties file :"
                         + ioException);
      System.exit(0);
    }
     catch (InterruptedException interruptedException) {
      System.out.println(" Failed to open properties file :"
                         + interruptedException);
      System.exit(0);
    }
  }
}
```

RMI Naming

As with any well-thought-out distributed computing paradigm, RMI also has a means to bind objects to names and look up object references via a name. As we saw in Chapter 16's sections "RMI Registration" and "RMI Lookup," both RMI/JRMP and RMI/IIOP had distinct ways to communicate with a naming service. Of course, RMI/IIOP used the CosNaming service interfaces as shown in Figure 16.6. RMI/JRMP used the built-in RMI Registry interfaces as shown in Figure 16.5.

RMI Naming System Interfaces

Chapter 16 demonstrates how to utilize a naming service for both RMI/JRMP and RMI/IIOP. The RMI Registry provides a simple mechanism for interfacing with a naming service, but it is dependent on RMI/JRMP, which is a Java-centric means for distributing objects. RMI/IIOP uses a CosNaming server, and thus you can both create RMI/IIOP clients to communicate with CORBA servers implemented in another language and implement RMI/IIOP servers that can offer their services to a language-independent community of CORBA clients. The CosNaming service running under such a scenario can conceivably be any service that implements the CORBA Naming Service interface and supports the special ORB extensions required of RMI/IIOP.

JNDI RMI SPI

An RMI Registry JNDI SPI that works with RMI/JRMP is shipped with J2EE products and is separately downloadable for use with the J2SE v1.2. RMI/IIOP-based applications can use a CosNaming JNDI SPI. Because our sample RMI/IIOP applications are dependent on the `tnameserv` CosNaming service provided with RMI/IIOP, our RMI/IIOP applications also depend on use of the CosNaming SPI provided by Sun to work with the `tnameserv` CosNaming service.

NOTE

An RMI/JRMP registry JNDI SPI provided by Sun is available for download from `http://java.sun.com/products/jndi/serviceproviders.html`. It can be used with the J2SE v1.2 platform using the JNDI v1.2 standard extension.

NOTE

Under the `examples\src\ejava\jndich19` directory, two sets of files exist to illustrate use of RMI with JNDI. A `runrmicontext.bat` file, a `jndich19rmiContext.properties` file, a `Sample.java` RMI interface, and a `SampleJRMPServerUsingNamingContext.java` RMI/JRMP server and registrar exist to illustrate use of the JNDI RMI Registry SPI with the RMI Registry. The `runrmicontext.bat` sample script assumes that the `RMICONTEXT_HOME` environment variable is set to the root directory of an RMI/JRMP JNDI SPI installation. A `runrmiiiopcontext.bat` file, a `jndich19rmiiiopContext.properties` file, the same `Sample.java` RMI interface, and a `SampleRMIIIOPServer.java` RMI/IIOP server and registrar exist to illustrate use of the JNDI CosNaming SPI with the `tnameserv` CosNaming server. The `runrmiiiopcontext.bat` sample script assumes that the `RMI_IIOP_HOME` environment variable is set to the root directory of your RMI/IIOP installation (as described in Chapters 15 and 16).

The `Sample.java` RMI interface in Listing 19.8 exports a simple "Hello-World" example RMI method implemented by both the RMI/JRMP server (`SampleJRMPServerUsingNamingContext`) of Listing 19.9 and the RMI/IIOP server (`SampleRMIIIOPServer`) of Listing 19.10. The `runrmicontext.bat` file included on the CD copies the `jndich19rmiContext.properties` file over to the `jndi.properties` file used by the `SampleJRMPServerUsingNamingContext` program and by the generic JNDI examples of Listings 19.1 through 19.3. Similarly, the `runrmiiiopcontext.bat` file included on the CD copies the `jndich19rmiiiopContext.properties` file over to the `jndi.properties` file used by the `SampleRMIIIOPServer` program, as well as by the generic JNDI examples of Listings 19.1 through 19.3.

LISTING 19.8 A Sample RMI Interface (`Sample.java`)

```
package ejava.jndich19;
import java.rmi.Remote;
import java.rmi.RemoteException;

public interface Sample extends Remote
```

continues

LISTING 19.8 Continued

```
{
  String sayHi(String s)
    throws RemoteException;
}
```

After reading in a set of properties from the property file, the `SampleJRMPServerUsingNamingContext.main()` method creates an instance of a `SampleJRMPServerUsingNamingContext` object, creates an `InitialContext` with the set of read properties, and then calls the `bindWithDifferentNames()` method. The `bindWithDifferentNames()` method binds a reference to the RMI/JRMP server to the initial context using a host of different names read from the property file. In addition to two simple names, the server is also bound to two compound names.

LISTING 19.9 A Sample RMI/JRMP Server (`SampleJRMPServerUsingNamingContext.java`)

```
package ejava.jndich19;
import java.rmi.server.UnicastRemoteObject;
import java.rmi.Naming;
import java.rmi.NotBoundException;
import java.rmi.RemoteException;
import java.util.Hashtable;
import java.util.Properties;
import java.net.MalformedURLException;
import java.rmi.AlreadyBoundException;
import java.io.FileInputStream;
import java.io.IOException;
import javax.naming.Context;
import javax.naming.InitialContext;
import javax.naming.NamingException;
import java.rmi.RMISecurityManager;


public class SampleJRMPServerUsingNamingContext
    extends  UnicastRemoteObject
  implements Sample
{
  public SampleJRMPServerUsingNamingContext()
    throws RemoteException
  {
    super();
  }

  public String sayHi(String s)
```

```
  throws RemoteException
{
  return "You Send !:"+ s;
}

public void bindWithDifferentNames(Context  context)
  throws NamingException, MalformedURLException,
    AlreadyBoundException
{
  Properties properties = (Properties) context.getEnvironment();
  String namingServerURL =
    (String) properties.get("java.naming.provider.url");
  String simpleName1 = (String) properties.get("SIMPLE_NAME1");
  String simpleName2 = (String) properties.get("SIMPLE_NAME2");

  // binding this object with different Names
  context.bind(namingServerURL + simpleName1, this);
  System.out.println("Bound As :" + namingServerURL + simpleName1);
  context.bind(namingServerURL + simpleName2, this);
  System.out.println("Bound As :" + namingServerURL + simpleName2);

  String compoundName1 = (String) properties.get("COMPOUND_NAME1");
  String compoundName2 = (String) properties.get("COMPOUND_NAME2");

  context.bind(compoundName1, this);
  System.out.println("Bound as :" + compoundName1);
  context.bind(compoundName2, this);
  System.out.println("Bound as :" + compoundName2);
}

public static void main(String[] args)
{

  if(args.length  == 0){
     System.out.println("Usage : java -Djava.security.policy"+
      "=rmi.policy ejava.jndich19.SampleJRMPServerUsingNamingContext"
      +" jndich19rmiContext.Properties");
    System.exit(0);

  }
  String propertiesFileName = args[0];
  try{
    FileInputStream fin = new FileInputStream(propertiesFileName);
    Properties properties = new Properties();
     properties.load(fin);
```

continues

LISTING 19.9 Continued

```
        if ( System.getSecurityManager() == null ) {
          System.setSecurityManager (new RMISecurityManager());
        }

        SampleJRMPServerUsingNamingContext serverObject =
          new SampleJRMPServerUsingNamingContext();
        // get initial context
        Context namingContext = new InitialContext(properties);
        // bound the objects with different names
        serverObject.bindWithDifferentNames(namingContext);

        System.out.println("Bound : Waiting for clients...");
      }
      catch (IOException ioException) {
        System.out.println("Failed to open properties :" + ioException);
        System.exit(0);
      }
      catch (AlreadyBoundException alreadyBoundException) {
        System.out.println("Already Bound :" + alreadyBoundException);
        System.exit(0);
      }
      catch (NamingException namingException) {
        System.out.println(" Naming Error: " + namingException);
        namingException.printStackTrace();
        System.exit(0);
      }
  }
}
```

The `SampleRMIIIOPServer` class is very similar to the `SampleJRMPServerUsingNamingContext` class. After reading in a set of properties from the property file, the `SampleRMIIIOPServer.main()` method creates an `InitialContext` with the set of read properties, creates an instance of a `SampleRMIIIOPServer` object, and then calls the `bindWithDifferentNames()` method. The `bindWithDifferentNames()` method binds a reference to the RMI/IIOP server to the initial context using two simple names read from the property file.

LISTING 19.10 A Sample RMI/IIOP Server (`SampleRMIIIOPServer.java`)

```
package ejava.jndich19;
import javax.rmi.PortableRemoteObject;
import java.rmi.Naming;
```

```
import java.rmi.NotBoundException;
import java.rmi.RemoteException;
import java.util.Hashtable;
import java.util.Properties;
import java.net.MalformedURLException;
import java.rmi.AlreadyBoundException;
import java.io.FileInputStream;
import java.io.IOException;
import java.rmi.RMISecurityManager;
import javax.naming.Context;
import javax.naming.NameNotFoundException;


public class SampleRMIIIOPServer extends  PortableRemoteObject
  implements Sample
{


  public SampleRMIIIOPServer()
    throws RemoteException
  {
   super();
  }

  public String sayHi(String s)
    throws RemoteException
  {
    return "You Send !:"+ s;
  }

  public void bindWithDifferentNames(Context context)
    throws NamingException
  {
    Properties prop = (Properties) context.getEnvironment();
    String namingServerURL = (String) prop.get(
                             "java.naming.provider.url");
    String simpleName1 = (String) prop.get("SIMPLE_NAME1");
    String simpleName2 = (String) prop.get("SIMPLE_NAME2");

    // binding this object with different Names
    context.bind(namingServerURL + simpleName1, this);
    System.out.println("Bound As :" + namingServerURL + simpleName1);
    context.bind(namingServerURL + simpleName2, this);
```

continues

Listing 19.10 Continued

```
    System.out.println("Bound As :" + namingServerURL + simpleName2);
  }

  public static void main(String[] args)
  {

    if(args.length  == 0){
       System.out.println("Usage : java -Djava.security.policy"+
        "=rmi.policy ejava.jndich19.SampleRMIIIOPServer "+
        " jndich19rmiiiop.Properties ");
      System.exit(0);

    }
    String propertiesFileName = args[0];
    try{
      FileInputStream fin = new FileInputStream(propertiesFileName);
      Properties properties = new Properties();
      properties.load(fin);
      if ( System.getSecurityManager() == null ) {
        System.setSecurityManager (new RMISecurityManager());
      }
      Context namingContext = new InitailContext(p);
      SampleRMIIIOPServer serverObject = new SampleRMIIIOPServer();
      serverObject.bindWithDifferentNames(namingContext, properties);
      System.out.println("Bound : Waiting for clients...");
    }
    catch (IOException ioException) {
      System.out.println("Failed to open properties :" + ioException);
      System.exit(0);
    }
    catch (NamingException namingException) {
      System.out.println("Failed to bind :"+ namingException);
      System.exit(0);
    }
  }
}
```

Running the `.bat` files for either the RMI/JRMP or the RMI/IIOP examples will register a server instance to two different names with their respective naming services (RMI Registry or CosNaming Service) using the appropriate JNDI SPI. After a server is bound to two different names, the `SampleLookupExample`, `SampleListAndSearchExample`, and `SampleBindingExample` programs are all run to illustrate use of the generic JNDI API with either the RMI Registry or the CosNaming system.

The following are the RMI Registry JNDI SPI properties of interest in the `jndich19rmiContext.properties` file on the CD that accompanies this book:

```
# Sun RMI Registry system SPI context factory
java.naming.factory.initial=
➥com.sun.jndi.rmi.registry.RegistryContextFactory

# RMI Registry system root context
java.naming.provider.url=rmi://localhost:1099/

# CompoundName properties
jndi.syntax.separator="."
jndi.syntax.escape = "\"
jndi.syntax.beginquote =""","'"
jndi.syntax.endquote=""","'"
jndi.syntax.reservednames: ".:", "..."
jndi.syntax.codeset= ISOLatin1
jndi.syntax.locale = US_EN

# These properties are used by the SampleJRMPServerUsingNamingContext
SIMPLE_NAME1=SampleServer
SIMPLE_NAME2=SampleServer2
COMPOUND_NAME1=Samples.SampleServer6
COMPOUND_NAME2=Samples.Servers.SampleServer5
```

The following are the RMI/IIOP CosNaming JNDI SPI properties of interest in the `jndich19rmiiiopContext.properties` file provided with the book:

```
# Sun CosNaming system SPI context factory
java.naming.factory.initial=com.sun.jndi.cosnaming.CNCtxFactory

# CosNaming system root context
java.naming.provider.url=iiop://localhost/

# CompoundName properties
jndi.syntax.separator="."
jndi.syntax.escape = "\"
jndi.syntax.beginquote =""","'"
jndi.syntax.endquote=""","'"
jndi.syntax.reservednames: ".:", "..."
jndi.syntax.codeset= ISOLatin1
jndi.syntax.locale = US_EN

# These properties are used by the SampleRMIIIOPServer
SIMPLE_NAME1=SampleServer
SIMPLE_NAME2=SampleServer2
COMPOUND_NAME1=Samples.SampleServer6
COMPOUND_NAME2=Samples.Servers.SampleServer5
```

DNS

At the time of this book's writing, no JNDI SPI for the domain name service existed. This section thus focuses on a description of the DNS and describes existing intermediate means for Java applications to perform some minimal DNS name management functionality. Although we feel that an understanding of DNS is important for any enterprise Java developer, the bad news is that the level of support via Java is currently limited to half-baked, simple lookups. The good news is that after a JNDI SPI is implemented, you will only have to be aware of the same JNDI API that you've already familiarized yourself with for the other naming services.

The Domain Name System

The DNS provides a translation of the hierarchically defined machine hostnames that we are all familiar with (for example, `www.yahoo.com`) to and from IP addresses (for example, `204.71.200.68`). DNS names have a syntax convention and map to IP addresses that are logical addresses of network devices or hosts. As discussed in earlier chapters, these IP addresses are used by network routing elements to determine how to deliver IP-based messages to a host machine. By using human-readable and structured names, the task of the developer is simplified and less dependent on a priori knowledge of the internals of routing tables and machine configurations.

The names in DNS adhere to the syntax convention of case-insensitive name components separated by dots (`.`). Parsing of the names occurs from right to left with the rightmost name component corresponding to a top-level domain context. Many organizations use the set of top-level domain names presented in Table 19.2.

TABLE 19.2 Top-Level DNS Names

Name	*Description*
`com`	Commercial entities
`edu`	Four-year collegiate educational institutions
`net`	Network access providers and administrators
`gov`	U.S. federal government organizations
`mil`	U.S. military organizations
`org`	Miscellaneous and nonprofit organizations
`int`	International organizations

Additionally, a country code can also serve as a top-level domain name, such as the code `US` for United States–based organizations. Names are then created according to this standard format:

```
<Entity Name>.<Locality>.<State Code>.US
```

For example

```
AssuredTech.Leesburg.VA.US
```

However, few commercial U.S. organizations adhere to this standard; they utilize the top-level domain names of Table 19.2. U.S. state- and city-level organizations to a certain extent do use the `US` country code and their state code for such things as K–12 schools (`K12`), community colleges (`CC`), state government organizations (`STATE`), and libraries (`LIB`). Country codes are used by many organizations outside of the U.S., such as `co.uk` for corporations in the United Kingdom and `ac.uk` for United Kingdom academic institutions.

A subdomain is prepended to a top-level domain name with a dot as a separator to formulate a "registered" domain name. Thus, `yahoo.com` is a registered domain with `yahoo` as the subdomain and `com` as the top-level domain. Regionally designated authority to grant "registered" domain names is provided by Internet Resource Registries such as with Network Solutions, Inc.'s management of all `.com`, `.net`, and `.org` top-level domains.

An organization that has registered a domain name with an Internet Resource Registry can then create various subdomains for the registered domain name. These subdomains can be organized in any way according to the organization's liking such as `sales.myCorp.com` and `products.myCorp.com`. Hostnames for machines within these subdomains can then be assigned. Thus, `joeSalesman.sales.myCorp.com` and `elPresidente.myCorp.com` may be valid, fully qualified domain names adhering to the following format:

```
<Hostname>.<Optional One or More Dot-Separated Sub Domains>.<Registered
Domain Name>
```

A DNS server can run DNS software offered by various COTS packages on various platforms. A popular implementation for UNIX systems is the Berkley Internet Name Domain (BIND) package, which has also been ported to Windows platforms (`http://www.isc.org/bind.html`). When establishing a domain name, the Internet Resource Registry of the U.S. (Network Solutions, Inc., at `http://www.networksolutions.com`) requires that primary and secondary IP addresses be designated for a primary and backup DNS server. The designated DNS servers must then be configured to map hostnames and IP addresses for hosts and subdomains within its domain. Each host in the domain must be configured to know the IP addresses of the local DNS servers or be configured to refer to a Dynamic Host Configuration Protocol (DHCP) to help locate the local DNS servers.

When a TCP/IP request is made with a hostname, the TCP/IP protocol consults the DNS server with which it has been configured to look up the IP address with the associated hostname. If a DNS server cannot resolve a hostname to an IP address, it forwards the request to another DNS server. If none of the DNS servers can resolve the hostname, a root DNS server is finally consulted that uses the top-level domain name to consult master DNS servers for a top-level domain. These master DNS servers map the full domain name to an IP address or return the fact that they could not resolve the hostname.

This whole DNS lookup process may seem as though it would be very time-consuming. However, each DNS server is typically configured with a cache in which each cache entry has a "time to live" parameter associated with it for refreshing a new hostname to IP address mapping (typically refreshed every one to two days). Each DNS server also has a timeout value associated with it and returns the fact that it could not resolve the name even though it is possible that it could have been given enough time. A subsequent request may indeed return a resolved IP address because the DNS server may have had more time to reply and make use of more information in its cache. When surfing the Net, you might observe this behavior from time to time when you see that a Web page request proves unfruitful one instance but then proves fruitful with a new request shortly thereafter.

Java-Based DNS Interfacing

The primary way to interact with the DNS via Java right now is by use of the `java.net.InetAddress` class to look up an IP address given a hostname. Three static methods defined on `InetAddress` can be used to return `InetAddress` object instances:

- `InetAddress getByName(String hostName)` returns a handle to an `InetAddress` object given an IP Address in the form *`X.X.X.X`* (for example, `209.207.135.133`) or a machine name `String` (for example, `www.assuredtech.com`).
- `InetAddress[] getAllByName(String hostName)` returns a handle to an array of all known `InetAddress` objects for a particular `hostName` defined as in the `getByName()` call.
- `InetAddress getLocalHost()` returns a handle to an `InetAddress` object for your local host machine.

After an `InetAddress` object is returned, the following calls can be used to obtain host naming and IP address information for use by your applications:

- `String getHostName()` returns a `String` defining the hostname associated with this IP address by performing a DNS lookup.
- `String getHostAddress()` returns a `String` containing the IP address in the form *`X.X.X.X`*.
- `byte[] getAddress()` returns a byte array of the IP address in network order with `byte[0]` as the most significant byte.

Thus, the `InetAddress.getHostName()` call is where the DNS lookup really transpires. All three static `InetAddress` methods and the `getHostName()` method map to native calls from your Java platform implementation to your specific machine's DNS TCP/IP client libraries. The configuration of which DNS servers to contact is platform-specific. On Windows NT, for example, DNS is configured from the Network icon accessible from the Control Panel. DNS configuration is then configured from within the Network Control Panel, Protocols tab, TCP/IP Properties, and DNS tab.

DCOM Naming

Although DCOM provides APIs that do support naming of DCOM classes and some support for stateful DCOM object naming, the mapping of these APIs to Java-based programs has produced a somewhat cumbersome, DCOM-equivalent naming service interface. In this section we briefly describe how DCOM class naming and DCOM object naming can be accomplished. Given the importance and growth of Java, however, you should expect to see better support for Java-based registration and lookup of stateful DCOM objects in the future.

DCOM Class Naming with CLSIDs and ProgIDs

DCOM Class Identifiers (CLSIDs) are used to uniquely identify a particular DCOM class. The DCOM class identified by a CLSID refers to a collection of DCOM interfaces implemented by that class. The DCOM `com.ms.win32.Ole32.CoCreateInstance()` API call uses this CLSID when looking up and registering DCOM objects with the Microsoft Windows Registry. As shown in Chapter 18, "DCOM Communications," Java-based DCOM server objects can be registered for distributed access using the `javareg` utility with the `/surrogate` parameter. The Java-based DCOM server also needs to be defined with a `static final` CLSID `String`. General DCOM clients can obtain a pointer to the DCOM object using the CLSID passed as a parameter to the `CoCreateInstance()` DCOM API call. Java-based DCOM clients using the Microsoft JVM can simply instantiate an instance of the DCOM object (for example, `QueryManager`) with the `new` operator and then cast the object to a DCOM interface (for example, `IQueryManager`):

```
IQueryManager query = (IQueryManager) new com.beeshirts.QueryManager();
```

With the creation of a `new` DCOM object reference, the Microsoft JVM will use the CLSID associated with this DCOM object to make the `CoCreateInstance()` call for you. The CLSID identifies those unique Interfaces Identifiers (IIDs) supported by this particular DCOM class. The casting to a particular interface by the client also cues the Microsoft JVM to call `QueryInterface()` to determine whether such an interface is supported by this DCOM class and to obtain the interface reference.

The Windows Registry stores the hostname of the remote implementation, as well as the remote implementation classname used during a call to `CoCreateInstance()`. Direct calls to the `CoCreateInstanceEx()` call permit passing of a particular hostname. The COM libraries make calls to the Service Control Manager (SCM) to activate the remote object. The SCM on the client machine makes a call to the SCM on the server machine. The server SCM then uses COM libraries to activate the remote object and return the remote reference.

Of course, CLSIDs don't really fall under the category of "human readable." Program identifiers (ProgIDs) can be used to define a human-readable name for a DCOM class. ProgIDs follow the format *<Program>.<Component>.<Version>*. The DCOM `com.ms.win32.Ole32.CLSIDFromProgID()` API call takes ProgIDs that map to CLSIDs. Such a CLSID can then be used with the `CoCreateInstance()` API call to obtain a handle to the object as shown here:

```
String name = "QueryManager.Application";
myGuid = // set appropriate Guid type
type = // set type of COM Server
com.ms.com._Guid objCLSID = com.ms.win32.Ole32.CLSIDFromProgID(name);
Object comObject =
    com.ms.win32.Ole32.CoCreateInstance(objCLSID, null, type, myGUID);
```

DCOM Object Naming with Monikers

CLSIDs and ProgIDs are useful only for registering and looking up DCOM classes and interfaces. Because DCOM objects are stateless by default, a different mechanism is needed in order to register actual stateful object instances to be retrieved later by a distributed DCOM client. To a certain extent, DCOM monikers provide this capability. Monikers in DCOM can be used to obtain a handle to an object previously created.

The interface used to define a moniker is the `com.ms.com.IMoniker` interface, as shown in Listing 19.11. If a client has a handle to an `IMoniker` interface, the client can refer to an existing server. The `IMoniker` object consults the COM libraries' running object table (ROT) to find an underlying reference to the actual running server. If `IMoniker` can not find a server in the ROT, it will create a handle to a new one from a persistent store. `IMoniker` objects derive from a `com.ms.com.IPersistStream` object and can be persisted themselves.

LISTING 19.11 The `com.ms.com.IMoniker` Interface

```
package com.ms.com;
public interface IMoniker extends com.ms.com.IPersistStream
{
   public String GetDisplayName(IBindCtx pbc, IMoniker pmkToLeft);
   public IMoniker ParseDisplayName(IBindCtx pbc, IMoniker pmkToLeft,
                              String pszDisplayName, int[] pchEaten);
   public IUnknown BindToObject(IBindCtx pbc, IMoniker pmkToLeft,
                              _Guid riidResult);
   public IUnknown BindToStorage(IBindCtx pbc, IMoniker pmkToLeft,
                              _Guid riid);
   public IMoniker Reduce(IBindCtx pbc, int dwReduceHowFar,
                              IMoniker[] ppmkToLeft);
   public IMoniker ComposeWith(IMoniker pmkRight,
```

```
                                boolean fOnlyIfNotGeneric);
    public IEnumMoniker Enum(boolean fForward);
    public boolean IsEqual(IMoniker pmkOtherMoniker);
    public int Hash();
    public boolean IsRunning(IBindCtx pbc, IMoniker pmkToLeft,
                             IMoniker pmkNewlyRunning);
    public long GetTimeOfLastChange(IBindCtx pbc, IMoniker pmkToLeft);
    public IMoniker Inverse();
    public void CommonPrefixWith(IMoniker pmkOther,
                                 IMoniker[] ppmkPrefix);
    public void RelativePathTo(IMoniker pmkOther,
                               IMoniker[] ppmkRelPath);
    public boolean IsSystemMoniker(int[] pdwMksys);
}
```

The `BindToObject()` call on an `IMoniker` object executes the bind to a stateful DCOM object. Some predefined `IMoniker` objects are equipped with the COM libraries. Of course, the semantics of the `BindToObject()` call are specific to the object implementing the `IMoniker` interface. `IMonikers` can also be associated with a binding context similar to the fashion in which names can belong to a naming context.

`IMoniker` objects have human-readable display names retrievable from the `GetDisplayName()` call. Displayed moniker names are of this general form: *<TypeName>*:*<InstanceName>*. The `ParseDisplayName()` API call can be used to parse a moniker's display name into a DCOM object instance `IMoniker` interface. The ProgID used in the display name is converted to a CLSID, and then an `IMoniker` reference associated with this CLSID type is returned.

Conclusions

Naming services fulfill a basic distributed enterprise communications need for mapping between names in a context and object references. Given an object reference, a server can bind this object to a name in a naming service, and given that name, a client can look up the object reference in the naming service. JNDI is a core component of the J2EE that provides a standard interface for enterprise Java applications to access naming services. JNDI naming-service providers exist for file systems, RMI applications, and CORBA programs. Mapping Internet DNS names to IP addresses is also possible from within Java. Finally, DCOM also provides a means for mapping between names and object references using its communications paradigm.

Beyond mere mapping between names and objects, characteristics about such objects can also be associated with an extended form of naming system known as a directory or trading system. The next chapter describes how naming systems are extended to offer more sophisticated forms of object registration by object attributes and lookup by object attributes.

Directory and Trading Services

CHAPTER

20

IN THIS CHAPTER

- Directory and Trading Services in a Nutshell 634
- JNDI Directory Services 636
- NIS as a Directory Service 645
- NDS as a Directory Service 646
- LDAP as a Directory Service 648
- CORBA as a Trading Service 664
- Jini as a Trading Service 673
- Microsoft Active Directory Services 686

This chapter describes the concept and application of directory and trading services. Directory services are one means for looking up objects in different naming contexts given a set of object attributes. Similarly, trading services provide a framework for objects to identify themselves in a distributed system, provide facilities for looking up and discovering other services, and provide services to remote objects. Example use of directory services in JNDI, the CORBA Trading Service, and Jini as a trading service is illustrated in this chapter. We also present a brief description of what you can expect in the future from Microsoft's Active Directory Service implementation for use with COM- and DCOM-based objects.

In this chapter, you will learn:

- The basic concepts used to describe what a directory service and a trading service are.
- The architecture and use of JNDI as a standard directory service API.
- An overview of the Network Information System (NIS) and Novell Directory Service (NDS) directory services and how they can be used with JNDI.
- A description of the Lightweight Directory Access Protocol (LDAP) and how it is used with JNDI.
- A description of the CORBA Trading Service and how to use it for basic object service trading.
- A description of Jini and how to use it for object service trading in a dynamic discovery-based network.
- An overview of how the Microsoft Active Directory Service will be utilized by COM- and DCOM-based applications with Windows 2000.

Directory and Trading Services in a Nutshell

A directory service can be viewed as a type of naming service augmented with the capability to perform more sophisticated searches for objects. Directory service searching can be based on attributes of that object with search filter criteria and search controls. Directory services also allow for the modification of object attributes. Thus whereas naming services provide a sort of telephone White Pages approach to associating names with objects, directory services provide a telephone Yellow Pages approach by associating attributes with the object of interest.

Akin to naming services, directory services typically have a hierarchical structure in which a directory object has a context in some directory structure. Thus, each context will contain zero or more subcontexts and zero or more named directory objects. The directory object corresponds to some enterprise resource such as a file, a printer, or a person. This directory object itself is manifested in a directory service as a collection of attributes describing this object and perhaps even contains an object reference or some serialized object. An attribute of a directory object has an identifier and one or more values. A directory object in a directory service tree can be retrieved by its name or via use of a set of search criteria expressed as a function of the directory object's name and attributes.

Thus, for example, a directory service search for a particular user may first involve formulating a query given a particular last name and geographical location such as city, state, and country. The search result from this query may yield one or more directory objects matching this criteria, each with a collection of attributes. Example attributes in this resultant collection for a particular user may include an attribute with a `lastName` ID and associated last name value, as well as an attribute with a `reference` ID and an associated distributed object reference value. The fact that an attribute can have only one ID but one or more values is typically used in scenarios in which those values are synonymous, such as a `firstName` attribute ID being associated with the values `Robert`, `Rob`, or `Bob`.

Directory services are used in many distributed enterprise applications in which a set of distributed objects or information useful to other distributed objects may be registered, unregistered, and queried based on a set of descriptive attributes. LDAP directories of security certificates, NDS printing and network services, and NIS system information are all sample uses of directory services. When directory services are used to add, delete, modify, and search for attributes of directory objects, they bear a striking resemblance to database services. However, directory services are by and large used in more of a retrieval-only fashion versus updates and typically lack the transaction semantics and large-scale data warehouse support that databases tend to offer.

Directory services also are similar to trading services. The OMG's CORBA Trading Service provides a means for CORBA servers to register their services with an independent trader process along with a set of descriptive attributes. A CORBA client consults the trader for a suitable CORBA server using some search criteria over the set of attributes provided by the CORBA servers offering their services. The CORBA client may then invoke the services of these CORBA servers. Thus, the CORBA Trading Service is sort of a sophisticated directory service in which the directory objects contain attributes and service type information on distributed objects, as well as handles to the distributed objects themselves.

Sun's new Jini technology is essentially a trading service in which descriptive information about remote processes or devices is registered with a lookup service. Jini clients can then search for such services using a service template description and obtain a set of matching service items from such a search. Proxy objects returned from these searches can represent handles to remote processes or devices. Jini also adds a mechanism for Jini services and clients to dynamically discover Jini lookup services used for trading.

Finally, the Microsoft Active Directory Service (ADS) provides the standard means by which COM- and DCOM-based applications can take advantage of directory service functionality. Of course, such technology is Microsoft platform-dependent. However, any Java-based COM/DCOM clients and servers you build will at least need to be familiar with ADS due to COM and DCOM's integration with such a product.

JNDI Directory Services

In addition to a standard naming service interface, JNDI also offers a Java-based interface to directory services. Thus, the same standardization advantages offered to Java applications for interfacing with naming services also exist for interfacing with directory services. Using the extended directory service API capabilities available through JNDI, Java clients can perform more complicated object and attribute lookups based on certain object properties than was the case with pure naming service interfacing. Furthermore, because the JNDI directory service API inherits all the JNDI naming service APIs, directory service clients inherit naming service functionality as well.

Directory Contexts

The pure JNDI naming service client API user previously obtained a handle to a `javax.naming.InitialContext` object in the preceding chapter for naming services, but the JNDI directory service client API user obtains a handle to a `javax.naming.directory.InitialDirContext` object. As can be seen from Figure 20.1, the `InitialDirContext` class inherits from the `InitialContext` class and implements the extended set of directory service interface operations from the `javax.naming.directory.DirContext` interface. As you'll soon see, use of the `InitialDirContext` class will enable API clients to be able to bind object attributes to names, search for objects based on such attributes as well as more sophisticated search control criteria, and modify attributes. Note that we have shown operation signatures in Figure 20.1 so that we could fit all relevant classes and interfaces into one diagram.

A handle to an `InitialDirContext` can be obtained in the same fashion as was done with obtaining a handle to an `InitialContext`. However, now you will have a handle to an object implementing the `DirContext` interface versus the pure `Context` interface as shown here:

```
Properties properties = new Properties();
// Set properties in some fashion
DirContext dirContext = new InitialDirContext(properties);
```

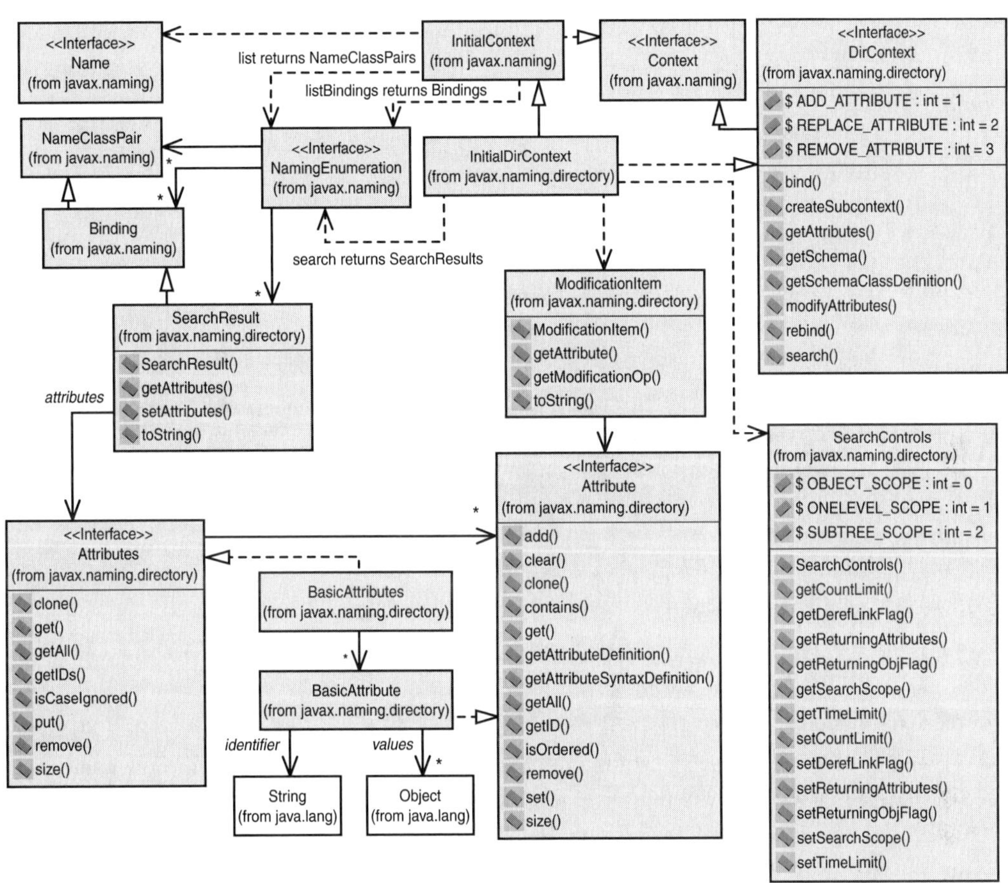

FIGURE 20.1

Core JNDI directory entities.

Directory Object Attributes

After you obtain a handle to a directory context, you can bind objects to the directory service or perhaps create special subcontexts identifiable with attributes. In either case, you will need to create one or more attributes that get associated with such objects or subcontexts. The `javax.naming.directory.BasicAttribute` class that implements the `javax.naming.directory.Attribute` interface represents an encapsulation of a basic attribute about an object in the directory service. Each `BasicAttribute` has a `String` name identifier and can have zero or more `Object` attribute values. The `javax.naming.directory.Attributes` interface and the `javax.naming.directory.BasicAttributes` class, which implements that interface, encapsulate a basic collection of `Attribute` instances. A directory object can be described using one or more attributes encapsulated by such an `Attributes` collection construct.

Creating attributes and collections of attributes is rather straightforward. For example, to create an attribute with a name, name-value pair, or name and set of values, we have the following examples:

```
BasicAttribute at1 = new BasicAttribute("name"); // Name only
BasicAttribute at2 = new BasicAttribute("building", "A"); // Name/value
BasicAttribute at3 = new BasicAttribute("floor", "5");
BasicAttribute at4 = new BasicAttribute("room", "506");
BasicAttribute at5 = new BasicAttribute("IP", "209.207.135.133");
BasicAttribute at6 = new BasicAttribute("Port"); // Name only
at6.add("8020"); // Add a port value to attribute at6
at6.add("8021"); // Add another valid port value to attribute at6
```

To add such attributes to an attribute collection as well as a few extra attributes, we can create a `BasicAttributes` instance and add attributes to it as such:

```
Attributes bindAttrs = new BasicAttributes(true);
bindAttrs.put(at1);
bindAttrs.put(at2);
bindAttrs.put(at3);
bindAttrs.put(at4);
bindAttrs.put(at5);
bindAttrs.put(at6);
bindAttrs.put("color", "yes");
bindAttrs.put("maxSize", "C");
```

As shown in Figure 20.1, other fairly intuitive operations also exist on objects implementing the `Attribute` and `Attributes` interfaces. In addition to adding new attributes, the `Attributes` interface allows one to remove an attribute, retrieve its contents, determine its size, and clone its contents. The `Attribute` interface implements methods to clear all of its values, get one or more of its values, remove its values, get its identifier, and determine the status of its size and contents.

Directory Schemas

The `Attribute` interface also offers two not-so-intuitive operations that return a `DirContext` object. The `getAttributeSyntaxDefinition()` and `getAttributeDefinition()` methods return a syntactical definition and schema definition of an attribute, respectively, both in the form of a `DirContext` object. The exact structure of such definitions will be directory service specific. You will similarly notice `getSchemaClassDefinition()` and `getSchema()` methods on the `DirContext` class itself. The `getSchema()` method returns the schema of the associated named object, and the `getSchemaClassDefinition()` method returns a collection of schema objects for the associated named object. The exact structure of the returned `DirContext` objects from these operations is also directory service specific.

Schemas describe the structure of an object or attribute and can be useful for dynamically querying and manipulating the directory service structure based on schema information. Although such dynamic directory service interfacing can be useful, you should be aware that because the returned `DirContext` values describing these schemas are directory service specific, you will most likely compromise some aspects of the standardized directory-access nature of your applications.

Directory Object Binding

Binding a name and object to the directory service with a collection of attributes is performed via either a `bind()` or a `rebind()` call to the `DirContext`. The only difference between `bind()` and `rebind()` is that `bind()` can throw a `NameAlreadyBoundException` if an object of that name is already bound to the directory service, whereas `rebind()` simply overwrites the original binding. However, both calls may throw an `InvalidAttributesException` if an attribute that is required to be bound with the name is missing. For example, we might have the following bind to a `Printers` subcontext for a particular directory service:

```
Attributes bindAttrs = // Attributes as set earlier
Printer printerObj = // Example Serializable printer object
DirContext printerContext = (DirContext) dirContext.lookup("Printers");
printerContext.bind("Printer.AI.HP550", printerObj, bindAttrs);
```

Basic Directory Searches

Searching for objects in a directory context can be accomplished in various ways through the JNDI directory service API using one of the `search()` methods on the `DirContext` class. As a first example, to search the directory-tree context for objects that have a certain set of attributes, we can simply create a set of attributes that should be matched and do the following:

```
BasicAttribute atr1 = new BasicAttribute("building", "A");
BasicAttribute atr2 = new BasicAttribute("floor", "5");
Attributes where = new BasicAttributes(true);
where.put(atr1);
where.put(atr2);

NamingEnumeration enum = dirContext.search("Printers", where);
```

As you'll see shortly, the `NamingEnumeration` object contains the results of your search.

If you are interested only in retrieving certain attribute values from the `search()` command, you can filter down the result list with an additional `String` array of attribute names. Such a filtering capability is similar to the `SELECT` clause in a SQL statement. For example

```
BasicAttribute atr1 = new BasicAttribute("building", "A");
BasicAttribute atr2 = new BasicAttribute("floor", "5");
Attributes where = new BasicAttributes(true);
```

```
where.put(atr1);
where.put(atr2);
String select[] = {"IP", "Port"};

NamingEnumeration enum = dirContext.search("Printers", where, select);
```

Directory Search Results

Note that if you knew the name of the directory object a priori, you can retrieve its set of attributes directly using this:

```
Attributes attributes = printerContext.getAttributes("Printer.AI.HP550");
```

In lieu of this, your use of the `search()` method will yield a `NamingEnumeration` object containing a set of `javax.naming.directory.SearchResult` objects, each of which matches the criteria submitted to the `search()` method. The `SearchResult` class extends the `javax.naming.Binding` class described in the preceding chapter. Thus, not only can the bound object name and object be retrieved (by virtue of inheriting from the `Binding` class), but the entire set of `Attributes` associated with that object also can now be obtained from the `SearchResult` instance. For example, the following `while` loop would examine each `SearchResult` object returned via such a `NamingEnumeration` and would print each contained `Attribute` identifier `String` and set of attribute values:

```
while (enum != null && enum.hasMore()) {

  SearchResult sr = (SearchResult) enum.next();
  System.out.println(" Result Name :" + sr.getName() );
  Attributes attrs = sr.getAttributes();

  if(attrs == null) {
    System.out.println(" No Attributes :");
  }
  else {
    for(NamingEnumeration ne = attrs.getAll();ne.hasMoreElements(); ){
      Attribute attribute = (Attribute)ne.next();
      String id = attribute.getID();

      for (Enumeration vals = attribute.getAll();
                        vals.hasMoreElements();){
        System.out.println(id + ": " + vals.nextElement());
      }
    }
  }
  System.out.println();
}
```

Directory Searches Using Search Controls and Filters

A `javax.naming.directory.SearchControls` object can be passed into a few of the `search()` methods to further refine the scope and set of results returned from a search. A `SearchControls` object can be constructed with a set of control parameters or can be constructed with no parameters, indicating that the default search controls should be used. For each search-control parameter type that can be passed into the nondefault `SearchControls` constructor, there also exists a getter and setter on the `SearchControls` class. Table 20.1 shows each search-control parameter type and its Java type, a description of the parameter, the associated getter/setter, and the default value if no value is set. If a `null` `SearchControls` object or a `SearchControls` object created with the default constructor is passed into the `search()` method, the default search control values are used.

TABLE 20.1 Directory Search Controls

Search Control	*Description*	*Getter and Setter*	*Default*
Search Scope (`int`)	If set to `ONELEVEL_SCOPE`, then search one level of the context. If set to `SUBTREE_SCOPE`, then search entire context subtree. If set to `OBJECT_SCOPE`, then search named object only.	`getSearchScope` `setSearchScope`	One level scope
Result Count Limit (`long`)	Maximum number of entries to return in a result.	`getCountLimit` `setCountLimit`	Max count limit
Search Time Limit (`int`)	Maximum time to spend searching (in milliseconds).	`getTimeLimit` `setTimeLimit`	Max time limit
Result Attributes (`String []`)	Specifies array of attributes to return from a search.	`getReturningAttributes` `setReturningAttributes`	Return all attributes
Return Object Flag (`boolean`)	Indicates whether the bound object should be returned.	`getReturningObjFlag` `setReturningObjFlag`	`False`
Dereference Flag (`boolean`)	Indicates whether dereferencing of links should occur.	`getDerefLinkFlag` `setDerefLinkFlag`	`False`

Whenever a `SearchControls` object is passed to a `search()` method on the `DirContext`, a filter expression `String` must also be passed as an argument. The exact syntax of the filter expression becomes more apparent when cast in the light of a specific directory service SPI, but suffice it to say for now that the search filter `String` (as defined by RFC 2254 found at `ftp://ftp.isi.edu/in-notes/rfc2254.txt`) may contain a series of name-value pairs as well as search criteria expressible in something similar in role to a SQL `WHERE` clause. Each search expression of the filter `String` is typically enclosed by parentheses and uses the search filter symbols listed in Table 20.2.

TABLE 20.2 Directory Search Filter Symbols

Symbol	*Description*
=	Equality of attributes
~=	Approximate equality of attributes
<=	Attribute is less than or equal to value
>=	Attribute is greater than or equal to value
!	Negation of an associated expression evaluation
&	The logical `AND` of two associated expressions
|	The logical `OR` of two associated expressions
*	A wildcard value used in expressing values
\	An escape character used inside values expressions

As a simple example, we might construct a `String` filter like this:

```
String filter = "(&(building=A)(floor=*))" ;
```

And then we might create and use a set of `SearchControls` like this:

```
SearchControls searchControls = new SearchControls();
String[] resultAttributes = {"name", "building", "floor", "room"};
searchControls.setReturningAttributes(resultAttributes);
searchControls.setCountLimit(2);
NamingEnumeration searchResults =
    dirContext.search("Printers", filter, searchControls);
```

The filter `String` argument may also be constructed such that variables in the filter `String` are expressed in the form of `{i}`, in which `i` is an array index number. The array for which this value is an index refers to an `Object[]` array parameter passed to the `search()` method along with the `SearchControls` object and filter `String`. For example

```
String filter = "(&(building={0})(floor={1}))" ;
Object [] filterArgs = {"A", "5"};
SearchControls searchControls = new SearchControls();
NamingEnumeration searchResults =
    dirContext.search("Printers", filter, filterArgs, searchControls);
```

Directory Object Attribute Modification

There are two primary ways to add, replace, and remove attributes associated with an already-bound directory object. The first way involves calling `modifyAttributes()` on the `DirContext` with a modification operation type and set of attributes to be modified according to this modification operation type. The second way involves creating an array of `Serializable` `ModificationItem` objects, each of which is composed of a modification operation type and attribute. In this way another `modifyAttributes()` method can be called with this array of `ModificationItem` objects to perform a batch update with a different modification operation per attribute. The modification operation types that can be performed are defined by `DirContext.ADD_ATTRIBUTE` to add an attribute, `DirContext.REPLACE_ATTRIBUTE` to replace the attribute, and `DirContext.REMOVE_ATTRIBUTE` to remove the attribute.

As an example of modifying an attribute collection using the same modification operation, we have this:

```
Attributes attrs = new BasicAttributes(true);
attrs.put("floor","4");
attrs.put("room","404");

printerContext.modifyAttributes("Printer.AI.HP550",
                                DirContext.REPLACE_ATTRIBUTE, attrs);
```

As an example of performing a batch of modification updates using `ModificationItem` objects, we have this:

```
ModificationItem mod1 = new ModificationItem(
                              DirContext.REPLACE_ATTRIBUTE,
                              new BasicAttribute("room", "408"));
ModificationItem mod2 = new ModificationItem(
                               DirContext.REMOVE_ATTRIBUTE,
                               new BasicAttribute("color"));
ModificationItem mod3 = new ModificationItem(
                               DirContext.ADD_ATTRIBUTE,
                               new BasicAttribute("status", "online"));

ModificationItem modItems[] = {mod1, mod2, mod3};

printerContext.modifyAttributes("Printer.AI.HP550", modItems);
```

Directory Events

The JNDI naming event infrastructure described in Chapter 19, "Naming Services," is also extended for directory service events. Figure 20.2 depicts this fact via the addition of a `javax.naming.event.EventDirContext` interface that extends the naming service–specific `EventContext` interface. Two new general types of the `addNamingListener()` method have been added to the `EventDirContext`. The first general form takes a `SearchControls` object and search filter `String`, as was the case with the directory `search()` methods, only now the search filter and controls are used to identify those object attributes at the associated named directory object whose events must be directed toward the associated `NamingListener`. Similarly, the second general form of the `addNamingListener()` method also takes an `Object[]` array of filter arguments to be used in conjunction with the search filter `String` to identify indexed directory service objects, as was also the case with the directory `search()` methods.

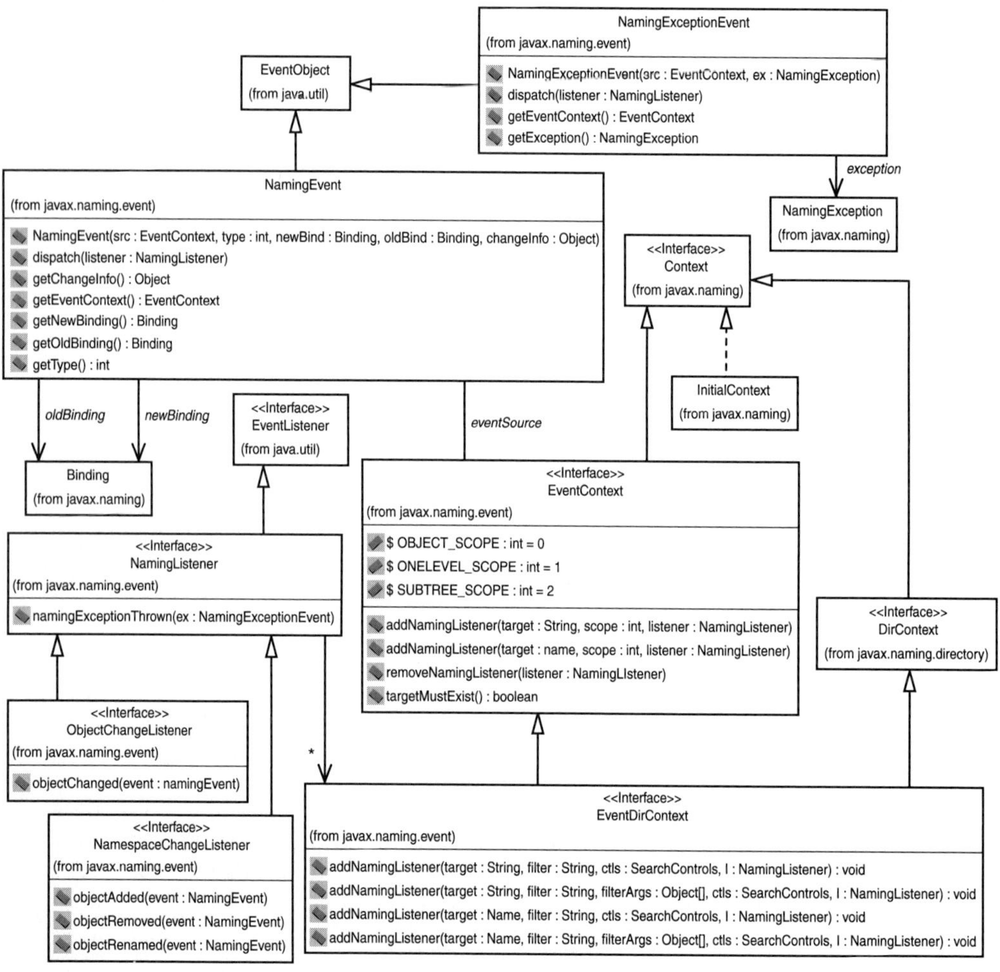

FIGURE 20.2

JNDI directory service events.

Thus, if we wanted to create a printer event listener that implemented the `ObjectChangeListener` interface and add it to our directory service that implemented the `EventDirContext`, we might have something like this:

```
SearchControls searchControls= new SearchControls();
searchControls.setSearchScope( SearchControls.SUBTREE_SCOPE );

EventDirContext eventContext = // Construct a directory event context
ObjectChangeListener printerEventManager = // Construct a listener
eventContext.addNamingListener("Printer.AI.HP550", "(status=*)",
                               searchControls, printerEventManager);
```

NIS as a Directory Service

The Network Information System (NIS) is a directory service (formerly referred to as the Yellow Pages, or YP) developed by Sun Microsystems in the 1980s and widely used in UNIX-based platforms. NIS was designed to allow for the centralized administration of resources shared by a network of machines. Machines in an NIS network share an NIS domain and speak to an NIS domain server to look up and update network information (for example, passwords). NIS also allows clients access to files and other system resources available over a local area network. NIS+ is a later version of NIS providing enhancements to security and other services.

JNDI NIS SPI

A JNDI SPI exists for NIS and is downloadable from the JavaSoft Web site at `http://www.javasoft.com/products/jndi/serviceproviders.html`. Because we illustrate use of the JNDI Directory Service API capabilities in more depth for the LDAP SPI later in this chapter, and because use of the NIS SPI requires NIS server access, we won't go into a detailed explanation of sample NIS use here. However, the CD does contain a simple NIS lookup example under the `examples\src\ejava\jndich20` directory.

NOTE

Under the `examples\src\ejava\jndich20` directory, three files exist to illustrate use of NIS with JNDI. In this directory, a `runniscontext.bat` file, a `jndich20NISContext.properties` file, and a `SampleNISExample.java` file are provided to illustrate use of the JNDI NIS SPI with a remote NIS service. Note that you will need to have NIS running on your network somewhere to run this example and have access to that service from your client program. Of course, our sample `runniscontext.bat` file would be useful only in running your NIS client from a Windows-based machine. The `runniscontext.bat` file copies the `jndich20NISContext.properties` file to the `jndi.Properties` filename looked for by the `SampleNISExample`. Note that you must also set the `NIS_PKG_HOME` environment variable to the root directory of your NIS JNDI SPI installation before invoking the `runniscontext.bat` script file.

A `SampleNISExample.java` file in the `examples\src\ejava\jndich20` directory simply reads a target NIS lookup name of interest from the command line, reads in a JNDI properties file, instantiates an instance of the `SampleNISExample`, and calls a method that lists the contents of the NIS server given the target lookup name. Two key JNDI properties to be set for the NIS SPI example are the NIS context factory and the NIS server URL properties:

```
#  Factory Context property for NIS
java.naming.factory.initial=com.sun.jndi.nis.NISCtxFactory

# NIS Server URL
java.naming.provider.url=nis://sampleYPServer/tracking.tshirts.com
```

NDS as a Directory Service

The Novell Directory Service (NDS) is a popular directory service for managing enterprise network resources and network user information. NDS's multiplatform support and its easy-to-use GUI administration toolkit have made it fairly popular with network administrators. NDS servers allow NDS clients to obtain access to such resources as networks, file servers, print servers, and database servers from a centrally managed location. Using NDS, administrators can enable access, limit access, and disable access to such resources by users in an easily configurable fashion.

JNDI NDS SPI

Novell currently offers a JNDI SPI for Java applications to interface with the NDS at `http://developer.novell.com/ndk/download.htm`. As with the NIS SPI, we also defer an in-depth illustration of the JNDI Directory Service API until the LDAP section in this chapter because use of the NDS SPI will require access to an NDS server. However, we will highlight some key points for NDS access via the NDS SPI here with a more complete example contained on the CD under the `examples\src\ejava\jndich20` directory.

NOTE

Under the `examples\src\ejava\jndich20` directory, three files exist to illustrate use of NDS with JNDI. In that directory, a `runndscontext.bat` file, a `jndich20NDSContext.properties` file, and a `SampleSearchExampleNDS.java` file are provided to illustrate use of the JNDI NDS SPI with a remote NDS server. Note that you will need to have NDS running on your network somewhere to run this example and have access to that service from your client program. Of course, our sample `runndscontext.bat` file would be useful only in running your NDS client from a Windows-based machine. The `runndscontext.bat` file copies the `jndich20NDSContext.properties` file to the `jndi.Properties` filename looked for by the `SampleSearchExampleNDS`. Note that you must also set the `NDS_HOME` environment variable to the root directory of your NDS JNDI SPI installation before invoking the `runndscontext.bat` script file.

The first thing to note about configuring a Java-based JNDI NDS client, such as the `SampleSearchExampleNDS` Java client on the CD, is that you will need to configure a few key properties such as the NDS context factory, the URL of your NDS server, and a distinguished name identifying the root context of your NDS server. For example:

```
#  NDS Factory Context property
java.naming.factory.initial=
➥com.novell.service.nds.naming.NdsInitialContextFactory

# NDS Server URL with format of...
#             nds://<treeName>/[fullyDistinguishedName]
java.naming.provider.url=nds://BeeShirtsTree/


# NDS Distinguished Name
NDS_ENTRY_DN=tshirts
```

After connecting to an `InitialDirContext` object using such properties, you can search for a set of basic NDS attributes perhaps by listing the `GivenName`, `Surname`, `PhoneNumber`, `Description`, and `EMail Address` of the NDS server contents using something along these lines:

```
DirContext context = new InitialDirContext(properties);
String entryDN = (String) properties.get("NDS_ENTRY_DN");

BasicAttribute atr1 = new BasicAttribute("Description");
BasicAttribute atr2 = new BasicAttribute("EMail Address");
Attributes matchAttrs = new BasicAttributes(true);
matchAttrs.put(atr1);
matchAttrs.put(atr2);

String resultAttributes[] = {"GivenName", "Surname", "PhoneNumber",
                             "Description","EMail Address"};
NamingEnumeration searchResults
      = context.search(entryDN, matchAttrs, resultAttributes);
```

Or you might search for NDS entries using a set of `SearchControls` as shown here:

```
DirContext context = new InitialDirContext(properties);
String entryDN = (String) properties.get("NDS_ENTRY_DN");
String filter = "(&(surname=Carter)(givenname=*))" ;

SearchControls searchControls = new SearchControls();
String[] resultAttributes = {"GivenName", "Surname", "PhoneNumber"};
searchControls.setReturningAttributes(resultAttributes);
searchControls.setCountLimit(2);

NamingEnumeration searchResults
      = context.search(entryDN, filter, searchControls);
```

LDAP as a Directory Service

The Lightweight Directory Access Protocol (LDAP) is implemented by servers that store user, organizational, file, and network resource information in the form of a directory service. LDAP is a lighter-weight version of the X.500's Directory Access Protocol (DAP) standard and offers efficiencies by being tailored for information retrieval versus updates and by operating over the TCP/IP protocol. Due to its lightweight and open-standards nature, LDAP is becoming a very popular directory-service alternative.

A fully defined name of a directory object in an LDAP directory structure, including its context, is referred to as a *distinguished name* (DN). Each component of a distinguished name is referred to as a relative distinguished name (RDN). Each RDN represents a directory-service entry and has one or more attributes. Each attribute of an RDN is described by a type and a value. Multiple attributes within an RDN are separated by a plus sign (+). For example, each RDN may be expressed in the following terms:

```
rdnComponent1=value1 + rdnComponent2=value2 + ... + rdnComponentN=valueN
```

RDNs within a DN are separated by commas (`,`) or semicolons (`;`) and typically proceed from right to left in terms of highest-level context to lower-level context. Thus, a root context of an LDAP system will be positioned in the rightmost portion of a DN, and each subcontext is separated by commas or semicolons. For example, a DN may be generally expressed in these terms:

```
rdnN, ..., rdn2, rdn1
```

The LDAP context structure is typically described in a hierarchical, treelike format following a top-down geographical and organizational description. That is, the LDAP root context is typically followed by a country subcontext, followed by an organizational subcontext, which in turn is followed by an individual/resource subcontext (that is, people or computing resource). Because of this geographical and organizational hierarchical convention, a set of standard RDN component type names have been defined as shown in Table 20.3.

TABLE 20.3 LDAP Standard RDN Type Names

RDN Type	*Description*
C	Country name
ST	State or province name
L	Locality or city name
STREET	Street address
O	Organization name
OU	Organizational unit name
CN	Common name

As an example of an LDAP DN defined using such conventions, we might have this:

```
CN=Paul J. Perrone, OU=Consulting, O=Assured Technologies,
➥L=Leesburg, ST=Virginia, C=US
```

In addition to providing a standard naming model, the Internet Engineering Task Force (IETF) standards body also defines a standard API for interfacing with an LDAP server. The LDAP API supports most of the basic directory service functionality, including the following:

- Bind (connect/authenticate) to an LDAP directory server.
- Unbind (disconnect) from an LDAP directory server session.
- Add a new directory object entry.
- Delete a directory object entry.
- Modify a directory object entry.
- Rename a directory object entry.
- Search for directory object entries.
- Compare an entry with particular attribute values to determine whether it contains those values.

Although version 2 of the LDAP standard defined much of what is in current use today with respect to LDAP implementations, the LDAP v3 standard has defined several enhancements that make LDAP more generic for use. LDAP v3 style conventions define generic approaches for submitting LDAP requests, retrieving responses, and setting behavioral controls.

LDAP Interfaces

The IETF has defined a standard Java API for performing LDAP v2 and LDAP v3 operations. The LDAP Java API defines a set of Java-based interfaces to LDAP enabling you to build Java applications that can communicate with LDAP servers and invoke some of the basic directory service functionality outlined earlier for LDAP. More information on the most current Java API standard is available at `http://www.ietf.org/html.charters/ldapext-charter.html`. Although the IETF has defined a standard Java API to LDAP, the Mozilla Organization provides the source code and SDK for the Netscape Directory Service implementation of the IETF Java LDAP standard API. More information on the Mozilla Organization's release of the LDAP SDK is available at `http://www.mozilla.org/directory`, and specific Java API binding information is available at `http://www.mozilla.org/directory/javasdk.html`. It should be noted that although the Mozilla Organization does implement a very clean and freely downloadable Java LDAP API, the package suffixes for such constructs follow Netscape Directory SDK suffixes, such as `netscape.ldap`, `netscape.ldap.util`, and `netscape.ldap.controls`.

The core class utilized by the LDAP Java API and implemented by the Mozilla Organization's distribution is the `LDAPConnection` class. An `LDAPConnection` object can be used to perform all the basic operations available to an LDAP client, including binding to and unbinding from LDAP connections, and searching for LDAP entries, as well as adding, deleting, modifying, comparing, and renaming LDAP entries. Additionally, these are the other core classes and interfaces that compose the LDAP Java API and that are implemented by the Mozilla Organization distribution:

- `LDAPv2`: An interface summarizing all the basic operations available in LDAP v2.
- `LDAPv3`: An interface extending the `LDAPv2` interface and providing additional LDAP v3 type operations.
- `LDAPConstraints`: A class encapsulating a set of generic operation constraints such as operation time limits and maximum number of server hops.
- `LDAPSearchConstraints`: A subclass of `LDAPConstraints` encapsulating a set of search preferences.
- `LDAPControl`: A class encapsulating LDAP v3 information that can be used to control a particular LDAP operation.
- `LDAPEntry`: A class encapsulating an LDAP entry.
- `LDAPAttribute`: A class encapsulating the name and values of an attribute in an LDAP entry.
- `LDAPAttributeSet`: A class encapsulating a collection of LDAP attributes.
- `LDAPMessage`: A base class for LDAP requests and responses.
- `LDAPResponse`: An LDAP response from an LDAP operation.
- `LDAPSearchResult`: An LDAP result from an LDAP search operation.
- `LDAPSearchResults`: A collection of LDAP results from an LDAP search operation.
- `LDAPModification`: A class describing the changes to be made to an LDAP entry.
- `LDAPModificationSet`: A collection of LDAP modifications.
- `LDAPExtendedOperation`: An LDAP v3–style extended operation.
- `LDAPExtendedResponse`: An LDAP v3–style response to an extended operation.

As a simple example illustrating the use of such an API, the following snippet demonstrates how you might use the `LDAPConnection` class to go about connecting to a particular LDAP server host on a particular port, authenticating yourself to that LDAP server, and then issuing a search operation using a filter and set of `LDAPSearchConstraints`:

```
LDAPConnection client = new LDAPConnection();

String ldapHost = "ldap.myserver.com";
```

```
int    ldapPort = 389;
client.connect( ldapHost, ldapPort );

int ldapVersion = 3;
String bindDN = "cn=Joe L. Dapp";
String password = "ldappwd";
client.authenticate( ldapVersion, bindDN, password );

LDAPSearchConstraints constraints = client.getSearchConstraints();
constraints.setMaxResults( 100 );
constraints.setTimeLimit( 1000 );
LDAPSearchResults results =
    client.search("ou=People", 0, "(&(sn=Carter)(givenname=*))",
                  null, null, constraints );
```

JNDI LDAP SPI

Although the Java LDAP API is a standard and tends to offer you support for the latest and greatest in LDAP API features, there also exists a JNDI SPI available for use with LDAP. Not only is there a JNDI SPI for LDAP, but there also exists a special JNDI `javax.directory.ldap` package for supporting some of the more sophisticated LDAP v3 features. The LDAP JNDI SPI is freely downloadable from the Sun Web site, and the extended `javax.directory.ldap` API libraries, of course, come with the Java 2 platform JNDI component.

NOTE

An LDAP JNDI SPI provided by Sun is available for download from `http://java.sun.com/products/jndi/serviceproviders.html`.

To illustrate use of the JNDI directory service interface, we will first demonstrate various basic directory service operations with the LDAP SPI and an LDAP directory service. We use the Netscape Directory Service as our LDAP server. If you are interested in running our examples with such a server, consult Appendix A, "Software Configuration," for details on installing and configuring such a server. Regardless of what LDAP server you decide to use, the LDAP SPI will make use of some basic property types that we store in a `jndich20ldapContext.properties` file on the CD:

```
# Sun's JNDI LDAP SPI Context Factory:
java.naming.factory.initial= com.sun.jndi.ldap.LdapCtxFactory

# LDAP Server URL
java.naming.provider.url=ldap://localhost:389/o=airius.com
```

```
# Example LDAP Authentication Information
java.naming.security.authentication=simple
java.naming.security.credentials=administrator
java.naming.security.principal=cn=Directory Manager
```

NOTE

Under the `examples\src\ejava\jndich20` directory, a `runjndildapcontext.bat` file can be run on a Windows OS to demonstrate use of the LDAP JNDI SPI. The `jndich20ldapContext.properties` file is used to establish a set of JNDI SPI–specific properties. Finally, a `SampleSearchExample` class and a `SampleNamingListener` class are used to illustrate JNDI LDAP SPI usage. Note that the `LDAP_HOME` environment variable must be set to the root directory of your LDAP JNDI SPI installation in order for our `runjndildapcontext.bat` example script to work properly. Of course an LDAP directory server must also be running at the URL defined by the `java.naming.provider.url` property specified in the `jndich20ldapContext.properties` file.

Listing 20.1 presents a basic demonstration of using the JNDI SPI directory service functionality with an LDAP SPI. To use this example, you must first configure and copy the `jndich20ldapContext.properties` file to a `jndi.Properties` file in the directory in which you'll execute the example. The `SampleSearchExample.main()` method reads property information from the `jndi.Properties` file and instantiates an instance of the `SampleSearchExample` JNDI LDAP SPI test driver class. The `main()` method then executes eight different sample driver methods on the `SampleSearchExample` object. Each driver method creates a connection to the LDAP server via the `getInitialContext()` method, which passes the read-in properties to an `InitialDirContext` constructor. Subsequently, the following eight methods illustrate different uses of the JNDI directory service API:

- `addAnEventListenerTotheContext()`: Simply demonstrates how to add a `NamingListener` (defined in Listing 20.2) to an `EventDirContext` given a particular LDAP name, filter, and `SearchControls`.
- `getEveryAttributeUsingSearch()`: Creates two `BasicAttribute` objects that are added to a `BasicAttributes` object and used to search a directory service context. The `NamingEnumeration` of `SearchResult` objects returning every attribute per entry is then traversed and displayed.
- `getSelectedAttributesUsingSearch()`: Performs the same basic search as the last `getEveryAttributeUsingSearch()` call but filters out which attributes per entry are returned in the `SearchResult` objects.

- `searchUsingFilterUsingSearch(filter)`: Searches the directory service context by creating a set of `SearchControls` and using a filter `String` passed into the method. The `NamingEnumerations` of `SearchResult` objects are traversed and displayed.
- `getEveryAttributeUsingGetAttributes()`: Retrieves the set of `Attributes` associated with a particular directory object name and prints its contents.
- `addANewAttribute()`: Demonstrates how to add an attribute by adding `Attribute` objects to an `Attributes` object and then calling `modifyAttributes()` with the `Attributes` object to add on the directory service context.
- `removeAttributes()`: Demonstrates how to remove an attribute by creating a `ModificationItem` array with a `BasicAttribute` element and then calling `modifyAttributes()` with the `ModificationItem` containing the attribute to remove.
- `replaceAttributes()`: Demonstrates how to replace an attribute by creating a `ModificationItem` array with two `BasicAttribute` elements and then calling `modifyAttributes()` with the `ModificationItem` containing the attributes to replace.

LISTING 20.1 Sample LDAP Search (`SampleSearchExample.java`)

```
package ejava.jndich20;
import javax.naming.directory.DirContext;
import javax.naming.directory.InitialDirContext;
import javax.naming.NamingException;
import javax.naming.directory.Attributes;
import javax.naming.directory.BasicAttribute;
import javax.naming.directory.Attribute;
import javax.naming.directory.BasicAttributes;
import javax.naming.directory.ModificationItem;
import java.util.Properties;
import java.io.IOException;
import java.io.FileInputStream;
import javax.naming.NamingEnumeration;
import javax.naming.directory.SearchResult;
import java.util.Enumeration;
import javax.naming.directory.SearchControls;
import javax.naming.event.EventDirContext;
import javax.naming.event.EventContext;


public class SampleSearchExample
{
  DirContext context = null;
  Properties properties = new Properties();
```

continues

LISTING 20.1 Continued

```
public SampleSearchExample(Properties p)
{
  super();
  properties = p;
}

public SampleSearchExample(String propertiesFileName)
  throws IOException
{
  // Open a file input stream for the associated properties
  // fileName.
  FileInputStream propertiesFileStream =
    new FileInputStream(propertiesFileName);
  // Now load the file input stream into the JNDI environment
  // properties.
  // This of course assumes that the file input stream is in a valid
  // Properties format.
  properties.load(propertiesFileStream);
}

public DirContext getInitialContext()
  throws NamingException
{
  // Create initial context if it is not already created
  if (context == null) {
    System.out.println("Properties :" + properties);
      // Read in a set of default parameters.
    context = new InitialDirContext(properties);
    System.out.println("Context is :" + context);
  }
  return context;
}

public static void printSearchResults(Attributes attrs)
  throws NamingException
{

    if(attrs == null) {
      System.out.println(" No Attributes :");
    }
    else {
      for(NamingEnumeration ne = attrs.getAll();
        ne.hasMoreElements(); ){
```

```
        Attribute attribute = (Attribute)ne.next();
        String id = attribute.getID();
        for (Enumeration vals = attribute.getAll();
          vals.hasMoreElements();){
          System.out.println(id + ": " + vals.nextElement());
        }
      }
    }
}

public static void printSearchResults(NamingEnumeration enum)
  throws NamingException
{
  while (enum != null && enum.hasMore()) {
    SearchResult sr = (SearchResult)enum.next();
    System.out.println(" Result Name :" + sr.getName() );
    Attributes attrs = sr.getAttributes();
    if(attrs == null) {
      System.out.println(" No Attributes :");
    }
    else {
      for(NamingEnumeration ne = attrs.getAll();
        ne.hasMoreElements(); ){

        Attribute attribute = (Attribute)ne.next();
        String id = attribute.getID();
        for (Enumeration vals = attribute.getAll();
          vals.hasMoreElements();){
          System.out.println(id + ": " + vals.nextElement());
        }
      }
    }
     System.out.println();
  }
}

public void searchUsingFilterUsingSearch(String filter)
{
  try{
    DirContext context = getInitialContext();
    SearchControls searchControls = new SearchControls();
    String[] resultAttributes = {"cn", "sn", "telephonenumber" };
    searchControls.setReturningAttributes(resultAttributes);
    // set the number of results
```

continues

LISTING 20.1 Continued

```
     searchControls.setCountLimit(10);

      // Search for objects with those matching attributes
      NamingEnumeration searchResults
        = context.search("ou=People ", filter,
          searchControls);
      SampleSearchExample.printSearchResults(searchResults);

    }
    catch(NamingException namingException){
      namingException.printStackTrace();
    }
}
  public void addANewAttribute()
  {
    try{
      DirContext context = getInitialContext();
      Attribute objclasses = new BasicAttribute("objectclass");
      objclasses.add("top");
      objclasses.add("person");
      objclasses.add("organizationalPerson");
      objclasses.add("inetOrgPerson");
      Attribute cn = new BasicAttribute("cn", "John Doe");
      Attribute sn = new BasicAttribute("sn", "Doe");
      Attribute telephonenumber = new BasicAttribute("telephonenumber",
        "777777777");
      Attribute givenNames = new BasicAttribute("givenname", "John");
      //Specify the dn we are adding
      String dn = "uid=jdoe, ou=People";
      Attributes organization = new BasicAttributes();
      organization.put(objclasses);
      organization.put(cn);
      organization.put(sn);
      organization.put(telephonenumber);
      organization.put(givenNames);
      context.createSubcontext(dn, organization);



    }
    catch(NamingException namingException){
      namingException.printStackTrace();
    }
```

```
    }

    public void replaceAttributes()
    {
      try{
        DirContext context = getInitialContext();
        ModificationItem modificationItems[] = new ModificationItem[2];
        modificationItems[0] = new ModificationItem(
          DirContext.REPLACE_ATTRIBUTE,
          new BasicAttribute("sn", "Carter") );
        modificationItems[1] = new ModificationItem(
          DirContext.REPLACE_ATTRIBUTE,
          new BasicAttribute("telephonenumber", "111111111111") );

        context.modifyAttributes("uid=scarter, ou=People ",
          modificationItems);

        String filter = "(&(sn=Carter)(mail=*))";

        searchUsingFilterUsingSearch(filter);

      }
      catch(NamingException namingException){
        namingException.printStackTrace();
      }

    }

    public void removeAttributes()
    {
      try{
        DirContext context = getInitialContext();
        ModificationItem modificationItems[] = new ModificationItem[1];

        modificationItems[0] = new ModificationItem(
          DirContext.REMOVE_ATTRIBUTE,
          new BasicAttribute("telephonenumber") );

        context.modifyAttributes("uid=jdoe, ou=People ",
          modificationItems);

        String filter = "(&(sn=Doe)(givenname=*))";

        searchUsingFilterUsingSearch(filter);
```

continues

LISTING 20.1 Continued

```
    }
catch(NamingException namingException){
      namingException.printStackTrace();
    }

  }

  public void getSelectedAttributesUsingGetAttributes()
  {
    try{
      DirContext context = getInitialContext();
      // search for the object with attribute value uid is scarter
      // and has the attribute givenname
      String resultAttributes[] = {"uid",
                              "givenname",
                              "sn",
                              "telephonenumber"
                              };
      // ignore name case
      // Search for objects with those matching attributes
      Attributes searchResults
        = context.getAttributes("uid=scarter,ou=People ",
        resultAttributes);
      SampleSearchExample.printSearchResults(searchResults);

    }
    catch(NamingException namingException){
      namingException.printStackTrace();
    }

  }


  public void getEveryAttributeUsingGetAttributes()
  {
    try{
      DirContext context = getInitialContext();
      // search for the object with attribute value uid is scarter
        // ignore name case, Search for objects with those matching attributes

      Attributes searchResults
        = context.getAttributes("uid=scarter, ou=People");
      SampleSearchExample.printSearchResults(searchResults);
```

```
  }
  catch(NamingException namingException){
    namingException.printStackTrace();
  }

}

public void getEveryAttributeUsingSearch()
{
  try{
    DirContext context = getInitialContext();
    // search for the object with attribute value uid is scarter
    // and has the attribute givenname
    BasicAttribute atr1 = new BasicAttribute("uid", "scarter");
    BasicAttribute atr2 = new BasicAttribute("givenname");
    Attributes matchAttrs = new BasicAttributes(true);
    matchAttrs.put(atr1);
    matchAttrs.put(atr2);
    // ignore name case
    // Search for objects with those matching attributes
    NamingEnumeration searchResults
      = context.search("ou=People", matchAttrs);
    SampleSearchExample.printSearchResults(searchResults);

  }
  catch(NamingException namingException){
    namingException.printStackTrace();
  }

}

public void getSelectedAttributesUsingSearch()
{
  try{
    DirContext context = getInitialContext();
    // search for the object with attribute value uid is scarter
    // and has the attribute givenname
    BasicAttribute atr1 = new BasicAttribute("uid", "scarter");
    BasicAttribute atr2 = new BasicAttribute("givenname");
    Attributes matchAttrs = new BasicAttributes(true);
    matchAttrs.put(atr1);
    matchAttrs.put(atr2);
```

continues

LISTING 20.1 Continued

```
      String resultAttributes[] = {"uid",
                              "givenname",
                              "sn",
                              "telephonenumber"
                              };
      // ignore name case
      // Search for objects with those matching attributes
      NamingEnumeration searchResults
        = context.search("ou=People", matchAttrs,
        resultAttributes);
      SampleSearchExample.printSearchResults(searchResults);

    }
     catch(NamingException namingException){
      namingException.printStackTrace();
    }

  }

  public void addAnEventListenerTotheContext(){
    try{
      DirContext context = getInitialContext();
      SearchControls searchControls= new SearchControls();
      searchControls.setSearchScope( SearchControls.SUBTREE_SCOPE );
      EventDirContext eventContext =
        (EventDirContext)context.lookup("");
      eventContext.addNamingListener("ou=People,uid=scarter",
        "(objectclass=*)", searchControls, new SampleNamingListener());
    }
    catch(NamingException namingException){
      namingException.printStackTrace();
    }

  }


  public static void main(String[] args)
  {

    // get System properties
    Properties p = System.getProperties();
    // Set name of properties file to use in initializing the simple
    // lookup.
    String propertiesFileName = "jndi.Properties";
```

```
    SampleSearchExample sampleSearchExample = null;
    try {
      // Instantiate an instance of this NamingClient
        sampleSearchExample =
          new SampleSearchExample(propertiesFileName);
    } catch (IOException ioException) {
      System.out.println("Error :" + ioException);
      System.exit(0);
    }

    sampleSearchExample.addAnEventListenerTotheContext();
    sampleSearchExample.getEveryAttributeUsingSearch();
    sampleSearchExample.getSelectedAttributesUsingSearch();

    // Ask for objects with attribute sn == Carter and which have
    // the "mail" attribute.
    String filter = "(&(sn=Carter)(mail=*))" ;
    sampleSearchExample.searchUsingFilterUsingSearch(filter);


    sampleSearchExample.getEveryAttributeUsingGetAttributes();

    sampleSearchExample.addANewAttribute();
    sampleSearchExample.removeAttributes();
    sampleSearchExample.replaceAttributes();
  }
}
```

LISTING 20.2 Sample Directory Service Event Listener (`SampleNamingListener.java`)

```
package ejava.jndich20;
import javax.naming.event.NamespaceChangeListener;
import javax.naming.event.ObjectChangeListener;
import javax.naming.event.NamingEvent;
import javax.naming.event.NamingExceptionEvent;
import javax.naming.NamingException;

public class SampleNamingListener  implements NamespaceChangeListener,
  ObjectChangeListener
{

  public void objectAdded(NamingEvent namingEvent)
```

continues

LISTING 20.2 Continued

```
  {
    System.out.println(" Object Added :");
    System.out.println("Change information :"
                       + namingEvent.getChangeInfo());
    System.out.println("New binding :"+ namingEvent.getNewBinding());
  }

  public void objectRemoved(NamingEvent namingEvent)
  {
    System.out.println(" Object Removed :");
    System.out.println("Old binding :"+ namingEvent.getOldBinding());
  }

  public void objectRenamed(NamingEvent namingEvent)
  {
    System.out.println(" Object Renamed :");
    System.out.println("Old binding :"+ namingEvent.getOldBinding());
    System.out.println("New binding :"+ namingEvent.getNewBinding());
  }

  public void objectChanged(NamingEvent namingEvent)
  {
    System.out.println(" Object Changed :");
    System.out.println("Change information :"
                        + namingEvent.getChangeInfo());
    System.out.println("Old binding :"+ namingEvent.getOldBinding());
    System.out.println("New binding :"+ namingEvent.getNewBinding());

  }

  public void namingExceptionThrown(NamingExceptionEvent
                                  namingExceptionEvent)
  {
   System.out.println(" NamingException Event :");
   NamingException namingException = namingExceptionEvent.getException();
   System.out.println(" Exception :"+ namingException);
  }
}
```

JNDI LDAP V3 API Extensions

The `javax.naming.ldap` package contains a set of JNDI API classes and interfaces that support some of the LDAP v3 extended set of operations and controls. Figure 20.3 depicts the classes and interfaces composing the `javax.naming.ldap` package. The `LDAPContext` interface extends the basic directory service operations supported by the `DirContext` interface with additional LDAP v3 style operations. The concrete `InitialLdapContext` class implements the `LDAPContext` interface and is the primary class used to invoke LDAP v3–style functionality.

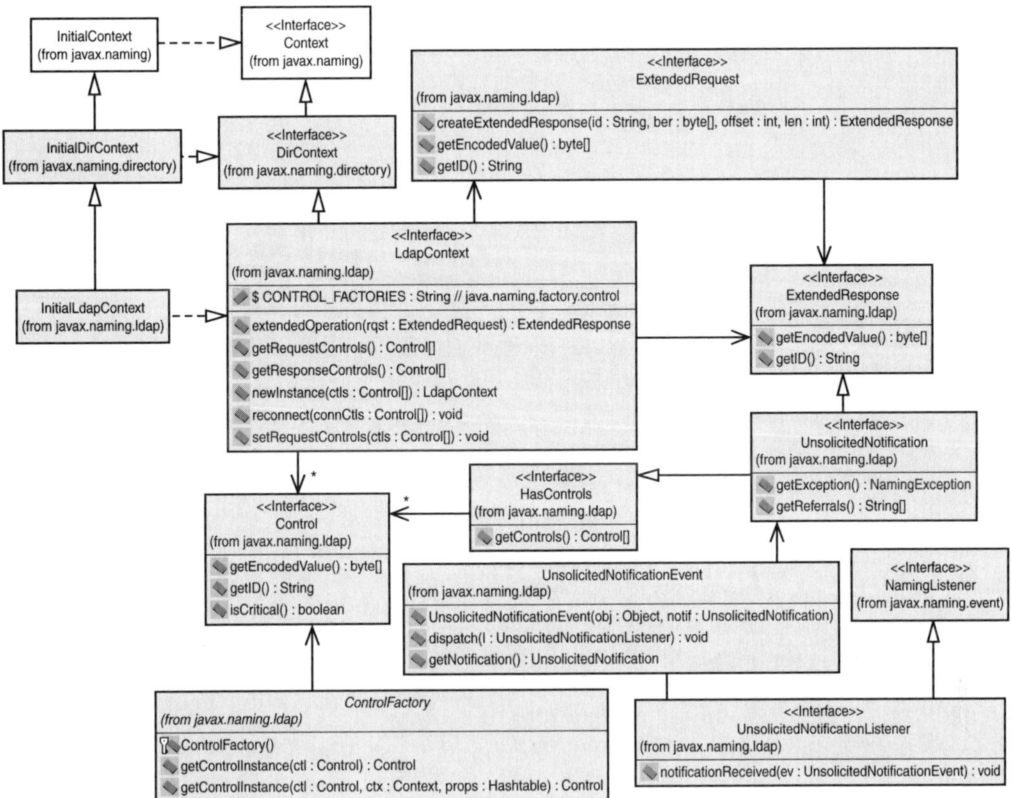

FIGURE 20.3
JNDI LDAP v3 extensions.

The `extendedOperation()` method on the `LDAPContext` is used to issue LDAP v3 style `ExtendedRequest` objects and receive LDAP v3 style `ExtendedResponse` objects. A service provider implements these interfaces for particular extended operations, and the API user then uses such concrete classes to interact with the `LDAPContext`. An `ExtendedRequest` service provider implementation uses the generic nature of LDAP v3 to create a generic request object consisting of a sequence of name-value pairs that are to be sent to the LDAP v3 server. Similarly, the `ExtendedResponse` service provider implementation returns a generic response object consisting of a sequence of names and values received from the LDAP v3 server.

Service provider objects that implement the `Control` interface encapsulate generically defined controls used to control the behavior of the extended request and response behavior of the LDAP v3 server. Such `Control` objects can be set onto the `LDAPContext` itself. They can also be returned from an `UnsolicitedNotification` object received from the LDAP server for unsolicited extended responses by virtue of the fact that the `UnsolicitedNotification` interface extends the `HasControls` interface. When an event is generated due to an `UnsolicitedNotification`, an `UnsolicitedNotificationEvent` object is created and can be dispatched to an object implementing the `UnsolicitedNotificationListener` interface to be used with the JNDI event-handling infrastructure.

CORBA as a Trading Service

The directory services we have examined thus far all provide a service in which names and attributes information can be registered with a directory server potentially in some hierarchically organized structure. Directory service clients can then list, look up, and search for such attribute information as well as bound objects using a set of search criteria. The CORBA Trading Service (also called CosTrading) is a CORBAservice that is very similar in concept to a directory service. However, the CORBA Trading Service implies more than just support for registering descriptive attributes about an object and support for searching for such objects using some intelligent search criteria. Rather, the CORBA Trading Service also provides support for registering type and interface information about a particular object, as well as support for allowing other federations of trading services to pool their registered objects such that they are available to any clients of the federation. Although such functionality is not necessarily precluded from being used with a directory service, the CORBA Trading Service provides explicitly defined interfaces for such support.

In CORBA Trading Service lingo, a *service exporter* is a CORBA service that exports a service offer to the trading service, which includes either a reference to the distributed service being offered or proxy information that can be used to obtain the service object reference during requested use of the service. The exporter also registers some attribute information about the service being offered. A *service importer* is a trading service client that can look up references or proxies to a service of interest based on a search expression akin to a SQL query or an LDAP query. The service client then has the handle it needs to the CORBA service of interest and can make distributed calls on that object in the typical fashion of CORBA remote invocation. Furthermore, given the federated capabilities offered by the CosTrading interfaces, a particular CORBA Trading Service may be able to satisfy a service client's request by returning a handle to a service that was registered with another trading service which is part of the current trading service's federation.

CORBA Trading Service Components

At the highest level of detail, one of five major trading service components can be supported by a particular trading service implementation. An `org.omg.CosTrading.TraderComponents` base interface provides hooks for which to obtain handles to these five major trading service components, as shown in Figure 20.4. A call to `ORB.resolve_initial_references("TradingService")` will return a handle to a `TraderComponents` object. This can then be used to obtain handles to any of the five major components of a trading service, shown as sub-interfaces of the `TraderComponents` interface in Figure 20.4. If any particular component is not implemented, the *`XXX`*`_if()` call on `TraderComponents` will return a null value.

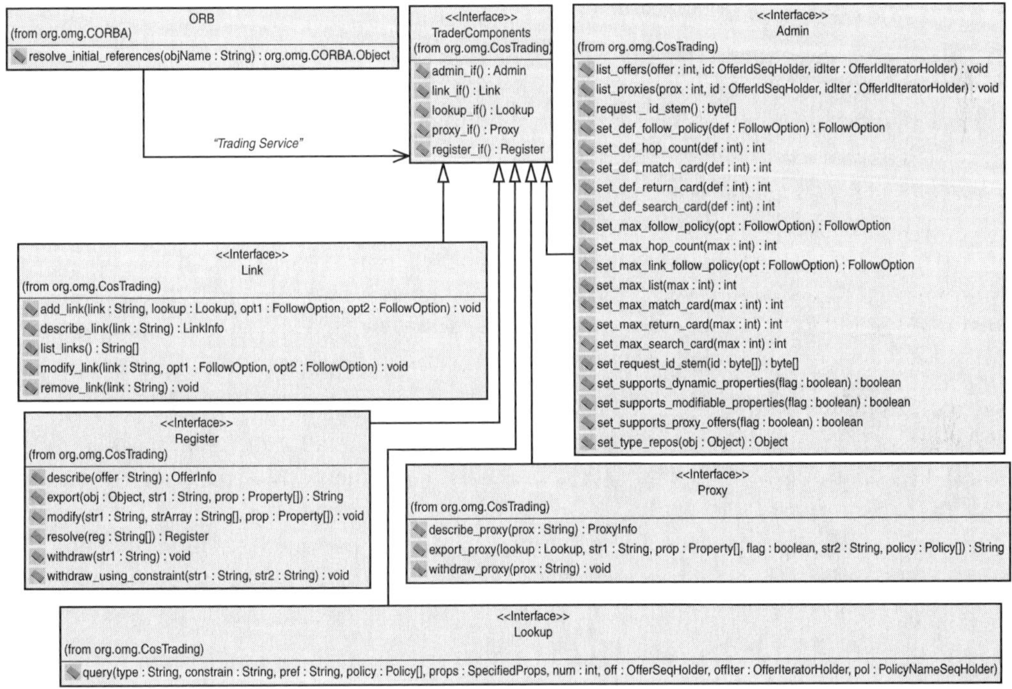

FIGURE 20.4

CORBA Trading Service components.

The `org.omg.CosTrading.Lookup` interface is used to query the trading service for desired service matches. Because it is a core component of the trading service, it may even be the object that is returned from the `ORB.resolve_initial_references()` call. The `org.omg.CosTrading.Register` interface is used by service exporters to export their services, as well as modify and withdraw their services. The `org.omg.CosTrading.Proxy` interface is used to export delayed references to services by service exporters such that the reference to the service will be determined only on a per-demand basis from service clients. The `org.omg.CosTrading.Link` interface is used to add and remove trading services from a trading service federation. Finally, the `org.omg.CosTrading.Admin` interface can be used to set various trading service properties and obtain more detailed information about the current registered services.

The goal of this section is to merely illustrate how one can use the CORBA Trading Service to perform basic object registration and discovery in the context of the other directory and trading services presented in this chapter. Therefore, we do not go into the details behind federating traders via the `Link` interface, deferring references via the `Proxy` interface, or managing the trading service via the `Admin` interface. Rather, we aim to describe the basic and most common use of the CORBA Trading Service via a description and illustration of the `Lookup` and `Register` interfaces from a service exporter and service importer point of view.

Service Exporting

Figure 20.5 depicts the primary components involved with exporting a service to a CORBA Trading Service. The `MyExporter` class in the diagram represents your home-grown class that is responsible for exporting one or more `MyCORBAService` objects also of your own creation. After obtaining a reference to a default `TraderComponents` object such as a `Lookup` object, you can use such an object to obtain references to other supported trading service interfaces such as the `Register` interface using the `TraderComponents.register_if()` call inherited by the `Lookup` interface. However, before you export your objects to the trading service, you should define the interfaces supported by your `MyCORBAService` objects with the trading service.

To describe your service interfaces, you must obtain a handle to an `org.omg.CosTradingRepos.ServiceTypeRepository` object via a call to the `type_repos()` method also supported by your initial reference to either the `Lookup` or the `Register` interface objects. The `type_repos()` interface and a set of interfaces used to determine the level of support for certain operation types are inherited by the `Lookup` and `Register` interfaces from the `org.omg.CosTrading.SupportAttributes` interface. The `ServiceTypeRepository` then offers you a set of interfaces available for adding, describing, listing, removing, and managing various service type interfaces registered with the trading service.

As an example, to add a service type to the `ServiceTypeRepository`, you would need to supply an array of `org.omg.CosTradingRepos.ServiceTypeRepositoryPackage.PropStruct` objects to the `ServiceTypeRepository.add_type()` method. Each `PropStruct` object would need to be populated with the name of the attribute, the mode in which the attribute may be gotten or set using `org.omg.CosTradingRepos.ServiceTypeRepositoryPackage.PropertyMode` identifiers, and the `CORBA::TypeCode` identifying the type of object. After building up an array of `PropStruct` objects describing each attribute of an interface, this `PropStruct` array is then used along with a `String` identifying the name for the new type, an identifier `String` describing the interface, and an array of `String` objects used to indicated any base type names of this type.

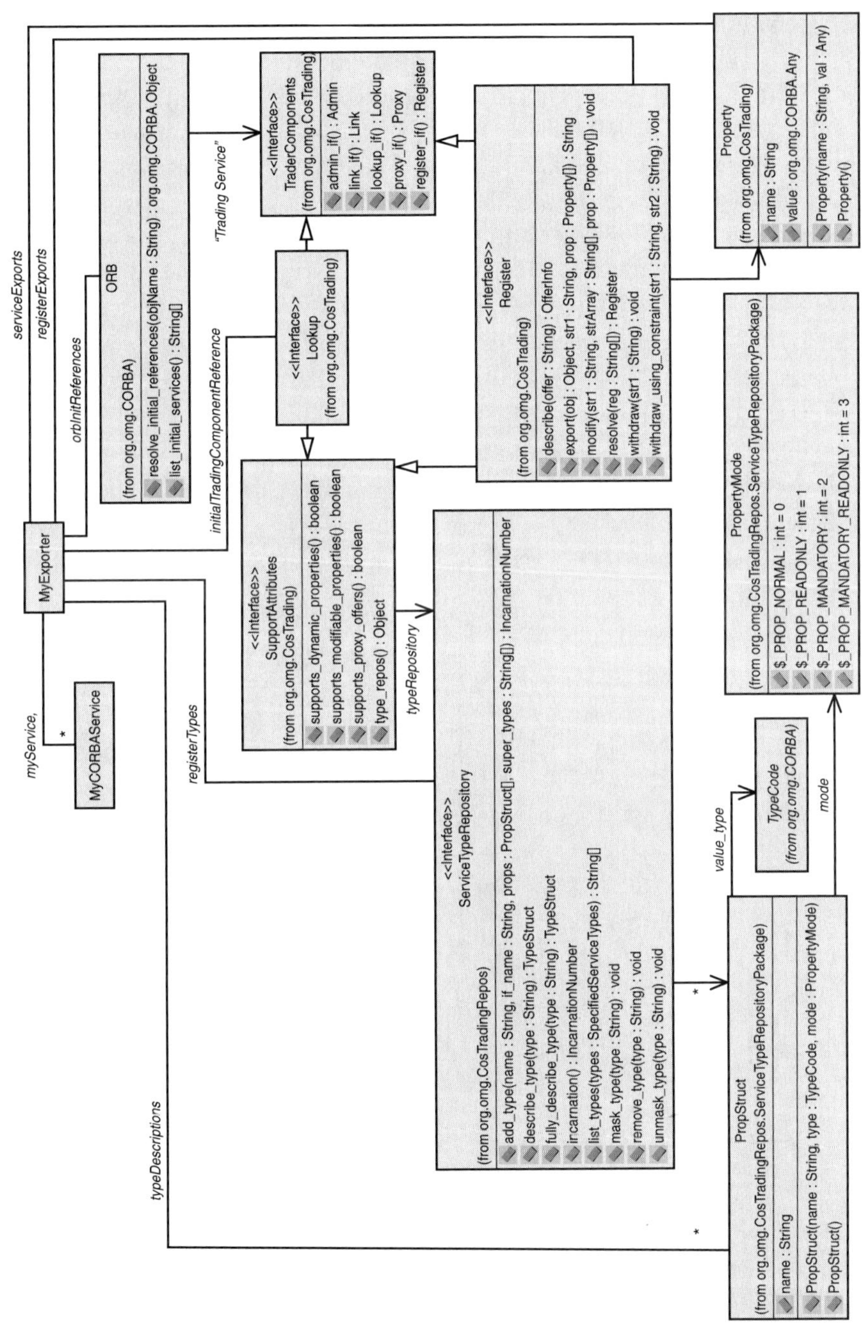

FIGURE 20.5
CORBA Trading Service exporting.

After a service type is registered describing the type of objects that will be exported to the trading service, your service exporter can export the object service instances themselves. You accomplished this by calling `export()` on the `Register` interface with the object instances you want to export (that is, your `MyCORBAService` objects), the service type name registered with the `ServiceTypeRepository` with which the object is associated, and an array of `org.omg.CosTradingRepos.ServiceTypeRepositoryPackage.Property` objects. Each `Property` object simply defines a set of name-value pairs describing particular attributes about the object. Note that each attribute name in the `Property` object will typically correspond to a property name associated with this type of object via one of the `PropStruct` objects created and registered with the `ServiceTypeRepository` for this service type.

Service Importing

Figure 20.6 depicts the primary components involved with the client import of a service from a CORBA Trading Service. The `MyImporter` client obtains a handle to the `Lookup` interface in the same fashion, as does an exporter. However, the client does not need to obtain a `Register` interface handle. The client may need to obtain a handle to a `ServiceTypeRepository` object, however.

The client can list all the service types in a `ServiceTypeRepository` by calling `list_types()` with a given `org.omg.CosTradingRepos.ServiceTypeRepositoryPackage.SpecifiedServiceTypes` instance. The `all_dummy()` method on the `SpecifiedServiceTypes` instance can be called with no parameter indicating that all service types should be listed or called with a number designating the fact that only those service types registered since a particular export incarnation number should be listed. Furthermore, given a particular service type name `String`, a `describe_type()` call on the `ServiceTypeRepository` object can be made to return a `org.omg.CosTradingRepos.ServiceTypeRepositoryPackage.TypeStruct` instance that describes the particular type requested. The `TypeStruct` object contains the interface name `String` of the type, a `String` array of super type names, the `PropStruct` array describing the registered type, the incarnation number associated with the type when it was added, and a `boolean` type indicating whether the type is deprecated.

Of course, the primary operation of interest to an importer is the `query()` method on the `Lookup` interface. It unfortunately also happens to have a rather complex operation signature, which is perhaps one of the key reasons why the CORBA Trading Service has been a difficult standard to adopt in practice. A type name parameter to a query method specifies the desired type to be retrieved. In addition to a type name parameter, a constraint `String`, a preferences `String`, an array of policies, a specification of desired properties, and a number indicating how many results should be returned are used as input to the `query()` method. Additionally, three CORBA holders to contain output values are also passed into the `query()` method, including a holder of a returned offer sequence, an offer iterator, and a sequence of policy limits that were applied to the requested query.

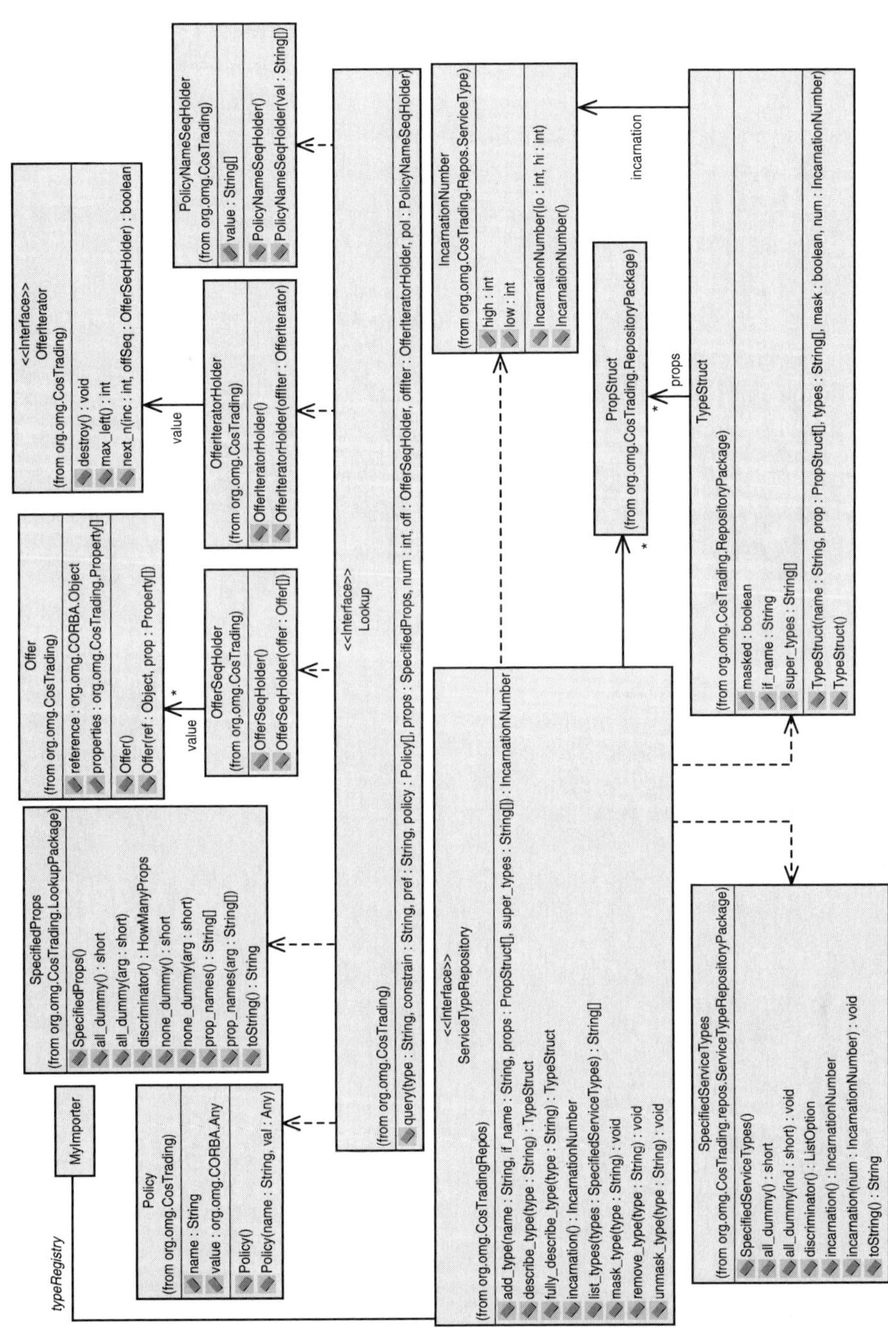

FIGURE 20.6
CORBA Trading Service importing.

A constraint `String` captures search criteria specified in a standard trading service constraint language. Different constraint languages (such as SQL) implemented by your particular trading service implementation can be designated between << >> in the beginning of the `String`. The default constraint language used by CosTrading is specified in Appendix B of the CORBA Trading Service standard. Similarly, a preference `String` is also passed to the `query()` method, which can be used to designate the order in which results are returned from the query. If no preference is supplied, the order in which service matches are found is returned.

An array of `org.omg.CosTrading.Policy` values is passed into the `query()` method to specify name-value pairs in which each name defines a particular policy that should be followed by the trading service when returning results. Although standard policy type names are defined in the CORBA Trading Service standard, CosTrading implementers may also define proprietary value-added query policy types.

An `org.omg.CosTrading.LookupPackage.SpecifiedProps` object can be used to specify that all properties (`all_dummy()`) or a selected set of property names (`prop_names()`) are to be returned from the query. The integer input into the `query()` statement designates how many results to return.

TIP

All of these input values to the `query()` command make issuing a query to the `Lookup` service rather complicated. To make it easier to understand how to use such parameters, it may help to compare a few of the individual parameters to elements of a SQL statement, which may be more familiar to you. For example, the constraint `String` may be viewed as similar in role to the `WHERE` portion of a SQL statement. The preferences `String` is similar in role to a SQL `ORDER_BY` clause. The service name itself is akin in role to specifying a SQL `FROM` clause. The specified properties may be viewed as similar in role to a SQL `SELECT` statement. Although role similarities exist, of course all querying is done in the context of a type-safe object-oriented paradigm, and there are indeed still differences between the two querying paradigms.

The values returned in the `org.omg.CosTrading.OfferSeqHolder` object are in an array of `org.omg.CosTrading.Offer` objects. Each `Offer` object contains a reference to the associated CORBA service (the `MyCORBAService` objects in Figure 20.5) and an array of `Property` objects associated with this service. The `org.omg.CosTrading.OfferIteratorHolder` contains a returned `org.omg.CosTrading.OfferIterator` object, which may be used to traverse the list of offered objects. Finally, if any limits were applied by the trading service during the query, an `org.omg.CosTrading.PolicyNameSeqHolder` object will contain an array of policy name `Strings` indicating those policies that were applied.

CORBA Trading Example

We have developed a basic CORBA Trader export and import example that is provided on the CD. Although we don't explicitly list the example here in the interest of conserving space and because it is slightly beyond the scope of this book, we encourage you to examine the sample code. We will describe the example's basic structure here. The example illustrates how to export a collection of CORBA objects to a trading service from a server-side object and how to look up and import these services from the client side. A few simple classes are used to illustrate the concepts and mechanisms involved in using the CORBA Trading Service. Because of the complexity involved with many of the CORBA services such as the CORBA Trading Service, finding a suitable mix of COTS that can be used with Java is difficult. We have developed the example using a COTS Trading Service implementation that works with the Visibroker for Java Orb COTS product.

NOTE

Under the `examples\src\ejava\jndich20\tradingExample` directory, six files exist to illustrate use of the CORBA Trading Service: `Customer.idl`, `CustomerImpl.java`, `CustomerServer.java`, `CustomerTradingClient.java`, `CustomerInfo.txt`, and `runtrading.bat`. The `runtrading.bat` file can be used as an example Windows script for building and executing the example. A `VISIGENIC_HOME` environment variable must be set to the root installation directory of your Visibroker for Java Orb installation (see Appendix A). An `OPEN_FUSION_HOME` environment variable must be set to the root directory of your OpenFusion installation.

The `Customer.idl` file is the sample IDL file that we use with the example. We've purposely kept the IDL interface straightforward so that we can focus on the salient features of using a CORBA Trading Service. The IDL interface simply exposes a few read-only attributes of a customer, which, when run through an IDL-to-Java compiler, produce the `_CustomerImplBase.java` skeleton utilized by our customer implementation class contained in the `CustomerImpl.java` file. The `CustomerImpl` class thus simply implements all the attribute retrieval methods exposed by the IDL, as well as a collection of attribute setter methods used by the server-side code.

Note that when you use the `runtrading.bat` file, the following IDL-to-Java compilation command generates the `_CustomerImplBase.java` class utilized here:

```
%VISIGENIC_HOME%\bin\idl2java Customer.idl
```

The CustomerServer class in the CustomerServer.java file serves as our trading service exporter of Customer CORBA objects. When the CustomerServer is run from the command line, its main() method first initializes itself with the ORB and resolves an initial reference to the CORBA Trading Service. The default reference is narrowed to a Lookup object reference, and we subsequently obtain a handle to a Register object using the register_if() call inherited by the Lookup object. A call to the addServiceTypesToTradingService() method from main() registers the type information about a Customer with the trading service's service type repository. A call to registerCustomerObjects() from main() then exports a collection of Customer CORBA objects with the trading service register. After all objects have been exported, the main() method waits for client requests with the server blocking input from the standard user input stream.

The addServiceTypesToTradingService() method first obtains a handle to the ServiceTypeRepository from the Lookup service's inherited type_repos() method. A PropStruct object is then filled out with a single customer ID attribute name, mode, and type. After a PropStruct object is created, it is passed in as an array along with a service type name, an interface name, and super type information (none to provide here) to the add_type() method on the ServiceTypeRepository. Note that we could have passed more attribute type information to the service type repository, but we use only one attribute here to keep the example simple.

The registerCustomerObjects() method first calls the getAllCustomers() method to obtain a Hashtable of Customer object references. The getAllCustomers() method accomplishes this task by reading and parsing the list of customers present in the CustomerInfo.txt file on the CD. The first line of CustomerInfo.txt is ignored, but each subsequent line contains customer information and is used to instantiate and initialize a new Customer CORBA object reference. Each Customer object is added to the Hashtable using its customer ID as a reference. The CustomerInfo.txt file looks something like this:

```
CUSTOMER_ID, FIRSTNAME, LASTNAME, STREET, CITY, STATE, ZIP, EMAIL
120, Sam, Mellone, 123 Sam Drive, Edison, NJ, 12345, 1234567890
121, Jerry, Joe, 123 Oracle Drive, Ellicot City, NJ, 12346, 1234567190
122, Joseph, Kowel, 123 HP Drive, Ocean City, NJ, 12347, 1234567290
123, Vincent, Frenz, 123 Sun Drive, Indus Vally, NJ, 12348, 1234567390
124, Margarate, Jarevy, 123 Palm Drive, Apple City, NJ, 12349, 1234567490
```

After the Hashtable of Customer objects is returned, the registerCustomerObjects() method cycles through the collection of returned customers and creates a Property element containing customer_id as the Property name and the actual customer ID value as the Property value. The Property (in the form of an array) along with the service type name and the Customer object reference are then exported to the Register object.

The CustomerTradingClient.java file contains the code for a CORBA Trading Service importer. When the CustomerTradingClient is executed from the command line, it too must go through the initial sequence of ORB initialization and obtaining handles to trading service Lookup and Register object interfaces. Subsequently, a listAllServiceTypes() is called to list all the available services in the trading service. The schema of the Customer type is then displayed with the describeAType() method. One or more Customer objects with an ID greater than 123 is then queried for and accessed within the queryAndDisplayCustomers() method. Finally, the service type is removed from the service type repository. All actions actually demonstrate basic interaction with the trading service apart from simply importing a service.

The listAllServiceTypes() method in the CustomerTradingClient example uses an instance of the SpecifiedServiceTypes interface to list all types in the service type repository with a call to ServiceTypeRepository.list_types() method. Each returned type is then output to standard output. The describeAType() method on CustomerTradingClient calls describe_type() on the ServiceTypeRepository and displays the contents of the returned TypeStruct describing the particular type.

The queryAndDisplayCustomers() method in CustomerTradingClient first creates a Policy and SpecifiedProps object. The SpecifiedProps object is initialized to indicate no properties to specify. After the output Holder classes are created, the query() method on Lookup is called. The content of the Offer returned from the query() method is then accessed to obtain a handle to the Customer object. The contents of the returned Customer object are then accessed and displayed.

Finally, as a simple illustration of how to use the trading service, a call to ServiceTypeRepository.remove_type() removes the particular service type interface that was registered with the trading service.

Jini as a Trading Service

Jini is a collection of Java APIs and components that is currently being heavily marketed and touted by Sun as the next-generation technology for building distributed systems. Jini is a lightweight layer of Java code that rests atop the Java 2 platform. Thus, Jini can run on top of the J2SE and J2EE, as well as the J2ME. Jini depends on Java's Remote Method Invocation (RMI) distributed communications infrastructure. Jini and RMI together offer a set of APIs and infrastructure for building distributed services that can dynamically register traits about themselves and register their availability to the Jini community such that Jini network clients can dynamically discover and use those services.

The most significant types of distributed Jini-based services that Sun has in mind are those services offered by embedded devices on a network. Thus, with proper Jini-enabling, devices such as printers, phones, PDAs, pagers, and storage devices can all offer their services to a dynamic network in a Jini-standard fashion. Jini clients such as other embedded devices, PCs, and enterprise servers can plug into this dynamic network and immediately obtain access to the Jini services made available to the enterprise network community.

Because Jini sits atop the Java RMI infrastructure and provides auxiliary distributed object communications services, the analogy can be made between Jini and RMI to that of a few CORBAservices and the CORBA ORB. As you'll soon see, Jini offers a programming model to provide distributed event, transaction, and leasing services that have overlapping logical role analogies to the CORBA Events, Transactions, and Licensing Services, respectively. The core functionality of Jini, however, revolves around its dynamic discovery, lookup, and network community joining behavior. The lookup behavior is analogous to the roles that would be played by a CORBA Trading Service in a CORBA distributed object community. Although there exists a clear overlap in terms of roles between the Jini paradigm and the CORBA paradigm, there are a few distinct design differences. CORBA is language independent and Jini is defined in terms of the Java language. Furthermore, although object passing-by-value semantics are part of the CORBA specification, the Java platform makes mobile objects much easier to implement precisely because of its language and Java platform dependence.

Jini Component Architecture

The basic logical and physical component architecture of Jini and Jini's architectural context are shown in Figure 20.7. The logical architecture depicted in the left half of the diagram shows Jini's dependence on the Java 2 platform and how Jini services are built atop the Jini platform. The right half of the diagram shows the physical architecture components (that is, Java packages) used by Jini and the development kits with which these components are distributed. Arrows are used to demonstrate how each physical component roughly relates to the logical architecture components.

Jini depends on many of the new security and distributed communication mechanisms in the Java 2 platform. RMI and its support for activatable objects are one key feature used by Jini. The Java 2 security model provides a set of fine-grained access-control mechanisms on which both RMI and Jini depend (as you'll see in Chapter 26, "Basic Java Security," and Chapter 27, "Advanced Java Security"). Finally, Java's basic networking, object serialization, utility, and core language components all are also utilized by the Jini platform.

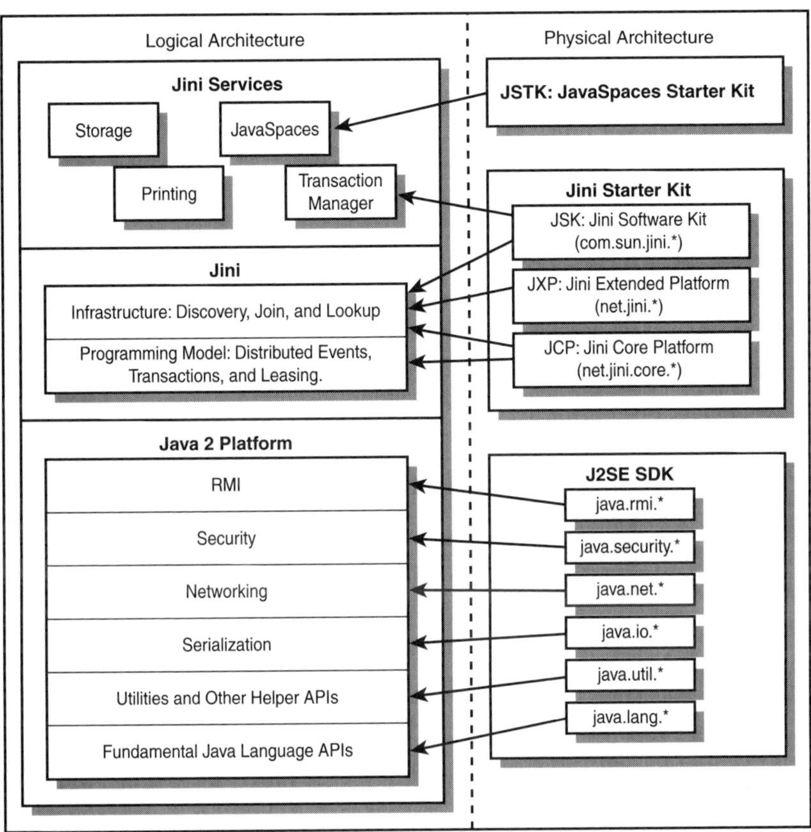

FIGURE 20.7
Jini component architecture.

Jini itself is partitioned into three collections of Java packages, all of which are currently distributed by Sun with the Jini Starter Kit. These are the package collections:

- The Jini Core Platform (JCP) distribution contains those Java packages below `net.jini.core` that encapsulate the core Jini specification standard classes and interfaces.
- The Jini Extended Platform (JXP) distribution contains packages below `net.jini` aside from `net.jini.core.*` that encapsulate the Jini specification standard classes and interfaces to provide additional Jini functionality and utilities.
- The Jini Software Kit (JSK) contains packages below `com.sun.jini` offered by Sun as a specific implementation of the key services defined in the JCP and JXP specifications.

Jini Programming Model

The Jini programming model is composed of three major distributed service APIs for distributed events, distributed leasing, and distributed transactions. The distributed event programming model offers a set of interfaces that extend the JavaBeans event model to provide a means for remote objects to be notified of asynchronously generated events from other distributed objects.

The distributed leasing model provides a set of interfaces that can be used to require distributed objects to obtain a lease for use of a particular distributed resource. Leases have a timeout associated with them before which they must be either renewed or cancelled by the holder. If the lease is not renewed or cancelled, access to the distributed resource expires, and the resource is released from the holder. Leasing is used by higher-level Jini services to clean up resources no longer in use by potentially failed distributed objects.

Finally, the distributed transactions programming model is used to provide services for coordinating distributed operations that either all must occur atomically (commit) or none must occur at all (rollback).

Jini Infrastructure

The Jini infrastructure represents the quintessential layer of Jini utilized by distributed objects to first discover a community of Jini services, join a Jini community, and look up a particular Jini service. Objects first must locate a Jini community using a discovery protocol. The discovery process may involve simply finding local Jini communities via a multicast request, receiving notification from newly formed communities via multicast announcements, or simply binding to a known Jini lookup service. Each Jini community may have a group name and is composed of one or more Jini lookup services belonging to that group.

Jini services join those Jini communities that they have discovered and have an interest in joining. When a Jini service joins a Jini community's lookup service, it provides a service item to the lookup service. These service items contain a collection of meta-data attribute information describing the Jini service, as well as a service proxy object. The service proxy object is simply a serializable Java object that is downloaded to clients of the Jini service. Operations invoked on the service proxy object may actually be handled by the proxy object itself or marshaled as requests to a remote back-end device proxy and unmarshal any responses (for example, service proxy as an RMI client).

Lookup services are used by Jini clients to locate Jini services. The clients first fill out a service template describing the service of interest. The service template can be filled out with a service identifier, a set of base Java class types, and a set of service meta-data attributes. A lookup call using this service template is invoked on the lookup service, which subsequently returns a set of service matches containing one or more service items that matched the service template. With a set of matching service items in hand, the client can then extract the service proxy item of interest and begin distributed computing with that object.

Jini Tools and Configuration

Jini services are created using the Jini infrastructure and programming model. The Jini lookup service is really itself a Jini service; it is provided with the JSK distribution and is referred to with the codename "reggie." The JSK also contains a transaction management service with a codename "mahalo." Finally, Sun also provides a Jini service called JavaSpaces as a product that can be used to store and retrieve Java objects in a distributed network. The JavaSpaces product is downloadable separately via a JavaSpaces Starter Kit, and it adheres to the codename "outrigger."

NOTE

Building Jini-enabled systems requires a couple of tools that are freely downloadable from the Sun Web site. However, we should note that use of Jini in commercial applications still did incur licensing fees payable to Sun at the time of this book's writing (`http://www.sun.com/jini/licensing/licenses.html`).

After installing a Java 2 platform such as the J2SE, you'll need to download the Jini System Software Starter Kit from Sun at `http://developer.java.sun.com/developer/products/jini`. The Jini System Software Starter Kit contains the distribution packages for the JCP, JXP, JSK, and other tools you'll need in order to get started. You will need to register with the Java Developer's Connection if you haven't already done so (it's free) and also accept the terms of the Sun Community Source License (SCSL) agreement to download the starter kit.

You can also download the Java Technology Core Platform Compatibility Kit to ensure that your Jini service can pass a compatibility test to function as a service living up to the Jini specifications. With all the proper tools installed, you'll lastly have to set some environment variables (`PATH` and `CLASSPATH`) before you begin development. The J2SE compiler and runtime binary should be in your `PATH`, and the J2SE runtime libraries should be in your `CLASSPATH` when you're creating Jini services. Additionally, at least the following three files provided with the Jini distribution should be included in your `CLASSPATH` when you're creating Jini services: `jini-core.jar` (JCP files), `jini-ext.jar` (JXP files), and `sun-util.jar` (a subset of JSK files).

Developing Jini services involves setting up a runtime infrastructure on which Jini communities depend, as well as creating the actual Jini service. Setting up a runtime environment for Jini involves the following basic tasks:

- *Configure HTTP Servers:* Configure and start simple HTTP servers on hosts that will serve downloadable Java code. Automatic downloading of code between clients and servers is a feature actually provided by the underlying RMI libraries. Code that may need downloading includes the core Jini components and any Jini service code. The HTTP servers need only support simple `GET` operation functionality, and the Jini starter kit itself comes equipped with a very slender server in the `tools.jar` file provided with the distribution.
- *Configure RMI Activation Daemons:* Configure and start an RMI activation daemon on hosts that will serve activatable Java code. This is yet another artifact of the underlying RMI toolkit; the RMI activation daemon is used to allow RMI activatable server objects to be activated (that is, started and brought into memory) on an as-needed basis from RMI client requests. Activatable objects include the Jini lookup service, the Jini transaction manager, and any Jini services.
- *Configure and Start a Lookup Service:* The RMI registry may be used as a lookup service. However, the Jini lookup service provides a much richer set of features that enable it to perform Jini infrastructure services. Because the Jini infrastructure is the key feature of Jini, the Jini lookup service is recommended rather than the RMI registry. The Jini lookup service server is located in the `reggie.jar` file, and the client-side access code is in the `reggie-dl.jar` file provided with the Jini distribution. The Jini lookup service must have an RMI activation running on the same host machine it is running. The RMI activation daemon activates the Jini lookup service and needs to know which system resources the lookup service is allowed to access. Thus, the Jini lookup service must be started with an associated security policy file (a Java 2 security feature) telling the activation daemon which system resources the lookup may access and how it may access them. You can also pass in a list of group names designating to which Jini clusters the lookup service belongs. Finally, the Jini lookup service must be started with a codebase parameter indicating via a URL the location of RMI client class files needed for using the lookup service. Thus, this URL points to a machine where you've typically run a Web server to serve up the subset of Jini lookup service code needed by lookup clients, for example, `http://www.assuredtech.com/jini/reggie-dl.jar`.
- *Configure Optional Transaction Manager:* You can also optionally configure and start a Jini transaction manager service that comes packaged with the JSK. The server-side code for the transaction manager is in `mahalo.jar`, and the client-side code is in `mahalo-dl.jar`.

Jini Class Architecture and Development Process

Using Jini technology requires that you build both a server side and a client side, as is the case with all distributed object communication development paradigms. Our server side in this case involves building the Jini service implementation, a Jini service proxy to that service, and any connectivity needed to a back-end device or process. The Jini client simply must look up and utilize such a service.

Figure 20.8 illustrates the core class architecture behind a Jini service, and Figure 20.9 illustrates the core class architecture behind a Jini client. Although many other classes and interfaces exist throughout the many Jini packages, we have presented only those class and interfaces that will most commonly be used by enterprise developers looking to Jini-enable their enterprises and take advantage of the trading service features of Jini. We also present only those constructs that we will use to describe the basic development process involved in building a Jini-based application and that we will use in an example included on the CD.

Each class and interface of Figure 20.8 is described here in the context of how it is used to build a Jini-enabled service. Creating a Jini service can be a straightforward process. The basic tasks (with entities from Figure 20.8 in parentheses) for creating a Jini service are as shown here:

- *Define Jini Service Interface:* Define a Jini service interface (`MyJiniService`) with all distributable method signatures defined.
- *Implement Jini Service Proxy:* Implement a Jini service proxy class (`MyJiniServiceProxy`) that implements the `Serializable` interface, implements the Jini service interface, and implements a default no-argument constructor (for serializeability). Note that the service proxy is what gets downloaded to the Jini client machine. The proxy can talk with any back-end process (`MyRemoteProcess`) using any communications technique or protocol whose interface can be downloaded to the client machine. Thus, for example, the proxy can act as a basic TCP/IP, RMI, or CORBA client to a corresponding back-end process.
- *Implement Remote Process Interface:* If the remote process interface (`MyRemoteProcess`) that can be called by your Jini service proxy does not already exist, you will need to create it during this step. The remote process may be an interface to a piece of hardware such as a printer or PDA, or it can be an interface to just about any other enterprise resource.
- *Implement the Jini Service Registrar:* A Jini service registrar (`MyJiniServiceRegistrar`) should be implemented to create the Jini service proxy and register the proxy with any discovered lookup services.

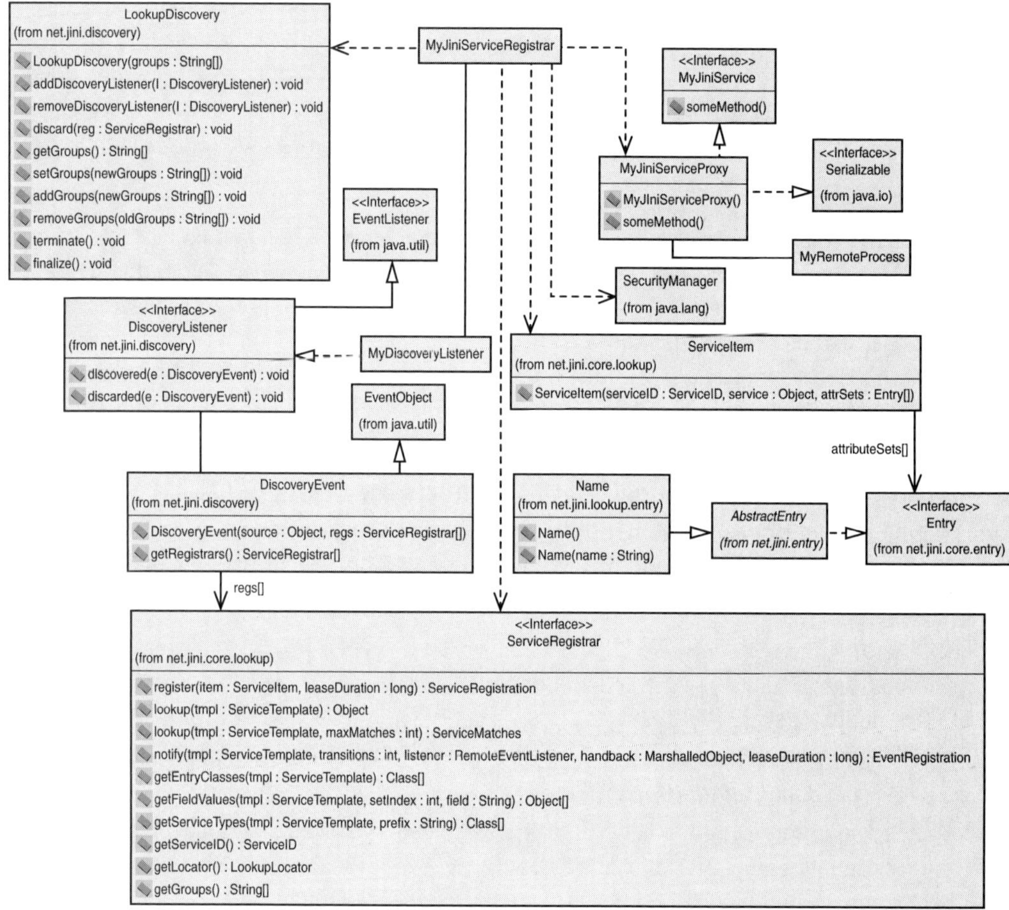

FIGURE 20.8
The Jini service architecture.

Because the implementation of the Jini Service Registrar is a somewhat more-involved process, we further expand on the tasks involved with Jini Service Registrar implementation here:

- *Create Jini Service Proxy:* Create an instance of a service proxy object (`MyJiniServiceProxy`).
- *Create a Jini Service Item Description:* Create a service item (`net.jini.core.lookup.ServiceItem`) that contains a reference to the service proxy object and a description of the Jini service's attributes (`net.jini.core.entry.Entry` array of `net.jini.lookup.entry.Name` objects).

- *Establish a Security Manager:* The registrar should also create a Security Manager (`SecurityManager`) instance to enable use of Java 2.0 application security features.
- *Discover a Lookup Service:* Implement a discovery process to locate one or more lookup services on the network by using multicast requests (using `net.jini.discovery.LookupDiscovery`, `net.jini.discovery.DiscoveryListener`, and `net.jini.discovery.DiscoveryEvent`), relying on multicast announcements (using the same classes as with multicast requests), or directly connecting to a lookup service (using `net.jini.core.discovery.LookupLocator`). Using multicast requests, the registrar will add (call `LookupDiscovery.addDiscoveryListener()`) with a listener representative (`MyDiscoveryListener`) that implements a discovery listener interface (`DiscoveryListener`).
- *Select a Lookup Service:* Implement the selection of one or more discovered lookup services to join. Note that when a discovery event (`DiscoveryEvent`) is received from the discovery infrastructure by an object (`MyDiscoveryListener`) that implements the discovery listener interface, then that listener object can filter which callbacks should be made onto the registrar for the discovered lookup service. The list of Jini lookup services (`net.jini.core.lookup.ServiceRegistrar`) that were discovered can then be retrieved from the discovery event passed to the discovery listener (`DiscoveryEvent.getRegistrars()`).
- *Join a Lookup Service:* Implement the joining process by registering the service item (`ServiceItem`) with the lookup service of interest (`ServiceRegistrar.register()`).
- *Provide Additional Services:* Optionally use a richer set of Jini services such as distributed event, leasing, and transaction services.

Jini clients that want to utilize the published Jini services are even simpler to create. Figure 20.9 presents the basic classes and interfaces used to build a Jini client.

The basic steps for creating a Jini client are shown here (with entities from Figure 20.9 in parentheses):

- *Discover a Lookup Service:* Implement the discovery process to locate a lookup service as was the case with the service registrar. Uses discovery listener (`MyClientDiscoveryListener`) as before to obtain a list of discovered lookup services (`ServiceRegistrar`).
- *Create a Jini Service Template:* Implement the creation and initialization of a service template (`net.jini.core.lookup.ServiceTemplate`) defining how items in a lookup service should be matched with the desired items designated by the template.
- *Look Up a Jini Service:* Implement the lookup of a Jini service using the service template (`net.jini.core.lookup.ServiceRegistrar.lookup()`).

- *Handle Jini Service Lookup Matches:* Implement the handling of service matches (`net.jini.core.lookup.ServiceMatches`) from a lookup to obtain a reference to the service proxy object.
- *Use the Jini Service:* Implement usage of the service proxy object that represents the client interface to the Jini service.

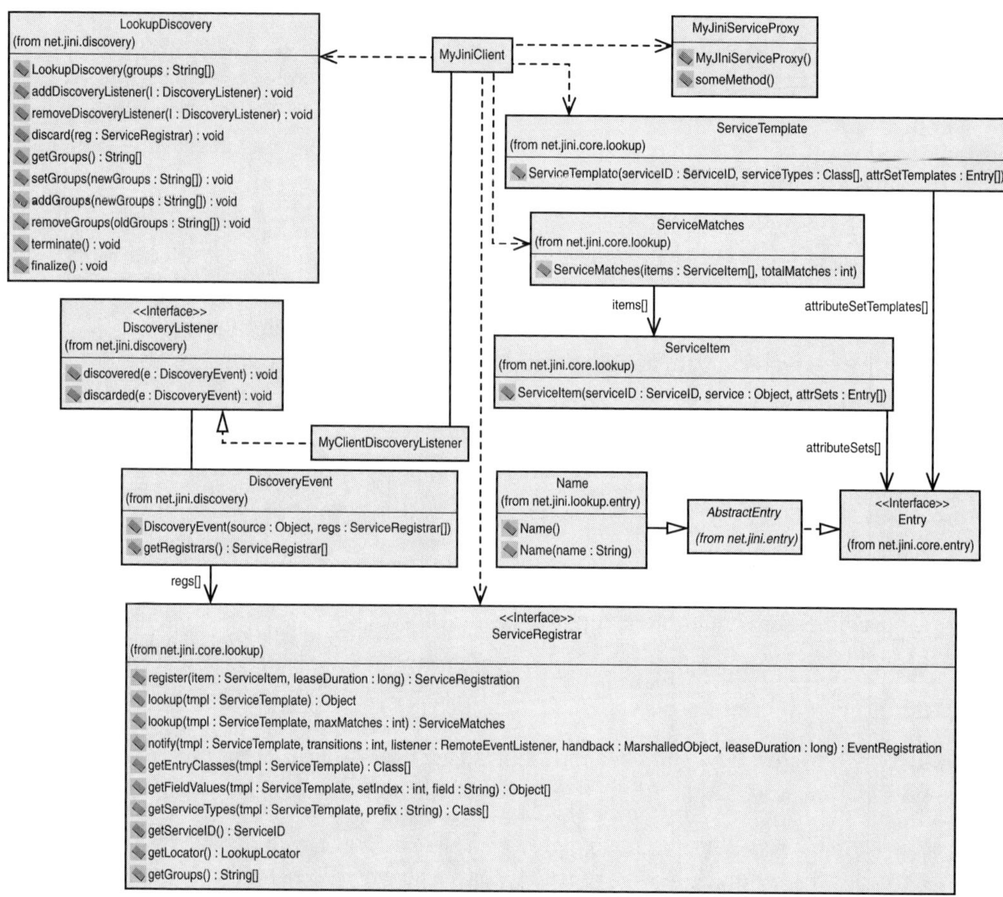

FIGURE 20.9
The Jini client architecture.

Jini Service Example

We have developed a basic Jini service example, which is provided on the CD. As with the CORBA Trading Service example, we also don't explicitly list the example here in the interest of conserving space and because it is slightly beyond the scope of this book. However, we encourage you to examine the sample code, and we describe the example's basic structure here. The Jini example illustrates how a Jini service registrar can discover lookup services in its community and then register a Jini service with a discovered lookup service. The example also shows how a Jini client can discover a lookup service and then look up a reference to registered Jini services.

NOTE

Under the `examples\src\ejava\jndich20\jiniexample` directory, 11 files exist to illustrate creation of a Jini service: `Customer.java`, `CustomerServiceProxy.java`, `CustomerActivatableInterface.java`, `CustomerActivatable.java`, `CustomerServiceRemote.java`, `CustomerDiscoveryListener.java`, `CustomerJINIClient.java`, `ClientDiscoveryListener.java`, `CustomerInfo.txt`, `rmi.policy`, and `runjiniexample.bat`. As described earlier in the chapter, you will also need to download the Jini SDK to run this example. The `runjiniexample.bat` file assumes that you've installed the Jini SDK in a root directory identified by a `JINI_HOME` environment variable.

The `Customer.java` file contains a `Customer` interface defining getter methods for customer information and is implemented by the `CustomerServiceProxy` Jini proxy in the `CustomerServiceProxy.java` file. The `CustomerServiceProxy` is serializable so that it can be downloaded to a Jini client. The proxy acts as an RMI client to an RMI server existing somewhere else on a network. The `CustomerServiceProxy` is instantiated with a reference to that RMI server.

The `CustomerActivatableInterface.java` file contains the `CustomerActivatableInterface` RMI interface to the `CustomerActivatable` activatable RMI server object in the `CustomerActivatable.java` file. The `CustomerActivatable` server implements the needed semantics for supporting activatable RMI servers, including the implementation of a constructor that takes activation and marshaled object information used during the reconstruction of the object from a non-active state. `CustomerActivatable` stores all customer information in an underlying `java.util.Hashtable` and implements getters and setters for all customer attributes.

The `CustomerServiceRemote` class in the `CustomerServiceRemote.java` file implements the Jini service registrar functionality. When started from the command line, the `CustomerServiceRemote.main()` method will first create a security manager instance and then call a `static registerCustomers()` method on itself to perform all discovery, joining, and registration steps. The static registerCustomers() method first retrieves a collection of customer information returned as a Vector of Hashtable objects returned from the CustomerServiceRemote.getAllCustomers() call. After a CustomerServiceRemote object is instantiated, each Hashtable of customer information is then passed as a parameter in a call to registerACustomerService() on the CustomerServiceRemote object. The getAllCustomers() creates the Vector of Hashtable objects from a parsed list of customer information read from a CustomerInfo.txt file assumed to be in the current working directory. Note that our runjiniexample.bat file will relocate such a file for you from the examples\src\ejava\jndich20\jiniexample directory.

When CustomerServiceRemote.registerACustomerService() is called with a Hashtable of customer information, a Name is constructed using a customer's ID, which is then in turn used to create a single-element array of Entry objects. A ServiceItem is then constructed with the Entry array, and a reference to a CustomerServiceProxy object is returned from the CustomerServiceRemote.getProxy() call. The getProxy() call creates and registers an activatable RMI server (note that this is a regular RMI registration process and not a Jini registration process). The RMI server handle is then used in the construction of a CustomerServiceProxy object. Subsequently, inside of the CustomerServiceRemote.registerACustomerService() method, a handle to a LookupDiscovery object is constructed indicating no preference for a particular discovery process group. The LookupDiscovery object is then used to add a CustomerDiscoveryListener object implemented in the CustomerDiscoveryListener.java file. The CustomerDiscoveryListener object is constructed with a handle to the CustomerServiceRemote object and the ServiceItem object created by the CustomerServiceRemote object.

The CustomerDiscoveryListener is called by the Jini discovery process (encapsulated by LookupDiscovery) whenever it discovers a lookup service in the available community. The discovered() method implementation will make a callback onto the CustomerServiceRemote.registerWithLookupService() method when it is invoked by the discovery process for each discovered lookup service represented by a ServiceRegistrar object. The registerWithLookupService() method will then register the ServiceItem with the lookup service for a requested MAX_LEASING_TIME.

On the client side, we have the CustomerJINIClient.java file implementing the Jini client functionality. The CustomerJINIClient.main() method also creates a security manager instance and then creates an instance of a CustomerJINIClient object before blocking for user input from the standard input stream. The CustomerJINIClient constructor first creates a ServiceTemplate object with a specified array of Customer class types to look for. This ServiceTemplate is stored in a private variable. The client discovery process that follows then invokes a newly created `LookupDiscovery` object to add a `ClientDiscoveryListener` instance. The `ClientDiscoveryListener` class is contained in the `ClientDiscoveryListener.java` file.

When the Jini discovery process discovers a lookup service in the client's community, it then calls `lookForThisService()` on the `CustomerJINIClient` for each instance of a `ServiceRegistrar` (that is, lookup service) that is discovered. When `lookForThisService()` is called, the `ServiceRegistrar` is used to look up any customers that match the criteria stipulated in the `ServiceTemplate` created earlier with an additional constraint of returning only `MAX_MATCHES` number of matches in the `ServiceMatches` object. For each item that has a match, the `CustomerServiceProxy` object is accessed to invoke the various getter methods defined on its `Customer` interface. The proxy in turn makes such calls to the remote RMI server.

The `runjiniexample.bat` file included with this example will help you configure and run this example. Because Jini requires a fairly extensive runtime environment, it will pay for you to understand the `runjiniexample` fairly well. You'll first be establishing `PATH` and `CLASSPATH` environment variables for your development and Jini environment as shown here:

```
if "%EJAVA_HOME%" == "" goto invalidHome1
if "%JAVA_HOME%" == "" goto invalidHome2
if "%JINI_HOME%" == "" goto invalidHome3


set CLASSPATH=%JAVA_HOME%\jre\lib\rt.jar;.;
set JINI_LIB=%JINI_HOME%\lib
set JINI_CLASSES=%JINI_LIB%\jini-core.jar;
➥%JINI_LIB%\jini-examples.jar;%JINI_LIB%\jini-ext.jar;
set JINI_CLASSES=%JINI_CLASSES%;%JINI_LIB%\mahalo.jar;
➥%JINI_LIB%\reggie.jar;%JINI_LIB%\sun-util.jar;
set JINI_CLASSES=%JINI_CLASSES%;%JINI_LIB%\tools.jar;

set CLASSPATH=%CLASSPATH%;%JINI_CLASSES%;%EJAVA_HOME%\examples\classes

set PATH=%JAVA_HOME%\bin;%PATH%
```

The `rmi.policy` file and `CustomerInfo.txt` file will then be copied to your working directory:

```
copy %EJAVA_HOME%\examples\src\ejava\jndich20\jiniexample\rmi.policy
➥ %EJAVA_HOME%\examples\classes

copy
➥ %EJAVA_HOME%\examples\src\ejava\jndich20\jiniexample\customerInfo.txt
➥ %EJAVA_HOME%\examples\classes
```

After compiling the files and creating the necessary RMI stubs and skeletons, the HTTP server for downloading classes can be started (using the Windows `start` command for spawning new processes):

```
start %JAVA_HOME%\bin\java -jar %JINI_HOME%\lib\tools.jar -dir .
➥ -verbose -port 8080
```

Next, the RMI activation daemon is started:

```
start %JAVA_HOME%\bin\rmid
```

The Jini lookup service can then be started:

```
start java -jar %JINI_LIB%\reggie.jar
➥ http://localhost:8080/reggie-dl.jar
➥ %JINI_HOME%\example\lookup\policy.all
➥ C:\temp\reggie_log1 public
```

Finally, the Jini service and Jini client are started:

```
start %JAVA_HOME%\bin\java
➥ -Djava.rmi.server.codebase=http://localhsot:8080/
➥ -Djava.security.policy=rmi.policy
➥ ejava.jndich20.jiniexample.CustomerServiceRemote

%JAVA_HOME%\bin\java
➥ -Djava.security.policy=rmi.policy
➥ ejava.jndich20.jiniexample.CustomerJINIClient
```

You'll notice a healthy distribution of "pause" statements in our `runjiniexample.bat` file. This is because when automatically running such services, we need to ensure that previous services are fully up and running before subsequent services are started. You should also note that if you run this example more than once, you may have to first clean up the lookup service's log file manually before running the example again.

Microsoft Active Directory Services

The Microsoft Active Directory Service (ADS) is a directory service that comes pre-installed with the Windows 2000 operating system. In fact, ADS is probably the most significant addition to the Windows 2000 operating system. The ADS maintains user, security, and network resource information used on a Windows 2000 network. Administration of Windows networks and network resources is all managed by an ADS running on a Windows 2000 server. ADS also provides a GUI interface for managing user information, managing network resources such as printers, and managing distributed applications. ADS employs a DNS naming hierarchy and ADS servers act as domain controllers for a network.

ADS stores elements in its structure as ADS objects. Each object is defined by a set of attributes and is also uniquely identified by a globally unique identifier (GUID) assigned by the ADS server. Each object also has a schema defining its structure in an LDAP-compatible fashion. ADS objects can assume different name formats as well, including LDAP-style distinguished names, GUIDs, security principal names, secure identifiers, and user login names. ADS objects are published to an ADS server to expose their information to a Windows network domain. ADS servers can be organized in various federated domain configurations.

DCOM components can use the ADS by storing their activation and connection information in the ADS. Updates to such information can then be propagated and made available to interested DCOM clients on the Windows network. Standard ADS connection information interfaces exist for DCOM applications, as well as for RPC and Winsock applications. DCOM servers publish connection information using a DCOM-specific class storage mechanism inside the ADS.

In addition to a direct LDAPv2- and LDAPv3-compliant C API to the ADS, the Active Directory Service Interface (ADSI) provides a means for exposing application programming interfaces to ADS objects as COM objects. Behind the scenes of the ADSI, a Service Provider Interface (SPI) also offers a COM interface to various types of concrete directory service implementations. ADSI SPIs currently exist for connectivity to LDAP, NDS, Novell NetWare 3.x, Windows NT/2000, and Microsoft Internet Information Service Web Server metabases. Thus, whereas ADS represents a concrete implementation of a directory service, the ADSI offers an interface to it as well as potentially other concrete directory service implementations. ADSI interfaces are offered in Java, C++, C, and Visual Basic. The Java-based ADSI interfaces are defined in the `com.ms.adsi` package and are downloadable from the Microsoft Web site. Because use of the interfaces in `com.ms.adsi` returns COM-based ADSI interfaces, use of the Microsoft JVM with such an API is required.

Conclusions

Directory services represent key components of many enterprise systems for storing enterprise resource–related information. Directory service clients can search a directory service using a user-friendly querying methodology. NIS, NDS, and LDAP all represent common directory service types with a large amount of industry support. JNDI offers a standard Java-based interface to directory services that can be used with directory services such as NIS, NDS, and LDAP. Additional APIs specific to more advanced LDAP v3 features are also part of the JNDI API.

The CORBA Trading Service adds to the directory service concept by providing support for associating distributed CORBA object references to the type of object attribute information that would be found in a directory service. The CORBA Trading Service is unfortunately a somewhat-complicated framework to use. Jini is a type of trading service that adds support for dynamically discovering lookup services on a network by both servers and clients. Although Jini has a simpler API, configuring the runtime infrastructure required for Jini can be somewhat tedious.

Finally, the Microsoft ADS provides a directory service implementation and standard interface for COM- and DCOM-based applications. Of course, use of the Microsoft ADS is platform dependent.

Activation Services

CHAPTER

21

IN THIS CHAPTER

- Activation Services Overview 690
- RMI Activation Framework 692
- CORBA Activation Framework 694
- CORBA Lifecycle Service 697
- DCOM Activation Framework 699
- JavaBeans Activation Framework 700
- Web and Application Activation Frameworks 702

Activation services are fundamental enterprise component services used to automatically activate objects in memory from some dormant state based on a component client's request. This chapter describes the basic concepts behind activation services and gives specific descriptions of the predominant activation service models encountered in enterprise Java development endeavors. Because activation services are largely transparent to the enterprise engineer, our coverage is necessarily overview material by nature. However, knowledge of the concepts and a basic understanding of activation service models provide the architect, designer, and developer with insight into an important set of behaviors occurring "under the hood" that allow one to better understand the capabilities and limits of particular enterprise component frameworks.

In this chapter, you will learn:

- The basic concept of activation services and how they generically operate.
- The architecture of RMI's activation framework.
- The architecture of CORBA's POA activation framework.
- The architecture of CORBA's LifeCycle Service extended activation-like framework.
- The architecture of DCOM's activation framework.
- The basic JavaBeans Activation Framework (JAF) architecture for transforming MIME typed data to and from active objects.
- The basic types of Web-enabled and application-enabled framework activation services.

Activation Services Overview

As depicted in Figure 21.1, an activation service is a component of software responsible for bringing other software from an inactive dormant state into an active in-memory state. The process of transitioning software from an inactive state to an active state is referred to as activation. Inactive software, such as a Java class file, may thus become active when it is instantiated as an object. A stored component may become active when it is allocated its own thread and brought into memory. Similarly, an entire program may be activated when it is spawned as its own process. Such examples apply mainly to transitioning software from some persistent storage mechanism into active memory. However, activation frameworks also include services that transition software into active memory from a dormant state in some other medium, such as from an I/O stream.

Given such a broad definition, as you can imagine, there are indeed many instances of activation services in computing platforms because the process of bringing code into memory from some dormant state, such as from a hard disk or floppy disk, is a fundamental aspect of everyday computing life. For example, components of an operating system that fork and execute a process are a form of activation service. Virtual machines must also provide an activation service because they operate on top of an operating-system platform and often take control of the activation of software away from the operating system directly. The Java Virtual Machine's class loader, for example, is a type of activation service.

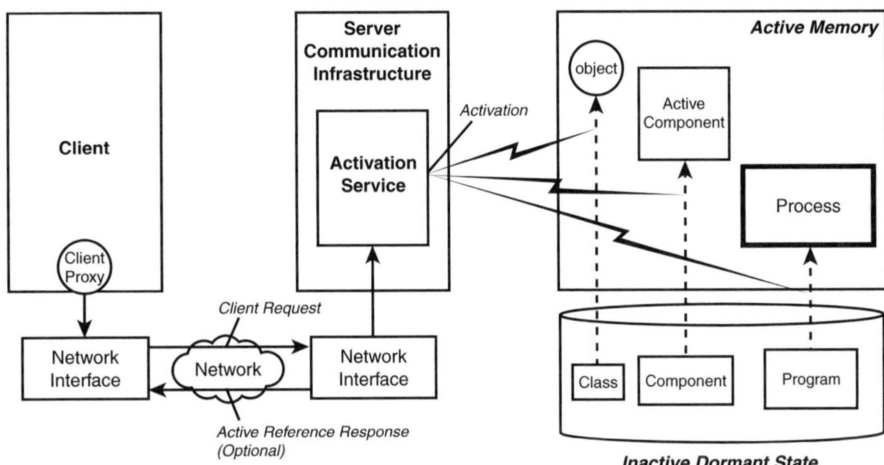

FIGURE 21.1
Activation services.

However, most of the time when we speak of activation services with respect to distributed enterprise systems, there is also an implied client initiating the activation request from a remote network location. On the server side of HTTP request handling, Web server software brings HTML pages and possibly a set of Web client scripting instructions into memory from a file system on the Web server. Though not client request initiated per se, a MIME type handler embedded in your Web client browser may spawn an Adobe Acrobat process based on a MIME type that was associated with an HTTP response.

Perhaps most common are distributed component-based activation services that work with some server-side communications infrastructure. Component-based software has provided a model of development that has made building enterprise systems a much more economical solution than other development paradigms. Thus, it should come as no surprise that many activation service models have been implemented to handle distributed client requests on enterprise components. Such services may optionally return active references to a client proxy or may maintain the active reference on the server side. Understanding how such activation services operate helps you understand one of the most important components operating under the hood of a distributed enterprise solution. Understanding how activation works will help you make better enterprise component design decisions by enabling you to know what are both the true benefits and the limits of your component-based enterprise solution.

RMI Activation Framework

Before Java 2, RMI was without an activation service framework. RMI servers could be created only by already-active server registrars and other RMI servers in Java 1.1. Of course, you can still create servers this way in Java 2. Server registrars register object references with associated names in an RMI registry. Other RMI servers can return references to newly created RMI servers from remote calls onto their methods. In either case, the lifetime of the RMI server is bound to the lifetime of the JVM process in which it was created. Clients that go down and reactivate themselves can obtain handles to the same server instances again only if either an RMI registry or another RMI server process can return such a handle to the client when the client comes back to life.

Calls made from RMI client to RMI server take place over the TCP/IP socket associated with the RMI server. The JVM process's RMI runtime handles creating or selecting a thread in which the active RMI object instance can run. The RMI runtime hands this object to that thread and delegates the call to the object. No assumptions can be made by the RMI server object with respect to which thread it is allocated. The RMI runtime may or may not allocate it the same thread in which it can handle successive calls. Multiple client calls to the same RMI server object may also be invoked concurrently by separate threads allocated to handle that call onto the server object. Thus, the RMI server object's implementation must guarantee its own thread safety.

Although the same threading model applies to RMI servers in Java 2, RMI servers have the option of utilizing a new activation framework built into RMI in Java 2 for handling client requests. As you saw in Chapter 16, "RMI Communications," activatable RMI server objects can be implemented such that they are brought into memory only upon client request. Activatable server objects can also be made inactive and be reactivated any number of times. RMI's activation service is implemented by a separately running process known as the remote method invocation daemon (`rmid`). One `rmid` process runs per host machine that wants to offer RMI activation services for its local RMI servers. Calls to RMI servers on that host machine which are currently inactive result in a request from the `rmid` process to activate the server and return a live handle that can be used to talk to the activated object. As you also saw in Chapter 16, APIs to the `rmid` are provided in the `java.rmi.activation` package.

Figure 21.2 represents the basic RMI activation service architecture via a conceptual diagram with a few genuine APIs interspersed. In Chapter 16, we demonstrated how an RMI registrar registers an activatable object with a running `rmid`. The registrar created an activation descriptor for an activatable object and then registered this descriptor with the activation system. The activation descriptor contained the ID of a JVM group, class information, the URL location of the class, and any marshaled object data to be used for initializing the object on activation. During an RMI client request on an activatable object that is currently inactive, the following basic sequence occurs:

1. *RMI client attempts reference*: An RMI client must first look up a remote object from the RMI registry or obtain a handle from another remote object. The client uses an RMI interface to that remote object implemented by an RMI stub which in turn has an association with a faulty remote reference. The faulty remote reference for an activatable object contains an activation ID that has a handle to an RMI activator. The RMI activator represents the interface to an RMI activation daemon sitting on the host machine from where the activatable object will be activated.
2. *Remote reference faults to activator reference*: During an RMI client's remote request of an RMI object, if the faulty remote reference object's remote reference value is null, it uses the activation ID to ask the remote activation daemon to activate the object and return a remote reference to an activated object.
3. *Activator looks up activation info*: The activator uses the activation ID information to look up an activation descriptor that has been registered with the activation daemon on that machine.
4. *Activator accesses/spawns JVM process*: The activator uses the JVM group ID to either obtain a handle to a proxy for an already-running JVM process, or spawn a new JVM process associated with that group ID if it is not already running.
5. *Activator requests activated object*: The activator then tells the activation group JVM process to activate the object in its process memory and passes it any necessary activation information from the associated activation descriptor, as well as the activation ID.
6. *JVM process loads activatable class*: The activation group JVM process's RMI runtime uses the class and URL location information to load the class that supports being instantiated as an activatable server object.
7. *JVM process instantiates activatable object*: The activation group JVM process's RMI runtime then passes the activation ID and marshaled object information to the activatable object during its instantiation. The marshaled object state can be used to initialize the state of the activatable object.
8. *Activated remote reference is returned*: A remote reference to this activated object is then propagated from the activation group JVM process to the activator and back to the faulty remote reference.
9. *RMI client has remote reference*: The faulty remote reference now has a handle to an activated RMI server object, and the call made by the client can now proceed as usual.

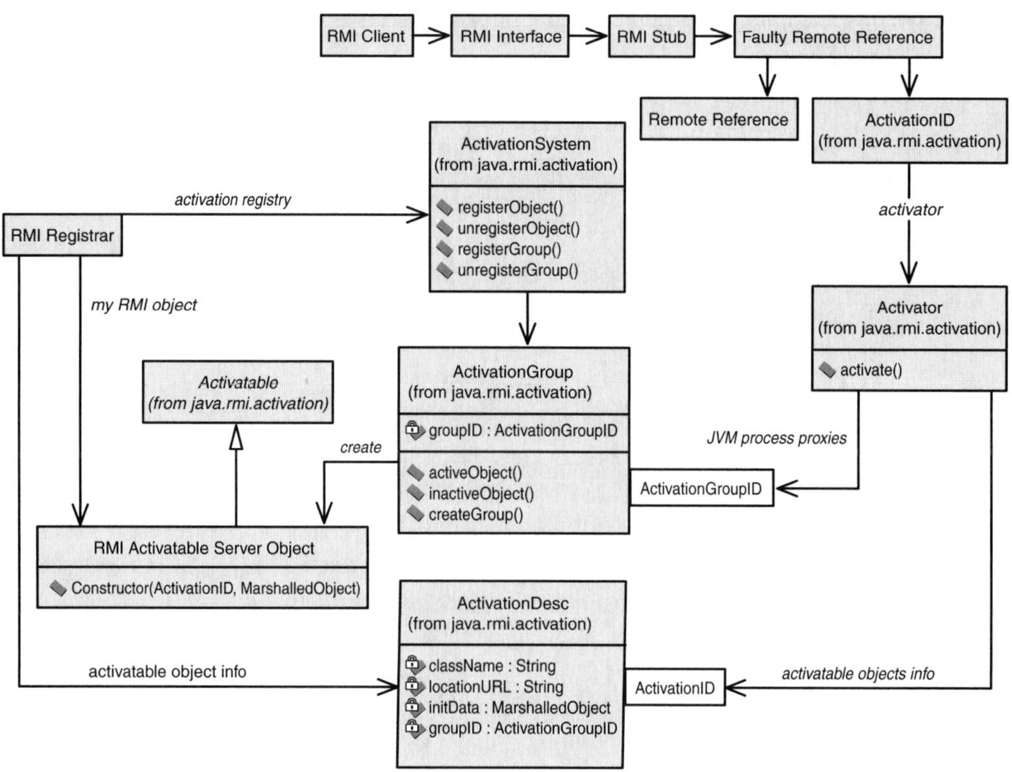

FIGURE 21.2
The RMI activation service architecture.

CORBA Activation Framework

The CORBA object adapter is CORBA's version of an activation service. As we have discussed in Chapter 14, "Modeling Components with CORBA," and Chapter 15, "CORBA Communications," the older Basic Object Adapter (BOA) in CORBA was deprecated in favor of the Portable Object Adapter (POA). The BOA specification had many holes, which led to CORBA server implementations that were not portable across ORB vendor products. The POA was defined in such a way that different server object implementations can remain portable across various ORB vendor products. Because the POA now represents the de facto standard that enables activation in CORBA, we focus on the POA here.

Because CORBA is simply a set of specifications, certain implementation details regarding the CORBA activation model vary from vendor to vendor. Thus, for example, the exact model that is supported for allocating threads to active server objects is left up to the vendor implementations. The CORBA specifications naturally focus on interfaces that need to be defined to enable vendor interoperability. CORBA specifications also offer the applications that utilize them the capability to use different vendor products without, ideally, any modifications.

Although precise thread models are undefined, the POA specification does define a thread model policy identification mechanism that indicates whether a single-threaded model or ORB-controlled threading model is supported. If a POA supports only a single-threaded model, requests are managed by a single thread allocated for a servant object, and that servant object can be implemented in a thread-unaware fashion. In an ORB-controlled model of threading, the POA is responsible for creating, allocating, and destroying threads that are associated with servants. Specific thread model behavior to be expected and ways to configure an ORB-controlled thread model are vendor-specific.

Figure 21.3 depicts the CORBA activation service architecture employed by the POA via a conceptual diagram with some CORBA entities interspersed. Central to this architecture is the POA interface used to register CORBA server implementations and objects (aka servants). Depending on the servant retention policy of the POA, an active set of servants can be retained in an active object map. A servant manager can be used by the POA to activate a particular servant. A specific type of servant manager known as a servant activator will actually carry out such a task when the servants will be retained in an active object map. Another type of servant manager known as a servant locator can be used when the servant will not be retained and is used only for a single request.

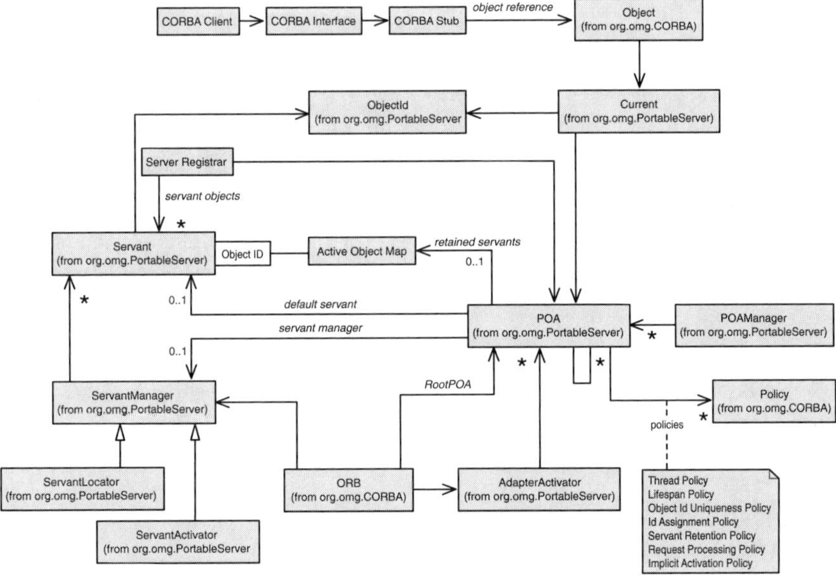

FIGURE 21.3

The CORBA activation service architecture.

Although object references are still held by the client, an underlying object ID is used by a POA to uniquely identify servants. A new current execution context object can be used to associate a POA and object ID for a CORBA object.

An initial reference to a root POA can be obtained from the ORB using the `ORB.resolve_initial_references("RootPOA")` call. Adapter activators can also be associated with a POA so that ORBs can create POA instances when a particular child POA does not exist. A POA manager can be used to manage POAs in a collection and deactivate particular POAs. With a POA reference in hand, server registrars register servants with a particular POA governed by a set of POA policies. After registration of a servant with a POA, the following general sequence of steps to activate a servant that is currently inactive occurs during CORBA client requests:

1. *CORBA client attempts reference*: A CORBA client attempts to reference a remote CORBA servant object with an underlying object reference.
2. *ORB obtains POA reference*: A portable execution context is associated with the object reference. The portable current execution context associates the reference with a particular POA. The server-side ORB can use an adapter activator to instantiate an instance of the referenced POA if it does not exist.
3. *POA obtains object ID*: The server-side POA yields an object ID from the portable current execution context.
4. *POA looks for cached object instance*: The POA looks in its active object map for an active instance associated with the object ID if a retain policy is in effect for this POA.
5. *POA requests servant from servant manager*: If POA cannot find an active servant associated with the object ID, it will ask the servant manager to activate the object. This is also referred to as asking the servant manager to incarnate the object.
6. *Servant manager loads servant information*: The server manager then must load the servant implementation and data using the object ID. The object ID can contain class location information and information indicating where initialization data can be loaded from.
7. *Servant manager instantiates servant*: The servant manager then creates an active instance of the servant object associated with the object ID.
8. *POA obtains servant handle*: The POA receives the created instance back from the servant manager and inserts the servant reference in its active object map if the servant was retrieved from the servant activator.
9. *POA invokes servant*: The POA then makes the requested call on the active object.
10. *CORBA client request satisfied*: The CORBA client is then returned any results from a distributed object invocation.

CORBA Lifecycle Service

The activation of CORBA objects in some server-side memory to be readied for the reception of CORBA client requests involves more than just loading a class's implementation from persistent storage and instantiating an object instance of that implementation. Apart from typical means of instantiating and activating CORBA objects, a standard means for creating, deleting, copying, and moving CORBA objects is defined as a CORBAservice in the CORBA Life Cycle Service Specification. Object creation and deletion involves the instantiation or destruction of an object by a client in some remote server. Copying objects allows for object references to be duplicated within a domain, whereas moving objects allows for the relocation of objects within a domain.

Core Life Cycle Service interfaces are defined in the `org::omg::LifeCycle` CORBA module. Support for creating, deleting, copying, and moving of objects in a deep manner spanning multiple objects and involving sophisticated relationships is provided in the `org::omg::CompoundLifeCycle` module. Figure 21.4 depicts the CORBA Life Cycle Service architecture with operation signatures shown for only a few of the core Life Cycle Service interfaces.

Factory patterns are alive and at play in CORBA environments. Factory objects can be used by CORBA clients to create instances of new CORBA server objects. The core Life Cycle interfaces enable a CORBA client to find factories as well as use a generic factory to create new CORBA server object instances. An encapsulation of an object that supports life-cycle operations of being copied, moved, and deleted is also provided by the Life Cycle Service. These are the core Life Cycle interfaces supporting this functionality:

- `FactoryFinder` can be used to return an array of factories that can be used to create object instances given a key name of the factory. Factories can be user-defined or of the `GenericFactory` type.
- `GenericFactory` can be used as a generic factory to create object instances given an object key name and a collection of name value pairs for use in a general fashion by the generic factory. The `GenericFactory` can also be asked whether it supports a particular object to create.
- `LifeCycleObject` is implemented by objccts that want to allow themselves to be copied, moved, and deleted. A `FactoryFinder` and set of search criteria passed to a `LifeCycleObject` copy operation are used to find a remote factory that is needed to create an object on the server platform. The `LifeCycleObject` copy is then returned from this copy operation. A `FactoryFinder` and set of search criteria passed to a move operation can be used to move an object to a remote server platform. A particular `LifeCycleObject` can also be deleted from memory using a remove operation on that object.

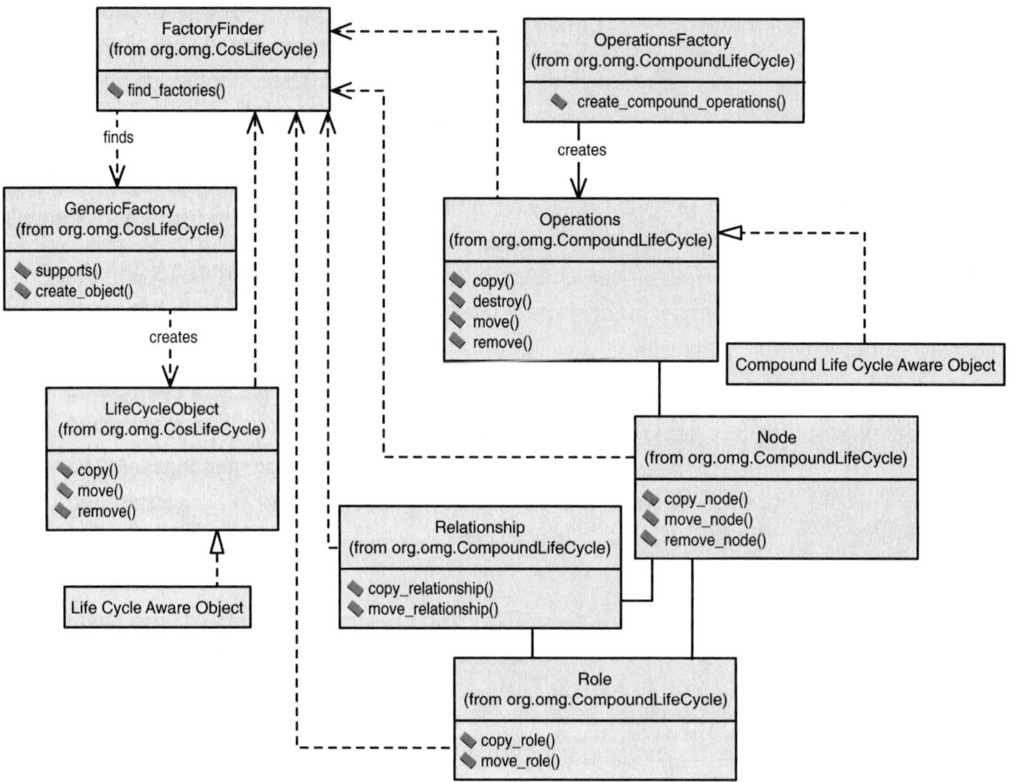

FIGURE 21.4
The CORBA Life Cycle Service architecture.

The compound Life Cycle interfaces enable you to define objects in such a way that complex relationships between themselves and other objects can be modeled to enable deep copies, moves, creations, and deletions. The compound life-cycle service relies on the CORBA Relationship Services to model complex relationships between distributed CORBA objects. Graphs of objects are modeled in which nodes correspond to objects and the relationships between such nodes are explicitly encapsulated with interfaces. The roles that nodes play in these relationships are also modeled. The Compound Life Cycle service uses these same notions to enable copies, moves, creations, and deletions. These are the key Compound Life Cycle interfaces:

- `OperationsFactory` is used as a factory to create objects implementing the compound life-cycle interfaces encapsulated by the `Operations` interface.

- `Operations` allows for the copying, moving, and destruction of a graph of objects. A remove operation also enables for the removal of a particular group of objects beginning with a starting node.
- `Node` provides a generic interface for representing nodes in a relationship that can be copied, moved, and removed.
- `Relationship` provides an interface for representing relationships that can be copied or moved during the copying and moving of nodes.
- `Role` provides an interface for representing roles of node relationships that can be copied or moved during the copying and moving of nodes.

DCOM Activation Framework

When creating instances of local COM objects, COM libraries use Class Identifiers (CLSIDs) to load dynamic link libraries looked up via the Windows registry and then create an instance of the COM object. DCOM requires additional mechanisms to support distributed object activation, as depicted in Figure 21.5. A Service Control Manager (SCM) on a client machine uses a server name in addition to a CLSID to contact a remote DCOM server machine's SCM. The remote SCM is then responsible for initiating activation of the DCOM object on that machine. Server names can be associated with a DCOM object either via configuration of the client's registry or via a parameter used with a DCOM API call during DCOM object instantiation by a client. Beginning with Windows 2000, the Active Directory Service (ADS) will be capable of storing all activation information related to COM and DCOM objects.

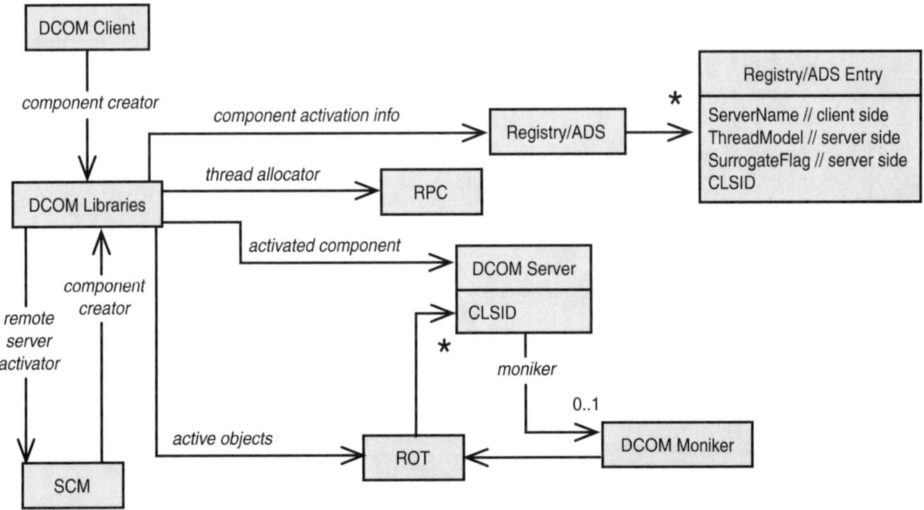

FIGURE 21.5
The DCOM activation service architecture.

If a server name is associated with a DCOM object explicitly using a tool such as the `javareg` utility described in Chapter 18, "DCOM Communications," then the DCOM client can transparently obtain access to the remote DCOM server. The server name is stored in the Windows registry under the `HKEY_CLASSES_ROOT\APPID\<appID>` entry with the `RemoteServerName` value equal to the DNS name of the server machine. The CLSID is stored in the `HKEY_CLASSES_ROOT\CLSID\<clsid>` entry with the `AppId` value equal to `<appID>`.

On the server side, a CLSID key in the Windows registry specifies which Windows binary dynamic link library (DLL) to load during activation. An `APPID` key in the registry must specify a `DIISurrogate` value indicating that the DLL to be loaded for this DCOM object is to be loaded into a surrogate process to handle distributed DCOM client requests. The approach for allocating a thread to this newly created DCOM instance is designated by a threading model flag in the Windows registry associated with the component. In a single threaded apartment (STA) model, a DCOM object is allocated to one thread and calls to multiple objects in that thread block until other calls are finished. In a multithreaded apartment (MTA) model, a DCOM object instance is allocated a thread that was created by DCOM's underlying RPC mechanism.

If monikers are used by DCOM servers to give themselves a name and enable themselves to be persisted for later use, a few more activation mechanisms become relevant. When monikers are created by DCOM servers, they not only pass handles to such objects to their DCOM clients, but also register such moniker instances using DCOM libraries. The server-side DCOM libraries manage the list of objects currently persistable via monikers in a running object table (ROT). Monikers look up object instances in the ROT associated with their named moniker value. When objects are in the ROT, pointers to such objects can be returned, whereas objects that are not in the ROT are newly created by the moniker. Newly created objects can have their state restored using whatever mechanism the particular moniker type was designed to support. That is, the moniker may read the object's state from a file, from a database, and so forth.

JavaBeans Activation Framework

The JavaBeans Activation Framework (JAF) is a framework for building applications which can automatically activate objects that can manipulate data received via an input stream. The JAF accomplishes this task by providing support for identifying the type of data received via an input stream, identifying the types of operations that are available on the data, and automatically instantiating (that is, activating) a JavaBean component that can handle a particular operation that needs to be performed on that data. Thus the JAF is a type of activation service whose dormant inactive state of an object rests within a data input stream, as opposed to in some persistent storage mechanism. The JAF is useful to applications that want to map data identified by MIME types into Java objects supporting operations on that particular data type. The JAF also enables the reverse process of streaming an object back into a byte stream from its active object state. As an auxiliary service, the JAF can provide services to map filename extensions to and from MIME types.

The JAF `javax.activation` package is a standard Java extension that can work with the Java 1.1 platform and J2SE. The JAF is also equipped with the J2EE platform because the J2EE JavaMail package depends on the JAF. JavaMail depends on the JAF for handling MIME type data that is sent within email messages. Aside from the underlying dependence on the JAF by JavaMail, most other J2EE applications will not have much interaction with the JAF. However, we briefly highlight the architecture of JAF here so that you can better understand it in the context of other activation services. Furthermore, a basic understanding of JAF will help comprehend an underlying component utilized by the J2EE JavaMail component, which we discuss further in Chapter 22, "Messaging Services."

The basic architecture of the JAF is shown in Figure 21.6. The basic responsibilities of the core JAF components shown in Figure 21.6 are as shown here:

- `DataHandler`: The `DataHandler` is the primary interface used by JAF clients to access data in different formats and to invoke conversion between an underlying byte stream and activated Java object type via a specific `DataContentHandler`. The `DataHandler` can by and large use the remaining APIs shown in Figure 21.6 transparently for the JAF client.
- `DataContentHandlerFactory`: The `DataContentHandlerFactory` takes a MIME type as a parameter and returns a specific `DataContentHandler` factory that can handle that MIME type.
- `DataContentHandler`: The `DataContentHandler` is responsible for reading data streams into objects and for writing objects to streams.
- `DataSource`: A `DataSource` offers a handle to data that has an associated object name and MIME type. Handles to input and output streams attached to an underlying data medium (for example, files and URLs) may also be obtained from the `DataSource`.
- `CommandMap`: A `CommandMap` maps MIME types to a collection of commands that can be performed on that data.
- `CommandInfo`: The `CommandInfo` encapsulates information about a particular command, including the name of the command class and the command name. The actual JavaBean object instance that can implement such a command is also returned.
- `CommandObject`: The `CommandObject` interface is implemented by JAF-aware JavaBean objects that can operate on MIME typed data.

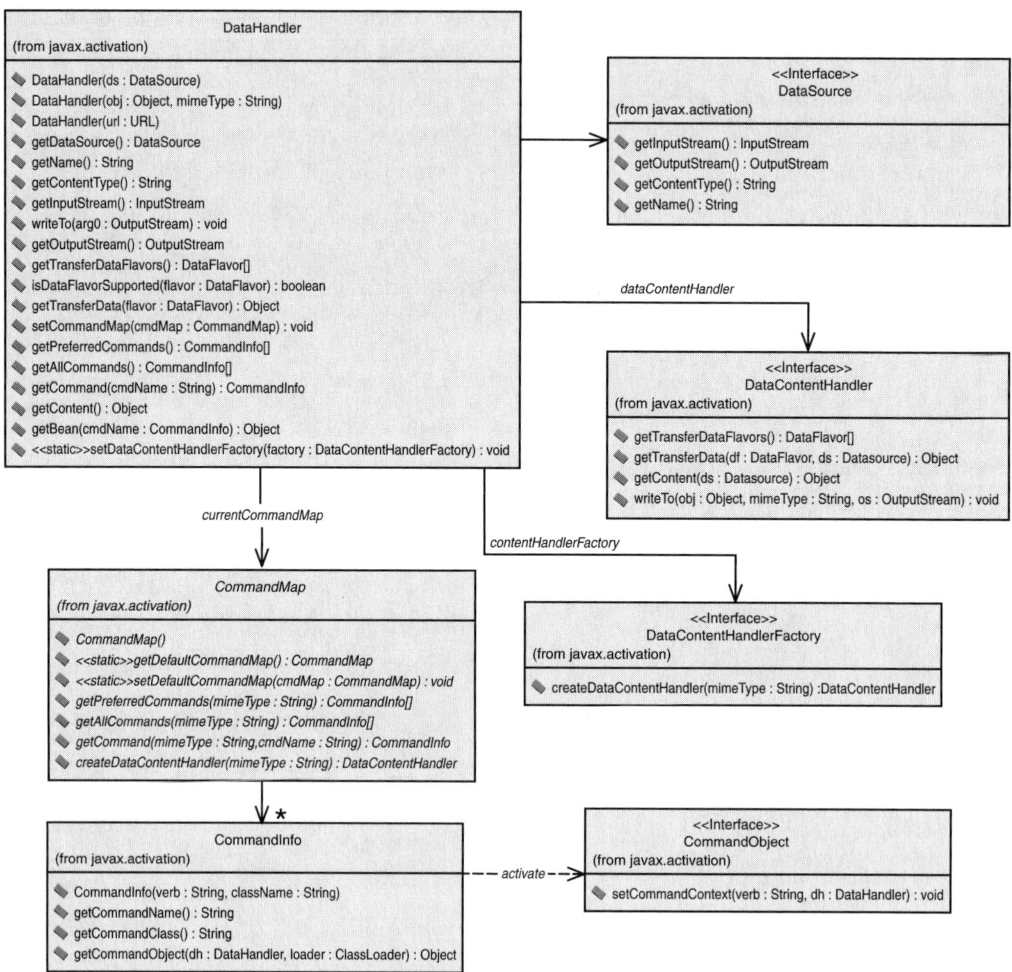

FIGURE 21.6
JavaBeans activation service architecture.

Web and Application Activation Frameworks

The activation services described thus far in this chapter focused on component-based activation services primarily to support a communications enabling infrastructure (RMI, CORBA, and DCOM) or to support content handling (JavaBeans Activation Framework). Many other types of activation services exist in the context of enabling your enterprise infrastructure for distributed Web or application access. The J2EE in particular employs various activation models for Web-enabling your enterprise via Java Servlets and JavaServer Pages and for application enabling your enterprise via Enterprise JavaBeans.

We discuss such activation models when we describe these various topics in Part VI, "Enterprise Web Enabling," and Part VII, "Enterprise Applications Enabling." Nevertheless, we highlight a broader range of Web- and application-enabling activation frameworks here:

- *Web Client MIME Handler Activation:* When a MIME type/subtype field is specified in an HTTP response from a Web server, the Web client browser is responsible for associating that type/subtype with a particular application handler. A plug-in application component may be used to handle the associated data within the Web browser, or a separate application process may be spawned to handle the associated data. Most Web browsers come prewired with a few application handlers and also allow the user to associate MIME type/subtype names with an application handler that can be run inside or external to the browser.
- *Web Client Applet Activation:* `APPLET` tags can be embedded in an HTTP response stream's HTML-based response body. When such tags are parsed, Applet-enabled browsers spawn a separate Java Virtual Machine (JVM) to display the applet inside of the Web browser window. The classes located at a particular URL, indicated via an associated `CODEBASE` tag, are loaded, instantiated, initialized, and started by the Web browser's JVM instance.
- *Web Client Script Processing Activation:* Scripting languages can also be delivered from Web server to Web browser in the response body of an HTTP response. Such languages contain instructions that must also be loaded and interpreted by a Web browser that supports execution of such languages in a runtime engine suitable for that language. For example, client-side JavaScript instructions can be run inside of a Web browser after the scripting instructions are loaded and initiated by a JavaScript runtime engine.
- *Web Server File-Stream Activation:* Web servers have activation mechanisms that must load HTML and certain scripting-language files into an HTTP response body based on HTTP requests for that information.
- *Web Server Process Activation:* Web servers may also spawn separate processes to generate HTTP responses for them. Based on an HTTP request, a particular process may be spawned that returns data to the Web server that can be sent back to the Web client. Common Gateway Interface (CGI) based applications are examples of applications that are spawned as separate processes by a Web server.
- *Web Server Script Engine Activation:* Web servers may also start a separate runtime engine to handle certain server-side scripting language instructions via separate threads in that runtime environment.

- *Web Server Servlet Activation:* Java Servlets can receive Java-based Web requests that a J2EE-based Web server submits to a Java Servlet container engine that runs inside of a JVM. Servlet HTTP request-handling code can run inside of the JVM as separate threads and return HTTP responses to the Web server for delivery back to the Web client. Servlet containers and the Web server both play a role in servlet activation.
- *Web Server JSP Activation:* JavaServer Pages (JSPs) are scripting language–like elements having a Java syntax that are typically converted into servlets for handling HTTP requests and generating HTTP responses. JSPs require a JSP compilation engine to process JSP code.
- *Application Server EJB Activation:* Enterprise JavaBeans (EJBs) are components that run inside of an application server to implement business logic–oriented behavior. EJBs must be activated by an EJB container and server.

Conclusions

Activation services are fundamental services implemented by many enterprise component-based platforms for transforming some dormant state of an object into active memory with a resulting object being ready to handle client requests. Many activation services perform these operations automatically for clients to handle client requests on a per-demand basis. The distributed object communications paradigms studied in Part III, "Distributed Enterprise Communications Enabling," including RMI, CORBA, and DCOM, all provide some form of activation service to distributed clients that bring a distributed object into active memory based on a client's request to access that object. The CORBA LifeCycle Service also offers value-added activation-like services by not only providing standard object creation interfaces using standard factory services, but also providing interfaces for copying and moving active objects around a distributed network environment. The JavaBeans Activation Framework provides activation of objects based on underlying MIME data streams and is utilized by the J2EE's JavaMail component. Finally, various Web and application activation services also exist in various forms using activation models for the J2EE Web and Enterprise JavaBean components discussed later in the book.

Messaging Services

CHAPTER

22

IN THIS CHAPTER

- Messaging Overview 706
- MOM 711
- Java Message Service 714
- CORBA Messaging 747
- JavaMail 757

Passing messages between applications in a distributed system is a very common service for an enterprise information system. In an abstract sense, this is precisely what happens when one makes a distributed object call using such communication models as CORBA, RMI, and DCOM. Messaging services can be distinguished from these remote procedure–oriented communication models by the added layer of abstraction that is provided above a communications paradigm to uncouple the connection between distributed message sender and receiver. Rather, an intermediate service exists between a message producer and message consumer that handles the delivery of messages from producer to consumer. Furthermore, producers do not block on messages they deliver. Rather, messages are sent asynchronously by the producer. This chapter describes a few key and standard methods for creating Java enterprise applications that tap the services of messaging service APIs and frameworks.

In this chapter, you will learn:

- The basic concepts behind messaging services and variations in message service models.
- The ideas behind Message Oriented Middleware (MOM) as a more traditional means for exchanging messages between MOM-aware applications.
- The architecture and sample use of the Java Message Service (JMS) as a standard API and provider framework that enables the development of portable, message-based Java applications that can be used with the J2EE.
- The architecture of CORBA-based means for sending asynchronous messages using the CORBA Event Service, CORBA Notification Service, and CORBA Messaging specifications.
- The architecture and example use of the JavaMail API for sending and receiving email messages via the Internet that can also be used with the J2EE.

Messaging Overview

A messaging service is software that provides support for passing messages between distributed applications in a reliable, asynchronous, loosely coupled, language-independent, platform-independent, and often configurable fashion. Messaging services accomplish this task by encapsulating messages that are sent between a sender and a receiver and providing a software layer that sits between distributed messaging clients. A messaging service also provides an interface for messaging clients to use that isolates the underlying message service implementation such that heterogeneous clients can communicate using a programmer-friendly interface. Such an infrastructure can also be viewed as an event notification type service in which messages are events and the delivery of these messages between messaging clients acts as sort of an event notification mechanism. Event notification types of messaging systems, however, are typically designed to handle lighter weight messages than are message oriented middleware applications developed for more general purpose message passing. In this section, we explore the various facets of messaging services utilized by enterprise systems.

Message Service Locality

Figure 22.1 and Figure 22.2 depict two types of messaging service implementations. Figure 22.1 shows the most common type of messaging service implementation, in which some middleware software implements the functionality of a messaging service to receive asynchronously generated messages from a message producer and route them to a message consumer. A messaging client utilizes the services of the centralized messaging service in a transparent fashion via a messaging client interface. Figure 22.2 depicts a messaging service implementation in which the messaging software is embedded directly into a thick messaging client.

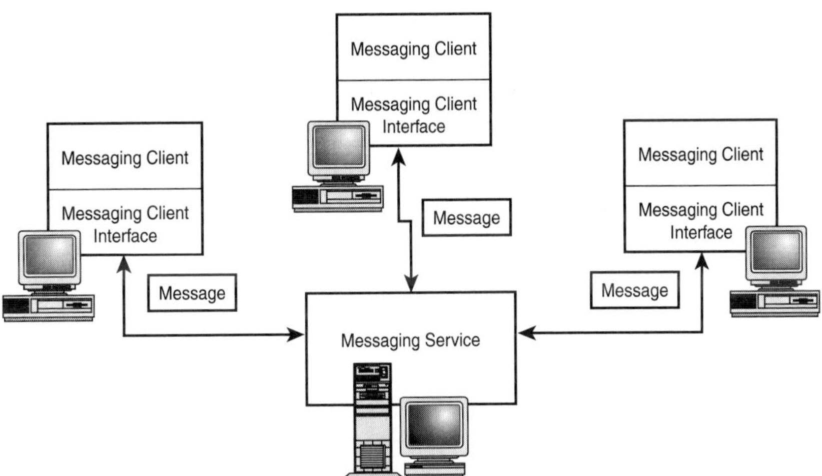

FIGURE 22.1
Messaging middleware.

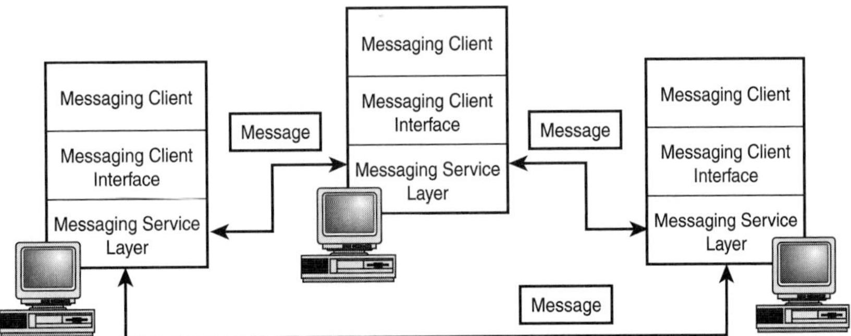

FIGURE 22.2
Messaging thick client software.

Most of our discussions here assume use of messaging middleware. Messaging middleware enhances the reliability and availability of a messaging service by virtue of a focus on the use of centrally managed persistent and redundant mechanisms in the middleware. Messaging middleware also alleviates the need for clients to manage connections to multiple messaging service endpoint locations by allowing a connection between a messaging client and a messaging service middleware server.

Point-to-Point Messaging

Figure 22.3 depicts one type of messaging service used for point-to-point communication between a message producer and a message consumer. A message producer sends a message to a particular consumer identified by some name (for example, "Foo"). This name actually corresponds to some queue in the message service used to store the message until it can deliver the message to the consumer associated with that queue. The queue may be persistent to help guarantee the delivery of a message even in the event of a message service failure. That is, a persistent queue can be read by a backup message service instance and used to deliver messages to a message consumer even if the primary message service fails.

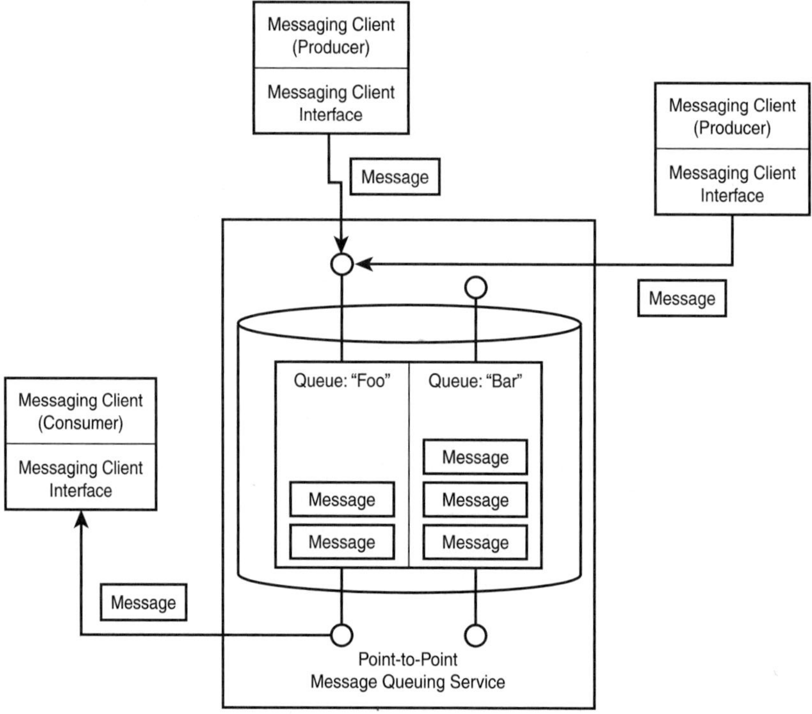

FIGURE 22.3

The point-to-point message queuing service.

Publish-Subscribe Messaging

Figure 22.4 depicts another popular model of messaging known as a publish-subscribe messaging service. With publish-subscribe, a message publisher publishes a message to a particular topic. Multiple subscribers can register to receive messages that have been published to a particular topic. Topics can be hierarchically arranged and can further enable the publication of messages and subscriptions to receive messages within a particular topic context. For example, we might subscribe to receive only those messages published specifically to the "Stocks" topic or subscribe to receive all of those messages published to the "Stocks" topic and its subtopics, such as "OTC."

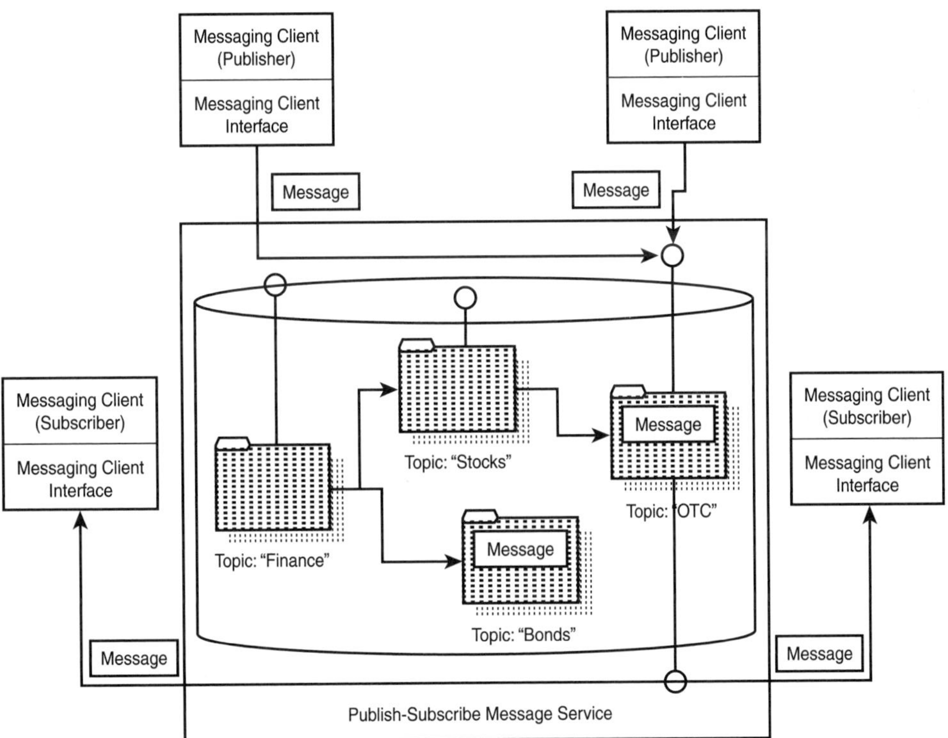

FIGURE 22.4
The publish-subscribe messaging service.

Push and Pull Messaging Models

Messaging services can also be distinguished according to their implementation of a message push or message pull model. A push model of messaging is the most typical style, in which a message producer sends a message to a messaging service, which pushes the message to the message consumer as shown in Figure 22.5. A pull model of messaging involves a consumer asking a message service to receive a message, at which point the message service pulls the message from the message producer as shown in Figure 22.6.

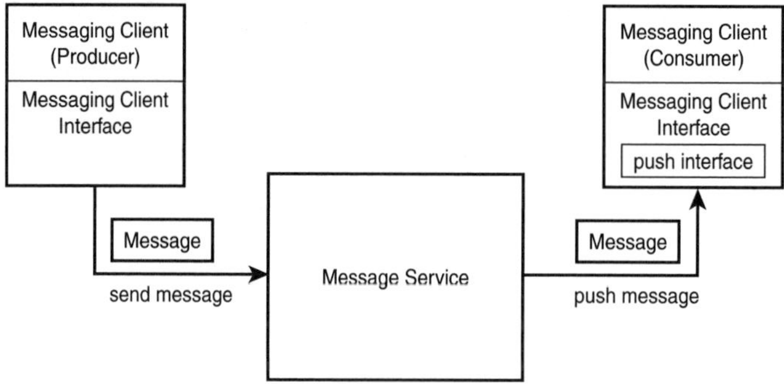

FIGURE 22.5
The messaging push model.

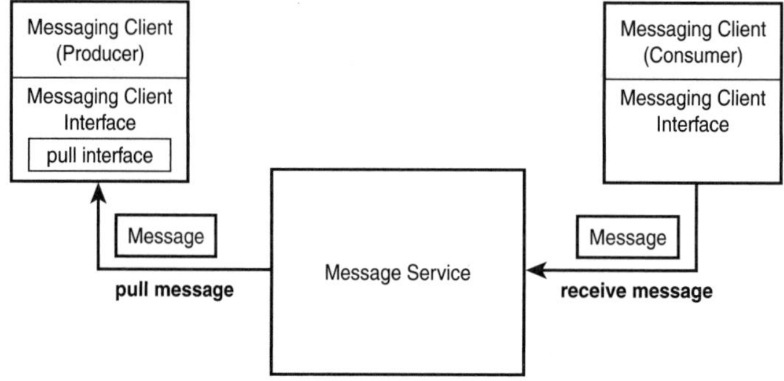

FIGURE 22.6
The messaging pull model.

Message Filtering, Synchronicity, and Quality

In the event that a message consumer desires to receive only certain messages based on some function of the message attributes, a message filtering scheme may be employed. Message filtering involves distinguishing between which messages should be delivered and which messages should not be delivered to a message consumer as a function of some filtering criteria. The filtering criteria are described in some language (for example, SQL) and can refer to attributes and values of a message. Thus, for example, you may subscribe to messages from a "Stocks" topic but filter out those messages whose "StockSymbol" attribute does not match the stock symbols in your stock portfolio.

Although various models of messaging exist, all messaging services share a common attribute of asynchronicity. Messages are sent by message producers to message consumers and do not require that the message producer block processing until the message is received. Typical remote method invocation protocols, however, such as RMI and CORBA, by default implement calls such that the distributed client does block until the call completes (that is, synchronous calls). Asynchronous calls thus offer a certain level of time-independence for the message producers and consumers.

As we've already alluded, a message service can also provide a certain level of assurance associated with message delivery. Reliability and availability of message delivery provide a Quality of Service (QoS) that can often be specified at various levels. Mission-critical messages may have a higher QoS than regular messages delivered. Many messaging services will provide a means to designate the QoS at the connection, message-type, and individual-message level.

Email Messaging

Of the various types of messaging services that exist, the delivery and reception of email messages is perhaps one of the most familiar and widely used types of messaging. An email server queues messages that have been sent to specific email addresses such that the email messages can be later retrieved by an email user. Email client software contains a transport mechanism for sending mail to a mail server. The mail server places such email in a message store such that it can be downloaded by email client software later. Email messaging thus typically serves as a point-to-point type of messaging service that uses a pull model of messaging. We discuss a few of the more popular types of email messaging service standards later in the chapter when we discuss the use of the JavaMail service.

MOM

The terms *Message Oriented Middleware* (MOM) and *Messaging Service* are nearly synonymous. MOM is simply an implementation of a messaging service albeit in a fashion that is standard for a particular type of MOM system. A MOM API defines how distributed applications should utilize an underlying MOM message channel or queue for communicating messages to one another. Messages are passed between applications via MOM in a way that does not block the sender of that message. That is, the sender can send a message and allow the MOM to ensure that it gets to the intended receiver without waiting for a response from the receiver.

MOM implementations can implement one or more types of messaging models. For example, one MOM implementation may employ simple point-to-point or push and pull models of messaging. Another MOM implementation may implement a more sophisticated publish-and-subscribe model and perhaps provide a server to manage message queuing in a centralized fashion and using redundant middleware server processes for enhanced reliability and availability.

MOM has historically been so popular that various organizations have been created and have gotten involved in providing standardization of MOM approaches. The Message-Oriented Middleware Association (MOMA) is a consortium of vendors, users, and interested parties that promote interoperability between MOM products. The Business Quality Messaging (BQM) organization focuses on providing standardization of MOM products for business-critical and highly reliable distributed and Internet-based commercial applications.

Although the efforts of such organizations help standardize MOM, MOM is not the only thing needed for enterprise applications. Other enterprise services and infrastructure such as standard communications, naming, transactions, and application-enabling frameworks are all key ingredients for building distributed enterprise applications. The Object Management Group (OMG) provides standards for MOM-based applications in the context of its CORBA model for building enterprise applications. OMG MOM-like functionality comes in the form of numerous specifications such as the CORBA Event Service, CORBA Notification Service, and CORBA Messaging. Because MOM is such a core part of an enterprise application, Sun's Java Message Service provides a standard MOM API for Java-based applications usable in a J2EE context. Though not traditionally labeled as MOM, email messaging has also been standardized on the Internet via various email protocols, and Sun's JavaMail service provides a Java interface to such a system.

MOM vendors abound and the MOMA standard has helped drive standard interfaces to such products. Companies such as PeerLogic, Inc., provide their PIPES Platform product for dynamic applications that want to communicate with other applications on a network using reliable messaging protocols. Veri-Q Inc. provides its VCOM product for reliable and secure messaging that can be developed using Java interfaces. IBM's MQSeries product is a popular messaging system for building platform-independent MOM systems. The Microsoft Message Queue Server (MSMQ) is a Microsoft platform-specific messaging solution integrated with the Windows NT platform.

As an example of MOM messaging using the IBM MQSeries product, a number of classes and interfaces can be used from the `com.ibm.mq` package libraries to perform basic message queuing. Message queuing first involves connecting to a middleware messaging server:

```
// Set up MQ environment hostname and channel (default port 1414)
MQEnvironment.hostname = "suppliers.BeeShirts.com";
MQEnvironment.channel  = "ServerChannel";

// Create a connection to the queue manager using MQ environment
MQQueueManager mqQueueManager = new MQQueueManager("SupplierManager");
```

We then open a specific queue on the message queue server:

```
// Set up the options on the queue we wish to open...
int openOptions = MQC.MQOO_INPUT_AS_Q_DEF | MQC.MQOO_OUTPUT ;
```

```
// Now specify the queue that we wish to open, and the open options...
MQQueue systemDefaultLocalQueue =
    mqQueueManager.accessQueue("SYSTEM.DEFAULT.LOCAL.QUEUE",
                               openOptions, null, null, null);
```

A particular message to send is also encapsulated using MOM APIs:

```
// Define a simple MQ message, and initialize it in UTF format...
MQMessage helloWorld = new MQMessage();
helloWorld.writeUTF("Hello World!");

// specify the message options as default
MQPutMessageOptions putMessageOptions = new MQPutMessageOptions();
```

The particular message is then added to the queue:

```
// put the message on the queue
systemDefaultLocalQueue.put(helloWorld,putMessageOptions);
```

On the message consumer side, we connect to a message queue in a fashion similar to the message producer. We then retrieve the message from the queue:

```
// First define an MQ message buffer to receive the message into...
MQMessage receivedMessage = new MQMessage();

// Set the get message options using default options...
MQGetMessageOptions getMessageOptions = new MQGetMessageOptions();

// Get the message off the queue with a max size of 1024...
systemDefaultLocalQueue.get(receivedMessage, getMessageOptions, 1024);

// Display the UTF message text
System.out.println("The message is: " + receivedMessage.readUTF());
```

On both sides of a message queuing application, the queue and connection to the centralized queue manager should be closed:

```
// Close the queue
systemDefaultLocalQueue.close();
// Disconnect from the queue manager
mqQueueManager.disconnect();
```

As you can see, use of MOM APIs for messaging can be rather straightforward with the help of MOM objects to provide a high-level interface to messaging. As you'll see in the next section, the Java Message Service also provides a means for interfacing with messaging systems and thus implements a standard Java-based interface to MOM.

Java Message Service

Java Message Service (JMS) is a Java API that defines how messaging clients can interface with underlying messaging service providers in a standard fashion. JMS also provides an interface that underlying messaging service providers implement to provide JMS services to clients. Thus, JMS follows the familiar model of providing both an application programmer interface and a service-provider interface to implement standard services akin to the model followed by JDBC, JNDI, and many other Java enterprise component interfaces.

The J2EE specification requires that the JMS API be included with a J2EE implementation, but a J2EE implementation is currently not required to provide any underlying service-provider implementation for JMS. JMS defines interfaces with transaction semantics that may be dependent on the Java Transaction Architecture and Java Transaction Service if transactions are supported. JMS also defines interfaces in which initial factory objects used to create JMS connections are retrieved from a naming service via JNDI.

JMS provides both a point-to-point and a publish-subscribe model of messaging. Point-to-point messaging is accomplished by the implementation of message queues to which a producer writes a message to be received by a consumer. Publish-subscribe messaging is accomplished by the implementation of a hierarchy of topical nodes to which producers publish messages and to which consumers can subscribe.

JMS provides a core abstract messaging architecture that is extended by both the point-to-point message queuing model and the publish-subscribe model. In this section, we cover the core JMS architecture, basic point-to-point message queuing model, and basic publish-subscribe model. We also illustrate the point-to-point and publish-subscribe models with concrete examples.

Core JMS Architecture

The core architecture behind JMS is depicted in Figure 22.7. Here we see that JNDI is used to create an initial context to a JMS connection factory that is then used to create connections to JMS-based service providers. Given a JMS connection, a particular session context can be retrieved to create message producers and message consumers. Messages sent from a producer to a consumer are associated with a particular endpoint destination. At the consumer end of a messaging session, filtering of messages can be achieved using a message selector `String`.

JMS Connections

Figure 22.8 depicts the detailed architecture behind JMS connections. JMS connections represent a connection between a JMS client and a JMS service provider's messaging server. The JMS connection-related interfaces shown here are base interfaces that are further extended for the two messaging models of JMS.

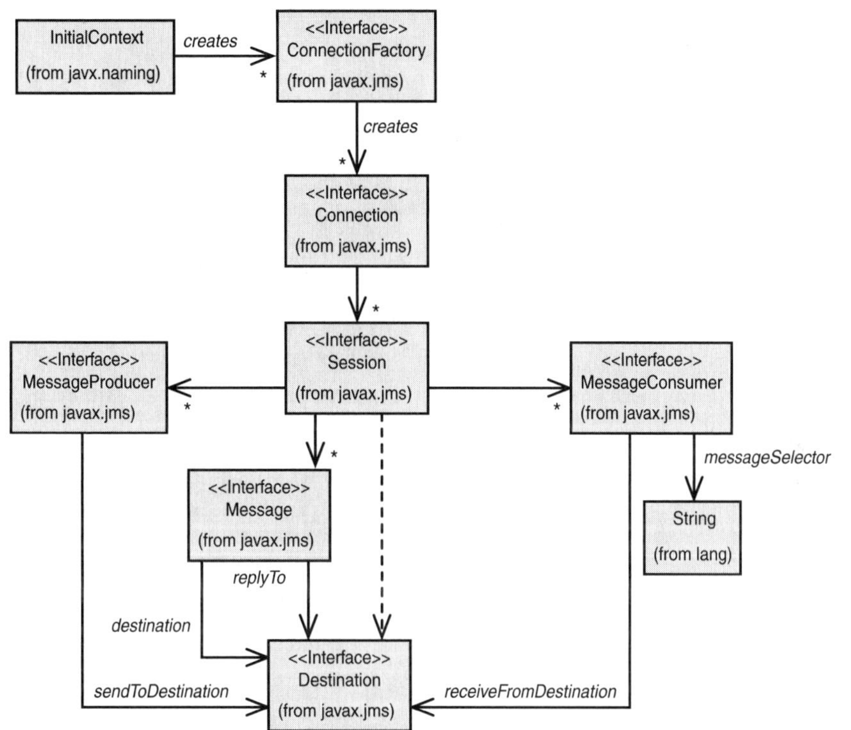

FIGURE 22.7
The JMS core architecture.

A `ConnectionFactory` interface is a marker interface used to create a connection to a particular JMS service provider's message service. JNDI is used to look up a handle to an initial `ConnectionFactory` object managed by a JMS service provider. Sub-interfaces of `ConnectionFactory` and objects that implement the `ConnectionFactory` interface provide methods for returning specific `Connection` object instances.

> **The J2EE and JMS**
>
> J2EE components can obtain handles to JMS connection factory objects via JNDI and subsequently obtain JMS `Connection` handles. Such a mechanism will be demonstrated in Chapter 37, "Advanced Enterprise JavaBeans Serving," when we describe how Enterprise JavaBeans obtain JMS connection factory handles from their middle-tier container/server environments.

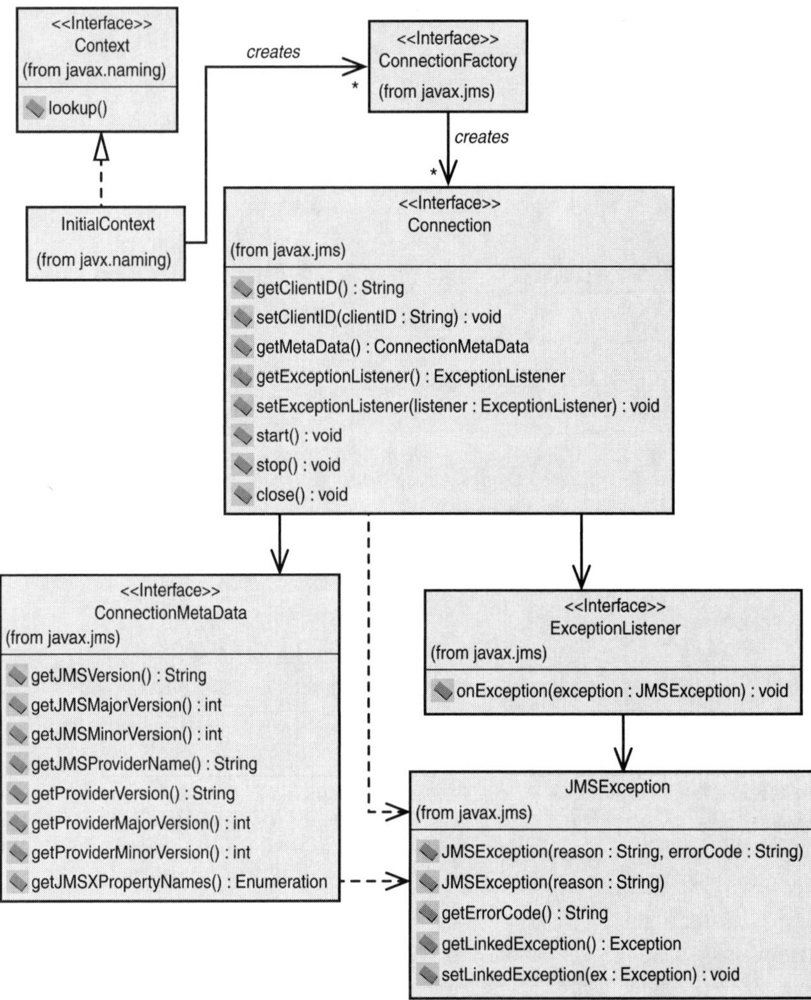

FIGURE 22.8
JMS connections.

A `Connection` interface encapsulates a JMS client's connection with a JMS service-provider instance. When a connection is created, it is in a "stopped" mode. That is, the consumers associated with the connection do not receive messages until `Connection.start()` is called. `Connection.stop()` can be used to return the connection to stopped mode. The `Connection.close()` method is called when the JMS client is finished with the connection and wants to clean up resources.

It should be noted that the JMSException class is an exception that is thrown by nearly every JMS API method call. It is also the root class for all other JMS exceptions. A JMSException can have a JMS service provider–specific error code String associated with it. A JMSException can also return its link to a lower-level exception that was responsible for the higher-level messaging exception.

A JMS client can be notified of asynchronously occurring exceptions that are associated with the connection. The JMS client can register an object implementing the ExceptionListener interface with the connection by calling the Connection.setExceptionListener() method. The ExceptionListener implements the single onException() method to be notified of the JMSException occurring on the connection. The listener may be retrieved by a call to Connection.getExceptionListener().

A JMS service provider–specific client ID associated with a connection can be retrieved with Connection.getClientID() and set with Connection.setClientID(). Typically, the client ID will be associated with a connection by the JMS service provider when creating the connection using the ConnectionFactory. If the JMS client attempts to set the client ID using setClientID(), an IllegalStateException should be thrown in the event that the ID set by the client is not permitted by the JMS service provider. If the client does attempt to set a client ID, it should be set immediately upon connection creation before any further actions are taken.

Meta-data about the connection can also be returned from the Connection object using the getMetaData() call. The ConnectionMetaData object that is returned can return the named version, major version numbers, and minor version numbers for both the JMS API and the service-provider code being used. Additionally, an enumeration of JMS properties associated with the connection can be returned from the ConnectionMetaData object.

JMS Sessions

Figure 22.9 depicts the core relations involved in JMS sessions. A JMS session is associated with a connection and represents a context within which messages are created. Messages can be encapsulated in their own transaction context by virtue of the session context.

The Session interface encapsulates the context within which JMS messages are created and received. The Session interface also extends the java.lang.Runnable interface, signifying that each session runs in the context of a single thread. Although it may not be immediately apparent in examining the Connection interface, a connection is used to create Session object instances. Objects implementing sub-interfaces of the Connection interface actually create object instances implementing sub-interfaces of the Session interface. The Session.close() method is used to close a session resource when the JMS client is finished with its use.

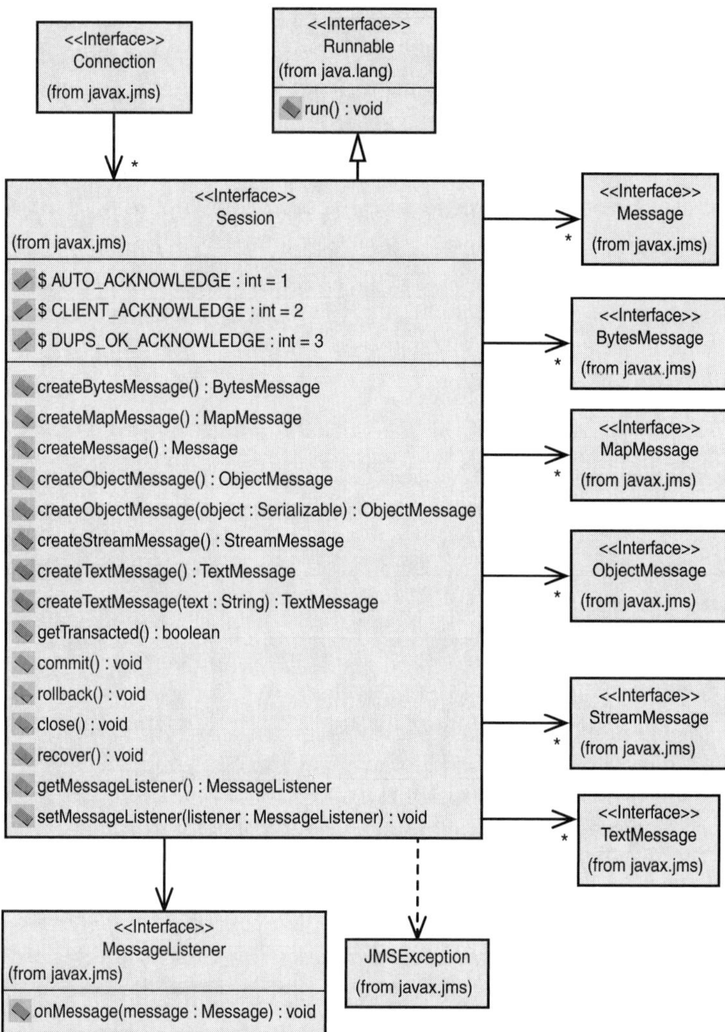

FIGURE 22.9
JMS sessions.

A set of `createXXXMessage()` methods on the `Session` interface are used to create instances of messages that are to be associated with a session. Messages that are created using the same `Session` object are optionally stored in the same session context until they are committed for delivery using the `Session.commit()` method if the particular `Session` object instance is transaction-sensitive. If `Session.rollback()` is called, the messages created within the context of this session are not sent. Such commit and rollback semantics ensure either that messages created within the same session context are all sent or that none are sent. The `Session.getTransacted()` method can be called to determine whether a session is transaction-aware via the return of a `boolean` value.

`Session` objects that are not transaction-aware require an acknowledgment that a message was received. Such messages are then marked as sent and will not be redelivered. Messages in transaction-aware sessions are delivered when they are sent and do not wait for a commit or rollback command to be issued on the session. Optionally, a `Session.recover()` method may be called to stop the current delivery of messages and restart the message delivery process for all messages that have yet to be acknowledged as delivered. Three `static public` constants designate the mode in which messages are sent:

- `AUTO_ACKNOWLEDGE`: The session automatically acknowledges that a message was received by the client.
- `CLIENT_ACKNOWLEDGE`: The session requires that the client explicitly acknowledge that it has received a message.
- `DUPS_OK_ACKNOWLEDGE`: The session acknowledges that a message was received by a client, but the overhead that it assumes to ensure that duplicate messages were not delivered is relaxed. Thus, duplicate messages may be sent to the client in the event of some failure.

Finally, a `MessageListener` interface implementation can also be associated with a `Session` object. The `MessageListener` implements an `onMessage()` method that takes a `Message` object as a parameter for any message that is received by this `Session` object. The `Session` object's `setMessageListener()` and `getMessageListener()` set and get the `MessageListener`, respectively.

JMS Messages

Figure 22.10 depicts the core interfaces and conceptual relations of the base JMS `Message` type. The `Message` interface is the root interface for all messages that flow through a JMS-based messaging system. The `Destination` interface is a marker interface used to represent an endpoint of message delivery. Because `Message` objects may have relationships to a destination and reply-to location, conceptual relationships with a `Destination` interface are shown in the diagram. Similarly, because a delivery mode for a message also exists, a conceptual relationship to a `DeliveryMode` interface is also shown.

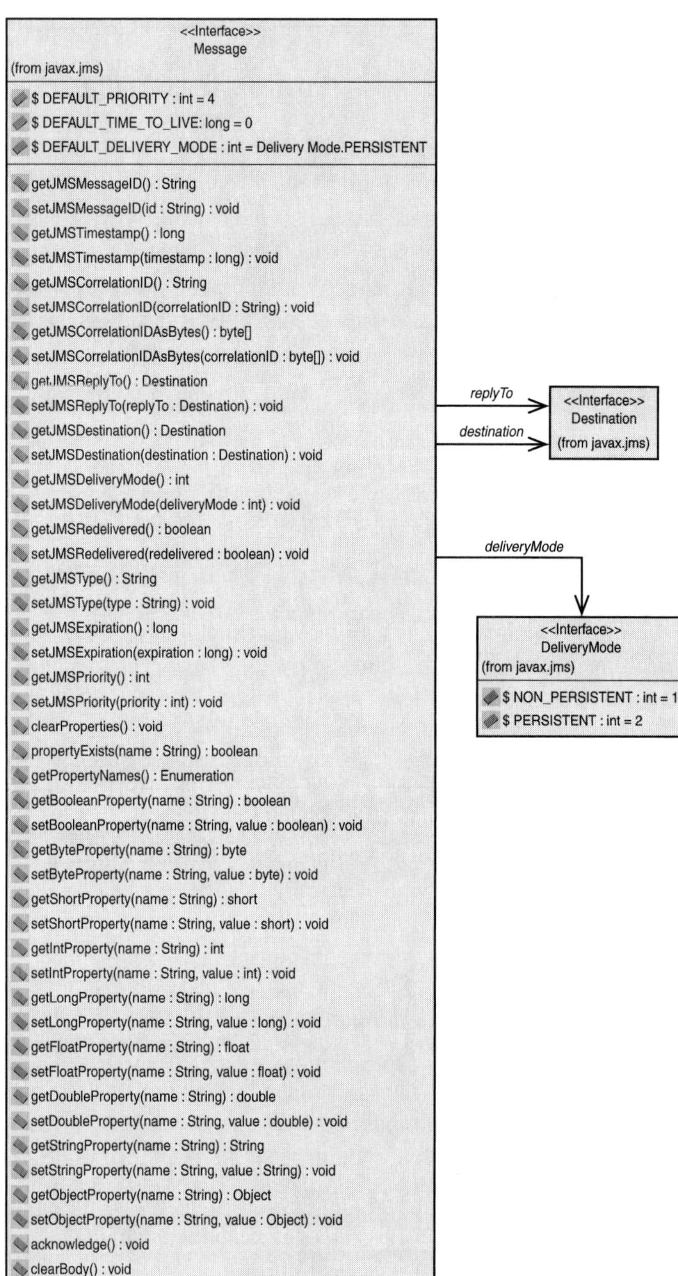

FIGURE 22.10
The JMS base message type.

These are the major elements of a message encapsulated by the `Message` interface:

- *Header*: The header is a collection of control information items used for routing and identification of messages.
- *Body*: The actual data content of the message.
- *Properties*: Optional application-specific properties of a message used to support an extensible set of message types.

Header information can be get or set using a standard getter and setter syntax of `getXXX()` and `setXXX()` where *XXX* is the name of a header property. Standard header properties defined as getters and setters on the `Message` interface are listed here:

- `JMSMessageID`: Unique ID associated with the message and beginning with the prefix `ID:`.
- `JMSTimestamp`: The time at which a message was sent.
- `JMSCorrelationID`: An identifier that can be used to link one message to another.
- `JMSCorrelationIDAsBytes`: A correlation identifier as an array of bytes.
- `JMSReplyTo`: A destination location to which a reply to this message should be sent.
- `JMSDestination`: A destination location to which a message is being sent.
- `JMSDeliveryMode`: The delivery mode of the message supported by the message service provider defined by `DeliveryMode.PERSISTENT` if the message is to be stored persistently during messaging or by `DeliveryMode.NON_PERSISTENT` if the message is to be cached in memory during messaging.
- `JMSRedelivered`: Indicates whether or not the message was sent in a previous transmission but has not yet been acknowledged.
- `JMSType`: The type of message.
- `JMSExpiration`: The time at which the message is to be considered expired. A default value of `0` indicates no expiration.
- `JMSPriority`: The priority of a message with `0` as the lowest priority and `9` as the highest priority.

By calling `Message.acknowledge()`, a client can acknowledge that the associated message and all previous messages associated with a session were received. The last message in a group of messages that is acknowledged designates that all previous messages were received in that group.

Provider-specific properties of a message can be get and set onto a message using a host of `getXXXProperty()` and `setXXXProperty()` methods, respectively, where *XXX* specifies the property type. Each property has a name identified by a `String` and a value of its specific type.

The existence of a named property can be tested using `Message.propertyExists(String)`. The `Message.getPropertyNames()` method returns an `Enumeration` of property names defined for this message. Property types supported are `boolean`, `byte`, `short`, `int`, `long`, `float`, `double`, and `String`.

This is the generic form of getter:

```
XXX getXXXProperty(String name) throws JMSException;
```

The `getObjectProperty()` method is the only exception to this rule. It allows retrieval of the types `Boolean`, `Byte`, `Short`, `Integer`, `Long`, `Float`, `Double`, and `String`.

This is the generic form of setter:

```
void setXXXProperty(String name, XXX value) throws JMSException;
```

The `setObjectProperty()` method is the only exception to this rule. It allows setting of the types `Boolean`, `Byte`, `Short`, `Integer`, `Long`, `Float`, `Double`, and `String`.

Property values are set before a message is sent and are in read-only mode when received by a client. A value written as a `byte`, `short`, `int`, or `long` can be read as a value of its own type or higher precision in the same type family. Thus, a `short`, for example, can be read as a `short`, an `int`, or a `long`. Values written as a `float` can be read as a `float` or `double`. All values can be read as a `String`, and `String` objects can possibly be read as another value of a particular type if they can be parsed into that type.

All properties can be removed from a message using the `Message.clearProperties()` method. When `clearProperties()` is called, the properties are no longer in read-only mode. If a client attempts to read a property when it is read-only, a `MessageNotWriteableException` is thrown.

Properties whose names begin with the `JMS_<provider_name>` prefix are reserved for the JMS service provider's defined properties. Properties whose names begin with the `JMSX` prefix are reserved for standard JMS properties. The properties `JMSXGroupID` and `JMSXGroupSeq` are required, but the remaining properties defined with the `JMSX` prefix are optional. The names of supported JMSX properties can be gotten from a call to `ConnectionMetaData.getJMSXPropertyNames()`. These are the standard JMSX properties:

- `JMSXGroupID`: Identifier for a group of messages.
- `JMSXGroupSeq`: Message sequence number for a message in a message group.
- `JMSXUserID`: User ID of the message sender.
- `JMSXAppID`: Identifier of the application that sent the message.
- `JMSXProducerTXID`: Identifier of the transaction that sent the message.

- `JMSXConsumerTXID`: Identifier of the transaction that received the message.
- `JMSXDeliveryCount`: Number of attempted deliveries of this message.
- `JMSXRcvTimestamp`: Time at which the message was sent to the consumer by the JMS service provider.
- `JMSXState`: Identifier for the state of a message in a service provider's message repository: waiting = `1`, ready = `2`, expired = `3`, and retained = `4`.

Five types of messages that extend the `Message` interface correspond to five types of message body data, as shown in Figure 22.11. Byte data is encapsulated by the `BytesMessage`, a `Serializable` object is encapsulated by the `ObjectMessage`, a `String` message is encapsulated by the `TextMessage`, key and value pairs are encapsulated by the `MapMessage`, and I/O streams are encapsulated by the `StreamMessage`. Individual methods on the message sub-interfaces define getters and setters for the type-specific data body, but a generic `clearBody()` method to clear the data body of a message and place it in write-only mode exists on the base `Message` interface.

These are the various message body specialization types:

- `BytesMessage`: Interface encapsulates a message whose body is a collection of bytes. Various `readXXX()` and `writeXXX()` methods defined in the `BytesMessage` interface are used to read and write specific types from and to the underlying byte stream, respectively. A `BytesMessage.reset()` call resets the pointer to the underlying byte stream and renders the object in read-only mode.
- `StreamMessage`: Interface encapsulates a message whose body is an underlying I/O stream of information. Various `readXXX()` and `writeXXX()` methods also exist on the `StreamMessage` interface to read and write specific types from and to the underlying stream, respectively. A `StreamMessage.reset()` call resets the pointer to the underlying stream and renders the object in read-only mode.
- `MapMessage`: Interface encapsulates a message whose body is an underlying collection of key and value pairs. A collection of `getXXX(String)` methods returns a typed value from the `MapMessage` given a particular `String` name. A collection of `setXXX(String, XXX)` methods sets a typed value into the `MapMessage` with a particular `String` name. The `getMapNames()` method returns an `Enumeration` of `String` key names associated with the `MapMessage`. The `itemExists(String)` method returns a `boolean` value indicating whether a particular `String` named value exists in the `MapMessage`.
- `ObjectMessage`: Interface encapsulates a message whose body is an underlying `Serializable` object. Has `getObject()` and `setObject()` methods.
- `TextMessage`: Interface encapsulates a message whose body is an underlying `String` value. Has `getText()` and `setText()` methods.

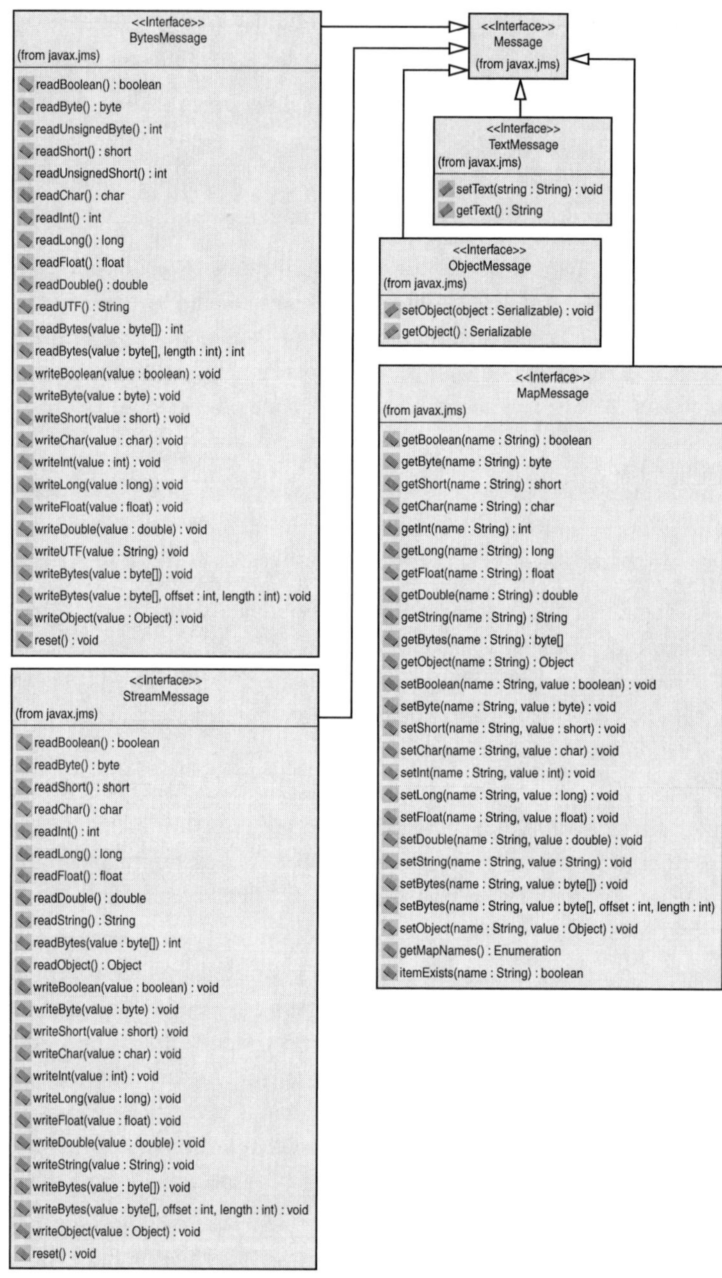

FIGURE 22.11

The JMS message body specialization types.

Message Producers, Consumers, and Selectors

JMS provides base encapsulations for message producers and consumers as shown in Figure 22.12. Message producers generate messages in a session context that are to be received by message consumers. Message consumers can filter which messages they receive using a message selector.

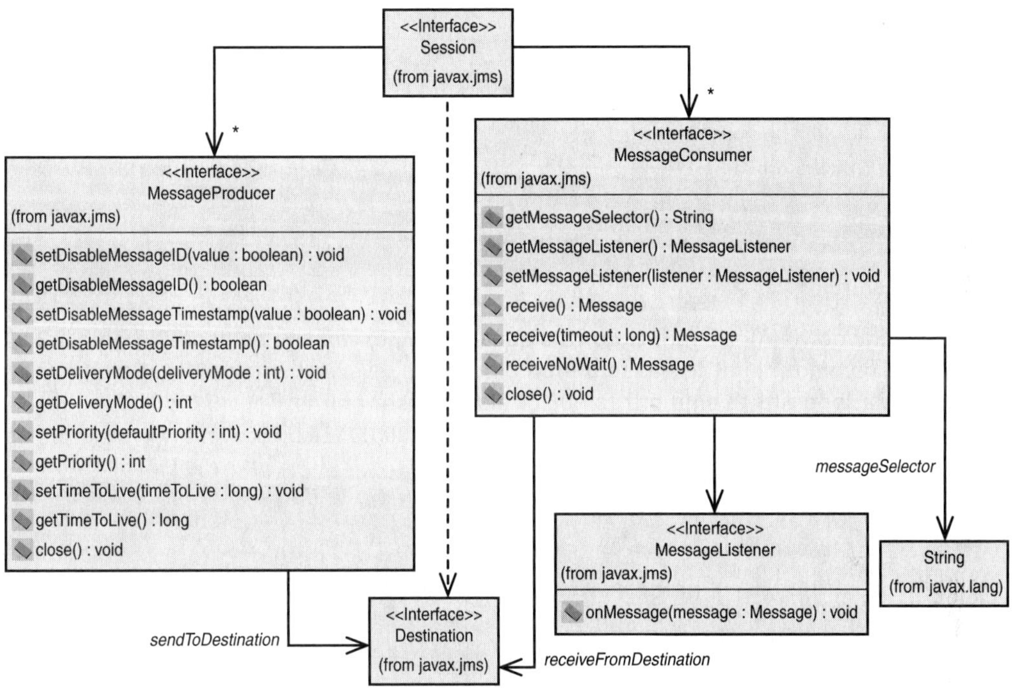

FIGURE 22.12
JMS message producers, consumers, and selectors.

The `MessageProducer` interface is the base interface for producers of messages. `MessageProducer` objects are created by passing a `Destination` for a message as an argument to a message producer creation method on a `Session` object. As you'll soon see, the actual method name and producer type that is returned is a function of the JMS messaging model being employed. Methods on the `MessageProducer` interface permit the setting and getting of a producer's default delivery mode, the associated message priority, and the time (in milliseconds) for which a message in the message system has to live. Setters also exist for disabling message ID and timestamps along with getters of these values.

The MessageConsumer interface is the base interface for consumers of messages. MessageConsumer objects are created by passing a Destination as an argument to a message consumer creation method on a Session object. As with the MessageProducer, method names and the message consumer type will vary per the particular JMS messaging model being used. The MessageConsumer also allows a MessageListener to be registered with it to independently receive messages for the MessageConsumer. The MessageConsumer.close() method is used to close the resources used to implement the message consumer by the service provider.

Various methods on the MessageConsumer are defined to receive messages from a destination. The MessageConsumer.receive() method blocks until a particular message is received for use by the consumer or until the MessageConsumer is closed. The MessageConsumer.receive(long) method can be used to specify a timeout in milliseconds for which the message consumer should wait to receive a message. MessageConsumer.receiveNoWait() can be called to receive a message only if it is immediately available and without blocking.

A MessageConsumer.getMessageSelector() call returns a String object defining a message selector. Message selectors define a filter that is used to determine which messages should be routed to a message consumer. For example, a particular message consumer may be interested only in receiving messages from a system administrator with a JMSXUserID property of admin. A message selector String is expressed in SQL92 syntax and can refer only to header and property information in a message. A selector is expressed using the following types of expression elements:

- *Literal*: A String in single quotes, a numeral, and boolean identifiers.
- *Identifier*: A sequence of letters and digits beginning with a letter that refers to a header name or property name in a message.
- *Whitespace*: A space, a tab, a form feed, or an end of line.
- *Expression*: Conditional, arithmetic, and Boolean expressions.
- *Brackets*: The () brackets group elements.
- *Operators*: Logical operators NOT, AND, OR. Comparison operators =, >, >=, <, <=, <>. Arithmetic operators unary +, unary -, *, /, +, -.
- BETWEEN: Use of BETWEEN operator to specify a range using *expression* [NOT] BETWEEN *expression* and *expression*.
- IN: Use of IN to specify inclusion in a set using *identifier* [NOT] IN (*literal*, *literal*, ...).
- LIKE: Use of LIKE to specify similarity in a pattern using *identifier* [NOT] LIKE *pattern*.
- IS: Use of IS for identifier IS [NOT] NULL.

Point-to-Point Message Queuing Model

Figure 22.13 depicts the basic JMS architecture elements that support point-to-point message queuing. The message queuing architecture is really an extension of the core JMS architecture with features to specifically implement message queuing behavior. Connection factories, connections, sessions, message producers, message consumers, and endpoint destinations are all extended with point-to-point message queuing model interfaces. Thus, by understanding the core JMS architecture presented earlier, you can most rapidly understand the specific point-to-point message queuing specializations presented here.

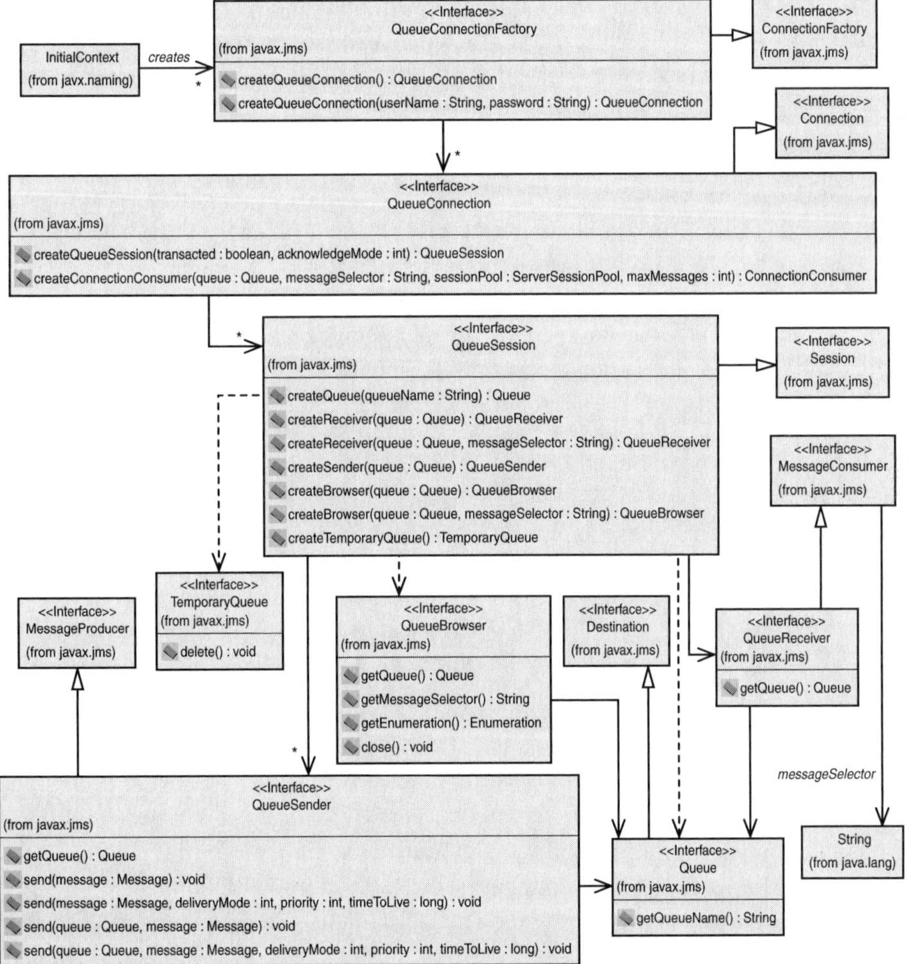

FIGURE 22.13
JMS point-to-point message queuing.

JMS clients use JNDI to obtain an initial reference to a named QueueConnectionFactory object. One of the QueueConnectionFactory.createQueueConnection() methods is used to create an instance of a QueueConnection object. The createQueueConnection() method can be called with a username and password or by using the parameterless version of the method with a default user identity assumed.

The QueueConnection interface is a type of Connection interface that represents a connection to a JMS point-to-point messaging queue service. The createConnectionConsumer() method is not used by regular JMS clients and is primarily used by an application server to manage queue service connections. The createQueueSession() method is called by JMS clients to create a QueueSession instance. Whether or not transactions are to be implemented by the QueueSession object is designated by a boolean parameter to createQueueSession(). Also, the acknowledgment mode is specified in the call to createQueueSession() using one of the static session identifiers, such as Session.AUTO_ACKNOWLEDGE, Session.CLIENT_ACKNOWLEDGE, or Session.DUPS_OK_ACKNOWLEDGE. The QueueSession interface extended from the Session interface implements various message queuing specific entity creation methods.

QueueSession.createQueue() creates an instance of a Queue object given a provider-specific name for that queue. Most service-provider implementations will provide other means for creating named queues, but this interface can be used by JMS clients for creating queues. The Queue interface encapsulates an interface to a queue destination using JMS's point-to-point messaging queue model and has a getQueueName() method to return the queue name. The QueueSession.createTemporaryQueue() method creates a TemporaryQueue object. The TemporaryQueue is deleted when its QueueConnection is closed.

The QueueSession.createBrowser() methods create an instance of a QueueBrowser object associated with a particular message queue. The QueueBrowser can be used to passively observe the contents of a particular message queue without modifying the queue contents. If the QueueBrowser was created with a message selector, only those messages identified in the message selector expression will be viewable. The getEnumeration() method returns the list of messages associated with the queue and perhaps refined by the message selector.

The QueueSession.createSender() method creates a QueueSender message producer that is used to send messages to a Queue. Messages can be sent to a Queue using the various QueueSender.send() methods. Variations of these methods enable the delivery of messages to the QueueSender object's associated Queue or to a newly specified Queue object passed to the send() method. Delivery modes, priorities, and time to live for a message can also be specified during calls to QueueSender.send(). Messages to send to a Queue can be created using the various message-creation methods defined on the Session interface from which QueueSession extends.

The `QueueSession.createReceiver()` methods create a `QueueReceiver` message consumer used to receive messages from a `Queue`. A variation of the `createReceiver()` method also permits the specification of a message selector to filter out which messages are received by the `QueueReceiver`. Above and beyond the built-in message consuming methods provided by the `QueueReceiver` interface's base `MessageConsumer` interface, a `QueueReceiver.getQueue()` method returns a handle to the associated `Queue`.

Extending the BeeShirts.com Example Data Model

Before we introduce a concrete example illustrating how JMS can be used in an enterprise application, we need to extend our BeeShirts.com model beyond what has been introduced thus far in the book. Figure 22.14 depicts our addition of a `SUPPLIER` table to persist data related to a BeeShirts.com business-to-business (B2B) partner that supplies particular T-shirts retailed by BeeShirts.com. The BeeShirts.com server software sends asynchronous messages to a JMS server that handles distributing these messages to the appropriate supplier. A `SUPPLIER` table contains contact information for a supplier, as well as a flag indicating whether the `SUPPLIER` is currently an active supplier. To support the relationship between a supplier and a requested T-shirt item, the `TSHIRT` table is also augmented with a foreign key to reference the particular `SUPPLIER`.

NOTE

The complete data model can be found in Appendix A, "Software Configuration," but here we only introduce an augmentation to the model above and beyond what has already been introduced. Appendix A also contains scripts for configuring the database to support the schema assumed by this book, as well as for configuring the database with some sample data.

Recall that the `TSHIRT` table first presented in Figure 10.1 of Chapter 10, "Advanced JDBC," was defined with a `PICTURE_FRONT` and `PICTURE_BACK` column that assumed SQL `BLOB` types. We defined the `TSHIRT` table in that way to illustrate advanced SQL type access via JDBC 2.0. Figure 22.14 depicts the `TSHIRT` table representation as it is used throughout all other chapters except Chapter 10. Here, the `TSHIRT` table's `PICTURE_FRONT` and `PICTURE_BACK` columns assume SQL `VARCHAR` types.

Point-to-Point Message Queuing Example

We present a brief examplehere to illustrate the use of JMS point-to-point message queuing. Our example implements a `QueueSupplier` that would typically sit on the server-side of BeeShirts.com. It submits `OrderRequest` objects to `Queue` objects managed by a JMS service provider that correspond to T-shirt suppliers. A T-shirt supplier implements a `QueueConsumer` that plucks `OrderRequest` objects from the `Queue`.

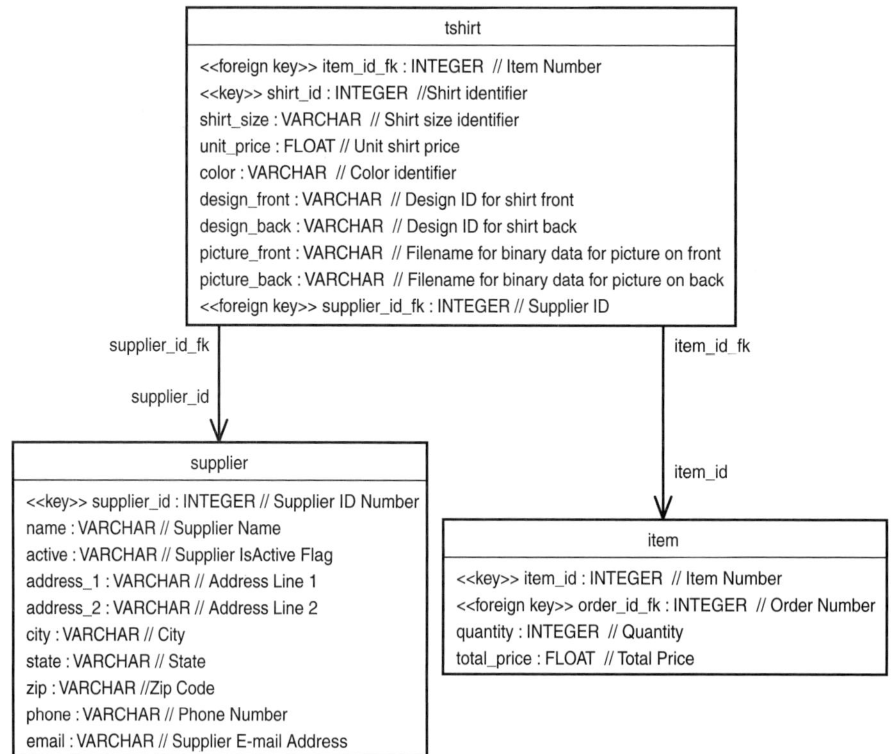

FIGURE 22.14
The BeeShirts.com supplier, T-shirt, and items data model.

NOTE

The sample code strewn throughout this section leaves out some exception handling and other non-essential features in the interest of simplifying the description. The complete set of code examples for this JMS message queue example can be found on the CD-ROM in the `examples\src\ejava\messagech22\jms` directory. The `QueueSupplier.java` and `QueueConsumer.java` files implement this example, and an `OrderRequest.java` and `OrderManager.java` class are also used. The `runqueue.bat` file can be used as a sample script for executing the example. The `CLOUDSCAPE_LIB` environment variable must be set to the library directory for your Cloudscape database installation as described in Appendix A. The `jmsch22.properties` file is used to configure the example.

Note that we use the JMS service-provider implementation equipped with the BEA WebLogic Server product. The `WEBLOGIC_HOME` environment variable must be set to the root directory of your WebLogic installation to run our example scripts. See Appendix A for instructions on configuration of the BEA WebLogic Server.

Note also that for all JMS examples, the `[EJAVA_HOME]\examples\classes` directory should be in your `CLASSPATH` as it is set in our example script files. You will also want to clean your `[EJAVA_HOME]\examples\classes` directory before running our example scripts.

Order Request

An `OrderRequest` class implements a `Serializable` object encapsulating a BeeShirts.com T-shirt order request message. The `OrderRequest` has a size, the design of the T-shirt front, the design of the T-shirt back, a T-shirt color, and an order quantity. Aside from a set of public `OrderRequest` attributes, an `OrderRequest.toString()` prints the order request contents:

```
package ejava.msch22.jms;
import java.io.Serializable;

public class OrderRequest implements Serializable
{
  public String size;
  public String designFront;
  public String designBack;
  public String color;
  public int    howMany;

  public String toString()
  {
    return "Size :"+ size + " Design Front :" + designFront
      + " Design Back :" +  designBack + " Color :" +color
      +" How Many : "+howMany;
  }
}
```

Order Manager

We won't list the details behind the `OrderManager` JDBC helper class here because its single `getNewOrders()` method is a rather long method that has nothing to do with demonstrating JMS. The `getNewOrders()` method implementation can be found on the CD. After reading a set of database connection properties from the `Properties` object passed to it, it creates a JDBC connection. A list of distinct BeeShirts.com suppliers is then queried from the database. For each distinct supplier, the T-shirt supply information is queried for that supplier, and the number of T-shirts of the desired kind available from that supplier is retrieved. If the number of available shirts is less than a maximum value, an `OrderRequest` object is created with a queue name associated with that supplier. The queue name serves as a key to the `Hashtable` for each `OrderRequest` entry, and the `Hashtable` is returned from the `getNewOrders()` method call.

Queue Supplier

The `QueueSupplier.main()` method reads a set of properties from the `jmsch22.properties` filename passed in from the command line and uses these properties in a call to obtain a `Hashtable` of new BeeShirts.com order requests using the `OrderManager.getNewOrders()` call. For each queue name in the `Hashtable` of orders, a queue is created and an order request is sent within the `createAQueueAndSendOrder()` method. The `QueueSupplier.main()` method is shown here:

```
public static void main(String[] args)
{
  if (args.length != 1) {
    System.out.println("Usage: "+
      "java ejva.messagech22.jms.QueueServicer jmsch22.properties");
    return;
  }
  Properties properties = new Properties();
  String fileName = args[0];

    // Load properties
    FileInputStream fin = new FileInputStream(fileName);
    properties.load(fin);
    fin.close();
    // Get new orders from database using order manager class
    Hashtable newOrders = OrderManager.getNewOrders(properties);
    Enumeration keys = newOrders.keys();
    // For each order, get order request and send to consumer
    while(keys.hasMoreElements()){
      String queueName = (String)keys.nextElement();
      OrderRequest orderRequest =
        (OrderRequest)newOrders.get(queueName);
      createAQueueAndSendOrder(properties,queueName,orderRequest);
    }
  // exception handling excluded here...
}
```

The `createAQueueAndSendOrder()` method called from `main()` first creates an `InitialContext` reference with a call to `getInitialContext()` using the properties object created in `main()`. A new `QueueSupplier` instance is then created given the properties, context reference, and queue name. The `QueueSupplier.send()` then sends the message. The `QueueSupplier.close()` and `Context.close()` methods close up resources before returning. The `createAQueueAndSendOrder()` method is shown here:

```
private static void createAQueueAndSendOrder(Properties properties,
  String queueName, OrderRequest orderRequest)
{
    InitialContext context = getInitialContext(properties);
    QueueSupplier queueSupplier =
      new QueueSupplier(properties, context, queueName);
    queueSupplier.send(orderRequest);
    queueSupplier.close();
    context.close();

   // Exception handling here...
}
```


The `getInitialContext()` method simply creates and returns a JNDI `InitialContext` reference using the properties passed to the `getInitialContext()` method. The properties that are read in from the `jmsch22.properties` file specify WebLogic's JNDI SPI with a `JNDI_FACTORY` property set to `weblogic.jndi.WLInitialContextFactory` and a `JNDI_PROVIDER_URL` set to the IP address and port on which the WebLogic naming service is running (for example, `t3://localhost:7001/`). After the context is retrieved, the `QueueSupplier.context` variable is set. The `getInitialContext()` method is shown here:

```
private static InitialContext getInitialContext(Properties properties)
     throws NamingException
{
  Hashtable env = new Hashtable();
  String jndiFactory = (String)properties.get("JNDI_FACTORY");
  String providerURL  = (String)properties.get("JNDI_PROVIDER_URL");
  env.put(Context.INITIAL_CONTEXT_FACTORY, jndiFactory);
  env.put(Context.PROVIDER_URL, providerURL);
  return new InitialContext(env);
}
```

The `QueueSupplier` constructor is where all messaging queue initialization is performed on the supplier side. A reference to a WebLogic JMS `QueueConnectionFactory` is first looked up from the JNDI context using the `JMS_FACTORY_FOR_QUEUE` property of `javax.jms.QueueConnectionFactory`. A `QueueConnection` and `QueueSession` are then created. The `Queue` is created and bound to JNDI if it cannot be looked up using JNDI. Finally, a `QueueSender` is created. The `QueueConnectionFactory`, `QueueConnection`, `QueueSession`, `Queue`, and `QueueSender` objects are all saved as private variables in this `QueueSupplier` class. The `QueueSupplier` constructor is shown here:

```
public QueueSupplier(Properties defaultProperties, Context context,
  String queueName)
  throws NamingException, JMSException
{
  properties = defaultProperties;
  String jmsFactoryName = (
     String)properties.get("JMS_FACTORY_FOR_QUEUE");
  // Create Queue Connection Factory
  queueConnectionFactory = (QueueConnectionFactory)
    context.lookup(jmsFactoryName);

  // Create Queue Connection to The Factory
  queueConnection = queueConnectionFactory.createQueueConnection();

  // Create Session to the Connection
  queueSession = queueConnection.createQueueSession(false,
    Session.AUTO_ACKNOWLEDGE);

  try {
    // if already created queue
    queue = (Queue) context.lookup(queueName);
  } catch (NamingException namingException) {
    // if needed to create new Queue
    queue = queueSession.createQueue(queueName);
    // bind the queue with a name
    context.bind(queueName, queue);
  }
  // Create Receiver
  queueSender = queueSession.createSender(queue);
}
```

The `QueueSupplier.send()` method sends an object to a JMS queue. In our sample case, the object is always the `OrderRequest` object called from the `createAQueueAndSendOrder()` method. To illustrate two types of message sending, if the object passed to `send()` was a `String`, we create a `TextMessage` and send it using our `QueueSender`. Otherwise, we create an `ObjectMessage` with the object and send it using our `QueueSender`:

```
public void send(Object newMessage)
     throws JMSException
{
  if(newMessage instanceof String){
    TextMessage sendingMessage = queueSession.createTextMessage();
    queueConnection.start();
    sendingMessage.setText((String)newMessage);
    queueSender.send(sendingMessage);
  }else {
```

```
        ObjectMessage sendingMessage = queueSession.createObjectMessage();
        queueConnection.start();
        sendingMessage.setObject((Serializable)newMessage);
        queueSender.send(sendingMessage);
    }
  }
```

Finally, our `QueueSupplier.close()` method simply cleans up `QueueSender`, `QueueSession`, and `QueueConnection` resources:

```
  public void close()
       throws JMSException
  {
    queueSender.close();
    queueSession.close();
    queueConnection.close();
  }
```


Queue Consumer

Our sample `QueueConsumer` represents a T-shirt supplier that the BeeShirts.com application, represented by the `QueueSupplier`, talks to. The `QueueConsumer` has a queue named `PureShirts` that the `QueueSupplier` uses to place an order request with the T-shirt supplier. The `QueueConsumer.main()` method reads a set of properties from the `jmsch22.properties` filename passed in from the command line. A JNDI context is then created with these properties with a call to `getInitialContext()`. The `QueueConsumer` is then constructed with the properties and JNDI context as parameters. The `QueueConsumer` then receives messages until the user exits the program and the `QueueConsumer.quitFromReceiving` flag is set. Finally, `QueueConsumer.close` resources are cleaned up, along with the JNDI context. The `QueueConsumer.main()` method is shown here:

```
   public static void main(String[] args)
       throws Exception
  {
    if (args.length != 1) {
      System.out.println("Usage: "+
        "java ejva.messagech22.jms.QueueConsumer jmsch22.properties");
      return;
    }
    // Load properties
    Properties properties = new Properties();
    String fileName = args[0];

      FileInputStream fin = new FileInputStream(fileName);
      properties.load(fin);
      fin.close();
```

```
        // Exception handling excluded...

        // Create initial context and queue consumer
        InitialContext context = getInitialContext(properties);
        QueueConsumer queueConsumer =
          new QueueConsumer(properties, context);
        System.out.println(" Queue Client is ready to receive Message");
        // Wait for messages to receive, until user quits from program.
        synchronized(queueConsumer) {
          while (! queueConsumer.quitFromReceiving) {
              queueConsumer.wait();
              // Exception handling excluded...
          }
        }
        queueConsumer.close();
        context.close();
        System.exit(0);

      // Exception handling excluded...
  }
```

The `getInitialContext()` method used to obtain a handle to the initial WebLogic JNDI context for `QueueConsumer` is identical to the `getInitialContext()` method for the `QueueSupplier`. The `QueueConsumer` constructor looks up the `QueueConnectionFactory`, creates a `QueueConnection`, creates a `QueueSession`, and looks up or creates a `Queue` in a fashion also similar to the `QueueSupplier`. The `QUEUE_NAME` property is retrieved from the `jmsch22.properties` file and is initially set to `PureShirts`. The `QueueConsumer` then creates a `QueueReceiver` and registers itself as a `MessageListener` with the `QueueReceiver`. The `QueueConnection` is then initialized to start receiving messages. The `QueueConsumer` constructor initialization is shown here:

```
  public QueueConsumer(Properties defaultProperties, Context context)
    throws NamingException, JMSException
  {
    properties = defaultProperties;
    String jmsFactoryName =
        (String)properties.get("JMS_FACTORY_FOR_QUEUE");

    // Create Queue Connection Factory
    queueConnectionFactory = (QueueConnectionFactory)
      context.lookup(jmsFactoryName);

    // Create Queue Connection to The Factory
    queueConnection = queueConnectionFactory.createQueueConnection();
```

```
    // Create Session to the Connection
    queueSession = queueConnection.createQueueSession(false,
      Session.AUTO_ACKNOWLEDGE);

    String queueName = (String)properties.get("QUEUE_NAME");
    try {
      queue = (Queue) context.lookup(queueName);
    } catch (NamingException namingException) {
      // if not created, create new queue
      queue = queueSession.createQueue(queueName);
      // bind the queue with a name
      context.bind(queueName, queue);
    }

    // Create Receiver
    queueReceiver = queueSession.createReceiver(queue);
    // Register QueueConsumer as Message Listener
    queueReceiver.setMessageListener(this);
    // Start Receiving Message
    queueConnection.start();
  }
```


Because the `QueueConsumer` is a message listener by virtue of implementing `MessageListener`, it must implement the `onMessage(Message)` method. The `QueueConsumer.onMessage()` is called when the JMS service provider receives an `OrderRequest` from the `QueueSupplier`. The `onMessage()` method will first display information from the received `Message` header and then display the message body information, depending on whether it is a `TextMessage` or an `ObjectMessage`. After it receives a message, we induce an exit from the program by setting the `QueueConsumer.quitFromReceiving` flag to `true`. The `onMessage()` implementation is shown here:

```
  public void onMessage(Message message)
  {
    try {
      // print information about the message
      System.out.println(message.getJMSMessageID());
      System.out.println("MessageID :" + message.getJMSMessageID() +
                          " for " + message.getJMSDestination());
      System.out.print("Message Expires        ");
      if (message.getJMSExpiration() > 0) {
          System.out.println( new Date( message.getJMSExpiration()));
      }
      else{
          System.out.println("never  Expires ");
```

```
        }
        System.out.println("Priority :" + message.getJMSPriority());
        System.out.println("Mode    : " + (
          message.getJMSDeliveryMode() == DeliveryMode.PERSISTENT ?
          "PERSISTENT" : "NON_PERSISTENT"));
        System.out.println("Reply to :       " + message.getJMSReplyTo());
        System.out.println("Message type :   " + message.getJMSType());
        if (message instanceof TextMessage) {
          String receivedMessage = ((TextMessage)message).getText();
          System.out.println("Received Message :" + receivedMessage);

        } else if(message instanceof ObjectMessage){
          String receivedMessage = message.toString();
          System.out.println("Received Message :" + receivedMessage);
        }
        quitFromReceiving = true;
        notifyAll(); // notify to main Thread to leave from the program
      }
      catch (JMSException jmsException) {
        jmsException.printStackTrace();
      }
    }
```

Finally, all `QueueReceiver`, `QueueSession`, and `QueueConnection` resources are closed:

```
public void close()
     throws JMSException
{
  this.queueReceiver.close();
  this.queueSession.close();
  this.queueConnection.close();
}
```

Publish-Subscribe Model

Figure 22.15 depicts the basic JMS architecture elements that support publish-subscribe messaging. The publish-subscribe messaging architecture is also an extension of the core JMS architecture with features specialized to suit a publish-subscribe messaging model. Connection factories, connections, sessions, message producers, message consumers, and endpoint destinations are all extended with publish-subscribe message model interfaces.

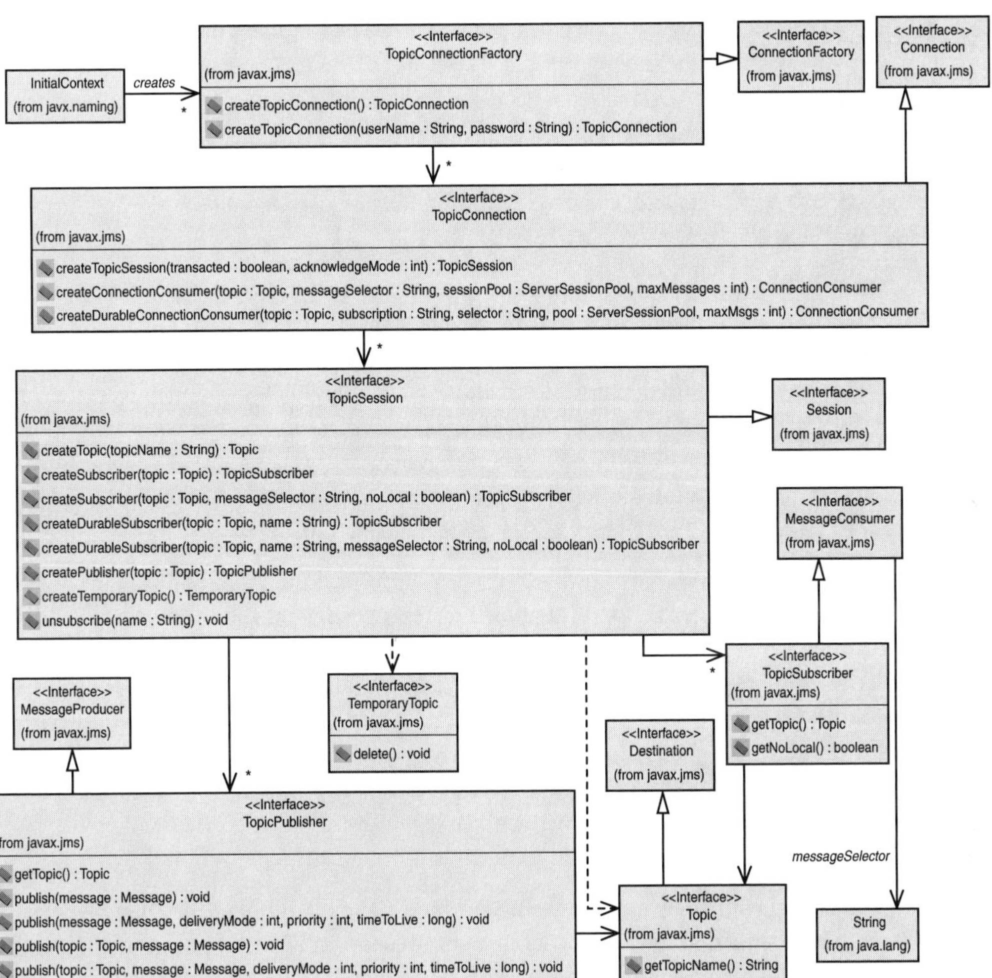

FIGURE 22.15
JMS publish-subscribe messaging.

JMS clients use JNDI to obtain an initial reference to a named `TopicConnectionFactory` object. The `TopicConnectionFactory.createTopicConnection()` methods are used to create an instance of a `TopicConnection` object. The `createTopicConnection()` method can be called with a username and password or by using the parameterless version of the method with a default user identity assumed.

The TopicConnection interface is a type of Connection interface that represents a connection to a JMS publish-subscribe messaging service. The createConnectionConsumer() and createDurableConnectionConsumer() methods are not used by regular JMS clients and are primarily used by an application server to manage publish-subscribe message service connections. The createTopicSession() method is called by JMS clients to create a TopicSession instance. Session transactions and acknowledgment mode are also established during the creation of a TopicSession.

TopicSession.createTopic() creates an instance of a Topic object given a provider-specific name for a topic. As with creating queues using QueueSession, the creation of named topics is something that will be provided using other means by most service-provider implementations. The Topic interface encapsulates a topic destination to which publishers publish messages and from which subscribers subscribe to receive messages. Different service providers will implement a hierarchy of topic names differently, but a Topic.getTopicName() can be used to obtain the String representation of the topic. The TopicSession.createTemporaryTopic() method creates a TemporaryTopic object. The TemporaryTopic is deleted when its TopicConnection is closed.

The TopicSession.createPublisher() method creates a TopicPublisher message producer that is used to publish messages to a particular Topic. Messages can be published to a Topic using the various TopicPublisher.publish() methods. Variations of these methods enable the publishing of messages to a TopicPublisher object's associated Topic or to a newly specified Topic object passed to the publish() method. Delivery modes, priorities, and time to live for a message can also be specified during calls to TopicPublisher.publish(). Messages to publish to a Topic can be created using the various message-creation methods defined on the Session interface from which TopicSession extends.

Two types of TopicSubscriber creation methods exist on TopicSession. The TopicSession.createSubscriber() methods create nondurable TopicSubscriber instances. Nondurable TopicSubscribers are those subscribers who receive notification only of published messages to which they have subscribed while the subscriber is active. Durable subscribers are those who can receive messages later even after they were temporarily unavailable; they can be created using the TopicSession.createDurableSubscriber() calls. Durable subscribers have a name associated with the published messages stored for their deferred notification. Versions of TopicSession.createSubscriber() and TopicSession.createDurableSubscriber() exist to also enable use of message selector filters and a boolean noLocal flag indicating that messages published by their own connection should be ignored.

Publish-Subscribe Example

We present a brief example here to illustrate the use of JMS publish-subscribe messaging. Our example implements a `TopicSupplier` implemented on the BeeShirts.com server side to publish `OrderRequest` objects to a `TshirtsSupplier` topic name. A `TopicConsumer` mimics a sample T-shirts supplier's `TopicSubscriber` which subscribes to receive `OrderRequest` messages.

NOTE

The sample code strewn throughout this section leaves out some exception handling and other non-essential features in the interest of keeping the description simple. The complete set of code examples for this JMS message publish-subscribe example can be found on the CD-ROM in the `examples\src\ejava\messagech22\jms` directory. The `TopicSupplier.java` and `TopicConsumer.java` files implement this example, and an `OrderRequest.java` and `OrderManager.java` class are also used. The `runtopic.bat` file can be used as a sample script for executing the example. The `CLOUDSCAPE_LIB` environment variable must be set to the library directory for your Cloudscape database installation as described in Appendix A. The `jmsch22.properties` file is used to configure the example.

Note that we use the JMS service-provider implementation equipped with the BEA WebLogic Server product. The `WEBLOGIC_HOME` environment variable must be set to the root directory of your WebLogic installation to run our example scripts. See Appendix A for instructions on configuration of the BEA WebLogic Server.

Note also that for all JMS examples, the `[EJAVA_HOME]\examples\classes` directory should be in your `CLASSPATH` as it is set in our example script files. You will also want to clean your `[EJAVA_HOME]\examples\classes` directory before running our example scripts.

Topic Supplier

The `TopicSupplier.main()` method reads in properties from the `jmsch22.properties` file and retrieves the `Hashtable` of orders from the `OrderManager.getNewOrders()` call. For each key name in the `Hashtable`, a call to `createATopicAndPublishOrder()` is made with an extracted `OrderRequest`:

```
public static void main(String[] args)
     throws Exception
{
  if (args.length != 1) {
    System.out.println("Usage: java ejava.messagech22.TopicSupplier"+
     " jmsch22.Properties");
```

```
        return;
      }

      Properties properties = new Properties();
      String fileName = args[0];
        // Read properties file info
        FileInputStream fin = new FileInputStream(fileName);
        properties.load(fin);
        fin.close();

        // Get The Orders if any
        Hashtable newOrders = OrderManager.getNewOrders(properties);
        Enumeration keys = newOrders.keys();
        // For each order, create order request and publish it
        while(keys.hasMoreElements()){
          String key = (String)keys.nextElement();
          OrderRequest orderRequest =
            (OrderRequest)newOrders.get(key);
          createATopicAndPublishOrder(properties,orderRequest);
        }

        // Exception handling excluded here...
    }
```

The `TopicSupplier.createATopicAndPublishOrder()` method obtains a JNDI context via a call to `getInitialContext()` in the same fashion as was performed by the `QueueSupplier` and `QueueConsumer`. Subsequently, a `TopicSupplier` instance is created and a call to `send()` on that instance is made to publish a message to a topic. Finally, the `TopicSupplier.close()` and `Context.close()` methods are called to clean up resources. The `createATopicAndPublishOrder()` is shown here:

```
public static void createATopicAndPublishOrder(Properties properties,
   OrderRequest orderRequest)
{
     InitialContext context = getInitialContext(properties);
     TopicSupplier topicSupplier =
       new TopicSupplier(properties, context);
     topicSupplier.send(orderRequest);
     topicSupplier.close();
     context.close();
   // Exception handling excluded...
}
```

Inside the `TopicSupplier` constructor, a `TopicConnectionFactory` is looked up from the JNDI context with a property filename of `JMS_FACTORY_FOR_TOPIC` mapping to a value of `javax.jms. TopicConnectionFactory`. The `TopicConnectionFactory` is then used to create a

TopicConnection, which in turn is used to create a TopicSession. A Topic is then created and bound to JNDI if it cannot be looked up using JNDI. The topic name used is TshirtsSuppliers read from the property TOPIC_NAME. Finally, a TopicPublisher is created. The TopicConnectionFactory, TopicConnection, TopicSession, Topic, and TopicSender objects are all saved as private variables in this TopicSupplier class. The TopicSupplier constructor is shown here:

```
public TopicSupplier(Properties defaultProperties, Context context)
  throws NamingException, JMSException
{
  properties = defaultProperties;
  String jmsFactoryName =
      (String)properties.get("JMS_FACTORY_FOR_TOPIC");
  // get TopicFactory
  topicConnectionFactory = (TopicConnectionFactory)
    context.lookup(jmsFactoryName);
  // Get TopicConnection
  topicConnection = topicConnectionFactory.createTopicConnection();
  // Get Session for the Connection
  topicSession = topicConnection.createTopicSession(false,
        Session.AUTO_ACKNOWLEDGE);
  topicName = (String)defaultProperties.get("TOPIC_NAME");
  try {
    // determine if topic by this name already exists
    topic = (Topic) context.lookup(topicName);
  } catch (NamingException namingException) {
    // if not there create new topic
    topic = topicSession.createTopic(topicName);
    // bind the topic with a name
    context.bind(topicName, topic);
  }
  topicPublisher = topicSession.createPublisher(topic);
}
```

The TopicSupplier.send() method publishes an object to a JMS topic. In our sample case, the object is always the OrderRequest object called from the createATopicAndPublishOrder() method. The published ObjectMessage is published using the created TopicPublisher, which publishes messages to the TshirtsSuppliers topic name:

```
public void send(Object newMessage)
     throws JMSException
{
  if(newMessage instanceof String){
    TextMessage sendingMessage = topicSession.createTextMessage();
    topicConnection.start();  // start Sending
    sendingMessage.setText((String)newMessage); // set the Text message
```

```
      topicPublisher.publish(sendingMessage); // send Message
    }else {
      ObjectMessage sendingMessage = topicSession.createObjectMessage();
      topicConnection.start();   // start Sending
      sendingMessage.
        setObject((Serializable)newMessage); // set Object Message
      topicPublisher.publish(sendingMessage); // send message
    }
  }
```

Finally, the `TopicSupplier.close()` method closes its `TopicPublisher`, `TopicSession`, and `TopicConnection` resources:

```
  public void close()
       throws JMSException
  {
    topicPublisher.close();
    topicSession.close();
    topicConnection.close();
  }
```

Topic Consumer

The sample `TopicConsumer` represents a T-shirt supplier that subscribes to receive orders from the `TshirtsSuppliers` topic. The `TopicConsumer.main()` method reads a set of properties from the `jmsch22.properties` filename passed in from the command line. A JNDI context is then created with these properties with a call to `getInitialContext()`. The `TopicConsumer` is then constructed with the properties and JNDI context as parameters. The `TopicConsumer` receives messages until the user exits the program and the `TopicConsumer.quitFromReceiving` flag is set. Finally, `TopicConsumer.close()` ensures that all resources are cleaned up along with the JNDI context. The `TopicConsumer.main()` method is shown here:

```
 public static void main(String[] args)
       throws Exception
  {
    if (args.length != 1) {
      System.out.println("Usage: "+
        "java ejva.messagech22.jms.QueueClient jmsch22.properties");
      return;
    }
    Properties properties = new Properties();
    String fileName = args[0];
      // Read properties file
      FileInputStream fin = new FileInputStream(fileName);
      properties.load(fin);
```

```
    fin.close();
    // Create context and topic consumer
    InitialContext context = getInitialContext(properties);
    TopicConsumer topicConsumer =
      new TopicConsumer(properties, context);
    System.out.println(" Topic Client is ready to receive Message");
    // Wait for messages to be received, until user quits from program.
    synchronized(topicConsumer) {
      while (! topicConsumer.quitFromReceiving) {
        try {
          topicConsumer.wait();
        }
        catch (InterruptedException interruptedException){

          System.out.println(" Error :"+ interruptedException);
          interruptedException.printStackTrace();
        }
      }
    }
    topicConsumer.close();
    context.close();
    System.exit(0);

    // Exception handling here...
}
```


The `getInitialContext()` method to obtain a handle to the initial WebLogic JNDI context for a `TopicConsumer` is identical to the `getInitialContext()` method for the `QueueSupplier`. The `TopicConsumer` constructor also looks up the `TopicConnectionFactory`, creates a `TopicConnection`, creates a `TopicSession`, and looks up or creates a `Topic` in a fashion similar to the `TopicSupplier`. That is, the `TOPIC_NAME` property used is retrieved from the `jmsch22.properties` file and is set to `TshirtsSuppliers`. The `TopicConsumer` then creates a `TopicSubscriber` and registers itself as a `MessageListener` with the `TopicSubscriber`. The `TopicConnection` is then initialized to start receiving published messages. The `TopicConsumer` constructor initialization is shown here:

```
public TopicConsumer(Properties defaultProperties, Context context)
  throws NamingException, JMSException
{
  properties = defaultProperties;
  String jmsFactoryName =
      (String)properties.get("JMS_FACTORY_FOR_TOPIC");
  // Create Queue Connection Factory
  topicConnectionFactory = (TopicConnectionFactory)
    context.lookup(jmsFactoryName);
```

```
    // Create Queue Connection to The Factory
    topicConnection = topicConnectionFactory.createTopicConnection();
    // Create Session to the Connection
    topicSession = topicConnection.createTopicSession(false,
      Session.AUTO_ACKNOWLEDGE);
    String topicName = (String)properties.get("TOPIC_NAME");
    try {
      topic = (Topic) context.lookup(topicName);
    } catch (NamingException namingException) {
      // create topic, if not created
      topic = topicSession.createTopic(topicName);
      // bind the topic with a name
      context.bind(topicName, topic);
    }
    // Create Receiver
    topicSubscriber = topicSession.createSubscriber(topic);
    // Register TopicClient as Message Listener
    topicSubscriber.setMessageListener(this);
    // Start Receiving Message
    topicConnection.start();
  }
```

Because the `TopicConsumer` is a message listener implementing a `MessageListener`, it must implement the `onMessage(Message)` method. The `TopicConsumer.onMessage()` is called when the JMS service provider receives an `OrderRequest` published by the `TopicSupplier`. The `onMessage()` method will first display information from the published `Message` header and then display the message body information depending on whether it is a `TextMessage` or an `ObjectMessage`. After it receives a message, we induce an exit from the program by setting the `TopicConsumer.quitFromReceiving` flag to `true`. The `onMessage()` implementation is shown here:

```
  public void onMessage(Message message)
  {
    try {
      // print information about the message
      System.out.println(message.getJMSMessageID());
      System.out.println("MessageID :" + message.getJMSMessageID() +
                            " for " + message.getJMSDestination());
      System.out.print("Message Expires        ");
      if (message.getJMSExpiration() > 0) {
          System.out.println( new Date( message.getJMSExpiration()));
      }
      else{
          System.out.println("never  Expires ");
      }
```

```
      System.out.println("Priority :" + message.getJMSPriority());
      System.out.println("Mode    : " + (
        message.getJMSDeliveryMode() == DeliveryMode.PERSISTENT ?
        "PERSISTENT" : "NON_PERSISTENT"));
      System.out.println("Reply to :       " + message.getJMSReplyTo());
      System.out.println("Message type :   " + message.getJMSType());

      if (message instanceof TextMessage) {

        String receivedMessage = ((TextMessage)message).getText();
        System.out.println("Received Message :" + receivedMessage);
      } else if(message instanceof ObjectMessage){

        String receivedMessage = message.toString();
        System.out.println("Received Message :" + receivedMessage);
      }

      quitFromReceiving = true;
      notifyAll(); // notify to main Thread to leave from the program
    } catch (JMSException jmsException) {
      jmsException.printStackTrace();
    }
  }
```

Finally, all `TopicReceiver`, `TopicSession`, and `TopicConnection` resources are closed:

```
  public void close()
       throws JMSException
  {
    topicSubscriber.close();
    this.topicSession.close();
    this.topicConnection.close();
  }
```

CORBA Messaging

The CORBA paradigm also provides its own form of messaging services. The most mature form of asynchronous messaging in CORBA is embodied in the CORBA Event Service. The CORBA Event Service defines basic interfaces for pushing and pulling event messages between suppliers and consumers via a CORBA Event Service middleware process. The CORBA Notification Service extends the CORBA Event Service to support more sophisticated filtering of messages, a publish-subscribe model of messaging, and the capability to define the QoS. The CORBA Messaging specification defines an asynchronous messaging model utilized at the method invocation and ORB level and also defines QoS standards. This section briefly covers these various CORBA-oriented options to messaging.

CORBA Event Service

The CORBA Event Service is a CORBAservice that provides basic messaging facilities via encapsulation of events that can be generated by objects and delivered to other objects. The CORBA Event Service handles the mechanisms for delivering the event from an event supplier object to an event consumer object after the event has been generated. A standard event channel object is used between suppliers and consumers to handle the reception of events from suppliers and delivery of these events to consumers. An event channel exists for each communication path that can exist between suppliers and consumers.

Two models for event communication via the event channel are the "push model" and the "pull model." The push model of events is used when a supplier pushes an event to the event channel object, which is then passed onto the consumer by the event channel. The pull model of events is used when a consumer attempts to pull an event from the event channel object, which pulls events from suppliers.

The event channel creates distributed proxy objects for both suppliers and consumers. Thus, a supplier will actually obtain a handle to a consumer proxy object that is managed by the event channel. Similarly, a consumer will obtain a handle to a supplier proxy that is managed by the event channel. Point-to-point events can also be implemented when consumers provide direct object references to suppliers known as push consumers and when suppliers provide direct object references to consumers known as push suppliers.

Typically, the events passed to an event channel object have unknown types from the event channel's perspective. A typed event can be created by describing the event with IDL. The event channel can then allow consumers to register for notification of events of a specific type.

Push Model

The Java mapping for the CORBA Event Service basic push-model architecture is shown in Figure 22.16. The left side of the diagram shows the supplier and its interfaces to the consumer proxy. The right side shows the consumer and its connection to the supplier proxy. The middle part shows the ORB and CORBA event channel.

Suppliers and consumers bind to a particular `EventChannel` object using one of three static `bind()` calls on an `EventChannelHelper`. Using these various bind calls, a default `EventChannel` may be used, a named `EventChannel` can be referenced, or a named `EventChannel` on a particular host can be referenced. Thus, a supplier might connect to an `EventChannel Foo` to which consumers attach and receive event messages from suppliers.

One way to understand the CORBA Event Service architecture is in the context of an event sequence. This is the basic sequence of events for a push supplier using the push model of Figure 22.16:

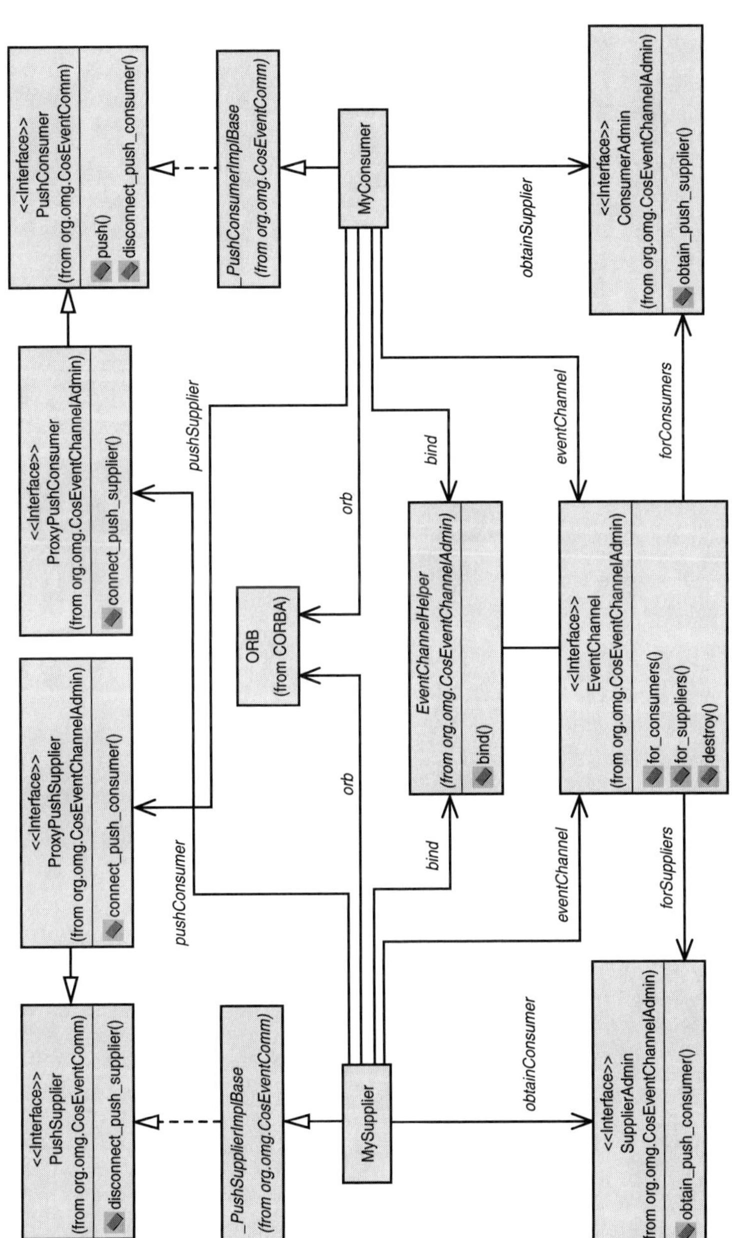

FIGURE 22.16

The CORBA events push model.

1. Bind to the ORB and event channel:

   ```
   org.omg.CORBA.ORB orb = org.omg.CORBA.ORB.init(args, null);
   EventChannel eventChannel = EventChannelHelper.bind(orb);
   ```

2. Obtain a push consumer proxy from the event channel:

   ```
   SupplierAdmin admin = eventChannel.for_suppliers();
   ProxyPushConsumer pushConsumer = admin.obtain_push_consumer();
   ```

3. Create a push supplier:

   ```
   MySupplier pushSupplier = new MySupplier();
   ```

4. Connect the supplier to the event channel:

   ```
   pushConsumer.connect_push_supplier(pushSupplier);
   ```

5. Create a CORBA message. The CORBA event message is a CORBA object:

   ```
   HelloImplementation msg = new HelloImplementation();
   ```

6. Create an `Any` event object with the CORBA message:

   ```
   org.omg.CORBA.Any pushMessage = orb.create_any();
   pushMessage.insert_Object(msg);
   ```

7. Push the message to a consumer:

   ```
   pushConsumer.push(pushMessage);
   ```

The basic sequence of events for a push consumer using the push model of Figure 22.16 is shown here:

1. Bind to the ORB and event channel:

   ```
   org.omg.CORBA.ORB orb = org.omg.CORBA.ORB.init(args, null);
   EventChannel eventChannel = EventChannelHelper.bind(orb);
   ```

2. Obtain a push supplier proxy from the event channel:

   ```
   ConsumerAdmin admin = eventChannel.for_consumers();
   ProxyPushSupplier pushSupplier = admin.obtain_push_supplier();
   ```

3. Create a push consumer:

   ```
   MyConsumer pushConsumer = new MyConsumer();
   ```

4. Connect the consumer to the event channel:

   ```
   pushSupplier.connect_push_consumer(pushConsumer);
   ```

5. Receive the call from the event channel when a message is received in an implementation of `push()`:

   ```
   public void push(Any pushMsg){
     org.omg.CORBA.Object object = pushMsg.extract_Object();
     Hello msg = HelloHelper.narrow(object);
   }
   ```

NOTE

We have included a simple CORBA Event Service push-model example on the CD in the `examples\src\ejava\messagech22\corbaevents` directory. The `PushSupplier.java` and `PushConsumer.java` files implement a push supplier and push consumer, respectively. The `Hello.idl` file defines a simple hello world CORBA message object implemented by `HelloImplementation.java`. The sample `runpushmodel.bat` script illustrates how to run such an example with the Visigenics Visibroker for Java CORBA Event Service implementation. Note that the `VISIGENIC_HOME` environment variable must be set to the root directory of your Visibroker installation as described in Appendix A.

Pull Model

The CORBA Event Service basic pull-model architecture is shown in Figure 22.17. We again have placed the supplier and its interfaces to the consumer proxy on the left side of the diagram. The right side contains the consumer and its connection to the supplier proxy. The middle portion shows the ORB and CORBA event channel. As with the push model, pull suppliers and pull consumers can bind to a particular `EventChannel` object using one of three static `bind()` calls on an `EventChannelHelper`. A default `EventChannel` can be assumed, a named `EventChannel` can be referenced, or a named `EventChannel` on a particular host can be referenced.

This is the basic sequence of events for a pull supplier using the pull model of Figure 22.17:

1. Bind to the ORB and event channel:

   ```
   org.omg.CORBA.ORB orb = org.omg.CORBA.ORB.init(args, null);
   EventChannel eventChannel = EventChannelHelper.bind(orb);
   ```

2. Obtain a pull consumer proxy from the event channel:

   ```
   SupplierAdmin admin = eventChannel.for_suppliers();
   ProxyPullConsumer pullConsumer = admin.obtain_pull_consumer();
   ```

3. Create a pull supplier:

   ```
   MySupplier pullSupplier = new MySupplier();
   ```

4. Connect the supplier to the event channel:

   ```
   pullConsumer.connect_pull_supplier(pullSupplier);
   ```

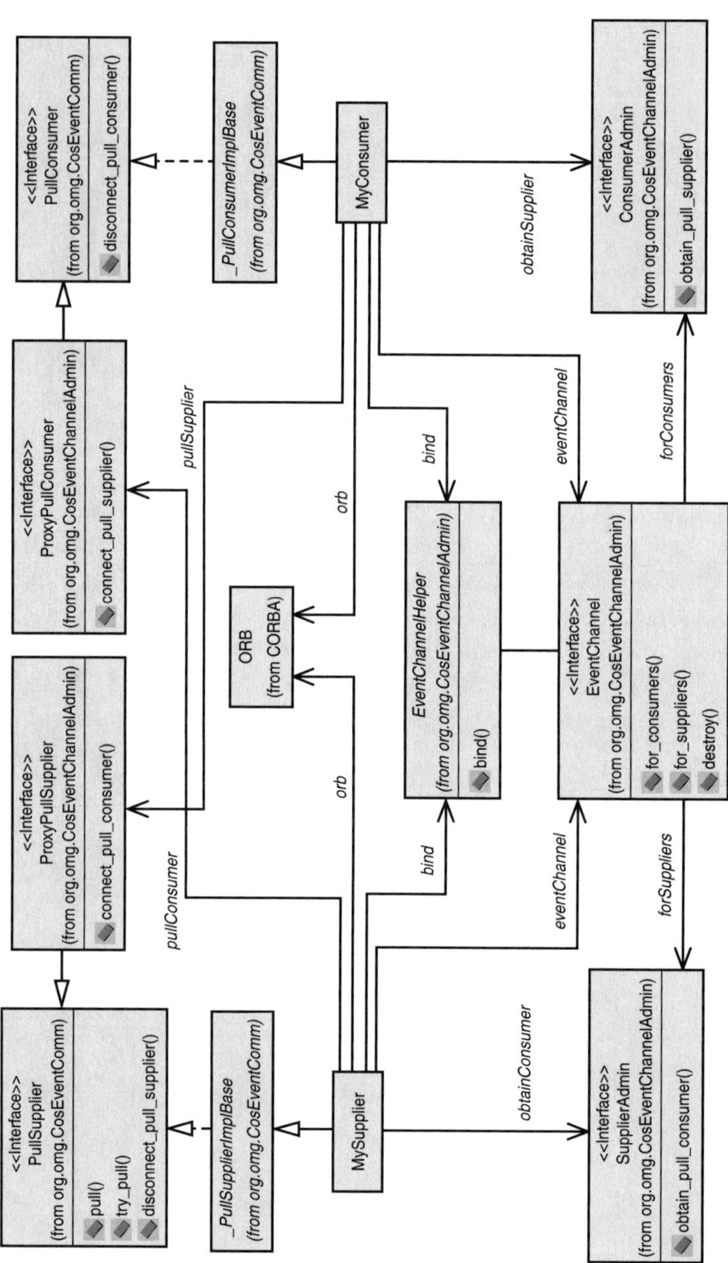

FIGURE 22.17
The CORBA events pull model.

5. Implement a `pull()` interface for consumers to pull messages:

```
public org.omg.CORBA.Any pull(){
  org.omg.CORBA.Any pullMsg = orb.create_any();
  HelloImplementation msg = new HelloImplementation();
  pullMsg.insert_Object(msg);
  return pullMsg;
}
```

6. Implement a `try_pull()` interface for consumers to pull a message only if one is available:

```
public org.omg.CORBA.Any
   try_pull(org.omg.CORBA.BooleanHolder isAvail){
  // Attempt to get a message.
  // Return a message only if available.
}
```


The basic sequence of events for a pull consumer using the pull model of Figure 22.17 is shown here:

1. Bind to the ORB and event channel:

```
org.omg.CORBA.ORB orb = org.omg.CORBA.ORB.init(args, null);
EventChannel eventChannel = EventChannelHelper.bind(orb);
```

2. Obtain a pull supplier proxy from the event channel:

```
ConsumerAdmin admin = eventChannel.for_consumers();
ProxyPullSupplier pullSupplier = admin.obtain_pull_supplier();
```

3. Create a pull consumer:

```
MyConsumer pullConsumer = new MyConsumer();
```

4. Connect the consumer to the event channel:

```
pullSupplier.connect_pull_consumer(pullConsumer).
```

5. Connect Call the `try_pull()` or `pull()` interface on the pull supplier proxy and convert it to the message type:

```
org.omg.CORBA.BooleanHolder holder
    = new org.omg.CORBA.BooleanHolder();
org.omg.CORBA.Any pullMsg = pullSupplier.try_pull(holder);
org.omg.CORBA.Object obj = pullMsg.extract_Object();
Hello hello = HelloHelper.narrow(obj);
```

NOTE

We have included a simple CORBA Event Service pull-model example on the CD in the `examples\src\ejava\messagech22\corbaevents` directory. The `PullSupplier.java` and `PullConsumer.java` files implement a pull supplier and pull consumer, respectively. The `Hello.idl` file defines a simple `hello world` CORBA message object implemented by `HelloImplementation.java`. The sample `runpullmodel.bat` script illustrates how to run such an example with the Visigenics Visibroker for Java CORBA Event Service implementation. Note that the `VISIGENIC_HOME` environment variable must be set to the root directory of your Visibroker installation as described in Appendix A.

CORBA Notification Service

The CORBA Notification Service specification is an extension to the CORBA Event Service specification. A conceptual model of the CORBA Notification Service is depicted in Figure 22.18. The CORBA Notification Service enables consumers to filter events that they are to receive using configurable filter object APIs. A proxy object for the consumer filters out undesired events before they are sent to the consumer. Filtering of events is described using a flexible constraint-based grammar. Suppliers can also be notified when consumers change their filtering criteria.

A new `EventChannel` object groups new `ConsumerAdmin` and `SupplierAdmin` objects in such a way that the attributes of the `EventChannel` can be inherited by the admin interfaces. Similarly, `ProxySupplier` and `ProxyConsumer` objects are grouped by the admin interfaces and inherit their behavioral attributes. `ProxySupplier` and `ProxyConsumer` interfaces serve as base interfaces to push and pull suppliers and consumers.

The CORBA Notification Service also adds a more sophisticated publish-and-subscribe framework for suppliers and consumers. Suppliers can publish structured events with certain descriptive attributes (that is, collections of name and value pairs). Consumers who have subscribed to events per a set of attributes that matches the published event will be notified of such events when they are published by the supplier. Whereas the CORBA Event Service allows for a minimalist publish-and-subscribe framework via the registration by consumers to receive specific event types, the CORBA Notification Service builds on such a concept with a more sophisticated means for objects to be notified based on the attributes of an event.

The capability to specify QoS properties in a standard fashion is also an important extension to the Event Service provided by the CORBA Notification Service. The QoS can be specified to designate the relative level of assurance that should be accompanied with the delivery of events. Event reliability, connection reliability, event priorities, and event expiration times are just a few examples of key QoS attributes that can be associated with a filtered event and set by both a supplier and a consumer.

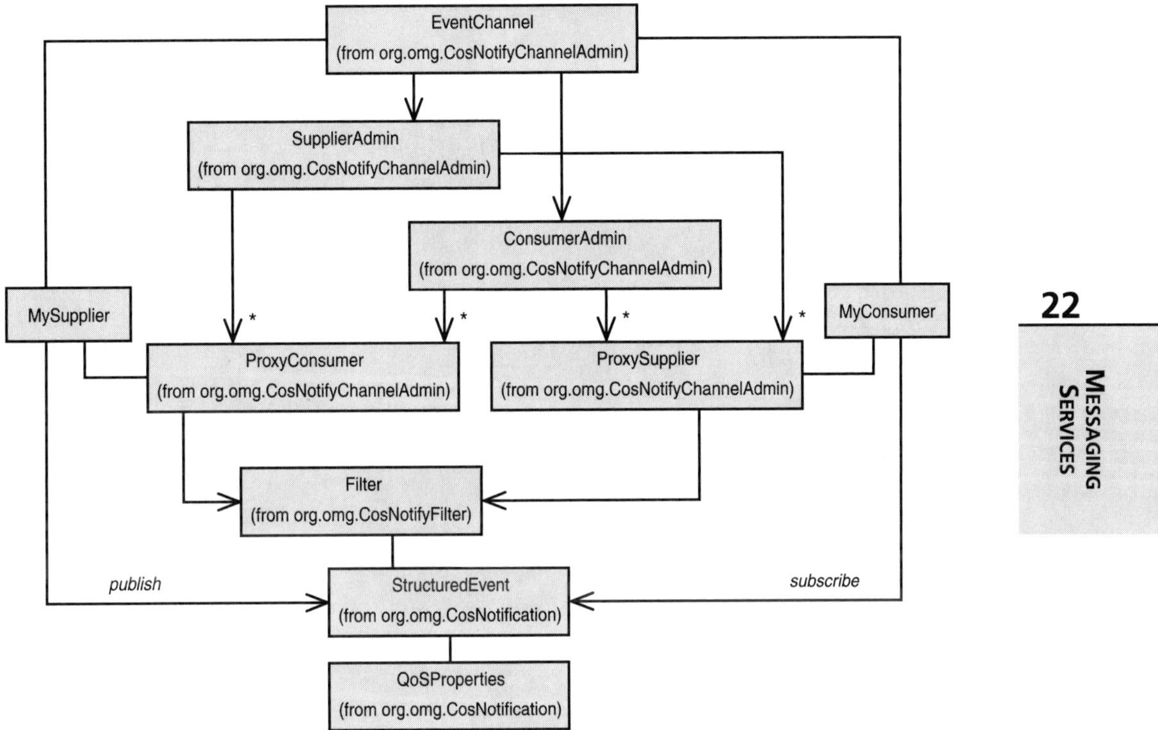

FIGURE 22.18
A CORBA Notification Service conceptual design.

CORBA Messaging Specification

In addition to the CORBA Event Service and CORBA Notification Service, several vendors have helped develop a CORBA Messaging specification. The CORBA Messaging specification, as depicted in Figure 22.19, defines several extensions to the standard CORBA framework, a new `Messaging` module, and a new `MessageRouting` module. Unlike the Event and Notification services, CORBA Messaging outlines standards that deal primarily with specifying how generic method calls on objects can be made asynchronously by clients. Typical CORBA calls rely on a client thread either to block while it waits for a distributed object invocation to return from a synchronous call or to continue processing while polling for a response from a deferred synchronous call. With CORBA Messaging, clients can make asynchronous calls on a server object. A callback to be made on the client when processing is finished may be implemented using standard callback interfaces. Alternately, a client may poll a server for results using standard interfaces.

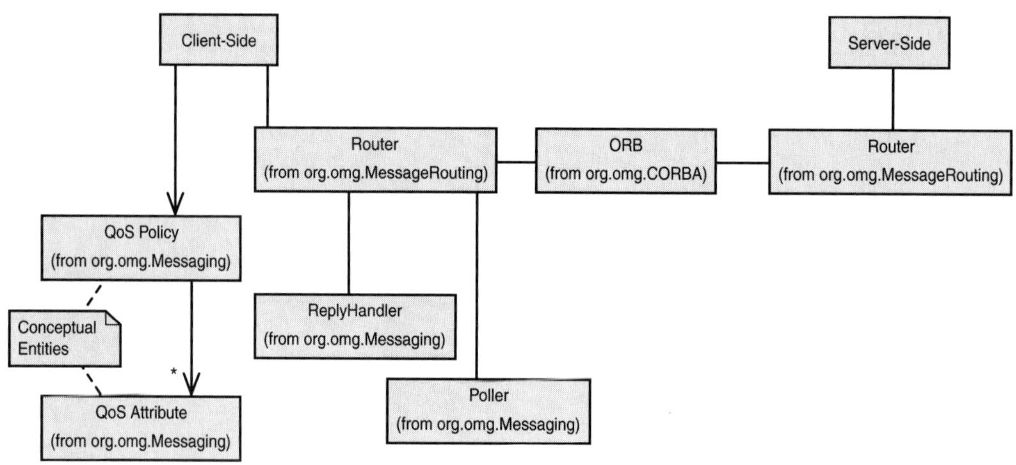

FIGURE 22.19
A CORBA Messaging conceptual design.

Many of the enhancements provided via a new Messaging module enable the standard specification for the QoS of a message, including message routing, synchronization, timeout, and priority. The QoS can be set via a host of new policy configuration interfaces. Although a default QoS can be established, the QoS can also be associated on a call-by-call basis.

Asynchronous method invocations can be implemented by programming the client to supply a `ReplyHandler` interface handle (part of the `Messaging` module) to a server. The server side can then invoke a callback on this interface when the remote call on the server has been completed. Asynchronous method invocations can also be implemented by programming the client to use the `Poller` interface that is also part of the `Messaging` module. The client can poll the server for a result using the standard `Poller` interface.

Software that sits between a client and a server that supports such a messaging paradigm in an interoperable fashion implements the `MessageRouting` module entities. Routing code may sit on the client side and server side of an interaction. Routing code enables implementations to remain unaware of the fact that a time-independent mechanism for returning messages to clients is being implemented. Thus, routing code alleviates the server from needing to know about `ReplyHandler` and `Poller` interfaces.

JavaMail

The various messaging services described so far in this chapter have a generic enterprise application nature. Email messaging systems also have a very important albeit application-specific role in the enterprise. JavaMail provides a way to interact with an email messaging system. Using JavaMail, enterprise applications can both send and receive email messages via the Internet. The J2EE includes the JavaMail API but does not require that any specific mail service provider implementations be equipped with a J2EE-based product. It is because of JavaMail's dependence on the Java Activation Framework (JAF) that the JAF is also required with the J2EE. In this section, we briefly cover the basic concepts involved in understanding email messaging systems, describe the JavaMail API, and then delve into a specific JavaMail API example.

Email Messaging Systems

Although email messaging systems can have various underlying protocol implementations, by far the most popular implementations are those defined by the Internet protocol suite. Email is typically sent from an email client using a standard Internet transport protocol. Email is then stored in a message store and later retrieved by email clients with the help of another standard Internet protocol.

Email Messages

An email message has a header and a body. Email headers are text-based name/value pairs identifying characteristics of a message, such as the sender email address, destination email address(es), subject information, and sent date. Most email addresses adhere to the format `UserName@HostName.DomainName`, such as `pperrone@babbage.assuredtech.com`. If a specific hostname for a mail server is excluded, DNS attributes associated with the domain name by the DNS can be referenced to determine the specific mail server name to which the email message should be delivered.

The body of a mail message is defined by the Multipurpose Internet Mail Extensions (MIME) standard. MIME message bodies have multiple parts to them that can assume different multimedia forms, including text, audio, images, and file attachments. MIME has a set of standard headers defined for it that includes content encoding format for any binary data and content type fields such as those defined in Table 13.1 of Chapter 13, "Web Communications." In addition to the types defined in Chapter 13, a `multipart` MIME type can be defined to identify the fact that multiple parts of a message are embedded into the message itself. The body of such a multipart message then contains one or more body parts, each with its own content type.

The multipart MIME type can be associated with various subtypes. The `mixed` subtype indicates that the body parts are independent and packaged in a particular sequence. An `alternative` subtype designates that the body parts represent alternative versions of one another, with the last body part being the most desirable form. A `digest` subtype changes the value of a body part from one type to a type that is more readable. The `parallel` subtype designates that the order of the body parts is irrelevant.

SMTP

The Simple Mail Transfer Protocol (SMTP) is a protocol that operates above TCP/IP and is used as a messaging transport for sending and receiving email messages. SMTP servers listen on a default port of 25. SMTP clients communicate with SMTP servers using a simple set of text-based commands. After establishing a connection, SMTP clients first issue a command to identify their email address in order to receive responses. The SMTP client then issues a command to identify the destination address. If the SMTP server accepts the sender and receiver identification commands, it acknowledges each command with an `OK` response. Another command sent by the client then signifies the beginning of the email message body, which is terminated with a period (`.`) on a line by itself. SMTP is purely an email transport protocol.

No queuing mechanism is implied by SMTP itself. This is why SMTP is often used in conjunction with another messaging service that provides queuing of the email sent to a receiver by a sender for later retrieval by the receiver. The POP and IMAP protocols both provide such support.

POP

Post Office Protocol Version 3 (POP3) describes a standard mechanism for queuing mail messages for later retrieval by receivers. POP3 servers also operate over TCP/IP and listen on a default port of 110. After an initial handshake between a client and a server, a sequence of text-based commands can be exchanged. POP3 clients authenticate themselves with a POP3 server using a password-based authentication method with a username and password. Authentication in POP3 occurs over an unencrypted session. A series of commands from the POP3 client may then be issued to the POP3 server, such as the request of status for the client's mailbox queue, requests for listing mailbox queue contents, and requests to retrieve the actual messages.

POP represents a store-and-forward type of messaging service that forwards email to the POP client on request and deletes it from the POP server queue. Many hosts are set up to let you use SMTP to send mail and POP3 to receive email messages.

IMAP

The Internet Message Access Protocol (IMAP) is an email message queuing service that represents an improvement over POP's store-and-forward limitations. IMAP also uses a text-based command syntax over TCP/IP with IMAP servers typically listening on the default port 143.

IMAP servers enable IMAP clients to download header information for an email and do not impose the requirements for downloading entire messages from the server to client as does POP. Folders of email messages can also be remotely maintained and managed on the IMAP server. IMAP servers provide a queuing mechanism to receive messages and must also be used in conjunction with SMTP's capability to send messages.

JavaMail Architecture Overview

The top-level architecture of the JavaMail system is depicted in Figure 22.20. Sessions with a mail server are encapsulated by the `Session` object. A `Session` object can be used to obtain a handle to a message `Store` service (for example, POP or IMAP server) and a message `Transport` service (for example, SMTP server). The `Store` and `Transport` services both extend a generic `Service` object. A mail `Store` can store messages in one or more mail `Folder` objects. A hierarchy of `SearchTerm` objects can be used to search for messages in a folder using sophisticated search criteria based on email message attributes.

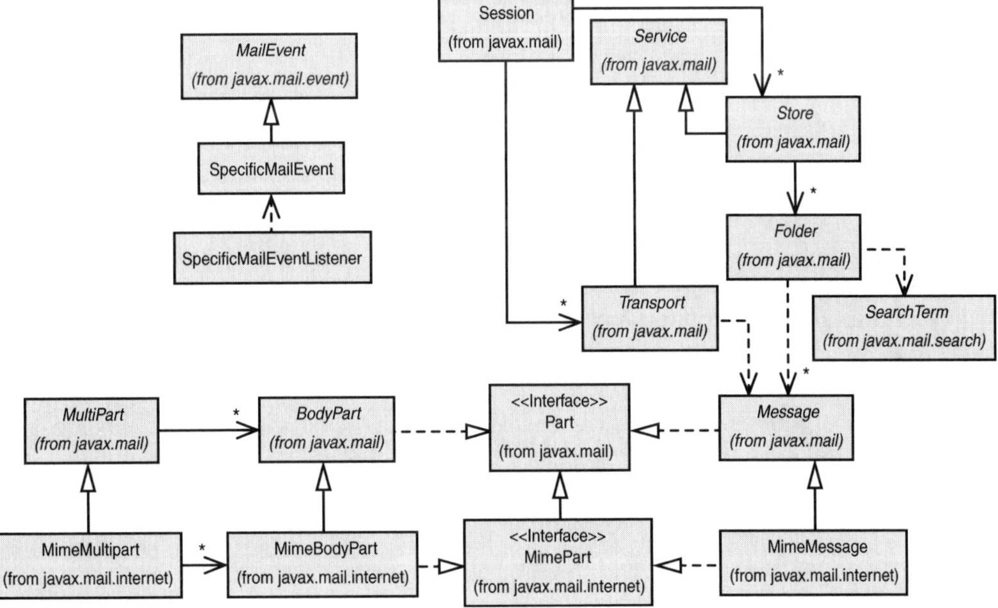

FIGURE 22.20
The JavaMail architecture.

Email messages are encapsulated by the `Message` object and by using a concrete `MimeMessage` object to encapsulate email messages on the Internet. `Multipart` objects encapsulate messages with multiple `BodyPart` elements. Concrete `MimeMultipart` and `MimeBodyPart` message implementations also exist. The `Part/MimePart` interfaces define a set of common operations implemented by both `BodyPart/MimeBodyPart` and `Message/MimeMessage` objects.

JavaMail also defines an event model for mail-system event handling. Mail-system events are implemented as specific mail event objects. Specific mail event listeners are also defined for each mail event type.

All of this mail-system interface functionality is implemented across four packages provided with JavaMail:

- `javax.mail`: Defines the basic JavaMail utilities and mail message system abstractions.
- `javax.mail.internet`: Defines a concrete implementation of the JavaMail abstractions for an Internet mail system using MIME messages.
- `javax.mail.event`: Defines mail-system events and listeners.
- `javax.mail.search`: Defines a hierarchy of search items used to express search criteria when searching for messages in mail folders.

JavaMail Generic Parts

Figure 22.21 depicts the basic architecture of an abstract email messaging part. The `Part` interface defines a set of operations that can be performed on a mail message part. Objects that implement a part have data content that can be returned as a Java object using the `Part.getContent()` call, as a message-specific stream using the `Part.getInputStream()` call, and as a `javax.activation.DataHandler` object using the `Part.getDataHandler()` call. The `DataHandler` class is utilized from the JAF (discussed in Chapter 21, "Activation Services") and allows access to data in different formats, discovers how to manipulate data, and can solicit data manipulation help from content handlers. Various getters and setters for common attributes of a message part are also defined on the `Part` interface. Message headers that are associated with a part can be get and set on the `Part` interface. A name/value pair field of a header is represented by the `Header` class.

JavaMail Generic Messages

Figure 22.22 represents the abstract JavaMail message architecture. The abstract `Message` class encapsulates an email message. A `Message` implements the `Part` interface and defines additional attributes above and beyond what the `Part` interface defines. Attributes specific to an email message have setters and getters and include a subject, sent date, and received date. Various endpoint address attributes are also associated with a `Message` and include message "from" addresses, recipient addresses, and "reply-to" addresses. Each address is encapsulated by the `Address` object, which defines an address type and value for the address. When a `Message` object is retrieved by an application from a message store, not all of its attribute values will be populated. Attributes of a message are often retrieved as an application requests them from the `Message` interface.

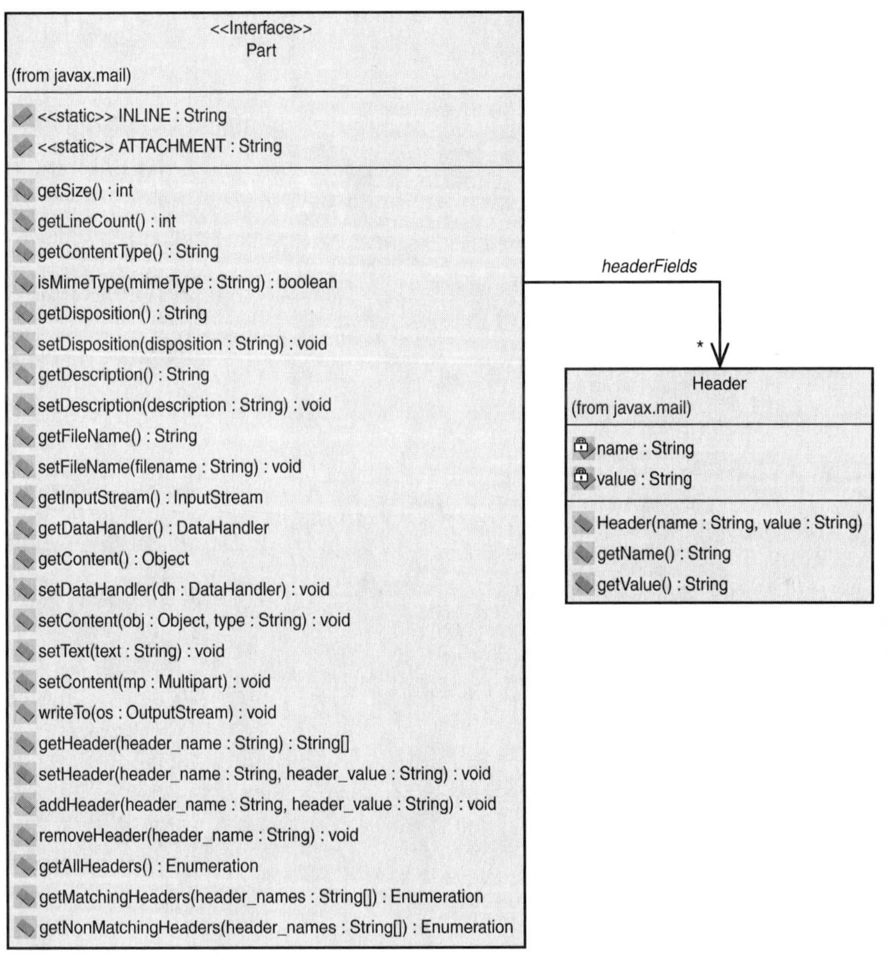

FIGURE 22.21
JavaMail parts.

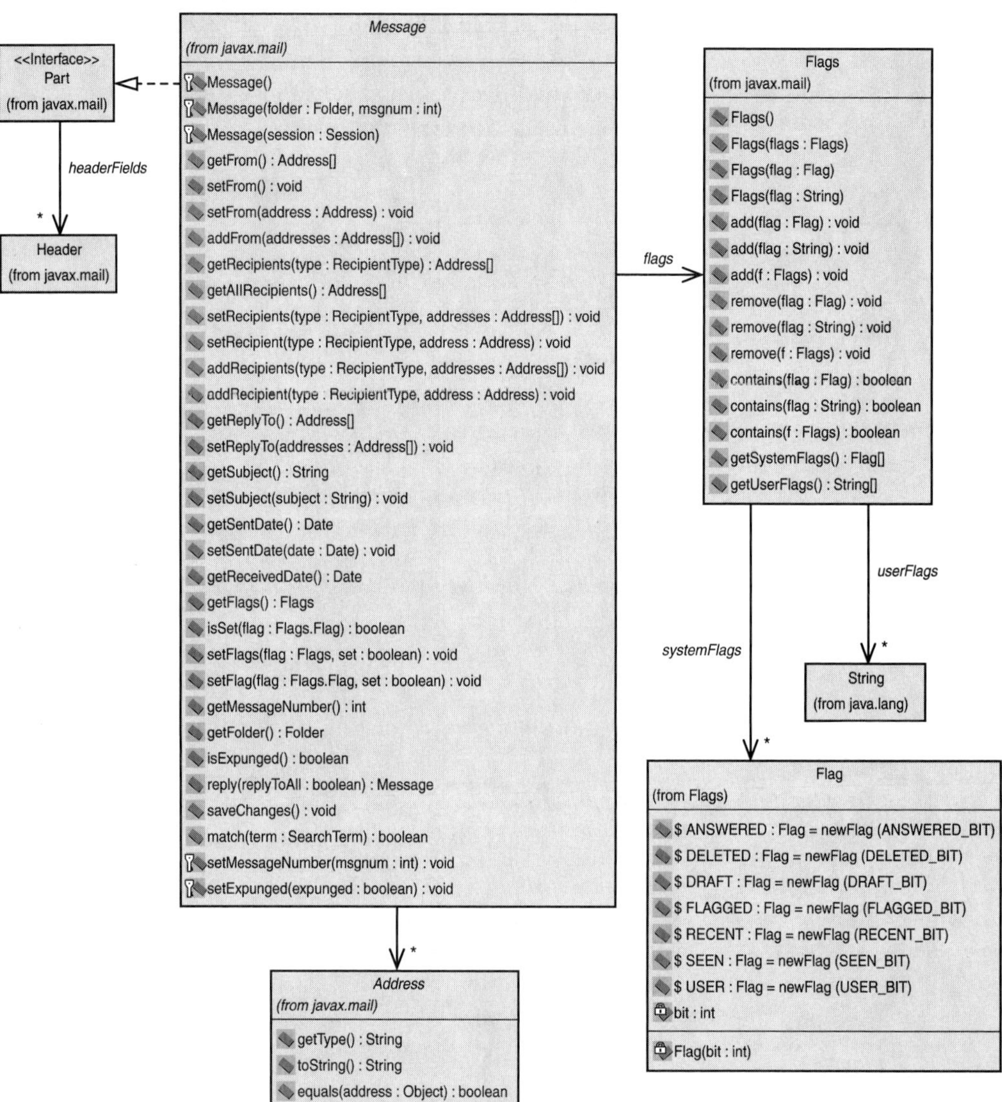

FIGURE 22.22
JavaMail messages.

Message objects also have flags associated with them that indicate the state of the message in a message store. The `Flags` class encapsulates this state of a message. User-defined flags can be added and removed as `String` objects to a `Flags` object. A set of system-defined flags can also be identified using the `Flag` class, which is an inner class to the `Flags` class. The system flags that describe a message's state as defined by the `Flag` class are listed here:

- `ANSWERED`: Message has been answered.
- `DELETED`: Message has been deleted.
- `DRAFT`: Message is a working draft.
- `FLAGGED`: Message has been flagged with no particular meaning associated with the flag.
- `RECENT`: Message is recent.
- `SEEN`: Message has been examined.
- `USER`: Message can have user-defined flags associated with it.

JavaMail Multipart Messages

Multipart message abstractions are also defined by the JavaMail API, as shown in Figure 22.23. The `Multipart` abstract class contains multiple parts of a message. Each message part that belongs to a `Multipart` message is encapsulated by the abstract `BodyPart` class, which implements the `Part` interface. Aside from methods to add, remove, and retrieve `BodyPart` elements from a multipart message, the `Multipart` class can also return the MIME content type via the `getContentType()` method.

The protected `Multipart.setMultipartDataSource()` method is set by concrete subclasses of a `Multipart` message to establish the data source of body-part data for the `Multipart` object. The `MultipartDataSource` interface is implemented by classes as a means to separate data-source location and protocol from the simple matter of reading `BodyPart` elements for the `Multipart` message. The `MessageAware` interface may also be implemented by a data source to return a context for the message. A `MessageContext` class encapsulates this message context by returning a handle to the part and message containing the message content, as well as the mail session in which the message is being manipulated.

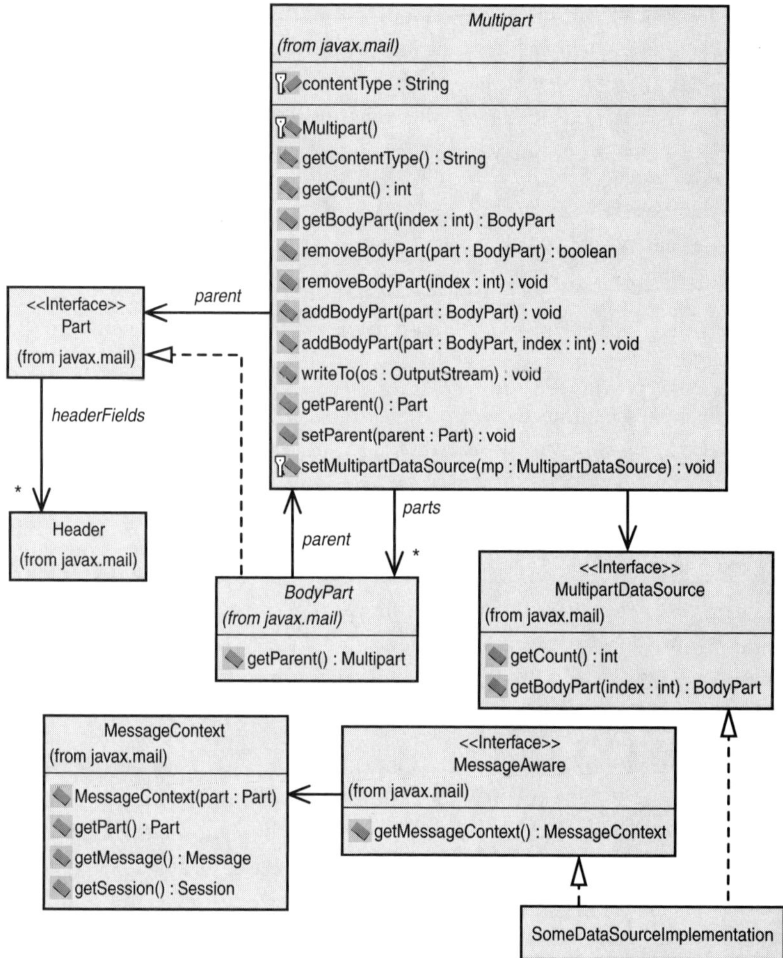

FIGURE 22.23
JavaMail multipart messages and data sources.

JavaMail MIME Messages

The `MimePart` interface shown in Figure 22.24 extends the `Part` interface with additional semantics provided to work with parts of a MIME message. Individual header lines, the MIME content ID, MIME encoding, the MIME MD5 message digest, and MIME content language tags can all be retrieved from a `MimePart` object. Additionally, lines to the header, content language tags, and content text can also be set on a `MimePart` object.

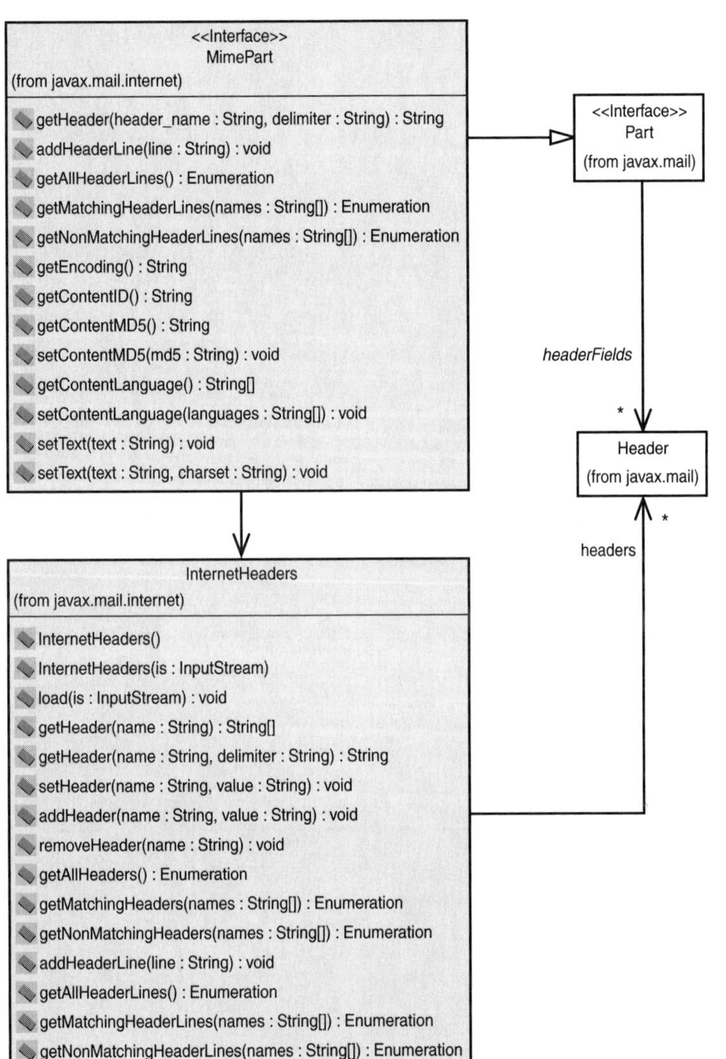

FIGURE 22.24
JavaMail MIME parts.

`MimePart` objects are associated with `InternetHeaders`. The `InternetHeaders` class represents a collection of individual `Header` fields and provides much of the helper functionality needed by objects that implement `MimePart` interfaces. The `InternetHeaders` class reads `Header` field information from an underlying `InputStream`. The `InternetHeaders` object, mainly used by service providers, transparently provides functionality to the API user via the `MimePart` objects that utilize it.

The `MimeMessage` class shown in Figure 22.25 implements a concrete MIME-style email message by extending the abstract `Message` class and implementing the `MimePart` interface. A `MimeMessage` may be created with an associated mail `Session` object and then have its attributes populated.

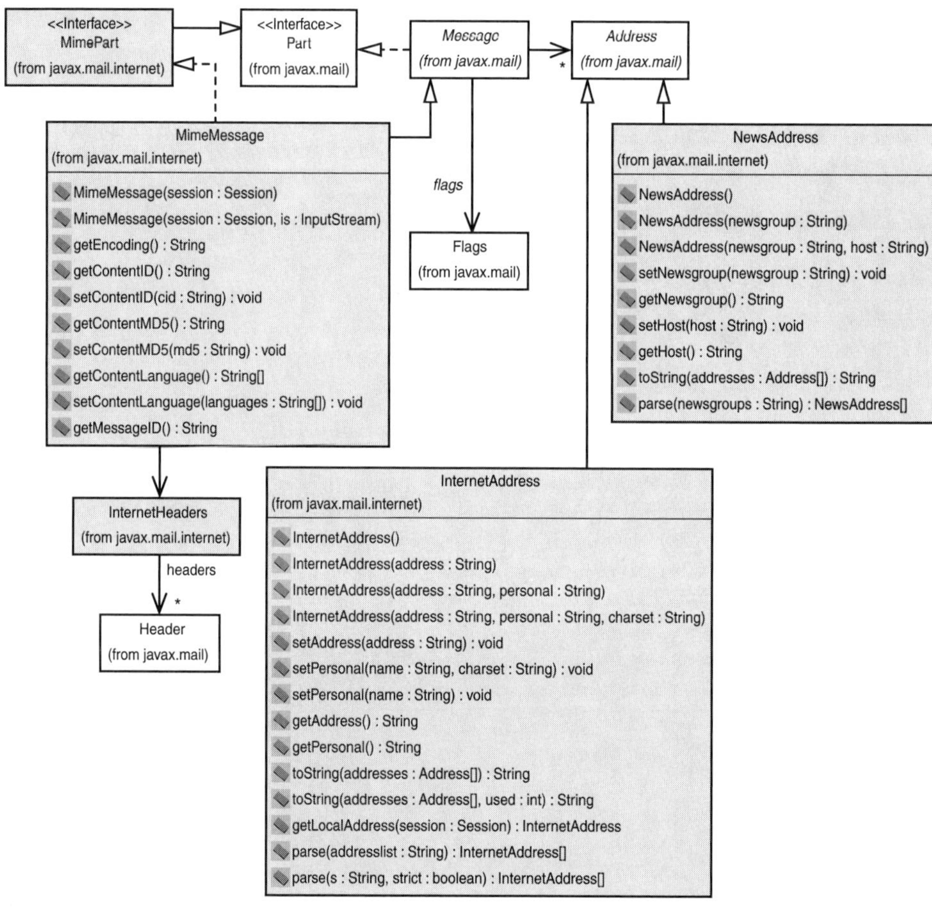

FIGURE 22.25

JavaMail MIME messages.

Two Internet-specific types of addresses provide concrete implementations of the abstract `Address` class, as shown in Figure 22.25. The `InternetAddress` class provides a means for encapsulating a user's Internet email address. The `NewsAddress` provides a means to encapsulate an Internet newsgroup address.

The `MimeMultipart` class shown in Figure 22.26 provides a concrete implementation of the abstract `Multipart` class for MIME multipart data. The `MimeMultipart` object's data source may be a `MimePartDataSource` object that implements a particular data source using a `MimePart` object. The `MimeBodyPart` class provides a concrete implementation of an abstract `BodyPart` class for MIME type messages and implements the `MimePart` interface. `MimeBodyPart` objects are contained inside of `MimeMultipart` object messages.

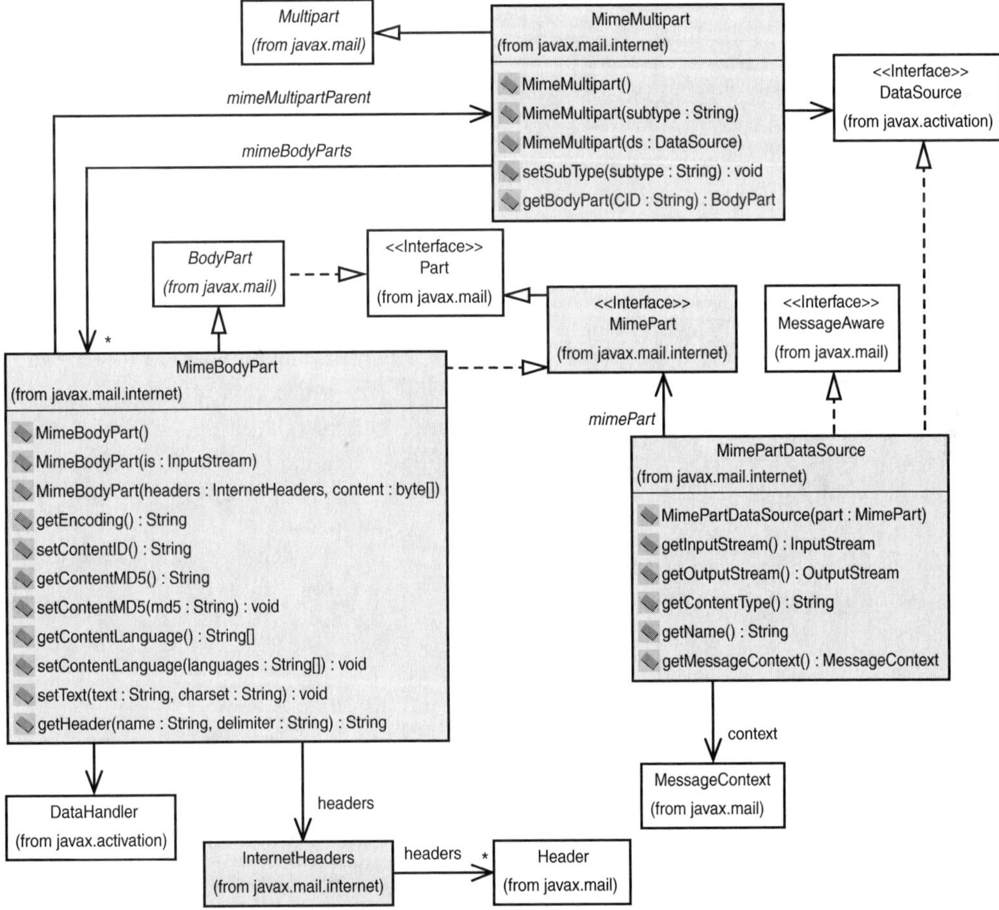

FIGURE 22.26
JavaMail multipart MIME messages and MIME data sources.

JavaMail Event Architecture

Figure 22.27 depicts the event architecture utilized by the JavaMail APIs. The JavaMail event model follows the basic Java event model architecture with events specializing in the `EventObject` class and event listeners extending the `EventListener` class. A base `MailEvent` class encapsulates a general event occurring somewhere in the mail system. Event listener interfaces that have more than one method defined have an associated event listener adapter class defined. Event listener adapters provide a set of empty method implementations as a convenience for classes wanting to extend a listener without implementing every method. The various event/listener combinations defined for JavaMail events are shown here:

- *Connection Event Model*: Manages mail session connection opening, closing, and disconnect events.
- *Folder Event Model*: Manages mail folder creation, deletion, and renaming events.
- *Store Event Model*: Manages mail message notification events.
- *Transport Event Model*: Manages mail communication delivery, nondelivery, and partial-delivery events.
- *Message Count Event Model*: Manages message folder addition and deletion events.
- *Message Changed Event Model*: Manages message content change events.

Creating Mail Sessions

Before a JavaMail client can interact with an email messaging system, it must establish a mail session with a mail server. The entities involved in establishing a JavaMail session are depicted in Figure 22.28. The `Session` class encapsulates a session with a mail server. We display only a subset of the total methods on the `Session` class of Figure 22.28 in order to focus on the interfaces relevant to this section. Additional methods on the `Session` class are covered in subsequent sections.

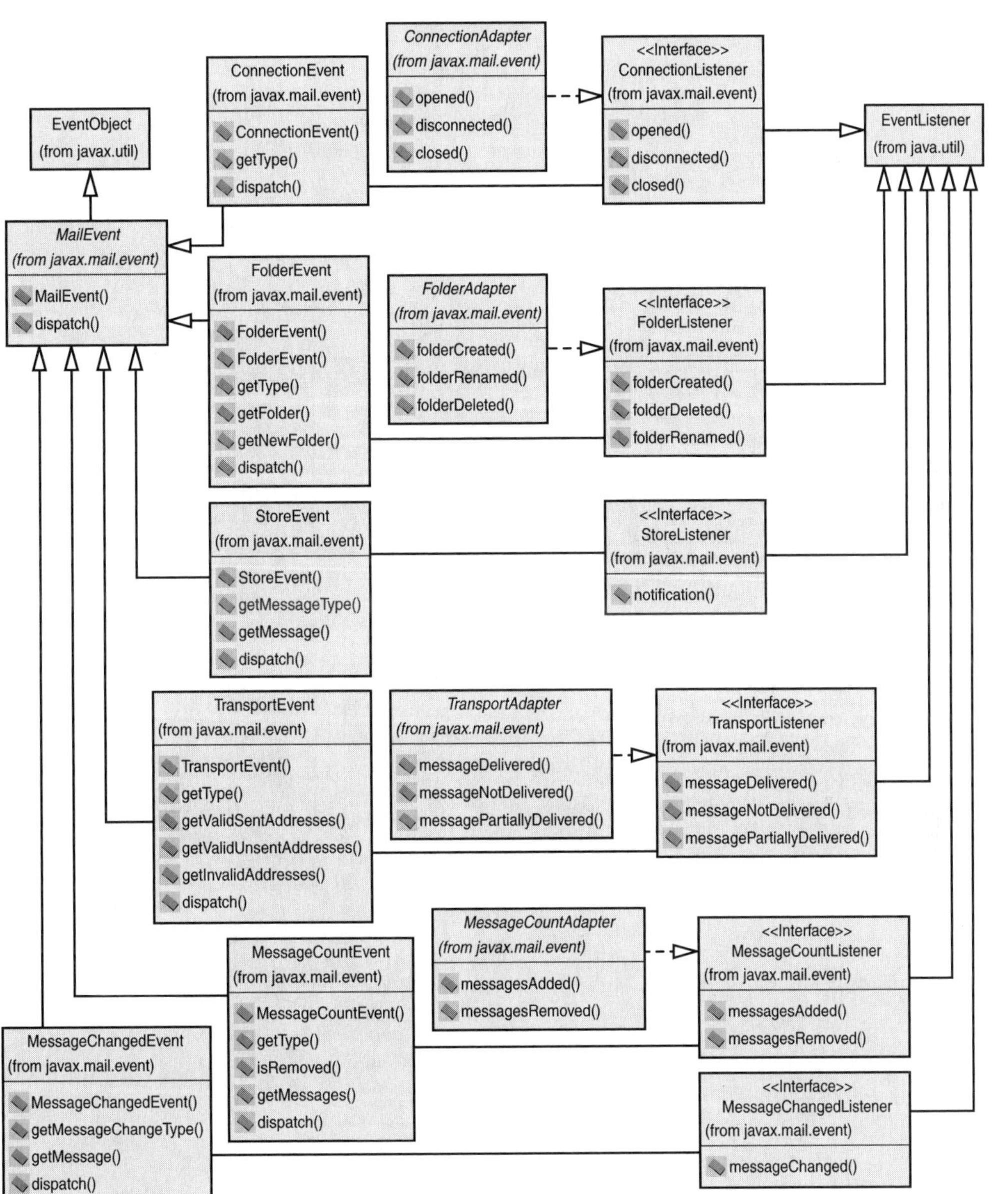

FIGURE 22.27
JavaMail events.

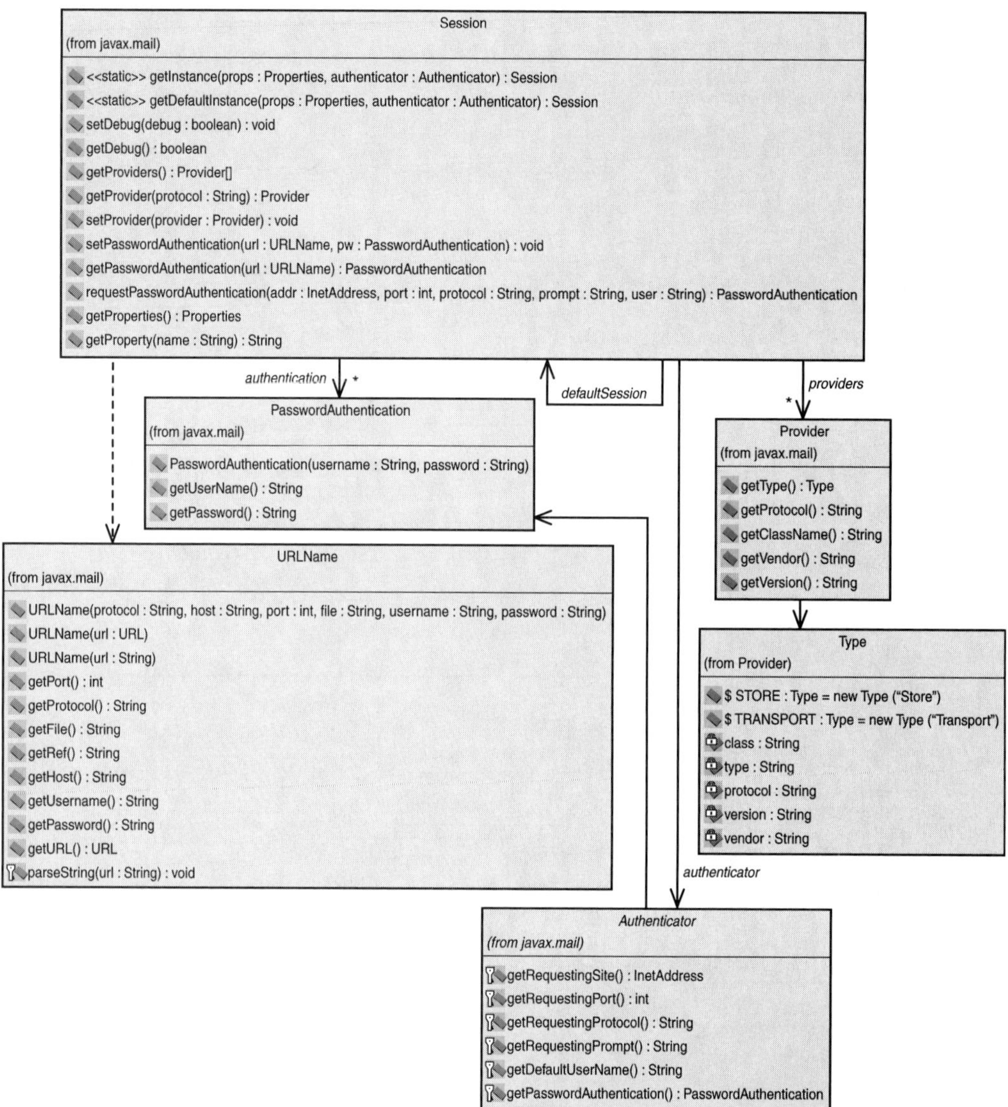

FIGURE 22.28
JavaMail sessions.

A handle to a `Session` is obtainable from a JNDI context if an application environment, such as the J2EE, has been used to register such objects. Two static methods on the `Session` class can also be used to obtain a `Session` instance. The `getDefaultInstance()` method is used to return an instance of a mail session that can be shared by other applications running on the same platform. The `getInstance()` method can be used to create a mail session that is unique and not shared with other applications. Both methods take a `Properties` object as an argument that can have values set with a set of standard property elements. When created, `Session.getProperty()` can return an individual property given a name, and `Session.getProperties()` can return the entire `Properties` collection associated with the session. These are the various session property element types and their descriptions:

- `mail.store.protocol`: Protocol for accessing message store.
- `mail.transport.protocol`: Default protocol for email message transport communications.
- `mail.host`: Default mail server. The `localhost` is the default otherwise.
- `mail.user`: Default user for connecting to mail server. The `user.name` system property is the default.
- `mail.protocol.host`: Protocol-specific mail server host. The `mail.host` system property is the default.
- `mail.protocol.user`: Protocol-specific default username for connecting to the mail server. The `mail.user` system property is the default.
- `mail.from`: Address of sender. The current *`userName@hostName`* is the default.
- `mail.debug`: Initial debug mode. The default is `false`.

The J2EE and JavaMail

J2EE components can obtain handles to JavaMail `Session` objects via JNDI. Such a mechanism will be demonstrated in Chapter 37 when we describe how Enterprise JavaBeans obtain JavaMail session object handles from their middle-tier container/server environments.

The creation of a `Session` object also involves the use of an optional `Authenticator` parameter. The abstract `Authenticator` class is subclassed by service providers to implement objects that know how to authenticate a user with a mail server. If a null `Authenticator` is used to create a `Session` object using the `Session.getDefaultInstance()` method and the default instance was already created, then the `Authenticator` object must match the instance used to create the original session. The `Authenticator` is primarily utilized by the mail messaging service environment as a callback to request user authentication information.

The PasswordAuthentication class is used to encapsulate a username and password, which can be set onto the Session object using setPasswordAuthentication(URLName, PasswordAuthentication) for later use in the session or by other applications. The URLName encapsulates the data elements of a URL that, in this case, is used to associate a mail server URL with the password authentication information.

The Session class's getProvider() and setProvider() methods allow a Provider object to be retrieved and set, respectively. The Provider object encapsulates a handle to an underlying mail service provider implementation. Providers are typically configured in standard files named javamail.providers and javamail.default.providers. Such files are searched for in the java.home\lib directory first and then referenced in the META-INF directory of a JAR file in the CLASSPATH. Default files are always referenced after other files have been referenced. Values for providers correspond to the private attributes defined in the package private Provider.Type class, as shown in Figure 22.28.

Message Stores

Figure 22.29 depicts the basic architecture of JavaMail message stores and their relation to generic JavaMail services. The Service class is an abstract class encapsulating common mail messaging service functionality. Service instances are created by Session objects and have a URLName associated with them. Service objects can be connected to and disconnected from TCP/IP sockets. Connection listeners can also be added to and removed from Service objects to be notified of connection events.

The Store class encapsulates access to a message store. A Store object contains one or more folders, represented by the Folder class, that hold mail messages. The Store.getDefaultFolder() method returns a Folder corresponding to the default root folder of the message store. Two Store.getFolder() methods also allow a folder to be retrieved using either a String form of the folder name or a URLName. Store listeners and folder listeners can also be added to and removed from Store objects such that clients can be notified of store and folder events, respectively.

The Session object defines various getStore() methods that enable you to retrieve a handle to a Store. The Session.getStore() method returns a Store object defined in the mail.store.protocol property. Other versions of the Session.getStore() methods also return Store objects associated with a String name, a URLName, and a Provider specification. The Session.getFolder() can be used to return a closed mail Folder object given the folder URLName.

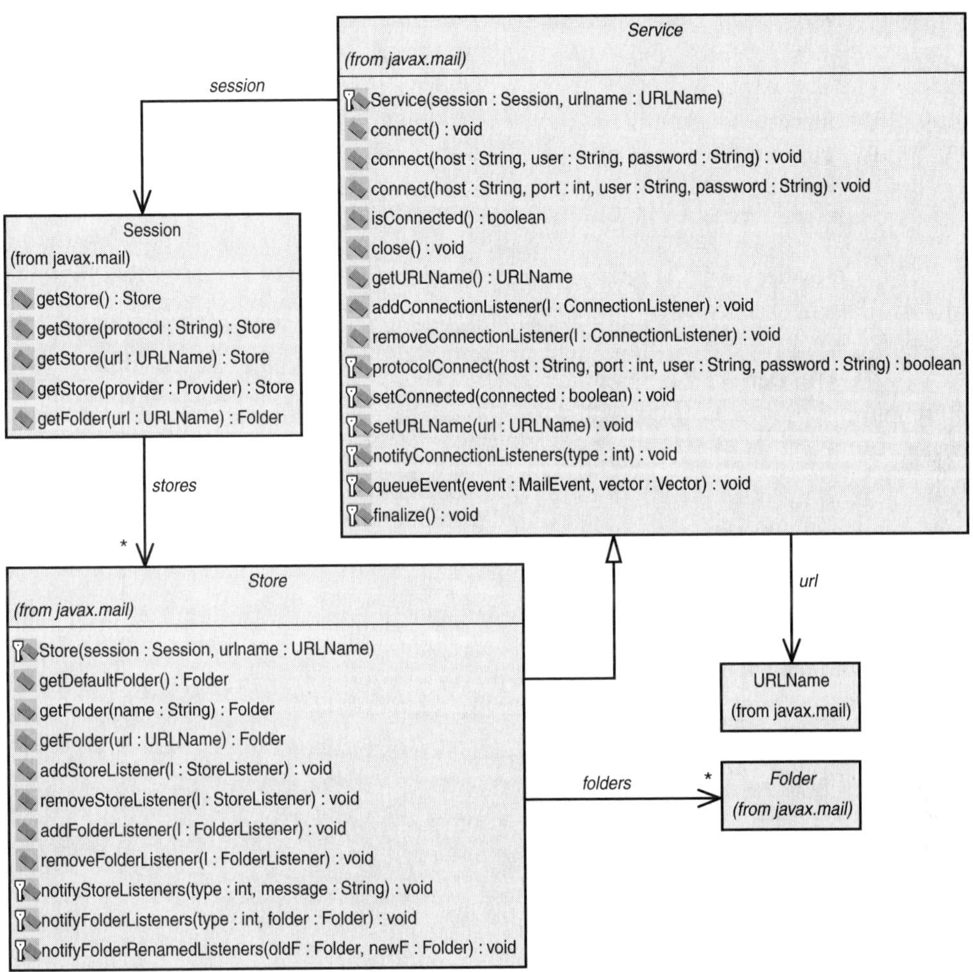

FIGURE 22.29

The JavaMail message store service.

Message Store Folders

The `Folder` class, shown in Figure 22.30, encapsulates mail folders in a message store. There are many methods on the `Folder` class. We don't delve into all of these methods here, but we do provide you with a good idea of how each method is generally used. The contents of a folder can include messages as well as other folders.

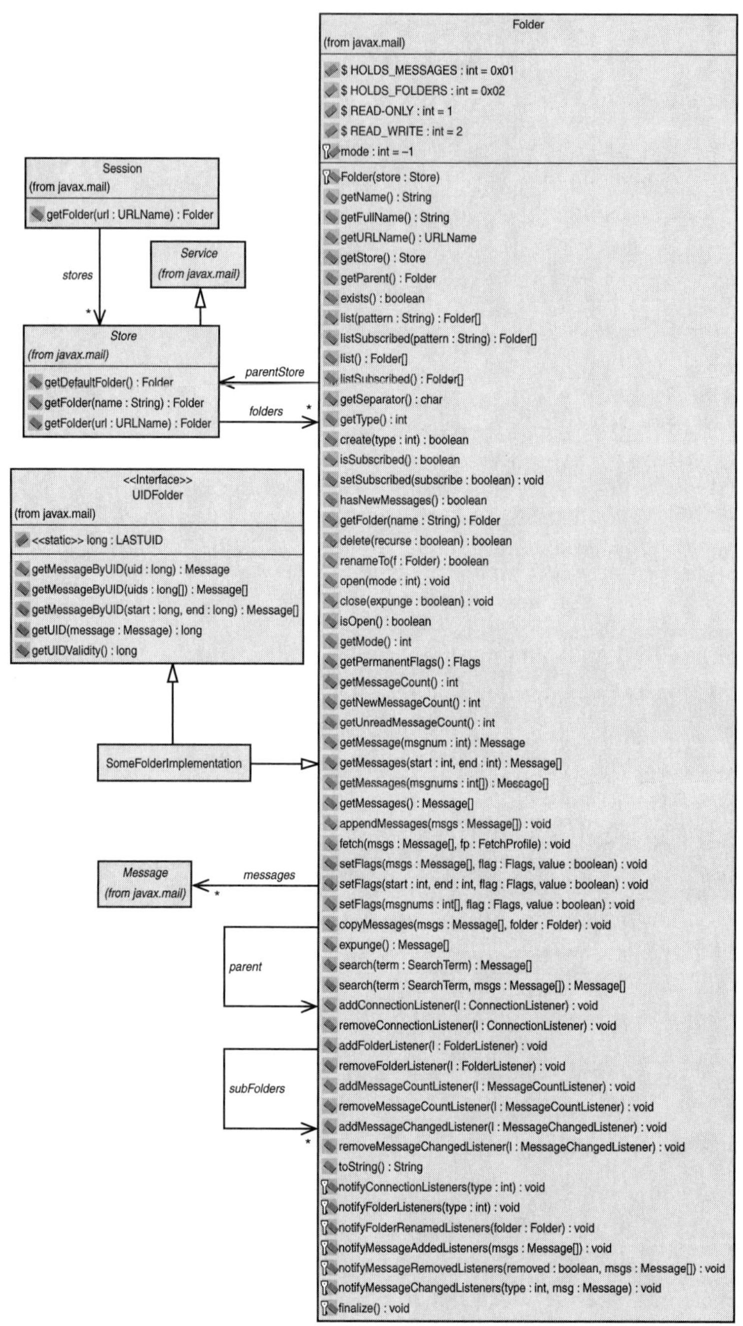

FIGURE 22.30
JavaMail folders.

Folder names are implementation-dependent, with folder elements in a hierarchy delimited by an implementation-specific character indicated by `Folder.getSeparator()`. The folder name `INBOX` is reserved to mean the primary folder in which mail messages are received.

Because a `Folder` object is returned from folder retrieval methods regardless of whether the folder exists in the mail store, a `Folder.exists()` method can be used to determine whether the folder does indeed exist. When a `Folder` object is retrieved, it is initially closed. The `Folder.open()` method opens the folder for access. Folders can also be closed, deleted, renamed, and tested for their current state using various intuitively named methods on the `Folder` object. The name of the `Folder` can be retrieved in various forms using methods such as `getName()`, `getFullName()`, and `getURLName()`. The containing message store and any parent folder of the `Folder` object can be obtained with calls to `getStore()` and `getParent()`, respectively. A `Folder` object also supports interfaces for notifying listeners of folder events, connection events, message count events, and message change events.

The capability of a `Folder` to contain folders and messages is indicated by the `Folder.getType()` method returning a static bit field set with the `HOLDS_FOLDERS` and/or `HOLDS_MESSAGES` bits. The `getMode()` method returns the mode of the folder such as the `READ_ONLY` or `READ_WRITE` constants. The flags that are supported by a folder can be returned from the `getPermanentFlags()` method call.

Various methods exist to manage the messages in the folders as well. The total number of messages, new messages, and unread messages can be obtained via the `getMessageCount()`, `getNewMessageCount()`, and `getUnreadMessageCount()` methods, respectively. An individual message can be retrieved with the `getMessage()` call, whereas groups of messages can be obtained with the `getMessages()` call. Messages can be appended to the folder with the `appendMessages()` method and can be copied to a folder with the `copyMessages()` method. Messages that have been marked for deletion are removed when the `expunge()` method is called. Flags on messages are set with the various `setFlags()` method variations.

The `UIDFolder` interface can also be implemented by those concrete folder implementations that offer the capability to retrieve messages given a unique ID (UID) for a message. Each UID is a `long` type and is assigned to each message in a folder. The `getUIDValidity()` method is used to obtain a folder UID that must be greater than a folder UID returned from a previous mail session if the message UIDs are now different for the current session.

You'll note that a series of methods exists on the `Folder` object to list its contents. The `Folder.list()` method simply returns the `Folder` objects contained by the `Folder`. The `Folder.list(String)` method returns the `Folder` objects contained by the `Folder` that match the `String` parameter name pattern. The `%` wildcard character matches any character except hierarchy separators, and the `*` wildcard character matches any character. The `listSubscribed()` methods can similarly be used to return a list of subscribed `Folder` objects contained by the current `Folder` object.

Messages within a folder can also be searched for given a particular search pattern. Both `Folder.search()` methods take a `SearchTerm` parameter describing the criteria that should be used to return a set of matching `Message` objects. A version of the `search()` method also takes a set of `Message` objects to be used as the messages to be searched. Figure 22.31 shows the hierarchy of classes that can be used to formulate a search expression with each class element described here:

- `SearchTerm`: Base search term used to describe search criteria in a search expression
- `AndTerm`: Logical `AND` operator used in a `SearchTerm`
- `OrTerm`: Logical `OR` operator used in a `SearchTerm`
- `NotTerm`: Logical `NEGATION` operator used in a `SearchTerm`
- `FlagTerm`: Comparison operator for message flags
- `ComparisonTerm`: Generic comparison operator
- `DateTerm`: Base comparison operator for dates
- `ReceivedDateTerm`: Comparison for the message received dates
- `SentDateTerm`: Comparison for the message sent dates
- `IntegerComparisonTerm`: Base comparison using integers
- `MessageNumberTerm`: Comparison for message numbers
- `SizeTerm`: Comparison for message size
- `AddressTerm`: Base comparison for message addresses
- `FromTerm`: Comparison for from addresses
- `RecipientTerm`: Comparison for recipient addresses
- `StringTerm`: Base comparison using `String` objects
- `AddressStringTerm`: Comparison for message addresses expressed as `String` objects
- `FromStringTerm`: Comparison for message from addresses expressed as `String` objects
- `RecipientStringTerm`: Comparison for message recipient addresses expressed as `String` objects
- `BodyTerm`: Comparison for message body elements
- `HeaderTerm`: Comparison for message header elements
- `MessageIDTerm`: Comparison for message ID elements
- `SubjectTerm`: Comparison for message subject elements

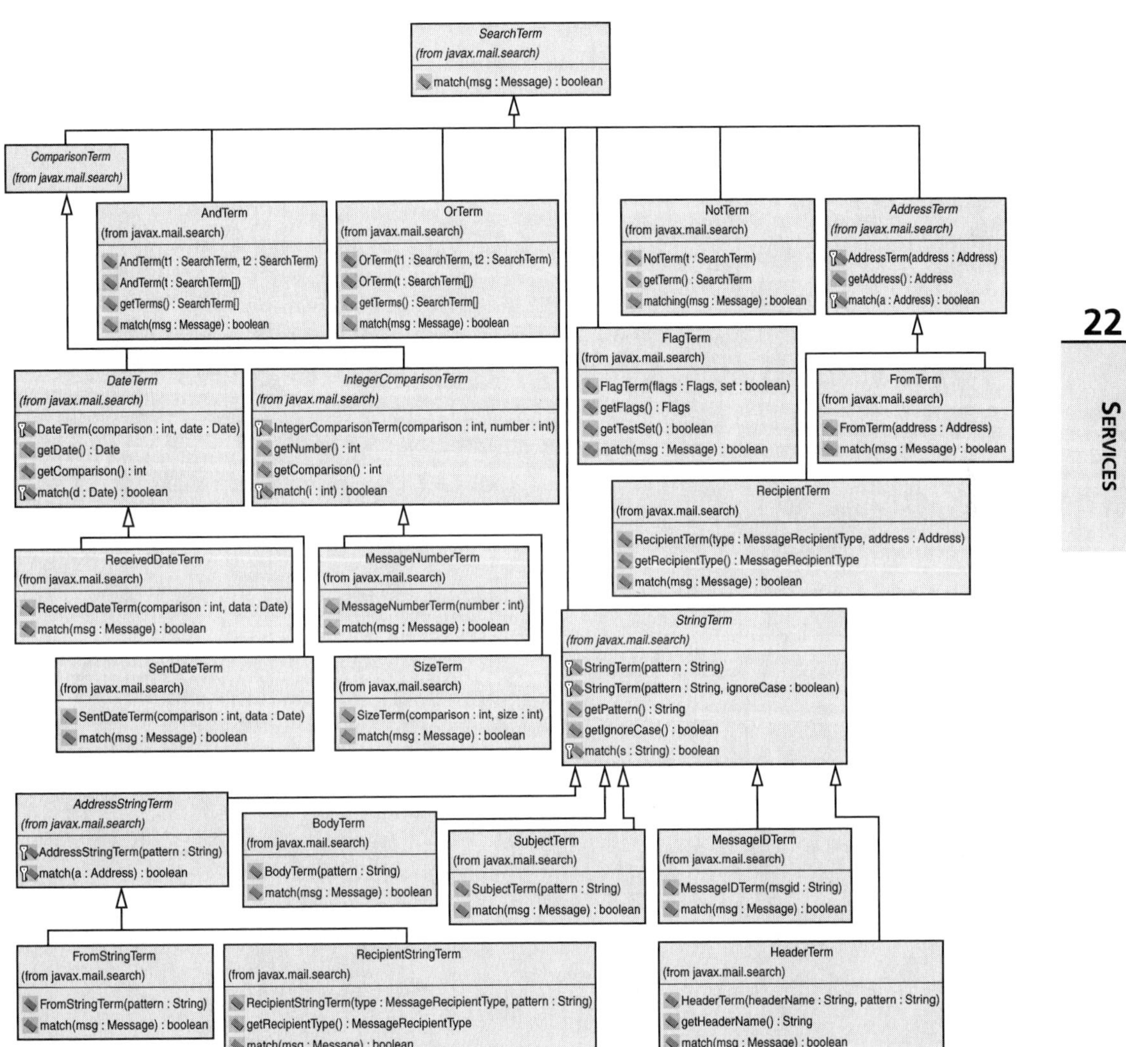

FIGURE 22.31
JavaMail folder search terms.

Message Transports

Figure 22.32 depicts the architecture used to send messages using JavaMail transport services. The abstract `Transport` class is implemented by service providers to provide message transport functionality. The `Transport` class extends the `Service` class and provides additional methods for sending messages, as well as for notifying listeners of transport events.

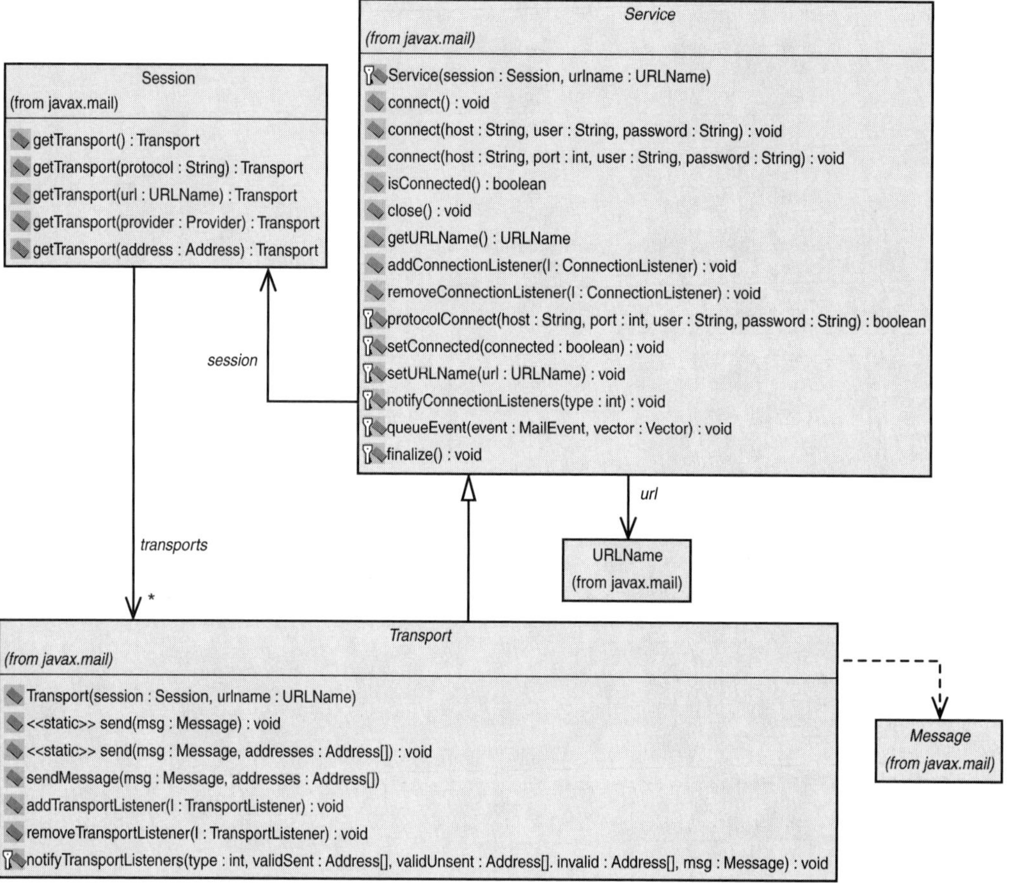

FIGURE 22.32
The JavaMail message transport service.

The `Session` object defines several `getTransport()` methods that enable you to retrieve a handle to a `Transport` object. The parameterless `Transport.getStore()` method returns a `Transport` object defined by the `mail.transport.protocol` property. Other versions of the `Session.getTransport()` methods also return `Transport` objects associated with a `String` name, a `URLName`, and a `Provider` specification.

JavaMail Example

Now that we've examined the JavaMail architecture and infrastructure, we're ready to look at a JavaMail example. We've created a single `MailClient` class to demonstrate the capability to connect to a mail server, read messages from a message store, send a message via a mail transport, and search for messages in the message store. As you'll see, all of this work is accomplished rather easily with the JavaMail API.

NOTE

The sample code strewn throughout this section leaves out some exception handling and other non-essential features in the interest of simplifying the description. The complete set of code examples for this JavaMail example can be found on the CD-ROM in the `examples\src\ejava\messagech22\mail` directory. The `MailClient.java` file implements this example and a `mailch22.properties` file that's used to configure the example. A `run.bat` file can be used as a sample script for executing the example.

Note that we also use a POP3 provider with our JavaMail example code. The POP3 v1.1.1 provider can be downloaded from `http://java.sun.com/products/javamail/pop3.html`. The `POP3_HOME` environment variable used in our `run.bat` sample script must be set to the root directory of your POP3 provider installation. Because the POP3 v1.1.1 provider was only compatible with JavaMail v1.1.3, you'll also need to download the JavaMail standard extension from `http://java.sun.com/products/javamail/` and the Java Activation Framework v1.0.1 from `http://java.sun.com/beans/glasgow/jaf.html`. The POP3 v1.1.1 provider that we utilize is not compatible with JavaMail v1.1.2 and thus cannot be used with the JavaMail API equipped with the J2EE v1.2 reference implementation. In order to use the `run.bat` script, a `MAIL_HOME` and `JAF_HOME` environment variable must be set to the root directory of your JavaMail and Java Activation Framework installation, respectively.

The `MailClient.main()` method first loads a set of properties from the properties file passed into the command line. The file `mailch22.properties` equipped with the CD contains a set of sample properties that can be configured for your environment and used with the `MailClient` program. The `MailClient.main()` method then instantiates an instance of a `MailClient` object, calls `connectToMailServer()` to connect to a mail server, calls `readMessages()` to read messages from the server, calls `sendAMessage()` with a set of message data properties to send a message to a user, and searches for email that match address "from" and "subject" strings. The `main()` method with exceptions excluded for simplicity is shown here:

```
public static void main(String[] args)
{
  // Read properties from property file
  if(args.length != 1){
    System.out.println("Error: should be"+
      " java ejava.messagech22.mail.MailClient mailch22.properties ");
```

```
    }
      Properties properties = new Properties();
      FileInputStream fileInputStream = new FileInputStream(args[0]);
      properties.load(fileInputStream);
      fileInputStream.close();
      // Exception handling code left out of listing here...

      // Create new MailClient
      MailClient mailClient = new MailClient(properties);

      // Connect to mail server
      mailClient.connectToMailServer();

      // Read messages from server
      mailClient.readMessages();

      // Read from, to, cc, subject, and body elements from properties
      String from = (String)properties.getProperty("MESSAGE_FROM");
      String to = (String)properties.getProperty("MESSAGE_TO"); ;
      String cc = (String)properties.getProperty("MESSAGE_CC");;
      String subject =
        (String)properties.getProperty("MESSAGE_SUBJECT");
      String body = (String)properties.getProperty("MESSAGE_BODY");;

      // Send a message to the server with property data
      mailClient.sendAMessage(from,to,cc,subject,body);

      // Search for Email with matching from and subject fields
      mailClient.searchFrom(from,subject);

      // Exception handling code left out of listing here...
  }
```

Various private attributes are defined for the `MailClient` class as shown here:

```
// Default set of properties
private Properties defaultProperties;
// SMTP host name
private String  SMTPHost;
// Message store host name
private String  MessageStoreHost;
// Message Store Server port  -1 is for default Port
private int MessageStorePort  = -1;
// Email User name
private String  userName;
// Email user password
private String  password;
```

```
// we read the messsges only from inbox.
private final String  INBOX = "INBOX";
// read messages from message store server
private final String  MSG_STORE_MAIL="pop3";
// read messages from smtp mail.
private final String  SMTP_MAIL="smtp";
// mail Header types
private final String MAIL_HEADER = "X-Mailer";

// Mail session handle
private Session mailSession;
// Mail message store handle
private Store   mailStore;
// Mail folder handle
private Folder  mailFolder;
```


The MailClient constructor called by main() uses the set of properties passed to it to establish a few of the private MailClient attributes as shown here:

```
public MailClient(Properties properties)
{
  // Read properties from properties object
  defaultProperties = properties;
  SMTPHost = (String)defaultProperties.get("SMTPHOST");
  MessageStoreHost = (String)defaultProperties.get("STOREHOST");
  userName = (String)defaultProperties.get("USERNAME");
  password = (String)defaultProperties.get("PASSWORD");
  String portString = (String)defaultProperties.get("STOREPORT");
  if(portString != null){
      MessageStorePort = Integer.parseInt(portString);
      // Exception handling code left out of listing here...
  }
}
```

The connectToMailServer() method called by main() first retrieves a non-authenticated SMTP session handle. A message store handle of the type defined in the MSG_STORE_MAIL private attribute is then retrieved from the Session object. Finally, a connection to a message store is created given the message store hostname, host port, username, and password information read in from the properties file and set as attributes onto the MailClient object. The connectToMailServer() method is shown here:

```
  public void connectToMailServer()
      throws NoSuchProviderException,
      AuthenticationFailedException , MessagingException
{
```

```
    // Retrieve session object with the mail.smtp.host property
    Properties sessionProperties = new Properties();
    sessionProperties.put("mail.smtp.host", this.SMTPHost);
    mailSession = Session.getDefaultInstance(systemProperties, null);

    // Get a message store that implements the protocol specified
    mailStore = mailSession.getStore(this.MSG_STORE_MAIL);

    // Connects to message store host/port with user name and password
    mailStore.connect(MessageStoreHost, MessageStorePort,
       userName, password);
  }
```

At various instances throughout our program, we want to print the contents of a message. The `MailClient.printMessage()` method demonstrates how to do this by first reading the contents of a `Message` object and then printing each element to standard output as shown here:

```
  public void printMessage( Message  message)
    throws MessagingException
  {
    // Get various data elements from message
    if(message != null){
     // Get various data elements from message
     String subject = message.getSubject();
     Date sentDate = message.getSentDate();
     int messageSize    = message.getSize();
     String[] headers = message.getHeader(this.MAIL_HEADER);
     Address[] mailFrom = message.getFrom();
     Address[] allRecipients = message.getAllRecipients();
     InputStreamReader inputStream = null;
     try{
       inputStream =
        new InputStreamReader(message.getInputStream());
     }
     catch(IOException ioException){
      System.out.println("Error: " +ioException);
      return;
     }

     // Print out various elements that were read from message
     System.out.println("Message Subject :"+subject);
     System.out.println("Message Date: "+sentDate);
     System.out.println("messageSize :"+messageSize);
     System.out.println("Headers :");
     for(int i = 0; headers != null && (i<headers.length); i++){
      System.out.print(headers[i]);
```

```
        }
        System.out.println();
        System.out.println("From :");
        for(int i = 0; i < mailFrom.length; i++){
         System.out.print("Address :" +mailFrom[i].toString());
        }
      }
    }
```

A private `MailClient.createFolder()` method is used in subsequent code to create a handle to the `INBOX` mail folder in the message store, and then it stores this handle in a private `mailFolder` attribute. We attempt to retrieve the `INBOX` folder as shown here:


```
private void createFolder() throws MessagingException
{
  // Get INBOX folder
  mailFolder = mailStore.getFolder(INBOX);
  if(mailFolder == null){
     throw new NullPointerException("Unable to get Inbox folder");
  }
}
```

After the mail folder handle is obtained, we can open the folder and retrieve a count of the number of available messages using a private `MailClient.openFolder()` method as defined here:

```
private int openFolder() throws MessagingException
{
  // Open folder for read-only access
  mailFolder.open(Folder.READ_ONLY);
  // Get number of inbox messages
  int numberOfMessagesInInbox = mailFolder.getMessageCount();

  if(numberOfMessagesInInbox == 0){
    System.out.println("No Messages");
    mailFolder.close(true);
  }

  return numberOfMessagesInInbox;
}
```

The `readMessages()` method called from `main()` first creates a folder and then opens the folder using the `createFolder()` and `openFolder()` methods. A vector of `Message` objects is then retrieved from the mail folder. Each message not yet seen is then printed using the `printMessage()` method, and read messages are marked for deletion. The `readMessages()` folder is shown here:

```
public void readMessages() throws MessagingException
{
  createFolder();
  if( openFolder() == 0 ) return; // Return if no messages

  // Retrieve the messages
  Message[]  newMessages = mailFolder.getMessages();
  // Print each message that hasn't been seen
  for (int i = 0; i < newMessages.length; i++)
  {
    if (!newMessages[i].isSet(Flags.Flag.SEEN)){
      printMessage(newMessages[i]);
      // Mark message to delete
      newMessages[i].setFlag(Flags.Flag.DELETED, true);
    }
  }

  // close folder and store
  this.mailFolder.close(true);
  this.mailStore.close();
}
```

The `sendAMessage()` method called from `main()` takes a collection of message elements and uses them to create a message that it sends. A `MimeMessage` is first created using the SMTP session object. The various elements of a message are then set before the message object is sent over the messaging transport. The `sendAMessage()` method is shown here:

```
public void sendAMessage( String from,
  String messageTo, String messageCCTo,
  String subject , String body)
  throws Exception
{
   // construct a message using SMTP session
   Message message = new MimeMessage(mailSession);

   boolean parseStrict = false;
   // set from whom message is
   message.setFrom(InternetAddress.parse(messageTo, parseStrict)[0]);
   // set recipients of message
   message.setRecipients(Message.RecipientType.TO,
                  InternetAddress.parse(messageTo, parseStrict));
       message.setRecipients(Message.RecipientType.CC,
                  InternetAddress.parse(messageCCTo, parseStrict));
   // set subject
   message.setSubject(subject);
   // set header
```

```
    String mailer = "sendMessage";
      message.setHeader("X-Mailer", mailer);
    // set date
      message.setSentDate(new Date());
    // set body
    message.setText(body);
    // send message
    Transport.send(message);
    System.out.println("\nMail was sent successfully.");
}
```


The searchFrom() method called from main() first creates a folder using the createFolder() method and then opens a folder using the openFolder() method. The searchFrom() method then creates and combines a set of search items for a message subject, a message sender address, and the current date. The mail folder is then searched using the newly created search-term criteria. Each message that matches the criteria is then returned. The searchFrom() method is shown here:

```
public void  searchFrom(String fromAddress, String subject)
  throws MessagingException
{
  createFolder();
  if( openFolder() == 0 ) return; // Return if no messages

  // Create a new subject term
  SearchTerm searchTerm = new SubjectTerm(subject);
  // Create a new from source term
  FromStringTerm fromStringTerm = new FromStringTerm(fromAddress);
  // Combine from and search term
  searchTerm = new OrTerm(searchTerm, fromStringTerm);
  // Create a new date term (today's)
  ReceivedDateTerm receivedDateTerm =
    new ReceivedDateTerm(ComparisonTerm.EQ, new Date());
  // Combine date term
  searchTerm = new OrTerm(searchTerm,receivedDateTerm);
  // Induce search for messages
  Message[]  newMessages = mailFolder.search(searchTerm);
  if(newMessages == null || newMessages.length == 0){
    System.out.println(" no message matches search Criteria");
  }
  // Print each found message
  for (int i = 0; i < newMessages.length; i++)
  {
    if (!newMessages[i].isSet(Flags.Flag.SEEN)){
      printMessage(newMessages[i]);
    }
  }
```

```
    // Close folder and store
    this.mailFolder.close(true);
    this.mailStore.close();
  }
```

To run the MailClient example, you can use the sample run.bat script equipped with the example to determine which environment variables are needed and how to execute the MailClient executable class. A single parameter to MailClient is required, which takes the name of the properties file used with the example. The mailch22.properties file has entries for each property used for the example. The various properties used for the example are shown here and should be customized for your own mail server configuration and desired message data:

```
# You need to change these properties below as needed

# SMTP Host, your mail smtp server
SMTPHOST=smtp.beeshirts.com
# POP3 Host, your mail pop3 server
STOREHOST=pop.beeshirts.com
# POP3 port for POP3 Server, default port is 110
STOREPORT=110

# Username on mail server
USERNAME=testuser
# Password on mail server
PASSWORD=password

# Message FROM
MESSAGE_FROM=myname@beeshirts.com
# Message TO
MESSAGE_TO=ccmyname@beeshirts.com
# Message CC
MESSAGE_CC=myname@beeshirts.com

# Message Subject
MESSAGE_SUBJECT=Test
# Messasge Body
MESSAGE_BODY=Hi There
```

Conclusions

We have explored the primary ways to connect Java enterprise applications with a messaging system in this chapter. Messaging services provide a means for message producers to send messages to message consumers in an asynchronous and time-independent fashion. Message consumers can also pull messages from a messaging service at their convenience, receive messages directly queued to them from a messaging service, or receive messages to which they've subscribed based on a topic name. Messaging services provide all of this functionality in a manner that enhances the underlying reliability and availability of applications that tap their services.

Although various MOM implementations can be used for messaging in Java applications, JMS provides a standard Java-based messaging API and SPI framework that can be used to tap into different messaging implementations. Furthermore, JMS is part of the J2EE standard suite of enterprise components. CORBA also provides a set of standards that enable one to build CORBA-based messaging applications including the CORBA Event Service, the CORBA Notification Service, and the CORBA Messaging specification. Finally, the JavaMail APIs, also part of the J2EE standard, offer Java applications a means for sending and receiving email messages using a standard Java API and framework.

Transaction Services

CHAPTER

23

IN THIS CHAPTER

- Transactions 791
- Transaction Services 795
- Object Transaction Service 801
- Java Transactions API 804
- JTA Transaction Manager Interface 807
- JTA Application Interface 809
- JTA and X/Open XA 810
- Java Transactions Service 812

We introduced the topic of transactions in Chapter 8, "Enterprise Data," within the context of database management systems. Chapter 8 discussed the basic concept of transactions, the ACID principles for transactions, and standards for distributed transaction processing. Chapter 10, "Advanced JDBC," built on this conceptual database transaction groundwork with specific application to JDBC. Updatable result set change visibility and transaction isolation levels can be managed using the JDBC 2.0 API. Furthermore, middle-tier transaction management interfaces support distributed transactions via the JDBC 2.0 specification. The transaction material of Chapters 8 and 10 just scratched the surface of concepts and which interfaces are exposed for interacting with transactions in the context of databases. And to a certain extent, given the broad range of issues and discussion that could surround the topic of transactions, this chapter is only able to scratch a little bit more off of the transactions topical surface.

In this chapter, we describe more than the mere application of transactions to databases. We explore those services used to manage transactions in a distributed enterprise system. Distributed objects need to coordinate and define boundaries for access to shared resources. Transaction services provide such support. This chapter expands on the transaction problem and generic transaction service architecture, the CORBA Object Transaction Service (OTS), the Java Transactions API (JTA), and the Java Transaction Service (JTS). As you'll see, the JTS is a Java mapping of the OTS.

The JTA and OTS/JTS are all core underlying components that can be utilized by J2EE-based servers. The J2EE specification, in fact, requires that certain APIs defined by the JTA be incorporated into J2EE-compliant servers. Although the J2EE's declarative model for using transactions simplifies application programming, much of the literature and declarative programming conventions describing transaction usage with the J2EE is described in the context of JTA and OTS/JTS constructs and concepts. A basic understanding of the underlying transactions framework will help you make better decisions as an enterprise developer to determine what the best model for declaring transactions is for your components, as well as perhaps being useful for creating standalone distributed enterprise applications.

In this chapter, you will learn:

- The concept of transactions and the problems encountered by distributed objects with transaction management.
- How transaction services solve the problems encountered by distributed objects with transactions.
- The CORBA Object Transaction Service as a standard distributed transaction service solution.
- The Java Transactions API for specifying local Java interfaces between a transaction manager and the various distributed entities involved in a transaction.

- The JTA high-level transaction manager interface for allowing an application server to control the boundaries of an application under control of an application server.
- The JTA high-level application interface that allows a transaction-savvy application to delineate transaction boundaries.
- The JTA mapping of the X/Open XA standard protocol that enables a resource manager to take part in a transaction controlled by an external transaction manager.
- The Java Transactions Service for implementation of the OTS via a Java mapping, as well as the implementation of a Transaction Manager supporting the JTA specification.

Transactions

Recall from Chapter 8 in the discussion of transactions that we covered ACID principles. ACID stands for Atomicity, Consistency, Isolation, and Durability. Guaranteeing that your enterprise system adheres to the ACID principles is an important first step in understanding the need for transactions.

Atomicity for a collection of operations can be very important for enterprise applications. For example, as illustrated in Figure 23.1, our BeeShirts.com application may desire to place a customer's order with a particular T-shirt supplier. The customer's order and associated credit-card information may then be used to charge the customer's account. If for some reason the order cannot be placed (for example, an item is out of stock), we would not want to charge the customer's account. Likewise, if for some reason the customer's account could not be charged (for example, the customer exceeded his maximum credit), we would not want to place the order with the supplier. Some means for treating these individual operations as an atomic and inseparable operation needs to be provided. In enterprise applications, much more complicated requirements for atomicity can exist when many individual operations can have such a codependence.

Consistency of system state is also important for enterprise applications. As shown in Figure 23.2, the placement of an order without the charging of an order can lead to the display of inconsistent information. It could be particularly troublesome to a customer visiting your e-commerce site if she sees that her account has been charged for an order that does not exist. Similarly, it could be particularly troublesome to the e-commerce storefront owner to discover that an order has been placed with one of his suppliers but that a customer was never charged. Thus, consistency of system state is a key requirement for your applications. This involves making sure that state embedded in different distributed objects and database elements is consistent.

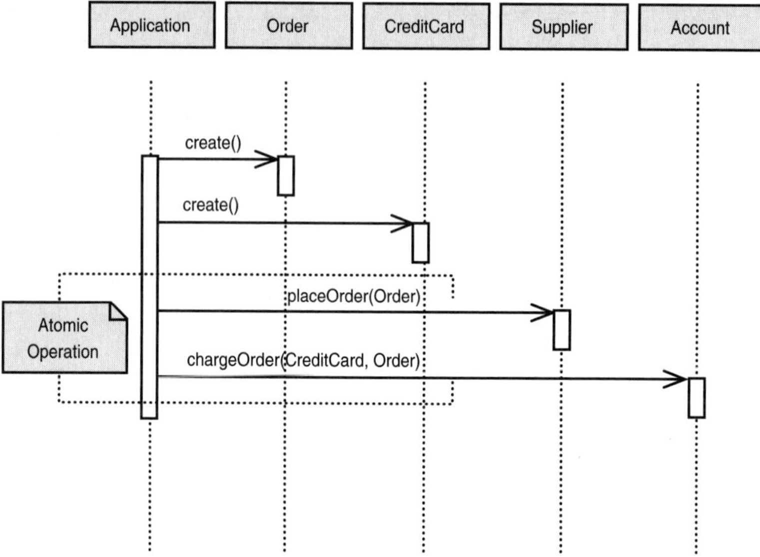

FIGURE 23.1
Transaction atomicity.

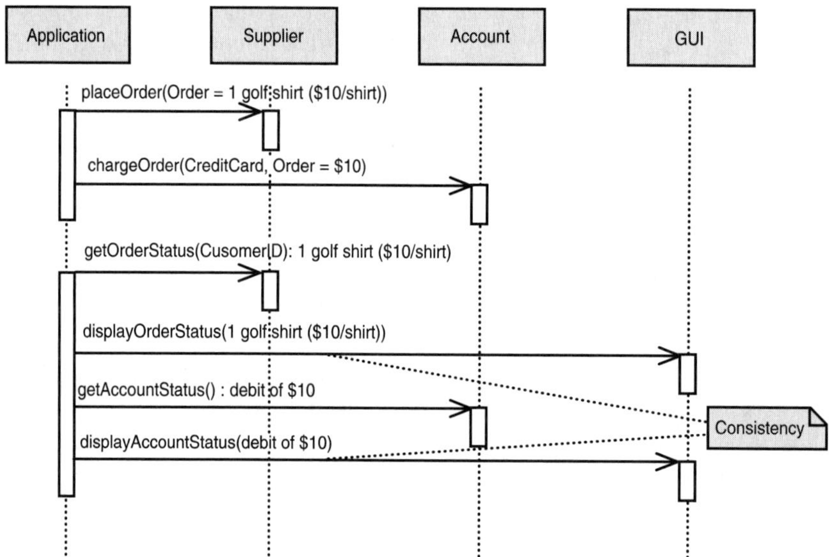

FIGURE 23.2
Transaction consistency.

The isolation of dependent operation changes to the system should be restricted to the application inducing the operations. Figure 23.3 illustrates the case in which an application `Bar` does not see the effect of a placed order by an application `Foo` until the changes can be committed by `Foo`. Isolation of change is thus important to present a consistent and accurate view of the system to other applications. Applications like `Bar` can then see changes only when they are committed.

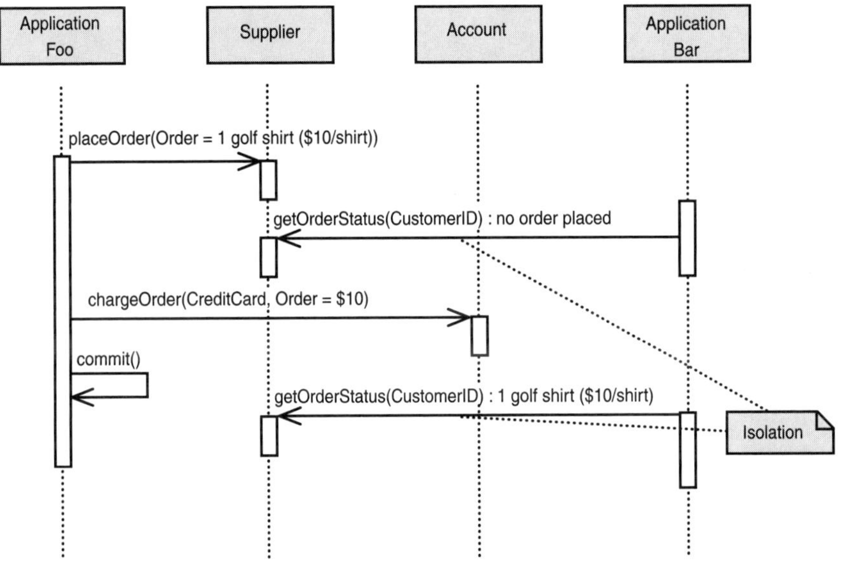

FIGURE 23.3
Transaction isolation.

Finally, Figure 23.4 depicts the need for ensuring durability or dependability of system state changes. If a failure occurs during the processing of operations before a change can even be committed or rolled back, a certain level of assurance must be provided that the system will still remain in a stable state when it comes back online. Durability of a system ensures that the system still behaves appropriately even in the event of system failure during the processing of inseparable operations.

A transaction, as depicted in Figure 23.5, is a sequence of processing steps that either must all take place or must have no individual step take place at all. We can commit the transaction and make it permanent when all steps occur as an inseparable operation. When no steps are allowed to occur because one or more steps failed, we say that the transaction must be rolled back to the original system state. By building your enterprise systems with transactions, you can guarantee that your system follows the ACID principles.

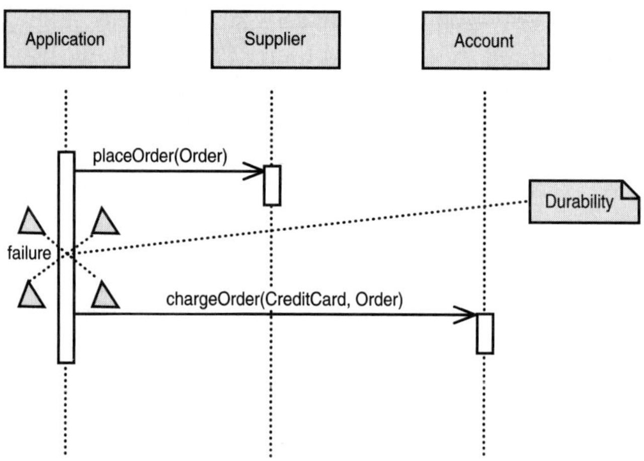

FIGURE 23.4
Transaction durability.

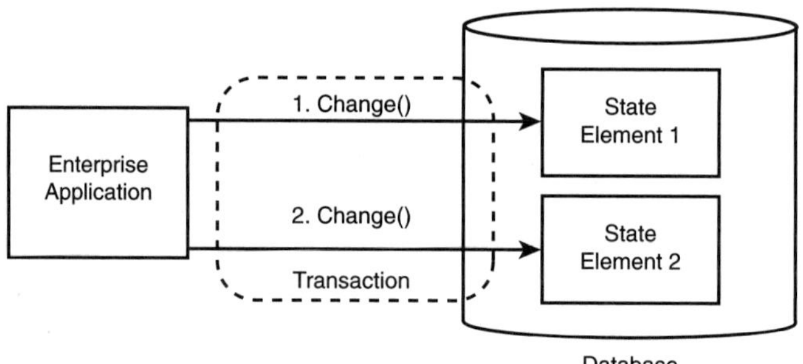

FIGURE 23.5
Transactions.

Distributed transactions are particularly important for enterprise applications. Transactions may need to encapsulate operations that affect the state of the system where the elements making up the state reside in multiple distributed system locations as illustrated in Figure 23.6. Such a distributed system state may rest in a database or perhaps within another enterprise resource such as a distributed communications server.

Transactions may also need to encapsulate operations invoked by different distributed applications as illustrated in Figure 23.7.

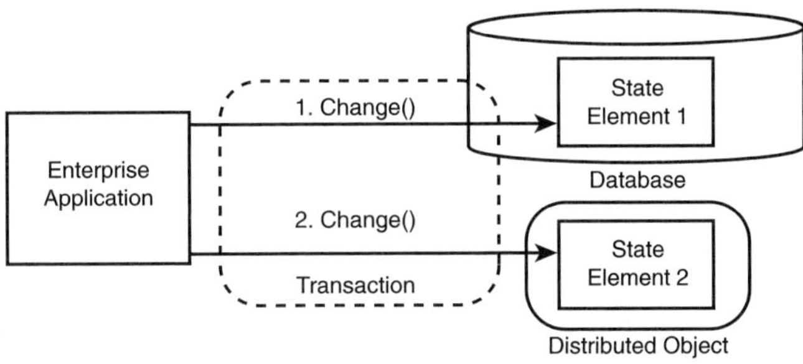

FIGURE 23.6
Distributed transaction state.

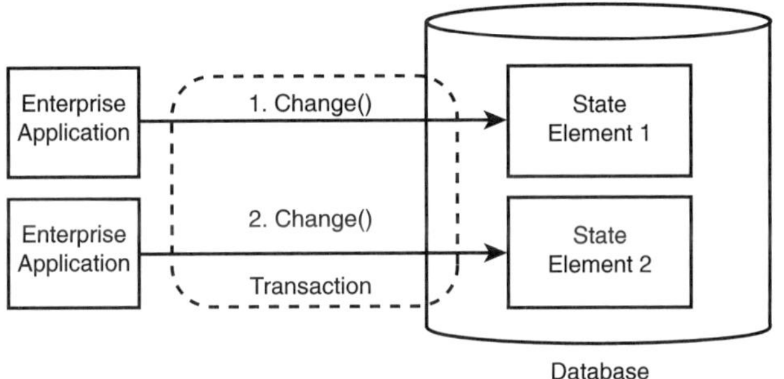

FIGURE 23.7
Distributed transaction applications.

Transaction Services

Guaranteeing that your enterprise applications employ transactions and adhere to ACID principles can require a lot of hand-coding overhead. It is true that you could conceivably identify every scenario in your system in which a collection of operations must occur within a transaction and subsequently write code to commit or rollback depending on the outcome of processing. For a few simple transactional scenarios, this may be a reasonable approach. However, for even moderately more complex applications, the number of transaction scenarios and number of operations per transaction scenario add a significant burden to your set of programming tasks and keep you from focusing on application logic.

Furthermore, the large-scale distribution of both application and state in an enterprise system mandates a need for sophisticated distributed transaction management services. The heterogeneity of platforms on which these applications run can further complicate matters as you strive to implement a standard distributed transaction processing methodology. As we saw in

Chapter 8, standards such as the X/Open Distributed Transaction Processing Model (as shown in Figure 8.2) provide a common framework within which transactions may operate in a heterogeneous distributed environment. The standard propagation of transaction context information between distributed applications enables a standard mechanism within which distributed transaction applications may operate.

Transaction services are middleware services that facilitate the provision of transaction semantics and ACID principle behavior for your enterprise applications. Transaction services provide an API for programmers to use that enables them to encapsulate which operations should be contained within a transaction. The J2EE relies on an underlying transaction service infrastructure with an exposed programmatic interface and also provides a means to declaratively define transactional semantics for enterprise components using separate descriptor files, as you'll see in the Web-enabling and application-enabling parts of this book.

Transaction Attributes

Declarative programming of transactions involves defining transaction attributes for components or their individual operations. The container then manages transactional processing for the component by using an underlying transaction service. The J2EE enables the declaration of transactional attributes for application components such as Enterprise JavaBeans. These are the latest standard transaction attribute classifications defined by the J2EE, with the older Enterprise JavaBean standard style analogues shown in parentheses (such as those used by WebLogic Server v4.5):

- `Required` (`TX_REQUIRED`): The component is required to operate inside of a transaction. If the calling client provides a transaction context within which the component operation is invoked, that transaction context is used. Otherwise, the container environment will provide a new transaction context within which the operation runs and will then attempt to commit the transaction when the operation completes.
- `RequiresNew` (`TX_REQUIRES_NEW`): The container creates a new transaction when the component is invoked and attempts to commit the transaction when the operation completes. Any transactions that were propagated by the calling client will be suspended and then resumed when the operation completes.
- `NotSupported` (`TX_NOT_SUPPORTED`): The container will not support the operation of a component within a transaction context. Any transaction context that was propagated by the calling client will be suspended and then resumed when the operation completes.
- `Never` (some `TX_BEAN_MANAGED` similarities): The container requires that the client does not propagate a transaction context for use with the invoked component operation. Otherwise, an exception will be thrown. In such cases, the component may manage its own transaction programmatically.

- `Supports` (`TX_SUPPORTS`): The container itself will not create any new transaction context within which the component may operate. However, any transaction context that was propagated by the calling context can be used with the called component. That is, the operation of the component will process within the context of the propagated transaction.
- `Mandatory` (`TX_MANDATORY`): The container requires that the client propagate a transaction context for use with the invoked component operation. Otherwise, an exception will be thrown.

Transaction Isolation Levels

Transaction services also allow for the specification of isolation levels. The isolation level defines how and when changes made to data within a transaction are visible to other applications accessing that data. Isolation levels range from rigidly restricting visibility of changes to not limiting visibility of changes at all. We defined and introduced the concept of isolation levels in Chapter 10 in the context of JDBC updates to databases. However, because isolation levels can also apply to concurrent transactions involving general back-end enterprise information systems (EISs), we redefine transaction isolation levels here to incorporate the broader definition of transactions:

- `TRANSACTION_NONE`: Transactions are not supported at all when identified by this isolation level.
- `TRANSACTION_READ_UNCOMMITTED`: This level allows other transactions to see state changes made by this transaction before a commit has been issued.
- `TRANSACTION_READ_COMMITTED`: This level does not allow other transactions to see state changes made by this transaction until a commit has been issued (that is, does not allow "dirty reads"). Also referred to as `ReadCommitted` in the J2EE design guidelines for general EIS transactions.
- `TRANSACTION_REPEATABLE_READ`: In addition to `TRANSACTION_READ_COMMITTED` level support, this level also does not allow a transaction to read data more than once and observe different data values because some other transaction made state changes to that data in the meantime (that is, does not allow "nonrepeatable reads" or "dirty reads"). Also referred to as `RepeatableRead` in the J2EE design guidelines for general EIS transactions.
- `TRANSACTION_SERIALIZABLE`: In addition to `TRANSACTION_REPEATABLE_READ` level support, this level does not allow a transaction to read a collection of data more than once satisfying a particular predicate condition. It also does not allow a transaction to observe newly added data because some other transaction added data satisfying the same predicate condition in the meantime (that is, does not allow "phantom reads," "nonrepeatable reads," or "dirty reads"). Also referred to as `Serializable` in the J2EE design guidelines for general EIS transactions.

Transaction Models

Transaction services can also support different models for encapsulating operations in a transaction. Simple transactions need to simply define the beginning of a transaction at some stage of processing and then conclude with either committing or aborting (that is, rolling back) the transaction. More complicated models of transaction processing also exist, however. The primary models for transaction processing are illustrated in Figures 23.8 through 23.10.

The flat transaction model depicted in Figure 23.8 relies on simple begin, commit, and abort functionality of a transaction service. A transaction context is created by a transaction service and encapsulates all operations until the transaction is committed or aborted.

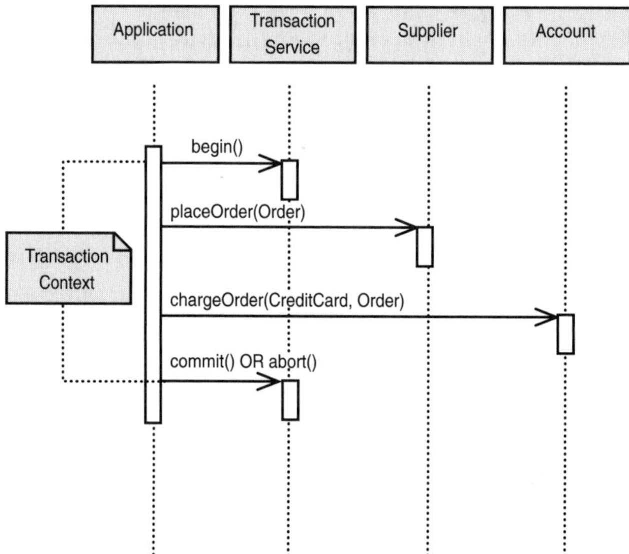

FIGURE 23.8
The flat transaction model.

The chained transaction model depicted in Figure 23.9 allows for one to persistently save a portion of the work accomplished up until a certain point. Rollback to the beginning of the chained transaction is allowed if the chained transaction follows the "saga model."

The nested transaction model depicted in Figure 23.10 allows transactions to be nested within other transactions. A nested subtransaction can be committed or aborted individually. Thus, complex transactions can be decomposed into more manageable subtransactions. Subtransactions can commit or rollback without requiring the entire transaction to commit or rollback.

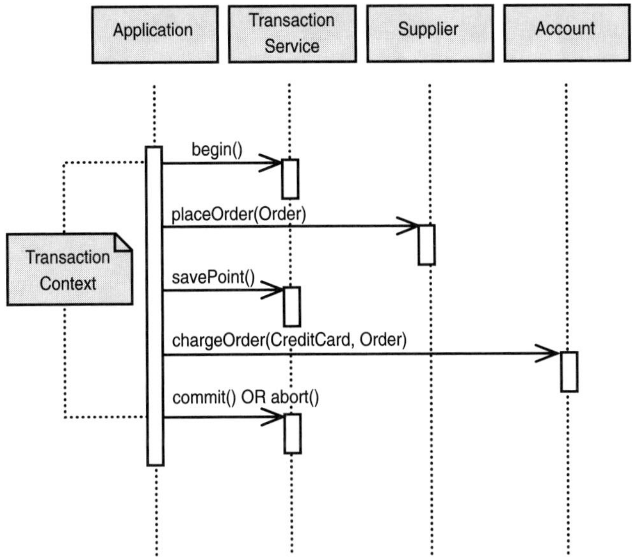

FIGURE 23.9
The chained transaction model.

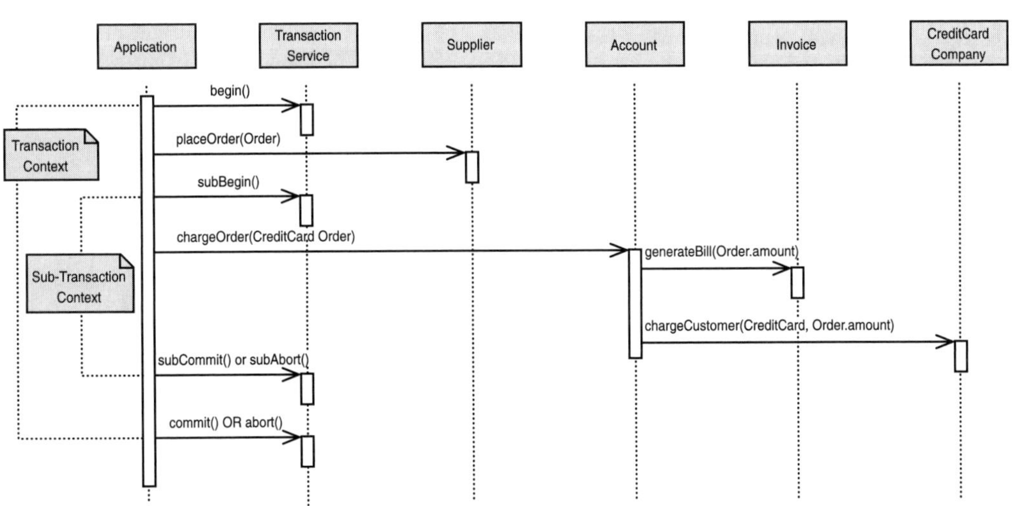

FIGURE 23.10
The nested transaction model.

X/Open Distributed Transaction Processing Standard

Chapter 8 described the standard X/Open Distributed Transaction Processing (DTP) model utilized by the Java transactions architecture for providing a standard distributed transaction processing framework (see Figure 8.2). An X/Open resource manager (RM) is used to describe a management process for any shared resource but is most often used to mean a DBMS. The X/Open transaction manager (TM) is the module responsible for coordinating transactions among the various distributed entities. A TX interface between application programs and TMs enables applications to initiate the begin, commit, and rollback of transactions, as well as to obtain the status of transactions. RMs participate in distributed transactions by implementing a transaction resource interface (XA) to communicate information needed by TMs for coordinating transactions.

TMs are often configured to manage a particular domain of distributed RMs and applications. Communication resource managers (CRMs) provide a standard means for connecting distributed transaction managers to propagate transaction information between different transaction domains for more widely distributed transactions. The standard interface between TMs and CRMs is defined by an XA+ interface, whereas communication resource manager to application program interfaces are defined by three different interfaces known as TxRPC, XATMI, and CPI-C.

Two-Phase Commit Protocol

A TM can guarantee that all steps in a distributed transaction are atomically completed using information from the distributed RMs. A TM accomplishes this using a two-phase commit protocol. The two-phase commit protocol helps guarantee ACID principles by ensuring that all RMs commit to transaction completion or rollback to an original state in the event of a failure. These are the two-phase commit protocol steps:

- *Phase One—Commit Preparation*: A prepare for commit message is first sent to each resource manager (for example, DBMS) with updated data involved in a transaction. Each resource manager then persists a description of the updates it has made within the context of the current transaction. Resource managers can also opt to abort the transaction at this stage, and then the whole transaction can be aborted by the transaction manager.
- *Phase Two—Actual Commit*: If the transaction was not aborted, the transaction manager will send a commit message to all resource managers involved in the transaction. The resource managers will then commit their updates.

Object Transaction Service

The CORBAservice known as the Object Transaction Service (`ftp://www.omg.org/pub/docs/formal/97-12-17.pdf`) defines interfaces to implement transactional behavior for distributed CORBA objects. Distributed CORBA objects can participate in transaction via an ORB and the OTS. The OTS supports both flat and nested transactions. Because OTS relies on the X/Open DTP standard, non–CORBA-based applications can also interoperate with OTS. OTS is defined primarily in the `org::omg::CosTransactions` module, but an auxiliary `org::omg::CosTSPortability` module also defines two interfaces defined for portable transaction context propagation.

OTS currently represents perhaps the only CORBAservice that has been wholeheartedly adopted by the J2EE distributed computing services paradigm. As you'll see later in the chapter, the Java Transaction Service is simply a Java mapping of the OTS.

Core OTS Types

As with other CORBA specifications, the OTS depends on a set of fundamental types. Two IDL `enum` types and three IDL `struct` types define the most important types defined in the `CosTransactions` IDL module. The Java mapping for these types is depicted in Figure 23.11. The five types of interest are listed here:

- `Status`: `Status` is an IDL `enum` that identifies the various states of a transaction.
- `Vote`: `Vote` is an IDL `enum` that identifies the responses from resource managers after the commit preparation phase (Phase One) of a two-phase commit protocol.
- `otid_t`: `otid_t` is an IDL `struct` that is a transaction identifier. It is based on the X/Open notion of a transaction ID referred to as XID.
- `TransIdentity`: `TransIdentity` is an IDL `struct` that encapsulates a handle to a transaction. A `TransIdentity` has an `otid_t` transaction identifier as well as a handle to its transaction coordinator and terminator.
- `PropagationContext`: `PropagationContext` is an IDL `struct` that encapsulates transaction context information to be propagated between distributed entities involved in a transaction. A transaction timeout and current transaction identity are part of the context. A sequence of parent transaction identities in a nested transaction can also be included. Implementation-specific data can also be added to a propagation context.

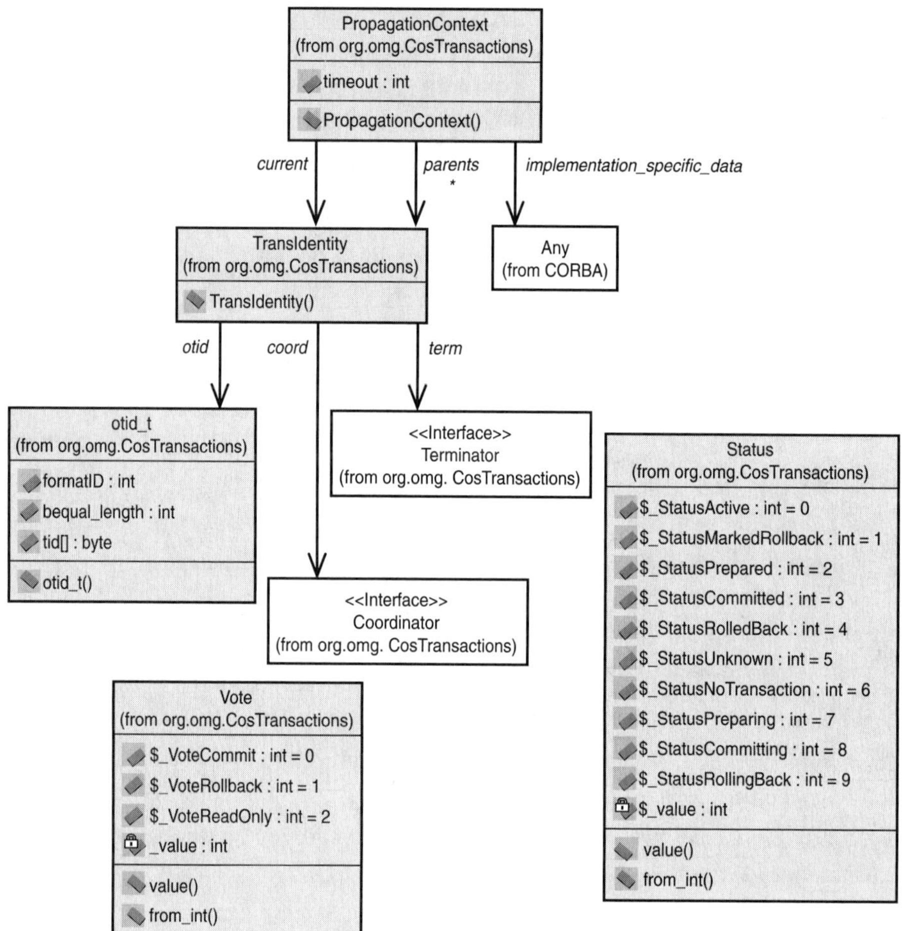

FIGURE 23.11
Basic OTS types.

OTS Interfaces

The primary OTS interfaces involved in encapsulating access to transactional objects, resources, and their coordination are shown in Figure 23.12. A transaction coordinator manages communication with transactional objects and resources that participate in transactions. Each interface of Figure 23.12 is described here:

- `TransactionalObject`: This marker interface is implemented by those objects that want to participate in a transaction. An ORB will automatically propagate the transaction context of a client thread when a method on a `TransactionalObject` implementation is invoked.

- `Synchronization`: The `Synchronization` interface is used to notify `TransactionalObject` instances before a commit is prepared (that is, `before_completion()`) and after a commit or rollback operation is performed (that is, `after_completion()`) during a two-phase commit protocol.
- `Resource`: The `Resource` interface is implemented by resources that participate in a two-phase commit protocol.
- `SubtransactionAwareResource`: This sub-interface of the `Resource` interface is implemented by resources that participate in a two-phase commit protocol that employs a nested transaction model.
- `Coordinator`: The `Coordinator` interface can be used to create transactions and manage their behavior, obtain transaction status and information, compare transactions, register resources and synchronization objects, and create subtransactions in a nested transaction.
- `RecoveryCoordinator`: When a `Resource` is registered with the `Coordinator`, a `RecoveryCoordinator` handle is returned to enable the handling of certain recovery scenarios. The resource can ask the coordinator to replay the transaction completion sequence if it did not receive a transaction completion request within a certain transaction timeout.

Figure 23.13 depicts those OTS interfaces used to create and manage transactions. We have already described the `Coordinator` interface, but the interfaces that rely on the `Coordinator` interface are also shown here. APIs such as the `Current` interface can be utilized by application programs to manage transactions at a higher level. The transaction management interfaces depicted in Figure 23.13 are described here:

- `Terminator`: A `Terminator` interface is used to commit or rollback a transaction. Thus, although a transaction may have been created by another application, this interface provides a mechanism to terminate the transaction from another application.
- `Control`: The `Control` interface provides a handle to manage a transaction context that can be propagated between applications. Can return a handle to a transaction coordinator or terminator to accomplish these tasks.
- `Current`: `Current` is a frontline IDL interface for applications to use when creating transactions. `Current` provides operations to begin, commit, rollback, suspend, and resume transactions. The status of a transaction can also be obtained from the `Current` object. The current transaction context can be obtained from the initial ORB references.
- `TransactionFactory`: A transaction can also be created with a `TransactionFactory`. Operations exist to create a new transaction with a particular timeout value and to re-create an existing transaction given a propagation context.

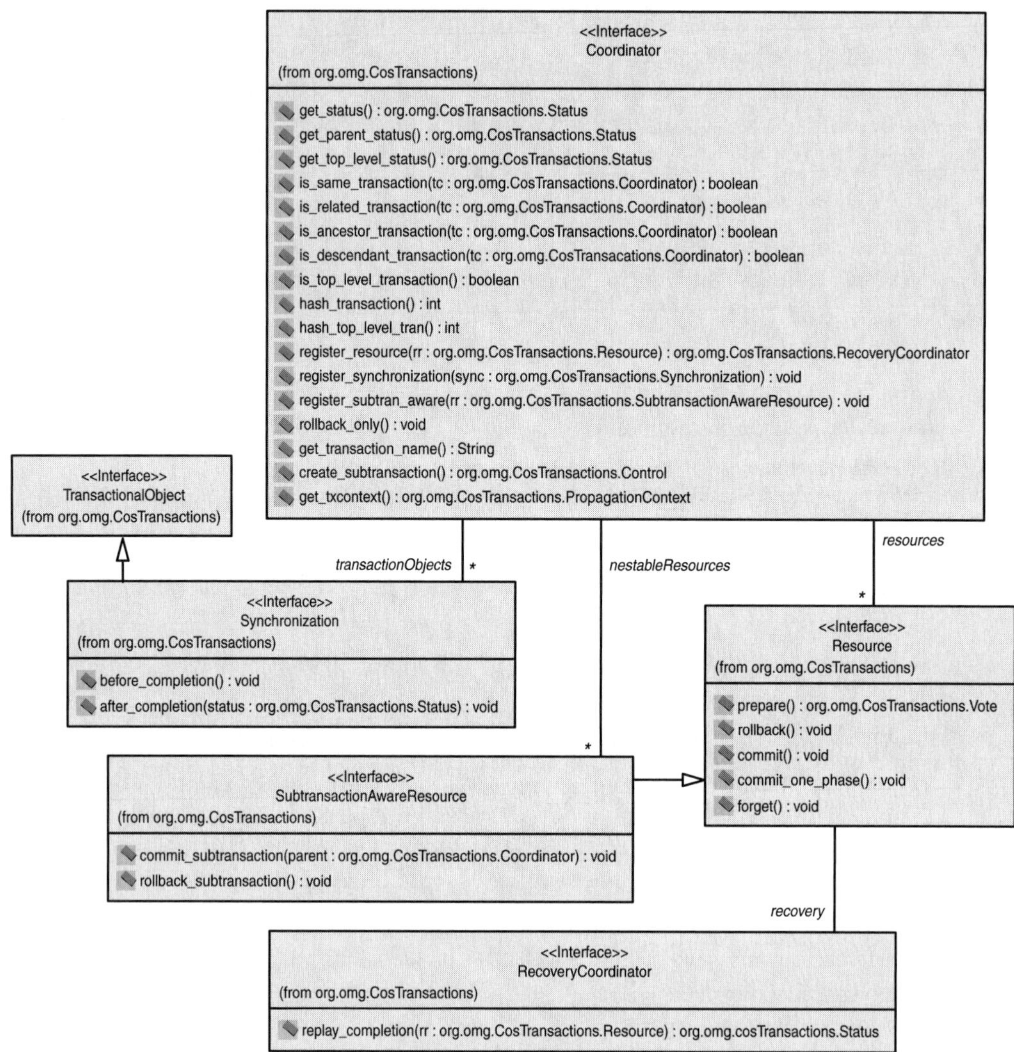

FIGURE 23.12

OTS coordination, resource, and transactional object interfaces.

Java Transactions API

The Java Transaction API (JTA) specifies standard interfaces for Java-based applications and application servers to interact with transactions, transaction managers, and resource managers (`http://java.sun.com/products/jta/`). The JTA model follows the basic X/Open

DTP model described earlier in this chapter and Chapter 8, as depicted in Figure 8.2. The main components of the JTA architecture are shown in Figure 23.14. The JTA components in this diagram are defined in both the `javax.transaction` and the `javax.transaction.xa` packages. Three main interface groupings of the JTA are also shown, including JTA transaction management, JTA application interfacing, and JTA XA resource management. The relation to the Java Transaction Service (JTS) is also shown in this diagram.

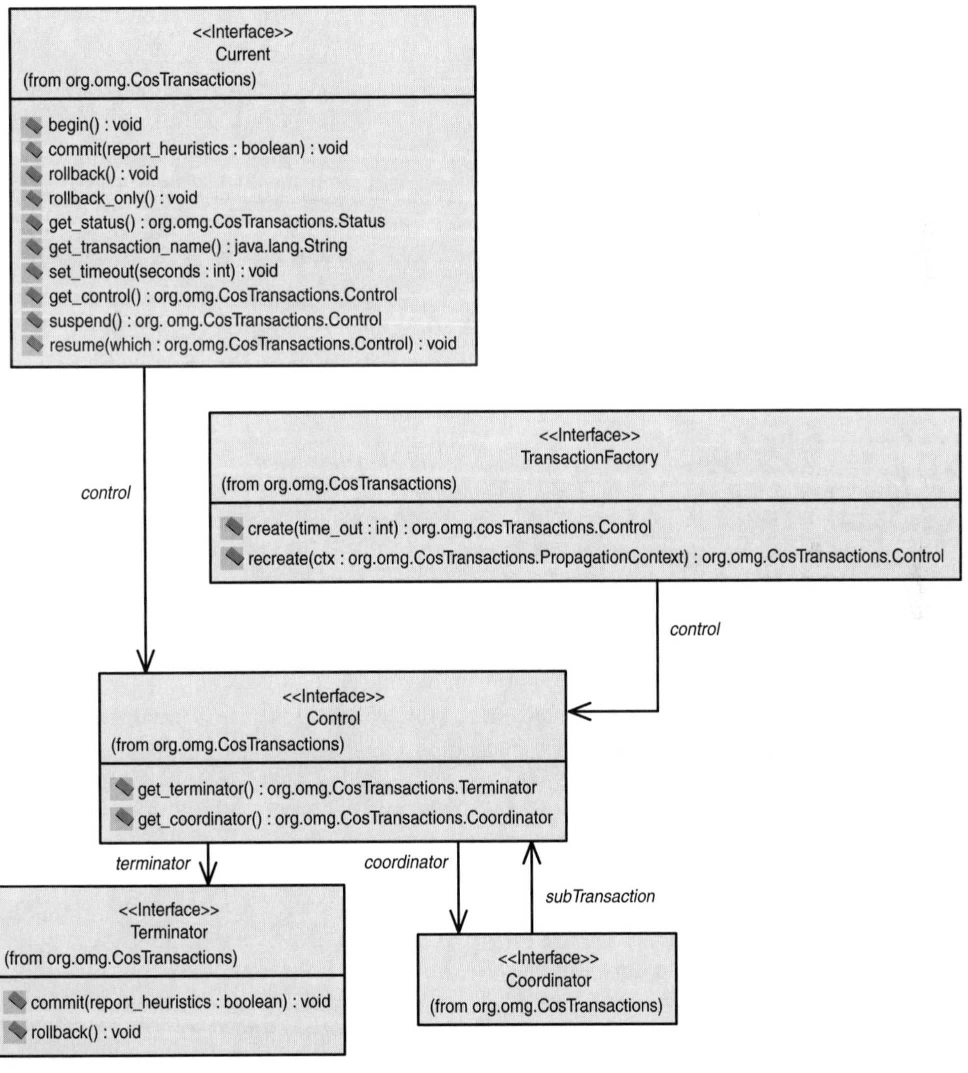

FIGURE 23.13
OTS transaction creation and management interfaces.

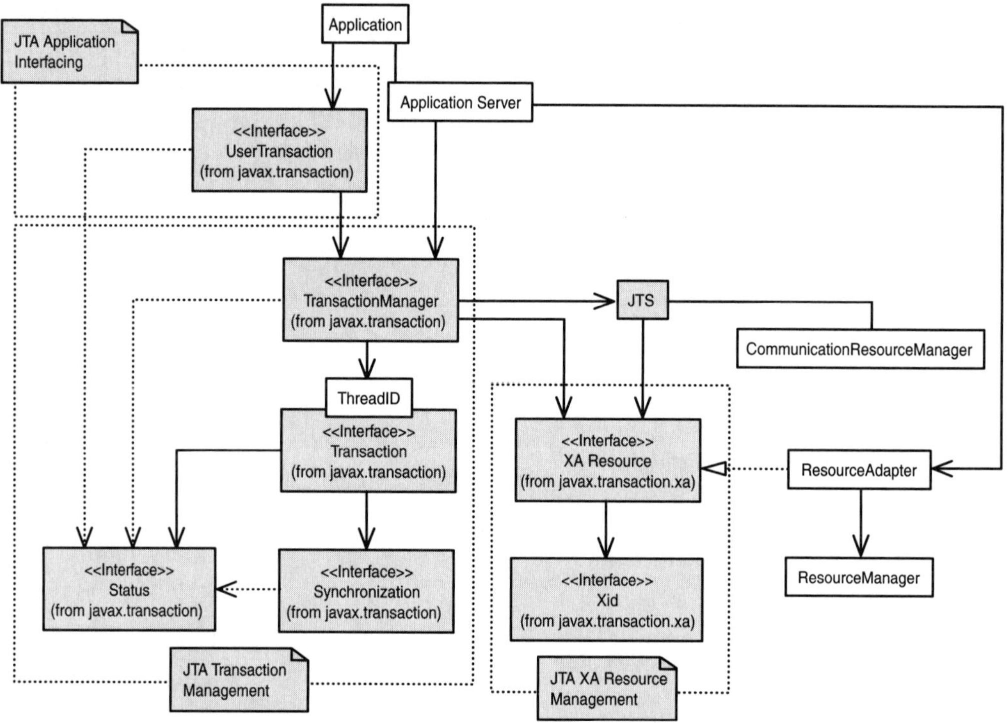

FIGURE 23.14
The JTA architecture.

JTA transaction management provides a set of interfaces utilized by an application server to manage the beginning and completion of transactions. Transaction synchronization and propagation services are also provided under the domain of transaction management. The JTA `Transaction`, `TransactionManager`, `Synchronization`, and `Status` interfaces all belong to the realm of JTA transaction management. An application server will typically implement a container environment within which enterprise application components can run and utilize the services of transaction management.

An application server environment such as with the J2EE can provide a declarative model for applications to utilize transaction management services. JTA application interfacing also provides a programmatic interface to transaction management for use by applications. An application uses the `UserTransaction` interface for this very purpose.

The X/Open XA resource management interface provides a standard means for transaction managers to interact with resources (for example, a DBMS) involved in a distributed transaction. A resource adapter, such as JDBC, implements the `XAResource` interface that is also used by an application server environment.

Finally, the Java mapping of OTS known as the JTS provides a lower-level interface to a distributed transaction service. A JTS implementation will propagate transaction context to other transaction managers via standard X/Open communications resource manager interfaces.

The JTA interfaces are required as a part of the J2EE. JTA application interfacing must be implemented by a J2EE server. JTA XA resource management interface implementations are not currently required but are encouraged. Furthermore, no specific protocol for transaction propagation interoperability across J2EE servers has been defined. However, a future version of the J2EE specification will require OTS-based interfaces and therefore require standard protocol interoperability via IIOP.

JTA Transaction Manager Interface

The JTA supports a standard interface to transaction management services. An application server accesses these services primarily through the `TransactionManager` and `Transaction` interfaces. Figure 23.15 depicts these interfaces and two other key JTA interfaces utilized by an application server to interact with an underlying transaction manager.

The `Status` interface defines a set of static constants that indicate the state of a transaction. The `Synchronization` interface is provided to enable notification before a commit is prepared (that is, `beforeCompletion()`) and after a commit or rollback operation is performed (that is, `afterCompletion()`). A call to `Transaction.registerSynchronization()` can register a `Synchronization` object with a transaction associated with a current thread so that the `beforeCompletion()` and `afterCompletion()` calls can be made by a transaction manager.

The `Transaction` interface, as the name implies, encapsulates a transaction. A `Transaction` is created by a transaction manager and enables operations to be invoked on a transaction that is associated with a target transactional object. A `Transaction` object can be told to `commit()` or `rollback()`. A `Transaction` object can also be told to only enable rollbacks to be performed on a transaction using the `setRollbackOnly()` call. The constant `Status` of a transaction can be obtained via a call to `Transaction.getStatus()`. You'll learn more about the `enlistResource()` and `delistResource()` methods in a subsequent section.

The `TransactionManager` interface is used by an application server to manage transactions for a user application. The `TransactionManager` associates transactions with threads. The methods `begin()`, `commit()`, and `rollback()` on a `TransactionManager` are called by an application server to begin, commit, and rollback transactions for a current thread, respectively. The `TransactionManager` also supports a `setRollbackOnly()` method to designate the fact that only a rollback will be supported for the current thread's transaction. A `setTransactionTimeout()` method also defines a timeout for a transaction in terms of seconds, and a `getStatus()` method returns the static constant `Status` of the current thread's transaction.

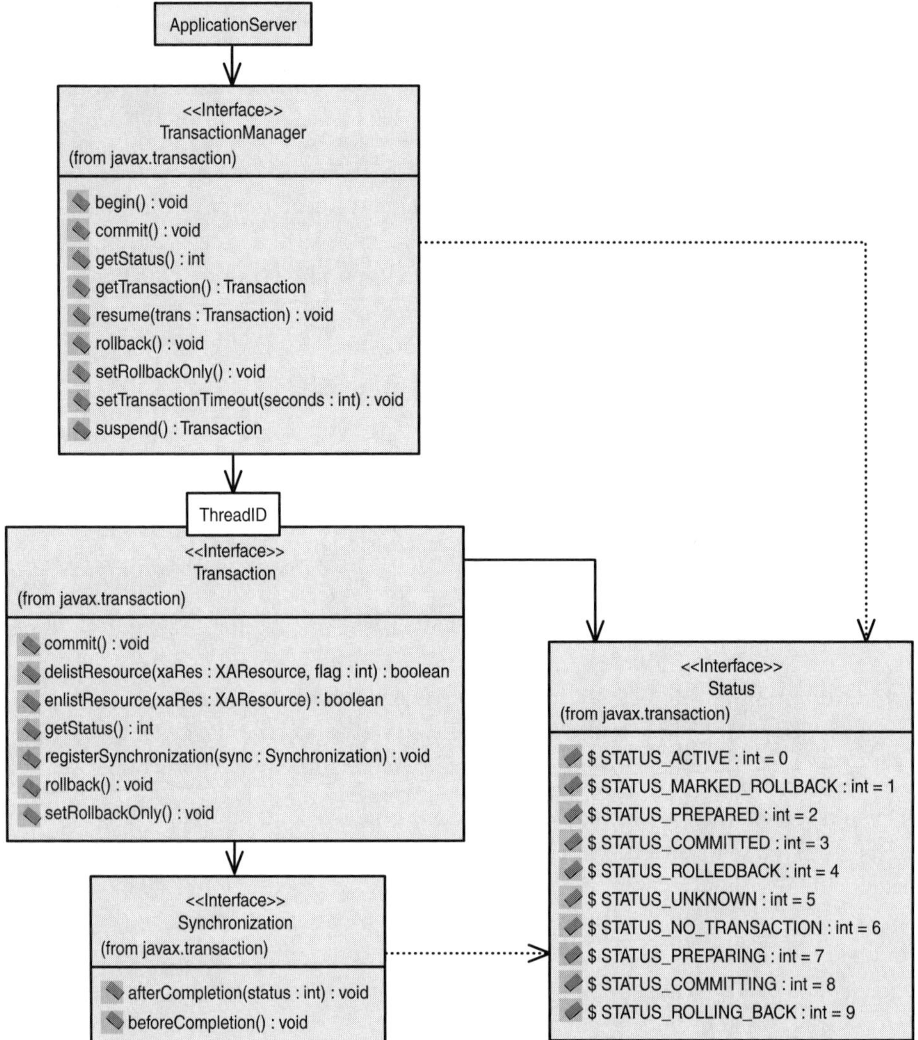

FIGURE 23.15
JTA transaction management.

A handle to the current thread's transaction can be obtained by calling `TransactionManager.getTransaction()`. By calling `TransactionManager.suspend()`, you can suspend the current transaction and also obtain a handle to the `Transaction` object. The `TransactionManager.resume()` method can resume the current transaction.

JTA Application Interface

The JTA application interface consists of the `javax.transaction.UserTransaction` Java interface. `UserTransaction` is used by an application to control transaction boundaries. Figure 23.16 depicts this interface and the relation between it, an application, and the underlying JTA transaction management architecture.

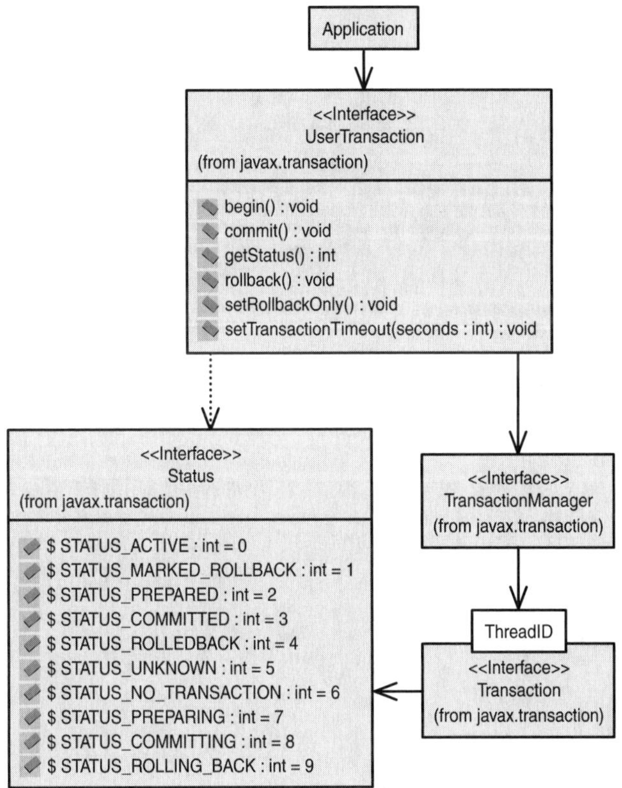

FIGURE 23.16
JTA user application interfacing.

The `UserTransaction.begin()` method can be called by an application to begin a transaction that gets associated with the current thread in which the application is running. An underlying transaction manager actually handles the thread to transaction association. A `NotSupportedException` will be thrown by the `begin()` call if the current thread is already associated with a transaction and there is no capability to nest the transaction.

The UserTransaction.commit() method terminates the transaction associated with the current thread. The UserTransaction.rollback() method induces an abort of the current transaction associated with the current thread. With a call to UserTransaction.setRollbackOnly(), the transaction associated with the current thread can only be aborted.

A timeout associated with the transaction can be set by calling UserTransaction.setTransactionTimeout() with an int value in seconds. Finally, the constant Status of a transaction can be yielded from the UserTransaction.getStatus() call.

J2EE application server components (that is, Enterprise JavaBeans) by and large can rely on the declarative and container-managed transaction semantics, but they can also utilize the UserTransaction interface if the component programmatically manages its own transactions. Java Web components (that is, Java Servlets and JavaServer Pages) can also utilize the UserTransaction interface to demarcate transactions. A handle to a UserTransaction may be gotten from a JNDI lookup or directly from the container environment in the case of Enterprise JavaBeans.

For example, you might retrieve the UserTransaction via JNDI using this:

```
UserTransaction trans
    = (UserTransaction) JNDIcontext.lookup("java:comp/UserTransaction");
```

Or you may obtain the UserTransaction directly from the container context using this:

```
UserTransaction trans = containerContext.getUserTransaction();
```

The transaction can then be demarcated programmatically using this:

```
trans.begin();

  // Do some work...

if( ALL_IS_OK )
  trans.commit();
else
  trans.rollback();
```

JTA and X/Open XA

The XA interface defined by the X/Open group (http://www.opengroup.org) specifies the interface to distributed resource managers as accessed by distributed transaction managers in the X/Open standard DTP model. The JTA encapsulates this interface using the XAResource and Xid interfaces depicted in Figure 23.17. The XAResource interface is utilized by a transaction manager to manage distributed transactions among resources.

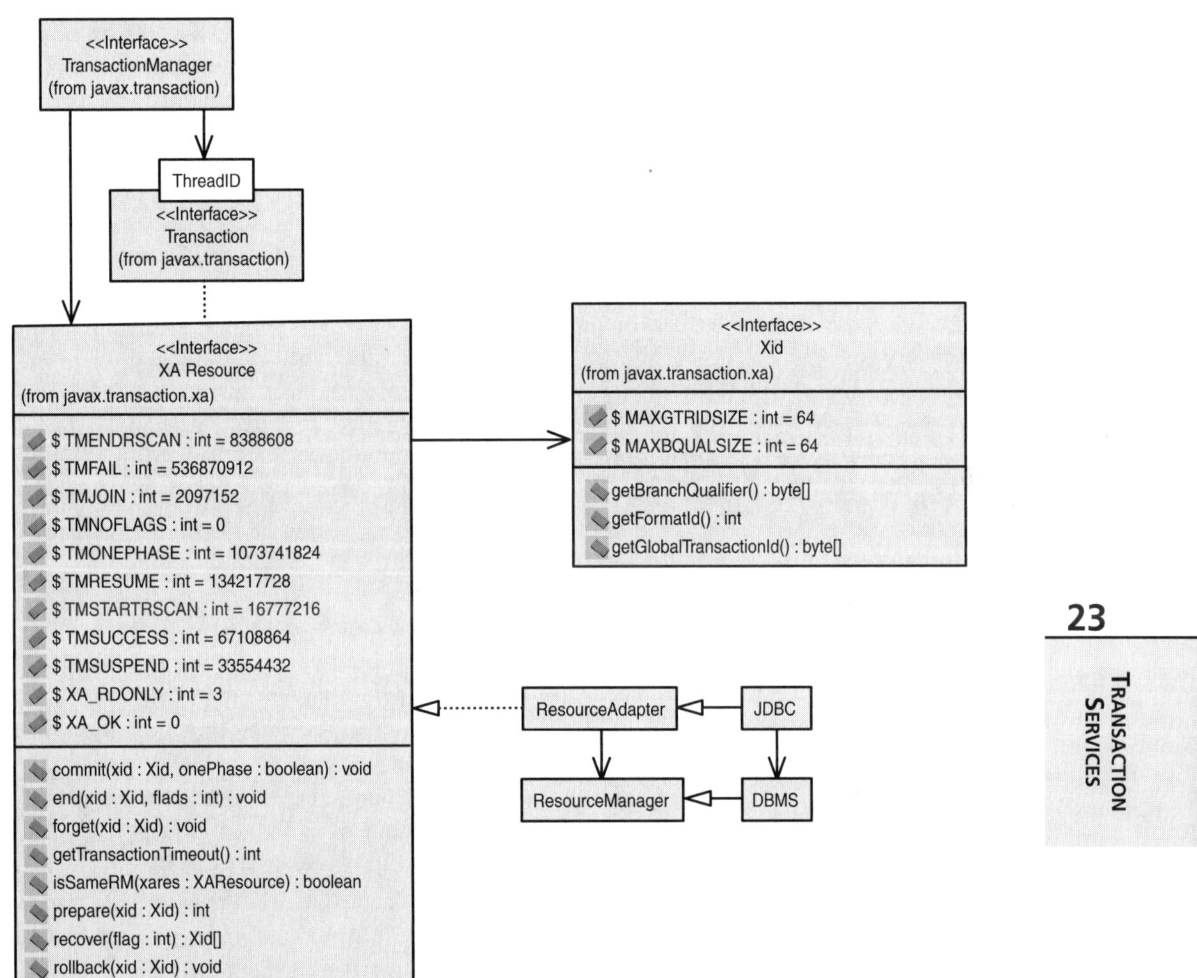

FIGURE 23.17
JTA resource management interfaces.

The `Xid` interface is an identifier for a distributed transaction specified in X/Open standard parlance. The standard X/Open format identifier, global transaction identifier bytes, and branch identifier bytes may all be retrieved from the `Xid` interface. Additionally, two static constants define characteristics of a transaction.

The XAResource interface is a Java mapping of the standard X/Open interface between a transaction manager and a resource manager. A resource manager's resource adapter must implement the XAResource interface to enable a resource to participate in a distributed transaction. A sample resource manager is a DBMS and a sample resource adapter is the JDBC interface to a DBMS. A transaction manager obtains an XAResource handle for every resource that participates in a distributed transaction.

The XAResource.start() method is used to associate a distributed transaction with a resource. In addition to the Xid, one of the XAResource static constant flags TMJOIN, TMRESUME, or TMNOFLAGS is used to, respectively, indicate whether the caller is joining an existing transaction, the caller is resuming a suspended transaction, or no flags are to be set. The XAResource.end() method is called to disassociate the resource from the transaction. In addition to an Xid, the end() call uses a flag TMSUSPEND, TMRESUME, TMFAIL, or TMSUCCESS to, respectively, indicate whether the transaction is suspended, is resumed, is to be rolled back, or is to be committed. The XAResource also provides methods to commit, prepare for a commit, rollback, recover, and forget about distributed transactions. The transaction timeout can also be set and retrieved from the XAResource.

Java Transactions Service

Figure 23.18 presents the system context in which the JTS architecture operates. JTS (http://java.sun.com/products/jts/) is a Java mapping of the OTS. Therefore, the JTS API is by and large defined by the org.omg.CosTransactions and org.omg.CosTSPortability packages. Java-based applications and Java-based application servers access transaction management functionality via the JTA interfaces. The JTA interacts with a transaction management implementation via JTS. Similarly, the JTS can access resources via the JTA XA interfaces or can access OTS-enabled non-XA resources. JTS implementations can interoperate via CORBA OTS interfaces. JTS supports a flat transaction model. JTS can support, but is not required to support, a nested transaction model.

There is no specified mechanism for an OTS-based transaction manager and an ORB to locate one another. The javax.jts.TransactionService interface is provided to facilitate a transaction manager and an ORB being able to locate one another. It is the only non-OTS standard interface defined by JTS and defines a single method.

The TransactionService.identifyORB() method is called by an ORB during initialization to let a transaction manager be aware of the ORB identity and attributes. The TSIdentification interface defined as an extension to the standard CORBA framework by the OTS is used by a JTS implementation to register Sender and Receiver objects with an ORB. Sender objects are registered with an ORB during initialization so that the ORB can issue a callback on the transaction service during the propagation of a transaction context from the transaction service.

`Receiver` callback objects are also registered with the ORB to receive propagated transaction contexts. A `Sender` can also receive context propagation replies, and a `Receiver` can send propagation replies.

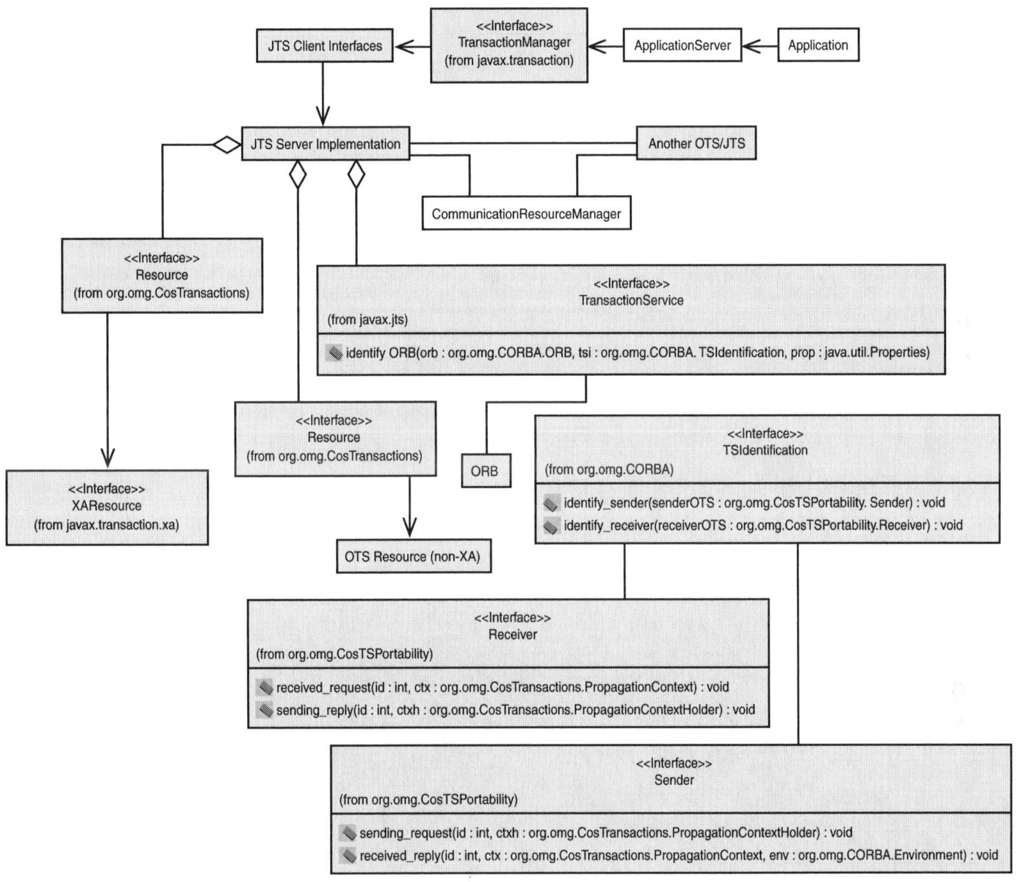

FIGURE 23.18
The JTS system context.

Conclusions

The need for transaction semantic support in distributed enterprise applications very frequently arises in the context of managing transactions that involve DBMS resources. There is a distinct and standard model for providing transaction service support to Java enterprise applications. The transaction services model available to Java enterprise applications revolves around the standard CORBA OTS and X/Open DTP models. The OTS is a CORBAservice for transactions, and the JTS is the Java mapping of this standard model. The JTA defines standard interfaces with the OTS/JTS, between applications and the transaction service, between transaction managers and application servers, and between transaction managers and X/Open XA-compliant resource managers.

Transaction services in Java are thus one of the J2EE components that is perhaps most in sync with other industry-standard transaction models. Because transaction services are one of the core components of a middle-ware architecture, many vendors will be able to better support the J2EE standard. Furthermore, interoperability with other DTP frameworks is better enabled. As you'll discover later in the book, interfacing with such transaction services is tremendously simplified for the application programmer when the J2EE declarative model for component transaction specification is used.

Enterprise Systems Assurance

PART V

IN THIS PART

24 High-Assurance Enterprise Applications 817

25 Security Basics 837

26 Basic Java Security 855

27 Advanced Java Security 879

28 CORBA Security 937

High-Assurance Enterprise Applications

CHAPTER

24

IN THIS CHAPTER

- What Is Assurance? 818
- General Assurance Process 821
- To Be Assured or Not to Be Assured? 825
- Security 827
- Reliability 829
- Availability 831
- Maintainability 833
- Safety 834

High assurance deals with enhancing the security, reliability, availability, maintainability, and perhaps safety of your enterprise system. This chapter provides an overview of the concept of assurance, its importance in enterprise applications, practical guidelines for pursuing assurance, and some general approaches used to provide assurance. This chapter may not be of interest to the entire readership of this book, but we feel that it is key for an enterprise development team to understand the issues involved in assurance, why it is important, and how to practically pursue it. Although enterprise architects will most likely find this chapter useful, we also encourage the enterprise developer to look it over.

In this chapter, you will learn:

- The concepts of assurance for security, reliability, availability, safety, and maintainability
- An overview of the general assurance process and how to practically trade off assurance for deployment
- An overview of the problems and solutions for providing security in enterprise applications
- An overview of the problems and solutions for providing reliability in enterprise applications
- An overview of the problems and solutions for providing availability in enterprise applications
- An overview of the problems and solutions for providing maintainability in enterprise applications
- An overview of the problems and solutions for providing safety in enterprise applications

What Is Assurance?

Your first encounter with a particular enterprise development effort will typically involve being introduced to what the project aims to provide in the way of information technology functionality for the enterprise. Subsequently, you'll begin to unravel the requirements and features being targeted for deployment into the enterprise. More often than not, you will focus on the functional and behavioral requirements that must be incorporated by the project. This is largely because, by its very definition, enterprise development aims to infuse information technology into the corporation and put it to work by providing some business advantage to the corporation. Such business advantages may include enhancing the productivity of its employees, enhancing the productivity of product or service output, increasing revenue received from customers, or minimizing the cost of its operations.

With such fundamental business-critical issues at hand, issues of software assurance can sometimes be overlooked. That is, you might engage in a development process that perhaps sacrifices the quantity or even presence of coding documentation and thus are left with difficult-to-maintain code. Or perhaps in the rush to deploy your new online e-commerce Web site, you didn't carefully examine your overall approach to providing a secure solution. Maybe you've even elected to use a particular technology for your online Web-based storefront because you were familiar with the technology or it was free. And then perhaps you soon become painfully aware that when more than five customers log on to your Web site, your server solution crashes, rendering your store completely unavailable. Providing assurance for your enterprise means solving these types of problems and more.

In general, providing assurance for your enterprise solutions means providing a secure, reliable, available, maintainable, and perhaps safe solution. All such marks of assurance correspond to providing high levels of satisfaction for their related probabilistic counterparts:

- *Security*: The likelihood that your system will operate in a secure and security-breach–free fashion. High assurance here means providing a secure system.
- *Reliability*: The likelihood that your system will operate correctly and as intended. High assurance here means providing a reliable system.
- *Availability*: The likelihood that your system will be operational and offering service. Scalability of your system to support growth in usage is one aspect of availability. High assurance here thus means providing an available and scalable system.
- *Maintainability*: The likelihood that your system will be capable of being maintained, upgraded, and extended for future growth. High assurance here means providing a maintainable system.
- *Safety*: The likelihood that your system will operate in a safe and accident-free manner. High assurance here means providing a safe system.

Who Should Provide Assurance?

That said, how does one provide high assurance for an enterprise system? Many proposed solutions have been defined separately from an actual enterprise system. That is, an abstract model of a system is assumed or defined, and then an assurance solution for that model is provided. In practice, this is a difficult thing to do and, quite frankly, it has led to many weird and unusable solutions. This is not necessarily due to any deficiency on the part of the assurance solutions provider; it is simply due to the fact that providing an abstract model of complex systems is very difficult, prone to leaving out key considerations, and in many cases completely impractical. Using such models as a guideline and not as a blueprint for providing assurance solutions, however, can be useful.

Assurance is literally an integral part of the architecture and development of an enterprise solution. Practically speaking, it is difficult to effectively separate the provision of assurance from the development of your enterprise systems. A very practical and comprehensive knowledge of how to build an enterprise system is needed to provide practical assurance solutions.

Unfortunately, not to overuse the "practice" theme, but "in practice" people with both combinations of skills are very rare.

For example, when a car, a house, or an office tower is built, assurance must be an integral part of development. Would you want to buy a car or house that does not have locks to access it? Would you want to enter an office tower that uses a less-than-sturdy material to support the building? Although assurance can be baked into discrete components of an overall solution (for example, you could buy a lock from a known locksmith), the integrated application of these components to provide an integrated assurance solution needs to be in the hands of the actual car, house, or office-tower architecture, engineering, and construction teams. The architects and engineers in particular should have practical assurance considerations on the blueprint.

The same principles hold true for enterprise systems development. The enterprise architects and developers must be cognizant of and provide the overall assurance solution. They may select small and well-defined components to purchase from other assurance vendors (for example, license RSA encryption technology), but the integrated application of these components, the overall assurance solution, and the decision-making process must rest in the hands of the enterprise architect and development team.

Dilemma of Assurance and Delivery Costs

So how do an enterprise architect and a development team both develop an enterprise system and provide enterprise assurance for that system? Costs associated with failing to deliver a system to a customer or perhaps failing to place some product into the marketplace in a timely fashion can often be devastating for an enterprise. A delay reaching the marketplace before the competition can lead to irrecoverably lost market share. Missed deadlines and frequent delays for delivery to customers can lead to lost contracts, fees, and exposure to legal liability.

Such delivery pressures can force members of the enterprise development team to compromise on the time needed to employ effective software assurance measures. Yet, failure to meet acceptable levels of software assurance can also cost the corporation. A diminished future revenue base can result from prospective customer awareness of software assurance failures. Assurance failures will be even more likely to directly affect the satisfaction of current customers using the problematic software and thus may lead to a more imminent loss of revenue. Failure to develop a maintainable product can cost the corporation by making future development extensions and product growth very costly and prohibitive. Security holes or safety-related software failures can lead to direct costs via exposure to legal liability. Security and safety-related failures could also have more significant intangible costs via harm to human beings, other living things, and the environment.

Of course, costs are incurred for accomplishing assurance goals too. Providing for enterprise systems assurance involves a cost for analyzing problems and weaknesses, as well as designing, implementing, testing, validating, deploying, and maintaining assurance solutions.

The question before the corporation is one of minimizing overall cost given the goals of assurance versus time-to-market. In rapid development or time-to-market–sensitive scenarios, decisions that trade-off delivery time and assurance implementation are usually based on gut feelings and past experiences. These are particularly problematic compromises for the development of distributed enterprise systems that frequently affect many users and significant amounts of corporate resources.

General Assurance Process

The diagram in Figure 24.1 depicts a high-level overview of a process for providing enterprise software assurance. This process can be generally applied to all forms of software assurance, including assurance for security, reliability, availability, maintainability, and safety. The general flow involves the identification of assurance problems with a system or product, assessing the risk of these problems, generating risk-reduction plans, and then assessing the residual risk with such plans in place, as well as the cost of the risk-reduction plan. Although many assurance processes recommend rigid rules, expensive procedures, and expensive tools for accomplishing many of these steps, the corporation experiencing complicated delivery time constraints and lacking any significant assurance program in place may need to employ a simplified procedure. Specifically, such corporations may decide to simply capture intermediate process results and information in a series of simple technical memos or perhaps establish a simple data repository.

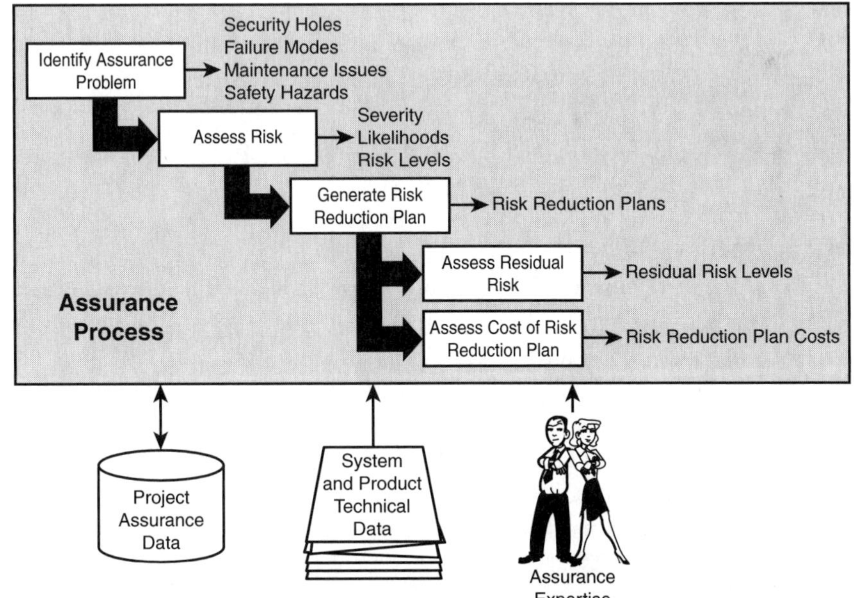

FIGURE 24.1
The general assurance process.

The inputs to such an assurance process of most use are typically previous project expertise and data on assurance issues. Of course, system and product technical data for the current system or product under analysis must be utilized for specific determination of assurance issues. Outside expertise and information on potential assurance pitfalls may also be utilized.

Identify the Assurance Problem

Various techniques can be used for identifying assurance issues. However, with the use of previous project assurance data, system and product technical data, and perhaps some outside assurance mentoring, a practical solution for many corporations is to simply direct their technical engineering staff to identify potential assurance problems via the generation of technical memos. Depending on the size of the project, one or more project members on a part-time basis can help collect this data into a centralized repository and help coordinate the timely flow of the remaining assurance process steps. An identified assurance problem should be expressed in terms of one or more causes that lead to one or more possible effects. Following are assurance problems needing identification by the technical staff:

- *Security Problems*: Security holes, weaknesses, and potential threats
- *Reliability Problems*: Potential failure modes, potential bottlenecks, and code-usage assumptions
- *Availability Problems*: Potential single points of failure, denial of service possibilities, scalability concerns, and code-usage assumptions
- *Maintainability Problems*: Difficult-to-maintain designs, code dependencies, code modules lacking encapsulation, software configuration, processing distribution, and extensibility to future demands
- *Safety Problems*: Hazardous scenarios, safety-critical code modules, and fail-safe components

Assurance Problem Models

To best identify particular assurance problems, it is usually beneficial to at least have some concept in mind for how problems of that type may occur. As an enterprise developer, you are usually in an excellent position to provide such insight because you know how your particular systems are built and are perhaps used to hearing how they have also failed on occasion via bug or defect reports. Nevertheless, in general, the assurance error model classification adapted from some earlier work by one of the authors (Paul Perrone) is presented here. In most cases the errors may occur throughout various aspects of the system, such as during communication of data and applications, during the storage of data and applications, or perhaps while such data and applications are being used. Of course, in an object-oriented system, the distinction between data and applications blur because an object can encapsulate both data and application code. Nevertheless, we distinguish between data and application in the general error model presented here:

- *Corrupted Data Errors*: Data can be corrupted (for example, during communication, while in storage, or even while being used).
- *Corrupted Application Errors*: Your application might be corrupted to perform certain operations incorrectly (for example, during mobile code communication, while in storage, or even while being used).
- *Incorrect Data Reference Errors*: Your application might be corrupted to reference the wrong data.
- *Incorrect Application Reference Errors*: Your application might be corrupted to execute the wrong set of operations.
- *Delayed Data Delivery Errors*: Data may be delayed for delivery during communications or during an attempt to access results.
- *Delayed Application Processing Errors*: Your application may be experiencing processing delays.
- *A Priori Data Creation Errors*: Data enters your system corrupted to begin with.
- *A Priori Application Creation Errors*: Applications enter your system corrupted to begin with.

Many assurance problems can be classified according to such a general error model. As you'll see later in this chapter, such an error model and other assurance problem models can help you more rapidly think about potential problems that may exist with your system.

Assess Risk

Upon identification of an assurance problem, a risk assessment should be performed. This is often difficult for corporations under the rapid development gun due to a lack of resources for gathering and assembling meaningful concrete data and statistics. Thus, the best way for many corporations to assess such risk is to employ a simplified set of evaluation steps like these:

- *Evaluate Severity*: Severity is the estimated cost of the possible damaging consequences resulting from the effects of an identified assurance problem. These costs might consider lost customer base, costs for repairs, and liability costs. Usually, qualitative severity levels are assumed, such as "not so bad," "bad," "really bad," or "catastrophic."
- *Evaluate Assurance Failure Likelihood/Rate:* The likelihood of an identified assurance problem leading to an actual failure over some unit of system operational time should also be estimated. These measures are also usually expressed qualitatively, such as "unlikely," "possible," "likely," or "going to happen."

- *Evaluate Assurance Failure Occurrence*: The more time a system is spent in operation and the more it is used, the greater the amount of risk exposure exists for any potential assurance problem to be revealed. Adjusting the previously defined assurance failure likelihood for a presumed time that the system is used can help provide a more realistic assessment of how often the problems will crop up.
- *Evaluate Risk Level*: The level of risk that can be associated with an identified assurance problem may be estimated by combining the severity level with the estimated number of assurance failure occurrences. This can also be accomplished qualitatively using a risk matrix, as shown in Figure 24.2.

Occurrence Level	*Severity Level*			
	Catastrophic	*Critical*	*Marginal*	*Negligible*
Frequent	Business-Critical (>$10M)	Business-Critical (>$10M)	Very High ($1M - $10M)	High ($100K - $1M)
Probable	Business-Critical (>$10M)	Very High ($1M - $10M)	High ($100K - $1M)	Significant ($10K - $100K)
Occasional	Very High ($1M - $10M)	High ($100K - $1M)	Significant ($10K - $100K)	Moderate ($1K - $10K)
Remote	High ($100K - $1M)	Significant ($10K - $100K)	Moderate ($1K - $10K)	Low (<$1K)
Improbable	Significant ($10K - $100K)	Moderate ($1K - $10K)	Low (<$1K)	Low (<$1K)

Levels are similar to those exemplified by MIL-STD-882C; Military Standard System Safety Program Requirements; January 19, 1993

FIGURE 24.2
A risk assessment decision matrix example.

Generate Risk-Reduction Plan

Risk-reduction planning involves establishing assurance solutions to potential assurance problems. Security measures, code reviews, testing techniques, rollback mechanisms, fail-safe error detection, and component-based development are all examples of techniques employed to provide a higher-assurance system. A key consideration during risk-reduction planning is to determine common design guidelines and common assurance frameworks to help provide a reusable platform on top of which a higher assurance system can be provided while minimizing the costs associated with providing assurance.

Thus, a common set of risk-reduction plans can help one to more rapidly address common assurance problems. In fact, an assurance problem model can often be used to provide general guidelines for selecting a general risk-reduction approach. You as the enterprise architect and developer are again a key player in this regard. You'll need to select approaches that have worked for your particular application before and perhaps reuse existing solutions and code already created or being used on your project. Although some assurance solutions embrace a one-shot cure for all your assurance woes, in practice only smaller and well-defined assurance solutions have really been of any use. Furthermore, such assurance solutions require cognizant enterprise architecture and development teams to hook the components together and into the enterprise for them to yield any practical advantages.

Assess Cost of Risk-Reduction Plan

The cost of the risk-reduction plans should be estimated and should include any additional expenses needed to commonly apply a plan to similar assurance problems (for example, extra COTS product licenses). Costs should include expenses for analyzing assurance problems as well as for designing, implementing, testing, deploying, and maintaining assurance solutions. Any assurance costs spent on employing assurance expertise should also be evaluated and incorporated into the overall risk-reduction plan cost. However, any additional time required by non-experts for developing risk-reduction plans to account for learning-curve time should be considered when generating the cost of internal plan development. Thus, at times it may pay to use assurance expertise with breadth of enterprise systems development experience and who offer assurance as part of an overall enterprise systems solution package. By engaging the help of expertise who offer assurance as part of an overall enterprise systems solution, you avoid risking any conflicts of interest or wasted resources for providing costly assurance solutions in scenarios in which time-to-market deems it impractical.

Assess Residual Risk

Putting an assurance plan in place will often not completely negate an assurance problem. Thus, the residual risk remaining even with assurance mechanisms in place via proposed risk-reduction plans should be evaluated. The previously defined risk assessment procedures involving severity levels, likelihood levels, and risk levels can be used during these risk assessment steps as well. The severity will often be the same, but the assurance failure likelihood levels and associated risk levels should demonstrate a decrease in risk with the risk-reduction plan in place.

To Be Assured or Not to Be Assured?

Given the data you might extract from an assurance process, the question before you is this: "Should you be assured or should you not be assured?" That is, given the residual risk of certain plans, does it make sense for you to pursue those plans, or do you let the assurance problem latently exist? To find the answer to this question you must consider the costs associated with potentially failing to deploy your enterprise application. Only then can you make an intelligent decision.

Failed Delivery Costs

Although there are costs associated with employing assurance and benefits associated with reducing corporate risk, there are also costs associated with delayed and aborted deliveries. These failed delivery costs can also be estimated in terms of a risk level for the corporation.

The delivery failure severity may be estimated as a function of the costs arising from failing to deliver a system or product on time. Costs due to stipulated contractual obligations regarding fees associated with delayed deliveries or missed deadlines may be included in such an estimate. Delivery failure severity costs may also be associated with the loss of market share resulting from a delayed time-to-market. As can be imagined, any exact quantitative costs would be difficult to assess. The use of qualitative severity levels is more useful for rapid cost assessment.

The likelihood of a delivery failure may also be estimated along with the delivery failure occurrence level. The delivery failure occurrence level can be estimated by combining the likelihood of a delivery failure with the number of proposed deliveries. Different delivery schedules you make may warrant different severity levels and can be evaluated separately to help determine how risk levels vary per delivery. Finally, the risk level can be generated for a set of failed deliveries via a risk assessment decision matrix by intersecting a severity level with an occurrence level as shown in Figure 24.2.

Making Decisions

The assurance and delivery risk levels and associated costs can now be used to determine the practicality of particular assurance plans. An identified assurance problem will have some assessed initial risk value which should be significantly greater than associated risk reduction plans, residual risk, and failed delivery risk. For a particular risk-reduction plan to be practical, the following general relation must hold

```
  (initial risk)
        >
  (proposed risk-reduction plan cost)
+ (residual risk)
+ (failed delivery risk for pursuing plan)
```

Although the truth of this rule can help guide the decision to pursue a particular assurance plan, the falsity of this rule does not necessarily justify ignoring the pursuit of an assurance plan. Rather, the reuse of an enterprise assurance plan to address multiple identified risks may be used to make the pursuit of particular plans practical. Thus, a particular risk-reduction plan will be practical if the following relation holds:

```
 (total initial risk for set of problems)
              >
  (proposed risk-reduction plan cost)
+ (total residual risk)
+ (failed delivery risk for pursuing plan)
```

These procedures help bridge the gaps among technical staff, project management, corporate management, and legal departments by providing a common interface language for explaining problems and technical decisions: *risk* and *cost*. For example, corporate management may be inclined to give project management risk budgets for constraining the overall allowable assurance risk to be assumed by a project based on the support possible from corporate liability coffers. Project management may also be inclined to give assurance budgets to the project technical staff to constrain the overall cost of assurance plans.

Management can also use such a framework to plan deployment increments. Thus, corporations may decide to ship a product under exposure to an assurance problem for early releases that presumably may be in operation for only a small amount of time relative to longer-term plans for future releases. Another increment or delivery that follows soon thereafter may permit just enough time to reduce the assurance risk via pursuit of an assurance plan while also minimizing future failed delivery cost risk. Consciously or subconsciously, this is the decision process employed by many successful corporations that understand the balance between high-assurance and time-to-market demands for deploying enterprise applications.

Security

Computer security problems have gained more attention over the years as the dependence on information technology by enterprise applications has increased. Because enterprise systems are used to implement enterprise business processes, if the security of an enterprise system is breached, the very business of that enterprise may be jeopardized.

Security Assurance Problem Models

Computer security involves protecting your system against attacks by malicious human beings. When your system has a vulnerability due to some security hole, a hacker may attempt to expose that hole. An attack brought about by such a hacker may result in an outcome that presents a cost to your enterprise in some form. For example, stolen corporate secrets may result in your competitor beating you to the market with a product idea. A hacker may also be able to corrupt your Web-based storefront by attacking your Web server in such a way that customers can no longer make purchases from your site. As a general security assurance problem model, we have the following general classifications:

- Security-critical data and applications corrupted by a hacker.
- Security-critical data and applications referenced by an unintended being.
- Hacker provides data or an application to another individual or organization representing your identity.
- Security-critical data and applications referenced by an untrusted being.
- Security-critical delivery of data or applications to an intended receiver is delayed or denied due to a hacker.

Security Risk-Reduction Plans

For each general class of security assurance problems, there also exists a broad range of risk-reduction plans that have been implemented over the years to address such problems. As a general security risk-reduction model we have the following:

- *Integrity:* Protecting data and applications against corruption and ensuring accuracy.
- *Confidentiality:* Protecting sensitive and private data and applications. Sometimes also referred to as privacy.
- *Authorization/Access Control:* Protecting valued resources from access by unauthorized users.
- *Identity:* Ensuring that data or an application can be securely associated with your individual or organizational identity.
- *Authenticity:* Requiring that data or an application be accessible to only a particular identity.
- *Security-Critical Availability:* Although availability is a separate assurance quality in and of itself, denial-of-service attacks due to hackers are often also protected by security-critical availability solutions.
- *Nonrepudiation:* Providing evidence that an intended receiver actually received a message sent from you or that a particular sender actually sent a message that you received.
- *Auditing:* Creating evidence of valued resource access.

Because security represents one of the key assurance problem types that has been addressed by the Java platform and enterprise computing solutions, we have dedicated the remaining chapters in this part of the book to security, beginning with Chapter 25, “Security Basics,” describing computer security in general. Subsequently, techniques that have been built into the Java platform are individually addressed and described in Chapter 26, “Basic Java Security,” and Chapter 27, “Advanced Java Security.” This will enable you to make the most effective use of the free and standard Java security mechanisms that can be used straight out of the box and in your enterprise Java applications. Furthermore, because CORBA represents a key distributed computing model that is being integrated with the enterprise Java computing model, we also present a few key facets about the CORBA security model and approach in Chapter 28, "CORBA Security."

Reliability

The reliability of an enterprise system is a measure of how correctly it is behaving. That is to say, given some enterprise system functionality that must be performed, reliability measures the bug-free level of that functionality. Much like you would say that a car which breaks down every two weeks is unreliable, software that has bugs in it is also unreliable.

Reliability, of course, presumes that one does know what the correct behavior of the system is supposed to be. If the software you do implement is correct but has left out core features, one can make the argument that your software is unreliable by virtue of its lack of completeness because the correct behavior is absent. Because of the difficulty in being able to express what the correct behavior of software is supposed to be, measuring software reliability is also difficult.

Reliability Assurance Problem Models

Problems that lead to a failure of correct or complete behavior are virtually infinite. Classification of reliability problems is therefore very difficult. Thinking in terms of the error model introduced earlier, however, we can identify a few sample reliability problems for illustration:

- Incorrect file formats are being sent to a printer due to an unknown requirement.
- An incorrect legacy database view is utilized by an application.
- Component A calls component B with some data values that component B was never designed to handle, and the call fails.
- Class A calls class B with an object type that class B was never designed to handle, and the call fails.
- A class throws exceptions at runtime when one of the classes it depends on is updated with a new incompatible interface.
- During the processing of some set of operations, a failure may result in an inconsistent system state.
- There is corrupted data in a database due to a program flaw.
- A corrupted program on the hard disk leads to a general memory protection fault.
- An incorrect SQL statement leads to an excessive or incorrect amount of data being returned from a query.

- An application fails as soon as it gets fielded when an older Web server version than the one with which it was developed is used at the deployment site.
- A program references a memory location outside its allowed address space due to a pointer problem.
- A blocking call to a distributed application hangs forever due to a failure on the distributed application's side.

Reliability Risk-Reduction Plans

Finding a solution to the very general problem of unreliable software is difficult. In practice, some of the more successful approaches to building reliable software that we have found are these:

- *Object-Oriented Behavioral Definition and Analysis:* To know what you are to build, it helps to follow a process in which the key behaviors of a system are defined and then analyzed to generate analysis models. Thus, use of case analysis and other object-oriented analysis techniques will be useful here.
- *Interface Specification:* Interfaces between your system and other systems and users need to be defined. This includes things such as detailed legacy system interfaces and database definitions.
- *Component-Based Architectural Analysis and Design:* After the behavior is analyzed, the architecture of your system design partitioned into cooperating components will help ensure that contracts between system components will work and that an integrated view of the system is maintained. Furthermore, component contracts and interfaces can be defined here to ensure cooperation among components.
- *Detailed Object-Oriented Design:* The guts of a component design adhering to some contractual interface should pursue an object-oriented design in which other reliable classes and objects already developed can be reused. Encapsulation of data, modularity of design, a reduction of class dependency, and class cohesion are all fundamental OO design principles that should be pursued to enhance reliability.
- *Object-Oriented Programming:* An object-oriented coding effort also helps ensure class cohesion, minimal code dependency, protection of data, type safety, and other OO paradigms that help one to build reliable code.
- *Testing:* Software testing at the unit level should always be performed, as well as testing at the system level to ensure compliance with known behavioral definitions. Levels of testing generally include unit testing of a class, component interface testing, system interface testing, and integrated system testing.

- *Software Version Specification and Checking:* The versions of any COTS (commercial off the shelf) and non-COTS software assumed to be used during deployment should match up with software being used during development.
- *COTS Evaluation:* It generally pays to evaluate a COTS product in some practical fashion before you stake your enterprise on its use.
- *Transaction Management:* This helps ensure that a system either performs a set of operations as a unit or rolls the system back to a previous state.
- *Watchdog Timers:* These are used to send out a heartbeat message every so often from one process to another process, letting the other process know that it is alive.
- *Checksums/Signatures:* Precomputing a checksum or signature over some data or an application can be used to help ensure that the intended data or application is being utilized by your system at some other point in time of system operation.
- *N-Version Software:* Diverse and perhaps similar versions of the same software are used to implement behavior such that when one fails, the other can be used instead.

Availability

What about when your system goes down? E-commerce applications such as an online stock-brokerage site often make the news when their services are not available to their customers when needed. Availability of a system at the time when the services are demanded is crucial for many enterprise systems. If a service demand from an enterprise system cannot be met when it is requested, the entire reason for an enterprise system's existence is affected. Certainly, the enterprise user is affected, which may result in a decline of customer satisfaction or employee productivity.

Availability Assurance Problem Models

The reliability or correct behavior of a system may also affect its availability. For example, a failed communications connection may be the result of a reliability problem and also cause a client connected to that communications session a temporary lack of availability. In fact, many of the reliability problems described in the preceding section already carry over to this section as well. However, availability assurance problems also have additional issues, such as these:

- During the course of system processing, a failure occurs, resulting in an inconsistent system state rendering the system unavailable.
- Access to a shared resource at the same time by two processes can result in a deadlocked state.
- Limited system resource utilization can lead to starved-out processes if another process hogs the resources or dies and does not release access to the resource.

- The system shuts down when a certain number clients attempt to access your back-end server system.
- The system shuts down when certain clients excessively tax the resource limitations of your back-end server system.
- A single point of system failure results in the shutdown of your entire application.

Availability Risk-Reduction Plans

Because availability and reliability problems can sometimes be the same, similar risk-reduction models will also apply. Above and beyond that, designing an enterprise system to be available can involve various considerations and techniques. Solutions that offer one to build an available system are discussed to an extent in the chapters of Part IV, "Common Services for Distributed Enterprise Communications." Availability also is discussed in the context of web enabling in Part VI, "Enterprise Web Enabling" and in the context of general enterprise application development in Part VII, "Enterprise Applications Enabling." Many of the specific availability techniques assumed or employed in those chapters assume such common features as these:

- *Rollback Techniques*: Help roll the system back to a stable state as opposed to allowing the system to be in an inconsistent state (similar to transaction management)
- *Concurrency Management*: Manages concurrent access to some shared resource via use of resource locking
- *Licensing*: Associates a license with a particular process such that it has a license only to use a particular resource for a certain amount of time unless it requests and is granted renewal
- *Thread/Process Management*: Allows for the effective management of multiple requests from multiple clients in a scalable fashion by creating new threads and processes to handle requests
- *Load-Balancing*: Allows for the effective management of multiple requests from multiple clients by distributing the load across multiple processors
- *Load-Testing*: Tests the limits of the load your system can handle due to multiple client requests and particularly heavy resource demands from individual clients
- *Resource Management*: Associates a maximum level with particular resources such that limits of individual resource usage can be imposed
- *Fail-over Management*: Allows another process or processor to take over operation when one fails

Maintainability

Maintainability of a system is often overlooked when you are trying to get a product out the door and into the marketplace. Yet it is a crucial aspect of system assurance if you ever desire to grow your system beyond what it is today and enable yourself to effectively address assurance problems as they arise. For example, if you have a system that is difficult to maintain, a software bug can bring your system down and keep it down if the bug is difficult to track down. Thus, solutions to maintainability problems also enhance availability. Furthermore, if you beat your competitor to market with version 1.0 of your product but your product is difficult to grow or maintain, then your competitor may produce a better product than yours before you can ever get to version 2.0.

Maintainability Assurance Problem Models

Maintainability problems crop up in varied ways, but a large number of programs boil down to the development team itself. Because maintainability of an application often has more to do with poor design decisions and coding practices than anything else, the practices of a development team will dictate how maintainable a code base is. These are some common maintainability assurance problems:

- One or more programmers leave your company, and their coding style is nearly incomprehensible to other programmers. An upgrade or a bug fix for your product may become a moot point.
- Some application with 500,000 lines of code is not documented in any form. It's a nearly impossible code base to maintain.
- A program is written by and large in functional form such that most code is in one file as a collection of functions. It is very difficult to understand code not broken up into digestible modules.
- Each module in an application has dependencies on 50 to 100 other modules. A change in one of those modules ripples into changes that must be made to many other modules.
- An application at a remote customer site or in the field goes down and is hard to reach for maintenance.

Maintainability Risk-Reduction Plans

Because many maintainability problems stem from programming problems, many of the solutions naturally focus on design and programming practices. Following are a few of the more significant maintainability risk-reduction plan practices:

- *Coding Standards*: Coding standards help developers on the same project more rapidly understand code they have never seen before.

- *Code Documentation*: Documented code helps other developers maintain and reuse code that is important for the business-critical growth of your product.
- *Design Documentation Standards*: Standards for higher-level design documentation used to describe the structure and behavior of code are also significant for people to be able to understand an even moderately complicated design. In particular, the use of industry standard notations and diagram conventions, such as UML, are extremely important.
- *Object-Oriented Programming*: OOP solves an enormous number of problems with respect to maintainability. These include modularity of code, reduced code dependencies, and ease of understanding.
- *Remote Administration*: Remote administration support built into your applications may be essential for sites that are geographically dispersed or hard to reach.

Safety

Though perhaps not as common as other assurance problems, safety issues can also sometimes plague an enterprise system. For example, if your enterprise system is a railway enterprise system, it may be responsible for safety-critical operations such as controlling the movement of trains over a railway network. A central computer-aided dispatch center may perform vital operations that dictate the authority of movement for a train over a particular segment of track. If this central computer-aided dispatch center falsely authorizes movement of that train to encroach on the territory of another train, a safety hazard exists. The design of a safe solution may thus involve relocating where safety-critical decisions are made throughout the enterprise system, such as moving safety-critical processing onboard the train or perhaps on the wayside network of switches and signals.

Safety Assurance Problem Models

Safety assurance problems are related to system errors that can lead to hazardous situations. Hazardous situations in turn lead to the potential for an accident in which some human is hurt or killed or in which some valued resource (for example, the environment or expensive machinery) is damaged. These are some examples of safety assurance problems:

- Corrupted or incorrectly referenced safe-distance data between trains may lead to a train collision.
- Corrupted or incorrect reference of an application may cause the malfunction of laser eye-surgery devices.
- Delayed delivery of storm-positioning information to an airplane may lead to severe flight stability problems.
- Uploading of wrong data for a patient's record may lead to an incorrect surgical operation being performed.

Safety Risk-Reduction Plans

Given the sometimes emotional, political, and costly nature of safety assurance problems, the measures employed to reduce safety risk are often significant and involved. The cost to an enterprise for a safety failure can be catastrophic in terms of both direct cost and cost for its reputation, not to mention the social issues involved. Safety risk-reduction plans sometimes strive toward providing fail-safe solutions if possible (for example, stop a train or turn a laser-surgery device off). However, the first step to safety assurance solutions involves the detection of safety-critical errors. The primary risk-reduction plans involved in the safety-critical aspects of a system are these:

- *Formal Specification*: The safety-critical aspects of specifications and requirements should be rigidly defined.
- *Formal Verification*: The formal verification of specifications, design, code, and a deployed system helps ensure correctness and completeness.
- *Information Coding*: Encoding techniques such as Cyclic Redundancy Checking (CRC) help protect safety-critical data and applications from corruption.
- *Object Identification*: Identifiers associated with safety-critical objects can be used to help ensure that the correct objects are being used at the right time.
- *Operation Identification*: Identifiers associated with safety-critical operations can be used to help ensure that the correct operations are being performed at the right time.
- *Object Timestamps*: Timestamps on safety-critical objects can be used to ensure that data is fresh and not outdated.
- *Watchdog Timers*: Watchdog timers are also commonly used here to ensure that applications are still alive.
- *Command Feedback*: The delivery of messages to safety-critical outputs and reading them back in can ensure that such external systems are still alive and functioning.
- *Vital Fail-Safe Hardware*: For systems that can fail-safe, a piece of vital hardware is usually employed to limit a safety-critical output to a safe state.

Conclusions

Assurance deals with enhancing the security, reliability, availability, maintainability, and perhaps safety of your enterprise system. More often than not, assurance is overlooked due to time-to-market pressures or perhaps a lack of understanding of the problems involved. Yet assurance should be in the hands of the enterprise architects and developers. Very often, they best know what problems do exist and how they can be effectively solved. Unfortunately, political pressures to keep such problems under wraps may also affect whether assurance issues make it to the surface.

It is for these reasons that a practical and acceptable assurance process with architects and developers as key players and leaders must be pursued. Problem identification and the generation of risk-reduction plans are key facets of an assurance process that needs enterprise development involvement. Casting such problems in the light of risk, as well as rapidly trading off the cost of pursuing a plan with the cost of not pursuing a plan, can help optimize decision making for everybody involved. Furthermore, guidelines for problem identification and solution provisioning for all facets of assurance should be grown over time within an enterprise software development organization. Eventually, an assurance-savvy enterprise software development organization will emerge and be able to provide more cost-effective assurance solutions to always make pursuit of assurance the most economically viable option.

Security Basics

CHAPTER

25

IN THIS CHAPTER

- The Basic Security Model 838
- Cryptography 839
- Authentication and Nonrepudiation 844
- Secure Socket Layer (SSL) 848
- Access Control 849
- Domains 851
- Auditing 852
- Policies and Administration 852

Out of all assurance facets described in Chapter 24, "High-Assurance Enterprise Applications," enterprise security represents perhaps the most important and widely needed assurance requirement. Because enterprise systems pertain to large-scale systems with large business needs, the cost associated with a breach of security in an enterprise system can be high. Furthermore, because security problems are human-induced problems, the range of possible problems is as limitless as the human mind. Security thus becomes a big problem to solve.

Because of the significant technical complexity and significant amount of risk implicit with the security problem and because security is a key component of the Java and CORBA security models, we focus the remainder of this part of the book on enterprise security. Specifically, we describe and demonstrate how Java and CORBA security work. This chapter prepares you with the conceptual background that will help you best understand the notions and terminology expressed in Chapter 26, "Basic Java Security," Chapter 27, "Advanced Java Security," and Chapter 28, "CORBA Security."

In this chapter, you will learn:

- About the basic model for providing security for enterprise applications.
- About the mechanisms available for encrypting and decrypting data.
- About the mechanisms for securely authenticating users and other systems and means for proving their involvement with security-critical actions.
- About the Secure Socket Layer (SSL) as a common means for providing encryption and authentication services over TCP/IP.
- About the mechanisms for controlling user/system access to security-critical resources.
- About the mechanisms for providing domains of control in a security environment.
- About the auditing of security-sensitive events.
- About security policy establishment and means for administering these policies and their associated domains.

The Basic Security Model

In the preceding chapter, we provided an overview of the general assurance problems and risk-reduction plans that relate to security. Figure 25.1 depicts the basic security model that results from such problems and assurance-provisioning mechanisms. At the top of the diagram we have a resource provider offering some security-critical data or application resources. Such resources are security-critical because a malicious being, such as the hacker depicted at the bottom of the diagram, can corrupt, reference (that is, access), replace, delay access to, or deny access to such resources. A security service provider, depicted on the left side of the diagram, attempts to protect such resources from attack by providing protection services such as integrity, confidentiality, authorization and access, identity, authenticity, availability, nonrepudiation, and auditing protection services. Such services attempt to thwart the best efforts of a hacker from accomplishing their goals. The right side of the diagram shows the beneficiary of such security services, which include the following:

- *Integrity Verification*: The beneficiary has some verification that the data or application is accurate.
- *Confidentiality Preservation*: The beneficiary has some assurance that confidentiality of the data or application has been preserved.
- *Authorization/Access Permission*: Properly authorized permission to access security-critical data, application, or other resource has been provided.
- *Identity Verification*: The beneficiary has some verification that the identity associated with the data or application source is who they say they are.
- *Authenticity Permission*: Properly authenticated permission to access some data, application, or other resource has been provided.
- *Availability of Service*: The beneficiary has access to the data, application, or other resource when he or she expects to have access.
- *Nonrepudiation Evidence*: The beneficiary has some evidence regarding from whom the data or application comes or has some evidence that an intended receiver actually received data sent.
- *Auditing Evidence*: The beneficiary has some evidence of security-critical operations that take place in the system.

Cryptography

Cryptography not only provides integrity and confidentiality protection, but also is a key technology used by other security service components such as identity, authenticity, and nonrepudiation protection mechanisms. Because cryptography is such a fundamental component of a security solution, some mistakenly think that providing a secure solution means to provide a solution using cryptography alone. This, as we have just seen in the preceding section, is not the case.

Classes of Cryptography

So what is cryptography, you ask? Cryptography is the basic science behind the process of taking some data or perhaps some code and running it through a cryptographic engine to generate some cryptographic material. Sometimes the process of generating cryptographic material is referred to in general as cryptographic processing because it takes a stream of input data and generates a stream of bits that may represent some scrambled form (also called cipher text) of the original input data (also called clear text) or perhaps may represent some token (also called message digest) generated uniquely for a particular input sequence. Different classes of cryptographic engines exist, and different algorithms that implement these different engine classes have varying characteristics such as performance, security, licensing cost, and strength or quality of protection (QOP).

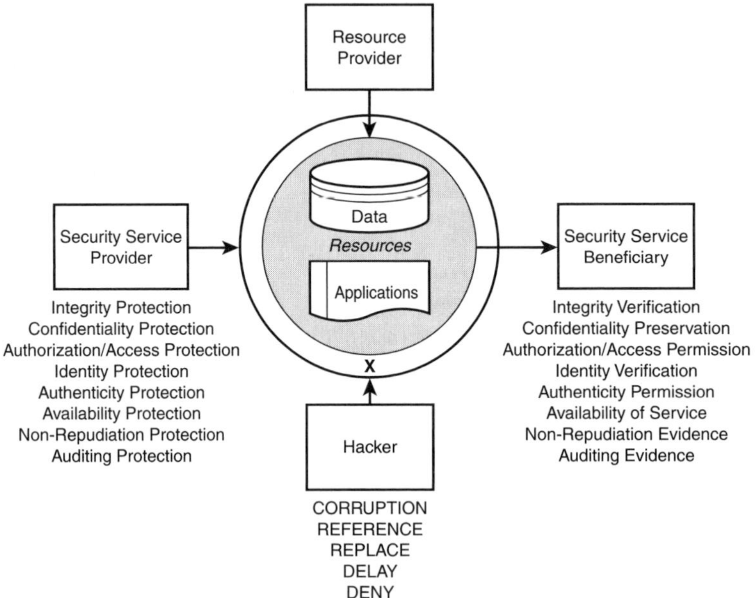

FIGURE 25.1
The basic security model.

As shown in Figure 25.2, if the output of the cryptographic engine represents some uniquely generated message digest, such a message digest can be used and sent to a receiver along with the data over which it was generated. The receiver can then run the received data through an identical cryptographic engine and generate its own message digest. If the received message digest matches the newly generated message digest, the received data can be presumed to be accurate, and integrity is thus provided. The associated cryptographic engine is said to implement a message digest algorithm.

If the output of the cryptographic engine represents some cipher text data, we can send such information over a communications network or perhaps store it somewhere and be assured that confidentiality of the data is preserved. A reverse process can then run the data through another cryptographic engine and convert the cipher text data into its clear text original form. Only cryptographic engines that have some secret key and know the algorithm to run can perform the reverse cryptographic process. The cipher text creation process in this context is referred to as encryption and the cipher text conversion to clear text is referred to as decryption. Very often, however, the entire process is simply referred to as encryption.

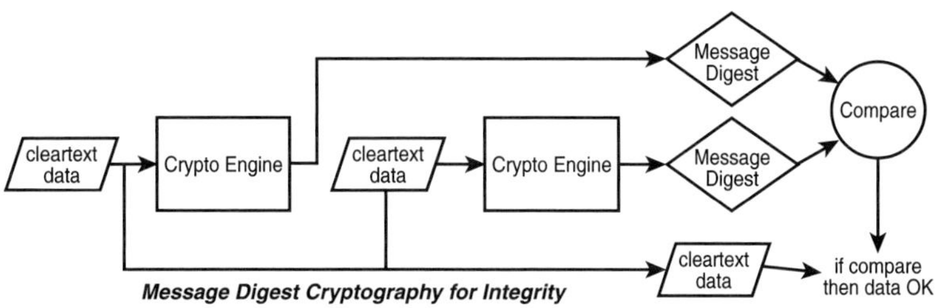

FIGURE 25.2
A message digest crypto for integrity.

As you'll see, two types of keys can be used to perform the encryption process: symmetric keys and asymmetric keys. With symmetric key encryption, both encryption and decryption occur using the same secret key. As shown in Figure 25.3, secret symmetric keys can be used to maintain confidentiality only if no one else obtains access to the secret key. With asymmetric encryption, the two ends use keys with different values. One end uses a private key that must be kept secret and must not be given to anyone else. The other end uses a public key that can be freely distributed.

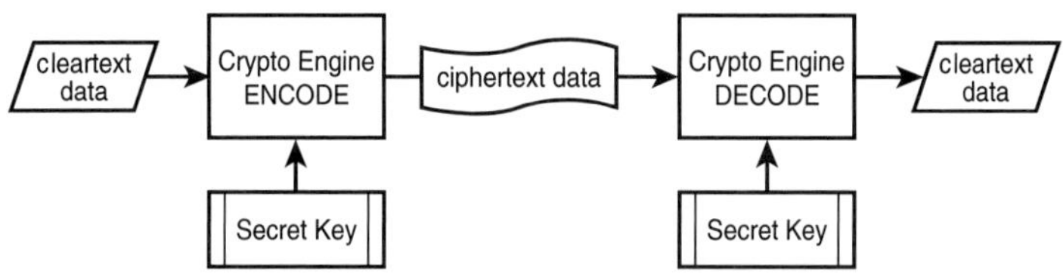

FIGURE 25.3
Symmetric key crypto for confidentiality.

If a private key is used to encrypt some data as shown in Figure 25.4, a public key must be used to decrypt the data. In such a scenario, because the public key is freely distributed, no confidentiality is maintained. Rather, the data encrypted with the private key can be guaranteed to be signed by the holder of that key because no one else is supposed to have access to that key. Thus, identity is provided in such a scenario. Furthermore, because a piece of data is encrypted with your private key, it is possible to implement certain nonrepudiation algorithms under such circumstances in which receivers may be able to prove that a particular data item was sent by you.

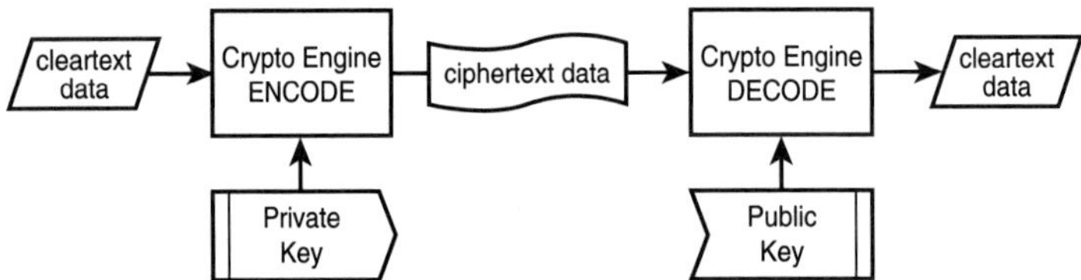

FIGURE 25.4
Asymmetric key crypto for identity and nonrepudiation.

Figure 25.5 illustrates the fact that if a public key is used to encrypt some data, a private key must be used to decrypt the data. Thus, confidentiality can be provided because only the holder of the private key can decrypt the data.

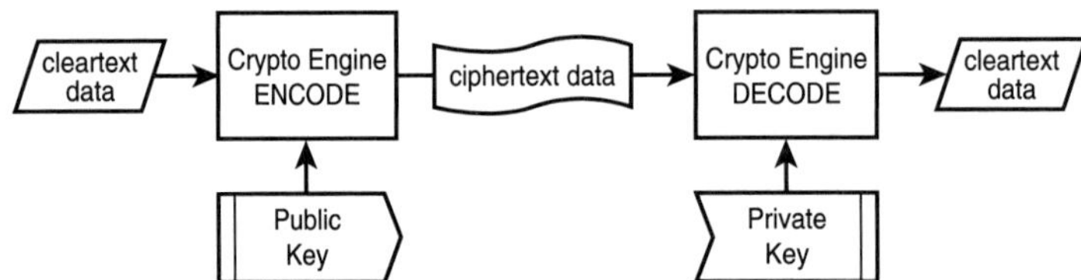

FIGURE 25.5
Asymmetric key crypto for confidentiality.

Message Digests

A message digest algorithm is a one-way function that generates a unique set of output bits based on a sequence of input bits. Different sequences of input bits generate a unique pattern of output bits within some probabilistic measure. Message digest algorithms come in various flavors:

- *MD2*: Message Digest #2 is a slow but very secure message digest algorithm producing 128-bit digest values.
- *MD4*: Message Digest #4 is faster but fairly insecure and also generates a 128-bit digest value.
- *MD5*: Message Digest #5 is a more secure version of MD4 but with speed advantages and also produces a 128-bit digest value.

- *SHA*: The Secure Hash Algorithm produces a 160-bit digest value.
- *SHA-1*: Secure Hash Algorithm 1 is a modification of SHA, overcoming a minor security flaw with SHA.
- *MAC*: The Message Authentication Code uses a secret key along with a message digest algorithm to create message digests.

Symmetric Keys

Symmetric key (also called secret key) algorithms typically perform very well and can lead to very strong encryption possibilities. The main drawback with symmetric keys is that both sides of the encrypted stream need to have the same key. This presents a problem in terms of sharing keys and poses a greater risk that someone could obtain a handle to your secret key. In practice, secret keys are usually first exchanged using an asymmetric key algorithm. Such key agreement or key exchange algorithms enable one to use a more powerful and secure asymmetric key algorithm to confidentially exchange a secret key and then use the secret key throughout the remainder of an encrypted communications session. These are some of the most common symmetric key algorithms:

- *DES*: The Data Encryption Standard uses a 56-bit secret key that is strong but possible to crack.
- *Triple-DES*: Triple DES strengthens DES by performing the DES algorithm three times with three different DES keys.
- *RC2 and RC4*: Can be used with up to 2,048-bit keys and provides for a very secure algorithm.
- *RC5*: Uses a configurable key size.

Asymmetric Keys

As shown in Figures 25.4 and 25.5, asymmetric keys can be used for providing identity, confidentiality, and to a certain extent nonrepudiation. Asymmetric key algorithms (also called public key algorithms) are generally more computationally intensive than symmetric and message digest algorithms. However, because asymmetric keys permit one to hold a private key that does not need to be distributed to other participants in an encryption session, the security of asymmetric keys is hard to compromise. Public keys can be freely distributed to those members of a community who want either to encrypt data using your public key and send you confidential messages or to verify the fact that an encrypted message supposedly sent from you was indeed sent from you. When you encrypt data using your private key, the generated cipher text data is sometimes referred to as a signature, because only the identity of the private key holder could have created such a pattern of bits. Following are some of the most common asymmetric key algorithms:

- *DSA*: The Digital Signature Algorithm uses keys of any length but is commonly restricted to keys between 512 bits and 1,024 bits via the Digital Signature Standard (DSS).
- *RSA*: The Rivest Shamir Adleman algorithm uses keys that can vary in length.
- *Diffie-Hellman*: The Diffie-Hellman algorithm is used as a key exchange algorithm in which a secret key is generated and securely exchanged so that both parties can participate in a particular encrypted session.

Authentication and Nonrepudiation

In security systems, the term *principal* is used to mean an individual, an organization, or some other sender or receiver of messages. Identity protection in secure systems provides a way to uniquely identify a principal. Principal identification is a fundamental security operation utilized by many other security-protection mechanisms. For example, in determining whether access to a particular resource is allowed, the identity of the principal desiring access must be determined. Such principal identification itself must be performed in a secure manner. That is, we just can't have someone saying that he is of a particular identity. He could then identify himself as a principal with more system privileges than he actually has and obtain access to certain parts of a system to which he should not have access. Thus the assignment of principal identity itself in a system is a security-critical operation.

Authentication represents the means by which principals securely identify themselves to a system. To accomplish this task, they usually must interact with some principal authenticator process or login module that takes certain secret information that only a particular principal would know or perhaps be able to generate. With such information in hand, the authenticator will determine whether a principal should be granted access to the system and perhaps (depending on the authentication technique) return a set of credentials defining the rights ascribed to that principal. Such credentials may be valid only for a particular session or perhaps for use within a certain security context. The security context in which valid credentials are defined may be a function of whatever thread or process from which the principal (or proxy for that principal) is acting.

Optionally, principals may allow other intermediate objects to delegate their credentials to calls on other objects on their behalf. Thus, object A making a call on object B may authenticate itself with object B first, and then object B might call object C and delegate the credentials of object A to object C. As a more explicit example of where delegation can be useful, consider a BeeShirts.com CORBA client that interfaces with a CORBA-based query server providing a common interface to many backend database-related constructs such as customer, order, and credit-card objects. Now suppose that the CORBA client makes a call on the CORBA query server and its credentials get passed to the server (this assumes that the client already was authenticated and given credentials). Now the server will make calls to the database-related constructs such as a credit-card object, and it needs certain credential information before it satisfies the query server's request. Delegation would allow the query server to pass the credentials of the CORBA client onto the credit-card object so that the operation can be performed on behalf of the CORBA client. This may be important, because perhaps certain client identities (for example, an administrator) may be allowed access to certain credit-card data to which other identities (for example, a customer) may not have access. Without delegation, the credit-card object would see all calls as being made by the identity of the query server. Thus, credit-card data access control will not be as fine-grained.

Authentication Types

Various techniques for securely allowing principals to identify themselves and authenticate themselves with a system have evolved over the years, including these:

- Password-based identity and authentication
- Physical token–based identity and authentication
- Biometrics-based identity and authentication
- Certificate-based identity and authentication

Password-Based Identity and Authentication

Perhaps the most common and familiar form of authentication is password-based authentication. With password-based authentication, a principal ID (for example, a user ID) and password are entered into the system and passed to a principal authenticator, who determines whether the associated password matches its stored version of that particular principal's password. Password-based identification is very easy to implement and is thus very common. However, a password is similar to a secret key in that both of the ends of a secure session must have a copy of the secret value (that is, the key or password). The password must also be transmitted from the principal's location to the principal authenticator's location, which may expose itself to being stolen by a hacker if the path between principal and principal authenticator does not provide confidentiality protection.

Kerberos is a particular type of password-based authentication system in which a user password is known to a Kerberos-based server. Because both the Kerberos-based server and the principal know the password, they can encrypt and decrypt messages sent between them using the password as a secret symmetric key.

Physical Token–Based Identity and Authentication

Physical token–based authentication techniques offer a powerful but more costly and thus less common authentication solution. Physical token–based authentication techniques typically involve using a physical item such as an automatic teller machine (ATM) card as principal identification. Smart cards are ATM-like cards with embedded miniprocessors on them that can be used to provide a more configurable means of physical token identity.

Biometrics-Based Identity and Authentication

Biometrics-based authentication solutions are even less common than physical token–based solutions, but they can provide a very powerful and difficult-to-crack identity and authenticity solution. Biometrics involves using some physical aspect of a person (for example, fingerprint or retinal characteristics of an eye) to identify that person. Needless to say, a hacker would be hard-pressed to mimic such identity unless, of course, the hacker could hijack someone's finger or eye. All such security is, however, predicated on the fact that the digital representation of this biometric information cannot be stolen. Once such information is obtained, then a hacker may be able to use it to bypass the security of a biometrics-based solution. This is problematic, since new fingers and eyes are not easily adapted for users, whereas a new password or physical token can be easily created.

Certificate-Based Identity and Authentication

Certificate-based authentication techniques are another authentication technique that has grown in popularity over recent years. A certificate is simply a block of data containing information used to identify a principal. Information in the certificate includes the principal's public key, information about the principal, dates in which the certificate is valid, information about the issuer of a certificate, and a signature generated by the certificate issuer.

As previously mentioned, a signature can be generated using a private key over some block of data to produce another block of data known as the signature. The generator of this signature using the private key is referred to as the signer. This signature can then be decrypted only using the public key of the signer, thus providing assurance in the identity of the signer.

Certificates come in handy when you're sending your public key to other entities so that they can identify information that you send to them which was encrypted with your private key. Certificates also facilitate other entities being able to send information to you that only you can decrypt with your private key. Without a certificate, hackers could send some other entity a public key that they say is yours but that is really not, and then sign messages to that entity (for example, an e-commerce Web site) with a private key corresponding to the public key that they falsely claim is yours.

Different certificate implementations have evolved with different formats, but the X.509 v3 certificate standard represents one of the more popular certificate types. The X.509 standard can be used to sign certificates using various signature algorithms. X.509 certificates contain version and serial-number information, information identifying the signature algorithm and its parameters, the CA identity and signature, the dates of validity, and the principal identity and public key.

The Public Key Cryptography Standards (PKCS) define a binary format that can be used for storing certificates. PKCS itself is defined using formats identified by a number, such as PKCS #1 and PKCS #2. PKCS #7, for example, defines the cryptographic message syntax, and PKCS #8 defines the private key information syntax. Certificates are also sometimes stored using the Privacy Enhanced Mail (PEM) ASCII format.

A certificate is signed by a third party known as a Certificate Authority (CA) such that if that CA says that the associated public key in the certificate is yours, then the receiving entity can be assured that the public key is indeed yours and not one from some hacker. Of course, the same problem exists for initially providing a public key associated with the CA to a receiving entity. Such a problem can be made simpler, however, by using a common CA (such as Verisign) whose public key has been given to a community of users in a secure fashion. This one-time secure provision of a CA's public key used to verify certificates from multiple principals is certainly simpler than attempting to securely provide a public key for each principal in the community. Tools such as Web browsers also often come preconfigured with the certificates of many common and trusted CAs.

Furthermore, certificates can be chained such that you might send your certificate to some receiving entity in which your certificate was signed by CA-bar and CA-bar's certificate, which was signed by CA-foo. If the receiving entity trusts CA-bar's signature, it can trust your public key. Otherwise, it can consult the CA-bar certificate that was chained with yours and determine whether it trusts CA-foo's signature. If it trusts CA-foo, it can trust CA-bar's signature and therefore can trust your public key. The moral of this story, however, is that there always must be a trusted foo-like signer somewhere in the certificate chain for the receiving entity to trust your public key.

Certificates are typically requested from a certificate server at the site of a CA. A certificate signing request (CSR) is sent to the CA's certificate server by you along with some other information used to identify yourself as required by the CA. Very often the CA's certificate server will provide a Web-based interface for submitting CSRs. The CA staff will then process your CSR and generate a public and private key pair for you if they grant your request. They will most likely send you a public key via email but should require that you retrieve your private key from them via some secure means such as through a secure Web connection download.

CAs also can maintain a certificate revocation list (CRL) that manages the list of certificates that have been revoked before their validity dates have expired. Entities may consult such CRLs periodically to be able to determine whether your certificate is still valid.

After you obtain your own private key and as you build up a collection of public keys and certificates from other principals, you'll need to store this information somewhere. Because your private key represents security-critical data, the storage mechanism should itself be secured. A key store represents a mechanism for storing private keys, public keys, and certificates. Web browsers and Web servers that support certificates come equipped with secured key stores. Furthermore, the Java 2 platform has a proprietary secured key store with which it comes equipped, referred to as the Java Key Store (JKS).

Nonrepudiation

Nonrepudiation (NR) provides a way to prove that certain principals sent or received a particular message. NR tokens providing this evidence are generated and verified according to the following two general ways that NR is used:

- Generation and verification of an NR token for a message sent by a principal. Thus, the principal cannot deny sending a particular message.
- Generation and verification of an NR token for a message received by a principal. Thus, the principal cannot deny receiving a particular message.

When another principal obtains an NR token generated according to one of the preceding two scenarios, he essentially has evidence that the particular action occurred. Such evidence can be presented to some arbitrator or NR authority later in the event of a dispute over whether such actions occurred. NR involves the use of asymmetric keys to generate the NR tokens used as proof of principal identity.

Secure Socket Layer (SSL)

The Secure Socket Layer (SSL) is a communications protocol layer created by the Netscape Communications Corporation that rests atop the TCP/IP protocol stack. SSL provides secure services over TCP/IP, such as confidentiality through data encryption, integrity via a MAC algorithm, and optional authenticity and nonrepudiation of both a socket client and a socket server. While operating over TCP/IP, SSL can also operate under other TCP/IP-based protocols such as HTTP and IIOP. Thus, SSL can be viewed as a layer that operates between TCP/IP and higher-level communications protocols such as HTTP and IIOP to provide a secure communications solution.

SSL v1 was never publicly used, but SSL v2 was introduced by Netscape with version 1 of Netscape Navigator. SSL v3 currently represents the most current SSL standard in wide use. The Transport Layer Security (TLS) protocol developed by the Internet Engineering Task Force (IETF) extends the SSL v3 protocol with enhancements to the authentication aspects of the SSL algorithm. The Wireless Transport Layer Security (WTLS) protocol, as its name implies, is a version of TLS used in wireless communications.

The basic Netscape SSL v3 algorithm is described here:

- An SSL Client connects to an SSL Server.
- The SSL Client sends a client hello message to the SSL Server containing the SSL version, any crypto methods supported by the client, and a random byte stream.

- The SSL Server sends a server hello message to the SSL Client containing the SSL version, the selected crypto method, a session ID, and a random byte stream.
- The SSL Server sends a server X.509 certificate to the SSL Client.
- (Optional Client Authentication) The SSL Server sends a certificate request to the SSL Client.
- The SSL Client authenticates the SSL Server using the server certificate by checking the validity date on the certificate, determining whether the signing CA is trusted, verifying the signature, and possibly determining whether the domain name of the server certificate matches the domain name of the server.
- The SSL Client generates a premaster secret key and encrypts it with the server public key.
- The SSL Client sends the encrypted premaster secret key to the SSL Server.
- (Optional Client Authentication) The SSL Client sends a client X.509 certificate and another signed piece of data to the SSL Server.
- (Optional Client Authentication) The SSL Server authenticates the SSL Client using the client certificate by checking the validity date on the certificate, determining whether the signing CA is trusted, and verifying the signature.
- The SSL Client and SSL Server both then use the premaster secret to generate a master secret.
- The SSL Client and SSL Server both independently generate a secret session key from the master key.
- The SSL Client and SSL Server exchange change cipher specification messages indicating that any subsequent messages should be encrypted using the secret session key.
- The SSL Client and SSL Server exchange a handshake-finished message encrypted with the session key indicating that the SSL session can now begin.

Access Control

In this book we use the terms *access control* and *authorization* interchangeably. Having access control protection means providing a means for limiting access by principals to valued resources based on their identity. Their identity may also be associated with security attributes such as a set of classification levels, privileges, permissions, or roles that can be used to provide more fine-grained access control decision making. Access control comes in many flavors, including discretionary, role-based, mandatory, and firewall types of access control. We briefly present these various forms of access control here.

Discretionary Access Control

Although some principal Foo may have access to your file system, principal Bar may not. Such a Boolean decision-making process can be alleviated by using permissions. That is, perhaps giving specific permission to principal Bar for read-only access and full access to principal Foo more closely models the access control protection you desire. Because principals can also identify a particular group, such permissions and privileges as previously described can be used to establish access control for groups of individuals. Such access control based on principal (that is, individual or group) identity is sometimes referred to as discretionary access control. Discretionary access control mechanisms typically maintain a list of principals and their associated permissions in an access control list (ACL). ACLs can be stored in a file or database and help make the administration of access control a fairly simple task.

Role-Based Access Control

A particular system-usage role can be associated with a collection of users. For example, an administrative role may be assigned to one or more system administrators responsible for maintaining your enterprise server. Roles are mapped to a particular principal or to a particular user group. When roles are mapped to a principal, the principal name involved with a particular role-sensitive operation is compared with the principal name extracted from the role to determine whether the operation is permitted to proceed. When roles are mapped to a group, a group associated with a principal involved with a particular role-sensitive operation is compared with the group extracted from the role to determine whether the operation is permitted to proceed. Such role-based access control requires that a list of roles be maintained and that mappings from role to user or user group be established.

Mandatory Access Control

Apart from using some explicit permission or privilege per individual or group, other certain access-control techniques are based on a classification level that a principal assumes. A classification level specifies the level of trust associated with that principal (for example, Top Secret, Confidential, Unclassified). Classification levels specified for principals have an implicit level of trust in which higher classification levels (for example, Top Secret) signify a higher level of trust than lower classification levels (for example, Unclassified). A classification level is also associated with a valued resource designating the minimum classification level needed by a principal to access that resource. If the principal's classification level is higher than or equal to the valued resource's classification level, the user can obtain access to the resource. This type of access control is sometimes referred to as mandatory access control. Mandatory access control techniques alleviate the need for maintaining ACLs because the access decision logic is built into the classification scheme. Rather, only a hierarchy of classification levels needs to be defined.

Firewall Access Control

A firewall is a mechanism by which access to particular TCP/IP ports on some network of computers is restricted based on the location of the incoming connection request. If the request is made from outside of the network, access may be restricted, but if it is made from within the network, access may be granted. Firewalls can also limit requests made from within its protected network to IP addresses outside of the network. Sometimes, however, such outgoing requests are routed around the firewall restrictions using a proxy server. Proxy servers used with firewall restrictions limit access to outgoing IP addresses in a more fine-grained fashion.

Domains

Access control can also be defined per some domain of protection. That is, various host machines or processes that all have the same access control policy may be grouped into a security domain (also called a realm or security policy domain). Thus, a set of permissions may be granted for one domain and another set of permissions may be granted to another domain. A security domain may also refer to a location where mobile code comes from (that is, a codebase). Thus, by specifying a set of permissions for a particular domain, you might actually be specifying a set of permissions to be granted to mobile code coming from a particular URL. Such permissions dictate what access to valued resources is permitted for such mobile code running on your local machine. Such is the case with Java security, as you'll see in Chapters 26 and 27.

Code in a domain may trust other code in the same domain to invoke certain operations on one another that would not be permitted for code that sits outside of the domain. The domain is thus termed a *trusted domain*. Trusted domains are also sometimes referred to as *trusted computing bases*. Thus, for example, you may not require an encrypted SSL session for database access from within a trusted domain but may require it for code that wants to access the database from outside the trusted domain.

Domains can also be partitioned into subdomains in which one or more subdomains are contained within an enclosing domain. The permissions applied to the outer domain may thus be inherited by the subdomains. Subdomains may further restrict which permissions apply to themselves, but they cannot generally specify permissions that are less restrictive than the enclosing domain.

Domains can also be federated. Federations of domains grant access to each other's resources at the domain level. For example, a domain named `sales.mysite.com` may grant one set of permissions to a domain named `accounting.mysite.com` but grant another set of more restrictive permissions to a domain named `partner.othersite.com`.

As a final note, when a particular security mechanism is used across multiple security domains, that security mechanism itself forms a domain of security. To distinguish this domain from security policy domains, the term *security technology domain* is used.

Auditing

Auditing involves logging security-critical operations that occur within a security domain. Auditing of such operations may be useful in trying to track down the sequence of events that led to a hack or perhaps in determining the identity of the hacker. Auditing is usually performed during authentication (logins), logouts, trusted resource access (for example, file access), and any modification of the security properties of a system.

This is the typical information logged during a security audit:

- Audit event type
- Timestamp of the event
- Identity of the principal initiating the event
- Identification of the target resource
- Permission being requested on the target resource
- Location from which the resource request is made

Because audit logs are used to provide evidence with respect to security-critical operations, the audit process and log itself tend to be security-critical. Thus they too must be protected in some way from hackers corrupting, denying, or perhaps replacing log information. Audit logs are thus often maintained behind a trusted computing base and possibly encrypted for added confidentiality.

Policies and Administration

Whereas a security solution selects a set of security mechanisms to use in a security domain, the security policy represents the particular state in which these mechanisms are configured. If the particular security approach has provided security mechanisms that are not very configurable, the range of security policies you can define for such mechanisms will obviously be limited.

For example, suppose that a particular access control protection solution you have defined in software has hard-coded method signatures on some access control class for each type of permission being requested. Thus, for a particular permission request, you'll need to add a call from code to make such a request. Although this solution provides an access control solution, a solution that enables you to define such permission in a file would be more configurable and enable the creation of policies to more manageable. Such is a key difference between Java 1.1 security and Java 1.2/2.0 security, as you'll see in Chapters 26 and 27.

Both security administration APIs and GUIs to manage such policies are sometimes provided to make the administration of security for a domain more manageable. Security administration tasks and associated policies that are commonly provided relate to the aforementioned security-protection mechanisms previously mentioned and include the following:

- Administration of the quality of protection (QOP) for cryptographic functions employed by a security domain.
- Administration of which principals can be authenticated with a domain.
- Administration of certificates, private keys, and public keys in a key store.
- Administration of issuing certificates if you are a CA.
- Administration of CRLs if you are a CA.
- Administration of which individuals belong to which groups.
- Administration of permissions associated with particular principals.
- Administration of classification levels associated with particular principals and resources.
- Administration of other domain permissions and privileges.
- Administration of which security-critical operations need to be audited.
- Generation of audit log reports.
- Generation of reports on the state of security in the system.

Conclusions

Security protection in an enterprise comes in the form of integrity verification, confidentiality preservation, authorization, identity verification, authenticity permission, availability of service, nonrepudiation evidence, and auditing evidence. Given the importance and complexity of security for an enterprise, a wide range of techniques and models for security have been developed over the years to provide for such diverse protection requirements. This chapter has armed you with the conceptual background and terminology you'll need as an enterprise architect or developer to understand such security provisioning techniques. In particular, much of the groundwork has been laid in this chapter for you to best understand the Java security techniques described in Chapters 26 and 27, as well as the CORBA security model described in Chapter 28. The Java and CORBA security models, after all, affect you the most as an enterprise Java architect and developer.

Basic Java Security

CHAPTER

26

IN THIS CHAPTER

- The History of Security in Java 856
- Java Security Architecture 859
- Byte Code Verifier 862
- Class Loader 864
- Security Manager 868
- Java Cryptography Architecture 873

The Java 2 security model is relied on for building secure distributed enterprise Java applications in general. Later in the book, you'll discover how specific features of the J2EE security model help employ security for Web and application enabling that alleviates the programmer from having to know too much about Java security APIs. Nevertheless, the Java 2 security model implementation represents a bedrock of components and tools that any serious enterprise Java architect or developer must comprehend. Building standalone CORBA or RMI Java server applications that operate outside of the J2EE application enabling model, for example, will still be necessary in practical enterprise Java deployment scenarios. Furthermore, the J2EE security model terminology and conceptual framework depend on the Java 2 security model, and thus an understanding of Java 2 security underpinnings will help you better understand the limits of and how to use J2EE-specific security features.

Some aspects of Java security discussed in this and the next chapter may simply serve as an information refresher if you have already familiarized yourself with Java security features. However, if you are new to the Java 2 security model, reading this chapter and the next chapter will be of the most use to you because we focus on specific Java 2 security features. Java 1.1 security features that have been replaced by Java 2 security features are largely ignored in these chapters in the interest of focusing our discussion.

In this chapter, you will learn:

- About the historical context for the evolving security model in Java.
- An overview of the Java security model as provided by the Java 2 platform.
- About the role of the JVM's byte code verifier in providing security.
- About the security aspects of the JVM's class loader.
- About the security aspects of the JVM's security manager.
- About the basic cryptographic infrastructure provided with the Java platform.

The History of Security in Java

One of the original ways in which Java was promoted for use by developers was for creating Java applets. Java applets enable code to be downloaded directly into a Web browser. This technology was one of the first that turned the Web browser into a framework that could support the execution of applications downloaded over the Web. Such a framework made many promises in terms of providing a new paradigm for computing starkly contrasted with the traditional way of desktop computing. With desktop computing, your applications were loaded and executed by you on your machine. Whenever updates to the application software were needed, you had to obtain such distributions from such sources as CDs and disks and load the updates yourself. Java applets promised a new paradigm in which mobile code would be downloaded dynamically to your Web browser and automatically updated whenever you revisited the Web site from where the code was downloaded. However, network performance has helped curb such grand visions by limiting the size of Java applets that users consider reasonable to download and therefore limiting the complexity of applications downloaded. Furthermore, the performance of JVM implementations equipped with Web browsers has also hampered the proliferation of Java applets on the Internet. Nevertheless, because Java applets brought mobile code into the limelight, Sun wisely considered security early in developing the Java APIs. After all, if you are now downloading mobile Java code from some remote Web site onto your local machine, how much access to your local machine would you want to relinquish to such code? Many traditional desktop applications require access to your local file system, but do you really want a Java applet downloaded from some malicious Web site to have access to your file system?

Thus, security was a key consideration for Java from day one. Enterprise applications can benefit from these security features as well. Although early models for Java security addressed Java applet issues, Java applications can now take advantage of the more sophisticated security model available in the Java 2 platform for enhancing the security of your distributed enterprise services.

The evolution of the Java security model introduced with each major Java version release is depicted in Figures 26.1 through 26.3. The Java version 1.0 platform provided a very limited security model known as the "sandbox" model, as shown in Figure 26.1. In the sandbox model, only local code had access to all the valuable resources (for example, files, new network connections) that are exposed and accessed by the Java Virtual Machine (JVM). Code downloaded from remote sources such as applets would have access only to a limited number of resources. Thus, file-system access and the capability to create new connections would be limited for remote code. This was a primary concern for JVM implementations equipped with Web browsers.

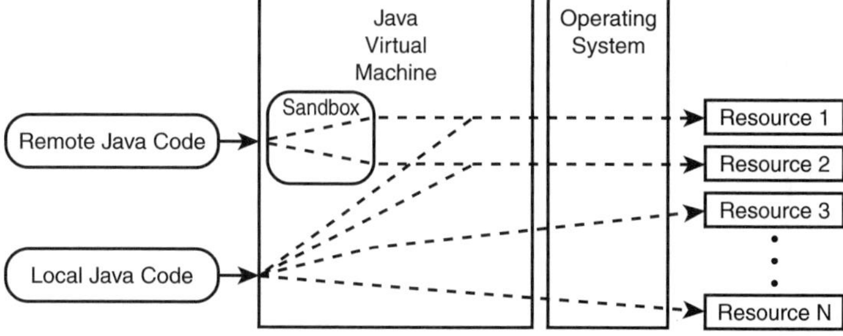

FIGURE 26.1
The Java 1.0 sandbox security model.

The Java 1.0 security model was somewhat too restrictive, however. The vision for providing downloadable applications over the Web was being stifled by the fact that such applications could not perform key operations such as file access or create new network connections. If Web-browser vendors treated remote code like local code, the path would have been opened for malicious code to corrupt the local machine. Such an all-or-none model was replaced in Java 1.1 when a trusted security model was employed, as depicted in Figure 26.2.

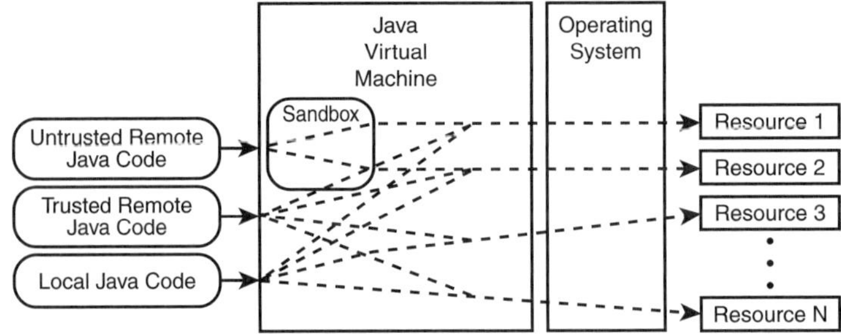

FIGURE 26.2
The Java 1.1 trusted code security model.

With the trusted code model, you could optionally designate whether code "signed" by certain providers would be allowed to have the full resource access it desired. Thus, you might actually trust that some Java code from Microsoft would be able to run inside of your browser with full access to your system resources much like you trust Microsoft when you install one of its many products on your system. Code or applet signing permits a company like Microsoft to sign its applet in such a way that you can verify that this code indeed came from this company. Thus, the signed applet would be granted access to all of your system resources, whereas untrusted code could still be confined to the sandbox.

The Java 2 platform (also called Java 1.2) really has paved the way for application security with a finer-grained security model, as depicted in Figure 26.3. Now local and remote code alike can be confined to utilize only particular domains of resources according to configurable policies. Thus, some Java code Foo may be limited to access resources confined by one domain, whereas some other Java code Bar may have access to a set of resources confined by some other domain. Domains of access and configurable security policies make the Java 2 platform much more flexible. Furthermore, relieving us from the distinction between remote and local code allows for better support of the more widely applicable enterprise application security problems instead of simply focusing on mobile code and Java applet security problems.

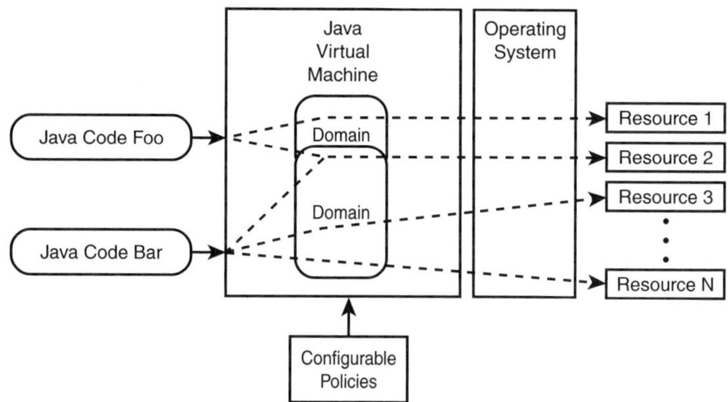

FIGURE 26.3
Java 1.2/2 configurable and fine-grained access security model.

Java Security Architecture

Figure 26.4 depicts the primary components that compose the standard set of APIs and mechanisms used to provide security for Java 2–based applications. In the lower half of the diagram are the core Java 2 security architecture and Java Cryptography Architecture (JCA), which together compose the Java 2 security platform that comes with the Java 2 platform. In the upper half of the diagrams are the standard Java security extensions shipped separately from the Java 2 platform but still dependent on different aspects of the Java 2 platform. Although many COTS packages external to the components shown here are available, the components in Figure 26.4 represent what Sun designates as those components that provide a standard interface. Various service-provider implementations of different aspects of these components that adhere to the interface standards defined by the Java security extension components are indeed available. Let's take a brief look at each of these components in more detail before we explore the details behind them in this chapter and the next chapter.

Core Java 2 Security Architecture

The core Java 2 security architecture in context of the rest of the Java 2 platform, operating system, resources, and Java code running atop the Java 2 platform is shown in Figure 26.5. The pieces of this architecture that form the core of Java Security are the byte code verifier, class loader, security manager, access controller, permissions, policies, and protection domains. The byte code verifier verifies that the byte codes being loaded from Java application code external to the Java platform adhere to the syntax of the Java language specification. The class loader is then responsible for actual translation of byte codes into Java class constructs that can be manipulated by the Java runtime environment. In the process of loading classes, different class loaders may employ different policies to determine whether certain classes should even be loaded into the runtime environment. The class loader and the Java 2 platform classes themselves help limit access to valued resources by intercepting calls made to Java platform API and delegating decisions as to whether such calls can be made to the security manager. Java 1.0 and 1.1 made exclusive use of a security manager for such decision making, whereas Java 2 applications can use the access controller for more flexible and configurable access control decision making. Finally, execution of code would not be possible without the beloved runtime execution engine.

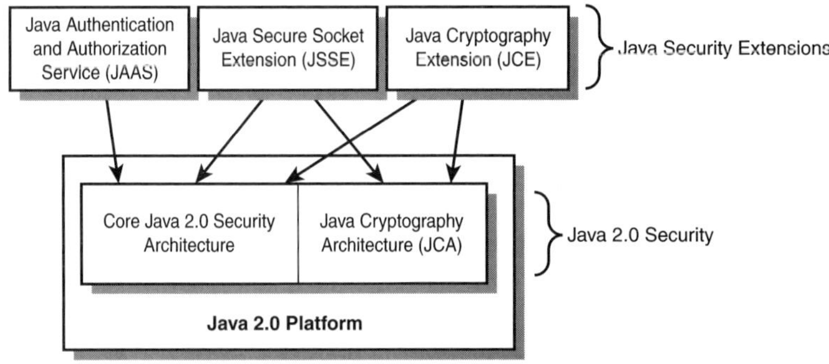

FIGURE 26.4
Java security architecture standard components.

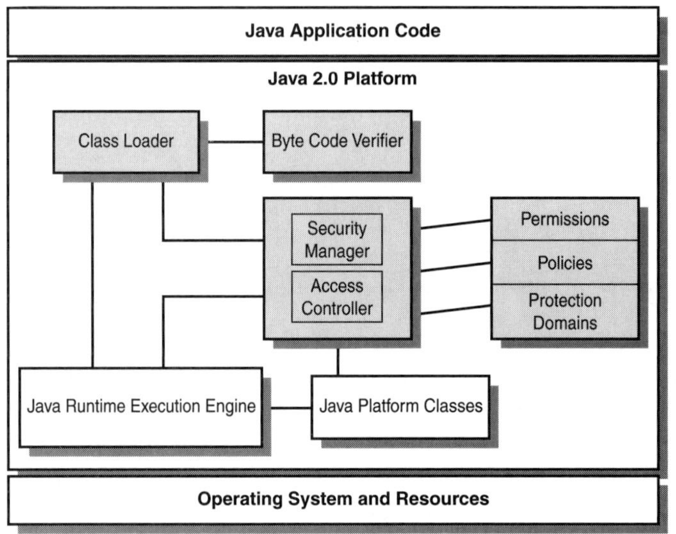

FIGURE 26.5
The core Java security architecture.

Access control is the most significant addition to the Java 2 security platform, helping extend the security model to allow configurable and fine-grained access control. Java 2 permissions encapsulate configurable and extendable ways to designate access limitations and allowances that may be associated with valued resources. Java 2 policies provide the mechanisms needed to actually associate such permissions with valued resources in a configurable fashion. Finally, means for encapsulating domains of access control are also provided with the core Java 2 security model.

The `java.security` package contains the classes and interfaces that define the core Java security architecture. The `java.security.acl` package also contained access control classes and interfaces that were core to the Java 1.1 security architecture, but they have been superseded as of Java 2 by newer access control constructs. Finally, other security-related classes are embedded throughout the entire collection of Java platform packages. Along the way in this chapter and the next, we highlight which classes play a role in supporting the core Java security architecture.

Java Cryptography Architecture

The Java Cryptography Architecture (JCA) provides an infrastructure for performing basic cryptographic functionality with the Java platform. The scope of cryptographic functionality includes protecting data against corruption for the sake of data integrity using basic cryptographic functions and algorithms. Cryptographic signature generation algorithms used for identifying sources of data and code are also built into the JCA. Because keys and certificates are a core part of identifying data and code sources, APIs are also built into the JCA for handling such features.

Although the JCA is part of the built-in Java security packages as are the core Java 2 security architecture features, we distinguish the JCA from such core APIs largely due to the JCA's underlying service provider interface. That is, different cryptographic implementations can be plugged into the JCA framework, whereas Java applications can still adhere to the same basic JCA interfaces. Sun does equip a default set of cryptographic functions with the JCA, however.

Java Cryptography Extension

The terms *encryption* and *cryptography* are sometimes used interchangeably. However, Sun adheres to the definition of *cryptography* that designates the provision of the basic data integrity and source identity functions supported by the JCA. *Encryption* is used to mean those functions used to encrypt blocks of data for the added sake of confidentiality until the data can be subsequently decrypted by the intended receiver. The Java Cryptography Extension (JCE) is provided as a Java security extension for these auxiliary encryption purposes.

Although most would logically argue that encryption is a core aspect of any secure system, Sun has purposely made JCE an extension to the Java platform largely due to U.S. export restrictions on encryption technology. If Sun were to include the JCE as a core part of the Java platform, exportability of the Java platform itself would be hampered. Furthermore, although many commercial-grade encryption technologies have been developed by third parties, the JCE provides a standard service provider and application programmer interface model. Thus, different commercial-grade encryption implementations can be used and still can provide the programmer with the same API to the different underlying implementations.

Java Secure Socket Extension

Because SSL happens to be one of the more commonly used encryption-based protocols for integrity and confidentiality, Sun has developed the Java Secure Socket Extension (JSSE) as an extension to the Java security platform. The JSSE provides a standard interface along with an underlying reference implementation for building Java applications with SSL. Different commercial-grade underlying SSL implementations can be used with the JSSE and still provide the same interface to the applications developer. The JSSE is also more generically defined to provide a standard interface to support other secure socket protocols such as the Transport Layer Security (TLS) and Wireless Transport Layer Security (WTLS) protocols.

Java Authentication and Authorization Service

The Java Authentication and Authorization Service (JAAS) extension to the Java security platform was developed to provide a standard way for limiting access to resources based on an authenticated user identity. Thus, standard APIs for login and logout are provided in which a standard interface for passing around secure user credentials and context makes it possible to swap in and out different underlying authentication model implementations. Thus, whether you use Kerberos or Smart Cards, the same API is provided.

Byte Code Verifier

Before the class loader bothers to register a class that it loads with the Java runtime environment, it passes the loaded Java class byte codes to the byte code verifier (also called the class file verifier). The byte code verifier then analyzes the byte code stream for the Java class and verifies that this byte stream adheres to the Java language rules defined for classes. The byte code verifier accomplishes this task in two phases. In phase one of byte code verification, the internals of the Java class byte stream itself are analyzed. In phase two, verifications of references to other classes from this class are made.

Phase two verification occurs when the classes to which a class refers are actually referenced at runtime. Not only will the references be verified for correctness, but the relationship rules involving that reference also will be verified. For example, a referenced method on another class will be checked to see whether that method is visible (that is, public, package, protected, or private) to the current class.

The following verification checks are typically performed by the byte code verifier:

- Verify that class bytes begin with the `0xCAFEBABE` byte stream.
- Verify that the byte stream is neither truncated nor padded with extra bytes.
- Verify that class bytes adhere to the correct format for the class itself, methods, fields, and other components of a Java class.
- Verify that there are no overflows of operands on the stack.
- Verify that there are no underflows of operands on the stack.
- Verify that proper visibility (public, package, protected, or private) of methods and field variables is defined and honored.
- Verify that final classes are not subclassed.
- Verify that final methods are not overridden.
- Verify that final variables are assigned an initial value and not modified.
- Verify that methods are invoked with the correct number and types of arguments.
- Verify that field variables of the class are assigned with values of the correct type.
- Verify that no local variable is accessed before it has an assigned value.
- Verify that the class has one superclass (except, of course, for `java.lang.Object`).

Although Java 1.1 did not verify classes that were loaded from the `CLASSPATH` and always verified classes that were loaded from outside the `CLASSPATH`, this behavior could be slightly modified with parameters passed to the `java` and `jre` commands. The `-verify` flag could induce verification of classes on the `CLASSPATH` as well. The `-noverify` flag could turn off verification of classes not on the `CLASSPATH`. The default verification of all classes not on the `CLASSPATH` could also be indicated with the `-verifyremote` flag.

Java 2 verifies all classes except the classes that are part of the core Java platform suite. Although the standard `java` executable command documentation for Java 2 does not explicitly list the `-verify`, `-noverify`, and `-verifyremote` options as valid command flags, some JVM implementations may indeed support use of the flags.

Class Loader

The class loader is one of the key components of a Java virtual machine responsible for managing the loading of Java class byte codes into the Java runtime environment. The class loader is responsible for:

- Loading Java class byte codes from an input stream (for example, file or network).
- Inducing the byte code verifier to verify these byte codes.
- Inducing the security manager and access controller to verify access to resources.
- Handing the classes off to the Java runtime execution engine.

The class loader component is actually composed of one or more individual class loaders. A primordial class loader is baked into the Java virtual machine and is responsible for loading the core Java platform classes. Other class loaders can be implemented by adhering to a standard class loader interface. However, such class loaders are subject to more stringent security verifications than is the primordial class loader. Different class loader implementations are provided to enable different ways to load classes from different input streams and using different policies.

Class Loader Architecture and Security

Figure 26.6 depicts the basic class loader architecture assumed by the Java security model. As a generic rule enforced by the standard class loader interface framework, when asked to load a class from an input stream, a class loader first checks its cached collection of classes to determine whether the class is already loaded. If it is loaded, the class loader can return the class without further processing. The security manager and access controller can then be consulted to determine whether access to the particular class is allowed. The primordial class loader is then consulted first to determine whether it can load the class. In Java 1.2, the primordial class loader loads core Java platform classes, whereas the Java 1.1 primordial class loader also loads classes from the `CLASSPATH`. In Java 1.2, auxiliary class loaders are consulted to load classes from the `CLASSPATH` as well as remote classes.

If the class is not loaded by the primordial class loader, the class is then read from the input stream. The actual type of input stream used depends on the type of class loader. An input stream connected to a local file medium location or to a network medium location requires a class loader that can read classes from such mediums. The bytes read from the input stream are then fed through the byte code verification process. If successful byte code verification is performed, a `java.lang.Class` object is created that is used to describe the class for the virtual machine. Before the class is created, the security manager is conferred with again to determine whether creation of such a class is permitted. Finally, if the class is loaded, the class is then cached with its collection of other loaded classes.

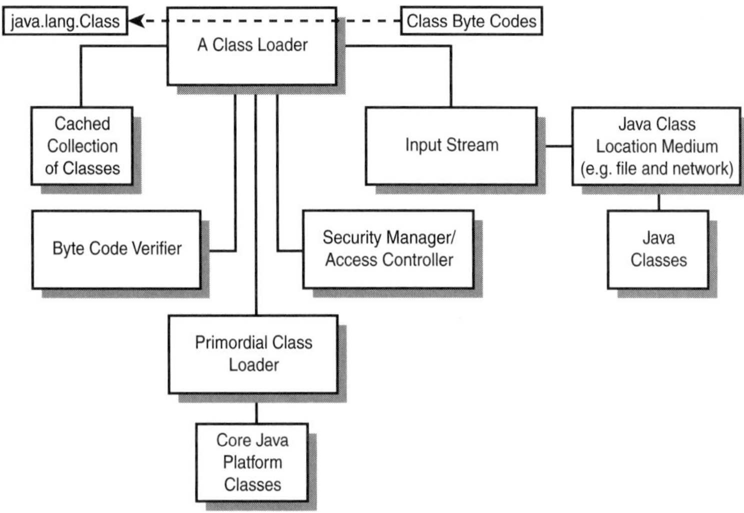

FIGURE 26.6
The class loader architecture.

When a class loaded by the class loader refers to another class, the same basic process for finding the referenced class is followed. Thus, you can see that a particular class loader will consult only the primordial class loader, its own cached collection of classes, and its associated input stream for a class to load. Different class loader instances within the same virtual machine thus do not consult one another to load classes. This separation of class loaders results in a separation of name spaces such that different implementations of classes with the same fully qualified name may live in different class loaders. This provides a security advantage in that a malicious class loader cannot corrupt the classes used by another class loader in the same virtual machine by purposely loading a malicious class into that class loader's name space.

Class Loader Interfaces

In addition to the primordial class loader that is part of the Java platform, other common and predefined class loaders also exist. Perhaps one of the first common class loader types to be implemented was the applet class loaders. Applet class loaders were implemented by Web browser vendors to provide support for loading classes, which form the code of an applet, from the network via HTTP from within a Web browser. Applet class loaders typically determine where to load these classes from based on a `CODEBASE` tag that accompanies an applet tag in an HTML file.

Although no standard API for an applet class loader exists, Figure 26.7 shows the standard base class loader class and three standard class loader implementations that come equipped with the Java platform. These standard class loader types are briefly described here:

- `java.lang.ClassLoader`: Represents the base class loader from which other class loaders should be extended. Core interfaces exist on the `ClassLoader` for loading classes, defining classes, finding classes, obtaining resource handles, and accessing class libraries. The `loadClass()` method is the single-most-important method on the `ClassLoader` responsible for performing the actual load of a class.
- `java.security.SecureClassLoader`: The `SecureClassLoader` was introduced in Java 2 as a base class that offers the capability to associate classes with permissions and a code source. A code source identifies the URL and certificate associated with a class.
- `java.net.URLClassLoader`: This class loader was also introduced in Java 2 to load classes from a list of URLs. The URLs can be either jar files or directories.
- `java.rmi.server.RMIClassLoader`: Left over from Java 1.1, the `RMIClassLoader` is used by RMI applications during marshaling and unmarshaling of classes passed as parameters or return values. The `RMIClassLoader` loads classes from the network using a list of URLs.

The `URLClassLoader` class may offer all you need in a class loader that can load classes from the network via HTTP or from the file system. However, you may indeed encounter a situation in which you need to implement your own class loader. For example, you may desire to load classes from a database or perhaps via some other protocol besides HTTP. In such a situation, you should still subclass `ClassLoader`, `SecureClassLoader`, or `URLClassLoader`. You'll then want to overload a few of the protected methods of the class you are extending.

Whereas Java 1.1 style class loader implementations often overrode the protected `ClassLoader.loadClass(String, boolean)` method, Java 2 style class loader implementations are encouraged to override the protected `ClassLoader.findClass(String)` method. This is because most of the generic class loading logic can still be utilized by leaving the `loadClass()` method as is. The `loadClass()` method calls the `findClass()` method after preliminary calls are made, such as determining whether the class is already loaded and checking with the primordial class loader. The `findClass()` method can thus be specialized to look for the class on the specialized input stream that your class loader implementation desires to search for classes matching the fully qualified classname as an input parameter. If you have a block of data you've read from your input stream, you can then run this class through the byte code verifier, as well as create an instance of a `Class` object by calling the `defineClass()` method. For example:

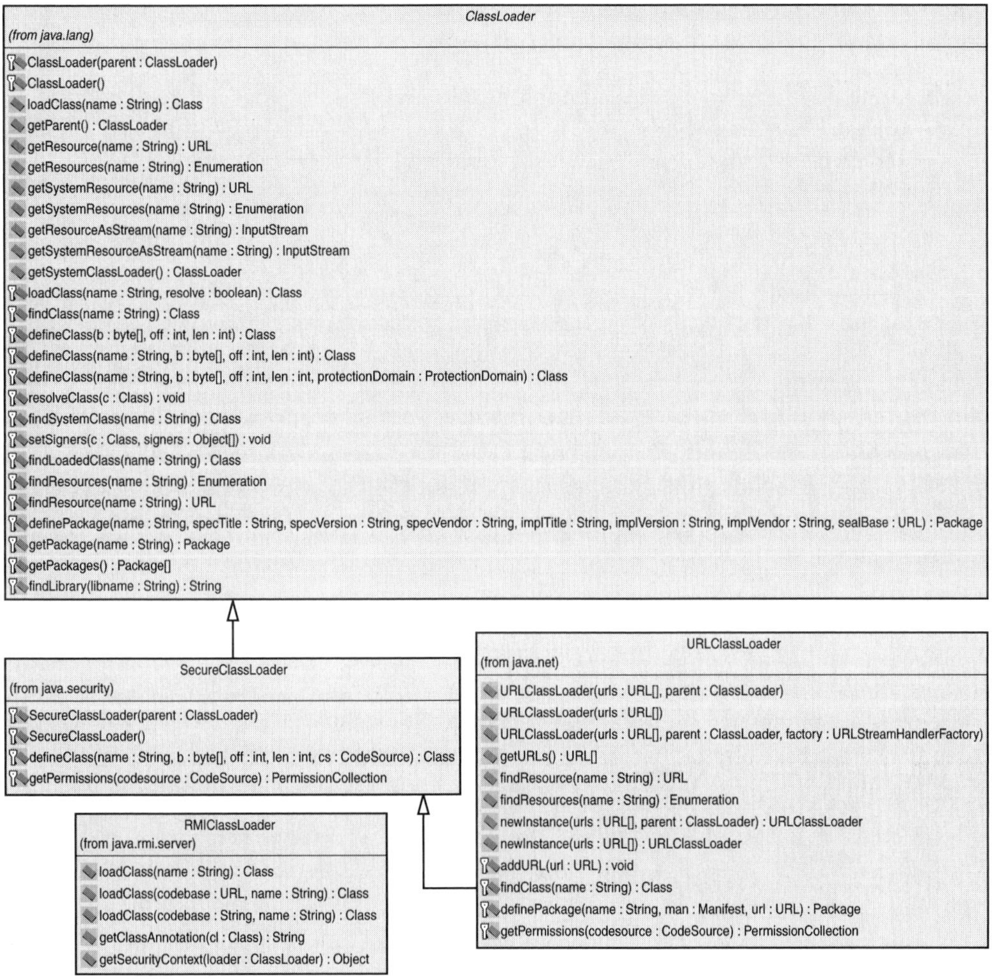

ClassLoader
(from java.lang)

ClassLoader(parent : ClassLoader)
ClassLoader()
loadClass(name : String) : Class
getParent() : ClassLoader
getResource(name : String) : URL
getResources(name : String) : Enumeration
getSystemResource(name : String) : URL
getSystemResources(name : String) : Enumeration
getResourceAsStream(name : String) : InputStream
getSystemResourceAsStream(name : String) : InputStream
getSystemClassLoader() : ClassLoader
loadClass(name : String, resolve : boolean) : Class
findClass(name : String) : Class
defineClass(b : byte[], off : int, len : int) : Class
defineClass(name : String, b : byte[], off : int, len : int) : Class
defineClass(name : String, b : byte[], off : int, len : int, protectionDomain : ProtectionDomain) : Class
resolveClass(c : Class) : void
findSystemClass(name : String) : Class
setSigners(c : Class, signers : Object[]) : void
findLoadedClass(name : String) : Class
findResources(name : String) : Enumeration
findResource(name : String) : URL
definePackage(name : String, specTitle : String, specVersion : String, specVendor : String, implTitle : String, implVersion : String, implVendor : String, sealBase : URL) : Package
getPackage(name : String) : Package
getPackages() : Package[]
findLibrary(libname : String) : String

SecureClassLoader
(from java.security)

SecureClassLoader(parent : ClassLoader)
SecureClassLoader()
defineClass(name : String, b : byte[], off : int, len : int, cs : CodeSource) : Class
getPermissions(codesource : CodeSource) : PermissionCollection

URLClassLoader
(from java.net)

URLClassLoader(urls : URL[], parent : ClassLoader)
URLClassLoader(urls : URL[])
URLClassLoader(urls : URL[], parent : ClassLoader, factory : URLStreamHandlerFactory)
getURLs() : URL[]
findResource(name : String) : URL
findResources(name : String) : Enumeration
newInstance(urls : URL[], parent : ClassLoader) : URLClassLoader
newInstance(urls : URL[]) : URLClassLoader
addURL(url : URL) : void
findClass(name : String) : Class
definePackage(name : String, man : Manifest, url : URL) : Package
getPermissions(codesource : CodeSource) : PermissionCollection

RMIClassLoader
(from java.rmi.server)

loadClass(name : String) : Class
loadClass(codebase : URL, name : String) : Class
loadClass(codebase : String, name : String) : Class
getClassAnnotation(cl : Class) : String
getSecurityContext(loader : ClassLoader) : Object

FIGURE 26.7
Standard class loader APIs.

```
public MyClassLoader extends ClassLoader
{
  protected Class findClass(String className){
    byte[] buffer = getMyData(className);
    Class returnClass = defineClass(className, buffer, 0, buffer.length);
    return returnClass;
  }
```

```
  private byte[] getMyData(String className){
    // This arbitrarily named method contains the logic
    // needed to retrieve the named class from the input stream
    // associated with your class loader implementation. Thus, this
    // method may read some data from a TCP/IP socket, for example,
    // given the name of a class and then return the bytes (byte codes)
    // associated with the read Java class.
  }
  ...
  // Implement other methods as needed
  ...
}
```

An explicit request to load a class using your custom class loader can be accomplished using the static `forName(String, boolean, ClassLoader)` method on `java.lang.Class`. The `String` parameter specifies the fully qualified classname to load, the `boolean` flag indicates whether the class should be initialized, and the `ClassLoader` parameter designates the class loader to use. Thus, you might explicitly load a class using your custom class loader and instantiate an instance of the class given the following call:

```
MyClassLoader myClassLoader = new MyClassLoader();
Class myQueryServerClass = Class.forName("com.beeshirts.QueryServer",
                                          true, myClassLoader);
QueryServer myQueryServer
                    = (QueryServer) myQueryServerClass.newInstance();
```

Every reference to unloaded classes from the `myQueryServer` object can then use the class loader with which it was loaded. Of course, you can also call `loadClass()` on an instance of your custom class loader and use it to load the class initially, as shown here:

```
MyClassLoader myClassLoader = new MyClassLoader();
Class myQueryServerClass
                  = myClassLoader.loadClass("com.beeshirts.QueryServer");
QueryServer myQueryServer
                  = (QueryServer) myQueryServerClass.newInstance();
```

Security Manager

The security manager component of the core Java security architecture is responsible for determining whether certain requests to access particular valued resources are to be allowed. To make this decision, the security manager considers the source (that is, Java class) making the request. Because access to many valued resources must first pass through the core Java classes from a Java class making the request, the core Java classes take the opportunity to first ask the security manager whether the request is allowed. If access is denied, a `java.lang.SecurityException` is thrown. If access is permitted, the call will proceed as normal.

Each Java virtual machine process instance allows only one security manager instance to exist (that is, a singleton). After the security manager is instantiated, the JVM can be configured such that the security manager cannot be replaced. It thus exists for the lifetime of the Java virtual machine process. Many Java virtual machines embedded in Web browsers will instantiate a security manager instance before the first Java applet is ever loaded and not permit the security manager to be replaced. Thus, the security manager in Web browsers cannot be replaced by a malicious Java applet. A malicious Java applet could, after all, replace the security manager with its own security manager instance that relaxes restrictions on which valued resources can be accessed.

Although Java applets run in a Java virtual machine process that has already instantiated a security manager, regular Java applications you create don't have the benefit of this fact. In Java 1.1, creating your own security manager was a tad tedious. Java 2 makes creating your own security manager for a Java application much simpler and makes it easily configurable. This is because a default and configurable security manager that is rich enough in flexible feature support for many applications can be used with Java 2 applications. Thus, as you'll see, use of a security manager to protect access to valued resources can also be provided for Java applications in the enterprise.

Use of the default security manager can be specified from the command line during startup of your Java applications. The `java.security.manager` property can be passed to the Java virtual machine as a system property specifying use of the default security manager in the following fashions:

```
java -Djava.security.manager MyApplication
java -Djava.security.manager=default MyApplication
```

Security Manager Interfaces

Figure 26.8 shows the `java.lang.SecurityManager` class encapsulating the key interface to the security manager currently instantiated in the Java machine process. The `java.lang.System.getSecurityManager()` method returns a handle to the currently instantiated `SecurityManager` object. If no security manager is instantiated, a null value is returned. The `java.lang.System.setSecurityManager()` call takes a `SecurityManager` input parameter and first checks to see whether the existing security manager is allowed to be replaced by the calling class. If the security manager does not exist or if the class is allowed to replace the existing security manager, the operation proceeds and returns. Otherwise, a `SecurityException` is thrown.

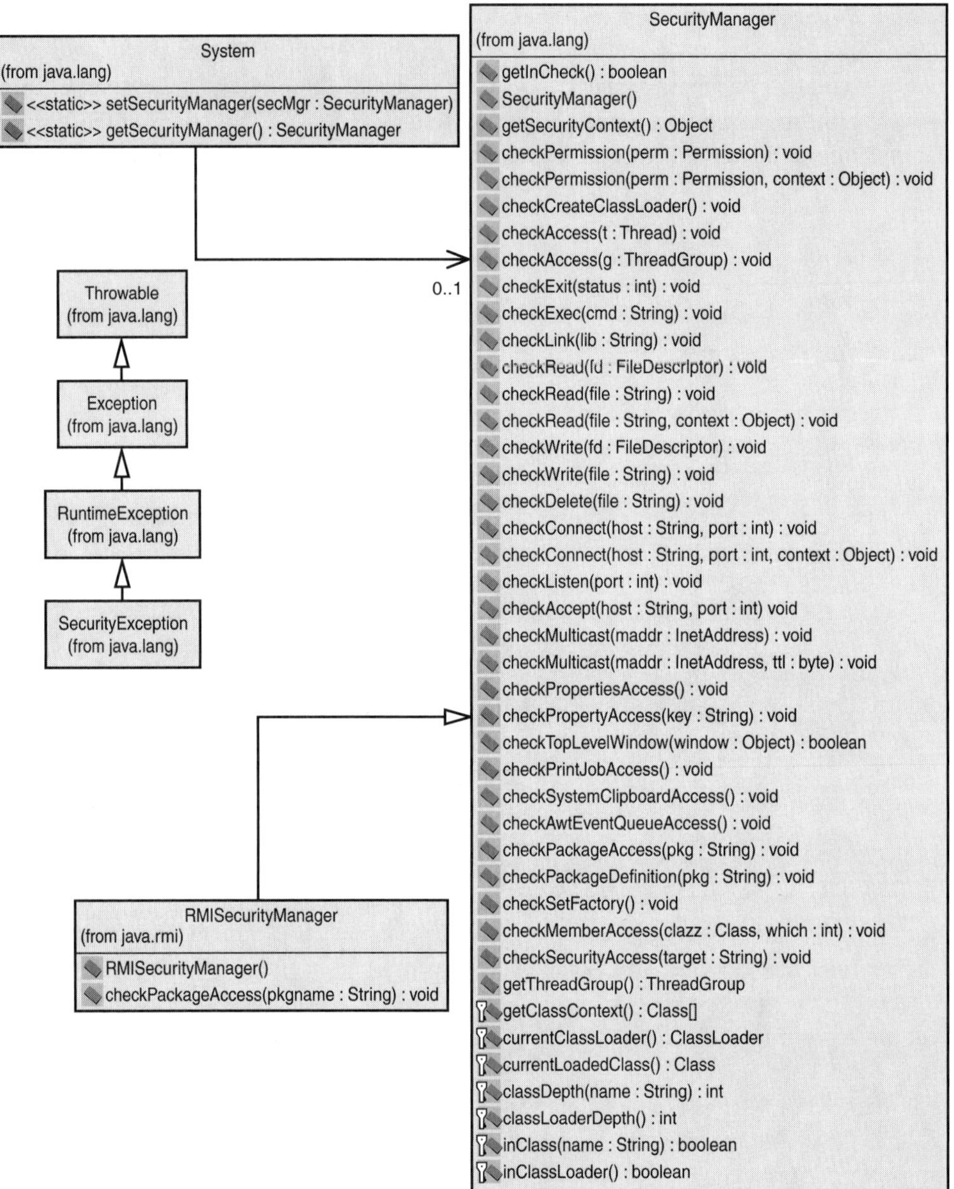

FIGURE 26.8

Security manager classes.

The SecurityManager class is mainly populated with public checkXXX() style methods. Each checkXXX() method is defined to check whether access is allowed for a particular valued resource. If access is not allowed, the checkXXX() methods will throw SecurityException objects. Most of these methods are left over from the Java 1.0 and 1.1 versions of the SecurityManager. Java 2 has introduced the checkPermission() method, which is a more generic form of the other checkXXX() methods. In fact, each checkXXX() method now calls the generic checkPermission() method under the hood of Sun's Java 2 platform implementation. The checkPermission() method in turn calls the java.security.AccessController class.

The AccessController was added in Java 2 to provide the fine-grained and configurable access control functionality that is central to the new security model. Although the SecurityManager is still maintained for backward compatibility with existing applications and to serve as a primary security management interface, the AccessController really subsumes the responsibility for algorithmic access checking that was once the province of the SecurityManager. In the next chapter we describe the AccessController in more detail and detail how the functionality of the Java 2 access control mechanisms replaces most of the SecurityManager API calls. Because we discuss the legacy SecurityManager calls in the next chapter in context of Java 2 access control, we do not cover the SecurityManager API calls here. We do, however, briefly outline how a SecurityManager might be customized by your applications in a Java 1.1 fashion.

Custom Security Managers

Java 1.1 required that a SecurityManager be extended to provide your own custom application-specific access control policies. Implementing your own SecurityManager is no longer recommended for Java 2–based applications, however. Instead of writing code that overrides the methods of a SecurityManager, we demonstrate customization of access decision making in Chapter 27, "Advanced Java Security," via configuration of security permissions and policies. Because the Java 2 platform discourages SecurityManager subclassing, all the protected SecurityManager methods (with the exception of getClassContext()) have been deprecated in Java 2.

Classes like the java.rmi.RMISecurityManager class introduced in Java 1.1 and shown in Figure 26.8 simply override the methods that relate to modified behavior for specific valued resource access checking. Thus, an overridden SecurityManager in Java 1.1 that extends a few file access checking operations might look like this:

```
public class CustomSecurityManager  extends SecurityManager
{
  public CustomSecurityManager()
  {
    super();
  }
```

```
  public void checkRead(String fileName)
  {
    if(fileName != null && fileName.endsWith(".java")){
    throw new SecurityException(" You are not allowed to read  "
        +" file names ending with .java");
    }
    super.checkRead(fileName);
  }

  public void checkWrite(String fileName)
  {
    if(fileName != null && fileName.endsWith(".java")){
      throw new SecurityException(" You are not allowed to write  "
        +" file names ending with .java");
    }
    super.checkWrite(fileName);
  }

  public void checkDelete(String fileName)
  {
    if(fileName != null && fileName.endsWith(".java")){
      throw new SecurityException(" You are not allowed to delete  "
        +" file names ending with .java");
    }
    super.checkDelete(fileName);
  }
}
```

To set this security manager as the security manager to use for your application's Java virtual machine process, you would call `System.setSecurityManager()` with an instance of this `CustomSecurityManager` sometime early in the process of starting your application (like perhaps inside the `main()` method of your application) like this:

```
System.setSecurityManager(new CustomSecurityManager());
```

At some point when your application attempts to access a file, the Java virtual machine will call your custom security manager for you under the hood. For example, the `java.io.FileInputStream` class calls `checkRead()` on the `SecurityManager`, which would actually use your registered `CustomSecurityManager` object. Your application code may also need to make such calls explicitly as exemplified here:

```
public void myFileAccessMethod(String fileName){
  SecurityManager secMgr = System.getSecurityManager();
  if(secMgr != null){
    secMgr.checkRead(fileName);
  }
  // If got this far, then can proceed on with method...
}
```

If the preceding explicit `checkRead()` call throws a `SecurityException`, the `myFileAccessMethod()` call will be terminated before the rest of the method can proceed and will return with the `SecurityException` thrown. Because the `SecurityException` class extends the `java.lang.RuntimeException` class, the fact that the `myFileAccessMethod()` can throw such an exception does not need to be explicitly declared in the method signature.

Java Cryptography Architecture

The Java Cryptography Architecture (JCA) equipped with the Java platform was first introduced with Java 1.1. The JCA provides basic cryptographic functions used for the following primary purposes:

- To protect data communicated or stored for integrity.
- To identify a principal associated with data that has been communicated or retrieved from storage.
- To provide support for generating keys and certificates used to identify data sources.
- To provide a framework for plugging different cryptographic algorithms from different service providers.

You should not assume too much by the word *cryptography* in JCA. The JCA is not really useful for encrypting data communicated or stored for decryption by an intended receiver. Such cryptographic functionality used to provide confidentiality is possible with the JCE. Because of U.S. export restrictions, the JCE is shipped separate from the Java platform, whereas the JCA does not have such limitations. Furthermore, although SSL represents one of the more popular crypto-related protocols in the Internet era, it also is not packaged with the JCA. Rather, SSL interface support is provided separately from the Java platform in the JSSE package.

This section provides an overview of the architecture of JCA. More detailed explanation and example uses of different components of the JCA are presented in the next chapter.

The Architecture of JCA

The JCA is composed of a number of classes and interfaces that implement basic cryptographic functionality. These are the Java 2 platform packages which contain classes and interfaces that make up the JCA:

- `java.security`: The set of core classes and interfaces for the JCA plug-and-play service provider framework and cryptographic operation APIs. Note that this package also contains core Java security architecture classes and interfaces.
- `java.security.cert`: A set of certificate management classes and interfaces.

- `java.security.interfaces`: A set of interfaces used to encapsulate and manage DSA and RSA public and private keys.
- `java.security.spec`: A set of classes and interfaces used to describe public and private key algorithm and parameter specifications.

Figure 26.9 depicts the top-level architecture of the JCA with a mixture of actual Java classes and conceptual classes (that is, not real code-based classes, but simply representative of concepts). At the top of the diagram, we have the `java.security.Security` class mainly responsible for managing a collection of Cryptographic Service Providers (CSPs). A CSP represents a service provider that implements one or more cryptographic functions that adhere to the cryptographic interfaces defined in the JCA. Information about each CSP is encapsulated by the `java.security.Provider` abstract class. CSPs (shown as `SomeCSPImpl` in Figure 26.9) extend the `Provider` abstract class with specific implementations of methods on the `Provider` class.

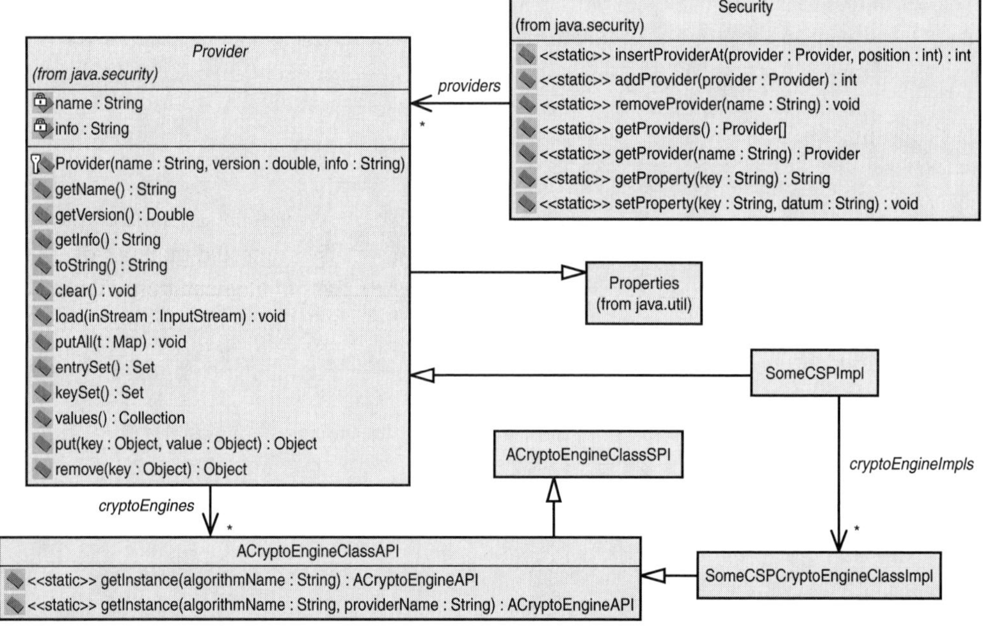

FIGURE 26.9
The top-level architecture of JCA.

Each CSP will implement one or more cryptographic engines. A cryptographic engine represents a particular cryptographic algorithm and set of parameters to that algorithm which perform some cryptographic functionality. For example, the MD5 message digest algorithm defined in Chapter 25, "Security Basics," is a particular algorithm and set of parameters used to generate an encrypted stream of data based on another stream of data. MD5 belongs to a general class of cryptographic engines referred to as a message digest cryptographic engine.

The various cryptographic engines (for example, `SomeCSPCryptoEngineImpl`) supplied by a CSP implement some standard cryptographic service provider interface (for example, `ACryptoEngineClassSPI`) provided by the JCA. Each service provider interface is extended by a cryptographic engine API (for example, `ACryptoEngineClassAPI`) used by the applications programmer. Each cryptographic engine API provides a static `getInstance(String)` method that takes the name of a particular algorithm name related to that engine class and returns a concrete instance of the requested cryptographic engine using that algorithm if it exists. Otherwise, a `java.security.NoSuchAlgorithmException` exception is thrown. A static `getInstance(String, String)` method on each cryptographic engine API specifies a particular CSP to use.

Cryptographic Engines

The `java.security.MessageDigest` abstract class is an example of a cryptographic engine API, whereas the `java.security.MessageDigestSpi` abstract class represents the cryptographic service provider interface that must be implemented. The protected methods of `MessageDigestSpi` will be visible and relevant only to the CSP's implementation. Figure 26.10 shows the various standard cryptographic engine types defined by the JCA. These cryptographic engine APIs and their helper classes rest at the core of how the JCA is used by enterprise application developers. The next chapter describes how to use many of the more practical cryptographic engines provided by the JCA. The primary functionality provided by each cryptographic engine type in Figure 26.10 is described here:

- `MessageDigest`: Creates and verifies message digests.
- `Signature`: Creates and verifies digital signatures.
- `KeyPairGenerator`: Generates public and private key pairs.
- `KeyFactory`: Converts between secure keys and key specifications.
- `KeyStore`: Modifies information in a secure key storage repository.
- `CertificateFactory`: Generates certificates and certificate revocation lists.
- `AlgorithmParameters`: Encodes crypto algorithm parameters.
- `AlgorithmParameterGenerator`: Creates crypto algorithm parameters.
- `SecureRandom`: Creates random numbers.

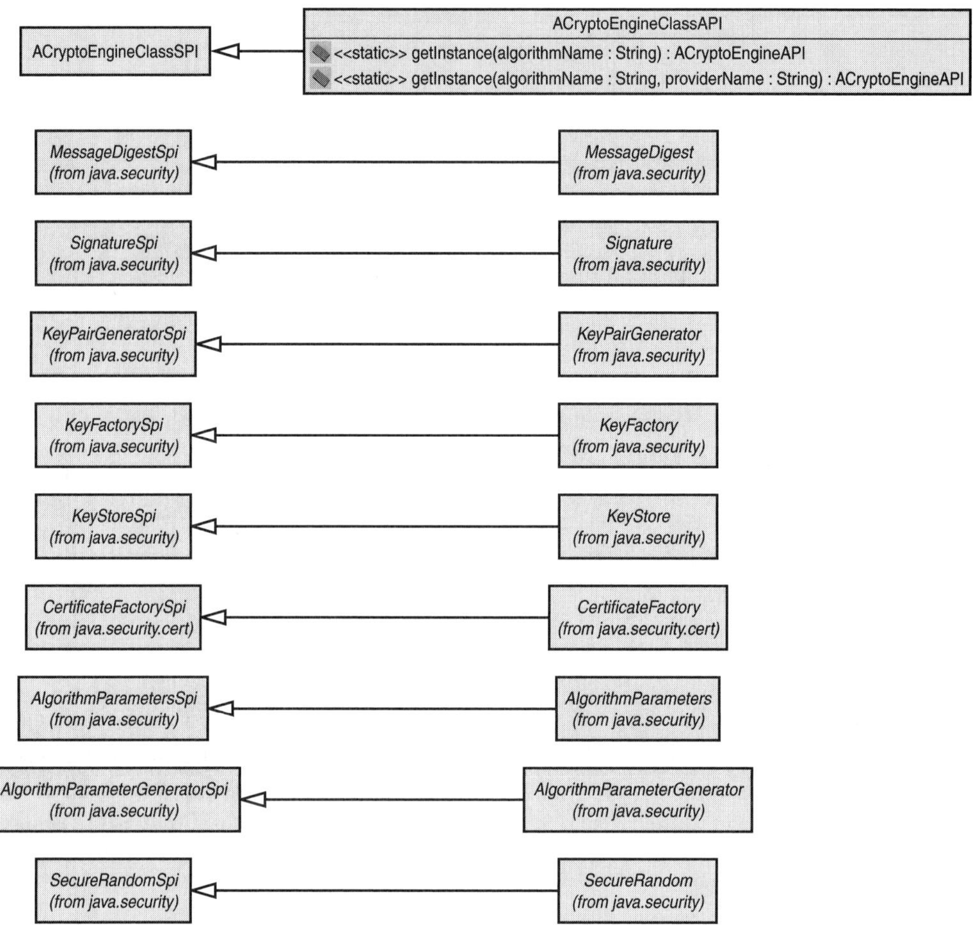

FIGURE 26.10

JCA cryptographic engine classes.

Cryptographic Service Providers

The JCA shipped with the Java platform comes equipped with a default CSP implemented by Sun. The `String` name used with the JCA APIs to designate this default provider is "`SUN`". The default Sun CSP implementation provides support for the following cryptographic engine and algorithm combinations:

- MD5 message digest algorithm
- SHA-1 message digest algorithm
- DSA for signatures

- DSA key pair generator
- DSA algorithm parameters
- DSA algorithm parameter generator
- DSA key factory
- JKS key store (JKS involves a proprietary algorithm)
- X.509 certificate factory
- SHA1PRNG pseudo-random number generator algorithm (an IEEE standard)

You can install a CSP for use with your Java runtime environment by simply placing a JAR or ZIP file with the classes that implement the JCA CSP interfaces somewhere on your CLASSPATH. You will then need to configure the `java.security` file under the root directory of your Java installation in the `<JavaRootInstall>\lib\security\` directory. In that file, you need to add the fully qualified classnames of your CSPs that extend the `Provider` class. The order of preference specifies which CSP to use in the event that an algorithm selected for use is implemented by another CSP. For example, the following `java.security` file entries specify that Sun's default CSP is preferred before Sun's RSA JCA CSP implementation:

```
# List of providers in order from most to least preferred CSP
security.provider.1=sun.security.provider.Sun
security.provider.2=com.sun.rsajca.Provider
```

CSPs can also be added and removed programmatically from within your JVM process. Only trusted applications can perform such operations, however. A trusted application here refers to an application running without a security manager installed or an application that has been granted permission to add and remove CSPs. We discuss how to configure such permissions in the next chapter. However, suffice it to say here that adding and removing CSPs with the `Security` class is rather straightforward, assuming the fact that your application has the proper permissions:

```
// Install SunJCE CSP by first creating a Provider instance
Provider providerSunJce = new com.sun.crypto.provider.SunJCE();
// Then add provider using Security class and obtain preference number
int providerPreferenceJCE = Security.addProvider(providerSunJce);

// Or set the preference number yourself increasing preference numbers
// of any providers already installed at that preference level
Provider providerATI = new com.assuredtech.security.JCAProvider();
int providerPreferenceATI = Security.insertProviderAt(providerATI, 1);

// A provider can be removed dynamically using Security class
// For example, to remove default Sun CSP
Security.removeProvider("SUN");
```

Conclusions

The Java security architecture provides a standards-based interface for Java developers to create secure Java applications. The core Java security architecture is composed of a byte code verifier, one or more class loaders, and a security manager/access control framework. The byte code verifier provides support for low-level object corruption checking. The class loader provides further protection in terms of authenticity of trusted code. The security manager and access control, of course, provide authorization protection.

Also part of the Java 2 platform, the JCA provides plug-and-play service provider–based protection of data and programs for integrity and identity. Extensions to the Java platform such as the JCE and JSSE provide protection for confidentiality, whereas the JAAS provides for enhanced authenticity and authorization protection. In terms of major security architecture components currently not supported by Java, any standard interfaces for nonrepudiation and security auditing are currently lacking. The next chapter describes practical usage of access control and JCA constructs for integrity and identity. We also discuss any architectural considerations of the Java security extensions such as the JCE, JSSE, and JAAS.

Advanced Java Security

CHAPTER

27

IN THIS CHAPTER

- Permissions 880
- Security Policies 891
- Java Access Control 896
- Principal Identification 906
- Protecting Objects 916
- Signing Code 924
- Java Security Extensions 929

Java security provides a collection of APIs and tools for infusing security into your Java applications. Infrastructure for providing fine-grained and configurable access control are built into the core Java security architecture via use of Java 2 permissions, policy files, and access controller functionality. Cryptography for information integrity and principal identity are built into the Java Cryptography Architecture (JCA) via use of message digests, signatures, keys, and certificates. Furthermore, industry-standard cryptography for confidentiality and authenticity can be provided using the Java Cryptography Extension (JCE), Java Secure Socket Extension (JSSE), and Java Authentication and Authorization Service (JAAS). This chapter describes the core Java security architecture and JCA in more detail and explains how to use such infrastructure in your enterprise Java applications. We also introduce the JCE, JSSE, and JAAS security extensions to Java.

In this chapter, you will learn:

- About the permission APIs available to the Java security programmer
- About the security policy APIs available to the Java security programmer
- About the security domains and the access control mechanisms available in the Java security framework
- About a means for principal identification via keys and certificates, as well as a means for managing keys and certificates in Java
- About a means for protecting information via message digests, signatures, and signed objects
- How to sign code for secure Java application privileges
- About the basic architecture of the Java security extensions, including the JCE, JSSE, and JAAS
- About conclusions that discuss the security risks that still exist apart from relying on the Java security features

Permissions

As part of the new Java 2 security model for providing fine-grained and configurable access control, a hierarchy of extendable permissions APIs has been added to the Java platform. Permission objects encapsulate the concept of a permission to access some valued resource. Permissions have names referring to a target resource for which a permission is to be granted or denied. Permissions also have a series of actions which scope the set of operations that may be performed on that target resource. Permissions are classified according to types using subclasses from base permission types in the Java API. Thus, for example, a file permission extends the concept of an abstract permission such that the target name represents one or more filenames or directories and the action list represents actions that may be performed on targets, such as “read” or “write.” These new Java 2 permission objects replace the permission-related constructs in the `java.security.acl` package.

Permissions Architecture

Figure 27.1 shows the basic architecture of Java 2 permissions. At the root of the permissions architecture is the `java.security.Permission` abstract class, which conceptualizes a permission to access some valued resource. A `Permission` object has a target name of a valued resource (for example, a filename) that is retrieved via the `getName()` method. A `Permission` object can also return a `String` defining the set of actions that are desired to be performed on the target resource. The actions' `String` is typically a comma-separated list of actions related to a target. For example, actions such as “read, write” might be the set of actions related to a particular target filename. The `implies(Permission)` method on the `Permission` class is used to indicate whether the `Permission` object passed in as a parameter is granted if the current `Permission` object is granted. The `checkGuard()` method on the `Permission` object is implemented by virtue of the fact that the `Permission` object implements the `java.security.Guard` interface to be described later in this chapter.

Subclasses of `Permission` can also implement the `newPermissionCollection()` method to return an object that extends the `java.security.PermissionCollection` abstract class. The `PermissionCollection` object is used to encapsulate a collection of one or more `Permission` objects and includes methods to add permissions and return the list of permissions it contains. Adding permissions to a `PermissionCollection` object is allowed only if it is not read-only. Read-only access can be set with the `setReadOnly()` method and tested with the `isReadOnly()` method. For certain subclasses of `Permission`, it may be necessary to store them as a homogeneous collection of permissions so that a call to `implies()` on the `PermissionCollection` object can make sense for that particular permission type. Whereas the `PermissionCollection` represents a collection of `Permission` objects of the same type, the `java.security.Permissions` class encapsulates a collection of heterogeneous permissions. The `Permissions` class accomplishes this by storing permissions of the same type into their own separate `PermissionCollection` objects.

Permission Types

The `Permission` class contains several subclasses, as shown in Figure 27.1. In the interest of conserving space, we've left the operation signatures of such classes out of the diagram. However, all the classes simply overload methods defined on the base `Permission` class. Although each class does define its own constructors, most classes have two constructors of the form *`Constructor`*`(String name)` taking a permission name parameter or *`Constructor`*`(String name, String actions)` taking a permission name and action `String`. A description of how to use each permission subclass, including example constructor usage, is presented in Table 27.1.

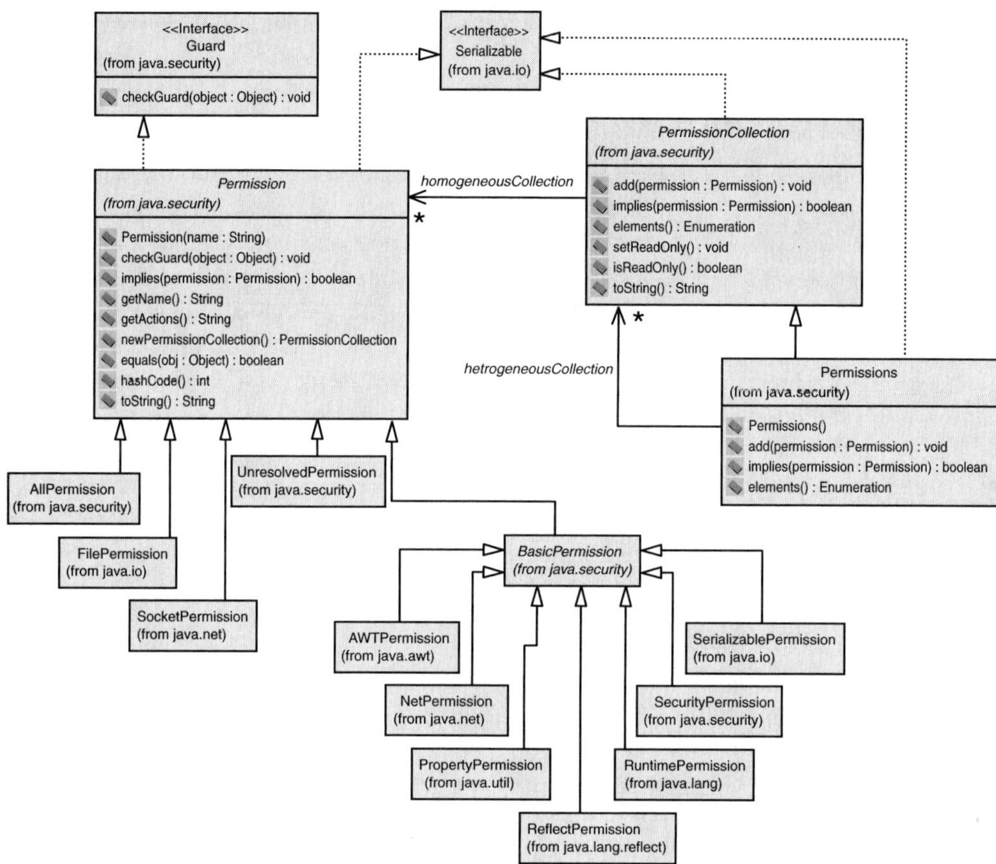

FIGURE 27.1
The Java 2 permissions architecture.

TABLE 27.1 Java Security Permission Types

Permission Type (and Package)	*Permission Usage*	*Description*
`AllPermission` (`java.security`)	`AllPermission ap = new AllPermission();`	Grant permission to every resource.
`FilePermission` (`java.io`)	`FilePermission fp = new FilePermission("C:\\temp\\sampleFile.txt", "read");`	Give permission to read a file.

Permission Type (and Package)	*Permission Usage*	*Description*
	`FilePermission fp = new FilePermission("C:\\temp", "read");`	Give permission to read directory information (not every file in the directory).
	`FilePermission fp = new FilePermission("C:\\temp\\*", "read");`	Give permission to read every file in the directory.
	`FilePermission fp = new FilePermission("C:\\temp\\-", "read");`	Give permission to read every file in and under the directory.
	`FilePermission fp = new FilePermission("<<ALL FILES>>", "read");`	Give permission to read every file on the file system.
	`FilePermission fp = new FilePermission("C:\\temp\\test.exe ", "read, write, delete, execute");`	Give permission to read, write, delete, and execute a file.
`SocketPermission` (`java.net`)	`SocketPermission sp = new SocketPermission("www.beeshirts.com", "accept");`	Give permission to accept connection from a single domain name.
	`SocketPermission sp = new SocketPermission("205.277.44.44", "accept, connect");`	Give permission to accept connection from and connect to a particular IP address.
	`SocketPermission sp = new SocketPermission("*.com", "accept, connect");`	Give permission to accept/connect for any domain name that ends with `.com`.

continues

TABLE 27.1 Continued

Permission Type (and Package)	*Permission Usage*	*Description*

	`SocketPermission sp = new`
	` SocketPermission( "*.beeshirts.com:80",`
	`                    "accept, connect");`
		Give permission to accept/connect on port 80 under `beeshirts.com` domain.

	`SocketPermission sp = new`
	` SocketPermission("*.beeshirts.com:1024-",`
	`                    "accept, connect");`
		Accept/connect on the unreserved ports.

	`SocketPermission sp = new`
	` SocketPermission("*.beeshirts.com:-1023",`
	`                   "accept, connect");`
		Accept/connect on the reserved ports.

	`SocketPermission sp = new`
	` SocketPermission(`
	`   "www.beeshirts.com:4000:4020",`
	`    "accept, connect");`
		Accept/connect on ports 4000 to 4020.

	`SocketPermission sp = new` ` SocketPermission( "*", "accept, connect");`	Accept/connect every machine on every port.

	`SocketPermission sp = new`
	` SocketPermission( "",`
	`                 "accept, listen, connect");`
	`SocketPermission sp = new`
	` SocketPermission("localhost",`
	`                 "accept, listen, connect");`
		Accept/connect/listen only on localhost.

`UnresolvedPermission`
 	
`(java.security)`
	`String type = // class name of permission`
	`String name = // permission name`
	`String actions = // permission action list`
	`java.security.cert.Certificate[] certs=`
	` // certificates of signed permission class`
	`UnresolvedPermission up = new`
	` UnresolvedPermission( type, name,`
	`                       actions, certs);`
		When a permission object is to be created for permissions that have yet to be associated with a particular `Permission` subclass, the

Permission Type (and Package)	*Permission Usage*	*Description*
		`UnresolvedPermission` object is used as a placeholder until the actual permission type is created.

`BasicPermission` (`java.security`)	`// BasicPermission is abstract base`
	`// class for subclasses such as...`
	
	`BasePermissionSubClass bp = new`
	` BasePermissionSubClass("com.ati.*");`
		An abstract base class that does not have actions and designates simply that you do or do not have permissions to access an associated resource. Main utility is the way that permissions are named using dot-separated hierarchy and wildcards.

`AWTPermission.` (`java.awt`)	`AWTPermission awtp = new` ` AWTPermission("accessClipboard");`	Give permission to access system clipboard.
	`AWTPermission awtp = new` ` AWTPermission("accessEventQueue");`	Give permission to access the system event queue.
	`AWTPermission awtp = new` ` AWTPermission("listenToAllAWTEvents");`	Give permission to listen to all AWT events.
	`AWTPermission awtp = new AWTPermission(` `        "showWindowWithoutWarningBanner");`	Give permission to show the windows without any warning banner (e.g., Trusted/Untrusted Applet).

continues

TABLE 27.1 Continued

Permission Type (and Package)	*Permission Usage*	*Description*
`NetPermission` (`java.net`)	`NetPermission np = new NetPermission( "requestPasswordAuthentication");`	Give permission to get password from registered system authenticator.
	`NetPermission np = new NetPermission( "setDefaultAuthenticator");`	Give permission to register authenticator used to get authentication information.
	`NetPermission np = new NetPermission( "specifyStreamHandler");`	Give permission to designate a stream handler when creating URL.
`PropertyPermission` (`java.util`)	`PropertyPermission pp = new PropertyPermission( "java.*", "read, write");`	Give permission to get and set properties that start with `java.`.
	`PropertyPermission pp = new PropertyPermission("*", "read");`	Give permission to get every property.
`reflectPermission` (`java.lang.reflect`)	`ReflectPermission rp = new ReflectPermission("suppressAccessChecks");`	Give permission for access methods and fields in a class for public, default package, protected, and private elements on reflected objects.
`RuntimePermission` (`java.lang`)	`RuntimePermission rp = new RuntimePermission("createClassLoader");`	Give permission to create a new class loader.

Permission Type (and Package)	Permission Usage	Description
	`RuntimePermission rp = new RuntimePermission("getClassLoader");`	Give permission to get the current class loader.
	`RuntimePermission rp = new RuntimePermission("setSecurityManager");`	Give permission to change current security manager.
	`RuntimePermission rp = new RuntimePermission("createSecurityManager");`	Give permission to create new security manager.
	`RuntimePermission rp = new RuntimePermission("exitVM");`	Give permission to exit from a JVM.
	`RuntimePermission rp = new RuntimePermission("setFactory");`	Give permission to set different socket factory.
	`RuntimePermission rp = new RuntimePermission("setIO");`	Give permission to change standard I/O streams.
	`RuntimePermission rp = new RuntimePermission("modifyThread");`	Give permission to change the state of a thread.
	`RuntimePermission rp = new RuntimePermission("stopThread");`	Give permission to stop a thread.
	`RuntimePermission rp =new RuntimePermission("modifyThreadGroup");`	Give permission to modify the thread group.
	`RuntimePermission rp = new RuntimePermission("readFileDescriptor");`	Give permission to read from a file descriptor.
	`RuntimePermission rp = new RuntimePermission("writeFileDescriptor");`	Give permission to write to a file descriptor.
	`RuntimePermission rp = new RuntimePermission("loadLibrary.myLibrary");`	Give permission to load a new dynamic shared library.

continues

TABLE 27.1 Continued

Permission Type (and Package)	*Permission Usage*	*Description*
	`RuntimePermission rp = new RuntimePermission("queuePrintJob");`	Give permission to start a print job.
	`RuntimePermission rp = new RuntimePermission("accessDeclaredMembers");`	Give permission to access declared members.
	`RuntimePermission rp = new RuntimePermission( "defineClassInPackage.myPackage");`	Give permission to define classes in a package.
	`RuntimePermission rp = new RuntimePermission( "accessClassInPackage.myPackage");`	Give permission to access classes in a package.
`SecurityPermission (java.security)`	`SecurityPermission sp =new SecurityPermission("getPolicy");`	Give permission to get security policy information.
	`SecurityPermission sp = new SecurityPermission("setPolicy");`	Give permission to set a security policy.
	`SecurityPermission sp = new SecurityPermission("setSignerKeyPair");`	Give permission to set new signed key pair.
	`SecurityPermission sp = new SecurityPermission("getSignerPrivateKey");`	Give permission to get a private key.
	`SecurityPermission sp = new SecurityPermission( "addIdentityCertificate");`	Give permission to add new certificate.
	`SecurityPermission sp = new SecurityPermission( "removeIdentityCertificate");`	Give permission to remove security identity.
	`SecurityPermission sp = new SecurityPermission("printIdentity");`	Give permission to get the security identity.

Permission Type (and Package)	*Permission Usage*	*Description*
	`SecurityPermission sp = new SecurityPermission("setIdentityInfo");`	Give permission to set security identity information.
	`SecurityPermission sp = new SecurityPermission("getProperty.myKey");`	Give permission to get the security property using a given key.
	`SecurityPermission sp = new SecurityPermission("setProperty.myKey");`	Give permission to set a security property using a given key.
	`SecurityPermission sp = new SecurityPermission("setSystemScope");`	Give permission to change system scope.
	`SecurityPermission sp = new SecurityPermission( "removeProviderProperty.myProviderName");`	Give permission to remove a provider property.
	`SecurityPermission sp = new SecurityPermission( "putProviderProperty.myProviderName");`	Give permission to add a new property to the provider.
	`SecurityPermission sp = new SecurityPermission( "clearProviderProperties.myProviderName");`	Give permission to clear all the provider properties.
	`SecurityPermission sp = new SecurityPermission( "removeProvider.myProviderName");`	Give permission to remove a provider.
	`SecurityPermission sp =new SecurityPermission( "insertProvider.myProviderName");`	Give permission to insert new provider.

continues

TABLE 27.1 Continued

Permission Type (and Package)	*Permission Usage*	*Description*
`SerializablePermission` (`java.io`)	`SerializablePermission sp = new SerializablePermission( "enableSubclassImplementation");`	Give permission to implement subclasses of object input and output streams for serialization.
	`SerializablePermission sp = new SerializablePermission( "enableSubstitution");`	Give permission to substitute objects during serialization.

Custom Permission Types

Although the standard permission types already encapsulate permissions for most of the predefined valued resources with which a Java Virtual Machine (JVM) can interact, the creation of application-specific permissions may be necessary from time to time. Customization is accomplished simply by extending one of the permission types. Typically, you will want to extend either the `Permission` class or the `BasicPermission` class. If you are extending the `Permission` class, implementing the `implies()`, `equals()`, `getActions()`, and `hashCode()` methods will be your primary concern, as well as implementing any permission-specific constructors. If you are extending the `BasicPermission` class, you can rely on the default implementation of methods that `BasicPermission` provides or provide implementation for such methods yourself. You will want to implement both constructor forms defined in the `BasicPermission` class, however, for taking a name and name/actions pair as parameters even if you do not make use of actions. For example

```
public class BeeShirtsPermission extends BasicPermission
{

  public BeeShirtsPermission(String name){...}

  public BeeShirtsPermission(String name, String actions){...}

  // Will rely on BasicPermission default method implementations
}
```

Security Policies

Although permissions to access valued resources from a JVM are encapsulated by the Java API hierarchy for permissions, the management of such permissions in a configurable fashion is encapsulated by the new Java 2 security policy infrastructure. Security policies provide a programmer-friendly way to configure which permissions are granted to which resources. Although a minimalist API exists to encapsulate security policy configuration, a default policy management framework is provided with the Java 2 platform to enable the configuration of security policies for a Java application without any additional tools. Such a default security policy management framework provides a mechanism for you to define security policies using a simple ASCII policy file format. Furthermore, a GUI-based policy tool utility can also be used to manipulate the security policy file.

As you'll see shortly, a policy file can be used to define which permissions are granted to certain domains of protection. A domain of protection is defined by a URL indicating where the code to be subject to a particular set of security policies comes from. A domain of protection can also be defined by one or more identities that define whom the code comes from.

Security Policy File Format

In the default implementation of security policy management with the Java 2 platform, a security policy is defined in an ASCII text file. A security policy file defines an optional key-store entry, and one or more permissions grant entries of the following general form:

```
[keystore "keystore_URL", "keystore_type";]

grant [SignedBy "list of names"] [, CodeBase "URL"]
{
    permission permission_class_name [ "name" ] [, "actions"]
                                     [, SignedBy "list of names"];
    permission ...
};

grant ...
```

Keywords used in the policy file, designated by boldface words in the preceding lines, are case-insensitive. Each policy file entry specified for a security domain begins with the `grant` keyword and contains one or more permission definitions for the particular domain of protection. Each permission entry begins with the `permission` keyword and is followed by the fully qualified permission classname. Permission target names and a comma-separated list of actions also follow a permission designation. The `SignedBy` field following the permission is optionally provided with a comma-separated list of alias names that indicate who must have signed the Java code for the permissions class. As you'll see in a later section, Java code may be signed such that you can securely verify that such code is from the intended supplier. The keystore entry designates which URL and type of storage mechanism to consult for signed classes.

Each grant entry delimiting a domain of protection can also contain a SignedBy field designating the fact that code being executed in the JVM associated with the grant entry must be signed by the named signers. A CodeBase field may also be associated with a grant entry to relate a set of permissions with a resource location from where the code is loaded. A code base URL that ends with / indicates all Java class files in a particular directory. A code base URL that ends with /* indicates all Java class files and JAR files in a particular directory. A code base URL that ends with /- indicates all Java class files and JAR files in a particular directory and its subdirectories.

Custom permission types and each of the standard Java permission types listed in Table 27.1 can be defined in a security policy file of the previously mentioned format. We discuss code signing in a later section. As an example (excluding concern for permissions code security), the following security policy file entries represent valid grant permission entries using a few of the same standard Java permission usage examples of Table 27.1:

```
grant
{
 permission java.io.FilePermission "C:\\temp\\sampleFile.txt", "read";
 permission java.io.FilePermission "C:\\temp", "read";
 permission java.io.FilePermission "C:\\temp\\*", "read";
 permission java.io.FilePermission "<<ALL_FILES>>", "read";
 permission java.io.FilePermission "C:\\temp\\test.exe ",
                                   "read, write, delete, execute";
};

grant CodeBase "http://code.beeshirts.com/-"
{
 permission java.net.SocketPermission "www.beeshirts.com", "accept";
 permission java.util.PropertyPermission "java.*", "read, write";
 permission java.lang.RuntimePermission "setSecurityManager";
};
```

Referencing Properties in Policy Files

You'll notice that in the preceding policy file example, a system-dependent file separator (\\) was used in the policy file definitions. Usage of such constructs makes your policy file system-dependent. You might consider it desirable to use the standard Java file.separator system property instead to refer to such a construct in order to keep your security policy file system-independent. You can refer to such properties and others defined for your currently running JVM process using a simple convention in your security policy file. The convention simply requires that you encapsulate properties between two curly braces preceded by a dollar sign as shown here:

```
${aProperty}
```

The JVM will expand such a property when it reads the security policy file. For example, the standard `user.home` and `file.separator` Java system properties can be referenced in your security policy file to grant file read permissions to all files from a user's home directory as shown here:

```
grant
{
 permission java.io.FilePermission "${user.home}${file.separator}* ",
                                                "read";
}
```


Using Security Policy Files

Now that you know how to define policies in a security policy file, you may be wondering where to create such files and how to make your Java applications use the policies defined in such files.

A default system security file is defined relative to the root directory of your Java install and is contained in `[JAVA_HOME]\lib\security\java.security`. That file contains two entries created during the installation of your Java environment that indicate where a default Java system security policy file and user-specific security policy file are installed:

```
policy.url.1=file:${java.home}/lib/security/java.policy
policy.url.2=file:${user.home}/.java.policy
```

The system security policy file is referenced first. If it is not present, the user security policy file is referenced. If neither file is present, a most-restrictive security policy is assumed akin to the Java 1.0 sandbox model. Additional policies can be referenced in the `java.security` file using incremental `policy.url.X` indices (that is, `policy.url.3` and so on). These index numbers specify the search order for which the JVM should attempt to load security policy files. As soon as a file is located, the search stops and that policy file is used.

If you want to define a policy file to be read from your own application-specific location, you can pass in the `-Djava.security.policy` system property to the command line when starting your Java application. Such a property is used to define the location of your own security policy file as exemplified here:

```
java -Djava.security.policy=beeshirts/beeshirts.policy
➥ -Djava.security.manager com.beeshirts.MySecureServer
```

Note that the `-Djava.security.manager` property designates that the default system security manager should be used as opposed to an application installing its own security manager. As a final note, if you desire to disable the capability for applications to define their own policy files, a `policy.allowSystemProperty` property in the `java.security` file can override the default value of `true` by setting the property to `false`.

Security Policy Tool

The Java 2 environment also comes equipped with a GUI-based tool for editing security policy files if hand-editing ASCII files is not to your liking. The `policytool` program is located under the root directory of your Java installation in `[JAVA_HOME]\bin\policytool`. Figure 27.2 shows what the `policytool` looks like after you have selected an entry of a particular policy file for editing. You can also create and save new policy files. When the policy file is open, you can add, remove, and edit individual permissions with an easy-to-understand GUI. Adding permissions is particularly simple, as shown in Figure 27.3. Here we see that drop-down lists of permission types, candidate names, and candidate actions can simplify adding permissions to an entry.

NOTE

Feel free to experiment with the `policytool` by creating your own policy file or perhaps creating and modifying a new copy of the `checkPermissionsPolicy` file on the CD in the `examples\src\ejava\jsecuritych27` directory. Note that other policy files in the same directory depend on code-signing procedures explained later in the chapter.

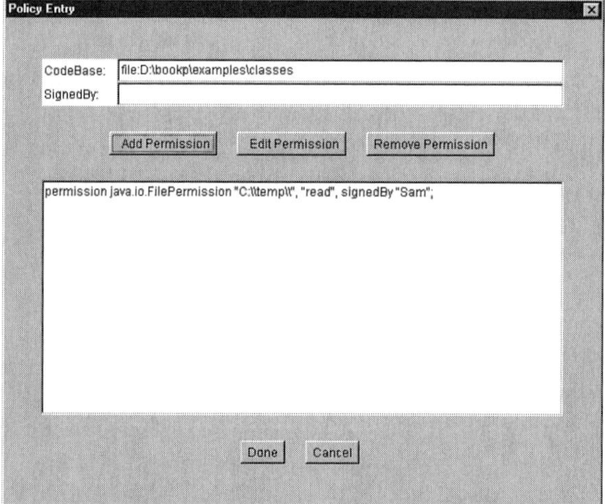

FIGURE 27.2

Viewing an entry with the Java security policy tool.

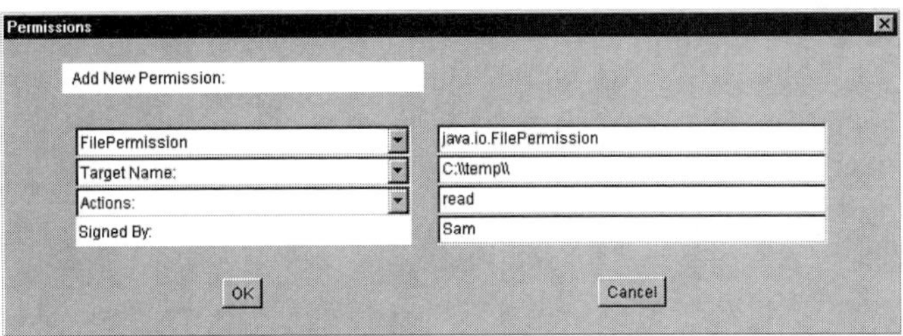

FIGURE 27.3
Adding permissions with the Java security policy tool.

Security Policy APIs

A minimalist API does exist for encapsulating security policies. The `java.security.Policy` abstract class implements a static `getPolicy()` method returning a handle to the current installed policy, and the static `setPolicy()` method allows one to set a new system-wide security policy. The `getPolicy()` method can be invoked if the `SecurityPermission getPolicy` allows it to be, and the `setPolicy()` method can be invoked if the `SecurityPermission setPolicy` allows it to be.

When you're setting a new security policy, the new policy must extend the `Policy` class and implement the `getPermissions()` and `refresh()` methods. The `getPermissions()` method takes a `java.security.CodeSource` object defining the code base URL and signed by certificates (to be discussed later) and returns the defined permissions allowed for such a code source as a `PermissionCollection` object. The `refresh()` method simply must refresh the policy information from the underlying policy storage mechanism associated with the newly defined `Policy` implementation.

Alternatively, the default policy implementation to use with your JVM instance can be specified with a `policy.provider` property in the `java.security` file:

```
policy.provider=com.assuredtech.security.GenericPolicy
```

As a final note, if a new policy object is not set using `Policy.setPolicy()` or if the `policy.provider` property is set, the default security policy provided by Sun is used. Sun's implementation of the default security policy that extends the `Policy` class and reads policy information from the previously mentioned policy files is contained in the class `sun.security.provider.PolicyFile`.

Java Access Control

Access control in Java 2 is managed by a new access controller construct. As we mentioned in the preceding chapter, the SecurityManager interfaces of Java 1.1 are still maintained for backward compatibility, but all checkXXX() methods defined on the SecurityManager can now delegate to the new java.security.AccessController class. The SecurityManager can implement such delegation by calling the generic checkPermission(Permission) methods now defined on the SecurityManager for every checkXXX() previously defined. The SecurityManager.checkPermission() method can then delegate calls to the AccessController.checkPermission() method. For example, for an implementation of the SecurityManager.checkRead(String fileName) method, we might have this:

```
checkPermission( new FilePermission(fileName, "read") );
```

And the corresponding SecurityManager.checkPermission(Permission permission) method might look like this:

```
java.security.AccessController.checkPermission( permission );
```

Thus, whereas permissions and policies help encapsulate and configure access levels to valued resources, the access control mechanisms in Java provide the infrastructure between Java code making calls to valued resources and the actual implemented access control for such resources. That is, Java access control provides the mechanisms in the Java security architecture that uses permissions and policies to actually allow or disallow access to valued resources.

Access Control Architecture

Figure 27.4 presents the architecture of access control in Java 2. At the top of this architecture is the SecurityManager revealing only the two checkPermission() methods new in Java 2 that simply delegate calls to AccessController and the AccessControlContext classes. The AccessController represents a decision maker for determining access allowance or denial (checkPermission()), a manager for designating which code should run as privileged (doPrivileged()), and a way to obtain a handle to the current access control context for use in other contexts (getContext()). The AccessControlContext class encapsulates the context pertinent to access control such as a particular stack state of execution. Thus, contexts can obtain handles to AccessControlContext objects from other contexts to determine whether access is permitted in that context.

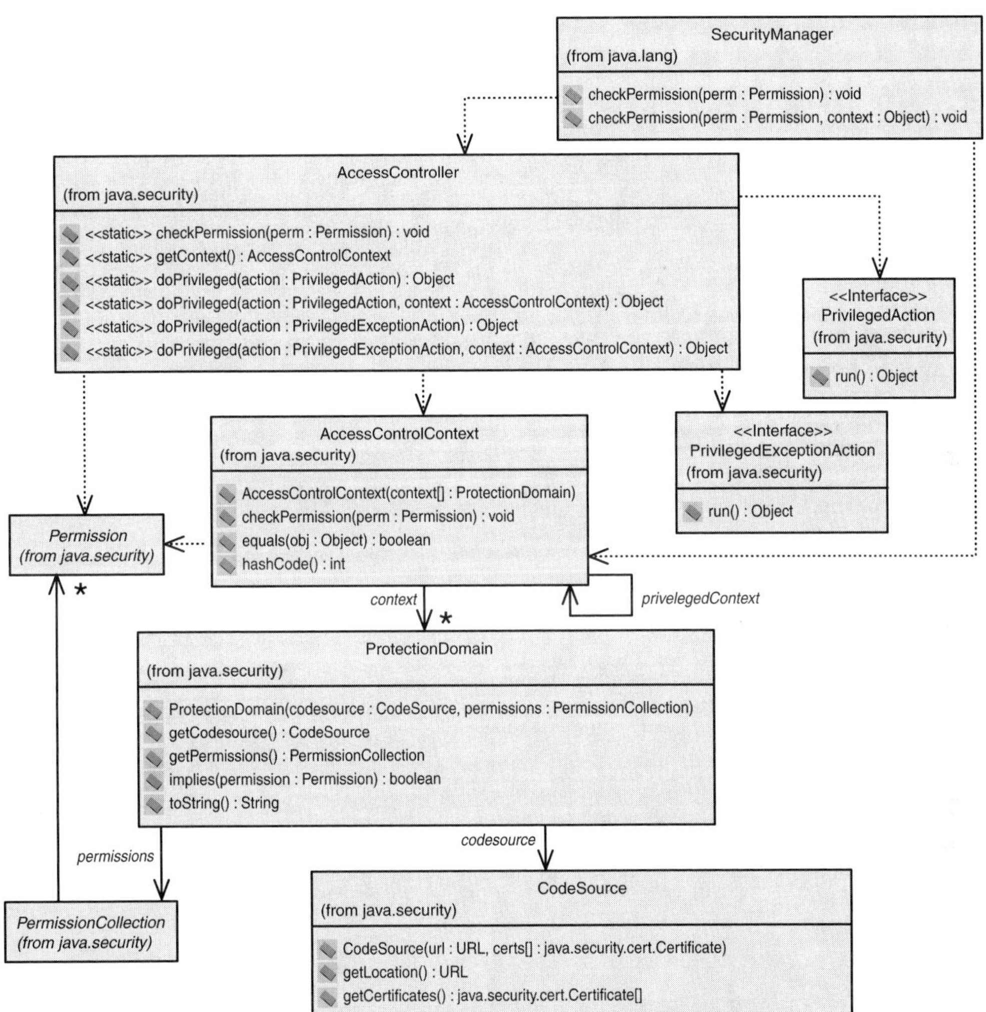

FIGURE 27.4
The Java 2 access control architecture.

An `AccessControlContext` can have one or more `ProtectionDomain` objects. Each `ProtectionDomain` object encapsulates the permissions granted to a particular code base. A `ProtectionDomain` can thus be viewed as one grant entry in a policy file in which the entry has one or more permissions, a potential code base, and a potential set of code-signing alias names. A `ProtectionDomain` object stores such permissions in a `PermissionCollection` object and the code base in a `CodeSource` object. The `CodeSource` object encapsulates the `CodeBase` location in a URL and the `SignedBy` entries in an array of `Certificate` objects.

Thus, code from the same code source and signed by the same signers belongs to the same protection domain. Thus, when `checkPermission()` is called on an `AccessControlContext` object, it checks the permissions associated with the collection of `ProtectionDomain` objects associated with its context.

The `doPrivileged()` methods on the `AccessContoller` can be used to perform certain actions as a privileged caller. Access control decisions will short-circuit permission checking if the calling code action was called from a `doPrivileged()` call assuming that the calling domain was allowed to execute such operations. Normal use of the `doPrivileged()` operation uses the `PrivilegedAction` interface to mark privileged operations that do not throw exceptions:

```
AccessController.doPrivileged( new PrivilegedAction()
  {
    public Object run()
    {
      // some privileged action
      // perhaps return some value or return null
    }
  }
);
```

If your privileged operation does throw an exception, you will want to use the `PrivilegedExceptionAction` interface as shown here:

```
AccessController.doPrivileged( new PrivilegedExceptionAction()
  {
    public Object run() throws SomeException
    {
      // some privileged action that throws some exception
      // perhaps return some value or return null
    }
  }
);
```

Both forms of the `doPrivileged()` method also take an `AccessControlContext` object as a second argument to designate a particular context to use for restricting privileges.

Because the `getContext()` method exists on `AccessController`, a current `AccessControlContext` can be retrieved and used later to check the permissions associated with one context from another context by calling `checkPermission()` on that `AccessControlContext`. The `SecurityManager` also has a `checkPermission(Permission, Object)` method which takes an `AccessControlContext` object as an argument and performs the same exact check. For example

```
// Store AccessControlContext for use in another context
AccessControlContext acc = AccessController.getContext();
 ...
 // Change context
 ...
FilePermission myPermission = new FilePermission("MyFile.txt", "read");
// Call check permission on context directly...
acc.checkPermission(myPermission);
// ...or call check permission on security manager which does
//    same thing as above method call...
(System.getSecurityManager()).checkPermission(myPermission, acc);
```


Guarded Objects

When resource access needs to be provided to an object in a different thread, a `java.security.GuardedObject` can be used to protect access to that resource as depicted in Figure 27.5. The sender in this case creates a `GuardedObject` with the `Object` encapsulating an interface to that resource and another object that implements the `java.security.Guard` interface. An object that implements the `Guard` interface is responsible for taking the resource object as a parameter to a `checkGuard()` call, and it throws a `SecurityException` if access is not allowed. After a `GuardedObject` is constructed, a receiver in another thread will have to first call `getObject()` on the `GuardedObject` to obtain access to the resource object. The `GuardedObject` then calls `checkGuard()` on the `Guard` implementation. Because the `java.lang.Permission` class implements the `Guard` interface, it can be used in situations as shown here:

```
// Create the guarded object in one thread
Socket sock = new Socket("myHost.com", 8000);
SocketPermission perm = new SocketPermission "myHost.com:8000",
➥"connect,accept");
GuardedObject gObject  = new GuardedObject(sock, perm);
  . . .
// Now need to use gObject from another thread
// This will throw exception if this thread is not allowed access
Socket mySock = (Socket) gObhect.getObject();
```

`SecurityManager` to Access Control Mapping

Now that you have an understanding of the basic role assumed by the `AccessController` and `AccessControlContext` classes, it should be apparent to you not only how such access control constructs can provide every function call provided by the `SecurityManager`, but also how it extends such calls to be more generic. Such generality is provided by virtue of the `checkPermission()` methods implemented on both the `AccessController` and the `AccessControlContext` classes. Table 27.2 shows how the `SecurityManager` calls map to calls on the new access control constructs.

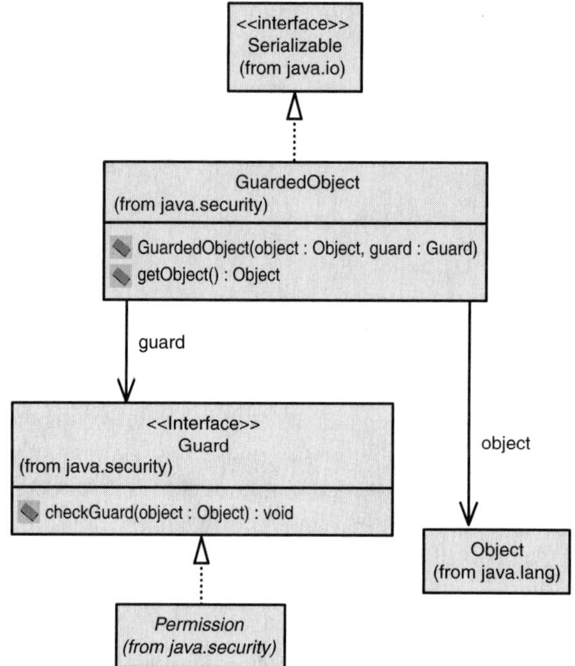

FIGURE 27.5
Guarded objects.

TABLE 27.2 `SecurityManager` to Access Control Mapping

`SecurityManager` *Call*	`AccessController` *or* `AccessControlContext` *Call(s)*
`checkPermission(Permission perm)`	`AccessController.checkPermission(perm)`
`checkPermission(Permission perm, Object ctx)`	`((AccessControlContext) ctx).checkPermission(perm)`
`checkAccess(Thread t)`	`AccessController.checkPermission(new RuntimePermission("modifyThread"))`
`checkAccess(ThreadGroup g)`	`AccessController.checkPermission(new RuntimePermission("modifyThreadGroup"))`
`checkExit(int status)`	`AccessController.checkPermission(new RuntimePermission("exitVM"))`
`checkExec(String cmd)`	`AccessController.checkPermission(new FilePermission(cmd, "execute"))`

SecurityManager *Call*	AccessController *or* AccessControlContext *Call(s)*
`checkLink(String lib)`	`AccessController.checkPermission(new RuntimePermission("loadLibrary."+lib))`
`checkRead(FileDescriptor fd)`	`AccessController.checkPermission(new RuntimePermission("readFileDescriptor"))`
`checkRead(String file)`	`AccessController.checkPermission(new FilePermission(file, "read"))`
`checkRead(String file, Object ctx)`	`((AccessControlContext) ctx).checkPermission(new FilePermission(file, "read"))`
`checkWrite(FileDescriptor fd)`	`AccessController.checkPermission(new RuntimePermission("writeFileDescriptor"))`
`checkWrite(String file)`	`AccessController.checkPermission(new FilePermission(file, "write"))`
`checkDelete(String file)`	`AccessController.checkPermission(new FilePermission(file, "delete"))`

`checkConnect(String host, int port)`	`if (port == -1) {`
	`((AccessControlContext) ctx).checkPermission(new SocketPermission(host,"resolve"));`
	`}else {`
	`((AccessControlContext) ctx).checkPermission(new SocketPermission(host+":" +port,"connect"));`
	`}`

`checkConnect(String host, int port, Object ctx)`	`if (port == -1) {`
	`AccessController.checkPermission(new SocketPermission(host,"resolve"));`
	`}else {`
	`AccessController.checkPermission(new SocketPermission(host+":"`
	`➥ +port,"connect"));`
	`}`

continues

TABLE 27.2 Continued

`SecurityManager` *Call*	`AccessController` *or* `AccessControlContext` *Call(s)*

`checkListen(int port)`	`if (port == 0) {`
	`AccessController.checkPermission(new`
	`SocketPermission("localhost:1024-",`
	`"listen"));`
	`}else{`
	`AccessController.checkPermission(new`
	`SocketPermission("localhost:"`
	`+port,"listen"));`
	`}`

`checkAccept(String host, int port)`	`AccessController.checkPermission(new` `SocketPermission(host+":"+port,"accept"))`

`checkMulticast(InetAddress maddr)`	`AccessController.checkPermission(new`
	`SocketPermission(maddr.getHostAddress(),`
	➥ `"accept,connect"))`

`checkMulticast(InetAddress maddr,`
`byte ttl)`
	`AccessController.checkPermission(new`
	`SocketPermission(maddr.getHostAddress(),`
	➥ `"accept,connect"))`

`checkPropertiesAccess()`	`AccessController.checkPermission(new` `PropertyPermission("*", "read,write"))`
`checkPropertyAccess(String key)`	`AccessController.checkPermission(new` `PropertyPermission(key,"read"))`

`checkTopLevelWindow(Object window)`	`AccessController.checkPermission(new`
	`AWTPermission(`
	`"showWindowWithoutWarningBanner"))`

`checkPrintJobAccess()`	`AccessController.checkPermission(new` `RuntimePermission("queuePrintJob"))`
`checkSystemClipboardAccess()`	`AccessController.checkPermission(new` `AWTPermission("accessClipboard"))`
`checkAwtEventQueueAccess()`	`AccessController.checkPermission(new` `AWTPermission("accessEventQueue"))`

SecurityManager *Call*	AccessController *or* AccessControlContext *Call(s)*
`checkPackageAccess(String pkg)`	`AccessController.checkPermission(new RuntimePermission( "accessClassInPackage." + pkg))`
`checkPackageDefinition(String pkg)`	`AccessController.checkPermission(new RuntimePermission( "defineClassInPackage." + pkg));`
`checkSetFactory()`	`AccessController.checkPermission(new RuntimePermission("setFactory"))`
`checkMemberAccess(Class clazz, ➥ int which)`	`AccessController.checkPermission(new RuntimePermission("accessDeclaredMembers"))`
`checkSecurityAccess(String target)`	`AccessController.checkPermission(new SecurityPermission(target))`

By examining Table 27.2, you can also deduce how permission entries set in a security policy file will affect calls to the `SecurityManager.check`*`XXX`*`()` methods. For example, if the entry

```
permission java.io.FilePermission "C:\\temp\\sampleFile.txt", "read";
```

appears in your security policy file, then the following `SecurityManager` call associated with the same code base will return without throwing an exception:

```
(System.getSecurityManager()).checkRead("C:\\temp\\sampleFile.txt");
```

Also, the following `SecurityManager` call associated with the same code base will throw a security access control exception:

```
(System.getSecurityManager()).checkWrite("C:\\temp\\sampleFile.txt");
```

Fine-Grained and Configurable Access Control Example

Given the fine-grained and flexible configuration of permissions via a security policy file and an understanding of how the access controller can provide security for your applications, the example of Listing 27.1 can be run in various modes to illustrate how simple making a Java application utilizing such features can be. Before we run this example under different scenarios, take a quick look at Listing 27.1.

NOTE

The following access control example is contained on the CD in the `examples\src\ejava\jsecuritych27` directory. A `CheckPermissions.java` file contains the sample code, and a `checkPermissionsPolicy` file contains a sample set of security permissions. You should, of course, compile the example before running it.

The `CheckPermissions.main()` method first attempts to read a number of system properties and subsequently creates a file input stream associated with a file read in from the `myFile` system property. Files and the `java.home` and `os.home` system properties all represent valued resources that can be protected by default Java security permissions. When you run this example with no security manager (the default), it will run fine because no security checks are performed. You simply specify an arbitrary file for which to check read permissions using the `myFile` system property. To run the example without a security manager, simply type this:

```
java -DmyFile=D:\bookp\testfile.txt ejava.jsecuritych27.CheckPermissions
```

NOTE

You'll need to create or identify your own file to use with this example. This file needs to be specified using the `myFile` system property as shown above.

If you then run the program by loading a security manager, the program will throw a runtime `AccessControlException` when the system property `java.home` is attempted to be read. `AccessControlException` objects would also be thrown for attempted access to `os.home` and when an attempt is made to read the file. This is because the default security manager and security policies that come equipped with a JDK distribution restrict access to such system properties. Thus, an exception will be thrown when you run this:

```
java -Djava.security.manager -DmyFile=D:\bookp\testfile.txt
➥ ejava.jsecuritych27.CheckPermissions
```

LISTING 27.1 Access Control Permissions Check Example (`CheckPermissions.java`)

```
package ejava.jsecuritych27;
import java.io.FileInputStream;
import java.io.IOException;
import java.io.FileNotFoundException;
import java.security.AccessControlException;
```

```
public class CheckPermissions
{
  public static void main(String[] args)
  {
    // check whether the application has permission to read
    // properties.

    String operatingSystem = (String)System.getProperty("os.name");
    String javaVersion = (String)System.getProperty("java.version");
    try{
      String javaDirectory = (String)System.getProperty("java.home");
      String userHomeDir = (String)System.getProperty("user.home");
      String myFile = (String)System.getProperty("myFile");
      FileInputStream fin = new FileInputStream(myFile);
    }
    catch(FileNotFoundException fne){
      System.out.println("File not found Exception "+fne);
      System.exit(0);
    }
    catch(AccessControlException ace){
      System.out.println("Security Access Control Exception "+ace);
      System.exit(0);
    }
  }
}
```


If you now use the `checkPermissionsPolicy` file of Listing 27.2, all desired permissions will be granted and the program can be run successfully. With `EJAVA_HOME` defined to be the root directory for your sample code (see Appendix A, "Software Configuration"), your command to test this example might look like this:

```
java -Djava.security.manager -Djava.security.policy=
➥%EJAVA_HOME%\examples\src\ejava\jsecuritych27\checkPermissionsPolicy
➥ -DmyFile=D:\bookp\testfile.txt
➥ ejava.jsecuritych27.CheckPermissions
```

LISTING 27.2 Sample Security Policy File (`checkPermissionsPolicy`)

```
grant{
 permission java.util.PropertyPermission  "java.home" , "read";
 permission java.util.PropertyPermission  "user.home" , "read";
 permission java.util.PropertyPermission  "myFile", "read";
 permission java.io.FilePermission "${myFile}", "read";};
};
```

Principal Identification

By using Java security policy files, we saw that access control decisions could sometimes be based on the identity of the principal that signed code needed permission to run in a JVM. The JCA provides a means by which the identity of principals can be encapsulated and managed. Certificate, key store, and CRL interfaces in the Java 2 platform provide one means by which principal identity can be encapsulated, stored, and managed. To support such interfaces, interfaces for public and private keys also need to be supported. Thus, a core set of interfaces related to asymmetric keys are also provided by the JCA. Because the JCA is designed to satisfy U.S. export restrictions, use of such keys with the JCA is not employed for encryption of data for confidentiality. Rather, the JCE provides support for encryption of data for confidentiality.

Java 2 deprecates a few legacy identity constructs and tools used with the JDK 1.1. The `java.security.Certificate` interface and `java.security.Identity`, `java.security.IdentityScope`, and `java.security.Signer` classes have been deprecated in favor of newer Java 2 classes and interfaces provided to support principal identification. Furthermore, new key management classes and additions to existing key-related classes have been added in Java 2.

Although many of the JDK 1.1–related identity entities have been deprecated, the `java.security.Principal` interface first introduced in JDK 1.1 is still being maintained. The `Principal` interface represents the concept of a principal such as a person or organization. Aside from defining a `getName()` method that returns a `String` name form of the principal, methods for requiring `equals()`, `hashCode()`, and `toString()` semantics are also defined on the `Principal` interface.

Keys

Figure 27.6 depicts the basic and core architecture behind keys and how they are created using the JCA. The `java.security.Key` interface defines three methods corresponding to three aspects of a key. The `getAlgorithm()` method returns a `String` name of the algorithm used to encode a key (for example, `DSA` or `RSA`). The `getFormat()` method returns a `String` name of the particular format in which the key was encoded (for example, `X.509` and `PKCS#8`). The `getEncoded()` method returns a `byte` array containing the key in its encoded format. The `java.security.PublicKey` interface extends the `Key` interface to represent public keys, whereas the `java.security.PrivateKey` interface extends the `Key` interface to represent private keys. A `java.security.KeyPair` class that can be constructed with both a `PublicKey` and a `PrivateKey` simply offers a way to group the two keys as a pair.

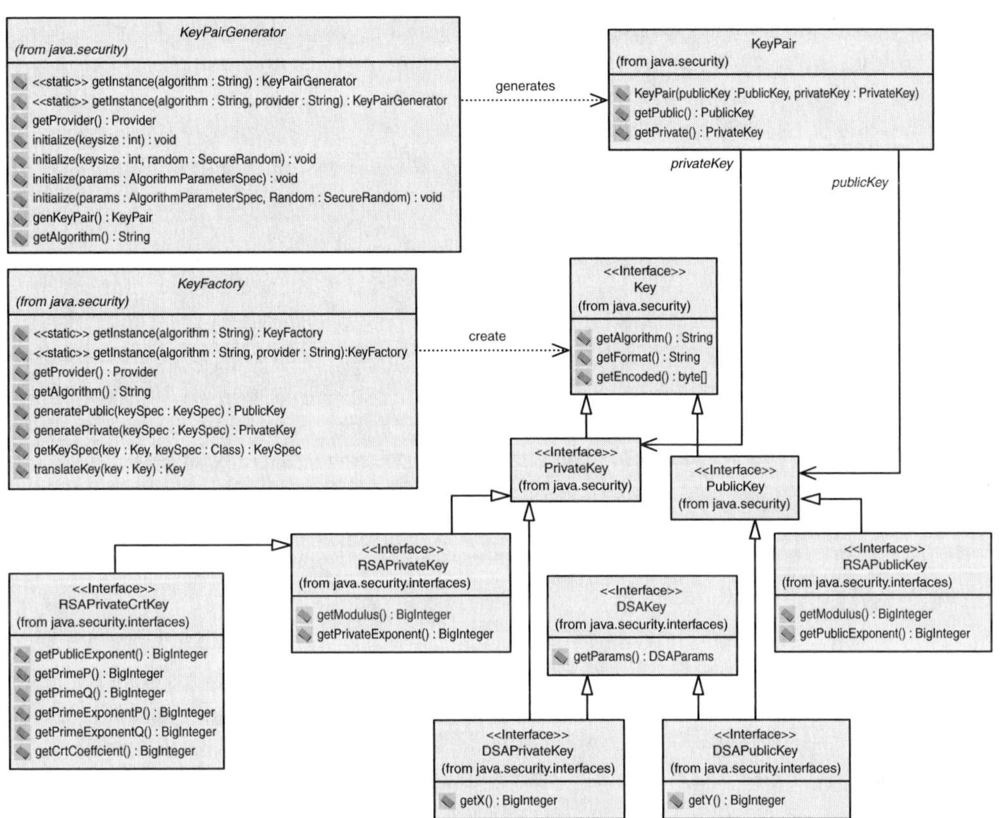

FIGURE 27.6
The JCA keys architecture.

The `java.security.KeyPairGenerator` class can be used to generate pairs of public and private keys. Because the `KeyPairGenerator` is a cryptographic engine (see Chapter 26, "Basic Java Security"), it provides two `static getInstance()` methods that support the creation of a particular cryptographic engine instance. The `getInstance(String)` method takes the name of a particular algorithm and returns an instance in accordance to the provider preference order as mentioned in Chapter 26. The `getInstance(String, String)` method takes the name of a provider as well, to specify exactly which provider's implementation to use.

After obtaining a `KeyPairGenerator` object, you can initialize the engine to generate keys according to a particular strength. Key strength can be specified as an integer defining the bit length of the key and also by the designation of other algorithmic parameters encapsulated by classes that implement the `java.security.spec.AlgorithmParameterSpec` interface. Finally, the `KeyPairGenerator.getKeyPair()` method returns the randomly generated `KeyPair` object containing the public and private keys of interest.

The JCA provides standard interfaces for DSA and RSA keys in the `java.security.interfaces` package. A `DSAPublicKey` and `RSAPublicKey` interface both extend the `PublicKey` interfaces with additional algorithm-specific operations. Similarly, a `DSAPrivateKey` and `RSAPrivateKey` interface extend the `PrivateKey` interface. An `RSAPrivateCrtKey` interface extends the `RSAPrivateKey` with additional RSA algorithmic constraints. Finally, the `DSAPublicKey` and `DSAPrivateKey` interfaces extend a common `DSAKey` interface.

The `java.security.KeyFactory` cryptographic engine can be used to translate keys between different compatible key types. That is, for example, a DSA key can be translated into an X.509 key and vice versa. This is accomplished by use of a `java.security.spec.KeySpec` implementation of the desired key type from which to translate. Then a `KeyFactory` can be created with a particular compatible key algorithm to which you want to translate the existing key. The various key specifications supported by the JCA out of the box are defined in the `java.security.cert` package and include `EncodedKeySpec`, `PKCS8EncodedKeySpec`, `X509EncodedKeySpec`, `DSAPublicKeySpec`, `DSAPrivateKeySpec`, `RSAPublicKeySpec`, `RSAPrivateKeySpec`, and `RSAPrivateCrtKeySpec`.

Certificates

Figure 27.7 depicts the basic architecture of security certificates provided with the JCA. Fundamental to this architecture is the new `java.security.cert.Certificate` abstract class, which encapsulates an interface to a certificate associating a principal with a public key. Core interfaces on the `Certificate` class include the `getEncoded()` interface returning a byte array of the certificate in its encoded form. The `verify(PublicKey)` interface can be used to verify that a certificate was signed by the private key associated with the given public key. If the certificate was not signed by such a private key, the `verify()` method throws a `java.security.InvalidKeyException`.

A few common certificate revocation list (CRL) operations are encapsulated by the `java.security.cert.CRL` abstract class. Specific CRL implementations subclass this abstract `CRL` class.

The `java.security.cert.CertificateFactory` class is a JCA cryptographic engine that can generate both certificates and CRLs. The type of `Certificate` and `CRL` implementation depends on the type of `CertificateFactory` created during a call to `getInstance()` (for example, `X.509`). A single `Certificate` or `Collection` of `Certificate` objects can be created with an `InputStream` using either the `generateCertificate()` or `generateCertificates()` method, respectively. Similarly, a single `CRL` or `Collection` of `CRL` objects can be created with an `InputStream` using either the `generateCRL()` or the `generateCRLs()` method, respectively. In both cases, the `InputStream` contains the certificate- or CRL-specific data that will be used to instantiate `Certificate` or `CRL` objects of that associated type.

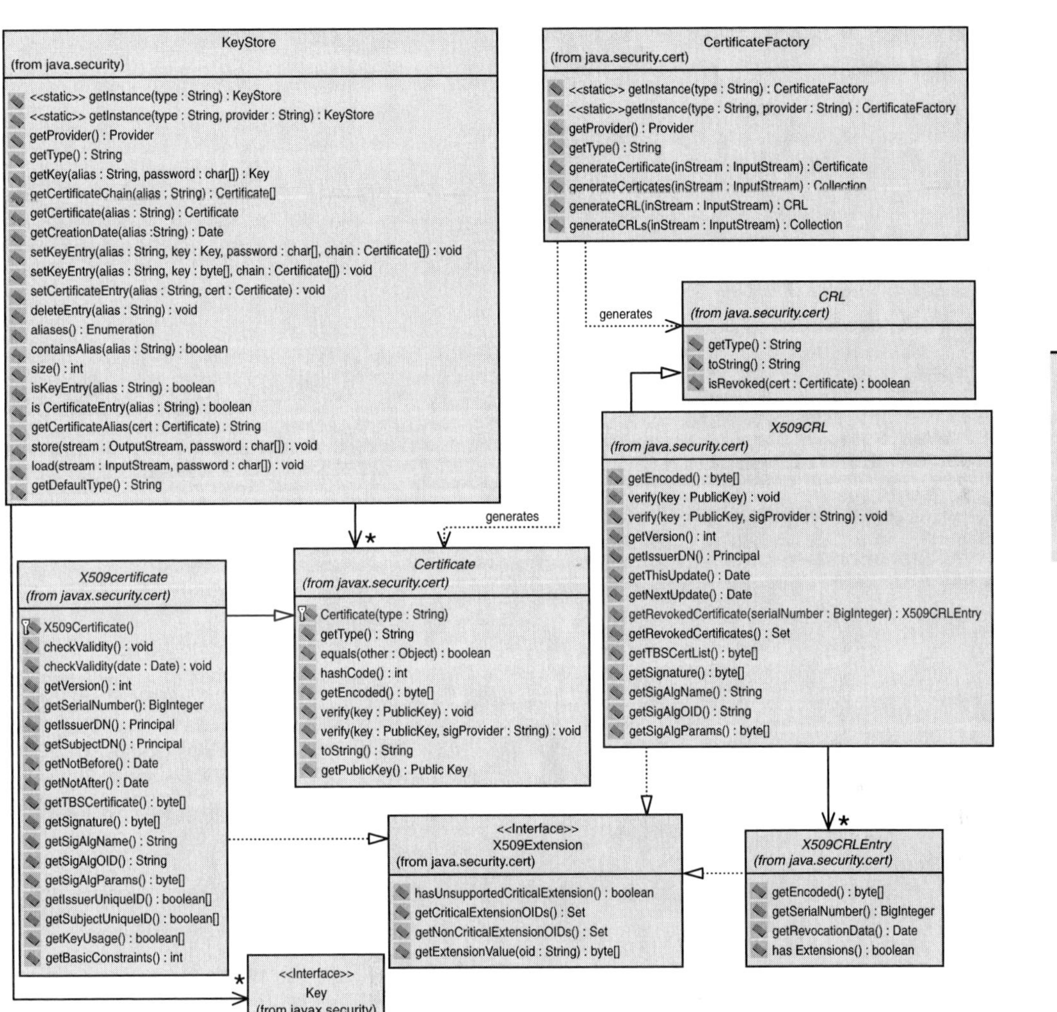

FIGURE 27.7
The JCA certificates architecture.

The JCA also provides a set of standard interfaces and classes for interacting with X.509-based certificates and CRLs. The `java.security.cert.X509Extension` defines a few methods for retrieving specific attributes common to X.509-related entities. The `java.security.cert.X509Certificate` abstract class encapsulates a standard interface to X.509 certificates. The `X509Certificate` extends the basic `Certificate` class to implement a number of certificate attribute retrieval methods for X.509-specific certificates. The `java.security.cert.X509CRL` class extends the `CRL` class to offer specific operations and attribute retrieval of X.509 CRLs.

Finally, the `java.security.cert.X509CRLEntry` class encapsulates an interface to a revoked X.509 certificate.

Key and Certificate Storage

The `java.security.KeyStore` class encapsulates an interface to a stored collection of certificates and keys. Because the `KeyStore` is a cryptographic engine, a particular provider's algorithm specific to a particular certificate and key storage implementation must be generated from one of the `getInstance()` methods. Sun provides a default proprietary key store with the Java platform referred to as `JKS`.

Private key entries stored in a `KeyStore` can be obtained only with a valid key-store alias name and password using the `KeyStore.getKey()` method. Certificate entries in a `KeyStore` can be obtained with just the key-store alias name because the `Certificate` contains only the public key. Each certificate and private-key entry in the key store has its own unique alias name. Before an in-memory `KeyStore` object can be used to manage key and certificate information, it must be loaded from an `InputStream` with a password using the `KeyStore.load()` method. Thus, the key-store format stored in a file using Sun's proprietary key store can be loaded using a `FileInputStream`. The `KeyStore` object also provides a varied number of other methods useful for managing key-store entities.

The Java 2 platform supplies a default file-based key-storage mechanism and a tool to manage this store from the command line. This `keytool` command-line utility partially replaces the `javakey` utility equipped with JDK 1.1. The `keytool` utility can be used to manage X.509 certificates and associated private keys. Some of the operations that `keytool` supports specified via command line options are listed here:

- `genkey`: Generate a public and private key pair and store it in the key store along with a self-signed certificate
- `selfcert`: Generate a self-signed certificate to store in the key store
- `import`: Import X.509 or PKCS#7 certificates from a file into the key store
- `export`: Export certificates from the key store to a file
- `printcert`: Print the contents of a certificate store in a separate file
- `list`: List the contents of the key store
- `certreq`: Generate a certificate signing request in PKCS#10 format
- `keyclone`: Clone an entry in the key store
- `delete`: Delete an entry from the key store
- `storepasswd`: Change the password used to access the key store
- `keypasswd`: Change the password used to access a particular private key in the key store
- `identitydb`: Read in JDK 1.1–style identity information

Using Keys and Certificates

Given some of the tools and APIs available for managing keys and certificates, a wide range of principal identification functions can be performed with your enterprise applications. For one, certificates play a vital role during authentication of access to your servers or when you need to present certificates for authentication as a client to other processes. Interfacing with a CRL may also be necessary if your process needs to be made cognizant of revoked certificate privileges. Finally, it may be necessary to import and export certificates to and from files and key stores if you make use of certificates during authentication.

As an example of importing and exporting certificates, let's first use the `keytool` command-line utility to generate a key pair inserted into a new key store named `developmentStore` in your working directory and with an alias of `Development` as shown here:

```
keytool -genkey -keystore developmentStore -alias Development
```

The `keytool` will prompt you for further information as shown here:

```
Enter keystore password:  bshirts
What is your first and last name?
  [Unknown]:  Sam Mellone
What is the name of your organizational unit?
  [Unknown]:  Development
What is the name of your organization?
  [Unknown]:  BShirts
What is the name of your City or Locality?
  [Unknown]:  Reston
What is the name of your State or Province?
  [Unknown]:  VA
What is the two-letter country code for this unit?
  [Unknown]:  US
Is <CN=Sam Mellone, OU=Development, O=BShirts, L=Reston, ST=VA,
➥ C=US> correct?
  [no]:  y

Enter key password for <Development>
        (RETURN if same as keystore password):
```

A key pair identified by the alias `Development` and stored in a key-store file named `developmentStore` should now be present in your current working directory. The newly created key store's password was entered as `bshirts` in the preceding transcript of events.

Listing 27.3 presents some code used to export this recently created certificate to a certificate file and import the certificate into another key store. The `main()` method of `ImportingAndExportingCertificates` is executed with a property filename as an argument when the following command is issued:

```
java ejava.jsecuritych27.ImportingAndExportingCertificates
➥ keystore.Properties
```

NOTE

The following certificates example is contained on the CD in the `examples\src\ejava\jsecuritych27` directory. An `ImportingAndExportingCertificates.java` file contains the sample code, and the `keystore.Properties` file contains a configurable set of properties used by the code. The `developmentStore` and `productionStore` key store files created above are also included on the CD.

LISTING 27.3 Sample Key and Certificate Usage (`ImportingAndExportingCertificates.java`)

```
package ejava.jsecuritych27;
import java.security.KeyStore;
import java.security.KeyStoreException;
import java.util.Properties;
import java.io.FileInputStream;
import java.io.IOException;
import java.security.cert.X509Certificate;
import java.security.NoSuchProviderException;
import java.security.KeyStoreException;
import java.security.Principal;
import java.io.FileOutputStream;

public class ImportingAndExportingCertificates
{

  public ImportingAndExportingCertificates()
  {
    super();
  }

  public  X509Certificate
    exportACertificateFromAKeyStore(
      KeyStore keyStore, String keyStoreFile, String password,
      String alias )  throws Exception
  {
    X509Certificate certificate = null;
    FileInputStream fin  = new FileInputStream(keyStoreFile);
    // load the keyStore
    keyStore.load(fin,password.toCharArray());
    // get Certificate for the given alias
    certificate =  (X509Certificate)keyStore.getCertificate(alias);
    // to print principal
    Principal principal = certificate.getIssuerDN();
```

```
  System.out.println(" Principal :" + principal.getName());
  fin.close();

  return certificate;
}

public  void importACertificateToAKeyStore(
  X509Certificate certificate, KeyStore keyStore,
  String keyStoreFile, String password,
    String alias ) throws Exception
{
  FileInputStream fin  = new FileInputStream(keyStoreFile);
  // load keyStore
  keyStore.load(fin,password.toCharArray());
  // import certificate
  keyStore.setCertificateEntry(alias, certificate);
  fin.close();
  FileOutputStream fout = new FileOutputStream(keyStoreFile);
  keyStore.store(fout,password.toCharArray());
}

public static KeyStore getKeyStore(
  String storeName, String storeProvider)
  throws NoSuchProviderException, KeyStoreException
{
    return KeyStore.getInstance(storeName,storeProvider);

}

public static void main(String[] args)
{
  if(args.length == 0){
    System.out.println("Usage : java "+
      "ejava.jsecuritych27.ImportingAndExportingCertificates "+
      "keystore.properties ");
    System.exit(0);
  }

  String fileName = args[0];
  Properties p = new Properties();
  try{
    FileInputStream fin = new FileInputStream(fileName);
    p.load(fin);
    String keyStoreName = (String)p.get("KEY_STORE_NAME");
    String keyStoreProvider = (String)p.get("KEY_STORE_PROVIDER");
    String importKeyStoreFileName =
                        (String)p.get("IMPORT_FILE_NAME");
```


continues

LISTING 27.3 Continued

```
      String exportKeyStoreFileName =
                              (String)p.get("EXPORT_FILE_NAME");
      String exportAlias = (String)p.get("EXPORT_KEY_ALIAS");
      String importAlias = (String)p.get("IMPORT_KEY_ALIAS");

      String exportKeyStorePassword =
        (String)p.get("EXPORT_KEY_STORE_PASSWORD");
      String importKeyStorePassword =
        (String)p.get("IMPORT_KEY_STORE_PASSWORD");
      fin.close();
      ImportingAndExportingCertificates importExport =
        new ImportingAndExportingCertificates();
      // get KeyStore
      KeyStore keyStore =
        importExport.getKeyStore(keyStoreName, keyStoreProvider);

      // export a certificate
      X509Certificate readCertificate =
        importExport.exportACertificateFromAKeyStore(keyStore,
             exportKeyStoreFileName,
             exportKeyStorePassword,   exportAlias);

       // get KeyStore
       keyStore =  getKeyStore(keyStoreName, keyStoreProvider);
       // import certificate into a another keyStore
       importExport.importACertificateToAKeyStore( readCertificate,
              keyStore,
              importKeyStoreFileName, importKeyStorePassword,
              importAlias ) ;
    }
    catch(IOException e){
      System.out.println(" Error :" +e);
      e.printStackTrace();
      System.exit(0);
    }
    catch(Exception ex)
    {
      System.out.println(" Error :" +ex);
      ex.printStackTrace();
      System.exit(0);
    }
  }
}
```

The following properties in the `keystore.Properties` file are then read inside of the `main()` method:

```
#name of the key store, we use the key store that comes with jdk "jks"
KEY_STORE_NAME=JKS
#keystore provider, the provider who implemented key store
KEY_STORE_PROVIDER=SUN

#export KeyStore password
EXPORT_KEY_STORE_PASSWORD=bshirts
#import KeyStore password
IMPORT_KEY_STORE_PASSWORD=bshirts

#export key Alias
EXPORT_KEY_ALIAS=Development
#import key Alias
IMPORT_KEY_ALIAS=Production

#export Key File Name
EXPORT_FILE_NAME=developmentStore
#import key file Name
IMPORT_FILE_NAME=productionStore
```


The `main()` method then calls `getKeyStore()` with the key-store name and provider (`JKS` and `SUN`) read in from the properties file to create the default key-store instance provided with the Java 2 platform.

The `exportACertificateFromAKeyStore()` method is then called with the key-store instance, key-store filename (`developmentStore`), key-store password (`bshirts`), and key alias name (`Development`). These values are used to load the key store with a call to `KeyStore.load()`, retrieve the X.509 certificate from the keystore using `KeyStore.getCertificate()`, print the principal name on the X.509 certificate, and then return a handle to the certificate.

The `main()` method then calls `importACertificateToAKeyStore()` method with the newly exported certificate, key-store instance, new key-store filename (`productionStore`), key-store password (`bshirts`), and key alias name (`Production`). The new key-store file is then loaded, and the certificate exported earlier from `developmentStore` is now imported into the `productionStore` key store with an alias name of `Production`. The import is accomplished in memory by calling `KeyStore.setCertificateFactory()` with the alias and certificate and then is committed to file by streaming the key-store file using `KeyStore.store()`.

Protecting Objects

When sending data and objects from point A to point B across a network or when storing data and objects to some medium and later retrieving them, some security issues arise that the JCA is designed to address:

- How can we be certain as receivers of this data or object that the information has not been corrupted in some fashion?
- How can we be certain as receivers of this data or object that it is from an intended or trusted source?

Message digests in the Java security API address the first issue, and signatures and signed objects in the Java security API address the second issue. In this section, we discuss how to use message digests, signatures, and signed objects to solve these particular security issues.

Message Digests

Java provides built-in support for creating and verifying message digests. When you have some data you want to protect from corruption while it's being sent to a receiver or being stored for later retrieval, you can use a few JCA APIs to create a message digest that can be sent or stored with the data. A retriever of that data can then use the JCA APIs to create their own message digest that is compared with the retrieved message digest. If the newly generated message digest and retrieved digest are equal, the message can be assumed to be uncorrupted. Of course, the probability of there being an undetectable corruption is a function of both the message digest algorithm and its parameters.

NOTE

A more cohesive version of the message digest snippets strewn throughout this section can be found on the CD in the `MessageDigestExample.java` file under the `examples\src\ejava\jsecuritych27` directory.

Figure 27.8 depicts the primary message digest–related classes that you will interface with as a developer. The static `getInstance()` methods on the `java.security.MessageDigest` class can be used to return an instance of a particular `MessageDigest` implementation. The `MessageDigest.getInstance(String)` method takes the name of a particular algorithm (for example, `MD5` or `SHA-1`) and returns an instance associated with the provider which implements that algorithm according to the provider preference order, as mentioned in Chapter 26. The `MessageDigest.getInstance(String, String)` method takes the name of a provider as well (for example, `SUN`) to specify exactly which provider's implementation to use. For example

```
String ALGORITHM_USED = "SHA-1";
MessageDigest messageDigestAlgorithm = null;
try{
   // JDK1.2 comes with two algorithms for message digest,
   // they are SHA-1 and MD5
   // We are using SHA-1.
   messageDigestAlgorithm =
     MessageDigest.getInstance(ALGORITHM_USED);
 }catch(NoSuchAlgorithmException noae){
   System.out.println("Error :"+noae);
   noae.printStackTrace();
   System.exit(0);
 }
```

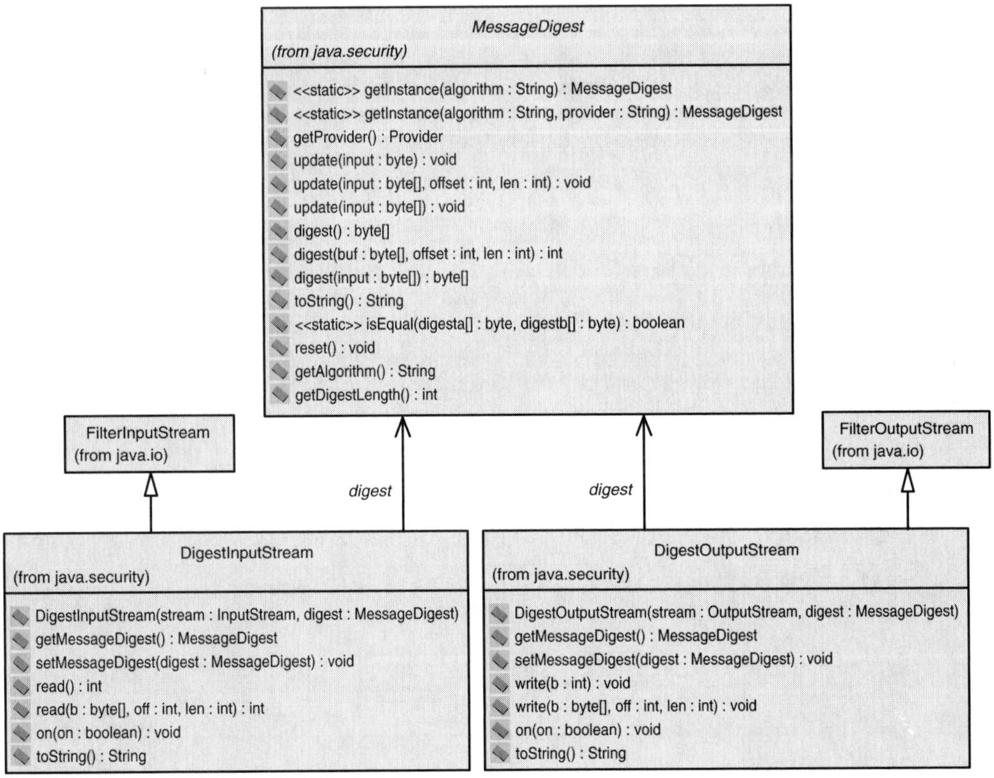

MessageDigest
(from java.security)

<<static>> getInstance(algorithm : String) : MessageDigest
<<static>> getInstance(algorithm : String, provider : String) : MessageDigest
getProvider() : Provider
update(input : byte) : void
update(input : byte[], offset : int, len : int) : void
update(input : byte[]) : void
digest() : byte[]
digest(buf : byte[], offset : int, len : int) : int
digest(input : byte[]) : byte[]
toString() : String
<<static>> isEqual(digesta[] : byte, digestb[] : byte) : boolean
reset() : void
getAlgorithm() : String
getDigestLength() : int

FilterInputStream
(from java.io)

FilterOutputStream
(from java.io)

digest

digest

DigestInputStream
(from java.security)

DigestInputStream(stream : InputStream, digest : MessageDigest)
getMessageDigest() : MessageDigest
setMessageDigest(digest : MessageDigest) : void
read() : int
read(b : byte[], off : int, len : int) : int
on(on : boolean) : void
toString() : String

DigestOutputStream
(from java.security)

DigestOutputStream(stream : OutputStream, digest : MessageDigest)
getMessageDigest() : MessageDigest
setMessageDigest(digest : MessageDigest) : void
write(b : int) : void
write(b : byte[], off : int, len : int) : void
on(on : boolean) : void
toString() : String

FIGURE 27.8
The message digest class.

The `MessageDigest.update()` methods take the data byte(s) to be protected as a parameter. The `update()` methods can be called as many times as needed. The message digest algorithm will simply continue to compress the data it receives into an underlying digest. The accumulated digest can then be retrieved using the `MessageDigest.digest()` method. The `MessageDigest.digest()` method can also be called with a set of data bytes that are to be accumulated in generating the digest before the digest is returned. Such calls are useful if you want to pass in the data to be compressed and receive the digest all in one operation. For example

```
// Message to send or store
String message = "12345678901234:12/2001:SamMellone";

byte[] messageInBytes = message.getBytes();
byte[] digestValue = null;
if(messageDigestAlgorithm != null){
  // make sure it is empty
  messageDigestAlgorithm.reset();
  // update the message to digest
  messageDigestAlgorithm.update(messageInBytes);
  // get digest Value from MessageDigest
  digestValue = messageDigestAlgorithm.digest();
}
```

After the data has been stored or sent to some location, a retriever or receiver of that data can use the same `update()` and `digest()` calls to generate a new message digest over the data. The `MessageDigest.isEqual()` method can then be used to compare the contents of the retrieved/received digest with the newly generated digest. If no corruption was detected, the `isEqual()` call returns `true`. Otherwise, a `false` value is returned.

```
// Read message that was sent or stored. If all was OK, the below
// message should be = "12345678901234:12/2001:SamMellone"
String message = // received message

// Read received digest as well that comes with message
byte[] receivedDigest = // received message digest

byte[] messageInBytes = message.getBytes();
byte[] digestValue = null;
if(messageDigestAlgorithm!= null){
  messageDigestAlgorithm.reset();
  messageDigestAlgorithm.update(messageInBytes);
  digestValue = messageDigestAlgorithm.digest();
  boolean trueIfEqual
    = messageDigestAlgorithm.isEqual(digestValue , receivedDigest);
}
```

Also shown in Figure 27.8 are `java.security.DigestInputStream` and `java.security.DigestOutputStream` classes. These classes can be used to facilitate how the data to be compressed is input and output from the message digest algorithm. Thus, manipulating data to be compressed as bytes can be avoided. The `DigestOutputStream(OutputStream, MessageDigest)` constructor is called with a target output stream and a `MessageDigest` object. If you construct an output stream with the `DigestOutputStream` object, then whenever calls are made to that output stream which write data to it, the `MessageDigest` object is called with `update()` invocations. Compression of calls to the `MessageDigest` object can be turned on and off with the `DigestOutputStream.on(boolean)` call. After the stream is completely written, the computed digest can be retrieved from the `MessageDigest` as usual via the `MessageDigest.digest()` call.

The reverse process occurs with the `DigestInputStream` object. It is constructed with an `InputStream` and `MessageDigest` object. If you then construct another input stream with the `DigestInputStream` as a parameter and invoke read calls on the input stream, this will result in `update()` calls being made to the `MessageDigest` as well. The `on()` method on `DigestInputStream` can also be used here to dictate whether the data being read should be compressed. Finally, the `MessageDigest.digest()` and `MessageDigest.isEqual()` methods can be used to obtain and verify the digest, respectively.

Signatures

Although using message digests helps protect data against corruption and therefore helps provide data integrity, it may be desirable to know from whom your data is coming. That is, the principal identity of the message sender may need to be securely provided to a receiver such that the receiver can be certain the data is from a trusted sender. For example, as an e-commerce vendor, you may be interested in knowing that the credit card information being sent to you from a particular customer is actually from that customer. Much like a customer signs a receipt acknowledging a credit card purchase in real life, a digital signature may be desirable to identify the signer of a credit card purchase over the Internet. Otherwise, someone else could simply use your stolen credit card information and make purchases from an e-commerce vendor over the Internet with no proof of identity provided. Figure 27.9 presents the interface to the `Signature` object used for creating and verifying signatures.

NOTE

A more cohesive version of the signature snippets strewn throughout this section can be found on the CD in the `SignatureExample.java` file under the `examples\src\ejava\jsecuritych27` directory.

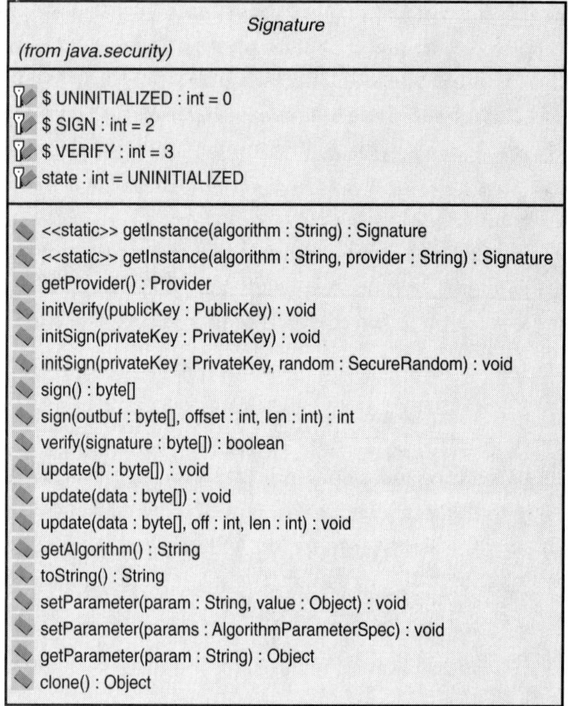

FIGURE 27.9
The signature class.

Because the `Signature` class is a cryptographic engine, it has the standard `getInstance()` static methods used to create instances of a particular provider's signature engine objects. As an example using the default Sun JCA provider, we have the following:

```
String ALGORITHM_NAME = "DSA";
Signature signature = null;
 try{
   // JDK comes with algorithm DSA
   signature = Signature.getInstance(ALGORITHM_NAME);
 }catch(NoSuchAlgorithmException noae)
 {
   System.out.println("Error :"+noae);
   noae.printStackTrace();
 }
```

Making a signature on the sender's side is then a matter of initializing the signature-creation process by calling `initSign()` on the `Signature` object with the sender's `PrivateKey`. You can optionally tweak the randomness of this initial seeding process as well using a form of the `initSign()` that takes a random value. Calls to `update()` on the signature can be performed with the message bytes that are to be signed. Then a call to `sign()` on the signature actually generates the byte stream containing the signature. As an example, here we first generate a random public and private key pair so that we can use the private key to later sign the message:

```
String ALGORITHM_NAME = "DSA";
KeyPairGenerator keyPairGenerator = null;
try{
  // JDK comes with algorithm DSA
  keyPairGenerator = KeyPairGenerator.getInstance(ALGORITHM_NAME);
}catch(NoSuchAlgorithmException noae)
{
  System.out.println("Error :"+noae);
  noae.printStackTrace();
}

//initialize keypairGenerator with a given Strength
int KEY_PAIR_STRENGTH = 512;
keyPairGenerator.initialize(KEY_PAIR_STRENGTH);
// Generate KeyPair
KeyPair keyPair = kPairGenerator.generateKeyPair();
// get private key from KeyPair
PrivateKey privateKey = keyPair.getPrivate();
PublicKey sendersPublicKey = keyPair.getPublic();
```

The private key can then be used to sign a message as shown here:

```
// Message to send or store
String message = "12345678901234:12/2001:SamMellone";

byte[] messageInBytes = message.getBytes();
byte[] digestValue = null;

try{
    // initialize signature with private Key
    signature.initSign(privateKey);
    // update message to the signature
    signature.update(messageInBytes);
    digestValue = signature.sign();
 }
 catch(InvalidKeyException invE){
  System.out.println(" Error :"+invE);
  invE.printStackTrace();
 }
 catch(SignatureException se){
  System.out.println(" Error :"+se );
  se.printStackTrace();
 }
```

The receiver of the message will need the `PublicKey` of the sender to be able to verify that the message came from a sender that the receiver trusts. This can be accomplished by packing the public key in a certificate that the receiver can import into its local key store. After the receiver has a `PublicKey`, it can then call `initVerify()` on a `Signature` object with the `PublicKey` as a parameter. The receiver can then call `update()` on the `Signature` object as usual with the message bytes it receives. The receiver must finally call `verify()` on the `Signature` object with the received message signature that it receives from the sender to verify whether the message was sent from that sender. For example

```
// Read message that was sent or stored. If all was OK, the below
// message should be = "12345678901234:12/2001:SamMellone"
String message = // received message
// Read received signature as well that comes with message
byte[] receivedDigest = // received message signature

byte[] messageInBytes = message.getBytes();
byte[] digestValue = null;
if(signature != null){
 try{
  // initialize verification
  signature.initVerify(sendersPublicKey);
  signature.update(messageInBytes);
  boolean trueIfVerified = signature.verify(receivedDigest);
 }
 catch(InvalidKeyException inve)
 {
  System.out.println("Error :"+inve);
  inve.printStackTrace();
 }
 catch(SignatureException se){
  System.out.println(" Error :"+se );
  se.printStackTrace();
 }
```

Signed Objects

A signed object in Java 2 lingo refers to a simple way to sign entire objects using a private key, serializing that object, and then sending it to a receiver. The receiver can then verify that the object is from the intended sender using the sender's public key. Figure 27.10 depicts the interface for the `java.security.SignedObject` class. The constructor of a `SignedObject` must be called with a `Serializable` object to be signed with a `PrivateKey` using a particular `Signature` engine object also passed into the constructor. This `SignedObject` is created on the sending side as shown here:

```
CreditCard creditCard = // create some Serializable object
PrivateKey privateKey = // sender's private key
Signature signature = // create new signature
SignedObject signedObject = null;
try{
    // Create a signed object using a privateKey
    signedObject =
      new SignedObject(creditCard, privateKey, signature);
 }
 catch(InvalidKeyException invE){
  System.out.println(" Error :"+invE);
  invE.printStackTrace();
 }
 catch(SignatureException se){
  System.out.println(" Error :"+se );
  se.printStackTrace();
 }
```

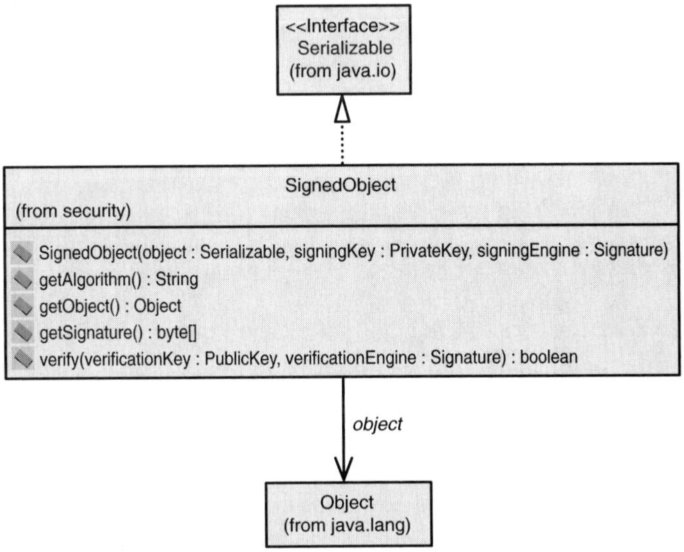

FIGURE 27.10
The signed object class.

Because the `SignedObject` and its payload are `Serializable`, it can be communicated to a receiver using any of various serialization techniques. After the `SignedObject` is reconstructed on the receiver side, the `verify()` method on the `SignedObject` can be called to determine whether a trusted sender has signed the object. The receiver passes in the `PublicKey` of the presumed sender and a `Signature` engine object in order for verification to occur. The object to be accessed can be retrieved using the `SignedObject.getObject()` method. As an example on the receiving side, we then have this:

```
PublicKey sendersPublicKey = // sender's public key
Signature signature = // create new signature
SignedObject signedObject = // a received signed object
try{
    boolean isTrueIfVerified =
       signedObject.verify(sendersPublicKey, signature);
    if(isTrueIfVerified){
      CreditCard creditCard =
           (CreditCard) signedObject.getObject();
      // now rest assured knowing that can use signed credit card
    }
 }
 catch(InvalidKeyException inve)
 {
  System.out.println("Error :"+inve);
  inve.printStackTrace();
 }
 catch(SignatureException se){
  System.out.println(" Error :"+se );
  se.printStackTrace();
 }
}
```

Signing Code

Signatures and signed objects in Java are used for much more than signing data and discrete objects. Signing an entire program can be effected using the code-signing support built into Java. Code signing in Java once almost exclusively meant applet code signing. In Java 1.1, signed applet code could be executed within a Web browser if the signer of that code was recognized as a trusted source. If the trusted source was verified, the Web browser let the applet code access valued resources that lay outside of the original sandbox restrictions. Mismatching between applet signing tools equipped with the JDK and applet signing tools equipped with Web-browser vendors such as Netscape did cause some signed-code compatibility problems, however.

What we as enterprise developers are concerned with here is how to sign Java application code. Such a need may arise if you simply want to verify that an entire application you receive for use in your enterprise has been signed by a trusted source. You may also want to download a jar file of component code from a Web site for use in your application and desire to subject it to the same identity source verification process. Furthermore, with the mobile capabilities inherent with Java code, you may also want to subject code that is automatically loaded by your applications during runtime to some sort of identity check. This section describes how to sign code and verify signed code that you use in your Java enterprise applications.

The JAR Signer Tool

As an enterprise developer, you have no doubt used the `jar` utility mentioned in Chapter 4, "Java Foundations for Enterprise Development," to create JAR files before. After your create a JAR file, you can sign this file with your own principal identification keys using a utility called `jarsigner`. The Java 2 `jarsigner` utility replaces one aspect of the `javakey` tool used in JDK 1.1. The `jarsigner` utility is a command-line utility that can be used to both generate signed JAR files and verify signed JAR files. These are the command-line options available for use with the `jarsigner` utility:

- `keystore`: Specifies the key-store URL
- `storetype`: Designates the key-store type
- `storepass`: Designates the key-store password
- `keypass`: Designates a private key password
- `sigfile`: Designates the filename base to use when generating signature files
- `signedjar`: Designates the name of the signed JAR file
- `verify`: Indicates that the named JAR file is to be verified as opposed to signed
- `certs`: Designates that certificate information should be included with the verification process
- `verbose`: Indicates that extra information should be displayed during operations
- `internalsf`: Indicates that a DSA file should not include a copy of signature file information
- `sectionsonly`: Indicates that a signature file should not include a manifest

Code Signing Process

These are the general steps involved with a principal signing code to identify themselves with that code:

1. Compile the code to be signed into class files.
2. Create a JAR file from class files.
3. Sign the JAR file.
4. Export a public key certificate.

On the receiving end, a Java application that wants to accept code only from a trusted source that has signed the code must carry out these steps:

1. Import the certificate as a trusted certificate.
2. Create a policy file indicating that such a principal should be trusted for certain permissions.
3. Load the trusted code with your Java application. (Access will be determined by the policy file.)

Code Signing Example

As a simple example of signing code, suppose we have the simple `BShirtsClient` application of Listing 27.4, which simply implements a `logIt()` method that writes some information to a log file. A `main()` method to test this functionality is provided; it reads a log filename as an argument and calls the `logIt()` method with a simple startup message.

NOTE

The following code-signing example is contained on the CD in the `examples\src\ejava\jsecuritych27` directory. A `BShirtsClient.java` file contains the sample code, `codeSignPolicy` policy file, and a `codeSigner.bat` script file.

LISTING 27.4 Sample Class File to Sign (`BShirtsClient.java`)

```
package ejava.jsecuritych27;
import java.io.PrintWriter;
import java.io.FileOutputStream;
import java.io.*;
import java.io.IOException;
import java.util.Date;


public class BShirtsClient
{
  private String logFile;
  public static PrintWriter logWriter;
  public BShirtsClient(String logFileName)
    throws IOException , FileNotFoundException, SecurityException
  {
    this.logFile = logFileName;
    logWriter = new PrintWriter(new FileOutputStream(logFile));
  }
```

```
  public void hasPermissionToWrite()
      throws Exception
  {
    logWriter = new PrintWriter(new FileOutputStream(logFile));
  }

  public static void logIt(String logInfo)
  {
    logWriter.println(logInfo);
  }

  public static void close()
  {
   logWriter.close();
  }

  public static void main(String[] args)
  {
    if(args.length == 0){
      System.out.println("Error :" +
        "java -Djava.security.manager "+
        "-Djava.security.policy=signedCodePolicy "+
        " ejava.jsecuritych27.BShirtsClient <logFile> ");
      System.exit(0);
    }
    String logFileName = args[0];
    try{
      BShirtsClient bshirtsClient = new BShirtsClient(logFileName);
      BShirtsClient.logIt(" Started Application :"+ new Date());
      BShirtsClient.close();
    }
    catch(FileNotFoundException fne){
      System.out.println("Error : "+fne);
    }
    catch(SecurityException se){
      System.out.println("Error : "+se);
    }
    catch(IOException ie){
      System.out.println("Error : "+ie);
    }
  }
}
```

A sample codeSignPolicy file equipped with the example designates which permissions are actually allowed for this code for a particular code signer. The codePolicyFile also designates the key store URL that our example application consults for code signer information. The key store at the specified location thus must be loaded with the appropriate code signer information as we will demonstrate shortly. Because our sample code need only write to a log file, it needs the appropriate file write permission for that file. You should modify the codeSignPolicy file to reference a file on your system as well as change the appropriate key store location, but the sample file equipped with the CD contains this:

```
keystore "file:/D:/bookp/examples/classes/myKeyStore";
grant signedBy "BShirts"
 {
  permission java.io.FilePermission "C:\\temp\\bshirts.log", "write";
};
```

The actual steps to take in signing the code are contained in the codeSigner.bat file on the CD, but they are also summarized here:

1. Set EJAVA_HOME and JAVA_HOME environment variables as appropriate for your environment (see Appendix A):

   ```
   set EJAVA_HOME=D:\bookp
   set JAVA_HOME=D:\jdk13
   ```

2. Compile the code:

   ```
   %JAVA_HOME%\bin\javac -d "%EJAVA_HOME%\examples\classes"
   ➥ BShirtsClient.java
   ```

3. Generate the jar file:

   ```
   %JAVA_HOME%\bin\jar -cvf Code.jar
   ➥ ejava\jsecuritych27\BShirtsClient.class
   ```

4. Generate the certificate:

   ```
   %JAVA_HOME%\bin\keytool -genkey -alias codeSign
   ➥ -keystore bshirtsStore -keypass bshirtsp
   ➥ -dname "cn=bshirts" -storepass 524316
   ```

5. Sign the jar file:

   ```
   %JAVA_HOME%\bin\jarsigner -keystore bshirtsStore
   ➥ -storepass 524316 -keypass bshirtsp
   ➥ -signedjar SignedCode.jar Code.jar codeSign
   ```

6. Export the certificate for use by the receiver:

   ```
   %JAVA_HOME%\bin\keytool -export -keystore bshirtsStore
   ➥ -storepass 524316 -alias codeSign -file BShirts.cer
   ```

The user of such code would typically perform the following steps on their own target application environment. However, for this example, we demonstrate the steps to take in granting trusted access to the signed code on the Java application side in `codeSigner.bat` assuming the same machine, directory, and files for simplicity in illustration:

1. Import the certificate:

```
%JAVA_HOME%\bin\keytool -import -alias BShirts -file BShirts.cer
➥ -keystore myKeyStore -storepass ij#kgl
```

2. The Java application can then be run using the signed JAR file with permissions granted through an associated security policy file:

```
%JAVA_HOME%\bin\java -Djava.security.manager
➥ -Djava.security.policy=codeSignPolicy
➥ ejava.jsecuritych27.BShirtsClient
➥ C:\\temp\\bshirts.log
```


Java Security Extensions

Now that we have seen some of the core features of Java security and the Java Cryptography Architecture, let's take a quick look at the extensions to Java security that come packaged separately from the Java 2 platform. The Java security extensions include the Java Cryptography Extension (JCE), Java Secure Socket Extension (JSSE), and the Java Authentication and Authorization Service (JAAS).

The JCE is the most mature extension of the three being available as version 1.2 at the time of this writing. However, both the JSSE and the JAAS were just released as version 1.0 at the time of this writing. Because all three extensions are still relatively young and because they are not an official part of the Java platform, we describe only the roles that each extension plays in providing a standard Java security API, as well as the top-level architecture of each extension. In this fashion, you as an enterprise developer can be in a better position to understand how to pursue use of such extensions if the need arises.

Java Cryptography Extension

The JCE is provided as a Java security extension for providing functions used to encrypt blocks of data for the sake of confidentiality until it can be subsequently decrypted by the intended receiver. Such functionality can be contrasted with the cryptography support offered by the JCA. The JCA primarily provides support for protecting data for integrity via message digests and provides a means for principal identification of data, objects, and code using signatures, keys, and certificates. Recall that the data, objects, or code itself was never encrypted. This is where the JCE steps in. Thus, whereas the JCA relies on an asymmetric public and private key infrastructure for secure identity (of principals), the JCE relies on a symmetric key infrastructure for secure confidentiality. In fact, the JCE symmetric key infrastructure class has many analogues to JCA asymmetric key infrastructure classes.

Encryption is arguably an extremely important security function to provide, but Sun has decided to not include encryption with the Java platform so that U.S. export restriction on encryption technology doesn't hamper global use of the Java platform. Of course, other third-party Java-based encryption products have come into being to fill this market gap. To provide a standard interface to such encryption technologies, the JCE uses a service-provider architecture similar to the JCA that provides a standard API to encryption functionality, but it allows for the use of different underlying encryption library providers. The latest JCE download and more information on the JCE can be found at `http://java.sun.com/products/jce/`.

The following packages compose the JCE v1.2 architecture:

- `javax.crypto`: The set of core classes and interfaces for the JCE plug-and-play service provider framework and cryptographic operation APIs.
- `javax.crypto.interfaces`: A set of interfaces used to encapsulate and manage Diffie-Hellman keys.
- `javax.crypto.spec`: A set of classes used to key algorithm and parameter specifications.

Figure 27.11 depicts the core architecture for the JCE. Note that we are not showing overloaded methods or method signatures in this diagram in order to keep the discussion brief. At the top of the diagram, we see five new cryptographic engine classes, each with the standard static `getInstance()` methods. Below that, we have a `SecretKey` designating a symmetric key, a `SealedObject`, Diffie-Hellman key interfaces, and helper classes for working with ciphers. The following list describes the role of each major API class or interface in the JCE architecture:

- `Cipher`: A cryptographic engine that provides the basic interface for encrypting and decrypting blocks of data bytes.
- `NullCipher`: A subclass of `Cipher` that provides a basic interface that does not encrypt or decrypt data (that is, cipher text and clear text are equal).
- `CipherInputStream`: An input stream class used to read cipher data from a decrypting `Cipher` object and enable chaining of an input stream with another input stream.
- `CipherOutputStream`: An output stream class used to write cipher data to an encrypting `Cipher` object and enable chaining of an output stream with another output stream.
- `SecretKey`: A marker interface for secret symmetric keys.
- `KeyAgreement`: A cryptographic engine that provides an interface for implementing a key exchange algorithm in which keys are first exchanged and a secret key is eventually created.
- `KeyGenerator`: A cryptographic engine that implements a symmetric key generator. Its asymmetric key generator analogue is the `KeyPairGenerator`.

- `SecretKeyFactory`: A cryptographic engine that can be used to translate keys between different compatible secret key types. Its asymmetric key generator analogue is the `KeyFactory`.
- `Mac`: A cryptographic engine that implements a Message Authentication Code algorithm for checking message integrity using secret symmetric keys.
- `SealedObject`: A class for protecting the confidentiality of an object using symmetric keys. Its asymmetric analogue is the `SignedObject`.
- `DHKey`, `DHPublicKey`, and `DHPrivateKey`: Base, public key, and private key interfaces for Diffie-Hellman keys, respectively.

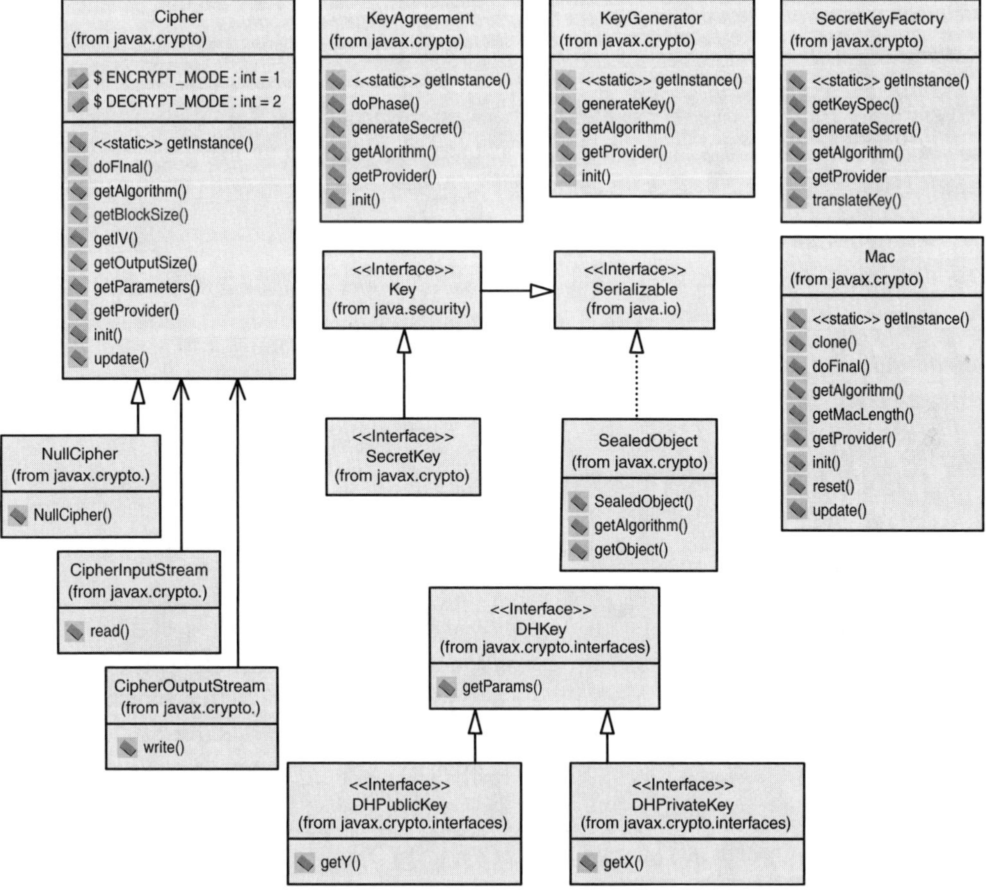

FIGURE 27.11
The JCE architecture.

Java Secure Socket Extension

Chapter 25, "Security Basics," described a few of the more popular secure socket protocols. The JSSE provides a standard API to secure socket protocols such as Secure Socket Layer (SSL). The JSSE also supports an API to the Transport Layer Security (TLS) and Wireless Transport Layer Security (WTLS) secure socket protocols. These are the specific protocol versions that are supported:

- SSL version 2 and 3
- TLS version 1
- WTLS version 1

Such versions are supported only by virtue of the JSSE API. At the time of this writing, Sun provided a reference implementation for only a subset of these protocols (SSL v3 and TLS v1). As with the other security extensions, the JSSE architecture follows the same adapter model of providing an API and a service provider interface for different underlying implementations to plug into the JSSE. The JSSE v1.0 download and more information on JSSE is available at `http://java.sun.com/products/jsse/`.

The following packages compose the JSSE v1.0 architecture:

- `javax.net.ssl`: This package contains the set of core classes and interfaces for the JSSE APIs.
- `javax.net`: This package is not specific to the JSSE but is needed to support basic socket and server socket factory functionality. We suspect that such a package will be deprecated in the future and instead utilize similar functionality in the Java platform.
- `javax.security.cert`: This package is also not specific to the JSSE but is needed to support basic certificate management functionality. We also suspect that such a package will be deprecated in the future and instead utilize similar functionality already present in the Java platform.

The JSSE class architecture is primarily useful for its encapsulation of SSL socket and SSL server socket objects and factories. SSL session handles can also be useful. Finally, SSL binding and handshake event and listener APIs are also provided. Figure 27.12 depicts this core architecture of the JSSE. Note that we are not showing overloaded methods or method signatures in this diagram in order to keep the discussion brief. The following list describes the role of each major API class or interface in the JSSE architecture:

- `SSLSocket`: A socket that supports SSL, TLS, and WTLS secure socket protocols
- `SocketFactory`: A factory for `Socket` objects
- `SSLSocketFactory`: A factory for `SSLSocket` objects

- `SSLServerSocket`: A server socket that supports SSL, TLS, and WTLS secure socket protocols
- `ServerSocketFactory`: A factory for `ServerSocket` objects
- `SSLServerSocketFactory`: A factory for `SSLServerSocket` objects
- `SSLSession`: An interface to an object encapsulating an SSL session
- `SSLSessionContext`: An interface to an object encapsulating a collection of SSL sessions identified with a session ID
- `SSLBindingEvent`: An event class encapsulating SSL session binding and unbinding events
- `SSLBindingListener`: A listener interface implemented by objects wanting to be made aware of SSL session binding and unbinding events
- `HandshakeCompletedEvent`: An event class encapsulating the fact that an SSL handshake has completed
- `HandshakeCompletedListener`: A listener interface implemented by objects wanting to be made aware of SSL handshake completion events

Java Authentication and Authorization Service

The JAAS extension to the Java security platform was developed to provide a standard way for limiting access to resources based on an authenticated user identity. JAAS APIs for login and logout also provide a standard technique for authenticating users and passing around secure context and credential information. Different underlying authentication and authorization models can be plugged into the JAAS service provider interface model while enabling API users to have a stable and standard interface. The JAAS v1.0 download and more information on JAAS are available at `http://java.sun.com/products/jaas/`.

The following packages compose the JAAS v1.0 architecture:

- `javax.security.auth`: Contains base classes and interfaces for authentication and authorization
- `javax.security.auth.callback`: Contains a framework of classes and interfaces defining a contract between an application and security service that enable the security service to pass certain authentication information to the application
- `javax.security.auth.login`: Contains classes used for login to a security domain
- `javax.security.auth.spi`: Currently contains one interface that is implemented by JAAS service providers

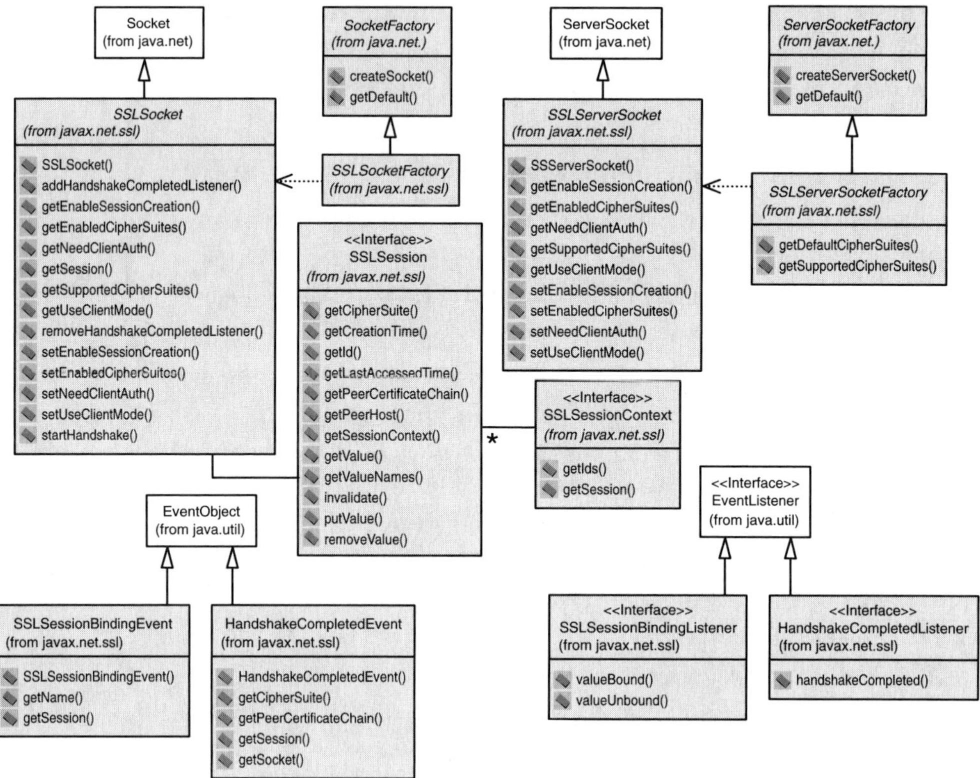

FIGURE 27.12
The JSSE architecture.

Figure 27.13 depicts the core architecture of the JAAS. Note that we are not showing overloaded methods or method signatures in this diagram in order to keep the discussion brief. The following list describes the role of each major API class or interface in the JAAS architecture depicted in Figure 27.13:

- `Subject`: Represents an individual or organization with multiple principal identities and therefore public and private credentials.
- `LoginContext`: Provides a basic API for subjects to log in and log out.
- `LoginModule`: Defines an interface to be implemented by service providers that support JAAS.
- `Configuration`: Encapsulates an entity used to configure an application with particular login modules.
- `Policy`: Encapsulates the system's policy for authorization.

- `AuthPermission`: Encapsulates permissions used during authentication.
- `CallbackHandler`: Defines an interface to be implemented by applications if they want to allow the authentication service to pass it information.
- `Callback`: Specifies a marker interface implemented by objects that are passed to a `CallbackHandler` implementation. A `Callback` object contains data to be given to an application.

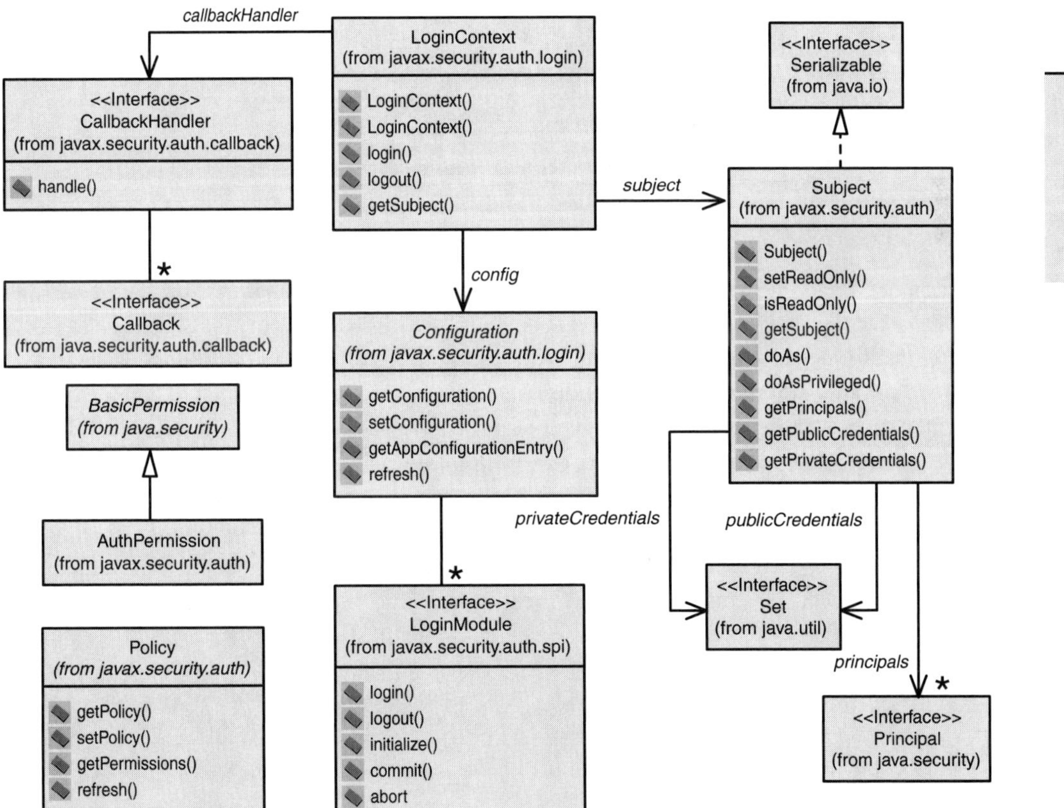

FIGURE 27.13
The JAAS architecture.

Conclusions

Because security is an involved problem with many facets of protection that must be provided, the Java security architecture is proportionately involved. Yet given the security protection built into the platform, Java provides a relatively simple API to these protection mechanisms. Java-based access control is greatly simplified in Java 2 versus Java 1.1 by the provision of a new fine-grained and configurable policy file–based permissions architecture. The JCA provides a rich set of APIs for implementing cryptographic protection for integrity and identity using industry-standard cryptographic techniques involving message digests, signatures, keys, and certificates. The management of keys and certificates is also made easier in Java 2 security. Finally, a set of standard security extensions for providing crypto-based confidentiality via the JCE, SSL interfacing via the JSSE, and authentication and authorization standards via the JAAS now also beef up the standard Java security model. Even with all the APIs and infrastructure provided, however, interfaces and standard support for nonrepudiation and auditing are not present in the architecture.

Furthermore, the protection mechanisms that are provided represent security-critical infrastructure that must themselves be protected against attack lest the very security of the Java architecture be compromised. Many such holes have been exploited and resolved over the years, but more are certain to crop up. A key consideration is to secure the environment where your JVM runs. In enterprise applications, this is less of a problem than is the case with applets, because the JVM may operate behind a firewall. This may not always be the case, however. For example, the security of your Java application may be compromised if your security policy file is open to attack via another route than your JVM, such as simply through open operating-system access. Thus, Java security can provide the mechanisms you need to protect against attacks embedded in Java code running in a JVM, but the provision of true enterprise security will also involve protecting that JVM and its operating environment as well.

CORBA Security

CHAPTER

28

IN THIS CHAPTER

- CORBA Security Overview 939
- Authentication 946
- Delegation 951
- Authorization 952
- Auditing 954
- Nonrepudiation 956
- Encryption 960
- Security Policies 962
- Security Administration 963

One of the OMG CORBAservice components that relates to assurance is the CORBA Security Service. The CORBA Security Service, like other CORBA services, is defined to function primarily atop the ORB layer. However, CORBA Security also defines some changes to the ORB layer as well to enable interoperability and enhanced security. The CORBA Security Service is defined in the OMG Security Service Specification. The idea behind the Security Service Specification was that by using components that implement the Security Service Specification, CORBA-based enterprise applications could gain the advantages of standards-based security protection including protection for identity, authenticity, nonrepudiation, authorization, auditing, integrity, and confidentiality.

In practice, however, the Security Service Specification is very complicated, and not many fully compliant COTS-based Java implementations are available. Even those products that have been developed are not widely used by CORBA applications programmers due to the complexity of the CORBA Security interface. However, interoperability with CORBA is a fundamental component of the J2EE specification. Although CORBA Security interoperability is not well-defined in v1.2 of the J2EE specification, in future versions of the specification it reportedly will be. In particular, the Enterprise JavaBeans (EJB) to CORBA Mapping specification described in Chapter 37, "Advanced Enterprise JavaBeans Serving", defines a few minimal guidelines for providing interoperability (including security interoperability) between J2EE EJB environments and other non-J2EE client/server environments. Furthermore, because this book focuses on how to build enterprise Java applications that not only use the J2EE features but also use features that satisfy broader enterprise Java development requirements, it is important to consider how CORBA Security can be used inside Java application components.

Given all of these considerations, we have decided to include this chapter on CORBA Security. Because CORBA Security has current minimal COTS support and not a very large usage base, we don't demonstrate how it can be used right now in your applications; it was still largely impractical to use at the time of this book's writing. However, because of the future push toward greater J2EE and CORBA interoperability and expected enhancements to CORBA that will make a service like CORBA Security simpler to use, we present an overview of CORBA Security in this chapter. We also discuss and present key interfaces and conceptual code snippets so that you can speak the language and understand the concepts involved with CORBA Security.

In this chapter, you will learn:

- About the CORBA Security Service Specification and architecture.
- About authentication using the CORBA Security Service.
- About the CORBA Security Service's delegation of credentials.
- About the means for authorizing users and access control in the CORBA Security model.

- About the means for auditing security-sensitive activities under the CORBA Security model.
- About CORBA Security Service nonrepudiation mechanisms.
- About support for integrating underlying data encryption for CORBA Security.
- About the mechanisms for defining specific CORBA Security policies.
- About current support for the administration of CORBA Security.

CORBA Security Overview

CORBA Security defines standard interfaces to services that operate on top of and to a certain extent are part of an ORB that provides security protection for your CORBA objects. CORBA Security provides security protection for identity, authenticity, nonrepudiation, authorization, auditing, integrity, and confidentiality. CORBA Security is defined in the CORBA Security Service Specification.

Digesting the CORBA Security Service Specification

The latest CORBA Security Service Specification (CSSS) from December 1998 is a very complex specification and is 386 pages in length. Because the specification is part of its parent CORBAservices specification, it has its own chapter number of 15. The following is a breakdown of the CORBA Security Service Specification (`ftp://ftp.omg.org/pub/docs/formal/98-12-10.pdf`) with notes indicating those sections that might be of interest to you and those that probably will not:

- *Section 15.1*: This is an introduction to security in general.
- *Section 15.2*: This section offers a specification overview that includes different specification packaging options for levels of compliance.
- *Section 15.3*: This section provides a reference model defining those elements of a system that need to be secured. That is, the CORBA security assurance problem model is presented.
- *Section 15.4*: This section covers the architecture of CORBA Security. This section is of use for understanding the big picture of how security is provided. That is, the CORBA security risk reduction model is presented.
- *Section 15.5*: This section presents the security API. This is perhaps the most useful section for you to examine because it discusses the API available for CORBA Security interfacing.
- *Section 15.6*: This section describes the administration interface. This section is of some interest, but most COTS vendors do not provide much in the way of administration support.

- *Section 15.7*: This section describes the service provider interface. This section will be of almost no interest to you as an enterprise developer.
- *Sections 15.8–15.15*: These sections describe security protocol interoperability. They will also most likely not be of interest because they discuss ORB-to-ORB interoperability issues for security protocols.
- *Appendixes A–I:* The IDL interfaces defined in Appendix A are of interest. The guidelines for implementing CORBA Security solutions in Appendix G may also be of interest to architects.

CORBA Security Packages

Because the CSSS is a fairly complicated work, vendors may be able to implement only certain pieces of the specification at a time. The CSSS describes a standard set of security specification packages that group certain features of the specification such that vendors can claim incremental compliance using a standard terminology. The CORBA Security packages are defined here:

- *Security Functionality Level 1 Package:* Defines minimal security interfaces for applications that are largely security unaware.
- *Security Functionality Level 2 Package:* Defines application and administrative programming interfaces for building security-aware applications and also much of the functionality of interest to enterprise developers.
- *Nonrepudiation Package:* Defines interfaces for providing nonrepudiation services for your application.
- *Security Replaceability Package:* Defines interfaces for supporting plug-in security services using CORBA interceptors and plug-in security service interfaces.
- *Common Secure Interoperability (CSI) Packages:* Defines three levels of support describing how interoperable one ORB is with another ORB for security interaction. CSI Level 0 defines an interoperable secure identity passing scheme with no delegation allowed. CSI Level 1 allows delegation. CSI Level 2 signifies that the ORB supports all Security Service functionality.
- *SECIOP Package:* Indicates the information an ORB may generate and use passed in an IOR via GIOP and IIOP for security with SECIOP enhancements.
- *Security Mechanism Packages:* Defines which underlying identity, authenticity, and confidentiality mechanisms are used that are relevant to ORB interoperability. For example, Kerberos and SSL are two security mechanisms used for passing around secure identity and ensuring confidentiality via encryption.

- *SECIOP and DCE-CIOP:* Such a package is of interest only if you are using DCE security services and the DCE-CIOP protocol.

CORBA Security Architecture

Many of the security packages defined in the CSSS actually map closely to IDL modules and therefore to packages in the Java binding for CORBA Security. For example, the following CORBA Security IDL modules and how they map to associated Java packages (listed next in the form of *IDL_Module ~ Java_Package*) will be of primary interest to our discussion throughout this chapter:

- `org::omg::Security` ~ `org.omg.Security`: Contains core and common CORBA Security types as needed by various security packages.
- `org::omg::SecurityLevel1` ~ `org.omg.SecurityLevel1`: Contains an interface defined for minimal CORBA Security support for application interfacing as defined by the Security Functionality Level 1 security package.
- `org::omg::SecurityLevel2` ~ `org.omg.SecurityLevel2`: Contains the large majority of interfaces relevant to CORBA Security Service application interfacing as defined by the Security Functionality Level 2 security package.
- `org::omg::NRService` ~ `org.omg.NRService`: Contains the interfaces used for nonrepudiation application interfacing as defined by the Nonrepudiation security package.
- `org::omg::SecurityReplaceable` ~ `org.omg.SecurityReplaceable`: Contains the interfaces for enhancing vendor interoperability used for service-provider interfacing as defined by the Security Replaceability security package.
- `org::omg::SecurityAdmin` ~ `org.omg.SecurityAdmin`: Contains system administration and security policy–related interfaces used for administrative interfacing as defined by the Security Functionality Level 2 security package.

The core interfaces depicted in Figure 28.1 scope the CORBA Security architecture presented in our discussion throughout the remainder of this chapter. Security features supported by the architecture of Figure 28.1 and to be discussed further in subsequent sections include these:

- Support for authenticating a client proxy with a CORBA Security domain using a principal authenticator (`PrincipalAuthenticator`) and obtaining credentials (`Credentials`) for that object.
- Support for transparent transmission of credentials from a current secure execution context (Current) via a security context (`SecurityContext`) over the wire from client-side secure invocation (`SecClientSecureInvocation` and `Vault`) to server-side secure invocation (`SecTargetSecureInvocation`) with delegation of credentials as an option.

- Support for access control decision making (`AccessDecision`) based on the required rights (`RequiredRights`) for authorized access.
- Support for nonrepudiation of messages sent or received from a principal by generating tokens and verifying evidence associated with that principal's credentials (`NRCredentials`).
- Support for determining whether certain events should be audited (`AuditDecision`) and then potentially logging the event to an audit log (`AuditChannel`).
- Support for configuring cryptographic quality of protection levels (`QOPPolicy`) according to integrity and confidentiality.
- Support for the configuration of various security policy types (`Policy` sub-interfaces).

NOTE

Throughout this chapter we present a series of figures and code snippets that utilize CORBA Security types and interfaces in terms of their Java mappings from CORBA IDL. Whereas the CSSS describes such CORBA Security entities in terms of IDL, we felt that it would be more appropriate and intuitive for Java programmers to understand CORBA Security in terms of how they would use it in a Java application. Thus, the figures and code snippets you see in this chapter reference classes and interfaces that have been generated from the IDL-to-Java mapping of the CORBA Security Service IDL.

Core CORBA Security Interfacing

Before we delve into any specific interfaces describing how security protection is provided for CORBA applications, we will quickly examine some of the core structures and types on which the actual security interfaces depend. Many such types are defined in the general `org::omg::Security` IDL module. Aside from core CORBA IDL dependence, the Security IDL module also minimally depends on the `TimeBase` IDL module.

Table 28.1 depicts a few of the most important core security types utilized by the rest of the CSSS interfaces. All of these types are encapsulated in the `org::omg::Security` module, which means that Java mappings of these types belong to the `org.omg.Security` package. The table presents each IDL entity, giving a brief description of the entity and stating what the entity looks like in its mapped Java form.

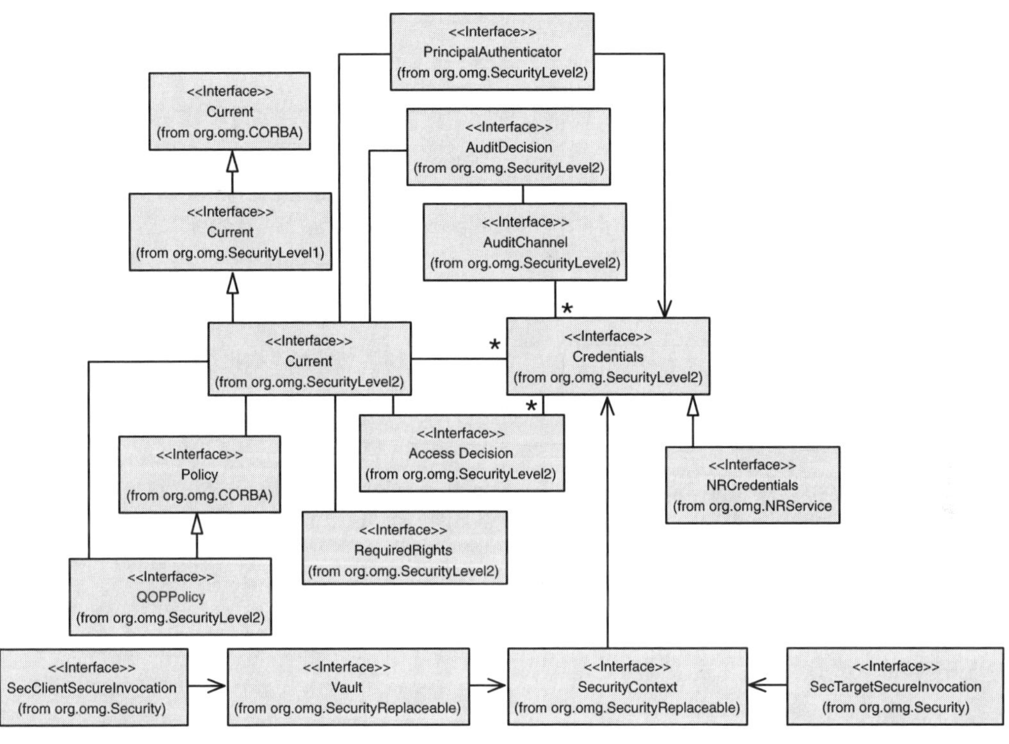

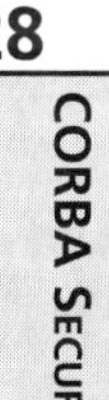

FIGURE 28.1
CORBA Security architecture.

TABLE 28.1 Core Security Types

IDL Entity	*Description*	*Java Mapping*
Basic Types		
typedef string SecurityName;	A security name used for various purposes	java.lang.String
typedef sequence<octet> Opaque;	Secure block of bytes	byte[]

continues

IDL Entity	Description	Java Mapping
Extensible Families		

struct ExtensibleFamily {
unsigned short family_definer;
unsigned short family;
};
	Used to save information on whether a particular data type is extensible	final public class
		ExtensibleFamily{
		  public short
		   family_definer;
		  public short
		   family;
		   ...}

Mechanism Types		
typedef string MechanismType;	Mechanism type name	java.lang.String

struct SecurityMechandName{
 MechanismType mech_type;
 SecurityName security_name;
};
	Associates a mechanism name with a security name	final public class
		SecurityMechandName{
		  public String
		   mech_type;
		  public String
		  security_name;
		  ...
		}

typedef sequence<MechanismType>
  MechanismTypeList;
	A collection of mechanism types	final public class
		MechanismTypeListHolder{
		  public String[]
		    value;
		 ...
		}

typedef sequence
 <SecurityMechandName>
   SecurityMechandNameList;
	A collection of security mechand names	Final public class
		SecurityMechandNameListHolder
		{
		public org.omg.Security.
		➥SecurityMechandName[]
		 value;
		 ...
		}

IDL Entity	*Description*	*Java Mapping*
Security Attribute Types		
typedef unsigned long SecurityAttributeType;	ID different security attributes with a set of constants also defined for various security attributes	int

struct AttributeType {
  ExtensibleFamily
    attribute_family;
  SecurityAttributeType
    attribute_type;
};
	Associate an extensible family and security attribute	final public class
		 AttributeType {
		  public org.omg.Security.
		➥ExtensibleFamily
		     attribute_family;
		  public int attribute_type;
		 ...
		}

struct SecAttribute {
 AttributeType Attribute_type;
 Opaque defining_authority;
 Opaque value;
};
	Associate a value and authority with security attribute	final public class
		SecAttribute {
		  public org.omg.
		 Security.AttributeType
		     attribute_type;
		  public byte[]
		    defining_authority;
		  public byte[]
		     value;
		  ...
		}

typedef sequence <SecAttribute>
  AttributeList;
	Collection of security attributes	Final public class
		  AttributeListHolder {
		 Public
		org.omg.Security.SecAttribute
		 value[];
		  ...
		}

continues

<table>
<tr><th>IDL Entity</th><th>Description</th><th>Java Mapping</th></tr>
<tr><td colspan="3">Timebase Types</td></tr>
<tr><td><pre>// from TimeBase
typedef unsigned long
 long   TimeT;

// from Security
typedef TimeBase::TimeT TimeT;</pre></td><td>Store time in long form</td><td><pre>long</pre></td></tr>
<tr><td><pre>// from TimeBase
struct IntervalT {
  TimeT lower_bound;
  TimeT upper_bound;
};

// from Security
typedef TimeBase::IntervalT
    IntervalT;</pre></td><td>Store time interval</td><td><pre>final public class
     IntervalT {
  public long
          lower_bound;
  public long
          upper_bound;
...
}</pre></td></tr>
<tr><td><pre>// from TimeBase
typedef short TdfT;
struct UtcT {
  TimeT time;
  unsigned long inacclo;
  unsigned short inacchi;
  TdfT tdf;
};

// from Security
typedef TimeBase::UtcT UtcT;</pre></td><td>Store universal time</td><td><pre>final public class
      UtcT {
  public long time;
  public int inacclo;
  public short inacchi;
  public short tdf;
...
}</pre></td></tr>
</table>

Authentication

Authentication APIs using the CORBA Security model involves use of components from the Security, SecurityLevel1, and SecurityLevel2 security packages. A principal authenticator represents a frontline interface for CORBA clients to use when authenticating themselves with the CORBA Security Service. After authenticating themselves, clients are given a set of credentials that are stored along with their current security context. When the client makes a remote invocation on a CORBA server, its security context is passed along with the marshaled call parameters to the server-side ORB. The target server's Security Service can use this information to determine whether the client should be allowed to make the call and optionally allow the server object to obtain access to the client's credential information that was passed along with the security context. Figure 28.2 depicts the core architecture of the Java-mapped CORBA entities that have relevance to such a CORBA Security authentication process.

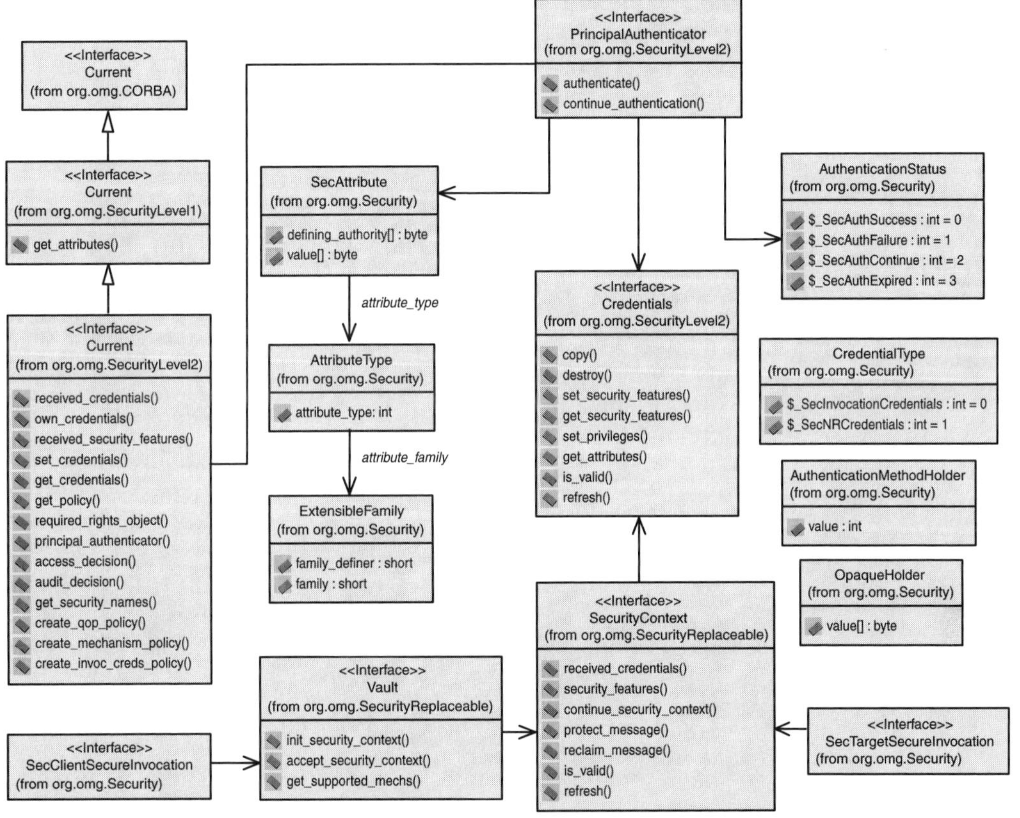

FIGURE 28.2
CORBA Security authentication.

In addition to using a few of the aforementioned core Security types, CORBA Security for authentication requires a few additional types from the `org::omg::Security` module:

```
// The vendor will define the values for AuthenticationMethod, with
// respect to what orb supports...e.g. password or certificate, etc.
// Maps to a Java int. Showing Holder value in Figure 28.2.
typedef unsigned long AuthenticationMethod;
```

```
// Maps to AuthenticationStatus class in Figure 28.2.
enum AuthenticationStatus {...};

// Maps to AuthenticationStatus class in Figure 28.2.
enum CredentialType {...};
```

Such types are utilized by the `org::omg::SecurityLevel2::PrincipalAuthenticator` interface's `authenticate()` and `continue_authenticate()` methods.

The `continue_authenticate()` call is a variation of `authenticate()` when a multistep authentication process is required. The `authenticate()` call is the primary interface needed for CORBA authentication. The IDL interface for this call looks like this:

```
Security::AuthenticationStatus authenticate (
  in Security::AuthenticationMethod method,
  in Security::SecurityName security_name,


  in Security::Opaque auth_data,

  in Security::AttributeList privileges,

  out Credentials creds,

  out Security::Opaque continuation_data,

  out Security::Opaque auth_specific_data
);
```

The Java mapping (including a description of each input and output parameter added by us) for this call looks like this:

```
// Returns status of authentication
org.omg.Security.AuthenticationStatus authenticate(

    // Designates type of authentication (e.g. password-based)
    int method,

    // Principal ID name
    java.lang.String security_name,

    // Authentication data (e.g. a password)
    byte[] auth_data,

    // Requested privileges
    org.omg.Security.SecAttribute[] privileges,
```

```
    // Returned credentials
    org.omg.SecurityLevel2.CredentialsHolder creds,

    // Returned information needed for continue_authenticate() calls
    org.omg.Security.OpaqueHolder continuation_data,

    // Returned info specific to authentication method
    org.omg.Security.OpaqueHolder auth_specific_data
  );
```

The org::omg::SecurityLevel2::Current object contains security-related state information associated with the current thread execution context (that is, a security context). The org::omg::SecurityLevel1::Current interface is a parent interface for org::omg::SecurityLevel2::Current containing minimal security context information useful for security-unaware applications that can utilize a SecurityLevel1-compliant ORB. The org:::omg::SecurityLevel2::Credentials object encapsulates the credentials returned from authentication and associated with the Current object.

The basic sequence of events for authentication via CORBA Security using such objects follows these general lines, with conceptual snippets of code given to illustrate each point:

1. Obtain a reference to the SecurityCurrent object representing the current security execution context:

```
ORB orb = ORB.init(args, null);
org.omg.CORBA.Object currentReference =
  orb.resolve_initial_references("SecurityCurrent");
org.omg.SecurityLevel2.Current current
   = org.omg.SecurityLevel2.CurrentHelper.narrow(currentReference);
```

2. Obtain a reference to PrincipalAuthenticator:

```
org.omg.SecurityLevel2.PrincipalAuthenticator principalAuthenticator
  = current.principal_authenticator();
```

3. Create the data needed for authentication and holders for the output of authentication:

```
// Create security name (principal and domain example here)
String securityName = "Sam@BEESHIRTSREALM.COM";
// Specify authentication method using vendor-specific
// identifiers. For example, ORB Vendor may define
// password-based authentication as constant value 1.
int authenticationMethod = 1;
// Set password value
String passwordValue = "MyPassword";
byte[]  authorizationData = passwordValue.getBytes();
// Define requested privileges (some methods may not support)
org.omg.Security.SecAttribute[] privileges
  = new org.omg.Security.SecAttribute[0];
```

```
// Create holders for output values
org.omg.SecurityLevel2.CredentialsHolder credentials
  = new org.omg.SecurityLevel2.CredentialsHolder();
org.omg.Security.OpaqueHolder continuationData
  = new org.omg.Security.OpaqueHolder();
org.omg.Security.OpaqueHolder authSpecificData
  = new org.omg.Security.OpaqueHolder();
```

4. The CORBA client now authenticates itself with a `PrincipalAuthenticator` object:

```
org.omg.Security.AuthenticationStatus status
  = principalAuthenticator.authenticate(
        authenticationMethod, securityName, authorizationData,
        privileges,credentials,continuationData, authSpecificData);
```

5. The authentication process returns a `Credentials` object and is associated with the client's `Current` object, as well as returned in a `CredentialsHolder` object parameter to the `authenticate()` method.
6. The client then makes remote invocations on security-sensitive target CORBA servers.

So how is authentication information used and communicated under the hood during such invocations? The following basic steps highlight just such a process during remote invocations on security-sensitive servers:

1. An `org::omg::Security::SecClientSecureInvocation` object handles secure invocations by a security-aware ORB on the client side.
2. An `org::omg::SecurityReplaceable::Vault` object is called by the `SecClientSecureInvocation` object.
3. The Vault creates an `org::omg::SecurityReplaceable::SecurityContext` object used to encapsulate a security context with a read-only collection of `Credential` objects and a `Current` object.
4. The `org::omg::SecurityReplaceable::SecurityContext` objects have methods enabling them to be serialized and sent over the wire.
5. An `org::omg::Security::SecTargetSecureInvocation` on the target server-side ORB deserializes `SecurityContext` and retrieves the credentials associated with the client.
6. The target server side now has the credentials it needs that were created during principal authentication to identify the client object. Based on such client identity from the credentials, the target can then use some policy to determine whether the client has permission to perform the invocation (per our authorization discussion later in the chapter).
7. Server objects running in secure mode can also retrieve and access the credentials associated with the invocation.

Delegation

CORBA Security supports three modes of operation for delegation of credentials during security-sensitive object invocations, as illustrated in Figure 28.3. Recall from Chapter 25, "Security Basics," that delegation pertains to issues regarding how some Object A's credentials propagate during a call to some Object C by some Object B when Object A first calls Object B. With a "No Delegation" mode of CORBA Security, the client's identity is not delegated, and thus an Object A's credentials would not propagate to Object C in this example. With a "Simple Delegation" mode, Object A's credentials would get propagated to Object C. With "Composite Delegation," both Object B's and Object A's credentials propagate to Object C.

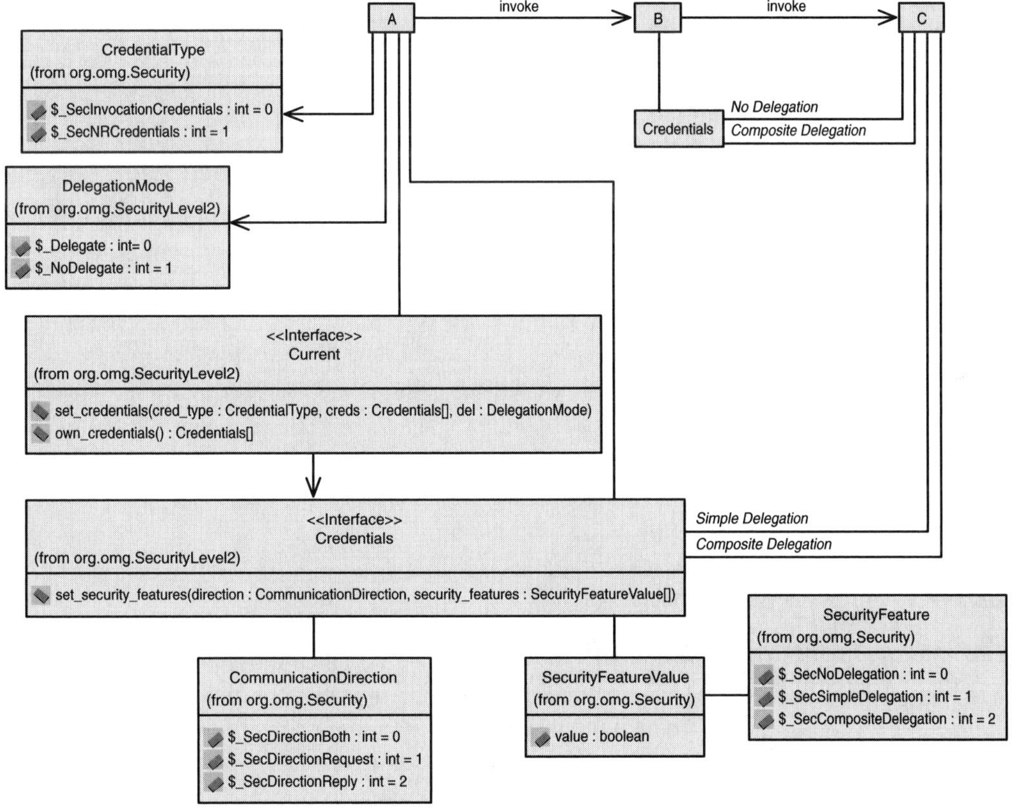

FIGURE 28.3
CORBA Security delegation.

Object A can turn delegation on by calling `set_credentials()` on a `Current` object reference using the `org::omg::Security::DelegationMode enum Delegate` value. Thus, Object A would then let Object B use Object A's credentials during delegation:

```
org.omg.SecurityLevel2.Current current
  = org.omg.SecurityLevel2.CurrentHelper.narrow(
      orb.resolve_initial_references("SecurityCurrent"));

org.omg.SecurityLevel2.Credentials[] ownCredentials
  = current.own_credentials();

org.omg.Security.CredentialType credentialType
  = org.omg.Security.CredentialType.SecInvocationCredentials;

org.omg.SecurityLevel2.DelegationMode delegationMode
 = org.omg.SecurityLevel2.DelegationMode.Delegate;

current.set_credentials(credentialType, ownCredentials, delegationMode);
```

The `DelegationMode enum NoDelegate` value can be used to turn delegation off for Object A. In such a mode, Object A would not let Object B use Object A's credentials during delegation.

```
org.omg.SecurityLevel2.DelegationMode delegationMode
 = org.omg.SecurityLevel2.DelegationMode.NoDelegate;

current.set_credentials( credentialType, ownCredentials, delegationMode);
```

As a final note, the particular mode of delegation for the set of credentials can also be established via the `Credentials.set_security_feature()` interface. Here, a `SecurityFeature` value defined according to the direction of invocation (that is, `request`, `reply`, or `both`) can be set on a particular `Credentials` object to establish whether no delegation, simple delegation, or composite delegation is supported.

Authorization

Authorization in CORBA follows a role-based access control model in which ACLs are maintained that describe which rights are required for particular operations, which roles are assigned to which principal identities, and which rights get associated with which roles. For particular calls on the server side, a target invocation may use the received client credential information and information about the operation being invoked to consult a CORBA Security access decision-making object for a yes or no answer regarding whether the operation is to be permitted. The required rights for such operations can also be determined a priori using the CORBA Security Service. Figure 28.4 shows some of the key objects involved in CORBA Security authorization.

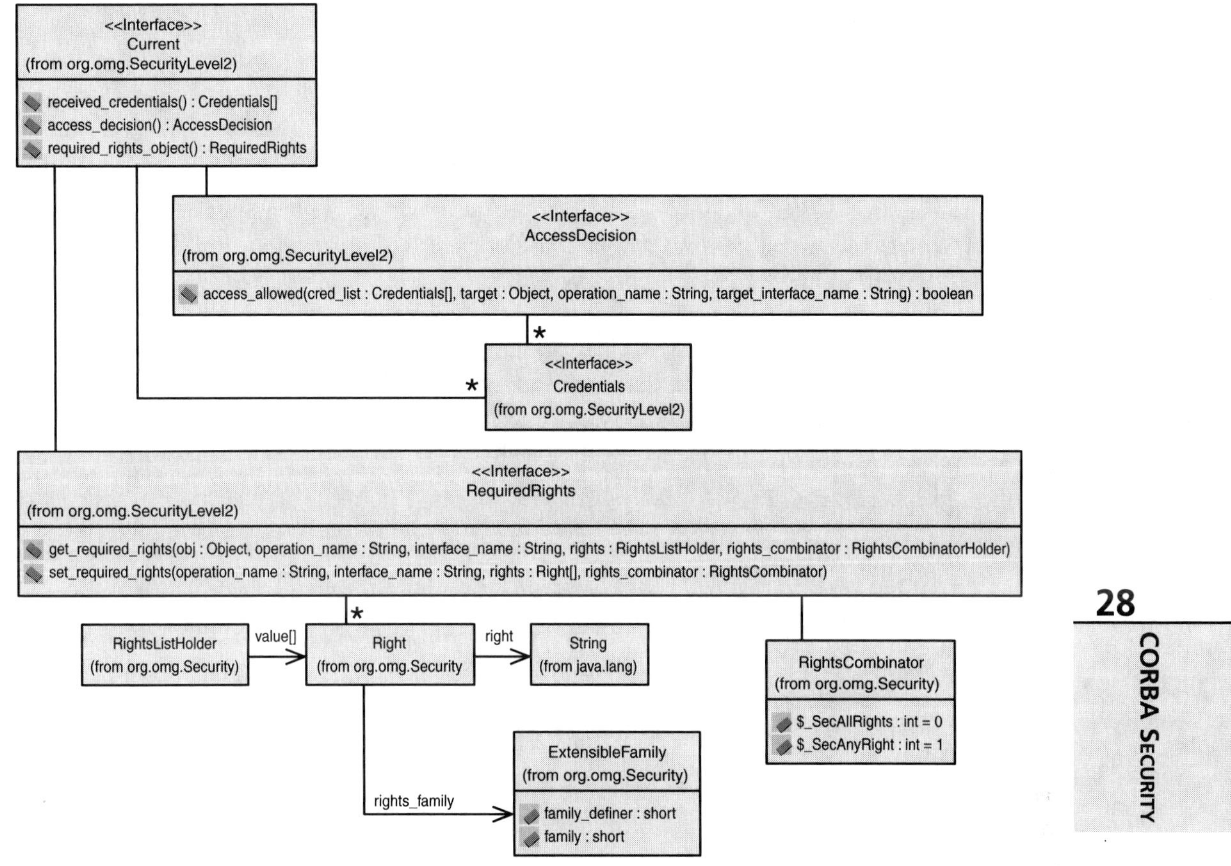

FIGURE 28.4
CORBA Security authorization.

On the target object side of a particular invocation, a target server asks the `Current` object for an `org::omg::SecurityLevel2::AccessDecision` object. The `AccessDecision` object can be used to determine whether access should be allowed for a particular operation. To accomplish this task, the `AccessDecision` object will need the credentials associated with the invoking client object that contains the privilege information it needs to make the decision. The received client credentials can be yielded from a call to the `Current.received_credentials()` call. For example:

```
org.omg.SecurityLevel2.AccessDecision accessDecision
  = current.access_decision();
```

```
org.omg.SecurityLevel2.Credentials[] credentialsList
  = current.received_credentials();

boolean  allowed =
  accessDecision.access_allowed(credentialsList,
    targetObject, "someOperationName, "TargetServer" );
```

If you desire a priori knowledge of the required rights level associated with such an operation, you can use the `org::omg::SecurityLevel2::RequiredRights` object to return a set of rights required for performing a particular operation. After a `RequiredRights` reference is retrieved from the `Current` object, a `required_rights()` call can be made on the `RequiredRights` object specifying the target object, the target object name, and the name of the target object interface. The `required_rights()` call returns a list of `Right` objects via a `RightsListHolder` object and a `RightsCombinator` object via a `RightsCombinatorHolder` object. These two objects can then be used to determine the particular rights information required for an operation.

```
org.omg.SecurityLevel2.RequiredRights
  requiredRights  = current.required_rights_object();

org.omg.Security.RightsListHolder  assignedRights
  = new org.omg.Security.RightsListHolder();
org.omg.Security.RightsCombinatorHolder rightsCombinator
  = new org.omg.Security.RightsCombinatorHolder();

requiredRights.get_required_rights(targetObject, "someOperationName",
  "TargetServer", assignedRights, rightsCombinator);
```

Auditing

Auditing of security-critical operations under the CORBA Security Service requires one to make an audit decision to first determine whether an audit is needed based on a particular audit event. If an audit is needed, the audit event data, the invoking principal's credentials, and the time are all written to an audit channel. Figure 28.5 depicts the CORBA interface constructs that implement such auditing functionality.

An `org::omg::SecurityLevel2::AuditDecision` object must first be obtained on the target server side from the `Current` object using `Current.audit_decision()`. The received client credentials must also be obtained from the `Current` object. An `org::omg::Security::AuditEventType` object is then constructed to encapsulate a particular event type that may be logged. This event type, along with an array of event type selectors, is passed to the `AuditDecision.audit_needed()` call. Here's a conceptual example:

```
// Get Current object as did in Authentication section of chapter
org.omg.SecurityLevel2.Current current = // Get "SecurityCurrent"
org.omg.SecurityLevel2.AuditDecision auditDecision
```

```
  = current.audit_decision();
org.omg.SecurityLevel2.Credentials[] receivedCredentials
  = current.received_credentials();

org.omg.Security.ExtensibleFamily eventFamily
  = new  org.omg.Security.ExtensibleFamily(0, 0);
short eventType = org.omg.Security.AuditAll.value;
org.omg.Security.AuditEventType auditEventType
  = new   org.omg.Security.AuditEventType(eventFamily, eventType);
org.omg.Security.SelectorValue[]  selectors
  = new org.omg.Security.SelectorValue[1];

boolean auditNeeded
  = auditDecision.audit_needed(auditEventType,selectors);
```

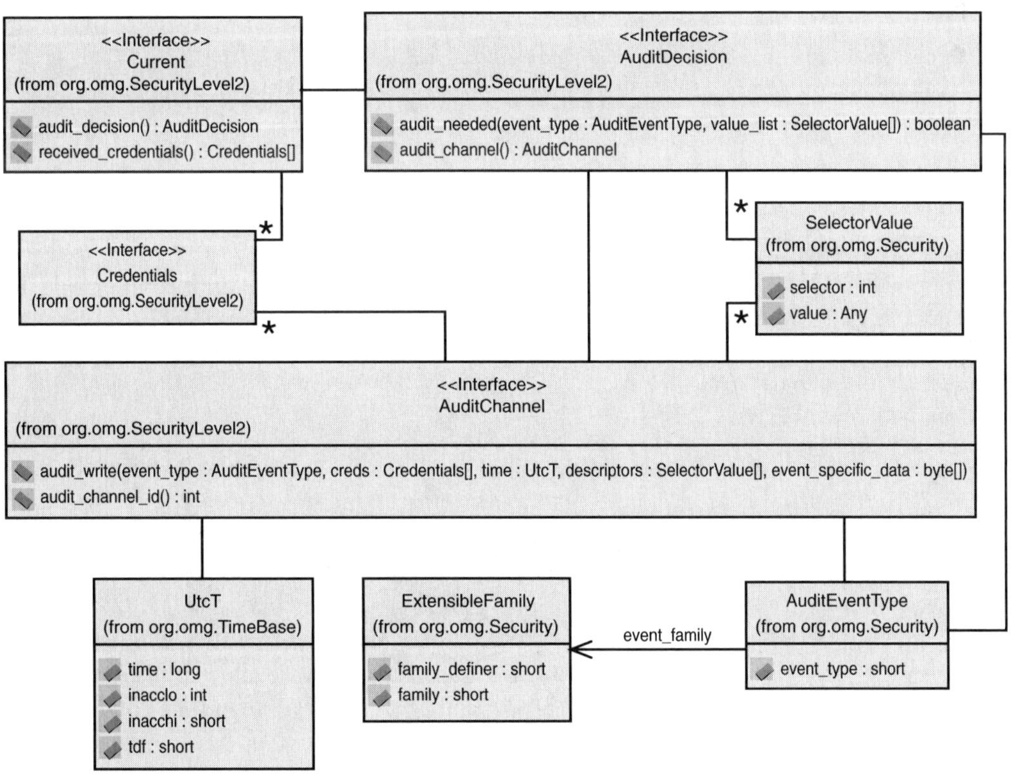

FIGURE 28.5
CORBA Security auditing.

If the returned value from an AuditDecision.audit_needed() call indicates that an audit should be performed, an AuditChannel object should be obtained from the AuditDecision object. This AuditChannel object's audit_write() call should then be called with the audit event, the received client credentials, the timestamp, event selectors, and other event-specific information. The audit_write() call will then write such information to the specific audit log. For example:

```
if(auditNeeded){
  org.omg.SecurityLevel2.AuditChannel currentAuditChannel
    = auditDecision.audit_channel();
  int currentAuditChannelID = currentAuditChannel.audit_channel_id();
  String data = "called someOperationName";
  byte[] eventSpecificData = data.getBytes();
  org.omg.TimeBase.UtcT time =
    new  org.omg.TimeBase.UtcT();

  currentAuditChannel.audit_write(auditEventType,
    receivedCredentials, time, selectors, eventSpecificData);
}
```

Nonrepudiation

CORBA Security also provides a set of interfaces for performing nonrepudiation (NR) of operation invocations. The generation of an NR token associated with received data from some principal can be used later to prove that the principal sent such data. This is accomplished using evidence that can be used later in case of a dispute. NR can also be used to prove that some principal received data as well. Figure 28.6 shows the core CORBA Security objects involved with providing an NR service.

An org::omg::NRService::NRCredentials object can be used to generate and verify NR tokens. The NRCredentials object inherits from the regular Credentials object. A returned set of credentials from the Current object may be narrowed to a NRCredentials object when NR support is in place. The NRCredentials.generate_token() call generates an NR token associated with a block of data passed to it and including principal identity information extracted from the NRCredentials object. The block of data is some message that one side of the NR process says it received or sent. Evidence received by the generate_token() call can be used later with the NR token to verify that the data was sent or received. As an example of token generation using the NRCredentials.generate_token() call, we have this

```
org.omg.NRService.NRCredentials[] receivedCredentials
    = (org.omg.NRService.NRCredentials[])current.received_credentials();

org.omg.NRService.NRPolicyFeatures[] nrPolicyFeatures
    = receivedCredentials[0].get_NR_features();

org.omg.NRService.EvidenceType evidenceType
    = org.omg.NRService.EvidenceType.SecProofofReceipt;

boolean includeDataInToken = true;
boolean generateRequest = true;
boolean inputBufferComplete = true;

// request everything
org.omg.NRService.RequestFeatures requestFeatures
    = new org.omg.NRService.RequestFeatures();
// data for which evidence is generated.
String received = "Hi There";
byte[] receivedData = received.getBytes();

// nrToken will be filled by the call
org.omg.Security.OpaqueHolder nrToken
             = new   org.omg.Security.OpaqueHolder();
// evidenceCheck will be filled by the call
org.omg.Security.OpaqueHolder evidenceCheck
            = new org.omg.Security.OpaqueHolder();

// generate token:
//      during token generation it uses credential information
receivedCredentials[0].generate_token( receivedData, evidenceType,
            includeDataInToken, generateRequest, requestFeatures,
            inputBufferComplete, nrToken,  evidenceCheck);
```

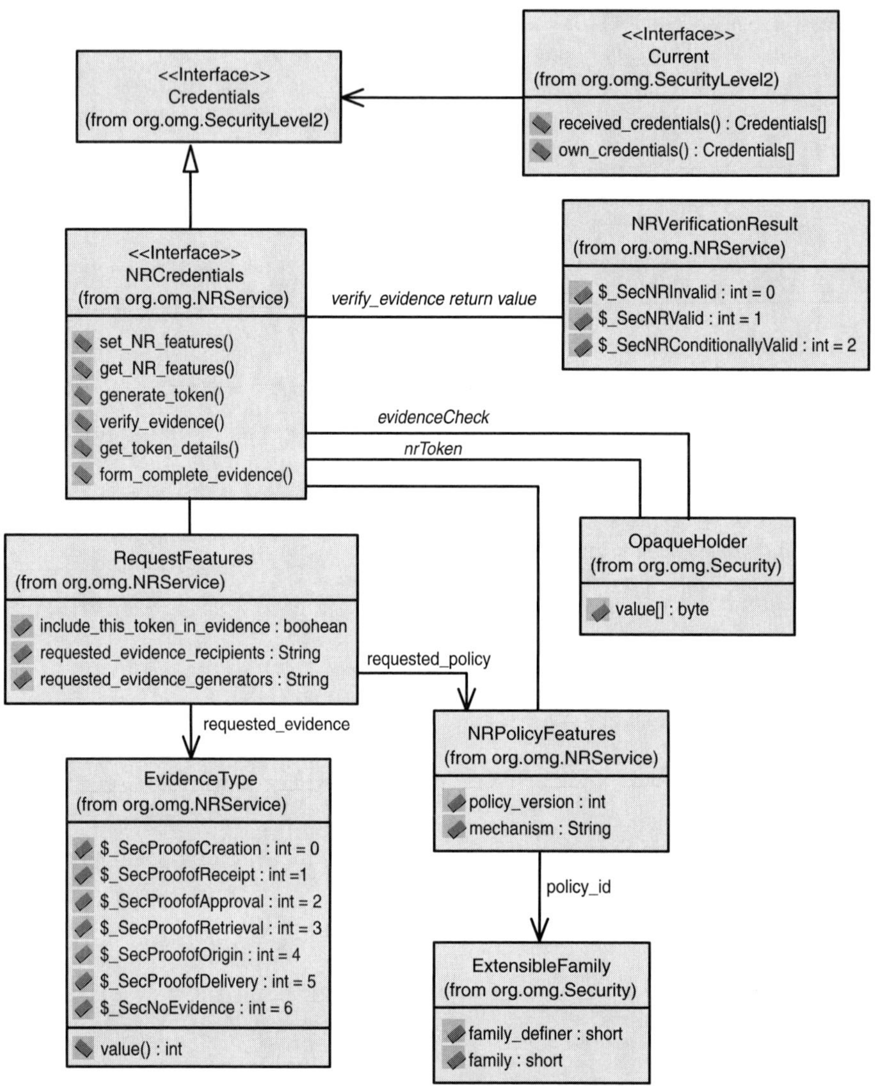

FIGURE 28.6
CORBA Security nonrepudiation.

The return `nrToken` and `evidenceCheck` values in the preceding snippet are returned in an `Opaque` object stored in the `OpaqueHolder`. The identity information of the principal associated with the received `NRCredentials` is also used during the creation of the NR token so that the principal identity can be bound to the received data.

Verification of evidence assumes that you have an NR token and evidence to verify that a particular action previously occurred. The `NRCredentials.verify_evidence()` call takes both the NR token and the evidence check value created during a prior `generate_token()` call. A returned `NRVerificationResult` object can then be used to determine whether the NR token was considered valid, invalid, or conditionally valid by the partner object. As an example of verification, we have this:

```
boolean checkGeneratedEvidence = true; // to check evidence
boolean formCompleteEvidence = true; // complete evidence requested
boolean tokenBufferComplete = true; // token buffer complete

// use token you got during generate token
byte[] inputToken = nrToken.value;
// use check value you got during generate token
byte[] evidenceCheckValue = evidenceCheck.value;

// All the following values are output values...
// output token
org.omg.Security.OpaqueHolder outputToken
      = new org.omg.Security.OpaqueHolder();
// data associated with evidence
org.omg.Security.OpaqueHolder dataIncludedInEvidence
      = new org.omg.Security.OpaqueHolder();
// evidence complete
org.omg.CORBA.BooleanHolder evidenceComplete
      = new org.omg.CORBA.BooleanHolder();
// is Trusted time used
org.omg.CORBA.BooleanHolder trusedTimeUsed
      = new org.omg.CORBA.BooleanHolder();
// complete evidence before time
org.omg.CORBA.LongHolder completeEvidenceBefore
      = new org.omg.CORBA.LongHolder();
// complete evidence after time
org.omg.CORBA.LongHolder compleEvidenceAfter
      = new org.omg.CORBA.LongHolder();

// All of that for the following evidence verification call
org.omg.NRService.NRVerificationResult verificationResult
      = receivedCredentials[0].verify_evidence(
          inputToken, evidenceCheckValue, formCompleteEvidence,
          tokenBufferComplete, outputToken, dataIncludedInEvidence,
          evidenceComplete, trusedTimeUsed,  completeEvidenceBefore,
          compleEvidenceAfter);
```

In the case of a dispute, the CSSS discusses the concept of arbitration, as well as evidence storage and retrieval, but has not defined any clear specification for such services. In fact, the whole NR interface suite in our opinion is very difficult to understand and even has many holes in terms of support that is lacking. Such holes will lead to application developer hand-coded solutions and nonstandard vendor solutions to fulfill undefined interface needs and thus in turn lead to a lack of interoperability.

Encryption

CORBA objects are understood to need cryptographic support for both integrity and confidentiality. Integrity protection would mean use of something like message digests, whereas confidentiality protection would include the use of key-based encryption. A quality of protection (QOP) level can be set for both requests and responses, indicating whether any protection, integrity protection, confidentiality protection, or both integrity and confidentiality protection are assumed. The underlying interfacing that takes place for providing a requested QOP is transparent to the API developer. Figure 28.7 depicts such QOP specification interfaces for defining the QOP in a particular current execution context.

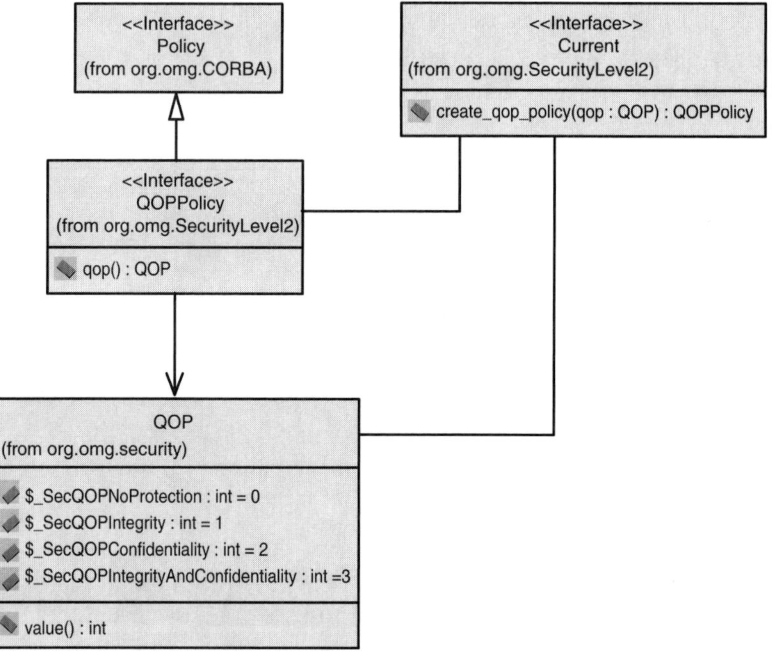

FIGURE 28.7
CORBA Security encryption protection.

Various underlying protocols that operate below the CORBA Security Service layer (for example, SSL) are by and large utilized transparently to the applications developer. Various common security interface protocols supported by the CSSS are SSL, Kereberos, SPKM, ECMA, and DCE-IOP (Distributed Computing Environment Inter-ORB Protocol). However, specifications for use of such secure protocols in the CSSS are defined at the ORB-to-ORB level to ensure interoperability between Orbs supporting such protocols. Thus an ORB from vendor A using SSL could theoretically talk to an ORB from vendor B using SSL.

The level of ORB-to-ORB interoperability is defined according to a Common Secure Interoperability (CSI) level. CSI Level 0 defines an interoperable secure identity passing scheme with no delegation allowed. CSI Level 1 allows delegation of identity for the principal that initiated an operation. CSI Level 2 signifies that the ORB supports all Security Service functionality, and thus all the information that can be passed along with a security context such as privileges is also communicated between Orbs.

No standard API for configuring and initializing secure protocols for use with an application is described in the CSSS. Although the QOP interfaces can be used to specify some abstract distinction between integrity and confidentiality, the particular initialization of SSL, for example, is vendor specific. For example, to configure your server-side CORBA environment for SSL using the Inprise Visigenics SSL solution, you would follow these steps:

1. Establish an `ORBServices` property during ORB initialization to select the vendor-specific SSL libraries.
2. Obtain a handle to a vendor-specific SSL certificate manager.
3. Use a proprietary certificate manager interface to configure the SSL protocol.
4. Initialize the BOA or POA to use connections pulled from an SSL pool for invocation requests.
5. When an SSL Client connection is made and client authentication is required, use an `SSLCurrent` object to obtain client certificate information used for authentication.

Clients of such a server can then make invocations on such a server with invocation requests and replies being encrypted via SSL. As an example of configuring your client-side CORBA environment for SSL using the Inprise Visigenics SSL solution, we have the following steps:

1. Establish an `ORBServices` property during ORB initialization to select the vendor-specific SSL libraries.
2. Obtain a handle to a vendor-specific SSL certificate manager if client authentication will be required.
3. Use a proprietary certificate manager interface to configure the SSL protocol.
4. Bind to the CORBA server.
5. Use an `SSLCurrent` object to obtain server certificate information for server authentication.

Security Policies

The CSSS security domain is defined according to which security policy governs that domain. Security policies for the various protection mechanisms of CORBA Security can be defined using a standard set of CORBA Security policy interfaces that inherit from the base `org::omg::CORBA::Policy` interface. The basic policy architecture used in establishing policies for different CORBA Security protection schemes is shown in Figure 28.8.

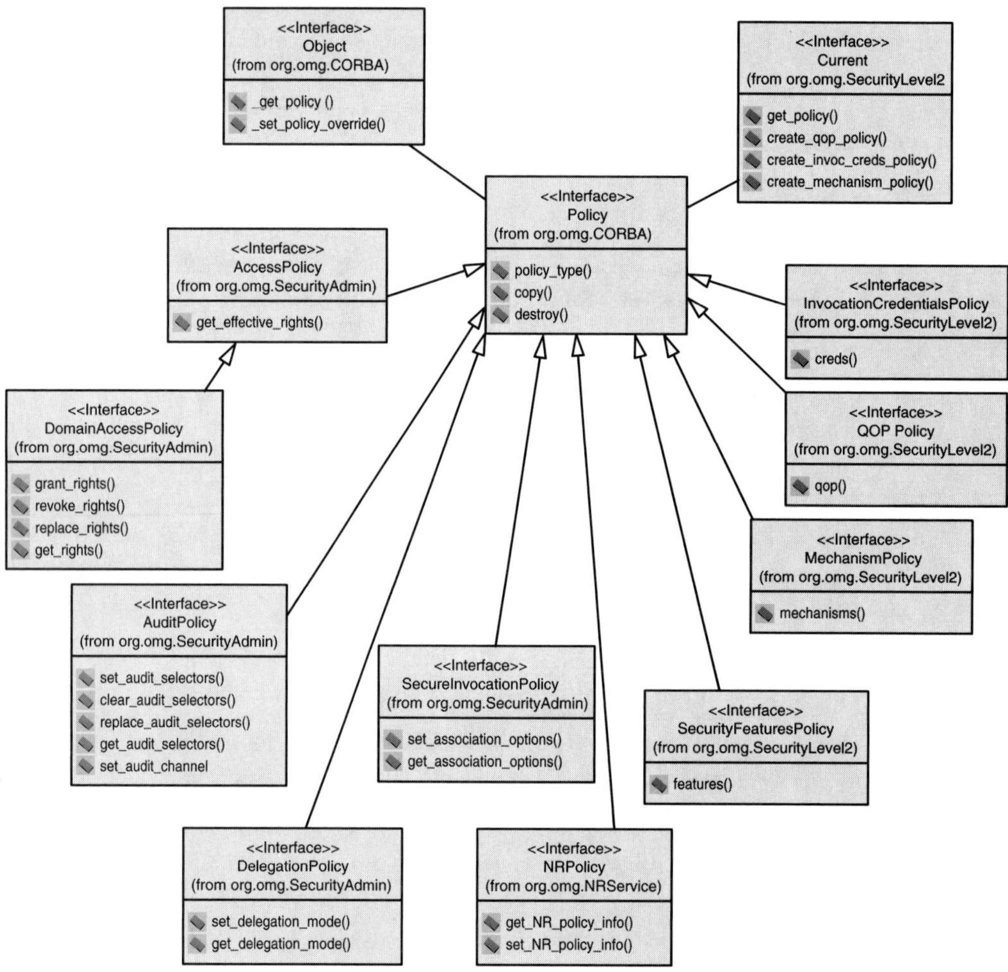

FIGURE 28.8
CORBA Security policies.

The CORBA policy interface serves as the base interface from which all other security policy–related interfaces extend. Policies for a particular distributed CORBA object can be retrieved and set onto that object using the `get_policy()` and `set_override_policy()` methods inherited from the `org::omg::CORBA::Object` interface. Policies from a current execution context can be obtained using `get_policy()` on the `Current` object. The suite of currently defined security related policy types includes the following:

- `org::omg::SecurityAdmin::AccessPolicy` is used for access control policies by returning a list of rights given some credential information.
- `org::omg::SecurityAdmin::DomainAccessPolicy` extends `AccessPolicy` and is used for granting, revoking, and replacing rights in a particular security domain.
- `org::omg::SecurityAdmin::AuditPolicy` is used for auditing policies.
- `org::omg::SecurityAdmin::DelegationPolicy` is used for establishing delegation policies.
- `org::omg::SecurityAdmin::SecureInvocationPolicy` is used for establishing policies related to secure invocations.
- `org::omg::NRService::NRPolicy` is used for establishing nonrepudiation policies.
- `org::omg::SecurityLevel2::SecurityFeaturesPolicy` is used for security feature policies.
- `org::omg::SecurityLevel2::MechanismPolicy` is used for establishing specific security mechanism policies and for using `Current.create_mechanism_policy()`.
- `org::omg::SecurityLevel2::QOPPolicy` is used for quality of protection policy information and for using `Current.create_qop_policy()`.
- `org::omg::SecurityLevel2::InvocationCredentialsPolicy` is used for invocation credentials requirement policies and for using `Current.create_invoc_creds_policy()`.

Security Administration

Support for administration of security policies in a domain can take advantage of the base class inheritance from the `org::omg::CORBA::Policy` interface. Thus, any generic interface defined for administering the `Policy` interface can apply to the CORBA Security policies. The problem is that standard support for even generic policy administration is lacking. The `org::omg::CORBA::DomainManager` interface can be used to retrieve security policies for access of their information, but it offers little use beyond that. It seems that support for any significant policy administration interfaces was deferred to the CORBA facilities layer.

A System Management Common Facilities specification has an expressed goal of providing support for such common system functions. The Policy and Security Management components of that specification in particular apply. However, pursuit of the System Management Common Facilities specification has been minimal. Thus, the only practical solution for many companies interested in managing the security policies encapsulated by the `SecurityAdmin` package and the `Policy` interfaces as shown in Figure 28.8 is to develop their own interface support.

Conclusions

The CORBA Security Service Specification is very complex. This has led to minimal levels of support by vendors. Of course, even when such products are provided, the method signatures and other aspects about the CORBA Security API are a difficult thing for enterprise developers to adopt. The CORBA Security Service Specification needs and is getting some help to make it a more palatable enterprise object security solution.

Nevertheless, it is a fairly well-rounded solution. Security for identity, authenticity, authorization, nonrepudiation, and auditing have all been considered. Interoperability among vendor solutions to provide encryption support has also been considered. However, configuration of such encryption support tends to be vendor specific. Furthermore, although the specification defines the concept of security administration, actual standard security administration interfaces are few and far between.

It is true that CORBA Security is defined with a complicated specification and currently forces application developers to comprehend some extremely complex API method signatures. However, the concepts behind CORBA Security and the future use of CORBA Security model features with the J2EE make it an important architecture to at least understand.

Enterprise Web Enabling

PART VI

IN THIS PART

29 Web Browsers and Servers in the Enterprise 967

30 Traditional Web Programming and Java 985

31 XML 1009

32 Java Servlets 1067

33 JavaServer Pages 1135

Web Browsers and Servers in the Enterprise

CHAPTER

29

IN THIS CHAPTER

- Web Browsers 968
- Web Browser Security 971
- Java Plug-in 973
- Web Servers 976
- Web Server Security 979
- Web Server Availability 982

We described the basic approach to developing Web-based Java applets in Chapter 4, "Java Foundations for Enterprise Development," and the basic communications infrastructure of the Web and HTTP in Chapter 13, "Web Communications." This chapter builds on those concepts with an introduction to the two primary computing platforms used to Web-enable an enterprise: Web browsers and Web servers. Understanding the basic architecture of Web browsers and Web servers, as well as understanding the common problems and solutions encountered with their use, is fundamental to understanding how to Web-enable an enterprise using the Java enterprise technologies discussed in subsequent chapters. This chapter thus simply provides a basic conceptual framework for you to understand how Web browsers and servers are constructed, as well as the most significant facts for you to consider with their use in an enterprise.

In this chapter, you will learn:

- The architecture of Web browsers and the types of Web browsers most commonly used in the enterprise.
- The problems and solutions of Web browser security.
- The Java Plug-in software for using an alternative Java Virtual Machine inside of a Web browser.
- The architecture of Web servers and the types of Web servers most commonly used in the enterprise.
- The problems and solutions of Web server security.
- The options for building highly available Web server applications.

Web Browsers

A Web browser is an application whose primary role is to transform GUI requests into HTTP requests and to transform HTTP responses into GUI display content. HTTP requests are, of course, sent to Web servers, and HTTP responses are received from Web servers. Requests for Web content are cast in the form of URLs that identify remote resource media accessible via the Internet. Web responses are often in the form of Web page documents with multimedia and HTML-based presentation content such as text, static and animated images, hyperlinks, GUI components, audio clips, and video clips. Additionally, referenced documents of various types managed by external handlers, Java applets, and executable browser script language commands (for example, JavaScript) can also be returned in an HTTP Web response.

Because HTTP is the standard protocol for the World Wide Web (WWW), Web browsers become the GUI windows to the WWW. However, current Web browser GUI component types, the bandwidth for most HTTP connections, and the nature of HTTP itself constrain the GUI designs of current Web browser–based document content. Some Web browsers may take advantage of more sophisticated GUI component interactions, but often at the cost of standards compliance or additional bandwidth consumption. It is for these reasons that the state of the art for most Web browser Web pages tends to be limited to supporting a set of core multimedia features for use over the Internet and limited Web page presentation features with the bulk of presentation being HTML related.

Web Browser Architecture

Figure 29.1 presents a basic conceptual architecture for Web browsers to provide a glimpse into their underlying structure. At the heart of a Web browser is a main controller process, which manages the caching and state management of information, manages stimulation of Web request and response handling, invokes the configuration of browser properties, and drives the basic presentation of Web page content. Request handlers map GUI-based requests into HTTP network requests, and response handlers map HTTP responses into GUI-based events and requested display content. Each request and response drives the I/O of HTTP data to and from a network interface. An HTTP protocol is used for unsecured connections, and HTTPS is used for HTTP with SSL-based connections.

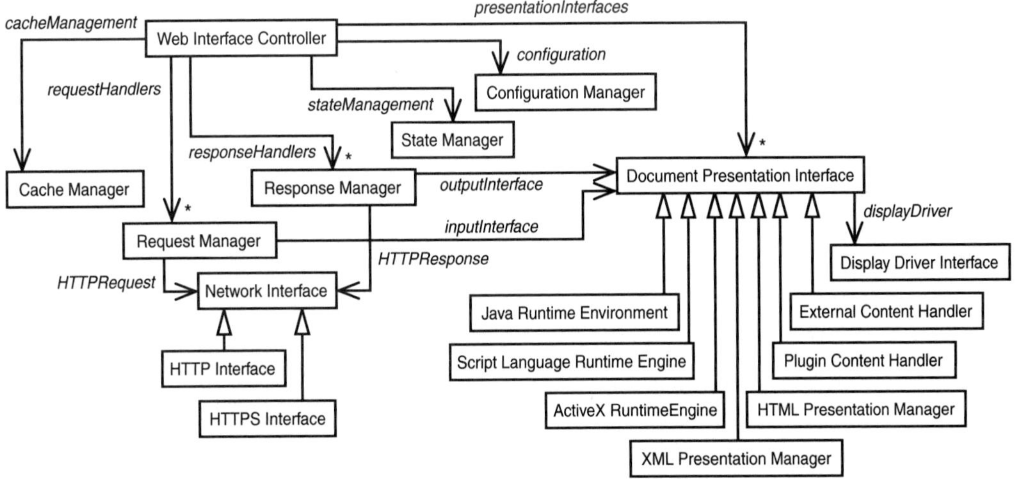

FIGURE 29.1
The Web browser architecture.

A cache manager is often employed within Web browser architectures to store previous request and response data in an effort to avoid making unnecessary network requests. A state manager may also be employed to provide some management of session information using cookies or to facilitate some other form of session tracking. Furthermore, a configuration manager may be used to configure the properties and behavior of a Web browser.

A document presentation interface is used to drive the actual display of GUI-based browser content. Web browsers typically support one or more of the following types of document presentation interfaces:

- *HTML Presentation Manager*: All Web browsers have some form of HTML-based presentation manager to output HTML display content and receive user inputs via HTML entities such as input forms and hyperlinks.
- *XML Presentation Manager*: A few current Web browser implementations and more Web browsers in the future are expected to support parsing of XML documents. We describe XML in more detail in Chapter 31, "XML".
- *Java Runtime Environment*: A Java runtime environment may be embedded into a Web browser to execute Java applets, as well as to invoke the services of downloaded JavaBean components.
- *ActiveX Runtime Engine*: A Microsoft ActiveX runtime engine is embedded into Microsoft browsers to execute downloaded ActiveX/COM components.
- *Scripting Language Runtime Engine*: One or more runtime scripting language engines may also be used to execute scripting commands that were embedded into HTML pages (for example, JavaScript).
- *External Content Handler*: External content handlers may be used to dynamically execute the content of retrieved URL information in an application that runs in a process external to the Web browser (for example, Adobe Acrobat PDF viewer).
- *Plug-In Content Handler*: Alternatively, certain content handlers can execute the content of retrieved URL information directly within a Web browser window in a separate thread via a content handler plug-in.

Web Browser Implementations

Various Web browser implementations exist, but the Netscape Navigator (NN) and Microsoft Internet Explorer (IE) Web browser products are by far the most popular. NN runs on various platforms, whereas IE is targeted for Microsoft platforms. Both browsers support the latest and greatest in HTML presentation standards, as well as various extensions to HTML. Both browser implementations also support a JavaScript scripting language runtime environment and a Java applet execution environment. Despite the presence of standards, NN and IE do differ in feature support. Thus, it is often a challenge for developers of Web page content to determine the lowest common denominator of support across both NN and IE. However, by designing to such a lowest common denominator, you can help ensure a maximal level of Web client base support.

Another interesting Web browser implementation is the HotJava browser from Sun. Implemented entirely in Java, it provides a customizable environment for extending the browser implementation following the configurable JavaBeans component model. The HotJava browser has built-in support for managing HTML, JavaScript, and Java runtime environment (JRE) applet presentation environments. Additionally, HotJava can also support various IE- and NN-specific extensions to the standard HTML specifications.

Web Browser Security

Web browsers expose their host machines to a wide range of security risks. Because of the growth in usage and the widely distributed nature of the WWW, the use of Web browsers introduces exposure to a whole new slew of risks for client machines that have never before been seen by industry. Hackers now take advantage of an easier means to funnel malicious code to client machines, as well as a greater opportunity for tapping security-critical resources and information on client machine environments. It is for these reasons of enhanced risk exposure that Web browser and document presentation manager implementations often consider security from the outset of product development. This section briefly examines the security problems associated with Web browser usage and security solutions to these problems.

Web Browser Security Problems

Security-critical resources on the machine in which a Web browser sits can be maliciously corrupted, referenced, or replaced by malicious content executing within a Web browser. Access to client machine resources can also be denied or delayed by malicious Web browser content. The following is a partial list of the more significant types of security problems that can plague a Web browser environment:

- *Exposed HTML Presentation Manager Flaw Attacks*: Flaws in certain HTML presentation manager implementations can be exploited. This may result in privacy and confidentiality concerns, as well as cause denial of service via exploited memory management faults.
- *Exposed Runtime Engine Flaw Attacks*: Flaws in scripting language, Java, and ActiveX runtime engine implementations can be exploited to perform operations on a client's machine to tap security-critical resources.
- *Java Applet and ActiveX Component Attacks*: Without proper controls, malicious Java applets and Microsoft ActiveX components that have been downloaded by a user may be used to access security-critical resources on the client machine.
- *External Content Handler Attacks*: External content handlers can be used to spawn infected documents (for example, Microsoft Word documents with a Word Macro virus).

- *Plug-in Content Handler Attacks*: Malicious plug-in content handlers that are downloaded and installed into a Web browser environment have complete access to the client machine's security-critical resources.
- *Client Information Request Attacks*: Malicious Web sites may solicit security-critical information from users (for example, credit-card information and passwords).
- *Sensitive HTTP Requests and Response Data*: Certain HTTP requests and responses may contain certain security-critical data that needs protection over the wire.
- *Client Privacy Violations*: Certain machine, configuration, and session information sent from a Web browser to a Web server can be used to disseminate certain private information about a Web user.
- *Falsified Client Identification*: Malicious Web users can falsely identify themselves as a particular Web user to a Web site.

Web Browser Security Solutions

Web browser and document presentation manager implementers, as well as developers of Web browser content, can address the security issues that plague Web browsers in various ways. The integrity and confidentiality of Web browser requests and responses are both addressed to various degrees by Web browser implementations. The authorization, identity, and authenticity of Web users and visited sites also play a key role in Web browser security solutions. Various means for providing secure Web browser environments based on the previously mentioned Web browser security problems are listed here:

- *Browser Implementation Updates*: Users should frequently update their browsers with the latest patches.
- *Java Security Restrictions*: Java has been built with security in mind as a primary design consideration. The Java 1.0 security sandbox model, Java 1.1 signed applet code restrictions, or Java 1.2/2.0 fine-grained access control restrictions may all be used to limit which and how security-critical resources can be accessed.
- *Authenticode Restrictions*: ActiveX code can be signed using Microsoft's Authenticode technology.
- *Java Plug-in Updates*: The security of an embedded Java runtime environment implementation can be enhanced by using a more rigorously tested JVM implementation that can be added to your Web browser environment using the Java Plug-in.
- *Runtime Engine Disabling*: As a more draconian measure, scripting-language engines and Java runtime engines can often be disabled within a Web browser's configuration.
- *External Content Handler Security*: Users need to manage the security inside of their external content handlers and should be wary of the external documents they download and spawn. Users can run a virus checker on documents before activating them with a content handler.

- *SSL Confidentiality*: SSL is built into many Web browsers to enable secure transfer between Web browser and server.
- *SSL Client Authentication*: A client-side certificate can be sent to a Web server during SSL handshaking to authenticate a particular client's identity.
- *SSL Server Authentication*: A server-side certificate can be sent to a Web browser during SSL handshaking to authenticate a particular server's identity.
- *Anonymizer Sites*: In the name of privacy, certain Web sites exist that can redirect your Web requests to other Web sites after removing certain privacy-related information from the HTTP request.

Java Plug-in

The Java Plug-in defines an approach for enabling the use of an alternative Java runtime environment inside of a Web browser instead of using the browser's built-in JRE. This is particularly useful for enabling your Web browsers used throughout an enterprise to take advantage of the latest JRE platform, APIs, and enhancements. The latest JDK v1.2.2, for example, can be downloaded to your enterprise users' Web browsers simply by use of a few special tags inside of an HTML document. Both Java applets and JavaBean components can thus be downloaded for use in a Web browser and can take advantage of the latest JDK library releases. After the libraries are downloaded, they are stored on the user's local hard disk and are simply used whenever the need for such alternative libraries is designated from within a Web page.

Installing the Java Plug-in into a Web Browser

Use of the Java Plug-in focuses on the definition of special tags in an HTML document that direct a Web browser to use a special JRE to process the downloaded Java code. The specification of such tags differs from browser to browser. After a Java Plug-in is installed inside of a user's Web browser environment, subsequent demands for such a JRE are forwarded to the user's local machine installation. Updates to the JRE are less time-consuming after the initial installation time. However, initial installation may require download times over a local area network that are anywhere from 3 to 10 minutes. Wide area network download times, such as over the Internet, are significantly longer.

Use of the Java Plug-in with IE relies on IE's built-in extension mechanism for augmenting IE with additional COM and ActiveX components that can be called from within a Web page. A pair of `<OBJECT>` and `</OBJECT>` tags is inserted into an HTML document to designate the use of an IE extension mechanism. If no Java Plug-in has been installed yet, and the user visits a site which designates that a Java Plug-in should be used, an IE browser first asks the user whether it is acceptable to download and install a signed ActiveX component. If the user answers Yes, a Java Plug-in ActiveX wrapper is downloaded to the Web browser that in turn manages the download and install of the new JRE.

Netscape's built-in plug-in mechanism is used to extend the NN browser to download and install native code to be used as a browser plug-in. The <EMBED> and </EMBED> tags are inserted into an HTML document to designate the use of an NN plug-in. If no Java Plug-in is yet loaded, an empty plug-in picture is displayed within the browser window, and the user is asked to download the appropriate plug-in. The user then downloads and installs the Java Plug-in for NN by following the instructions.

Designating the Use of a Java Plug-in JRE

As we just mentioned, the installation of a Java Plug-in JRE can be initiated via the specification of the appropriate tags in a Web page. The Java Plug-in HTML Specification at `http://java.sun.com/products/plugin/1.2/docs/tags.html` defines the syntax needed within a Web page for designating the use of the Java Plug-in with an associated Java applet or JavaBean component. The Java Plug-in HTML Converter tool is also available and can be used to automatically mark up HTML documents with the necessary tags for using the Java Plug-in (`http://java.sun.com/products/plugin/1.2/features.html`). We only briefly describe the syntax of such tags from within an HTML document here to give you a flavor for what referencing the Java Plug-in from within a browser environment looks like. We encourage you to examine the Java Plug-in HTML Specification for more information and to use the Java Plug-in HTML Converter for ease of mapping your Java applet tags to Java Plug-in–style tags.

For example, suppose that we wanted to run a Java applet inside of a Web browser and use the Java Plug-in. A normal Java applet tag designation, such as the format described in Chapter 4, may be defined as shown here:

```
<APPLET
  codebase = "."
  code     = "com.beeshirts.MyApplet.class"
  archive = "MyApplet.jar"
  width    = 400
  height   = 300
>
<PARAM NAME = "sample_value" VALUE = "123">
</APPLET>
```

We might then decide that our applet should operate inside of a JRE v1.2.2 environment and therefore require the use of a Java Plug-in HTML Specification as shown here:

```
<OBJECT
    classid="clsid:8AD9C840-044E-11D1-B3E9-00805F499D93"
    codebase="http://java.sun.com/products/plugin/1.2.2
➥/jinstall-1_2_2-win.cab#Version=1,2,2,0"
    width="400"
    height="300">
```

```
    <PARAM NAME="type" VALUE="application/x-java-applet;version=1.2.2">
    <PARAM NAME="codebase" VALUE=".">
    <PARAM NAME="code" VALUE=" com.beeshirts.MyApplet.class">
    <PARAM NAME="archive" VALUE="MyApplet.jar">
    <PARAM NAME="sample_value" VALUE="123">
  <COMMENT>
    <EMBED
      pluginspage="http://java.sun.com/products/plugin/1.2
➥/plugin-install.html"
      type="application/x-java-applet;version=1.2.2"
      width="400"
      height="300"
      codebase="."
      code="com.beeshirts.MyApplet.class"
      archive="MyApplet.jar"
      sample_value="123"
    >
      <NOEMBED>
  </COMMENT>
        No Java 2.0 support is possible for this applet.
      </NOEMBED>
    </EMBED>
</OBJECT>
```

In this rather convoluted tag sequence, multiple needs were satisfied. We've encapsulated all information within an IE `OBJECT` tag pair such that IE can use its extension mechanisms to process the applet. Per the Java Plug-in HTML Specification, certain standard applet tags map to `OBJECT` attributes, and others map to `PARAM` tags within an `OBJECT` tag scope. Additionally, the statically defined `classid` and `codebase` values within the `OBJECT` tag attributes are defined to point to the appropriate Java Plug-in ActiveX component wrapper to use. Such a wrapper may be downloaded from the `codebase` if it is not already loaded onto the client's machine.

The necessary tags for use of the Java Plug-in within NN browsers are defined within the `COMMENT` tags shown above. IE ignores the `COMMENT` tags, and NN will not recognize the leading `OBJECT` tag. Thus, the information within the `EMBED` tags is interpreted only by NN browsers. As you can see, the various `APPLET` tag elements also map to attributes of the `EMBED` tag. The special `pluginspage` attribute defines the location from which to locate the special Java Plug-in for NN browsers. The location from which to load a Java Plug-in can actually be defined to be a particular Web site within the domain of an enterprise, but we have shown only standard locations from the Sun site here.

Web Servers

A Web server is a server-side application whose primary role is to handle or delegate HTTP requests and to generate or route HTTP responses. Web servers come in various flavors and can support various needs. The most simplistic form of Web server may simply receive `GET` or `POST` requests, read a local file based on a requested URL, and stream the file data back to the Web client. Higher-end enterprise-class Web servers support concurrent requests from a scalable number of clients, implement some form of secure access control, and support various APIs for extending the functionality of a Web server to dynamically generate Web documents in an application-specific fashion. This section briefly describes a generic architecture for Web servers and highlights those commercial Web server implementations currently pervading the marketplace.

Web Server Architecture

Figure 29.2 presents a basic conceptual architecture of a Web server. The Web server controller serves to represent the main process controller context in which a Web server runs. A Web server controller typically manages a pool of threads that are used to handle requests from clients as they are received. A Web handler thread is allocated to manage a particular client request and response. Each request and response passes through a network interface. The HTTP protocol is used for unsecured connections, and HTTPS is used for HTTP with SSL-based connections.

A Web server controller may also maintain session management information between successive requests from a client such that statefulness for the otherwise stateless HTTP protocol may be implemented. Caches of response information may also be maintained by a Web server such that successive instances of the same request may be used to rapidly generate a cached response. The behavior of the Web server will often be manageable through some means of configuring the server environment. Management of the Web server environment may also include the specification of ACLs limiting access to server-side resources for particular Web users. Furthermore, most Web server environments will also provide some mechanism for logging Web server requests and responses.

Interfaces that can generate Web-based documents according to HTTP requests are central to a Web server architecture. Web servers typically support one or more of the following types of document-serving interfaces:

- *File Request Handler*: Most Web servers have file request handlers that map a URL to a file (for example, an HTML file) local to the Web server that is to be read and sent back to the client in an HTTP response stream.
- *CGI Engine*: The Common Gateway Interface (CGI) provides a standard interface mechanism for spawning external processes implemented in any language to handle HTTP requests and generate HTTP responses.

- *ISAPI*: The Internet Server Application Program Interface (ISAPI) defines an interface for calling Microsoft platform DLLs to handle HTTP requests and generate HTTP responses.
- *NSAPI*: The Netscape Server Application Programming Interface (NSAPI) defines an interface for calling binary libraries to handle HTTP requests and generate HTTP responses.
- *Script Language Runtime Engine*: Script language runtime engines allow scripting language commands, such as JavaScript and VBScript, stored in HTML files to be executed within the Web server's process space. Such commands are used to generate dynamic HTML content to be sent back to the requesting client.
- *Java Servlet Engine*: Java Servlet engines allow Java code adhering to a particular interface to be executed within the Web server's process space to handle HTTP requests and generate HTTP responses.
- *JSP Engine*: JavaServer Pages (JSP) engines are used to compile special Java scripting language commands into executable Java Servlet content, which is then executed within a Web server's process space to handle HTTP requests and generate HTTP responses.

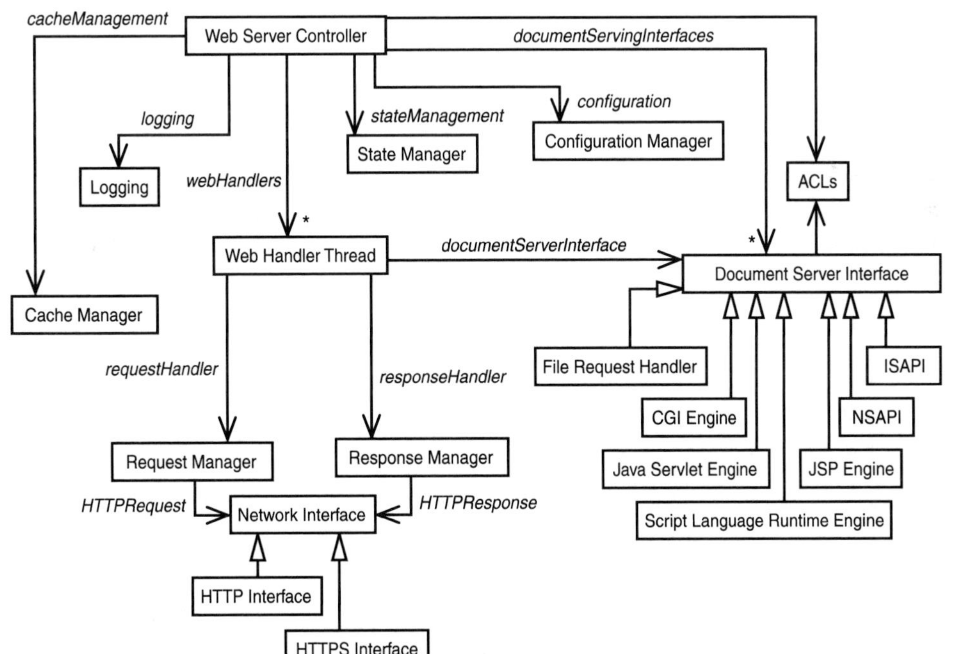

FIGURE 29.2
The Web server architecture.

Web Server Implementations

Web server implementations can be extremely simplistic in nature or support various sophisticated enterprise-class features. Web servers may be started from the command line and be configured from a simple text file, or they may come equipped with a nifty GUI interface for starting, stopping, creating, deleting, and configuring server instances. We've already seen an example of a simple Web server implementation such as the one used in Chapter 16, "RMI Communications," for dynamic RMI code downloading. However, more sophisticated Web servers are needed for commercial and enterprise-class applications.

Netscape provides the Netscape FastTrack Server for low-end Web server applications. The Netscape Enterprise Server (NES) is used in many scalable Web server applications with security requirements. NES provides a fancy GUI for managing and configuring Web server applications and offers many extensions for document serving. Document serving interfaces offered by NES include file serving, CGI, NSAPI, JavaScript runtime, and Java Servlet support.

The Microsoft Internet Information Server (IIS) is used on server-side Microsoft platforms as the Microsoft platform-specific solution for Web serving. IIS is tightly integrated with Windows NT and Windows 2000 platforms and can be used with Microsoft's other enterprise solutions. IIS provides document serving interfaces such as file serving, CGI, ISAPI, and the Active Server Pages (ASP) scripting environment.

The Java Web Server (also called Jeeves) is a Web server implemented completely in Java and thus offers a platform-independent Web server solution. The Java Web Server provides document serving interfaces for file serving, CGI, and Java Servlets.

The BEA WebLogic Server is an enterprise-class Web server and is also largely built on top of the Java platform. Web servers that come equipped with BEA WebLogic Server v5.0 follow the J2EE model and offer an environment for both Java Servlets and JSPs. In addition to file serving and CGI support, the BEA WebLogic Server also supports basic NSAPI and ISAPI document serving interfaces.

The Apache Web Server is a freeware server and has been developed according to the open source shareware model of development. Apache operates on UNIX and Windows platforms and is actually used in many enterprise-class Web serving applications. The Apache Web Server not only includes basic file serving and CGI support, but has also been extended for use with various scripting languages and Java Servlets.

Many other Web server implementations exist beyond the core products mentioned here. The J2EE enables you to create Web server–based applications with Java Servlet and JSP technology that is independent of the underlying Web server vendor implementation. J2EE-compliant Web server implementation vendors are required to provide J2EE-compliant container environments within which Java Servlet and JSP components run. These container environments are standardized versions of the previously mentioned document serving engines for such technologies. Many of the Web server implementations mentioned here either have already implemented or have begun to implement J2EE-compliant container environments. Even if a particular Web server vendor's J2EE Web environment is not up to snuff, many vendor implementations make it easy for you to plug in third-party Web container environments. For example, the JRun Servlet engine from Live Software has been a popular separately purchasable Java Servlet environment of choice for use with some of the Web server vendor products mentioned previously.

Web Server Security

The security of a Web server environment is crucial for the practical usage of Web-enabling technology in most enterprise environments. Web servers often act as an entry point into the operations of an enterprise when used to generate interfaces that enable enterprise employees to engage in some sort of business with the enterprise via the Web. Web servers also act as business-to-consumer (B2C) and e-commerce portals for customers to conduct Web-based business transactions with an enterprise. Such a portal by way of the Web exposes both the operations and the business of an enterprise to a global network of people, some of whom may be malicious. This is why Web-based security of Web serving environments must be a fundamental consideration when one is Web-enabling the enterprise with a Web server environment. This section briefly examines the security problems associated with Web server usage and security solutions for these problems.

Web Server Security Problems

Security-critical resources on the server end of a Web connection are plentiful. Enterprise applications and data both represent key resources of an enterprise that must be secured. Security-critical resources on the machine in which a Web server sits or those resources that can be directly affected by the operations of a Web server can be maliciously corrupted, referenced, or replaced under the direction of a malicious hacker. Access to enterprise system resources can also be denied or delayed by malicious Web server hackers. The following is a partial list of the more significant types of security problems that can plague a Web server environment:

- *Exposed Implementation Flaw Attacks*: Flaws in the implementation of a Web server product or a document server interface may be subject to exploitation by hackers.
- *Denial-of-Service Attacks*: Malicious inundation of HTTP or lower-level TCP/IP requests to a Web server can bring the operations of the server to a grinding halt.
- *Credential Sniffing*: Passwords and other credential information sent in the clear or over weak encryption links to a Web server can be captured and utilized later by a hacker.

- *Server Information Request Attacks*: Malicious Web users may be inclined to solicit security-critical information from enterprise Web servers.
- *Server Command Request Attacks*: Malicious Web users may also submit commands to an enterprise Web server to perform some security-critical operation.
- *Sensitive HTTP Requests and Response Data*: Certain HTTP requests and responses may contain certain security-critical data that needs protection.
- *Back Door Service Attacks*: Certain processes and services (such as SMTP, FTP, Telnet, and DNS) can provide security holes that when exploited can be used to corrupt Web server processing.
- *Platform Machine Attacks*: Flaws in operating systems and environments are primarily breached by way of a breach of physical security and direct access to a system. Nevertheless, other means do exist, such as when a Web server system is also used for potentially unsecure purposes such as WWW browsing and email reading.

Web Server Security Solutions

Web server and document serving interface implementers, as well as developers of Web document server interface logic, can address the security issues that plague Web serving in various ways. The integrity and confidentiality of Web server requests and responses are both addressed to various degrees by Web server and document serving interface implementations. The authorization, identity, and authenticity of Web users and visited sites also play a key role in Web server and application security. Various means for providing secure Web server environments based on the previously mentioned Web server security problems are listed here:

- *Server Implementation Updates*: Always maintain awareness of patches to exposed server security holes and obtain updates appropriately. This includes patches to both the Web server implementation itself and document server interface implementations (for example, a new Java Servlet engine patch).
- *SSL Confidentiality*: SSL is built into many Web servers to enable secure transfer between Web browser and server.
- *SSL Client Authentication*: A client-side certificate can be sent to a Web server during SSL handshaking to authenticate a particular client's identity.
- *User Authentication*: In addition to SSL client certificate authentication, certain application-specific and more fine-grained authentication techniques may be employed to authenticate the identity and role of a particular user.
- *SSL Server Authentication*: A server-side certificate can be sent to a Web browser during SSL handshaking to authenticate a particular Web server's identity.

- *Firewalls*: Filtering of IP address access to a Web server can restrict access to a server from users within unauthorized IP domains. More sophisticated firewalls can also help limit the effects of a denial-of-service attack.
- *Access Control Lists*: Many Web servers use access control lists to restrict which Web resources, such as URLs and document serving interface applications, are available for access by certain identities and roles.
- *Security Auditing*: Many Web servers provide logging of incoming HTTP requests and associated IP addresses useful for security auditing. Additionally, higher-level application-specific auditing of security-critical activities will also be a key concern in the design of a secure Web server application.
- *Server Redundancy*: Redundancy of server processes and threads can help limit the effects resulting from denial-of-service attacks by switching over to redundant servers in the event of a malicious attack.
- *Auxiliary Service Reduction*: Auxiliary processes and services running on the same machine as a Web server should be turned off and removed if possible to close off the potential for an attack via a back door.
- *Secure Document Serving Interface Logic*: Because the document serving interface logic has access to back-end enterprise resources, the security of these applications must also be secured. That is, interfaces such as CGI, Java Servlets, JSPs, and server-side scripting language commands all must be implemented in such a way that the security of the system is not compromised. Such assurances are not only specific to the type of interface, but also often application-specific.
- *Secure Web Server Architecture*: A significant technique for providing security in an enterprise application is to have an integrated enterprise architecture with security considered as one key aspect of that architecture. The Web server tier can be maintained separately from an application server architecture tier. All security-critical operations of an enterprise (for example, database, EAI access, credential storage) can then be managed behind the wall of an application server with the Web server tier acting primarily as a Web presentation layer. This is the approach advocated in this book for building enterprise systems.
- *Server Analysis Tools*: Some tools do exist to independently analyze a Web server offline and at runtime for security weaknesses and suspicious behavior. Because such tools are typically created based on some abstraction of system architecture and behavior, the utility of such tools for many practical and application-specific scenarios can be limited.
- *Platform Security*: The security of your operating system and environment should also be secured. Employing credential-based access to a Web server platform and limiting use of a platform for strict Web serving purposes can greatly aid in the security of your Web server environment.

Web Server Availability

Without the availability of service provided by a Web server, the e-commerce and business operations of an enterprise can be tremendously affected. We also alluded to the importance of Web server availability in the preceding section when we briefly discussed the problem associated with denial-of-service due to a malicious attack. Web service unavailability not only may be induced by malicious denial-of-service attacks, but also may be the result of excessive client load requests or perhaps due to a flawed architecture design to account for Web server scalability.

Building highly available Web server applications can be accomplished within the design of different parts of a Web server architecture. The Web server controller and handler framework implementation itself can be designed to support multiple client requests and offer redundancy management services for availability. The Web document server interface engines can also be designed with availability in mind. Finally, the application-specific design of the logic operating inside of a particular document server interface engine can affect the availability of a Web-enabled enterprise application.

Thread pooling is one common technique for achieving availability and is provided by most enterprise-class Web server environments. Pools of handler threads inside Web servers and document serving engines are created and left in a hot state ready to handle a request at any moment. A management facility receives a client request and hands it off to a separate thread to manage the request. Thread pools offer an efficient means for handling requests within a single process.

Multiple Web server processes may also be used to operate in a clustered configuration to balance received Web requests among multiple processes. These processes may run on the same or different machines in a network. In addition to load balancing support, such configurations are also useful for purposes of redundant fail-over. That is, when one process or hardware platform fails, another process on another machine may take over. Additionally, clustering may also occur at the level of document server interface engines. Thus, diversely redundant Web servers from different vendors may be used with different document server interface engines (for example, Java Servlet engines) cooperating in a heterogeneous server cluster.

The easiest way to build clustered processes is to provide a stateless load balancing configuration. That is, a request is received, and it is sent to a particular Web server handler without any regard for any maintained session state. More sophisticated clustered processes can persist Web server session state or document server interface engine state such that it can be loaded by another process in the clustered environment. Such environments not only enable the development of more sophisticated Web server applications, but also allow for the support of fail-over to redundant processes in the event of the failure of another process in the cluster.

Conclusions

Web browsers and Web servers are the platforms used to Web-enable an enterprise. Enterprise users utilize GUI-based Web browsers to submit Web requests from Web servers and receive Web document responses that are to be displayed within the client-side Web browser environment. Issues of security and the means by which Java applets can operate inside of a Web browser are key concerns that can be addressed by the enterprise systems architect via various techniques. Additionally, the selection of a scalable, secure, and highly available Web server is paramount to effective enterprise Web-enabling. This chapter briefly explored the architecture of Web browsers and Web servers with a particular focus on the key issues and options that face the enterprise systems architect and designer in determining how to Web-enable an enterprise.

Traditional Web Programming and Java

CHAPTER

30

IN THIS CHAPTER

- HTML Programming 986
- CGI Programming 995
- Scripting Languages 1001
- Active Server Pages 1006
- Java-Based Web Programming 1007

Traditional Web programming involves the construction of static HTML documents, CGI programming, and scripting language–based code. Such techniques have traditionally provided rapid Web-enabling solutions at the expense of true enterprise-system class support. J2EE's Java Servlet and scripting-based technologies via JSP offer the best of many worlds to enterprise Java developers. This chapter first describes fundamental concepts of HTML that are pertinent to all forms of Web enabling. It then describes traditional models for Web-based programming and provides a context for understanding the differences between these models and the Java-based models for Web programming. Finally, an introduction to the key Java-based Web programming models is presented.

In this chapter, you will learn:

- The basics behind HTML document structures and components for Web-based interactions
- The basic approach for implementing CGI programs
- The basic use of JavaScript, VBScript, and other Web-based scripting techniques for client and server-side Web enabling
- The basic capabilities and constraints behind using Active Server Pages (ASP) as a Web-enabling technique
- The main differences between J2EE-based Web programming techniques and traditional Web programming techniques

HTML Programming

The Hypertext Markup Language (HTML) is a way to describe how information and certain user-interface controls are to be displayed and handled within a Web browser. HTML documents (*aka* Web pages) can embed formatted text, images, audio, video, and executable content directly in an HTML data stream. Cognizant Web browsers receiving such data can then offer the embedded informational media as an Internet-based user interface. HTML documents that are sent to a Web browser are interpreted to display a GUI and receive input events from the user that are then sent to a Web server.

Standard and industry-wide use of HTML didn't truly start to take shape until HTML 2.0 was created in 1994. HTML 3.0 was introduced in 1995 but proved to be unwieldy. Thus, an updated HTML 3.2 superseded 3.0 in 1997. HTML 3.2 also introduced support for Java applets. HTML 4.0 support for dynamic client-side HTML, embedded objects, and style sheets was introduced in 1998 and was the latest HTML standard at the time of this writing.

In Chapter 13, "Web Communications," we also reviewed the basics behind HTML interaction and gave a brief history of HTML's evolution from a communications point of view. We'll now expand on HTML in this chapter to describe the features of HTML that you as an enterprise developer need to be familiar with in order to Web-enable an enterprise. We do not assume that you will necessarily need to focus on the actual screen layout and display characteristics of HTML. Rather, we assume that the mechanisms involved in HTML interface controls that affect back-end server processing and Web-session management will be important to understand. To understand such concepts, a basic understanding of HTML document structure is also required. We will thus focus in this section on HTML topics that are most widely applicable to enterprise Web enabling.

HTML in General

HTML document data can be partitioned into two general styles of HTML data content. HTML structure control and display elements describe how an HTML document is to be presented and manipulated by the browser. HTML forms describe how data is to be extracted from a user and submitted back to the Web server.

All such elements are described in an ASCII text–based data stream using case-insensitive HTML tags. HTML tags are enclosed within angle brackets, < and >. Some tags stand by themselves whereas others have leading and trailing tags with data inserted in between, such as a `<TAG>` leading tag and `</TAG>` trailing tag.

The various tags also may have attributes embedded within the initial tag, usually in the form of name-value pairs, such as `<TAG NAME1=VALUE1 NAME2=VALUE2 ... >`. Colors specified using a hexadecimal identifier or color name and sizes specified in numbers of pixels or percentages of a displayed page are common examples of attributes embedded in various HTML tags.

The general structure of an HTML document includes a heading and body. As an alternative to displaying a single HTML page inside of an HTML body, frames may also be used to display and control different windows within the same HTML page. We describe each element of the following sample HTML document structure in the sections that follow:

```
<HTML>

  [<HEAD>
    [<META Meta-Information about the HTML Document>]
    [<TITLE>
      [HTML Document Title]
    </TITLE>]
  </HEAD>]

  [<BODY name=value ...>
    The Body of your HTML Document here...
```

```
    Document display elements:
      Use formatted text, tables, inline images, and hyperlinks.

    <!-- Comments inserted here -->

    <FORM>
      Solicit user input here...
      <INPUT name=value ...>
      <INPUT name=value ...>
    </FORM>
  </BODY>]

  [<FRAMESET name=value ...>
    The set of embedded frame windows here...
    <FRAME name=value ...>
    <FRAME name=value ...>
  </FRAMESET>]

</HTML>
```

HTML Structure Control and Display Elements

The basic elements and controls used to structure an HTML document for use by the Web browser to display a Web interface are described in more detail here. HTML structure control includes the fundamental HTML document description tags to identify components of an HTML document. The basic HTML structure display elements include formatted text, tables, inline images, and hyperlinks. Each of the following subsections describes one of the basic controls and elements that can be used to display an HTML document.

HTML Tags

The `HTML` tags inform a browser that the information contained within the `<HTML>` and `</HTML>` tags is an HTML document. HTML documents referenced as files have a `.html` or `.htm` file extension. For example

```
<HTML>
  <!-- HTML Document goes here! -->
</HTML>
```

Headings

The `HEAD` tags inform a browser that the information contained within the `<HEAD>` and `</HEAD>` tags is header information associated with an HTML document. Such header information is used by your browser as nondisplayable control information:

```
<HTML>
 <HEAD>
```

```
  <!-- HTML Document Header info goes here! -->
 </HEAD>
  <!--Body of document -->
</HTML>
```

Meta-Data

Meta tags indicated by the <META> tag designate information that describes some feature of your HTML document. Such information is not displayed by your Web browser. Rather, the information is associated with your HTML document and is often inserted to enable search engines to learn more about the nature of your particular HTML page. Meta tags can designate any name-value pair of meta information using <META NAME="*MetaTagName*" CONTENT="*MetaTagValue*">. Here's an example of a valid generic name-value meta tag pair:

```
<HTML>
 <HEAD>
   <!--META information about the document -->
   <META NAME="keywords" CONTENT="shirts, tshirts, t-shirts">
 </HEAD>
</HTML>
```

Meta tags can also be used to control the behavior of a Web browser by virtue of encoding HTTP header information into an HTML document using <META HTTP-EQUIV="*HTTPName*" CONTENT="*HTTPValue*">. As an example to encode the HTTP charset header name to a particular value, we have this:

```
<HTML>
 <HEAD>
   <META HTTP-EQUIV="charset" CONTENT="iso-8859-1">
 </HEAD>
</HTML>
```

Titles

The TITLE tags inform a browser that the information contained within the <TITLE> and </TITLE> tags designates a title for the HTML document. Titles are often displayed in the title bar of a browser window when the associated HTML document is loaded. Titles are also often the information that is displayed by search engines and hot-lists, so titles often are descriptive enough to convey the content of a particular HTML document. For example

```
<HTML>
 <HEAD>
  <!--Document Title -->
  <TITLE>    BEESHIRTS.COM  </TITLE> </HEAD></HTML>
```

Body

The BODY tags inform a browser that information contained within the <BODY> and </BODY> tags designates the portion of an HTML document that is to be displayed in a browser window. You can also set the background, text, and link color default for your document by setting name-value pairs according to the following standard names within the initial <BODY> tag:

- <BODY BGCOLOR=*some_color*> to set the background color.
- <BODY LINK=*some_color*> to set the link color.
- <BODY VLINK=*some_color*> to set the link color after it has been followed.
- <BODY ALINK=*some_color*> to set the link color when it is clicked.
- <BODY TEXT=some_*color*> to set the text color.

For example, to set the default background color to white and the text color to black using hexadecimal notation for those colors inside of a BODY tag, we have this:

```
<HTML>
 <BODY BGCOLOR="#FFFFFF" TEXT= "#000000">
   <!-- HTML Document Body goes here! -->
 </BODY>
</HTML>
```

Linking

Hyperlinks are inserted into documents such that user clicks on those links can enable new HTTP requests to be generated or allow one to reference components of an HTML document. The <A HREF> and </A> tags enclose the part of a document that is highlighted as a hyperlink. When you enclose text or some other data within <A HREF="*AssociatedURL*"> and </A>, the associated URL can be invoked via a click on the highlighted text or data between the tags. For example

```
<HTML>
 <BODY>
  <A HREF="hockey.html">Click here for sale on Hockey Shirts</A>
 </BODY>
</HTML>
```

You can also name a location inside of an HTML document to be referenced relative to that HTML document by enclosing text and data within the <A NAME="*TargetName*"> and </A> tags. This location can also be hyperlinked relatively within a document by use of the <A HREF="*#TargetName*"> and </A> tags. For example

```
<HTML>
 <BODY>
   <A HREF="#custom_graphics"> Custom Graphics </A><BR>
```

```
    <A HREF="#hand_oven_designs"> Hand Oven Designs </A><BR>
    The BR tag is a line break as we'll learn in the next section.<BR>
       ...
    <!-- Often more space between HREF and the target than shown here -->
    <A name="custom_graphics">Custom Graphics </A><BR>
       ...
    <!-- Often more space between HREF and the target than shown here -->
    <A name="hand_oven_designs"> Hand Oven Designs </A><BR>
  </BODY>
<HTML>
```

Formatting

Various HTML formatting tags can also be inserted into HTML documents. These are some of the more common place formatting tags:

- `<I>` and `</I>` to italicize text
- `<B>` and `</B>` to boldface text
- `<BR>` for a line break
- `<H1>` and `</H1>` to specify the largest heading, `<H2>` and `</H2>` for the second-to-largest heading, and so on, and `<H6>` and `</H6>` for the smallest heading
- `<P>` and `</P>` for a paragraph
- `<P ALIGN=alignment>` to specify the alignment of a paragraph as `LEFT`, `RIGHT`, or `CENTER`
- `<UL>` and `</UL>` for a bulleted item list
- `<OL>` and `</OL>` for a numbered item list
- `<LI>` and `</LI>` before each numbered list item to add a number
- `<!-- Comments -->` to insert uninterpreted comments into HTML document
- `<HR SIZE=optional_height WIDTH=optional_width>` to insert a horizontal line (*aka* horizontal rule)

Inline Images

Images are also commonly added to HTML documents for display within the HTML page. The `IMG` tag designates such image insertion. `<IMG SRC="ImageName">` designates from where such an image file can be obtained relative to the current HTML page's URL. An `ALIGN` name-value attribute pair can be inserted within the `IMG` tag to indicate whether the image is to be positioned to the `TOP`, `BOTTOM`, `MIDDLE`, `LEFT`, `RIGHT`, or `CENTER` of the screen. For example

```
<HTML>
 <BODY>
  <IMG SRC="ejavashirt.gif" ALIGN=CENTER>
 </BODY>
</HTML>
```

Tables

The TABLE tags inform a browser that information contained within the <TABLE> and </TABLE> tags is to be displayed as a table of information in an HTML document. The <TR> and </TR> tags block off a row in the table. The <TD> and </TD> tags block off a table cell in each row. The <TH> and </TH> tags contain table header cells. For example

```
<HTML>
 <BODY>
  <TABLE>

     <TR>
      <TD><BR></TD>
      <TD>Small</TD>
      <TD>Medium</TD>
     </TR>

     <TR>
    <TH> Tennis Pro Shirt</TH>
        <TD> Yes </TD>
        <TD> Yes </TD>
     </TR>

     <TR>
    <TH> Millennium Shirt</TH>
        <TD> Yes </TD>
        <TD> Yes </TD>
     </TR>

  </TABLE>
 </BODY>
</HTML>
```

Frames

An HTML frame enables one to partition how HTML information is displayed within the same browser window. A collection of frames can be indicated between <FRAMESET> and </FRAMESET> tags. Each frame within the FRAMESET tags can then be indicated via a <FRAME> tag. Other FRAMESET tags can also be nested within outer FRAMESET tags. Various name-value pairs defined within frames and frame sets are as shown here:

- <FRAMESET ROWS="*row_size_init, row_size_end*"> to designate the size in rows of a frame set either in pixels or as a percentage size of a document.
- <FRAMESET COLS="*col_size_init, col_size_end*"> to designate the size in columns of a frame set either in pixels or as a percentage size of a document.
- <FRAME SRC="*AssociatedURL*"> to define the URL of the document to be read for display in this frame.

- <FRAME NAME="*FrameName*"> to identify the frame with a name.
- <FRAME SCROLLING="*YesOrNo*"> to indicate whether the frame should display scroll bars ("yes") or not ("no"). Can also be set to the default value of "auto" to turn scrollbars on and off depending on screen sizing.
- <FRAME NORESIZE> to disable the capability to resize the frame.
- <FRAME MARGINHEIGHT=*margin*> to indicate the top and bottom frame margins.
- <FRAME MARGINWIDTH=*margin*> to indicate the left and right frame margins.

As an example of using frames with nested frame sets, we have the following HTML frame-set snippet with a layout as shown in Figure 30.1:

```
<HTML>
    <FRAMESET  ROWS = "145,100%" BORDER="0" FRAMESPACING="0"
➥                    FRAMEBORDER="NO">
     <FRAME SRC="top.html" NAME="ftop" SCROLLING="NO" MARGINWIDTH="17"
➥                    MARGINHEIGHT="10" NORESIZE>
       <FRAMESET   COLS = "190,100%"   BORDER="0" FRAMESPACING="0"
➥                   FRAMEBORDER="NO">
         <FRAME SRC="left.html" NAME="fleft" SCROLLING="NO" NORESIZE>
         <FRAME SRC="main.html" NAME="fmain" NORESIZE>
       </FRAMESET>
   </FRAMESET>

</HTML>
```

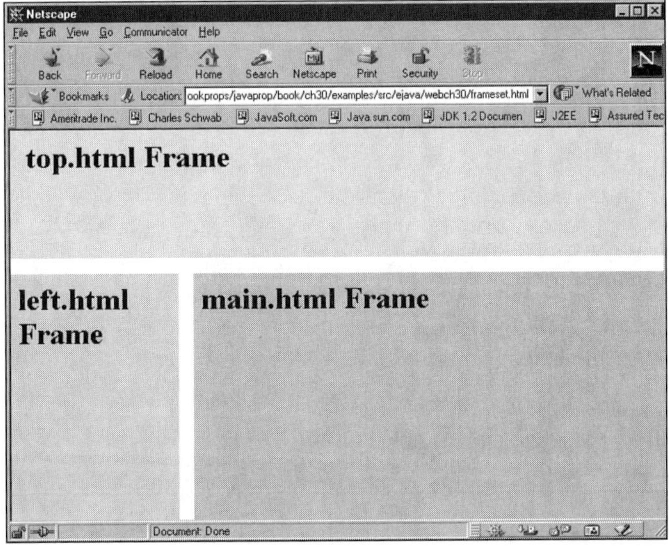

FIGURE 30.1
An HTML frame-set example.

HTML Forms

HTML forms provide a means by which user input can be solicited from within a Web browser's display of an HTML document and subsequently transmitted to the Web server inside of an HTTP request. HTML forms are thus one of the more important features of HTML for Web-enabling enterprise developers to understand. HTML forms are designated between `<FORM>` and `</FORM>` tags in a document. `FORM` tags can also have attributes embedded inside of the leading tag, such as `<FORM METHOD="MethodType" ACTION="ActionValue" ENCTYPE="EncodingType">`. The three `FORM` attributes are defined in this way:

- `METHOD="MethodType"` designates the HTTP request method. The `GET` method passes user input via a URL string that gets added to the resource identification field of an HTTP request. The `POST` method passes user input via name-value pairs in the request body of an HTTP request.
- `ACTION="ActionValue"` designates the action to be performed. A URL as the action value specifies to what base URL information is to be sent. A `mailto` directive can indicate to what email address information is to be sent.
- `ENCTYPE="EncodingType"` designates the method in which the input information is encoded via a MIME type and subtype. The default encoding format is `application/x-www-form-encoded`.

As an example of a basic `FORM` specification for posting data to a particular URL, we have this:

```
<FORM
       METHOD = "POST"
       NAME="contactForm"
       ACTION="http://www.beeshirts.com/cgi-bin/contact">
  <!--Add input elements here -->
</FORM>
```

Whereas `FORM` tag attributes specify how information is to be sent via an HTTP request, input elements between leading and trailing `FORM` tags describe how that information is actually obtained from the user interface. The HTML input element describes UI input components inside of an `<INPUT>` tag. Input elements necessarily designate a type of input component with a `TYPE` attribute, as in `<INPUT TYPE="InputType">`. Input elements also are uniquely identified by a `NAME` attribute, as in `<INPUT NAME="ElementName">`. The various input element `TYPE` components are listed here:

- `TEXT`: Defines a GUI text-box component. A `VALUE` attribute specifies initial text to display in the box. `SIZE` and `MAXLENGTH` attributes specify the size and maximum number of characters to allow in a text box. If no `TYPE` is specified for an `INPUT`, the `TEXT` component is assumed.

- PASSWORD: Defines a GUI text-box component that does not display the text as it is input.
- SUBMIT: Defines a button that submits the form when clicked. A VALUE attribute specifies the button label.
- RESET: Defines a button to clear all form data. A VALUE attribute specifies the button label.
- IMAGE: Defines an image that can also be used to submit form data. An SRC attribute describes the image URL.
- HIDDEN: Defines an input element that is not displayed but is used to store document information in name-value pairs that is submitted with the rest of the form data. Hidden fields are often used to store session information.
- CHECKBOX: Defines a GUI check-box component. A CHECKED attribute can indicate that the box is initially checked.
- RADIO: Defines a GUI radio button. A CHECKED attribute can indicate that the radio button is initially selected.

For example, to post data from a TEXT field to a particular URL on the clicking of a displayed SUBMIT button, we might have this:

```
<FORM
       METHOD = "POST"
       NAME="contactForm"
       ACTION="http://www.beeshirts.com/cgi-bin/contact">
   <INPUT type="TEXT" size="50" name="email" value="">
   <INPUT type="SUBMIT" Name="Send" Value="Submit">
</FORM>
```

A text-area GUI component can also be displayed within an HTML page by the insertion of <TEXTAREA> and </TEXTAREA> tags within enclosing <FORM> and </FORM> tags. Leading text-area tags are defined using the syntax <TEXTAREA NAME="*ElementName*" ROWS="*characters_tall*" COLS="*characters_wide*">. The NAME attribute uniquely identifies the component. The ROWS and COLS attributes can define the number of rows and columns for the text area. Any information within the <TEXTAREA> and </TEXTAREA> tags represents initially displayed data.

CGI Programming

The Common Gateway Interface (CGI) defines a standard interface contract between a Web server and a Web-enabled application. This interface allows Web servers to delegate the responsibility for generating HTTP responses to independent CGI-capable applications. Such applications can thus be used to dynamically generate HTTP responses. This may be contrasted with a Web server's typical support for reading statically defined HTML files and sending back their contents in an HTTP response stream.

Whenever an HTTP request is made and references a URL that refers to a CGI application, the Web server spawns the application, passing it inputs via environment variables, as well as through standard input. Results from the CGI application can then be returned via standard output to the Web server. If the CGI application supports generation of HTTP response header information, the Web server can then simply send the entire response back to the Web browser without further processing. Otherwise, the Web server may need to prepend HTTP response header information to the CGI application's generated HTTP response body.

We described the basic flow of a CGI request and response scenario involving a Web browser, Web server, and CGI process in Chapter 13 in the context of pure communications-level HTTP requests and responses. Such a scenario can now be described at a higher level above pure HTTP communications in terms of a user's interaction with HTML GUI components embedded inside of a Web browser. An HTML form captures input data entered into Web-based `INPUT` components with a `METHOD` of either `GET` or `POST` and an `ACTION` designating a target CGI application URL (for example, `http://www.beeshirts.com/cgi-bin/contact`). A `SUBMIT` type of `INPUT` component packages data into an HTTP request to be sent to a CGI application referenced in the target URL. At this point, the same basic flow of CGI behavior described in Chapter 13 applies.

Example CGI Program

Listing 30.1 presents a Java program that can be called as a separate CGI program. The `SampleCGIExample.main()` method on this application instantiates an instance of a `SampleCGIExample` object and saves any standard input arguments passed to it when it is run from the command line by a Web server. The `SampleCGIExample.generateResponseFile()` method called from the `SampleCGIExample` constructor then generates an HTML header in the `generateHTMLHeader()` call, generates an HTML body in the `generateHTMLBody()` call, and generates closing HTML tags in the `generateHTMLClose()` method call. All calls output HTML document syntax to the standard output stream.

This particular CGI example happens to generate HTTP response header information in the `generateHTMLHeader()` call and thus can be output directly to the Web browser output stream without requiring the Web server to prepend any header information. The `generateHTMLHeader()` also creates the first portion of the HTML document using `HTML`, `TITLE`, and opening `BODY` tags. The `generateHTMLBody()` method calls `generateHashtableFromString()` to parse data passed to the application via the standard input stream as a string of `name=value` pairs separated by an ampersand (`&`) and translates this `String` into a `Hashtable` of keyed values. The `generateHTMLBody()` call then formats this data into an HTML table embedded into the output HTML document. The `generateHTMLClose()` call closes the HTML output document by adding trailing `BODY` and `HTML` tags.

NOTE

The basic CGI program example is contained on the CD in the `examples\src\ejava\webch30` directory.

LISTING 30.1 Java-Based CGI Program (*SampleCGIExample.java*)

```
package ejava.webch30;
import java.util.Hashtable;
import java.util.StringTokenizer;
import java.util.Enumeration;
/**
  * This example takes data from Standard input and
  * converts the Standard input Data into HTML file.
  */
public class SampleCGIExample
{
  private String[] receivedArgs;

  public SampleCGIExample(String[] args)
  {
   receivedArgs = args;
    generateResponseFile();
  }

/**
  * generate HTML file
  */
  public void generateResponseFile()
  {
    generateHTMLHeader();
    generateHTMLBody(receivedArgs);
    generateHTMLClose();
  }
/**
  * to generate HTMLHeader
  */
  private void generateHTMLHeader()
  {
    System.out.println ("Content-Type: text/html\n" +
        "\n" +
```

continues

LISTING 30.1 Continued

```
        "<!DOCTYPE HTML PUBLIC \"-//W3C//DTD HTML 3.2//EN\">\n" +
        "<HTML>\n" + "<HEAD>\n" + "<TITLE>The CGI Example "
         +" </TITLE>\n"  +  "<!--");
    System.out.println ("-->\n" + "</HEAD>\n" +
        "\n" + "<BODY>\n" + "<H1>I received following Data from client
</H1>" );
  }
/**
  * To generate HTML Body
  */
  private void generateHTMLBody(String[] data) {
    System.out.println("<BR>");
    // 0th element in data is the input String from the Client
    Hashtable receivedValues = generateHashtableFromString(data[0]);
    if(receivedValues == null){
      System.out.println("No data Received ");
    }else{
      Enumeration keys = receivedValues.keys();
      System.out.println("<TABLE>");
      while(keys.hasMoreElements()){
        System.out.println("<TR>");
        String key = (String)keys.nextElement();
        String value = (String)receivedValues.get(key);
        System.out.println("<TD>"+key+ " </TD> <TD>  "+value +"</TD>");
        System.out.println("</TR>");
      }
      System.out.println("</TABLE>");
    }
    System.out.println("<BR>");
  }
/**
  * it converts the input String to a hashtable using delimiters
  */
  private Hashtable generateHashtableFromString(String inString)
  {
     if(inString == null){
      return null;
     }
     StringTokenizer stringTokens = new StringTokenizer(inString, "&");
     Hashtable returnTable = new Hashtable();
     while(stringTokens.hasMoreElements()){
      String subString = stringTokens.nextToken();
      StringTokenizer subTokens = new StringTokenizer(subString, "=");
      String name = subTokens.nextToken();
```

```
      String value = "";
      if(subTokens.hasMoreElements()){
        value = subTokens.nextToken();
      }
      returnTable.put(name, value);
     }
     return returnTable;
  }
  /**
    * close html tags
    */
  private void generateHTMLClose() {
    System.out.println("</BODY>\n</HTML>");
  }

  public static void main(String[] args){
    SampleCGIExample cgiExample =
      new SampleCGIExample(args);

  }
}
```

Many Web server environments designate a particular directory for storing CGI-based applications. A common directory name used is `cgi-bin`. You might thus first compile and store your `SampleCGIExample` Java class file in the `cgi-bin` directory for a particular Web server root directory using this:

```
javac -d <WebServerRoot>/cgi-bin ejava.webch30.SampleCGIExample
```

Because the Java class is not directly executable without a JVM instance first being invoked from the command line, the Web server will also need another helper script file that calls the application, such as the following directly executable UNIX script call also added to the `cgibin` directory:

```
#!/bin/sh
java ejava.webch30.SampleCGIExample
```

If such a directly executable script or one like it is stored in a file called `CGIShellExample` in the `cgi-bin` directory, as an example, then the following `FORM` tag attributes can be used in an HTML document when pointing a browser to invoke the dynamic behavior of a CGI application:

```
<FORM  METHOD = "POST" NAME="contactForm"
➥ ACTION="http://www.beeshirts.com/cgi-bin/CGIShellExample">
  <!--Insert Form INPUT types here -->
</FORM>
```

Note that different Web servers will have different configuration requirements and techniques for hooking into CGI applications, but it is usually as simple as the basic technique described previously. We simply wanted to illustrate the basic concept of how a CGI application can be invoked over the Web here.

Stateful CGI Applications

Each request to a CGI application spawns a new process, and there is no direct means for persisting state across application invocations. CGI programmers have to hand-code such mechanisms themselves. One programmatic approach for preserving state is to embed some session identifier information into an HTML `HIDDEN INPUT` field and use this identifier to refer to a client's sessions state that is stored on the server side in some persistent store. More state information can also be embedded into a `HIDDEN` field and referenced, but there is a practical limit on how much information you would want to be stored in such fields because it would have to be transmitted in every HTTP request and response.

When a Web client begins a Web-based interaction session with a Web server, a session ID can be generated on the server side and stored inside of an HTML form's `INPUT` tag whose type is `HIDDEN` (for example, `<INPUT TYPE="HIDDEN" NAME="SessionID" VALUE="id8245">`). The server side can also persist such client session ID information in a database, a file, or perhaps a separate running process. When the HTML form submits an HTTP request to the Web server, the `HIDDEN INPUT` field data associated with this form and containing the session ID can be sent to the Web server. A CGI application can use this session ID to look up other client session information persisted in the database, file, or separate process. As long as the session ID is always generated on the server side and stored in a `HIDDEN INPUT` field and always sent back to the Web server via an HTML form `GET` or `POST`, the Web client session can be tracked.

As we alluded, session IDs are not the only way in which state can be embedded into a CGI-based interaction. Depending on the amount of state needed for the application, only the state used for subsequent transactions needs to be embedded into a `HIDDEN INPUT` field. If this state is minimal, it may always be stored in a `HIDDEN INPUT` field, sent to the Web client in HTTP responses, and then sent back to the Web server in HTTP requests. The need to persistently store session information in a back-end database, file, or separate process may thus be alleviated.

CGI Pros and Cons

CGI-based Web enabling is a good solution in that back-end applications written in any language can be communicated with by writing a CGI wrapper application that adheres to the CGI requirements and talks to the back-end application on behalf of the Web server. It is also a rather simple programmatic paradigm for many developers to rapidly Web-enable applications and provide dynamically generated Web content. It is for precisely these reasons that CGI has been a popular Web-enabling technique since the early days of the World Wide Web.

But CGI is not a very good solution for Web-enabling scalable enterprise applications. A major disadvantage lies in the need to spawn separate processes to handle Web client requests. As the number of client requests increases, the load on server-side system process resources becomes burdensome. Furthermore, the performance of the standard input and output interface stream technique itself can be very slow. Stateful applications are also not readily available to CGI applications out of the box without a significant hand-coding effort. Thus, although CGI-based applications can be useful for rapid prototyping and for quickly Web-enabling stateless applications with small user bases, CGI-based applications for the enterprise requires significant amounts of hand-coding and still offers only limited scalability.

Scripting Languages

Scripting languages provide another popular solution for programming both client-side and server-side Web behavior. Figure 30.2 shows how scripting languages can be used for Web enabling on both the client and the server side. Scripting language code that is embedded into HTML documents that are sent to a Web browser are processed by client-side script runtime engines that can interpret scripts embedded within special `<SCRIPT>` and `</SCRIPT>` HTML tags. Scripting language code is also supported by most Web servers, often by the provision of server-side runtime engines that process scripts embedded into HTML documents before they are sent to the Web browser. Server-side script processing involves interpreting script language code embedded within special server script HTML tags and dynamically generating content that is output to an HTML document stream before it is sent to a Web browser. Server-side scripting languages are also used in CGI application development.

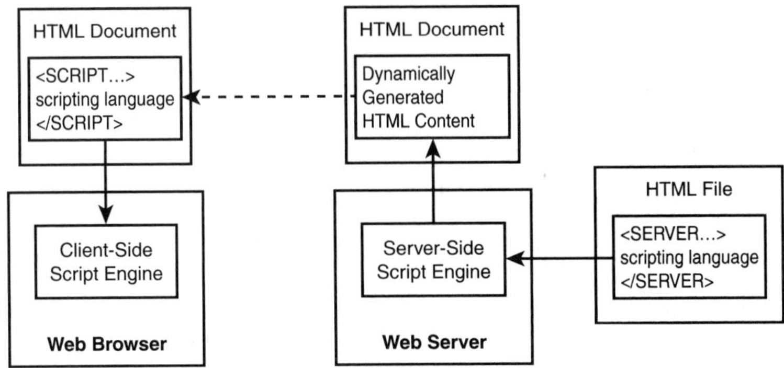

FIGURE 30.2
Scripting languages on the Web.

Scripting language Web solutions on the client side are good for performing data and input validation and for displaying basic messages. On the server side, however, pure scripting solutions to Web enabling have scalability, maintainability, and performance problems when used for anything besides dynamic Web presentation logic. Because scripting languages are not OO by nature, the lack of inheritance and encapsulation leads to limitations for true enterprise class usage when they're used to implement business and interface logic. However, scripting languages are often employed in development scenarios in which the language is already known or can be easily understood due to the language's inherent simplicity. A few of the more common client- or server-side scripting language solutions for Web enabling are JavaScript, VBScript, and Perl, which we'll briefly cover throughout the remainder of this section.

JavaScript

JavaScript is a scripting language that can be run on both the client and the server side. JavaScript was created by Netscape with client-side JavaScript executed in its Netscape Navigator Web browser and server-side JavaScript executed in its Netscape Enterprise Server Web server. Microsoft's Internet Explorer Web browser and Internet Information Server Web server also process JavaScript but refer to it as JScript. JavaScript is now standardized by the European Community Manufacturers Association (ECMA). Despite standardization, there are still some differences between Netscape's JavaScript and Microsoft's JScript implementations.

Despite the name and some syntactic similarities, JavaScript and Java are distinctly different languages. JavaScript does, however, have some object-based support. Although support for inheritance and encapsulation is nonexistent in JavaScript, manipulating information as objects and programmatic association of data and functions to objects are possible.

On the client side, JavaScript can be embedded directly into an HTML document and recognized by Web browsers that can read JavaScript contained within `SCRIPT` tags. `SCRIPT` tags are defined according to the most basic format:

```
<SCRIPT language="SomeScriptingLanguage">
   // Scripting language source inserted here.
</SCRIPT>
```

Here, *`SomeScriptingLanguage`* is a predefined name of the scripting language source code that is inserted between the `SCRIPT` tags. If no script language is defined, JavaScript is assumed as the default language. As an example of defining JavaScript code between `SCRIPT` tags, we have this:

```
<SCRIPT language="JavaScript">

  // Declare variables
  var hrsWorked, overtime;
```

```
  hrsWorked = 42;

  if (hrsWorked > 40){
    overtime = hrsWorked - 40;
    // Dynamically write to browser
    document.write(" Overtime : " + overtime);
  }

</SCRIPT>
```

JavaScript may also be embedded into `INPUT` tags as attributes that designate certain actions to take. JavaScript is thus very useful for client-side data validation. For example, a client-side JavaScript function that validates whether an email input field has been entered can be called when a `SUBMIT` action is invoked. This is accomplished by specifying an `onSubmit` attribute in an `INPUT FORM` as shown here:

```
<HTML>
 <HEAD>
 <TITLE> Contact </TITLE>
  <SCRIPT LANGUAGE="JavaScript">
   <!-- Write function to check whether the email fields are empty -->
   function checkKeyFields(){
      // Read value from INPUT email field
      var emailField = document.contactForm.email;
      if(emailField.value == ""){
        // Generate a pop-up alert message
        alert("Email Field Should be filled ");
        return (false);
      }
      // now submit form
      return(true);
   }
  </SCRIPT>
 </HEAD>

 <BODY>
 <FORM
       METHOD = "POST"
       NAME="contactForm"
       ACTION="http://www.beeshirts.com/cgi-bin/contactAP"
       onSubmit="return(checkKeyFields())">
   <INPUT size="50" name="email" value="">
   <INPUT type="SUBMIT" Name="Send" Value="Submit">
 </FORM>
 </BODY>
</HTML>
```

Because many Web programmers have come to learn JavaScript through their client-side Web page development efforts, the tendency to use JavaScript on the server side and employ the same knowledge along with opportunities for code reuse has made server-side JavaScript a popular solution for some developers. Server-side JavaScript inserted into an HTML file between special SERVER tags can be read by a server-side JavaScript runtime engine and dynamically generate information to be displayed in an HTML document using the following:

```
<SERVER>
  write("Hi There!"); // Write to client document
  var clientName = Client.name;
  write("Client is :"+clientName); // Write to client document
</SERVER>
```

Nevertheless, use of JavaScript on the server side is fraught with perils. For one, the lack of any real OO support for inheritance and encapsulation violates much of the foundational success that object-oriented programming languages offer in terms of scalability, reusability, and maintainability (see Chapter 2, "Object-Oriented Software Development for the Enterprise"). Server-side JavaScript runtime engines also provide minimal inherent scalability from a resource management and concurrency management point of view.

JavaScript does support a means to call interface JavaScript code with Java code. Both client-side and server-side Java-JavaScript interfacing adds some flexibility to JavaScript as a bridging technology. However, the interface between Java and JavaScript runtime environments also can add significant and at times buggy overhead when data types are being transferred between runtime environments.

VBScript

A subset of the Visual Basic programming language can also be used as a scripting language via VBScript in both the client and the server side. VBScript is Microsoft's preferred scripting approach for Web enabling on the client and server side. VBScript can be interpreted by the Microsoft Internet Explorer for client-side Web browser processing and using the Microsoft Internet Information Server for server-side Web server processing. Server-side VBScript is primarily used by the Microsoft Active Server Pages technology to be explored in a bit more detail later in this chapter. On the client side, embedded VBScript is identified between SCRIPT tags as shown here:

```
<SCRIPT language="VBScript">
  sub UseVBScript_DoClick
    MsgBox "DoClick from VBScript"
  end sub
</SCRIPT>
```

Because VBScript leverages much of the existing developer knowledge of Visual Basic and Basic, it has significant developer support. The simplicity of VBScript has also enabled it to become a popular Web-enabling solution.

Perl

As a final note, the Perl language has also been used for Web enabling on the server side. Because Perl is considered to be a simple language to understand and has a syntax familiar to many UNIX scripting gurus, it is often used for quick Web-enabling solutions. Furthermore, Perl as a language has also been around since 1987 and has thus gained considerable development support over the years. However, the scalability and enterprise applicability of Perl on the server side are extremely limited, as is the case with many server-side scripting solutions.

Although some support exists for calling Perl scripts directly from within a Web server's process space (for example, the Apache Web server) as well as from within an HTML document, many Web servers use Perl scripts within a CGI application. A Perl script file is placed inside of a CGI directory and then referenced within a URL like any other Web page or CGI application. Thus a URL, such as `http://www.BeeShirts.com/cgi-bin/hello.pl`, may reference a Perl script like this:

```
#  File name : hello.pl

# Main part of Perl script calls write_document subroutine and exits
&write_document();
exit(0);

# This subroutine calls print_html subroutine
sub write_document
{
 @print_html();
}

# This subroutine generates HTML to an output stream
sub print_html
{
 print "Content-type: text/html" , "\n";
 print  " <HTML>";
 print  "    <BODY>";
 print  "       <H1> Hello World </H1>";
 print  "    </BODY>";
 print  " </HTML>";
 print << EOF;
}
```

Active Server Pages

Active Server Pages (ASP) is Microsoft's answer to Web-enabling applications using a server-side scripting language technique. ASP requires use of Microsoft's Internet Information Server (IIS) Web server to process server-side ASP files upon a Web request and to dynamically generate Web response content. IIS uses a special Windows platform–specific dynamic link library (`ASP.DLL`) to process ASP files. ASP files having the `.asp` extension contain special ASP commands that are processed by the IIS Web server to generate dynamic content.

ASPs can be created using server-side scripting languages such as VBScript and JScript, although VBScript is by far the most popular language used in ASP implementations. ASPs are HTML files that contain embedded scripting language code in which the first line in an ASP identifies the language used as follows:

```
<%@ LANGUAGE="VBSCRIPT" %>
```

ASP commands embedded in the HTML document are encapsulated by `<%` and `%>` tags. As a simple example of using an ASP `Response` object to write data to a client Web HTTP response output stream, we have this:

```
<%@ LANGUAGE="VBSCRIPT" %>

 <%
   set aCustomer = Server.CreateObject("Customer");
   customerID = aCustomer.customerID;
 %>

<HTML>
<BODY>
  <% Response.Write("Hi There!") %>
  Customer  ID is  <% Response.Write(customerID) %>
</BODY>
</HTML>
```

The preceding snippet not only illustrates ASP's method for writing to a client output stream using a `Response.write()` command, but also demonstrates how a COM object, such as a `Customer` COM object, can be created, manipulated, and used to generate data for display in a dynamically generated Web page. ASP code can not only access COM objects directly, but also be used to access databases and other system resources using standard scripting language syntax.

ASPs thus provide the same advantages as other scripting language–based server-side Web programming paradigms in the context of a Microsoft Web server platform-specific architecture. Because the `ASP.DLL` is needed to transform HTML pages sprinkled with server-side ASP commands into dynamic HTML response content, ASPs rely on a server-side Microsoft platform. Some COTS products do exist to transform ASPs into an intermediate format usable on other platforms. However, the added overhead required by such a process is typically necessary only if an existing legacy of ASPs have been developed in the first place on a Windows platform and then need to be run on another platform such as UNIX.

Java-Based Web Programming

We have described various non–Java-based Web-enabling techniques thus far in this chapter so that you as a developer tasked with Web-enabling your enterprise can best understand the alternative technologies that are available and sometimes used in the enterprise. You can then better trade-off the advantages and disadvantages of these other technologies with the recommended J2EE-based Web-enabling techniques of Java Servlets and JavaServer Pages (JSPs) to be described in this book. Java Servlets and JSPs are not only part of the J2EE and therefore germane to this book's topical discussion, but they also represent the most optimal option for Web-enabling most enterprise systems. Servlets and JSPs offer advantages of platform independence, rapid application development, performance, and the capability to use a familiar Java paradigm that other Web-enabling technologies cannot offer.

J2EE Servlets provide a way to allow Web servers to hand off Web requests to Java-based code by starting such code as a separate thread, handing request data to the servlet, and then receiving response data. Servlets have numerous advantages over CGI-based applications in that servlet requests are handled by a separate thread inside of a running JVM process as opposed to having a separate process for each request. Servlets can also easily maintain state between requests and provide built-in APIs to session management facilities. Servlets also share data among multiple servlet instances as an added advantage over CGI.

Although many server-side scripting language approaches to Web enabling support stateful sessions and threaded processing, servlets offer the rich OO API of Java that scripting languages inherently do not support. Thus the maintainability and reusability of code across enterprise Java applications can be provided by virtue of a Java Servlet–based approach to Web enabling. Servlets also running on top of J2EE also offer platform and COTS server independence that no other non-Java scripting-based Web-enabling technology can provide. We describe servlets in much more detail in Chapter 32, "Java Servlets."

JSP is a Java-based scripting language approach for Web enabling. JSPs are server-side HTML documents with embedded JSP commands as is the case with ASP. JSPs are converted into Java Servlets as they are processed by a J2EE-based Web server. Although JSPs may initially seem like an undesirable Web programming solution given the disadvantages of other scripting language–based solutions, JSP technology in J2EE servers focuses on the use of JSP as a strictly presentation-layer description of Web-page content. All the enterprise-critical business and interface logic rests in either a servlet or an Enterprise JavaBean. Thus, the maintainability and reuse pertinent to business and interface logic can rest inside more OO-based constructs, and JSPs can be used to describe the Web screen presentation in a fashion more familiar to Web page development personnel. JSPs also offer an advantage of platform and COTS Web server independence not offered by other scripting-based Web-enabling solutions. We describe JSPs in more detail in Chapter 33, "JavaServer Pages."

Java-based Web enabling not only offers an effective means to generate Web content, but also has technology built-in to generate and parse XML documents. XML is fast becoming the standard data-exchange technology used not only across the Web, but also in business-to-business transactions, other client-to-server interactions, and server-to-server interactions. Java's built-in support for XML thus gives you an added advantage for Web-enabling applications and other enterprise interfaces straight out of the J2EE box. We describe XML's use with Java in Chapter 31, "XML."

Conclusions

Traditional Web-enabling techniques have focused on the generation of static HTML pages, CGI programming, and non-Java client- and server-side scripting solutions. The popularity of many of these approaches has been fostered by the simplicity with which they can be implemented. In the early days of Web enabling and in modern-day Web applications with small user bases, such techniques have been sufficient. However, Web enabling of a scalable enterprise application requires a solution offering decent performance, scalability, reusability, and maintainability without sacrificing the requirement for rapid development. Java-based servlet and JSP Web-enabling approaches offer such a solution. The remainder of this part of the book presents servlets, JSPs, and XML as key Web-enabler technologies using Java. The foundations of HTML also presented in this chapter will arm you with the conceptual and practical information you need in order to understand how to employ such Web-enabling techniques.

XML

CHAPTER

31

IN THIS CHAPTER

- XML Overview 1010
- XML Formatting 1012
- DTD Declaration 1018
- Hyperlinking in XML 1025
- XML Style Sheets 1029
- Simple API for XML 1031
- Document Object Model 1047
- Java and XML 1061

The eXtensible Markup Language (XML) has quickly caught on in industry as the most widely adopted standard for describing and exchanging data in a platform-, language-, and protocol-independent fashion. XML and its auxiliary specifications are used to describe data XML document representations, describe constraints for XML document types, describe links between XML documents and resources, and describe automated transformations and formatting of XML documents. Two key API standards are also defined that facilitate standard interfacing with XML documents and parsers from Java. Although the J2EE is currently dependent on XML only for defining standard application deployment descriptions, the J2EE will require XML APIs in a future specification as an integral part of enterprise data exchange with the J2EE. In the meantime, a standard Java extension for XML can be used to build XML-enabled enterprise applications.

In this chapter, you will learn:

- An overview of what XML is and the standards defined to support it.
- The basic structure of well-formed XML documents.
- The structure and usage of a Document Type Definition (DTD) to validate particular XML document types.
- The basic utility behind the XML Linking Language (XLink) and the XML Pointer Language (XPointer) for linking XML document data to external resources as well as other XML document data.
- The basic utility behind the XML Stylesheet Language (XSL) for automated transformations of XML documents as well as automated formatting of XML documents.
- The architecture and usage of the Simple API for XML (SAX) for interfacing with XML parsers and documents using the Java API for XML Parsing (JAXP) standard extension.
- The architecture and usage of the Document Object Model (DOM) API for interfacing with XML parsers and documents using the JAXP.
- The relationship between Java enterprise APIs and XML, the J2EE and XML, and the use of XML for describing J2EE application deployment properties.

XML Overview

XML is a markup language used to describe how data should be represented in an I/O stream. An XML document is a block of data structured according to the rules of XML syntax. As depicted in Figure 31.1, an XML document is often thought of with respect to its transfer between applications. A sending application may create an XML document directly or utilize a special XML document builder to produce an XML document that is sent over a network in a communications-protocol–independent fashion. A receiving application may then take advantage of an XML parser to parse the XML document stream into a form that can be easily manipulated by the application. The application may be less likely, although it is possible, to parse the document itself. A key point to note here is that XML documents can be exchanged between applications regardless of the application's implementation language and host platform.

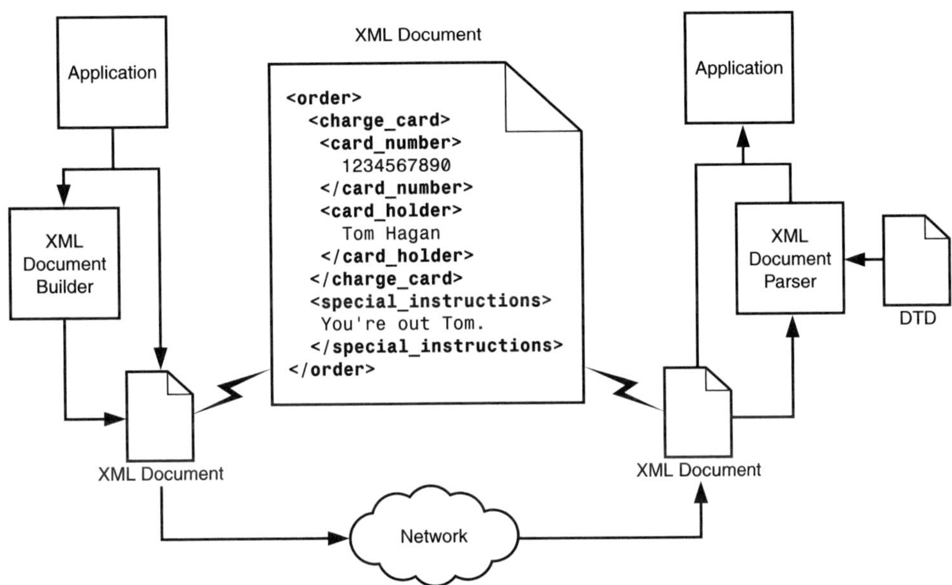

FIGURE 31.1
Basic XML usage.

In addition to a standard syntax for describing document data representation, a standard way to define the semantic meaning of a particular type of XML document is also possible via an XML Document Type Definition (DTD). A DTD describes the basic structure and rules for particular XML document classifications. Thus, whereas XML document syntax rules are akin to an underlying data serialization format, a DTD is akin to a schema definition of the document data. As an example, the contents of an XML document may contain a hierarchical set of order data in an online e-commerce application, but a DTD defines the standard structure that must be adhered to by an XML document that contains order data.

The World Wide Web Consortium (W3C) is the standards body that works to define the syntax of XML documents and the syntax of DTDs (`http://www.w3.org/XML/`). XML is defined as a simplified subset of the more complicated Standard Generalized Markup Language (SGML). XML's markup tag syntax has a similar appearance to HTML, but it provides a much richer, more flexible, and extensible set of language conventions. The W3C also defines a set of supporting standards that augment the capabilities offered by use of XML. These are the most significant W3C standard specifications:

- *Extensible Markup Language (XML)*: Defines the basic syntax of XML and DTDs (`http://www.w3.org/TR/REC-xml`).
- *XML Linking Language (XLink)*: Defines how resources are referenced from within XML documents (`http://www.w3.org/TR/xlink/`).
- *XML Pointer Language (XPointer)*: Defines a mechanism for addressing different portions of an XML document (`http://www.w3.org/TR/xptr`).
- *Extensible Stylesheet Language (XSL)*: Defines how XML documents can be transformed into other document types, as well as how XML documents should be formatted (`http://www.w3.org/TR/xsl`).
- *Extensible Hypertext Markup Language (XHTML)*: Defines HTML v4.0 in terms of an XML application (`http://www.w3.org/TR/xhtml1`).

Above and beyond the general language-oriented specifications, the W3C also maintains a standard API definition for interfacing with XML documents via the Document Object Model (DOM) specification. An independent group from industry has also defined an API model for XML document interfacing known as the Simple API for XML (SAX) standard. In addition to the broadly defined standards for XML and auxiliary specifications, many other organizations are involved in defining standard DTDs for specific vertical markets. The Organization for the Advancement of Structured Information Standards (OASIS) in particular is involved in promoting the adoption of XML standards within specific industries. JavaSoft has also defined a few standard DTDs for use with the J2EE and will continue to integrate XML standards into the J2EE platform.

XML Formatting

An XML document is a structured collection of ASCII-based markup tags. Each tag either defines some information used to describe how the document is to be interpreted or describes some data contained within the document. The basic structure and syntax of an XML document is shown here:

```
<?xml version="1.0" encoding="ISO-8859-1" standalone="yes" ?>

<!-- A comment -->

<!-- Begin root document element scope below -->
<RootElement>

  <!-- Begin sub element scope below -->
  <SubElement1>
    <!-- A sub element value -->
    SubElement1_Value
```

```
  </SubElement1>
  <!-- Close sub element scope -->

  <!-- Begin sub element with attributes in tag below -->
  <SubElement2 attribute1="value1" attribute2="value2">
    <!-- Another sub element value -->
    SubElement2_Value
  </SubElement2>
  <!-- Close another sub element scope -->

  <!-- Begin another sub element scope below-->
  <SubElement3>

    <!-- A sub element value with entity references -->
    &quot; Foo &#38; Bar &CorpAddress; &quot;

    <!-- A processing instruction with data -->
    <?ProcessingInstructionName SomeData MoreData?>

    <!-- Unparsed character data -->
    <![CDATA[ Don't Parse This Stuff ]]>

  </SubElement3>
  <!-- Close another sub element scope -->

  <!-- An empty marker element below -->
  <EmptyElement1/>

  <!-- Another empty marker element below -->
  <EmptyElem2></EmptyElem2>

</RootElement>
<!-- Close root document element scope -->
```

NOTE

Snippets are strewn throughout this section from a concrete XML document that contains the data associated with a BeeShirts.com order. The order not only contains order-related data, but also contains an ordered item sub-element and a charge-card sub-element. The `xmlDocument.xml` file on the CD in the `examples\src\ejava\xmlch31` directory contains a cohesive collection of these snippets.

Comments

Comments represent information useful to someone examining the source document only and are not parsed by XML tools. Comments are added to XML documents between the `<!--` and `-->` character sequences. Comments can be placed anywhere in the XML document.

Here's an example of a comment:

```
<!-- Definition of order data follows below -->
```

XML Declaration

An XML declaration is added to identify the associated block of data as an XML document. XML declarations are defined between the `<?xml` and `?>` case-sensitive character sequences. The XML standard version number is identified within the declaration using `version="versionNumber"`. Furthermore, the text encoding format of the document can optionally be defined within the declaration using `encoding="encodingFormat"`, and the dependence on any other documents defined external to the current document can also optionally be defined with the declaration using `standalone="yes/no"`.

As an example of a most basic XML declaration, we might have this:

```
<?xml version="1.0"?>
```

Elements

Container elements contain data values or other XML elements. Elements have a case-sensitive name that is defined within < and > characters, such as `<ElementName>`. Element boundaries are defined within a start tag, such as `<ElementName>`, and an end tag, such as `</ElementName>`. Element names begin with a letter, underscore (_), or colon (`:`). Element names are subsequently constructed with letters, numbers, underscores (_), colons (`:`), hyphens (`-`), or periods (`.`). Elements can be nested within one another but cannot overlap. An XML document can have only one root element that contains all other elements. Namespaces of XML element scope may be separated with colons (`:`) between each namespace.

As an example of a base order element containing order data and a nested order item element, we have this:

```
<order>
  <order_id> 123 </order_id>
  <customer_id> 101 </customer_id>
  <order_date> 10/19/99 </order_date>
  <ship_instruct> Leave stuff at back door if no answer </ship_instruct>
  <ship_date> 11/10/99 </ship_date>
  <ship_charge> $3.80 </ship_charge>
```

```
  <paid_date> 11/01/99 </paid_date>

  <item>
    <item_id> 1001 </item_id>
    <quantity> 10    </quantity>
    <total_price> $78.99 </total_price>
  </item>
    ...
</order>
```

An empty element designates a place in a document where some action should occur without containing any data values or other XML elements. Empty element names are defined within < and /> characters. Empty elements can also be defined within a start tag followed immediately by an end tag with no data between the tags.

For example, adding an empty element to our order data, we might have this:

```
<order>
       ...
  <ship_weight/>
       ...
</order>
```

Attributes

Attributes are name and value pairs associated with elements, and they serve to describe some information about the element. Attributes are defined within the start tag of an element as one or more whitespace-separated sequences of *name*="*value*" pairs. Attribute values must be within quotation marks, and attribute names within the same element start tag must be unique. Namespaces of XML attributes may also be separated with colons (:) between each namespace.

As an example, a charge-card sub-element of an order element may define a card type attribute:

```
<order>
             ...
  <charge_card card_type="credit">
    <card_number> 12345678901234 </card_number>
    <expired_date> 10/10/2000 </expired_date>
    <card_confirmation_number> 0987654321 </card_confirmation_number>
      ...
  </charge_card>
</order>
```

Entity References

Entity references are special identifiers and character sequences that refer to a value that is expanded by an XML parser whenever the entity is referenced (in a fashion similar to a C/C++ macro). Certain predefined entity references have special identifiers reserved and are used within the & and ; characters. For example, & defines an ampersand, ' defines an apostrophe, " defines a quote, < defines a less-than symbol, and > defines a greater-than symbol. To reference a special character in an XML document, you can also refer to that character using its Unicode decimal representation between &# and ; characters. Hexadecimal representations of Unicode characters can be defined within &#x and ; characters. For example:

```
<!-- The tilde (~) symbol in hexadecimal and decimal form     -->
<!--                             &#x007E          &#126         -->

<!-- The medical Rx symbol in hexadecimal and decimal form    -->
<!--                             &#x211E          &#8478        -->

<!-- The less than (<) symbol in hexadecimal and decimal form -->
<!--                                &#x003C          &#60        -->
```

A user-defined entity is an XML mechanism that associates an identifier with some user-defined data to be expanded. A user-defined entity reference in an XML document can refer to a user-defined entity with the entity identifier incorporated within & and ; characters. The entity reference acts to replace every instance of an entity reference within an XML document with the data associated with the user-defined entity. An entity must be declared within a DTD before it is referenced. We discuss entity declaration in the next section on DTDs.

For example, if we assume that a set of card-name entities, such as VISA, MC, and AMEX, has been defined, our sample charge card may reference one of these entities within a card name as shown here:

```
<order>
             ...
  <charge_card card_type="credit">
    <card_name> &VISA; </card_name>
             ...
  </charge_card>
</order>
```

Processing Instructions

A processing instruction embedded in an XML document can be used by an application to tell it to perform some operation and use some optional data during that operation. A processing instruction is defined within <? and ?> character sequences. Within such a tag, a processing instruction name identifier may be optionally followed by processing instruction parameter data. Processing instruction names should not begin with the reserved word `xml`.

For example, if we assume that our XML order document wants to trigger an external application to validate an order passing in credit-check and check-customer flags, we might have this:

```
<order>
         ...
  <?OrderValidation creditCheck checkCustomer?>
</order>
```

Unparsed Character Data

Because all character data within an XML document is parsed by an XML document parser, a special notation must be used when it is necessary to tell the XML document parser not to parse certain data in the document and pass it directly to an application. Unparsed character data is contained within `<![CDATA[` and `]]>` character sequences.

For example, our charge-card data may want to embed binary data representing a customer signature directly into the document stream as shown here:

```
<order>
         ...
  <charge_card card_type="credit">
         ...
    <card_signature> <![CDATA[0xA72938B72F79C8DE]]> </card_signature>
  </charge_card>
</order>
```

Well-Formed XML Documents

A document that adheres to the syntax of XML per the XML v1.0 specification is said to be "well-formed." The basic syntax of an XML document is defined according to the basic formatting rules presented thus far. If a document is not well-formed, it is not considered to be an XML document. In fact, the examples that have been inserted throughout this section are elements of a well-formed `xmlDocument.xml` on the CD. Thus, a well-formed document is simply a document that is created according to the syntax rules that apply to XML. If the rules of XML syntax are violated, the document is not well-formed.

Thus, the requirements for creating XML documents are more stringent than those for creating HTML documents. While our `xmlDocument.xml` file is an example of a well-formed XML document, the lackadaisical fashion in which HTML documents can be specified will not be permitted for XML documents. For example, this would not be well-formed XML document body syntax, but a web browser will read and parse it as HTML correctly:

```
<HTML>
  <BODY>
    <H1>I'll use proper tags here.</H1>
    <H2>Here I will not.
    <H3>But here I will again.</H3>
<!-- I won't close the BODY and HTML tags either -->
```

We make the analogy here between a Java file and an XML file. If you adhere to the syntax rules of Java, you will be able to successfully compile your code. If not, you will receive a compiler error when you attempt to compile such code and will have to fix the syntax errors in your code for it to be well-formed Java source code. Similarly, you will have to fix a syntax error in your XML file for it to be considered a well-formed XML document.

DTD Declaration

The fact that a document can be defined as a well-formed XML document simply indicates that the document follows the rules of XML syntax. But what about semantics? That is, although the sample order document of the preceding section may be a well-formed XML document, what does the document mean? We could just as easily replace the root element name `order` with the name `customer` and the document would still be a well-formed XML document. But an application that reads such data would certainly want to distinguish between a `customer` and an `order`. After all, a `customer` object may be manipulated by an e-commerce application to maintain customer address information and data for use in delivering an order. An `order` object, on the other hand, may be manipulated to induce the actual order of a set of items and may additionally require that a customer's credit card be associated with the order data.

A Document Type Definition (DTD) is a structured collection of ASCII-based declarations which define the semantic constraints that apply to a particular type of XML document. A DTD is essentially a set of meta-information that defines the required structure and characteristics of an XML document for the document to be considered a valid type of particular XML document. The tags required, relationships among tags, valid attribute values, and named entities are all defined within a DTD. The basic top-level structure of a DTD with its four different types of DTD declarations is shown here:

```
<?xml version = "1.0"?>

<!-- A comment -->

<!-- Begin Root Element DTD below -->
<!DOCTYPE RootElementName SYSTEM "URL" [
  <!--  DTD elements inserted below -->

  <!-- DTD Element Declarations -->
```

```
  <!ELEMENT ... >

  <!-- DTD Attribute Declarations -->
  <!ATTLIST ... >

  <!-- DTD Entity Declarations -->
  <!ENTITY ... >

  <!-- DTD Notation Declarations -->
  <!NOTATION ... >

]>
<!-- End Root Element DTD -->
```

Document Type Definition Header

A DTD, if present, must be declared in the beginning of an XML document after the XML declaration. The root-containing element name for the XML document is used to identify the XML document type for which the DTD defines structure and characteristics. The `<!DOCTYPE` and `>` characters delimit the boundaries of the DTD's definition. A DTD and root element name are thus defined using the following delimiters:

```
<!DOCTYPE RootElementName [...]>
```

A DTD stored at some external URL may also be referenced with a system identifier and utilized by the current DTD using the following general form:

```
<!DOCTYPE RootElementName SYSTEM "SystemURL"[...]>
```

A public identifier may also be used with a system identifier to reference an external DTD. The public identifier may be used by an application to determine the alternative location of the DTD. Otherwise, the application will use the system identifier URL. This is the general form of use for public identifiers with system identifiers:

```
<!DOCTYPE RootElementName PUBLIC "PublicIdentifier" "SystemURL"[...]>
```

Element Declarations

An element declaration within a DTD defines the characteristics of a named element as it should exist within the XML document. Element declarations are defined within `<!ELEMENT` and `>` characters and have one of the following general forms:

- *Empty Content*: The named element is defined to have no content and is therefore an empty element if it has this form:

  ```
  <!ELEMENT ElementName EMPTY>
  ```

- *Any Content*: The named element is defined to have any content, and therefore the DTD allows any content defined for the named element if it has the following form:

  ```
  <!ELEMENT ElementName ANY>
  ```

- *Content Model*: A particular content model is defined to constrain the contents of the named element with an appended question mark (?) designating that the model is optional, an appended asterisk (*) designating that the model may contain zero or more of the model elements, and an appended plus symbol (+) designating that the model may contain one or more of the model elements. The basic format for the content model is this:

  ```
  <!ELEMENT ElementName (exactly_one_content_model)>
                <!-- OR -->
  <!ELEMENT ElementName (optional_content_model)?>
                <!-- OR -->
  <!ELEMENT ElementName (zero_or_more_content_model)*>
                <!-- OR -->
  <!ELEMENT ElementName (one_or_more_content_model)+>
  ```

The content model definition within an element declaration itself has various valid formats and may employ the following format conventions:

- A single element, such as `SubElement`, can be defined to indicate that an element contains one other element:

  ```
  <!ELEMENT ElementName (SubElement)>
  ```

- Commas between named elements indicate that the elements must be contained in the sequence specified:

  ```
  <!ELEMENT ElementName (SubElement1, SubElement2, SubElement3)>
  ```

- A plus symbol (+) can be used to indicate that an element contains one or more elements named `SubElement`:

  ```
  <!ELEMENT ElementName (SubElement+)>
  ```

- An asterisk (*) can be used to indicate that an element contains zero or more elements named `SubElement`:

  ```
  <!ELEMENT ElementName (SubElement*)>
  ```

- A question mark (?) can be used to indicate that an element optionally contains an element named `SubElement`:

  ```
  <!ELEMENT ElementName (SubElement?)>
  ```

- Optional character data within an element that can be parsed is indicated as shown here:

  ```
  <!ELEMENT ElementName (#PCDATA)*>
  ```

- An OR relation symbol (|) can be used to indicate that zero or more elements (as well as possibly parsed character data) can be contained within an enclosing element:

```
<!ELEMENT ElementName (#PCDATA | SubElement1 | SubElement2)*>
```

Notation Declarations

A notation declaration is used to define a specific type of data external to an XML document. A named data type is associated with a data type value. The format for a notation declaration follows this form:

```
<!NOTATION DataTypeName SYSTEM "DataTypeValue">
```

Entity Declarations

An entity declaration is used to associate an entity name with data. Entity declarations are defined within `<!ENTITY` and `>` characters and have the following basic forms:

- *Internal Entity*: A defined entity name can be associated with some data value that is used in an XML document to replace each user-defined entity reference of the form `&EntityName;` with the `EntityDataValue`. The internal entity declaration has the following form:

  ```
  <!ENTITY EntityName "EntityDataValue">
  ```

- *External XML Entity*: A defined entity name can be associated with an XML document defined at some external URL to replace each entity reference of the form `&EntityName;` with the XML document at the URL. The external XML document entity is parsed when read. The external XML entity declaration has this form:

  ```
  <!ENTITY EntityName SYSTEM "URL">
  ```

- *External Binary Entity*: A defined entity name can be associated with a binary block of data defined at some external URL to replace each entity reference of the form `&EntityName;` with the binary data defined at the URL of the data type defined in a data type name. For example, if the data type name has a defined value of GIF87A, a GIF file may be referenced at the URL. The external binary entity is not parsed by the XML parser and may only be referenced in an element's attribute. The external binary entity declaration has this form:

  ```
  <!ENTITY EntityName SYSTEM "URL" NDATA DataTypeName>
  ```

- *Parameter Entity*: A defined DTD entity name can be associated with a value that is used only within a DTD (as opposed to an XML document). The DTD entity name is preceded by a percent sign (%) and is referenced within the DTD using `%DTDEntityName;` to expand the entity to its associated entity data value within the DTD. The parameter entity has the following form:

  ```
  <!ENTITY % DTDEntityName "DTDEntityDataValue">
  ```

Attribute Declarations

Attribute declarations define the characteristics of attributes that are associated with a named element. The attribute name along with an attribute type and default value may all be specified for an attribute. One or more attributes can be characterized within `<!ATTLIST` and `>` characters according to this general form:

```
<!ATTLIST ElementName
  AttributeName1 AttributeType1 DefaultAttributeValue1
  AttributeName2 AttributeType2 DefaultAttributeValue2
                           ...
  AttributeNameN AttributeTypeN DefaultAttributeValueN
  >
```

Each attribute associated with a named element, such as `ElementName`, must be identified by its name, such as `AttributeName1` and `AttributeName2`. The attribute type may be defined according to one of the following general forms:

- *Identifiers*: An `ID` attribute value is an identifier that is unique throughout an XML document. Only one `ID` attribute can exist per element.
- *Identifier References*: An `IDREF` attribute value refers to an `ID` attribute value elsewhere in an XML document. An `IDREFS` attribute value refers to one or more whitespace-separated ID attribute values in the document.
- *Entities*: An `ENTITY` attribute value must be the name of an entity. `ENTITIES` are whitespace-separated `ENTITY` values.
- *Character Data*: A `CDATA` attribute value is a string of text that may be expanded from embedded markup data in the string.
- *Name Tokens*: An `NMTOKEN` attribute value is a single string word with no expanded markup data in the string. `NMTOKENS` are whitespace-separated `NMTOKEN` values.
- *Enumerated Types*: An enumerated type can define the set of valid values that an attribute may assume within parentheses. Value options are separated within the parentheses by an `OR` symbol (|). For example: `(Value1 | Value2 | Value3)`.

Default attribute values are defined according to one of the following general forms:

- *Required Values*: An attribute must have a defined value in the document if the `#REQUIRED` identifier is defined as the default value.
- *Implied Values*: An attribute does not need to have a defined value in the document if the `#IMPLIED` identifier is defined as the default value.
- *Defined Default Values*: An attribute value will have the default value defined between quotation marks, such as `"AttributeValue"`, if a value is not defined in the document.
- *Fixed Values*: An attribute value does not need to be defined but must have the fixed value defined within quotation marks in the expression `#FIXED "AttributeValue"`.

Valid XML Documents

A valid XML document is one that satisfies the rules defined within the DTD. This, of course, presumes that both the XML document and the DTD have a well-formed syntax. Validity may apply to only the declarations defined within the XML document, to both external and internal declarations, or none at all.

DTD Example

In this section, we present a concrete example of a DTD that can be used to validate an XML order document. Note that we will first add a `DOCTYPE` header at the top of our XML order document instance to reference a DTD defined externally at a URL. Here, the URL simply references our `order.dtd` file presumed to be in the current working directory. The `dtdAndXmlDocument.xml` file contains a reference to the external `order.dtd` file and must designate that the XML document no longer stands alone in the XML declaration. The `dtdAndXmlDocument.xml` file is shown in Listing 31.1.

> **NOTE**
>
> The `dtdAndXmlDocument.xml` file on the CD in the `examples\src\ejava\xmlch31` directory contains the sample XML document and referenced DTD associated with a BeeShirts.com order shown here. The `order.dtd` file in the `examples\src\ejava\xmlch31` directory contains the actual order DTD.

LISTING 31.1 XML Order Document with DTD Reference (`dtdAndXmlDocument.xml`)

```
<?xml version="1.0" standalone="no"?>

<!-- DTD of Order Document follows below -->
<!DOCTYPE order SYSTEM "order.dtd">

<!-- Definition of order data follows below -->
  <order>
    <order_id> 123 </order_id>
    <customer_id> 101 </customer_id>
    <order_date> 10/19/99 </order_date>
    <ship_instruct>Leave stuff at back door if no answer</ship_instruct>
    <ship_date> 11/10/99 </ship_date>
    <ship_charge> $3.80 </ship_charge>
    <paid_date> 11/01/99 </paid_date>
    <ship_weight/>
```

continues

LISTING 31.1 Continued

```
    <item>
      <item_id> 1001 </item_id>
      <quantity> 10    </quantity>
      <total_price> $78.99 </total_price>
    </item>
    <charge_card card_type="credit">
      <card_name> &VISA; </card_name>
      <card_number> 12345678901234 </card_number>
      <expired_date> 10/10/2000 </expired_date>
      <card_confirmation_number> 0987654321</card_confirmation_number>
      <card_signature>
         <![CDATA[0xA72938B72F79C8DE]]>
      </card_signature>
    </charge_card>
    <?OrderValidation creditCheck checkCustomer?>
  </order>
```

Listing 31.2 presents our sample `order.dtd` DTD file used to validate an order XML document, such as the one in our `dtdAndXmlDocument.xml` file. Note first that we've defined top-level element content models for an `order`, an `item`, and a `charge_card`. Note that the order element contains both the `item` and the `charge_card` element. The `card_signature` element in our `charge_card` element is optional.

We've also defined entities for `VISA`, `MC`, and `AMEX` credit card strings, as well as a parameter entity for `PD` that is referenced within the `charge_card` element definition. Most entities have parseable data values identified by the `#PCDATA` type. A couple of key things should also be noted about the elements within the order document. The `ship_weight` element within our `order` element optionally has content. Finally, note that our `charge_card` element has a required `card_type` attribute.

LISTING 31.2 XML Order DTD (`order.dtd`)

```
<!-- Define Top-Level Element for order -->
<!ELEMENT order (order_id, customer_id, order_date, ship_instruct,
                ship_date, ship_charge, paid_date, ship_weight, item,
                charge_card )>
<!ELEMENT item (item_id, quantity, total_price)>
<!ELEMENT charge_card (card_name, card_number, expired_date,
                      card_confirmation_number, card_signature?)>

<!-- Define entities -->
<!ENTITY VISA "Visa Credit Card">
```

```
<!ENTITY MC "Master Card Credit Card">
<!ENTITY AMEX "American Express Credit Card">
<!ENTITY % PD "(#PCDATA)">

<!-- Define Elements for order -->
<!ELEMENT order_id (#PCDATA)>
<!ELEMENT customer_id (#PCDATA)>
<!ELEMENT order_date (#PCDATA)>
<!ELEMENT ship_instruct (#PCDATA)>
<!ELEMENT ship_date (#PCDATA)>
<!ELEMENT ship_charge (#PCDATA)>
<!ELEMENT paid_date (#PCDATA)>
<!ELEMENT ship_weight (#PCDATA)*>

<!-- Define Elements for Item -->
<!ELEMENT item_id (#PCDATA)>
<!ELEMENT quantity (#PCDATA)>
<!ELEMENT total_price (#PCDATA)>

<!-- Define elements for charge card and use PD entity -->
<!ELEMENT card_type %PD;>
<!ELEMENT card_name %PD;>
<!ELEMENT card_number %PD;>
<!ELEMENT expired_date %PD;>
<!ELEMENT card_confirmation_number %PD;>
<!ELEMENT card_signature %PD;>

<!-- define attributes for charge_card -->
<!ATTLIST charge_card card_type CDATA  #REQUIRED>
```

Hyperlinking in XML

Hyperlinking in XML involves the association of URLs to resources (for example, images and XML documents), as well as defining the relationship between resources. Linking specifications in XML was once referred to as the eXtensible Linking Language (XLL) and is now divided into two separate specifications: XLink and XPointer. The XML Linking Language (XLink) defines how resources are referenced from within XML documents and is embodied within an evolving W3C specification (`http://www.w3.org/TR/xlink/`). The XML Pointer Language (XPointer) defines a mechanism for addressing different portions of an XML document and is also embodied within an evolving W3C specification (`http://www.w3.org/TR/xptr`).

CAUTION

Both the XLink and the XPointer specifications are currently evolving and subject to much change. Although a detailed discussion of XML linking is beyond the scope of this book, we at least want to give you an idea of the nature of XLinks and XPointers. You will certainly run across such terminology in the course of understanding how to use XML in an enterprise environment, and you may even run across concrete examples of their usage. We should note that at the time of this book's writing, support for XLink and XPointer was very limited. In particular, XPointer support was virtually non-existent due to its complexity and certainty for change.

XLinks

Central to the topic of linking in XML is the concept of a resource. A resource is an addressable piece of information such as the type of information addressed by a URL (for example, files, images, and applications). A link is a relationship between resources. A local resource is a resource embedded inside of an XML link element. A remote resource is the actual resource information pointed to by an XML link.

Linking elements are XML elements that include links. A linking element defines a link as an attribute using the `xlink:type` attribute name. XLink defines several standard `xlink:type` attribute values:

- `simple`: Defines an association between a local resource and a remote resource.
- `extended`: Defines associations among multiple resources.
- `locator`: Defines addresses to remote resources. An extended link must have at least one `locator` element type defined.
- `arc`: Defines rules for traversing between the links contained by an extended link element.
- `title`: Defines a human-readable description of an extended link.
- `resource`: Defines the local resources for an extended link. If an extended link defines a `resource` element type, it is called an inline link.

Simple Links

A simple link associates a local resource with a remote resource. Simple link information is embedded inside of an XML element akin to the way an attribute is embedded inside of an element. The form of the link (that is, `"simple"`) and URL reference are both embedded into the XML element. This is the general form of a simple link:

```
<ElementName xlink:type="simple" xlink:href="URL"> ...</ElementName>
                    <!-- OR -->
<ElementName xlink:type="simple" xlink:href="URL"/> <!-- Empty -->
```

The `xlink:type` attribute of an element is thus defined as `"simple"` and the URL of the resource is defined after an `xlink:href` attribute. For example:

```
<homepage xlink:type="simple" xlink:href="http://www.beeshirts.com/">
  BeeShirts Home
</homepage>

<beeShirtsLogo xlink:form="simple" xlink:href="images/beeshirts.gif"/>
```

Simple links thus have a familiar HTML flavor. A simple link can be associated with XML element data such that, when it's viewed by an application such as a Web browser, clicking on the link can induce a reference to the remote resource. Likewise, a simple link to a remote resource, such as an image, may be used by an application to display the resource directly within (that is, `"inline"`) the viewed XML document page.

Link Semantics and Behavior Attributes

In addition to defining a link attribute and its associated URL, the title and role of a remote resource may optionally be described as attributes. The `xlink:title` attribute describes the remote resource's title in a human-readable fashion. The `xlink:role` attribute describes the purpose of the remote resource in a fashion useful to an application.

The behavior of a link may also optionally be defined as an attribute inside the element. An `xlink:show` attribute is used to describe how an endpoint resource is to be displayed when referenced. If the `xlink:show="new"` value is specified, a new window will be created to display the remote resource. If the `xlink:show="replace"` value is specified, the window used to load the current link is used to display the remote resource. If the `xlink:show="embed"` value is specified, the window used to load the current link is used to display the remote resource inline.

An `xlink:actuate` attribute is used to describe the latency between parsing of a link and the actual reference of the remote resource. If the `xlink:actuate="onLoad"` value is specified, the application should immediately load the remote resource upon loading of the link. If the `xlink:actuate="onRequest"` value is specified, the application should load the remote resource upon activation of the link (for example, a click on the link).

Extended Links

Simple links have a single association between a local resource and a remote resource. Extended links are more generic links that can associate multiple resources with one another. If one of the links is local, the extended link is said to be inline. If all the links are remote, the extended link is said to be "out-of-line."

An extended link is identified within an XML element using the "extended" value for an xlink:type attribute. A local resource is embedded inside of an extended link as an element whose xlink:type attribute value is equal to "resource". A remote resource that exists outside of an extended link (perhaps in another XML document) is represented as an extended link element's sub-element with an xlink:type attribute value of "locator". Such locator-type elements can identify a remote resource URL as an xlink:href attribute, as well as include the other standard attributes used with links, including link semantic and behavior attributes.

For example, a sweaters XML document that defines a local resource sweater advertisement may be associated with three different remote resources that target a particular sweater-style homepage URL. An application may use xlink:role attributes to determine which target remote resource to reference depending on some particular customer preference criteria. Customer profile data may indicate a preference for "classic" or "sporty" styles of sweaters, and the application will select a suitable target remote reference based on this knowledge. An XML document supporting such extended link functionality might look like this:

```
<sweaters xlink:type="extended" xlink:title="BeeShirts.com Sweaters">
  <sweaterAd xlink:type="resource" xlink:role="sweaters">
    BeeShirts.com has sweater styles to suit you
  </sweaterAd>
  <default
    xlink:type="locator"
    xlink:href="http://www.beeshirts.com/sweaters/standard/"
    xlink:role="standard"/>
  <option
    xlink:type="locator"
    xlink:href="http://www.beeshirts.com/sweaters/classic/"
    xlink:title="Classic Sweater Style"
    xlink:role="classic"/>
  <option
    xlink:type="locator"
    xlink:href="http://www.beeshirts.com/sweaters/sports/"
    xlink:title="Sporty Sweater Style"
    xlink:role="sports"/>
</sweaters>
```

Extended links have many traversal possibilities among the resources it identifies. The xlink:type attribute with a value of "arc" can be defined within a sub-element of an extended link element to identify a particular traversal rule. Link traversal behavior for an arc-type element can be defined with the link behavior xlink:show and xlink:actuate attributes. Arcs also define xlink:from and xlink:to attributes to identify the "from" resource and "to" resource directionality of link traversal. The values of xlink:from and xlink:to attributes are the values that have been assigned to a defined resource's `xlink:role` attribute. For example, we might define a set of arcs identifying the traversal from a local resource selection to a particular remote resource selection inside of our `sweaters` XML document such as the one shown here:

```
<sweaters xlink:type="extended" xlink:title="BeeShirts.com Sweaters">
     ...
  <selection
    xlink:type="arc"
    xlink:from="sweaters"  xlink:to="classic"
    xlink:show="replace" xlink:actuate="onRequest"/>
</sweaters>
```

XPointers

Extended pointers (XPointers) define a means for identifying and addressing sections of an XML document. HTML defines a means for tagging portions of a document and then referencing those internal relative links within a URL by using the convention evident in `http://www.beeshirts.com/myPage.html#myRelativeLink`. XPointers provide a means to reference XML documents in a much more resolute and flexible form. XPointers also provide a way to reference ranges of XML document data.

A particular element with an `ID` attribute type can be referenced using an XPointer syntax of `xpointer(id("`*`MyElementID`*`"))` or simply using *`MyElementID`*. For example, an element named `order` with an `ID` attribute of `jshmoe4867` can be referenced as

```
http://www.beeshirts.com/orders/BoaShirts.xml#jshmoe4867
```

or as

```
http://www.beeshirts.com/orders/BoaShirts.xml#xpointer(id("jshmoe4867"))
```

Nested sub-elements may also be referenced in various ways. For example, the 16th child element of the 3rd child element may be discovered using this:

```
http://www.beeshirts.com/orders/BoaShirts.xml#/3/16
```

XML Style Sheets

The eXtensible Stylesheet Language (XSL) is used to describe how particular XML documents can be transformed into other XML documents, as well as to describe how XML documents should be formatted. XSL is managed by a separate working group within the W3C. The XSL Transformations (XSLT) portion of the XSL specification defines how XML documents can be mapped into other XML documents and other document formats (for example, HTML, PDF, and text). The XSL formatting portion of the XSL specification defines how XML documents can be formatted and laid out within an XML document presentation interface.

CAUTION

The XSL specification is currently evolving and subject to much change. Although XSL is beyond the scope of this book, we at least want to give you an idea of the nature of XSL transformations and XSL formatting. You will certainly run across XSL terminology in the course of understanding how to use XML in an enterprise environment.

XSL formatting is defined using a collection of XSL formatting objects and properties. Formatting objects tell an application that can understand XSL formatting notation where to place XML document portions in a cohesive XML-based page. Formatting objects and properties are standard names for elements and attributes of elements that can be read by a formatting application. You can recognize XSL formatting object notation in a document if you see any elements that begin with the `fo:` namespace prefix.

XSL transformations define a set of rules to apply when transforming an XML document into another format or type of XML document. XSLT borrows heavily from concepts of style sheets used in HTML documents. Style sheets, such as Cascading Style Sheets (CSS), are a collection of rules attached to HTML documents that affect how its fonts, borders, backgrounds, and other style properties are displayed within a Web browser.

Similarly, an application capable of reading XML and XSL reads an XML document and an XSL style sheet and then produces a new XML document based on the instructions present within the XSL style sheet. XSL applications parse the source XML document into a hierarchical tree-based description of the document and build another tree-based description of the target document. XSL applications can also be specialized to produce non-XML documents such as HTML and plain-text documents.

XSL style sheets are described in the form of XML documents themselves. XSL style sheets contain templates that describe what pattern of a tree-based XML document representation to search for in a source document. When a pattern is matched, the XSL style sheet contains an associated output template pattern to apply in generating the target document. The template output usually describes new XML syntax and data to generate.

The XSL style sheet root XML element has a name of `xsl:stylesheet` and a version attribute defined using an `xmlns:xsl` attribute. Template rules within an XSL style sheet document are elements with an attribute type of `xsl:template`. An `xsl:match` attribute inside of the `xsl:template`-type element defines which elements of an XML document need to be matched. Instructions for processing a particular matched template are described as sub-elements of the `xsl:template`-type element with names that begin with the prefix `xsl:`. All other contents of an `xsl:template`-type element are the XML syntax and data that is output to the target XML document stream. Therefore, an XSL style sheet document may follow this basic form:

```
<?xml version="1.0"?>
<xsl:stylesheet xmlns:xsl="http://www.w3.org/1999/XSL/Transform">

  <xsl:template match="elementName">
    <!-- Action for element named elementName -->
      <!-- Select sub-elements named myElement -->
      <xsl:apply-template select="myElement"/>
      <!-- Insert output style in here -->
  </xsl:template>

</xsl:stylesheet>
```

A source XML document designates a particular XSL style sheet to use in transforming itself via a processing instruction declaration that resembles its XML declaration and is of the following form:

```
<?xml version="1.0"?>
<?xml-stylesheet type="text/xml" href="XSLdocumentName.xsl"?>
<!-- Rest of XML document description below -->
           ...
```

Simple API for XML

The Simple API for XML (SAX) is used for parsing XML documents via a programmatic interface implemented using a standard set of parse event listeners. SAX is an API standard that was developed by a community of individuals participating in a XML-DEV mailing list group. The standard interfaces to SAX are defined in an `org.xml.sax` Java package. The Java API for XML Parsing (JAXP) is a standard Java extension from JavaSoft (`http://java.sun.com/xml/`) that provides a reference implementation of these standard interfaces. JAXP also defines a few non-SAX-standard abstractions in a `javax.xml.parsers` package used as a SAX parser instance factory and SAX parser helper class. Additionally, another collection of three simple helper classes that are rarely used have been defined in an `org.xml.sax.helpers` package.

NOTE

Throughout the architecture description and sample code in this section, we assume use of the JAXP v1.0 implementation. At the time of this writing, the J2EE reference implementation came equipped with the SAX standard abstractions from the JAXP but did not come equipped with the abstractions contained in the `javax.xml.parsers` package. Future versions of the J2EE are expected to require incorporation of a fully implemented JAXP specification. Refer to Appendix A, "Software Configuration," to determine how to obtain the appropriate JAXP implementation for use with our examples.

continues

The sample code found in this section can be found on the CD in the `examples/src/ejava/xmlch31` directory. We also include a simple `runsax.bat` script example on the CD to demonstrate how to compile and execute the code presented in this section. An `XMLLIB_HOME` environment variable is assumed to reference the root directory of your JAXP library installation. Note that the `runsax.bat` script uses the `dtdAndXmlDocument.xml` file on the CD. However, you must ensure that the `dtdAndXmlDocument.xml` file properly references the `order.dtd` in the `DOCTYPE` declaration as described in the `dtdAndXmlDocument.xml` file comment and shown here:

```
<!--
    For rundom..bat, DOCTYPE line should be...
       <!DOCTYPE order SYSTEM "file:order.dtd">

    For runsax.bat, DOCTYPE line should be...
       <!DOCTYPE order SYSTEM "order.dtd">
-->

<!-- DTD of Order Document follows below -->
<!DOCTYPE order SYSTEM "order.dtd">
```

SAX Architecture

Figure 31.2 depicts the top-level architecture of Java-based SAX classes and interfaces (excluding exceptions). Most classes and interfaces come from the standard `org.xml.sax` package. Two additional classes defined in the `javax.xml.parsers` package are also utilized to define a provider-independent means for creating parser handles as well as a non–SAX-standard parser helper class. A `Parser` interface defines a standard interface to a SAX parser for initiating the parsing of XML documents. The SAX `Parser` interface can notify parse event-handler objects during the parsing of XML documents and the generation of parse events. Standard SAX abstractions also exist for an XML document content input source, XML element attribute list, and XML document event location information.

Core SAX Objects

Before we delve into the primary application interfaces, let's look at a few of the core and most basic SAX standard objects. Figure 31.3 depicts these key elements. The most basic elements can be partitioned into exception-related classes, a document event location helper, a document element attribute list, and a document content input source abstraction.

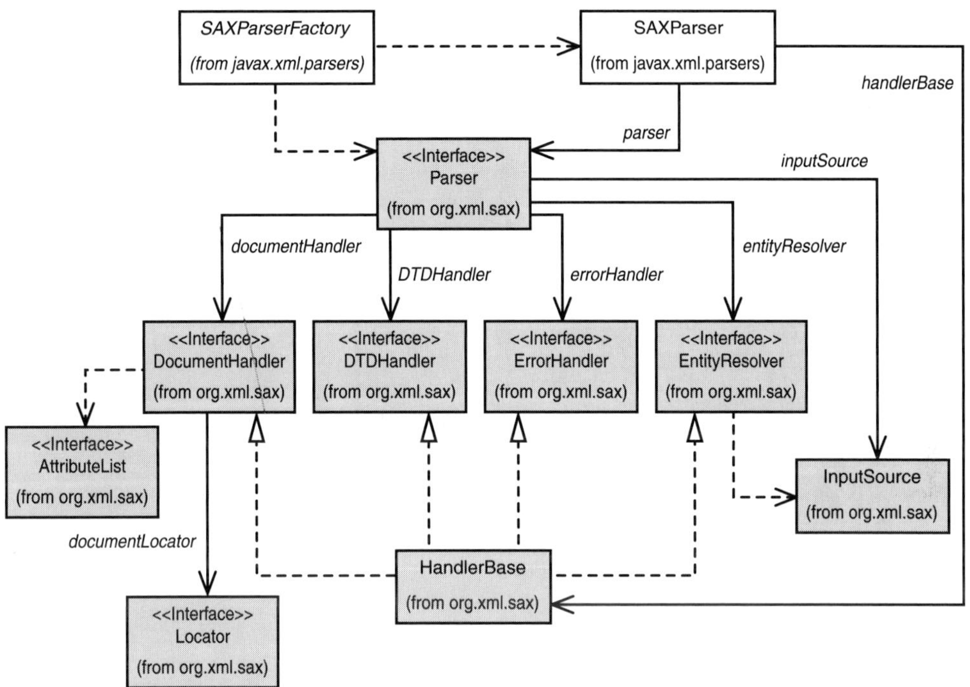

FIGURE 31.2
The SAX class architecture.

The `Locator` interface represents the location of some event in an XML document. Information about the location of an event in a document can be obtained from a `Locator`, including a public identifier of the element, a system identifier (for example, URL), and the line and column numbers in the document.

Two exception classes are used to encapsulate errors occurring during processing of XML documents. The `SAXException` class encapsulates a generic SAX error condition containing a nested root exception. The `SAXParseException` class encapsulates a generic error during parsing of an XML document. Information about the location of the error can also be obtained from a `SAXParseException` using the same type of information that is obtained from a `Locator` object.

The `AttributeList` interface is implemented by a parser provider and describes an interface to an XML element's list of attributes. The `AttributeList.getLength()` method returns the number of attributes contained by the list. Although the order of attributes in an `AttributeList` is arbitrary, the `String` version of names, types, and values of attributes may be retrieved by an index number using the `getName(int)`, `getType(int)`, and `getValue(int)` methods, respectively. The type and value of a named attribute may also be retrieved using the `getType(String)` and `getValue(String)` methods, respectively.

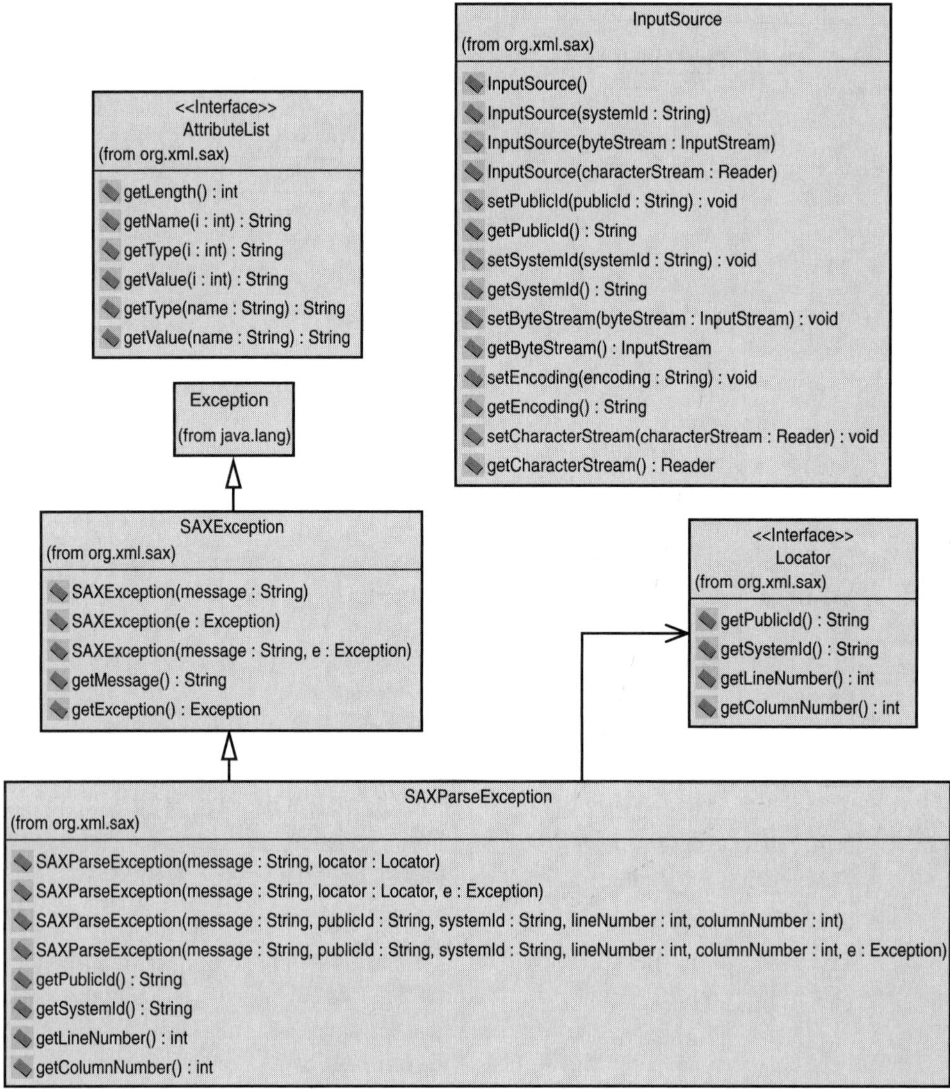

FIGURE 31.3
Core SAX objects.

The `InputSource` class encapsulates a source of XML document data input. Public identifiers, system identifiers, a byte stream, a character stream, and encoding all have associated setters and getters on the `InputSource` class. Public and system identifiers of an input source are optional and have semantics that are specific to an application. A character stream representation of the XML content takes preference over use of a byte-stream representation if both are specified. The system identifier is used as a URI in creating an input stream connection if neither a character stream nor a byte stream is specified. Finally, the encoding format of an input stream can also be specified.

SAX Application Handler Interfaces

Figure 31.4 represents the abstractions used by applications to receive notification of XML document parsing events from a SAX XML document parser. The four interfaces shown represent interfaces that are implemented by applications to receive such events. Object implementations of these interfaces are registered with an XML parser. A default implementation of these interfaces is defined within a `HandlerBase` class.

The `DTDHandler` is implemented by application classes that handle events related to DTD processing. Specifically, events related to notation and unparsed entity declarations can be received, and the associated information can be stored for later reference when parsing an associated XML document. The `DTDHandler.notationDecl()` method is implemented to receive notification of the declaration of a notation in a parsed DTD. An application uses this information for later reference and includes the name of the notation, an optional public identifier for the notation, and an optional system identifier (for example, URL). The `DTDHandler.unparsedEntityDecl()` method can be implemented to receive notification of a declaration of an unparsed entity in the DTD. The unparsed entity's name, optional public identifier, optional system identifier, and associated notation name may be passed into this method. Listing 31.3 shows a sample `DTDHandler` implementation via a `SampleDTDHandler` class that simply prints information when its implemented methods are called.

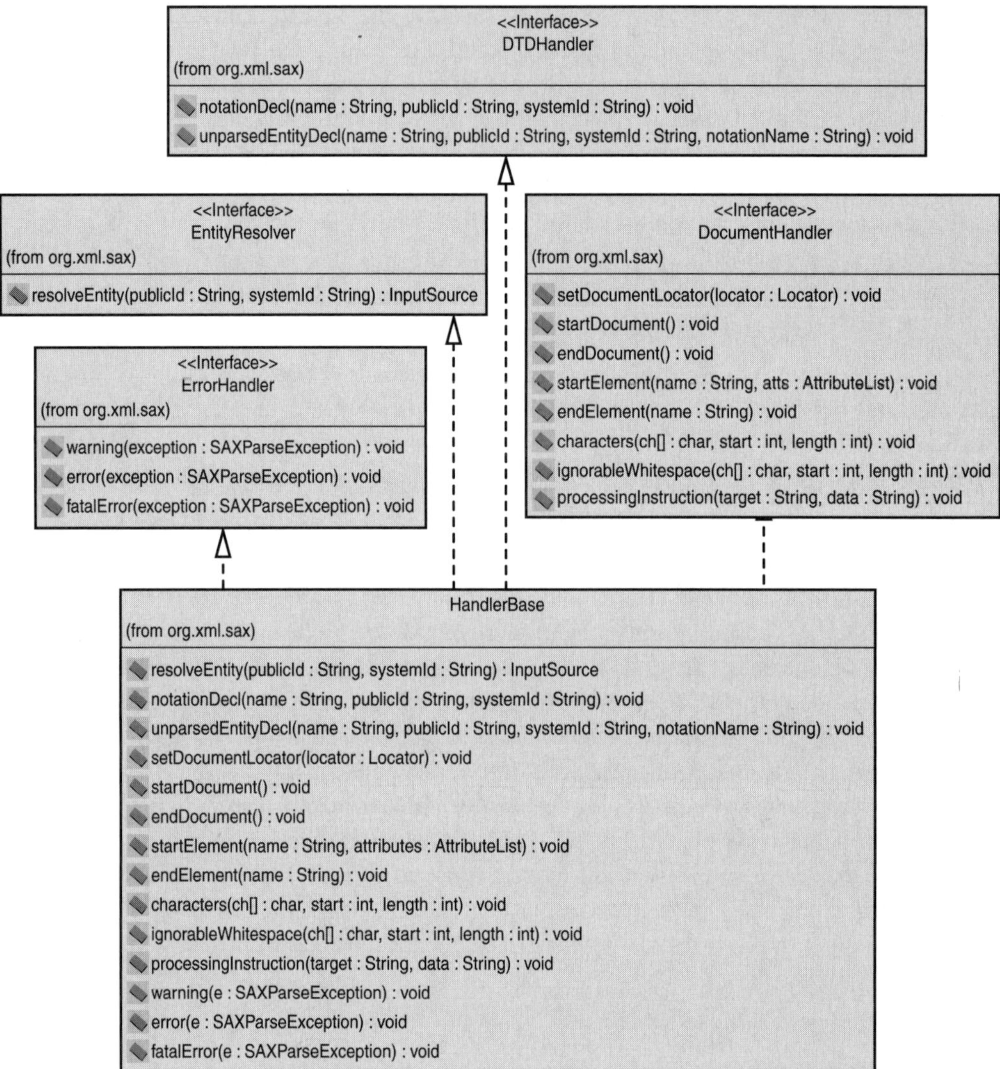

FIGURE 31.4
SAX application handlers.

LISTING 31.3 DTD Handler (`SampleDTDHandler.java`)

```
package ejava.xmlch31;
import org.xml.sax.DTDHandler;
import org.xml.sax.SAXException;

/**
  * implements DTDHandler to receive DTD events from parser
  */
public class SampleDTDHandler implements DTDHandler
{

  /**
  * receive information about DTD entity information.
  */
  public void notationDecl(String name, String publicID,
    String systemID)
    throws SAXException
  {
    System.out.println(" Notation Name :" +name +
      " publicID :" +publicID + "System ID :  " +systemID);
  }

  /**
  * receive information about a DTD unparsed entity
  */
  public void unparsedEntityDecl(String name, String publicID,
    String systemID, String notationName)
    throws SAXException
  {
    System.out.println(" Entity :" + name +" public ID :" + publicID +
      "System ID :" +systemID + "Notation Name :" + notationName);
  }
}
```

The `EntityResolver` interface is implemented by application classes that resolve external entities. The single `EntityResolver.resolveEntity()` method is implemented to receive a public identifier and system identifier of the external entity being referenced. The application creates and returns an `InputSource` object associated with the external XML content. If a `null` value is returned, it is assumed that the system identifier URL form can be used to identify the external entity location. A parser calls this method before it attempts to open an external entity. Listing 31.4 shows a sample `EntityResolver` implementation via a `SampleEntityResolver` class that simply prints information when its implemented methods are called.

LISTING 31.4 Entity Resolver (`SampleEntityResolver.java`)

```
package ejava.xmlch31;
import org.xml.sax.EntityResolver;
import org.xml.sax.SAXException;
import org.xml.sax.InputSource;
import java.io.IOException;
import java.net.URL;
import java.io.InputStream;
import org.xml.sax.SAXParseException;

/**
  * Implements EntityResolver. If it sees a specific
  * systemID, it creates a different InputSource to
  * read data.
  */

public class SampleEntityResolver  implements EntityResolver
{

  /**
  * to resolve each entity, resolveEntity is called by parser
  */
  public InputSource resolveEntity(String publicID,
                                  String systemID)
    throws SAXException, IOException
  {
    System.out.println("Public ID :" + publicID);
    System.out.println("System ID :" + systemID);

    String urlString =
      "http://www.beeshirts.com/
➥examples/src/ejava/xmlch31/XMLDocument.xml";

    if (systemID.equals(urlString)) {
       // return input source
       URL url = new URL(urlString);
       InputStream inputStream = url.openStream();
       return new InputSource(inputStream);
     } else {
       // return null and require default systemID
       return null;
     }
  }
}
```

The `ErrorHandler` interface is implemented by applications that need to handle warnings, errors, and fatal errors that can occur during XML parsing. A parser passes a `SAXParseException` during a call to an appropriate `ErrorHandler` method, and the application decides how to handle the exception. The application may also throw a `SAXException` when one of these methods is called. Listing 31.5 shows a sample `ErrorHandler` implementation via a `SampleErrorHandler` class that simply prints information when its implemented methods are called.

LISTING 31.5 Error Handler (`SampleErrorHandler.java`)

```
package ejava.xmlch31;
import org.xml.sax.ErrorHandler;
import org.xml.sax.SAXException;
import org.xml.sax.SAXParseException;

/**
  * implements Error Handler
  */

public class SampleErrorHandler implements ErrorHandler
{

  /**
  * it receives the errors of type recoverable Errors
  */
  public void error(SAXParseException saxParseException)
    throws SAXException
  {
    printException(saxParseException);
  }

  /**
  * to receive the Fatal or non recoverable Error
  */
  public void fatalError(SAXParseException saxParseException)
    throws SAXException
  {
    printException(saxParseException);
  }

  /**
  * To receive warnings from the parser
  */
  public void warning(SAXParseException saxParseException)
```

continues

LISTING 31.5 Continued

```
    throws SAXException
  {
    printException(saxParseException);
  }

  private void printException(SAXParseException saxParseException)
  {
    System.out.println(saxParseException);
    System.out.println("Column # :"
                       + saxParseException.getColumnNumber());
    System.out.println("Line # : " + saxParseException.getLineNumber());
    System.out.println("System ID :"+ saxParseException.getSystemId());
    System.out.println("Public ID :"+saxParseException.getPublicId());
  }
}
```

The `DocumentHandler` interface is the primary interface implemented by applications that need to handle most XML document parsing–related events. The `DocumentHandler.startDocument()` method is called when parsing of an XML document begins, and `DocumentHandler.endDocument()` is called when parsing ends. When the parser encounters the start tag of an XML document element, the `DocumentHandler.startElement()` method is called. The element name and element's attribute contents will be passed as parameters to the `startElement()` method. Any `IMPLIED` attribute values will be omitted from the `AttributeList` object passed into `startElement()`. For each `startElement()` method call, a `DocumentHandler.endElement()` method will be called with an element name indicating that the end of the element was parsed. The `endElement()` method is also called for empty elements. The `DocumentHandler.setLocator()` method can be used by an application to obtain a `Locator` object from a parser such that the location of events in an XML document, within the scope of element boundaries, can be inferred.

The `DocumentHandler.characters()` method is called by a parser to notify an application of an array of characters that have been retrieved from an XML document element's character data. The `DocumentHandler.ignorableWhitespace()` method is used to report whitespace characters read from an XML document element. Any processing instructions embedded in an XML document can be received by an application using the `DocumentHandler.processingInstruction()` method. The processing instruction name and associated parameter data are passed as parameters to the `processingInstruction()` method. Listing 31.6 shows a sample `DocumentHandler` implementation via a `SampleDocumentHandler` class that simply prints information when its implemented methods are called.

LISTING 31.6 Document Handler (SampleDocumentHandler.java)

```
package ejava.xmlch31;
import org.xml.sax.DocumentHandler;
import org.xml.sax.SAXException;
import org.xml.sax.Locator;
import org.xml.sax.AttributeList;
import org.xml.sax.Parser;
import org.xml.sax.SAXParseException;
import java.io.File;

/**
  * An example document handler
  */
public class SampleDocumentHandler  implements DocumentHandler
{

/**
  * to receive the character data for each element
  */
  public void characters(char[] value, int start, int length)
      throws SAXException
  {
    String newValue = new String(value);
    System.out.println(" Present Char Chunk :" +
      newValue.substring(start,start+length) );
  }

  /**
  * to receive information about end of the document
  */
  public void endDocument()
    throws SAXException
  {
    System.out.println("End of Document ");
  }

/**
  * to receive information about end of an element in the document
  */
  public void endElement(String elementName)
    throws SAXException
  {
    System.out.println(" End of  Element :"+elementName) ;
```

continues

LISTING 31.6 Continued

```
  }

/**
  * Receive notification of ignorable whitespace in element content.
  */
  public void ignorableWhitespace(char[] value, int start , int length)
    throws SAXException
  {
    String newValue = new String(value);
    if(length > 0){
        System.out.println(" ignorable Value is :"
                             + newValue.substring(start,start+length-1) );
    }
  }

/**
  * The Parser will invoke this method once for each processing
  * instruction found
  */
  public void processingInstruction(String target, String data)
    throws SAXException
  {
    System.out.println("Processing Instruction Target :"+target);
    System.out.println("Processing Instruction data :"+data);
  }

  /**
  * To get information about the document Locator
  */
  public void setDocumentLocator(Locator locator)
  {
    System.out.println("Column , Current Event  Ends  :"+
      locator.getColumnNumber());
    System.out.println("Line , Doc Event Ends :" +locator.getLineNumber());
    System.out.println(" public ID for current Event :"
                        +locator.getPublicId());
    System.out.println("Public System ID :" +locator.getSystemId());
  }

/**
  *  To receive the information about starting of document
  */
  public void startDocument()
    throws SAXException
```

```
  {
    System.out.println(" The parser started parsing document :");
  }

/**
  * Info about started parse of new element
  */
  public void startElement(String elementName ,
    AttributeList attributeList)
    throws SAXException
  {
    System.out.println(" Element :"+elementName +" Started ");
    int totalAttributes = attributeList.getLength();
    for(int i = 0; i < totalAttributes; i++){
      String name = attributeList.getName(i);
      String type = attributeList.getType(i);
      String value = attributeList.getValue(i);
      System.out.println("Attribute Name :" + name +
        " Type : "+ type +" Value :" +value);
    }
  }
}
```

As a final note, the `HandlerBase` class provides a default implementation for all four of the XML document event handler interfaces. Applications extend this class when they want to override this default behavior.

SAX Parser Interfaces

Figure 31.5 depicts the detail for those interfaces implemented by SAX parser providers. A parser factory is used to create parser instances, and two parser abstractions can be used for interfacing with a SAX parser. The `Parser` interface is the SAX-standard parser interface. The `SAXParser` class is a JAXP wrapper to a standard SAX parser interface. Both parser abstractions can be used to initiate the parsing of an XML document content stream.

The `Parser` interface is implemented by SAX parser providers. Applications register `DocumentHandler`, `DTDHandler`, `EntityResolver`, and `ErrorHandler` objects with the `Parser` object's appropriately named setter methods. The `Parser.parse()` methods are called to ask the `Parser` to begin parsing an XML document either from an `InputSource` or from a URL `String`, depending on the version of the `parse()` method that is called. The `Parser.locale()` method is called to use a particular `java.util.Locale` (see Chapter 4, "Java Foundations for Enterprise Development") object when errors and warnings are reported.

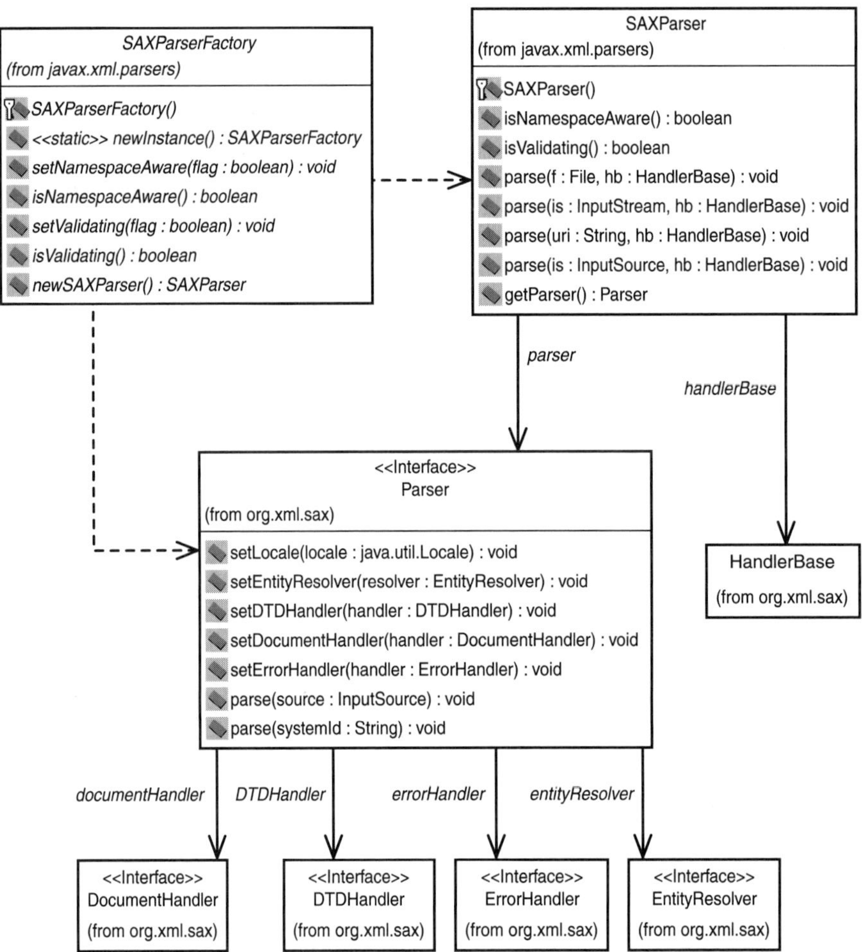

FIGURE 31.5
SAX parser interfaces.

The `SAXParser` class is a helper class that wraps a regular `Parser` object and provides a set of methods that implement a more convenient way of initiating the parsing of an XML document. Aside from methods for determining XML namespace awareness and DTD validation capability, the `SAXParser` also defines various methods that help initiate the parsing of a document. The `SAXParser.parse()` methods all take a `HandlerBase` object as an argument along with a reference to an XML document content stream in the form of a `File` reference, an `InputStream`, an `InputSource`, or a URL `String` location. The `SaxParser.getParser()` method can be used to obtain a reference to the underlying standard `Parser` interface object.

The SAXParserFactory abstract class can be used to configure and create Parser objects. A SAX parser provider supplies a concrete implementation of the SAXParserFactory class, and the definition of this class is defined via the javax.xml.parsers.SAXParserFactory system property. The static SAXParserFactory.newInstance() method is used to return an instance of this concrete factory implementation. DTD validation capability and XML namespace awareness of parsers can all also be set and checked using appropriately named methods on a SAXParserFactory object instance. Finally, new instances of SAXParser objects can be created by calling the newSAXParser() method.

Listing 31.7 presents a SAX sample driver class to tie together a complete sample usage of SAX. The SaxExample class takes an XML document filename from the command line via a main() method and induces the parsing of this document. A SaxParserFactory is first created and then used to create a validating SAXParser object. The SAXParser object is then used to obtain a handle to the standard Parser object. The handlers of Listings 31.3 through 31.6 are then set onto the Parser. Lastly, the Parser is told to parse the XML document.

LISTING 31.7 SAX example (SaxExample.java).

```
package ejava.xmlch31;
import javax.xml.parsers.SAXParserFactory;
import javax.xml.parsers.SAXParser;
import org.xml.sax.SAXException;
import org.xml.sax.Locator;
import org.xml.sax.AttributeList;
import org.xml.sax.Parser;
import org.xml.sax.SAXParseException;
import java.io.File;

/**
  * An example to induce the parsing of an XML document
  */
public class SaxExample
{
  public static void main(String[] argv)
  {
    if(argv.length  != 1){
      System.out.println(" Usage : "+
        "java ejava.xmlch31.SaxExample <xmlfile> ");
      System.exit(0);
    }
```

continues

LISTING 31.7 Continued

```
    try {
        String xmlFileURI = "file:" +
               new File (argv [0]).getAbsolutePath ();
      // Get Parser Factory
      SAXParserFactory saxParserFactory =
        SAXParserFactory.newInstance ();
      // set Document Validation true
      saxParserFactory.setValidating (true);
      // get SAX parser from Factory
      SAXParser saxParser = saxParserFactory.newSAXParser();
      // get a Parser from Factory
      Parser  parser = saxParser.getParser();

      // set Document Handler to receive document Handler Events
      parser.setDocumentHandler (new SampleDocumentHandler());
      // set DTD Handler to receive DTD events from Parser
      parser.setDTDHandler(new SampleDTDHandler());
      // set EntityResolver to receive EntityResolver Events.
      parser.setEntityResolver(new SampleEntityResolver());
      // set ErrorHandler to receive Errors and warnings.
      parser.setErrorHandler(new SampleErrorHandler());
      // parse document
      parser.parse (xmlFileURI);
    }
    catch (SAXParseException saxParseException) {
      System.out.println (" Parsing error"
            + ", at line " + saxParseException.getLineNumber ()
            + ", in file  " + saxParseException.getSystemId ());
        System.out.println("    " + saxParseException.getMessage ());
      saxParseException.printStackTrace();
    }
    catch (SAXException saxException) {
        saxException.printStackTrace ();
    }
    catch (Throwable throwable) {
        throwable.printStackTrace ();
    }
  }
}
```

NOTE

Note that the older version of JAXP equipped with the J2EE reference implementation did not include the `javax.xml.parsers.SAXParserFactory` or `javax.xml.parsers.SAXParser` classes. Rather, an `org.xml.sax.helpers.ParserFactory` class is used to create a reference to a new standard SAX `Parser` object. For example, when using the J2EE reference implementation, in our Listing 31.7 example we would replace the lines that retrieve a `SAXParser` object from the `SAXParserFactory` and then a `Parser` from the `SAXParser` with a call to

```
Parser parser = ParserFactory.makeParser();
```

Document Object Model

The Document Object Model (DOM) was developed by the W3C to provide a standard set of language-independent interfaces to manipulate XML and HTML documents. We are mainly interested in the DOM Level 1 specification (`http://www.w3.org/TR/REC-DOM-Level-1/`) in terms of the definitions it provides for a set of basic interfaces to manipulate XML documents. These interfaces are defined using the OMG CORBA IDL notation. A Java binding for such interfaces is also presented in the specification and is the style of interface that we focus on in this section. A DOM Level 2 specification (`http://www.w3.org/TR/DOM-Level-2/`) is also under development to define mechanisms for the dynamic access and modification of XML document content, structure, and style.

The standard Java-binding interfaces to DOM map to an `org.w3c.dom` Java package. The JAXP from JavaSoft provides a reference implementation of the DOM Level 1 interfaces. Additionally, JAXP also defines a few non-DOM-standard abstractions in a `javax.xml.parsers` package used as a DOM parser instance factory and DOM parser class.

NOTE

Throughout the architecture description and sample code in this section, we assume use of the JAXP v1.0 implementation. At the time of this writing, the J2EE reference implementation came equipped with the DOM standard abstractions from the JAXP, but it did not come equipped with the abstractions contained in the `javax.xml.parsers` package. Future versions of the J2EE are expected to require incorporation of a fully implemented JAXP specification. Refer to Appendix A of this book to determine how to obtain the appropriate JAXP implementation.

continues

The code snippets strewn throughout this section can be found in the DOMExample.java file on the CD in the examples/src/ejava/xmlch31 directory. We also include a simple rundom.bat script example on the CD to demonstrate how to compile and execute the code presented in this section. An XMLLIB_HOME environment variable is assumed to reference the root directory of your JAXP library installation. Note that the rundom.bat script uses the dtdAndXmlDocument.xml file on the CD. However, you must ensure that the dtdAndXmlDocument.xml file properly references the order.dtd in the DOCTYPE declaration as described in the dtdAndXmlDocument.xml file comment and shown here:

```
<!--
    For rundom..bat, DOCTYPE line should be...
       <!DOCTYPE order SYSTEM "file:order.dtd">

    For runsax.bat, DOCTYPE line should be...
       <!DOCTYPE order SYSTEM "order.dtd">
-->

<!-- DTD of Order Document follows below -->
<!DOCTYPE order SYSTEM "file:order.dtd">
```

Figure 31.6 shows how DOM views the parsing of XML documents. A DOM parser maps an XML document into a treelike hierarchical structure of nodes in the form of a document object model. Each node in a DOM corresponds to some abstraction of an XML document component (for example, an element, a comment, CDATA). DOM permits applications to access such a model in terms of either a flat or an object-oriented view. In an object-oriented view, applications access each node in terms of a type-safe abstraction of actual components of an XML document (that is, Element, Comment, CDATA). In a flat view, applications access each node in terms of a non-type-safe generic representation of each node (that is, some generic Node abstraction).

DOM Architecture

Figure 31.7 depicts the top-level architecture of Java-based DOM classes and interfaces. Most classes and interfaces come from the org.w3c.dom package. Two additional classes defined in the javax.xml.parsers package are also utilized to define a provider-independent means for creating parser handles as well as a non-DOM-standard parser class. The DocumentBuilder DOM parser is created by a DocumentBuilderFactory and is used to create an XML Document object encapsulation from an XML content stream. After that, the Document and various types of DOM Node objects can be used to access the XML document contents in terms of XML document components.

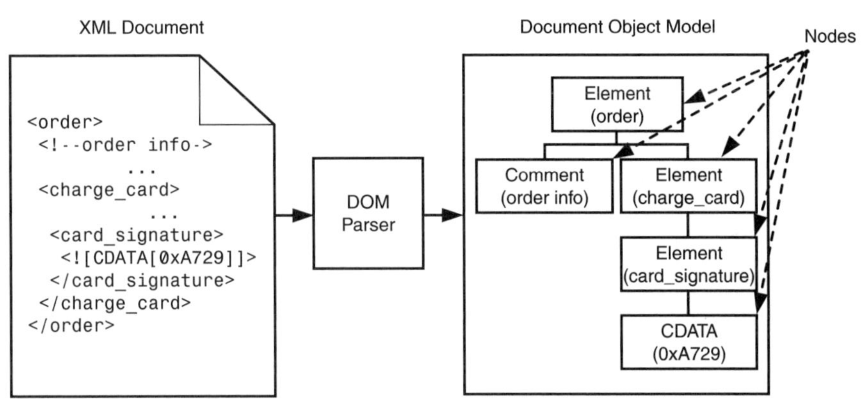

FIGURE 31.6
The Document Object Model.

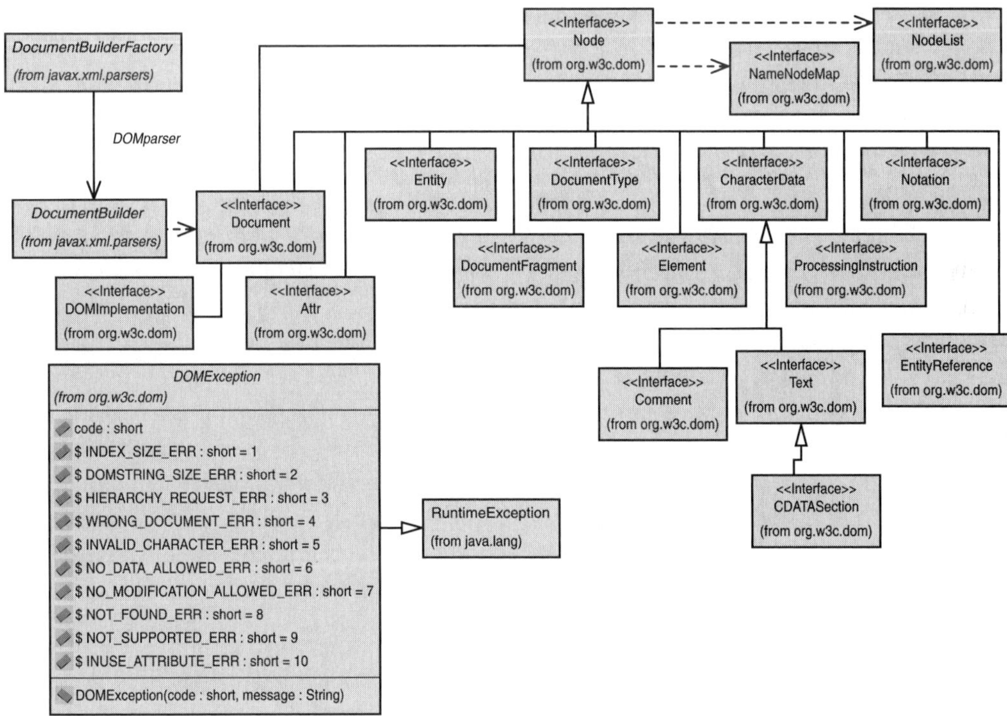

FIGURE 31.7
The DOM class architecture.

Also shown in this diagram is the only standard abstraction defined for DOM exceptions. The `DOMException` abstract class is a base class for exceptions thrown by the DOM objects. In addition to a message `String`, a `DOMException` can be created with `short` value exception code assigned according to one of the predefined `DOMException` static `short` constant values.

DOM Nodes

Figure 31.8 depicts the main abstractions involved in generic DOM nodes. A node interface and two node collection interfaces serve as the base generic interfaces for manipulating DOM in a flat-view fashion. Nodes also provide a handle to the object-oriented XML document that they contain and serve as the base interface for object-oriented XML document components.

The `Node` interface is the base interface for all DOM nodes and can be used as the generic abstraction for all nodes in a hierarchical document object model. Nodes are contained inside of XML documents, and the `Node.getOwnerDocument()` method returns a handle to a `Document` object that represents the XML document containing the node. The `Node` also provides interfaces to get the node name `String` using `getNodeName()`, as well as to get and set the node value in the form of a `String` using `getNodeValue()` and `setNodeValue()`. The `getNodeType()` method returns a `short` value code that identifies the type of `Node` according to one of the static short constant values defined by the `Node` interface.

The parent node of a `Node` object can be obtained using `Node.getParentNode()` method. The `Node.getChildNodes()` method returns a `NodeList` object containing a collection of `Node` objects that represent the children of a node. The `NodeList` interface provides a simple means for traversing a list of nodes with a `getLength()` method returning the length of the list and an `item(int)` method returning an individual indexed `Node`. The `Node.getFirstChild()` and `Node.getLastChild()` methods return the first and last child node objects, respectively. Children of the node can also be inserted, removed, replaced, and appended using appropriately named `Node` methods. The existence of any child nodes can be tested using the `hasChildren()` method. The `Node` object's sibling nodes immediately preceding and following it in its parent's child node list can be retrieved using the `getPreviousSibling()` and `getNextSibling()` calls.

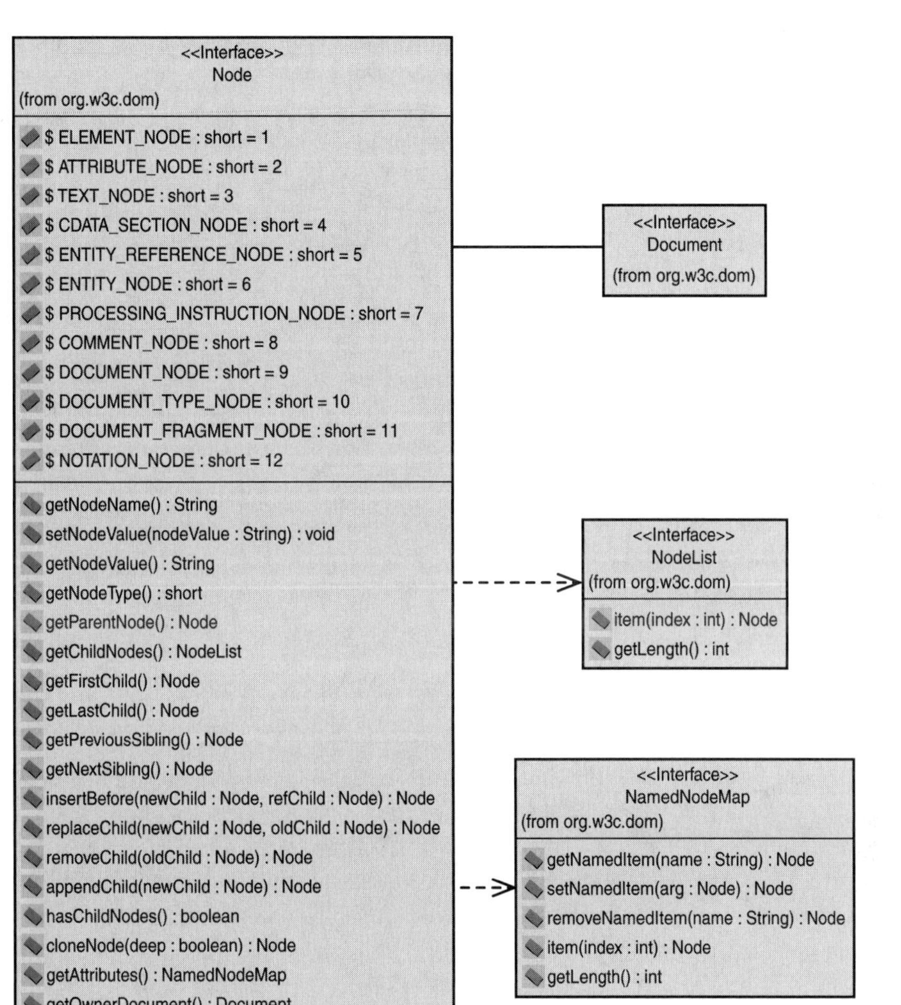

FIGURE 31.8
DOM nodes.

As an example, the `DOMExample` on the CD has a `printNodeNameAndValue()` method that illustrates some sample usage of a `Node` interface when invoked:

```
/**
 * This method prints the Node Name and Node Value
 */
public static void printNodeNameAndValue(Node node)
  throws DOMException
{
 System.out.println("Name :" + node.getNodeName());
 System.out.println("Value :"+ node.getNodeValue());
 if(node.hasChildNodes()){
  NodeList nodeList = node.getChildNodes();
  // print all child node information.
  for(int i = 0; i< nodeList.getLength(); i++){
    Node item = nodeList.item(i);
    System.out.println(" Node Name :"+item.getNodeName());
    System.out.println(" Node Value :" +item.getNodeValue());
    PrintNodeNameAndValue(item);
  }
 }
}
```

The attributes of a node can be returned using the `Node.getAttributes()` method. The returned `NamedNodeMap` object represents a collection of `Node` objects that can be referenced via a `String` name. The `NamedNodeMap` also allows its elements to be referenced by an index number.

DOM Node Types

Figure 31.9 presents the various interface extensions to the base `Node` extension. All the subinterfaces of `Node` are concrete type-safe interfaces to some component of an XML document. Object instances that implement these interfaces can be used to access and manipulate the various parts of an XML document in terms of an object-oriented abstraction. The `Node` subinterfaces are defined here with accompanying code-snippet methods to illustrate usage taken from the `DOMExample` file:

- `Notation`: Encapsulates a notation in a DTD. A public identifier and system identifier may be obtained via this interface. For example:

  ```
  public static void printNotationInformation(Notation notation)
  {
      System.out.println("Notation System ID :"
                         + notation.getSystemId());
      System.out.println("Notation Public ID :"
                         + notation.getPublicId());
  }
  ```

- `Entity`: Encapsulates an XML entity with getters for any associated public identifier, system identifier, and notation name. For example:

```
public static void printEntityInformation(Entity entity)
{
    System.out.println("Entity Name :"+ entity.getNotationName());
    System.out.println("Entity System ID :" + entity.getSystemId());
    System.out.println("Entity Public ID :"+entity.getPublicId());
}
```

- `EntityReference`: A marker interface for an entity reference.
- `ProcessingInstruction`: Encapsulates a processing instruction whose target name and data can be read. Additionally, data can also be set for the instruction. For example:

```
public static void printProcessingInstructionInformation(
    ProcessingInstruction processingInstruction)
{
    System.out.println("Data   :"
                       + processingInstruction.getData());
    System.out.println("Target   :"
                       + processingInstruction.getTarget());
}
```

- `CharacterData`: Encapsulates character data read from the document. Operations for getting, setting, adding, deleting, inserting, and replacing data in the character data stream are provided. For example:

```
public static void printCharacterData(
    CharacterData charData)
{
    System.out.println("Character Data  :"+ charData.getData());
}
```

- `Comment`: A type of character data extended as a marker interface for a comment in an XML document.
- `Text`: A type of character data that can be broken up into two regions of textual content.
- `CDATASection`: A type of textual character data extended as a marker interface for textual CDATA content.
- `Attr`: Encapsulates an attribute in an element including the retrieval of the attribute's name and value. Additionally, the attribute can be set. If the attribute was originally set in the parsed XML document, the `getSpecified()` method returns `true`. For example:

```
public static void printAttributeInformation(Attr attribute)
{
    System.out.println("Attribute Name :"
                       + attribute.getName());
    System.out.println("Is it specified :"
```

```
                         + attribute.getSpecified());
    System.out.println(" Attribute Value :"
                         + attribute.getValue());
}
```

- `Element`: Represents an element in an XML document. An `Element` can be used to retrieve a tag name and get, set, and remove named element attribute values. Additionally, a list of sub-elements returned in a `NodeList` object can also be obtained from an `Element`. The `Document.getDocumentElement()` method returns the root element for an XML document. The `Document.getElementsByTagName()` returns a node list of elements matching a specified tag name in a document. The `Element.normalize()` method is used to transform any `Text` nodes within an `Element` into a normal format in which only XML document component markup separates `Text` data.
- `DocumentType`: The `Document.getDocumentType()` method retrieves a `DocumentType` object that encapsulates information related to a top-level DTD description. The name, external entities, and notations defined within a DTD can all be accessed from the `DocumentType` object. For example:

```
public static void printDocumentTypeInformation(DocumentType
    documentType) throws SAXParseException
{
    String documentName = documentType.getName();
    System.out.println("Document Name :"+ documentName);
    //get all the entities that are defined for document.
    NamedNodeMap entities = documentType.getEntities();
    printNameNodeMap(entities); // to be defined later in section
}
```

- `Document`: A handle to an XML document. Provides a set of `create`*`XX`*`()` methods to create instances of other components of an XML document. Additionally, a set of getters is used to retrieve some of the top-level XML document components. For example:

```
public static void printDocument(Document document)
   throws SAXParseException
{

    DocumentType documentType = document.getDoctype();
    printDocumentTypeInformation(documentType);
    Element element = document.getDocumentElement();
    printNodeNameAndValue(element) ;
    NamedNodeMap attributes = element.getAttributes();
    printNameNodeMap(attributes); // to be defined later in section
}
```

- `DocumentFragment`: A marker interface used to encapsulate a portion of an XML document tree.

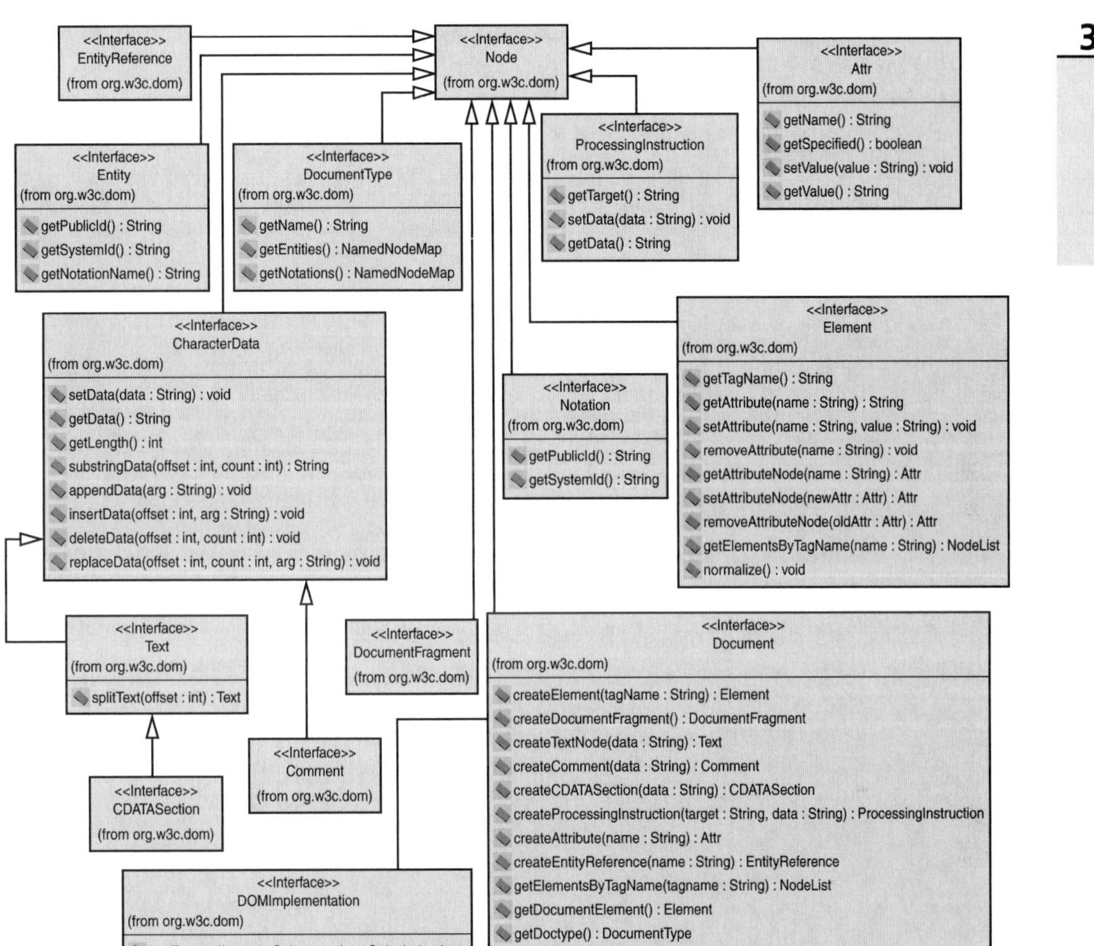

FIGURE 31.9
DOM node types.

In addition to the various `Node` sub-interfaces, we also show the `Document.getImplementation()` method and returned object in Figure 31.9. The `DOMImplementation` interface has one method that is used to determine whether a particular feature was implemented by the DOM parser provider. The `hasFeature()` method takes a feature `String` name (that is, `XML` or `HTML`) and a DOM specification version `String` (that is, `1.0`) and expects a `boolean` value indicating whether the feature is supported for the particular specification version.

A few of the Node sub-interface snippets that were presented utilized a DOMExample.printNameNodeMap() method. The DOMExample.printNameNodeMap() method cycles through a NameNodeMap and, depending on the Node type, will print some descriptive information about the specific Node instance. The printNameNodeMap() method is defined here:

```
public static void printNameNodeMap(NamedNodeMap values)
  throws SAXParseException
{
  int length = values.getLength();
  for(int i = 0; i<length; i++){
    Node node = values.item(i);
    short nodeType = node.getNodeType();
    switch(nodeType){
      case Node.ATTRIBUTE_NODE:
        {
          System.out.println(" This is an attribute :");
          Attr attribute = (Attr)node;
          printAttributeInformation(attribute);
          printNodeNameAndValue(node);
          break;
        }
      case Node.CDATA_SECTION_NODE:
        {
          System.out.println("This is a CDATA section :");
          CDATASection cdataSection = (CDATASection)node;
          printCharacterData(cdataSection);
          printNodeNameAndValue(cdataSection);
          break;
        }
      case Node.COMMENT_NODE:
        {
         System.out.println("This is a comment :");
         Comment comment = (Comment)node;
         printCharacterData(comment);
         printNodeNameAndValue(comment);
         break;
        }
      case Node.DOCUMENT_FRAGMENT_NODE:
        {
         DocumentFragment documentFragment = (DocumentFragment)node;
         System.out.println("This is a document fragment :");
         printNodeNameAndValue(node);
         break;
        }
      case Node.DOCUMENT_NODE:
```

```
  {
    System.out.println("This is a document :");
    Document document = (Document)node;
    printNodeNameAndValue(node);
    break;
  }
case Node.DOCUMENT_TYPE_NODE:
  {
    System.out.println("This is a document type :");
    DocumentType documentType = (DocumentType)node;
    printNodeNameAndValue(node);
    break;
  }
case Node.ELEMENT_NODE:
  {
    System.out.println("This is an element :");
    Element element = (Element)node;
    printNodeNameAndValue(node);
    break;
  }
case Node.ENTITY_NODE:
  {
   System.out.println("This is an entity :");
   Entity entity = (Entity)node;
   printEntityInformation(entity);
   printNodeNameAndValue(node);
   break;
  }
case Node.ENTITY_REFERENCE_NODE:
  {
    System.out.println("This is an entity reference :");
    EntityReference entityReference = (EntityReference)node;
    printNodeNameAndValue(node);
    break;
  }
case Node.NOTATION_NODE:
  {
    System.out.println(" This is a notation :");
    Notation notation =(Notation)node;
    printNotationInformation(notation);
    printNodeNameAndValue(node);
    break;
  }
case Node.PROCESSING_INSTRUCTION_NODE:
  {
    System.out.println("This is a processing instruction :");
```

```
                ProcessingInstruction processingInstruction
                  = (ProcessingInstruction)node;
                printProcessingInstructionInformation(
                   processingInstruction);
                printNodeNameAndValue(node);
                break;
              }
            case Node.TEXT_NODE:
              {
                System.out.println("This is text :");
                Text text = (Text)node;
                printNodeNameAndValue(node);
                break;
              }
            default:
              {
               System.out.println("This is not a defined node.");
               break;
              }
          }
       }
    }
```

DOM Parsing

Figure 31.10 depicts the main entities involved in creating and initiating DOM parsing. A DOM parser factory is used to create parser instances. The parser is then used to parse a particular data stream and generate an XML document object. The DOM parser factory and parser are both from the non-DOM-standard `javax.xml.parsers` package.

The `DocumentBuilder` abstract class is extended by DOM parser service providers to parse data streams into XML documents encapsulated by the `Document` interface. Aside from methods for determining XML namespace awareness and DTD validation capability, the `DocumentBuilder` also defines some methods that help initiate the parsing of a document. The `DocumentBuilder.parse()` methods all take an XML document content stream in the form of a `File` reference, an `InputStream`, an `InputSource`, or a URL `String` location and return an XML `Document` object instance. The `newDocument()` method simply creates an empty instance of a new `Document` object. A SAX `ErrorHandler` and `EntityResolver` may also be associated with a `DocumentBuilder`.

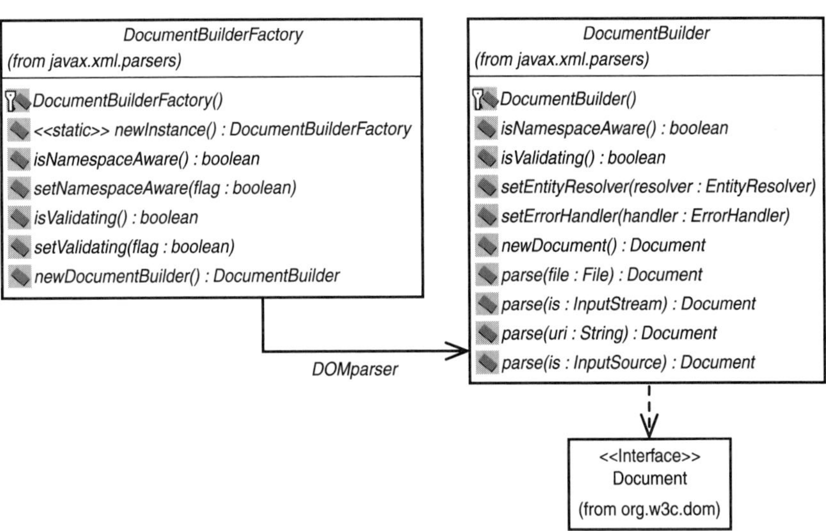

FIGURE 31.10
DOM parser interfaces.

The `DocumentBuilderFactory` abstract class can be used to configure and create DOM parser `DocumentBuilder` objects. A DOM parser provider provides a concrete implementation of the `DocumentBuilderFactory` class, and the definition of this class is defined via the `javax.xml.parsers.DocumentBuilderFactory` system property. The `static DocumentBuilderFactory.newInstance()` method is used to return an instance of this concrete factory implementation. DTD validation capability and XML namespace awareness of parsers can all be set and checked using appropriately named methods on a `DocumentBuilderFactory` object instance. New instances of `DocumentBuilder` objects can be created via a call to the `newDocumentBuilder()` method.

As an illustration of how to kick off DOM parsing, the `main()` method of the `DOMExample` should be invoked when `DOMExample` is being executed from the command line with a sample XML document. The `DOMExample.main()` method then creates a new instance of a `DocumentBuilderFactory` object, creates a new `DocumentBuilder` object, turns on parser validation, and induces the parsing of the XML document stream. After the root document element is normalized, the document is told to print itself via a call to `DOMExample.printDocument()`. The `main()` method is shown here:

```
public static void main(String[] argv)
{
  if(argv.length  != 1){
    System.out.println(" Usage :"+
     " java ejava.xmlch31.DOMExample <xmlfile> ");
```

```
      System.exit(0);
    }

    try{
      String xmlFileURI = "file:" +
        new File (argv [0]).getAbsolutePath ();
      // get new instance of Document Factory
      DocumentBuilderFactory documentBuilderFactory
        = DocumentBuilderFactory.newInstance();
      // get new Document Builder
      DocumentBuilder documentBuilder
        = documentBuilderFactory.newDocumentBuilder();
      documentBuilderFactory.setValidating(true);
      Document document = documentBuilder.parse(xmlFileURI);
      // normalize document
      document.getDocumentElement ().normalize ();
      printDocument(document);
      System.out.println ("Root element is" +
                          document.getDocumentElement().getNodeName());
    }catch (SAXParseException saxParseException) {
      System.out.println (" Parsing error"
              + ", at line " + saxParseException.getLineNumber ()
              + ", in file  " + saxParseException.getSystemId ());
      System.out.println("   " + saxParseException.getMessage ());
      saxParseException.printStackTrace();
    }catch (SAXException saxException) {
        saxException.printStackTrace ();
    }catch (Throwable throwable) {
        throwable.printStackTrace ();
    }
  }
```

NOTE

Note that the older version of JAXP equipped with the J2EE reference implementation did not include the `javax.xml.parsers.DocumentBuilderFactory` or `javax.xml.parsers.DocumentBuilder` classes. Rather, a `com.sun.xml.tree.XmlDocument` class is used to create a reference to a parsed standard DOM `Document` object. For example, when we're using the J2EE reference implementation, in our `DOMExample.main()` method we would replace the lines that create a `DocumentBuilder` and retrieve a `Document` object with a call to

```
Document document = XmlDocument.createXmlDocument(xmlFileURI);
```

In fact, the `XmlDocument` class has various methods named `createXmlDocument()` that are akin to the `DocumentBuilder.parse()` methods.

Java and XML

So with all of this talk about XML, you might be wondering what relevance it has to Java and Java enterprise systems in particular. XML documents provide a standard way to represent data that is exchanged between applications implemented in any language, on any platform, and via any communications protocol. XML document data structure definition thus fulfills a role similar to the role fulfilled by Java's underlying object serialization format definition. However, Java's object serialization format is Java-language specific albeit platform and communications-protocol independent. By using XML formats to represent data, Java applications can now communicate serialized object information to and from applications implemented in other languages. This fact is perhaps the root reason for why XML is useful to Java-based applications.

Although XML is still a relatively new technology compared to the other technologies referenced in this book, the growing use and support of XML makes it an attractive technology with which Java can integrate. As more COTS products are developed using XML data representations for data interchange and as standard XML DTDs are defined, Java enterprise systems can integrate with and take advantage of these software products and standard releases.

Despite XML's language independence, we of course advocate the development of enterprise applications using Java for all the reasons stemming from Java's advantages and features touted throughout this book. However, from a practical perspective, not all COTS software vendors will want to offer interfaces to their products that permit only Java-based product clients. CORBA interfaces may fill the void somewhat, but CORBA interfaces lack the simple, flexible, and extensible data object exchange by value semantics provided by XML.

The Java Enterprise APIs and XML

Java interfaces to XML documents, DTDs, and auxiliary standards thus further enable Java's utilization within heterogeneous and distributed computing environments. XML can be used by Java enterprise systems for business-to-business (B2B), Web-based business-to-consumer (B2C), and enterprise application integration (EAI) applications. As an example of just a few of the Java enterprise system–related components that can be integrated with XML, we list the following XML/Java points of current and future potential integration:

- *Java Serialization*: Use of Java serialization APIs, SAX APIs, and DOM APIs can be used to transform XML document data content to and from an I/O stream. Future extensions to Java serialization APIs will have specific XML input and output stream abstractions. This, of course, facilitates XML document exchange across different language-based applications.

- *JDBC*: XML documents can be used to represent data in a database, schemas in a database, and results of database queries. XML can thus be used in conjunction with JDBC query formulation and result-set processing. JDBC is an ideal candidate API for providing additional abstractions for queries and query results described as XML documents.
- *CORBA*: XML documents can be used to pass object state by value, as well as for input and output parameters during distributed CORBA calls. Java-based CORBA servers and clients can thus use XML to parse objects that have been passed by value, as well as parse input and output parameters to distributed method calls. CORBA is thus a good candidate to provide abstractions and potentially new fundamental data types that facilitate describing parameters via XML. The currently complex objects-by-value specification can also benefit from XML-based object-by-value semantics.
- *RMI*: XML documents can be used with RMI in a fashion similar to the way XML is used with CORBA. Additionally, mobile Java code can be described in an XML representation.
- *JNDI*: Because naming and directory services often provide hierarchical structures for associating names and attributes with objects, XML provides a natural way to describe such structure. JNDI is thus another good candidate API to be extended with abstractions that provide an XML-based means for JNDI lookups, searches, and service/object registrations.
- *JMS*: Messages in JMS can be described using an XML format. XML documents essentially are analogues for messages. JMS would certainly benefit from a set of abstractions that allow direct creation, submission, and reception of messages in the form of XML documents.
- *Java Servlets*: Servlets can be used to receive XML-based Web requests and can also be used to generate XML-based responses.
- *JavaServer Pages*: In addition to the input of Web requests and output of Web responses in the format of XML documents, JavaServer Pages (JSP) will also benefit from the mapping of JavaServer Pages directly into XML-based pages.
- *Enterprise JavaBeans*: Enterprise JavaBeans (EJBs) will benefit from services to receive and generate XML documents for B2B, B2C, and EAI purposes.

The J2EE and XML

Because Java Servlets and JavaServer Pages can currently use XML to generate XML-based documents, the J2EE can immediately benefit from using XML. The J2EE also currently uses XML as the data representation format for describing how Java Servlets, JSPs, and EJBs are to be deployed within a J2EE server environment. A future version of the J2EE specification will also require inclusion of SAX and DOM APIs and implementations in addition to additional

XML API extensions outlined within a Java Specification Request (http://java.sun.com/aboutJava/communityprocess/jsr/jsr_005_xml.html) as part of the Java Community Process.

The J2EE reference implementation currently comes equipped with an older version of the JAXP with implementations of SAX and DOM parsers. However, the only current requirement for J2EE-based servers is that they be capable of parsing XML to support its requirement for providing XML-based deployment descriptions. Although you can use the XML abstractions that come equipped with a particular J2EE-compliant server, use of abstractions that work with the latest version of the JAXP will offer the most in terms of interoperability with future J2EE specification upgrades.

J2EE Application Deployment Descriptions in XML

When J2EE applications are being created, XML-based deployment descriptors can be defined at the component level when modules are created and at the module level when applications are created. Java Servlet and JSP Web components can thus have an XML-based deployment descriptor defined for them when a collection of such components is used to build a module. Similarly, EJB components can also have an XML-based deployment descriptor when assembling these components into modules. The modules, in turn, can also have an XML-based deployment descriptor defined for them when assembled into a cohesive J2EE application. Chapter 32, "Java Servlets," Chapter 33, "JavaServer Pages," and Chapter 36, "Modeling Components with Enterprise JavaBeans," all present XML-based component-level deployment descriptors as they relate to the specific J2EE component types and content of those chapters. A generic J2EE application deployment description that is defined by a J2EE standard DTD with the name `J2EE:application` is presented next.

Listing 31.8 presents the standard DTD to describe the semantics and form of XML documents used as deployment descriptors during creation of J2EE applications. We have logically ordered the sequence of elements presented in the DTD of Listing 31.8 as opposed to the alphabetical ordering used for the standard DTD. Furthermore, we have also added our own comments to describe each element in the standard.

LISTING 31.8 J2EE Application DTD (http://java.sun.com/j2ee/dtds/application_1_2.dtd)

```
<!--
  The application element defines the root element of a J2EE
  application deployment descriptor. The icon and description
  elements are optional. One or more module elements must be defined.
```

continues

LISTING 31.8 Continued

```
  Zero or more security roles can be defined.
-->
<!ELEMENT application (icon?, display-name, description?, module+,
                       security-role*)>
<!--
  Defines optional small-icon and optional large-icon URLs for GIF or
  JPEG files that represent application icons.
-->
<!ELEMENT icon (small-icon?, large-icon?)>
<!--
  Defines a GIF or JPEG URL for a large icon.
-->
<!ELEMENT large-icon (#PCDATA)>
<!--
  Defines a GIF or JPEG URL for a small icon.
-->
<!ELEMENT small-icon (#PCDATA)>
<!--
  Provides a displayable and machine readable application name.
-->
<!ELEMENT display-name (#PCDATA)>
<!--
  Provides a human readable description of an application.
-->
<!ELEMENT description (#PCDATA)>
<!--
  A module defines a type of module (java, web, or ejb) and an optional
  alternate deployment descriptor URL.
-->
<!ELEMENT module ((ejb | java | web), alt-dd?)>
<!--
  Defines a URL for an application client module.
-->
<!ELEMENT java (#PCDATA)>
<!--
  Defines a URL and root context for a web module.
-->
<!ELEMENT web (web-uri, context-root)>
<!--
  Defines the URI of a web application module relative to the
  application package.
-->
<!ELEMENT web-uri (#PCDATA)>
<!--
```

```
  Defines the root context of a web application.
-->
<!ELEMENT context-root (#PCDATA)>
<!--
  Defines the URI of an EJB module relative to the application package.
-->
<!ELEMENT ejb (#PCDATA)>
<!--
  Used to define the URL of an alternate deployment descriptor
  to be used when deploying an application. Is an optional element.
  If not specified, the deployment descriptor from the application's
  JAR file is used.
-->
<!ELEMENT alt-dd (#PCDATA)>
<!--
  Defines an optional security role description as well as a role name.
-->
<!ELEMENT security-role (description?, role-name)>
<!--
  Defines the name of a security role.
-->
<!ELEMENT role-name (#PCDATA)>
<!--
  A set of ID attributes are defined for each element in the application
  deployment descriptor to allow an easy way to reference elements.
-->
<!ATTLIST alt-dd id ID #IMPLIED>
<!ATTLIST application id ID #IMPLIED>
<!ATTLIST context-root id ID #IMPLIED>
<!ATTLIST description id ID #IMPLIED>
<!ATTLIST display-name id ID #IMPLIED>
<!ATTLIST ejb id ID #IMPLIED>
<!ATTLIST icon id ID #IMPLIED>
<!ATTLIST java id ID #IMPLIED>
<!ATTLIST large-icon id ID #IMPLIED>
<!ATTLIST module id ID #IMPLIED>
<!ATTLIST role-name id ID #IMPLIED>
<!ATTLIST security-role id ID #IMPLIED>
<!ATTLIST small-icon id ID #IMPLIED>
<!ATTLIST web id ID #IMPLIED>
<!ATTLIST web-uri id ID #IMPLIED>
```

Thus, the DTD of Listing 31.8 is used to define the standard structure for deployment descriptors used in deploying J2EE applications. To utilize such a standard, valid J2EE application deployment descriptors must contain the following DOCTYPE reference:

```
<!DOCTYPE application
  PUBLIC "-//Sun Microsystems, Inc.//DTD J2EE Application 1.2//EN"
  "http://java.sun.com/j2ee/dtds/application_1_2.dtd"
>
```

With such a standard DTD definition, you'll see in Chapters 32, 33, and 36 how specific module types can be combined into a cohesive J2EE application. Specifically, Web modules for Java Servlets and EJB modules can be created from individual Java Servlet and EJB components. These different module types can then be used with deployment descriptors defined using XML documents that adhere to the preceding DTD to assemble and deploy J2EE applications.

Conclusions

XML is used to describe how data should be represented in an I/O stream. Such a standard data representation format enables open exchange of information between disparate applications implemented in different languages, on different platforms, and over various communication protocols. DTDs define a standard way to define a standard type of XML document. XML, DTDs, XLink, XPointers, XSL, SAX, and DOM all facilitate interoperability and a certain degree of interface uniformity among enterprise applications using a wide range of flexible, extensible, and powerful standards. Java's integration with XML is thus of primary significance if Java and the J2EE are to be useful in integrating with enterprise applications. The J2EE currently uses XML to define a standard way to describe J2EE-based application deployments and is earmarked to require full support for XML-based APIs in the future in order to facilitate B2B, B2C, and EAI with the J2EE. For now, the JAXP standard XML parsing APIs can be used.

Java Servlets

CHAPTER

32

IN THIS CHAPTER

- Servlet Architecture 1068
- Servlet Interfaces 1071
- Servlet HTTP Interfaces 1078
- Request Processing 1086
- Response Generation 1095
- Session Management 1103
- Servlet Deployment 1110
- Servlet Configuration 1122
- Servlet Service Management 1126

Java Servlets provide one of the core means for Web-enabling enterprises using Java technology. Custom J2EE-compliant Java Servlet components are built by application developers to handle business-specific requests and generate responses via HTTP and the Web. Stateful HTTP behavior can also be provided using a simple collection of Java Servlet APIs. J2EE-based Web containers make it easy to configure, deploy, and build robust Web applications using Java Servlets. This chapter describes how to build Web-enabled Java enterprise systems using Java Servlets inside of J2EE Web container environments. Our discussion centers around a description of the rich Java Servlet API abstractions and sample usage of these APIs in the context of a BeeShirts.com e-commerce storefront. We also describe how to configure and deploy this application in the context of a J2EE Web server environment.

In this chapter, you will lcarn:

- The architecture of J2EE-based Java Servlet Web component and container frameworks.
- The basic Java Servlet API framework abstractions and sample usage.
- The HTTP-based Java Servlet API framework abstractions and sample usage.
- The basic and concrete HTTP Java Servlet request and request dispatch abstractions as well as sample usage.
- The basic and concrete HTTP Java Servlet response abstractions as well as sample usage.
- The Java Servlet HTTP session and cookie management abstractions and sample usage.
- The J2EE standard Web application deployment descriptor format and procedures for deployment.
- The configuration of J2EE standard Web applications using deployment descriptors.
- The management services provided by J2EE Web application containers and how to configure and utilize such services.

Servlet Architecture

Java Servlets are Java components that are created by developers to handle requests and generate responses and that adhere to a component interface standard. Although Java Servlets define a generic request and response framework paradigm, a specific extension of the framework is provided for handling HTTP requests and generating HTTP responses via the Web. Java Servlet components operate inside of a Java Servlet container environment standardized by the Java Servlet Specification, v2.2 (`http://java.sun.com/products/servlet/2.2/`) for J2EE compliance. The J2EE Web component-container framework must also support the Java Servlet v2.2 API (`http://java.sun.com/products/servlet/2.2/javadoc/`). This section explores the logical, physical, and dynamic architecture of such J2EE-compliant Java Servlets.

Servlet Logical and Physical Architecture

Figure 32.1 depicts the Java Servlet architecture assumed by J2EE-based Web applications and v2.2 of the Java Servlet Specification. As can be seen from the diagram, HTTP requests and responses are built atop generic servlet requests and responses. A custom Java Servlet is built by an enterprise Web applications developer to specialize an HTTP servlet abstraction, which in turn specializes a generic servlet framework. Abstractions for managing data associated with the same user across multiple requests from that user are also possible via HTTP session management and cookies.

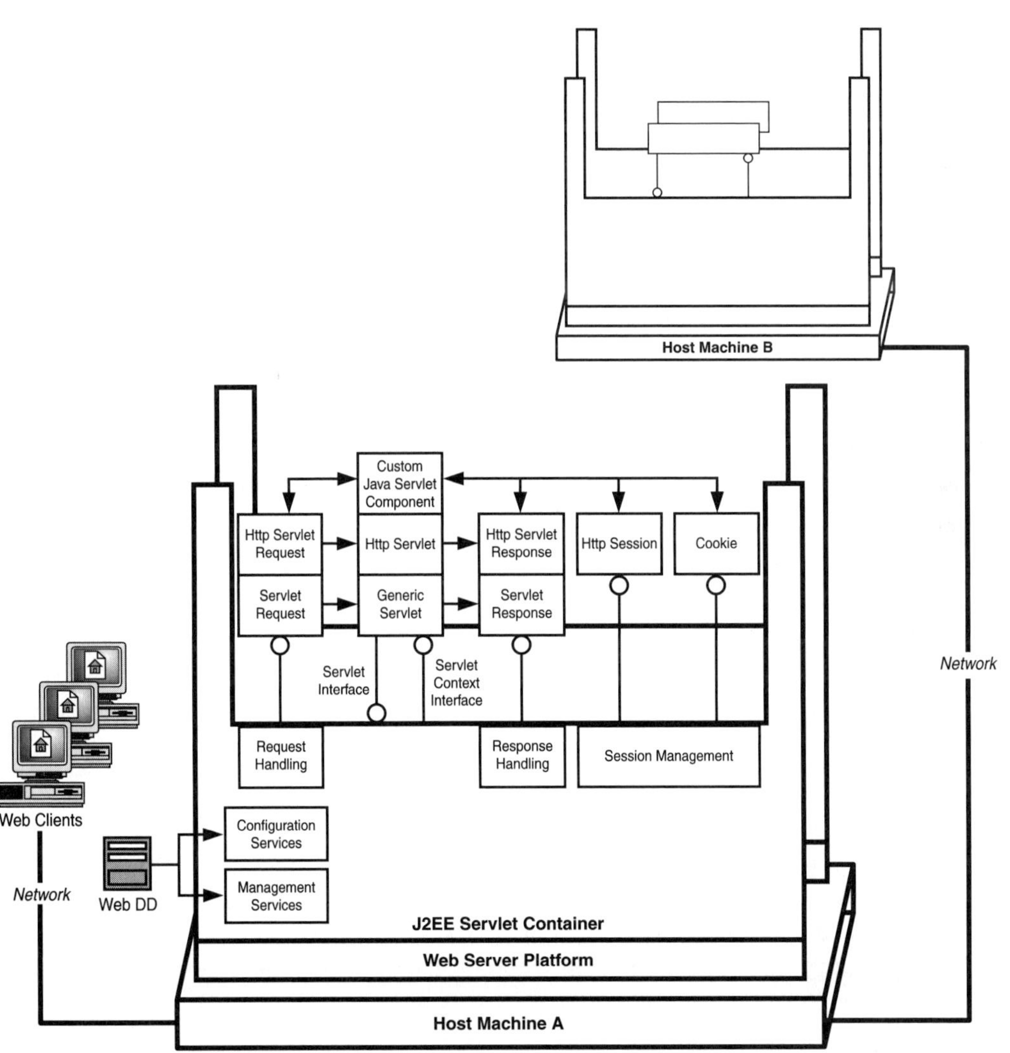

FIGURE 32.1
The Java Servlet architecture.

The J2EE-compliant Java Servlet container provides an environment in which Java Servlets take advantage of various services that make creating Web server applications simple and robust. The container environment provides the implementation of an abstraction layer above an underlying HTTP communications paradigm and Web server platform implementation architecture. A J2EE servlet container may be installed into a COTS Web server product using an extension mechanism provided by the Web server, such as ISAPI or NSAPI. The container environment also provides a simple means for configuring Java Servlet applications, as well as for providing various management services to Java Servlet applications in a declarative fashion using special Web application XML-based deployment descriptors. Finally, although a J2EE servlet container environment may apply to a single process on a single machine, we also depict the possibility for supporting distributable servlet environments across multiple processes and host machines as shown in Figure 32.1.

Servlet Lifecycle

Understanding the lifecycle of a servlet is useful in understanding the dynamic behavior of the Java Servlet architecture. The basic lifecycle of a Java Servlet in the context of a concrete HTTP request and response handling scenario is as given here:

1. The container loads a Java `Servlet` class either when the servlet's services are requested by a Web client or when the Web server is started.
2. The container will also either create a `Servlet` object instance based on a client request or create multiple instances of a `Servlet` object and add these instances to a servlet instance pool.
3. The container calls a servlet's initialization method, `HttpServlet.init()`, upon servlet instantiation.
4. The container constructs an `HttpServletRequest` and `HttpServletResponse` object to encapsulate a particular HTTP request received from a Web client and the response to be generated by the servlet.
5. The container passes the `HttpServletRequest` and `HttpServletResponse` objects to the `HttpServlet.service()` method. A custom Java Servlet then has access to such HTTP request and response interfaces.
6. The custom Java Servlet reads HTTP request data from the `HttpServletRequest` object, accesses any state information from an `HttpSession` or `Cookie` object, performs any application-specific processing, and generates HTTP response data using the `HttpServletResponse` object.
7. When the Web server and container shuts down, the `HttpServlet.destroy()` method is called to close any open resources.

Servlet Interfaces

The classes and interfaces defined in the `javax.servlet` package encapsulate an abstract framework for building components that receive requests and generate responses (that is, servlets). Abstractions for these servlets, requests, and responses are all encapsulated within this package. Additionally, an interface to the servlet's container context is also defined within this package. This section describes the base exceptions and basic component and container abstractions that form the servlet framework. Although the material presented in this section is necessarily abstract, we do illustrate how to utilize some of the interfaces defined in this section via sample code snippets toward the end of the section.

Servlet Exception Abstractions

Before we delve into the detailed architecture and APIs of servlets, let's take a quick look at the base exception types used with servlets. Figure 32.2 shows two exception classes used with Java Servlets. The `javax.servlet.ServletException` class is a simple root exception type that can be thrown by servlets. The `ServletException` can be constructed and associated with both an exception message and a root exception object.

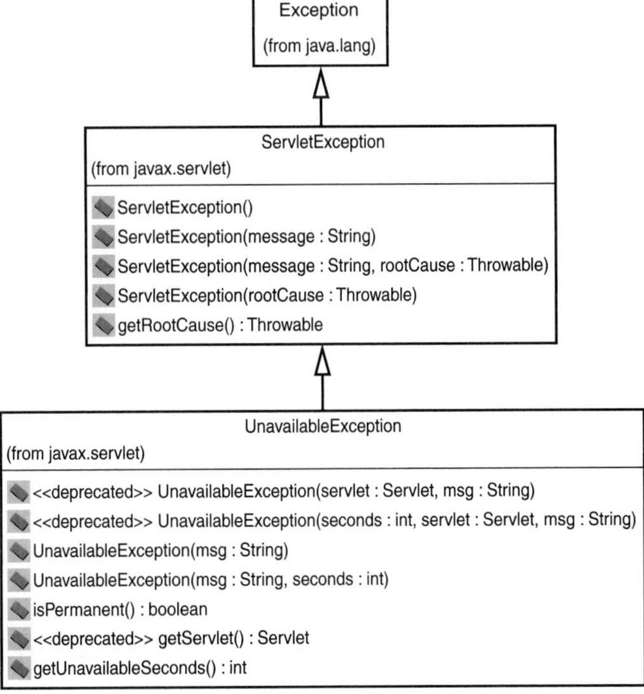

FIGURE 32.2
Servlet exceptions.

The `javax.servlet.UnavailableException` is a type of `ServletException` thrown when a particular servlet is not available to handle requests. If an exception is constructed with the `UnavailableException(String)` constructor receiving an exception message as a parameter, then the servlet is assumed to be permanently unavailable. If an exception is constructed with the `UnavailableException(String, int)` constructor receiving an exception message as a parameter and `int` value, then the servlet is assumed to be temporarily unavailable for an estimated number of seconds as indicated by the `int` parameter value. Zero or a negative number of seconds can be used to indicate that no unavailability time estimate can be provided. The state of servlet availability and number of unavailable seconds can also be retrieved from an `UnavailableException` object. The `getUnavailableSeconds()` method will return a negative number if the servlet is permanently unavailable or unable to estimate how long it will be unavailable.

Base Servlet Framework Abstractions

Figure 32.3 shows the core entities involved in defining the base Java Servlet interface framework contained within the `javax.servlet` package. These entities define the basic abstract framework from which all concrete Java Servlet request and response paradigms (that is, HTTP communications) are extended. Base servlet and servlet configuration interfaces are implemented by a generic servlet class that represents an abstract view of a Java Servlet component. Servlets operate inside of a servlet container context that controls the lifecycle of a servlet and provides a servlet with configuration and management services. We only display the method signatures for those base servlet entities used to encapsulate servlet components and containers in Figure 32.3 and defer a detailed discussion of requests and responses until a later section.

Base `Servlet` Interface

The `javax.servlet.Servlet` interface is the base interface for all Java Servlets. The `Servlet.init()` method is called once by a servlet component's container when the servlet is instantiated. When the servlet container is ready to take the servlet out of service, the container calls the `Servlet.destroy()` method, giving the servlet an opportunity to clean up any resources before it becomes dormant. The `init()` method takes a `javax.servlet.ServletConfig` object as a parameter that contains initialization information from the container environment. The `Servlet.getServletConfig()` method may subsequently be used to return a handle to the `ServletConfig` object. Additional information about a servlet, such as author and version information, may also be obtained from a `Servlet` instance using the `getServletInfo()` method.

The `Servlet.service()` method is called by a servlet's container to handle requests and generate responses during regular operational usage of the servlet. A `javax.servlet.ServletRequest` object is passed to the `service()` method containing all servlet request information to be read from an input stream. A `javax.servlet.ServletResponse` object is also passed to a `service()` method and is used to generate response information from within the servlet by way of writing information to an output stream.

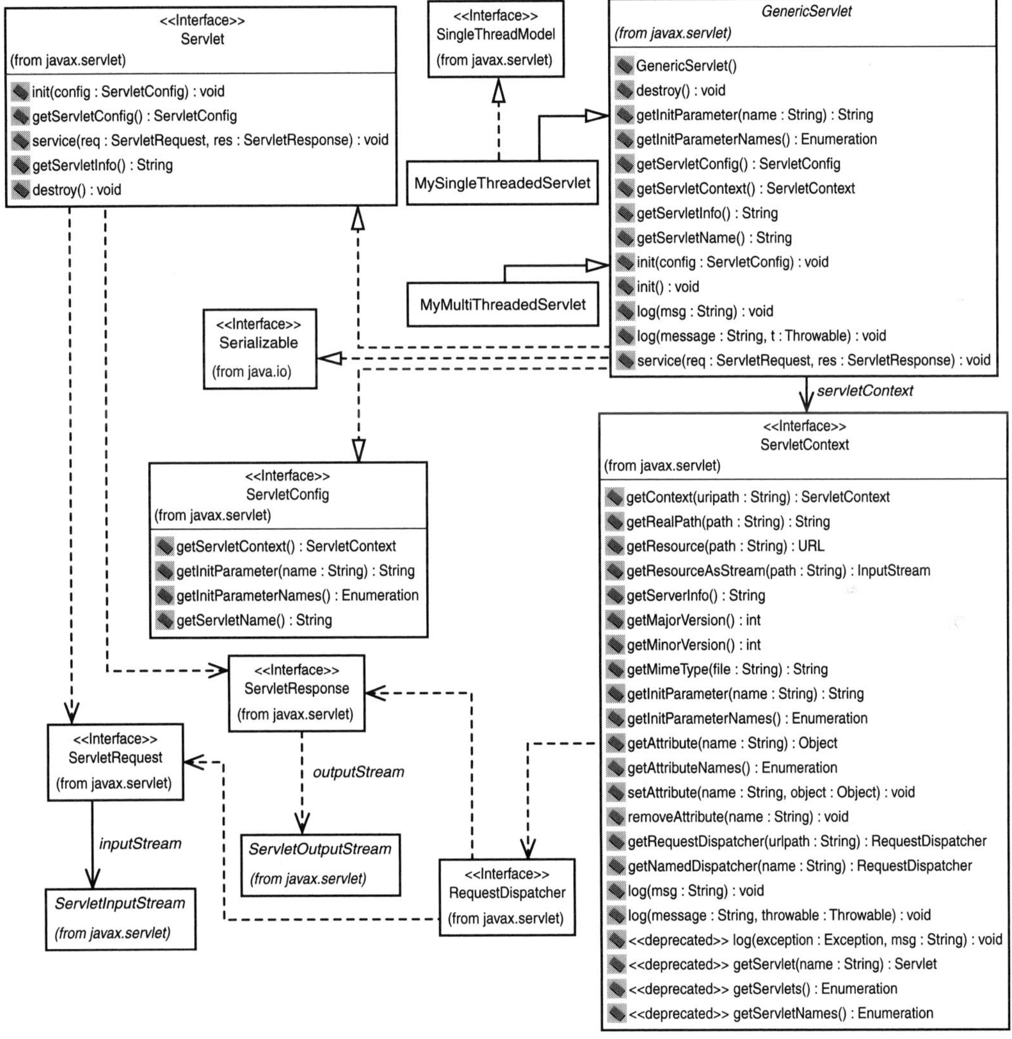

FIGURE 32.3
Base servlet interfaces.

Because containers may allow more than one thread to call a `Servlet` object instance's `service()` at the same time, the implementer of a particular `Servlet` must provide for the thread safety of the servlet. However, a particular `Servlet` implementation may also implement the `javax.servlet.SingleThreadModel` marker interface, which indicates that the servlet container should guarantee that only one thread be allowed to call the `service()` method of a `Servlet` at one time.

`ServletConfig` Interface

The `ServletConfig` interface is implemented by servlets that want to receive initialization information from the servlet container environment. Named initialization parameter value strings can be retrieved from the `ServletConfig.getInitParameter()` method by passing in the name of the parameter. The entire `Enumeration` of initialization parameter `String` names can be retrieved from the `ServletConfig.getInitParameterNames()` method. Any name for a servlet can also be retrieved from the `ServletConfig.getServletName()` method. Finally, a handle to the servlet's context can be retrieved from the `Servlet.getServletContext()` method.

`GenericServlet` Class

The abstract `javax.servlet.GenericServlet` class provides a default implementation for much of the `Servlet` and `ServletConfig` interfaces that it implements. The `GenericServlet` class also defines a convenience `init()` method definition and defines two `log()` methods used to write log messages and exception information to an underlying servlet log destination. Concrete subclasses of `GenericServlet` define specific request and response handling mechanisms (for example, HTTP request and response handling). Most application developers will actually extend subclasses of the `GenericServlet` class (for example, `HttpServlet`), but service providers are only required to define an implementation for the abstract `GenericServlet.service()` method.

`ServletContext` Interface

The `javax.servlet.ServletContext` interface provides a handle to a servlet's container context. Within a single JVM process, only one `ServletContext` instance exists to encapsulate the servlet context environment. However, a particular servlet container implementation may contain multiple servlet contexts across multiple processes and host machines. The servlet context is specified relative to a root context for a particular URL. Thus, a particular root context of `http://www.beeshirts.com/customers` may serve as the root context for a particular servlet context that will receive any requests sent to the `/customers` context on the `www.beeshirts.com` host machine. The `ServletContext.getContext()` method may be used to obtain a handle to another `ServletContext` object on the same Web server by passing in the absolute pathname of a server's document root beginning with a slash (`/`). A `null` value may be returned from the `getContext()` call if permission to the other `ServletContext` is not allowed. We talk about `RequestDispatcher` objects later in the chapter, but suffice it to say for now that the `ServletContext` also serves as the entry point from which Web requests can be dispatched to other servlets within the same servlet context via its `getRequestDispatcher()` and `getNamedDispatcher()` calls.

Resources and underlying system pathnames can be retrieved from the container environment given a pathname relative to the servlet's context. The real path of a particular path relative to a servlet's context can be obtained from the `ServletContext.getRealPath()` method. By passing in a virtual path to this method, the real path associated with the underlying operating system environment can be returned in `String` form. A URL to a particular resource may be made available to a servlet by calling `ServletContext.getResource()` with a path relative to a servlet's context. A resource may also be retrieved in the form of an `InputStream` object via a call to the `ServletContext.getResourceAsStream()` with a path relative to the servlet's context.

Various product information about a servlet's container environment may also be obtained through `ServletContext` calls. The `ServletContext.getServerInfo()` method returns a `String` of servlet container and server information of the format *`ServerName`*`/`*`VersionNumber`* `(`*`OptionalInformation`*`)`. The major and minor version of the container's supported Java Servlet API may also be obtained from calls to `getMajorVersion()` and `getMinorVersion()` on a `ServletContext` object.

Configuration information about the container environment is obtained in various ways from `ServletContext`. MIME type mappings that have been configured for a particular Web server environment will be used to return the appropriate MIME type/subtype `String` from a call to `ServletContext.getMimeType()` given a particular filename. Configuration parameter values for a container environment can be returned from the `ServletContext.getInitParameter()` method given a named configuration parameter. The names of all container-wide parameters can also be returned from a call to `Servlet.Context.getInitParameterNames()` in the form of an `Enumeration` of `String` names.

In addition to configuration parameters, a collection of named `java.lang.Object` types can be associated with a container environment as attributes of the `ServletContext` environment. These attributes can be shared by other servlets in the context and can be set, gotten, and removed using the `ServletContext` object's `setAttribute()`, `getAttribute()`, and `removeAttribute()` methods, respectively. An `Enumeration` of `String` names for all attributes can also be retrieved via the `getAttributeNames()` call.

The `ServletContext.log()` methods are used to write log messages and exception information to an underlying servlet log destination. This presumes that the servlet container environment will allow for some way to specify the name and type of log to generate. A log file is typically assumed here as the type of logging medium.

As a final note, the `ServletContext getServlet()`, `getServletNames()`, and `getServlets()` methods have all been deprecated. Although the methods were once used to obtain handles to other servlets and servlet names within a particular context, the methods now return null values and empty `Enumeration` objects. The methods are preserved for binary compatibility but will be removed in a future API specification.

Servlet Framework Examples

The servlet framework APIs presented thus far are not typically used alone to build fully functional Java Servlets. Rather, the HTTP extensions presented in the next section provide the means for building Web-based servlets. Nevertheless, an `ejava.servletsch32.ServletHelper` class that we equip with our sample software for this chapter on the book's CD does demonstrate some basic usage of the servlet framework abstractions presented thus far. The `ServletHelper` class will be used by HTTP servlet sample code presented in subsequent sections to provide some common utilities for the sample servlets.

NOTE

All the sample code strewn throughout this chapter is contained on the CD under the `examples\src\ejava\servletsch32` directory. Because the code on the CD represents a moderately large amount of Web-based BeeShirts.com storefront code, we do not present all the code in this chapter. Rather, we describe the basic structure of such code and present snippets from that code germane to chapter topics as they are discussed.

The `printServletContextInformation()` method defined on the `ServletHelper` class demonstrates use of a few `javax.servlet.ServletContext` methods. The `printServletContextInformation()` simply retrieves and logs a set of attributes, parameters, version information, path information, and resource information as shown here:

```
public static void printServletContextInformation(
  ServletContext servletContext) throws ServletException
{
  // Get attribute names from servlet context
  Enumeration attributes = servletContext.getAttributeNames();
  // For each attribute, print name and value to log
  while(attributes.hasMoreElements()){
    String attributeName = (String)attributes.nextElement();
    Object attribute = servletContext.getAttribute(attributeName);
    servletContext.log("Attribute :" +attributeName +
      " Attribute :" + attribute);
  }
```

```
    // Get parameter names from context
    Enumeration parameters = servletContext.getInitParameterNames();
    // For each parameter, print name and value to log
    while(parameters.hasMoreElements()){
      String parameterName = (String)parameters.nextElement();
      Object parameterValue = servletContext.getAttribute(parameterName);
      servletContext.log("Parameter :" +parameterName +
        " Parameter Value :" + parameterValue);
    }

    // Get and log real path
    String servletPath = servletContext.getRealPath("/");
    servletContext.log("Servlet Path :"+servletPath);
    // Get and log server info
    String serverInformation = servletContext.getServerInfo();
    servletContext.log("Server Information  :"+serverInformation);
    // Log major and minor version of API
    servletContext.log("Major Version :"
        + servletContext.getMajorVersion());
    servletContext.log("Minor Version :"
        + servletContext.getMinorVersion());

    // Get and log resource info
    try{
      java.net.URL resource = servletContext.getResource("/");
      servletContext.log("Resource : " +resource);
    }
    catch(MalformedURLException malformedURLException){
      servletContext.log(" Error :" +malformedURLException);
    }
  }
```

The `printServletConfigInformation()` method defined on the `ServletHelper` class demonstrates use of a few `javax.servlet.ServletConfig` methods. The `printServletConfigInformation()` retrieves a `ServletContext` object from a `ServletConfig` object, retrieves and prints `ServletConfig` parameters, and calls the `printServletContextInformation()` method as shown here:

```
  public static void printServletConfigInformation(
    ServletConfig servletConfig) throws ServletException
  {
    // Retrieve servlet context and log message
    ServletContext servletContext = servletConfig.getServletContext();
    servletContext.log("Servlet Initial Parameters Names:");
    // Retrieve parameter names from ServletConfig
    Enumeration enumeration = servletConfig.getInitParameterNames();
```

```
    // For each parameter, log the name and value
    while(enumeration.hasMoreElements()){
      String parameterName = (String)enumeration.nextElement();
      String value = servletConfig.getInitParameter(parameterName);
      servletContext.log("Parameter :" +parameterName +
        " Parameter Value :"+value);
    }

    // Now print the ServletContext information
    servletContext.log("Servlet Context information :");
    printServletContextInformation(servletConfig.getServletContext());
  }
```

Servlet HTTP Interfaces

The `javax.servlet.http` package defines a concrete extension of the basic servlet framework for HTTP-based servlets. HTTP-based servlets are, of course, used in Web-based scenarios in which HTTP requests flow into Web servers, which in turn generate HTTP responses. This section describes the basic HTTP servlet component type and the means by which application-specific components extend the HTTP servlet. We then present the basic structure of a sample BeeShirts.com e-commerce storefront based on HTTP servlets.

Base HTTP Servlet Framework Abstractions

Figure 32.4 presents the collection of core interfaces and classes in the `javax.servlet.http` package. The entities in this package extend the abstract entities in the `javax.servlet` package to provide a concrete framework for handling HTTP requests and generating HTTP responses. Note that we only display the method signatures for the base HTTP servlet component type class in Figure 32.4. We defer a detailed discussion of HTTP servlet requests, responses, stateful sessions, and event handling until later sections in this chapter.

The `javax.servlet.http.HttpServlet` abstract class specializes the `GenericServlet` class to specifically deal with HTTP requests and responses. HTTP requests and responses are encapsulated by the `javax.servlet.http.HttpServletRequest` and `javax.servlet.http.HttpServletResponse` interfaces, respectively.

Cookies that are associated with HTTP requests and responses are encapsulated by the `javax.servlet.http.Cookie` class. Stateful HTTP session information managed by a servlet container environment can also be encapsulated within a `javax.servlet.http.HttpSession` interface. Objects interested in discovering when they are bound to an HTTP session implement the `javax.servlet.http.HttpSessionBindingListener` interface and receive notification by way of `javax.servlet.http.HttpSessionBindingEvent` objects.

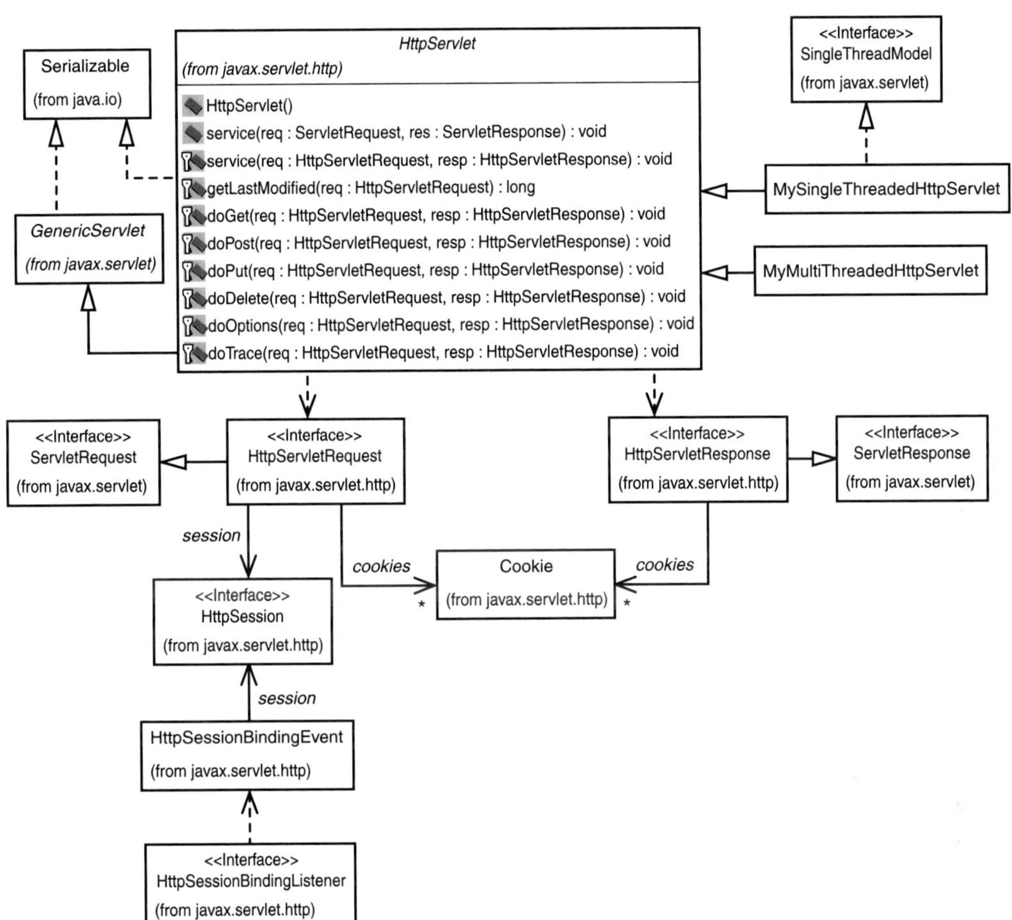

FIGURE 32.4
Base HTTP servlet interfaces.

`HttpServlet` Class

The `HttpServlet` class is extended by application-specific servlet classes to handle HTTP requests and generate HTTP responses. Application-specific classes override one or more of the `HttpServlet` methods, as well as its base `GenericServlet` class methods. The `init()`, `destroy()`, and `getServletInfo()` methods inherited from the `GenericServlet` class are the most common types of methods implemented by application-specific classes. We also show a custom `MySingleThreadedHttpServlet` class in Figure 32.4 that extends the `HttpServlet` class and implements the `SingleThreadModel` to clue the container into allowing only a single thread to access the servlet object at one instant. Otherwise, a servlet such as `MyMultiThreadedHttpServlet` simply extends the `HttpServlet` class.

Recall from Chapter 13's discussion of HTTP requests that an HTTP request can come in one of many flavors defined by the request method field of an HTTP request. The request method is an identifier for the type of HTTP request being made. One of the `doXXX()` methods defined on `HttpServlet` is called by a servlet container environment on `HttpServlet` instances when the container receives an associated HTTP request method type. Each `doXXX()` method receives an `HttpServletRequest` and `HttpServletResponse` as input parameters used to handle HTTP requests and generate HTTP responses. One of the following `HttpServlet` method types is invoked under the specified HTTP request method scenarios:

- `doGet()`: Called when HTTP `GET` or `HEAD` request method types are received by the Web server. `GET` requests are used to retrieve a limited amount of data from a Web server. `HEAD` requests are similar to `GET` requests, but require only header information to be returned in an HTTP response.
- `doPost()`: Called when HTTP `POST` request method types are received by the Web server. `POST` requests are also used to retrieve data from a Web server, but without the restriction on the amount of data to be returned. As an example, `POST` requests can contain data posted by an HTML `INPUT FORM`.
- `doPut()`: Called when HTTP `PUT` request method types are received by the Web server. `PUT` requests are used to upload data to a Web server.
- `doDelete()`: Called when HTTP `DELETE` request method types are received by the Web server. `DELETE` requests are used to delete data from a Web server.
- `doOptions()`: Called when HTTP `OPTIONS` request method types are received by the Web server. `OPTIONS` requests are used to retrieve the configuration options supported by a Web server.
- `doTrace()`: Called when HTTP `TRACE` request method types are received by the Web server. `TRACE` requests are used to ask the Web server to return the HTTP header information sent by the client for debugging purposes.

Of the six methods defined previously, typically there is ever a need for application-specific overriding only of the `doGet()`, `doPost()`, `doPut()`, and `doDelete()` methods.

Recall that the `service(ServletRequest, ServletResponse)` method defined on the parent `GenericServlet` class is used to handle general requests from the servlet container context environment and generate responses for the environment. The `HttpServlet.service(HttpServletRequest, HttpServletResponse)` method is called by the `HttpServlet.service(ServletRequest, ServletResponse)` method to specifically handle HTTP requests and generate responses, and there is generally no reason to override either form of method. The `service(HttpServletRequest, HttpServletResponse)` form of method is implemented by the Servlet API to dispatch specific requests to one of the `doXXX()` method types depending on the received HTTP request method types.

The `HttpServlet.getLastModified()` method is called by servlet containers to determine the last time in which the state of a servlet was modified. Containers may use this information to aid in enabling Web browser and Web server caches to operate more efficiently by being able to determine whether they need to issue a request to a servlet or whether they can rely on a previously cached response. Given a particular `HttpServletRequest`, the time in milliseconds since midnight January 1, 1970, is returned to indicate the last time of change. Unknown state change times result in a negative return value.

BeeShirts.com Java HTTP Servlet Examples

The `HttpServlet` class serves as the base class from which we can build Web-enabled Java Servlets. We have in fact developed a Web-enabled BeeShirts.com e-commerce storefront using Java Servlets and placed the sample code on the CD. Because the example is moderately large for inclusion in this book, we won't be inserting all the source code in the chapter but will be providing core snippets from such code as relevant topics are introduced. Figure 32.5 does, however, provide a logical diagram of the various HTTP servlet and HTML pages used to service requests and generate responses for this sample code.

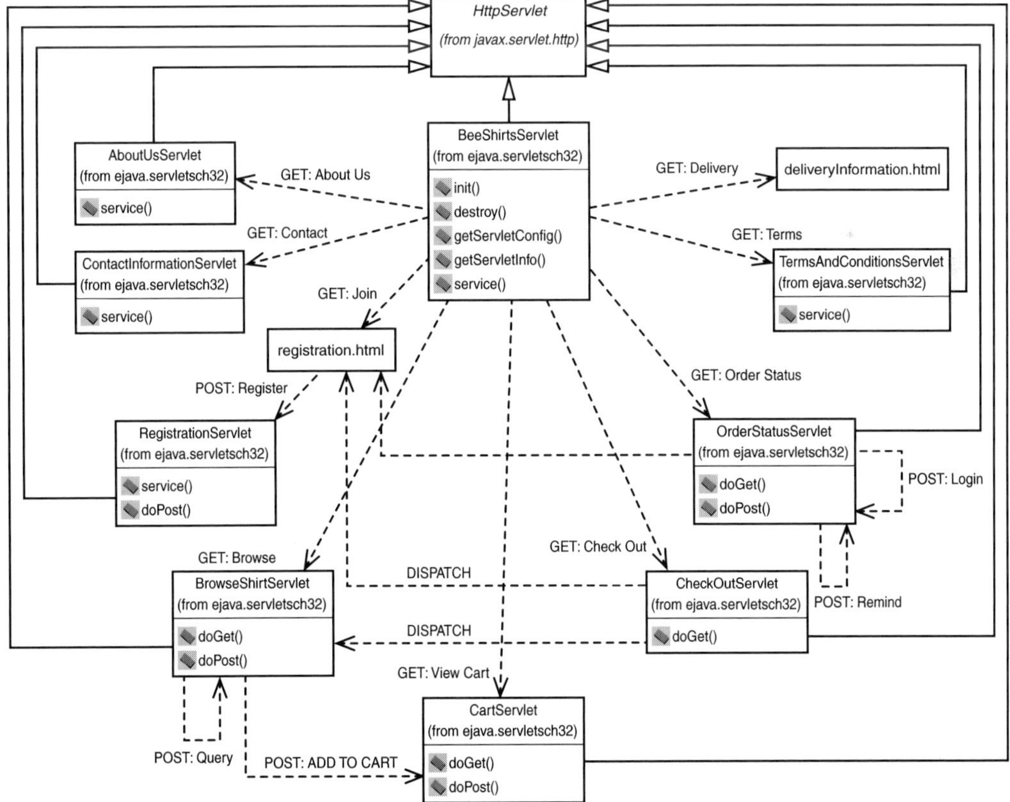

FIGURE 32.5
BeeShirts.com Java Servlets and HTML.

All the classes shown in Figure 32.5 extend the `javax.servlet.http.HttpServlet` class and override one or more of the `HttpServlet` methods. The various servlets also define a few private application-specific methods not shown in the diagram. The `BeeShirtsServlet` class serves as the root servlet for the BeeShirts.com e-commerce storefront. Arcs drawn between the `BeeShirtsServlet` and other servlets and HTML pages are followed when requests are made from one resource to another. The arcs are labeled with the type of HTTP request made and the HTML button label that induced the request.

As you can see with the main `BeeShirtsServlet` of Figure 32.6, the basic BeeShirts.com screens are divided into three sections. For all servlets, the top portion of the screen displays the BeeShirts.com logo and the left side of the screen displays the main set of button controls. The center page area changes for each servlet requested.

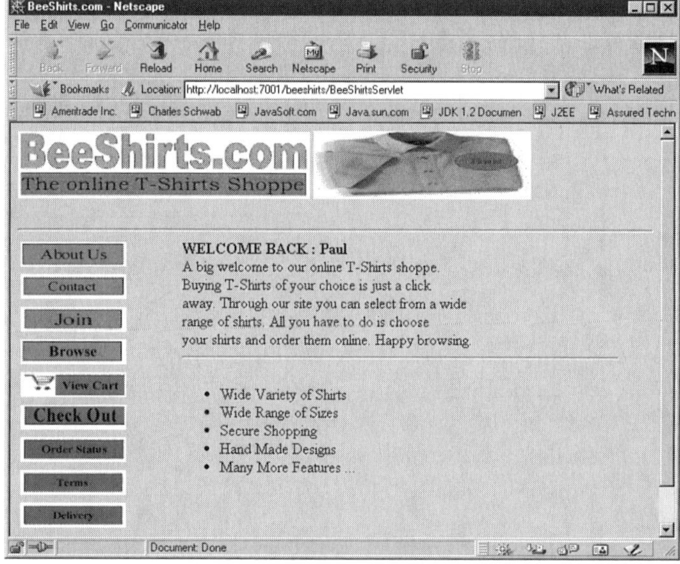

FIGURE 32.6
The BeeShirts.com root screen.

Figure 32.7 shows some of the problem domain entities used by the BeeShirts.com Java Servlets. The classes shown in Figure 32.7 actually correspond to entities that map from persisted elements of our BeeShirts.com database. We saw how entities such as `Order` and `Customer` could be mapped from a database via JDBC in previous chapters. We will demonstrate how such mapping can occur in the context of Enterprise JavaBean entity beans in a subsequent chapter. However, for simplicity here, we simply implement the entities shown in Figure 32.7 as classes that we load with dummy data and data received from Web browser interaction. Most of the BeeShirts.com entities displayed in Figure 32.7 also contain a few helper methods to extract the contents of the objects in the form of HTML tables for use with these examples.

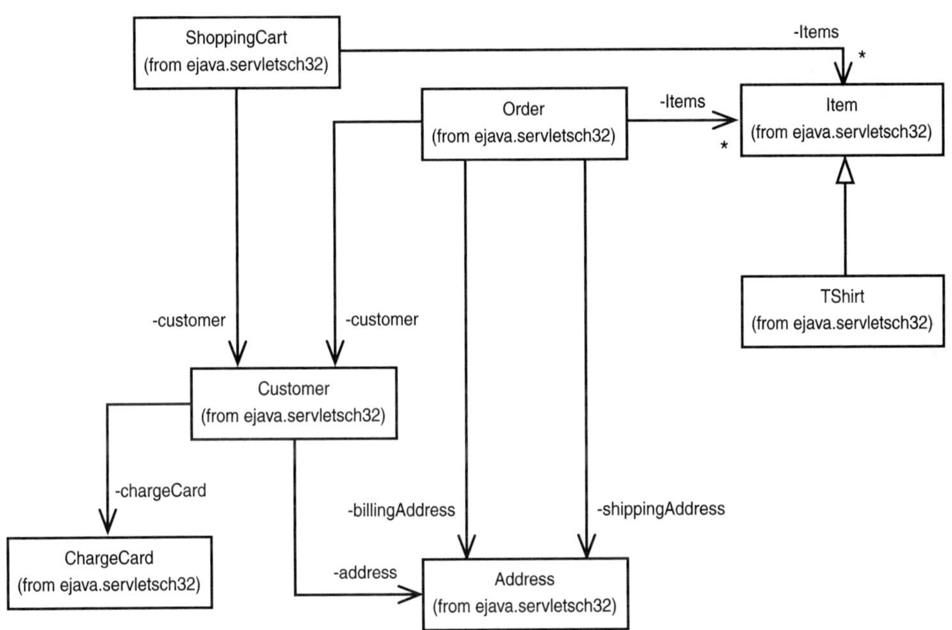

FIGURE 32.7
BeeShirts.com entities.

Now that you've gotten a taste for the basic structure of the BeeShirts.com storefront, let's examine the main elements of BeeShirts.com business logic as implemented with Java Servlets. The BeeShirts.com servlets and two HTML files shown in Figure 32.5 are described here:

- `BeeShirtsServlet`: Handles the initial BeeShirts.com site requests as the root servlet that generates the starting page as shown in Figure 32.6. This servlet also creates a session object for the user and checks to see whether the user has a cookie. If the user has a cookie, this servlet displays a personalized `WELCOME BACK` message.
- `AboutUsServlet`: Handles the HTTP request generated from clicking the About Us button and displays some simple BeeShirts.com information.
- `ContactInformationServlet`: Handles the HTTP request generated from clicking the Contact button and displays some simple contact information.

- `registration.html`: Contains a static HTML page referenced from the Join button that displays a registration form and Register button. Performs some minimal field validation functions via JavaScript. It posts data to the `RegistrationServlet`.
- `RegistrationServlet`: Handles the HTTP `POST` generated by clicking the Request button from the `registration.html` page. This servlet creates a `Customer` object and associates this object with an HTTP session. It also generates a personalized cookie to be sent back to the customer's Web browser. The registration information is also displayed.
- `BrowseShirtsServlet`: Handles the HTTP `GET` generated from clicking the Browse button and allows a user to query for the T-shirts they might be interested in purchasing. After selecting some query criteria, this servlet submits an HTTP `POST` to itself with form data after the user has selected some T-shirt search criterion. The posted query data is used to display search results. The user is given the option to add a shirt to his shopping cart.
- `CartServlet`: Handles the HTTP `POST` from the `BrowseShirtsServlet` ADD TO CART button. It will first create a `ShoppingCart` object in the HTTP session if none was created yet and will subsequently add the posted T-shirt data to the `ShoppingCart` object. It also handles the HTTP `GET` request from the View Cart button and displays the items, if any, from the `ShoppingCart` stored in the session.
- `CheckOutServlet`: Handles the HTTP `GET` request generated from clicking the Check Out button. If a `Customer` object is not associated with the session, the user is redirected to the `registration.html` page. If the cart is empty, the user is redirected to the `BrowseShirtsServlet`. Otherwise, the servlet simply displays what is in the current shopping cart.
- `OrderStatusServlet`: Handles the HTTP `GET` generated from clicking the Order Status button. The generated response then provides fields for accepting a username and password, as well as displaying Login and Remind buttons. When the Login button is pressed, the user information is posted to the servlet itself. The HTTP `POST` then stimulates the display of a dummy order status. For this chapter's example, we require the entry of a `sam@sam.com` email address and `sam` password value to retrieve dummy order status data since we defer illustrating database connectivity until a subsequent chapter. If the user enters invalid login information five times in a row, the user is then directed to `registration.html`. If the user clicks the Remind button, the user is told that she will be emailed her password information. Clicking the Remind button also results in the HTTP `POST` to `OrderStatusServlet`.
- `TermsAndConditionsServlet`: Handles the HTTP request generated from clicking the Terms button and displays some simple order terms-and-conditions information.
- `deliveryinformation.html`: Contains a static HTML page referenced from the Delivery button and displays some canned delivery information.

The `BeeShirtsServlet` class defines methods for `init()`, `destroy()`, `getServletConfig()`, and `getServletInfo()`. The `init()` method is used to receive and store a private `ServletConfig` object. The basic structure of the `BeeShirtsServlet`, excluding request and response handling code, is shown here:

```
public class BeeShirtsServlet extends  HttpServlet
{
  private ServletConfig servletConfig;
  public static final String  SERVLET_NAME = "/BeeShirtsServlet";

/**
  * This is the first method the Web Server calls and it is called once.
  */
  public void init (ServletConfig config)
    throws ServletException
  {
    servletConfig = config;
  }

/**
  * This is the last method WebServer calls and it is called only once.
  */
  public void destroy()
  {
  }

/**
  * return the Configuration information about the Servlet
  */
  public ServletConfig getServletConfig()
  {
    return servletConfig;
  }

/**
  * Return Servlet Information
  */
  public String getServletInfo()
  {
    return "BeeShirts.com Welcome page Servlet";
  }

  // ...more code to display here in subsequent sections...

}
```

Request Processing

Handling requests is the first order of business when one is developing servlets. The servlet container encapsulates requests for application-specific servlets and enables manipulation of requests in a programmer-friendly fashion. As we discussed in Chapter 13, "Web Communications," HTTP requests have many elements that can be sent from a client to a server. Request parameters, attributes, header values, and body data all have programmatic interfaces defined via Java Servlet request handling abstractions. Abstractions also exist to encapsulate the forwarding of requests from one servlet to another Web resource. This section describes these various request processing abstractions and demonstrates how such processing is implemented via snippets from our BeeShirts.com example.

Request Handling Abstractions

Figure 32.8 depicts many of the major API elements and method signatures related to handling servlet and HTTP requests. Servlet container environments create and pass servlet request objects to `Servlet` objects in the abstract servlet framework model and pass HTTP servlet request objects to an `HttpServlet` in the more concrete HTTP paradigm. An abstraction for a servlet request exists at the basic servlet framework level that is extended by a more concrete HTTP servlet request. Access to the input stream for data sent from the client via a request body is encapsulated at the abstract servlet framework level.

`ServletRequest` Interface

The `javax.servlet.ServletRequest` interface encapsulates a generic request sent to a Java Servlet. When a request is received by the underlying container environment from a distributed client, the servlet container creates a `ServletRequest` object to encapsulate the data sent in the request. The `ServletRequest` is then passed as a parameter to the target servlet's `service()` method. `ServletRequest` objects contain request parameter data, attributes, and an associated input stream from which request data is read.

As a first step in understanding the type of request received, a servlet can issue inquisitive calls on a `ServletRequest` object. The `ServletRequest.getProtocol()` is used to retrieve the name and version of the protocol used to deliver the request (for example, `HTTP/1.1`). The `ServletRequest.getScheme()` method can be used to retrieve the name of the scheme used in the request (for example, `http`, `ftp`). The fact that the channel over which the request was made is secure can be determined via the `ServletRequest.isSecure()` call. Additionally, the encoding format of the request is yielded from the `ServletRequest.getCharacterEncoding()` call, and the MIME type/subtype of the request body is returned from the `ServletRequest.getContentType()` call. The locale preference information of the client as retrieved from the request is determined from either the `ServletRequest.getLocale()` method or the `ServletRequest.getLocales()` method in the form of an `Enumeration` of `Locale` objects in decreasing order of preference.

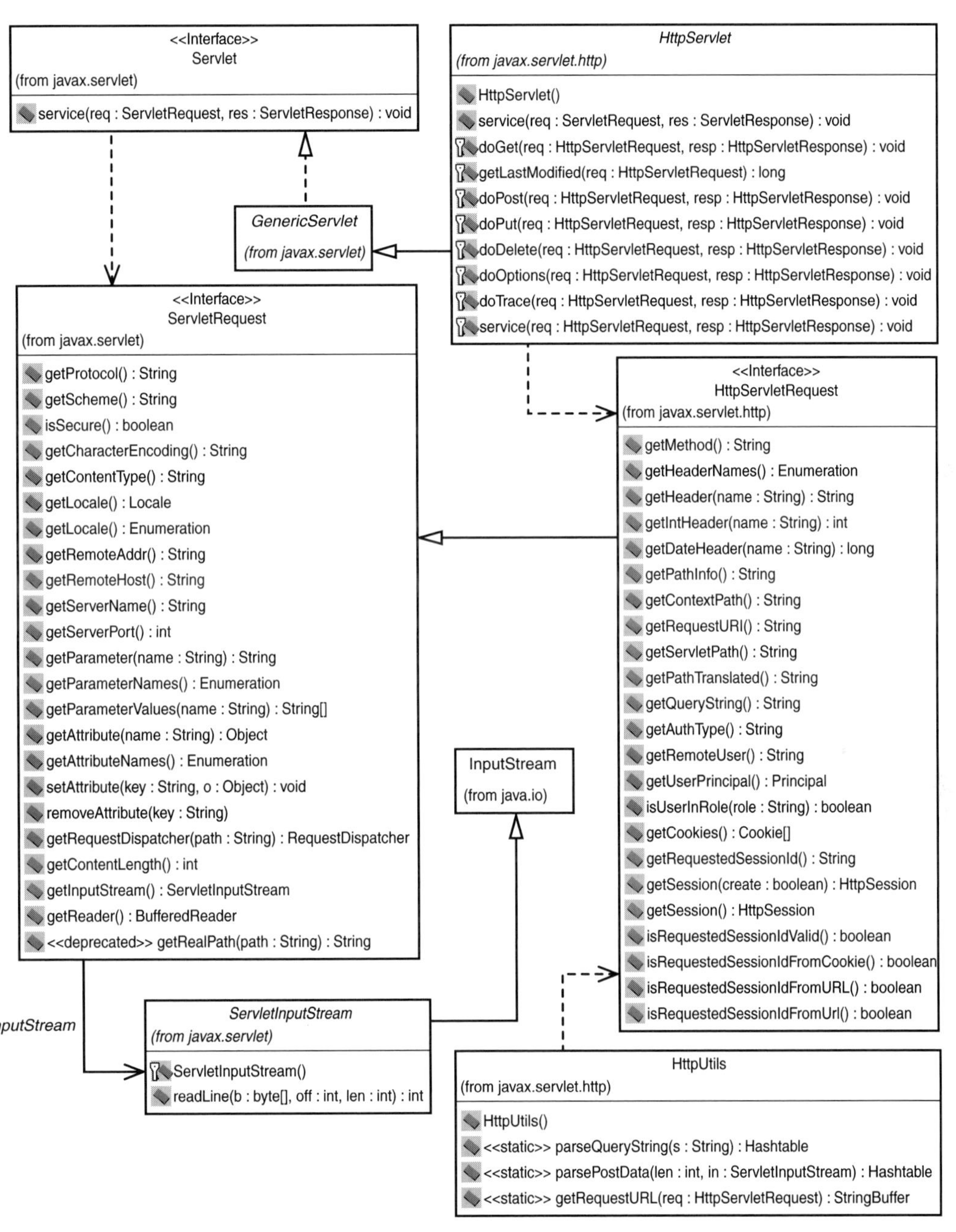

FIGURE 32.8
Handling HTTP servlet requests.

Certain socket-level information about the request can also be determined from ServletRequest. The ServletRequest.getRemoteAddr() call returns the IP address of the client, and the ServletRequest.getRemoteHost() returns the hostname of the client if it can be determined via DNS. Server-side socket information can also be determined from the request with the ServletRequest.getServerName() and ServletRequest.getServerPort() methods returning the server name and port number at which the request was received, respectively.

Parameters of requests are String values that can be identified by a String name. HTTP request parameters are sent in a request query String or via form post data. The first parameter value of a named type can be returned from the ServletRequest.getParameter() call, whereas zero or more String values of a named type can be retrieved from the ServletRequest.getParameterValues() call. An Enumeration of String names for all parameters in a request is obtained via the ServletRequest.getParameterNames() method call.

Attributes of a request are often added to a ServletRequest object by a servlet container environment. An attribute can be any Object value that has a String name. Attributes can also be set onto a ServletRequest using the setAttribute() method call. Attribute values are retrieved from the ServletRequest via the getAttribute() call. Attributes are removed from the ServletRequest using the removeAttribute() call. Finally, the names of all attributes can be retrieved using the ServletRequest.getAttributeNames() call to return an Enumeration of String names.

The request body contains data from which application-specific information can be read and used by the servlet. The number of bytes in the request body data stream can be obtained via the ServletRequest.getContentLength() call. The ServletRequest.getBufferedReader() call can be made to retrieve a handle to a BufferedReader I/O stream form of the data. Alternatively, the ServletRequest.getInputStream() call can be made to retrieve a handle to a special ServletInputStream helper object that is used to read data from the input stream as lines of binary data. Either the getInputStream() or the getBufferedReader() method may be called during a particular request service call, but not both.

ServletInputStream Class

The abstract javax.servlet.ServletInputStream class extends the java.io.InputStream class and provides the readLine() method definition as a means for reading bytes of information from a request body one line at a time. A byte array into which data should be read, a beginning offset into that array, and a number of bytes to read are all passed as parameters to the readLine() method. When protocols such as HTTP are used, data from the HTTP request body can be retrieved via the ServletInputStream. The BufferedReader returned from the ServletRequest.getBufferedReader() call can also be used to read such request body data.

HttpServletRequest Interface

The javax.servlet.http.HttpServletRequest interface extends the ServletRequest interface to specifically encapsulate HTTP requests. The servlet container creates an HttpServletRequest object when an HTTP request is received and passes this object to the public HttpServlet.service() method call. The HttpServlet object then ultimately calls an appropriate HttpServlet.do*XXX*() method. The exact do*XXX*() method to be called is driven by the HTTP request method type received, which may also be determined from the HttpServletRequest.getMethod() call.

Specific HTTP request header information can also be read from the HttpServletRequest object. The getHeaderNames() method will return an Enumeration of String names for the various HTTP request headers received. The getHeader() method retrieves the String value of a header given the header name. Certain header values that can be converted to an int value can also be retrieved using the getIntHeader() method given the header name. Headers that correspond to dates can be retrieved in terms of milliseconds since January 1, 1970, GMT using the getDateHeader() method.

Various portions of information from the target URI path of the requested resource can be retrieved using the HttpServletRequest object. The getRequestURI() method is used to return the entire requested URI field extracted from the HTTP request data excluding any URI query parameter data. The getContextPath() method can be used to retrieve that part of the request URI that corresponds only to the context of an HTTP request. The getServletPath() method is used to return only that portion of the requested URI used to identify the servlet to be called relative to the root servlet context. The getQueryString() method returns any data contained within the query parameter String portion of a requested URI. Finally, the getPathTranslated() method is used to retrieve any data between the servlet pathname and the query String within the requested URI.

Certain security-related information associated with an HTTP request can be extracted from the HttpServletRequest when needed. Methods such as getAuthType(), getRemoteUser(), getUserPrincipal(), and isUserInRole() can all be used in the context of providing secure servlet access to be discussed later in this chapter. We also defer discussion until a later section of various servlet session and cookie management facilities that can be tapped from HttpServletRequest object methods.

HttpUtils Class

The javax.servlet.http.HttpUtils class provides a set of static methods that can be used by a servlet application to retrieve URL, URL parameter, and post data from HTTP requests into a more easily managed form. The static HttpUtils.getRequestURL() method is used to take an HttpServletRequest object and extract the URL from the request in the form of a StringBuffer. Only the URL protocol, server hostname, server port number, and server path are extracted from the HTTP requested URL.

The static `HttpUtils.parseQueryString()` method can be used to convert a `String` of name/value parameters embedded in a URL to a `Hashtable` of the name/value pairs. Recall that parameters in a URL are an ampersand (`&`) separated set of name/value pairs of the following form: *`name1=value1&name2=value2&...`*. If two names embedded in a URL `String` are of the same value, the `Hashtable` entry associated with that name is associated with an array of `String` values. Before values are added to the `Hashtable`, the URL-encoded form of the values is decoded (for example, the + values are converted to spaces).

The static `HttpUtils.parsePostData()` is used to parse data sent from an HTML form encoding according to the `application/x-www-form-urlencoded` MIME type/subtype via an HTTP `POST` request. A `ServletInputStream` object containing this data and the length of the input stream are submitted to `parsePostData()`, which returns a `Hashtable` of the parsed name/value pairs. As with the `parseQueryString()` method, the `parsePostData()` method also converts similarly named values into an array of values and decodes the URL encoded format of the `String` before it populates the `Hashtable`.

Servlet Request Dispatching Abstractions

Figure 32.9 depicts the basic entities involved in dispatching requests received by one servlet to another resource (for example, another servlet). This may involve forwarding a servlet request using a special request dispatcher object. It may also involve the inclusion of output from another resource within the output of the initial target resource.

`RequestDispatcher` Interface

The `javax.servlet.RequestDispatcher` interface is used to encapsulate an object that is used to dispatch requests from a client to another server resource such as a servlet or JavaServer Page. As you'll see in a later section, servlets and JSP Web components can be named using deployment descriptor properties. A request dispatcher associated with these named components can be obtained using the `ServletContext.getNamedDispatcher()` method.

`RequestDispatcher` objects can also be created from `ServletContext.getRequestDispatcher()` method calls by passing in a URL pathname (beginning with `/`) for a resource relative to the root servlet context. The returned `RequestDispatcher` object can then be used as a handle to forward a `ServletRequest` object to the associated resource URL path. A call to `ServletContext.getContext()` can be used to obtain a `ServletContext` object for another servlet context environment. The returned `ServletContext` can then be used to obtain a `RequestDispatcher` object for forwarding requests to resources in that foreign context. Alternatively, the `ServletRequest.getRequestDispatcher()` method may also be used to obtain a `RequestDispatcher` object.

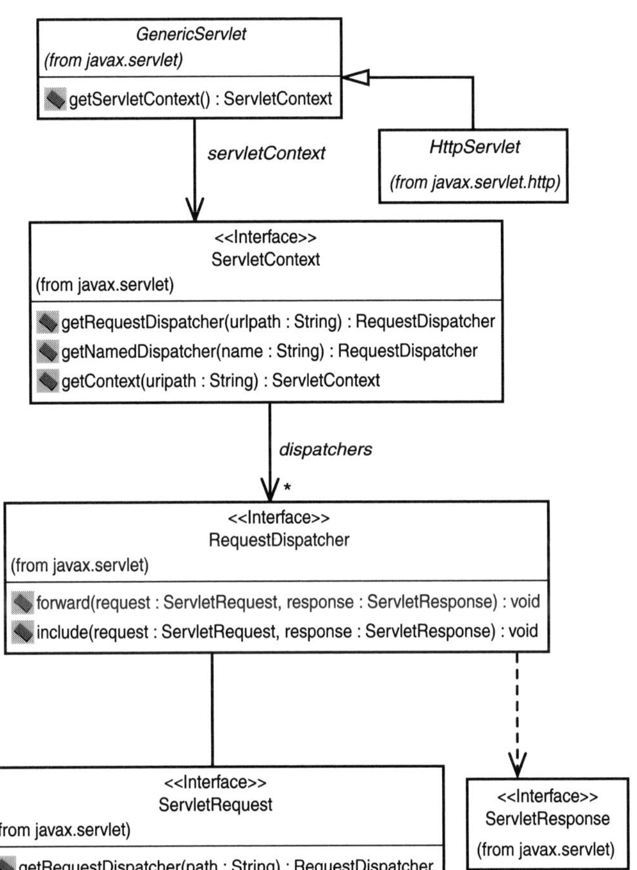

FIGURE 32.9
Forwarding HTTP servlet requests.

After a `RequestDispatcher` handle is obtained, one of two methods on the `RequestDispatcher` may be called. The `RequestDispatcher.forward()` method is used to forward a servlet request to another resource. Thus, the initial servlet may process the servlet request in some way first before it redirects the request to another URL. Although the request may be preprocessed in some way, no output to the servlet response stream may be performed before the request is forwarded. Alternatively, the `RequestDispatcher.include()` method is used to include the contents of a targeted resource with the output of the current servlet.

Request Handling Examples

The `service()` method of the `BeeShirtsServlet` is the initial point of entry into our BeeShirts.com e-commerce servlet storefront. When the `BeeShirtsServlet` deployed to a particular Web server is referenced from within the URL of a Web browser, the `service()` method receives an `HttpServletRequest` from the servlet container environment. The `BeeShirtsServlet.service()` method first extracts some server information from the HTTP request as shown here:

```
public void service (HttpServletRequest servletRequest,
  HttpServletResponse servletResponse)
  throws ServletException, IOException
{
  // Extract server information from HTTP request
  String serverInfo = ServletsHelper.getServerInfo(servletRequest);

// ...more code to be described in later sections...

}
```

The static `ServletsHelper.getServerInfo()` method simply extracts info from the `HttpServletRequest` and returns a concatenated form of the server hostname, server port, and context path:

```
public static String getServerInfo(HttpServletRequest servletRequest)
{
  String serverHost = servletRequest.getServerName();
  int serverPort = servletRequest.getServerPort();
  String context = servletRequest.getContextPath();

  return serverHost +":"+serverPort + context;
}
```

As exemplified in the `doGet()` request handling method of the `CheckOutServlet`, we also need to redirect the user to another servlet from within the `CheckOutServlet` on occasion. The `CheckOutServlet.doGet()` method first retrieves `Customer` information from the HTTP session and then invokes a special `redirectRegistrationScreen()` method if no `Customer` information was stored in the session. Subsequently, if no `ShoppingCart` information is stored in the session object, a special `redirectBrowseScreen()` method is invoked. Otherwise, the current user's shopping-cart information is displayed. The `doGet()` method is defined this way:

```
public void doGet(HttpServletRequest servletRequest,
 HttpServletResponse servletResponse)
 throws ServletException, IOException
{
// Get stored customer session information
  Customer customer = getCustomerFromSession(servletRequest);
```

```
    // If no stored customer info, redirect to registration screen
    if(customer == null){
      redirectRegistrationScreen(servletRequest, servletResponse);
    }

    // Get stored shopping cart information
    ShoppingCart cart = getShoppingCartFromSession(servletRequest);

    // If no stored cart info, redirect to browse screen
    if(cart == null){
      redirectBrowseScreen(servletRequest, servletResponse);
    }
    else{ // Else display the cart info and request card info
       displayTheCartAndTakeUserCardInformation(servletRequest,
                                               servletResponse, cart);
    }
  }
```


The CheckOutServlet.redirectRegistrationScreen() method first obtains a RequestDispatcher object associated with the registration.html page. The RegistrationServlet.REGISTRATION_HTML constant is used to identify the /registration.html page. The request and response parameters are then submitted to the RequestDispatcher.forward() method to be redirected as shown here:

```
  private void redirectRegistrationScreen(
    HttpServletRequest servletRequest,
    HttpServletResponse servletResponse)
      throws ServletException, IOException
  {
    // First retrieve servlet context handle
     ServletContext ctx = getServletContext();
     // Obtain dispatcher handle to registration.html
     RequestDispatcher dispatcher =
        ctx.getRequestDispatcher(RegistrationServlet.REGISTRATION_HTML);
     // Forward to registration.html
     if(dispatcher != null){
       dispatcher.forward(servletRequest, servletResponse);
     }
  }
```

Similarly, the CheckOutServlet.redirectBrowseScreen() method is used to create a RequestDispatcher object associated with the BrowseShirtsServlet and the Web request is redirected to that servlet as shown here:

```
  private void redirectBrowseScreen(HttpServletRequest servletRequest,
    HttpServletResponse servletResponse)
      throws ServletException, IOException
```

```
{
   RequestDispatcher dispatcher
      = getServletContext().getRequestDispatcher(
                                 BrowseShirtsServlet.SERVLET_NAME);
   if(dispatcher != null){
     dispatcher.forward(servletRequest, servletResponse);
   }
}
```

We encourage you to examine all the HTTP request handling semantics defined for the BeeShirts.com storefront code on the CD. For the most part, requests to BeeShirts.com servlets serve as triggers to stimulate the servlet to generate a response. Data sent within the request is used minimally. The `ServletsHelper.getServerInfo()` method and retrieval of session information represent the most frequent uses of `HttpServletRequest` objects. However, there are a few more sample uses of request information by the BeeShirts.com servlets. These nontrivial usage scenarios are described here:

- `RegistrationServlet`: The `RegistrationServlet.doPost()` method receives information posted from the Register button inside the `registration.html` page. The `registration.html` page posts user registration form data from a collection of `INPUT TEXT` fields. The `RegistrationServlet.doPost()` method calls the private `RegistrationServlet.registerNewCustomer()` method to extract this form data by using `HttpServletRequest.getParameterValues()` calls using a set of `String` name constants as shown here:

  ```
  String firstName =
    (String)servletRequest.getParameterValues(Customer.FIRST_NAME)[0];
  String lastName =
    (String)servletRequest.getParameterValues(Customer.LAST_NAME)[0];
      ...
  String state =
    (String)servletRequest.getParameterValues(Address.STATE)[0];
  String zip_code =
    (String)servletRequest.getParameterValues(Address.ZIP_CODE)[0];
  ```

- `BrowseShirtsServlet`: Recall that the `BrowseShirtsServlet doGet()` method displays a query form for users to submit an HTTP `POST` to the `BrowseShirtsServlet` with shirt size and color query criteria. The servlet's `doPost()` method must retrieve this information from the received `HttpServletRequest` like this:

  ```
  String queriedSize = servletRequest.getParameter(SHIRT_SIZE);
  String queriedColor = servletRequest.getParameter(SHIRT_COLOR);
  ```

- `CartServlet`: A `POST` from the `BrowseShirtsServlet` induced by the ADD TO CART buttons that are associated with each shirt passes along a `Tshirt` ID and quantity to the `CartServlet.doPost()` method. The `CartServlet.doPost()` method extracts this information and uses it to locate Tshirt objects from within an HTTP session and add them to the user's ShoppingCart. The retrieval of the POST data is rather straightforward:

```
// Get shirt ID from POST
String selectedShirtIDString =
  servletRequest.getParameterValues(TShirt.SHIRT_ID)[0];
// Get number of shirts from POST
String numberSelectedString =
 servletRequest.getParameterValues(TShirt.ORDERED_FIELD)[0];
```

- OrderStatusServlet: A POST to OrderStatusServlet.doPost() is sent from within the OrderStatusServlet.doGet() method response. The POST results from a user clicking a Login or Remind button. The extraction of the relevant data from the HttpServletRequest object for either post from within the doPost() method is shown here:

```
// Check whether the user is asking to remind him/her
// This occurs when Remind button is pressed
String[] remindValues  =
  servletRequest.getParameterValues(EMAIL_LOOKUP_FIELD_NAME);

if(handleRemindRequest(remindValues,
                       servletRequest, servletResponse)){
  return;
}

// Otherwise user hit Login button
// Get email and password info
String emailAddress =
  servletRequest.getParameterValues(EMAIL_FIELD_NAME)[0];
String password =
  servletRequest.getParameterValues(PASSWORD_FIELD_NAME)[0];
```


Response Generation

You saw in the preceding section how Web requests can be encapsulated and used by application-specific servlets via a core set of Java Servlet abstractions. You can then implement application-specific usage of this request information and any additional business logic within the confines of your application-specific servlet. At some point, you must also generate a servlet response. The Java Servlet framework offers a set of servlet response abstractions that are used for this purpose. Responses to Web clients contain response headers and contain response body data that can be buffered in various ways depending on your specific application. We describe the Java Servlet response abstractions in this section, as well as illustrate some basic examples for usage of these abstractions in the context of our sample BeeShirts.com e-commerce storefront.

Response Handling Abstractions

Figure 32.10 depicts the basic set of abstractions involved in encapsulating servlet responses. A basic protocol-independent servlet response abstraction is used to encapsulate a set of basic response operations to a client. An output stream for sending data in such a response body is provided as its own abstraction. A concrete HTTP-specific extension of the servlet response abstraction is also provided. The HTTP servlet response abstraction provides many operations specific to the HTTP response protocol and also defines a collection of response type constants.

`ServletResponse` Interface

The `javax.servlet.ServletResponse` interface encapsulates an object used to send responses from a servlet to a client. The actual creation of a `ServletResponse` object is performed by the servlet container and passed as a parameter to the `Servlet.service()` method. `ServletResponse` objects have various base interfaces defined that allow one to obtain a handle to a response body data stream, configure the format of a response, and tune the performance of a response.

The `ServletResponse.getOutputStream()` method is used to obtain a handle to a `ServletOutputStream` object used to write binary data to an HTTP response body. Alternatively, the `getWriter()` method can be used to obtain a handle to a `PrintWriter` object for writing character text data to a response body. Either the `PrintWriter` or the `ServletOutputStream` object can be used to write response data, but not both. The particular format of character data can be established by first calling `setContentType()` with the MIME type/subtype and character encoding format to be used (for example, `text/html; charset=ISO-8859-4`). The `getCharacterEncoding()` method can be used to retrieve the value of the `charset` to send the response (for example, `ISO-8859-4`). The `Locale` of the `ServletResponse` can be read and set using the `getLocale()` and `setLocale()` methods, respectively.

The size of a response body is important to consider when trading off performance and memory utilized on the server and client. The desired buffer size to be used for the response body can be set using the `setBufferSize()` method. The buffer size actually allocated can be retrieved using the `getBufferSize()` method. By establishing the buffer size for servlet responses, applications can better manage server performance and memory resource utilization trade-offs. Furthermore, smaller buffer sizes allow servlet clients to receive response data sooner. Any buffer-size setting must occur before the writing of content to an output stream. Additionally, any servlet header field for specifying content length (for example, `Content-Length` for HTTP responses) can also be set using the `setContentLength()` method.

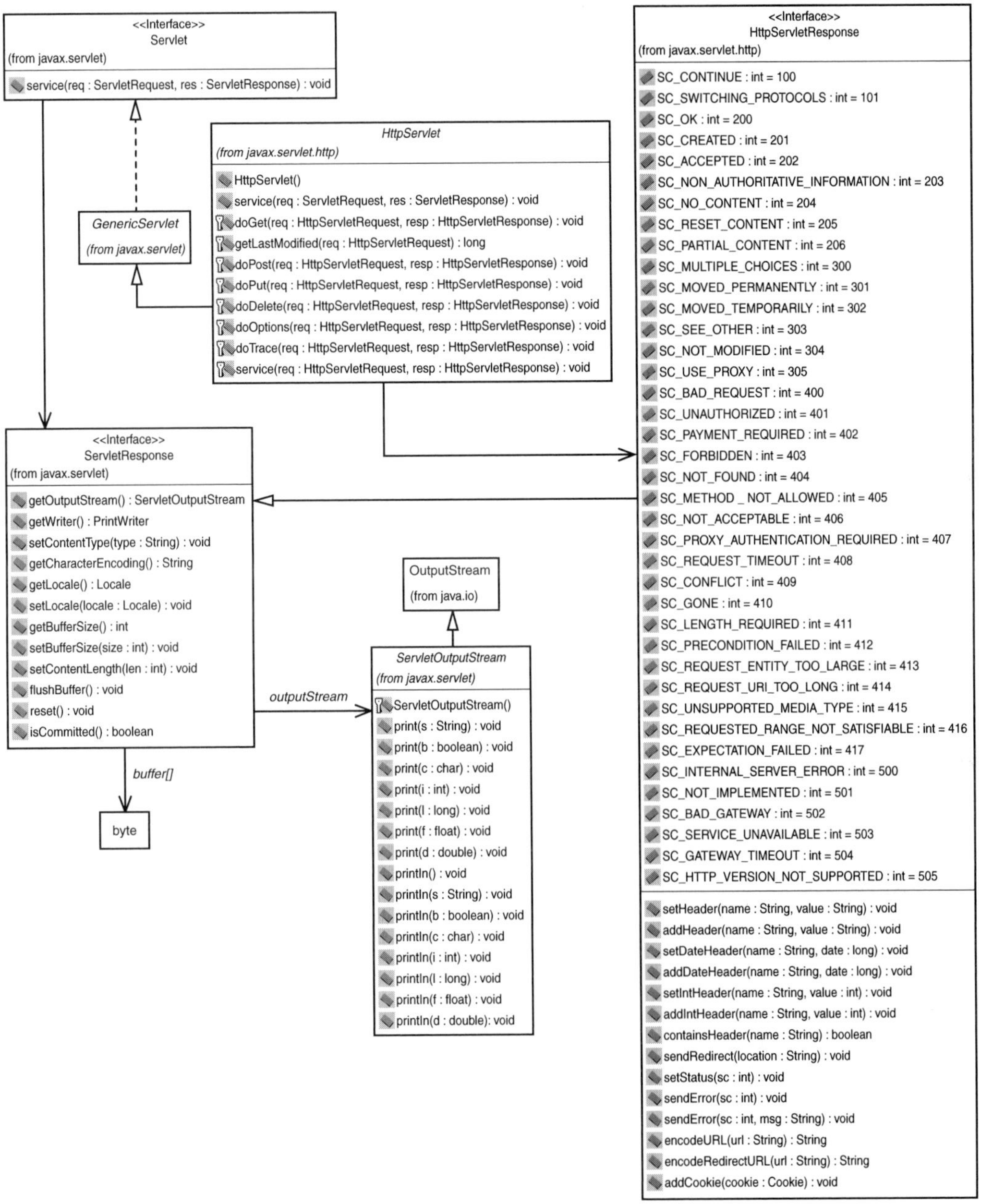

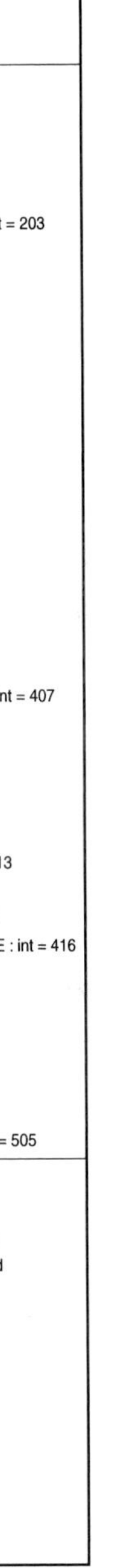

FIGURE 32.10

Generating HTTP servlet responses.

The data from a response buffer can be flushed to the client with a call to flushBuffer(). Such a call commits all header and status information as well. The status of whether such a commit has taken place is determined from a call to isCommitted(). If a response has yet to be committed, a call to reset() will clear all response data, headers, and status information written from the response buffer.

ServletOutputStream Class

The abstract javax.servlet.ServletOutputStream class extends the OutputStream class to encapsulate an interface to a servlet output stream. A collection of print() and println() methods is defined on the ServletOutputStream class to facilitate writing information to a servlet response body stream. The print() methods write information to the servlet output stream with no carriage-return line-feed added. The println() methods write information to the servlet output stream with a carriage-return line-feed added. Various fundamental Java types and Java String objects can be written to the output stream using print() and println(). The parameterless println() method simply writes a carriage-return line-feed to the stream.

HttpServletResponse Interface

The javax.servlet.http.HttpServletResponse interface extends the basic ServletResponse interface with specific HTTP response semantics. An HTTP servlet container creates an HttpServletResponse object and passes it along with an HttpServletRequest to an HttpServlet.service() method. The application-specific HttpServlet then uses the HttpServletResponse to create the HTTP response information to be sent back to the HTTP client. The sendRedirect() method can also be used to send a redirect response to an HTTP client that redirects the client to request information from another specified URL String. Although absolute URLs can be passed to the sendRedirect() method, the servlet container environment will convert any URLs specified in relative form to an absolute URL.

The HttpServletReponse exposes a collection of methods specifically meant to deal with HTTP response header writing. The setHeader() method is used to write a particular header value to be associated with a header name. The addHeader() method is used to add multiple values that are to be associated with a particular header name. Similarly, the setDateHeader() and addDateHeader() methods can be used to write date values associated with a named header, and the setIntHeader() and addIntHeader() methods can be used to write int values to a header. The containsHeader() returns a boolean value indicating whether a particular named header exists in the response stream.

The setStatus() method is used to write status information into the HTTP response header if no error has occurred. Otherwise, the setError() methods are used to set error messages in the HTTP response header. In both cases, an HTTP response code is used as encapsulated by one of the static public final int attribute values in the HttpServletResponse interface, as shown in Figure 32.10. Recall from our discussion in Chapter 13 that the response codes defined in RFC 1945 may be broadly classified as informational (100-199), successes (200-299), redirection (300-399), client request errors (400-499), and server-side errors (500-599).

Response Handling Examples

As previously mentioned, the BeeShirtsServlet.service() method is the initial point of entry into our BeeShirts.com e-commerce servlet storefront. After extraction of a String of server information from the HttpServletRequest, the service() method manages the writing of response data back to the client via the HttpServletResponse object. This response consists of the construction of some initial document response type and header data, the writing of the response body, and the closing of the document response tags and stream as shown here:


```
public void service (HttpServletRequest servletRequest,
  HttpServletResponse servletResponse)
  throws ServletException, IOException
{
  // Extract server information from HTTP request
  String serverInfo = ServletsHelper.getServerInfo(servletRequest);

  String sessionCookie = // session management shown in later section

  // Create initial document type and headers
  PrintWriter printWriter =
    ServletsHelper.createInitialDocumentResponse(servletResponse);

  // Write the body of the page to the stream
  writePageBody(printWriter, serverInfo, sessionCookie);

  // Close with BODY and HTML closing tags
  ServletsHelper.createClosingDocumentResponse(printWriter);
}
```

The common means by which the initial document response is created is encapsulated within the BeeShirts.com ServletsHelper.createInitialDocumentResponse() method. This method sets the common context type for the document (that is, text/html), obtains a handle to a PrintWriter, and writes the common initial document DOCTYPE, HTML, HEAD, TITLE, and BODY tags as shown here:

```
public static PrintWriter createInitialDocumentResponse(
      HttpServletResponse servletResponse)
  throws IOException
{
  // Set common text/html content type for all of our documents
```

```
    servletResponse.setContentType(CONTENT_TYPE);
    // Retrieve the PrintWriter handle
    PrintWriter printWriter = servletResponse.getWriter();
    // Print common DOCTYPE, HTML begin tag, HEAD, and TITLE tags
    printWriter.println(
      "<!DOCTYPE HTML PUBLIC \"-//W3C//DTD HTML 4.0 Transitional//EN\">"
      + "\n <HTML> \n <HEAD> \n <TITLE> "
      + "\n BeeShirts.com </TITLE>\n </HEAD>\n");
    // Print common BODY begin tags
    printWriter.println( "<BODY ALINK=\"#FFCC66\"  BGCOLOR=\"#ffcc66\" "+
      " LINK=\"#FFFFFF\" VLINK=\"#FFFFFF\"> " );

    return printWriter;
  }
```

Similarly, the `ServletsHelper.createClosingDocumentResponse()` method can be used to close the `PrintWriter` stream after closing `BODY` and `HTML` tags are written as shown here:

```
  public static void createClosingDocumentResponse(
    PrintWriter printWriter)
  {
    printWriter.println(" </BODY> ");
    printWriter.println( "</HTML>" );
    printWriter.close();
  }
```

The `BeeShirtsServlet.writePageBody()` method implements some of the custom layout and page body logic specific to this root servlet. The `writePageBody()` first invokes the `ServletsHelper.writePageTopArea()` method to write the top area of the Web page common to all BeeShirts.com servlets, which consists of the BeeShirts.com logo. The lower half of the screen is then partitioned into two areas, with the left side corresponding to the common selection of buttons as created by the `ServletsHelper.writePageLeftArea()` method. The center page area is then written by the custom `BeeShirtsServlet.writePageCenterArea()` method. The `writePageBody()` method is shown here:

```
  private void writePageBody(PrintWriter printWriter,
    String serverInfo, String cookieValue)
  {
    // Write common top portion of page
    ServletsHelper.writePageTopArea(printWriter);

    // Partition lower page portion into one row of two TABLE columns
    printWriter.println("<TABLE BORDER=0 COLS=2 WIDTH=\"100%\" >");
    printWriter.println(" <TR> ");
```

```
    // Write the common left-hand portion of the page
    ServletsHelper.writePageLeftArea(printWriter, serverInfo);

    // Write this servlet's specific center of the page info
    writePageCenterArea(printWriter, cookieValue);

    // Close with TABLE end tags
    printWriter.println("</TR>");
    printWriter.println("</TABLE> <br> ");
  }
```


The `BeeShirtsServlet.writePageCenterArea()` method generates the welcome page body of our root servlet as shown here:

```
  private void writePageCenterArea(PrintWriter printWriter,
    String cookieValue)
  {
    // Write the body of the page
    printWriter.println("<TD  > ");
    // If the cookie session value is valid, then user has visited
    // the site before, so display a welcome message...
    if(cookieValue != null){
      printWriter.println("   <STRONG> WELCOME BACK : "
                          + cookieValue +"</STRONG> <BR>");
    }
    String msg = "";
    try{
      // Get initial context and lookup welcome message via JNDI
        // Note: This concept discussed in subsequent section
      InitialContext ctx = new InitialContext();
      msg = (String) ctx.lookup("java:comp/env/WelcomeMessage");
    }
    catch(NamingException namingException){
      namingException.printStackTrace();
    }
    // Print the root screen promo and welcome...
    printWriter.println(msg + "</TD>");
  }
```

We also encourage you to examine all the HTTP response handling semantics defined for the BeeShirts.com storefront code on the CD. Almost all the responses from the BeeShirts.com servlets manage display of the top and left portions of the BeeShirts.com screens with custom development for the center area of the screen. In between HTTP request handling and HTTP response generation, some session management takes place, as we describe in a subsequent section. However, in general, BeeShirts.com servlet response generation follows the same basic pattern. For your edification in understanding the code on the CD, we describe the basic response generation scenarios here:

- `BeeShirtsServlet`: When a `GET` or `POST` request is made, this servlet generates the display of a welcome message and a welcome-back message to users with cookies wherein most of the presentation display is generated within the `writePageCenterArea()` method.
- `AboutUsServlet`: When a `GET` request is made, this servlet generates the display of some information about the BeeShirts.com Web site with most of the presentation display generated within the `writePageCenterArea()` method.
- `ContactInformationServlet`: When a `GET` request is made, this servlet generates the display of some contact information at BeeShirts.com with most of the presentation display generated within the `writePageCenterArea()` method.
- `registration.html`: When a `GET` request is made, this static HTML page generates a form with `INPUT TEXT` fields for entering user registration information. Also generates some minimal JavaScript data field validation code.
- `RegistrationServlet`: When a `POST` request is made, this servlet creates a `Customer` object from the `POST` data sent from `registration.html` and adds this info to the session via the `registerNewCustomer()` method and also creates a personalized cookie for the user. The success or failure status of the attempted registration is then generated with most of the presentation display generated from within the `writePageCenterArea()` method.
- `BrowseShirtsServlet`: When a `GET` request is made, an HTML `FORM` used to query for T-shirts is generated with most of the presentation encapsulated within the `writePageCenterAreaForForm()` method. When a `POST` request is made, the result of the `T-Shirt` query is generated with most of the presentation encapsulated within the `writePageCenterAreaResults()` method.
- `CartServlet`: When a `GET` request is made, the contents of the current `ShoppingCart` object are generated via the `displayItemsInTheCart()` method, or a message indicating that the cart is empty is generated via the `displayNoItemsInTheCart()` method. When a `POST` message is received to add a T-shirt to the `ShoppingCart`, the `displayAddedOrFailedToAdd()` method is called to generate most of the presentation response for such a scenario.
- `CheckOutServlet`: When a `GET` request is received, the user may be redirected to the `registration.html` page or `BrowseShirtsServlet` as described in the preceding section. However, if neither redirection scenario occurs, the user and cart information is generated via the `displayTheCartAndTakeUserCardInformation()` method.

- `OrderStatusServlet`: When the `GET` request is received, an HTML `INPUT FORM` is generated via the `writePageBodyForLoginForm()` and `writePageCenterAreaForLoginForm()` methods. The form provides a means for accepting login information sent via a Login button and for requesting a password information reminder sent via a Remind button. When an HTTP `POST` is received, the `handleRemindRequest()` determines whether the user clicked the Remind button and will call the `writeEmailReminderPage()` method to generate a message indicating that the user's password will be mailed to him. If the Login button was clicked and incorrect login data was sent by the `POST` method, the user will be told he has erred via the `informUserThatLoginFailed()` method and will be presented with another login form. If the Login button was clicked and the user attempted to log in more than five times, the `askTheUserToRegister()` method will redirect the user to the `registration.html` page. Because we defer illustration of connectivity to a database from a J2EE server application until our EJB discussion, this chapter's `OrderStatusServlet` requires that the user enter in a canned `sam@sam.com` email address and `sam` password to induce a successful login. A set of canned order data is then generated via the `constructOrderForThisCustomer()` method and displayed with the `showUserOrders()` method.
- `TermsAndConditionsServlet`: When a `GET` request is made, this servlet generates the display of some terms and conditions about BeeShirts.com purchases with most of the presentation display generated within the `writePageCenterArea()` method.
- `deliveryinformation.html`: When a `GET` request is made, this static HTML page generates the display of some dummy delivery information.

Session Management

The communications paradigm of HTTP, as discussed in Chapter 13, is a stateless paradigm sans any higher-level augmentation on the client and server side to support stateful sessions. State can be managed over HTTP using such mechanisms as URL rewriting, hidden HTML variables, and cookies. Regardless of the means by which stateful HTTP sessions can be provided, the Java Servlet API provides an abstraction for this mechanism. Once a session is created, the API developer can bind objects to an HTTP session during the handling of one HTTP request and subsequently retrieve these objects during a subsequent request from the same user. The servlet container environment shields the programmer from the need to know the details behind the underlying implementation of session management.

Apart from satisfying the need to store and retrieve objects related to the same Web client user session, cookies, as a particular session management implementation type, also satisfy another need. Cookies are sometimes used to store information on the client side for an extended period beyond a single user session for later retrieval by the server side. For example, an e-commerce storefront may induce your Web browser to store some information about you on your client machine such that a visit to that site later will result in the site being able to recognize you individually. This permits the site to be able to customize the Web presentation of the storefront to your interests (as well as perhaps permit certain violations of your privacy). The Java Servlet framework thus also offers an abstraction for manipulating cookies explicitly to facilitate such functionality on the server side. This section describes cookie and HTTP session abstractions, as well as presenting some sample uses of these abstractions within the context of our BeeShirts.com storefront.

Session Management Abstractions

Figure 32.11 presents the abstractions provided by the Java Servlet API for managing Web-based sessions within the context of HTTP servlets. At the core of this framework lies an HTTP session abstraction for manipulating session information across multiple requests from the same user. An abstraction for manipulating cookies is also provided. Finally, a means for listening to and generating events related to the binding and unbinding of objects from an HTTP session is also provided.

`HttpSession` Interface

The `javax.servlet.http.HttpSession` interface encapsulates the concept of an HTTP session associated with a particular Web client's access of a Web server over multiple requests within some scope of time. Because the `HttpSession` is associated with a particular Web client user, information associated with the user can be maintained by associating the information with an `HttpSession` object. The servlet container environment may actually implement the management of sessions underneath the hood using one of the HTTP session management techniques discussed in Chapter 13. However, the servlet applications developer will still have the same consistent and easy-to-use interface to manage session information via the `HttpSession` object.

The `HttpServletRequest.getSession()` object returns the current `HttpSession` object associated with the request and creates one if none yet exists. Optionally, the `HttpServletRequest.getSession(boolean)` method may be used to do the same thing, but it will return a `null` value if a `false` value was used as a method parameter and if no session yet exists. The `HttpSession.isNew()` method indicates whether the client is aware of an HTTP session. The `isNew()` method returns `true` if the client is not yet session-aware.

The `HttpServletRequest` object can also be used to determine the nature of session management. A call to `isRequestedSessionIdFromCookie()` indicates whether the received session ID came from a cookie, whereas the `isRequestedSessionIdFromURL()` method indicates whether the received session ID came from a rewritten URL. The `isRequestedSessionIdValid()` method indicates whether the current request received an ID that could be associated with a valid session. The servlet container implementation-dependent session ID value may be returned from a call to `HttpSession.getId()`.

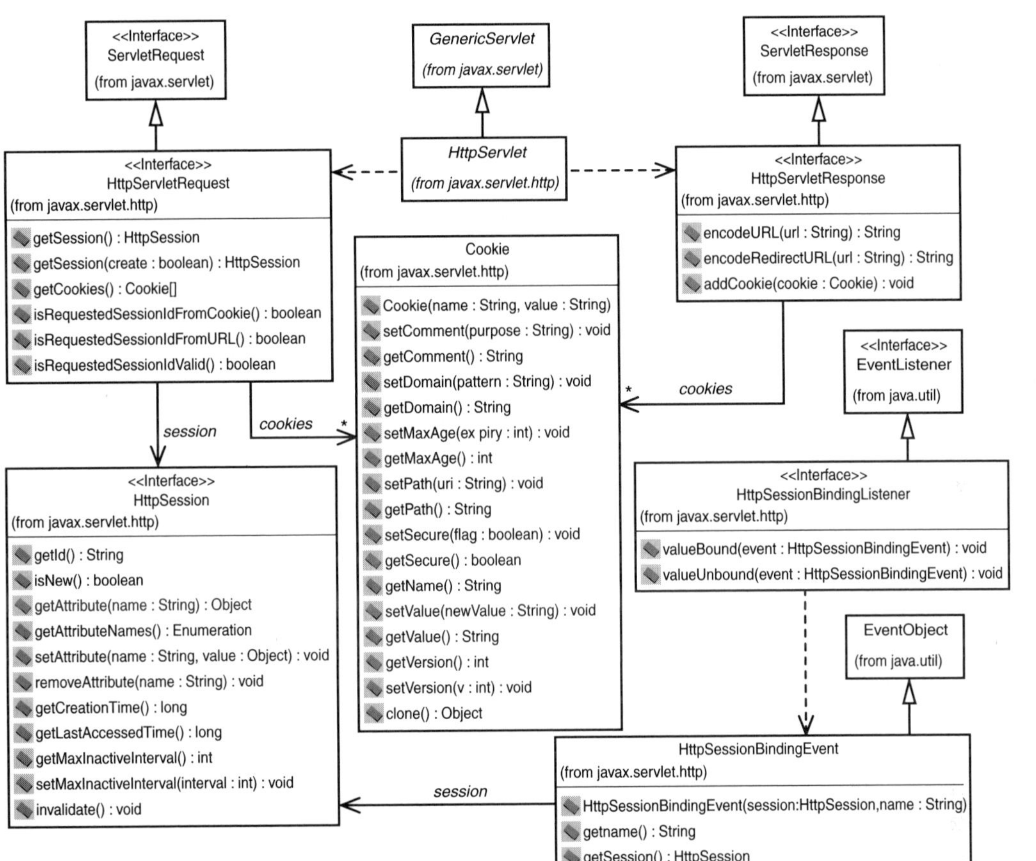

FIGURE 32.11
HTTP session management.

When URL rewriting is being used for session management, it is important to properly embed session ID information into URLs that are sent back to the Web client. The `HttpServletResponse.encodeURL()` method takes a URL `String` parameter and encodes a session ID into the `String`. If the Web client supports cookies or session management is disabled, the returned `String` is unchanged. URLs created by a servlet should use this method just in case a particular Web client does not support cookies for session management. Similarly, before using the `sendRedirect()` method, the `encodeRedirectURL()` should be used to create a URL that can modify the URL to send with session ID information.

The maximum inactive interval for which a session is to be maintained by a servlet container environment can be managed via the `HttpSession` object. The `setMaxInactiveInterval()` method is used to designate the number of seconds between requests that must pass before a servlet container will render a session invalid. A negative number passed to `setMaxInactiveInterval()` is used to designate that no time limit should be set. The `getMaxInactiveInterval()` method may be used to retrieve this value. Of course, a session may be invalidated beforehand with a call to `invalidate()`. Any objects that were associated with a session are unbound when the session becomes invalid.

Two methods on the `HttpSession` object are used to determine certain statistical timing information related to a user's session. The time when the session was created is returned from `getCreationTime()`, whereas the time that has passed since the Web client last accessed the server can be determined from `getLastAccessedTime()`. Both times are expressed in terms of milliseconds since January 1, 1970, GMT.

`HttpSession` objects have named attribute values associated with them. The attribute names are in `String` form and the attribute values assume a general `Object` form. An `Enumeration` of all attribute name `String` objects can be retrieved via a call to the `getAttributeNames()` method. Attributes can furthermore be read, set, and removed using the `getAttribute()`, `setAttribute()`, and `removeAttribute()` methods, respectively.

`HttpSessionBindingEvent` and `HttpSessionBindingListener`

The `javax.servlet.http.HttpSessionBindingEvent` class is used to create an event that indicates that a particular attribute has been bound to or unbound from a session. The `HttpSession` object to which the object was bound and the name of the attribute object are both associated with an `HttpSessionBindingEvent` object. The `javax.servlet.http.HttpSessionBindingListener` interface is implemented by those objects wanting to be notified of `HttpSessionBindingEvent` instances. The `valueBound()` and `valueUnbound()` methods are used to listen for both session binding and unbinding events, respectively.

Cookie Class

The `javax.servlet.http.Cookie` class encapsulates a Web cookie used to store information sent between Web browsers and servers inside of HTTP requests and responses. Although many modern browsers support cookies, some limitations may be imposed by your browser on what it can support. The `Cookie` class supports both v0 of the Netscape cookie specification and the v1 RFC2109 cookie specification. Some browsers may support only v0 of the cookie specification, however. The version supported by a cookie (0 or 1) can be determined and set via the `Cookie.getVersion()` method. A browser is expected to be capable of handling 20 cookies from each Web server and a minimum of 300 cookies total. Browsers may limit the size of a cookie to 4KB per cookie.

Cookies can be constructed with both a name and a value. The name of the cookie can also subsequently be read via the `getName()` method. The value can also be set and read using `setValue()` and `getValue()`. The cookie name can be composed only of ASCII alphanumeric characters.

The Cookie class also provides support for getting and setting various other security, comment, and lifetime expiration data. A comment that describes the purpose of the cookie can be set or read using the setComment() and getComment() methods. Comments are not supported for v0-style cookies. The security of the cookie can be specified using the setSecure() method and determined from the getSecure() method. Cookie security simply indicates whether the cookie is to be transmitted over a secure protocol. The getMaxAge() and setMaxAge() methods are used to read and set the maximum number of seconds for the cookie's validity. A negative age number indicates that the cookie will be deleted when the Web client browser exits. Zero seconds implies that the cookie should be deleted immediately.

After a Cookie object is first created on the server side, it should be added to an HttpServletResponse object using the HttpServletResponse.addCookie() method. Multiple cookies can be added to an HttpServletResponse object. The Cookie objects that have been sent back from the Web client during subsequent requests can be retrieved from the HttpServletRequest.getCookies() method call. The URL path to which the Web client should return a cookie can be specified via the setPath() method. All server resources in or below the path of the specified return path can use the cookie for session management. The getPath() method returns this path value. Similarly, the domain within which the cookie is visible can be specified and read via the setDomain() and getDomain() methods, respectively. The domain name format begins with a dot and defines that domain within which the cookie is visible (for example, .beeshirts.com).

Session Management Examples

Our BeeShirts.com application uses both HttpSession and Cookie objects for state management over HTTP. The registration.html page sends a POST request to the RegistrationServlet where the creation of a cookie is first induced. The RegistrationServlet.doPost() method first calls the RegistrationServlet.registerNewCustomer() method to create a Customer object that is added to the user's HttpSession as shown here:

```
private String registerNewCustomer(HttpServletRequest servletRequest)
  throws ServletException
{
  // Exclude code here to extract following data from servletRequest:
    // firstName, lastName, middleName, password, phone, eMail,
    // address_1, address_2, city, state, zip_code

  ...

  // Create an Address object from POST data
  Address address = new Address(address_1, address_2, city,
                                state,zip_code);
```

```
    // Create a Customer object from Address object and POST data
    Customer customer = new Customer(firstName, lastName, middleName,
                                     address, phone, eMail, password);
    // Get session and add Customer object to session
    HttpSession session  = servletRequest.getSession();
    session.setAttribute(Customer.CUSTOMER_OBJECT, customer);

    // Return user's first name
    return firstName;
  }
```

The `RegistrationServlet.doPost()` method retrieves the user's first name from the `registerNewCustomer()` method and creates a `Cookie` with the standard name of `BEESHIRTS` and the user's first name as the cookie value. After setting the maximum age of the cookie to six months, the cookie is added to the `HttpServletResponse` to be sent back to the client as shown here:

```
  public void doPost(HttpServletRequest servletRequest,
    HttpServletResponse servletResponse)
    throws ServletException, IOException
  {
      ...
      // Create Customer object in session from POST data
      String firstName = registerNewCustomer(servletRequest);
      // Get session object and the cookie name value
      HttpSession session = servletRequest.getSession(false);
      String cookieValue
          = (String)session.getAttribute(ServletsHelper.COOKIE_NAME);
      // If no cookie, then add user's first name to cookie
      if(cookieValue == null){
        // create Cookie for this customer
        // ServletsHelper.COOKIE_NAME equals "BEESHIRTS"
        Cookie cookie = new Cookie(ServletsHelper.COOKIE_NAME, firstName);
        cookie.setMaxAge(SIX_MONTHS_IN_SECONDS);
        servletResponse.addCookie(cookie);
      }
    ...
  }
```

Our BeeShirts.com `BeeShirtsServlet` front page uses the `HttpServletRequest` object to obtain cookie information from the Web client. The `BeeShirtsServlet.service()` method calls a `BeeShirtsServlet.manageSession()` method to extract a value for a cookie like this:

```
  public void service (HttpServletRequest servletRequest,
    HttpServletResponse servletResponse)
    throws ServletException, IOException
  {
```

```
    ...
    // Extract session information
    String sessionCookie = manageSession(servletRequest);
    ...
}
```

The BeeShirtsServlet.manageSession() method first extracts or creates an HttpSession object, as well as retrieving any cookies received from the HttpServletRequest. The ServletsHelper.getOurCookieValue() method is then called to search the array of Cookie objects for the standard BEESHIRTS cookie value. If the returned cookie value is not null, the cookie value is then added to the HttpSession object. The cookie value or null value is then returned from the manageSession() method as shown here:


```
private String manageSession(HttpServletRequest servletRequest)
{
  // Create a Session each time the user comes to this site.
  HttpSession session =  servletRequest.getSession(true);

  // Get any cookies from servlet request
  Cookie[]  cookies = servletRequest.getCookies();

  // Retrieve value for standard BEESHIRTS cookie if present,
  // otherwise will return a null value.
  String cookieValue = ServletsHelper.getOurCookieValue(cookies);
  System.out.println("Cookie Value :" +cookieValue);
  // If cookie value is present, then add this to the HttpSession
  if(cookieValue != null){
     session.setAttribute(ServletsHelper.COOKIE_NAME, cookieValue);
  }

  // Return cookie value if present...or null if not present
  return cookieValue;
}
```

The cookie value returned from the manageSession() method is ultimately used by the BeeShirtsServlet.writePageCenterArea() method to display a personalized welcome-back message to the user as shown here:

```
private void writePageCenterArea(PrintWriter printWriter,
  String cookieValue)
{
  ...
  if(cookieValue != null){
    printWriter.println("   <STRONG> WELCOME BACK : " +
      cookieValue +"</STRONG> <BR>");
  }
  ...
}
```

We encourage you to examine all the session management handling semantics defined for the BeeShirts.com storefront code on the CD. Information stored in a session includes customer information, order information, shopping-cart information, current T-shirt search query results, and number of failed login attempts. The cookie previously described also is used to store a personalized username for subsequent logins. These are the basic session management scenarios employed by the examples on the CD:

- `BeeShirtsServlet`: Saves the user's `Cookie` value if present to the `HttpSession` via the `manageSession()` method called from `service()`.
- `RegistrationServlet`: Retrieves the user's `Cookie` value from the `HttpSession` inside of `doPost()` to determine whether a new `Cookie` should be created. Saves a `Customer` object to the `HttpSession` via the `registerNewCustomer()` method called from `doPost()`. Also extracts this `Customer` object later from the `HttpSession` to print customer information from within the `writePageCenterArea()` method.
- `BrowseShirtsServlet`: Saves a `Vector` of `TShirt` objects created from a browse query result to the `HttpSession` from within the `writePageCenterAreaResults()` method called from `doPost()`.
- `CartServlet`: Retrieves the user's current `ShoppingCart` and `Vector` of `TShirt` objects from the `HttpSession` via the `doPost()` method. Each `TShirt` selected to be added to the shopping cart is added to the `ShoppingCart` object, and the updated `ShoppingCart` object is added to the `HttpSession` object from within the `doPost()` method. The `doGet()` method retrieves the `ShoppingCart` object from the `HttpSession` object to display its contents.
- `CheckOutServlet`: The `doGet()` method induces the retrieval of both `Customer` and `ShoppingCart` information from the `HttpSession` object to effect a customer checkout.
- `OrderStatusServlet`: The `doPost()` method induces the retrieval and update of an integer value from the `HttpSession` object that is used to indicate the number of attempted failed logins. A canned object of `Customer` information is also added to the `HttpSession` from within the `constructDefaultUserInformation()` method during an attempted login. The `constructOrderForThisCustomer()` method also uses the `HttpSession` object to retrieve the canned `Customer` information and also saves `Order` information to the `HttpSession`. The display of user order information retrieved from the `showUserOrders()` method accesses this stored `Order` object from the `HttpSession`.

Servlet Deployment

A J2EE Web application may be composed of Java Servlet classes, JavaServer Page components, auxiliary Java classes, HTML files, image files, sound files, Java code that is downloadable to clients, and meta information used to describe the Web application. All of these files are collected into a Web application ARchive (WAR) file, which is simply a JAR file having a `.war` extension and embodying a standard directory structure.

The WAR file includes the Web application deployment descriptor used to configure a Web application for a particular deployment environment. After a WAR file is created to compose a Web application, one or more of such Web applications, EJB applications, and application clients can be composed into a J2EE application along with a J2EE application deployment descriptor as described in Chapter 31, "XML." This section describes the Web application deployment descriptor format, procedures for creating Web applications, procedures for creating J2EE applications that contain Web applications, and how to deploy such applications into a J2EE server environment.

Web Application Deployment Descriptor Format

A special deployment descriptor is defined for configuring and deploying Web-based applications. XML-based deployment descriptors are defined at the servlet level during creation of modules that contain Java Servlets. These modules in turn can also be combined into a J2EE application using the application deployment descriptor syntax described in Chapter 31. The XML-based component-level deployment descriptor for describing Web components, such as Java Servlets, has a structure defined by the DTD shown in Listing 32.1. Note that we have added our own comments to describe each element in the standard shown in Listing 32.1.

LISTING 32.1 Web Component DTD (`http://java.sun.com/j2ee/dtds/web-app_2_2.dtd`)

```
<!-- The web-app element defines the root element of a J2EE
  web application deployment descriptor. Icon, display name,
  description, distributable, welcome file lists, login
  configuration, and session configuration elements are optional.
  Zero or more context parameter, servlets, servlet mappings,
  MIME mappings, error pages, tag libraries, resource references,
  security constraints and roles, environment entries, and EJB
  references are also allowed. -->
  <!ELEMENT web-app (icon?, display-name?, description?, distributable?,
                    context-param*, servlet*, servlet-mapping*,
                    session-config?, mime-mapping*, welcome-file-list?,
                    error-page*, taglib*, resource-ref*,
                    security-constraint*, login-config?, security-role*,
                    env-entry*, ejb-ref*)>
<!-- Defines optional small-icon and optional large-icon URLs for GIF or
  JPEG files that represent Web application icons. -->
  <!ELEMENT icon (small-icon?, large-icon?)>
```

continues

LISTING 32.1 Continued

```
<!-- Defines a GIF or JPEG URL for a small 16x16 pixel icon. -->
  <!ELEMENT small-icon (#PCDATA)>
<!-- Defines a GIF or JPEG URL for a large 16x16 pixel icon. -->
  <!ELEMENT large-icon (#PCDATA)>
<!-- Defines a displayable Web application name. -->
  <!ELEMENT display-name (#PCDATA)>
<!-- Defines an element used to provide a description of something. -->
  <!ELEMENT description (#PCDATA)>
<!-- If present in a deployment descriptor, this element
  defines the fact that the Web application can be used
  in a distributed servlet container environment. -->
  <!ELEMENT distributable EMPTY>
<!-- Defines a set of initialization parameters for use by
  a Web container (e.g. servlet context). While a name and value
  are required, a description of each parameter is optional. -->
  <!ELEMENT context-param (param-name, param-value, description?)>
<!-- The name of an initialization parameter. -->
  <!ELEMENT param-name (#PCDATA)>
<!-- The value of an initialization parameter. -->
  <!ELEMENT param-value (#PCDATA)>
<!-- Defines an element that contains a set of declarative properties
  of a servlet. If the component is a JSP, then the properties apply to
  the compiled form of a JSP (i.e. a servlet). An icon, display name,
  description, and startup flag are optional. The servlet name and
  component class or file name are required. Zero or more init parameters
  and security roles for a servlet are also specified here. -->
  <!ELEMENT servlet (icon?, servlet-name, display-name?, description?,
                    (servlet-class|jsp-file), init-param*,
                    load-on-startup?, security-role-ref*)>
<!-- The name of a servlet is defined within this element. -->
  <!ELEMENT servlet-name (#PCDATA)>
<!-- The fully qualified name of a Java Servlet class. -->
  <!ELEMENT servlet-class (#PCDATA)>
<!-- The full path to a JSP file inside of a Web application. -->
  <!ELEMENT jsp-file (#PCDATA)>
<!-- Defines a set of initialization parameters for use by
  a Web component (e.g. servlet init params). While a name and value
  are required, a description of each parameter is optional. -->
  <!ELEMENT init-param (param-name, param-value, description?)>
<!-- The presence of this element indicates that this servlet
  should be loaded upon Web application startup. Optional content
  of this element consists of a number designating the startup order
  number for this servlet. -->
  <!ELEMENT load-on-startup (#PCDATA)>
```

```
<!-- Defines a mapping between a URL pattern and a servlet.
  That is, the associated servlet is used whenever a URL defined
  according to the associated pattern is referenced. -->
  <!ELEMENT servlet-mapping (servlet-name, url-pattern)>
<!-- Defines a URL pattern that is related to a servlet.
  Servlets which are absolutely referenced are always matched
  first. However, a pattern beginning with "/" and ending with
  "/*" can be mapped to servlets which handle other requests
  defined within or below that URL subtree. A pattern defined in terms
  of an extension, such as "*.", can be mapped to servlets which handle
  unmatched requests related to the associated extension. -->
  <!ELEMENT url-pattern (#PCDATA)>
<!-- Defines configuration parameters for session management. -->
  <!ELEMENT session-config (session-timeout?)>
<!-- Defines the minutes that must pass before a session times out. -->
  <!ELEMENT session-timeout (#PCDATA)>
<!-- Used to define mappings between extensions and MIME types. -->
  <!ELEMENT mime-mapping (extension, mime-type)>
<!-- Defines a resource extension String name (e.g. "html"). -->
  <!ELEMENT extension (#PCDATA)>
<!-- Defines a MIME type/subtype (e.g. "text/html"). -->
  <!ELEMENT mime-type (#PCDATA)>
<!-- Contains an ordered list of welcome file elements. -->
  <!ELEMENT welcome-file-list (welcome-file+)>
<!-- Defines a default file name (e.g. "index.html"). -->
  <!ELEMENT welcome-file (#PCDATA)>
<!-- Describes a JSP tag library (see Chapter 33). -->
  <!ELEMENT taglib (taglib-uri, taglib-location)>
<!-- Describes a JSP tag library URI (see Chapter 33). -->
  <!ELEMENT taglib-uri (#PCDATA)>
<!-- Describes a JSP tag library location (see Chapter 33). -->
  <!ELEMENT taglib-location (#PCDATA)>
<!-- Maps between an error code or exception to an error page URL. -->
  <!ELEMENT error-page ((error-code | exception-type), location)>
<!-- Defines an HTTP error code (e.g. 401). -->
  <!ELEMENT error-code (#PCDATA)>
<!-- Defines a fully qualified Java exception class name. -->
  <!ELEMENT exception-type (#PCDATA)>
<!-- Defines the URL of a Web resource. -->
  <!ELEMENT location (#PCDATA)>
<!-- Defines a reference to an external resource (e.g. database). -->
  <!ELEMENT resource-ref (description?, res-ref-name, res-type,
                          res-auth)>
<!-- Defines the name of the resource factory. -->
  <!ELEMENT res-ref-name (#PCDATA)>
```

continues

LISTING 32.1 Continued

```
<!-- Defines the fully qualified Java type of the data source. -->
  <!ELEMENT res-type (#PCDATA)>
<!-- Indicates if the servlet authenticates itself with the resource
  or if the container should authenticate: SERVLET or CONTAINER -->
  <!ELEMENT res-auth (#PCDATA)>
<!-- Associates security constraints with Web resources. -->
  <!ELEMENT security-constraint (web-resource-collection+,
                              auth-constraint?, user-data-constraint?)>
<!-- Defines a Web resource name, URL pattern, and set of HTTP method
  types to scope what security constraints apply to Web resources. -->
  <!ELEMENT web-resource-collection (web-resource-name, description?,
                                    url-pattern*, http-method*)>
<!-- Defines the name of a Web resource grouping. -->
  <!ELEMENT web-resource-name (#PCDATA)>
<!-- Defines an HTTP method (e.g. GET, POST, etc...). -->
  <!ELEMENT http-method (#PCDATA)>
<!-- Defines security quality of service for communications. -->
  <!ELEMENT user-data-constraint (description?, transport-guarantee)>
<!-- Defines whether the communication stream should be unprotected
  (NONE), protected for integrity (INTEGRAL), or protected for
  confidentiality (CONFIDENTIAL). -->
  <!ELEMENT transport-guarantee (#PCDATA)>
<!-- Defines the user roles permitted to access this resource. -->
  <!ELEMENT auth-constraint (description?, role-name*)>
<!-- Defines a user role name. -->
  <!ELEMENT role-name (#PCDATA)>
<!-- Defines the authentication method, domain/realm name, and
  the attributes needed for a form login mechanism. -->
  <!ELEMENT login-config (auth-method?,realm-name?,form-login-config?)>
<!-- Configures the type of authentication method used. Can be BASIC,
  DIGEST, FORM, or CLIENT-CERT based type of authentication. -->
  <!ELEMENT auth-method (#PCDATA)>
<!-- Defines a realm (i.e. security domain) name for authorization. -->
  <!ELEMENT realm-name (#PCDATA)>
<!-- Defines a login and error page used for form-based login. -->
  <!ELEMENT form-login-config (form-login-page, form-error-page)>
<!-- Defines a URL for a resource used to receive login data. -->
  <!ELEMENT form-login-page (#PCDATA)>
<!-- Defines a URL resource used to indicate unsuccessful logins. -->
  <!ELEMENT form-error-page (#PCDATA)>
<!-- Defines a security role used in Web security constraints. -->
  <!ELEMENT security-role (description?, role-name)>
<!-- This value is used within the servlet element to reference
  a particular secure role using a servlet security role-name. -->
```

```
  <!ELEMENT security-role-ref (description?, role-name, role-link)>
<!-- Defines the role-name of a security role specified in one of the
  security-role elements. -->
  <!ELEMENT role-link (#PCDATA)>
<!-- Declares an environment configuration parameter for
  a J2EE application environment. -->
  <!ELEMENT env-entry (description?, env-entry-name,
                       env-entry-value?, env-entry-type)>
<!-- Defines the name of an environment entry parameter. -->
  <!ELEMENT env-entry-name (#PCDATA)>
<!-- Defines the value of an environment entry. -->
  <!ELEMENT env-entry-value (#PCDATA)>
<!-- Defines a fully qualified Java type for a particular environment
   value. Acceptable values are: java.lang.Boolean, java.lang.String,
  java.lang.Integer, java.lang.Double, java.lang.Float -->
  <!ELEMENT env-entry-type (#PCDATA)>
<!-- Defines a reference to an EJB interface (see Chapter 36). -->
  <!ELEMENT ejb-ref (description?, ejb-ref-name, ejb-ref-type,
                    home, remote, ejb-link?)>
<!-- Defines the JNDI name of the EJB reference. -->
  <!ELEMENT ejb-ref-name (#PCDATA)>
<!-- Defines the Java class type of the referenced EJB. -->
  <!ELEMENT ejb-ref-type (#PCDATA)>
<!-- Defines the fully qualified name of the EJB home interface. -->
  <!ELEMENT home (#PCDATA)>
<!-- Defines the fully qualified name of the EJB remote interface. -->
  <!ELEMENT remote (#PCDATA)>
<!-- Defines an EJB name to an EJB in a J2EE application package.
  Indicates that this EJB is linked to another EJB. -->
  <!ELEMENT ejb-link (#PCDATA)>
<!-- A set of ID attributes are defined for each element in the Web
  application deployment descriptor to allow an easy way to
  reference elements. -->
  <!ATTLIST web-app id ID #IMPLIED>
  <!ATTLIST icon id ID #IMPLIED>
  <!ATTLIST small-icon id ID #IMPLIED>
  <!ATTLIST large-icon id ID #IMPLIED>
  <!ATTLIST display-name id ID #IMPLIED>
  <!ATTLIST description id ID #IMPLIED>
  <!ATTLIST distributable id ID #IMPLIED>
  <!ATTLIST context-param id ID #IMPLIED>
  <!ATTLIST param-name id ID #IMPLIED>
  <!ATTLIST param-value id ID #IMPLIED>
  <!ATTLIST servlet id ID #IMPLIED>
  <!ATTLIST servlet-name id ID #IMPLIED>
```

continues

LISTING 32.1 Continued

```
<!ATTLIST servlet-class id ID #IMPLIED>
<!ATTLIST jsp-file id ID #IMPLIED>
<!ATTLIST init-param id ID #IMPLIED>
<!ATTLIST load-on-startup id ID #IMPLIED>
<!ATTLIST servlet-mapping id ID #IMPLIED>
<!ATTLIST url-pattern id ID #IMPLIED>
<!ATTLIST session-config id ID #IMPLIED>
<!ATTLIST session-timeout id ID #IMPLIED>
<!ATTLIST mime-mapping id ID #IMPLIED>
<!ATTLIST extension id ID #IMPLIED>
<!ATTLIST mime-type id ID #IMPLIED>
<!ATTLIST welcome-file-list id ID #IMPLIED>
<!ATTLIST welcome-file id ID #IMPLIED>
<!ATTLIST taglib id ID #IMPLIED>
<!ATTLIST taglib-uri id ID #IMPLIED>
<!ATTLIST taglib-location id ID #IMPLIED>
<!ATTLIST error-page id ID #IMPLIED>
<!ATTLIST error-code id ID #IMPLIED>
<!ATTLIST exception-type id ID #IMPLIED>
<!ATTLIST location id ID #IMPLIED>
<!ATTLIST resource-ref id ID #IMPLIED>
<!ATTLIST res-ref-name id ID #IMPLIED>
<!ATTLIST res-type id ID #IMPLIED>
<!ATTLIST res-auth id ID #IMPLIED>
<!ATTLIST security-constraint id ID #IMPLIED>
<!ATTLIST web-resource-collection id ID #IMPLIED>
<!ATTLIST web-resource-name id ID #IMPLIED>
<!ATTLIST http-method id ID #IMPLIED>
<!ATTLIST user-data-constraint id ID #IMPLIED>
<!ATTLIST transport-guarantee id ID #IMPLIED>
<!ATTLIST auth-constraint id ID #IMPLIED>
<!ATTLIST role-name id ID #IMPLIED>
<!ATTLIST login-config id ID #IMPLIED>
<!ATTLIST realm-name id ID #IMPLIED>
<!ATTLIST form-login-config id ID #IMPLIED>
<!ATTLIST form-login-page id ID #IMPLIED>
<!ATTLIST form-error-page id ID #IMPLIED>
<!ATTLIST auth-method id ID #IMPLIED>
<!ATTLIST security-role id ID #IMPLIED>
<!ATTLIST security-role-ref id ID #IMPLIED>
<!ATTLIST role-link id ID #IMPLIED>
<!ATTLIST env-entry id ID #IMPLIED>
<!ATTLIST env-entry-name id ID #IMPLIED>
<!ATTLIST env-entry-value id ID #IMPLIED>
<!ATTLIST env-entry-type id ID #IMPLIED>
```

```
<!ATTLIST ejb-ref id ID #IMPLIED>
<!ATTLIST ejb-ref-name id ID #IMPLIED>
<!ATTLIST ejb-ref-type id ID #IMPLIED>
<!ATTLIST home id ID #IMPLIED>
<!ATTLIST remote id ID #IMPLIED>
<!ATTLIST ejb-link id ID #IMPLIED>
```

The DTD of Listing 32.1 is used to define the standard structure for deployment descriptors used in deploying J2EE Web applications. To utilize such a standard, valid J2EE Web application deployment descriptors must contain the following DOCTYPE reference:


```
<!DOCTYPE web-app PUBLIC "-//Sun Microsystems, Inc.//DTD Web Application
➥ 2.2//EN" "http://java.sun.com/j2ee/dtds/web-app_2_2.dtd">
```

You'll in fact note that the general structure of our web.xml deployment descriptor file equipped with the CD and used to configure the BeeShirts.com servlet application adheres to the following top-level form:

```
<?xml version="1.0" encoding="UTF-8"?>
<!DOCTYPE web-app PUBLIC "-//Sun Microsystems, Inc.//DTD Web Application
➥ 2.2//EN" "http://java.sun.com/j2ee/dtds/web-app_2_2.dtd">
<web-app>
  <servlet>
    ...
  </servlet>
  ...
  <servlet>
    ...
  </servlet>

  <servlet-mapping>
    ...
  </servlet-mapping>
  ...
  <servlet-mapping>
    ...
  </servlet-mapping>

  <env-entry>
    ...
  </env-entry>
  ...
  <env-entry>
    ...
  </env-entry>
</web-app>
```

NOTE

At the time of this writing, the BEA WebLogic Server v5.0 and v5.1 required that you specify an older Web API version number in the DOCTYPE reference of a web.xml file. The BEA WebLogic Server also did not support use of the standard <session-config> element in a web.xml file. The DOCTYPE reference for BEA WebLogic is defined as such:

```
<!DOCTYPE web-app PUBLIC "-//Sun Microsystems, Inc.//DTD Web Application
➥ 1.2//EN" "http://java.sun.com/j2ee/dtds/web-app_2_2.dtd">
```

We thus have placed three sample XML files in the examples\src\ejava\servletsch32 directory. The weblogic-web.xml file defines the BEA WebLogic version of the web.xml file for use with our examples. The j2ee-web.xml file defines the J2EE reference implementation's version of the web.xml file for use with our examples. During execution of our sample compilation and deployment scripts for each implementation, the proper XML file is copied to the standard web.xml file name. The web.xml file on the CD is simply a snapshot of the standard Web XML deployment descriptor for use with our examples and is identical to j2ee-web.xml.

Web Application Deployment Procedures

The process for deploying J2EE applications involves one of establishing environment variables, configuring server properties, compiling Java code, creating XML-based deployment descriptors, packaging archive files, and deploying archives to a J2EE server environment. Although we focus on the deployment of our J2EE-based Java Servlet application in this section, the process described here can be generalized to the deployment of JSP and EJB applications as well. Appendix A, "Software Configuration," provides instructions for how to install and perform the basic configuration of both a J2EE reference implementation server and a BEA WebLogic Server used to deploy our J2EE-based Web applications. However, the procedure for deploying J2EE-based Web applications assumes the following general steps:

1. *Set J2EE Server Environment Variables*: Environment variables must often be set for running a J2EE server environment and will vary per vendor implementation and operating-system platform. For example, we set root installation directories for the J2SE (JAVA_HOME), J2EE reference implementation (J2EE_HOME), and BEA WebLogic Server (WEBLOGIC_HOME) as described in Appendix A.
2. *Configure J2EE Server Properties*: Configuration properties for most J2EE server implementations can be set to suit your particular network and operating environment. For example, we modify the J2EE reference implementation's [J2EE_HOME]\config\

web.properties file such that the http.port property is set equal to 7001. We also set the BEA WebLogic Server's [WEBLOGIC_HOME]\weblogic.properties file such that a weblogic.httpd.webApp.beeshirts property is set to reference a WAR file that we will generate for BEA WebLogic (that is, [WEBLOGIC_HOME]/myserver/servletsch32.war). Appendix A describes these configuration properties in more detail.

3. *Compile J2EE Web Application Code*: All J2EE Web component code must be compiled using a standard Java compiler.
4. *Create a J2EE Web Application Deployment Descriptor*: An XML-based deployment descriptor is created according to the Web application DTD defined previously. We include a Web application deployment descriptor for our BeeShirts.com servlet-based storefront on the CD in the file named web.xml. Many products create this file for you from a GUI-based configuration tool.
5. *Package J2EE Web Application Code*: The Web deployment descriptor, all compiled J2EE servlet classes, all HTML files, all image files, and all other Web resources need to be packaged into a Web application archive file with a .war extension. J2EE-based products may supply command-line or GUI-based utilities, or both, for this purpose.
6. *Start the J2EE Server*: The J2EE-compliant server must generally be started or already be started at this stage. The exact mechanism for starting a server is often vendor-dependent but can be as simple as invoking a single startup command from the command line.
7. *Create a J2EE Application Deployment Descriptor*: A J2EE application deployment descriptor must be created to collect one or more Web, EJB, and application client modules into a cohesive J2EE application. We have included an application.xml file for our application deployment descriptor on the CD. Many products will create this file for you automatically or via a GUI-based configuration tool.
8. *Package J2EE Application Code*: The application deployment descriptor, Web applications, EJB applications, and application clients need to be packaged into an Enterprise ARchive (EAR) file with a .ear extension. Many products also create this archive for you automatically or via GUI-based development tools.
9. *Deploy the J2EE Web Application Code*: Finally, the integrated J2EE application is deployed to the J2EE server environment for access by enterprise application clients. This step also is often automated via GUI tools.

Web Application Directory Structure

The root Web application context is defined within a Web server after the host address for that server (for example, http://www.beeshirts.com/myRootContext). Files that are served directly to the client, such as HTML and image files, can be placed directly under the root Web application context. Files that are not directly served to the client are placed under a `WEB-INF` directory that sits under the root Web application context. The contents under the `WEB-INF` directly are not publicly available and are subject to the management constraints of the J2EE server environment. A `web.xml` file under `WEB-INF` contains the Web application deployment descriptor information. All Java Servlets and auxiliary Java classes are rooted under the `WEB-INF\classes` directory. JAR files with `.jar` file extensions that contain Java Servlets and auxiliary Java classes are placed under the `WEB-INF\lib` directory.

This entire directory structure is typically contained within a WAR file. A WAR file also contains a `Manifest.mf` file under a `META-INF` directory. For example, a `servletsch32.war` file created for our sample Web application contains the following file structure:

```
\*.gif
\*.jpg
\*.html
\WEB-INF\web.xml
\WEB-INF\classes\ejava\servletsch32\*.class
\META-INF\Manifest.mf
```

J2EE Reference Implementation Server Startup and Deployment

The J2EE reference implementation comes packaged with a J2EE-compliant Java Servlet v2.2 and JSP v1.1 container environment. This Java Servlet and JSP reference implementation was developed by the Apache Software Foundation's Jakarta project and is sometimes referred to by its codename of "Tomcat." When using the J2EE reference implementation server with our examples, you must first start the server. You must first change to the `[J2EE_HOME]\bin` directory on the machine on which you've installed the reference implementation. Then simply begin an instance of the server by executing the `j2ee` command from that directory. The `-verbose` option can be used to display more detailed server information to the screen as the server is running. The `-version` option can be used to display the current J2EE version number. The server may be stopped with the `-stop` option. Although the `-singleVM` option is the default JVM process option for running all applications in a single process, the `-multiVM` option may also be used to launch separate JVM processes for each deployed J2EE application.

Our `compilej2ee.bat` file equipped with the CD provides a Windows-based sample script for compiling, packaging, and deploying a J2EE application to a running J2EE reference implementation server. The `compilej2ee.bat` file uses the J2EE `packager` tool to create a Web application given a `web.xml` deployment descriptor and target WAR filename. The packager tool follows the most basic syntax for creating WAR files as shown here:

```
[J2EE_HOME]\bin\packager -webArchive web.xml warFileName.war
```

Alternatively, a `-classpath` *`classPath`* option can be used to designate the `CLASSPATH` for servlet and auxiliary Java classes. The `-classFiles` *`classFileList`* option designates that only certain class files in the colon-separated class file list are to be included in the WAR file. A root directory for all content files (for example, directly referenced image and HTML files) can also be specified on the command line. Finally, a `-contentFiles` *`contentFileList`* option can be used to designate that only certain content files in the colon-separated content file list are to be included in the WAR file.

We also use the packager tool in our `compilej2ee.bat` sample script to create a J2EE application EAR file. The packager tool used for creating EAR files given a WAR filename and other archive files, as well as given an enterprise application name, follows the basic syntax shown here:

```
[J2EE_HOME]\bin\packager -enterpriseArchive
➥ warFileName.war:[otherArchiveFiles]
➥ ApplicationName earApplicationFileName.ear
```

Alternatively, a `-alternativeDescriptorEntries` *`archiveFileName/xmlFileName`*`.xml:...` option can be used to reference alternate XML descriptors for each of the archives designated in the archive list.

Although the packager utility is supposed to create properly defined J2EE `application.xml` files, our `compilej2ee.bat` file provides a mechanism for using a canned `application.xml` file for assigning our J2EE application to the `beeshirts` root servlet context as shown here:

```
<application>
  <display-name>ServletApp</display-name>
  <description>Application description</description>
  <module>
    <web>
      <web-uri>servletsch32.war</web-uri>
      <context-root>beeshirts</context-root>
    </web>
  </module>
</application>
```

A J2EE reference implementation `deploytool` with no command-line arguments spawns a GUI-based deployment tool for creating J2EE application EAR files, as well as for deploying J2EE applications. The `deploytool` invoked with the `-deploy` option deploys an application contained by an associated EAR filename to a J2EE server running onto a named host machine according to the following form:

```
[J2EE_HOME]\bin\deploytool -deploy earFileName.ear serverHostName
```

The deploytool invoked with the -uninstall option can remove a named enterprise application from a J2EE server running on a specified host machine as follows:

```
[J2EE_HOME]\bin\deploytool -uninstall ApplicationName serverHostName
```

After the BeeShirts.com Web application is deployed according to the preceding guidelines, our root BeeShirtsServlet is accessed from a local machine using the URL http://localhost:7001/beeshirts/BeeShirtsServlet.

NOTE

You may have copied an orb.properties file to your [JAVA_HOME]\jre\lib directory if you have installed the standard RMI/IIOP extension per the instructions of Chapter 16, "RMI Communications." This orb.properties file must be removed in order to properly run the J2EE reference implementation server. Refer to Appendix A for more details.

BEA WebLogic Server Startup and Deployment

The BEA WebLogic Server is an enterprise-class server environment for creating and deploying J2EE-compliant Web and EJB applications. Our compileweblogic.bat file equipped on the CD contains a sample Windows script for compiling, packaging, and deploying our Web application to a BEA WebLogic Server. At the time of this writing, the BEA WebLogic Server v5.0 and v5.1 did not support deployment of J2EE application EAR files. Thus, our sample compileweblogic.bat file simply creates the appropriate web application directory structure populated with our example code, and then uses the jar command to create a servletsch32.war file mapped from this directory structure. This WAR file must be referenced by the weblogic.httpd.webApp.beeshirts property defined within the BEA WebLogic Server's [WEBLOGIC_HOME]\weblogic.properties file. The weblogic.properties file's weblogic.httpd.documentRoot property should also be set to myserver/ for our examples. The BEA WebLogic Server can then be started using the [WEBLOGIC_HOME]\startweblogic.cmd command script. Appendix A describes the general configuration procedures for the BEA WebLogic Server.

Servlet Configuration

Using the standard Web application deployment descriptor, we can configure our Java Servlet processing environment in a standard fashion. Although it can be argued that all the parameters established within the deployment descriptor are a form of application configuration, we are specifically referring to the configurable initialization and environment parameters of servlets and servlet container environments. Servlets can be configured with initialization parameters that are obtained via the `ServletConfig` interface implementation. Servlet containers can also be configured with initialization parameters obtained via the `ServletContext` interface implementation. Servlets can also reference global context configuration environment parameters that can be accessed via JNDI lookups under a standard environment context. This section describes these mechanisms for configuring your servlets and servlet container environments.

Individual Servlet Configuration

As shown earlier in Figure 32.3 and Figure 32.4, the `GenericServlet` class and `HttpServlet` subclass implement the `ServletConfig` interface for receiving initialization information from the servlet container environment. The `ServletConfig.getServletName()` value is retrieved from the Web deployment descriptor within a `<servlet-name>` element inside of a particular `<servlet>` element. The `ServletConfig.getInitParameterNames()` retrieve the `<param-name>` values from within an `<init-param>` sub-element of `<servlet>`. The `ServletConfig.getInitParameter()` method can be used with a parameter name defined within a `<param-name>` to retrieve a value defined within a parallel element named `<param-value>`. A sample snippet of a particular XML deployment descriptor document defining these values is shown here:

```
<web-app>
  ...
  <servlet>
    <servlet-name>OrderStatus</servlet-name>
    <servlet-class>ejava.servletsch32.OrderStatusServlet</servlet-class>
    <init-param>
      <param-name>email</param-name>
      <param-value>sam@sam.com</param-value>
    </init-param>
    <init-param>
      <param-name>lastName</param-name>
      <param-value>Mellone</param-value>
    </init-param>
    ...
  </servlet>
  ...
</web-app>
```

Thus, our `OrderStatusServlet` that is bound to the named `OrderStatus` servlet in the preceding snippet may be used to retrieve initial parameter values as such (calls are assumed to be made from within `OrderStatusServlet` here):

```
// Returns the name "OrderStatus"
String name = this.getServletName();
```

```
// Returns an Enumeration of String objects
// including "email", "lastName", etc...
Enumeration names = this.getInitParameterNames();

// Returns the paramValue "sam@sam.com"
String emailAddressFromParameter = getInitParameter("email");
```

Servlet Context Configuration

The `ServletContext` abstraction shown in Figure 32.3 encapsulates an interface to a servlet container environment that can also be configured via an XML deployment descriptor. The `ServletContext.getInitParameterNames()` retrieves the `<param-name>` values from within a `<context-param>` sub-element of `<web-app>`. The `ServletContext.getInitParameter()` method can be used with a parameter name defined within a `<param-name>` to retrieve a value defined within a parallel element named `<param-value>`. A sample snippet of a particular XML document defining these values is shown here:

```
<web-app>
  ...
  <context-param>
    <param-name>StoreName</param-name>
    <param-value>BeeShirts Site 105</param-value>
    <description>Designates the deployed web site.</description>
  </context-param>
  ...
  <context-param>
    ...
  </context-param>
  ...
</web-app>
```

For example, we could retrieve a `ServletContext` object and the initialization parameters from within a particular Java Servlet as shown here:

```
// Get the ServletContext from this current Servlet
ServletContext ctx = this.getServletContext();

// Returns an Enumeration of String objects
// including "StoreName", etc...
Enumeration names = ctx.getInitParameterNames();

// Returns the paramValue "BeeShirts Site 105"
String storeName = getInitParameter("StoreName");
```

The default timeout, in minutes, for a session can also be established for the container environment using the `<session-config>` and `<session-timeout>` elements as defined in our `web.xml` file:

```
<web-app>
  ...
  <session-config>
    <session-timeout>30</session-timeout>
  </session-config>
  ...
</web-app>
```

If we were to retrieve such information from an HttpSession object, we could use the following code snippet:

```
HttpSession session =  ...  // retrieve session object
// Returns a value of 1800 seconds = 30 minutes X 60 seconds/minute
int maxTimeoutInSeconds = session.getMaxInactiveInterval();
```


Servlet Application Configuration

Access to parameters of a servlet environment can return only String value parameters. A more generic means to access Java objects managed from within a servlet container environment is provided via JNDI lookup services through the J2EE container. A JNDI context can be created from within a Java Servlet and used to look up certain types of Java objects that have been configured via the servlet deployment descriptor. Environment configuration names defined in an <env-entry-name> element, values in an <env-entry-value> element, types defined in an <env-entry-type> element, and descriptions defined in a <description> element can all be defined inside <env-entry> elements within the servlet deployment descriptor file. The environment values are then read from within a servlet via the JNDI API. Such environment values can only be read and not modified at runtime. Acceptable types for these environment values are java.lang.Boolean, java.lang.String, java.lang.Integer, java.lang.Double, and java.lang.Float.

As an example, we have defined a configurable welcome message for the front page of our BeeShirts.com Web application from within an env-entry named WelcomeMessage as shown here:

```
<web-app>
  ...
  <env-entry>
    <description>
      Customizable description for the Application
    </description>
    <env-entry-name>WelcomeMessage</env-entry-name>
    <env-entry-value> A big welcome to our online T-Shirts shoppe.
➥ &lt;BR&gt;
          Buying T-Shirts of your choice is just a click
➥ &lt;BR&gt;
```

```
            away. Through our site you can select from a wide  &lt;BR&gt;
            range of shirts. All you have to do is choose      &lt;BR&gt;
            your shirts and order them online. Happy browsing. &lt;BR&gt;
            &lt;HR&gt;
            &lt;UL&gt;
            &lt;LI&gt;Wide Variety of Shirts
            &lt;LI&gt;Wide Range of Sizes
            &lt;LI&gt;Secure Shopping
            &lt;LI&gt;Hand Made Designs
            &lt;LI&gt;Many More Features ...
            &lt;/UL&gt;
    </env-entry-value>
    <env-entry-type>java.lang.String</env-entry-type>
  </env-entry>
</web-app>
```

Servlets access such environment variables by first creating an instance of a `javax.naming.InitialContext` object using the parameterless form of the `InitialContext` constructor. The servlet then performs a `lookup()` on the `InitialContext` with a name that begins with `java:comp/env`. The object returned from the `lookup()` is of the associated `<env-entry-type>`. Environment entry names can be also be named as subcontexts below `java:comp/env`, such as `java:comp/env/foo/bar`. Lookups via the `InitialContext` can thus be made with respect to relative and absolute context references as discussed in Chapter 19, "Naming Services."

As an example of programmatic access to a configurable object, the `WelcomeMessage` `<env-entry>` defined in the previous XML document can be retrieved from within a servlet as is the case from within our `BeeShirtsServlet` class's `writePageCenterArea()` method extracted as a snippet here:

```
String msg = "";
try{
  // Get initial context and lookup welcome message via JNDI
  InitialContext ctx = new InitialContext();
  msg = (String) ctx.lookup("java:comp/env/WelcomeMessage");
}
catch(NamingException namingException){
  namingException.printStackTrace();
}
```

Servlet Service Management

J2EE servlet containers provide various services that can be tapped by Java Servlet component implementations. These management services provide for an efficient, scalable, configurable, and dependably assured computing environment. To provide such management services, J2EE servlet containers often restrict what a servlet component can do by use of Java security restrictions, such as providing read/write-only file permissions, connect-only socket permissions (that is, cannot create server sockets), and read-only system property permissions. Servlet containers can thus effectively provide service management for thread pooling, servlet activation and instance pooling, transactions, security, availability, EJB object naming, and resource interface object naming. Although we have explored many of these services in a broader API context in previous chapters, we explore their specific application here to use with servlets inside of J2EE Web container environments.

Servlet Thread and Activation Service Management

The Java Servlet framework does not implicitly provide protection of a particular servlet instance for concurrent access by multiple client threads. A servlet container may activate a single instance of a particular servlet to handle a request from one Web client and hand that instance off to a thread that has been allocated for that Web client request. A subsequent call from another Web client to the same servlet type may cause the servlet container to use the same active servlet instance and hand that servlet object off to a different Web client handler thread. Many servlet container implementations will pull hot thread handlers from a thread pool to avoid the overhead associated with creating new threads per request.

Thread synchronization can be implemented by the servlet developer using synchronized blocks or methods as discussed in Chapter 4, "Java Foundations for Enterprise Development." However, declaring an entire `service()` or `doXXX()` method synchronized can add significant performance overhead if pending client requests must block until the current thread returns from such methods. Of course, synchronization of concurrent servlet requests need be a concern only for synchronizing shared state that is subject to modification. Thus, class and field attributes of a servlet class are often prime candidates to examine when considering how to make your servlets thread safe. Variables that are local to a servlet method, however, are of course local to the stack created by the invoking thread and are therefore automatically thread safe.

If you create a servlet that implements the `javax.servlet.SingleThreadModel` marker interface, this will serve as an indicator to the servlet container implementation that it should allow only one thread to invoke the `service()` or `doXXX()` methods at a time. Servlet container implementations often create pools of servlet instances that are allocated to Web client request threads as the requests are received. Most often, the size of these servlet instance pools is configurable as well. Thus, although implementing the `SingleThreadModel` interface can minimize concern over thread synchronization issues, you can also rest assured that performance degradation due to imposing single-threaded servlet access restrictions will be minimized via servlet instance pooling. Nevertheless, servlet instance pools do increase the memory overhead of a Web application. The trade-off will be yours to consider based on your specific application and your COTS servlet container implementation.

EJB and Resource Naming Service Management

Much like environment objects can be configured within an XML deployment descriptor and accessed by a servlet via JNDI, so too can EJB and resource interface objects. EJB client references can be defined within a Web application deployment descriptor inside of `<ejb-ref>` elements. Information such as the EJB reference name, class type, and interface names can be defined under this element. Servlets can then act as clients to these EJBs in a very straightforward fashion using the JNDI API with EJB reference names looked up under a standard `java:comp/env/ejb` root context name. We defer detailed discussion of EJB references from J2EE clients until Chapter 36, "Modeling Components with Enterprise JavaBeans," and Chapter 37, "Advanced Enterprise JavaBeans Serving."

Web applications can also be configured for access to resources in a simple manner as defined under `<resource-ref>` elements in the Web application XML deployment descriptor. Resources include JDBC data sources, JMS connections, JavaMail sessions, and URLs. Web applications can then obtain access to such resources using JNDI and a standard JNDI lookup naming convention. EJB applications can also access database management and messaging services in a fashion similar to Web applications. Although it is possible to access database management and messaging services from within a Web server tier, we defer much of our discussion on how such services are more commonly accessed to our EJB discussion in Chapter 36 and Chapter 37.

Servlet Transaction Service Management

Servlets can begin, commit, and rollback transactions using the `javax.transaction.UserTransaction` interface as described in Chapter 23, "Transaction Services." Using such an interface, servlets can access multiple shared resources and EJBs within the context of a single atomic transaction. A handle to a `UserTransaction` object is obtainable using JNDI with a lookup via the name of `java:comp/UserTransaction`. A servlet transaction may be begun only within a `service()` method thread, and the transaction must be committed or rolled back before returning from the `service()` method. Otherwise, the servlet container will abort the transaction. Thus, we might have access to and demarcation of a transaction as shown here:

```
public void service (HttpServletRequest servletRequest,
    HttpServletResponse servletResponse) throws ServletException
{
  try{
    InitialContext ctx = new InitialContext();
    UserTransaction transaction
      = (UserTransaction) ctx.lookup("java:comp/UserTransaction");
```

```
    transaction.begin();

    // Do some work involving shared resources...

    if( // Everything is OK? )
      transaction.commit();
    else
      transaction.rollback();
  }
  catch(...){
    // Handle exceptions
  }
}
```


Transaction context information must be propagated from process to process in a standard fashion for distributed transactions to be possible. A J2EE servlet container environment primarily concerns itself with such matters. However, the following rules may be assumed by Web component developers for transaction propagation in J2EE environments:

- *Servlet to EJB*: The transaction context of a JTA transaction must be propagated from a servlet to an EJB when both operate inside of a J2EE container environment.
- *Servlet to Data Resource*: A servlet's access to a resource (that is, DBMS via JDBC) can be managed within the context of a JTA transaction as long as the servlet did not create its own thread and instead has relied on the creation of the thread by the J2EE container.
- *Servlet to Web Server Resource*: Servlets are required to propagate transaction context to other Web resources only when requests are dispatched via a `RequestDispatcher`.
- *Web Client to Servlet*: Servlets are not required to handle a transaction context propagated by their Web clients.

JDBC connection resources are perhaps the most common type of resource that servlet developers encounter and must take into consideration when dealing with transactional environments. Servlet component developers should be particularly sensitive to the following rules related to JDBC connection handling:

- *Inter-Thread Sharing*: JDBC connections should not be shared between threads.
- *Class Attribute Storage*: JDBC connections should not be stored in `static` servlet class attributes.
- *Single Threaded Storage*: JDBC connections can be stored in servlet class instance attribute fields if the servlet implements the `SingleThreadModel`.
- *Multithreaded Storage*: JDBC connections should not be stored in servlet class instance attribute fields if the servlet does not implement the `SingleThreadModel`.

Servlet Security Service Management

The Java Servlet framework is integrated with many Java 2.0 security features and also augments the Java 2.0 security framework to provide an easy way to provide secure servlets. Servlet security deals with identity and authentication, authorization, integrity, and confidentiality. In particular, the J2EE Java Servlet framework provides a means to declaratively define security attributes in a Web application XML deployment descriptor that is used to configure the online operational security aspects of the associated servlets. Alternatively, certain features of the security framework are also exposed to servlets via APIs that enable more elaborate programmatic security provisioning by servlet application developers.

Servlet Authentication

The `<login-config>` element defined within the `<web-app>` element of the Web application XML deployment descriptor is used to define the particular authentication configuration used by a Web application. The `<auth-method>` sub-element of `<login-config>` defines the type of authentication used. Authentication of principals that access servlets is accomplished in one of four ways, including basic, digest-based, forms-based, and SSL client certificate–based authentication. These four authentication types, with their associated `<auth-method>` element value in parentheses, are defined here:

- *Basic Authentication* (`BASIC`): A Web server asks the Web client to authenticate the user within a particular domain identified by a string sent to the client. The `<realm-name>` sub-element of `<login-config>` defines this domain name string. The Web client responds with a username and password solicited from the Web user.
- *Digest-Based Authentication* (`DIGEST`): Although a username and password are used to authenticate a user as with basic authentication, an added layer of security is provided by encoding the password using a simple cryptographic algorithm.
- *Forms-Based Authentication* (`FORM`): Standard HTML forms for login and failed login can be defined using a forms-based authentication scheme within the `<form-login-config>` sub-element of `<login-config>`. When a user attempts to log in, standard field names of `j_username` and `j_password` are posted to a specified Web server URL using a standard action named `j_security_check`. As a sample snippet, the form within the referenced login HTML page may be defined as shown here:

```
<form method="POST" action="j_security_check">
  <input type="text" name="j_username">
  <input type="password" name="j_password">
</form>
```

- *SSL Client Certificate–Based Authentication* (`CLIENT-CERT`): Client authentication via SSL using client certificates is perhaps the most secure means for authentication. Because this form of authentication requires SSL over HTTP, this form of authentication is sometimes referred to as HTTPS-based client authentication.

Certain authentication-related information associated with an HTTP request can be extracted from the HttpServletRequest when needed. The getAuthType() method can be used to identify any secure authentication scheme used to protect access to the servlet (for example, BASIC, DIGEST, or null for "none"). The user identity name that was authenticated and associated with an HTTP servlet request (optionally null if no authentication) is obtained via a call to getRemoteUser(). Finally, a handle to an authenticated user in java.security.Principal form can be obtained from a call to getUserPrincipal().

Secure Servlet Communications

When a servlet request is sent to a Web server using a secure protocol, the ServletRequest.isSecure() method call can be used to return a boolean value indicating this fact. When SSL is used with HTTP, an array of javax.security.cert.X509Certificate objects is returned from a call to ServletRequest.getAttribute() using the attribute name javax.servlet.request.X509Certificate. The security of a cookie can also be specified using the Cookie.setSecure(boolean) method and determined from the Cookie.getSecure() method. Cookie security simply indicates whether the cookie is to be transmitted over a secure protocol.

Servlet Authorization

After a user has been identified using one of the previously defined authentication mechanisms, the authorization to servlet resources identified by URLs can be determined. Servlet authorization is based on a role-based access control technique. Security roles are mapped to principals or groups. When a request is made by a particular principal on a resource with an associated security role, the principal name or group to which the principal belongs is compared with the principal name or group associated with the required role to determine whether access to the resource is allowed.

A collection of security roles valid for a particular J2EE servlet environment can be defined within the XML deployment descriptor's <security-role> sub-element of the <web-app> element. The <security-role> simply defines a set of valid role names and optional descriptions in this way:

```
<web-app>
  <security-role>
    <description>Sytem Administration Role</description>
    <role-name>admin</role-name>
  </security-role>
  ...
</web-app>
```

Access to a particular servlet can then be restricted to access by users of a defined role using the <security-role-ref> sub-element of a <servlet> element. A <role-name> element defines a security role assumed by the application, and a <role-link> element refers to one of the servlet container-managed <security-role> element's <role-name> values as illustrated here:

```
<web-app>
  <servlet>
    <servlet-name>UserAccountManagement</servlet-name>
      ...
    <security-role-ref>
      <role-name>SystemAdmin</role-name>
      <role-link>admin</role-link>
    </security-role-ref>
  </servlet>
  ...
</web-app>
```

The role of a user associated with a particular HTTP servlet request can be determined via a call to the `HttpServletRequest.isUserInRole(String)` method with a role name parameter designating the security role defined within a Web deployment descriptor.

More sophisticated Web resource authorization can be specified with the <security-constraint> sub-element of <web-app>. A collection of Web resources can be specified and associated for access only by principals belonging to certain associated roles. Furthermore, the secure nature of the communications link over which access occurs can also be defined. As an example for limiting access to detailed user information stored on a Web server, we might have this:

```
<web-app>
    ...
  <security-constraint>
    <web-resource-collection>
      <web-resource-name>UserInfo</web-resource-name>
      <description>URL for all detailed user information</description>
      <url-pattern>/users/*</url-pattern>
      <http-method>POST</http-method>
    </web-resource-collection>
    <auth-constraint>
      <description>Only allow system administrator access</description>
      <role-name>admin</role-name>
    </auth-constraint>
    <user-data-constraint>
      <description>Require SSL session to get user info</description>
      <transport-guarantee>CONFIDENTIAL</transport-guarantee>
    </user-data-constraint>
  </security-constraint>
    ...
</web-app>
```

Servlet Availability Service Management

Web-enabling an enterprise opens the gateway to an enterprise system for access by a large Internet or intranet community. Although access to resources can be restricted to authorized users via security mechanisms, the demand for service by Web clients placed on a Web server can be significantly large for most Web-enabled enterprise applications. Thus, availability of service for Web-enabled applications built using servlets must be considered from the outset of design. Multiple Web client requests must not bring your Web-enabled enterprise interface to its knees. Furthermore, the scalability of Web client usage will need to be considered by any enterprise system that wants to expand its Web client base.

Fortunately for the Java Servlet developer, the management of such availability can be kept transparent to the developer and managed by a particular Java Servlet container and server implementation environment. Most Web servers and servlet container implementers support scalability and availability in part by providing efficient techniques for thread pooling and servlet instance pooling. As a client request is received by the server, the server framework handles the efficient allocation of system memory and thread resources to the request transparently to the servlet application developer. Transaction management services also provide a certain degree of availability by managing distributed access to shared distributed resources in a fashion that permits for the atomicity, consistency, isolation, and durability of operations.

More sophisticated means for providing highly available Web-enabled applications may also be provided by vendors that implement load-balancing, clustering, and failover techniques. Load-balancing and clustering basically involve the management of multiple JVM processes within the same machine or across different distributed machines to spread the load of client requests. In the event of a particular process or machine's failure, a failover technique may be employed to distribute client requests to another redundant JVM process or machine. Such features are relatively simple for stateless servlets, but the storage of `HttpSession` information in stateful Web applications makes such redundancy management more difficult. Vendors thus may have to guarantee the capability to persist `HttpSession` information or provide the capability to serialize and deserialize `HttpSession` information across different JVM processes.

J2EE servlet container environments that support distributable servlets can deploy instances of servlets to different JVM processes on the same machine or on other networked host machines in a standard fashion. A container environment can be viewed as a distributed environment domain that contains and manages multiple distributed JVM processes. An optional `<distributable>` element placed within the `<web-app>` element of a Web application's XML deployment descriptor designates the capability to run the Web application inside of a distributable servlet environment. By specifying that a Web application can operate in a distributable fashion, we are telling the servlet container environment that the Web application adheres to a few behavioral constraints to facilitate distribution. Web containers can then implement features of clustering and failover that would otherwise not be possible for nondistributable servlets.

The restrictions that must be adhered to by the servlets mainly revolve around the type of objects that are stored in an `HttpSession` object. Only `java.io.Serializable`, `javax.ejb.EJBObject`, `javax.ejb.EJBHome`, `javax.transaction.UserTransaction`, and `javax.naming.Context` objects may be stored in an `HttpSession` by a distributable servlet. Otherwise, an `IllegalArgumentException` may be thrown by the container when an attempted `HttpSession` storage operation is performed. By restricting such object types to being added to a servlet `HttpSession` object, the servlet container can guarantee the mobility of servlet session object state during failover or clustering.

Conclusions

We have covered the gamut of development topics that concern the Web-enabling of enterprise applications using Java Servlets. The J2EE Java Servlet architecture provides a component-container model that can result in a significant amount of simplified HTTP communications paradigm and management service abstraction for the servlet developer. We've explored means to manipulate HTTP requests, responses, sessions, and cookies via standard higher-level APIs. However, the Java Servlet API is very rich in support and can sometimes be cumbersome to digest for the Java newcomer. JavaServer Pages, as you'll see in the next chapter, can address this issue to a certain extent.

We have also explored the use of a J2EE server environment for the deployment of Java Servlet Web components. Deploying and configuring Java Servlets is simplified and standardized with the J2EE. J2EE servers also provide many management services, such as security and availability, that can be configurably managed from within the context of XML deployment descriptors. However, the extension of some of these declarative management features to certain enterprise applications can be limited. Nevertheless, you can always fall back on programmatic use of the various enterprise Java APIs that we have described in previous chapters.

JavaServer Pages

CHAPTER

33

IN THIS CHAPTER

- JSP Overview 1136
- JSP Language Basics 1142
- JSP Translation and Compilation Directives 1144
- Java Scripting from JSP 1149
- Java Abstractions of JSP 1152
- Standard Java Objects from JSP 1159
- Standard Java Actions from JSP 1164
- JSP Configuration and Deployment 1175
- Custom Java Actions and Tags from JSP 1181

JavaServer Pages (JSPs) are text documents interpreted by a JSP container that can contain a mixture of static HTML and scripting language commands for dynamically generating Web responses to Web requests and for communicating with server-side applications and data. JSPs are translated and compiled into Java Servlets but are easier to develop than Java Servlets and may be viewed as a technology for providing a way to Web-enable an enterprise via a programming paradigm more familiar to Web programmers. JSP developers can use a simplified scripting language–based syntax for embedding HTML into JSPs, for directing how JSPs are translated into Java Servlets, for embedding Java into JSPs, and for accessing standard objects and actions provided by JSP containers. The configuration and deployment of JSPs also has a simplified XML-based deployment descriptor approach akin to the approach provided for Java Servlets.

In this chapter, you will learn:

- The architecture and concepts behind use of JavaServer Pages.
- The basic language of JSPs and the basic structure of JSP documents.
- The commands used for directing translation and compilation of JSPs into Java Servlet implementation classes.
- The methodology and syntax for embedding Java code directly into JSPs.
- The APIs and standard objects used by JSPs for interacting with managed objects provided by the JSP container for manipulating requests, responses, sessions, and JSP information.
- The standard JSP scripting language tags and actions they invoke.
- The configuration and deployment of JSPs in a J2EE-compliant environment.
- The basic approach for providing custom JSP scripting language tags and associated actions.

JSP Overview

JavaServer Page technology provides a means for specifying special scripting language commands inside of a text-based document that are used on the server side to process requests from a client and to generate responses for the client. As is the case with Java Servlets, JSPs use HTTP as the default request/response communications paradigm and thus make JSPs ideal as a Web-enabling technology. HTML, XML, and other template data can be defined in a JSP and are sent directly to a Web client without any additional processing on the server side. However, JSP scripting language commands inserted into the same page are processed on the server side before a requested page is delivered back to a Web client.

JSP is often attractive to a Web-enabling enterprise developer because regular template data can be used directly within a JSP, the JSP scripting command language has a simple XML-like syntax, and Java code can be used within the page. JSP is also defined in a generic enough fashion that future versions of the specification will be able to support other embedded languages besides Java. However, the most recent JSP v1.1 standard requires use of only Java as the embedded scripting language. JSP v1.1 is required by the J2EE v1.2 and also depends on the Java Servlets v2.2 standard described in Chapter 32, "Java Servlets."

JSP Architecture

Figure 33.1 depicts the basic architecture of a JSP environment. The first thing to note is that JSP extends and depends on the Java Servlet API and implementation. Although JSPs are written by application developers, they are ultimately converted to Java Servlets. An implementation class of the JSP is actually an underlying servlet representation of the JSP. However, additional semantics are imposed on the implementation to satisfy the expected interface contract between the JSP container and the JSP implementation class. Thus, although developers create JSP components using a combination of HTML, XML, JSP command syntax, and an embedded scripting language (for example, Java), all the benefits provided to the Java Servlet component by its container environment are provided to the JSP component by its container environment. Because JSPs and Java Servlets are both generically viewed as Web components from a J2EE container's perspective, they share the same mechanisms for configuration and service management.

JSPs can also refer to request, response, and session management objects created by a container directly from the JSP. As you'll see in later sections, such objects can be used to perform request handling, response handling, and session management from within a JSP using the same APIs for such objects as were used with Java Servlets. JSPs thus reap all the benefits provided by Java Servlets and Web container environments, but they have the added advantage of being simpler and more natural to program for Web-enabling enterprise developers.

Phases of a JSP

Figure 33.2 depicts the various transformations that a JSP must go through before it can process requests online. A developer first creates a JSP using JSP syntax and the collection of request, response, and session management abstractions provided by the JSP API and programming model. A translation tool is then used to transform the JSP into Java Servlet implementation source code, which in turn is compiled into a Java Servlet implementation class file by a Java compiler tool. This translation and compilation process may be performed offline before or during deployment, or it may be performed online by the JSP container upon request of a particular JSP. The specific approach depends on a developer's preference and the specific JSP vendor tools provided. Finally, the compiled Java Servlet implementation class is activated by the JSP container in the same manner that a Java Servlet is activated. The activated JSP representative object is then capable of processing actual requests, responses, and session actions.

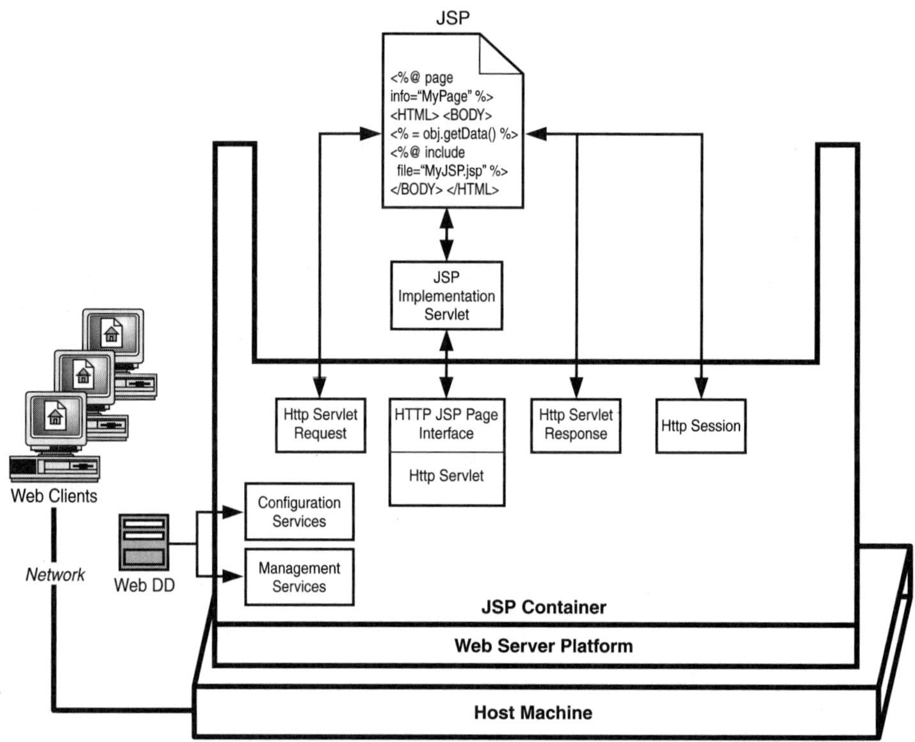

FIGURE 33.1

The JSP architecture.

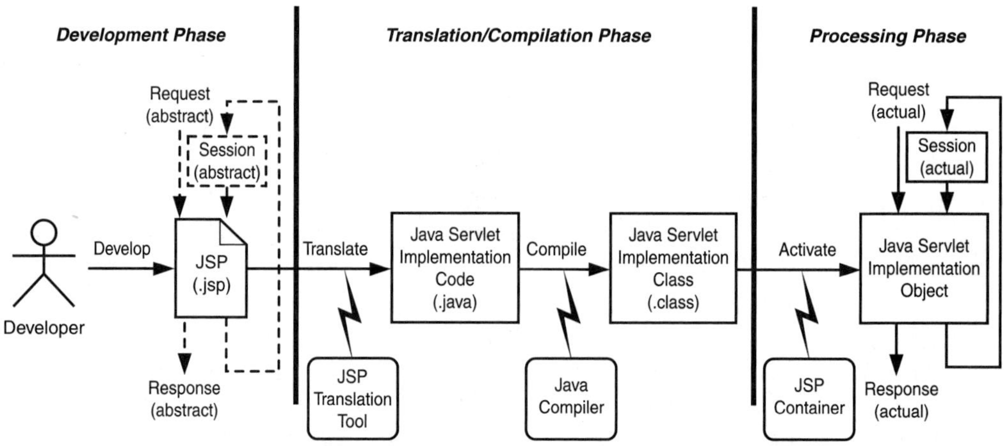

FIGURE 33.2

The phases of a JSP.

BeeShirts.com JSP Examples

We have created a JSP version of the Java Servlet–based BeeShirts.com e-commerce storefront that was presented in Chapter 32 and placed the new JSP code on the CD. Because this sample code is moderately large, we also won't be inserting all the source code from the CD into the chapter text but will be providing core snippets from such code as relevant topics are introduced. Figure 33.3 does, however, provide you with a logical diagram of the various JSPs used to service requests and generate responses for this sample code. These JSPs essentially provide the same functionality as the code from Chapter 32. We also utilize the images and BeeShirts.com entity classes (`Customer`, `Item`, and so on) developed in Chapter 32 as were illustrated in Figure 32.7.

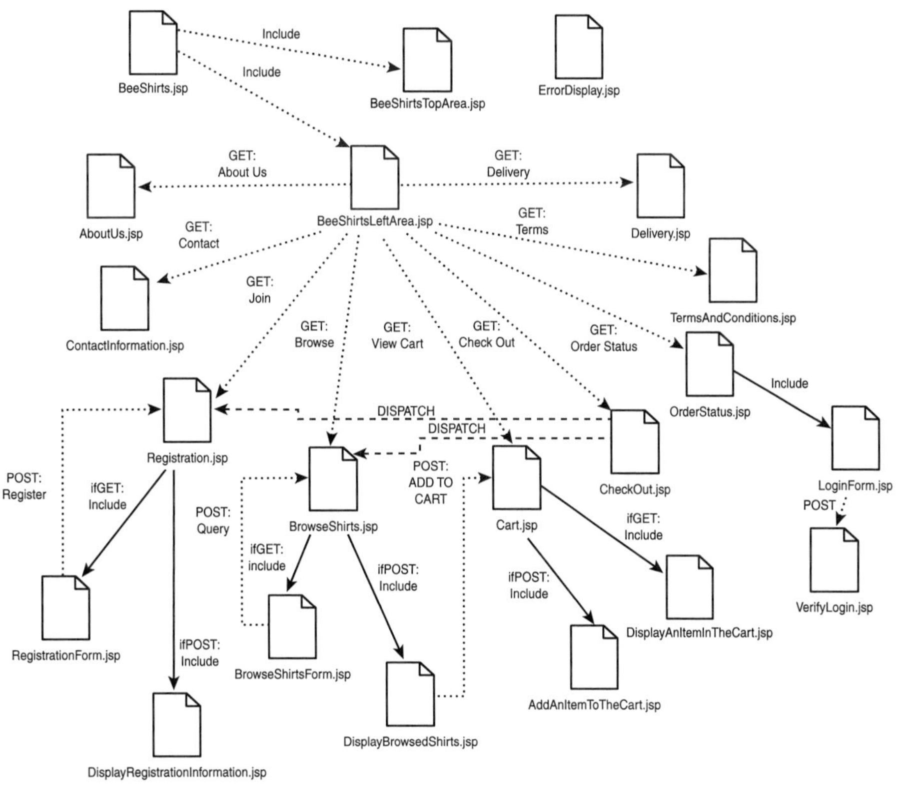

FIGURE 33.3
BeeShirts.com JSPs.

NOTE

All the sample code strewn throughout this chapter is contained on the CD under the `examples\src\ejava\jspch33` directory. Because the code on the CD represents a moderately large amount of Web-based BeeShirts.com storefront code, we do not present all the code in this chapter. Rather, we describe the basic structure of such code and present snippets from that code germane to chapter topics as they are discussed. We should also note that this code depends on some of the code from Chapter 32 stored on the CD under the `examples\src\ejava\servletsch32` directory.

The BeeShirts.com JSPs shown in Figure 33.3 and the Chapter 32 Java Servlet classes and HTML pages to which they relate are briefly defined here:

- `ErrorDisplay`: Is a global JSP to provide a standard page for displaying JSP errors as they occur. JSPs experiencing errors automatically are routed to this page.
- `BeeShirts`: Provides the root JSP that generates the BeeShirts.com starting page akin to the `BeeShirtsServlet` of Chapter 32.
- `BeeShirtsTopArea`: Is a special JSP to display the top logo portion of the BeeShirts.com Web page. This JSP is included by all the root page JSPs.
- `BeeShirtsLeftArea`: Is a special JSP to display the left portion of the BeeShirts.com Web page displaying the BeeShirts.com button options. This JSP is included by all the root page JSPs.
- `AboutUs`: Handles the request generated by clicking the About Us button and displays some simple BeeShirts.com information akin to the `AboutUsServlet` of Chapter 32.
- `ContactInformation`: Handles the request generated from clicking the Contact button and displays some simple contact information akin to the `ContactInformationServlet` of Chapter 32.
- `Registration`: Is referenced from the Join button and handles display of registration form or registration information. Will execute an included `RegistrationForm` JSP if a `GET` request is received and will execute an included `DisplayRegistrationInformation` JSP if a `POST` is received.
- `RegistrationForm`: Displays a registration form and submits a `POST` to the current `Registration` JSP when the Register button is clicked akin to the `registration.html` file of Chapter 32.
- `DisplayRegistrationInformation`: Displays the results of a user registration akin to the `RegistrationServlet` of Chapter 32.

- `BrowseShirts`: Is referenced from the Browse button and handles display of a browsing query form or display of browse result information. Will execute an included `BrowseShirtsForm` JSP if a `GET` request is received and will execute an included `DisplayBrowsedShirts` JSP if a `POST` is received.
- `BrowseShirtsForm`: Creates a display that allows a user to query for the T-shirts they might be interested in purchasing akin to the `BrowseShirtsServlet` of Chapter 32. Submits a `POST` to `BrowseShirts` when a Query button is clicked.
- `DisplayBrowsedShirts`: Displays search results from a browse query akin to the `BrowseShirtsServlet` of Chapter 32. Submits a `POST` to `Cart` when an ADD TO CART button is clicked.
- `Cart`: Is referenced from the View Cart button and handles display of current shopping-cart contents or display of a status message when an item is added to the cart. Will execute an included `DisplayItemsInTheCart` JSP if a `GET` request is received and will execute an included `AddAnItemToTheCart` JSP if a `POST` is received.
- `DisplayItemsInTheCart`: Handles the `GET` to display the current contents of the shopping cart akin to the `CartServlet` of Chapter 32.
- `AddAnItemToTheCart`: Handles the `POST` from the `DisplayBrowsedShirts` JSP ADD TO CART button to add a `TShirt` item to the shopping cart akin to the `CartServlet` of Chapter 32.
- `CheckOut`: Handles the `GET` request generated from the Check Out button and dispatches requests appropriately akin to the `CheckOutServlet` of Chapter 32.
- `OrderStatus`: Handles the `GET` request generated from clicking the Order Status button and includes the `LoginForm` JSP.
- `LoginForm`: Displays an order status login form akin to the `OrderStatusServlet` of Chapter 32. Whenever the Login or Remind button is clicked, a `POST` is sent to the `VerifyLogin` JSP.
- `VerifyLogin`: Handles the `POST` from either a Login or a Remind button being pressed akin to the `OrderStatusServlet` of Chapter 32.
- `TermsAndConditions`: Handles the request generated from clicking the Terms button and displays some simple terms and conditions information akin to the `TermsAndConditionsServlet` of Chapter 32.
- `Delivery`: Handles the request generated from the Delivery button and displays some canned delivery information akin to the `deliveryinformation.html` page of Chapter 32.

JSP Language Basics

JSPs contain a mixture of template data (for example, HTML and XML) interspersed with JSP elements. JSP elements are defined within begin and end tags and are the portions of a JSP that are translated and compiled by a JSP compiler into Java Servlets. These JSP elements are the portions of a JSP that represent the commands that are interpreted by JSP containers to service requests from clients. The template data, on the other hand, represents the commands that are ultimately interpreted by clients and therefore simply pass unaffected through the JSP compiler and container processing infrastructure. Figure 33.4 is a conceptual logical diagram that depicts the main components of a JSP and the hierarchy of JSP elements used to build JSPs.

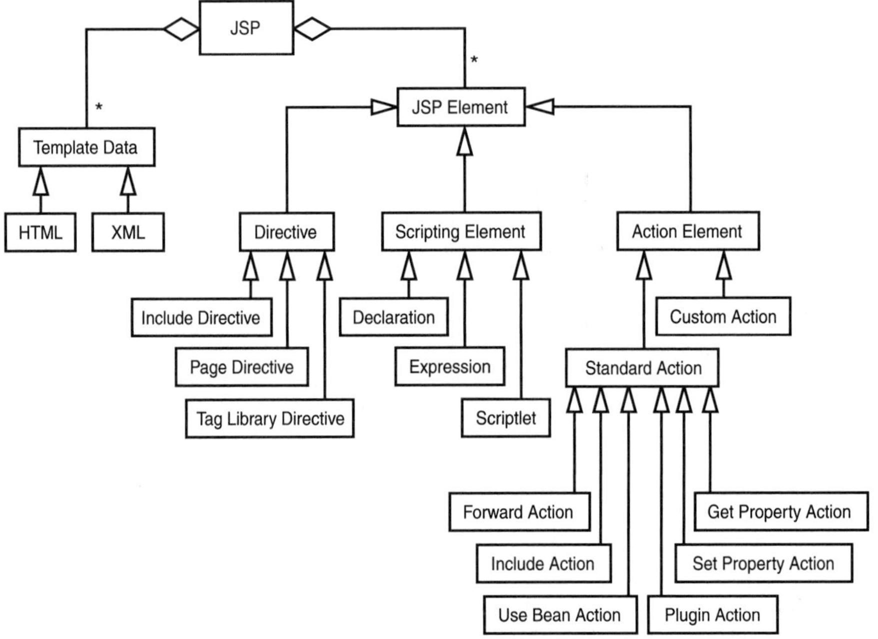

FIGURE 33.4
A concept diagram for components of a JSP.

Three main types of JSP elements are defined in the JSP specification. A directive element is interpreted at translation time and can be used to tell a JSP compiler to include other files in the compilation of a JSP, define attributes about the JSP page being translated, and define any libraries of custom elements used in the JSP. A scripting element is used to define any variable and method declarations, expressions to be evaluated, and blocks of commands known as scriptlets all in terms of the host language supported by the JSP container (for example, Java).

Finally, action elements are commands that have a purely taglike look to them but are implemented by the host language transparently to the JSP programmer. Either a set of custom actions can be defined or a set of standard actions can be used to forward requests to other resources, include responses from other resources, look up or create JavaBean objects for use within a JSP, set JavaBean property values, get JavaBean property values, and embed Java applets or JavaBeans directly into a JSP using the Java Plug-in syntax.

JSP Standard and XML-Based Elements

JSP elements can be interpreted by the JSP container. Elements should not be confused with tags. JSP elements represent a unit of interpretable JSP syntax with a start and end tag. JSP tags, on the other hand, simply represent a small piece of markup code that may be used inside of a JSP element and do not necessarily have start and end tags.

JSP elements have a syntax similar to XML elements and have start and end tags, have case-sensitive element names, can be empty elements, have optional attribute values, and have an optional element body. Although JSP element syntax is identical to XML in some cases, it is only similar to XML in other cases. The JSP specification does define a convention for expressing JSPs as XML documents, but it is not recommended that such a convention be used for hand-authoring of JSPs. Rather, due to the sometimes-awkward syntax that must result from expressing JSPs via XML, the XML representation of JSPs is primarily specified for implementation by JSP development tools. Furthermore, the specification is currently not completely well-defined and is not required to be supported by JSP v1.1 containers. When representing a JSP using XML, a `<jsp:root>` element along with an `xmlns:jsp` attribute is used to define the root of the XML-based JSP document that must be formatted according to a standard DTD.

Tags

Although we sometimes think of tags as discrete snippets of markup that define parts of a JSP or HTML page, the term *tags* as it relates to custom tag extensions is actually an important part of the JSP specification with a very specific meaning. Custom tags relate to custom actions that can be defined by developers using a special set of JSP tag extension Java classes and interfaces. These custom actions are implemented by custom Java-based tag handler classes that handle any custom tags inserted into a JSP. A collection of these tag handlers is referred to as a tag library, which can be referenced and utilized by JSPs using a special tag library directive. Furthermore, an XML-based tag library descriptor file can also be used to configure a particular tag library. We have much more to say about custom tags and actions in a later section.

Comments

Comments in JSP pages can be used to document JSP source code or used to embed information to be sent to the client. Comments that are to be ignored during processing and used to document JSP source code are included between `<%--` and `--%>` characters. Comments specific to the type of scripting language being used with the JSP may also be used within scripting elements. Thus, for Java-based JSP scripting, we would place documentation comments between `<% /**` and `**/ %>` characters. As an example of such comments, we have this:

```
<%-- JSP documentation comment --%>

<% /** Java-specific JSP documentation comment **/ %>
```

Comments that are to be sent to the client response stream are defined within `<!--` and `-->` characters. Such comments can also have data dynamically generated within them between `<%=` and `%>` characters that are inserted between client comment boundaries. For example:

```
<!-- Comment that gets sent to JSP client -->

<!-- Client comment with a dynamic expression: <%= a + b %> -->
```

Special Character Handling

Characters that are used as part of regular JSP language syntax may occasionally need to be inserted inside of quoted expressions and comments. Single quotes (`'`), double quotes (`"`), and back slashes (`\`) can all be escaped when they're prepended with a back slash. The `<%` and `%>` character sequences can be escaped via a back slash inserted in between their characters. For example, we can escape all such characters as shown here:

```
<MyElement attribute1=" \'escaped single quotes\' "
           attribute2=" \"escaped double quotes\" "
           attribute3=" \\escaped back slashes\\ "
           attribute4=" <\%escaped literals %\> "   />
```

JSP Translation and Compilation Directives

JSP directive elements (*aka* directives) direct a JSP compiler in how it should translate and compile JSPs into Java Servlet implementation classes. Directive elements define data for ultimate use by a JSP container and do not directly affect the output of information to the client response stream. Directives are thus independent of any particular request to be processed. Directive elements are defined according to this general form:

```
<%@ DirectiveTypeName attribute1="value1" attribute2="value2" ... %>
```

Here, the *`DirectiveName`* corresponds to the specific type of directives defined for the JSP v1.1 specification: `include`, `page`, and `taglib`. Each directive type has its own set of valid attributes that further define how the particular directive should be processed. Directives also have a special format for JSPs defined as XML documents that follows this form:

```
<jsp:directive.DirectiveTypeName attribute1="value1"
➥ attribute2="value2" ... />
```

include Directive

The include directive is used to insert a file into a JSP as the JSP is being translated into its implementation class. Files that can be included into a JSP may be a text file, an HTML file, or perhaps another JSP file. A JSP and its static include files are sometimes collectively referred to as a translation unit because they are all in the translation of JSPs. The include directive has one attribute named file whose value is a relative URL of the file to be included. URLs beginning with a slash (/) are relative to a JSP Web application context. Otherwise, the URL is defined relative to the JSP file. For example:

```
<%-- Relative to context --%>
<%@ include file="/sales/SalesTemplate.html" %>

<%-- Relative to current JSP file --%>
<%@ include file="CommonTopArea.jsp" %>
```

The XML version of the include directive also includes a flush attribute indicating whether the buffer should be flushed after inclusion. For example:

```
<jsp:directive.include file="/sales/SalesTemplate.html" flush="true"/>
```


NOTE

We present the XML-based representation of the various JSP elements throughout the chapter. As a developer, however, you will most likely be inclined to use the standard JSP syntax as do all of our JSP examples on the CD.

page Directive

One or more page directives are used to define information about a JSP file and any of its statically included files. JSP containers use page directives to determine the nature and characteristics of a JSP. A page directive has various standard attributes that can be defined only once in the JSP file and its static include files. The import attribute, however, can be defined more than once in the JSP translation unit. The valid page directive attributes are listed here:

- language: Specifies the type of scripting language that is used inside of the JSP. The only defined, required, and default value for this attribute in JSP v1.1 is java to indicate that Java-based language scripts will be used within the JSP.

- `extends`: Specifies a fully qualified class name of a superclass from which this JSP's implementation class is extended. This attribute should be used with caution and requires that the servlet superclass implement `service()`, `init()`, and `destroy()` methods appropriately for JSP processing as described later in this chapter.
- `import`: Specifies a comma-separated list of classes and packages used by the JSP. For Java-based scripting languages, this list is akin to Java `import` statements. The default and implicitly defined value is `java.lang.*, javax.servlet.*, javax.servlet.jsp.*, javax.servlet.http.*`.
- `session`: Specifies a value of `true` or `false` (the default is `true`) indicating whether this JSP uses an HTTP session.
- `buffer`: Specifies the minimum buffer size to be allocated for containing output stream response data. If `none` is specified, all data is output directly to an underlying `ServletResponse PrintWriter`. Otherwise, a value of the form *n*`kb` designates that *n* kilobytes are to be used for buffering. The default is `8kb`.
- `autoflush`: Specifies a value of `true` or `false` (the default is `true`) indicating whether the buffer should automatically be flushed when full. Otherwise, a buffer overflow exception will be thrown when the value is set to `false` and the buffer overflows.
- `isThreadSafe`: Specifies a value of `true` or `false` (the default is `true`) indicating whether the JSP is thread-safe. A value of `false` will induce the JSP container to dispatch client requests to JSPs one at a time by making the implementation class implement the `javax.servlet.SingleThreadModel` interface. A value of `true` will allow multiple requests to be dispatched to the JSP at a time, and the JSP therefore must provide thread safety.
- `info`: Specifies a string of information describing the JSP that relates to a call from `Servlet.getServletInfo()`.
- `errorPage`: Specifies a URL for a JSP that handles any `Throwable` exception objects that were uncaught by JSPs and made their way into the JSP container.
- `isErrorPage`: Specifies a value of `true` or `false` (the default is `true`) indicating whether the current JSP is an error page to handle uncaught JSP exceptions.
- `contentType`: Specifies a character encoding format for the JSP response. A MIME type is specified and an optional character set is specified after a charset name (for example, `text/html;charset=UTF-8`).

As an example of a few `page` directives, we have this:

```
<%-- Importing classes --%>
<%@ page import="java.util.Date, java.util.Enumeration" %>
```

```
<%-- Specify JSP page information and an error page --%>
<%@ page info="This JSP contains the BeeShirts.com root page"
        errorPage="ErrorDisplay.jsp" %>

<%-- Setting minimum buffer size and autoflushing --%>
<%@ page buffer="20kb" autoFlush="true" %>

<%-- Specify an output response type --%>
<%@ page contentType="text/plain;charset=UTF-8" %>
```

As an example of an XML form of JSP page directive, we have this:

```
<jsp:directive.page import="java.util.Date, java.util.Enumeration" />
```

`taglib` Directive

The `taglib` directive indicates that certain tags, such as custom tags, are being used in the JSP translation unit. The `taglib` directive essentially associates a prefix ID with a tag library location that is used by the JSP compiler. A `prefix` attribute is used to define the tag prefix ID that the JSP compiler should use to identify which tags in the JSP belong to an external library. The tag IDs `jsp`, `jspx`, `java`, `javax`, `servlet`, `sun`, and `sunw` are all reserved tag prefix IDs. A `uri` attribute is used to identify the location of the tag library as identified with the `prefix` attribute when parsing the JSP. Here's an example:


```
<%@ taglib uri="http://www.beeshirts.com/tags" prefix="beeshirts" %>
```

Thus, a tag library located at `http://www.beeshirts.com/tags` will be referenced whenever tags with the prefix of `beeshirts` are encountered in a JSP. The XML version of a `taglib` differs somewhat in that a root `<jsp:root>` element of the XML document representing the JSP is augmented with an `xmlns:` name space definition attribute identifying the tag library like this:

```
<jsp:root ... xmlns:beeshirts="http://www.beeshirts.com/tags" ... >
  ...
</jsp:root>
```

Directive Examples

The `BeeShirts.jsp` page first uses a `page` directive to describe the page and import any auxiliary libraries needed by its translation unit. Thereafter, the BeeShirts JSP then defines some basic HTML template data followed by another `page` directive to define an `errorPage` JSP and two `include` directives. The `include` directives simply include the `BeeShirtsTopArea.jsp` JSP within a top row of an HTML table and the `BeeShirtsLeftArea.jsp` JSP within a second row of the HTML table. The main welcome message body of the `BeeShirts.jsp` JSP is then displayed within a separate cell of the second row. The HTML template data and JSP directives for this `BeeShirts.jsp` JSP are shown here:

```
<%@ page info="BeeShirts Page" import=
    "javax.naming.InitialContext, javax.naming.NamingException,
     ejava.jspch33.JSPHelper"
%>

<HTML>
<HEAD>
  <TITLE>
    BeeShirts.com
  </TITLE>
</HEAD>
<BODY ALINK="#FFCC66"  BGCOLOR="#ffcc66" >
<%-- Add Error page to display Error --%>
<%@ page errorPage="ErrorDisplay.jsp" %>

  ...

<%-- Display the Top and Left part of JSP --%>
<TABLE BORDER=0 COLS=2 WIDTH=\"100%\" >
 <TR>
   <%@ include file="BeeShirtsTopArea.jsp" %>
 </TR>
 <TR>
   <%@ include file="BeeShirtsLeftArea.jsp" %>

   ...

  <TD  VALIGN=TOP>

<%-- Print welcome message --%>
   ...
  </TD>
 </TR>
</TABLE>
</BODY>
</HTML>
```

Note that we've excluded other code not shown in the preceding snippet at this point in the book because we have not yet covered certain topics. For the most part, our BeeShirts.com JSPs follow the same pattern as described previously with the use of a page directive at the top of each JSP, referencing of an error page, and the inclusion of the `BeeShirtsTopArea` and `BeeShirtsLeftArea` JSPs via `include` directives as was done with the `BeeShirts` JSP. JSPs using such directives include the `BeeShirts`, `AboutUs`, `ContactInformation`, `Registration`,

BrowseShirts, Cart, OrderStatus, TermsAndConditions, and VerifyLogin JSPs. All of these JSPs share the fact that they are front pages that directly receive HTTP requests. Additionally, the OrderStatus JSP also includes the LoginForm JSP directly following the inclusion of both the BeeShirtsTopArea and the BeeShirtsLeftArea JSPs.

Furthermore, as was illustrated in Figure 33.3, the Registration, BrowseShirts, and Cart JSPs all handle both GET and POST requests in a separate fashion. When a GET request type is received, the JSP includes one type of file, and when a POST request type is received, another course of action is taken. JSP scriptlets encapsulate the conditional logic, and the include directives sit outside of the scriptlet boundaries. We illustrate this here for the Registration JSP, but the same basic pattern applies to the BrowseShirts and Cart JSPs as well:

```
<%
   ...
  // if the request method type is not POST
  if( ... ){
%>
  <%@ include file="RegistrationForm.jsp"  %>
<%
  }
  else{
%>
  <%@ include file="DisplayRegistrationInformation.jsp"  %>
<%
  }
%>
```


Java Scripting from JSP

As a default and as the only JSP v1.1 language that can be fully inserted inside of a JSP, the Java language can be used as a scripting language. Use of Java as scripting language code inside of JSP enables more sophisticated manipulation of objects, creation of presentation content, and the capability to interface with a middle-tier server or DBMS. Scripting language code is inserted inside of JSP scripting elements. JSP scripting elements are defined within <% and %> character sequences. Scripting elements come in three flavors, including the capability to declare variables and methods (declarations), evaluate language statements (expressions), and implement scripting logic (scriptlets). We discuss each of these scripting element types in the subsections that follow.

Declarations

Declarations are scripting elements that are used to declare variables and methods that are used by the JSP. When a JSP is initialized by the JSP container, the declarations within a JSP are also initialized and made ready for use within the JSP. Declarations are defined within the <%! and %> character sequences. The declarations inserted between such tag boundaries are defined in a scripting language–specific way. For Java-specific declarations, one or more semicolon-separated Java variable and method declarations can be defined within a JSP declaration.

As an example, to declare a variable and method in a JSP, we have this:

```
<%-- Declare simple variable for this JSP --%>
<%!
    private static int MAX_FAILED_LOGINS = 5;
%>

<%-- Declare simple method for this JSP --%>
<%!
    public boolean haveExceededMaxLogins(int loginCounts){

      boolean maxLogins = (MAX_FAILED_LOGINS>=loginCounts);

      return maxLogins;
    }
%>
```

As another example, JSPs may declare the standard `jspInit()` and `jspDestroy()` methods to create specialized implementations for initializing and destroying resources associated with a particular JSP. Note, however, that implementing the standard `_jspService()` method is not permitted. Also note that defining your own nonstandard method beginning with `jsp`, `_jsp`, `jspx`, and `_jspx` is not permitted because such prefixes are reserved for standard JSP method definitions.

XML-based JSP files can also declare variables and methods if they insert them within a `<jsp:declaration>` element as exemplified here:

```
<jsp:declaration>
    private static int MAX_FAILED_LOGINS = 5;
</jsp:declaration>
```

Expressions

Expressions are scripting elements that define statements that are evaluated during request processing time. When expressions are evaluated, their evaluated output value is converted to a `String`. Expressions are defined within the <%= and %> character sequences. The expressions inserted between such boundaries are defined in a scripting language–specific way. Here's an example of a Java-specific expression:

```
<HTML>
  <BODY>
```

```
    Date Today: <%= new java.util.Date() %>
  </BODY>
</HTML>
```

Expressions are also used to generate more elaborate template data output. For example, our `DisplayItemsInTheCart` JSP extracts current shopping-cart data in the form of an HTML table and writes this table directly into the JSP as an expression as shown here:

```
<TD VALIGN=TOP>
  <%=cart.getCartAsHTMLTable()%>
</TD>
```

XML-based JSP files using expressions simply insert expressions inside of a `<jsp:expression>` element as shown here:

```
<HTML>
  <BODY>
    Date Today: <jsp:expression> new java.util.Date() </jsp:expression>
  </BODY>
</HTML>
```


Scriptlets

Scriptlets are more general-purpose scripting elements used to execute statements, declare variables and methods, evaluate expressions, and utilize JSP objects. Scriptlets are executed during the processing of JSP client requests with any output generated to the response output object. Scriptlets are defined within the `<%` and `%>` character sequences. Any code contained within such boundaries is expressed in terms of the host scripting language. As an example of a Java-based scriptlet taken from the `Registration` JSP, we have this:

```
<%
  String method = request.getMethod();

  // Include RegistrationForm if GET method request.
  // Include DisplayRegistrationInformation if POST method request.

  // if the request method type is not POST
  if(!method.equalsIgnoreCase(JSPHelper.POST_METHOD)){
%>
  <%@ include file="RegistrationForm.jsp"  %>
<%
 }
 else{
%>
  <%@ include file="DisplayRegistrationInformation.jsp"  %>
<%
 }
%>
```

XML-based JSP files rather straightforwardly encapsulate scriptlets within a `<jsp:scriptlet>` element as shown here:

```
<jsp:scriptlet>
  String method = request.getMethod();

  // Include RegistrationForm if GET method request.
  // Include DisplayRegistrationInformation if POST method request.

  // if the request method type is not POST
  if(!method.equalsIgnoreCase(JSPHelper.POST_METHOD)){
</jsp:scriptlet>
<jsp:directive.include file="RegistrationForm.jsp" />
<jsp:scriptlet>
 }
 else{
</jsp:scriptlet>
<jsp:directive.include file="DisplayRegistrationInformation.jsp" />
<jsp:scriptlet>
 }
</jsp:scriptlet>
```

Java Abstractions of JSP

A few new abstractions have been added to the Java Servlet API framework to support JSP. Many of these core new abstractions are contained within the `javax.servlet.jsp` package. The abstract classes and interfaces contained within this package are implemented within the JSP container environment and encapsulate post-translation JSP implementation objects. JSP programmers use many of these APIs via implicit object handles provided by the container and from within JSP scripting elements, as we describe in subsequent sections. We simply provide the API architecture and definitions here and defer examples for how to tap their services from within JSPs to sections that follow. Such abstractions are also used as the basis for creating custom JSP superclasses, as we describe toward the end of this section.

Page Context

The abstract `javax.servlet.jsp.PageContext` class, shown in Figure 33.5, encapsulates the context of a JSP. A `PageContext` object's primary role is to manage access to named objects belonging to particular scopes of visibility from within JSPs. Although the creation and initialization of a `PageContext` is usually transparent to the JSP programmer, as you'll see in subsequent sections, a JSP programmer will be able to obtain a handle to a `PageContext` representative from within a JSP and therefore make use of its many varied APIs.

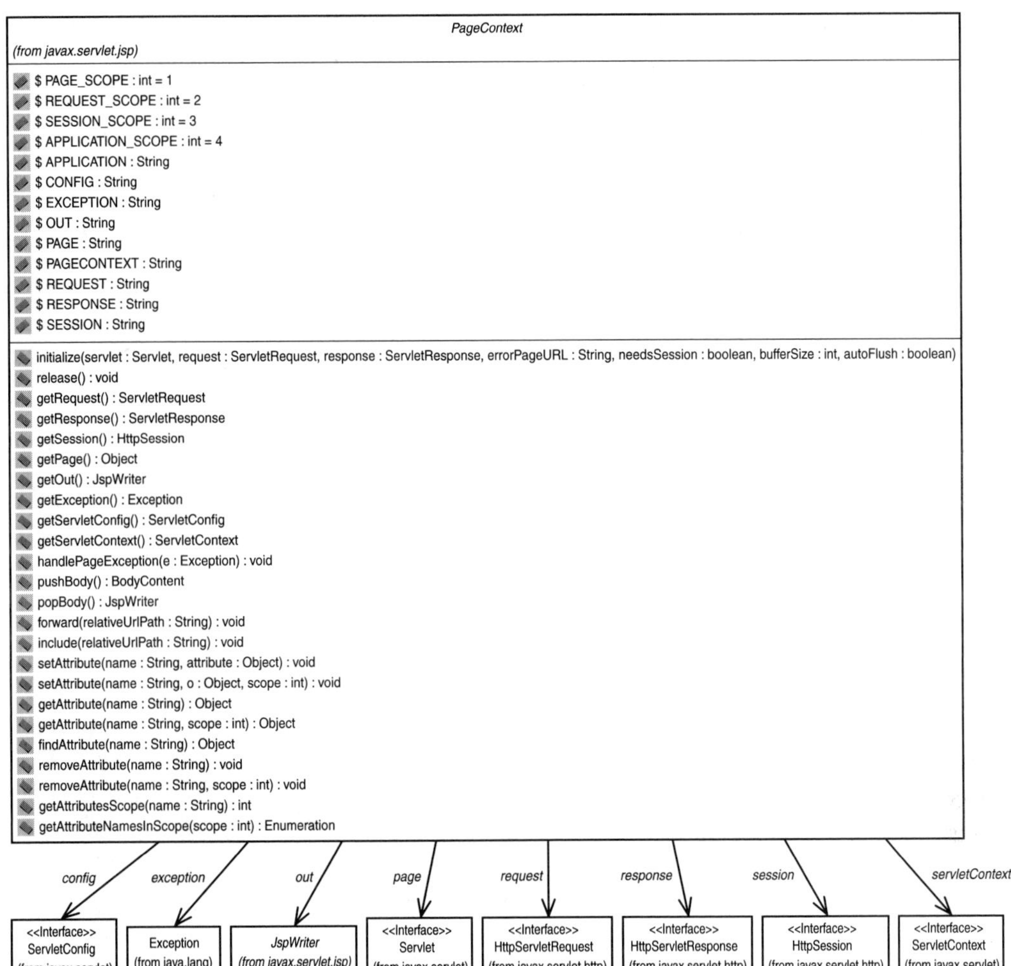

FIGURE 33.5
The JSP page context.

The `PageContext.initialize()` method is called such that the `PageContext` can be used by a JSP implementation class during request servicing. Much of the information passed to the `initialize()` method is taken directly from the page directive attributes for a particular JSP. This information includes a handle to the JSP implementation class servlet, a request object, a response object, the URL of an error page, a `boolean` indicator for whether a session is needed, the buffer size, and a buffer overflow auto flush indicator. The `PageContext.release()` method is also called to subsequently release such resources.

A series of methods can subsequently be called from within a JSP to obtain handles to and utilize many of the JSP implementation objects managed by the JSP container, such as the request object, the response object, the session object, the page implementation servlet object, an output response `JSPWriter` object, any propagated exception object, the servlet configuration object, and a servlet context object. The `PageContext.handlePageException()` method is used to pass an uncaught exception from a JSP to the page context, which handles forwarding the exception to any specified error page URL for the JSP or to a default error handler. A `PageContext` object's `forward()` and `include()` methods are also used to dispatch requests to other URLs.

The main function of a `PageContext` object is to manage access to objects that are referenceable from JSPs. The scope of each object is particularly important for considering object access and defines the scope within which an object reference is valid. The four valid types of object scope are identified by static constant `int` values on the `PageContext` object and are listed here:

- `PAGE_SCOPE`: Such objects are accessible only in the page in which they were instantiated. The lifetime of the object ends when the response is generated. Any such objects created with page scope are stored in the `PageContext` object. A named object is retrieved from `PageContext.getAttribute()`.
- `REQUEST_SCOPE`: The request associated with the page in which an object was created may be handled by other pages as well. Request objects are accessible from such pages that are handling the same request. The lifetime of the object ends when the request is processed. Any such objects created with request scope are stored in a request object of a subtype form of `javax.servlet.ServletRequest`. A named object is retrieved from `ServletRequest.getAttribute()`.
- `SESSION_SCOPE`: The session associated with the page in which an object was created may be associated with other pages as well. Session objects are accessible from such pages that are associated with the same user session. The lifetime of the object ends when the session terminates. Any such objects created with session scope are stored in a session object of the `javax.servlet.http.HttpSession` type. A named object is retrieved from `HttpSession.getValue()`.
- `APPLICATION_SCOPE`: Such objects are accessible in the Web application in which they were instantiated. The lifetime of the object ends when the application's `ServletContext` is destroyed. Any such objects created with application scope are stored in an application object of the `javax.servlet.ServletContext` type. A named object is retrieved from `ServletContext.getAttribute()`.

Each object is also associated with a case-sensitive `String` name that is used to uniquely identify an object within a translation unit. For example, a set of core implicit objects of JSP to which handles can be obtained all have `static String` names defined on the `PageContext` class. Each implicit object has a particular type defined as shown here in parentheses along with the `static String` implicit object ID name:

- `REQUEST` (`javax.servlet.ServletRequest` subclass): A request to a JSP valid only within the scope of a JSP request. For HTTP, this object maps to an object of the `javax.servlet.http.HttpServletRequest` type.
- `RESPONSE` (`javax.servlet.ServletResponse` subclass): A response from a JSP valid within the scope of the JSP page. For HTTP, this object maps to an object of the `javax.servlet.http.HttpServletResponse` type.
- `OUT` (`javax.servlet.jsp.JspWriter`): An object that writes data to the output response stream and is valid within the scope of the JSP page.
- `SESSION` (`javax.servlet.http.HttpSession`): A session for a JSP client using HTTP that is valid only within the scope of JSPs processing requests within the same session.
- `PAGECONTEXT` (`javax.servlet.jsp.PageContext`): The page context of a JSP that is valid within the scope of the JSP page.
- `PAGE` (`java.lang.Object`): A handle to the JSP's implementation class object that is valid for the scope of the JSP page. When Java is the scripting language, the `this` object name may also be used to refer to this object.
- `CONFIG` (`javax.servlet.ServletConfig`): A handle to JSP's configuration handler that is valid for the scope of the JSP page.
- `APPLICATION` (`javax.servlet.ServletContext`): A handle to the servlet context for the JSP's implementation object that is valid for the scope of the Web application.
- `EXCEPTION` (`java.lang.Throwable`): An exception that was not caught by a JSP and propagated into the JSP container environment and is valid only within the scope of a JSP error page.

Finally, getter, setter, and finder methods on the `PageContext` object are the methods used to manage access to such objects according to different object scopes. The `PageContext.getAttribute()` methods can be used to obtain a handle to a named object either in a default page scope if no scope is specified or in another scope if a constant `int` value identifying that scope is specified. Additionally, the scope of a particular named object can be retrieved from the `getAttributeScope()` method, and an `Enumeration` of `String` names for each attribute in a specified scope can be retrieved from a call to `getAttributeNamesInScope()`. The `findAttribute()` method can also be used to search for a named attribute in the order of page, request, session, and then application scope. Finally, the `setAttribute()` methods and `removeAttribute()` methods have method forms that can respectively set or remove named objects either in a default page scope or from a specified object scope.

Page Handles

Many handles to core JSP objects are directly derived from abstractions in the `javax.servlet` and `java.servlet.http` packages. Figure 33.6 depicts a few of the other abstractions used to encapsulate core JSP objects that are derived from the `javax.servlet.jsp` package. Abstractions for both JSP pages and JSP output streams are key new additions to the JSP suite of APIs. Furthermore, a `javax.servlet.jsp.JspException` is used to encapsulate many types of JSP-related exceptions, and a `javax.servlet.jsp.JspTagException` encapsulates an exception related to processing JSP tags.

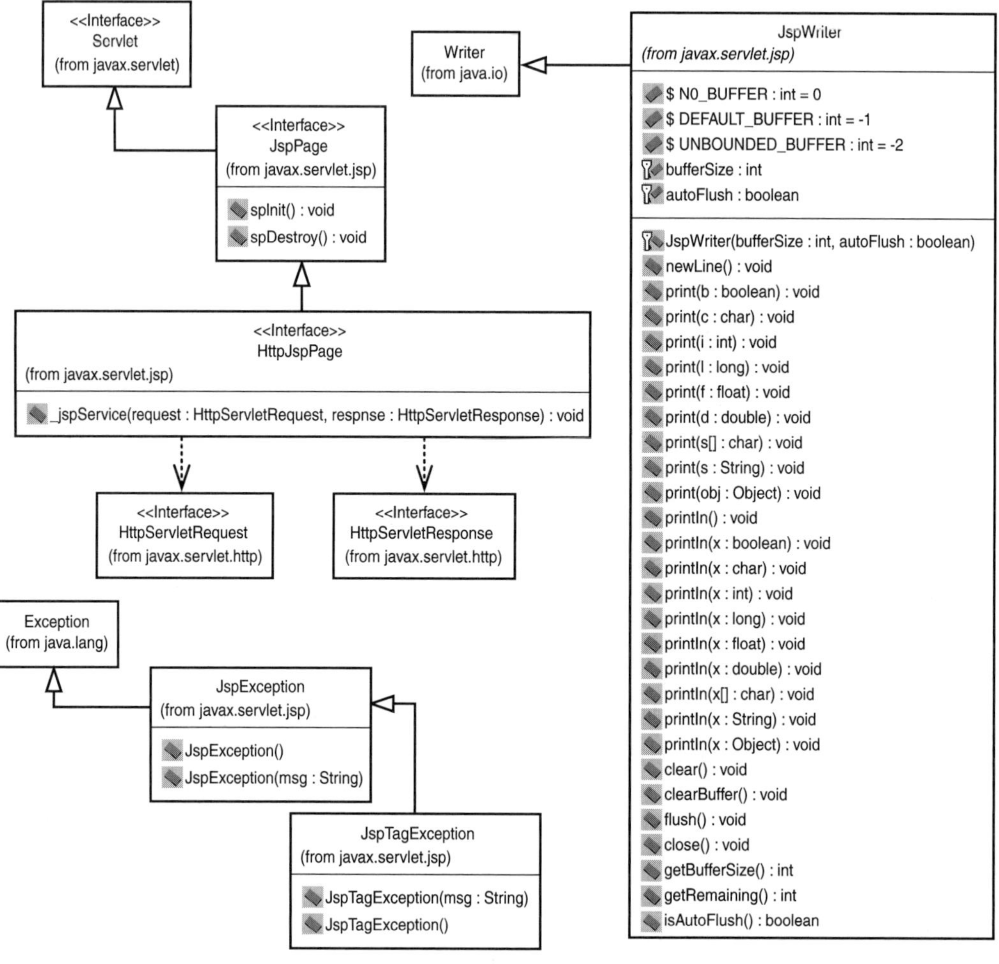

FIGURE 33.6
JSP core page handles.

The javax.servlet.jsp.JspPage interface extends the Servlet interface and is implemented by an implementation class of a JSP. The JspPage.jspInit() method is called by the JSP container when the JSP page is initialized. A subsequent call to getServletConfig() on the servlet object must return an initialized ServletConfig object. The JspPage.jspDestroy() method is called by the JSP container before the JSP is destroyed. The javax.servlet.jsp.HttpJspPage interface further extends JspPage to utilize HTTP communications semantics and defines a _jspService() method. The _jspService() method is automatically defined by the JSP compiler and contains the parsed and translated body of a JSP to service HTTP requests and generate HTTP responses.

The abstract javax.servlet.jsp.JspWriter class is associated with a PrintWriter of a ServletResponse and is very similar in functionality. The JspWriter delegates print() and println() calls directly to the PrintWriter object if buffering for the page is deactivated. If page buffering is activated, the JspWriter will otherwise manage buffering before it delegates calls to the PrintWriter and handle correct throwing of exceptions.

With respect to exceptions, in general, if an error occurs during the translation of a JSP into a Java Servlet, a request to such a page from an HTTP client will result in an HTTP 500 Server Error code being generated. When exceptions thrown within code are not caught by the JSP during a request, the uncaught exception is first added as an attribute by the JSP container to the javax.servlet.ServletRequest using the javax.servlet.jsp.jspException name. The request is then forwarded to a configured error page handler URL. The errorPage attribute of the page directive defines the particular error page handler URL for the current JSP. In our BeeShirts.com example, all uncaught exceptions result in the page being forwarded to the ErrorDisplay.jsp.

JSP Factories and Container Information

A few abstractions for obtaining a factory to create page contexts and handles to some minimal JSP container information are also provided in the javax.servlet.jsp package. Figure 33.7 illustrates these JSP factory and engine information abstractions.

The abstract javax.servlet.jsp.JspFactory class defines a means to create and destroy PageContext objects, as well as obtain a handle to some minimal JSP container information. The static getDefaultFactory() method is used to obtain a handle to the JspFactory object set by the JSP container. Only the container should use setDefaultFactory() when establishing this factory implementation. The JspFactory object handle can be used to obtain a handle to a PageContext object with page context initialization information passed to the getPageContext() method. The releasePageContext() is then used to release the PageContext object handle. Most JSP API developers will rely on other implicit object means to obtain PageContext handles as described in a later section.

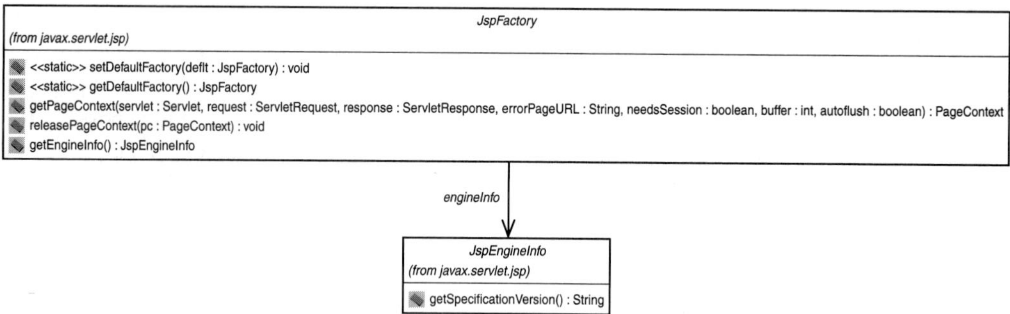

FIGURE 33.7
JSP factories and container information.

The `JspFactory.getEngineInfo()` method returns a handle to `javax.servlet.jsp.JspEngineInfo` object. Currently, the `JspEngineInfo` object simply returns the specification version number string supported by the underlying JSP container when its `getSpecificationVersion()` method is called.

Custom JSP Classes

For each JSP page, a JSP implementation class is created by the JSP compilation process for use inside of the container. Although the JSP compiler can create an implementation-dependent JSP implementation class, a JSP developer can also specify use of a specific superclass to use via the `extends` attribute of the `page` directive. Such an approach allows developers more controllability and visibility into creating JSPs but should be pursued with caution. Following is a basic set of rules to consider when building custom JSP classes that will be used with the `extends` attribute:

- Implement the `JspPage` interface or most likely the `HttpJspPage` interface for HTTP-based JSPs. Of course, all `Servlet` interface operations must also be implemented.
- Declare all methods implemented from the `Servlet` interface as `final`.
- Implement the `_jspService()` method as an `abstract` and non-`final` method.
- Implement the `service()` method to invoke `_jspService()`.
- Implement the `init(ServletConfig)` method to store the `ServletConfig` object and invoke `jspInit()`.
- Implement the `getServletConfig()` method to retrieve the `ServletConfig` object.
- Implement the `destroy()` method to invoke `jspDestroy()`.

Standard Java Objects from JSP

Many of the APIs presented in the preceding section can be utilized from within a JSP page in the form of objects created by a JSP container. In fact, JSP containers create and expose such objects, as well as objects encapsulating many of the Java Servlet APIs such as request, response, and session objects. JSPs can use this standard suite of objects from within JSP scripting elements by referring to them with a standard object name. This section describes these standard implicit objects and describes the scope within a JSP in which they are valid.

Implicit Objects

Implicit objects are handles to objects created by the JSP container for use within JSPs. Implicit objects thus do not have to be declared or created by JSP developers, but rather can be assumed to exist from certain vantage points of execution within a JSP. These vantage points define the scope in which such implicit objects are usable by JSPs. Although each implicit object has its own JSP object name, each object also has an implicit type that maps to a particular class or interface after JSP-to-servlet translation. The class or interface to which the implicit object is mapped indicates those methods that can be invoked on the implicit object. All objects relate to a `String` ID name stored by the `PageContext` object that defines their scope and additional semantics as defined in an earlier section. The standard set of implicit JSP objects, their `PageContext` ID name, and their target translation type or super-type definition are defined in Table 33.1.

TABLE 33.1 Implicit Objects, Their Names, and Their Types

Object Name	`PageContext` *ID*	*Type/Super-Type*
`request`	`REQUEST`	`javax.servlet.ServletRequest`
`response`	`RESPONSE`	`javax.servlet.ServletResponse`
`out`	`OUT`	`javax.servlet.jsp.PrintWriter`
`session`	`SESSION`	`javax.servlet.http.HttpSession`
`pageContext`	`PAGECONTEXT`	`javax.servlet.jsp.PageContext`
`page`	`PAGE`	`java.lang.Object`
`config`	`CONFIG`	`javax.servlet.ServletConfig`
`application`	`APPLICATION`	`javax.servlet.ServletContext`
`exception`	`EXCEPTION`	`javax.lang.Throwable`

Object Scope

The scope in which an object (such as an implicit object) is valid is defined in one of four ways. The way in which an object scope is defined directly relates to the valid types of object scope identified by `static` constant `int` values on the `PageContext` object as described earlier. Each type of object scope indicates which type of implicit object is used to store an object in that scope. Table 33.2 reiterates each object scope type identified from a `PageContext` constant and the implicit object that is used to store objects in that scope.

TABLE 33.2 Object Scope and Implicit Object Storage

`PageContext` *Scope*	*Implicit Object Storage*
`PAGE_SCOPE`	`pageContext`
`REQUEST_SCOPE`	`request`
`SESSION_SCOPE`	`session`
`APPLICATION_SCOPE`	`application`

JSP Object Manipulation Examples

With an understanding of directives, scripting elements, and implicit objects, you are now armed with the knowledge you need to comprehend most of the BeeShirts.com JSPs. Listing 33.1, in fact, is a cohesive snapshot of code that composes the BeeShirts front-page JSP. You'll notice a healthy sprinkling of template data mixed with JSP code. The JSP code is processed on the server side and generates HTML, which, along with the predefined template data, is the HTML that is interpreted by the client-side Web browser.

LISTING 33.1 BeeShirts.com Home Page JSP (`BeeShirts.jsp`)

```
<%@ page info="BeeShirts Page" import=
    "javax.naming.InitialContext, javax.naming.NamingException,
     ejava.jspch33.JSPHelper"
%>

<HTML>
<HEAD>
  <TITLE>
    BeeShirts.com
  </TITLE>
</HEAD>
<BODY ALINK="#FFCC66"  BGCOLOR="#ffcc66" >
<%-- Add Error page to display Error --%>
<%@ page errorPage="ErrorDisplay.jsp" %>
```

```
<%-- Get the server information --%>
<% String serverInfo = JSPHelper.getServerInfo(request); %>

<%-- Display the Top and Left part of JSP --%>
<TABLE BORDER=0 COLS=2 WIDTH=\"100%\" >
 <TR>
   <%@ include file="BeeShirtsTopArea.jsp" %>
 </TR>
 <TR>
   <%@ include file="BeeShirtsLeftArea.jsp" %>

<%-- Create session object and obtain cookie value --%>
<%
  // Create a session each time the user comes to this site.
  boolean createNew = true;
  session =  request.getSession(createNew);
  // check if it is the first time visiting and if has cookie
  Cookie[]  cookies = request.getCookies();
  String cookieValue = JSPHelper.getOurCookieValue(cookies);
  if(cookieValue != null){
     session.setAttribute(JSPHelper.COOKIE_NAME, cookieValue);
  }
%>
  <TD  VALIGN=TOP>
<%-- Print welcome message --%>
<%
  // If have cookie, then print welcome back message
  if(cookieValue != null){
     out.println("   <STRONG> WELCOME BACK : "
                 + cookieValue +"</STRONG> <BR>");
  }
  try{
    JSPHelper.initialContext = new InitialContext();
    String welcomeMessage =
      (String)JSPHelper.initialContext.
        lookup(JSPHelper.WELCOME_MESSAGE_ENV);
    // Print the root screen promo and welcome...
    out.println(welcomeMessage);
  }
  catch(NamingException namingException){
    namingException.printStackTrace();
  }
%>
  </TD>
</TR>
</TABLE>
</BODY>
</HTML>
```

After a page directive and some preliminary HTML, the BeeShirts JSP first makes a call to the `static getServerInfo()` method on a `JSPHelper` class used as a utility class with our examples. The `static JSPHelper.getServerInfo()` method simply extracts the server hostname, server port, and context path from the request object and returns a formatted `String` of this information as shown here:

```
public static String getServerInfo(HttpServletRequest request)
{
  String serverHost = request.getServerName();
  int serverPort = request.getServerPort();
  String context = request.getContextPath();
  String protocol = "HTTP://";
  String serverInfo = protocol+serverHost+":"+serverPort+context;
  return serverInfo;
}
```

NOTE

Hopefully you can now see how easy it is for JSPs to interact with Java code. Because JSPs get converted to Java code during translation and compilation, this JSP-Java interaction is extremely efficient as opposed to other solutions for interaction between other scripting languages and Java that are currently in the marketplace.

The returned `serverInfo String` from the `JSPHelper.getServerInfo()` method to the `BeeShirts` JSP is not actually used within the `BeeShirts.jsp` file, but it is in fact used by the included `BeeShirtsTopArea.jsp` and `BeeShirtsLeftArea.jsp` files. Because they are part of the same translation unit, they can refer to objects defined within parent JSPs such as the `BeeShirts` JSP.

The BeeShirts JSP then demonstrates how the `request` object can be used just like calls to an `HttpServletRequest` object, but now the call occurs within a JSP scriptlet. A handle to an `HttpSession` object is created and used to retrieve any `Cookie` values associated with the session. Recall from the preceding chapter that this same type of functionality was embedded within the `BeeShirtsServlet` class to extract the first name of a user stored in a `Cookie` if they had previously visited the site. Any extracted cookie value is then used to display a personalized `WELCOME BACK` message.

Also recall from the preceding chapter that the `RegistrationServlet` added the personalized cookie to the response stream during registration of a user. This functionality is now embedded in the `DisplayRegistrationInformation` JSP. That portion of the

DisplayRegistrationInformation JSP that creates a Cookie named BEESHIRTS with the value of the customer's first name is shown here:

```
<%-- Declare an easier-to-read reference to six months' time --%>
<%!
  private final int SIX_MONTHS_IN_SECONDS =  60*60*24*183;
%>

<%-- customer and address objects created above in this JSP --%>
<%
   // Set address onto customer object now
   customer.setAddress(address);

   // Get any cookie value named "BEESHIRTS" from chapter 32's
   // JSPHelper static constant COOKIE_NAME
   String cookieValue
       = (String)session.getAttribute(JSPHelper.COOKIE_NAME);

   // If no cookie, then add user's first name to cookie
   if(cookieValue == null){
     // create Cookie for this customer
     Cookie cookie = new Cookie(JSPHelper.COOKIE_NAME,
                                customer.getFirstName());
     // Set maximum age of cookie
     cookie.setMaxAge(SIX_MONTHS_IN_SECONDS);
     // Now add the cookie to the response stream
     response.addCookie(cookie);
   }
   // Output the customer info to the HTML page as a table
   out.println(customer.getCustomerAsHTMLTable());
%>
```


After the BeeShirts JSP retrieves and prints any WELCOME BACK message stored in the cookie, note that it uses Web component environment settings as was the case with this JSP's servlet counterpart. The BeeShirts JSP creates a handle to an InitialContext object, which is then used to look up a named welcome message String object. The JSPHelper.WELCOME_MESSAGE_ENV constant maps to the java:comp/env/WelcomeMessage value in our example, which refers to an <env-entry> element in our web.xml deployment descriptor as shown here:

```
<env-entry>
  <description>
    Customizable description for the Application
  </description>
  <env-entry-name>WelcomeMessage</env-entry-name>
  <env-entry-value> A big welcome to our online T-Shirts shoppe.
       ...
  </env-entry-value>
  <env-entry-type>java.lang.String</env-entry-type>
</env-entry>
```

Finally, the `BeeShirts` JSP uses the `out` object to print any specialized `WELCOME BACK` message, as well as the message looked up from the JNDI `java:comp/env/WelcomeMessage` named environment entry.

As a final example of implicit object usage with exception handling, our `ErrorDisplay.jsp` standard error handler JSP, shown in Listing 33.2, uses the exception object to print the contents of the received exception, as well as a stack trace for the exception. While exceptions are a rather ugly thing to display on a Web page, for our development purposes, it can be very informational. We thus print out such exception information in the `ErrorDisplay` JSP.

LISTING 33.2 BeeShirts.com Standard Error Page JSP (`ErrorDisplay.jsp`)

```
<%@ page isErrorPage="true" import="java.io.*" %>

<HTML>
<HEAD>
  <TITLE>
    BeeShirts.com Error Display Page
  </TITLE>
</HEAD>
<BODY ALINK="#FFCC66"  BGCOLOR="#ffcc66" >

<TABLE BORDER=0 COLS=2 WIDTH=\"100%\" >
 <TR>
  <TD  VALIGN=TOP>
   Error occurred in accessed page :
   <%=exception%>
   and exception occurred in :
   <%exception.printStackTrace(new PrintWriter(out)); %>
  </TD>
</TR>
</TABLE>
</BODY>
</HTML>
```

Standard Java Actions from JSP

JSP actions define specific operations that are to be performed as directed by a JSP using scripting language tags. JSP actions, in fact, are defined within JSPs using an XML syntax and thus have no need to define a special XML-based representation. Actions have a begin tag and end tag along with an action name to identify the specific type of action to be performed. Actions also can have a collection of name/value attribute pairs defined within the action. An optional body between the begin and end tags may contain other actions or parameters defined in terms of names and values. Because actions are implemented by Java classes underneath the hood, they can be as arbitrarily complex as scriptlets. However, JSP actions are specified using a taglike syntax that is more natural for many Web page developers who are used to using HTML and scripting languages.

Although we describe a means to create arbitrarily complex custom actions later in the chapter, this section describes a means to utilize a few standard actions defined for JSPs. Using these standard actions, you can do the following:

- Forward requests to other resources.
- Include responses from other resources.
- Embed applet and JavaBean tags into a page.
- Obtain server-side JavaBean reference identifiers.
- Set properties on a server-side JavaBean.
- Get properties from a server-side JavaBean.

`jsp:param` Action Sub-Elements

The `jsp:param` empty sub-element is used to define name/value pairs that have meaning specific to an enclosing action element. Names and values are defined as case-sensitive attributes of the `<jsp:param>` element. The value attribute can be either a string value or an expression evaluating to a string value. The `<jsp:param>` sub-element has the following general form:

```
<jsp:param name="paramName" value="paramValue|<%= expression %>" />
```

And as an example (excluding any enclosing elements), we have this:

```
<jsp:param name="FirstName" value="Julia" />
<jsp:param name="LastName" value="Perrone" />
```

`jsp:forward` Action

The standard `jsp:forward` action element is used to dispatch a request to another resource in the same Web application context, such as an HTML file, a JSP, or a servlet. The `jsp:forward` name is used as an XML element name and can be used to define either an empty element or an element with start and end tags. If start and end tags are used, the element can be defined with one or more `<jsp:param>` sub-elements used to add parameters to the forwarded request object. The relative URL of the resource to which the request will be dispatched is defined by a `page` attribute within the `<jsp:forward>` element. The page attribute can be defined in terms of a string or an expression that evaluates to a string and is described in terms of a URL relative to the JSP Web application context (if it begins with a `/`) or relative to the JSP file.

This action can be in either of these two forms:

```
<jsp:forward page="targetURL|<%= expression %>" />


<jsp:foward page="targetURL|<%= expression %>">
  <jsp:param name="param1" value="param1Value|<%= expression %>" />
  <jsp:param name="param2" value="param2Value|<%= expression %>" />
    ...
</jsp:forward>
```

We have the following associated examples:

```
<jsp:forward page="/OrderStatus" />


<jsp:forward page="/CustomerService/Feedback">
  <jsp:param name="user" value="pperrone" />
  <jsp:param name="email" value="pperrone@assuredtech.com" />
  <jsp:param name="message" value="Help Me!" />
</jsp:forward>
```

jsp:include Action

The standard `jsp:include` action element is used to include the output response from another resource into the output from the current JSP. If the other resource is a static file, the content is simply included with the current output response. If the other resource generates a dynamic response, the request dispatched to that resource is used to generate the dynamic response, which is included in the current JSP's output response. The `jsp:include` name is used as the XML element name and can be used to define either an empty element or an element with start and end tags. If start and end tags are used, the element can be defined with one or more `<jsp:param>` sub-elements used to add parameters to the dispatched request object for use by resources that generate dynamic content. The URL of the resource to which the request will be dispatched is defined after a `page` attribute within the `<jsp:include>` element. You must also include a mandatory `flush` attribute that must always be set to `true`, indicating that the output buffer is to be flushed.

This action can be in either of these two forms:

```
<jsp:include page="targetURL|<%= expression %>" flush="true"/>

<jsp:include page="targetURL|<%= expression %>" flush="true">
  <jsp:param name="param1" value="param1Value|<%= expression %>" />
  <jsp:param name="param2" value="param2Value|<%= expression %>" />
    ...
</jsp:include>
```

For example:

```
<jsp:include page="<%= copyrightPage.getPageName() %>" />
```

jsp:useBean Action

The standard `jsp:useBean` action element is used to associate a JavaBean object instance within a specified scope to an identifier. The identifier can then be used as an object reference to the newly retrieved object for subsequent method calls on the object. The `jsp:useBean` action first attempts to locate an object based on the value of an object identifier name, the type name, and the scope in which the object should be located. If it cannot find the specified object, a new object of a specified type will be created.

The `<jsp:useBean>` element has the following general form:

```
<jsp:useBean id="identifierName" scope="page|request|application|session"
          [    class="className"
             | type="typeName"
             | class="className" type="typeName"
             | beanName="beanName|<%= expression %>" type="typeName" ] />
```

Or if a body is to be associated with the action, we have this:

```
<jsp:useBean id="identifierName" scope="page|request|application|session"
          [    class="className"
             | type="typeName"
             | class="className" type="typeName"
             | beanName="beanName|<%= expression %>" type="typeName" ] >
    <other elements>
    ...
</jsp:useBean>
```

The `id` and `scope` attributes are individually specified, but the `class`, `type`, and `beanName` attributes must be defined according to one of the four combinations shown previously. The `jsp:useBean` attributes are defined here:

- `id`: Assumes a case-sensitive name value that is used to uniquely identify an object within a translation unit (that is, a JSP and its statically included pages). Is also synonymous with the name of the scripting variable that was declared with this object reference.
- `scope`: Assumes a value that is associated with an `id` attribute to specify the scope of the object. The valid object scope values are of the type `page`, `request`, `session`, and `application` as described in an earlier section. The `page` object scope is a default value.
- `class`: Assumes a case-sensitive fully qualified class name for the class of the object. If the object cannot be located, this class name will be used to instantiate an instance of the class with a public and parameterless constructor for the class.

- beanName: Assumes a case-sensitive fully qualified class name for location and possible instantiation of a JavaBean using the java.beans.Beans.instantiate() method. If the JavaBean is serialized, this name can be used to read a serialized form of the JavaBean with a class loader.
- type: Assumes a case-sensitive fully qualified name of the class, super-class of, or interface implemented by the class of the object. Allows for the distinct use of a special type with the object. If used with no class or beanName attribute, no object is newly instantiated.

If the object could not be located within the page context of the JSP, it may need to be instantiated by the container. If it has been instantiated instead of located, other elements within the body of the <jsp:useBean> element will be processed to initialize the object. Mainly, the <jsp:setProperty> action defined next is used in this context.

As an example of associating an object from a session scope to an identifier used to manage some system user information, we have the following sample cases:

```
<%-- Create object from class --%>
<jsp:useBean id="user"
             class="com.assuredtech.security.identity.User"
             scope="session" />

<%-- Create object from class in terms of other type --%>
<jsp:useBean id="user"
             class="com.assuredtech.security.identity.User"
             type="com.assuredtech.security.identity.Principal"
             scope="session" />

<%-- Create object from JavaBean name --%>
<jsp:useBean id="user"
             beanName="com.assuredtech.security.beans.User.ser"
             scope="session" />
```

The identifier returned from this action can then be subsequently used in the JSP as shown here within a scriptlet:

```
<%
    String userName = user.getName();
    if(userName.equals("root")){
      out.println("You are the root of all evil!");
    }
%>
```

jsp:setProperty Action

The standard jsp:setProperty action element is used to set the value of properties in a JavaBean object. A <jsp:setProperty> element has a name attribute that refers to the identifier of an object located or instantiated via a jsp:useBean action. Attributes are also defined that describe a mapping from named JSP request parameters to named JavaBean properties whose values are to be set.

The <jsp:setProperty> action element has the following general form:

```
<jsp:setProperty name="JavaBeanNameID"
    [  property="*"
     | property="JavaBeanPropertyName"
     | property="JavaBeanPropertyName"
         param="requestParameterName"
     | property="JavaBeanPropertyName"
         value="JavaBeanPropertyValue|<%= expression %>"] />
```

The name attribute is required, and the valid combinations of property attributes with param and value attributes are indicated in the preceding text. The attributes of the <jsp:setProperty> element are as shown here:

- name: Defined with a value describing the name of a JavaBean object identifier that has previously been defined within the id value of a <jsp:useBean> action element.
- property: Defined with a value that describes how named request parameter values can be used to set associated JavaBean property values. The property="*" form can be used to indicate that any named request parameters received by the current JSP are to be set into matching JavaBean properties that share the same name. The property="*propertyName*" form can be used to specifically designate the name of the JavaBean property that should be set. JavaBean properties that have types of boolean/Boolean, byte/Byte, char/Character, int/Integer, long/Long, double/Double, float/Float, or indexed arrays of these types can all be set using this action.
- param: Defined with a value that is the name of a request parameter to be used with a named property attribute value if the name of the JavaBean property differs from the name of the request parameter.
- value: Defined with a value that will be used to directly set a JavaBean property named by the property attribute. The value can be a String form of the JavaBean property type or an expression to be evaluated.

For example, suppose we have already defined a user id from a jsp:useBean action as illustrated in the preceding example. We can populate the property values of this JavaBean from request information in one of the following ways:

```
<%--
     Populate with userName and password request info.
     Thus, the userName and password request parameters will be set
     onto the userName and password JavaBean properties.
--%>
<jsp:setProperty name="user" property="userName" />
<jsp:setProperty name="user" property="password" />

<%--
     Populate using different names from request object.
     Thus, the user and pwd request parameters will be a set
     onto the userName and password JavaBean properties.
--%>
<jsp:setProperty name="user" property="userName" param="user"/>
<jsp:setProperty name="user" property="password" param="pwd"/>

<%--
    Populate with specific values.
    Thus, the userName and password JavaBean properties will
    be set with the specific tjefferson and UVA1819 values.
--%>
<jsp:setProperty name="user" property="userName" value="tjefferson"/>
<jsp:setProperty name="user" property="password" value="UVA1819"/>

<%--
    Populate with all request values that match.
    Thus, all of the request parameter values that match the JavaBean
    properties will be set onto those JavaBean properties.
--%>
<jsp:setProperty name="user" property="*" />
```

`jsp:getProperty` Action

The standard `jsp:getProperty` action element is used to retrieve the value of a named JavaBean property for display in a JSP. A `name` attribute identifies the JavaBean `id`, which needs to be previously established in the JSP by a `jsp:useBean` action. A `property` attribute refers to the name of the property on the JavaBean.

The `<jsp:getProperty>` action element has the following general form:

```
<jsp:getProperty name="JavaBeanNameID" property="JavaBeanPropertyName"/>
```

For example, using the same `user id` from a `jsp:useBean` action previously established, we have this:

```
<HTML>
  <BODY>
```

```
    Welcome back <jsp:getProperty name="user" property="userName" /> !
  </BODY>
</HTML>
```

jsp:plugin Action

The standard jsp:plugin action element is used to embed a JavaBean or Java applet within a JSP response page. When the JSP response is received by the Web client browser, the browser is directed to utilize the Java Plug-in technology in order to activate and display the JavaBean or Java applet. The <jsp:plugin> element handles the correct formatting and insertion of either OBJECT tags or EMBED tags as appropriate, depending on the Web client's particular browser requirements. The attributes defined within the <jsp:plugin> element either are derived from or directly map to attributes defined within the standard HTML APPLET, OBJECT, and EMBED tags described in previous chapters. Furthermore, two sub-elements of the <jsp:plugin> element are used to define JavaBean or Java applet parameters and alternative text displays.

NOTE

See Chapter 29, "Web Browsers and Servers in the Enterprise," for a discussion of the Java Plug-in technology. Chapter 29 and Chapter 4, "Java Foundations for Enterprise Development," also provide a better understanding for many of the various attribute tags used by the <jsp:plugin> element.

The <jsp:plugin> action element has the following general form:

```
<jsp:plugin
    type="bean|applet"
    code="componentClassName"
    codebase="codebaseURL"
    [ archive="commaSeparatedListOfJARs" ]
    [ name="componentInstanceName" ]
    [ width="widthInPixels" ]
    [ height="heightInPixels" ]
    [ align="bottom|top|middle|left|right" ]
    [ vspace="spaceLeftAndRightInPixels" ]
    [ hspace="spaceAboveAndBelowInPixels" ]
    [ jreversion="majorAndMinorVersionOfJRE" ]
    [ nspluginurl="NetscapeNavigatorPluginURL" ]
    [ iepluginurl="InternetExplorerPluginURL" ]
>
```

```
    [ <jsp:params>
      [ <jsp:param name="parameterName"
                   value="parameterValue|<%= expression %>" />
        <jsp:param name="parameterName"
                   value="parameterValue|<%= expression %>" />
          ...
      ]
      </jsp:params>
    ]

    [ <jsp:fallback>
         Alternative message if failed to load
      </jsp:fallback>
    ]

</jsp:plugin>
```

The `code`, `codebase`, `archive`, `name`, `width`, `height`, `align`, `vspace`, and `hspace` attributes of the `jsp:plugin` element all directly map from attributes of an `APPLET` tag as described in Chapter 4's discussion of Java applets as well as from the `EMBED` and `OBJECT` tags described in Chapter 29. Additionally, the remaining attributes of a `jsp:plugin` element are defined here:

- `type`: Indicates whether the component is a JavaBean or Java applet.
- `jreversion`: Defines the version number of the JRE that this component requires to run. The value of `1.1` is the default and refers to the JRE v1.1.
- `nspluginurl`: Defines the URL from which the Netscape Navigator JRE plug-in can be downloaded. This attribute is equivalent to the `pluginspage` attribute of the `EMBED` tag as described in Chapter 29.
- `iepluginurl`: Defines the URL from which the Internet Explorer JRE plug-in can be downloaded. This attribute is equivalent to the `codebase` attribute of the `OBJECT` tag as described in Chapter 29.

A body for the `jsp:plugin` action element can also define a `<jsp:params>` element that contains one or more `<jsp:param>` elements. Each `<jsp:param>` element then defines the `name` and `value` of parameters used to initialize the Java applet or JavaBean. This is, of course, akin to the `PARAM` tags within an `APPLET` tag. Finally, the `<jsp:fallback>` element within the `<jsp:plugin>` element can be used to display an alternative text message if the Java applet or JavaBean cannot be loaded in the Web client's browser. This is similar to the `ALT` attribute of an `APPLET` tag or to any text added within the body of an `APPLET` tag.

For example (analogous to the example from Chapter 29's Java Plug-in discussion), we have this:

```
<jsp:plugin
    type="applet" code="com.beeshirts.MyApplet.class" codebase="."
    archive="MyApplet.jar" name="MyGloriousApplet" jreversion="1.2"
    width="400" height="300" align="middle" vspace="10" hspace="10"
    nspluginurl="http://java.sun.com/products/plugin/1.2/
➥plugin-install.html"
    iepluginurl=" http://java.sun.com/products/plugin/1.2.2/
➥jinstall-1_2_2-win.cab#Version=1,2,2,0"
>
  <jsp:params>
    <jsp:param name="sample_value" value="123" />
  </jsp:params>
  <jsp:fallback>
     Cannot load Java Applet.
  </jsp:fallback>
</jsp:plugin>
```

Standard Action Examples

The `CheckOut` JSP provides a good example of a JSP making effective use of the `<jsp:forward>` type of action. As Listing 33.3 demonstrates, the `CheckOut` JSP first attempts to retrieve a `Customer` object from the session. If no `Customer` object is retrieved, the client is redirected to the `Registration` JSP. Subsequently, a `ShoppingCart` object is looked up in the session object. If no `ShoppingCart` is present, the client is redirected to the `BrowseShirts` JSP; otherwise, it's redirected to the `Cart` JSP.

33 JAVASERVER PAGES

LISTING 33.3 Check Out JSP (`CheckOut.jsp`)

```
<%@ page info="BeeShirts.com Browse Shirts Page"
  import=" ejava.jspch33.JSPHelper,
           ejava.servletsch32.Customer,
           ejava.servletsch32.ShoppingCart,
           java.util.Vector "  %>
<HTML>
<HEAD>
  <TITLE>
    BeeShirts.com
  </TITLE>
</HEAD>

<BODY ALINK="#FFCC66"  BGCOLOR="#ffcc66" >

<%
```

continues

LISTING 33.3 Continued

```
  // Get stored customer session information
   Customer customer = (Customer)session.getAttribute("customer");


   // If no stored customer info, redirect to Registration JSP
   if(customer == null){
%>
    <jsp:forward page="<%=JSPHelper.REGISTRATION_PAGE%>" />
<%
   }

   // Get stored shopping cart information
   ShoppingCart cart =
     (ShoppingCart)session.
       getAttribute(ShoppingCart.SHOPPING_CART_OBJECT);

   // If no stored cart info, redirect to BrowseShirts JSP
   if(cart == null){
%>
     <jsp:forward page="<%=JSPHelper.BROWSE_SHIRTS_PAGE%>" />
<%
   }
   else{ // Else redirect to Cart JSP
%>
     <jsp:forward page="<%=JSPHelper.CART_PAGE%>" />
<%
   }
%>
```

As another example, recall from our illustration of standard JSP objects earlier that the `DisplayRegistrationInformation` JSP used a `Customer` and `Address` object to set the user's first name as a cookie value into the client response object. The means by which the `DisplayRegistrationInformation` JSP retrieved these `Customer` and `Address` object references was via `jsp:useBean` actions. Because the `Customer` and `Address` objects are JavaBeans, we can also set properties onto these values. We set request parameters received from the `POST` created by the `RegistrationForm` JSP onto the `Customer` and `Address` properties as shown here:

```
<%-- Get handle to a Customer JavaBean --%>
<jsp:useBean id="customer"
  class="ejava.servletsch32.Customer"
  scope="session" >
  <jsp:setProperty name="customer" property="firstName"  />
  <jsp:setProperty name="customer" property="lastName"  />
```

```
    <jsp:setProperty name="customer" property="middleName"  />
    <jsp:setProperty name="customer" property="email"  />
    <jsp:setProperty name="customer" property="phone"  />
    <jsp:setProperty name="customer" property="password"  />
  </jsp:useBean>

  <%-- Get handle to an Address JavaBean --%>
  <jsp:useBean id="address"
    class="ejava.servletsch32.Address"
    scope="session" >
    <jsp:setProperty name="address" property="address_1"  />
    <jsp:setProperty name="address" property="address_2"  />
    <jsp:setProperty name="address" property="city"  />
    <jsp:setProperty name="address" property="state"  />
    <jsp:setProperty name="address" property="zipCode"  />
  </jsp:useBean>
```

JSP Configuration and Deployment

We described the general Web application deployment process, Web application deployment descriptor format, and specific deployment steps for our sample BeeShirts.com e-commerce storefront application in Chapter 32. From an application developer's perspective, the deployment of JSPs is very closely related to the deployment of Java Servlets. JSPs are viewed as generic Web components as are Java Servlets. The deployment descriptor format, the WAR file packaging, and the tools used to deploy such Web components do not differ between JSPs and Java Servlets. In fact, the same means as are available for Java Servlets exist for JSPs to configure JSPs, JSP context, and environment variables, as well as for managing thread, EJB access, resource access, transaction, security, and distributable container services. The only real difference lies in the initial translation of JSPs into Java Servlet implementation classes. Two options for translating JSPs to Java Servlets thus must be considered by application developers: first, the direct approach and second, the precompiled approach.

In the direct approach to JSP deployment, developers simply copy their JSP files to the root Web application context directory and rely on their J2EE vendor's JSP-compliant tools and Web servers to translate the JSP into a Java source file and then compile the Java source file into a Java class file. In the precompiled JSP approach, the developer often uses a tool to precompile the JSP into its target implementation class. The easiest approach is, of course, to let the JSP deployment and server tools consider how and when it will compile the JSP. However, there may be a noticeable performance hit when the JSP is first visited if the JSP server is implemented to translate and compile the JSP at runtime. Furthermore, such an approach also requires the use of a JSP compiler utility to be physically deployed to the Web server for runtime processing.

This section describes those special considerations for deploying JSPs using the basic Web application deployment model described in Chapter 32. We first describe a few key considerations when making JSP deployment descriptors and then move on to specific considerations for deploying a JSP in its direct form to a J2EE server, as well as by first precompiling the JSP. We use the J2EE reference implementation to provide an example of direct deployment of JSPs and the BEA WebLogic Server to provide an example of deploying precompiled JSPs.

JSP Deployment Descriptor Considerations

The same deployment descriptor format used for deploying Java Servlet components as defined by the Web application DTD (shown in Listing 32.1 of the preceding chapter) is used for deploying JSP components. Just a few small differences in how the deployment descriptor is created for JSPs deserve mentioning. For one, instead of using a `<servlet-class>` element to define a servlet class within each `<servlet>` element, a `<jsp-file>` element can be used. The `<jsp-file>` element is used to identify the filename for JSPs that are directly deployed without precompilation. The path to the JSP file relative to the root Web application context must also be specified as part of this element's value. For example, our JSP file `BeeShirts.jsp` is placed directly under the root Web application context directory in a `WAR` file, and thus we have an entry in our sample `web.xml` deployment descriptor file as shown here:

```
<web-app>
    ...
    <!-- BeeShirts page generates starting page for BeeShirts.com -->
    <servlet>
      <servlet-name>BeeShirts</servlet-name>
      <display-name>BeeShirts</display-name>
      <jsp-file>BeeShirts.jsp</jsp-file>
    </servlet>
    ...
</web-app>
```

If the JSP is precompiled into an implementation class, the `<servlet-class>` element can be used. If it is still desirable to refer to the JSPs using the JSP name or some other configurable URL pattern, a `<servlet-mapping>` element can be used. For example, we use a BEA WebLogic precompiler to translate and compile the `BeeShirts.jsp` file into a `_beeshirts` Java class file in the `ejava.jspch33` package, and then set deployment descriptor entries for this JSP in a `weblogic_app.xml` file on the CD like this:

```
<web-app>
   ...
  <!-- BeeShirts page generates starting page for BeeShirts.com -->
  <servlet>
    <servlet-name>BeeShirts</servlet-name>
    <display-name>BeeShirts</display-name>
```

```
    <servlet-class>ejava.jspch33._beeshirts</servlet-class>
  </servlet>
    ...
  <servlet-mapping>
    <servlet-name>BeeShirts</servlet-name>
    <url-pattern>BeeShirtsJSP</url-pattern>
  </servlet-mapping>
  ...
</web-app>
```

As just alluded, we in fact include two sample XML-based deployment descriptor files on the CD. The `web.xml` file is used to directly deploy the BeeShirts.com JSPs in their raw JSP file form to the J2EE reference implementation server. The `weblogic_app.xml` file is used to deploy JSPs that have been precompiled as Java Servlets to the BEA WebLogic Server.

JSP Configuration

In addition to defining basic `<servlet>` entry information for each JSP as illustrated previously, both sample XML deployment files also contain configuration information for the JSPs that can be read in one of two ways. The `BrowseShirts` JSP and `OrderStatus` JSP both have collections of `<init-param>` values associated with them that can be read via calls to `ServletConfig` akin to the way their servlet counterparts read such values in Chapter 32. We also define a collection of corresponding `<env-entry>` entries in each XML file as another means for reading configuration information into JSPs and any J2EE component for that matter.

NOTE

Although we include sample code in our JSPs for accessing configuration information from both `<init-param>` and `<env-entry>` elements in an XML deployment descriptor, we have coded the examples to utilize only the information retrieved from `<env-entry>`. This is because the products we have used to implement our sample JSP code at the time of this writing did not support use of `<init-param>` values. We have nevertheless left the code on the CD for accessing configuration information using `<init-param>` so that you can see how both forms of configuration information may be read.

As an example of using `<init-param>` entries, the `<servlet>` description for the `BrowseShirts` JSP follows this form:

```
<web-app>
    ...
  <!-- Form for querying for TShirts -->
```

```
  <servlet>
    <servlet-name>BrowseShirts</servlet-name>
    <display-name>BrowseShirts</display-name>
    <jsp-file>BrowseShirts.jsp</jsp-file>
    <init-param>
      <param-name>numberOfShirts </param-name>
      <param-value>8 </param-value>
      <description>Number Of Shirts to Read </description>
    </init-param>
    <init-param>
      <param-name>shirt_0 </param-name>
      <param-value>0,XL,White, 11.5, 123,145,shirtOne.jpg </param-value>
      <description>First Shirt Information </description>
    </init-param>
      ...
  </servlet>
    ...
</web-app>
```

Recall that the `DisplayBrowsedShirts` JSP is included as part of the `BrowsedShirts` translation unit. The `DisplayBrowsedShirts.getQueriedShirts()` scriptlet method is where access to such `<init-param>` values is performed with calls such as this:

```
javax.servlet.ServletConfig config = getServletConfig();
String nShirtsString = config.getInitParameter("numberOfShirts");
```

Such a call might also be made from directly within a JSP using the `config` implicit object in this way:

```
String nShirtsString = config.getInitParameter("numberOfShirts");
```

The same `BrowseShirts` configuration is also stored in the `<env-entry>` values displayed here:

```
<web-app>
    ...
  <env-entry>
    <env-entry-name>numberOfShirts </env-entry-name>
    <env-entry-value>8 </env-entry-value>
    <env-entry-type>java.lang.String</env-entry-type>
  </env-entry>
  <env-entry>
    <env-entry-name>shirt_0 </env-entry-name>
    <env-entry-value>
      0,XL,White, 11.5, 123,145,shirtOne.jpg
    </env-entry-value>
    <env-entry-type>java.lang.String</env-entry-type>
  </env-entry>
    ...
</web-app>
```

The DisplayBrowsedShirts.getQueriedShirtsFromEnvironment() scriptlet method implements the form of configuration that is utilized by our actual online JSP processing example. This method is where access to <env-entry> values is performed with calls to the InitialContext object stored within our JSPHelper class as such:

```
String nShirtsString = (String)
  JSPHelper.initialContext.lookup("java:comp/env/numberOfShirts");
```

As previously mentioned, the OrderStatus JSP also has configuration information defined for it. The VerifyLogin JSP, which is part of the OrderStatus JSP translation unit, contains a constructDefaultUserInformation() method that reads configuration information from the <init-param> entries for OrderStatus. The constructDefaultUserInformationFromEnvironment() method reads this information from the <env-entry> entries and is the method actually invoked by our sample code.

Direct JSP Deployment Procedure Considerations

The process for deploying JSP components follows many of the steps described in Chapter 32 to deploy Java Servlets. Setting J2EE server environment variables and configuring J2EE server properties are two initial steps that must be performed, as was the case in Chapter 32. The creation of XML-based deployment descriptors as well as the packaging and deployment of archives are also very similar. Our compilej2ee.bat file, in fact, contains sample scripts for automatically executing many of these steps for use with the J2EE reference implementation. This particular script deploys JSPs directly in their untranslated source form.

The first special consideration for deploying JSPs directly is to ensure that the JSP files are placed under the root context of the Web application. We accomplish this in our sample compilej2ee.bat script file by simply copying the .jsp files associated with this chapter's example to a root directory, named deploycontent, which contains a collection of Web content files. The content directory also includes other directly accessible content files, such as .gif, .jpg, and .html files. The J2EE reference implementation's packager utility is subsequently used to create a jspch32.war file from these content files in a deploycontent directory, any compiled Java classes in a deployclasses directory, and a web.xml deployment descriptor as illustrated here:

```
%J2EE_HOME%\bin\packager -webArchive -classpath deployclasses
                            deploycontent web.xml jspch33.war
```

We subsequently create a J2EE enterprise application named JspApp inside of a jspch32.ear enterprise application archive file using our newly created WAR file with a command of the following form:

```
call %J2EE_HOME%\bin\packager -enterpriseArchive  jspch33.war
                              JspApp  jspch33.ear
```

Before we deploy the jspch32.ear file, we also insert our own application.xml file into the EAR file from within the compilej2ee.bat script. The main body of our application.xml file simply defines the root context of beeshirtsjsp for our JSP-based Web application as shown here:

```
<application>
  <display-name>JspApp</display-name>
  <description>Application Description</description>
  <module>
    <web>
      <web-uri>jspch33.war</web-uri>
      <context-root>beeshirtsjsp</context-root>
    </web>
  </module>
</application>
```

Assuming that the J2EE reference implementation server was started (that is, by calling %J2EE_HOME%\bin\j2ee -verbose), the compilej2ee.bat script can then successfully deploy the EAR file using the deploytool utility as shown here:

```
%J2EE_HOME%\bin\deploytool -deploy jspch33.ear localhost
```

Finally, the root BeeShirts.com JSP can be accessed from a Web browser with this URL:

```
http://localhost:7001/beeshirtsjsp/BeeShirtsJsp
```

You'll notice a slight delay the first time each JSP is accessed due to the time it takes the J2EE reference implementation to translate and compile each JSP. Subsequent requests to the same JSP are processed much faster.

NOTE

You may have copied an orb.properties file to your [JAVA_HOME]\jre\lib directory if you have installed the standard RMI/IIOP extension per the instructions of Chapter 16, "RMI Communications." This orb.properties file must be removed in order to properly run the J2EE reference implementation server. Refer to Appendix A, "Software Configuration," for more details.

Precompiled JSP Deployment Procedure Considerations

The enterprise-class BEA WebLogic Server comes equipped with a compiler tool that we use from within a compileweblogic.bat file to precompile our BeeShirts.com JSP files. The java.weblogic.jspc program for precompiling JSPs using a specified package name is invoked from within compileweblogic.bat using this general command form:

```
java weblogic.jspc -package packageName JspFileName.jsp
```

As an example for compiling the BeeShirts JSP, we have this:

```
java weblogic.jspc -package ejava.jspch33 BeeShirts.jsp
```

After compiling and deploying each JSP implementation class as was done for Java Servlets in Chapter 32, we are ready to access our BeeShirts.com application from a Web browser. At the time of this writing, the BEA WebLogic Server v5.0 and v5.1 did not support deployment of J2EE application EAR files. Thus, our sample compileweblogic.bat file simply creates the appropriate web application directory structure populated with our example code and then uses the jar command to create a jspch33.war file mapped from this directory structure. This WAR file must be referenced by the weblogic.httpd.webApp.beeshirtsjsp property defined within the BEA WebLogic Server's [WEBLOGIC_HOME]\weblogic.properties file. The weblogic.properties file's weblogic.httpd.documentRoot value should also be set to myserver/ for our examples. The BEA WebLogic Server can then be started using the [WEBLOGIC_HOME]\startweblogic.cmd command script. Appendix A describes the general configuration procedures for the BEA WebLogic Server.

Custom Java Actions and Tags from JSP

In an earlier section, you saw how a few standard JSP actions can be used to make writing JSPs an easier task and more natural to developers used to writing scripting language–based Web-enabling code. JSP actions encapsulate a set of operations that are implemented behind the scenes in Java code. Such actions can then be used to provide a simple set of scripting tags and attributes describing an action to be performed. JSP also defines a mechanism for extending the capability of JSP actions by providing a mechanism to create your own custom actions and tags.

Actions defined in terms of a begin tag, attributes, an optional body, and an end tag can be implemented using a set of special Java classes and interfaces. A set of custom classes that extend these abstractions is then inserted into a class archive referred to as a tag library. Such libraries can be configured at deployment time and referenced from within JSPs using taglib directives. The custom classes are referred to as tag handlers and are simple nonvisible JavaBean components that implement a special tag handling interface contract. A JSP container can create or locate tag handler objects whenever an associated action is defined in the JSP. This section briefly describes the JSP tag extension abstractions and how they are used with tag libraries, tag library descriptor files, and taglib directives to extend the functionality available to JSP programs.

JSP Custom Tag Extension Abstractions

Abstractions from the `javax.servlet.jsp.tagext` package are used to create custom tag extensions. To create a custom tag handler, you must implement either the `javax.servlet.jsp.tagext.Tag` or the `javax.servlet.jsp.tagext.BodyTag` interfaces, or you must extend either the `javax.servlet.jsp.tagext.TagSupport` or the `javax.servlet.jsp.tagext.BodyTagSupport` classes. Figure 33.8 depicts these key tag extension abstractions and how they relate to custom tag handlers.

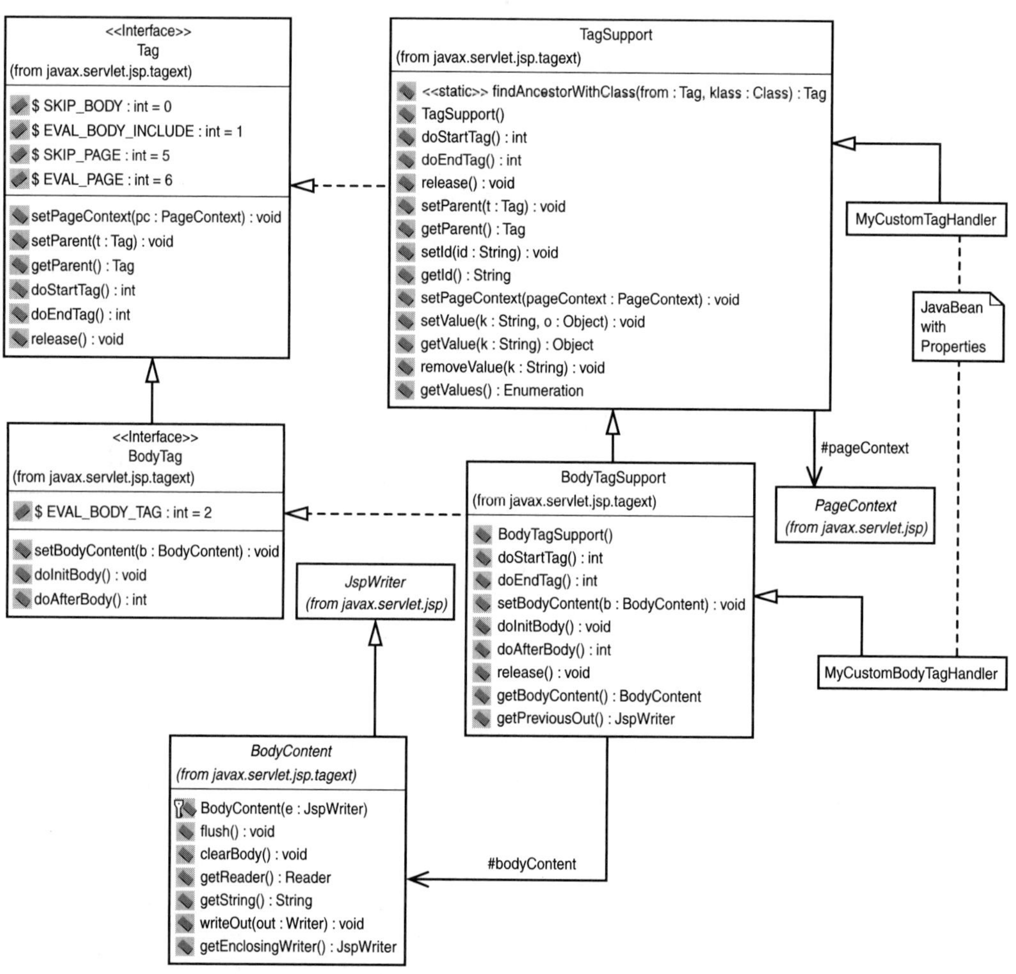

FIGURE 33.8
JSP custom tag extension abstractions.

The Tag interface defines a set of basic operations called by the container to manage a custom action defined within a JSP. A container will first set a PageContext object and any parent tags onto the Tag implementation when the container encounters an associated custom tag in the JSP. Any attributes of the custom action are then set according to the properties of a JavaBean component model onto the tag handler. The container then calls doStartTag() when it wants the tag handler to begin processing an action. A call to doEndTag() occurs when the container processes the end tag in the JSP. The TagSupport class is a utility class with some helper methods that can also be directly extended by a custom tag handler instead of implementing the Tag interface.

The BodyTag interface is used when a custom action can contain an action body. After starting a tag, a container calls the setBodyContent() method with a handle to a BodyContent object. The BodyContent object can be used to read the body data that has been output to an output stream by the container. The doInitBody() method is then called by the container to ask the tag handler to begin evaluating the body that is output to the output stream. The container then calls doAfterBody() as parts of the body are evaluated. The BodyTagSupport class is a utility class that implements the BodyTag interface and can also be extended by custom body tag handlers.

In addition to these basic custom tag extension abstractions, a collection of abstractions is also defined to describe meta information about libraries used to collect implementation classes. Figure 33.9 depicts these abstractions and their relations. The TagExtraInfo class is extended by a custom tag implementation to provide additional information about a custom tag library. A TagExtraInfo object can use TagData (name/value attribute pairs) to retrieve VariableInfo to describe any scripting variables created or modified by a tag. Information related to a particular custom tag is extracted from a TagInfo class. Attributes associated with that tag can then be extracted from a collection of associated TagAttributeInfo objects. Finally, a TagLibraryInfo object can be used to provide more information about the tag library itself.

Tag Libraries

A tag library is a collection of custom tag handler implementation classes. They are often packaged in a JAR file and can be stored under the WEB-INF/lib directory of a WAR file or can be stored in their unpackaged class form under the WEB-INF/classes directory of a WAR file.

A tag library descriptor (TLD) is an XML file used to describe the contents of a tag library. JSP containers use such files to interpret JSPs that have taglib references to custom tags defined in an associated tag library. The location of TLD file is defined by a <taglib> element within the <web-app> element of a web.xml deployment descriptor file. A <taglib> element contains a <taglib-uri> element that points to the location of the tag library classes. The

<taglib> element also contains a <taglib-location> element that points to the location of the TLD file to be associated with the tag library classes. For example:

```
<web-app>
   ...
  <taglib>
    <taglib-uri>/tag/BeeShirtsActions</taglib-uri>
    <taglib-location>/WEB-INF/tld/BeeShirts.tld</taglib-location>
  </taglib>
   ...
</web-app>
```

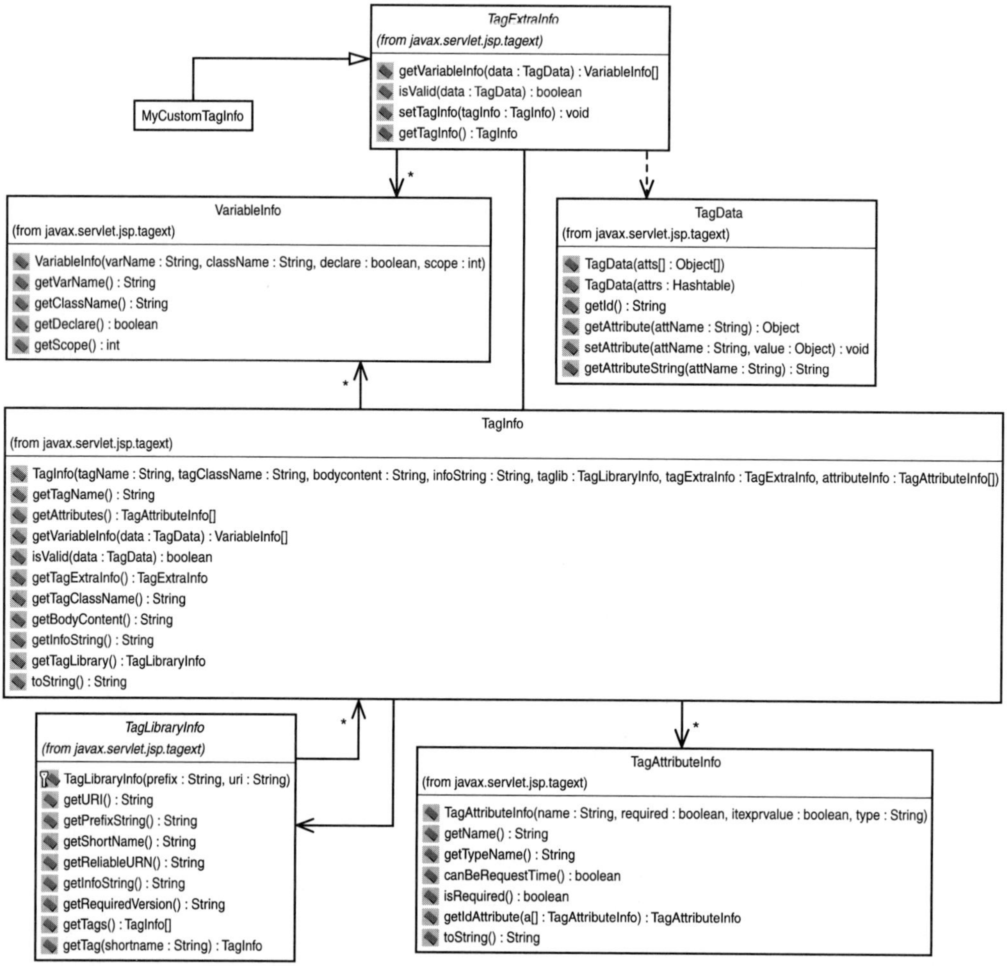

FIGURE 33.9

JSP custom tag library abstractions.

If no `<taglib>` location mapping is defined in the `web.xml` file, the `uri` attribute of a `taglib` directive may be used to define the location of the TLD file. However, a `taglib` directive in a JSP more commonly refers to a library that has been defined in a `web.xml` file as exemplified here:

```
<%@ taglib uri="tag/BeeShirtsActions" prefix="beeshirts" %>
```

Action code that follows from the `taglib` directive in the JSP may utilize custom actions defined in these libraries. For example, assume for now that a `displayOrder` action name associated with a custom `beeshirts` library is to be invoked from within a JSP. We might have something like this:

```
<beeshirts:displayOrder user="pperrone" password="thedoors4u" />
```

So how does the `displayOrder` name map to a specific custom tag handler class, you ask? The answer lies within the TLD file itself. A `name` element within a `tag` element within a TLD file defines the name of a particular tag library. Tag information associated with that name is also used within the TLD file to describe other information about the particular tag handler. We close here with a description of the TLD DTD in Listing 33.4. Note that we have augmented this TLD DTD with our own element descriptions and have included only the core content of the DTD in the interest of brevity.

LISTING 33.4 Abridged TLD File DTD (`http://java.sun.com/j2ee/dtds/web-jsptaglibrary_1_1.dtd`)

```
<!--
The taglib is the root of the TLD file with the following elements:
 tlibversion: Version number of tag library
 jspversion: Version number of JSP API needed
 shortname: Defines a default prefix mnemonic for tags from this library
 uri: Defines a URI identifying this tag library version
 info: Defines arbitrary info about the library
 tag: Defines one or more tag library descriptions
-->
<!ELEMENT taglib (tlibversion, jspversion?, shortname, uri?,
                  info?, tag+) >
<!ATTLIST taglib id ID #IMPLIED
          xmlns CDATA #FIXED
            "http://java.sun.com/j2ee/dtds/web-jsptaglibrary_1_1.dtd"
>
<!ELEMENT tlibversion (#PCDATA) >
<!ELEMENT jspversion  (#PCDATA) >
<!ELEMENT shortname      (#PCDATA) >
<!ELEMENT uri    (#PCDATA) >
```

continues

LISTING 33.4 Continued

```
<!ELEMENT info  (#PCDATA) >
<!--
The tag defines each tag library described in this TLD:
 name: Defines the unique tag name
 tagclass: Defines the javax.servlet.jsp.tagext.Tag implementation class
 teiclass: Defines a javax.servlet.jsp.tagext.TagExtraInfo subclass
 bodycontent: Defines the BodyContent type
 info: Describes the tag in more detail
 attribute: Describes zero or more attributes of the tag
-->
<!ELEMENT tag (name, tagclass, teiclass?, bodycontent?, info?, attribute*) >
<!ELEMENT name  (#PCDATA) >
<!ELEMENT tagclass (#PCDATA) >
<!ELEMENT teiclass (#PCDATA) >
<!ELEMENT bodycontent (#PCDATA) >
<!ELEMENT attribute (name, required? , rtexprvalue?) >
<!-- Defines true, false, yes, no if attribute is required -->
<!ELEMENT required    (#PCDATA) >
<!-- Defines true, false, yes, no if attribute can have expressions -->
<!ELEMENT rtexprvalue (#PCDATA) >
```

Conclusions

JavaServer Pages (JSPs) provide a Web programmer–friendly means to Web enable enterprise applications. JSPs enable direct embedding of HTML template data into server-side Web documents and use of a syntax that is more familiar to Web-oriented developers and to developers who may be less familiar with enterprise-class Java programming. The use of actions, tags, and implicit objects from directly within the JSP provides the Web developer with a more familiar script-based programming environment. However, arbitrarily complex Java code can also be inserted into JSPs as a scripting language and thus provides added benefit to those developers who know Java and want to mix its more powerful syntax with the simplicity of creating JSPs.

JSP is in the early stages of development and currently has a limited set of standard actions and tags for Web-enabling developers to use. However, JSP does provide a means to create custom tag libraries and actions. As more custom actions and tag libraries are defined by third-party vendors and standardized by the JSP specification, the growth in acceptance and use of JSP among Web-enabling developers will also increase. By employing JSPs as part of your Web-enabling enterprise solution now, you will gain advantages in more rapid application development, as well as in providing the basis for future use of more sophisticated third-party and standard JSP extensions.

As a final note, given the flexibility provided by JSPs in enabling the use of Java from directly within JSPs, one may be tempted to create overly complex Web-enabling code, but we generally recommend maintaining the pure presentation-oriented nature of the Web tier in this book. Although we wanted to highlight the capabilities of JSPs in this chapter, we generally advocate the use of JSPs for generating Web presentation logic and the glue logic needed to talk with enterprise business logic and data components. The chapters that follow describe the architecture and approach for developing such enterprise business logic and data components in the context of application server frameworks and Enterprise JavaBeans.

Enterprise Applications Enabling

IN THIS PART

34 Enterprise Application Platforms 1191

35 Application Servers and Enterprise JavaBeans 1207

36 Modeling Components with Enterprise JavaBeans 1231

37 Advanced Enterprise JavaBeans Serving 1315

38 Enterprise Application Integration 1355

Enterprise Application Platforms

CHAPTER

34

IN THIS CHAPTER

- Enterprise Platforms Overview 1192
- TP Monitor Platforms 1193
- OTMs 1195
- Generic Application Frameworks 1196
- Standard Java-Based Generic Application Framework 1198
- CORBAcomponents 1200
- Microsoft's Generic Application Framework 1202
- Application-Specific Platforms 1203
- Enterprise Application Management 1205

Enterprise application platforms provide off-the-shelf and standard reference architectures for building enterprise applications. Enterprise platforms provide enterprise applications with distributed accessibility, common distributed services, data-enabling services, Web-enabling services, and connectivity to legacy applications. Although no enterprise application platform is complete and offers all things to all types of applications, such frameworks provide excellent starting points for more rapidly building robust and distributed enterprise applications. This chapter covers the basic evolution of enterprise application platforms and the most basic architecture of such platforms for enabling scalable and dependable access to enterprise applications.

In this chapter, you will learn:

- The basic context of an enterprise application platform and its basic role in the enterprise.
- The basic services and architecture of Transaction Processing (TP) monitors.
- The basic services and architecture of Object Transaction Monitors (OTMs).
- The basic services and architecture of generic enterprise application frameworks sometimes referred to as application servers.
- The basic services and architecture of the Java-based generic enterprise application framework known as the J2EE.
- The basic services and architecture of the CORBA-based generic enterprise application framework known as CORBAcomponents.
- The basic services and architecture of the Microsoft Windows–based generic enterprise application framework known as the Microsoft Distributed Network Architecture (DNA).
- The basic role of application-specific enterprise frameworks as provided by Enterprise Resource Planning (ERP) systems, Product Data Management (PDM) systems, CORBA vertical facilities, and Java vertical facilities.
- The basic role of distributed enterprise application management services such as those provided by the Java Management Extension (JMX).

Enterprise Platforms Overview

As we've already discussed throughout the book, enterprise applications have particular needs that make rapidly building them a complicated proposition at times. We've discussed numerous methods for effectively building enterprise applications such as object-oriented and component-based development paradigms. We've also described many techniques and technologies for communications-enabling, providing common standard COTS services, providing systems assurance, and Web-enabling an enterprise system. Enterprise platforms can encapsulate all such development paradigms, techniques, technologies, and services inside of an integrated framework for building enterprise applications. Such frameworks often follow the component-container model of development advocated throughout this book.

Figure 34.1 depicts a high-level overview of an enterprise application framework and its context. At the center of the diagram is the framework itself with a set of services that it provides for use by enterprise application components. Interface contracts from component to framework and from framework to component often exist to provide well-defined responsibility boundaries. From an enterprise application client's perspective, they are able to tap the application-specific functionality of the enterprise application component with all the distribution, usability, scalability, assurance, and accessibility benefits enabled by the enterprise application framework. Such services are often provided transparent to the enterprise application component or are encapsulated by framework APIs. Enterprise application frameworks also often offer seamless connectivity to external enterprise systems and resources such as DBMSs. Finally, many frameworks provide a means to easily configure and deploy enterprise applications, as well as sometimes provide an integrated environment for developing enterprise application components.

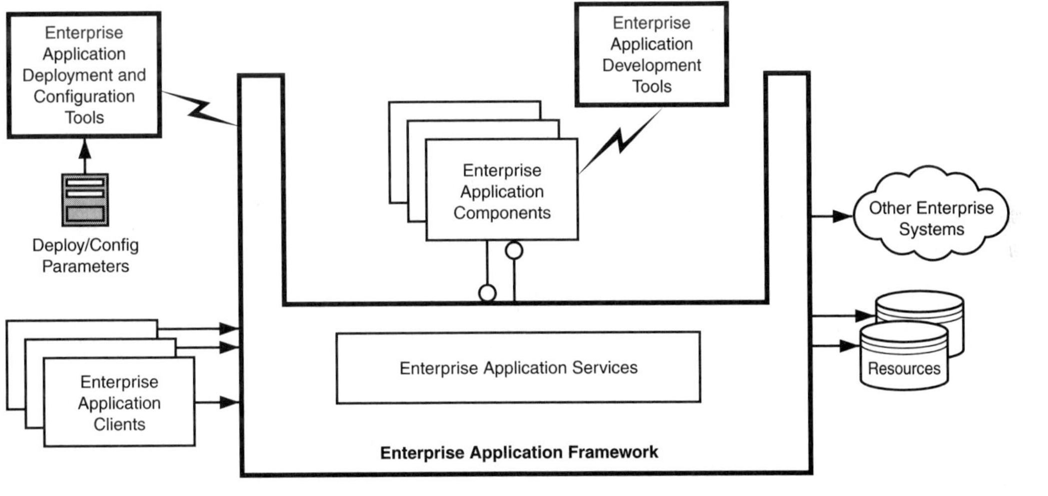

FIGURE 34.1
The enterprise application framework architecture.

TP Monitor Platforms

Transaction Processing (TP) monitors were one of the first types of enterprise platforms having significant commercial success whose services could be relied on and utilized by enterprise applications. The enterprise applications involved here are transaction-processing applications that have requirements to operate within the context of a transaction. TP monitors are operating environments that manage the transactional behavior of transaction-processing applications. TP monitors handle the creation, termination, and management of the transactional contexts for the transaction-processing application. Because effective transaction management involves the management of database connections, network resources, and operating-system resources, a TP monitor can offload a significant amount of coding effort that would otherwise need to be developed by applications programmers. Furthermore, because transaction-processing applications have enterprise class client request scalability requirements, TP monitors are designed to manage the scalability and availability of applications as well.

TP monitors are middle-tier servers that sit between a distributed transaction application client and resources (for example, DBMSs), as depicted in Figure 34.2. TP monitors provide the following services to transaction-processing applications that run inside of their environment:

- *Naming Service Support:* TP monitors often manage the mapping of a client's request of a named application service to the actual reference for that application running in the TP monitor's domain.
- *Connection Handling:* Client connections are multiplexed by a TP monitor process connection handler. The connection handler helps manage the utilization of network resources and funnels client requests to transaction processing applications.
- *Resource Handling:* A TP monitor can also be configured to use information embedded in a particular client request to an application and determine which resource (for example, DBMS) should be used to satisfy the request. Furthermore, standard interfaces to resources, such as the X/Open XA interface, can provide access to a heterogeneous variety of resources.
- *Availability Assurance:* TP monitors can provide for a more scalable client request base via load balancing across redundant servers. TP monitors can also often support fail-over to redundant processes in the event of a failure.

TP monitors were popular precursors to the application frameworks that we utilize in this book. Many TP monitors adopt the X/Open DTP standard. TP monitors thus function as transaction managers with additional services needed to build scalable enterprise-class transaction processing applications. However, the need to build enterprise class applications with more general needs aside from pure transaction processing alone has given rise to new terminology and to more generic application frameworks. Furthermore, the need for standards that support object- and component-based application models also has driven the evolution of TP monitors. You'll learn about a few of the more significant evolutions from TP monitoring models to more generic and standard application platforms throughout the remainder of this chapter.

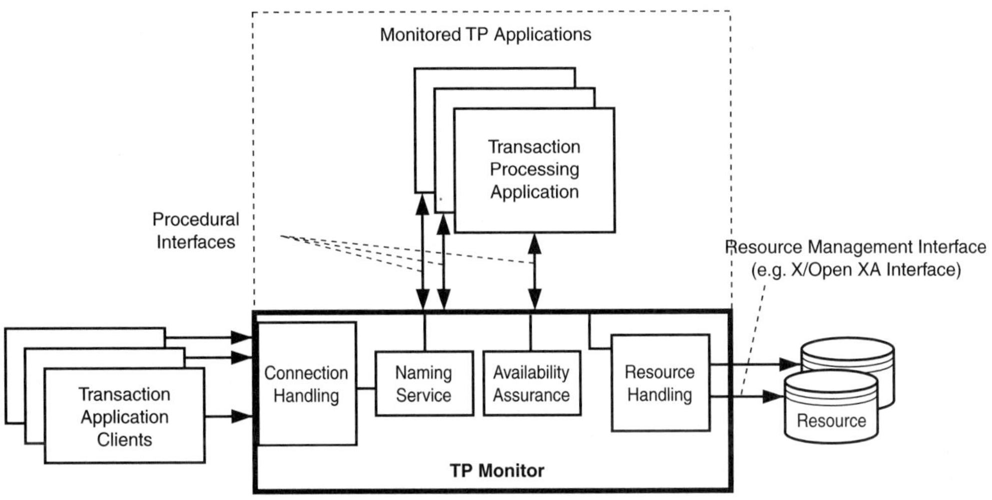

FIGURE 34.2
The transaction-processing monitor architecture.

OTMs

The popularity of TP monitor products has been indicative of the general need for assistance by organizations that want to build enterprise systems more rapidly and more robustly than was previously possible. However, the modern heterogeneous enterprise has also placed a higher premium on standard interoperability, as well as on use of object-oriented and component-based system development paradigms. The largely proprietary and remote procedure-oriented nature of the older TP monitors fell short in these regards. This has been the reason for the introduction of the Object Transaction Monitor (OTM) into the marketplace.

OTMs, as depicted in Figure 34.3, offer various features and services that make them an attractive solution for modern enterprise systems development. For one, OTMs extend the TP monitor concept to define and interact with object-oriented interfaces. OTMs are also constructed according to the component-container model of development and therefore provide TP monitor services to component-based enterprise applications. Thus, transaction services, connection handling services, naming services, resource management, and availability services can all be provided to components built on top of OTM frameworks. Because OTMs follow the component-container model, they also quite naturally augment the TP monitor suite of general services to provide a form of component activation service.

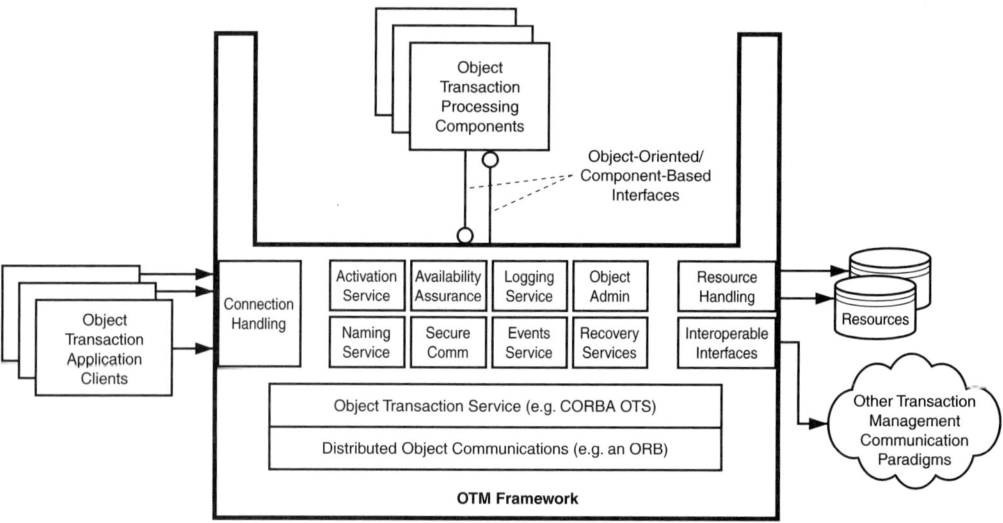

FIGURE 34.3
The Object Transaction Monitor architecture.

As another general rule, OTMs are also built on top of a distributed object computing paradigm such as CORBA. In fact, most popular OTM implementations today, such as Inprise's ITS and Iona's OrbixOTM products, are built on top of an ORB and also utilize CORBA Object Transaction Services. The core OTM products in the marketplace have also beefed up their product offerings with additional features and services for applications. These services include asynchronous event messaging services (for example, CORBA Event Service), secure communication services (for example, SSL), logging services, distributed object administration services, recovery and fault-tolerance services, and interoperability interfaces with other transaction monitoring and communication paradigms. Thus, as OTM products have matured, they have also grown in the scope of their enterprise application applicability.

Generic Application Frameworks

As more services are added to an OTM framework, any pure transaction processing application focus of the framework becomes blurred. Rather, the framework begins to serve as a more generic framework for building a more general class of enterprise applications. These more generic application frameworks have consequently assumed a new marketing term and have now become what we refer to as *application servers*. Although we have highlighted the evolutionary path of such application servers from TP monitors and OTMs, vendors from other market focuses have also beefed up their product offerings with application server–oriented features. Database vendors, such as Oracle and Sybase, have particularly been aggressive with building auxiliary application services atop their existing database management service frameworks. Web server vendors, such as Netscape and NetDynamics (now owned by Sun), have also evolved their Web-serving product suites to support more generic enterprise application serving capabilities. Of course, as perhaps the only example of a vendor who has attempted to grow an enterprise application framework out of an operating system, Microsoft has also defined an enterprise application service framework that is dependent on and integrated with the Microsoft Windows operating system.

Figure 34.4 depicts a generic architecture for such a convergence of enterprise application service provisioning. Although not all application server products contain all the services depicted in this diagram, most of the core services provided by any particular product have a representative set of services in the diagram. With such a generic set of enterprise application services provided by an enterprise application framework, enterprise application components can be more rapidly built and allow a developer to focus on the business logic of an application rather than on common application infrastructure services. Some enterprise application service products will also provide tools to facilitate the development, deployment, and configuration of enterprise applications within the enterprise application framework.

Many of the services depicted in Figure 34.4 have already been described in this book. However, the enterprise application framework provides a means to offer access and utilization of such services to enterprise application components in a fashion that simplifies enterprise application development. We have already seen an example of this with the enterprise Web-enabling interfaces described in the context of J2EE Java Servlets and JSPs in Part VI, "Enterprise Web Enabling." This part of the book begins to focus on the general enterprise application–enabling aspects of an enterprise system as provided by an enterprise application framework. In fact, we typically distinguish between products that provide Web-enabling services and products that provide more general enterprise application–enabling services because Web-enabling solutions can require less in the way of service support than can more generic enterprise application–enabling solutions.

Although we indeed have covered many of the services in Figure 34.4 throughout this book, a few new terms should jump out at you. For one, object persistence services within a data connectivity service suite of tools can help map application objects into relational database models. Enterprise application integration services may also be provided to enable connectivity to legacy and auxiliary enterprise applications from enterprise application components built atop the enterprise application framework. A set of management services for managing enterprise applications such as network and system administration, logging, and debugging services may also be provided within a framework. Furthermore, a set of configuration and deployment services is almost always provided to facilitate the configuration and deployment of enterprise application components that operate inside of the enterprise application framework environment. Generic enterprise application frameworks thus provide a platform for creating enterprise applications and allow an enterprise applications developer to focus on implementation of enterprise business logic and rules.

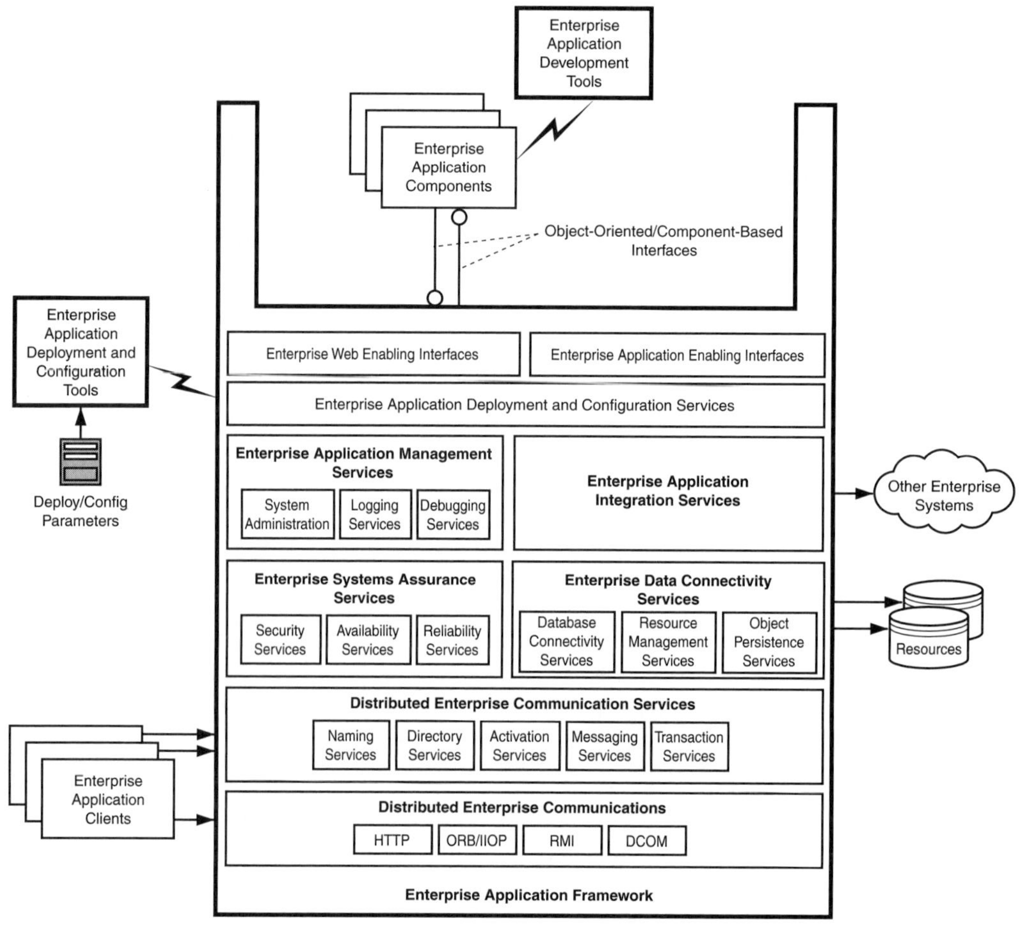

FIGURE 34.4

The generic application server framework architecture.

Standard Java-Based Generic Application Framework

As many vendor-specific enterprise application framework solutions began to enter the market, the threat of many divergent camps of enterprise application development solution provisioning was heightened. Enterprise application components developed for one framework would be able to operate only inside the confines of that framework vendor's product suite. Even though CORBA technologies for vendor interoperability were being used inside of the framework, there was no assurance that components which were developed for one vendor product would also work inside of another product. Sun Microsystems began to address this threat with the introduction of the Enterprise JavaBeans (EJB) specification in 1998.

The EJB specification defined a Java-based standard interface contract that exists between enterprise application components and enterprise application service framework products. Thus, EJBs implemented for one vendor's enterprise application service framework product solution could run atop another vendor's enterprise application service framework product solution. The interfaces remain fixed, but the underlying service provisioning implementations naturally vary from vendor to vendor. Sun later extended this concept to the more pervasive J2EE specification as described in Chapter 5, "Java Enterprise System Architecture with the J2EE." Figure 34.5 depicts the standard server-side enterprise application serving architecture defined by the J2EE specification. Java Servlets, JSPs, and EJBs can all be developed to utilize the Java enterprise APIs shown in Figure 34.5, which provide standard interfaces to many of the services of an application server framework.

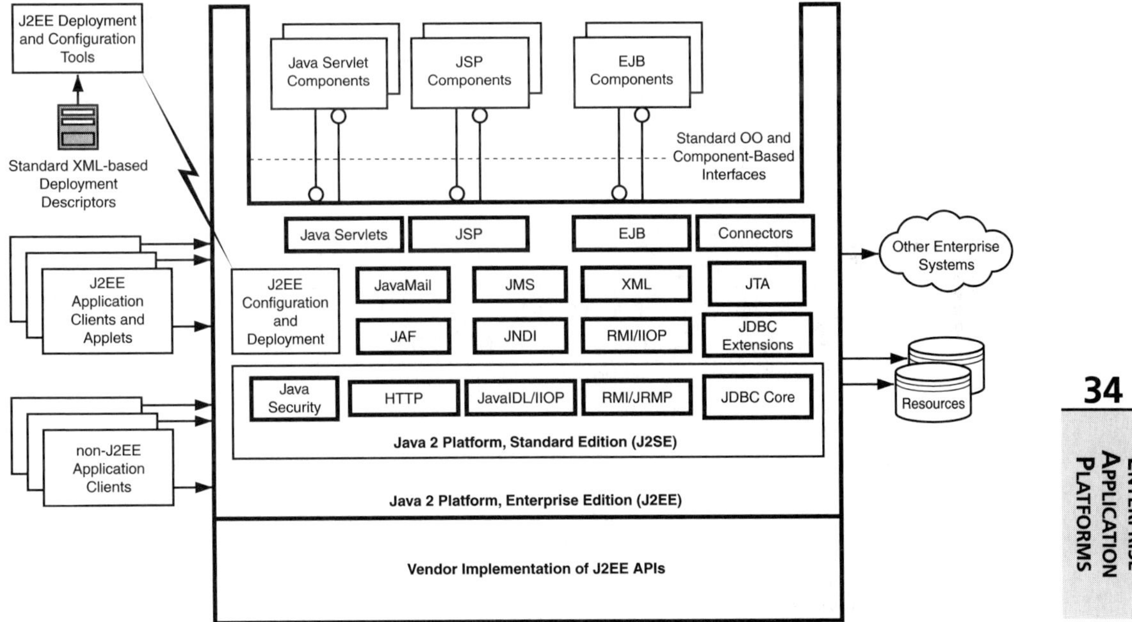

FIGURE 34.5
The J2EE standard application server framework architecture.

We have already described many of the APIs shown in Figure 34.5 throughout this book. Although not all the APIs depicted require that vendors provide complete implementations of the underlying services, future versions of the J2EE specification will require such full implementation compliance levels. Furthermore, XML APIs and APIs for implementing enterprise application integration connectivity such as that defined in the J2EE Connectors standards will also become a standard requirement in future J2EE specifications.

Because the J2EE incorporates the J2SE into its architecture, J2EE vendors can also implement application service products that are operating system and hardware platform-independent. However, some vendors may still indeed opt to take advantage of certain platform-specific optimization features within their application service implementations. Within the confines of the standard APIs, vendors in fact will primarily differentiate their product offerings based on levels of system assurance and performance. Vendors are also currently able to differentiate their products in terms of offering sophisticated development and deployment tools and tools that integrate J2EE-based applications with other enterprise systems, resources, and clients. Perhaps most significant is the fact that vendors currently and will most likely continue to define value-added functionality via APIs that lie outside of the standards. It is thus up to the applications developer to provide adapter logic for such APIs to fully enable migration between platform implementations. Nevertheless, the level of platform interoperability achievable through even the current set of J2EE specifications has never before been possible.

In addition to standard application service API specifications, the J2EE specification has also defined a standard format for describing how applications should be deployed via XML-based deployment descriptors. Additionally, standard means for building Java-based application clients and Java applets to connect with J2EE server-side applications are also defined. The effort to provide standard interfaces for enterprise application components has thus come a long way in a relatively short amount of time. Standards have already begun to spill over into other areas of application development that lie outside of pure server-component standardization. Only time will tell how fully vendors will embrace all of these standards. We suspect that as the scope of J2EE standardization grows, levels of compliance will be and should be established to provide a compromise for some vendors to allow their products to shine, as well as to lower the barrier of entry for newcomers.

CORBAcomponents

As Sun was defining a pure Java-based standard for creating enterprise applications via EJBs, the OMG was also hard at work to define a CORBA-based enterprise application framework. The CORBAcomponents specification defines language-independent standards for building enterprise components using existing and extended CORBA technology standards according to a new model of development referred to as the CORBAcomponents model. Because of the popularity of EJBs, the CORBAcomponents model also defines an explicit mapping to the EJB model and allows for the deployment of EJB components to CORBAcomponents-based frameworks. The CORBAcomponents model, however, is also touted to be extendable to other application server interface models as well and is certainly language-independent.

Figure 34.6 illustrates the architecture of the CORBAcomponents model and the new interface models that have emerged as a result. Interfaces to CORBAcomponents from a client perspective are still defined according to CORBA IDL and can also take advantage of the capability to utilize component activation service interfaces, as well as interface with facets or views of a component's overall interface. CORBAcomponents can be defined to connect to other CORBA enterprise objects via an interface syntax for the component known as receptacles. Component attributes, sources of events from components, and events that a component consumes can also be defined for a component and enable the container to manage configuration and event handling services for components. Additionally, a means for defining local interfaces to the container from the component and interfaces to components from containers is specified. As a final note on new interface models, the new Component Implementation Definition Language (CIDL) provides a means to describe the structure and state of component implementations that play a significant role for containers to provide object persistence services.

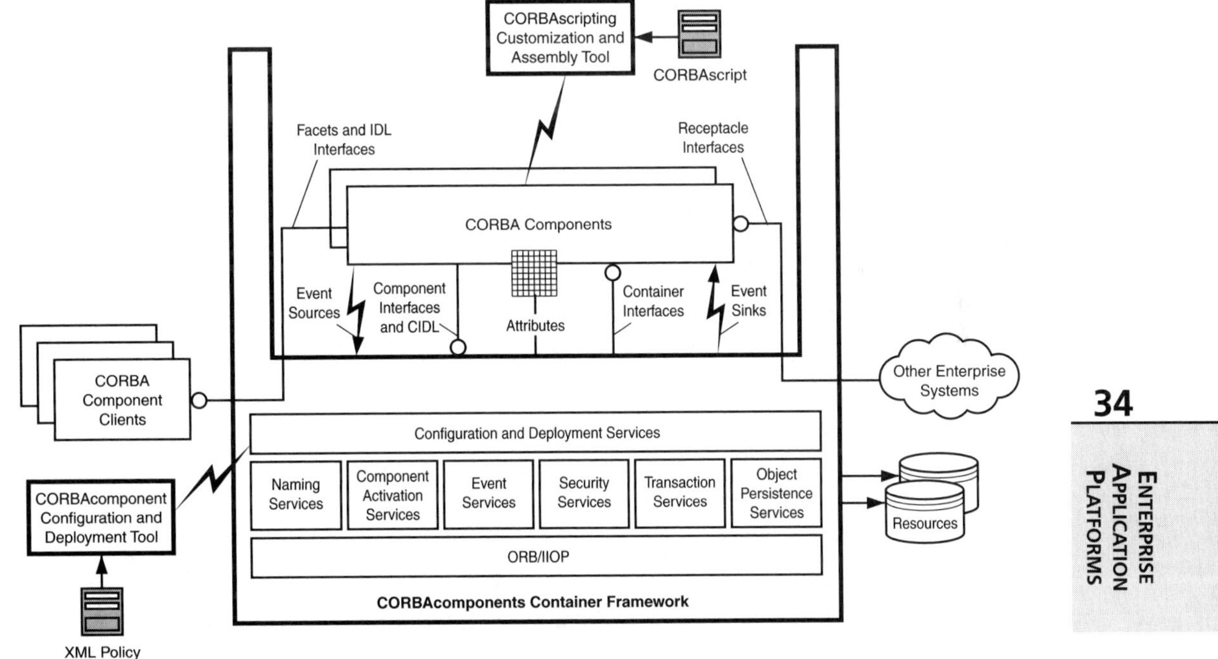

FIGURE 34.6
The CORBAcomponents framework architecture.

Configuration and deployment is also a concern for CORBAcomponents, and a standard means for configuring and deploying components via XML-based descriptors is specified in the CORBA Components specification. Such an approach and supporting tools simplify the capability for CORBAcomponents to use CORBAservices that are otherwise very difficult for application developers to use out of the box. Although XML descriptors can be used to describe how to configure and deploy a particular application, a complement to CORBA Components, known as the CORBA Component Scripting specification, is also being developed to provide a more elaborate means for customizing the business logic and assembly of components using easy-to-use scripting languages. All of these features make CORBAcomponents an interesting standard to monitor and watch for further development and signs of industry acceptance. Although CORBAcomponents has shown initial promise with its effort to define compatibility with the EJB model of development, only time will tell how compatible the technologies will remain in the future.

Microsoft's Generic Application Framework

It should come as no surprise to you that Microsoft also has defined its own enterprise application framework architecture and that it is tightly integrated with the Windows operating system. Although some people frown on such high levels of dependency and tight coupling, others argue that such a high level of integration and platform-dependent solutions has produced a more cohesive enterprise architecture for more immediate use by industry. Figure 34.7 depicts this Distributed Network Architecture (DNA) of Microsoft. Much of the platform services depicted in Figure 34.7 are in fact already embedded into the Windows 2000 server operating-system platform.

At the core of the Microsoft DNA vision is the Windows server-side operating-system environment with its touted support for building scalable, available, and secure enterprise applications. Above that, COM and DCOM serve as the fundamental models for local and distributed component-based development. COM+ has also been developed by Microsoft to support a more sophisticated container-component model of development for COM-based applications that can also take advantage of new configuration and deployment features. Additionally, HTTP-based communications and Web server development are made possible with the Internet Information Server (IIS) and Active Server Pages (ASP) technology.

A host of additional enterprise services are also provided by the Microsoft DNA. The Microsoft Active Directory Service (ADS) provides advanced naming and directory services. Messaging services are provided with Microsoft Message Queue Server (MSMQ) technology and a new event notification service provided with COM+. Database connectivity is provided with the ODBC database-independent interface, and a new in-memory database service provides for enhanced database access performance. Finally, the Microsoft Transaction Server (MTS) serves as the distributed transaction service for managing distributed transaction applications. With Microsoft's significant penetration of the marketplace via its operating-system platform, Microsoft's DNA is certain to be another enterprise application framework to keep an eye on for future developments.

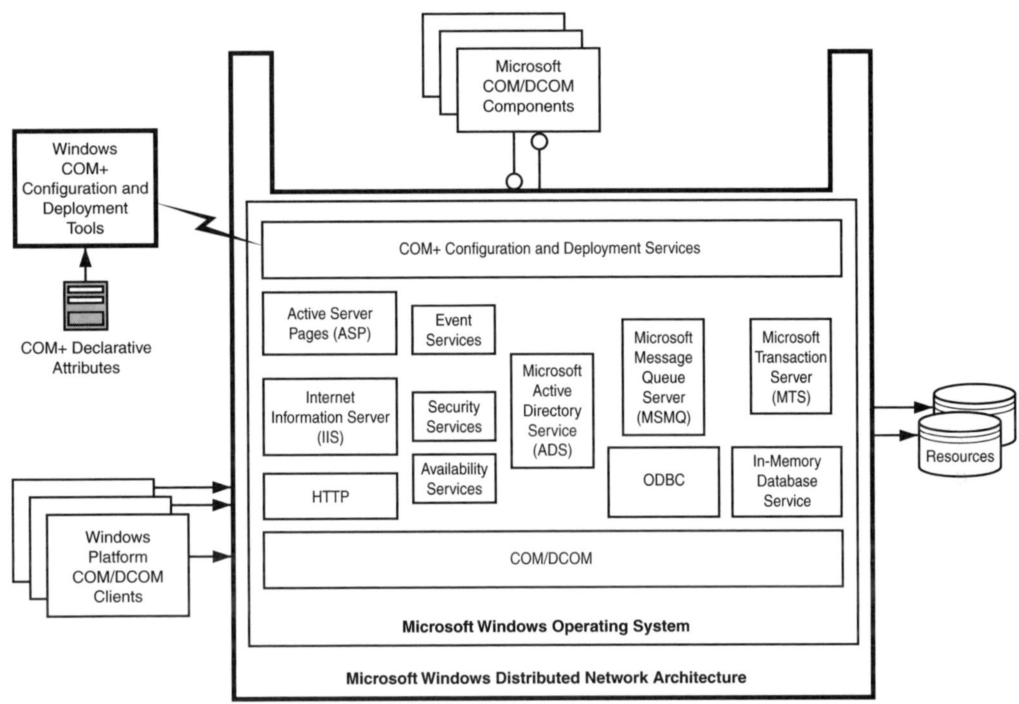

FIGURE 34.7
Microsoft Windows Distributed Network Architecture.

Application-Specific Platforms

Instead of supplying general platforms and frameworks for building enterprise applications, a few companies have earned their revenue by supplying more application-specific frameworks to use in enterprise application environments. Such frameworks are designed to facilitate one or more specific business activities of an enterprise and perhaps even within a specific application domain. Some of these application-specific frameworks build on existing generic enterprise application platforms, although others are built on proprietary platforms. The key advantage to using such platforms is that they are often more rapidly deployed when the abstract application model for which they've been built closely matches the actual enterprise application to which it is applied. The key disadvantage to using such platforms is the lack of extendibility and interoperability of such products.

The OMG has partially addressed the issue of application-specific interoperability within its suite of higher-level CORBA specifications. As we discussed in Chapter 14, "Modeling Components with CORBA," CORBAfacilities are specifications defined at a higher level than the CORBA ORB and CORBAservices specifications. CORBAfacilities defined at the vertical market level define standard interfaces to specific types of applications such that vendors who implement those specifications can provide a standards-based interface to an application-specific framework. Similarly, CORBA Domain Interfaces define standard interfaces to systems from certain industrial domains, such as manufacturing.

Enterprise Resource Planning (ERP) software is nonstandardized application-specific frameworks that have been very popular with enterprise IT departments. ERP software platforms, such as those by PeopleSoft, SAP, BAAN, and J.D. Edwards, are used to manage some specific aspect of a business such as parts purchasing, product planning, inventory management, order tracking, supply management, customer service, finance, quality management, and human resources. ERPs are often supplied with client software, server software, and a database connectivity solution all tightly integrated with one another. Although ERP software is catered to a specific business activity, customization of that business activity for a specific enterprise is often possible via some form of scripting and database configuration. Although ERPs have seen some success in industry due to the near-term benefits from their application, a lack of extendibility and interoperability of certain ERP products can lead to a stagnant and isolated enterprise systems solution.

Product Data Management (PDM) systems are another application-specific type of enterprise system mainly catering to the manufacturing domain and used to manage engineering design information as it evolves from initial concept to production and maintenance. Engineering information managed by PDM systems includes product part information, specifications, schematics, and so on. PDM system frameworks typically provide a generic set of business modeling libraries that can be customized for a particular PDM application. PDM systems include data persistence services, data classification and relationship management services, and software services for managing the flow of data and the tracking of operations performed on data.

Even Sun has ventured into the application-specific framework business and standards process with a collection of Java-based application-specific frameworks. As an example, the Java Electronic Commerce Framework (JECF) is used for supporting electronic commerce applications. The Java Telephony API (JTAPI) framework is used to provide a standard Java-based means for supporting telephony networks across a range of platforms.

Application-specific frameworks are very attractive to IT departments and to enterprise organizations that want to rapidly deploy a specific type of business enterprise application. However, organizations need to be wary of whether the abstract model for which the application-specific framework has been built can be customized well enough to sufficiently model the enterprise's actual business process. More often than not, such application-specific frameworks require extensive consulting time to assist with the customization and help with redefining the organization's business process to fit into the new model provided by the framework. Enterprises also need to be aware of the underlying architecture on which the application-specific framework has been built. Application-specific frameworks built atop CORBA and the J2EE may have a greater chance for extendibility and interoperability than those products built atop proprietary underpinnings.

Enterprise Application Management

This chapter described many of the enterprise application frameworks of the past, present, and imminent future. This book in general focuses on the specific Java-based enterprise application technologies and frameworks you can use to build enterprise systems. Although a detailed discussion of how these applications can be managed in a distributed enterprise network at runtime is beyond the scope of this book, it is nonetheless an important consideration and something that warrants some mention here. Enterprise application management deals with the management of enterprise applications across a heterogeneous distributed network for applications that range from scalable distributed applications to embedded enterprise applications. The management of such applications is greatly facilitated when they can be configured, monitored, shut down, restarted, and updated from a remote administration location.

Although many standard network management frameworks exist, Sun and a few key industry leaders have developed a Java-based standard via the Java Community Process. The Java Management Extension (JMX) specification defines a framework, a set of APIs, and services for managing distributed network services. An instrumentation-level standard defines a means for making any Java-based object resource capable of being managed by the JMX framework. An agent-level standard defines a means for building distributed agent containers of instrumented Java-based object resources. Agents provide services to such resources and communicate with distributed network management servers defined at a management-level standard. Finally, JMX also defines APIs to enable use of existing network management standards.

Enterprise application management thus may require some instrumentation considerations when you're building your enterprise applications so that they can be managed by a distributed network management framework such as JMX. Some enterprise-class J2EE environments indeed provide a means to manage Java Servlets, JSPs, and EJBs via a user-friendly GUI-based management interface. However, effective use of such services may require nonstandard instrumentation of your J2EE components. Future integration of JMX and the J2EE and the standardization of other administration services such as debugging and logging within the J2EE may provide further levels of portability between application servers.

Conclusions

The term *Enterprise Application Platform* may mean different things to different people depending on their concept of what an enterprise application is. In general, enterprise application platforms provide a set of services to enterprise applications often in a transparent and configurable fashion or via well-defined and higher-level APIs. The services provided are infrastructure services that reduce the amount of hand-coding by developers for creating such services and allow a developer to focus on the business logic of an enterprise application. We examined the evolution of generic enterprise application frameworks from TP monitors to OTMs, as well as from Web servers, from database servers, and even from operating systems (that is, Microsoft). We've also discussed the advantages and disadvantages of many application-specific frameworks and explored the basic features of enterprise application management service frameworks.

We of course focus on the Java enterprise–based approach to development in this book, which includes the standard J2EE enterprise application framework. Throughout the book we've already discussed many of the services under such a framework and learned about the Web-enabling aspects of such a framework, and we are now ready to explore the final leg of our journey. Chapter 36, "Modeling Components with Enterprise JavaBeans," and Chapter 37, "Advanced Enterprise JavaBeans Serving," describe the J2EE EJB approach to enterprise application enabling, and Chapter 38, "Enterprise Application Integration," describes enterprise application integration solutions. Chapter 35, "Application Servers and Enterprise JavaBeans," follows this chapter and provides a more in-depth conceptual framework to understand the subsequent chapters by describing the basic architecture of application servers with a specific focus on how EJB applies in such contexts.

Application Servers and Enterprise JavaBeans

CHAPTER

35

IN THIS CHAPTER

- Standalone Enterprise Applications 1208
- Application Server–Based Enterprise Applications 1210
- Application Server Architecture Provider Roles 1212
- Application Server Components 1214
- Application Server Client Interfaces 1218
- Application Server Client Implementations 1220
- Enterprise Application Configuration and Deployment 1225
- Application Service Management 1228

The preceding chapter provided a high-level view of how services can be provided by enterprise application platforms to make developing enterprise applications an easier task. This chapter gives more specific details behind how such services are provided to enterprise application components and who fulfills what role in these application server architectures. Throughout our discussions, we specifically focus on and introduce the notion of Enterprise JavaBeans (EJBs) and discuss how EJB application servers help application-enable an enterprise. We also introduce these concepts in the context of building a simple EJB server and client.

In this chapter, you will learn:

- The pros and cons of building enterprise applications in a standalone runtime environment.
- The architecture and pros and cons of building enterprise applications using an application server and EJBs.
- The partitioning of knowledge among architecture providers and the roles they assume when application servers are used.
- The basic approach for building enterprise application components to operate within an application server with a specific discussion and example of EJB component implementations.
- The basic approach for building enterprise application client interfaces to enterprise application components with a specific discussion of EJB client interfaces.
- The basic approach for implementing enterprise application clients including an example of EJB standalone and J2EE application clients.
- The features provided by application servers for configuring and deploying applications with a specific example of XML-based EJB deployment descriptors.
- The basic underlying approaches by application servers for providing management services to enterprise application components.

Standalone Enterprise Applications

Throughout Parts II, III, IV, and V of this book, we described the technologies that can be used to build Java enterprise applications. Direct use of these technologies typically requires an application architecture as depicted in Figure 35.1. Here we see a "standalone" enterprise application utilizing the APIs offered by a database connectivity solution (for example, JDBC), a distributed enterprise communications paradigm (for example, CORBA, RMI, DCOM), a set of distributed communications services (for example, JNDI, JMS, JTS), and an enterprise security assurance solution (for example, Java Security). Of course, all of our sample applications of these services built thus far in this book have used a Java runtime environment.

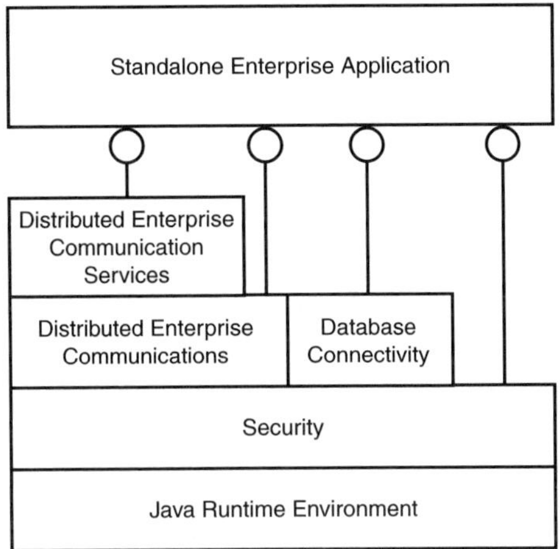

FIGURE 35.1
Standalone enterprise applications.

The sample Java enterprise applications we have built using these services have run in a standalone fashion without the use of any container environment or enterprise application framework. These applications are just plain old Java applications with which you are probably most familiar, and they operate using a JDK 1.1 or J2SE type of environment along with separately packaged standard Java extension APIs and implementations. Such standalone applications were often, in fact, the only option available to enterprise programmers using Java before the birth of application server environments.

Standalone enterprise applications, however, can require a lot of coding effort to make them fully functional in a multiuser, heterogeneous, distributed, secure, and scalable enterprise environment. Recall from Part III, "Distributed Enterprise Communications Enabling," that use of the communications-enabling technologies often requires the need to understand a special interface language, requires thread-safety design considerations, and requires an understanding of how to create scalable server implementations. Also recall from Part II, "Enterprise Data Enabling," that use of JDBC requires careful consideration of which drivers to use and how to create connection resources. The preceding chapter introduced some of the concepts for why application server frameworks, such as J2EE EJB frameworks, help alleviate some of these concerns, but this chapter further explains how such application server frameworks accomplish this task. Furthermore, we pursue this discussion in the context of EJB application servers with a supporting introductory-level EJB example.

Application Server–Based Enterprise Applications

Chapter 34, "Enterprise Application Platforms," described the various types of enterprise application frameworks that have evolved over the years and the types of services they provide for enterprise application developers. These application services essentially provide all the services shown under the standalone enterprise application depicted in Figure 35.1 and help alleviate some of the infrastructure coding that would otherwise be embedded within the standalone enterprise application. Figure 35.2 depicts another view of an application server architecture, including the primary elements that compose a functioning enterprise application serving environment. Specific relationships to J2EE and EJB concepts are also indicated in the diagram. These are the primary application server elements:

- *Enterprise Application Component:* The enterprise application component encapsulates the business logic and data of an enterprise application. Enterprise application components are written in a fashion that frees them from directly managing lower-level infrastructure services. The Enterprise JavaBean is the enterprise application component for J2EE-based environments.
- *Enterprise Application Module:* The enterprise application module contains one or more enterprise application components to form an individual enterprise service. Enterprise application modules also contain a module deployment descriptor for defining the configuration and deployment properties of the module. Such entities correspond to EJB modules packaged into JAR files in the J2EE environment along with XML-based EJB application module deployment descriptors.
- *Enterprise Application:* The enterprise application represents a cohesive collection of enterprise application modules, as well as perhaps Web application modules. Additionally, an enterprise application deployment descriptor contains any enterprise application assembly information. J2EE enterprise applications are composed of one or more Web and EJB modules represented by WAR and EJB JAR files packaged into an EAR file along with an XML-based J2EE application deployment descriptor.
- *Enterprise Application Container:* The enterprise application container provides the runtime environment in which enterprise applications operate. They also provide the interfaces and glue logic between enterprise application components and the services provided by an underlying application server implementation. To provide a means to deploy enterprise applications, containers also implement the configuration and deployment tools. Finally, containers also sometimes offer tools to enable the runtime deployment and management of enterprise applications. With J2EE containers, such as servlet, JSP, and EJB containers, no standard means for system management is provided. However, standards do exist for the set of Java enterprise APIs that need to be provided and for the means by which applications are deployed and configured using XML-based deployment descriptors.

- *Enterprise Application Server:* The enterprise application server provides the systems infrastructure functionality such as enterprise communication services (for example, ORBs), transaction management services, security and services in an integrated application server environment. In a J2EE environment, the application server provides the implementation of J2EE-based services and APIs. Currently, there are no standard interfaces defined between a J2EE container and application server. In fact, many times in the trade literature and even in this book, the terms *application server* and *container* are used to mean both the container and the server.

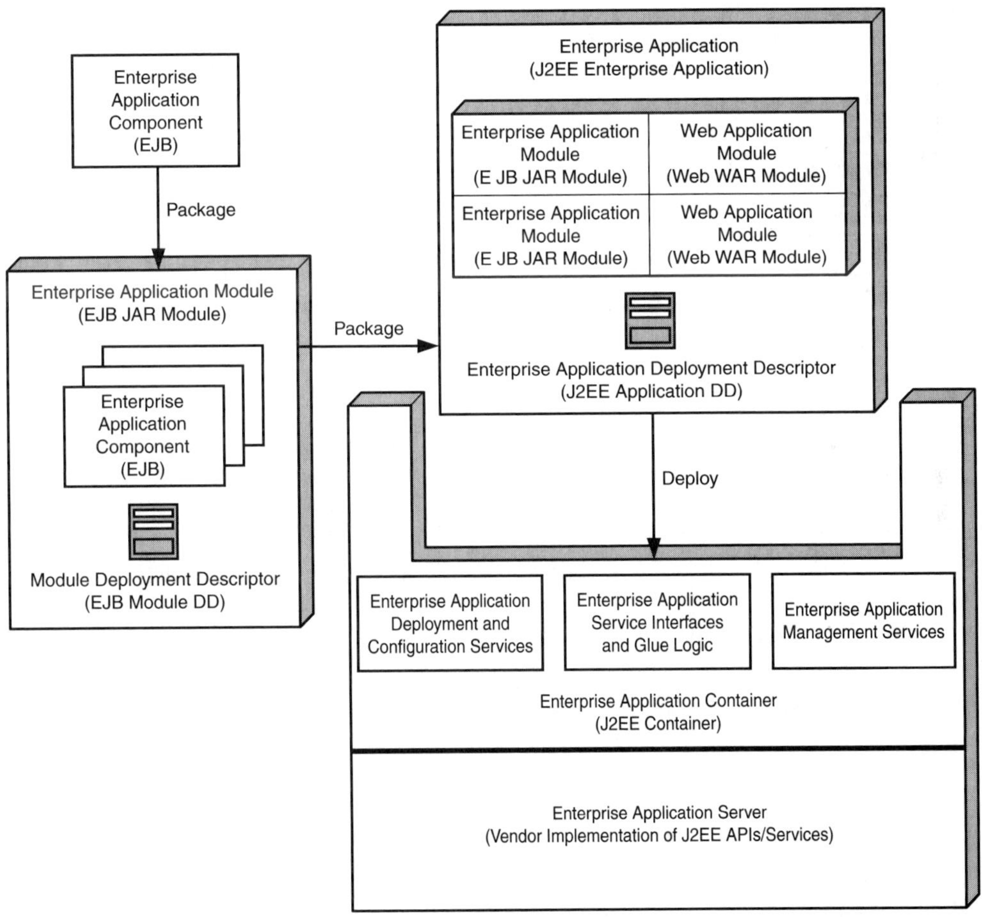

FIGURE 35.2
Primary application server architecture elements.

Regardless of certain marketing claims, application server frameworks do not negate the need for understanding the technologies described earlier in this book. For one, as you'll see, application server environments provide a means for configuring many of the services that we have described thus far and shield the developer from understanding all aspects of the Java enterprise APIs, but they do not completely negate the need to understand these APIs. Many application server frameworks, such as EJB, still at least require the developer to have an understanding of a subset of the APIs. Application servers often manage how associated objects are created, deleted, and allocated but still expose the main parts of an API for enterprise applications to utilize those services.

Furthermore, use of an application server at every distributed location within an enterprise where some application service must be provided will be completely impractical in many scenarios. Application servers often have a significant monetary cost associated with them and can require a powerful enough underlying platform that enterprise engineers will almost always opt for the use of standalone enterprise applications in many scenarios. However, application servers become the hubs and engines of the enterprise, whereas standalone applications become more suited for moderately scalable or perhaps embedded types of applications distributed throughout an enterprise.

Although one might argue on more theoretical grounds that such applications fall into the high-end desktop realm of J2SE applications or even the more embedded realm of J2ME applications, we contend based on practical experiences that such applications are still an integral part of building enterprise systems. Such standalone enterprise applications still have a need to use the various enterprise technologies described in this book and often require distributed communications, JNDI services, trading services, JMS services, transaction management services, security services, and database connectivity. The truly enterprise-class architect and developer will thus always need to understand and be able to employ the full suite of Java enterprise technologies for building Java enterprise applications in both standalone and application server–based environments such as the J2EE.

Application Server Architecture Provider Roles

Given the basic enterprise application server architecture elements defined in the preceding section, we can better understand who plays what role in providing such an architecture within an enterprise system. Figure 35.3 depicts the primary role players in providing the enterprise application server architecture elements defined in Figure 35.2. Some of the roles indicated in this diagram may actually be provided by software tools as opposed to actual people, or may perhaps be a combination of both people and tools. Furthermore, one or more roles may actually be implemented by one person/tool, or one or more people/tools may in fact implement one or more of the roles. However, defining such roles does provide a more natural encapsulation of what person/tool contains what engineering knowledge and how they provide that knowledge to an enterprise application server architecture. These primary application server architecture provider roles are listed here:

- *Enterprise Application Server Provider:* The enterprise application server provider is the provider of systems infrastructure functionality contained within an application server implementation. In a J2EE environment, the application server provider provides the implementation of J2EE-based services and APIs. Because no standard interfaces are defined between a J2EE container and an application server, the roles of container and application service provider are often the same.
- *Enterprise Application Container Provider:* The enterprise application container provider supplies the enterprise application runtime environment, service interfaces and glue logic, deployment and configuration services, and management services. As mentioned, the roles of container and application service provider are often the same.
- *Enterprise Application Component Developer:* The enterprise application component developer primarily represents a domain expert skilled in understanding the business logic and data needs of an enterprise application. Their main duty is to create enterprise application components and combine them into a cohesive module along with any deployment descriptor information on the structure and dependencies of the components. With respect to EJB and the J2EE, this person is also referred to as the EJB provider or bean provider. EJB providers create EJBs and package them into EJB JAR modules along with XML-based EJB application module deployment descriptors.
- *Enterprise Application Assembler:* The enterprise application assembler composes one or more enterprise application modules into a cohesive enterprise application. The application assembler also defines any application assembly deployment descriptor properties, as well as perhaps adding or altering the module-level deployment descriptors to provide assembly configuration information. In the J2EE world, this assembly process may involve collecting one or more Web and EJB modules into a cohesive enterprise application. Thus, WAR and EJB JAR files are packaged into an EAR file along with an XML-based J2EE application deployment descriptor.
- *Enterprise Application Deployer:* The enterprise application deployer takes an assembled enterprise application and deploys this application to the enterprise application container/server environment. Deployers are knowledgeable of the specific container/server and operating environment to which an application will be deployed. An enterprise application deployer may need to modify or add to existing module or application-layer deployment descriptor properties to accomplish this task. Although standard deployment descriptors exist for the J2EE, deployers often define additional vendor-specific deployment properties to support configuration of container/server-specific environment properties. Furthermore, deployers will also generate the appropriate stubs, skeletons, and implementation classes needed by a container to support use of the enterprise application components.

- *Enterprise Application System Administrator:* The enterprise application system administrator monitors and manages the runtime communications, database, security, and computing resources of an enterprise application operating within the enterprise application container/server environment. No standard system administration interfaces or services are defined for J2EE application environments at this time, but vendors may choose to provide their own vendor-specific services.

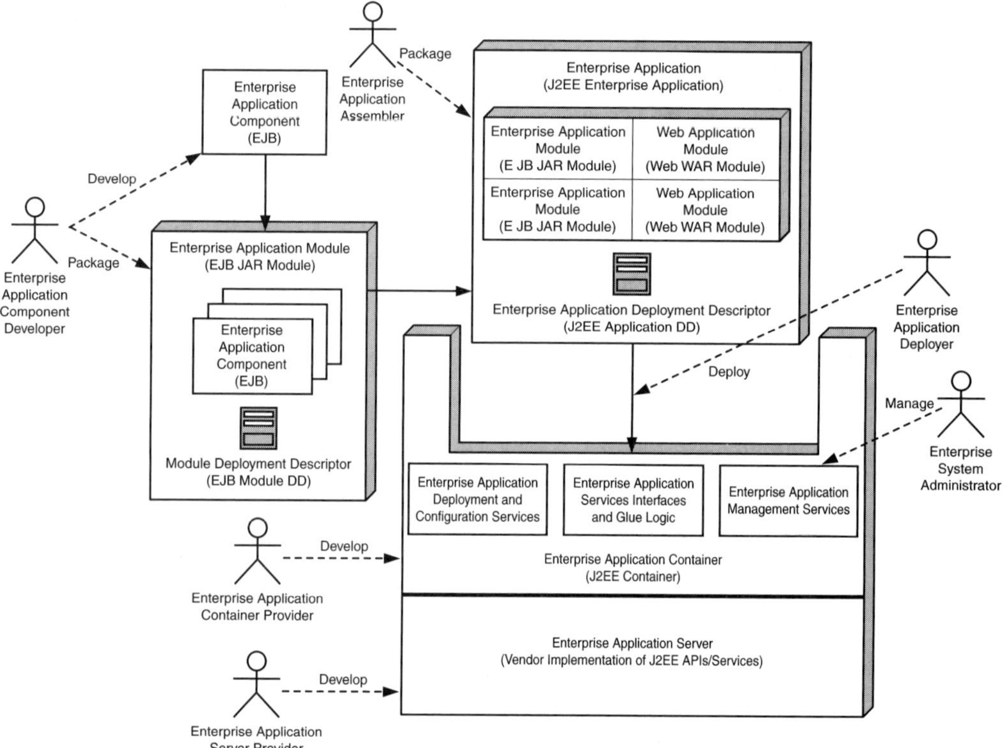

FIGURE 35.3

Application server element providers.

Application Server Components

One of the most attractive features of an application server is the capability it provides for enterprise software developers to be able to focus on developing the business logic and data for an enterprise application. Business logic and data are encapsulated within the enterprise application components that get plugged into an application server environment. For the J2EE, these enterprise application components are implemented as Enterprise JavaBeans. Thus, enterprise developers focus on defining the application logic and data within the component, and the application server handles how distributed clients access such components in a scalable and secure fashion. Application servers also implement much of the infrastructure logic that components use to access other enterprise systems and enterprise database resources.

Very often, application servers define an interface contract to which enterprise application components must adhere if they want to enable the application container/server environment to be able to manage the lifecycle of that component. Lifecycle management of components includes instance creation, instance destruction, state management, and perhaps database connectivity management.

As an example, Listing 35.1 depicts the basic logic provided for a simple credit-management bean that receives credit information from a client via its business-logic–specific `public createCreditRecord()` method and hands off the information to a server-side credit management handler. In this simplified example, we first call the application-specific `shouldUseChapter36Handler()` method to read a `Boolean` variable from a component configuration property name `java:comp/env/Handler` to determine whether a special handler (to be provided in Chapter 36, "Modeling Components with Enterprise JavaBeans") should be used. The default value for this chapter's example will direct the component to call its application-specific `handleNewCredit()` method, which simply prints the credit information that was received.

NOTE

All the sample code presented in this chapter is contained on the CD in the `examples\src\ejava\ejbch35\creditmgr` directory. This chapter's sample code also references the `CreditManagerHandler` class in the `examples\src\ejava\ejbch36\credit` directory. However, this Chapter 36 class is not invoked at runtime in the examples presented here, so it needs to be in the `CLASSPATH` only during compilation.

LISTING 35.1 EJB Enterprise Application Component (`CreditManagerSessionEJBean.java`)

```
package ejava.ejbch35.creditmgr;

import javax.ejb.SessionBean;
import javax.ejb.SessionContext;
```

continues

LISTING 35.1 Continued

```
import javax.naming.InitialContext;

public class CreditManagerSessionEJBean implements SessionBean
{
  private SessionContext ctx;

  // Standard interfaces

  public void setSessionContext(SessionContext aCtx){ ctx = aCtx; }

  public void ejbCreate(){ /* implement any creation logic */ }

  public void ejbRemove(){ /* implement any removal logic */ }

  public void ejbPassivate(){ /* implement any state persistence */ }

  public void ejbActivate(){ /* implement any state activation */ }

  // Application-specific interfaces

  /** Hand off info to credit management handler. */
  public void createCreditRecord(int customerID,
                                 String cardType,
                                 String cardName,
                                 String cardNumber,
                                 java.util.Date expirationDate,
                                 String defaultConfirmationNumber)
  {
    // If configured to use chapter 36's handler, then use it
    if(shouldUseChapter36Handler()){
      ejava.ejbch36.credit.CreditManagerHandler.handleNewCredit(
                         customerID, cardType, cardName, cardNumber,
                         expirationDate, defaultConfirmationNumber);
    }
    else{ // Otherwise, use default handler from this chapter
      this.handleNewCredit(customerID, cardType, cardName, cardNumber,
                            expirationDate, defaultConfirmationNumber);
    }
  }

  /** Determine if should use chapter 36's handler or default */
  private boolean shouldUseChapter36Handler()
  {
    // Local variable to store credit management handler flag
    boolean hasHandler = false;
```

```
    // Get initial context and determine if need use special handler
    try{
      InitialContext ctx = new InitialContext();
      Boolean handler = (Boolean) ctx.lookup("java:comp/env/Handler");
      hasHandler = handler.booleanValue();
    }
    catch(Exception namingException){
      System.out.println("No special handler defined. Using default.");
    }

    return hasHandler;
  }

  /** Default printout of credit data */
  private void handleNewCredit(int customerID,
                               String cardType,
                               String cardName,
                               String cardNumber,
                               java.util.Date expirationDate,
                               String defaultConfirmationNumber)
  {
    // Print out all credit information as the default functionality
    System.out.println("\nCREATE: Credit Information Record");
    System.out.println("  Customer ID: " + customerID);
    System.out.println(  "  Card Type: " + cardType
                       + "    Card Name: " + cardName);
    System.out.println("  Card Number :" +cardNumber);
    System.out.println(  "  Expire Date: " + expirationDate.toString()
                    + " Confirm Number: " + defaultConfirmationNumber);
  }
}
```

Although the application-specific logic of this particular component example is rather straightforward, it does also illustrate the component contract that must be honored for this particular type of EJB component. Our EJB component first indicates its capability to operate inside of an EJB container by implementing the `javax.ejb.SessionBean` interface. The `setSessionContext()` and various `ejbXXX()` methods defined on the EJB support this interface contract and enable the EJB to operate inside of a J2EE EJB container. Thus, by implementing a few simple methods and providing its own business logic, the EJB component becomes a first-class citizen of a J2EE enterprise application environment and can be managed by the EJB container.

Application Server Client Interfaces

Enterprise application components are written to provide some type of service to enterprise application clients. Thus, application server environments must define some way for clients to tap the services of these components. The mechanism by which application servers offer these services is via some distributed application service interface. These are the basic client interface problems that application servers must solve:

- *Distributed Business-Specific Interfaces:* The application service interface needs to expose only the business-specific operations defined on a component that have been defined to be distributable.
- *Distributed Business-Specific Naming and LifeCycle Management:* The application service interface must provide a means for clients to look up, create, and destroy component instances and references.
- *Interface Definition Language:* The application service interface must utilize some language for defining interfaces usable by clients.
- *Interface Communications Protocol:* The application service interface must utilize some underlying communications protocol usable by clients.

To satisfy these needs, J2EE application service frameworks define standards for creating client interfaces to EJB components. These corresponding standards include the following:

- *EJB Remote Interfaces:* EJB remote interfaces define the business-specific operations to be distributed by an EJB to its clients.
- *EJB Home Interfaces and JNDI:* EJB home interfaces define business-specific and standard means for creating and destroying EJB components, as well as for looking up certain EJB component instances. JNDI is also used to obtain initial EJB home interface handles.
- *Java and IDL:* Because EJB depends on RMI, Java-based EJB client interfaces can be defined. Additionally, CORBA IDL EJB client interfaces can also be defined via a CORBA-to-EJB mapping.
- *IIOP:* The standard protocol over which EJB clients communicate with EJB application server environments is IIOP. RMI/IIOP and a CORBA-to-EJB mapping both support this capability. JRMP may also be used for EJBs that communicate via standard RMI/JRMP. The actual underlying protocol, however, is transparent to both the EJB client and the component developer.

As an example of an EJB remote interface to our `CreditManageSessionEJBean` defined earlier, Listing 35.2 defines the one remote interface operation defined for our simple EJB. The extension of our interface from `javax.ejb.EJBObject` signifies that this is a remote EJB interface.

Because it is a remote interface and RMI interface language semantics are implied by EJB, the method also declares that it can throw a `java.rmi.RemoteException`. We should also note that `EJBObject` extends `java.rmi.Remote`.

LISTING 35.2 EJB Client Remote Interface (`CreditManagerSession.java`)

```
package ejava.ejbch35.creditmgr;

import javax.ejb.EJBObject;
import java.rmi.RemoteException;

/** Provides a means to take customer credit info into the system. */
public interface CreditManagerSession extends EJBObject
{

  /** Create a credit record for a customer. */
  public void createCreditRecord(int customerID,
                                 String cardType,
                                 String cardName,
                                 String cardNumber,
                                 java.util.Date expirationDate,
                                 String defaultConfirmationNumber)
         throws RemoteException;
}
```

The corresponding EJB home interface used to create an instance of a remote `CreditManagerSession` interface object is defined in Listing 35.3. Here we see a single `create()` method used to create an instance of our EJB from the client's perspective. The extension of this interface from `javax.ejb.EJBHome`, as you'll see in the next chapter, also inherits `remove()` methods that are used to destroy instances of the EJB object from the client's perspective.

LISTING 35.3 EJB Client Home Interface (`CreditManagerSessionHome.java`)

```
package ejava.ejbch35.creditmgr;

import javax.ejb.EJBHome;
import javax.ejb.CreateException;
import java.rmi.RemoteException;

public interface CreditManagerSessionHome extends EJBHome
{
  /** Create an instance of a credit manager. */
  CreditManagerSession create()
       throws CreateException, RemoteException;
}
```

Application Server Client Implementations

Application server clients may use the aforementioned interfaces to speak with enterprise application components operating inside of an application server either in a standalone fashion or perhaps inside of its own container environment. Standalone clients provide their own run-time environment and communicate with the application server tier using a distributed communications paradigm such as CORBA or RMI. Standalone application clients are also responsible for ensuring that they have communications and service libraries installed on their machine that are compatible with the application server's communications and service libraries. Some application server environments may also provide a container environment in which their clients can operate which helps guarantee that the client and server have compatible communications and service libraries, as well as providing a hook for more sophisticated client-server communications.

The same two general approaches apply to clients of J2EE EJBs. EJB clients operating in a standalone fashion include regular Java-based clients perhaps operating on top of a J2SE-based platform with the correct standard Java enterprise library extensions needed for communications with the EJB server. These libraries include JNDI v1.2, EJB v1.1 client libraries, RMI/IIOP v1.0 libraries, and possibly JMS v1.0 and JDBC 2.0 extension libraries. Standalone EJB clients may also be Web-tier Java Servlets or JSPs, as well as perhaps CORBA clients talking with an EJB server that supports a pure EJB-CORBA mapping.

EJB clients can also operate inside of a standard J2EE container environment. Such clients may be other EJBs, Java Servlets, JSPs, or J2EE application clients. J2EE application clients may be viewed simply as J2SE-based Java applications along with support for a minimal set of container environment requirements. J2EE application clients essentially require a J2SE run-time environment complete with Java IDL and core JDBC 2.0, as well as the provisioning of the standard Java enterprise JNDI v1.2, EJB v1.1 client, RMI/IIOP v1.0, JMS v1.0, and JDBC 2.0 extension libraries. Additionally, J2EE application clients have a minimalist standard XML-based deployment descriptor for configuring their operating environment.

As an example of an EJB application client that can run in both a standalone mode and a J2EE application client container environment, Listing 35.4 presents a client of our previously defined `CreditManagerSessionEJBean`. If the client is executed with the `-standalone` option flag, it will process the client code assuming a standalone environment; otherwise, it assumes that a J2EE application client environment is provided.

The `runStandaloneClient()` call needs to create a JNDI `InitialContext` as usual with initialization properties sent in from the command line as system environment properties. When using the J2EE reference implementation, the `org.omg.CORBA.ORBInitialHost` system property needs to be set to the hostname for the name service, and the `java.naming.factory.initialValue` system property defines the initial JNDI context factory class. When the BEA WebLogic server is being used, the `java.naming.provider.url` system property needs to be set to the hostname for the name service, and the `java.naming.factory.initial` system property defines the initial JNDI context factory class. After an initial context is created, the JNDI name of `CreditManagerHome` is used to locate the EJB's home interface object.

LISTING 35.4 EJB Client Implementation (`CreditManagerClient.java`)

```
package ejava.ejbch35.creditmgr;

import javax.naming.Context;
import javax.naming.InitialContext;
import javax.rmi.PortableRemoteObject;
import java.rmi.RemoteException;
import java.io.BufferedReader;
import java.io.IOException;
import java.io.InputStreamReader;

public class CreditManagerClient
{
  /** Main method determines if is standalone or J2EE client */
  public static void main(String[] args)
    throws Exception
  {
    // Create new client instance
    CreditManagerClient myClient = new CreditManagerClient();

    // If pass in "-standalone" flag, then run standalone client
    if( (args.length > 0) && (args[0].equalsIgnoreCase("-standalone")) ){
      myClient.runStandaloneClient();
    }
    else{ // Else run J2EE application client
      myClient.runJ2EEClient();
    }
  }

  /* Method to run client as a standalone client */
  public void runStandaloneClient()
  {
    try{
      // Get initial context for standalone client using
      //   system environment variables for context parameters
```

continues

LISTING 35.4 Continued

```
      Context context = new InitialContext();

      // Look up server reference using raw JNDI name
      Object object =
        context.lookup("CreditManagerHome");

      // Now run common client code
      runCommonClientBody(object);
    }
    catch(Exception exception){
      exception.printStackTrace();
    }
  }

  /* Method to run client as a J2EE application client */
  public void runJ2EEClient()
  {
    try{
      // Get initial context using container provided context
      Context context = new InitialContext();

      // Look up server reference using EJB reference from
      // the XML deployment descriptor
      Object object =
        context.lookup("java:comp/env/ejb/CreditManagerHome");

      // Now run common client code
      runCommonClientBody(object);
    }
    catch(Exception exception){
      exception.printStackTrace();
    }
  }

  /** Method to run code that is common for both client types */
  private void runCommonClientBody(Object creditManagerHomeRef)
    throws Exception
  {
    System.out.println("Class Type :"+
      creditManagerHomeRef.getClass().getName());

    // Narrow to credit manager reference
    CreditManagerSessionHome creditManagerHome =
      (CreditManagerSessionHome)
```

```
     PortableRemoteObject.narrow(creditManagerHomeRef,
              ejava.ejbch35.creditmgr.CreditManagerSessionHome.class);

  // Create handle to server object now using home factory
  CreditManagerSession creditManagerSession =
     creditManagerHome.create();

  // Solicit user information from input and send to CreditManager
   processCreditRecords(creditManagerSession);
}

/** Solicits user information from input and sends to EJB */
private   void processCreditRecords(CreditManagerSession mgr)
  throws Exception
{
  // Declare credit record variables
  int customerID = 0;
  String cardType = "";
  String cardName = "";
  java.util.Date expirationDate = new java.util.Date();
  String defaultConfirmationNumber = "";
  String cardNumber = "";

  // Loop forever to get input and send to manager until
  // escape from program with Ctrl-C
  while(true){
    // Solicit credit record variable information from user input
    System.out.println("    Enter a new credit record.");
    System.out.println("Enter Customer ID (####):" );
    customerID = Integer.parseInt(readStringFromInput());
    System.out.println("Enter Card Type  (CREDIT/DEBIT):");
    cardType = readStringFromInput();
    System.out.println("Enter Card Name  (VISA/MC/AMEX):");
    cardName = readStringFromInput();
    System.out.println("Enter Card Number (#############) :");
    cardNumber = readStringFromInput();
    System.out.println("Enter Expire Date  (MM/DD/YYYY):");
    String expirationDateString = readStringFromInput();

    // Create and format date using date formatter
    java.text.DateFormat dateFormat =
     java.text.DateFormat.getInstance();
    expirationDate =
     dateFormat.parse(expirationDateString+ " 0:0 PM EST" );
```

continues

LISTING 35.4 Continued

```
        // Now print info on client side
        System.out.println("\nCLIENT SIDE: Credit Information Record");
        System.out.println("  Customer ID: " + customerID);
        System.out.println(  "  Card Type: " + cardType
                          + "    Card Name: " + cardName);
        System.out.println("  Card Number :" +cardNumber);
        System.out.println(  "  Expire Date: " + expirationDate.toString()
                      + " Confirm Number: " + defaultConfirmationNumber);

        // Now send info to manager
        mgr.createCreditRecord(customerID, cardType, cardName, cardNumber,
                               expirationDate, defaultConfirmationNumber);
      }
    }

    /* Special helper to read a String from standard user input */
    public static String readStringFromInput()
    {
      String readValue = null;
      try{
        BufferedReader reader = new BufferedReader(
          new InputStreamReader(System.in));
        readValue = reader.readLine();
      }
      catch(IOException ioException){
        ioException.printStackTrace();
      }
      return readValue;
    }
}
```

The `runJ2EEClient()` method instantiates an `InitialContext` object using whatever system properties are set for it by the J2EE application container environment. A JNDI lookup is then performed using the EJB reference of `java:comp/env/ejb/CreditManagerHome` as configured by the J2EE application client's container environment and deployment descriptors.

Both client types then invoke the `runCommonClientBody()` method, which uses the home interface to create a `CreditManagerSession` remote interface object instance and then calls `processCreditRecords()`. The `processCreditRecords()` method simply solicits credit record data from the command line and invokes the EJB's remote `CreditManagerSession.createCreditRecord()` method after all data is input.

Enterprise Application Configuration and Deployment

Application server configuration and deployment involves establishing a set of properties that define how your enterprise applications should behave and interact at runtime. The establishment of these properties may be performed manually via setting of a text-based configuration file, or it may be performed via use of some GUI-based configuration and deployment tool. J2EE-based configuration, as you have already seen in Chapter 32, "Java Servlets," and Chapter 33, "JavaServer Pages," involves defining standard element values in an XML-based deployment descriptor file. Many J2EE vendor products also define GUI-based mechanisms for setting these deployment descriptors.

Server Configuration and Deployment Example

As an example of a standard XML-based deployment descriptor for our `CreditManagerSession` EJB, Listing 35.5 presents the standard `ejb-jar.xml` file containing this information. Meta-data about the EJB, the EJB's type information, and the EJB's class information are all defined in this file. This file is used along with compiled versions of the EJB's classes and interfaces to create an EJB JAR module. The EJB JAR module is then encapsulated within an EAR file, which is deployed to a J2EE-compliant EJB container/server.

NOTE

All XML files and sample build scripts for creating the EJB server application are provided on the CD in the `examples\src\ejava\ejbch35\creditmgr` directory. A `buildj2ee.bat` script file is used to build and deploy the EJB to the J2EE reference implementation server and also uses a server-specific `sun-j2ee-ri.xml` file in addition to the standard `ejb-jar.xml` file. You may have copied an `orb.properties` file to your `[JAVA_HOME]\jre\lib` directory if you have installed the standard RMI/IIOP extension per the instructions of Chapter 16, "RMI Communications." This `orb.properties` file must be removed in order to properly run the J2EE reference implementation server. Refer to Appendix A, "Software Configuration," for more details.

A `buildweblogic.bat` file is used to build and deploy the EJB to the BEA WebLogic Server and also uses a server-specific `weblogic-ejb-jar.xml` file in addition to the standard `ejb-jar.xml` file. WebLogic also requires that you add the `CreditManagerEJB.jar` file built for this example to the `weblogic.ejb.deploy` property list in the `[WEBLOGIC_HOME]\weblogic.properties` file. Appendix A describes the steps needed to configure J2EE reference implementation and BEA WebLogic servers. The next chapter also describes how to build EJB server applications in much more detail.

LISTING 35.5 EJB Server Configuration (`ejb-jar.xml`)

```
<?xml version="1.0" encoding="UTF-8"?>

<!DOCTYPE ejb-jar PUBLIC '-//Sun Microsystems, Inc.//
➥DTD Enterprise JavaBeans 1.1//EN'
➥ 'http://java.sun.com/j2ee/dtds/ejb-jar_1_1.dtd'>

<ejb-jar>

  <description>Credit Manager Server</description>
  <display-name>CreditManager</display-name>

  <enterprise-beans>
    <session>
      <description>Credit Manager EJB</description>
      <display-name>CreditManagerEJB</display-name>
      <ejb-name>CreditManagerEJB</ejb-name>
      <home>ejava.ejbch35.creditmgr.CreditManagerSessionHome</home>
      <remote>ejava.ejbch35.creditmgr.CreditManagerSession</remote>
      <ejb-class>
        ejava.ejbch35.creditmgr.CreditManagerSessionEJBean
      </ejb-class>
      <session-type>Stateless</session-type>
      <transaction-type>Container</transaction-type>
    </session>
  </enterprise-beans>

</ejb-jar>
```

Client Configuration and Deployment Example

As an example of a standard XML-based deployment descriptor for our `CreditManagerClient` J2EE application client, Listing 35.6 presents the standard `client.xml` file containing this information. Meta-data about the client and the EJB reference information are both defined in this file for the client. This file is used along with a compiled version of the client class to create a client JAR module, such as the `packager -applicationClient` command option for use with the J2EE reference implementation. A `Main-Class` attribute added to the client JAR file specifies the class name of the class (for example, `ejava.ejbch35.CreditManagerClient`) that provides the `main()` method implementation to be executed at startup. Finally, the client JAR file is then referenced from within a special J2EE application client launcher program provided with the J2EE reference implementation to execute the application client code using a command of this basic form:

```
[J2EE_HOME]\bin\runclient -client myApClient.jar
➥ -name [displayName] [apArguments]
```

NOTE

The `client.xml` file and sample build scripts for creating the EJB client application are provided on the CD in the `examples\src\ejava\ejbch35\creditmgr` directory. The J2EE reference implementation also uses a vendor-specific `sun-j2ee-ri-client.xml` file in addition to the standard `client.xml` file. The `buildj2ee.bat` file compiles the standalone client and builds the J2EE application client for use with the J2EE reference implementation. The `buildweblogic.bat` file compiles the standalone client for the BEA WebLogic server.

Additionally, the `runJ2EEApClient.bat` file executes the EJB client as a J2EE application client using the J2EE reference implementation server. The `runStandaloneJ2EEClient.bat` file executes the EJB client as a standalone client using the J2EE reference implementation server. The `runStandaloneWebLogicClient.bat` file executes the EJB client as a standalone client using the BEA WebLogic server.

LISTING 35.6 EJB Client Configuration (`client.xml`)

```
<?xml version="1.0" encoding="UTF-8"?>

<!DOCTYPE application-client PUBLIC '-//Sun Microsystems, Inc.//
➥DTD J2EE Application Client 1.2//EN'
➥ 'http://java.sun.com/j2ee/dtds/application-client_1_2.dtd'>

<application-client>

  <display-name>CreditManagerJ2EEClient</display-name>
  <description>Credit Manager Client</description>

  <ejb-ref>
    <ejb-ref-name>ejb/CreditManagerHome</ejb-ref-name>
    <ejb-ref-type>Session</ejb-ref-type>
    <home>ejava.ejbch35.creditmgr.CreditManagerSessionHome</home>
    <remote>ejava.ejbch35.creditmgr.CreditManagerSession</remote>
  </ejb-ref>

</application-client>
```

NOTE

When running the J2EE application client via our `runJ2EEApClient.bat` script, you will be prompted for a user name and password in a pop-up window. Enter `guest` for a user name and `guest123` for a password. These default authentication values are set in the `[J2EE_HOME]config\auth.properties` file.

Application Service Management

In addition to the ease with which enterprise application components can be built and with which clients can connect to these components, application servers also make it easy for enterprise application components to tap various enterprise services. Service mechanisms include data connectivity, communications enabling, security, availability, enterprise application integration, and more. Some of these services are transparently provided using declarative configuration parameters in a deployment descriptor file. Other services have their API exposed to the enterprise application component by the application server. Regardless of how the component accesses these services, the application server often creates, allocates, destroys, and generally manages the lifecycle of all underlying service-related objects.

J2EE-based servers are no different. For example, security and transaction management are provided as services to the EJB (as well as Web components) in a declarative fashion using configurable deployment descriptor properties. Access to such services can also be provided programmatically via exposed APIs. JDBC is another example in which the J2EE container/server will manage the creation and destruction of connections and the allocation of connections to J2EE components from a JDBC connection pool. J2EE components can then utilize the JDBC connection and statement APIs as usual.

We close the chapter here with a brief list of those services commonly managed by application servers with specific focus on EJB-based servers and how such service management is provided:

- *Distributed Communications Services:* Application servers transparently provide distributed communication support for server-side components. For example, EJB containers provide handler code for calls to server-side skeletons from client-side stubs. These handlers then delegate calls to EJB server component instances pulled from an EJB pool of instances and are allocated to their own thread, which is also often retrieved from a pool of threads. Thus, EJB server components can be implemented without worrying about managing server-side resources or threads.
- *State Management:* Application servers often handle the resolution of particular client requests to the state managed for that client on the server side. EJB stateful session objects provide a means to resolve requests from a particular client to particular server-side object instances. The passivation and activation of such state are also managed by the EJB container/server.
- *Database Connectivity:* Application servers often provide handles to pooled database connections via an API and may also provide object-relational data mapping services. EJBs provide direct access to the JDBC API from components with the capability to configure database resources via deployment descriptors. Although the JDBC API may be exposed, EJB servers handle the creation, destruction, and allocation of database connections from

a pool. EJB containers also provide an object-to-relational means for specifying how fields of an object automatically map to columns in a database table or view. Such mappings allow for a more object-oriented interface to EJBs, with the container handling the actual relational database inserts, deletes, queries, and updates.

- *Configuration Services:* Application servers also provide ways to define properties of an application that can be read from configuration files. JNDI is used in EJB application server environments for looking up environment configuration information specified in deployment descriptors. Component-specific initialization parameters can also be specified in deployment descriptors for the automatic initialization of components during activation.
- *Security:* Security in application servers can be specified declaratively and programmatically. Declarative security parameters in J2EE deployment descriptors can define required authentication mechanisms and authorization parameters. Security roles and how they map to groups and users can all be specified declaratively to implement the access control decision logic for defining who can access what EJB. Additionally, programmatic security interfaces provide for more sophisticated and application-specific access control when the limited J2EE security model does not suffice.
- *Availability:* Availability of service in application servers is provided primarily as a function of proper thread management, resource management, transaction management, and state management. J2EE-based servers provide both declarative and programmatic means for managing JTA/JTS-based transactions from within EJB server components and from within a few EJB client types. Additionally, EJB servers provide thread, resource, and state management to enable the capability to build scalable enterprise applications. Additionally, some application servers provide clustering and failover mechanisms.
- *Enterprise Application Integration and Connectivity:* Many application server products realize the importance not only for connecting to back-end enterprise data, but also for connecting to back-end enterprise business logic. At the time of this writing, no standard means for connecting to back-end enterprise applications from within J2EE environments was specified. EJBs can utilize technologies such as CORBA and XML for integrating with enterprise applications, but such technologies require additional hand-coding. EJB connectors are an up-and-coming technology to be employed within a future EJB and J2EE specification for automatically connecting to back-end enterprise systems.

Conclusions

In this chapter, you got a glimpse of how application server architectures partition the problem of building enterprise applications by partitioning an enterprise architecture into elements whose providers can encapsulate the proper level of knowledge needed to create those elements. Enterprise application container and server providers can thus focus on what they know best, which is to provide infrastructure and domain-independent services, and enterprise application component developers can focus on what they know best, which is the business logic and data specific to a particular domain. We also saw how EJB makes implementing such enterprise application server components a simple task. EJB clients talk to EJBs using standard interface patterns and can also operate inside of their own J2EE application client container environment. Finally, application servers and EJB can make configuring and deploying components and providing management services for components a simple matter of declaring properties in an XML file. Although standalone enterprise applications will still be key components of an enterprise system solution, enterprise application servers and EJB can provide your enterprise with a central hub to rapidly deploy the lion's share of your enterprise system's business logic and data handling.

Modeling Components with Enterprise JavaBeans

CHAPTER

36

IN THIS CHAPTER

- EJB Overview 1232
- EJB Configuration and Deployment Basics 1243
- Session Bean Server Components 1250
- Session Bean Client Interfaces 1263
- Session Bean Configuration and Deployment 1273
- EJB and JDBC 1277
- Entity Bean Server Components 1279
- Entity Bean Client Interfaces 1299
- Entity Bean Configuration and Deployment 1307

J2EE Enterprise JavaBeans (EJBs) provides a model for developing server-side enterprise application components that can make building portable and distributed enterprise applications an easier task than is required for building standalone enterprise applications. EJB containers/servers provide distributed communications-enabling services, data-enabling services, common distributed communication services, and systems assurance services for EJB components with minimal effort on the part of a developer to utilize these services. This chapter describes this J2EE EJB component model in terms of how to build these server-side enterprise application components, how clients to these components are created, and how these components can be configured and deployed using standard J2EE XML-based deployment descriptors.

In this chapter, you will learn:

- The basic architecture and concepts involved in building EJBs, including the concepts of session and entity bean types.
- The common approach for configuring and deploying all types of EJBs.
- The steps required for building server-side session EJB components, including stateless and stateful session beans.
- The steps required for building EJB clients to session beans.
- The steps required to configure and deploy session beans.
- The basic relation between EJB and JDBC and how JDBC access can be achieved from within EJB components.
- The steps required for building server-side entity EJB components, including bean-managed persistence and container-managed persistence entity beans.
- The steps required for building EJB clients to entity beans.
- The steps required to configure and deploy entity beans.

EJB Overview

Enterprise JavaBeans (EJBs) represents a powerful component model for building distributed, server-side, and Java-based enterprise application components. The Enterprise JavaBeans model can be starkly contrasted with the regular JavaBeans model described in Chapter 7, “Modeling Components with JavaBeans.” The JavaBeans model defines a means for building Java-based components for use in containers that have a nondistributed nature, have many client-side GUI semantics associated with them, and do not define standard operations to enable sophisticated life-cycle management of JavaBean components. The Enterprise JavaBeans model, on the other hand, defines a means for building Java-based components for use in containers that do offer distributed client connectivity, have exclusive server-side semantics associated with them, and define various standard operations to enable sophisticated life cycle management of Enterprise JavaBean components.

EJBs, in fact, have the following key features:

- Provide a model for defining server-side components.
- Provide a model for defining distributed client interfaces to the services provided by these components.
- Provide standard operations and semantics for allowing a container to create, destroy, allocate, persist, and activate component instances.
- Provide a standard model for defining a component that maintains a conversational session with a client with session management handled by the container.
- Provide a standard model for defining a component that encapsulates a data-source (for example, database) entry with object-to-relational data mapping being handled by the container.
- Provide a standard for defining configuration and deployment characteristics of a component independent of its implementation.
- Provide a standard model for declaratively defining the security attributes of a component.
- Provide a standard model for declaratively defining the transactions attributes of a component.
- Provide a standard component interface contract such that components can run in any vendor-compliant container/server that implements that standard interface contract.

The EJB component model is thus a very powerful model for building enterprise applications and is the focal point of the J2EE architecture. The J2EE v1.2 requires that all EJB v.1.1 APIs and implementations be included within J2EE EJB containers and that EJB v1.1 client APIs and implementations be included with J2EE Web containers and J2EE application clients. EJB v1.1 represents a significant advancement over EJB v1.0. EJB v1.1 compliance deprecates a set of `javax.ejb.deployment` package abstractions provided by EJB v1.0, requires standard XML-based deployment descriptors to be used, and requires use of EJB entity beans, whereas in EJB v1.0 they were optional.

EJB Architecture

Figure 36.1 depicts the basic architecture of EJB-based client-server enterprise applications. The client side of an EJB architecture contains the EJB interfaces needed for invoking business-specific methods on an EJB, as well as for managing handles to server-side objects. The server side of an EJB architecture contains the instances of the actual EJB component implementation as well as the container code that maps calls to and from clients and EJBs after appropriate service management infrastructure logic has been e XEcuted. RMI remote interface semantics are currently implied by these interfaces and thus enable RMI/JRMP, RMI/IIOP, and RMI-to-CORBA IDL mappings to be used as the interface mechanism.

The primary elements of these application-specific elements of an EJB architecture as depicted in the diagram are listed here:

- *EJB Clients*: EJB client applications utilize JNDI to look up references to home interfaces and use home and remote EJB interfaces to utilize all EJB-based functionality.
- *EJB Home Interfaces (and Stubs)*: EJB home interfaces provide operations for clients to create, remove, and find handles to EJB remote interface objects. Underlying stubs marshal home interface requests and unmarshal home interface responses for the client.
- *EJB Remote Interfaces (and Stubs)*: EJB remote interfaces provide the business-specific client interface methods defined for a particular EJB. Underlying stubs marshal remote interface requests and unmarshal remote interface responses for the client.
- *EJB Implementations*: EJB implementations are the actual EJB application components implemented by developers to provide any application-specific business method invocation, creation, removal, finding, activation, passivation, database storage, and database loading logic.
- *Container EJB Implementations (Skeletons and Delegates)*: The container manages the distributed communication skeletons used to marshal and unmarshal data sent to and from the client. Containers also may store EJB implementation instances in a pool and use delegates to perform any service management operations related to a particular EJB before calls are delegated to the EJB implementation instance.

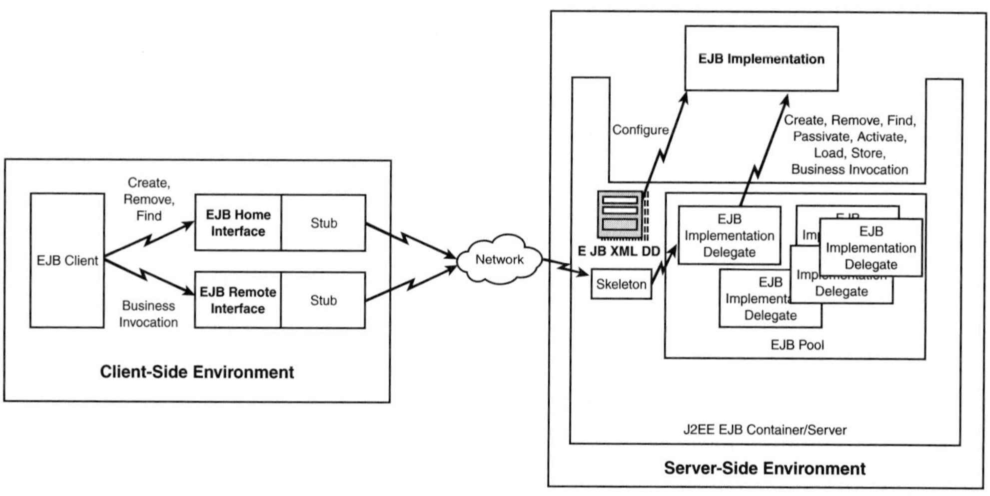

FIGURE 36.1
The EJB architecture.

EJB Types

EJBs are distinguished along two main functional roles. Within each primary role, the EJBs are further distinguished according to two subroles. By partitioning EJBs into roles, the programmer can develop an EJB according to a more focused programming model than would be the case if such roles were not distinguished. Such roles also allow the EJB container to determine how to best manage a particular EJB based on its programming model type.

These are the two main distinctions of EJBs:

- *Session Beans*: Session beans are EJBs that are created to perform some action on the enterprise system and possibly return results to the client. Session beans correspond to the controllers of a system exposed for manipulation to clients. Session beans may thus be thought of as the "verbs" of a particular problem domain for which they are implemented to solve. Session beans are particularly well-suited to encapsulate coarse-grained "frontline" service entry points into the system. The creation of fine-grained session bean service points is discouraged due to potential resource limitations when such applications must scale.
- *Entity Beans*: Entity beans are EJBs that are created to encapsulate some data contained by the enterprise system. Such data may be created, removed, or found by clients. Data may also be retrieved and updated by clients with EJB containers determining how any updates occur based on the transaction semantics for a particular entity bean. Entity beans also have special primary key classes defined for them that relate to the primary keys of an associated entity stored in the database. Entity beans correspond to some enterprise system entity. Entity beans may thus be thought of as the "nouns" of a particular problem domain for which they are implemented to solve. Because clients could potentially hold many entity references as the result of a find operation, many effective EJB designs will provide access to entity beans only from session beans and limit how many entity bean handles are returned to a client. Scalability can become severely ta XEd if an excessive number of entity bean remote object references are doled out to clients.

Within the realm of session beans, two further distinctions may be made:

- *Stateless Session Beans*: Stateless session beans represent those session EJBs created with no regard for the maintenance of any state between subsequent calls by a client. Stateless session beans thus represent pure input and output engines.
- *Stateful Session Beans*: Stateful session beans represent those session EJBs created to maintain state for a particular client between subsequent calls before some maximum amount of time has expired. Stateful session beans thus represent input and output engines that can utilize the state created by a client from a previous invocation.

Within the realm of entity beans, two distinctions also apply:

- *Bean-Managed Persistence (BMP) Entity Beans*: BMP entity beans represent those entity EJBs in which all code dealing with the insert, delete, querying, and update of data to a relational data source (for example, a database) is performed by the entity EJB developer.
- *Container-Managed Persistence (CMP) Entity Beans*: CMP entity beans represent those entity EJBs in which all code dealing with the insert, delete, querying, and update of data to a relational data source (for example, a database) is provided by the container EJB implementations. Containers primarily provide such an implementation by using deployment descriptor–based information to map EJB class fields to relational data table columns and then subsequently generate the SQL code using these mappings.

EJB Exception Types

Because EJB interfaces imply RMI semantics, all distributed EJB client interfaces extend from `java.rmi.Remote` and throw the `java.rmi.RemoteException` from each of their methods. In addition to `RemoteException` objects, EJBs can also throw other EJB-specific exceptions that relate to error and failure scenarios resulting from the invocation of EJB operations. Figure 36.2 depicts this EJB exception hierarchy. Those exceptions shown in Figure 36.2 that have been introduced for EJB-specific exception behavior are listed here:

- `EJBException`: This exception is thrown by an EJB when an application-specific method cannot be completed.
- `NoSuchEntityException`: This exception is thrown by an EJB when an application-specific method cannot be completed because a particular entity bean does not exist.
- `CreateException`: This exception is thrown when a particular EJB cannot be created.
- `DuplicateKeyException`: This exception is thrown when a particular entity EJB cannot be created when objects with the same key already exist.
- `RemoveException`: This exception is thrown when a particular EJB cannot be removed.
- `FinderException`: This exception is thrown when a collection of one or more entity EJBs cannot be found.
- `ObjectNotFoundException`: This exception is thrown when a singular entity EJB object cannot be found.

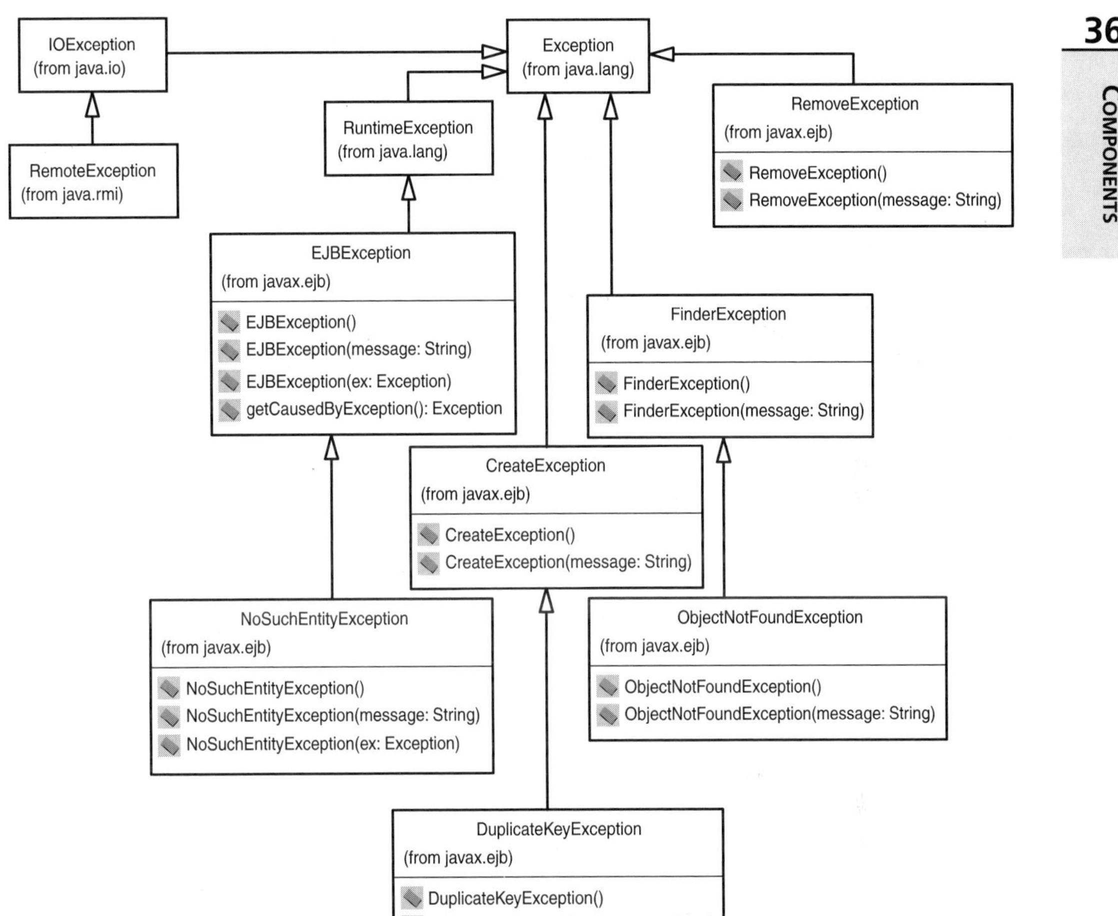

FIGURE 36.2
EJB exceptions.

EJB Development Considerations and Steps

The steps to developing EJBs may be partitioned along two main lines: server-side and client-side development. Although server-side development of distributed communications servers, such as CORBA and RMI, may take on a somewhat complicated nature at times, server-side development of EJBs is simplified because much of the communications, state management, resource allocation, and thread management infrastructure coding is provided by the container. These are the main steps employed for server-side EJB development:

1. *Implement EJB Standard Interfaces*: Any interfaces required by the standard EJB component model to enable container-based management of the EJB should be implemented.
2. *Implement EJB Business-Specific Interfaces*: Any business-specific interfaces provided by your EJB and any supporting helper and utility classes should be implemented.
3. *Create Client Remote Interfaces*: The remote interface for your EJB that defines all business-specific interfaces to the EJB should be created.
4. *Create Client Home Interfaces*: The home interface for your EJB that defines the application-specific methods for creating your EJB, as well as application-specific methods for finding your EJB (if it is an entity bean) should be created.
5. *Compile EJB Code*: The EJB implementation, home interface, and remote interface should be compiled.
6. *Configure Module Deployment Descriptors*: The standard EJB deployment descriptor should be configured to define the specific structural characteristics and dependencies of your EJB. Any deployment descriptors needed by your container/server provider should also be configured.
7. *Package EJB into EJB JAR Module*: The standard EJB deployment descriptor, any vendor-specific deployment descriptors, and one or more of your compiled EJB class files should be packaged into an EJB JAR module.
8. *Configure Application Deployment Descriptor*: A standard J2EE deployment descriptor should be configured for a cohesive collection of J2EE modules.
9. *Package EJB Modules into J2EE EAR Application*: The standard J2EE deployment descriptor and one or more EJB JAR files should be packaged into a J2EE EAR application.
10. *Deploy the J2EE Application*: The J2EE EAR application should be deployed to a J2EE-compliant application container/server environment.

On the client side, clients must simply be designed to utilize the proper EJB client interfaces and libraries. EJB client development proceeds along the following lines:

1. *Standard Client Library Verification*: The proper EJB client libraries must be established, including correct versions of the JNDI v1.2, EJB v1.1 client, RMI/IIOP v1.0, JMS v1.0, and JDBC 2.0 core extension libraries.
2. *EJB Client Interface Generation*: The properly compiled interfaces and stubs specific to a particular EJB must also be provided to an EJB client.

3. *Client Implementation*: The EJB client may be implemented to utilize any interfaces as appropriate.
4. *Client Code Compilation*: The EJB client code should be compiled.
5. *Configure Application Client Deployment Descriptors (Optional)*: Any standard J2EE application client deployment descriptor should be configured to define the specific configuration properties of your EJB client.
6. *Package Client into Application Client JAR (Optional)*: The standard J2EE Application Client deployment descriptor and compiled EJB client class files should be packaged into a J2EE application client JAR.
7. *Launch the J2EE Application Client (Optional)*: The J2EE application client may be launched within a special J2EE application client container environment.

BeeShirts.com EJB Application

We have created a back-end enterprise application serving framework for our BeeShirts.com example using EJBs and placed the code on the CD. The next chapter illustrates how such EJBs can be integrated with the BeeShirts.com e-commerce storefront presented in Chapter 32, "Java Servlets," and Chapter 33, "JavaServer Pages," but this chapter lays the foundation for providing a scalable enterprise application–enabled back end for BeeShirts.com using EJBs. Because our sample code is moderately large for inclusion in this book, we also won't insert all the source code in the chapter text but will provide core listings and snippets from the code as relevant topics are introduced. Figure 36.3 provides you with a logical diagram of the EJBs at play in our example.

NOTE

All the sample code strewn throughout this chapter is contained on the CD under the `examples\src\ejava\ejbch36` directory. Because the code on the CD represents a moderately large amount of BeeShirts.com enterprise application component code, we do not present all the code in this chapter. Rather, we will describe the basic structure of such code and present snippets from that code germane to chapter topics as they are discussed. We should also note that this code depends on some of the code from Chapter 32 stored on the CD under the `examples\src\ejava\servletsch32` directory and from Chapter 35 stored under the `examples\src\ejava\ejbch35` directory.

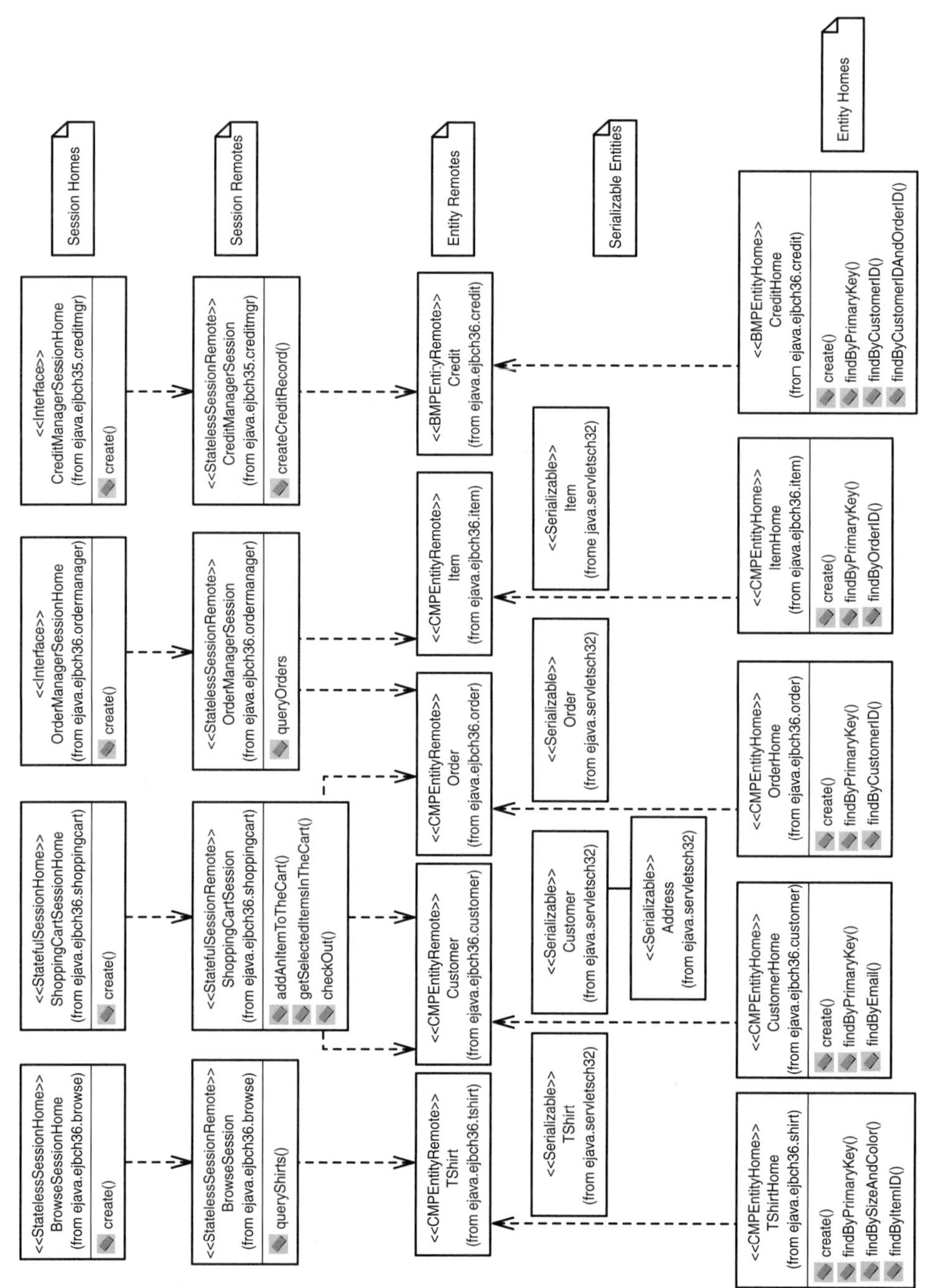

FIGURE 36.3

BeeShirts.com EJBs.

You'll note from Figure 36.3 that we depict only EJB home and remote objects in this diagram, along with a collection of `Serializable` entity objects from Chapter 32's code base. The session beans in the diagram represent the primary client interfaces to the BeeShirts.com EJB application. All entity beans are accessed behind the wall of session beans. Any data from an entity bean returned to the client is returned in the form of an associated `Serializable` entity object using classes from Chapter 32. Such a design helps reduce the number of client references to distributed entity objects, which can become too excessive for applications that need to scale. The BeeShirts.com EJBs and their helper objects are described here:

- `TShirt`: A container-managed persistence entity bean that encapsulates T-shirt data and provides a mechanism to read T-shirt image data as bytes from the server's file system. This EJB is defined by a `TShirt` remote interface, a `TShirtHome` home interface, and a `TShirtEJBean` implementation. Chapter 32's `Serializable TShirt` object is also used to encapsulate T-shirt result data sent back to an EJB client.
- `Item`: A container-managed persistence entity bean encapsulating item data from the database. This EJB is defined by an `Item` remote interface, `ItemHome` home interface, and `ItemEJBean` implementation. Chapter 32's `Serializable Item` object is also used to encapsulate item result data sent back to an EJB client.
- `Customer`: A container-managed persistence entity bean encapsulating customer and address data from the database. This EJB is defined by a `Customer` remote interface, `CustomerHome` home interface, and `CustomerEJBean` implementation. Chapter 32's `Serializable Customer` and `Address` objects are also used to encapsulate customer result data sent back to an EJB client.
- `Credit`: A bean-managed persistence entity bean encapsulating credit data from the database. This EJB is defined by a `Credit` remote interface, `CreditHome` home interface, `CreditEJBean` implementation, `CreditPrimaryKey` primary key class, `CreditDefinition` helper interface of schema constant names, and `CreditDBAccess` helper class that performs the actual database access calls.
- `Order`: A container-managed persistence entity bean encapsulating order data from the database. This EJB is defined by an `Order` remote interface, `OrderHome` home interface, and `OrderEJBean` implementation. Chapter 32's `Serializable Order` object is also used to encapsulate order result data sent back to an EJB client.
- `BrowseSession`: A stateless session bean with a `queryShirts()` method to manage the query for `TShirt` information via the `TShirt` entity bean and to map this data into a collection of `Serializable TShirt` objects to be returned to the client. This EJB is defined by a `BrowseSession` remote interface, `BrowseSessionHome` home interface, and `BrowseSessionEJBean` implementation.

- CreditManagerSession: A stateless session bean (from Chapter 35, "Application Servers and Enterprise JavaBeans") with a createCreditRecord() method to manage the insertion of credit information into the database by first consulting an ejava.ejbch36.credit.CreditManagerHandler, which in turn utilizes the Credit entity bean to perform the actual database insert. This EJB is defined by a CreditManagerSession remote interface, a CreditManagerSessionHome home interface, a CreditManagerSessionEJBean implementation, and a CreditManagerHandler helper class.
- ShoppingCartSession: A stateful session bean encapsulating the information associated with a user shopping session at BeeShirts.com. The addAnItemToTheCart() method is used to add selected T-shirt item identifiers to the user's shopping-cart state. The getSelectedItemsInTheCart() method is used to retrieve TShirt entity beans associated with the T-shirt item identifiers, convert their data into Serializable TShirt objects, and then return these Serializable objects in a collection. The checkout() method creates an Order entity bean entry, converts the user's T-shirt items stored in the session to Serializable TShirt objects, retrieves the associated user's Customer entity bean, and adds Serializable TShirt and Customer information to a Serializable Order object returned to the client. This EJB is defined by a ShoppingCartSession remote interface, ShoppingCartSessionHome home interface, and ShoppingCartSessionEJBean implementation.
- OrderManagerSession: A stateless session bean providing a queryOrders() method that first retrieves any Order entity beans associated with the customer, retrieves Item entity beans associated with those orders, retrieves TShirt entity beans associated with those items, and then creates a collection of Serializable Order objects containing Serializable Order and TShirt data to be returned to the client. This EJB is defined by an OrderManagerSession remote interface, OrderManagerSessionHome home interface, and OrderManagerSessionEJBean implementation.

NOTE

Each Chapter 36 sample BeeShirts.com EJB has its own directory under the examples\src\ejava\ejbch36 directory. Within each subdirectory, an ejb-jar.xml file is used as a standard EJB deployment descriptor, a sun-j2ee-ri.xml provides J2EE reference implementation–specific properties, and weblogic-ejb-jar.xml provides BEA WebLogic–specific properties. A weblogic-cmp-rdbms.xml file may be provided as well for BEA WebLogic–specific container-managed persistence bean properties.

continues

Within each Chapter 36 subdirectory exists a sample `buildj2ee.bat` script and `buildweblogic.bat` script for building each bean for the J2EE reference implementation and BEA WebLogic Server, respectively. A `buildj2eeall.bat` script and `buildweblogicall.bat` script are also provided in the `examples\src\ejava\ejbch36` directory; these call all `buildj2eejar.bat` or `buildweblogic.bat` scripts in each EJB directory and induce the deployment of the beans to the J2EE reference implementation and BEA WebLogic Server, respectively.

Each Chapter 36 bean directory also has a sample standalone EJB client named `TestClient`. A `runJ2EEClient.bat` and `runWebLogicClient.bat` file build and execute the `TestClient` for use with EJBs deployed to the J2EE reference implementation and BEA WebLogic Server, respectively. When using the `buildj2eeall.bat` script to deploy all EJBs to the J2EE reference implementation server, a special `runJ2EEClientWithAll.bat` script in each EJB directory can be used to build and execute the `TestClient` to test the associated EJB deployed along with the other beans on the server.

The only exception to all of these conventions for this chapter are the EJB client script file names and J2EE application client XML deployment descriptor file names added to the `examples\src\ejava\ejbch36\creditmgr` directory. These file names follow the naming convention for the credit manager EJB as defined in Chapter 35 but are modified here to enable the `CreditManagerSession` EJB to now talk with the database via the `CreditManagerHandler` introduced in this chapter.

Note that you may have copied an `orb.properties` file to your `[JAVA_HOME]\jre\lib` directory if you have installed the standard RMI/IIOP extension per the instructions of Chapter 16, "RMI Communications." This `orb.properties` file must be removed in order to properly run the J2EE reference implementation server. Refer to Appendix A for more details.

EJB Configuration and Deployment Basics

As explained in Chapter 5, "Java Enterprise System Architecture with the J2EE," and illustrated in Chapters 32 and 33, J2EE enterprise applications are composed of one or more individual J2EE modules. J2EE modules have deployment descriptors specific to the module type, and J2EE enterprise applications also have their own deployment descriptor format. We explored the J2EE enterprise application deployment descriptor format in Chapter 31, "XML," and the J2EE Web application module deployment descriptor in Chapter 32. In this chapter we introduce the EJB application module deployment descriptor. In this section we introduce the basics for understanding EJB deployment descriptors, deployed archives, and deployment procedures.

EJB Deployment Descriptor Top-Level Elements

J2EE EJB application module deployment descriptors are defined in XML files named ejb-jar.xml. Because configuring EJB deployment descriptors is more involved than configuring Web component deployment descriptors, we take a slightly different tack in describing the format and use of the EJB deployment descriptor. We in fact describe elements of the EJB deployment descriptor as they become relevant to the topic at hand throughout this chapter and the next chapter. We thus carve out pieces of the XML EJB module DTD and describe them as the elements they define become relevant. The top-level elements of an EJB deployment descriptor, shown in Listing 36.1, are containers used to define EJB application meta-data, EJB structure, assembly information, and the archive filename for any EJB client files.

LISTING 36.1 EJB DTD Top-Level Elements

```
<!-- The root element of EJB deployment for a single EJB JAR file. -->
  <!ELEMENT ejb-jar (description?, display-name?, small-icon?,
                     large-icon?, enterprise-beans, assembly-descriptor?,
                     ejb-client-jar?)>
<!-- Generally used to describe its containing element -->
  <!ELEMENT description (#PCDATA)>
<!-- Generally used as a name for display by tools. -->
  <!ELEMENT display-name (#PCDATA)>
<!-- A name for a small 16x16 pixel GIF or JPG file. -->
  <!ELEMENT small-icon (#PCDATA)>
<!-- A name for a large 32x32 pixel GIF or JPG file. -->
  <!ELEMENT large-icon (#PCDATA)>
<!-- Container for one or more entity and session bean descriptors. -->
  <!ELEMENT enterprise-beans (session | entity)+>
<!-- Contains definitions for security and transaction semantics
associated with the application in the ejb-jar file.
NOTE: We describe these elements in more detail in Chapter 37. -->
  <!ELEMENT assembly-descriptor (security-role*, method-permission*,
                                container-transaction*)>
<!-- Specifies a JAR file URL containing the client stub and interface
classes needed by EJB clients to use the EJBs in this ejb-jar file. -->
  <!ELEMENT ejb-client-jar (#PCDATA)>
```

EJB application module deployment descriptors defined according to the preceding top-level format must also include a standard DOCTYPE definition referencing the standard DTD. The basic top-level structure of an EJB deployment descriptor thus follows the sample form shown here:

```
<!DOCTYPE ejb-jar PUBLIC "-//Sun Microsystems, Inc.//
➥DTD Enterprise JavaBeans 1.1//EN"
➥ "http://java.sun.com/j2ee/dtds/ejb-jar_1_1.dtd">
```

```
<ejb-jar>
  <description> This is my BeeShirts.com EJB Application </description>
  <display-name> BeeShirts.com Application Service </display-name>
  <small-icon> beeshirtsSmall.jpg </small-icon>
  <large-icon> beeshirtsLarge.jpg </large-icon>
  <enterprise-beans>
    <session> ... </session>
    <session> ... </session>
    <entity> ... </entity>
    <entity> ... </entity>
      ...
  </enterprise-beans>
  <assembly-descriptor>
    ...
  </assembly-descriptor>
  <ejb-client-jar> beeshirtsClient.jar </ejb-client-jar>
</ejb-jar>
```

EJB JAR Files

An EJB JAR file represents the deployable JAR library that contains the server-side code and configuration of the EJB module. During deployment, the `ejb-jar.xml` file is placed under the `META-INF` directory of the EJB JAR file. Any entity and session beans defined within the `ejb-jar.xml` file must have the `.class` files for their implementations, home interfaces, remote interfaces, and any dependent classes archived inside of the EJB JAR file. As you'll see later in this chapter, the `ejb-jar.xml` file can be used to define references to other EJBs in other EJB JAR files from EJBs defined in the current EJB JAR file. If the `Class-Path` attribute in the EJB JAR file's `Manifest.mf` file includes any auxiliary EJB JAR file library URLs, then the current EJB JAR file does not need to include any EJB client stubs or interfaces from any associated auxiliary EJBs that its EJBs are dependent on.

Any client stub and interface classes needed to access the EJBs in a particular EJB JAR file can be placed in a separate EJB client JAR file. The URL of this EJB client JAR file can then be specified in the `ejb-jar.xml` file's `<ejb-client-jar>` element. Any EJB clients of the EJBs in the associated server-side EJB JAR file can then automatically receive downloaded interface and stub classes as they are needed if the EJB client's class loader can reach the URL defined within the `<ejb-client-jar>` element. If no automatic class downloading mechanism is supported or used by the client, the EJB client JAR libraries should be installed on the EJB client's machine.

EJB Deployment Procedures

As presented initially in Chapter 32, the process for deploying J2EE applications involves establishing environment variables, configuring server properties, compiling Java code, creating XML-based deployment descriptors, packaging archive files, and deploying archives to a J2EE server environment. We focus on the deployment of our J2EE-based EJB applications in this section. Appendix A, "Software Configuration," provides detailed instructions for how to install and perform the basic configuration of both a J2EE reference implementation server and a BEA WebLogic Server used to deploy our J2EE-based EJB applications. However, the general procedure for deploying J2EE-based EJB applications assumes the following general steps:

1. *Set J2EE Server Environment Variables*: Environment variables must be set for running a J2EE server environment and will vary per vendor implementation and operating-system platform. For example, we set root installation directories for the J2SE (`J2SE_HOME`), J2EE reference implementation (`J2EE_HOME`), and BEA WebLogic Server (`WEBLOGIC_HOME`) as described in Appendix A.
2. *Configure J2EE Server Properties*: Configuration properties for most J2EE server implementations can be set to suit your particular network and operating environment.
3. *Compile J2EE EJB Application Code*: All J2EE EJB implementation, home, remote, and dependent utility code must be compiled using a standard Java compiler.
4. *Create a J2EE EJB Application Deployment Descriptor*: An XML-based deployment descriptor is created according to the EJB application DTD defined throughout this chapter and the next chapter. We include an EJB application deployment descriptor for each individual BeeShirts.com EJB on the CD in the file named `ejb-jar.xml` per EJB. Many products create this file for you from a GUI-based configuration tool.
5. *Create Vendor-Specific Deployment Descriptors*: Because no standard means exists to bind J2EE standard EJB reference names to a J2EE server's JNDI-based naming service, a vendor-specific deployment descriptor mechanism is required to perform this mapping. This deployment descriptor must map EJB reference names used by J2EE components to the actual JNDI names associated with EJB home interfaces. Other vendor-specific properties may also be set for customizing both session and entity beans. Vendors often provide a GUI-based means to configure these files.
6. *Package J2EE EJB Application Code*: The EJB deployment descriptors, all compiled J2EE EJB implementation classes, all compiled J2EE EJB implementation interfaces, and all other compiled classes dependent on your EJBs need to be packaged into an EJB JAR file with a `.jar` extension. J2EE-based products may supply command-line and/or GUI-based utilities for this purpose.

7. *Start the J2EE Server*: The J2EE-compliant server must generally be started or already be started at this stage. The exact mechanism for starting a server is often vendor dependent but can be as simple as invoking a single startup command from the command line.
8. *Create a J2EE Application Deployment Descriptor*: A J2EE application deployment descriptor must be created to collect one or more Web, EJB, and application client modules into a cohesive J2EE application. Many products will create this file for you automatically or via a GUI-based configuration tool.
9. *Package J2EE Application Code*: The application and JNDI mapping deployment descriptor, Web applications, EJB applications, and application clients need to be packaged into an enterprise archive (EAR) file with a `.ear` extension. Many products also create this archive for you automatically or via GUI-based development tools.
10. *Deploy the J2EE Enterprise Application Code*: Finally, the integrated J2EE application is deployed to the J2EE server environment for access by enterprise application clients. This step is also often automated via GUI tools.

J2EE Reference Implementation Server Startup and Deployment

The procedure for starting and actually deploying EJB-based applications is almost identical to the procedure described for Java Servlets in Chapter 32. The J2EE reference implementation server is invoked with the `[J2EE_HOME]\bin\j2ee` command as usual. A `buildj2ee.bat` file included on the CD in the directory for each sample EJB of this chapter provides a Windows-based sample script for compiling and packaging J2EE EJBs on an individual basis. A `buildj2eeall.bat` file is also equipped with the CD in the root source code directory for this chapter; it provides a Windows-based sample script to call all individual `buildj2eejar.bat` files, packages the EJBs into an integrated enterprise application, and deploys the enterprise application.

The `buildj2ee.bat` and `buildj2eejar.bat` files use the J2EE `packager` tool to create an EJB application module given individual `ejb-jar.xml` deployment descriptors and target EJB JAR filenames. The packager tool follows the most basic syntax for creating EJB JAR files as shown here:

```
[J2EE_HOME]\bin\packager -ejbJar [root_dir]
➥ [classFileList] ejb-jar.xml ejbJarFileName.jar
```

The `[root_dir]` specifies an optional root directory from which all files are referenced, and `[classFileList]` specifies a colon-separated list of class files to include in the resulting `ejbJarFileName.jar` EJB JAR file.

We also use the packager tool to create J2EE application EAR files from these EJB JAR files. Each buildj2ee.bat file creates an EAR file for testing an individual EJB and the buildj2eeall.bat file creates an EAR file containing all of the EJBs. The packager tool command used for creating EAR files given our collection of EJB JAR filenames follows the same format as described in Chapter 32. Specifically, the packager command for creating EARs follows this form:

```
[J2EE_HOME]\bin\packager -enterpriseArchive
➥ ejbFileName.jar:[otherArchiveFiles]
➥ ApplicationName earApplicationFileName.ear
```

Although many folks may use the J2EE reference implementation's GUI-based deploytool to create properly packaged enterprise applications, we use the command-line utilities here to make explicit those steps that take place in building EJB applications. We thus also must provide a special vendor-specific sun-j2ee-ri.xml file that maps JNDI versions of the EJB names to the standard EJB names. This file also is used to configure certain aspects of session and entity beans specific to the J2EE reference implementation container.

As a last step, our sample buildj2ee.bat scripts and the buildj2eeall.bat script also spawn the deploytool to deploy the EJBs according to the following general command form:

```
[J2EE_HOME]\bin\deploytool -deploy earFileName.ear
➥serverHostName [optionalEJBClientJarFileName.jar]
```

BEA WebLogic Server Startup and Deployment

We also demonstrate how to use the BEA WebLogic Server as an enterprise class server capable of deploying J2EE-based EJB applications. Each EJB sample directory for this chapter also contains a special buildweblogic.bat file for building EJB application modules for deployment to the BEA WebLogic Server. Each script first compiles all Java classes and then copies the ejb-jar.xml file under the META-INF directory created below a special temporary WebLogic build directory. Special WebLogic-specific configuration and deployment parameters are defined in a weblogic-ejb-jar.xml file for all beans and a weblogic-cmp-rdbms-jar.xml file for entity beans. These descriptor files are also copied to the META-INF directory.

The buildweblogic.bat file then creates a standard JAR file out of all compiled classes and XML deployment descriptor files and subsequently calls a special WebLogic Server weblogic.ejbc program to create the EJB JAR file. The weblogic.ejbc program is a Java program that creates all necessary client- and server-side stubs, skeletons, and delegates for the EJB classes. The format for running weblogic.ejbc can be found at http://www.weblogic.com/docs50/classdocs/API_ejb/EJB_reference.html. The basic format of weblogic.ejbc used with our examples is shown here:

```
[JAVA_HOME]\bin\java -classpath [CLASSPATH]
                     -Dweblogic.home=[WEBLOGIC_HOME]
                      weblogic.ejbc
                     -compiler javac
                     [build_directory]\standardJarFileName.jar
                     [WEBLOGIC_HOME]\myserver\EJBJarFileName.jar
```

The `[CLASSPATH]` value after the `-classpath` flag specifies those class files and libraries to use during compilation with the Java compiler defined after the `-compiler` flag. The location and filename of the standard JAR file previously built with your compiled EJB classes and interfaces must also be provided on the command line (that is, `[build_directory]\standardJarFileName.jar`) along with the desired location and filename for the EJB JAR file to be created by `weblogic.ejbc` (that is, `[WEBLOGIC_HOME]\myserver\EJBJarFileName.jar`).

The individual `buildweblogic.bat` files can be invoked from this chapter's sample root directory using the `buildweblogicall.bat` file. Before deploying the beans, each EJB JAR file location and name must also be added to the `weblogic.properties` file's `weblogic.ejb.deploy` property. The BEA WebLogic Server can then be started using the `[WEBLOGIC_HOME]\startweblogic.cmd` command script. Appendix A describes the general configuration procedures for the BEA WebLogic Server.

J2EE Test Client Startup

We also include a `TestClient` Java file in each EJB directory on the CD. Each `TestClient` runs as a standalone EJB client to demonstrate the basic invocation of the EJBs with which it is associated. To start the `TestClient` for use with the J2EE reference implementation, the `runJ2EEClient.bat` sample script can be used, which simply invokes a Java startup command along these lines:

```
[JAVA_HOME]\bin\java -Dorg.omg.CORBA.ORBInitialHost=localhost
➥ -Djava.naming.factory.initialValue
➥=com.sun.enterprise.naming.SerialInitContextFactory
➥ [client package name].TestClient
```

The `runJ2EEClientWithAll.bat` file can also be used to start the `TestClient` application to test an EJB when it is deployed along with all other EJBs developed in this chapter.

A standalone EJB client to BEA WebLogic–based EJB servers may be started using the `runWebLogicClient.bat` file in each EJB directory. These scripts start the `TestClient` with a command along these lines:

```
[JAVA_HOME]\bin\java -Djava.naming.provider.url=t3://localhost:7001/
➥ -Djava.naming.factory.initial
➥=weblogic.jndi.WLInitialContextFactory
➥ -classpath [CLASSPATH] [client package name].TestClient
```

Session Bean Server Components

Session beans are EJB components designed to perform some action on the enterprise system on behalf of the client. Session beans are often designed to serve as the entry points or "front-line" EJBs for EJB clients. EJB clients interact with session beans in order to be provided with the functional behavior and services of the enterprise system that the clients desire to utilize. This section describes how to create session bean component implementations that adhere to the EJB component-container model contract that enables them to operate inside of an EJB container to expose its services to session bean clients.

We specifically present the rules and approach for building both stateless and stateful session beans in this section. Stateless session bean components are implemented assuming that no state will be maintained for a particular client between subsequent invocations on that bean over time. Stateless session bean implementations thus provide pure input-output request and response behavior for their clients. Stateful session beans assume that a client may revisit the same bean instance later and that the state preserved for that bean relates to a particular client's prior interaction with the bean. Stateful session bean implementations thus provide a stateful object interaction behavior to be utilized within the request and response behavior provided to their clients. The state of a session bean specifically relates to the values that a session bean object's field variables can assume, along with the state assumed by any objects referenced from the session bean.

Stateless Session Beans

Stateless session beans are designed not to require the preservation of state within the EJB that is specific to a particular EJB client. This does not imply that the EJB does not actually maintain any state within its fields or associated objects. However, it does imply that the state it maintains is not required to be accessed or utilized for a specific EJB client later. It also implies that the state is not important for access by another client later.

Such a designation allows an EJB container some flexibility in maximizing the efficiency in management of such EJBs. Because use of stateless session bean components implies that any of their instances created by the container can be used by any client at any time, the container can maintain a pool of such instances that are allocated to clients on an as-needed basis without regard to which instance belongs to which client. Containers can also easily create and destroy bean instances as needed to adjust for scalability and resource demands. Thus, although stateless session beans can have state, no assumptions are to be made by the programmer about the validity of that state between successive uses of that bean instance. EJB containers may create, destroy, and allocate stateless session beans for use as they please.

Stateless Session Bean Logical Component Architecture

Figure 36.4 depicts the basic architecture involved in creating stateless session bean components. At the top of the diagram, we have the `javax.ejb.EnterpriseBean` marker interface,

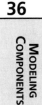

which is the base interface for all EJBs. The `EnterpriseBean` interface is extended by the `javax.ejb.SessionBean` interface, which is required to be implemented by all session EJB classes. Public, nonfinal, and non-abstract stateless session bean EJBs, such as `MyStatelessSessionEJBean` as shown in the diagram, must implement the `SessionBean` interface. Stateless session bean EJBs implement public, nonfinal, and nonstatic business-specific methods, such as `someMethod()` and `anotherMethod()` shown in the diagram. Session bean implementations must also have a public parameterless constructor and should not implement the `finalize()` method.

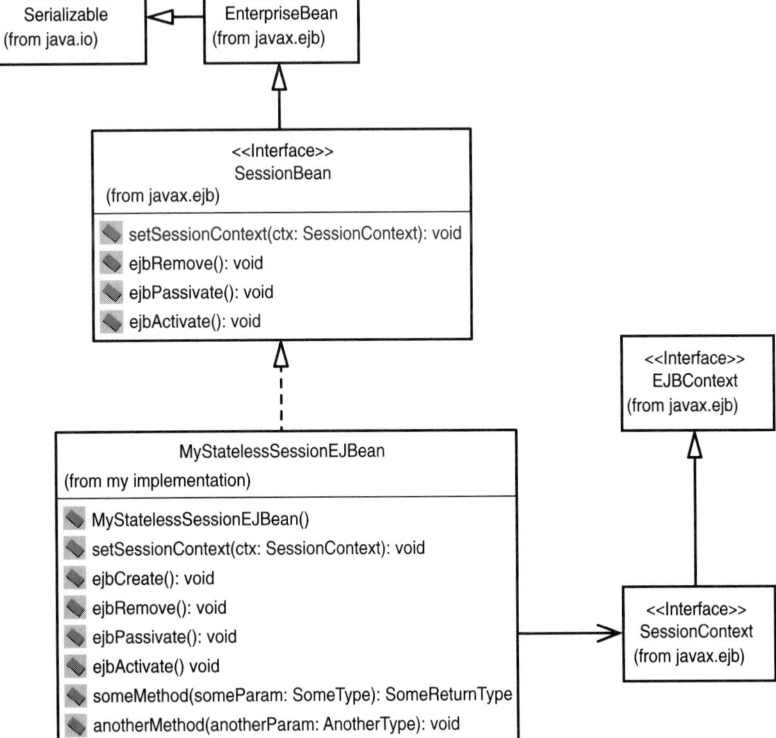

FIGURE 36.4
Stateless session EJBs.

Stateless Session Bean Context Setting

The `setSessionContext()` method defined on a stateless session bean is used to pass an instance of a `SessionContext` object to the EJB. It is also the first method defined on the `SessionBean` interface that is called by the container. A `SessionContext` object encapsulates an interface to the EJB session container context. The `SessionContext` interface extends a more generic EJBContext interface and provides hooks for session beans to access client interfaces to the EJB, transaction information, and security information. We have more to say about client interfaces later in this chapter and discuss EJB transactions and security in the next chapter.

Stateless Session Bean Creation and Removal

A key operation required by a custom stateless session bean, such as MyStatelessSessionEJBean, but not defined within the SessionBean interface is the ejbCreate() method. A single public, nonfinal, nonstatic, and parameterless ejbCreate() method must be defined on stateless session bean implementations with a void return type. This method is called by the EJB container when the container decides to create an instance of the stateless session EJB. The container may decide to do this when it wants to create an initial pool of bean instances, or it may do this when it receives a client's request. The ejbCreate() method is thus akin to a special type of constructor or initialization method implemented by EJBs.

The ejbRemove() method is called by a container on a session bean object when the container is about to decommission the bean instance from handling any more client requests. For stateless session beans, the container is solely responsible for determining when it will call ejbRemove() on a particular session bean instance. It is not bound in any way to the EJB client.

Stateless Session Bean Passivation and Activation

Because no assumptions are made about the importance of state in a stateless session bean, there is no assumed need to passivate and activate stateless session beans. That is, containers do not assume that a stateless session bean must close any open resources when it is to be removed from active memory (that is, passivated) and do not need to re-create any connections to open resources when brought back into active memory from persistent memory (that is, activated). Thus, the implementations for ejbPassivate() and ejbActivate() methods for stateless session beans are often simple empty implementations.

Stateless Session Bean Component Interface Rules Summary

The life cycle of a stateless session bean is thus implied by the methods it must support. The life cycle of a stateless session bean as managed by its EJB container proceeds according to these basic guidelines:

1. *Instantiate EJB*: The container calls Class.newInstance() with the name of your EJB to create a new instance of the stateless session bean when the container decides it is necessary.
2. *Set Context*: The container calls setSessionContext() on the EJB with a container managed SessionContext object.
3. *Call* ejbCreate(): The container then calls ejbCreate() on the EJB.
4. *Add EJB to Pool*: The container may now add the EJB to a pool of stateless session beans.

5. *Delegate Client Calls*: The container delegates EJB client calls on the stateless session bean to a stateless session bean instance it selects from a pool. Calls are delegated from a distributed skeleton layer to the actual EJB implementation object.
6. *Call* `ejbRemove()`: The container calls `ejbRemove()` on the EJB when it wants to destroy the stateless session bean that sits in the pool.

Stateless session beans are thus extremely simple EJBs to create. An EJB applications developer needs to worry only about implementing the rather simple `SessionBean` interface and creating business-specific methods. The standard operations of concern are the `setSessionContext()`, parameterless `ejbCreate()`, `ejbRemove()`, empty `ejbPassivate()`, and empty `ejbActivate()` methods. Stateless session bean implementations must simply receive a request via one of their business-specific methods, implement some functionality when that method is invoked, and return any response via any return type from that method call.

EJB containers for stateless session beans take care of the actual bean's instance creation and destruction, as well as determining when to allocate the bean to a client request. The container ensures that only one thread associated with a client's request is allocated to execute a bean instance's method at any instant in time. Containers are required to propagate a `java.rmi.RemoteException` to any clients that attempt to access a particular session bean when it is being accessed by another client instance. Although properly designed EJB clients will not ever be in such a situation, the container at least protects the integrity of your server-side component against such breaches of client etiquette.

Stateless Session Bean Example

The `CreditManagerSessionEJBean` presented in Chapter 35 was the first EJB presented in this book and was an example of a stateless session bean. Listing 36.2 presents another stateless session bean example in the form of those core snippets from the `BrowseSessionEJBean` implementation of a stateless session bean that are germane to our discussion here. The complete code listing is found on the CD. No standard `ejbXXX()` methods are needed for this bean, but a public `queryShirts()` method is provided for business-specific logic.

NOTE

EJB v1.1 deprecates (but still supports) the need to specify the throwing of `java.rmi.RemoteException` objects from EJB implementations. EJB home and remote interfaces must still specify that `RemoteException` objects may be thrown, however. While the BeeShirts.com EJB examples in this book are EJB v1.1 and J2EE v1.2 compliant, the EJB implementations still specify `RemoteException` objects to be thrown by our EJB implementations akin to the EJB v1.0 requirement. The new `javax.ejb.EJBException` should actually be thrown by pure EJB v1.1 implementations that need to throw system level exceptions.

LISTING 36.2 Stateless Session Bean Example (`BrowseSessionEJBean.java`)

```
package ejava.ejbch36.browse;

  ...// import statements excluded...

public class BrowseSessionEJBean implements SessionBean
{
  private SessionContext sessionContext;
  private TShirtHome tshirtHome; // Not specific to client session state

  // Standard interfaces
  public void setSessionContext(SessionContext aCtx)
  {
    sessionContext = aCtx;
  }
  public void ejbCreate(){ /* no creation logic */ }
  public void ejbRemove(){ /* no removal logic */ }
  public void ejbPassivate(){ /* no state persistence */ }
  public void ejbActivate(){ /* no state activation */ }

  /** Finds the TShirt Home Object...not specific to a client session */
  private void lookupTShirtHome() throws NamingException { ... }

  /** Find TShirt entity beans and create Serialized versions */
  public Vector queryShirts(String size, String color)
    throws RemoteException
  {
    // Create collections for entity beans and serialized objects
    Enumeration queriedShirts = null;
    Vector returnedShirts = new Vector();

    try{
      // First create TShirt Home object handle and set tshirtHome
      lookupTShirtHome();

      // Find a collection of TShirt entity beans in the database
      queriedShirts = tshirtHome.findBySizeAndColor(size, color);

      // While cycling through TShirt entity object collection...
      while(queriedShirts.hasMoreElements()){
        // Get TShirt entity bean
        ejava.ejbch36.tshirt.TShirt beanShirt =
          (ejava.ejbch36.tshirt.TShirt)queriedShirts.nextElement();

        // Create Serialized TShirt object from entity bean data
```

```
            ejava.servletsch32.TShirt clientShirt =
                new ejava.servletsch32.TShirt(
                  beanShirt.getID().intValue(),
                  beanShirt.getSize(),beanShirt.getColor(),
                  beanShirt.getDesignFront(),beanShirt.getDesignBack(),
                  beanShirt.getPictureFront(),beanShirt.getPictureBack(),
                  beanShirt.getUnitPrice());

            // Add the TShirt object to a return vector
            returnedShirts.addElement(clientShirt);
          }
        }

        ... // exception handling excluded here...

        // Return the Vector of Serialized TShirt objects
        return returnedShirts;
    }
}
```

The `BrowseSessionEJBean.queryShirts()` method first looks up a reference to the `TShirt` entity bean home interface from within `lookupTShirtHome()` and then uses that interface to query for a collection of `TShirt` entity beans that match the shirt size and color query parameters. We describe how to build entity beans later in the chapter, but suffice it to say that an `Enumeration` of `TShirt` entity bean remote interface objects is returned. For each entity bean in the `Enumeration`, the `queryShirts()` method creates an associated `Serializable TShirt` object instance and returns a `Vector` of these `Serializable TShirt` objects to the client.

Stateful Session Beans

Stateful session beans are session beans that preserve some state within the EJB specifically associated with its EJB client. The state (*aka* conversational state) of a stateful session bean refers to the data stored within the fields (that is, variables) of the bean instance, as well as within any objects the bean holds and those objects' fields and objects, and so on. When an EJB client accesses a stateful session bean at one instant and changes the state of the bean instance, that state must be preserved and assumed by the bean instance at some later instant in which the bean is accessed.

By creating a session bean that is stateful, the container must assume more responsibility and care in how it manages the bean, as opposed to the case with stateless session beans. For one, stateful session bean instances are associated with clients that create them and therefore cannot simply be plucked at random from a pool to service client requests. In fact, the creation and removal of a stateful session bean by a client is directly related to the creation and removal of stateful session bean instances on the server side. Furthermore, when resources become limited, a container may decide to serialize (*aka* passivate) one or more stateful session beans to persistent storage. As resources become available or perhaps upon client request, the passivated bean must be activated and brought into active memory. Thus, stateful session beans require additional special design considerations on the part of the bean developer.

Stateful Session Bean Logical Component Architecture

Figure 36.5 depicts the basic architecture involved in creating stateful session bean components. Public, nonfinal, and nonabstract stateful session bean implementations, such as `MyStatefulSessionEJBean`, must implement the `SessionBean` interface, which in turn extends the `EnterpriseBean` interface. Stateful session EJBs also implement public, nonfinal, and nonstatic business-specific methods, such as the `someMethod()` and `anotherMethod()` sample methods shown in the diagram. As a final note, session bean implementations must also have a public parameterless constructor and should not implement the `finalize()` method. Finally, stateful session beans may optionally implement the `javax.ejb.SessionSynchronization` interface to enable the bean to be notified of certain transaction management events. We defer discussion of most EJB transaction management issues until Chapter 37, "Advanced Enterprise JavaBeans Serving."

Stateful Session Bean Creation and Removal

Because state is important for stateful session beans, the initial state in which such a bean is created may be important. Thus, stateful session beans can be defined with one or more public, nonfinal, and nonstatic `ejbCreate(...)` methods that take zero or more input parameters and return a `void` type. The exact parameters that are passed into such methods are application specific, but the name of the method must be `ejbCreate`. Unlike the `ejbCreate()` invocation on a stateless session bean, stateful session bean `ejbCreate()` methods are bound to the EJB client that will continue to use that specific EJB instance. Note also that the container calls `setSessionContext()` on the stateful session bean before any `ejbCreate()` method is called, as was the case with the stateless session bean.

The invocation of an `ejbRemove()` method implemented by a session bean indicates that the client to which this session belongs has prevented the stateful session bean from servicing any more requests. The container may also invoke `ejbRemove()` on a bean when a configurable session maximum timeout has expired. However, because there is no guarantee that `ejbRemove()` will always be called in the event of a server failure or after certain critical exceptions, an auxiliary method to periodically attempt the cleanup of any unclosed resources may need to be provided by the applications developer.

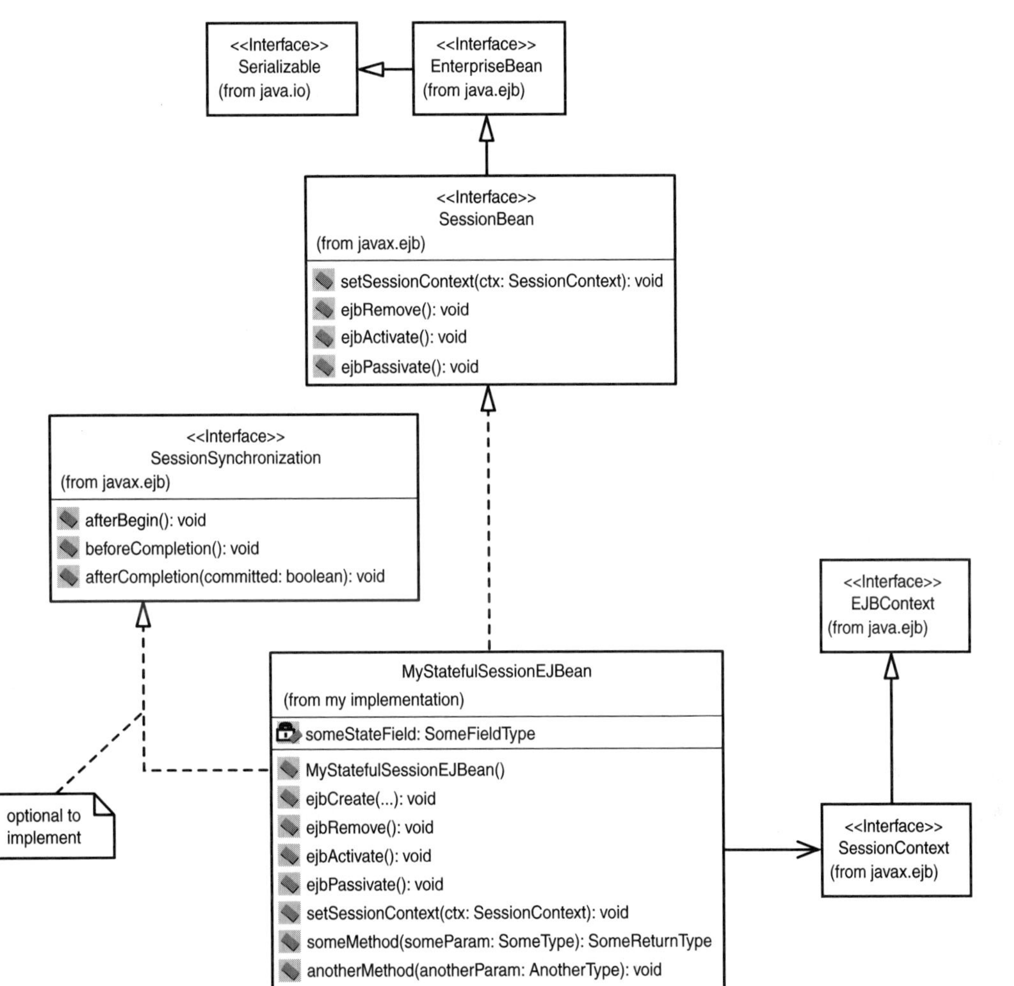

FIGURE 36.5
Stateful session EJBs.

Stateful Session Bean Passivation and Activation

Perhaps the most significant thing to consider when designing a stateful session bean are the ramifications of passivation and activation on your bean. As we stated earlier, a container passivates your session bean by serializing its contents and writing this information to some persistent storage mechanism. A container does this when active memory resources are becoming scarce and usually employs some sort of least recently used algorithm to determine which specific bean instances should be passivated (although the actual algorithm used is vendor specific). Before a container passivates your bean instance, it will call `ejbPassivate()` on your bean, which your bean must implement.

The implementation of `ejbPassivate()` must clean up any resources that cannot be serialized and persisted, such as database connections and open file handles. Any objects that remain unclosed after `ejbPassivate()` completes must be passivatable by the container. Passivatable objects include fundamental types, `Serializable` objects, objects set to null, or a collection of special enterprise Java object references. The special enterprise Java object references that are passivatable and that must also not be specified as transient objects in a session bean are EJB home and remote references, JNDI and session contexts, and `UserTransaction` references.

When a request for a passivated bean is made or perhaps when resources are again freed up, the container will activate the bean. That is, the container will deserialize the persisted state of the bean and reconstruct the bean in active memory with the state in which it was originally persisted. After the bean state is reconstructed, the container will call `ejbActivate()` on the stateful session bean implementation, which should reconstruct any resources that were closed during the call to `ejbPassivate()`. Alternatively, if a certain amount of time has expired while the bean was in persistent storage, the vendor may elect to remove the bean from persistent storage given some configurable time limit.

Stateful Session Bean Component Interface Rules Summary

Much like the stateless session bean, the life cycle of a stateful session bean is also implied by the methods it must support. However, because of its stateful nature, issues such as passivation and activation must be considered by the container. We present the basic guidelines that a container for a stateful session bean must consider (sans transaction management) here:

1. *Instantiate EJB*: The container calls `Class.newInstance()` with the name of your EJB to create a new instance of the stateful session bean when the EJB client induces the creation of such a bean.
2. *Set Context*: The container calls `setSessionContext()` on the EJB with a container-managed `SessionContext` object.
3. *Call* `ejbCreate(...)`: The container then calls the appropriate `ejbCreate(...)` on the EJB depending on the call that the EJB client used to create the EJB instance.
4. *Add EJB to Cache*: The container may now cache the stateful session EJB.
5. *Delegate Client Calls*: The container delegates EJB client calls to the stateful session bean whose reference is associated with the client. Calls from a client pass from client stub to the container's skeleton representation of the EJB and then to the EJB implementation itself.

6. *Call* `ejbPassivate()`: The container may decide to passivate the stateful session bean according to some container-specific policy (for example, least recently used algorithm). The container first calls `ejbPassivate()` and then serializes the state of the session bean to persistent storage.
7. *Retire Passive Beans*: The container may remove from persistent storage a session bean that has been passivated for an amount of time exceeding some configurable limit.
8. *Call* `ejbActivate()`: The container will activate any passivated beans when a client attempts to access such beans. Activated beans are brought from persistent storage into the active cache memory. The container first deserializes the state of the session bean and then calls `ejbActivate()` on the bean.
9. *Call* `ejbRemove()`: The container calls `ejbRemove()` on the EJB when the client attempts to remove the bean.

Stateful session beans thus require more design considerations than do stateless session beans. Aside from implementing the `SessionBean` interface, a collection of `ejbCreate(...)` methods can be specified to provide initial state to the bean. Furthermore, passivation and activation must be taken into consideration when defining the field objects of a stateful session bean, as well as when implementing the `ejbPassivate()` and `ejbActivate()` methods. Finally, as is the case for stateless session beans, EJB containers for stateful session beans ensure that only one thread associated with an EJB client request is allocated to e XEcute a bean instance's method at any moment in time.

Stateful Session Bean Example

Listing 36.3 presents a stateful session bean example in the form of those core snippets from the `ShoppingCartSessionEJBean` implementation of a stateful session bean that specifically relate to our discussion here. The complete code listing is found on the CD. Most standard `ejbXXX()` methods are not needed for this bean. An `ejbCreate(Hashtable)` method is defined, however, to populate the session bean with initial shopping-cart data. Furthermore, the `addAnItemToTheCart()`, `getSelectedItemsInTheCart()`, and `checkOut()` public business-specific methods do contain component logic and will be exposed to EJB clients.

LISTING 36.3 Stateful Session Bean Example (`ShoppingCartSessionEJBean.java`)

```
package ejava.ejbch36.shoppingcart;

  ... // import statements excluded here...

public class ShoppingCartSessionEJBean implements SessionBean
{
```

continues

LISTING 36.3 Continued

```
private SessionContext sessionContext;
private TShirtHome tshirtHome; // non-client specific state
private OrderHome orderHome; // non-client specific state
private ItemHome  itemHome; // non-client specific state
private CustomerHome customerHome; // non-client specific state
private Hashtable itemsInTheCart; // Client specific state!

private static final long FIVE_DAYS = 432000000;
private static final long THIRTY_DAYS = FIVE_DAYS*6;

// Standard interfaces
public void setSessionContext(SessionContext aCtx)
{
  sessionContext = aCtx;
}
public void ejbCreate(){ /* no creation logic */ }
public void ejbRemove(){ /* no removal logic */ }
public void ejbPassivate(){ /* no state persistence */ }
public void ejbActivate(){ /* no state activation */ }
public void ejbCreate(Hashtable initialCart) // Initial cart data
{
  itemsInTheCart = initialCart;
}

/** Look up TShirt Home object and set tShirtHome */
private void lookupTShirtHome() throws NamingException {...}

/** Look up Item Home and set itemHome*/
private void lookupItemHome() throws NamingException {...}

/** Look up Customer Home object and set customerHome */
private void lookupCustomerHome() throws NamingException {...}

/** Look up Order Home object and set orderHome */
private void lookupOrderHome() throws NamingException {...}

/** Add a particular item identified by ID and quantity to session */
public void addAnItemToTheCart(int shirtID, int quantity)
{
  // If no Hashtable created make one
  if(itemsInTheCart == null){
    itemsInTheCart = new Hashtable();
  }
  try{
```

```
    // Put the item ID and quantity into Hashtable (session state)
    itemsInTheCart.put(new Integer(shirtID), new Integer(quantity));
  }
  catch(Exception exception){
    exception.printStackTrace();
  }
}

/** For each item in session, return Vector of associated TShirts */
public Vector getSelectedItemsInTheCart()
  throws RemoteException
{
  // Create return Vector
  Vector  returnItemsInTheCart = new Vector();

  // For each ID in Hashtable (session state)
  Enumeration shirtIDs = itemsInTheCart.keys();
  while(shirtIDs.hasMoreElements()){
     Integer shirtID = (Integer)shirtIDs.nextElement();
     Integer quantity = (Integer)itemsInTheCart.get(shirtID);

    try{
      // Create TShirt Home object and set in tShirtHome
      lookupTShirtHome();
      // Find an associated TShirt entity bean
      ejava.ejbch36.tshirt.TShirt beanShirt
          = tshirtHome.findByPrimaryKey(shirtID);
      // Create and initialize a Serializable TShirt object
      //    with data from TShirt entity bean.
      ejava.servletsch32.TShirt clientShirt =
          new ejava.servletsch32.TShirt(
            beanShirt.getID().intValue(),
            beanShirt.getSize(),beanShirt.getColor(),
            beanShirt.getDesignFront(),beanShirt.getDesignBack(),
            beanShirt.getPictureFront(),beanShirt.getPictureBack(),
            beanShirt.getUnitPrice());
       clientShirt.setQuantity(quantity.intValue());
       clientShirt.setTotalPrice(
             quantity.intValue()*beanShirt.getUnitPrice());
       // Add Serializable TShirt object to return vector
       returnItemsInTheCart.addElement(clientShirt);
    }
    catch(NamingException namingException){
```

continues

LISTING 36.3 Continued

```
        namingException.printStackTrace();
      }
      catch(FinderException finderException){
        finderException.printStackTrace();
      }
    }

    // Return Vector of Serializable TShirt objects
    return returnItemsInTheCart;
  }

  /** Create an Order entity bean, get items from cart session,
      create relation to orders in Item entity beans, create
      Serialized TShirt for cart, look up Customer entity bean,
      create Serialized Order with Serialized Customer and
      TShirt object info. */
  public ejava.servletsch32.Order checkOut(int customerID)
    throws RemoteException { ...  }

  /** Helper method to get Serialized Customer based on
     Customer entity data. */
  private ejava.servletsch32.Customer getCustomer(int customerID)
    throws RemoteException { ... }

  /** Helper method to get a maximum order ID based on max ID in DBMS */
  private int getNextOrderID() { ... }

  /** Helper method to create an Item entity bean for each item
      in the cart session along with order ID information */
  private void createItemOrderRelationInDatabaseForSelectedItems(
      Integer orderID, Vector itemsSelected) { ... }

  /** Helper method to get a maximum item ID based on max ID in DBMS */
  private int getNextItemID() { ... }
}
```

The state variable of interest to clients in this example is the `Hashtable` variable called `itemsInTheCart`. The `addAnItemToTheCart()` method adds an entry to the `itemsInTheCart` `Hashtable` given an item ID and quantity. A subsequent call to the bean instance by a client on a method such as `getSelectedItemsInTheCart()` will utilize the `itemsInTheCart Hashtable`. After the `TShirt` entity bean is looked up based on each item ID in the `itemsInTheCart Hashtable`, a `Serializable TShirt` object is created and added to a `Vector` returned to the client. The `checkout()` method (not listed in Listing 36.3) also uses the stateful `itemsInTheCart Hashtable` by creating an `Order` entity bean and returning a `Serializable Order` object based on the items that have been added to the client's shopping-cart information stored in the `itemsInTheCart`.

Session Bean Client Interfaces

Now that we have seen how to build session bean components on the server side, let's explore how clients can tap the services provided by these components. Two main types of interfaces exist for client interfacing to a session bean: a session bean home interface and a session bean remote interface. The session bean home interface is used primarily as a factory to create references to session bean objects. The session bean remote interface then provides the client-side interface to the distributed session bean object's application-specific operations. Additionally, both home and remote interfaces provide a means to destroy client object references.

We describe how to build such interfaces and how clients access these interfaces in this section. We also describe the slightly different rules and semantics that exist for defining and using these interfaces as applied to both stateless and stateful session beans. Many of the concepts and abstractions described here also apply to entity bean interfacing, and we describe those similarities and the differences in a subsequent section.

Session Bean Remote Interfaces

A session bean remote interface defines the set of application-specific distributed operations that can be invoked on a particular session bean. Remote interfaces describe the client's view of the EJB akin to the way RMI remote interfaces describe the client's view of an RMI server. In fact, remote interfaces are essentially defined using RMI semantics and can be used with RMI/JRMP and RMI/IIOP. A CORBA mapping to such interfaces also exists, as we discuss in the next chapter. This section describes how to build and use session bean remote interfaces.

Session Bean Remote Interface Logical Architecture

Figure 36.6 depicts the basic logical architecture for building and using remote EJB client interfaces to distributed session EJBs. All application-specific interfaces to distributed EJB objects, such as `MySessionEJB` shown in the diagram, must extend the `javax.ejb.EJBObject` interface. `EJBObject` in turn extends `java.rmi.Remote`, which adds the distributed RMI semantics to remote EJB interfaces. Under the hood, remote interfaces make use of some container-provided stub implementation on the client side that handles the marshaling of calls to the distributed server-side skeleton. Skeletons in turn delegate calls to the actual server-side EJB component implementation such as the `MySessionEJBean` shown in the diagram. Runtime EJB containers are ultimately responsible for managing which bean instance is used and how calls are routed on the server side, but the result is that calls from an EJB client to application-specific EJB remote interface methods ultimately result in the invocation of an associated application-specific method on the server-side EJB component instance.

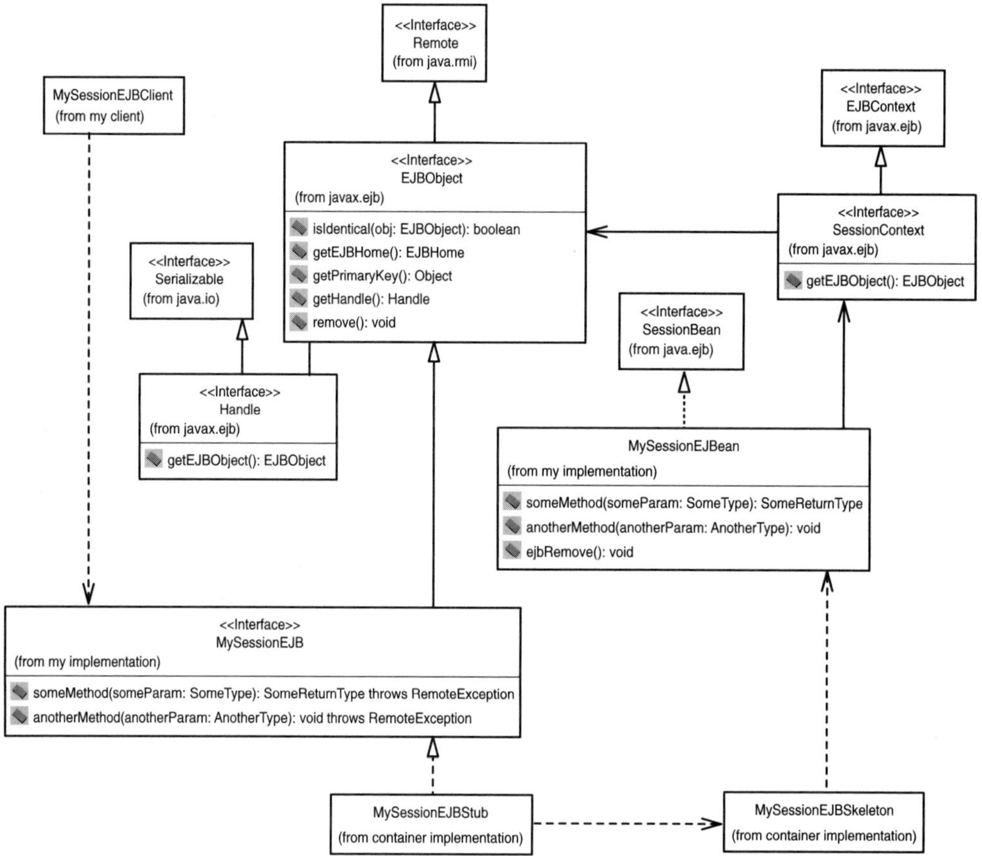

FIGURE 36.6
The session bean remote interface architecture.

Session Bean Application-Specific Remote Interfaces

An application-specific remote EJB interface must be created for each EJB component. This interface provides the distributed interface usable by EJB clients to invoke the application-specific logic of EJB components. For each distributable application-specific method on an EJB server-side component, such as `MySessionEJBean.someMethod()`, an associated application-specific method must be defined on the EJB client-side remote interface, such as `MySessionEJB.someMethod()`. As a side effect of their distributable nature, each method in the application-specific remote interface should also declare that it can throw a `java.rmi.RemoteException`. Of course, such rules apply only to those server-side component methods you want to be made distributable.

Session Bean Generic Remote Interfaces

In addition to application-specific interfaces on an EJB remote interface, a set of methods inherited from `EJBObject` can be invoked on a remote EJB object. In situations in which clients want to determine whether one remote EJB object is identical to another, the `EJBObject.isIdentical()` method can be called. The `EJBObject.getEJBHome()` method returns a handle to the home interface object that is used to create remote interface objects. Because session EJBs do not have primary keys, calling `EJBObject.getPrimaryKey()` on a remote interface for a session bean will result in a `RemoteException` being thrown.

The `EJBObject.getHandle()` method returns an object that implements the `javax.ejb.Handle` interface. The `Handle` object represents a persistent reference to a distributed remote EJB object. Because the `Handle` object is serializable, it can be serialized and persisted by the client and then reactivated later to obtain a reference to the remote EJB object via the call to `Handle.getEJBObject()`.

The `EJBObject.remove()` method is used by clients to destroy their reference to the remote EJB object. This method definitively destroys EJB object resources only on the client side. Containers will call `ejbRemove()` on a server-side stateful session bean instance when such a call is made. However, the invocation of `remove()` from the client side on a remote stateless session bean object does not induce the container to invoke `ejbRemove()` on a server-side bean instance because containers reuse stateless session bean instances for different client invocations.

As a final note, on the server side, a session bean can obtain a reference to an `EJBObject` with which it is associated by calling `getEJBObject()` on its `SessionContext` object. Bean components may want to obtain such a reference for use as input or output parameters in their application-specific methods. Be aware of the fact, however, that the `EJBObject` will be valid only between the time when `ejbCreate()` is called and the time when `ejbRemove()` is called on the bean instance. Also be aware that direct access to `EJBObject` references should be passed around with care. This is because no more than one client thread can utilize a single server-side bean instance at a time lest it induce a `RemoteException`. Thus, EJB server objects should pass around `EJBObject` instances that have been bound to server-side bean instances only when they can be certain that one client will utilize the `EJBObject` reference at a time.

Session Bean Remote Interface Examples

The remote interfaces of properly designed session beans should naturally imply the stateless or stateful session of the bean for an application. Our `BrowseSession` remote interface shown in Listing 36.4 defines the single distributable operation exposed by the `BrowseSessionEJBean` described in Listing 36.2. Note that no state to be maintained by the bean is implied by the very nature of its business-specific semantics. This stateless session bean call thus simply takes input from a client and returns output.

LISTING 36.4 Stateless Session Bean Remote Interface Example (`BrowseSession.java`)

```
package ejava.ejbch36.browse;

import javax.ejb.EJBObject;
import java.rmi.RemoteException;
import java.util.Enumeration;
import java.util.Vector;

public interface BrowseSession extends EJBObject
{
  /** Return Vector of Serializable TShirt objects
      based on queried shirt size and color */
  public Vector queryShirts(String size, String color)
    throws RemoteException;
}
```

The `ShoppingCartSession` remote interface, shown in Listing 36.5, relates to the distributed interfaces provided by the `ShoppingCartSessionEJBean` presented in Listing 36.3. Note that statefulness is implied by the application-specific business logic of these methods. Thus, a stateful session bean was indeed best suited for this bean implementation.

LISTING 36.5 Stateful Session Bean Remote Interface Example (`ShoppingCartSession.java`)

```
package ejava.ejbch36.shoppingcart;

import javax.ejb.EJBObject;
import java.rmi.RemoteException;
import java.util.Vector;

public interface ShoppingCartSession  extends EJBObject
{
  /** Add an item to this shopping session with an ID and quantity */
  public void addAnItemToTheCart(int shirtID , int quantity)
    throws RemoteException;
  /** Obtain a Vector of Serializable TShirt objects for the
      items stored in this shopping session */
  public Vector getSelectedItemsInTheCart()
    throws RemoteException;
  /** Check out of this shopping session by creating and returning
      an order for the items associated with this shopping session. */
  public ejava.servletsch32.Order checkOut(int customerID )
    throws RemoteException;
}
```

Session Bean Home Interfaces

Session bean clients use home interfaces to create initial references to session beans as well as remove these references. These references are, of course, implemented via the remote session bean interface objects. Clients should always use home interfaces to create references to EJBs because these provide the container with the opportunity it needs to manage how to allocate EJB bean instance resources. Furthermore, if a client bypasses use of home interfaces and uses an `EJBObject` handle retrieved via some other means, such as via a JNDI lookup, it runs the risk of causing a threading problem. This is again because no more than one client thread can utilize a single server-side bean instance.

Session Bean Home Interface Logical Architecture

Figure 36.7 depicts the architecture behind creating session bean home interfaces and how clients may use these interfaces. JNDI is used to obtain handles to application-specific EJB home interface objects, such as `MySessionEJBHome`, which must extend the standard `javax.ejb.EJBHome` interface. Application-specific EJB home interface objects are also implemented on the client side by stubs, which communicate with server-side skeletons, and the container, which creates, destroys, and delegates calls to session bean instances as appropriate. Home interfaces can also be used for persisting their handles for later reconstruction and for obtaining meta-data about the EJBs that they serve to create.

Session Bean Home Object Lookup

An EJB client must first obtain a handle to an EJB's home interface when it wants to create a new reference to the EJB. This task is accomplished via JNDI. Clients that operate inside of a J2EE container environment can utilize the default parameterless constructor of the `InitialContext` object and simply look up a handle to an EJB's home interface with a call to `InitialContext.lookup()`. The J2EE container handles establishing the system properties that should be assumed by the `InitialContext` object. The name passed to an `InitialContext.lookup()` can refer to an `<ejb-ref>` element in the client's XML-based deployment descriptor. The `<ejb-ref>` element defines the reference name that will be used in creating the name passed to `InitialContext.lookup()`, the type of EJB being referenced, the home information, the remote information, and the linking information as defined in Listing 36.6.

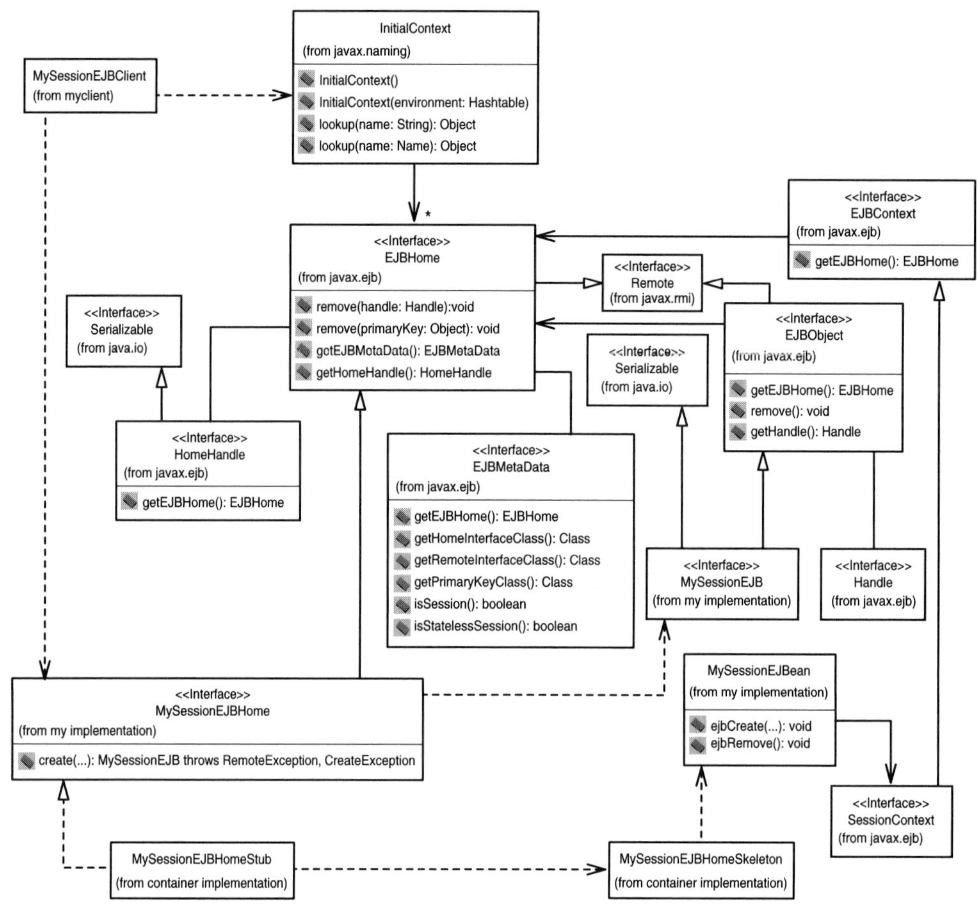

FIGURE 36.7

The session bean home interface architecture.

LISTING 36.6 EJB Reference DTD Elements

```
<!-- Serves to define a reference to an EJB from this J2EE component -->
  <!ELEMENT ejb-ref (description?, ejb-ref-name, ejb-ref-type, home,
                     remote, ejb-link?)>
<!-- Provides name to refer to an EJB typically prefixed with "ejb/" -->
  <!ELEMENT ejb-ref-name (#PCDATA)>
<!-- Specifies the type of referenced EJB: Entity, Session -->
  <!ELEMENT ejb-ref-type (#PCDATA)>
<!-- Specifies an ejb-name of an EJB to which this reference is
linked. The other EJB may be in the same JAR file or in another
JAR file which is in the same J2EE enterprise application. -->
  <!ELEMENT ejb-link (#PCDATA)>
```

As an example, our `ejb-jar.xml` file associated with the `ShoppingCartSessionEJBean` defines a reference to the `TShirt` EJB as shown here:

```
<ejb-jar>
    ...
  <enterprise-beans>
    <session>
        ...
      <ejb-ref>
         <ejb-ref-name>ejb/tshirt</ejb-ref-name>
         <ejb-ref-type>Entity</ejb-ref-type>
         <home>ejava.ejbch36.tshirt.TShirtHome</home>
         <remote>ejava.ejbch36.tshirt.TShirt</remote>
      </ejb-ref>
      ...
    </session>
  </enterprise-beans>
    ...
</ejb-jar>
```

Thus, our `ShoppingCartSessionEJBean` acts as an EJB client to the `TShirt` EJB and looks up a reference to the `TShirt` EJB's home interface object from within its `lookupTShirtHome()` helper method like this:

```
  /** Look up TShirt Home object */
  private void lookupTShirtHome()
    throws NamingException
  {
    if(tshirtHome == null){
      InitialContext context = new InitialContext();
      Object tshirtHomeRef =  context.lookup(EJBHelper.TSHIRT_REFNAME);
      tshirtHome = (TShirtHome)PortableRemoteObject.narrow(tshirtHomeRef,
        ejava.ejbch36.tshirt.TShirtHome.class);
      context.close();
    }
  }
```

TIP

Note that the use of the `javax.rmi.PortableRemoteObject.narrow()` call on returned home and remote interface objects helps guarantee maximum interoperability with all EJB container/server implementations, as opposed to simply casting returned objects. Containers using RMI/IIOP in particular require that returned objects be narrowed rather than cast by the client.

The name used for the lookup should prefix `java:comp/env/` to the name specified in the `<ejb-ref-name>` element for the client. The `EJBHelper.TSHIRT_REFNAME` value previously shown is defined within `ejava.ejbch36.EJBHelper` in this way:

```
public static String TSHIRT_REFNAME = "java:comp/env/ejb/tshirt";
```

EJB clients that operate outside of a J2EE container environment also use JNDI to create an `InitialContext` as described in Chapter 35. In fact, all the `TestClient` classes associated with each EJB in this chapter operate as a standalone EJB client. The `TestClient` associated with the `BrowseSession` EJB looks up a handle to the `BrowseSessionHome` object as shown here:

```
Context context = new InitialContext();
Object objectRef =
 context.lookup(EJBHelper.BROWSE_SESSION_HOME);

BrowseSessionHome browseSessionHome =
    (BrowseSessionHome)PortableRemoteObject.narrow(objectRef,
                     ejava.ejbch36.browse.BrowseSessionHome.class);
```

In the preceding snippet, system properties for the `InitialContext()` are assumed to have been defined during the launching of the `TestClient`. The `EJBHelper.BROWSE_SESSION_HOME` value previously shown is defined within `ejava.ejbch36.EJBHelper` as shown here:

```
public static String BROWSE_SESSION_HOME = "BrowseSessionHome";
```

Such standalone clients must use the JNDI name for the registered EJB home interface. Because this is container specific, it is extracted from a vendor-specific property file. The J2EE reference implementation's `sun-j2ee-ri.xml` file is used to configure such a value by mapping the `<jndi-name>` element that defines the JNDI name for the EJB home object to the `<ejb-name>` element that relates to an associated `<ejb-name>` element in an `ejb-jar.xml` file. The J2EE reference implementation mapping is shown next:

```
<j2ee-ri-specific-information>
   ...
  <enterprise-beans>
    <ejb>
      <ejb-name>BrowseSessionEJB</ejb-name>
      <jndi-name>BrowseSessionHome</jndi-name>
      ...
    </ejb>
  </enterprise-beans>
</j2ee-ri-specific-information>
```

A similar mapping is required for BEA WebLogic in the `weblogic-ejb-jar.xml` file as shown here:

```
<weblogic-ejb-jar>
    <weblogic-enterprise-bean>
```

```
      <ejb-name>BrowseSessionEJB</ejb-name>
         ...
      <jndi-name>BrowseSessionHome</jndi-name>
    </weblogic-enterprise-bean>
</weblogic-ejb-jar>
```

Session Bean Application-Specific Home Interfaces

A series of one or more `create(...)` methods are defined on the custom home interface to represent the different ways in which the associated EJB can be created. A single `create(...)` method must be defined on the home interface for each `ejbCreate(...)` method defined on the EJB implementation. Each version of a `create(...)` method returns an instance of the EJB's remote interface (for example, `MySessionEJB`) and contains zero or more input parameters related to the specific types of initialization parameters needed by the associated `ejbCreate(...)` methods. Each `create(...)` method must also be defined to throw a `java.rmi.RemoteException` and `javax.ejb.CreateException`. Additionally, each `create(...)` method must be defined to throw any application-specific exceptions that have been defined for its associated `ejbCreate(...)` method.

Because stateless session beans define only one parameterless `ejbCreate()` method, stateless session bean home interfaces can define only one parameterless `create()` method. Invoking `create()` on stateless session beans only induces a container to pull a bean instance from the pool and does not necessarily cause the container to call `ejbCreate()` on the bean at that moment. However, stateful session beans do induce the container to call `ejbCreate(...)` on a bean instance with any parameters passed into an associated home interface `create(...)` method.

Session Bean Generic Home Interfaces

As you saw in the preceding section, after a handle to an EJB object is obtained, a client can invoke `EJBObject.remove()` to release its hold on a particular session EJB. Clients can also call `remove(Handle)` inherited from `EJBHome` by the home interface object. The `Handle`, of course, needs to relate to the particular `EJBObject` that is to be removed. The specific rules for removal of stateless and stateful session beans are the same here as they were when `EJBObject.remove()` was being called. The `EJBHome.remove(Object)`, which takes a primary key as a parameter, is not valid for session home objects and will throw a `RemoteException` when invoked.

Much like an `EJBObject` object can persist its reference in a `Handle` object, `EJBHome` objects can persist their references in `javax.ejb.HomeHandle` objects. A call to `EJBHome.getHomeHandle()` will return this `Serializable` `HomeHandle` object. When a `HomeHandle` is persisted and later brought into active memory, the `HomeHandle.getEJBHome()` call can be used to return a reference to the reconstructed `EJBHome` object.

The EJBHome.getEJBMetaData() method is called to obtain a handle to a javax.ejb.EJBMetaData object, which provides a mechanism for clients to discover certain information about an EJB. EJBMetaData.getEJBHome() simply returns a reference to the home interface again. The getHomeInterfaceClass() and getRemoteInterfaceClass() methods return Class objects associated with the EJB's home and remote interfaces, respectively. The getPrimaryKeyClass() is useful only for entity beans. Finally, the isSession() method can be used to determine whether the EJB is a session bean or an entity bean if the method returns false, and the isStatelessSession() can be used to determine whether the EJB is a stateless session bean. If isSession() returns true and isStatelessSession() returns false, you may assume that the EJB is a stateful session bean.

As a final note, on the server side, a session bean can obtain a reference to an EJBHome object with which it is associated by calling getEJBHome() on its SessionContext object (as inherited from EJBContext). Bean components may want to obtain such a reference for the creation of their own beans.

Session Bean Home Interface Examples

The home interfaces of session beans are typically simple interfaces. Our BrowseSessionHome home interface shown in Listing 36.7 defines only a single parameterless create() method because it is a stateless session bean.

LISTING 36.7 Stateless Session Bean Home Interface Example (BrowseSessionHome.java)

```
package ejava.ejbch36.browse;

import javax.ejb.EJBHome;
import javax.ejb.CreateException;
import java.rmi.RemoteException;

public interface BrowseSessionHome extends EJBHome
{
  /** Parameterless creation of session bean */
  BrowseSession create() throws CreateException, RemoteException;
}
```

The ShoppingCartSessionHome remote interface shown in Listing 36.8 defines a parameterless create() method that results in the invocation of ShoppingCartSessionEJBean.ejbCreate(). A create(Hashtable) method is also defined to provide initial shopping-cart state to the ShoppingCartSessionEJBean.ejbCreate(Hashtable) method.

LISTING 36.8 Stateful Session Bean Home Interface Example (ShoppingCartSessionHome.java)

```
package ejava.ejbch36.shoppingcart;

import javax.ejb.EJBHome;
import javax.ejb.CreateException;
import java.rmi.RemoteException;

public interface ShoppingCartSessionHome  extends EJBHome
{
  /** Create session bean with default initial state */
  public ShoppingCartSession create()
    throws CreateException, RemoteException;
  /** Create session bean with initial shopping cart data */
  public ShoppingCartSession create(java.util.Hashtable initialCart)
    throws CreateException, RemoteException;
}
```

Session Bean Configuration and Deployment

Previously in the chapter, we introduced the basic top-level structure of an EJB application module deployment descriptor. The root <ejb-jar> element contained an <enterprise-beans> element, which could in turn contain a collection of <session> elements. Each <session> element is used to describe the configuration and deployment of an individual session bean. The <session> bean element DTD structure, shown in Listing 36.9, defines session bean meta-data, a unique name in the EJB JAR file, the bean's class and interface names, the type of session bean, configuration parameters, references to other EJBs and database connections, security semantics, and a transaction flag.

LISTING 36.9 EJB DTD Session Bean Elements

```
<!-- Container used to describe an individual session bean. -->
  <!ELEMENT session (description?, display-name?, small-icon?,
                     large-icon?, ejb-name, home, remote, ejb-class,
                     session-type, transaction-type, env-entry*,
                     ejb-ref*, security-role-ref*, resource-ref*)>
<!-- A description of the session bean -->
  <!ELEMENT description (#PCDATA)>
<!-- Description of the session bean's displayable name. -->
  <!ELEMENT display-name (#PCDATA)>
```

continues

LISTING 36.9 Continued

```
<!-- A name for a small 16x16 pixel GIF or JPG file. -->
  <!ELEMENT small-icon (#PCDATA)>
<!-- A name for a small 32x32 pixel GIF or JPG file. -->
  <!ELEMENT large-icon (#PCDATA)>
<!-- Specifies the name of an EJB unique to its ejb-jar file.
The code and JNDI names are independent from this name. -->
  <!ELEMENT ejb-name (#PCDATA)>
<!-- Fully qualified class name of the EJB home interface. -->
  <!ELEMENT home (#PCDATA)>
<!-- Fully qualified class name of the EJB remote interface. -->
  <!ELEMENT remote (#PCDATA)>
<!-- Fully qualified class name of the EJB implementation. -->
  <!ELEMENT ejb-class (#PCDATA)>
<!-- Specifies type of session bean: Stateful, Stateless -->
  <!ELEMENT session-type (#PCDATA)>
<!-- The Transaction management type: Bean, Container -->
  <!ELEMENT transaction-type (#PCDATA)>
<!-- Declares an environment configuration parameter for
a J2EE application environment. -->
  <!ELEMENT env-entry (description?, env-entry-name,
                      env-entry-value?, env-entry-type)>
<!-- Defines the name of an environment entry parameter. -->
  <!ELEMENT env-entry-name (#PCDATA)>
<!-- Defines the value of an environment entry. -->
  <!ELEMENT env-entry-value (#PCDATA)>
<!-- Defines a fully qualified Java type for a particular environment
value. Acceptable values are: java.lang.Boolean, java.lang.String,
java.lang.Integer, java.lang.Double, java.lang.Float -->
  <!ELEMENT env-entry-type (#PCDATA)>
<!-- Serves to define a reference to another EJB from this EJB. -->
  <!ELEMENT ejb-ref (description?, ejb-ref-name, ejb-ref-type, home,
                    remote, ejb-link?)>
<!-- Provides a name to refer to another EJB typically
prefixed with "ejb/" -->
  <!ELEMENT ejb-ref-name (#PCDATA)>
<!-- Specifies the type of referenced EJB: Entity, Session -->
  <!ELEMENT ejb-ref-type (#PCDATA)>
<!-- Specifies an ejb-name of another EJB to which this reference is
linked. The other EJB may be in the same ejb-jar file or in another
ejb-jar file which is in the same J2EE enterprise application. -->
  <!ELEMENT ejb-link (#PCDATA)>
<!-- This value is used within the EJB to reference
a particular secure role using a EJB security role-name. -->
  <!ELEMENT security-role-ref (description?, role-name, role-link)>
```

```
<!-- The EJB security role-name. -->
  <!ELEMENT role-name (#PCDATA)>
<!-- Defines the role-name of a security role specified in one of the
security-role elements. -->
  <!ELEMENT role-link (#PCDATA)>
<!-- Defines a reference to an external resource (e.g. database). -->
  <!ELEMENT resource-ref (description?, res-ref-name, res-type,
                         res-auth)>
<!-- Defines the name of the resource factory. -->
  <!ELEMENT res-ref-name (#PCDATA)>
<!-- Defines the fully qualified Java type of the data source. -->
  <!ELEMENT res-type (#PCDATA)>
<!-- Indicates if the bean performs authentication to a resource
or if the container performs authentication: Application, Container -->
  <!ELEMENT res-auth (#PCDATA)>
```

As an example, the session-related elements of our stateful `BrowseSession` bean's `ejb-jar.xml` file are shown in Listing 36.10. You'll note that in addition to standard meta-data and structural information about the EJB, it has defined `<ejb-ref>` elements for all the EJBs it accesses as a client to those beans. It also defines a `<resource-ref>` element to a data-source connection, as we describe in the next section.

LISTING 36.10 Example of EJB Session Bean Deployment Descriptor Information

```
<?xml version="1.0" encoding="UTF-8"?>

<!DOCTYPE ejb-jar PUBLIC '-//Sun Microsystems, Inc.//
➥DTD Enterprise JavaBeans 1.1//EN'
➥ 'http://java.sun.com/j2ee/dtds/ejb-jar_1_1.dtd'>

<ejb-jar>
  <description>no description</description>
  <display-name>CartJar</display-name>
  <enterprise-beans>
    <session>
      <description/>
      <display-name>ShoppingCartSessionEJB</display-name>
      <ejb-name>ShoppingCartSessionEJB</ejb-name>
      <home>ejava.ejbch36.shoppingcart.ShoppingCartSessionHome</home>
      <remote>ejava.ejbch36.shoppingcart.ShoppingCartSession</remote>
      <ejb-class>
        ejava.ejbch36.shoppingcart.ShoppingCartSessionEJBean
```

continues

LISTING 36.10 Continued

```
        </ejb-class>
        <session-type>Stateful</session-type>
        <transaction-type>Container</transaction-type>
        <ejb-ref>
           <ejb-ref-name>ejb/tshirt</ejb-ref-name>
           <ejb-ref-type>Entity</ejb-ref-type>
           <home>ejava.ejbch36.tshirt.TShirtHome</home>
           <remote>ejava.ejbch36.tshirt.TShirt</remote>
        </ejb-ref>
        <ejb-ref>
           <ejb-ref-name>ejb/item</ejb-ref-name>
           <ejb-ref-type>Entity</ejb-ref-type>
           <home>ejava.ejbch36.item.ItemHome</home>
           <remote>ejava.ejbch36.item.Item</remote>
        </ejb-ref>
        <ejb-ref>
           <ejb-ref-name>ejb/order</ejb-ref-name>
           <ejb-ref-type>Entity</ejb-ref-type>
           <home>ejava.ejbch36.order.OrderHome</home>
           <remote>ejava.ejbch36.order.Order</remote>
        </ejb-ref>
        <ejb-ref>
           <ejb-ref-name>ejb/customer</ejb-ref-name>
           <ejb-ref-type>Entity</ejb-ref-type>
           <home>ejava.ejbch36.customer.CustomerHome</home>
           <remote>ejava.ejbch36.customer.Customer</remote>
        </ejb-ref>
        <resource-ref>
           <res-ref-name>jdbc/demoPool</res-ref-name>
           <res-type>javax.sql.DataSource</res-type>
           <res-auth>Container</res-auth>
        </resource-ref>
      </session>
  </enterprise-beans>
      ...
</ejb-jar>
```

Vendor-specific deployment descriptor files to configure and deploy session beans for both the J2EE reference implementation and the BEA WebLogic implementation are also needed and are provided with the examples on the CD. Developers will most often use GUI-based deployment tools provided by vendors to develop such files, but we wanted to explicitly provide you with a sense of what they contain with our sample code on the CD.

NOTE

No information on the J2EE reference implementation's `sun-j2ee-ri.xml` file was readily available at the time of this book's writing. The GUI-based deployment tool for the J2EE reference implementation is the same `deploytool` utility we have been using in command-line mode. The GUI version of the `deploytool` is simply invoked from the command line using `[J2EE_HOME]\bin\deploytool`.

For more information on the `weblogic-ejb-jar.xml` file format, see the WebLogic EJB reference manual at `http://www.weblogic.com/docs50/classdocs/API_ejb/EJB_reference.html`. BEA WebLogic also provides a GUI-based `weblogic.ejb.ui.deployer.DeployerTool` (executed as a Java application) described at `http://www.weblogic.com/docs50/classdocs/API_ejb/EJB_deploy.html`.

EJB and JDBC

The need to connect to databases from within EJB is clearly one of the more significant features of the EJB specification. All J2EE-based components may need to talk with a database, and J2EE provides support for this need via JDBC. Vendors such as Oracle and a future J2EE specification will allow the use of SQLJ to provide database connectivity. However, our primary approach advocated in this book and assumed here is the use of JDBC. J2EE-compliant environments provide access to the JDBC API and a convenient means for configuring JDBC resources via the XML-based deployment descriptor and for connecting to JDBC resources via JNDI.

NOTE

Many of the concepts discussed here with respect to database connectivity from EJB assume a basic understanding of such topics as SQL, JDBC, relational/object translations, and embedded SQL via SQLJ. We encourage you to review our coverage of these topics, primarily in Chapters 8 through 10, at this time if you are a little rusty on the associated concepts.

JDBC driver configuration and data-source identification are accomplished via the XML-based deployment descriptor for J2EE modules. The `<resource-ref>` element can be defined for individual J2EE EJB session and entity beans, J2EE servlets and JSPs, and J2EE application clients. Zero or more JDBC resources may be configured per EJB, servlet, JSP, or application client within the J2EE deployment descriptor.

As an example of JDBC resource configuration for entity EJBs as extracted from the `ejb-xml.jar` file for our BeeShirts.com `Credit` entity bean, we have this:

```
<ejb-jar>
  ...
  <enterprise-beans>
    ...
    <entity>
      ...
      <resource-ref>
         <res-ref-name>jdbc/ejavaPool</res-ref-name>
         <res-type>javax.sql.DataSource</res-type>
         <res-auth>Container</res-auth>
      </resource-ref>
    </entity>
    ...
  </enterprise-beans>
  ...
</ejb-jar>
```

Utilizing such a data source from within an entity bean is then a simple matter of looking up the named data source from within the EJB and obtaining a handle to a `javax.sql.DataSource` object. The `DataSource` object, as described in Chapter 10, "Advanced JDBC," can then be used to obtain a `java.sql.Connection` object. The underlying container is responsible for determining how this `Connection` object is to be allocated to your bean and will most likely maintain a pool of connections. From that point on, the bean can use the `Connection` object to create JDBC statements and obtain results as usual. For example, the `ejava.ejbch36.EJBHelper` class provides a method to return a `Connection` object using the configured `DataSource` reference as shown here:

```
public static String BEESHIRTS_DATA_SOURCE
                                = "java:comp/env/jdbc/ejavaPool";

/** Get database Connnection for BeeShirts.com data source */
public static Connection getDBConnection()
  throws SQLException,  NamingException
{
  // Create initial context
  InitialContext initialContext = new InitialContext();
  // Look up DataSource object
  DataSource dataSource = (DataSource)
        initialContext.lookup(EJBHelper.BEESHIRTS_DATA_SOURCE);
  // Request Connection object from pool managed by DataSource
  Connection connection = dataSource.getConnection();
  // Close context
```

```
    initialContext.close();
    // Return Connection object
    return connection;
}
```

Because bean-managed entity beans must manage their own connectivity to the database, a means for connecting to a database via Java must be employed. Although we use JDBC resources only from within a bean-managed persistence entity bean EJB in this chapter, JDBC resources can also be explicitly accessed from session beans, Java Servlets, and JSPs. Session bean access to JDBC resources configured inside of zero or more `<resource-ref>` elements is located within the `<session>` sub-element of the `<enterprise-beans>` element in an EJB deployment descriptor and within the `<web-app>` element in the Web deployment descriptor. However, we tend to stray away from direct access to enterprise data stored in databases from Java Servlets and JSPs as a general design philosophy to avoid security problems and to maintain the Web server tier as a scalable presentation layer. Inside of the application-serving tier, we also avoid any direct database access from within session EJBs because that is the primary role filled by entity EJBs. However, the option is still available, and the means by which such resources are configured and accessed is the same.

Entity Bean Server Components

An entity bean is a class that represents a logical classification of data in a database. An entity bean class contains fields that map to elements of a database schema definition. Entity bean fields most easily map directly to columns of a database table, and the entity bean itself may be likened to an actual database table. Relations among entity beans may thus be analogous to relations among tables. Views and table joins may also be likened to an entity bean with the elements of those data sources mapping to the fields of an entity bean class.

NOTE

Many of the concepts discussed here with respect to entity beans assume a basic understanding of SQL, JDBC, and relation/object translations. We encourage you to review our coverage of these topics in Chapters 8 through 10 at this time.

Entity bean instances that contain populated values within their fields correspond to an actual entry within a data source. Thus, an entity bean instance may correspond to a particular row within a table or perhaps be related to the single result of a table join query. For example, our `Customer` BeeShirts.com entity bean class that encapsulates a customer directly relates to a `CUSTOMER` table in our sample database. Fields of the `Customer` entity bean directly relate to columns of the `CUSTOMER` database. An instance of a `Customer` entity bean contains the data for a particular customer whose field values directly correspond to the column values in the `CUSTOMER` table for a row associated with that customer.

Entity bean components can be developed in one of two ways by developers. Bean-managed persistence (BMP) entity beans contain code (typically JDBC code) created by developers to manage all database inserts, deletions, querying, and updates associated with a particular entity bean. Container-managed persistence (CMP) entity beans are defined in such a way by developers that the EJB containers can automatically provide all the code required for managing all database inserts, deletions, querying, and updates associated with the entity bean. Developers opt to use BMP entity beans most often when their container does not support CMP entity beans, when a particular data source is too complex to enable effective CMP entity bean mapping, or when the developer desires more control over how the data should be managed. Otherwise, CMP entity beans can significantly reduce the amount of hand-coding required to data-enable enterprise applications. This section describes the concepts involved in entity beans in general, as well as describing the specific approaches to building both BMP and CMP entity bean components.

Entity Bean Pooling

A particular server-side instance from a container's point of view may not always correspond to a particular data-source entry (for example, a row in a table) at all times. Entity bean container implementations often pool a limited number of server-side entity bean instances belonging to the same type in order to preserve resources and provide a scalable EJB client base. When the number of entity bean instances exceeds some maximum value, the container may begin to passivate and persist the state of some instances in order to reuse those instances to populate them with the state of other data-source entries. Thus, from a container's perspective, server-side entity bean instances may be viewed as hosts for data from particular data-source entries. These server-side instances can be distinguished from the distributed client-side instance stubs for such entity beans, which are of course under the management of the client application.

How a container manages server-side entity bean instance pooling is very much transparent to the entity bean developer. An entity bean developer designs a bean under the assumption that any actions on the bean relate to the state it contains and therefore relate to a particular data-source entry to which that state maps. When properly designed and when adhering to the specified entity bean component interface contract, the container will manage when and how instances of entity beans actually get allocated to particular data-source entries throughout the operation of the system.

Primary Keys

Although EJB containers may pool entity beans and reuse server-side entity bean instances to encapsulate different data-source entries at different times, there must be a way to uniquely identify a particular data-source entry. If the client-side handle were to simply refer to the server-side entity bean instance directly, there would be no guarantee that the instance is actually related to the correct data-source entry given the EJB container instance pooling and reuse policies.

Entity beans thus utilize the concept of a primary key. A primary key uniquely identifies the data-source entry that is associated with a particular entity bean instance. That is, although a particular entity bean instance can be allocated with different data-source entry values at different times by a container, the primary key provides a way to identify the particular data-source entry that should underlie an entity bean instance. When EJB clients create or look up particular data-source entries using entity bean interfaces, the container then associates a primary key with the EJB entity bean handle(s) returned to the client. Thus, for example, if a customer entity bean has a customer first and last name that represents a primary key for a customer entity bean, those two values should uniquely identify a row in a customer table for the container. From the programmer's point of view, however, it maps to a unique entity bean instance.

Bean-Managed Persistence Entity Beans

This section describes how to build entity beans using BMP entity bean component semantics. Many of the concepts and techniques used here also apply to CMP entity beans. However, BMP entity beans, as you will see, require a significant amount of hand-coding. In a certain sense, there is not much difference between using BMP entity beans and creating homegrown JDBC-based components. The difference lies in how the implementation of such JDBC logic is encapsulated. Specifically, standard methods on a BMP entity bean imply which JDBC statement types should be created and processed. Additionally, BMP entity beans can inherit the declarative transactional and security aspects of EJBs, as we describe in the next chapter.

BMP Entity Bean Logical Component Architecture

Figure 36.8 introduces the basic elements needed to construct a BMP entity bean. Public, nonfinal, and nonabstract entity bean implementations, such as `MyBeanManagedEntityEJBean`, must implement the `javax.ejb.EntityBean` interface, which in turn extends the `EnterpriseBean` marker interface. The `EntityBean` interface defines a set of operations that must be implemented by an entity bean to support the life cycle management contract required by the EJB container. Bean-managed entity EJBs can also implement public, nonfinal, and nonstatic business-specific methods, such as the `someMethod()` and `anotherMethod()` sample methods shown in the diagram. A bean-managed entity bean will also typically define some state in the form of field variables that contain cached versions of the data-source entry values. As a final note, entity bean implementations must also have a public parameterless constructor and should not implement the `finalize()` method.

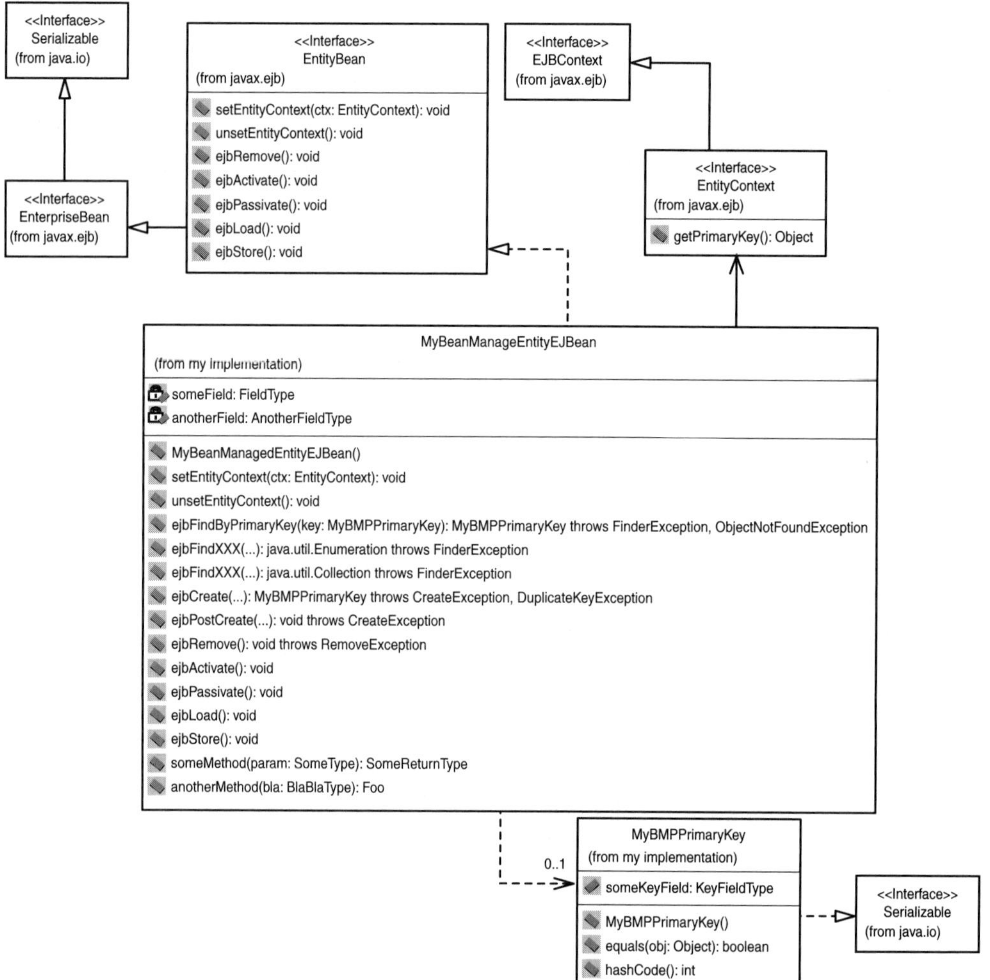

FIGURE 36.8
Bean-managed persistence entity EJBs.

BMP Entity Bean Context Setting and Unsetting

The `javax.ejb.EntityContext` interface is implemented by a container object that provides a handle to an entity bean's runtime context. `EntityContext` extends the more generic `EJBContext` and defines a method for obtaining a handle to a remote EJB interface handle, as well as for obtaining a handle to the bean instance's primary key. The `setEntityContext()` method on an `EntityBean` implementation is invoked by a container immediately after an instance of the bean is constructed. The bean should save this value in a field variable for later use. An entity bean will also find calling the `getPrimaryKey()` method useful in determining the primary key that this particular entity bean instance identifies.

An `unsetEntityContext()` method is also required to be implemented by entity bean implementations. A container will call this method when the entity bean instance is to be decoupled from the container context. That is, the container is about to terminate this bean instance from the bean pool, and the bean should take care to close any resources that were opened during a call to `setEntityContext()`.

BMP Entity Bean Finding

Whenever a client desires to locate particular existing entity bean instances that correspond to particular existing data-source entries, the container will invoke one of the `ejbFindXXX(...)` methods on the entity bean. The `ejbFindXXX(...)` methods fill a role similar to a SQL `SELECT` statement in database functionality. BMP implementations generally need to throw a `FinderException` during processing of these methods to indicate that an application error has occurred.

The `ejbFindByPrimaryKey()` method must be defined on all entity beans. An implementation of this method must take the primary key of an entity bean as an input parameter, verify that the associated data-source entry identified by the primary key exists in the database, and then return the primary key to the container. If the requested data-source entry does not exist, a BMP implementation may throw the `ObjectNotFoundException` subclass of `FinderException` to indicate that the requested object could not be found. Most likely, a BMP entity bean will formulate a `SELECT` statement query to issue to the database via JDBC to implement this method to verify that the data with the primary key exists in the database.

Zero or more additional `ejbFindXXX(...)` methods may also be defined that take zero or more business-specific input parameters and must attempt to locate any associated data-source entries in the database. For each located entry, a collection of primary keys associated with each entry should be returned from the `ejbFindXXX()` method. The collection may be returned in one of two forms. For JDK 1.1 and above compatibility, a `java.util.Enumeration` of primary key objects can be returned. For Java 2.0 and above compatibility, a `java.util.Collection` of primary key objects can be returned. A BMP implementation of these methods can utilize the JDBC API to issue a SQL `SELECT` statement as a function of the input parameters and bean type and then use the results to create a collection of associated primary key objects. If the underlying query results in no primary keys to return, an empty collection should be returned.

BMP Entity Bean Creation and Removal

Zero or more ejbCreate(...) methods with zero or more parameters may be defined on an entity bean. The optional ejbCreate() methods perform a function akin to database INSERT statements in that they create an entry in the data source associated with this entity bean type and populate it with any data established within the entity bean. Data can be established within the bean via the initialization of any field variables during construction, as well as by using any values passed as parameters to an ejbCreate(...) method. A container calls ejbCreate(...) on an entity bean due to a client-induced creation event on the bean.

The ejbCreate(...) methods must return an application-specific Java Object that represents the primary key for this newly created entity bean. The primary key class must be serializable, must provide a default parameterless constructor, must implement the equals() method, and must implement the hashCode() method as is illustrated with the MyBMPPrimaryKey class in Figure 36.8.

BMP entity beans must implement the necessary database connectivity logic to perform the database SQL INSERT within the ejbCreate(...) methods. The primary mechanism to accomplish this task is via the JDBC API, which can be configured via XML-based data-source configuration parameters. BMP entity beans may throw the CreateException to indicate that an entity bean cannot be created for some reason. BMP entity beans may also throw the DuplicateKeyException subclass of CreateException if an entity bean could not be created due to the existence of a data-source entry with the same primary key.

For each ejbCreate(...) method defined, the entity bean must also define an ejbPostCreate(...) method using the same input parameters. The ejbPostCreate() method is called by the container after it calls ejbCreate() and after the container associates an instance of the entity bean with the client reference. Thus, any initial actions your entity bean desires to perform using a fully associated entity bean instance can be done when this method is called. The ejbPostCreate(...) methods may also throw a CreateException to indicate an application error that has occurred during this method call.

When a client induces a remove action on an entity bean, the container calls the ejbRemove() method. The ejbRemove() method for an entity bean means that the associated data-source entry should be deleted from the database akin to a SQL DELETE statement in functionality. A BMP entity bean will need to obtain a handle to the primary key using its entity context's getPrimaryKey() method and then use the JDBC API to formulate a SQL DELETE statement for this particular data-source entry. A BMP implementation of ejbRemove() may also throw the RemoveException to indicate a general exception that has occurred during the attempted deletion operation.

BMP Entity Bean Passivation and Activation

The `ejbPassivate()` and `ejbActivate()` methods must be implemented for entity beans as they were for stateful session beans. The `ejbPassivate()` method is called by the container before it returns the entity bean to the pool of bean instances. This occurs most likely when the bean has been inactive for some period and perhaps will be selected for passivation according to a least recently used algorithm. The entity bean should clean up any resources and states that cannot be serialized to a passive persistent store. None of the bean's field values that relate to data-source entry elements should be persisted within this method, though.

The `ejbActivate()` method generally performs the inverse operations of `ejbPassivate()`. A container calls `ejbActivate()` when it needs to bring the state of a previously passivated bean into active memory due to some client demand on that bean. The BMP implementation must reestablish any resources that were closed during the call to `ejbPassivate()` and populate any data that was serialized during the call to `ejbPassivate()`. This data does not include the bean's field values that relate to data-source entry elements, however.

BMP Entity Bean Storing and Loading

Whereas `ejbPassivate()` and `ejbActivate()` relate to closing and opening any non–data-source related resources, the `ejbLoad()` and `ejbStore()` methods explicitly deal with the data-source information. A container will call `ejbStore()` and `ejbLoad()` on an entity bean whenever it wants the bean to synchronize the state of the database field data in the bean with the state of the associated data actually stored in the data source.

A container calls `ejbStore()` on a bean when it wants the bean instance to update the associated data-source entry with the state of the data in the bean instance. This operation thus satisfies a function similar to that of a SQL `UPDATE` in the database. However, the determination of when this update is performed is a function of the container's transaction management decision-making logic. A container will also call `ejbStore()` right before it makes a call to `ejbPassivate()`. BMP implementations will typically use JDBC to implement SQL `UPDATE` statements when `ejbStore()` is invoked.

A container calls `ejbLoad()` on a bean when it wants the bean instance to be updated with the latest state values of the associated data-source entry in the database. This operation thus updates the in memory bean instance representation of the database entry. A BMP implementation will typically call `getPrimaryKey()` on the associated entity context to first determine the specific data-source entry associated with this bean instance. The BMP implementation will then query the data-source entry's element values using JDBC and update the state of the bean. A container determines when `ejbLoad()` is called as a function of transaction management and also calls `ejbLoad()` before calls to `ejbRemove()` and after calls to `ejbActivate()`.

BMP Entity Bean Component Interface Rules Summary

The life cycle of an entity bean is significantly more complicated than that of a session bean and relies heavily on transaction management. Such complexity is part of the reason why entity bean support was not required by EJB v1.0–compliant implementations to lower the barrier for entry into the EJB marketplace. Although we defer discussion of transaction management with EJBs until the next chapter, we present the basic steps that a container for an entity bean must follow (without transaction management) here:

1. *Instantiate EJB*: The container calls `Class.newInstance()` with the name of your EJB to create a new instance of the entity bean when the container decides it needs an entity bean instance for its pool of entity beans.
2. *Set Context*: The container calls `setEntityContext()` on the EJB with a container-created `EntityContext` object.
3. *Add EJB to Pool*: The container may now add the entity bean to a pool of server-side entity bean instances of this same type. Note that these server-side instances are not yet related to a client-side reference.
4. *Call* `ejbFindXXX(...)`: The container may use any available bean instance from the pool to implement the functionality of a select method as induced by a client. The returned primary key or keys are used to create delegates of entity beans but are not instances of server-side entity beans themselves. Client-side references are associated with these delegates.
5. *Call* `ejbCreate(...)` *and* `ejbPostCreate(...)`: The container may use a bean instance's implementation of these methods to insert a new database entry into the database as induced by a client.
6. *Call* `ejbActivate()`: The container calls `ejbActivate()` whenever a client demands that a particular database entry be accessed in memory and requires the bean to allocate any needed resources.
7. *Call* `ejbLoad()`: A container calls `ejbLoad()` when it wants to synchronize the state of database-related fields with the field values of an entity bean instance.
8. *Delegate Client Calls*: The container delegates EJB client calls to the entity bean whose reference is associated with the client. Calls from a client pass from the client stub to the container's skeleton representation of the EJB and then to the server-side bean instance implementation itself.
9. *Call* `ejbStore()`: The container calls `ejbStore()` when it wants to synchronize the state of the entity bean's database-related fields with the database by means of a database update operation.

10. *Call* `ejbPassivate()`: The container calls `ejbPassivate()` whenever it wants to release the resources consumed by an entity bean so that the bean instance can be used to encapsulate another database entry.
11. *Call* `ejbRemove()`: A container calls `ejbRemove()` when a client induces the deletion of an associated database entry. This does not remove the bean instance from the pool, though.
12. *Unset Context*: A container calls `unsetEntityContext()` when a bean instance is about to be removed from the pool as determined by the container's management policy.

BMP entity beans thus require a significant amount of hand-coding to accomplish the desired effects of database connectivity. BMP entity beans provide implementations for the management of bean instance state and resources, as well as for the management of database data and connectivity. BMP entity beans manage bean instance state and resources through business-specific methods, as well as through the implementation of standard methods that effect resource closing (via `ejbPassivate`), resource opening (via `ejbActivate`), and state management (via `setEntityContext` and `unsetEntityContext`). BMP entity beans manage database data and connectivity through the implementation of standard methods that effect database entry querying (via `ejbFind`*XXX*), insertion (via `ejbCreate`), post-insertion (via `ejbPostCreate`), deletion (via `ejbRemove`), synchronization updates (via `ejbStore`), and in-memory synchronization (via `ejbLoad`). BMP entity beans provide this functionality through the use of a Java enterprise technology such as JDBC. BMP entity beans thus may be viewed as providing standard interfaces for JDBC-based code that want to operate inside of the J2EE EJB container environment.

BMP Entity Bean Example

The only example of a BMP entity bean in our BeeShirts.com application is the `Credit` EJB. Only the core portions of this `CreditEJBean` BMP entity bean are shown in Listing 36.11, with exception handling excluded from the listing for simplicity in presentation. The database entity creation, removal, finding, and updating logic of the `CreditEJBean` largely delegates to a helper class in this bean's directory on the CD called `CreditDBAccess`. Each `ejb`*XXX*`()` call that must perform some database-related activity first obtains a connection from our `EJBHelper` class, sets this connection onto `CreditDBAccess`, and then instructs `CreditDBAccess` to perform an insert, delete, select, or update operation, depending on the `ejb`*XXX*`()` method invoked on `CreditEJBean`. All credit information associated with the credit entity is stored in the `CreditEJBean` object's `creditInformation Hashtable` with key names taken from the `CreditDefinition` interface's constant names. Additionally, a `CreditPrimaryKey` class, shown in Listing 36.12, defines the primary key for this bean, which includes a customer ID, an order ID, and a card number.

LISTING 36.11 BMP Entity Bean Example (`CreditEJBean.java`)

```
package ejava.ejbch36.credit;

  ...// imports excluded here...

public class CreditEJBean  implements EntityBean
{
  private EntityContext entityContext;
  private Hashtable creditInformation; // Stores credit information

  /** Create CREDIT table entry based on initial creditInformation */
  public CreditPrimaryKey ejbCreate(Hashtable creditInformation)
    throws CreateException, RemoteException
  {
    CreditDBAccess dbAccess = new CreditDBAccess();
    Connection connection = null;
    ...
      // Get connection, set on CreditDBAccess, and perform INSERT
      connection = EJBHelper.getDBConnection();
      dbAccess.setConnection(connection);
      dbAccess.insert(creditInformation);
      ...
    // Create primary key and return
    CreditPrimaryKey primaryKey = new CreditPrimaryKey();
    primaryKey.customerID =
      ((Integer)creditInformation.
        get(CreditDefinition.CUSTOMER_ID)).intValue();
    primaryKey.orderID =
      ((Integer)creditInformation.get(CreditDefinition.ORDER_ID)).intValue();
    primaryKey.cardNumber =
       ((String)creditInformation.get(CreditDefinition.CARD_NUMBER));
    return primaryKey;
  }

  /** No need for post creation semantics */
  public void ejbPostCreate(Hashtable creditInformation)
    throws CreateException, RemoteException {  }

  /** No need for activation semantics */
  public void ejbActivate(){}

  /** No need for passivation semantics */
  public void ejbPassivate(){}

  /** Verify that primary key for Credit exists */
```

```
public CreditPrimaryKey ejbFindByPrimaryKey(
      CreditPrimaryKey primaryKey)
  throws FinderException, RemoteException
{
  if ((primaryKey == null)){
    throw new FinderException ("PrimaryKey should not be null");
  }


 // Throws exception if cannot load based on this key
  loadCreditData(primaryKey);

  return primaryKey;
}

/** Look up all primary keys for Credit objects with customer ID */
public Collection ejbFindByCustomerID(int customerID)
  throws FinderException,  RemoteException
{
  Connection connection = null;
  CreditDBAccess dbAccess = new CreditDBAccess();
  ...
    // Get/set connection, SELECT credit info from database
    connection = EJBHelper.getDBConnection();
    dbAccess.setConnection(connection);
    Vector results = dbAccess.select(customerID);
    // Return  Matching Primary Keys
    return results;
  ...
}


/** Look up primary keys for Credit with customer ID and order ID */
public Collection ejbFindByCustomerIDAndOrderID(
      int customerID, int orderID)
  throws FinderException,  RemoteException
{
  Connection connection = null;
  CreditDBAccess dbAccess = new CreditDBAccess();
  ...
   // Get/Set connection, SELECT credit information
    connection = EJBHelper.getDBConnection();
    dbAccess.setConnection(connection);
    Vector results = dbAccess.select(customerID, orderID);
```

continues

LISTING 36.11 Continued

```
      // Return  Matching Primary Keys
      return results;
    ...
  }

  /** Remove data source entry associated with this bean from DBMS */
  public void ejbRemove()
  {
    Connection connection = null;
    CreditDBAccess dbAccess = new CreditDBAccess();
      ...
      // Get/Set Connection, DELETE this credit info from DB
      connection = EJBHelper.getDBConnection();
      dbAccess.setConnection(connection);
      dbAccess.delete((CreditPrimaryKey)entityContext.getPrimaryKey());
     ...
  }

  /** Store EJB data to database */
  public void ejbStore()
  {
    Connection connection = null;
    CreditDBAccess dbAccess = new CreditDBAccess();
    ...
      // Get/Set connection, UPDATE credit info in DB
      connection = EJBHelper.getDBConnection();
      dbAccess.setConnection(connection);
      dbAccess.update(creditInformation);
     ...
  }

  /** Load EJB data from database */
  public void ejbLoad()
    throws RemoteException
  {
    // Get primary key
    CreditPrimaryKey primaryKey =
        (CreditPrimaryKey) entityContext.getPrimaryKey();
      ...
    // Now load the actual data based on primary key
    loadCreditData(primaryKey);
      ...
  }
```

```
  /** Private method to load credit data into bean using primary key */
  private void loadCreditData(CreditPrimaryKey primaryKey)
    throws RemoteException
  {
    Connection connection = null;
    CreditDBAccess dbAccess = new CreditDBAccess();
      ...
      // Get Connection, set connection, SELECT credit info
      connection = EJBHelper.getDBConnection();
      dbAccess.setConnection(connection);
      creditInformation = dbAccess.select(primaryKey.customerID,
        primaryKey.orderID, primaryKey.cardNumber);
     ...
  }

  /** Sets the EntityContext for the EJBean. */
  public void setEntityContext(EntityContext entityContext)
  {
    this.entityContext = entityContext;
  }

  /** Unsets the EntityContext for the EJBean. */
  public void unsetEntityContext()
  {
    entityContext = null;
  }

  /** Set credit information onto bean */
  public void setCreditInformation(Hashtable creditInformation)
  {
    this.creditInformation = creditInformation;
  }

  /** Retrieve credit info from bean. */
  public Hashtable getCreditInformation()
  {
    return creditInformation;
  }
}
```

LISTING 36.12 Primary Key Example (`CreditPrimaryKey.java`)

```
package ejava.ejbch36.credit;

import java.io.Serializable;

public class CreditPrimaryKey implements Serializable
{
  public int customerID;
  public int orderID;
  public String cardNumber;

  public int hashCode() { return super.hashCode(); }

  public boolean equals(Object object)
  {
    if(object instanceof CreditPrimaryKey){
      CreditPrimaryKey otherKey = (CreditPrimaryKey)object;
      if( otherKey.orderID == orderID
          && otherKey.customerID == customerID
          && otherKey.cardNumber.equals(cardNumber)){
        return true;
      }
      else{
        return false;
      }
    }else {
      return false;
    }
  }
}
```

We do not list the `CreditDBAccess` code here because it is rather long and contains only JDBC code not germane to the topic of EJB. We encourage you to take a look at the `CreditDBAccess` class on the CD, however. `CreditDBAccess` wraps all the actual JDBC calls to be performed by the `CreditEJBean`. Using the schema names from the `CreditDefinition` interface and data passed into its particular methods, it makes the appropriate JDBC calls joining both the `CREDIT_TABLE` and the `CARD_TYPE` database entities. The `CreditDBAccess` method has `select()`, `insert()`, `delete()`, and `update()` methods to perform the relational database operations related to these method names. A `Hashtable` used by these methods whose elements are named according to the `CreditDefinition` class identify both `CreditEJBean` data elements and database columns. The `Hashtable` is used during `CreditDBAccess` calls to `insert()` and `update()` and is returned from `select()` calls. The `CreditDBAccess.delete()` call is invoked only with the `CreditPrimaryKey`.

Container-Managed Persistence Entity Beans

As you have just seen, creating BMP entity beans can be quite a chore. Although the amount of hand-coding may be equivalent to what you would expect for implementing JDBC-based connectivity to access your enterprise data, EJB also provides a means to simplify the amount of effort required to create entity beans via its container-managed persistence (CMP) entity bean standards. With CMP, the container implements all the JDBC database access logic for you. The container thus handles the object-to-relational mapping necessary to transfer data from your EJB entity object to relational database entities and from the relational database entities to your EJB entity object. We describe how to create CMP entity bean components in this section. We primarily focus on those aspects of developing CMPs that differ from the development of BMPs and avoid reiterating discussion of the common concepts shared by CMPs and BMPs.

CMP Entity Bean Logical Component Architecture

Figure 36.9 depicts the basic architecture behind creating CMP entity bean components. A public, nonfinal, and nonabstract CMP entity bean implementation, such as `MyContainerManagedEntityEJBean`, must implement the `EntityBean` interface. CMP entity EJBs can also implement public, nonfinal, and nonstatic business-specific methods, such as the `someMethod()` and `anotherMethod()` sample methods shown in the diagram. Also note that entity bean implementations must also have a public parameterless constructor and should not implement the `finalize()` method.

CMP Entity Bean and Primary Key Container-Managed Fields

CMP entity beans must take additional care to define any fields that will be managed by the container as `public` and ensure that the associated types are serializable. These container-managed fields map directly to elements of the data-source entry associated with this CMP entity bean. For example, a container-managed field may map directly to a column in a particular database table. The container figures out which of the fields will be managed via a specification in the EJB deployment descriptor for this bean.

A primary key for a CMP entity bean may simply be specified as a single field of the CMP entity bean. CMP entity bean primary keys may also be uniquely defined using a separate class containing one or more public field names that map to field names of the CMP entity bean. Alternately, the bean provider may specify no primary key for a CMP entity bean. In such a case, the vendor's deployment tools should be used to select a primary key to be associated with that bean at deployment time.

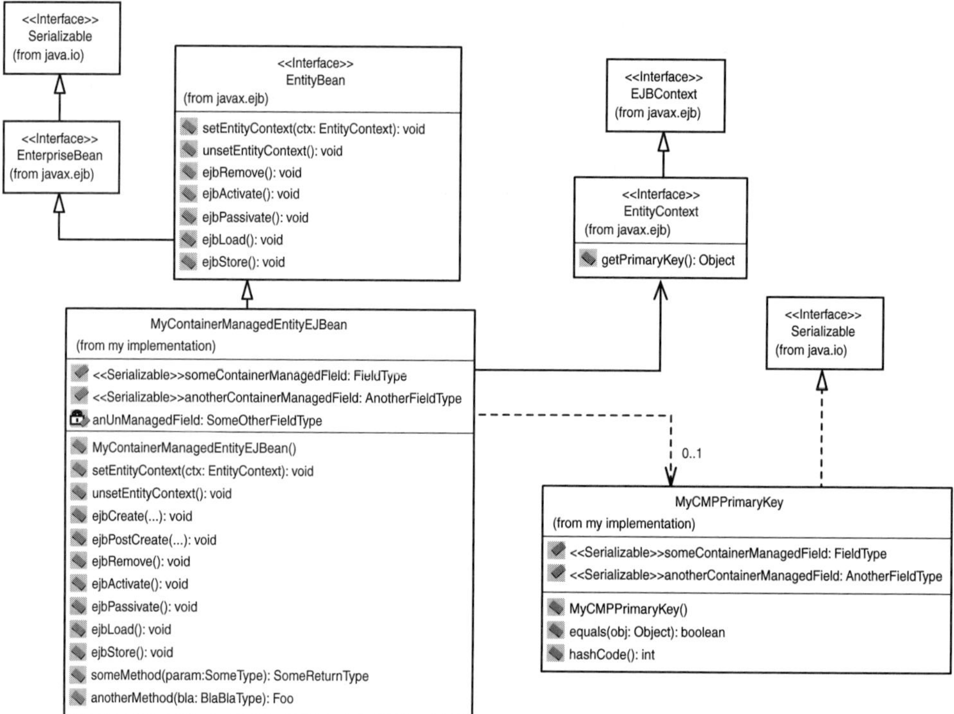

FIGURE 36.9
Container-managed persistence EJBs.

CMP Entity Bean Context Setting and Unsetting

Setting and unsetting the `EntityContext` associated with a CMP entity bean is accomplished using the `setEntityContext()` and `unsetEntityContext()` methods, respectively. Containers call these methods on CMP entity beans for the same reasons and during the same phases of a bean's life cycle as they do for BMP entity beans. However, CMP entity beans may not be as interested in using the `EntityContext` for its capability to return the bean's primary key because the container handles the resolution of data-source entry to bean instance. CMPs may, however, decide to manage the allocation and closing of resources tied to a bean instance from within the entity context setting and unsetting method.

CMP Entity Bean Finding

CMP entity beans relieve the programmer from having to define and write `ejbFindXXX(...)` methods. Rather, the container deduces how to implement such methods for the CMP entity bean by reading certain configuration information from the EJB deployment descriptors, as you'll soon see. The implementation of these methods is thus transparent to the developer.

These methods may be implemented by EJB vendor products within subclasses of the CMP entity bean or by separate entities to which the calls are delegated and results received. Regardless of the underlying implementation, the CMP bean developer need not worry about writing any code to support these operations.

CMP Entity Bean Creation and Removal

The `ejbCreate(...)` methods are also optional for CMP entity beans. Thus, the bean developer need not worry about implementing the actual database `INSERT` related code to support this method. Rather, the developer need only ensure that each container-managed field value is properly initialized with any default values and with values passed in as parameters to the `ejbCreate(...)` method. The container will initialize all container-managed field values to the Java language defaults (for example, `0` and `null`) before it calls this method. Such default value initialization may be all that is needed for a particular EJB and thus not require any special `ejbCreate(...)` implementation on the part of the bean developer. The bean developer should also either return a `null` value for the primary key from this method or declare a `void` return type because the container will handle the creation of a primary key.

CMP bean providers must also define `ejbPostCreate(...)` methods that match `ejbCreate(...)` methods in terms of parameters. The `ejbPostCreate()` method is called by the container after it calls `ejbCreate()` and after the container associates an instance of the entity bean with the client reference. Thus, any initial actions your entity bean desires to perform using a fully associated entity bean instance can be done when this method is called. Containers handle all primary key resolutions and throwing of EJB exceptions as appropriate.

The container calls `ejbRemove()` on a CMP right before it deletes associated data from the database. The bean developer need only focus on any actions that must be performed before the data is deleted from the database. The container implements all database deletion code and throws any EJB exceptions as appropriate.

CMP Entity Bean Passivation and Activation

The `ejbPassivate()` and `ejbActivate()` methods must be implemented by CMP entity bean developers as they were for BMP entity bean developers. Developers must thus clean up any non–data-source entry related resources within an `ejbPassivate()` method implementation. Developers must also reestablish any non–data-source entry related resources within an `ejbActivate()` method implementation.

CMP Entity Bean Storing and Loading

The container for CMP entity beans also handles most of the work that was previously implemented inside of `ejbLoad()` and `ejbStore()` BMP entity bean method calls. Containers manage the actual storage of data that was previously implemented within the `ejbStore()` call. CMP bean developers need worry only about readying any container-managed field values for persistence to the database, such as by deriving any recent updates that need to be reflected in the container-managed field values before they are persisted. CMP developers similarly need to worry only about reflecting any changes that were made to a bean's field values within the `ejbLoad()` method implementation. After a container handles updating the container-managed field values, the `ejbLoad()` method is called and the CMP entity bean implementation of this method may need to derive any changes to other state that result from this synchronization with the database.

CMP Entity Bean Component Interface Rules Summary

The life cycle of CMP entity beans is essentially identical to that of BMP entity beans. Thus, we do not reiterate the entity bean component life cycle guidelines here. The only difference is in who implements the functionality embedded inside of the entity bean life cycle methods. For CMP entity beans, the container implements much of this functionality, and for BMP entity beans, it is the bean developer's job.

CMP entity beans thus alleviate a significant amount of the hand-coding that was required by BMP entity beans in order to accomplish the desired effects of database connectivity. CMP entity bean providers simply ready beans for container-managed persistence operations within calls to the `ejbCreate()`, `ejbPostCreate()`, `ejbRemove()`, `ejbLoad()`, and `ejbStore()` methods. CMP entity bean developers should, however, manage bean instance state and resources through business-specific methods, as well as through the implementation of standard methods that effect resource closing (via `ejbPassivate`), resource opening (via `ejbActivate`), and state management (via `setEntityContext` and `unsetEntityContext`). Most often, the amount of coding that is performed within such methods is either extremely minimal or nonexistent. CMP entity beans thus may be viewed as providing standard interfaces for enabling a J2EE EJB container to implement object-relational mapping for an EJB and for providing the underlying database connectivity solution.

CMP Entity Bean Example

Listing 36.13 contains the core portions from our `TShirtEJBean` CMP entity bean implementation with non-germane portions of the complete code, such as exception handling, not listed here for simplicity in presentation. This `TShirtEJBean` simply defines its public field members to be managed by the container, entity context handling, `ejbCreate()` initialization semantics, other `ejb`*`XXX`*`()` methods not needing any implementation, and a series of business-specific getters and setters for its data. Additionally, a `public getImageBytes()` method is defined to retrieve an array of bytes for T-shirt image data stored on the local file system using the filenames contained within the `TShirtEJBean` object's respective image name fields. That's about it for the example! As you can see, CMP entity bean code implementations can be tremendously more simple than BMP entity bean code implementations. However, we have to specify more information about the CMP entity bean in its XML-based deployment descriptor, as you'll see in a subsequent section.

NOTE

Your particular EJB application server environment security restrictions must be configured such that `java.io.FilePermission read` access is permitted for the `TShirtEJBean.getImageBytes()` method to successfully complete.

LISTING 36.13 CMP Entity Bean Example (`TShirtEJBean.java`)

```
package ejava.ejbch36.tshirt;

  ...// imports excluded here...

public class TShirtEJBean  implements EntityBean
{
 // CMP fields
  public Integer SHIRT_ID;
  public String  SHIRT_SIZE;
  public String  COLOR;
  public String  DESIGN_FRONT;
  public String  DESIGN_BACK;
  public String  PICTURE_FRONT;
  public String  PICTURE_BACK;
  public Integer ITEM_ID_FK;
  public double  UNIT_PRICE;

  // Context
  private EntityContext ctx;

  // Set/get entity context
  public void setEntityContext(EntityContext aCtx) { ctx = aCtx; }
  public void unsetEntityContext(){ ctx = null; }

  // Initialize TShirt info only during creation
  public Integer ejbCreate(Integer shirtID, String size, String color,
    String designFront, String designBack,
    String pictureFront, String pictureBack, double unitPrice,
    Integer itemID)
    throws CreateException, RemoteException
  {
    SHIRT_ID = shirtID;
    SHIRT_SIZE = size;
    COLOR = color;
    DESIGN_FRONT = designFront;
    DESIGN_BACK = designBack;
    PICTURE_FRONT = pictureFront;
```

continues

LISTING 36.13 Continued

```
    PICTURE_BACK = pictureBack;
    UNIT_PRICE  = unitPrice;
    ITEM_ID_FK = itemID;
    return null;
  }

  // Not needed
  public void ejbPostCreate(Integer shirtID, String size, String color,
    String designFront, String designBack,
    String pictureFront, String pictureBack, double unitPrice,
    Integer itemID)
    throws CreateException, RemoteException  { /* No impl */ }

  // Standard methods not needing implementation...thank you CMP!
  public void ejbActivate(){}
  public void ejbPassivate(){}
  public void ejbRemove(){}
  public void ejbLoad(){}
  public void ejbStore(){}

  // Getters for our TShirt data
  public Integer getID(){ return SHIRT_ID; }
  public String getSize(){ return SHIRT_SIZE; }
  public String getColor(){ return COLOR; }
  public Integer getItemID(){ return ITEM_ID_FK; }
  public double getUnitPrice(){ return UNIT_PRICE; }
  public String getDesignFront(){ return DESIGN_FRONT; }
  public String getDesignBack() { return DESIGN_BACK;}
  public String getPictureFront(){ return PICTURE_FRONT; }
  public String getPictureBack(){ return PICTURE_BACK;}
  // Setters for our TShirt data
  public void setID(Integer shirtID){ SHIRT_ID = shirtID; }
  public void setSize(String size){ SHIRT_SIZE = size; }
  public void setColor(String color){ COLOR = color; }
  public void setItemID(Integer itemID){ ITEM_ID_FK = itemID; }
  public void setUnitPrice(double unitPrice){ UNIT_PRICE = unitPrice; }
  public void setDesignFront(String file){ DESIGN_FRONT = file; }
  public void setDesignBack(String file){ DESIGN_BACK = file; }
  public void setPictureFront(String file){ PICTURE_FRONT = file; }
  public void setPictureBack(String file){ PICTURE_BACK = file; }

  // Special method to read TShirt images as bytes given picture names
  public byte[] getImageBytes(String imageType)
  {
    if(imageType == null){ return null;}

    if(imageType.equals("PictureFront"))
```

```
➥{return readImage(PICTURE_FRONT);}
    else if(imageType.equals("PictureBack"))
➥{return readImage(PICTURE_BACK);}
    else{ return null; }

  }

  // Helper method to read byte array of data from named file
  private byte[] readImage(String fileName)
  {
    if( (fileName == null)||(fileName.equals("")) ){ return null;}

    // Set local variables
    File imageFile = null;
    FileInputStream fin = null;
    byte[] returnBytes = null;
    ...
      // Create File handle to fileName, read from FileInputStream
      imageFile = new File(fileName);
      int size = (int)imageFile.length();
      fin = new FileInputStream(imageFile);
      returnBytes = new byte[size];
      int length = fin.read(returnBytes);
    ...
    // Return the bytes read from the file
    return returnBytes;
  }
}
```

Entity Bean Client Interfaces

Building and using home and remote client interfaces for entity beans is very similar to building and using home and remote client interfaces for session beans. In fact, except for an additional type of finder method that needs to be added to the entity bean home interface definition, only a few subtle semantic differences exist. We describe how to build entity bean interfaces and how clients access these interfaces in this section.

Entity Bean Remote Interfaces

Entity bean remote interfaces encapsulate the client's view of an entity bean. The approach by which entity bean remote interfaces are developed is identical to that of session bean remote interfaces. Entity bean interfaces typically consist of getters and setters for retrieving and establishing data to be associated with an entity bean, but they can also have other arbitrary application-specific interfaces defined for them. This section describes how to build and use entity bean remote interfaces.

Entity Bean Remote Interface Logical Architecture

Figure 36.10 depicts the basic logical architecture for building and using remote EJB client interfaces to distributed entity EJBs. All application-specific interfaces to distributed EJB objects, such as `MyEntityEJB` shown in the diagram, must extend the `javax.ejb.EJBObject` interface. As with session beans, entity beans also employ underlying stubs, skeletons, and container management services for implementing distributed and managed access to server-side entity EJBs from client-side interfaces. The only real difference between entity bean and session bean remote interfaces lies in a few subtle semantic differences, as we discuss next.

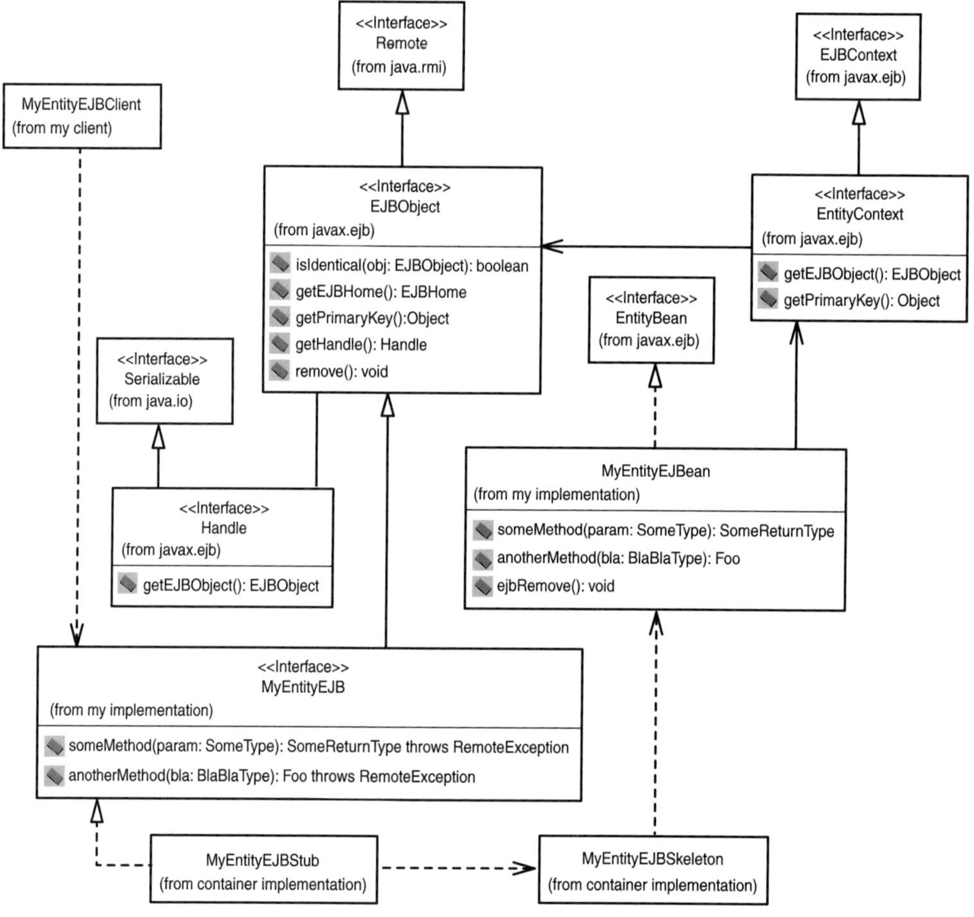

FIGURE 36.10

Entity bean remote interface architecture.

Entity Bean Application-Specific Remote Interfaces

As with session bean remote interfaces, an application-specific remote EJB interface must be created for each entity bean component. This interface provides the distributed interface used by entity bean clients to invoke the application-specific logic of entity beans. For each distributable application-specific method on an entity bean server-side component, such as `MyEntityEJBean.someMethod()`, an associated application-specific method must be defined on the EJB client-side remote interface, such as `MyEntityEJB.someMethod()`. As a side effect of their distributable nature, each method in the application-specific remote interface should also declare that it can throw a `java.rmi.RemoteException`. Of course, such rules apply only to those server-side component methods you want to be made distributable.

Entity Bean Generic Remote Interfaces

In addition to application-specific interfaces on an EJB remote interface, a set of methods inherited from `EJBObject` can also be invoked on a remote entity bean object. When clients want to determine whether EJB objects are identical to others, the `EJBObject.isIdentical()` method can be called. The `EJBObject.getEJBHome()` method returns a handle to the entity bean's home interface object that is used to create remote interface objects. The `EJBObject.getHandle()` method returns an object that implements the `javax.ejb.Handle` interface for serializing and persisting `EJBObject` references. Unlike session bean clients, entity bean clients can make a valid call to `EJBObject.getPrimaryKey()` on a remote interface to obtain the primary key object associated with the entity bean object.

A very important difference between session bean client interface and entity bean client interface semantics is the implication of calling the `EJBObject.remove()` method. For session beans, this method cleans up client references and possibly destroys a server-side stateful session object. For entity beans, a call to `remove()` will result in the deletion of an associated data-source entry from the database. Thus, entity bean clients must be particularly careful when using this method and make sure that they intend for the data to be deleted and not the object reference.

As a final note, on the server side, an entity bean can obtain a reference to an `EJBObject` with which it is associated by calling `getEJBObject()` on its `EntityContext` object. Bean components may want to obtain such a reference for use as input or output parameters in their application-specific methods. Entity bean developers must be careful, though, to be sure that any `EJBObject` references passed around in such a manner are not accessed by more than one client at one time to guarantee correct behavior for all clients.

Entity Bean Remote Interface Examples

Our sample remote interfaces corresponding to the two types of entity beans presented earlier really convey no new information past that for session bean remote interfaces. Nevertheless, Listing 36.14 is presented to show you the `Credit` remote interface for our BMP

CreditEJBean described in Listing 36.11. Listing 36.15 presents the TShirt remote interface for our CMP TShirtEJBean that was presented in Listing 36.13.

LISTING 36.14 BMP Entity Bean Remote Interface Example (Credit.java)

```
package ejava.ejbch36.credit;

import javax.ejb.EJBObject;
import java.rmi.RemoteException;
import java.util.Hashtable;

public interface Credit  extends EJBObject
{
  /** Set credit information onto the bean using key names
      taken from the CreditDefinition interface */
  public void setCreditInformation(Hashtable creditInformation)
    throws RemoteException;
  /** Get credit information from the bean accessible with key
     names from CreditDefinition interface. */
  public Hashtable getCreditInformation()
    throws  RemoteException;
}
```

LISTING 36.15 CMP Entity Bean Remote Interface Example (TShirt.java)

```
package ejava.ejbch36.tshirt;

import javax.ejb.EJBObject;
import java.rmi.RemoteException;

public interface TShirt extends EJBObject
{
  /** Getters for TShirt data **/
  public Integer getID() throws RemoteException;
  public String getSize() throws RemoteException;
  public String getColor() throws RemoteException;
  public Integer getItemID() throws RemoteException;
  public double getUnitPrice() throws RemoteException;
  public String getDesignFront() throws RemoteException;
  public String getDesignBack() throws RemoteException;
  public String getPictureFront() throws RemoteException;
  public String getPictureBack() throws RemoteException;
  /** Setters for TShirt data **/
  public void setID(Integer shirtID) throws RemoteException;
  public void setSize(String size) throws RemoteException;
```

```
  public void setColor(String color) throws RemoteException;
  public void setItemID(Integer itemID) throws RemoteException;
  public void setUnitPrice(double unitPrice) throws RemoteException;
  public void setDesignFront(String designFront) throws RemoteException;
  public void setDesignBack(String designBack) throws RemoteException;
  public void setPictureFront(String pictureFront)
    throws RemoteException;
  public void setPictureBack(String pictureBack) throws RemoteException;
  /** Read image as bytes given names: PictureFront or PictureBack **/

  public byte[] getImageBytes(String imageType) throws RemoteException;
}
```

Entity Bean Home Interfaces

Entity bean clients use home interfaces to create, find, and remove entity beans. Creation of entity beans actually relates to the insertion of a new entry into a data source (for example, a new row in a database table). Interfaces for finding entity beans provide a mechanism for querying for data-source entries with results returned in an object-oriented fashion (that is, in terms of entity bean objects). Removing an entity bean relates to the deletion of its associated data-source entry in the database. This section describes how to create and utilize entity bean interfaces to perform these basic functions as well as additional supporting functionality.

Entity Bean Home Interface Logical Architecture

Figure 36.11 depicts the architecture behind creating entity bean home interfaces and how clients may use these interfaces. To obtain handles to application-specific EJB home interface objects, such as `MyEntityEJBHome`, which must extend the standard `javax.ejb.EJBHome` interface, we use JNDI to look up named home references. Server-side skeletons and the container handle mapping calls from entity bean client stubs that implement application-specific home interfaces onto a particular entity bean instance. Home interfaces can also be used to persist their handles for later reconstruction and for obtaining meta-data about the EJBs that they serve to create.

Entity Bean Home Object Lookup

The means by which entity bean home objects are looked up by clients is identical to the means by which session bean home objects are looked up. JNDI is used whether your client operates inside of a J2EE container or outside of a container in a standalone fashion. If a client operates inside of a J2EE container, `<ejb-ref>` elements can be used to refer to EJB home interfaces during lookup. Entity beans that want to act as clients to other EJBs define `<ejb-ref>` elements within their `<entity>` element definition inside of an `ejb-jar.xml` file.

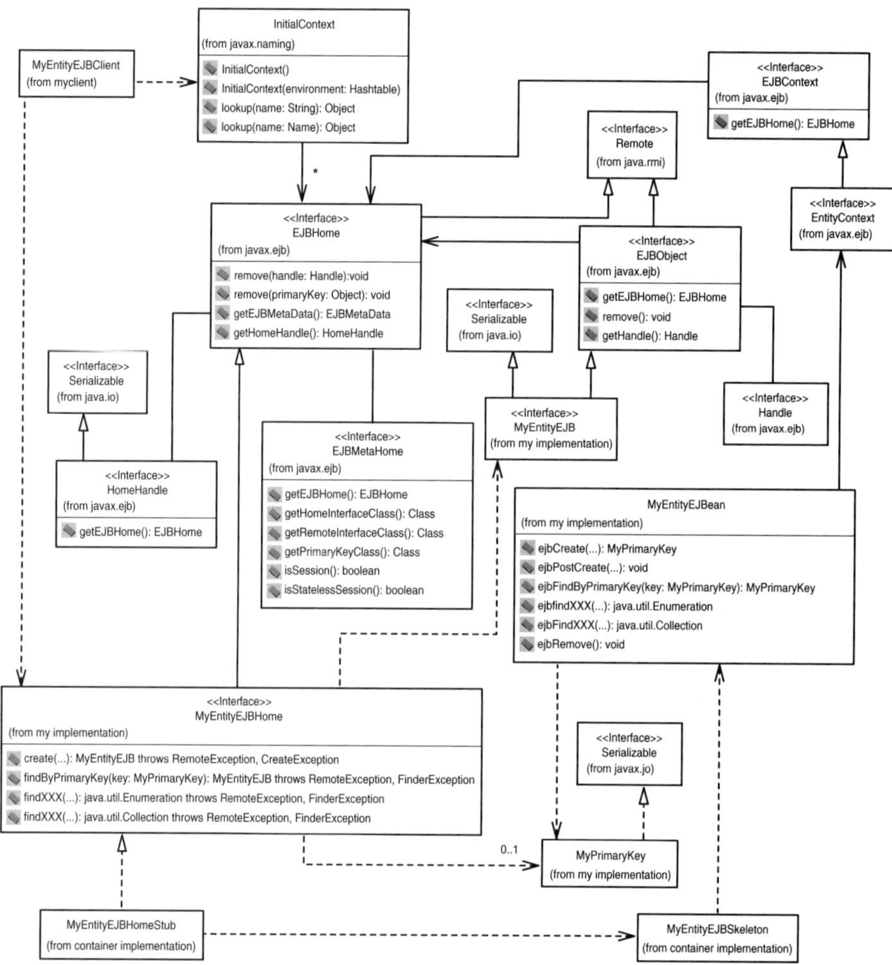

FIGURE 36.11

Entity bean home interface architecture.

Entity Bean Application-Specific Home Interfaces

A series of one or more `create(...)` methods are defined on the custom home interface to represent the different ways in which the associated entity bean data-source entry can be created. A single `create(...)` method must be defined on the home interface for each `ejbCreate(...)` method defined on the entity bean implementation. Each version of a `create(...)` method returns an instance of the entity bean's remote interface (for example, `MyEntityEJB`) and contains zero or more input parameters related to the specific types of initialization parameters needed by the associated `ejbCreate(...)` methods. Each `create(...)` method must also be defined to throw a `java.rmi.RemoteException` and `javax.ejb.CreateException`. Additionally, each `create(...)` method must be defined to throw any application-specific exceptions that have been defined for its associated `ejbCreate(...)` method.

The `create()` methods are not the only application-specific methods that can be defined on an entity bean home interface. A collection of finder methods are also defined that enable the client to query for existing entity beans. A `findXXX(...)` method on the entity bean home interface must exist for each `ejbFindXXX(...)` method that exists on the entity bean implementation. For CMP entity beans, because no `ejbFindXXX(...)` methods are explicitly defined on an entity bean implementation, the valid `findXXX(...)` methods can be determined from the entity bean deployment descriptor (as you'll learn in a subsequent section). Each `findXXX(...)` method defined on the entity bean client home interface should also declare that `RemoteException` and `FinderException` objects can be thrown back to the client.

All entity bean home interfaces must define at least one `findByPrimaryKey()` method because all entity beans must define an `ejbFindByPrimaryKey()` method. The `findByPrimaryKey()` method must be defined such that it returns a handle to an entity bean remote object (for example, `MyEntityEJB`). The container handles associating the primary key returned from the `ejbFindByPrimaryKey()` entity bean method to an actual bean instance and returned entity bean client remote interface stub. The other `findXXX(...)` methods must also be defined to match each associated `ejbFindXXX(...)` method and should have the same input and output parameters. The difference on the client side is that the `Enumeration` or `Collection` object returned from `findXXX(...)` contains implementations of entity bean remote objects as opposed to primary keys contained in the collections returned from associated `ejbFindXXX(...)` methods on server-side entity bean implementations.

Entity Bean Generic Home Interfaces

In addition to calling `EJBObject.remove()` on a remote entity bean object to delete an associated data-source entry, entity bean clients can also call `remove(Handle)` inherited from `EJBHome` by the home interface object. The `Handle`, of course, needs to relate to the particular `EJBObject` that is to be removed. Entity bean objects may also be removed by passing the primary key object associated with a particular entity bean to the `remove(Object)` method defined at the `EJBHome` level.

As with session beans, the `EJBHome.getEJBMetaData()` method is called to obtain a handle to a `EJBMetaData` object that provides a mechanism for clients to discover certain information about an entity bean. Entity bean `EJBMetaData` methods provide the same semantics as they do for session beans when calling `getEJBHome()` to return the home object, `getHomeInterfaceClass()` to return the home interface `Class`, `getRemoteInterfaceClass()` to return the remote interface `Class`, and `isSession()` to determine whether it is a session or an entity EJB. Additionally, the `getPrimaryKeyClass()` method can be called to return the `Class` object that represents the entity bean's primary key class. A call to `isStatelessSession()` always returns `false` for entity beans.

On the server side, an entity bean can extract a handle for its EJBHome object with a call to getEJBHome() on its EntityContext object (as inherited from EJBContext). Bean components may want to obtain such a reference for creating, finding, and removing entity beans of their own type.

Entity Bean Home Interface Examples

In addition to creation methods, our entity bean home interface examples include finder method definitions in them according to the way in which the entity bean objects can be selected. Listing 36.16 depicts the CreditHome BMP entity bean home interface associated with the CreditEJBean of Listing 36.11. Here, our create() method is mapped by the container to a call to our CreditEJBean.ejbCreate() method, and the findXXX(...) methods map to calls to associated CreditEJBean.ejbFindXXX(...) methods.

LISTING 36.16 BMP Entity Bean Home Interface Example (CreditHome.java)

```
package ejava.ejbch36.credit;

import javax.ejb.EJBHome;
import javax.ejb.CreateException;
import java.rmi.RemoteException;
import java.util.Hashtable;
import java.util.Enumeration;
import javax.ejb.FinderException;
import java.util.Collection;

public interface CreditHome extends  EJBHome
{
  /** Create a Credit entity given credit information whose
      keys are defined according to names from CreditDefinition */
  public Credit create(Hashtable creditInformation)
    throws CreateException, RemoteException;
  /** Find a Credit entity given its primary key */
   public Credit findByPrimaryKey(CreditPrimaryKey primaryKey)
    throws FinderException, RemoteException ;
  /** Find Credit entities given with the given customer ID */
  public Collection findByCustomerID(int customerID)
    throws  FinderException,  RemoteException;
  /** Find Credit entities given the customer ID and order ID */
  public Collection
        findByCustomerIDAndOrderID(int customerID, int orderID)
    throws  FinderException,  RemoteException;
}
```

Listing 36.17 presents the `TShirtHome` CMP home interface for the `TShirtEJBean` of Listing 36.13. Although it is apparent that the `create(...)` method maps to the `TShirtEJBean.ejbCreate()` method, just how the `findXXX(...)` methods are mapped or even defined may not be so apparent to you just yet. No `ejbFindXXX(...)` methods are defined on our `TShirtEJBean`. In the next section, we show how such methods are defined by the container after appropriate hints are given to the container during configuration and deployment of the CMP entity bean.

LISTING 36.17 CMP Entity Bean Home Interface Example (`TShirtHome.java`)

```
package ejava.ejbch36.tshirt;

import javax.ejb.EJBHome;
import javax.ejb.CreateException;
import java.rmi.RemoteException;
import javax.ejb.FinderException;
import java.util.Enumeration;

public interface TShirtHome extends EJBHome
{
  /** Create a TShirt entity given all of its field data */
  public TShirt create(Integer shirtID, String size, String color ,
    String designFront, String designBack,
    String pictureFront, String pictureBack, double unitPrice,
    Integer itemID)
    throws CreateException, RemoteException;
  /** Find a TShirt entity given its primary key */
  public TShirt findByPrimaryKey(Integer shirtID)
    throws FinderException, RemoteException;
  /** Find TShirt entities given a TShirt size and color */
  public Enumeration findBySizeAndColor(String size, String color)
    throws  FinderException, RemoteException;
  /** Find TShirt entities given a TShirt Item ID */
  public Enumeration findByItemID(Integer itemID)
    throws  FinderException, RemoteException;
}
```

Entity Bean Configuration and Deployment

We have already presented the basic top-level deployment descriptor and session bean elements in this chapter. As you saw previously, the root `<ejb-jar>` element contained an `<enterprise-beans>` element, which in turn contained a collection of `<session>` elements. As opposed to just `<session>` elements, the `<enterprise-beans>` element can also contain a collection of <entity> elements. Each <entity> element is used to describe the configuration and deployment of an individual entity bean. The <entity> bean element DTD structure, shown in Listing 36.18, defines entity bean meta-data; a unique name in the EJB JAR file; the bean's class, interface, and primary key names; the type of entity bean; configuration parameters; references to other EJBs and database connections; security semantics; and elements to assist in the object-relational mapping for CMP entity beans.

LISTING 36.18 EJB DTD Entity Bean Elements

```
<!-- Container used to describe an individual entity bean. -->
  <!ELEMENT entity  (description?, display-name?, small-icon?,
                     large-icon?, ejb-name, home, remote, ejb-class,
                     persistence-type, prim-key-class, reentrant,
                     cmp-field*, primkey-field?, env-entry*,
                     ejb-ref*, security-role-ref*, resource-ref*)>
<!-- A description of the entity bean -->
  <!ELEMENT description (#PCDATA)>
<!-- Description of the entity bean's displayable name. -->
  <!ELEMENT display-name (#PCDATA)>
<!-- A name for a small 16x16 pixel GIF or JPG file. -->
  <!ELEMENT small-icon (#PCDATA)>
<!-- A name for a small 32x32 pixel GIF or JPG file. -->
  <!ELEMENT large-icon (#PCDATA)>
<!-- Specifies the name of an EJB unique to its ejb-jar file.
The code and JNDI names are independent from this name. -->
  <!ELEMENT ejb-name (#PCDATA)>
<!-- Fully qualified class name of the EJB home interface. -->
  <!ELEMENT home (#PCDATA)>
<!-- Fully qualified class name of the EJB remote interface. -->
  <!ELEMENT remote (#PCDATA)>
<!-- Fully qualified class name of the EJB implementation. -->
  <!ELEMENT ejb-class (#PCDATA)>
<!-- Specifies if BMP or CMP type bean using: Bean, Container -->
  <!ELEMENT persistence-type (#PCDATA)>
<!-- Fully qualified class name of EJB's primary key if known
before deployment time. Otherwise, java.lang.Object should be used. -->
  <!ELEMENT prim-key-class (#PCDATA)>
<!-- Specifies if entity bean is reentrant: True, False -->
  <!ELEMENT reentrant (#PCDATA)>
<!-- Describes fields for CMP entity beans -->
  <!ELEMENT cmp-field (description?, field-name)>
<!-- Specifies name of a public field variable in CMP entity bean -->
  <!ELEMENT field-name (#PCDATA)>
<!-- Specifies the name of a public field variable in CMP entity bean
that corresponds to the primary key. This is used only if a separate
```

```
primary key class is not used. -->
  <!ELEMENT primkey-field (#PCDATA)>
<!-- Declares an environment configuration parameter for
a J2EE application environment. -->
  <!ELEMENT env-entry (description?, env-entry-name,
                       env-entry-value?, env-entry-type)>
<!-- Defines the name of an environment entry parameter. -->
  <!ELEMENT env-entry-name (#PCDATA)>
<!-- Defines the value of an environment entry. -->
  <!ELEMENT env-entry-value (#PCDATA)>
<!-- Defines a fully qualified Java type for a particular environment
value. Acceptable values are: java.lang.Boolean, java.lang.String,
java.lang.Integer, java.lang.Double, java.lang.Float -->
  <!ELEMENT env-entry-type (#PCDATA)>
<!-- Serves to define a reference to another EJB from this EJB. -->
  <!ELEMENT ejb-ref (description?, ejb-ref-name, ejb-ref-type, home,
                     remote, ejb-link?)>
<!-- Provides a name to refer to another EJB typically
prefi XEd with "ejb/" -->
  <!ELEMENT ejb-ref-name (#PCDATA)>
<!-- Specifies the type of referenced EJB: Entity, Session -->
  <!ELEMENT ejb-ref-type (#PCDATA)>
<!-- Specifies an ejb-name of another EJB to which this reference is
linked. The other EJB may be in the same ejb-jar file or in another
ejb-jar file which is in the same J2EE enterprise application. -->
  <!ELEMENT ejb-link (#PCDATA)>
<!-- This value is used within the EJB to reference
a particular secure role using a EJB security role-name. -->
  <!ELEMENT security-role-ref (description?, role-name, role-link)>
<!-- The EJB security role-name. -->
  <!ELEMENT role-name (#PCDATA)>
<!-- Defines the role-name of a security role specified in one of the
security-role elements. -->
  <!ELEMENT role-link (#PCDATA)>
<!-- Defines a reference to an external resource (e.g. database). -->
  <!ELEMENT resource-ref (description?, res-ref-name, res-type,
                          res-auth)>
<!-- Defines the name of the resource factory. -->
  <!ELEMENT res-ref-name (#PCDATA)>
<!-- Defines the fully qualified Java type of the data source. -->
  <!ELEMENT res-type (#PCDATA)>
<!-- Indicates if the bean performs authentication to a resource
or if the container performs authentication: Application, Container -->
  <!ELEMENT res-auth (#PCDATA)>
```

As an example, the entity-related elements of our CMP entity TShirt bean's ejb-jar.xml file are shown in Listing 36.19. You'll note that for the TShirt EJB, its <persistence-type> is marked as Container and a set of <cmp-field> elements defines the container-managed fields of this EJB. The primary key class field is indicated in the <primkey-field> as the SHIRT_ID field, which is of type java.lang.Integer as defined in the <prim-key-class> field.

LISTING 36.19 Example of EJB Entity Bean Deployment Descriptor Information

```
<?xml version="1.0" encoding="UTF-8"?>

<!DOCTYPE ejb-jar PUBLIC '-//Sun Microsystems, Inc.//
➥DTD Enterprise JavaBeans 1.1//EN'
➥ 'http://java.sun.com/j2ee/dtds/ejb-jar_1_1.dtd'>

<ejb-jar>
  <description>no description</description>
  <display-name>TSHIRT</display-name>

  <enterprise-beans>
    <entity>

      <description/>
      <display-name>TShirtEJB</display-name>
      <ejb-name>TShirtEJB</ejb-name>
      <home>ejava.ejbch36.tshirt.TShirtHome</home>
      <remote>ejava.ejbch36.tshirt.TShirt</remote>
      <ejb-class>ejava.ejbch36.tshirt.TShirtEJBean</ejb-class>
      <persistence-type>Container</persistence-type>
      <prim-key-class>java.lang.Integer</prim-key-class>
      <reentrant>False</reentrant>

      <cmp-field><field-name>SHIRT_ID</field-name></cmp-field>
      <cmp-field><field-name>SHIRT_SIZE</field-name></cmp-field>
      <cmp-field><field-name>COLOR</field-name></cmp-field>
      <cmp-field><field-name>DESIGN_FRONT</field-name></cmp-field>
      <cmp-field><field-name>DESIGN_BACK</field-name></cmp-field>
      <cmp-field><field-name>PICTURE_FRONT</field-name></cmp-field>
      <cmp-field><field-name>PICTURE_BACK</field-name></cmp-field>
      <cmp-field><field-name>ITEM_ID_FK</field-name></cmp-field>

      <primkey-field>SHIRT_ID</primkey-field>

    </entity>
  </enterprise-beans>
  ...
</ejb-jar>
```

Vendor-specific deployment descriptor files to configure and deploy entity beans for both the J2EE reference implementation and BEA WebLogic implementation are also needed and are provided with the examples on the CD. Developers will most often use GUI-based deployment tools provided by vendors to develop such files, but we wanted to explicitly provide you with a sense of what they contain with our sample code on the CD. No information on the J2EE reference implementation's `sun-j2ee-ri.xml` file was readily available at the time of this book's writing. For more information on the `weblogic-ejb-jar.xml` file and `weblogic-cmp-rdbms-jar.xml` file formats, see the WebLogic EJB reference manual at `http://www.weblogic.com/docs50/classdocs/API_ejb/EJB_reference.html`.

What is perhaps most important about these vendor-specific XML files, aside from the JNDI-to-EJB name mappings for all EJBs, is the object-to-relational mappings they contain for CMP entity EJBs. In the J2EE reference implementation's `sun-j2ee-ri.xml` file, a `<cmp>` element per CMP entity bean contains a set of `<sql-statement>` elements that are used to define the SQL that must be performed per CMP entity bean method. A method on the EJB implementation is identified within a `<method>` element that defines where the interface for the method is defined (for example, `Bean` or `Home`), the name of the method (for example, `ejbCreate`, `find`*`XXX`*), and the class types of any method parameters defined within `<method-param>` elements of an outer `<method-params>` element. Finally, a `<sql>` element defines the SQL statement that should be executed when the associated method is invoked.

Developers will most likely use the GUI-based `deploytool` (in `[J2EE_HOME]\bin`) to create such vendor-specific deployment descriptors. Nevertheless, we have included `sun-j2ee-ri.xml` files for all of our examples on the CD, with a snippet of the `sun-j2ee-ri.xml` file for our `TShirt` CMP entity bean shown here:

```
<j2ee-ri-specific-information>
    ...
  <enterprise-beans>
    <ejb>
     <ejb-name>TShirtEJB</ejb-name>
     <jndi-name>TShirtHome</jndi-name>
     <cmp>
       ...
      <sql-statement>
        <method>
         <ejb-name>Enterprise Bean</ejb-name>
         <method-intf>Bean</method-intf>
         <method-name>ejbCreate</method-name>
        </method>
        <sql>INSERT INTO "TSHIRT"  ( "COLOR" , "DESIGN_BACK" ,
➥ "DESIGN_FRONT" ,  "ITEM_ID_FK", "PICTURE_BACK" , "PICTURE_FRONT" ,
➥ "SHIRT_ID" , "SHIRT_SIZE" ) VALUES (  ?  ,  ?  ,  ?, ?  ,  ?  ,
```

```
➥ ? , ? , ? )
        </sql>
       </sql-statement>
   ...
    <sql-statement>
            <method>
            <ejb-name>Enterprise Bean</ejb-name>
              <method-intf>Home</method-intf>
              <method-name>findBySizeAndColor</method-name>
              <method-params>
                <method-param>java.lang.String</method-param>
                <method-param>java.lang.String</method-param>
              </method-params>
            </method>
            <sql>SELECT "SHIRT_ID" FROM   "TSHIRT"  WHERE SHIRT_SIZE ?
➥AND COLOR = ?
         </sql>
          </sql-statement>
       ...
      </cmp>
    </ejb>
  </enterprise-beans>
</j2ee-ri-specific-information>
```

A `weblogic-cmp-rdbms-jar.xml` file is used to define CMP entity mappings specific to BEA WebLogic's deployment environment. An `<attribute-map>` element maps names defined as CMP entity bean fields within `<bean-field>` elements to column names in the database within `<dbms-column>` elements. The database table is defined within a `<table-name>` element. Only a minimal amount of information needs to be defined for methods to be implemented by containers in the `weblogic-cmp-rdbms-jar.xml` file. A `<finder-list>` element contains a collection of `<finder>` elements, each of which corresponds to a `findXXX()` method to be defined on the CMP entity bean's home interface. A `<method-name>` element inside of `<finder>` defines the name of the method, and a `<method-params>` element defines method parameter class types inside of `<method-param>` sub-elements. Finally, a `<finder-query>` element defines the query that should be performed for the particular method using a special WebLogic Query Language (WLQL) as defined at `http://www.weblogic.com/docs50/classdocs/API_ejb/EJB_environment.html`.

Developers will most likely use the GUI-based `weblogic.ejb.ui.deployer.DeployerTool` (executed as a Java application) to create such vendor-specific deployment descriptors as described at `http://www.weblogic.com/docs50/classdocs/API_ejb/EJB_deploy.html`. Nevertheless, we have included `weblogic-ejb-jar.xml` and `weblogic-cmp-rdbms-jar.xml` files for all of our examples on the CD with a snippet of the `weblogic-cmp-rdbms-jar.xml` file for our `TShirt` CMP entity bean shown here:

```
<weblogic-rdbms-bean>
  <pool-name>ejavaPool</pool-name>
  <table-name>TSHIRT</table-name>

  <attribute-map>
    <object-link>
      <bean-field>SHIRT_ID</bean-field>
      <dbms-column>SHIRT_ID</dbms-column>
    </object-link>
    <object-link>
      <bean-field>SHIRT_SIZE</bean-field>
      <dbms-column>SHIRT_SIZE</dbms-column>
    </object-link>
    <object-link>
      <bean-field>COLOR</bean-field>
      <dbms-column>COLOR</dbms-column>
     ...
  </attribute-map>

  <finder-list>
    <finder>
      <method-name>findBySizeAndColor</method-name>
      <method-params>
        <method-param>java.lang.String</method-param>
        <method-param>java.lang.String</method-param>
      </method-params>
      <finder-query>
        <![CDATA[ ( & (= SHIRT_SIZE $0  ) (= COLOR $1) ) ]]>
      </finder-query>
    </finder>
    <finder>
      ...
    </finder>
  </finder-list>
    ...
</weblogic-rdbms-bean>
```

Conclusions

Enterprise JavaBeans provides a standard component model for developing distributed enterprise applications as components that operate inside of an EJB container environment. EJB session bean types include simple request and response handlers known as stateless session beans and also include stateful session beans to maintain state within a component on behalf of a particular distributed client over time. EJB entity bean types include components that encapsulate data and manage access calls to a database directly from within the component itself and also include components that are defined in such a way that an EJB container can implement all data access on behalf of the component. By developing Enterprise JavaBean components and their XML-based deployment information using the J2EE standards, the same code and deployment information can be used across different J2EE-compliant EJB application server platforms.

Investment protection of your enterprise business rules and data access logic may thus truly be preserved across hardware platforms, operating system platforms, and application server products. As you have also seen in this chapter, Enterprise JavaBeans provides a model for developing server-side enterprise application components that can make building portable and distributed enterprise communications-enabled and data-enabled applications an easier task than is required for communications-enabling and data-enabling standalone enterprise applications. The next chapter shows how EJBs can also be used to make it easier to provide systems assurance and common services for distributed enterprise applications designed using EJB components.

Advanced Enterprise JavaBeans Serving

CHAPTER

37

IN THIS CHAPTER

- EJB Transactions 1316
- EJB Security 1325
- EJB/Web Connectivity 1334
- EJB/CORBA Connectivity 1341
- EJB and XML 1343
- EJB and JMS 1346
- EJB and JavaMail 1351

The core benefit of using EJB was explored in the preceding chapter. There you saw how the EJB component model simplifies server-side distributed enterprise application component development. The EJB component model is also defined in such a way that EJBs can be run atop any vendor's application container/server product that is J2EE EJB compliant. Yet another benefit of EJB in this J2EE context is its capability to make the use of other Java enterprise technologies much easier for developers than is the case with such technologies in standalone environments. We specifically focus on use of various Java enterprise technologies from within the context of J2EE EJBs in this chapter and address those areas where hand-coding or vendor-specific help is a must, as well as where future improvement is expected. Furthermore, in the course of pursuing this discussion, we also present for you the integrated Web and EJB BeeShirts.com e-commerce enterprise application.

In this chapter, you will learn:

- The programmatic and declarative use of transactions with EJBs.
- The programmatic and declarative use of security with EJBs.
- The basic approach for integrating J2EE Web components and EJBs with BeeShirts.com serving as an integrated example.
- The basic approach for providing CORBA interfaces to EJBs and for talking with CORBA servers from EJBs.
- The means by which XML can be used to send and receive messages from within EJBs.
- The means by which EJBs can act as JMS message producers and be configured to receive JMS consumer messages.
- The means by which EJBs can send email via JavaMail.

EJB Transactions

We explored a wide range of Java-related transaction management concepts and services in Chapter 23, "Transaction Services." Transaction services for EJB components are implemented within the confines of the EJB container/server environment. EJBs can use such services either declaratively or programmatically. Only session beans can take advantage of programmatic bean-managed transaction demarcation through the use of a `javax.transaction.UserTransaction` object as well as through JDBC objects retrievable from the container environment. Session and entity EJBs can both take advantage of declarative container-managed transaction management services that are automatically provided by the container environment based on information configured by an assembler and deployer via the EJB's deployment descriptors.

This section explores how to provide both bean-managed and container-managed transaction demarcation for your EJBs. In either case, the model for EJB transaction management is simplified due to the flat transaction model assumed by the EJB v1.1 specification. J2EE EJB-compliant containers are in fact required to support only the JTA application interface implementation for the purposes of enabling bean-managed transaction demarcation. Implementation support for JTA transaction management interfaces, JTA interfaces with X/Open XA-compliant resource managers, and transaction context propagation interoperability via JTS is not required by the J2EE v1.2 specification. However, such support is encouraged and expected to be required by a future specification.

NOTE

This section contains a few simple code snippets that can be found in soft-copy form on the CD in the `examples/src/ejava/ejbch37/transactions` directory.

Bean-Managed Transaction Demarcation

Bean-managed transaction demarcation is allowed only for session EJBs. Entity beans must use container-managed demarcation, described in the next section. Session beans must indicate their bean-managed as opposed to container-managed transaction demarcation preference via setting the `<transaction-type>` element of its `<session>` EJB deployment descriptor to a value of `Bean` (as opposed to `Container`). Bean-managed transaction demarcation enables session beans to explicitly indicate where a transaction must begin, commit, and potentially roll back via calls to `UserTransaction` from within their methods. Session beans can obtain handles to `UserTransaction` objects from the EJB container by calling `getUserTransaction()` on its `SessionContext` object (as inherited from `EJBContext`). Alternately, a session bean can also obtain a handle to a `UserTransaction` object from the EJB container via a JNDI lookup using the name `java:comp/UserTransaction` as shown here:

```
// Acquire handle to JNDI context from container environment
Context jndiCtx = new InitialContext();

// Lookup UserTransaction from container environment
UserTransaction transaction
    = (UserTransaction) jndiCtx.lookup("java:comp/UserTransaction");
```

With a `UserTransaction` object in hand, calls to `begin()`, `commit()`, and `rollback()` can be used to programmatically demarcate transaction boundaries as you saw in Chapter 23. Between the boundaries of a `begin()` and `commit()`, all JDBC or other resource manager adapter access should be implemented that needs to occur in an atomic, consistent, isolated, and durable fashion. Given the flat transaction model required of EJBs, after a transaction is begun in such a fashion, another one should not be started until the current transaction is committed or rolled back. Furthermore, whereas stateful session beans can keep a transaction uncompleted across multiple calls on the same bean instance, stateless session beans must commit or roll back the transaction before the bean method in which it was invoked returns from the call.

As described in Chapter 23, a transaction's isolation level defines how and when changes made to data within a transaction are visible to other applications accessing that data. Manipulating transaction isolation levels from within an EJB is specific to a particular resource manager. For JDBC, the transaction isolation level can be gotten and set via calls to a `java.sql.Connection` object via `getTransactionIsolation()` and `setTransactionIsolation()` calls, respectively. Recall from the preceding chapter that JDBC `Connection` objects are obtained from calls to `getConnection()` on `javax.sql.DataSource` objects, which are in turn retrieved from JNDI lookups using `<resource-ref>` defined names.

For example, we might attempt to demarcate transactions within a session bean that periodically handles resolving data between a BeeShirts.com orders database and a separate database used to store orders sent to suppliers as shown here:

```
public class MySessionEJBean implements SessionBean
{
  private SessionContext ejbContext;

  public void setSessionContext(SessionContext aCtx)
  {
     ejbContext = aCtx;
  }

  public void resolveOrders(String supplierName)
  {
    UserTransaction transaction = null;

    try{
      // Get UserTransaction
      transaction = ejbContext.getUserTransaction();

      // Begin transaction
      transaction.begin();

      // Get context and data sources and connections
      InitialContext jndiCtx = new InitialContext();
      DataSource ordersDatabase
        = (DataSource) jndiCtx.lookup("java:comp/env/jdbc/Orders");
      DataSource suppliersDatabase
        = (DataSource) jndiCtx.lookup("java:comp/env/jdbc/Suppliers");
      Connection ordersConnection = ordersDatabase.getConnection();
```

```
      Connection suppliersConnection = suppliersDatabase.getConnection();

      // Possibly set isolation level for a connection
      suppliersConnection.setTransactionIsolation(
                              Connection.TRANSACTION_READ_COMMITTED);

      // Do work...
        // 1) Create JDBC statements from connections.
        // 2) Do a bunch of JDBC update-related work on statements.

      // If error occurs while doing work and doesn't throw exception...
      transaction.rollback();

      // Else if all is OK when done...end Transaction
      transaction.commit();

      // Close any connection and statements
    }
    catch(Exception e){
      // Error occurred while doing work...
      try{
        transaction.rollback();
      }
      catch(SystemException se){
        se.printStackTrace();
      }
      e.printStackTrace();
    }
  }
    ...
}
```


As an example of a stateful session bean that begins a transaction when an order is placed via one method and subsequently notifies the supplier in another method before the transaction is completed, we have this:

```
public class MySessionEJBean implements SessionBean
{
  private SessionContext ejbContext;
  private DataSource ordersDatabase = null;
  private DataSource suppliersDatabase = null;
  private Connection ordersConnection = null;
  private Connection suppliersConnection = null;

  public void setSessionContext(SessionContext aCtx)
        { ejbContext = aCtx; }
```

```
public void placeOrder(String orderID, Object orderInfo)
{
  UserTransaction transaction = null;

  try{
    // Get UserTransaction
    transaction = ejbContext.getUserTransaction();

    // Begin transaction
    transaction.begin();

    // Get context and data sources and connections
    InitialContext jndiCtx = new InitialContext();
    ordersDatabase
      = (DataSource) jndiCtx.lookup("java:comp/env/jdbc/Orders");
    ordersConnection = ordersDatabase.getConnection();

    // Do work...
      // 1) Create JDBC statements from connections.
      // 2) Update order database.

    // If error occurs while doing work and doesn't throw exception...
    transaction.rollback();
  }
  catch(Exception e){
    // Error occurred while doing work...
    try{
      transaction.rollback();
    }
    catch(SystemException se){
      se.printStackTrace();
    }
    e.printStackTrace();
  }
}


public void notifySupplier(String supplierName, String orderID)
{
  UserTransaction transaction = null;

  try{
    // Get UserTransaction
    transaction = ejbContext.getUserTransaction();
```

```
      // Get context and data sources and connections
      InitialContext jndiCtx = new InitialContext();
      suppliersDatabase
        = (DataSource) jndiCtx.lookup("java:comp/env/jdbc/Suppliers");
      suppliersConnection = suppliersDatabase.getConnection();

      // Possibly set isolation level for a connection
      suppliersConnection.setTransactionIsolation(
                              Connection.TRANSACTION_READ_COMMITTED);

      // Do work...
        // 1) Create JDBC statements from connections.
        // 2) Do a bunch of JDBC update-related work on
        //     order and suppliers database statements.

      // If error occurs while doing work and doesn't throw exception...
      transaction.rollback();

      // Else if all is OK when done...end Transaction
      transaction.commit();

      // Close any connection and statements
    }
    catch(Exception e){
      // Error occurred while doing work...
      try{
        transaction.rollback();
      }
      catch(SystemException se){
        se.printStackTrace();
      }
      e.printStackTrace();
    }
  }
   ...
}
```


Container-Managed Transaction Demarcation

Container-managed transaction demarcation is an option for session beans and a requirement for entity beans. A session bean must specify the value of `Container` in its `<transaction-type>` element within a `<session>` element in an EJB deployment descriptor, but no such option even exists for entity beans. The means by which a container determines how to demarcate transactions for a bean is via establishment of zero or more `<container-transaction>` elements within an `<assembly-descriptor>` element that can optionally be defined within the root `<ejb-jar>` element for an EJB module (see Listing 36.1 in Chapter 36, "Modeling Components with Enterprise JavaBeans"). Listing 37.1 shows such a `<container-transaction>` element DTD that associates a transaction attribute (as defined in Chapter 23) with one or more EJB methods.

LISTING 37.1 EJB DTD Container Transaction Elements

```
<!-- Associates a transaction attribute with one or more EJB methods.-->
  <!ELEMENT container-transaction (description?, method+,
                                   trans-attribute)>
<!-- Describes this transaction management specification. -->
  <!ELEMENT description (#PCDATA)>
<!-- Identifies particular method(s) for which this transaction
management specification applies. -->
  <!ELEMENT method (description?, ejb-name, method-intf?, method-name,
                    method-params?)>
<!-- Identifies the EJB name to which this specification applies. -->
  <!ELEMENT ejb-name (#PCDATA)>
<!-- Specifies if home or remote interface applies to this particular
specification via: Home, Remote. Used when interfaces have same method
names and need to differentiate. -->
  <!ELEMENT method-intf (#PCDATA)>
<!-- Identifies the EJB method(s) to which this specification applies.
If an asterisk (*) is used, then this particular specification applies
to all methods on the EJB. If another container-transaction is specified
for this EJB with a specific name, then the properties specific to that
method override those defined by an *. -->
  <!ELEMENT method-name (#PCDATA)>
<!-- Used to specify fully qualified parameter types associated with an
EJB method to which this specification applies. Providing this
information uniquely identifies a particular EJB method and overrides
any generic specification for a particular group of overloaded methods
or for the whole EJB. -->
  <!ELEMENT method-params (method-param*)>
<!-- Defines a fully qualified type for a method parameter. -->
  <!ELEMENT method-param (#PCDATA)>
<!-- Specifies the transaction attribute for the method(s) on
a particular EJB that are associated with this attribute. The valid
types are akin to those described in Chapter 23: Required, RequiresNew,
NotSupported, Never, Supports, Mandatory. -->
  <!ELEMENT trans-attribute (#PCDATA)>
```

Methods identified by such elements have transactions managed for them by the container according to the specified transaction attribute type. A session bean using such declarative transaction specifications must have all of its business-specific remote interface methods associated with a particular transaction attribute. An entity bean needs both its business-specific remote interface methods and its home interface methods associated with a transaction attribute. If no transaction attributes are specified for the EJB, such attributes must be defined either by default or manually at deployment time. Of course, if a particular resource manager (for example, DBMS) will not provide transaction coordination with your application server via its resource adapter (for example, JDBC), then a transaction attribute of `NotSupported` should be defined to turn off container-managed transaction demarcation and suspend client-managed transaction demarcation.

As an example, suppose that we've defined the following transaction-unaware bean for which we want to allow a container to manage transaction demarcation:

```
package ejava.ejbch37.transactions;

import javax.ejb.*;
import java.rmi.*;

public class MyEntityEJBean  implements EntityBean
{
  public void myMethod(){ /* Do something...*/  }
  public void myMethod(String foo){ /* Do something...*/ }
  public void myMethod(String foo, Object bar) {/* Do something...*/ }

  public void myOtherMethod(){ /* Do something...*/  }
  public void myOtherMethod(String foo){ /* Do something...*/ }
  ...
}
```

Now suppose that during assembly time, we decide the following about this bean's transaction semantics:

A. All remote methods should have a `Required` transactional attribute by default. That is, the container will demarcate a transaction if the client does not.

B. The remote `myMethod(String, Object)` method should have a `Never` transactional attribute associated with it. That is, the container won't demarcate a transaction; neither can the client or an exception will be thrown.

C. Both remote `myOtherMethod()` methods should have a `Supports` transactional attribute associated with them. That is, the container will not demarcate transactions, but the client may.

Given such transactional semantics, we would define our `ejb-jar.xml` file for this bean according to the basic structure shown here:

```
<ejb-jar>
   ...
```

```
  <enterprise-beans>
    <entity>
      <description>Transaction-unaware Bean</description>
      <ejb-name>MyEntityEJBean</ejb-name>
        ...
    </entity>
  </enterprise-beans>

  <assembly-descriptor>
    <container-transaction>
      <method>
        <ejb-name>MyEntityEJBean</ejb-name>
        <method-intf>Remote</method-intf>
        <method-name>*</method-name>
      </method>
      <trans-attribute>Required</trans-attribute>
    </container-transaction>

    <container-transaction>
      <method>
        <ejb-name>MyEntityEJBean</ejb-name>
        <method-intf>Remote</method-intf>
        <method-name>myMethod</method-name>
        <method-params>
          <method-param>java.lang.String</method-param>
          <method-param>java.lang.Object</method-param>
        </method-params>
      </method>
      <trans-attribute>Never</trans-attribute>
    </container-transaction>

    <container-transaction>
      <method>
        <ejb-name>MyEntityEJBean</ejb-name>
        <method-intf>Remote</method-intf>
        <method-name>myOtherMethod</method-name>
      </method>
      <trans-attribute>Supports</trans-attribute>
    </container-transaction>
  </assembly-descriptor>

</ejb-jar>
```

Although bean implementations should not attempt to perform any transaction demarcation or isolation setting themselves under container-managed demarcation, beans can call `getRollbackOnly()` and `setRollbackOnly()` on their `EJBContext` object. `EJBContext.`

`setRollbackOnly()` is used to set the current transaction state such that it can only roll back and never commit. The `EJBContext.getRollbackOnly()` method can be called to return a `boolean` value indicating if such a state was already set. Setting a transaction to rollback is useful only to inform the container that an application error has occurred within the current transaction, and that the state of the system affected by this transaction should thus be considered invalid. The container will then roll back the transaction when it is appropriate.

Stateful session beans can also be made a tad more transaction aware when they implement the `javax.ejb.SessionSynchronization` interface as shown in Figure 36.5. Stateful session beans that implement the `SessionSynchronization` interface's `afterBegin()`, `beforeCompletion()`, and `afterCompletion(boolean)` methods can be informed when the container has just begun a transaction, is about to complete a transaction, or has just completed the transaction with a `true` status if it committed, respectively.

On a final note, some vendors may also define their own specific transaction semantics for EJBs. For example, the BEA WebLogic `weblogic-ejb-jar.xml` file contains a `<transaction-descriptor>` element that contains a `<trans-timeout-seconds>` element to define the maximum time in seconds a transaction may exist between its beginning and completion. If this time expires before the transaction can be completed, the transaction will be rolled back.

EJB Security

Standard security mechanisms defined for EJBs are currently largely focused around providing a minimal set of constructs for EJB security access control. Although a mechanism for authenticating a user is implied by virtue of the fact that a particular user must be granted access to a particular EJB method, no standard means for authenticating a user is defined in EJB v1.1 and the J2EE v1.2. Such standard mechanisms are planned for the J2EE v1.3, however, and will most likely focus around use of the JAAS. Furthermore, a combination of container-specific and user-definable security mechanism is also currently needed to create a truly secure and practical security environment for EJBs. This section describes the standard programmatic and declarative means available and the additional mechanisms needed for providing practical EJB security.

NOTE

This section contains a few simple code snippets that can be found in soft-copy form on the CD in the `examples/src/ejava/ejbch37/security` directory.

Standard Programmatic EJB Security Mechanisms

Although bean-implemented security access control logic is not recommended by the EJB specification, in many practical cases it may be inevitable. The decision to implement your own security access control logic will largely be a function of which vendor-specific services your container and deployment tools can provide. Two primary main hooks into obtaining security information are provided via the `EJBContext` object (and two other methods are deprecated). Security-related calls to the `EJBContext` object are callable only from within the context of a business-specific method on an EJB. Otherwise, a `java.lang.IllegalStateException` will be thrown by the container to indicate that no security context exists.

The `EJBContext.getCallerPrincipal()` method is invoked by an EJB to obtain a handle to a `java.security.Principal` object. The `Principal` represents the particular principal identity on behalf of which the invoking EJB client is acting. A call to `Principal.getName()` by the bean can return a `String` object that is used in some business-specific security checking logic decision making. The `EJBContext.isCallerInRole(String)` method is used to ask the EJB environment whether the current principal associated with this security context is a member of the role passed in as a `String` to this method. A `boolean` return value indicates whether the caller is indeed in this role.

For example, if we have an EJB that allows a client to retrieve sensitive customer order data given a customer ID, we might restrict such access only to authorized users in the "admin" role or to the particular customer having that customer ID as a principal name as shown here:

```
public Object getMyOrder(String customerID)
{
  Object returnData = "";
  try{
    // Get principal from context and principal name
    java.security.Principal caller = ejbContext.getCallerPrincipal();
    String callerID = caller.getName();

    // If not in admin role and not the user associated with
    //   this order, then deny access...
    if(   (ejbContext.isCallerInRole("admin") == true)
        ||(callerID.equalsIgnoreCase(customerID)      ))
    {
      // Allow access to do security-critical stuff here...
    }
    else
    {
      // Access denied. Audit this event and return...
    }
  }
```

```
    catch(Exception e){
      e.printStackTrace();
    }
    return returnData;
  }
```

Standard Declarative EJB Security Mechanisms

Whenever a call to EJBContext.isCallerInRole() is made from within EJB code, an associated <security-role-ref> should be identified in the EJB's deployment descriptor for that bean. The <security-role-ref> element is defined within an <entity> element for entity beans and within a <session> element for session beans. Listing 37.2 shows the DTD for this security role reference and the optional reference to a role name defined during assembly as we describe next.

LISTING 37.2 EJB DTD Security Role References

```
<!-- Identifies a security role reference for this EJB.-->
  <!ELEMENT security-role-ref (description?, role-name, role-link?)>
<!-- Describes this security role. -->
  <!ELEMENT description (#PCDATA)>
<!-- Identifies a logical role name that this EJB uses. -->
  <!ELEMENT role-name (#PCDATA)>
<!-- Identifies a role defined in a security-role element. -->
  <!ELEMENT role-link (#PCDATA)>
```

The <role-link> element within an EJB's <security-role-ref> element is defined during EJB assembly to refer to a <role-name> defined within a particular <security-role> element as shown in Listing 37.3. All logical security roles defined for a particular EJB module are identified by <security-role> elements that sit within an <assembly-descriptor> element that can optionally be defined within the root <ejb-jar> element for an EJB module (see Listing 36.1 in Chapter 36). Additionally, a <method-permission> element is defined for each method in an EJB to define those security roles that can access such methods. The <method> element contained within the <method-permission> element is defined in the same manner as it was for transaction management (see Listing 37.1).

LISTING 37.3 EJB DTD Security Assembly Elements

```
<!-- Identifies those security roles defined for an EJB module.-->
  <!ELEMENT security-role (description?, role-name)>
<!-- Describes a security role or a method permission (see below). -->
  <!ELEMENT description (#PCDATA)>
```

continues

LISTING 37.3 Continued

```
<!-- Identifies a logical role name that this EJB module uses. -->
  <!ELEMENT role-name (#PCDATA)>
<!-- Identifies security roles permitted to access each EJB method.-->
  <!ELEMENT method-permission (description?, role-name+, method+)>
<!-- Identifies a logical role name that this EJB module uses. -->
  <!ELEMENT role-name (#PCDATA)>
<!-- Identifies particular method(s) for which this access control
specification applies (see transaction management Listing 37.X). -->
  <!ELEMENT method (description?, ejb-name, method-intf?, method-name,
                    method-params?)>
```

Thus, for our security-aware `getMyOrder()` method on the EJB shown in the preceding section, we can make the fact that it references the `admin` role relevant to assembly via its `ejb-jar.xml` file entry as shown here:

```
<ejb-jar>
   ...
  <enterprise-beans>

    <session>
      <description>Security Bean</description>
      <ejb-name>MySecureEJBean</ejb-name>
        ...
      <security-role-ref>
        <description> Bean references admin role. </description>
        <role-name>admin</role-name>
        <role-link>Administrator</role-link>
      </security-role-ref>
    </session>

  </enterprise-beans>

  <assembly-descriptor>
    <security-role>
      <description> Administrator role for bean mgt. </description>
      <role-name>Administrator</role-name>
    </security-role>
       ...
  </assembly-descriptor>
</ejb-jar>
```

As a final example of completely declarative security specification, say that we desire to add another method to our same `MySecureEJBean`, which is security unaware:

```
public void printOrderInfo(String orderID)
{
  // Assume that access to do security-critical stuff here
  //   is allowed by virtue of fact that container allowed
  //   method to be invoked...
}
```

Then we might be able to capitalize on our ability to declaratively limit access to such a method from only those users belonging to a special `ClassifiedPrinterUser` role as shown here:

```
<ejb-jar>
    ...
  <assembly-descriptor>
     ...

    <security-role>
      <description> Role for classified printer users. </description>
      <role-name>ClassifiedPrinterUser</role-name>
    </security-role>

    <method-permission>
      <role-name>ClassifiedPrinterUser</role-name>
      <method>
        <ejb-name>MySecureEJBean</ejb-name>
        <method-name>printOrderInfo</method-name>
      </method>
    </method-permission>

  </assembly-descriptor>

</ejb-jar>
```


Vendor-Specific Access Control Mapping

Although the roles specified by an assembler in the `<security-role>` elements of an `ejb-jar.xml` file define logical roles assumed by an EJB application, the container and deployment tools/people must map these roles to actual user groups and/or users in the operational system. Additionally, the container and deployment tools/people must manage how these roles relate to particular security domains from the operational system. Vendor-specific mappings from logical security roles to operational environment groups/users may be performed in an automated fashion without requiring the development of vendor-specific code.

As an example of vendor-specific mapping, the BEA WebLogic Server's GUI `DeployTool` can be used to map standard J2EE EJB defined role names to BEA WebLogic Server principal names. DeployTool populates the weblogic-ejb-jar.xml file's <security-role-assignment> element with one or more standard EJB <role-name> to WebLogic-specific <principal-name> mappings.

Declarative EJB security access control checking mechanisms provide a codeless way for determining whether a particular user in a particular role is allowed access to a particular method on a particular EJB. However, some enterprise applications may need to provide access control checking functionality in which access to a particular EJB method should be allowed based on some business-specific states and logic of the system associated with that user. For example, it may not simply be valid to say that all users belonging to a particular employee role have access or do not have access to particular getter and setter methods on some TimeSheet EJB that encapsulates employee timesheets in an enterprise human resource management application. Rather, you may want to implement a security checking mechanism that provides access control to such TimeSheet EJB getter and setter methods based on whether the identity of the invoking client matches some employeeID field state of the TimeSheet EJB. Although bean developers can use the standard programmatic EJB security access control checking mechanisms to implement the needed logic, some EJB container vendors may provide additional access control mechanisms to implement such features.

Vendor-Specific Identity and Authentication

Vendor-specific mappings from logical security role to operational environment groups/users may not require any vendor-specific code, but the exact means for how your container manages the access, addition, and removal of the operational groups/users within its auspices may indeed require vendor-specific code. For example, if your enterprise manages user profile information in a database, a vendor-specific means to access that information via JDBC may be required. However, you may also decide to use whatever means are provided by your particular vendor to automatically manage such information, which may not require specialized coding. Such methods might include a means to specify user profile information in a simple text file, an XML file, or an LDAP structure.

The BEA WebLogic Server, in fact, uses its weblogic.properties file as the default means for storing usernames and passwords. WebLogic also provides a means to manage identities stored by Windows NT, UNIX, LDAP structures, or a custom extendible identity management realm. The custom extendible identity management realm, however, involves the implementation of vendor-specific interfaces to support interoperation with the WebLogic security checking environment. The basic approach is to create a special realm class that implements methods to retrieve and modify user, group, and access control information. Thus, user profile information may be stored in a database and managed in a business-specific fashion under these interface implementations. Your operational environment–specific implementations of these interfaces are based entirely on vendor-specific interfaces. However, such built-in support provides a lot of flexibility in how you manage your specific operational user profiles. Furthermore, a proper adapter design pattern implementation (see Chapter 3, "Component-Based Software Development for the Enterprise") can be used to isolate vendor-specific library dependencies from your business-specific logic.

As previously mentioned, J2EE v1.3 will most likely incorporate JAAS for standard authentication to EJB servers. In the meantime, you'll have to rely on utilizing vendor-specific means for authenticating clients in EJB server environments. A principal identity name and set of credentials must somehow propagate from EJB client to EJB server for authentication to occur. BEA WebLogic accomplishes this via setting of `javax.naming.Context.SECURITY_PRINCIPAL` and `javax.naming.Context.SECURITY_CREDENTIALS` properties onto an `InitialContext` during initial connectivity with the EJB server from the client.

On the BEA WebLogic server side, if a custom realm is being used, special callbacks onto the custom realm implementation class are made to pass such principal and credential information to enable your code to provide custom authentication of such users with the system. An object returned by your code to the WebLogic container representing an authenticated user of the system is then associated with a server-side thread handler for the client. When subsequent requests are made from that same client associated with the thread, the client's credentials from its thread handler then can be used in the process of providing access control for EJBs.

EJB Security Authentication Model Limitations

Herein lies the rub with the current EJB framework. EJB designs with minimal or no security requirements may be portable, but implementation of commercially-viable and practical security mechanisms into your EJB-based designs may lead one down the path to creating non-portable server-side code without proper designs. Furthermore, a particular vendor's model for associating principal and credential information with a particular EJB invocation can lead to unforeseen problems with your EJB implementations if you do not consider this model carefully during EJB design. As an example, associating the security context with server-side thread representatives for EJB clients is somewhat disjointed with the EJB component and client modeling assumptions described in Chapter 36.

From my (that is, Paul Perrone's) own professional experience with designing and implementing sophisticated and production-ready EJB security mechanisms using EJB-compliant servers, I've had to create many design workarounds in practice and have made many suggestions directly to EJB vendors regarding how to better support security that suits EJB application serving models. The latest BEA WebLogic Server v5.1 release seems to have actually incorporated a few of these suggestions. Nevertheless, it is something to be cognizant of and plan for if you must incorporate enterprise security mechanisms into your EJB designs.

Extending the BeeShirts.com Example Data Model

As a final extension to the BeeShirts.com data model in this book, we add BeeShirts.com authentication information to the database. Figure 37.1 depicts our addition of an AUTHENTICATION table to encapsulate customer authentication information. Here we see that a customer is related to authentication information which contains the customer's BeeShirts.com password. An authentication type is also defined which, for our example code purposes, is always set to PASSWORD. The complete data model can be found in Appendix A, "Software Configuration," but here we only introduce an augmentation to the model above and beyond what has already been introduced. Appendix A also contains scripts for configuring the database to support the schema assumed by this book, as well as for configuring the database with some sample data.

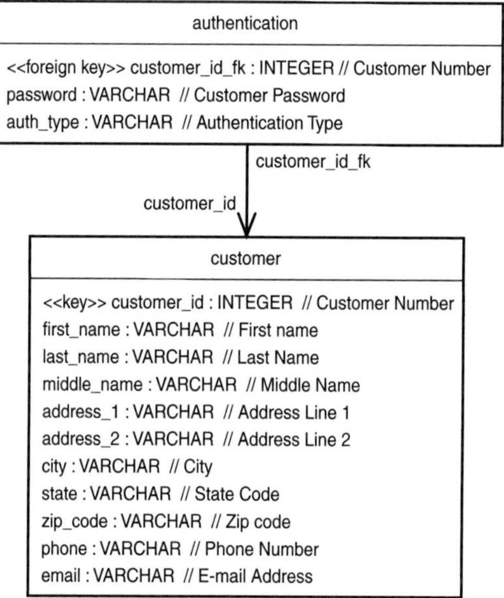

FIGURE 37.1
The BeeShirts.com authentication and customer data model.

BeeShirts.com Security

Our BeeShirts.com EJB code defined in Chapter 36 did not employ any security mechanisms. We have therefore provided a concrete example on the CD of how to implement a simplified authentication scheme for use with our BeeShirts.com EJBs. These authentication related EJBs have been placed under the `examples/src/ejava/ejbch37` directory on the CD for this chapter. You should first note that we added a container-managed persistent entity bean for encapsulating authentication information. An `Authentication`, `AuthenticationHome`, and `AuthenticationEJBean` define this bean provided in the `ejava.ejbch37.authentication` package. This bean has a customer ID `Integer` field/primary key, a password `String`, and an authentication type `String` (always set to `PASSWORD`).

NOTE

The authentication entity bean code is contained on the CD under the `examples/src/ejava/ejbch37/authentication` directory.

We have also added a stateless session bean for password-based login, for customer registration, and for reminding the user of a forgotten password. An `AuthenticationSession`, `AuthenticationSessionHome`, and `AuthenticationSessionEJBean` define this bean provided in the `ejava.ejbch37.authenticationsession` package. A `register()` method takes a `Serializable Customer` object as input, creates a `Customer` entity bean, and creates an `Authentication` entity bean based on this information. The `login()` method takes a user email and password as input, finds an associated `Customer` entity bean, finds an associated `Authentication` entity bean, compares the found password with the password submitted to this method, and returns a `Serializable Customer` object if the passwords match or throws a `FailedToLoginException` if the passwords do not compare. A `remindPassword()` method sends an associated password to a user's email address. As you'll see in the next section, such beans will come in handy when we're integrating our EJBs into the Web tier.

NOTE

The authentication session bean code is contained on the CD under the `examples/src/ejava/ejbch37/authenticationsession` directory.

CAUTION

Note that in an actual application, connectivity to the authentication session bean would probably occur over an encrypted session such as SSL. Furthermore, any password remind functionality that sends a password in the clear, although it may be common, also provides real-world security issues and should probably utilize some form of encrypted email, such as PGP, in a real application.

EJB/Web Connectivity

You saw an example of how to create both standalone Java clients and J2EE application clients to an EJB in Chapter 35, "Application Servers and Enterprise JavaBeans," and how to make one EJB serve as a client to another in Chapter 36. Our sample EJBs developed for Chapter 36 also have simple test clients on the CD for each EJB that demonstrate how to exercise the functionality of each bean. But you also may be wondering how one makes the business logic and data encapsulated behind a wall of EJBs accessible via the Web. The solution advocated by this book is to use Java Servlets or JSPs. As you'll discover, because Java Servlets and JSPs operate inside of a J2EE container environment, turning them into EJB clients is very similar to the process in which J2EE application clients and EJBs are turned into EJB clients.

BeeShirts.com: An Integrated J2EE Web and EJB e-Commerce Application

Given the BeeShirts.com J2EE JSPs of Chapter 33, "JavaServer Pages," and the J2EE EJBs of Chapters 35 and 36, we have integrated these two J2EE component tiers together and placed the resulting code on the CD for this chapter. We have also added the two session and entity beans from the preceding section into the mix to provide a means for authenticating and registering users with the system. As you'll see in subsequent sections of this chapter, parts of the architecture are also extended to demonstrate the use of JMS and JavaMail with EJB. Figure 37.2 depicts the architecture of this fully integrated BeeShirts.com e-commerce enterprise application.

The architecture of Figure 37.2 can be partitioned into four primary tiers:

- *Enterprise Client Enabled Tier*: The primary interface to our BeeShirts.com application is the Web interface introduced in Chapter 32, "Java Servlets," and Chapter 33. Through this interface, BeeShirts.com customers browse for T-shirts, add shirts to a shopping cart, register, place orders, and learn about BeeShirts.com business practices. A simple credit manager client to demonstrate J2EE application clients was introduced in Chapter 35 and is used by BeeShirts.com customer representatives to add customer credit-card information received via the phone.
- *Enterprise Web Enabled Tier*: Our Web presentation layer is composed of JSPs as described in Chapter 33. All BeeShirts.com Web requests and responses are handled at this layer with any business logic and data requests delegated to EJBs.
- *Enterprise Application Enabled Tier*: Our BeeShirts.com application business logic and data are encapsulated by EJBs at this tier. Our EJB infrastructure was introduced in Chapters 35 and 36.
- *Enterprise Data Enabled Tier*: Finally, our enterprise data tier contains all BeeShirts.com enterprise data in a database accessed by JDBC from BMP entity beans and via an EJB container for CMP entity beans. Most of our BeeShirts.com data schema was introduced in Chapter 9, "Basic JDBC," and Chapter 10, "Advanced JDBC," and subsequently embellished in Chapter 22, "Messaging Services," as well as in Figure 37.1.

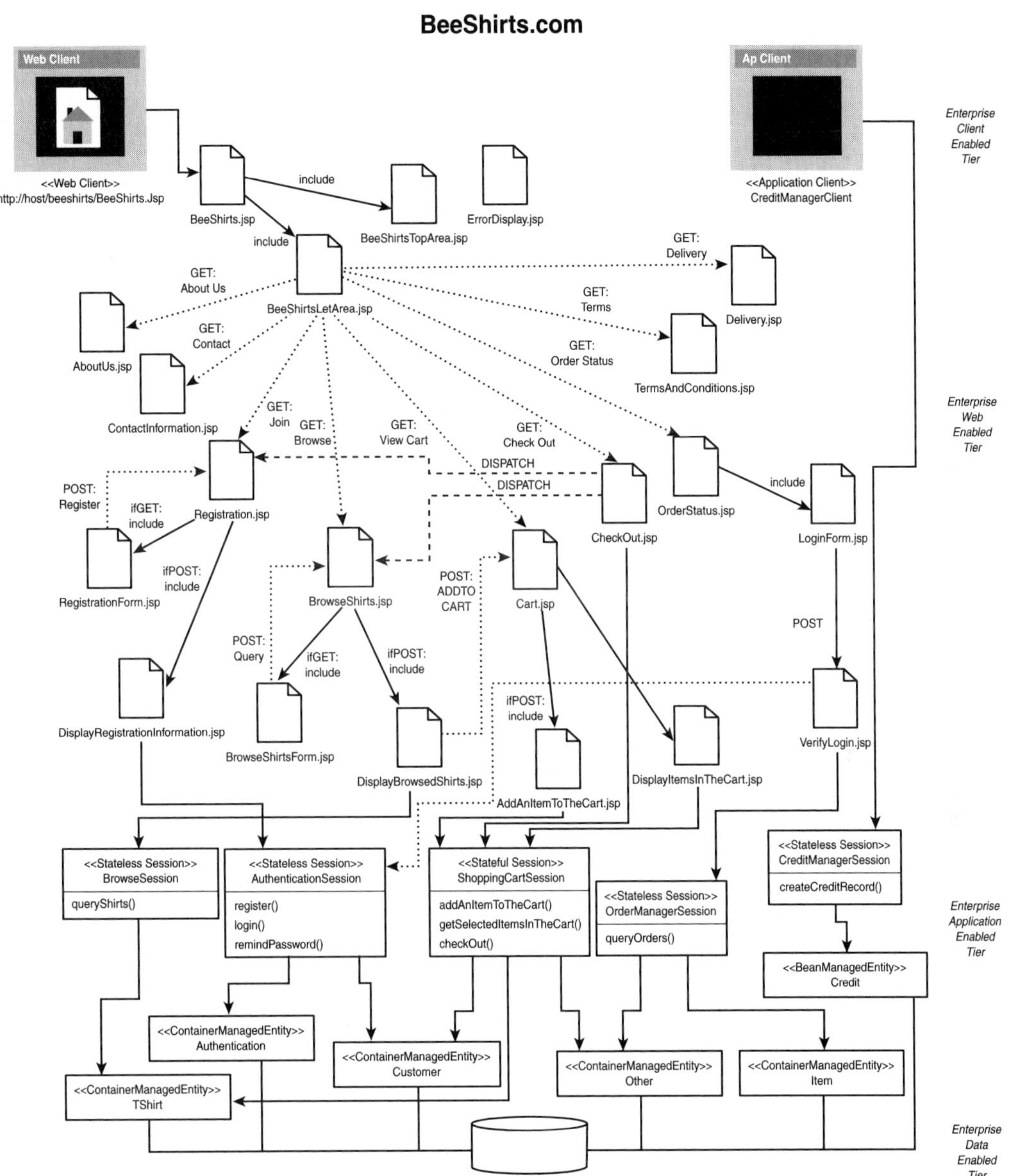

FIGURE 37.2

The BeeShirts.com e-commerce enterprise application.

The points of BeeShirts.com JSP/EJB integration are described here:

- *Customer Registration*: The `DisplayRegistrationInformation` JSP was engineered to now invoke the `AuthenticationSession` EJB's `register()` method with a `Serializable Customer` object before the user is officially registered with the system and added to the database.
- *T-Shirt Browsing*: The `DisplayBrowsedShirts` JSP was engineered to invoke the `BrowseSession` EJB's `queryShirts()` method to query for actual T-shirt data in the database.
- *Shopping-Cart Item Addition*: The `AddAnItemToTheCart` JSP was engineered to create a `ShoppingCartSession` EJB and add it to the JSP's session, if none was currently in the JSP session. The `AddAnItemToTheCart` JSP was then engineered to invoke the `ShoppingCartSession` EJB's `addAnItemToTheCart()` method to add selected item data to the shopping session.
- *Shopping-Cart Item Retrieval*: The `DisplayItemsInTheCart` JSP was engineered to use the `ShoppingCartSession` EJB stored in the JSP session to invoke that EJB's `getSelectedItemsInTheCart()` method for retrieving cart items from this shopping session.
- *Shopping-Cart Checkout*: The `Checkout` JSP was engineered to invoke the `ShoppingCartSession` EJB's `checkOut()` method to create an order for the customer based on the shopping cart session items and then display this order for the customer.
- *Customer Login*: The `VerifyLogin` JSP was engineered to invoke the `AuthenticationSession` EJB's `login()` method to effect a login and receive a serialized `Customer` object when a Login button is clicked.
- *Order Query*: The `VerifyLogin` JSP (included from the `OrderStatus` JSP) was engineered to invoke the `OrderManager` EJB's `queryOrders()` method to retrieve a collection of orders for this customer that will be displayed. Note that this occurs only if the customer can successfully log in.
- *Customer Password Reminding*: The `VerifyLogin` JSP was engineered to invoke the `AuthenticationSession` EJB's `remindPassword()` method to effect the emailing of a customer's password when a Remind button is clicked.

NOTE

Note that we have left some business logic within the `VerifyLogin` JSP to check whether the user has exceeded a certain number of attempted logins. As an interesting exercise for the reader, we encourage you to turn the `AuthenticationSession` bean into a stateful session bean and move this checking logic behind the wall of this bean to further enable the `VerifyLogin` JSP to focus on pure Web presentation.

Web/EJB Connectivity Approach and Examples

Now that we've seen *what* was integrated between our BeeShirts.com Web and EJB components, let's explore *how* this is accomplished. Whether from within a Java Servlet or a JSP scriptlet, the application code for looking up EJB home interface object handles is very straightforward. After a parameterless `javax.naming.InitialContext` object is created, a `lookup()` is performed on that context given an EJB reference name. EJB reference names follow the general form of `java:comp/env/ejb/MyEJBRefName`.

> **NOTE**
>
> The reengineered JSP code for talking with the EJBs has been placed on the CD under the `examples/src/ejava/ejbch37/webclient` directory. Note that we insert snippets from such code in this section.

We have added some methods to our `JSPHelper` class from Chapter 33 to assist with creating handles to EJBs. For example, this new `ejava.ejbch37.webclient.JSPHelper` class maintains a private `InitialContext` object created from within a `getInitialContext()` method and used to look up various EJB home objects as shown here for the `BrowseSessionHome` object:

```
package ejava.ejbch37.webclient;

  ...

public class JSPHelper
{
   ...
  private static String BROWSE_SESSION_REFNAME
     = "java:comp/env/ejb/browsesession";
  ...

  private static void getInitialContext()
    throws NamingException
  {

      initialContext = new InitialContext();
  }

  ...

  public static BrowseSessionHome getBrowseSessionHome()
    throws NamingException
  {
    if(browseSessionHome == null){
```

```
        getInitialContext();
        Object browseSessionHomeRef =
          initialContext.lookup(BROWSE_SESSION_REFNAME);
        browseSessionHome =
        (BrowseSessionHome)PortableRemoteObject.
          narrow(browseSessionHomeRef,
            ejava.ejbch36.browse.BrowseSessionHome.class);
        initialContext.close();
        System.out.println("Got Browse Session :"+ browseSessionHome);

      }

      return browseSessionHome;
    }
    ...
}
```

Our `DisplayBrowsedShirts` JSP invokes the `JSPHelper.getBrowseSessionHome()` method from inside of a `getQueriedShirts()` method defined within the JSP. At the top of the JSP, this `getQueriedShirts()` method is called to receive and display a `Vector` of `Serializable` `TShirt` objects. The EJB client invocations on the `BrowseSessionHome` and `BrowseSession` object interfaces are created like any other EJB client code. The reengineered `DisplayBrowsedShirts` JSP is shown here:

```
<%
  String postToPage = serverInfo+JSPHelper.CART_PAGE;
  String queriedSize = request.getParameter(SHIRT_SIZE);
  String queriedColor = request.getParameter(SHIRT_COLOR);
  Vector browsedShirts = getQueriedShirts( queriedSize, queriedColor);
  session.setAttribute(JSPHelper.BROWSED_SHIRTS, browsedShirts);
%>
<TD VALIGN=TOP>
<TABLE  bgcolor="#CCCC99" cellpadding="1" cellspacing="0" border="1">
<%
  if(browsedShirts.size() == 0){
%>
  <TR> <TD><STRONG> NO Shirts Match Your Query Criteria
       </STRONG> </TD> </TR>
<%
  }
%>
<TR> <TD COLSPAN=2> Queried For :</TD> </TR>
<TR> <TD> SHIRT_SIZE : </TD> <TD> <%=queriedSize%></TD> </TR>
<TR> <TD> SHIRT_COLOR : </TD> <TD> <%=queriedColor%></TD> </TR>
<TR> </TR>
```

```
<TR> </TR>
<TR> </TR>
<%
    for(int i = 0; i< browsedShirts.size(); i++){
      TShirt tShirt = (TShirt)browsedShirts.elementAt(i);
      out.println("<TR> <TD VALIGN=TOP COLSPAN=2> "+
        tShirt.getTShirtAsHTMLTableForBrowing(postToPage)+
        "</TD></TR>");
    }
%>
</TABLE>
</TD>

<%!
  private Vector getQueriedShirts(String queriedSize,
    String queriedColor)
  {
    Vector returnValue = null;
    try{
      if(browseSessionHome == null){
        browseSessionHome =
          JSPHelper.getBrowseSessionHome();
      }
      System.out.println("Got Browse Session ");
      BrowseSession browseSession
        =  browseSessionHome.create();
      System.out.println("Querying Browse Session ");
      returnValue =
       browseSession.queryShirts(queriedSize, queriedColor);
    }
    catch(RemoteException remoteException){
      remoteException.printStackTrace();
      return returnValue;
    }
    catch(NamingException namingException){
      namingException.printStackTrace();
      return returnValue;
    }
    catch(CreateException createException){
      createException.printStackTrace();
    }
    return returnValue;
  }
%>
```

The means by which EJB reference names are mapped to point to the correct EJBs is a function of configuring your web.xml file for the JSP or Java Servlet as well as a function of deployment time mapping of EJB names to JNDI names. Recall that the web.xml file has an <ejb-ref> element under the root <web-app> element. At a minimum, the <ejb-ref> element defines the EJB reference name within an <ejb-ref-name> element, the type of EJB being referenced within an <ejb-ref-type> element, the home interface class name within a <home> element, and the remote interface class name within a <remote> element.

As an example, an EJB reference to the BrowseSession bean utilized in the preceding code snippets is defined within the web.xml file for these examples this way:

```
<web-app>
   ...
 <ejb-ref>
        <description>A description of EjbRefName</description>
        <ejb-ref-name>ejb/browsesession</ejb-ref-name>
        <ejb-ref-type>Session</ejb-ref-type>
        <home>ejava.ejbch36.browse.BrowseSessionHome</home>
        <remote>ejava.ejbch36.browse.BrowseSession</remote>
  </ejb-ref>
   ...
</web-app>
```

With such elements defined, the remaining step is to define the mapping from <ejb-ref-name> to a JNDI name and JNDI name service host/port during deployment time in a vendor-specific fashion. Such an EJB reference to JNDI name mapping is needed if the Web application module (that is, deployed as WAR files) is not incorporated as part of the same J2EE enterprise application (that is, deployed as an EAR file) as was the EJB module (that is, deployed as EJB JAR files) containing the referenced EJB. If the Web application module and EJB module *are* part of the same deployed J2EE enterprise application, then a special <ejb-link> element within the <ejb-ref> element inside of the web.xml file can be defined to refer to the <ejb-name> of the particular EJB within the EJB module.

NOTE

The deployment descriptors and build scripts for creating the Web client module and for building the enterprise application for this integrated BeeShirts.com application are contained on the CD in the examples/src/ejava/ejbch37/webclient directory. The web.xml file contains the standard Web module descriptor. The weblogic_app.xml file contains standard Web module descriptor information for deploying the JSPs to BEA WebLogic. The application.xml and sun-j2ee-ri.xml files contain integrated JSP/EJB enterprise application deployment descriptors in the standard descriptor form and J2EE reference implementation–specific deployment information, respectively.

continues

A `buildj2ee.bat` sample Windows script induces the creation of all EJB JAR files by calling `buildj2eejars.bat`. It then creates a WAR file and creates the standard EAR file for the J2EE reference implementation. Note that you may have copied an `orb.properties` file to your `[JAVA_HOME]\jre\lib` directory if you have installed the standard RMI/IIOP extension per the instructions of Chapter 16, "RMI Communications." This `orb.properties` file must be removed in order to properly run the J2EE reference implementation server.

The `buildweblogic.bat` sample script is used to build all code for BEA WebLogic. Note that the `buildweblogic.bat` sample script independently copies our `Serializable` entity classes to the `[WEBLOGIC_HOME]\myserver\serverclasses` directory and does not package these files inside of the deployable WAR file. This step was taken due to a class casting issue that occurs as we have experienced with the BEA WebLogic v5.1 server when such classes are packaged inside of the WAR file. Appendix A, "Software Configuration," describes these build and deployment procedures in more detail.

Note also that we have included a WebLogic specific `weblogic.xml` file in the `examples/src/ejava/ejbch37/webclient` directory as well. This file contains JNDI name mappings for EJB references utilized by the web application code. At the time of this writing, BEA WebLogic did not provide a `PUBLIC` URL for use from within the `DOCTYPE` to reference the structure of this file and also did not provide a public name for this DTD. Thus, we had to use a `SYSTEM` URI to reference the DTD that sits in the `[WEBLOGIC_HOME]/classes/weblogic/servlet/internal/dd/weblogic-web-jar.dtd` file equipped with the BEA WebLogic installation. You thus must modify the `weblogic.xml` file to reference the correct root WebLogic installation directory for your environment. For example:

```
<!DOCTYPE weblogic-web-app SYSTEM 'file:D:/weblogic/classes/
➥weblogic/servlet/internal/dd/weblogic-web-jar.dtd'>
```


EJB/CORBA Connectivity

There are two perspectives from which we might consider using CORBA with EJBs. These two perspectives are EJB as CORBA client and EJB as CORBA server. Being able to implement either one involves a completely different set of problems. EJBs acting as CORBA clients can simply utilize the CORBA APIs provided by Java IDL as a standard API required for all J2EE environments. However, because J2EE-compliant EJB containers do not allow EJBs to create their own server sockets in order to enable the container to be able to manage system resources, EJBs cannot create and register their own CORBA servers. Rather, EJB developers must rely on the capability to offer CORBA interfaces to their EJB components to be provided by the container/server provider. This section briefly discusses the approach to creating CORBA clients and servers with J2EE-compliant EJBs.

EJBs as CORBA Clients

As we just mentioned, the Java IDL APIs come equipped as a standard part of all J2EE container/server environments. EJB component developers can thus create their own client interfaces to distributed CORBA servers operating in another environment that may or may not be another J2EE-compliant environment. Furthermore, the distributed CORBA server may even be implemented in another language. The means by which these CORBA clients are built follows the same technique described in Chapter 14, "Modeling Components with CORBA," and Chapter 15, "CORBA Communications." The only caveat for creating such CORBA clients from within EJBs is that callbacks to the client cannot be passed to the CORBA server unless the EJB container/server implements the EJB-to-CORBA mapping as described in the next section.

EJBs as CORBA Servers

The specification that must be followed by EJB container/server vendors wanting to provide CORBA interfaces to EJBs is defined in the Enterprise JavaBeans to CORBA Mapping specification (`http://java.sun.com/products/ejb/docs.html`). Although the J2EE v1.2 and EJB v1.1 does not require that vendors implement this specification, a future J2EE and EJB standard version will likely require its support. The EJB-to-CORBA mapping defines a standard means for EJB server environments to be able to better interoperate with other server environments because standard CORBA communication protocols, naming, transaction context propagation, and security context propagation are scoped within the specification.

Two main types of clients can access such CORBA-enabled EJB servers. An EJB/CORBA client is a Java-based client that uses JNDI for EJB home lookups, relies on RMI/IIOP, and uses the JTA `UserTransaction` API for any client-side transaction demarcation. A pure CORBA client implemented in any language can use CosNaming for EJB home lookups, relies on CORBA/IIOP and IDL-based interfaces, and uses the OTS for any client-side transaction demarcation. CORBA-compliant J2EE EJB servers provide support for these two types of clients in the following four key ways:

- *CORBA Distribution*: J2EE EJB servers provide support for pure CORBA/IIOP communication protocols. Remote and home interfaces for EJBs are mapped from Java to IDL in a standard fashion. Clients thus utilize such IDL to interact with CORBA-enabled EJB components narrowing any references as necessary. IDL mappings exist for all standard client-related abstractions in a `javax::ejb` module, such as `EJBHome`, `EJBObject`, `Handle`, `HomeHandle`, and `EJBMetaData`. IDL mappings must also be generated for any application-specific EJB home and remote interfaces. Furthermore, IDL mappings also exist for all EJB exceptions and must also be generated for any application-specific exceptions.

- *CORBA Naming*: A CosNaming-compliant naming service must be provided by a J2EE EJB server for clients to look up handles to `EJBHome` interface objects. EJB/CORBA clients can access this naming service via JNDI with a CosNaming SPI plug-in. Pure CORBA clients use the CosNaming service directly. When EJB JAR files are deployed to a server, they are deployed specifying the root CosNaming context from which the names defined in their `ejb-jar.xml` file are relative. Exactly how such a root context is defined is vendor specific.
- *CORBA Transactions*: A CORBA Object Transaction Service (OTS) implementation must be provided by a J2EE EJB server to enable support for CORBA clients to propagate their transaction context during client-managed transaction demarcation. The IDL for those EJBs that permit at least one method to be wrapped by client-side transaction demarcation (that is, transactional attributes of `Supports`, `Required`, or `Mandatory`) must be generated such that the EJB interfaces inherit from `CosTransactions::TransactionalObject`. EJB/CORBA clients can use the JTA `UserTransaction` object to demarcate their own transaction boundaries, whereas pure CORBA clients can use `CosTransactions::Current` for pure CORBA transaction demarcation.
- *CORBA Security*: Exactly how CORBA security context is propagated is a function of the specific CORBA security protocol that is used. Security context may be propagated via one of the standard CORBA Security mechanisms described in Chapter 28, "CORBA Security."

After a CORBA-compliant J2EE EJB server is used that adheres to the preceding requirements, EJB developers can deploy their beans to such servers and let the platform handle all CORBA connectivity. Developers can generate the IDL for their application-specific client interfaces using a standard Java-to-IDL mapping tool. From the client side, CORBA client development proceeds as usual with the proper IDL files in hand.

EJB and XML

Although J2EE deployment environments must utilize XML for parsing J2EE standard deployment descriptors, there is no explicit requirement for J2EE v1.2 servers to expose the XML API to developers. J2EE v1.3, however, is expected to require support for the Java API for XML Parsing (JAXP) as described in Chapter 31, "XML." Most J2EE container vendors either already offer such support or provide support through an older version of the JAXP. Nevertheless, these older JAXP versions differ only in their means for creating handles to parsers and in the way in which a parse is initiated. The bulk of XML API interfacing via either DOM (`org.w3c.dom` packages) or SAX (`org.xml.sax` package) has remained unaffected between older JAXP releases and the latest JAXP release.

Thus, you might safely take advantage of such APIs from within your EJBs to manipulate XML documents communicated between the EJB and its clients or between the EJB and other back-end servers. One of the easiest ways to accomplish this task is to send and receive XML documents over the wire as Java `String` objects. When the EJB is receiving an XML document over the wire, it can easily use standard JAXP libraries to parse the received `String` into a DOM `Document` object. However, when any application must create XML document `String` objects, a nonstandard mechanism must currently be implemented. An application can, of course, create the `String` object from scratch with proper insertion of brackets and other syntax items at the right points during construction of the document `String`, but such an XML document creation approach is prone to error. You may thus provide your own technique for creating the document using homegrown serialization APIs, or you may instead rely on some vendor-specific means.

As an example, the following snippet illustrates how one might go about creating a stringified XML document using the standard JAXP `org.w3.dom` and `javax.xml.parsers` libraries to create the initial document structure in an ordered fashion and then relying on a vendor-specific conversion of that document into a `String` in a few simple lines of code:

```
public String returnXML()
{
  String returnData = "";

  try{
     // get new instance of doc factory, and builder
    DocumentBuilderFactory documentBuilderFactory
      = DocumentBuilderFactory.newInstance();
    documentBuilderFactory.setValidating(false);
    DocumentBuilder documentBuilder
      = documentBuilderFactory.newDocumentBuilder();

    // Now get XML Document
    Document xmlDocument = documentBuilder.newDocument();
    // Set XML Document with data
    Element root = xmlDocument.createElement("CREDITINFO");
    Element cardelement = xmlDocument.createElement("CARD");
    root.setAttribute("CUSTOMER_ID", "08910");
    cardelement.setAttribute("CARD_TYPE",   "CREDIT");
    cardelement.setAttribute("CARD_NAME",   "VISA");
    cardelement.setAttribute("CARD_NUMBER", "1234567890");
    cardelement.setAttribute("EXPIRE_DATE", "11/27/00");
    xmlDocument.appendChild(root);
    root.appendChild(cardelement);
```

```
      returnData = xmlToString(xmlDocument);
    }
    catch(Exception e){
      e.printStackTrace();
    }

    // Return XML document as a String
    return returnData;
  }

  private String xmlToString(org.w3c.dom.Document xmlDocument)
  {
    // Write XML Document to StringWriter object and get as String
    java.io.StringWriter stringWriter = new java.io.StringWriter();

    try{
      // Write document as String using vendor-specific call
      com.sun.xml.tree.XmlDocument sunXmlDocument
        = (com.sun.xml.tree.XmlDocument) xmlDocument;
      sunXmlDocument.write(stringWriter);
    }
    catch(Exception e){
      e.printStackTrace();
    }

    return stringWriter.toString();
  }
```

Encapsulating the vendor-specific code that converts the standard `Document` object into a `String` within a single method will help reduce the amount of maintenance involved in porting your EJB. You also, of course, can implement such functionality yourself to assist with EJB portability. It is expected that standard XML serialization libraries will also be released by Sun in the future.

The receiving end of the stringified XML document sent over the wire in the preceding example can fully utilize the standard JAXP v1.0 libraries. As an example, we first simply need to parse the stringified XML document as usual and then traverse the DOM structure to extract the data we desire, as shown here:

```
  public String receiveXML(String document)
  {
    String returnData = "";

    try{
       // Create doc factory and builder
      DocumentBuilderFactory documentBuilderFactory
        = DocumentBuilderFactory.newInstance();
```

```
        documentBuilderFactory.setValidating(false);
        DocumentBuilder documentBuilder
          = documentBuilderFactory.newDocumentBuilder();

        // Parse document String using InputSource on StringReader
        StringReader ris = new  StringReader(document);
        org.xml.sax.InputSource is = new org.xml.sax.InputSource(ris);
        Document xmlDocument = documentBuilder.parse(is);

        // Get document data from parsed structure in elegant fashion
        Element documentElement = xmlDocument.getDocumentElement();
        NamedNodeMap namedNodeMap  = documentElement.getAttributes();
        Node node = namedNodeMap.getNamedItem("CUSTOMER_ID");
        String customerIDString = node.getNodeValue();
        NodeList nodeList = xmlDocument.getElementsByTagName("CARD");
        Node cardItem = nodeList.item(0);
        NamedNodeMap attributesMap = cardItem.getAttributes();
        Node cardTypeNode = attributesMap.getNamedItem("CARD_TYPE");
        Node cardNameNode = attributesMap.getNamedItem("CARD_NAME");
        Node cardNumberNode = attributesMap.getNamedItem("CARD_NUMBER");
        Node expirationDateNode =
            attributesMap.getNamedItem("EXPIRE_DATE");

        // Set attribute data from XML message
        int customerID = Integer.parseInt(customerIDString);
        String cardType   = cardTypeNode.getNodeValue();
        String cardName   = cardNameNode.getNodeValue();
        String cardNumber = cardNumberNode.getNodeValue();
        String expirationDateString = expirationDateNode.getNodeValue();
        returnData = customerID + ":" + cardType + ":" + cardName
                   + ":" + cardNumber + ":" + expirationDateString;
      }
      catch(Exception e){
        e.printStackTrace();
      }

      // Return a parsed concatenated String of the XML document info
      return returnData;
    }
```

EJB and JMS

EJBs provide a purely synchronous call model for clients. That is, clients invoke EJB remote methods, an associated EJB component instance method is invoked, the method returns, and any data is returned to the invoking client. We explored JMS's asynchronous calling mechanisms in Chapter 22. Such services allow a producer to submit a message to a queue or topic allowing a middleware messaging server to figure out how and when to send this to the distributed consumer object instance. Regardless, the messaging service eventually invokes a method on the consumer to receive the message. In the meantime, the producer has gone about its business and has not blocked waiting for a response as is the case with EJB synchronous calls.

You may be wondering whether it is possible or you may have encountered a situation already in which you would like to merge the ease of server component development provided by EJBs with the asynchronous calling nature of JMS. Unfortunately, as of the EJB v1.1 and J2EE v1.2 specification, there was no standard way to do this. In fact, the J2EE v1.2 specification requires only that vendors supply the JMS v1.0 API, but no underlying JMS messaging service implementation is required. EJB v2.0 and J2EE v1.3 will, however, define a standard way for EJBs to act as JMS consumers and thus support the capability to be invoked with asynchronous calls via JMS. However, a standard way for EJBs to act as JMS producers and nonstandard means for EJBs to act as JMS consumers is possible if your container provides a JMS implementation in addition to the required JMS API.

EJB as JMS Producer

Let's first cover the means by which EJBs can act as JMS producers. Recall from our Chapter 36 discussion that `<resource-ref>` elements defined within either an `<entity>` or a `<session>` element in an `ejb-jar.xml` file are used to define a reference to an external resource. EJBs must obtain handles to JMS connection factory objects via JNDI using names defined within `<resource-ref>` elements as is the case for obtaining JDBC `DataSource` objects. Either `javax.jms.QueueConnectionFactory` or `javax.jms.TopicConnectionFactory` objects are defined in these `<resource-ref>` elements. As an example of how to define such elements for enabling named access to a `TopicConnectionFactory` from an EJB, we have this:

```
<ejb-jar>
   ...
  <enterprise-beans>
    <session>
       ...
      <resource-ref>
         <description>Don and Judy Perrone's Shirts Supply</description>
         <res-ref-name>jms/donAndJudyShirts</res-ref-name>
         <res-type>javax.jms.TopicConnectionFactory</res-type>
         <res-auth>Container</res-auth>
      </resource-ref>
      ...
    </session>
  </enterprise-beans>
   ...
</ejb-jar>
```

Looking up such a reference from within an EJB is then a simple matter of looking up the named JMS connection factory resource reference like this:

```
try{
  Context context = new InitialContext();
  TopicConnectionFactory factory = (TopicConnectionFactory)
          context.lookup("java:comp/env/jms/donAndJudyShirts");
  TopicConnection topicConnection = factory.createTopicConnection();
  TopicSession topicSession =
    topicConnection.createTopicSession(false, Session.AUTO_ACKNOWLEDGE);
    ... // proceed as usual with JMS publishing
}
catch(Exception exception){
  // handle any exceptions
}
```

The code required to implement such JMS producer functionality then proceeds as described in Chapter 22. Such JMS producer functionality can come in handy with EJBs that want to communicate with auxiliary enterprise systems for B2B or enterprise application integration as we'll describe in the next chapter.

EJB as JMS Consumer

As mentioned previously, no current standard means is available for turning EJBs into JMS consumers. Recall that consumer listeners are created by calling `setMessageListener (MessageListener)` on a `MessageConsumer` listener representative. Defining your EJB component implementations to implement the `MessageListener` interface would be improper because that would bypass the required use of EJB remote and home interfaces by EJB clients to talk with your EJBs. It is also not possible to set your remote interface onto the `MessageConsumer` as a `MessageListener` because your remote interface must be extended from the `EJBObject` interface. Furthermore, management of transactions that embody both JMS and EJB operations is a tricky issue that is currently not required of J2EE vendors. Another means for hosting EJBs as JMS consumers is currently possible, however.

If your J2EE server vendor does implement JMS, as does the BEA WebLogic Server product on the CD, then there is a chance you will be able to effectively hand-code connectivity from JMS to an EJB. The means by which this is done simply involves creating an independent JMS consumer listener that delegates calls to the EJB. We include an example on the CD extended from the BEA WebLogic Server documented approach in which asynchronous calls are made to our `CreditManagerSession` EJB from a JMS delegate. The `JMSReceiver` class implements the `MessageListener` interface and registers itself as a JMS topic consumer. It then implements the `MessageListener.onMessage()` interface to receive a message and invoke an appropriate call onto our `CreditManagerSession` bean.

NOTE

All the sample code strewn throughout this section is placed on the CD in the `examples/src/ejava/ejbch37/creditmgr` directory. A standard `ejb-jar.xml` deployment descriptor file and WebLogic specific `weblogic-ejb-jar.xml` deployment descriptor file are also provided. Additionally, a `buildweblogic.bat` sample Windows script can be used to build our example for BEA WebLogic. This example depends upon the `Credit` EJB from Chapter 36. Thus, you will need to have built and deployed the `CreditEJB.jar` file (that is, run the `examples/src/ejava/ejbch36/credit/buildweblogic.bat` example script) before running this example. The `runJMSWeblogicClient.bat` file is used to initiate a client to this example. The `weblogic.properties` file for this example needs to have the following entries:

```
weblogic.ejb.deploy=\
  [WEBLOGIC_HOME]/myserver/CreditEJB.jar,\
  [WEBLOGIC_HOME]/myserver/CreditManager37EJB.jar
```


`JMSReceiver` also implements a vendor-specific `weblogic.common.T3StartupDef` interface. The `T3StartupDef` interface is implemented by special WebLogic startup classes that are created and invoked during startup of the BEA WebLogic Server. The `JMSReceiver.startup()` method required by `T3StartupDef` invoked during startup is in fact where we register the `JMSReceiver` as a message listener on a topic name passed in as an initialization parameter to `startup()`. The `JMSReceiver.startup()` method implementation is shown here:

```
public String startup(String name, Hashtable args) throws Exception
{
  // JMS_TOPIC_NAME from weblogic.properties info for startup class
  String topicName = (String)args.get("JMS_TOPIC");
  if ( topicName == null) {
    throw new RemoteException(" topicName="+topicName);
  }

  // Get context, look up connection factory,
  //    create connection/session
  Context context = new InitialContext();
  topicConnectionFactory = (TopicConnectionFactory)
    context.lookup("javax.jms.TopicConnectionFactory");
  topicConnection =
    topicConnectionFactory.createTopicConnection();
  topicSession =
    topicConnection.createTopicSession(false,
     Session.AUTO_ACKNOWLEDGE);
```

```
    // Look up topic and create one if does not exist
    try {
      topic = (Topic) context.lookup(topicName);
    }
    catch (NamingException namingException) {
      topic = topicSession.createTopic(topicName);
      context.bind(topicName, topic);
    }

    // Create subscriber, set self as message listener, start listening
    topicSubscriber = topicSession.createSubscriber(topic);
    topicSubscriber.setMessageListener(this);
    topicConnection.start();
    context.close();

    return "ok";
  }
```

The BEA WebLogic Server is informed about use of the `JMSReceiver` as a startup class and configured to pass in initialization parameters to `JMSReceiver.startup()` from within the `weblogic.properties` file for the server as shown here:

```
# Define JMSReceiver as startup class with init parameters shown here
weblogic.system.startupClass.JMSReceiver=\
  ejava.ejbch37.creditmgr.JMSReceiver
weblogic.system.startupArgs.JMSReceiver=\
  JMS_TOPIC=JMS_CREDIT_TOPIC
```

When the `JMSReceiver` receives a topic subscription posted to JMS by a producer, `JMSReceiver.onMessage()` is invoked with the `Message`. The `JMSReceiver` then parses this message data and uses it in a call to our `CreditManageSession` bean just like any other EJB client to our bean. The `onMessage()` method implementation is shown here:

```
  public void onMessage(Message message)
  {
    try{
      // Received text data
      String receivedData = ((TextMessage)message).getText();
      System.out.println("JMS Message Received: "+ receivedData);

      // This method parses data from the String and sets private
      //    credit data to be sent later on the JMSReceiver instance.
      extractValuesFromString(receivedData);

      // This method uses the private credit data to make a regular
      //    EJB call onto the CreditManagerSession bean.
```

```
      submitCreditDataToCreditManager();
    }
    catch(Exception exception){
      exception.printStackTrace();
    }
}
```

Our CreditManagerClient class introduced in Chapter 35 as an EJB client to the CreditManagerSession bean has been augmented on the CD for this chapter to support publishing an asynchronous JMS message to the EJB. The runJMSWeblogicClient.bat sample script on the CD can be used to run this client. A special -stringpublisher flag and JMS_TOPIC set equal to the JMS_CREDIT_TOPIC property are passed into the command-line startup of CreditManagerClient. This induces CreditManagerClient to invoke runJMSTopicProducer(), which creates the initial JMS connection, session, and message wrapper before invoking processCreditRecords(). The processCreditRecords() solicits credit data input from standard user input and publishes the message data to the topic listened to by JMSReceiver. The CreditManagerClient is thus simply a regular standalone JMS client as was demonstrated in Chapter 22.

EJB and JavaMail

We also explored the JavaMail v1.1 style of asynchronous messaging in Chapter 22. JavaMail provides APIs to send email via a messaging transport and retrieve email from a message store. The JavaMail v1.1 API is, in fact, required by J2EE v1.2 for EJB and Web containers. However, implementation support is required only for sending mail via a JavaMail Transport. The capability to receive email via a JavaMail Store is not required. For that matter, the capability to create threads used to receive notification of JavaMail Folder, Store, and Transport events will generally be forbidden by J2EE container environments. Thus, we focus on the simple means available for EJBs to send email via the JavaMail APIs. This, of course, will be the most common need for EJBs to use JavaMail anyway for notification of certain application-specific events.

The <resource-ref> elements defined within either an <entity> or a <session> element in an ejb-jar.xml file are also used to configure handles to JavaMail Session objects that serve as factory objects for Transport objects. EJBs can use JNDI to look up handles to these Session objects after they're configured.

NOTE

This section contains a few simple code snippets that can be found on the CD in the code contained within the examples/src/ejava/ejbch37/authenticationsession directory.

Our `AuthenticationSession` bean, in fact, defines a JavaMail factory reference from within its `ejb-jar.xml` file as shown here:

```
<ejb-jar>
   ...
  <enterprise-beans>
    <session>
       ...
      <resource-ref>
        <description>Mail Session Reference</description>
        <res-ref-name>mail/BeeShirtsMailSession</res-ref-name>
        <res-type>javax.mail.Session</res-type>
        <res-auth>Container</res-auth>
      </resource-ref>
      ...
    </session>
  </enterprise-beans>
    ...
</ejb-jar>
```

The distributed `remindPassword()` method implementation on our `AuthenticationSessionEJBean` class first finds a `Customer` entity bean based on an email address `String`, finds an `Authentication` entity bean based on a customer ID from `Customer`, and then invokes a `sendMail()` method on a special `MailSender` helper class as shown here:

```
  public boolean remindPassword(String email)
  {
        // get password and send Email
        lookupCustomerHome();
        System.out.println("Customer Home :"+customerHome);
        // uniqueness constraint on email attribute associated
        //   with customer in database enables us to get first and
        //   only customer associated with this email
        Enumeration customers = customerHome.findByEmail(email);
        Customer customerBean = null;
        if(customers.hasMoreElements()){
         customerBean = (Customer) customers.nextElement();
        }
        System.out.println("Customer Bean :" +customerBean);
        if(customerBean == null){
          return false;
        }

        // look up AuthenticationHome
        lookupAuthenticationHome();
        Authentication authenticationBean
```

```
            = authenticationHome.findByPrimaryKey(customerBean.getID());
          String password = authenticationBean.getPassword();
          // send email
          MailSender.sendMail(email,password);
        ...
    }
```

Finally, the `MailSender.sendMail()` utility method handles the `Session` lookup from the J2EE environment, creating the email message and sending it to the customer as shown here:

```
package ejava.ejbch37.authenticationsession;

  ...

public class MailSender
{
  /** send email to the user to remind them of their password */
  public static void sendMail(String toAddress, String password)
  {
    // Look up JavaMail Session reference
    Session session = null;
    try{
      InitialContext context = new InitialContext();
      session = (Session)
        context.lookup("java:comp/env/mail/BeeShirtsMailSession");
      session.setDebug(true);
    }
    catch(NamingException namingException){
      namingException.printStackTrace();
    }

    // Get Mail Session
   try {
    // Create E-mail Message
    Message message = new MimeMessage(session);
    message.setFrom(new InternetAddress("contact@beeshirts.com"));
    InternetAddress[] address = {new InternetAddress(toAddress)};
    message.setRecipients(Message.RecipientType.TO, address);
    message.setSubject("Password Reminder");
    message.setSentDate(new Date());
    message.setText("Your BeeShirts.com password :" + password);

    // Send E-mail Message
    Transport.send(message);
   }
   catch (MessagingException messagingException) {
```

```
        messagingException.printStackTrace();
      }
    }
}
```

Conclusions

This chapter illustrated how EJB relates to many of the key technologies described throughout the book thus far. In some instances, use of such technologies is simplified by the J2EE EJB container model. In other cases, the current state of J2EE and EJB specification development can still result in either the use of vendor-specific interfaces or a little hand-coding to make utilization of these technologies with EJB a reality. In all cases, future specifications are already in the works to make the use of these technologies much easier from within EJB and general J2EE container environments. However, let's summarize what is available now (at the time of this writing).

EJB transactions are perhaps integrated the best of all technologies mentioned in this chapter. EJB security can provide some minimal declarative access control support, but real-world code will almost certainly utilize hand-coded or vendor-specific authentication and more sophisticated access control models. We have also seen a good example of how easily the J2EE Web tier can integrate with the EJB application tier. Although EJB-to-CORBA mapping is fairly straightforward and standardized, integrating CORBA clients with an EJB framework still relies on support being provided by the container vendor. XML is not a current required J2EE API, but developers may tap the services of an XML parser to send stringified XML documents with minimal vendor specific or hand-coded help and receive stringified XML documents using standard JAXP calls. Finally, both JMS and JavaMail can be used to send messages in their specific messaging genre from within EJBs. Receiving messages via JMS, however, will require some hand-coding and perhaps a little vendor-specific support.

Enterprise Application Integration

CHAPTER

38

IN THIS CHAPTER

- Enterprise Application Integration Overview 1356
- EAI with JNI 1357
- EAI with Distributed Enterprise Communication Paradigms 1361
- EAI with Messaging Services and JMS 1365
- EAI with XML 1367
- EAI with J2EE Connectors 1368
- Embedded Applications Integration 1370

The integration of auxiliary and legacy enterprise applications with your Java enterprise applications is a problem that is generally addressed by enterprise application integration (EAI) solutions. EAI involves providing tools, techniques, and technologies for integrating enterprise data and application logic from disparate systems. EAI can be partitioned into those integration efforts internal to an enterprise and those that extend beyond a single enterprise into more business-to-business (B2B) specific arenas. This chapter describes how many of the Java enterprise technologies already described throughout the book can be put to work in providing internal and external EAI and B2B solutions. We also introduce a few new Java-based technologies that can be used for this same purpose.

In this chapter, you will learn:

- The general problems addressed by and solutions provided by EAI.
- The approach for integrating native code via the Java Native Interface (JNI) as an internal EAI solution.
- The approach for integrating applications via distributed communications technologies such as TCP/IP, HTTP, CORBA, RMI, and DCOM.
- The approach for integrating internal and external applications via JMS.
- The approach for integrating internal and external applications via XML.
- The architecture behind J2EE Connectors for EAI to be introduced with the J2EE v1.3.
- The embedded Java technologies that may be used to integrate embedded applications with your Java enterprise applications.

Enterprise Application Integration Overview

Although this book has focused on how to build new enterprise applications, many enterprise application development problems also involve integrating with auxiliary or legacy enterprise applications. A significant portion of overall development time can, in fact, revolve around integration with other enterprise applications. Figure 38.1 depicts a very simplified view of the problem and Enterprise Application Integration solution. Here we see a legacy/auxiliary enterprise application on the right side of the diagram that we want to integrate into our Java enterprise applications. EAI involves solving the problem regarding how to integrate the data and logic of such legacy/auxiliary systems into the framework of your current and future-generation enterprise systems.

NOTE

The Sun J2EE specifications and literature often refer to these legacy/auxiliary enterprise applications as enterprise information systems (EISs).

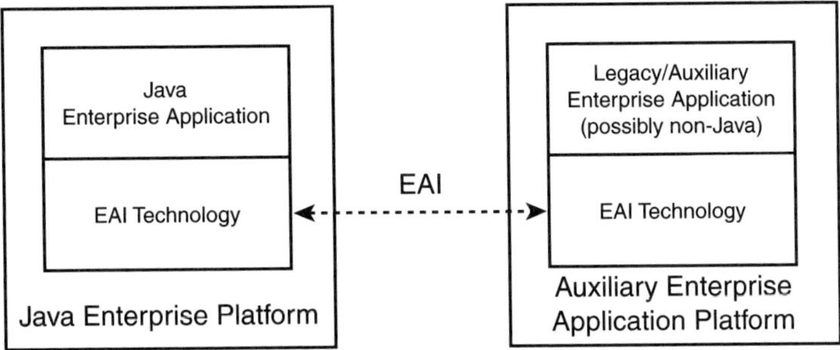

FIGURE 38.1
Enterprise application integration.

When legacy/auxiliary enterprise applications are internally managed by an enterprise, we have an internal EAI problem that can offer more flexibility and controllability over how a solution may be provided. When legacy/auxiliary enterprise applications sit external to an enterprise, these external EAI problems can become significantly more complicated because multiple enterprise organizations must agree and come to some consensus on how their systems will integrate. Such, however, are often the problems of business-to-business (B2B) applications that must decide how to exchange enterprise data.

EAI solutions involve various technologies, techniques, and products to enable one enterprise system to integrate with the data and logic of another. Although many EAI solutions involve the use of quasi-automated products for integrating one system with another, most techniques still require a significant amount of auxiliary engineering effort in addition to the need for the purchase of additional COTS products. Many EAI solutions also perform integration at the data level by transforming data from one enterprise system into data used by another enterprise system. Although use of such EAI solutions may be warranted in some cases, a discussion of their use is outside the scope of this book. What we instead will do in this chapter is describe how you might provide EAI for your Java enterprise applications using Java technologies and therefore many of the Java enterprise technologies we have already described in this book.

EAI with JNI

The Java Native Interface (JNI), as illustrated in Figure 38.2, is built into the standard Java platform and provides a means for enabling Java code to directly interact with shared binary libraries native to a particular operating system and hardware platform. This interaction occurs within the same JVM process in which calls made from Java classes to Java methods tagged as "native" get mapped to function calls in a shared binary library loaded into the same process space. At the Java level, pure Java code is often implemented above Java wrappers that provide the native code linkage from Java. Inside of the shared library, special JNI types are defined to map from the Java platform type system to the native platform and language type system. The languages used to implement these shared libraries to interface with Java are most often C or C++ based languages (although means for linking in assembly and other language-based libraries do exist).

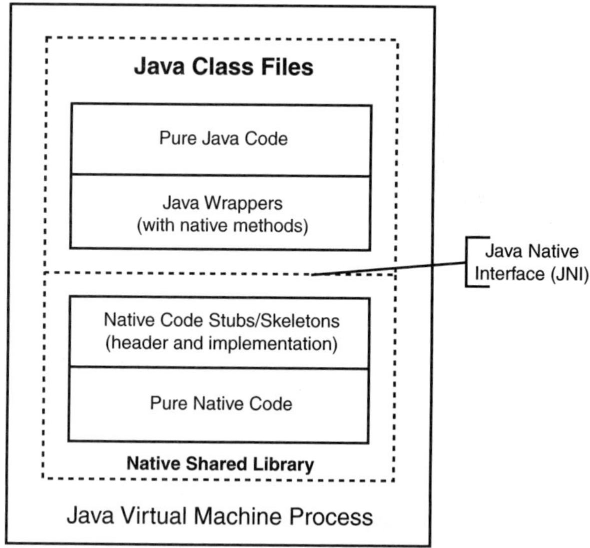

FIGURE 38.2
The Java Native Interface (JNI) architecture.

JNI can thus provide one means for you to integrate legacy application code implemented in other languages into your Java enterprise applications. A common scenario encountered by many organizations is the existence of legacy application code that can be used for a particular enterprise application. Rewriting that code in Java to integrate it with your Java enterprise environment may be too time-consuming or perhaps undesirable. The con with using JNI, however, is that memory and threading resources inside of Java and memory and threading resources inside of the shared library code are managed in disparate fashions. Thus, use of JNI must proceed with caution, and you must consider the ramifications of such resource impedance mismatch when using JNI. Nevertheless, JNI may often represent the simplistic and most direct route for integrating enterprise Java with legacy code. This is especially true if that legacy code is fairly stateless, consumes minimal memory resources, and relies on only a small amount of interaction across the JNI boundary.

Creating JNI-based bridges to native code from Java is simplified if the target native platform language is C or C++ due to the already-available support provided by the Java platform for such bridging. The steps involved with creating JNI-based bridges are listed here:

1. *Define a Java Wrapper Class:* The first step is to define a Java class that will isolate your interface to native code from your pure Java code. We assume the existence of a sample wrapper here for illustration purposes:

   ```
   package ejava.eaich38.jni;

   public class MyNativeWrapper {   ...   }
   ```

2. *Define System Library Loading:* We next need to create a standard Java class that loads the target shared library. A common means for doing this is to insert a `System.loadLibrary()` statement within a `static` initializer inside of your Java wrapper class. The name passed to `loadLibrary()` is often the extension-less form of your platform's library name. For example, as shown here inside of `MyNativeWrapper` on a Windows platform, we anticipate loading a `MyNativeLibrary.DLL` file like this:

   ```
   static
   {
     // Try to load native library.
     try{
       System.loadLibrary("MyNativeLibrary");
     }
     catch(UnsatisfiedLinkError error){
       System.out.println("Error loading library.");
       error.printStackTrace();
     }
   }
   ```

3. *Define Native Methods:* Your Java wrapper should then define as `native` those methods that will delegate to the external shared library function calls as shown here inside of our `MyNativeWrapper` class:

   ```
   public synchronized native void myNativeCall(String myParams)
       throws UnsatisfiedLinkError;
   public synchronized native int myOtherNativeCall(String hello)
       throws UnsatisfiedLinkError;
   public synchronized native int myOtherNativeCall(int hello)
       throws UnsatisfiedLinkError;
   public synchronized native int myOtherNativeCall(float hello)
       throws UnsatisfiedLinkError;
   ```

4. *Compile Java Wrappers:* Your Java wrappers must now be compiled using a standard Java compiler (for example, `javac`).

5. *Create Native Header Files:* The javah utility that comes with the J2SE SDK can be executed with the compiled Java wrapper class files to generate header files that implement the native method signatures. The javah utility is invoked with a list of fully qualified Java wrapper class names and a few options that offer a little control over how your header files are generated. As an example, using javah with our MyNativeWrapper class is as simple as shown here:

   ```
   javah ejava.eaich38.jni.MyNativeWrapper
   ```

6. *Create Native Language Implementation:* The javah command will generate a header file with a name that is an underscore-separated series of package name elements and the class name associated with the Java wrapper (for example, ejava_eaich38_jni_MyNativeWrapper.h). This file must be included by the implementation class, which must provide implementations of the prototype functions defined in the header file. The function names will look like the header filename with the exception that a Java_ name is used as a prefix, and the associated method name from which it is mapped is appended to the function name. Additional identifiers associated with method parameters may also be tacked onto the function names if methods are overloaded. For example, we might define a simple MyNativeWrapperImpl.c file as shown here:

   ```
   #include <jni.h>
   #include <stdio.h>

   #include "ejava_eaich38_jni_MyNativeWrapper.h"

   /** Impl each ejava.eaich38.jni.MyNativeWrapper.myOtherNativeCall() */
   JNIEXPORT jint JNICALL
      Java_ejava_eaich38_jni_MyNativeWrapper_myOtherNativeCall__F
     (JNIEnv *env, jobject object, jfloat myFloat)
   { printf("Called myOtherNativeCall(float)");  return 0;  };

   JNIEXPORT jint JNICALL
      Java_ejava_eaich38_jni_MyNativeWrapper_myOtherNativeCall__I
     (JNIEnv *env, jobject object, jint myInt)
   { printf("Called myOtherNativeCall(int)");  return 0;  };

   JNIEXPORT jint JNICALL
     Java_ejava_eaich38_jni_MyNativeWrapper_myOtherNativeCall
   ➥__Ljava_lang_String_2
     (JNIEnv *env, jobject object, jstring myString)
   { printf("Called myOtherNativeCall(String)"); return 0;  };

   /** Impl of ejava.eaich38.jni.MyNativeWrapper.myNativeCall() */
   JNIEXPORT void JNICALL
     Java_ejava_eaich38_jni_MyNativeWrapper_myNativeCall
   ```

```
    (JNIEnv *env, jobject object, jstring str)
  {
    jboolean strCopy;
    const char *strPtr = (*env)->GetStringUTFChars(env, str, &strCopy);
    printf("Called myNativeCall(%s)", strPtr);
    (*env)->ReleaseStringUTFChars(env, str, strPtr);
    return;
  };
```

7. *Compile Implementation and Create Shared Library:* The native language implementations then need to be compiled and any necessary shared libraries created. On a Windows platform, for example, we might compile our `MyNativeWrapper.c` implementation and generate a `MyNativeLibrary.DLL`.
8. *Execute the Java Application:* A Java application is then executed as normal. Note, however, that the shared library should be placed in the library path of your Java application. The library path search mechanism is platform-specific. For Windows platforms, we simply must make sure the `MyNativeLibrary.DLL` is in our `PATH`. Calls to such native methods may be as simple as shown here:

```
System.out.println("Beginning MyNativeWrapper Test");
MyNativeWrapper wrapper = new MyNativeWrapper();
wrapper.myNativeCall("Hello Bedford Falls!");
wrapper.myOtherNativeCall("Hello You Ole' Building and Loan!");
wrapper.myOtherNativeCall(4);
wrapper.myOtherNativeCall((float)4.0);
System.out.println("Ending MyNativeWrapper Test");
```


As a final note, we close our short JNI discussion here with a brief comment about how to properly define Java wrapper method signatures and how to manipulate the abstractions that funnel through to the native language side. This requires an understanding of how Java types and native language types map between one another. The `[JAVA_HOME]\include\jni.h` file defines the C language types that map from many Java-specific types. All fundamental Java types map to a C type of the same name with a `j` prepended (for example, `jint`, `jfloat`, `jboolean`). Additionally, special C language types are defined for particular Java object types, including `jstring` for a Java `String`, `jobject` for a Java `Object`, `jclass` for a Java `Class`, `jthrowable` for Java exceptions, and `j<type>Array` types for Java arrays of each Java fundamental type (for example, `jintArray` for arrays of fundamental `int` types).

EAI with Distributed Enterprise Communication Paradigms

In the preceding section, we briefly explored the use of JNI as an EAI solution suitable for fairly simple integration efforts involving well-defined auxiliary non-Java–based component interfaces. However, use of JNI represents a purely nondistributed approach to EAI.

Some enterprise environments, as illustrated in Figure 38.3, demand distributed access to services provided by particular auxiliary enterprise applications. Many of the distributed enterprise communications enabling paradigms described in Part III, "Distributed Enterprise Communications Enabling," will thus become applicable when such needs arise. Furthermore, a few of these distributed communication approaches can be implemented directly from the vantage point of a J2EE EJB component, as you saw in Chapter 37, "Advanced Enterprise JavaBeans Serving," or from J2EE Web components. This section briefly explains those approaches and considerations for using distributed enterprise communication paradigms when providing EAI connectivity between auxiliary or legacy enterprise applications and your Java enterprise applications.

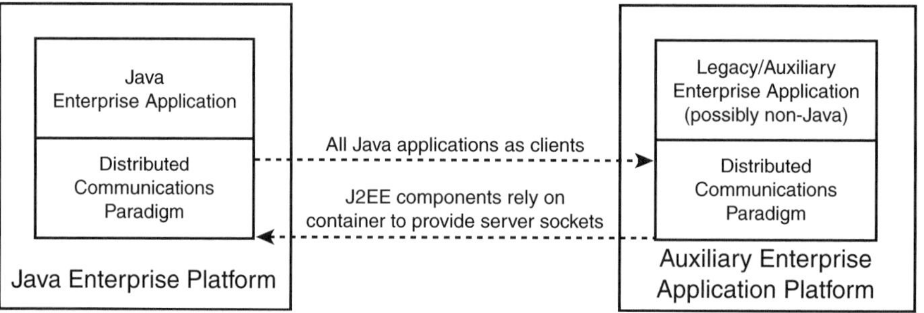

FIGURE 38.3
EAI with distributed communication paradigms.

EAI with TCP/IP

As you saw in Chapter 12, "Network Communications," use of TCP/IP in Java enterprise environments can be a costly solution in terms of time spent coding, but it may be the only distribution mechanism possible for certain environments. It is thus at least important to consider how TCP/IP can be used to connect auxiliary enterprise applications to your Java enterprise applications.

An auxiliary or legacy application may already provide or be adaptable to support a TCP/IP-based interface for tapping its services. However, TCP/IP-based support may not already be provided or a non-Java–based language may have been used to implement the auxiliary application. In such cases, JNI with Java-based TCP/IP or the native language with native socket libraries may be used to implement the auxiliary enterprise application distributed TCP/IP interface. In either case, any Java enterprise application, J2EE or standalone, can act as a TCP/IP client to this distributed auxiliary enterprise application interface using the `java.net` libraries described in Chapter 12. J2EE EJB components, however, would not be able to support a socket callback mechanism if it were needed without any container-provided support for such a feature.

In addition to EJB restrictions, TCP/IP-based EAI has plenty of other limitations. One notable limitation relates to the significant amount of hand-coding that must often be performed to implement custom marshaling and unmarshaling and other high-level protocol features. In general, TCP/IP will be useful only when the distributed auxiliary application requires a simple interface or when limited COTS makes employing an auxiliary distributed component technology impossible.

EAI with HTTP

Although HTTP has a focused Web-based applicability, HTTP can be useful in low-cost EAI solutions as well. Of course, any low-level programming of request and response handling via HTTP begins to lose its low-cost appeal if the EAI solution is anything but simple. Nevertheless, certain EAI solutions are indeed simple. In such cases, creating simple HTTP servers to implement `GET` functionality can be very straightforward.

Using the `java.net` libraries described in Chapter 12, a simple homegrown HTTP server can be made that creates a single `ServerSocket` object to block for incoming client requests using `accept()`. The returned client `Socket` objects can then be handed off to a custom server `Thread`, and the listener can go about its business listening for more incoming socket requests. The custom server `Thread`, however, can read HTTP request data from the client using the `InputStream` returned from `Socket.getInputStream()` and send any HTTP response data back to the client via an `OutputStream` returned from `Socket.getOutputStream()`. The custom server `Thread` must parse any HTTP request data and submit it to the legacy/auxiliary application and transform any response from the legacy/auxiliary application into HTTP response data. Thus, the custom server `Thread` must have intimate knowledge of how to parse HTTP request data and generate HTTP response data at the byte level, which is largely why such custom HTTP serving will often be practical only in the simplest of EAI cases. Of course, one of the COTS-based Web-enabling solutions of Part VI, "Enterprise Web Enabling," may be also be used on the legacy/auxiliary application end to offer EAI via HTTP.

On the HTTP client end of EAI, many options are available to our Java enterprise applications. Because HTTP and simple HTTP client abstractions are built into the J2SE, both standalone Java applications and J2EE-based components can easily tap the services of a legacy/auxiliary application integrated with HTTP. As mentioned in Chapter 13, "Web Communications," the standard `java.net.HttpUrlConnection` and `java.net.URL` classes can be used as the basis for building basic Web client functionality into Java applications. Connections can be created, HTTP requests can be issued, and HTTP responses can be received using these two abstractions.

J2EE container environments have life a little easier because handles to `java.net.URL` factories for URL connections can be obtained directly from JNDI using resource references. That is, say that we have a URL factory defined inside of a J2EE XML-based deployment descriptor as shown here:

```
<resource-ref>
  <description> My URL Connection Factory </description>
  <res-ref-name>url/MyHttpEAIServer</res-ref-name>
  <res-type>java.net.URL</res-type>
  <res-auth>Container</res-auth>
</resource-ref>
```

Then we can obtain a handle to such factories as shown here:

```
InitialContext ctx = new InitialContext();
java.net.URL myHttpEAIServer
    = (java.net.URL) ctx.lookup("java:comp/env/url/MyHttpEAIServer");
```

Of course, a container-specific way to associate such URL factory references to remote hosts and ports must also be provided. After that, your EJBs, Java Servlets, and JSPs are in business for integrating with a remote application over HTTP.

EAI with CORBA

The most significant technique for implementing EAI over a distributed communications paradigm is via CORBA. As described in Chapter 14, "Modeling Components with CORBA," and Chapter 15, "CORBA Communications," CORBA is a language- and platform-independent solution for enabling distributed communications. Thus, providing CORBA-based interfaces to auxiliary and legacy applications enables a very high level of EAI with other applications. On the legacy/auxiliary enterprise application side, a native language CORBA wrapper implementation around the application may be provided with distributed interfaces defined via CORBA IDL. Alternatively, JNI with Java can be used to bridge the auxiliary application locally with the distributed CORBA interface implemented via Java IDL or a commercial Java-based CORBA ORB implementation.

Regardless of whether Java is used as a bridging technology on the auxiliary enterprise application side, the interface to the application is via IDL. Therefore, we can speak to such applications from within standalone Java applications using Java IDL or a commercial ORB, and we can also speak to such applications from a J2EE EJB or Web component. J2EE components, however, cannot implement any sort of CORBA server callback mechanism due to the restrictions on creating server sockets in J2EE environments by a component. Of course, as described in Chapter 37, a CORBA-enabled EJB can be defined in J2EE container environments that support CORBA-to-EJB mappings.

EAI with RMI

RMI, as described in Chapter 16, "RMI Communications," can also be used as a distributed EAI-enabling paradigm in certain cases. The strong case for RMI on the Java enterprise application side is that maximum interoperability is guaranteed with all J2EE EJB environments because RMI is the standard EJB interface technology. Callbacks to EJBs over RMI are thus a matter of implementing regular EJB client interfacing on the legacy/auxiliary application side. RMI on the legacy/auxiliary application end means that JNI bridging will be needed if the application is implemented in another language. Although access from the Java enterprise application tier may be simplified in this scenario, access to your legacy/auxiliary application from other enterprise application environments is limited to Java-based applications that can use RMI.

EAI with DCOM

As a final note about distributed communications enabling, we feel compelled to mention the particular applicability of DCOM in such scenarios. If you are still puzzling over Chapter 17, "Modeling Components with COM/DCOM," and Chapter 18, "DCOM Communications," and wondering why we would ever talk about COM/DCOM in a Java enterprise book, then we hope the need can be finally clarified here when cast in the light of this chapter's EAI topic. When a Windows-based platform hosts your legacy/auxiliary enterprise application, DCOM may be your best bet for implementing connectivity of that application with your Java enterprise application environment. Use of DCOM on the auxiliary Windows-based application side to provide a distributed interface will allow you to easily use whatever libraries and languages were used to build the original application.

Although standalone Java-based COM/DCOM clients can be built on the Java enterprise side, you are also locked into Windows-based platforms if you use the Microsoft JVM. However, some J2EE container/server vendors offer COM connectivity as a value-added service above and beyond the standard J2EE requirements. Access to EJBs as COM objects is possible via some vendor products such as the BEA WebLogic Server equipped with this book. BEA WebLogic also allows for COM components to be made accessible from Java components via WebLogic's own RMI implementation. See `http://www.weblogic.com/docs50/classdocs/API_com.html` for more information on how the BEA WebLogic product equipped with this book integrates COM with its Web and application server products.

EAI with Messaging Services and JMS

The distributed communication paradigms used for EAI all depend on the capability to make synchronous calls onto the legacy/auxiliary enterprise applications that are to be integrated. Such an approach to EAI may be best suited for particular internal EAI projects as opposed to external EAI or B2B projects. When the need arises to perform external EAI, an asynchronous messaging scheme is almost always the best option. As described in Chapter 22, "Messaging Services," asynchronous messaging schemes allow for a greater level of decoupling between systems and also allow for the centralized management of reliable and robust message queuing by the messaging service provider. Of course, within J2EE and Java enterprise environments, JMS is the messaging service technology of choice. Although Chapter 22 describes how to implement standalone JMS consumers and producers, Chapter 37 describes the potential for using JMS with J2EE EJBs based on the current state of the J2EE v1.2 specification and based on a future J2EE v1.3 specification.

Figure 38.4 shows the basic architecture for using JMS in an EAI solution. Because of JMS's underlying Service Provider Interface (SPI)–based architecture, our Java enterprise applications can be built to readily integrate with any particular vendor's messaging service implementation that provides a JMS SPI implementation. Thus, if our auxiliary enterprise application is external to our organization, the particular messaging system provided by the auxiliary system may be easily integrated with our Java enterprise application. Furthermore, the options for integrating the legacy/auxiliary enterprise application (if that is indeed also your particular problem to solve) are constrained only by the availability of a messaging service interface for the auxiliary application language and platform. Of course, the auxiliary application may also decide to use JMS as its interface to an underlying messaging service provider.

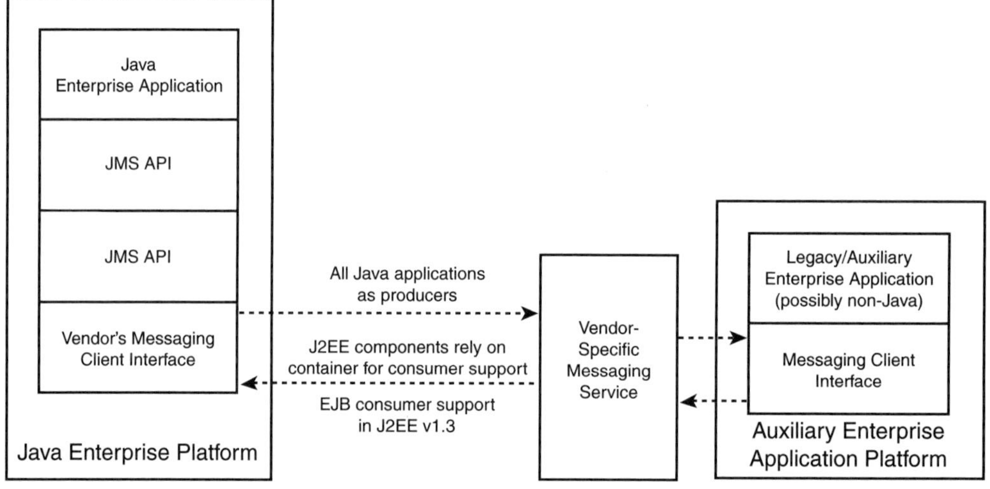

FIGURE 38.4
EAI with JMS.

With JMS, all Java enterprise applications can act as JMS producers with no problems. Java enterprise applications built as J2EE EJB components, however, currently have limitations with J2EE v1.2–based containers in terms of directly being able to host EJBs as JMS consumers. Rather, a separate JMS consumer delegate to an EJB is needed. The J2EE v1.3–based containers, however, will enable full integration between EJB and JMS.

EAI with XML

As described in Chapter 31, "XML," XML is the data representation technology of choice for Java enterprise environments. XML is also the emerging data representation technology of choice among most other enterprise application environments. XML is particularly attractive to EAI vendors and is almost always incorporated into EAI product vendor architectures. XML is used to represent the data that is transferred from one system to another and thus becomes the standard language used for passing messages when pursuing EAI. Standard DTDs for interpreting exchanged XML documents can be defined and shared between systems that want to be integrated. A means for transforming XML documents from one system's dialect to another system's dialect can also be achieved using technologies such as XSLT.

Figure 38.5 depicts the basic architecture for integrating your Java enterprise environment with a legacy/auxiliary enterprise application environment via XML. A legacy/auxiliary enterprise application must either already have or be extended with an XML document builder/parser for constructing and parsing XML documents. Such products are already very much commercially available for most platforms with APIs in various programming languages. Additionally, certain standardized ways of conducting B2B and EAI have already begun to result in commercially available libraries for encapsulating XML-based information in a fashion that is specific to a particular application. As a result, standard DTDs emerge for describing such documents, and standard ways of transforming documents from one dialect into another may be defined via an XSLT-like technology.

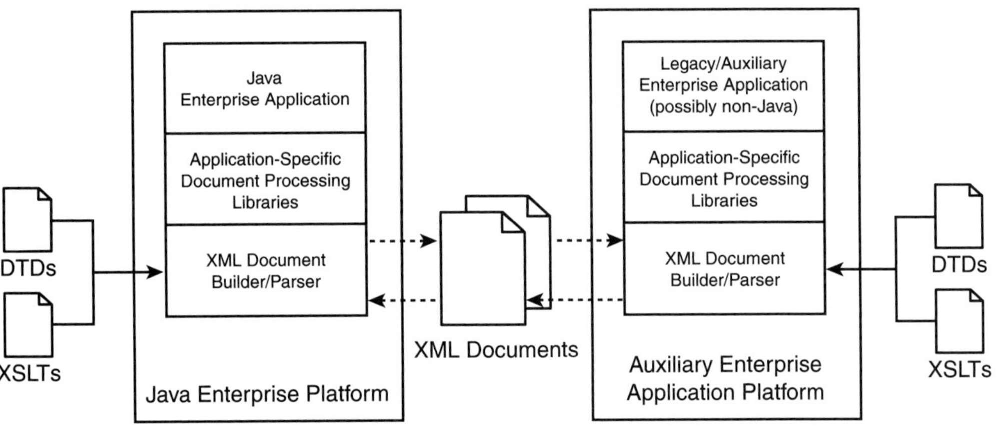

FIGURE 38.5
EAI with XML.

On the Java enterprise application side, you have already seen in Chapter 31 that standard Java libraries exist for creating and parsing XML documents using standard SAX or DOM interfaces. Chapter 37 also describes the capability to use XML for communication via EJBs operating within J2EE containers. Such Java enterprise applications are thus already largely readied for use of XML-based EAI now and will certainly be even more readied in the future as XML becomes more accessible to all J2EE-compliant container environments with version 1.3 of the J2EE specification.

The form of XML document that gets passed between enterprise applications will be application-specific. In some scenarios, you may actually have control over defining the XML document message formats via specification of DTDs that will be used on both enterprise application sides of the house to be integrated. In other scenarios in which XML document message formats are already defined, you may opt to integrate the enterprise application with those messaging standards, perhaps using some reusable document processing libraries. You may instead also define a set of transformations to be performed on the predefined XML documents using a technology like XSLT that can transform XML documents sent or received over the wire into a format that your enterprise application can understand.

The ease with which any XML document transformations and integration effort can be carried out will be a function of the type of XML document. XML used in a data-driven application will result in XML document formats that simply contain serialized representations of objects to be exchanged (for example, sending a serialized form of a credit object to an external credit vetting system). XML may also be used to encapsulate actual commands or method invocations incorporating such data as a command or method name, parameter names, and parameter values, and subsequently requiring a serialized response message associated with the particular method invocation. Finally, XML can also contain arbitrarily complicated query data, `CDATA`, and processing instructions used in more sophisticated XML-based applications.

Because XML can represent simple to arbitrarily complicated data, it is a prime EAI candidate for representation of data that must emanate from and be consumed by many different enterprise applications. In almost every regard, JMS as the messaging control technology and XML as the message representation technology are the perfect combination for external EAI and B2B. When CORBA as an underlying messaging communication paradigm implementation is added into the mix, maximum interoperability and platform flexibility are ensured.

EAI with J2EE Connectors

On the horizon to be incorporated into the J2EE v1.3 architecture are J2EE connectors. J2EE connectors, as illustrated in Figure 38.6, define a standard Connector Service Provider Interface to be implemented by legacy/auxiliary enterprise application vendors (aka "EIS" vendors per Sun terminology). EIS vendors provide resource adapters implementing the Connector

SPI to provide connectivity between the management services of a J2EE-based container/server and the vendor's EIS. By providing such resource adapters implementing standard SPIs, J2EE container providers can properly manage the services provided by EIS vendors using an interface that does not need to vary per vendor EIS. EIS vendors can also be guaranteed that their products will easily plug into any other vendor's J2EE-compliant server product.

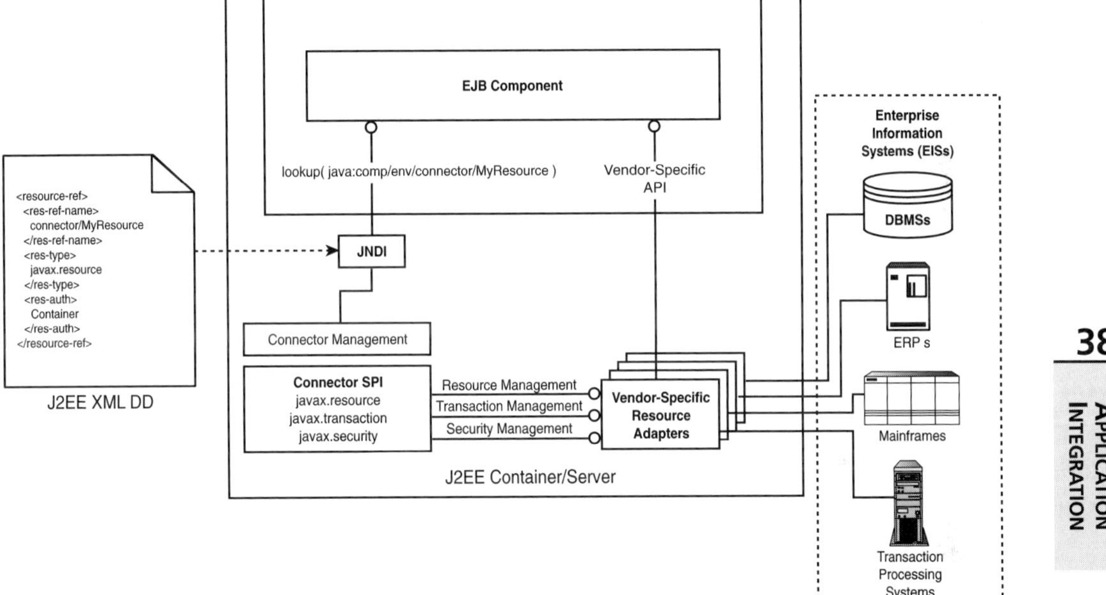

FIGURE 38.6
J2EE connector architecture.

The Connector SPI defines three main interface types that can be implemented by EIS vendors. A resource management interface allows a J2EE-based server to manage how connections to EISs are pooled and allocated to J2EE component clients on request. A transaction management interface allows a J2EE-based server to manage distributed transactions that involve multiple EISs. Finally, a security management interface manages secure access to the EIS from components inside of the J2EE container environment.

J2EE components, such as EJBs, initially obtain handles to vendor-specific resources via JNDI. Vendor-specific resource references will be configurable via a `<resource-ref>` element entry in a J2EE XML-based deployment descriptor using sub-elements such as `<res-ref-name>`

elements (for example, `connector/MyResource`) and `<res-type>` elements (that is, the class name of the resource object). J2EE components then look up such resources via an `InitialContext.lookup()` method using the `<res-ref-name>`. The J2EE container can then appropriately handle how such a resource will get allocated to a requesting component using the resource management connection pooling capabilities enabled by the underlying standard Connector SPI.

After the J2EE component has a handle to that resource, however, the API is vendor-specific. That is, the J2EE component uses whatever vendor-specific APIs they have defined for that resource when integrating the EIS with the J2EE-based enterprise application. The good news is, however, that J2EE components dependent on such EIS APIs will be able to be ported from one J2EE-compliant container/server vendor product to another if both container/server vendors and your EIS vendor support the Connector SPI. Thus, building J2EE-based enterprise applications will be made even more portable when J2EE Connector technologies are employed for EIS integration.

Embedded Applications Integration

Not all applications in an enterprise sit inside of desktop computers and workstations or inside of large server or mainframe platforms. A current and growing need in many enterprise systems is to also integrate their peripheral embedded applications into the mix. Embedded applications drive such devices in the enterprise system as printers, photo copiers, PDAs, cell phones, scanners, fax machines, ATMs, information kiosks, cash registers and checkout counters, remote automotive terminals, and traffic lights, to name a few. Embedded applications may be viewed as the bridge between the informational and physical universe of an enterprise. They are the I/O sensors and actuators of an enterprise that connect people, physical assets, and the environment with the enterprise. Embedded devices may connect with enterprise applications via standard Internet-based communication paradigms, CORBA, or perhaps via a wireless communication paradigm.

The very birth of Java was driven by the desire on the part of Sun to become involved in the embedded consumer electronics and associated embedded software market. Sun has continued with the pursuit of its interests and has as a result fostered many products, APIs, and platforms that focus on embedded Java applications. Although a detailed discussion of embedded Java technologies is beyond the scope of this book, we do want to close this chapter with a brief description of those Java technologies used in embedded applications that can be integrated with Java enterprise applications. The following list contains a brief description of the core embedded Java technologies that can be integrated with enterprise Java technologies:

- *Java 2 Platform, Micro Edition (J2ME):* The J2ME is the embedded platform counterpart to the large-scale J2EE platform. The J2ME contains a JRE and a minimal set of APIs needed for embedded applications. Community-defined profiles are used to specify additional APIs and libraries needed for specific application types. Two main classes of J2ME configuration are the Limited, Connected Device Configuration for embedded applications in the 128KB to 512KB memory range and the Connected Device Configuration for embedded applications with 512KB+ memory.
- *PersonalJava:* PersonalJava was an embedded application environment introduced before the J2ME and was specialized to satisfy higher-end embedded application needs such as those for PDAs, cell phones, and set-top boxes. PersonalJava is now being merged with the J2ME to represent one J2ME profile suitable in Connected Device Configurations for embedded "Personal" and "Web" applications.
- *EmbeddedJava:* EmbeddedJava, also introduced before the J2ME, provides a means to configure exactly which aspects of a JRE and which APIs are used by a particular embedded Java application. EmbeddedJava accomplishes this task by running the Java code that you want to embed through a set of filtering and compacting tools that generate native language code containing translated versions of all JRE and Java APIs used, as well as a translated version of your Java code. The native language code can then be compiled and linked into a minimalist binary executable for your embedded platform. EmbeddedJava was dependent on the Java 1.1 platform at the time of this writing.
- *JavaCard:* At the lowest level of Java embedding, the JavaCard technology provides the capability to embed the most minimal JRE and APIs into a processor and memory space small enough to fit onto a credit card. Such cards are used for secure identification of individuals and for commerce transactions such as are used for credit and debit cards.
- *Jini:* We have already described Jini in Chapter 20, "Directory and Trading Services," as a technology useful in building trading services for enterprise applications. Jini, in fact, is primarily touted for its applicability to embedded application environments as described by us in another paper (`http://www.assuredtech.com/papers/jini/embedded.pdf`). When a Jini-based discovery and trading service is provided for embedded applications, your enterprise applications can dynamically discover when its embedded peripherals are available and negotiate with a community of such devices for access to their services from enterprise applications. For example, your enterprise applications can dynamically negotiate access to network printing devices using Jini.
- *Java Communications API:* The Java Communications API is a standard Java extension defined in the `javax.comm` package to offer access to serial (RS-232) and parallel (IEEE 1284) communication ports from Java applications.

- *Minimum CORBA:* CORBA v3.0 includes a specification for minimum CORBA. Minimum CORBA, as the name implies, defines a minimum profile for CORBA that can be used in embedded applications. A real-time CORBA specification is also being defined for enabling determinism in managed resources critical to many embedded real-time applications. Resources needing real-time determinism include connection management, thread management, state management, and communications protocol.
- *Wireless Access Protocol (WAP)*: WAP defines a standard communications protocol suite for distributed communications between wireless devices. WAP specifically addresses how wireless devices can interface with the Internet.
- *Wireless Markup Language (WML)*: WML is a markup language used for textual display of Web pages on embedded devices. WML is specifically designed to be useful for representing data communicated over WAP.

Use of such technologies in embedded applications allows for maximum ease of integration between embedded applications and enterprise-scale applications. Enterprise applications can utilize TCP/IP, HTTP, CORBA, and RMI to directly communicate with embedded applications that utilize such technologies. Thus, use of Java in embedded applications and integration with enterprise applications truly enable you to permeate every vein of the enterprise to provide a fully caffeinated enterprise.

Conclusions

Enterprise Application Integration (EAI) of Java enterprise technologies with legacy/auxiliary enterprise applications is well supported by the host of Java enterprise technologies available today and is described throughout this book. Internal EAI solutions may utilize JNI and certain distributed communications enabling approaches such as CORBA, TCP/IP, HTTP, RMI, and DCOM. External EAI and B2B solutions may pursue a more loosely coupled solution that involves JMS for asynchronous message communications and XML for standard message representations and dialect transformations. J2EE connectors with commercial enterprise application vendor products and the integration of embedded applications with the enterprise are two other areas of EAI that enterprise system architects and developers must consider. As this book and chapter have thus pointed out, not only can building Java enterprise systems be made easy with Java enterprise technologies and the J2EE, but the integration of enterprise applications with these same technologies also is at your fingertips.

Appendixes

A Software Configuration 1375

B Additional Resources 1405

Software Configuration

APPENDIX

A

This appendix contains descriptions of how to configure the commercial off the shelf (COTS) and sample software equipped with this book on the accompanying CD. Because of the highly dynamic nature involved in vendor software releases, the information in this appendix is perhaps the most sensitive-to-change information in the book. Stay tuned for any updates to these instructions posted to `http://www.assuredtech.com/books/j2ee/software.html`.

Also note that much of the material in this appendix is very dry and reference-oriented by nature. We thus recommend that you not read this information in one sitting but rather refer to each section of this appendix as you encounter examples that depend on that section's contents. We describe how each chapter in the book with associated sample code on the CD relates to each section in this appendix (in the "Software Configuration per Chapter" section of this appendix).

Software on the CD

The software on the CD is placed into one of the directories depicted graphically in Figure A.1. At the leftmost side of this diagram, we see the root directory for the CD (`<CD_ROOT>`). `<CD_ROOT>` is not an actual directory name, but rather represents the top-level directory for all code on the CD and will be referred to throughout this appendix. The `cots` directory contains all COTS software equipped with the book on the CD. Other COTS software used in the book will be downloadable from various Web sites. The `webref` directory contains links to additional resources on the Web. The `examples` directory contains all the sample source code (in a `src` subdirectory) and COTS configuration scripts (in a `config` subdirectory).

The `src` directory under the `examples` directory represents the root of all Java source code (prefixed with the `ejava` package name). Each chapter with sample code stored in soft form on the CD has its own directory below the `ejava` directory. Finally, note that a special `classes` directory has been established on the CD. No compiled Java class files are stored in this directory, but it is left as a placeholder in the event that readers want to transfer the entire CD directory structure and contents into a working local directory on their host machines.

Note also that a sample `setenv.bat` file is contained on the CD in the `<CD_ROOT>\examples\config` directory that may be used to set environment variables for your particular environment. The `setenv.bat` file simply serves as a starter file that must be modified for your particular environment based on the instructions that follow in this appendix.

The CD also contains a nifty automatic startup feature and GUI for Windows platforms. The GUI can also be started by invoking the `<CD_ROOT>\Start.exe` application file. The resulting GUI window enables you to explore the CD example code, explore the COTS products on the CD, obtain access to online web resources, and discover other book, product registration, and support information.

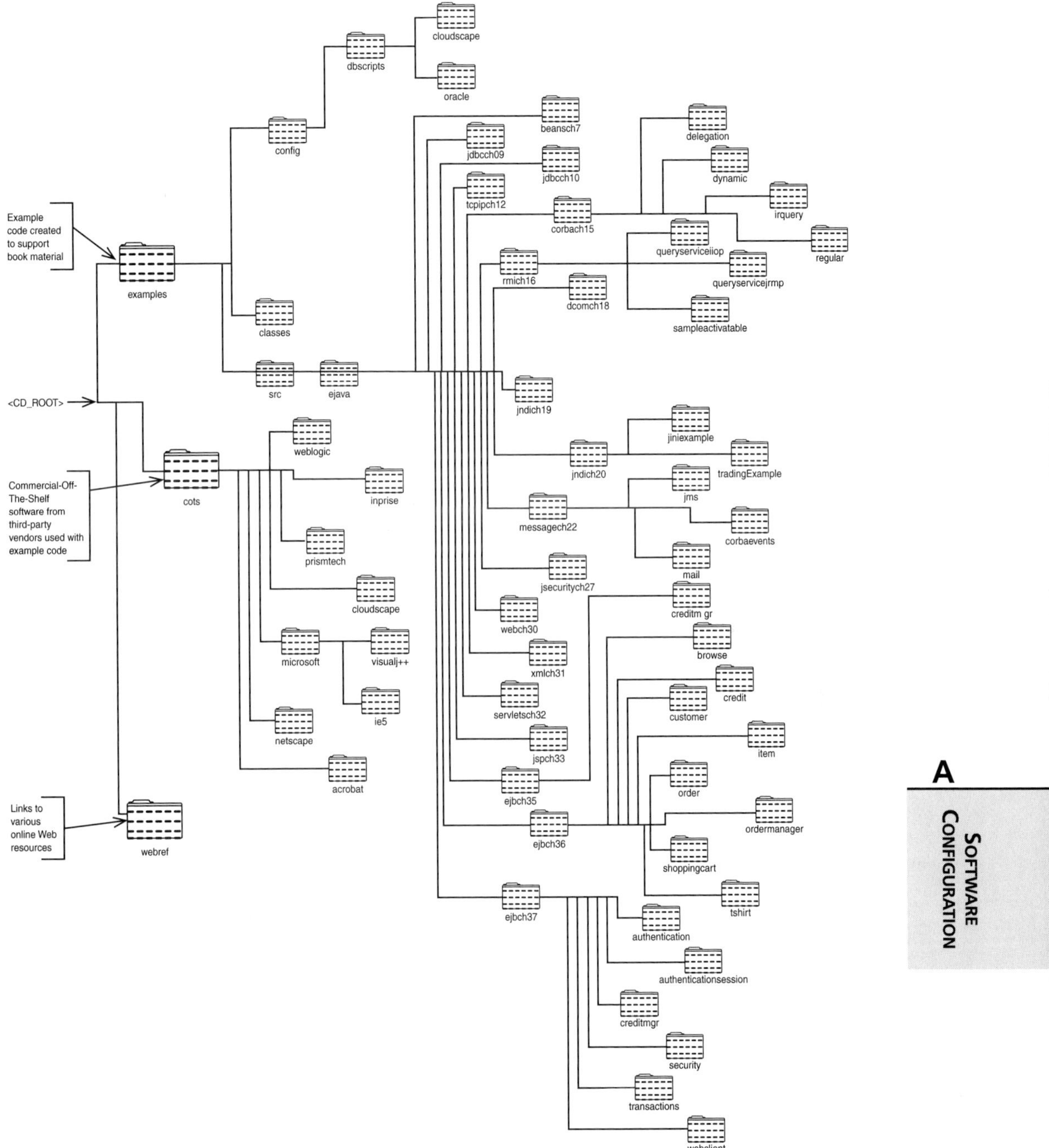

FIGURE A.1

The Building Java Enterprise Systems with J2EE *CD structure.*

A

SOFTWARE CONFIGURATION

Software Configuration per Chapter

This appendix describes general software configuration procedures that must be performed to run the sample code associated with chapters in the book. In general, the large majority of code examples in this book will work only after the following Common Software Configuration sections of this appendix have been successfully completed:

- J2SE Configuration
- J2EE Configuration
- Java Environment Variable Configuration
- Sample Software Configuration

Additionally, Table A.1 maps chapters of the book to the section titles of this appendix whose instructions are pertinent to that chapter. Note that in Table A.1, we repeat those sections relevant to a chapter for each chapter in the book. Of course, after a particular software configuration step is performed for one chapter, it will no longer be necessary to perform many of the same configuration steps for a subsequent chapter that is also dependent on those steps.

TABLE A.1 Appendix Section(s) Relevant to a Chapter

Chapter	*Configuration Step(s) Required*
Chapter 7	Common Software Configuration JavaBeans Configuration
Chapter 9	Common Software Configuration Database Configuration
Chapter 10	Common Software Configuration Database Configuration
Chapter 12	Common Software Configuration Database Configuration
Chapter 15	Common Software Configuration Database Configuration CORBA ORB Configuration RMI/IIOP Configuration
Chapter 16	Common Software Configuration Database Configuration RMI/IIOP Configuration
Chapter 18	Common Software Configuration Microsoft Java Configuration Database Configuration
Chapter 19	Common Software Configuration CORBA ORB Configuration

Chapter	*Configuration Step(s) Required*
	CORBA Services Configuration JNDI Configuration RMI/IIOP Configuration
Chapter 20	Common Software Configuration CORBA ORB Configuration CORBA Services Configuration JNDI Configuration LDAP Configuration Jini Configuration
Chapter 22	Common Software Configuration BEA WebLogic Server Configuration Database Configuration CORBA ORB Configuration CORBA Services Configuration JMS Configuration JavaMail Configuration
Chapter 27	Common Software Configuration
Chapter 30	Common Software Configuration
Chapter 31	Common Software Configuration XML Configuration
Chapter 32	Common Software Configuration BEA WebLogic Server Configuration Web Configuration
Chapter 33	Common Software Configuration BEA WebLogic Server Configuration Web Configuration
Chapter 35	Common Software Configuration BEA WebLogic Server Configuration Application Server Configuration
Chapter 36	Common Software Configuration BEA WebLogic Server Configuration Database Configuration Application Server Configuration
Chapter 37	Common Software Configuration BEA WebLogic Server Configuration Database Configuration Web Configuration Application Server Configuration JMS Configuration JavaMail Configuration

J2SE Configuration

Most of the examples in this book require a Java 2 Platform, Standard Edition (J2SE) version 1.2 compatible Java runtime environment (JRE) and software development kit (SDK). In fact, the J2EE v1.2 is dependent on the J2SE v1.2. The J2SE v1.2 SDK can be downloaded from `http://java.sun.com/products/jdk/1.2/`. Follow the instructions provided on that site for downloading and installing the J2SE v1.2 SDK for your particular platform. We should note that our sample helper scripts equipped with the book are catered for Windows environments but can be extended or mimicked for use with a Java SDK on any platform.

Our build scripts equipped with the CD typically assume that you have set the `JAVA_HOME` environment variable to the root directory of your J2SE installation. For example, at a Windows DOS prompt, you might set this variable like this:

```
set JAVA_HOME=C:\jdk1.2.2
```

The J2SE v1.3 cannot be used with the J2EE v1.2, but it can be used for many of the stand-alone Java applications described in this book. The J2SE v1.3 can be downloaded from `http://java.sun.com/products/jdk/1.3/`. Follow the instructions provided on that site for downloading and installing the J2SE v1.3 SDK for your particular platform.

J2EE Configuration

Part VI, "Enterprise Web Enabling," and Part VII, "Enterprise Applications Enabling," provide examples of how to run and deploy Web and EJB components inside the Java 2 Platform, Enterprise Edition version 1.2 reference implementation server. Those parts of the book also assume the use and availability of the J2EE version 1.2 APIs and SDK. The J2EE v1.2 software can be downloaded from `http://www.javasoft.com/j2ee/j2sdkee/`. Follow the instructions provided on that site for downloading and installing the J2EE SDK for your particular platform.

Our build scripts equipped with the CD typically assume that you have set the `J2EE_HOME` environment variable to the root directory of your J2EE installation. For example, at a Windows DOS prompt, you might set this variable as shown here:

```
set J2EE_HOME=C:\j2sdkee1.2
```

The `[J2EE_HOME]\bin\j2ee` command is used to start a J2EE server. The `[J2EE_HOME]\bin\packager` tool is used to create J2EE WAR, EJB JAR, EAR, and Application Client JAR files. The `[J2EE_HOME]\bin\deploytool` is used to initiate the deployment of J2EE packaged modules and enterprise applications using either a GUI or a command-line form of the tool. The documentation for how to use such tools with the J2EE reference implementation can be downloaded from `http://www.javasoft.com/j2ee/j2sdkee/`.

Java Environment Variable Configuration

Aside from the standard Java environment variables defined previously, the PATH and CLASSPATH environment variables must also be set. Our build script examples typically set these variables automatically when building or running an example. The PATH identifies the path for executable applications, and the CLASSPATH identifies the path for class files and archive files (that is, JAR files) to be used when initiating the JRE. See http://java.sun.com/products/jdk/1.2/docs/tooldocs/tools.html for more information specific to your particular platform.

Microsoft Java Configuration

The Microsoft Java Virtual Machine (MSJVM) is used to facilitate the creation of Java-based COM/DCOM applications. The MSJVM, also referred to as jview, comes with the Microsoft Java SDK version 3.2 or higher. You can download the latest Microsoft Java SDK from http://www.microsoft.com/java. Follow the instructions provided on that site for downloading and installing the Microsoft JVM SDK for use with the COM/DCOM examples in the book. To use our sample COM/DCOM scripts equipped on the CD, the MSDK_JAVA environment variable must be set to the root directory of a Microsoft SDK installation (we have used the Microsoft SDK for Java v3.2).

Microsoft Visual J++ version 6.0 or higher can be used to help create the COM/DCOM examples in the book. The Microsoft Visual J++ tool of most use to you will be the Professional Edition, with better support for building COM and DCOM applications than that found with other editions. An evaluation copy of Microsoft Visual J++ is provided on the CD in the <CD_ROOT>\cots\microsoft\visualj++ directory.

BEA WebLogic Server Configuration

The BEA WebLogic Server v5.1 is equipped with this book on the CD in the <CD_ROOT>\cots\weblogic directory. The BEA WebLogic Server, in fact, contains much of the J2SE- and J2EE-compliant software infrastructure that can be used to execute many of the examples provided on the CD. All BEA WebLogic documentation is rooted at http://www.weblogic.com/docs50/resources.html. The specific instructions for installing the BEA WebLogic Server are contained at http://www.weblogic.com/docs50/install/.

The root directory in which you install the BEA WebLogic Server on your machine corresponds to a WEBLOGIC_HOME environment variable assumed by the configuration scripts for our sample software. On a Windows platform, this environment variable may be set as exemplified here:

```
set WEBLOGIC_HOME= D:\weblogic
```

A special weblogic.properties Java properties file contained under the WEBLOGIC_HOME directory defines many of the properties we will need to modify throughout this book for proper operation with our examples. A complete description of all BEA WebLogic Server properties configurable in the weblogic.properties file is defined at http://www.weblogic.com/docs50/admindocs/properties.html.

A set of special scripts is contained under the WEBLOGIC_HOME directory for starting the BEA WebLogic server. On a Windows NT platform, the script to use is named startWeblogic.cmd. For UNIX platforms the script to use is named startWeblogic.sh, and for Windows NT platforms using the Microsoft SDK the script to use is called startWeblogicJView.cmd. These scripts can be configured to easily start a BEA WebLogic Server that references the weblogic.properties file. You will specifically need to set the JDK_HOME environment variable defined in the startWeblogic file to reference your [JAVA_HOME] directory. More information on starting the BEA WebLogic Server and on configuring these startWeblogic files can be found at http://www.weblogic.com/docs50/install/startserver.html.

Sample Software Configuration

Most of the sample code on this book's CD is compiled using standard Java compilation tools. Furthermore, a subset of the code on this book's CD can be executed after compilation using standard Java runtime execution tools. This book assumes a basic ability on the part of developers to compile and execute regular standalone Java code. Additional information on basic Java SDK usage can be found at http://java.sun.com/products/jdk/1.2/docs/index.html. Furthermore, specific instructions for use of the various Java SDK tools can be found at http://java.sun.com/products/jdk/1.2/docs/tooldocs/tools.html.

The directories under the <CD_ROOT>\examples\src directory contain the source code for all examples in this book. To compile such code, you must copy the directories from the CD onto your local working file system. Sample scripts included on the CD build the code assuming that you've copied this directory structure to mimic the structure shown in Figure A.1. The code rooted at <CD_ROOT> in that diagram thus must be copied to your local working environment rooted at a directory of your choice. However, it is important that the directory root be identified by an EJAVA_HOME environment variable. Thus, for example, if EJAVA_HOME is set as

```
set EJAVA_HOME=C:\books\j2ee
```

then the <CD_ROOT>\examples\src directory should be equivalent to C:\books\j2ee\examples\src on your local file system. All sample source code compilation and class file execution, of course, must occur within this local file system environment rooted at EJAVA_HOME.

We include many `.bat` script files on the CD for the plethora of software examples equipped with the book. If you've set your environment variables described in this appendix correctly, you should be able to use the `.bat` script files "as is" on Windows platforms. These script files can also serve as templates to create scripts for other platforms on which you are running this code (for example, UNIX and Macintosh).

Database Configuration

In this section, we present an integrated view of the sample BeeShirts.com data model used to configure our sample database. We also describe how to install and configure a database with our sample BeeShirts.com data. Note that because all of our examples in this book use JDBC as a database interface technology, the examples will work with any database that supports a JDBC-compliant driver interface. We have created database configuration scripts for use with both the Cloudscape DBMS and Oracle8i DBMS. These scripts can be used to configure either database with the BeeShirts.com schema and initial set of sample data.

Because Chapter 10, "Advanced JDBC," describes the latest JDBC 2.0 standard features, some of the JDBC 2.0 features demonstrated in Chapter 10 were not fully supported by all vendors, including both Cloudscape and Oracle. Chapter 9, "Basic JDBC," and all other chapters, however, utilize the most common JDBC features that most database vendors support.

BeeShirts.com Data Model

Figure A.2 depicts the data model used with the examples in this book. Chapter 8, "Enterprise Data," contains a description of the basic data model diagram conventions used to understand this diagram. These are the basic entities of this model:

- `CUSTOMER`: Contains BeeShirts.com customer data.
- `STATE`: Maps a state code to a state name.
- `AUTHENTICATION`: Contains customer authentication data.
- `CREDIT`: Contains keys to all credit-related data.
- `CHARGE_CARD_TYPE`: Contains customer charge-card data.
- `ORDERS`: Contains customer order data.
- `ITEM`: Contains order item data.
- `TSHIRT`: Contains T-shirt item data.
- `SUPPLIER`: Contains BeeShirts.com T-shirt supplier data.

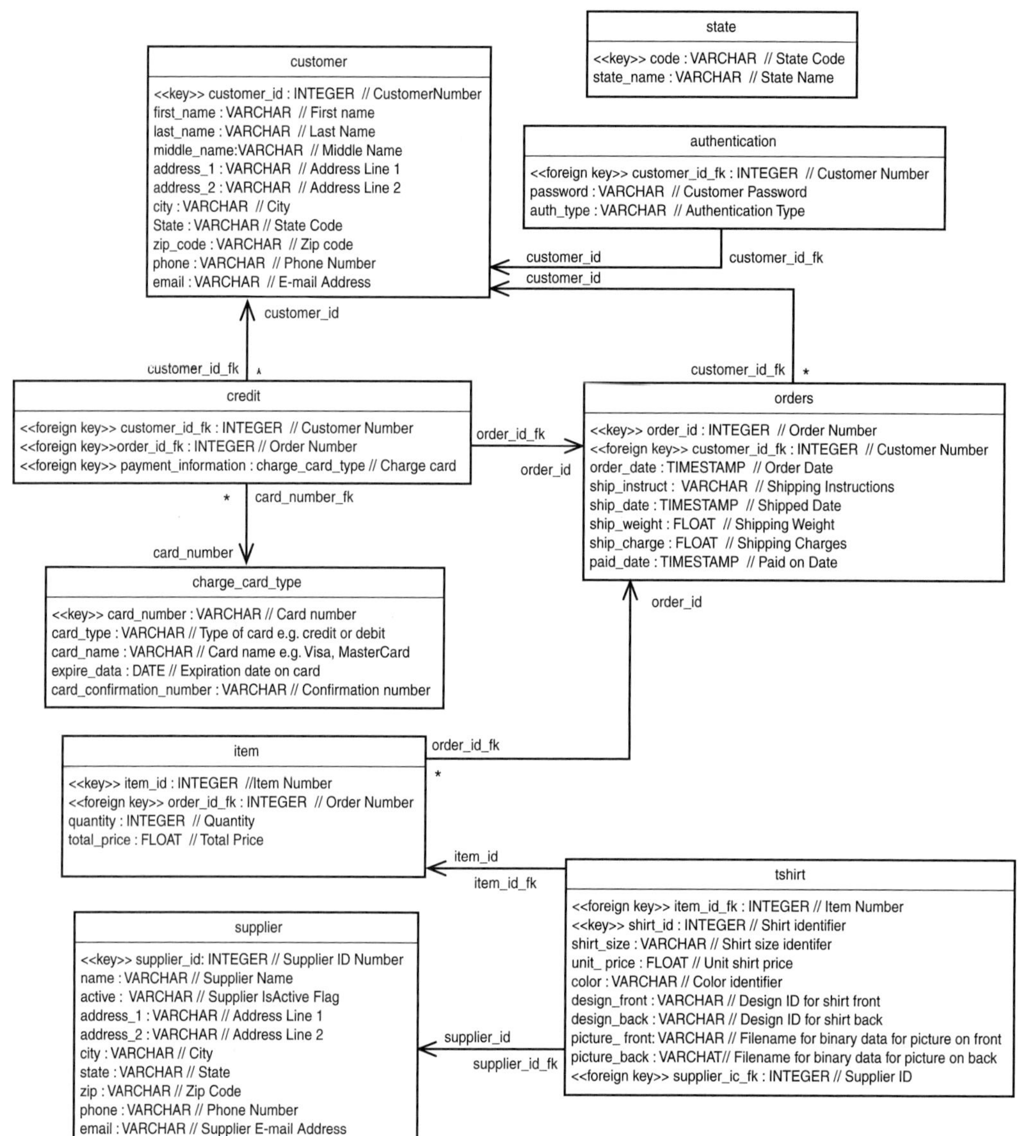

FIGURE A.2

The BeeShirts.com data model.

Cloudscape Database Configuration

The Cloudscape database is the primary database that we use with our examples throughout this book primarily because of its ease of configuration, its open integration with Java enterprise environments, and the Cloudscape Corporation's open policy for making Cloudscape accessible to developers and various SDKs. Cloudscape, in fact, comes equipped with both the BEA WebLogic Server and the J2EE reference implementation used by this book. The following steps describe how to use the Cloudscape database with our examples.

Cloudscape Software to Install

You can use the Cloudscape database contained in the `<CD_ROOT>\cots\cloudscape` directory on the CD, the database that comes equipped with the BEA WebLogic software provided with the CD, or the database that comes equipped with the J2EE reference implementation downloadable from Sun Microsystems. Cloudscape v1.5 is equipped with BEA WebLogic, and Cloudscape v3.0 is used with the J2EE reference implementation.

NOTE

Note that although the Cloudscape database is equipped with this book's CD as a separate installation package, we only describe how to configure the Cloudscape database equipped with the BEA WebLogic Server and the J2EE reference implementation. This is because you will need to configure such databases when you run our sample scripts that use either the BEA WebLogic Server or the J2EE reference implementation server. However, you may also opt to use the standalone Cloudscape database provided on the CD for use with the standalone Java enterprise examples contained on the CD.

Cloudscape Limitations

The Cloudscape version equipped with BEA WebLogic did not support any JDBC 2.0 features as described in Chapter 10. The Cloudscape version equipped with the J2EE reference implementation with the book's CD could support JDBC 2.0 scrollable result sets and batch updates, but it could not support any of the new SQL types that we use in our examples. We include scripts on the CD for configuring the Cloudscape database with sample BeeShirts.com data. These scripts do not define data structures that exemplify how to use Cloudscape with Chapter 10's new SQL type examples, however. The configuration steps for Oracle that follow the Cloudscape configuration steps presented here can be used to demonstrate Chapter 10's new SQL type examples.

Cloudscape Configuration Tool Startup with BEA WebLogic

The CloudView GUI configuration tool for Cloudscape equipped with BEA WebLogic requires that you set JAVA_HOME (for root J2SE install), WEBLOGIC_HOME (for root WebLogic install), and CLASSPATH environment variables before running it. As an example of setting such environment variables for Windows, we have this:

```
set JAVA_HOME=C:\jdk1.2.2
set WEBLOGIC_HOME=D:\weblogic
set CLASSPATH=%JAVA_HOME%\lib\dt.jar;%JAVA_HOME%\lib\tools.jar;
set CLASSPATH=%CLASSPATH%;
➥%WEBLOGIC_HOME%\eval\cloudscape\lib\cloudscape.jar
set CLASSPATH=%CLASSPATH%;%WEBLOGIC_HOME%\eval\cloudscape\lib\tools.jar
set CLASSPATH=%CLASSPATH%;%WEBLOGIC_HOME%\lib\weblogicaux.jar
```

The CloudView GUI tool is then invoked from the command line via this:

```
java COM.cloudscape.tools.cview
```

Alternatively, you can use the sample startWebLogicCloudview.bat Windows script file contained on the CD under the <CD_ROOT>\examples\config\dbscripts\cloudscape directory to invoke CloudView. You must set only the JAVA_HOME and WEBLOGIC_HOME environment variables before running this script.

Cloudscape Configuration Tool Startup with the J2EE Reference Implementation

You must first execute a special cloudscape script equipped with the J2EE reference implementation. You must invoke this command not only during installation, but also when you want to use Cloudscape with our examples after it has been installed. First change to the [J2EE_HOME]\bin directory and invoke the command as shown here:

```
cloudscape -start
```

The CloudView GUI configuration tool for Cloudscape equipped with the J2EE reference implementation requires that you set JAVA_HOME (for root J2SE install), J2EE_HOME (for root J2EE reference implementation install), and CLASSPATH environment variables before running it. As an example of setting such environment variables for Windows, we have the following:

```
set JAVA_HOME=C:\jdk1.2.2
set J2EE_HOME=C:\j2sdkee1.2
set CLASSPATH=%JAVA_HOME%\lib\dt.jar;%JAVA_HOME%\lib\tools.jar;
set CLASSPATH=%J2EE_HOME%\lib\j2ee.jar;
➥%J2EE_HOME%\lib\cloudscape\RmiJdbc.jar;%CLASSPATH%
set CLASSPATH=%J2EE_HOME%\lib\cloudscape\tools.jar;
➥%J2EE_HOME%\lib\cloudscape\client.jar;%CLASSPATH%
set CLASSPATH=%J2EE_HOME%\lib\cloudscape\cloudscape.jar;%CLASSPATH%
```

The CloudView GUI tool is then invoked from the command line via this:

```
java COM.cloudscape.tools.cview
```

Alternatively, you can use the sample `startJ2EECloudview.bat` Windows script file contained on the CD under the `<CD_ROOT>\examples\config\dbscripts\cloudscape` directory to invoke CloudView. You must set only the `JAVA_HOME` and `J2EE_HOME` environment variables before running this script.

Cloudscape Database, Sample Database Schema, and Sample Data Configuration

After the CloudView GUI tool is launched, the steps for configuring a Cloudscape database are generally the same. The general steps for Cloudscape database configuration using the CloudView GUI tool follow:

1. Select File, New, Database from the CloudView GUI menu.
2. Enter the name of the database to create. For the J2EE reference implementation, we set this value to `[J2EE_HOME]\cloudscape\beeshirtdb`. For BEA WebLogic, we set this value to `[WEBLOGIC_HOME]\eval\cloudscape\beeshirts`.
3. Select System on the lefthand tree view of the CloudView GUI and the Connection tab on the right side, and add the prefix, username, and password. For the J2EE reference implementation, the prefix should be set to `jdbc:rmi//localhost:1099/jdbc:cloudscape:`. For the BEA WebLogic server, the prefix should be set to `jdbc:cloudscape`. We set the username to `TSHIRTS` and the password to `TSHIRTS` for our examples. Click the OK button.
4. Select the database just created in the lefthand tree view.
5. Select the Scripts icon on the database tab and then choose to Open a Script.
6. Select `<CD_ROOT>\examples\config\dbscripts\cloudscape\createshirtsdb.sql`.
7. Execute this script by clicking the Execute icon on the tab.

The Cloudscape database should now be configured with the BeeShirts.com schema and data used with our examples throughout the book. Note that the `<CD_ROOT>\examples\config\dbscripts\cloudscape\removeshirtsdb.sql` script can also be executed to remove the database that was created.

Cloudscape Library Environment Variable

For all examples that use the Cloudscape database, the `CLOUDSCAPE_LIB` environment variable must be set to the directory of your Cloudscape JAR files. For the Cloudscape database that comes with the J2EE reference implementation, this directory is `[J2EE_HOME]\lib\cloudscape`. For the Cloudscape database that comes with the BEA WebLogic Server, this directory is `[WEBLOGIC_HOME]\eval\cloudscape\lib`.

For example, to set CLOUDSCAPE_LIB on a Windows platform with the J2EE reference implementation, you might have this:

```
set CLOUDSCAPE_LIB=C:\j2sdkee1.2\lib\cloudscape
```

To set CLOUDSCAPE_LIB on a Windows platform with BEA WebLogic, you might have this:

```
set CLOUDSCAPE_LIB=d:\weblogic\eval\cloudscape\lib
```

Sample Properties Files for Cloudscape Configuration

To use the BEA WebLogic Server or the J2EE reference implementation with Cloudscape, you'll need to set a few parameters enabling the application servers to communicate with the Cloudscape database. For BEA WebLogic, the [WEBLOGIC_HOME]\weblogic.properties file needs to have the following entries for use with the database:

```
# This connection pool uses the sample Cloudscape database shipped
# with WebLogic. Used by the EJBean, JHTML, JSP, and JMS examples.
weblogic.jdbc.connectionPool.ejavaPool=\
       url=jdbc:cloudscape:D:\\weblogic\\eval\\cloudscape\\beeshirts,\
       driver=COM.cloudscape.core.JDBCDriver,\
       initialCapacity=1,\
       maxCapacity=2,\
       capacityIncrement=1,\
       props=user=TSHIRTS;password=TSHIRTS;server=none

# Add a TXDataSource for the connection pool:
weblogic.jdbc.TXDataSource.weblogic.jdbc.jts.ejavaPool=ejavaPool
#
# Add an ACL for the connection pool:
weblogic.allow.reserve.weblogic.jdbc.connectionPool.ejavaPool=everyone
```

Note that the url parameter in the weblogic.properties file just shown must be set to the jdbc:cloudscape:[WEBLOGIC_HOME]\eval\cloudscape\beeshirts value as appropriate for your environment and as configured in the preceding section.

When you're using the J2EE reference implementation, the following entry must be present in the [J2EE_HOME]\config\default.properties file for use of Cloudscape:

```
jdbc.datasources=
➥jdbc/Cloudscape|jdbc:rmi:jdbc:cloudscape:beeshirtsdb;create=true;
```

Note that the J2EE reference implementation assumes that the beeshirtsdb database configured in the previous property is stored under the [J2EE_HOME]\cloudscape directory as described earlier in step 2.

For chapters that do not use the BEA WebLogic Server or the J2EE reference implementation and just use straight JDBC to talk with the database in standalone applications (that is, most chapters before Part VI and Part VII of the book), you'll need to ensure that any DRIVER_CLASS and DATABASE_URL properties assumed by those examples are valid. These properties are defined in the various Java properties files associated with each chapter that has database connectivity via JDBC. The following properties must be set for the Cloudscape version equipped with BEA WebLogic:

```
# JDBC Driver Class for Cloudscape
DRIVER_CLASS=COM.cloudscape.core.JDBCDriver
# Database URL for our example database with Cloudscape
#  Info supplied here relates to configuration steps described earlier
DATABASE_URL=jdbc:cloudscape:D:\\weblogic\\eval\\cloudscape\\beeshirts
```

Of course, the DATABASE_URL previously defined must reference the appropriate root directory of your WebLogic installation given in the jdbc:cloudscape:[WEBLOGIC_HOME]\\eval\\cloudscape\beeshirts property value.

Similarly, the DRIVER_CLASS and DATABASE_URL properties must be set as shown here when you're using the Cloudscape version equipped with the J2EE reference implementation:

```
# JDBC Driver Class for Cloudscape
DRIVER_CLASS=RmiJdbc.RJDriver
# Database URL for our example database with Cloudscape
#  Info supplied here relates to configuration steps described earlier
DATABASE_URL=jdbc:rmi:jdbc:cloudscape:beeshirtsdb
```

Cloudscape Database Starting with the J2EE Reference Implementation

Before running our standalone Java application examples with the J2EE reference implementation's version of Cloudscape, you must first execute a special cloudscape script equipped with the J2EE reference implementation. First change to the [J2EE_HOME]\bin directory and invoke the command as shown here:

```
cloudscape -start
```

Oracle Database Configuration

Oracle's latest database, Oracle8i, is an upgrade of their DBMS technology on the part of Oracle and employs a very Java-centric and CORBA-oriented enterprise architecture. We provide scripts for configuring our BeeShirts.com data for use with Oracle8i. We also provide a few additional scripts for configuring Oracle8i to work with a few of the advanced JDBC 2.0 features described in Chapter 10.

Oracle Software to Install

Before you download any Oracle database software, you will need to join Oracle's free Technet membership. Simply go to http://technet.oracle.com and answer all of Oracle's questions to become a registered Oracle Technet member.

The Oracle8i database server software that you may use with the examples in this book can then be downloaded from `http://technet.oracle.com`. Note that we have used the Enterprise Edition of Oracle8i, but the Standard Edition and Personal Editions may also be used. Note also that we have used the Windows NT version of Oracle with our examples, but that other operating-system platforms for your database installation can also be used.

Oracle Limitations

Oracle8i v8.1.5 had a few limitations at the time of this writing. Certain JDBC 2.0 features of Chapter 10 did not yet function, including scrollable result sets, updatable result sets, and batch updates. Chapter 10's advanced SQL type examples, all the Chapter 9 features, and the remaining database features utilized throughout the rest of the book, however, do function correctly with Oracle8i v8.1.5. Oracle8i v8.1.6 uses a JDBC driver that reportedly will function with the newer JDBC 2.0–compliant features described in Chapter 10, including scrollable result sets, batch updates, and all the new SQL types. Updatable result sets were reportedly still not supported by Oracle v8.1.6's JDBC driver at the time of this writing.

Oracle Database Installation

Installation of the Oracle database can proceed according to the instructions at `http://technet.oracle.com`. During installation, you will be asked to enter some information that will affect how our examples can work with the database. These are the main concerns with setting parameters:

- Global Database Name and SID should be `TSHIRTS`.
- Ensure that default database listener uses port `1521`.

The main steps involved in installing an Oracle8i database using the Oracle GUI-based installation utility follow:

1. Select the option to Install/Deinstall Products from within the Oracle install utility screen options.
2. It is acceptable to use the default product install path and Oracle home name for our examples. However, you may want to select a different installation path.
3. Select an actual database server to install when prompted.
4. Note that you can choose a minimal installation for use with our examples if you want.
5. When prompted, opt to install a starter database.
6. It is important that your sample global database name and SID are entered as `TShirts` (case-insensitive) when prompted.
7. A summary of selected options is displayed.
8. The status of your install is eventually displayed. Write down any initial passwords created during installation.

Oracle Database Sample Schema and Data Configuration

Before we configure the database with our sample schema and data, you'll need to set up an Oracle network client (that is, Net8 client) on your machine since we use SQL-Plus during configuration. You may set up a SQL network client as shown here:

1. Invoke the Network Administration's Net8 Easy Config application for configuring a SQL network client.
2. When prompted, make sure that you create a new net service name of `TSHIRTS`.
3. When prompted, select TCP/IP as your protocol.
4. When prompted, enter your machine's hostname (it can be `localhost`), and a port of `1521` (which is the default).
5. When prompted, enter a service name of `TSHIRTS`.

After configuring a SQL network client, you can use SQL-Plus to read the database configuration scripts that we have packaged with the CD to automatically create your database schema and load a set of sample data.

The `<CD_ROOT>:\examples\config\dbscripts\oracle\createshirtsdb.sql` file can be executed by SQL-Plus to configure the database as shown here:

1. Invoke the SQLPlus application. Note that SQLPlus can be run from the command line using `sqlplus`.
2. When prompted, enter `system` as a username, `manager` as a password, and `tshirts` as a host string.
3. Enter `@<CD_ROOT>\examples\config\dbscripts\oracle\createshirtsdb.sql` and press the Enter key. Alternately, you may enter `@<CD_ROOT>\examples\config\dbscripts\oracle\createshirtsdbforch10.sql` and press the `Enter` key to configure the database with the schema to be used with Chapter 10's new SQL type examples.

Your Oracle8i database should now be ready for use with our examples. Note that you can also remove the database by executing our `<CD_ROOT>\examples\config\dbscripts\oracle\removeshirtsdb.sql` script. You can remove the special Chapter 10 database by executing our `<CD_ROOT>\examples\config\dbscripts\oracle\removeshirtsdbforch10.sql` script.

Changing Properties Files for Oracle Configuration

Our configurable Java properties files on the CD for many examples typically contain two database entries, which may vary between database installations. The `DRIVER_CLASS` property can be set equal to `oracle.jdbc.driver.OracleDriver` if you are using the Oracle thin JDBC driver. The DATABASE_URL property may vary depending on your install but can be configured in our properties files with jdbc:oracle:thin:@localhost:1521:TSHIRTS. If you have installed your database on a remote machine, you will need to replace the localhost value with the hostname or IP address of the remote machine. Also note that the default database port of 1521 is assumed and that an SID of TSHIRTS is also presumed.

Additionally, when using the Oracle database with the BEA WebLogic Server, you'll also need to configure the [WEBLOGIC_HOME]\weblogic.properties file with the following entries:

```
# This connection pool uses the Oracle database.
# Used by the EJBean, JHTML, JSP, and JMS examples.
weblogic.jdbc.connectionPool.ejavaPool=\
       url=jdbc:oracle:thin:@localhost:1521:TSHIRTS,\
       driver= oracle.jdbc.driver.OracleDriver,\
       initialCapacity=1,\
       maxCapacity=2,\
       capacityIncrement=1,\
       props=user=TSHIRTS;password=TSHIRTS;

# Add a TXDataSource for the connection pool:
weblogic.jdbc.TXDataSource.weblogic.jdbc.jts.ejavaPool=ejavaPool
#
# Add an ACL for the connection pool:
weblogic.allow.reserve.weblogic.jdbc.connectionPool.ejavaPool=everyone
```

When using the Oracle database with the J2EE reference implementation server, you'll need to configure the [J2EE_HOME]\config\default.properties file with the following entry:

```
jdbc.datasources=
➥jdbc/Cloudscape|jdbc:oracle:thin:@localhost:1521:TSHIRTS;create=true;
```

Web Configuration

Various configuration variables and execution scripts can be used to build and execute the Web examples presented in Chapter 32, "Java Servlets," Chapter 33, "JavaServer Pages," and Chapter 37, "Advanced Enterprise JavaBeans Serving." These examples can be executed in either the J2EE reference implementation or the BEA WebLogic Server. This section describes these Web configuration procedures.

Web Configuration Properties for the J2EE Reference Implementation

For the J2EE reference implementation's Web server environment, a special [J2EE_HOME]\config\web.properties file needs to be modified. The HTTP port in that file needs to be set to 7001 for our examples as shown here:

```
http.port=7001
```

Web Configuration Properties for the BEA WebLogic Server

The BEA WebLogic Server's Web server is configured with configuration variables set inside of the `[WEBLOGIC_HOME]\weblogic.properties` file. The root context for running the Chapter 32 Java Servlet examples in the book needs to point to the `[WEBLOGIC_HOME]/myserver/servletsch32.war` WAR file created in Chapter 32 as exemplified here:

```
weblogic.httpd.webApp.beeshirts=
➥D:/weblogic/myserver/servletsch32.war
```

The root context defined in the `[WEBLOGIC_HOME]\weblogic.properties` file for running the Chapter 33 JavaServer Pages examples needs to point to the `[WEBLOGIC_HOME]/myserver/jspch33.war` WAR file created in Chapter 33 as exemplified here:

```
weblogic.httpd.webApp.beeshirtsjsp=
➥D:/weblogic/myserver/jspch33.war
```

Similarly, the root context defined in the `[WEBLOGIC_HOME]\weblogic.properties` file for running the Chapter 37 integrated JavaServer Pages and EJB examples needs to point to the `[WEBLOGIC_HOME]/myserver/jspch37.war` WAR file created in Chapter 37 as exemplified here:

```
weblogic.httpd.webApp.beeshirtsjsp=
➥D:/weblogic/myserver/jspch37.war
```

The Chapter 32, 33, and 37 examples also need to have a `weblogic.httpd.documentRoot` property from the `[WEBLOGIC_HOME]\weblogic.properties` file configured as exemplified here:

```
weblogic.httpd.documentRoot=D:/weblogic/myserver/
```

The Chapter 33 and Chapter 37 examples also need to have `weblogic.httpd.register` and `weblogic.httpd.initArgs` properties from the `[WEBLOGIC_HOME]\weblogic.properties` file configured as exemplified here:

```
weblogic.httpd.register.*.jsp=\
       weblogic.servlet.JSPServlet

weblogic.httpd.initArgs.*.jsp=\
       pageCheckSeconds=1,\
       compileCommand=c:/jdk1.2.2/bin/javac.exe,\
       workingDir=D:/weblogic/myserver,\
       verbose=true
```

Note also that we have included a WebLogic specific weblogic.xml file in the examples/src/ejava/ejbch37/webclient directory as well. This file contains JNDI name mappings for EJB references utilized by the web application code. At the time of this writing, BEA WebLogic did not provide a PUBLIC URL for use from within the DOCTYPE to reference the structure of this file and also did not provide a public name for this DTD. Thus, we had to use a SYSTEM URI to reference the DTD that sits in the [WEBLOGIC_HOME]/classes/weblogic/servlet/internal/dd/weblogic-web-jar.dtd file equipped with the BEA WebLogic installation. You thus must modify the weblogic.xml file to reference the correct root WebLogic installation directory for your environment. For example:

```
<!DOCTYPE weblogic-web-app SYSTEM 'file:D:/weblogic/classes/
➥weblogic/servlet/internal/dd/weblogic-web-jar.dtd'>
```

Web Configuration Scripts for the J2EE Reference Implementation

Throughout the Web chapters, we also include sample Windows scripts for building and deploying J2EE Web applications for use with the J2EE reference implementation. Before such J2EE reference implementation–specific scripts are run, you must change to the [J2EE_HOME]\bin directory in a separate window and issue the J2EE reference implementation server startup command (that is, j2ee).

You must also start up the Cloudscape database server (that is, [J2EE_HOME]\bin\cloudscape -start) before running the Web code used in Chapter 37. The sample scripts compile all Java code, package the Web module and EAR file, and deploy the Web module to a running J2EE server.

Note that you may have copied an orb.properties file to your [JAVA_HOME]\jre\lib directory if you have installed the standard RMI/IIOP extension per the instructions of Chapter 16, “RMI Communications.” This orb.properties file must be removed in order to properly run the J2EE reference implementation server.

Web Configuration Scripts for the BEA WebLogic Server

Throughout the Web chapters, we also include sample Windows scripts for building J2EE Web applications for use with the BEA WebLogic Server. The sample scripts compile all Java code as well as package and deploy a Web module (note that BEA WebLogic Server v5.1 version did not support EAR file deployment, however). Note that Chapter 37’s examples/src/ejava/ejbch37/webclient/buildweblogic.bat sample script independently copies our Serializable entity classes to the [WEBLOGIC_HOME]\myserver\serverclasses directory and does not package these files inside of the deployable WAR file. This step was taken due to a class casting issue that occurs as we have experienced with the BEA WebLogic v5.1 server when such classes are packaged inside of the WAR file.

The BEA WebLogic Server can then be started with the [WEBLOGIC_HOME]\startWeblogic.cmd script. Note that in order to enable the BEA WebLogic Server to compile JSP classes (used in Chapter 37), you must add the [JAVA_HOME]\bin directory to the PATH environment variable that is set from within the [WEBLOGIC_HOME]\startWeblogic.cmd script as exemplified here:

```
SET PATH=C:\jdk1.2.2\bin;%PATH%
```

Note also that the BEA WebLogic Server comes equipped with the java.weblogic.jspc JSP compiler tool that we use from within our Chapter 33 JSP build scripts. Instructions for how to use the WebLogic JSP compiler can be found at http://www.weblogic.com/docs50/classdocs/API_jsp.html#compiler.

Application Server Configuration

Various configuration variables and execution scripts can be used to build and execute the application serving examples presented in Chapter 35, "Application Servers and Enterprise JavaBeans," Chapter 36, "Modeling Components with Enterprise JavaBeans," and Chapter 37, "Advanced Enterprise JavaBeans Serving." These examples can be executed in either the J2EE reference implementation or the BEA WebLogic Server. This section describes these EJB application server configuration procedures.

Application Server Configuration Properties for the BEA WebLogic Server

The BEA WebLogic Server's EJB application server is configured via setting properties in the [WEBLOGIC_HOME]\weblogic.properties file. The build scripts used with our Part VII examples for BEA WebLogic create EJB JAR files that are copied to the [WEBLOGIC_HOME]\myserver directory. At the time of our creation of these examples, the BEA WebLogic Server v5.1 could not deploy EJBs inside of EAR files. Deploying EJBs as EJB JARs in BEA WebLogic requires configuring the weblogic.ejb.deploy property inside of the weblogic.properties file as exemplified here for the single EJB deployed in Chapter 35:

```
# Deploys EJBeans. Add the following entries as appropriately
# named with the root WEBLOGIC_HOME directory for your environment
weblogic.ejb.deploy=\
    D:/weblogic/myserver/CreditManagerEJB.jar
```

For Chapter 36, the [WEBLOGIC_HOME]\weblogic.properties file's weblogic.ejb.deploy property must be modified to reference the new beans created for that chapter as exemplified here:

```
# Deploys EJBeans. Add the following entries as appropriately
# named with the root WEBLOGIC_HOME directory for your environment
weblogic.ejb.deploy=\
      D:/weblogic/myserver/CreditEJB.jar,\
```

```
        D:/weblogic/myserver/CustomerEJB.jar, \
        D:/weblogic/myserver/TShirtEJB.jar,\
        D:/weblogic/myserver/ItemEJB.jar, \
        D:/weblogic/myserver/OrderEJB.jar, \
        D:/weblogic/myserver/BrowseEJB.jar, \
        D:/weblogic/myserver/OrderManagerEJB.jar, \
        D:/weblogic/myserver/ShoppingCartEJB.jar , \
        D:/weblogic/myserver/CreditManager36EJB.jar
```

For Chapter 37's integrated EJB and JSP example, the `[WEBLOGIC_HOME]\weblogic.properties` file's `weblogic.ejb.deploy` property must be modified to reference the two new beans created for that chapter as exemplified here:

```
# Deploys EJBeans. Add the following entries as appropriately
# named with the root WEBLOGIC_HOME directory for your environment
weblogic.ejb.deploy=\
        D:/weblogic/myserver/CreditEJB.jar,\
        D:/weblogic/myserver/CustomerEJB.jar, \
        D:/weblogic/myserver/TShirtEJB.jar,\
        D:/weblogic/myserver/ItemEJB.jar, \
        D:/weblogic/myserver/OrderEJB.jar, \
        D:/weblogic/myserver/BrowseEJB.jar, \
        D:/weblogic/myserver/OrderManagerEJB.jar, \
        D:/weblogic/myserver/ShoppingCartEJB.jar , \
        D:/weblogic/myserver/CreditManager36EJB.jar, \
        D:/weblogic/myserver/AuthenticationEJB.jar, \
        D:/weblogic/myserver/AuthSessionEJB.jar
```

Finally, for Chapter 37's integrated EJB and JMS example, the `[WEBLOGIC_HOME]\weblogic.properties` file's `weblogic.ejb.deploy` property must reference the two deployable beans for that example as exemplified here:

```
# Deploys EJBeans. Add the following entries as appropriately
# named with the root WEBLOGIC_HOME directory for your environment
weblogic.ejb.deploy=\
  D:/weblogic/myserver/CreditEJB.jar,\
  D:/weblogic/myserver/CreditManager37EJB.jar
```

Application Server Configuration Scripts for the BEA WebLogic Server

Throughout the EJB chapters, we also include sample Windows scripts for building J2EE EJB and enterprise applications for the BEA WebLogic Server. The scripts compile all Java code and package the EJB modules and Web module (for Chapter 37). The BEA WebLogic Server can then be started with the `[WEBLOGIC_HOME]\startWeblogic.cmd` script.

For Chapter 35 and Chapter 36, each EJB directory contains a `buildweblogic.bat` script to build the individual EJB associated with that directory. An associated `runWebLogicClient.bat` file can then be used to run the test client for that bean. Although each entity bean can be run and tested by itself, the session beans require any entity beans they depend upon to have already been deployed.

Additionally, a `buildweblogicall.bat` file in the `<CD_ROOT>\examples\src\ejava\ejbch36` directory can be used to build all the Chapter 36 EJBs for BEA WebLogic. The `<CD_ROOT>\examples\src\ejava\ejbch37\webclient\buildweblogic.bat` file can be used to build all the EJBs and the WAR file used by Chapter 37's examples that utilize the BEA WebLogic Server.

Application Server Configuration Scripts for J2EE Reference Implementation

We also include sample Windows scripts for building and deploying J2EE EJB and enterprise applications for the J2EE reference implementation server. Before such a script is run, you must change to the `[J2EE_HOME]\bin` directory in a separate window and issue the J2EE reference implementation server startup command (that is, `j2ee`). You must also initiate the Cloudscape database server using `[J2EE_HOME]\bin\cloudscape -start`. The J2EE reference implementation scripts compile all Java code; package the EJB modules, Web module (for Chapter 37), and EAR file; and then deploy the EAR file to a running J2EE server.

For Chapter 35 and Chapter 36, each EJB directory contains a `buildj2ee.bat` script to build the individual EJB associated with that directory. An associated `runJ2EEClient.bat` file can then be used to run the test client for that bean. Although each entity bean can be run and tested by itself, the session beans require any entity beans they depend on to have already been deployed.

Additionally, a `buildj2eeall.bat` file in the `<CD_ROOT>\examples\src\ejava\ejbch36` directory can be used to build all the Chapter 36 EJBs for the J2EE reference implementation. The `buildj2eeall.bat` file uses a `buildj2eejar.bat` file in each Chapter 36 EJB directory. A `runJ2EEClientWithAll.bat` file in each Chapter 36 EJB directory can also be used to test the associated EJB encapsulated by the deployed EAR file. The `<CD_ROOT>\examples\src\ejava\ejbch37\webclient\buildj2ee.bat` file can be used to build all the EJBs and the WAR file used by Chapter 37's examples that utilize the J2EE reference implementation. Chapter 37's `buildj2ee.bat` file uses a `<CD_ROOT>\examples\src\ejava\ejbch37\webclient\buildj2eejars.bat` file to create all EJB JAR files before creating a WAR and then an EAR file.

Note that you may have copied an `orb.properties` file to your `[JAVA_HOME]\jre\lib` directory if you have installed the standard RMI/IIOP extension per the instructions of Chapter 16. This `orb.properties` file must be removed in order to properly run the J2EE reference implementation server.

Note also that at the time of this writing, the J2EE v1.2 reference implementation did not support the use of composite primary keys. Thus, the `Credit` EJB and its `CreditPrimaryKey` composite primary key did not function properly. Thus, the `Credit` test client code and `CreditManagerSession` EJB would not function properly with the J2EE reference implementation. The J2EE v1.2.1 reference implementation will reportedly fix this bug. The BEA WebLogic Server can be used to fully demonstrate use of the `Credit` and `CreditManagerSession` EJB code.

JavaBeans Configuration

In addition to establishing your common software configuration environment for Chapter 7's sample code, you may optionally elect to utilize a JavaBeans container environment. Integrated Development Environments (IDEs) such as Symantec's Visual Café and Inprise/Borland's JBuilder tools provide container implementations within which your JavaBean can be manipulated during design-time. The JavaBeans Development Kit (BDK), downloadable from the Sun Web site at `http://java.sun.com/beans/software/bdk_download.html`, can also be used to provide an environment for creating JavaBean components and includes a reference JavaBean container known as the "BeanBox."

XML Configuration

BEA WebLogic and the J2EE reference implementation both include XML parsers under the hood to interpret J2EE XML-based deployment descriptors. However, the standard Java API for XML Parsing (JAXP) implementation can be downloaded from `http://java.sun.com/xml/download.html`. JAXP will come in handy particularly for code examples in Chapter 31, "XML."

CORBA ORB Configuration

The Java IDL ORB comes equipped with the J2SE installation and is ready to use with our examples. We have also included the Inprise Visigenics Visibroker for Java ORB on the CD to use with the CORBA related examples in the book which utilize features that are not supported by Java IDL. The Inprise Visigenics ORB is included on the CD in the `<CD_ROOT>\cots\inprise` directory and can be installed to a root directory on your local machine. You must simply set the `VISIGENIC_HOME` environment property that we use with our examples to the root directory of your Inprise Visigenic installation as exemplified here:

```
set VISIGENIC_HOME=D:\visigenics
```

CORBA Services Configuration

The Inprise Visigenics ORB product comes equipped with the CORBA Naming Service and CORBA Events Service used by our examples in the book. Additionally, Prism Technologies's OpenFusion suite of CORBAservices (including a CORBA Naming Service and CORBA Events Service) on the CD can be used with the Inprise Visigenics ORB. In particular, we use OpenFusion's CORBA Trading Service with our examples. The OpenFusion product suite is included on the CD in the `<CD_ROOT>\cots\prismtech` directory. You must set the `OPEN_FUSION_HOME` environment property that we use with our examples to the root directory of your Prism Technologies OpenFusion installation as exemplified here:

```
set OPEN_FUSION_HOME=C:\prismtech
```

You will also need to add the following line to the `[OPEN_FUSION_HOME]\bin\configure.bat` file (substituting the `[VISIGENIC_HOME]` value shown with the root directory of your Inprise Visigenic installation):

```
SET CPATH=[VISIGENIC_HOME]\lib\vbjorb.jar;
➥[VISIGENIC_HOME]\lib\vbjapp.jar;%CPATH%
```

You'll need to change to the `[OPEN_FUSION_HOME]\bin` directory and execute the `configure.bat` script file. A pop-up dialog then appears, and you must click the Next button until you are given the option to save your configuration to the registry. Thereafter, you must execute the `manager.bat` file in the `[OPEN_FUSION_HOME]\bin` directory. From within the resulting pop-up window, you then must click on the Trading Service option and subsequently elect to start the server when prompted. You can then use the `runtrading.bat` file equipped with the CORBA Trading Service sample code in Chapter 20, "Directory and Trading Services."

RMI/IIOP Configuration

You must download and install the RMI/IIOP standard extension for use with the J2SE v1.2 platform, whereas RMI/IIOP comes equipped with the J2SE v1.3 platform. The RMI/IIOP download package and instructions can be found at `http://java.sun.com/products/rmi-iiop/index.html`. You also must set an `RMI_IIOP_HOME` environment variable to the root directory for your RMI/IIOP installation when running any examples. Note that it is very important to make sure that the `orb.properties` file generated during this installation is copied properly to your `[JAVA_HOME]\jre\lib` directory. The installation program may attempt to copy this file to another directory that it perceives as the JRE library directory, so step through the installation process carefully. Note, however, that this `orb.properties` file must be removed when attempting to properly run the J2EE reference implementation server with the other examples in the book. The RMI/IIOP IDL-to-Java compiler can be downloaded from `http://developer.java.sun.com/developer/earlyAccess/idlc/index.html`. A single `idlc1_0_1ea.zip` file is downloaded which contains a single `idlj.jar` file that must be copied into the `[RMI_IIOP_HOME]\lib` directory.

JNDI Configuration

JNDI comes packaged with the J2EE APIs provided by both the BEA WebLogic Server and the J2EE reference implementation. JNDI can also be downloaded separately and run in a standalone J2SE v1.2 environment from `http://java.sun.com/products/jndi/`. The J2SE v1.3 environment comes with JNDI but cannot be used with the J2EE v1.2 environments. JNDI SPI implementations can be downloaded from `http://java.sun.com/products/jndi/serviceproviders.html`.

To run our sample JNDI software with the book, you'll need to set the `JNDI_HOME` environment variable to the root directory of your JNDI installation as exemplified here:

```
set JNDI_HOME=C:\unzipped\jndi1_2_1
```

To run our sample software that uses the file-system JNDI SPI, you'll need to set the `FSCONTEXT_HOME` environment variable to the root directory of your file-system SPI installation as exemplified here:

```
set FSCONTEXT_HOME = D:\unzipped\fscontext1_2beta2
```

To run our sample software that uses the RMI registry JNDI SPI, you'll need to set the `RMICONTEXT_HOME` environment variable to the root directory of your RMI registry SPI installation as exemplified here:

```
set RMICONTEXT_HOME= D:\unzipped\rmiregistry1_2_1
```

To run our sample software that uses the CORBA Naming Service JNDI SPI, you'll need to set the `COSCONTEXT_HOME` environment variable to the root directory of your CORBA Naming Service SPI installation as exemplified here:

```
set COSCONTEXT_HOME=D:\unzipped\cosnaming1_2_1
```

You'll also need to set the `RMI_IIOP_HOME` environment variable to the root directory of your RMI/IIOP installation for both the CORBA Naming Service and the RMI registry JNDI examples as exemplified here:

```
set RMI_IIOP_HOME=C:\rmi-iiop
```

To run our sample software that uses the LDAP JNDI SPI, the `LDAP_HOME` environment variable must be set to the root directory of your LDAP JNDI SPI installation as exemplified here:

```
set LDAP_HOME=C:\unzipped\ldap-spi
```

LDAP Configuration

Chapter 20 utilizes an actual LDAP server in addition to an LDAP SPI to provide directory service functionality examples through JNDI. We used the Netscape Directory Server v4.11 with our examples. The Netscape Directory Server can be downloaded from iPlanet.com at `http://www.iplanet.com/downloads/download/index.html`.

After you have downloaded and spawned the Netscape Directory Server GUI setup program, you must proceed with a set of configuration steps as described here:

1. Select the option to install as a Netscape Server when prompted by the Netscape Directory Server GUI installation program.
2. Select the Typical install option when prompted.
3. Select the installation directory of your choice when prompted.
4. Select the products that you want to install when prompted. The optional Netscape Directory Server Synch Service product is not necessary.
5. Select the first time configuration when prompted, unless you already have installed the Netscape Directory Server.
6. If this is your first-time installation, you may not have any existing data to import when the installation wizard prompts you for such data. No extra special data is needed to run our examples.
7. Establish your `localhost` as the server identifier and a port number of `389` when prompted. Also be sure to set the suffix as `o=Airius.com` when prompted.
8. Establish any administration ID and passwords that you like when prompted.
9. Provide the directory-manager name and password when prompted.

The Netscape Directory Server should now be set up. When you first install the Netscape Directory Server, no directory service data is loaded. For our examples in the book, we use some sample data that comes with Netscape Directory Server. This data is stored in an `Airius.ldif` stored file in the `[NETSCAPE_DIRECTORY_SERVER_HOME]\slapd-localhost\ldif` directory. To load such data, follow these steps:

1. Invoke the Netscape Console 4.1 application (from the Windows Start menu).
2. Select the lefthand tree node directory server on the `localhost`, and click the `Edit` button on the right side of the window.
3. A new window titled `Netscape Directory Server - localhost` should now appear.
4. Select the Console, Import menu item from that window.
5. Select the `[NETSCAPE_DIRECTORY_SERVER_HOME]\slapd-localhost\ldif\Airius.ldif` file for import.

Our examples from Chapter 20 may now be run, and they may utilize this default directory service data.

Jini Configuration

Jini is used in Chapter 20 as a trading service. The Jini Technology SDK can be downloaded from `http://developer.java.sun.com/developer/products/jini/`. We assume that the root directory of your Jini installation is identified by a `JINI_HOME` environment variable for Chapter 20's examples as exemplified here:

```
set JINI_HOME=D:\jini1_0_1
```

JMS Configuration

We use the JMS infrastructure provided with the BEA WebLogic Server with our Chapter 22 and Chapter 37 JMS examples. Thus, JMS will largely be configured for use after you have gone through the BEA WebLogic Server Configuration steps defined previously. You must add the `[EJAVA_HOME]\examples\classes` directory to the `JAVA_CLASSPATH` variable contained in the `[WEBLOGIC_HOME]\startweblogic.cmd` script before starting the BEA WebLogic Server for use with our JMS code. For example:

```
set JAVA_CLASSPATH=.\classes\boot;.\eval\cloudscape\lib\cloudscape.jar;
➥[EJAVA_HOME]\examples\classes
```

You will also want to clean your `[EJAVA_HOME]\examples\classes` directory before running our sample JMS execution scripts.

Finally, the BEA WebLogic Server is informed about the use of a special startup thread handler class (that is, `JMSReceiver`) in Chapter 37's integrated EJB and JMS example and is configured to pass in initialization parameters from within the `weblogic.properties` file for the server as shown here:

```
# Define JMSReceiver as startup class with init parameters shown here
weblogic.system.startupClass.JMSReceiver=\
  ejava.ejbch37.creditmgr.JMSReceiver
weblogic.system.startupArgs.JMSReceiver=\
  JMS_TOPIC=JMS_CREDIT_TOPIC
```

JavaMail Configuration

Our sample JavaMail code in Chapter 22 utilizes a POP3 provider. The POP3 v1.1.1 provider can be downloaded from `http://java.sun.com/products/javamail/pop3.html`. The `POP3_HOME` environment variable used in our sample scripts must be set to the root directory of your POP3 provider installation. Because the POP3 v1.1.1 provider is compatible only with

JavaMail v1.1.3, you'll also need to download the JavaMail standard extension from `http://java.sun.com/products/javamail/` and the Java Activation Framework v1.0.1 from `http://java.sun.com/beans/glasgow/jaf.html`. The POP3 v1.1.1 provider that we utilize is not compatible with JavaMail v1.1.2 and thus cannot be used with the JavaMail API equipped with the J2EE v1.2 reference implementation. To run our examples, a `MAIL_HOME` and `JAF_HOME` environment variable must be set to the root directory of your JavaMail and Java Activation Framework installation, respectively.

We do, however, utilize the JavaMail SMTP implementation provided with the J2EE reference implementation with the integrated EJB and JavaMail sample code of Chapter 37. The `AuthenticationSessionEJBean` class in the `examples\src\ejava\ejbch37\authenticationsession` directory sends an email message via JavaMail. In order to support this functionality, you will have to set the `<mail-host>` element defined in the `examples\src\ejava\ejbch37\authenticationsession\sun-j2ee-ri.xml` file to an appropriate SMTP server name (for example, smtp.*myHost*.com). The BEA WebLogic v5.1 Server does not support the JavaMail functionality presented in Chapter 37.

Additional Resources

APPENDIX

B

This appendix contains references to additional resources that can be used to augment the material presented in this book. For the latest list of such resources, contact Assured Technologies, Inc.'s information technology resources site at `http://www.assuredtech.com/resources`. The accompanying CD also includes a collection of Web resources, stored beneath the `webref` directory.

Object-Oriented and Component-Based Software Development

We list resources for additional information on object-oriented software development and component-based software development here:

Booch, Grady; *Object-Oriented Analysis and Design with Applications*, Second Edition; Benjamin-Cummings; Redwood City, CA; 1994.

Eriksson, Hans-Erik, and Magnus Penker; *UML Toolkit*; Wiley; New York; 1998.

Gamma, Eric, et al.; *Design Patterns: Elements of Reusable Object-Oriented Software*; Addison-Wesley; Reading, MA; 1995.

Hillside Group; *Patterns Home Page*; `http://hillside.net/patterns/`.

Jacobson, Ivar; *Object-Oriented Software Engineering: A Use Case Driven Approach*; Revised Printing; Addison-Wesley; Harlow, England; 1992.

Jacobson, Ivar, et al.; *The Object Advantage: Business Process Reengineering with Object Technology*; Addison-Wesley; Workingham, England; 1995.

Marchukov, Mark; *Component Software Resources*; `http://www.geocities.com/m_a_r_c_h/components.html`.

Rumbaugh, James, et al.; *Object-Oriented Modeling and Design*; Prentice Hall; Englewood Cliffs, NJ; 1991.

Software Engineering Institute, Carnegie Mellon University; *Component-Based Software Development/COTS Integration*; `http://www.sei.cmu.edu/str/descriptions/cbsd.html`.

Java Basics

We list resources for additional information on the Java language, basic Java APIs, and the J2SE here:

Flanagan, David; *Java in a Nutshell*, Second Edition; O'Reilly; Cambridge, MA; 1997.

Jaworski, Jamie; *Java 1.1 Developer's Guide*, Second Edition; Sams.net Publishing; Indianapolis, IN; 1997.

Sun Microsystems, Inc.; *Applet Tag*; `http://java.sun.com/products/jdk/1.1/docs/guide/misc/applet.html`.

Sun Microsystems, Inc.; *Java 2 SDK, Standard Edition*; http://java.sun.com/products/jdk/1.2/.

Sun Microsystems, Inc.; *Java 2 SDK, Standard Edition Documentation*; http://java.sun.com/products/jdk/1.2/docs/index.html.

Sun Microsystems, Inc.; *Java 2 Platform, Standard Edition, v1.2.2 API Specification*; http://java.sun.com/products/jdk/1.2/docs/api/index.html.

Sun Microsystems, Inc.; *Manifest File Format*; http://java.sun.com/products/jdk/1.2/docs/guide/jar/manifest.html.

J2EE Basics

We list resources for additional information on the J2EE and the BEA WebLogic Server product here:

BEA WebLogic; *BEA WebLogic Server v5.1 Documentation*; http://www.weblogic.com/docs50/resources.html.

Sun Microsystems, Inc.; *Java 2 Platform, Enterprise Edition*; http://www.javasoft.com/j2ee/.

Sun Microsystems, Inc.; *Java 2 Platform, Enterprise Edition, v1.2 Specification*; http://www.javasoft.com/j2ee/download.html#specs.

Sun Microsystems, Inc.; *JSR-000058 Java 2 Platform, Enterprise Edition 1.3 Specification (J2EE 1.3)*; http://java.sun.com/aboutJava/communityprocess/jsr/jsr_058_j2ee13.html.

User Interfacing

We list resources for additional information on Java user interfacing APIs here:

Sun Microsystems, Inc.; *Abstract Window Toolkit (AWT)*; http://java.sun.com/products/jdk/1.2/docs/guide/awt/index.html.

Sun Microsystems, Inc.; *Java 3D API*; http://java.sun.com/products/java-media/3D/.

Sun Microsystems, Inc.; *Java Foundation Classes (JFC)*; http://java.sun.com/products/jfc/index.html.

Sun Microsystems, Inc.; *JavaHelp*; http://java.sun.com/products/javahelp/.

Sun Microsystems, Inc.; *Java Media APIs*; http://java.sun.com/products/java-media/index.html.

Sun Microsystems, Inc.; *The Swing Connection*; http://java.sun.com/products/jfc/tsc/index.html.

JavaBeans

We list resources for additional information on JavaBeans here:

Sun Microsystems, Inc.; *JavaBeans Component API*; `http://java.sun.com/products/jdk/1.2/docs/guide/beans/index.html`.

Sun Microsystems, Inc.; *JavaBeans Specifications for Java 2*; `http://java.sun.com/beans/glasgow/`.

Sun Microsystems, Inc.; *InfoBus*; `http://java.sun.com/beans/infobus/`.

Database Development and JDBC

We list resources for additional information on database development and the JDBC API here:

Silberschatz and Korth; *Database System Concepts*; McGraw-Hill; New York; 1986.

Sun Microsystems, Inc.; *JDBC Data Access API*; `http://java.sun.com/products/jdbc/`.

Sun Microsystems, Inc.; *JDBC 1.X Specifications*; `http://java.sun.com/products/jdbc/download2.html`.

Sun Microsystems, Inc.; *JDBC 2.X Specifications*; `http://java.sun.com/products/jdbc/download.html`.

Sun Microsystems, Inc.; *JDBC 3.0 Specification JSR*; `http://java.sun.com/aboutJava/communityprocess/jsr/jsr_054_jdbc3.html`.

Sun Microsystems, Inc.; *SQL to Java Type Mapping*; `http://java.sun.com/products/jdk/1.2/docs/guide/jdbc/spec/jdbc-spec.frame8.html`.

General Distributed Communications and TCP/IP

We list resources for additional information on TCP/IP and distributed communications topics in general here:

Casad, Joe, and Bob Willsey; *Teach Yourself TCP/IP in 24 Hours*; Sams; Indianapolis, IN; 1999.

FreeSoft; *Internet Encyclopedia*; `http://freesoft.org/CIE/Topics/index.htm`.

Spurgeon, Charles; *Ethernet Web Site*; `http://www.ots.utexas.edu/ethernet/`.

Internet Engineering Task Force; `http://www.ietf.org`.

Stallings, William; *Data and Computer Communications*, Sixth Edition; Macmillan; New York; 1999.

Sun Microsystems, Inc.; *J2SE Networking Features*; `http://java.sun.com/products/jdk/1.2/docs/guide/net/index.html`.

CORBA

We list resources for additional information on CORBA in general as well as on Java-related CORBA technology here:

Distributed Object Computing Group, Washington University in St. Louis; *OMG CORBA Documents in PDF*; `http://tao.cs.wustl.edu/corba/`.

McCarty, Bill, and Luke Cassady-Dorion; *Java Distributed Objects*; Sams; Indianapolis, IN; 1999.

Object Management Group; *CORBA/IIOP Specification*; `http://www.omg.org/corba/corbaiiop.html`.

Object Management Group; *CORBA Services Specification*; `http://www.omg.org/library/csindx.html`.

Object Management Group; *IDL to Java Language Mapping*; `http://www.omg.org/corba/clchpter.html#ijlm`.

Object Management Group; *Java to IDL Language Mapping*; `http://www.omg.org/corba/clchpter.html#jilm`.

Object Management Group; *OMG Home Page*; `http://www.omg.org`.

Orfali, Robert, and Dan Harkey; *Client/Server Programming with Java and CORBA*, Second Edition; Wiley; New York; 1998.

Orfali, Robert, Dan Harkey, and Jeri Edwards; *Instant CORBA*; Wiley; New York; 1997.

Prism Technologies, Inc.; *OpenFusion Home Page*; `http://www.prismtechnologies.com/products/openfusion/main.htm`.

Sun Microsystems, Inc.; *Java IDL*; `http://java.sun.com/products/jdk/1.2/docs/guide/idl/index.html`.

RMI

We list resources for additional information on RMI via JRMP and IIOP here:

McCarty, Bill, and Luke Cassady-Dorion; *Java Distributed Objects*; Sams; Indianapolis, IN; 1999.

Sun Microsystems, Inc.; *RMI Specification*; `http://java.sun.com/products/jdk/1.2/docs/guide/rmi/spec/rmiTOC.doc.html`.

Sun Microsystems, Inc.; *Java Remote Method Invocation (RMI)*; `http://java.sun.com/products/jdk/rmi/`.

Sun Microsystems, Inc.; *RMI over IIOP*; `http://java.sun.com/products/rmi-iiop/`.

COM/DCOM

We list resources for additional information on COM/DCOM in general as well as on Java related COM/DCOM technology here:

Adler, Dan; "Using RMI and JDBC From Visual Basic"; *JavaReport*; November 1998.

Maso, Brian; *Visual J++ 6 from the Ground Up*; Osborne/McGraw Hill; New York; 1999.

McCarty, Bill, and Luke Cassady-Dorion; *Java Distributed Objects*; Sams; Indianapolis, IN; 1999.

Microsoft Corporation; *DCOM*; `http://www.microsoft.com/com/tech/dcom.asp`.

Sessions, Roger; *COM and DCOM*; Wiley; New York; 1998.

JNDI, Naming, Directory, Trading, and Jini Services

We list resources for additional information on JNDI, naming services, directory services, trading services, and Jini here:

Edwards, Keith W.; *Core Jini*; Prentice Hall PTR; Upper Saddle River, NJ; 1999.

Information Technology Division, University of Michigan; *Lightweight Directory Access Protocol*; `http://www.umich.edu/~dirsvcs/ldap/ldap.html`.

Internet Software Consortium; *ISC BIND*; `http://www.isc.org/bind.html`.

Jini Community; *Jini Community Home Page*; `http://www.jini.org`.

Kosovic, Douglas; *Trader Information Service*; `http://archive.dstc.edu.au/AU/research_news/odp/trader/trader.html`.

Microsoft Corporation; *Active Directory Architecture*; `http://www.microsoft.com/windows2000/library/howitworks/activedirectory/adarch.asp`.

Netscape Communications Corporation; *The String Representation of LDAP Search Filters*; `ftp://ftp.isi.edu/in-notes/rfc2254.txt`.

Perrone, Paul, and Krishna Chaganti; "Java Naming and Directory Service Interfaces"; *Distributed Computing*; October 1999 (online copy at `http://www.assuredtech.com/papers/jndi/dc99.pdf`).

Perrone, Paul, and Krishna Chaganti; "Jini in the Box"; *Embedded Systems Programming*; November 1999; cover story (online copy at `http://www.assuredtech.com/papers/jini/embedded.pdf`).

Prism Technologies, Inc.; *OpenFusion Home Page*; `http://www.prismtechnologies.com/products/openfusion/main.htm`.

Salamon, András; *DNS Resources Directory*; `http://www.dns.net/dnsrd/`.

Sun Microsystems, Inc.; *Java Naming and Directory Interface (JNDI)*; `http://java.sun.com/products/jndi/`.

Sun Microsystems, Inc.; *JNDI Service Providers*; www.javasoft.com/products/jndi/serviceproviders.html.

Sun Microsystems, Inc.; *JavaIDL Naming Service*; http://java.sun.com/products/jdk/1.2/docs/guide/idl/jidlNaming.html.

MOM, JMS, and JavaMail

We list resources for additional information on messaging systems and technology in general, JMS, and JavaMail here:

FreeSoft; *Mail*; http://freesoft.org/CIE/Topics/91.htm.

FreeSoft; *Post Office Protocol*; http://freesoft.org/CIE/RFC/1725/index.htm.

FreeSoft; *Simple Mail Transfer Protocol*; http://freesoft.org/CIE/RFC/821/index.htm.

Sun Microsystems, Inc.; *JavaMail API*; http://java.sun.com/products/javamail/.

Sun Microsystems, Inc.; *Java Messaging Service API*; http://java.sun.com/products/jms/.

Distributed Transactions, JTA, and JTS

We list resources for additional information on transaction services, the OTS, JTS, and JTA here:

Sun Microsystems, Inc.; *Java Transaction API (JTA)*; http://java.sun.com/products/jta/.

Sun Microsystems, Inc.; *Java Transaction Service (JTS)*; http://java.sun.com/products/jts/.

Vogel, Andreas, and Madhavan Rangarao; *Programming with Enterprise JavaBeans, JTS and OTS*; Wiley; New York; 1999.

General Assurance and Security

We list resources for additional information on assurance and security here:

Garfinkel, Simson, and Gene Spafford; *Web Security & Commerce*; O'Reilly; Cambridge, MA; 1997.

Oaks, Scott; *Java Security*; O'Reilly; Cambridge, MA; 1998.

Russell, Deborah, and G. T. Gangemi Sr.; *Computer Security Basics*; O'Reilly & Associates, Inc.; Cambridge, MA; 1991.

Perrone, Paul; *Global Safety Assurance: Concepts and Application to Train Control Systems*; University of Virginia; Charlottesville, VA; 1995.

Perrone, Paul; *Practical Enterprise Assurance*; `http://www.assuredtech.com/papers/assurance/pea.pdf`.

Venners, Bill; *Inside the Java Virtual Machine*; McGraw Hill; New York; 1998.

Sun Microsystems, Inc.; *Java Security API*; `http://java.sun.com/security/`.

Sun Microsystems, Inc.; *Java Security Architecture (JDK1.2)*; `http://java.sun.com/products/jdk/1.2/docs/guide/security/spec/security-spec.doc.html`.

Sun Microsystems, Inc.; *Java Cryptography Extension (JCE)*; `http://java.sun.com/products/jce/`.

Sun Microsystems, Inc.; *Java Secure Socket Extension (JSSE)*; `http://java.sun.com/products/jsse/`.

Sun Microsystems, Inc.; *Java Authentication and Authorization Service (JAAS)*; `http://java.sun.com/products/jaas/`.

Sun Microsystems, Inc.; *Permissions in the Java 2 SDK*; `http://java.sun.com/products/jdk/1.2/docs/guide/security/permissions.html`.

General Web, HTML, and Scripting

We list resources for additional information on general Web enabling and HTML here:

4GuysFromRolla.com; *General ASP Resources*; `http://www.4guysfromrolla.com/webtech/index.shtml`.

National Center for Supercomputing Applications (NCSA) at the University of Illinois at Urbana-Champaign (UIUC); *NCSA (at UIUC) Beginner's Guide to HTML*; `http://www.ncsa.uiuc.edu/General/Internet/WWW/HTMLPrimer.html`.

Sun Microsystems, Inc.; *Java Plug-In Product*; `http://java.sun.com/products/plugin/index.html`.

World Wide Web Consortium; *W3C Home Page*; `http://www.w3.org/`.

World Wide Web Consortium; *HTML 4 Specification*; `http://www.w3.org/TR/REC-html40/`.

World Wide Web Consortium; *HTTP—Hypertext Transfer Protocol*; `http://www.w3.org/Protocols/`.

XML

We list resources for additional information on XML here:

Sun Microsystems, Inc.; *Java Technology and XML*; `http://java.sun.com/xml/`.

Sun Microsystems, Inc.; *Java API for XML Parsing (JAXP) Downloads and Specifications*; `http://java.sun.com/xml/download.html`.

World Wide Web Consortium; *Extensible Markup Language (XML)*; `http://www.w3.org/XML/`.

World Wide Web Consortium; *Extensible Markup Language (XML) Specification*; `http://www.w3.org/TR/REC-xml`.

World Wide Web Consortium; *XML Linking Language (XLink)*; `http://www.w3.org/TR/xlink/`.

World Wide Web Consortium; *Extensible Stylesheet Language (XSL)*; `http://www.w3.org/Style/XSL/`.

World Wide Web Journal; "XML: Principles, Tools, and Techniques"; O'Reilly; Cambridge, MA; 1997.

Java Servlets and JSP

We list resources for additional information on Web enabling via Java Servlets and JSP here:

Sun Microsystems, Inc.; *Java Servlet API*; `http://java.sun.com/products/servlet/`.

Sun Microsystems, Inc.; *Java Servlet Specification*; `http://java.sun.com/products/servlet/2.2/`.

Sun Microsystems, Inc.; *JavaServer Pages*; `http://www.javasoft.com/products/jsp/`.

Sun Microsystems, Inc.; *JavaServer Pages Specification*; `http://www.javasoft.com/products/jsp/download.html`.

Application Serving and EAI

We list resources for additional information on application serving frameworks and EAI here:

IT Toolbox; *IT Toolbox for ERP*; `http://www.erpassist.com/`.

IT Toolbox; *IT Toolbox for EAI*; `http://eai.ittoolbox.com/`.

Microsoft Corporation; *Microsoft Windows DNA*; `http://www.microsoft.com/dna/`.

Sun Microsystems, Inc.; *JSR-000016 J2EE Connector Architecture*; `http://java.sun.com/aboutJava/communityprocess/jsr/jsr_016_connect.html`.

Sun Microsystems, Inc.; *Java 2 Platform, Enterprise Edition*; `http://www.javasoft.com/j2ee/`.

Enterprise JavaBeans

We list resources for additional information on Enterprise JavaBeans here:

Sun Microsystems, Inc.; *Enterprise JavaBeans*; http://java.sun.com/products/ejb/.

Sun Microsystems, Inc.; *Enterprise JavaBeans Specification*; http://java.sun.com/products/ejb/docs.html.

Sun Microsystems, Inc.; *EJB to CORBA Mapping Specification*; http://java.sun.com/products/ejb/docs.html.

Sun Microsystems, Inc.; *JSR-000019 Enterprise JavaBeans 2.0 Specification*; http://java.sun.com/aboutJava/communityprocess/jsr/jsr_019_ejb2.html.

INDEX

SYMBOLS

! (negation) symbol, directory search filter, 642

!-- --> character sequence, 1014

!--> tag, 991

<? ?> character sequence, 1016

% (wildcard character), folder lists, 775

& (logical AND) symbol, directory search filter, 642

< > (angle brackets), HTML tags, 987

: (colon), XML namespaces, 1015

| (OR relation)
- content model element declaration, 1021
- directory search filter, 642

? (question mark), content model element declaration, 1020

; (semicolon), RDNs/DNs, 648

\ (backslash)
- escape character, 642
- filenames, 606

// (forward slash), file names, 606

<= (less than or equal to) symbol, directory search filter, 642

>= (greater than or equal to) symbol, directory search filter, 642

= (equality) symbol, directory search filter, 642

~= (approximate equality) symbol, directory search filter, 642

*** (asterisk)**
- content model element declaration, 1020
- wildcard character
  - *folder lists, 775*
  - *directory search filter, 642*

+ (plus symbol), content model element declaration, 1020

, (comma)
content model element declaration, 1020
RDNs/DNs, 648
100BASE-FX, 331
100BASE-TX, 331
10BASE-2, 331
10BASE-5, 331
10BASE-F, 331
10BASE-T, 331
2D geometrical shapes, 136
2D images, 136
3D images, 136

A

<A HREF> tag, 990-991
<A> tag, 990
absolute() method, 253
abstract classes (class diagram notation), 34
Abstract Windowing Toolkit. *See* AWT
AbstractCollection class, 82
abstraction levels (databases), 175
abstractions
HTTP session managment, 1104-1107
JSPs
container information, 1157-1158
custom tag extension abstractions, 1181-1186
custom tag library abstractions, 1183
factories, 1157-1158
page context, 1152-1157
object-oriented software development), 24
AbstractList class, 84
AbstractMap class, 84
AbstractSequentialList class, 84
AbstractSet class, 84
access
databases, 203
DBMS, 114
IRs, 449
permissions, 242
security manager, 868
AccessController class, 871
checkPermission() method, 871
customizing, 871-873
default, 869
getSecurityManager() method, 869
instantiation, 869
RMISecurityManager class, 871
SecurityManager class, 869, 871
SecurityManager objects, 869
setSecurityManager() method, 869
Access Control, 861, 896
architecture, 896, 898
examples, 903-904
guarded objects, 899
mapping, 900-903
security, 828, 896, 898
SecurityManager, 899-903
access control lists, 981
access control mapping, 1329-1330
AccessControlContext object, 898
AccessControlException objects, 904
AccessController class, 871
AccessController.checkPermission() method, 896
accessibility (UI support), 135
Accessible interface, 135
AccessibleContext object, 135
AccessibleObject class, 78
Accounting Facility, 399
AcessDecision objects, 953
ACID (atomicity, consistency, isolation, durability), 177
ACTION attribute (<FORM> tag), 994
actions (JSPs)
action sub-elements, 1165
examples, 1173-1175
forward action, 1165-1166
getProperty action, 1170-1171
include action, 1166-1167
plugin action, 1171-1173
setProperty action, 1169-1170
useBean action, 1167-1168
Activatable class, 515
activatable object clients, 521-522
activatable object interface, 517
activatable server registrar, 519-521
activatable servers, 517-518
activation (servlets), 1127
activation groups, 520
activation services, 690
application frameworks, 702-704
communications, 117
CORBA framework, 694-696
CORBA lifecycle service, 697-699
DCOM framework, 699-700
JAF (JavaBeans Activation Framework), 700-701
overview, 690-691
RMI framework, 692-693
Web frameworks, 702-704
ActivationGroupDesc objects, 520
Active Directory Service Interface (ADSI), 687
Active Directory Service (ADS), 636, 686-687, 1202

Active Server Pages (ASPs), 1006-1007
ActiveX component attacks, 971
ActiveX Runtime Engine, 970
actuate attribute (XLink), 1027
adapter pattern, 51
adapters (object), 444
- BOA-based server registration, 444-445
- IDL server registration, 446-447
- POA-based server registration, 447-448

add() method, 149
addAnEventListenerTotheContext() method, 652
addANewAttribute() method, 653
addAuditListener() method, 151
addBatch() method, 274
addDateHeader() method, 1098
addHeader() method, 1098
adding
- attributes to collections, 638
- columns to RDBMS tables, 182
- property change listeners, 156
- rows
  - *RDBMS tables, 183*
  - *updateable result sets, 264*
- RowSetListener objects, 295
- services to containers, 149
- vetoable property change listeners, 158

addIntHeader() method, 1098
addNamingListener() method, 643
addPropertyChangeListener() method, 156, 166
Address Resolution Protocol (ARP), 333
addresses (IP), 332-333
addRowSetListener() method, 295
addVetoableChangeListener() method, 158
Admin interface, 666
administration
- CORBA Security, 963-964
- security, 852-853
- tools, 123

ADS (Microsoft Active Directory), 636, 686-687, 1202
ADSI (Active Directory Service Interface), 687
advanced data types (JDBC 2.0), 278
- advanced SQL types example, 288-294
  - *BLOB inserts/retrievals, 290-291*
  - *custom type inserts/retrievals, 292-294*
  - *structure inserts/retrievals, 291-292*
- BeeShirts.com data model example, 286-287
- custom types, 284-285
- Java objects, 278-279
- SQL, 280-284

advanced imaging, 136
afterLast() method, 253
aggregation (class diagram notation), 34
Algorithm Parameters (cryptographic engines), 875
AlgorithmParameterGenerator (cryptographic engines), 875
algorithms
- asymmetric keys, 843
- message digests, 842
- Netscape SSL v3, 848-849
- symmetric keys, 843

AllPermission permissions, 882
ALTER_TABLE statement, 182-183
analysis
- behavioral, 26
- interface, 27
- pattern identification, 47
- requirements, 26-27
- use-case, 27

analysis paralysis, 26
analyzeMetaData() method, 236-237
angle brackets (< >), HTML tags, 987
anonymizer sites, 973
ANSI92 entry levels, 242
ANSI92 full SQL compliance, 243
ANSI92 intermediate levels, 242
any content element declaration, 1020
Apache Web server, 978
APIs (application program interfaces), 73. *See also* servlets
- application server frameworks, 1212
- archive files, 90-91
- component, 44
- core Java language APIs, 73
- data types, 76-77
- date, 97-98
- garbage collection, 79-80
- history, 107
- J/Direct, 531
- Java, 50
- Java 2D, 136
- Java 3D, 136
- Java Advanced Imaging, 136
- Java API class files, 58
- Java Communications, 1371
- Java Enterprise, 108
- Java Media, 137
- Java Media Framework, 137

Java serialization, 1061
Java Shared Data Toolkit, 137
Java Sound, 137
Java Speech, 137
Java Telephony, 137
Java-based application frameworks, 1199
JAXP (Java API for XML Parsing), 120, 1031
JDBC. *See* JDBC
JTA, 117
language, 74
LDAP, 649
mathematical, 76-77
ODBC, 195
reflection, 77-78
SAX (Simple API for XML). *See* SAX
security policies, 895
standards Web site, 649
system, 74
thread, 96-97
threading, 93-96
time, 97-98
XML, 123, 1061-1062

appendMessages() method, 775

AppleContext object, 100

Applet class, 99, 500

applet clients, 109

APPLET property (JNDI contexts), 584

applet-based interfaces, 138

applets, 49, 99, 119, 138
Applet class, 99
AppletContext object, 100
AppletStub interface, 99
appletviewer tool, 64
attacks, 971
class downloads, 500
class loader, 865
defining
initial definition, 99, 101
lifecycle, 101, 103
destroy() method, 101
getAppletInfo() method, 102
getParameterInfo() method, 102
init() method, 101
referencing from Web pages, 103-104
security, 856-857
start() method, 101
stop() method, 101
storing, 103
Web browsers, 99
with CORBA connectivity. *See* Orblets

AppletStub interface, 99

appletviewer tool, 64

application assembler, 1213

Application Development Facility, 399

application layer (OSI communications layer model), 328

application modules, 1210

application program interfaces. *See* APIs

application programs (APs), 177

application servers, 1196
APIs, 1212
architecture, 1210-1211
availability, 1229
based enterprise applications, 1210-1212
client configuration/deployment example, 1226-1227
client implementations, 1220-1224
client interfaces, 1218-1219
components, 1214-1217
configuration services, 1229
configuring, 1225
database connectivity, 1228
deployment, 1225
distributed communication services, 1228
EJB activation, 704
EJB client home interface example, 1219
EJB client remote interface example, 1219
provider roles, 1212-1214
providers, 1213
security, 1229
server configuration/deployment example, 1225-1226
services, 1228-1229
state management, 1228

application services, 1228-1229

application system administrator, 1214

Application TCP/IP layer, 334-335

application-specific entity bean remote interfaces, 1301

application-specific frameworks, 1203-1205

application-specific home entity bean interfaces, 1304-1305

application-specific platforms, 1203-1205

application-specific remote session bean interfaces, 1264

application-specific session bean home interfaces, 1271

applications, 1210
activation frameworks, 702-704
application server-based enterprise, 1210-1212
BshirtsClient example, 926-929
business-to-business (B2B) integration, 122
CGI example, 996, 998-1000
client service enhancements (J2EE future), 122
component developer, 1213
components, 1210
connectivity, 121-122
container providers, 1213

containers, 1210
CORBA standalone, 419
deployers, 1213
deployment descriptions in XML, 1063-1066
DNS, 627
enabling, 17, 113
enterprise, 54-55
frameworks, 1196-1197
application integration services, 1197
architecture, 1197
configuration/deployment services, 1197
CORBA-based, 1200-1202
DNA (Distributed Network Architecture), 1202
Java-based, 1198, 1200
management services, 1197
object persistence services, 1197
handler interfaces (SAX)
document handlers, 1040-1043
DTD handler, 1035-1037
entity resolvers, 1037-1038
error handlers, 1039-1040
integration services, 1197
J2EE-based EJB container environments, 121
J2EE-based Web-enabling, 119
Java-based, 119
management, 1205
regedit.exe , 565
running, 1361
servers. *See* application servers
standalone, 121, 205
standalone enterprise, 1208-1209
stateful CGI, 1000
TCP/IP, 335
testing, 29
Web, 1119-1120
Web application deployment descriptors
format, 1111-1117
procedures, 1118-1119

approximate equality (~=) symbol, directory search filter, 642

APs (application programs), 177

arc attribute (XLink), 1026

architecture

access control, 896, 898
application frameworks, 1197
application servers, 1210-1211
BeeShirts.com example, 1334, 1336
BMP entity beans, 1281-1282
browsers, 969-970
class loader, 864-865
CMP entity beans, 1293
CORBA Security, 941-942
CORBAcomponents, 1201
core security architecture, 859, 861
databases, 175-176
DCOM, 529-530
distributed systems, 319-320
DNA, 1202
DOM, 1048, 1050
EJBS, 1233-1234
entity bean remote interfaces, 1300
home entity bean interfaces, 1303
InfoBus, 167-168
J2EE component-container, 108-110
Java Enterprise System (overview), 112-113
JavaBeans, 142-144
JavaMail, 759-760
JCA, 859-861, 873, 907
cryptographic engines, 875
CSPs, 874-877
encryption/cryptography distinction, 861, 873
functions, 873
Provider class, 874
Security class, 874
security package, 873
security.cert package, 873
security.interfaces package, 874
security.spec package, 874
JDBC, 200-204
Jini class, 679, 681-682
Jini components, 674-675
JMS, 714
connections, 714, 717
messages, 719-723
producers/consumers/selectors, 725-726
sessions, 717-719
JNDI, 580-582
JSPs (JavaServer Pages), 1137
ODBMSs, 186-187
ORB, 390
permissions, 881
RDBMSs, 179-180
remote session bean interfaces, 1263
RMI, 467-469
row sets, 295
runtime platform, 58
SAX, 1032
servlets, 1068-1070
session bean home interfaces, 1267
stateful session beans, 1256
stateless session beans, 1251
Web servers, 976-977

archives

APIs, 90-91
Attributes class, 91
JAR files, 60
jar tool, 63
structure, 62
JarEntry class, 90
JarInputStream class, 90
JarOutputStream class, 91

Manifest class, 90
manifest files, 60-62
ZipEntry class, 90
ZipInputStream class, 90
ZipOutputStream class, 91
arithmetic operators, 65
ARP (Address Resolution Protocol), 333
arp utility (TCP/IP), 336
ARPAnet, 330
Array class, 78
Array interface, 282
array properties (JavaBeans), 155
arrays
building, 68
defined, 68
SQL, 282-283
Arrays class, 82
ASCII text (HTML), 987
ASPs (Active Server Pages), 1006-1007
assembly (object-oriented software development process), 29
assembly-language programming, 20
assignment operators, 66
associations (class diagram notation), 33
assurance, 113, 818-819
a priori application creation errors, 823
a priori data creation errors, 823
availability, 819
models, 831-832
risk reduction plans, 832
problems, 822
corrupted application errors, 823
corrupted data errors, 823
costs, 820-821
delayed application processing errors, 823
delayed data delivery errors, 823
delivery pressures, 820
failed delivery costs, 826
failure likelihood/rate evaluations (risk assessments), 823
failure occurrence evaluations (risk assessments), 824
incorrect application reference errors, 823
incorrect data reference errors, 823
maintainability, 819
models, 833
problems, 822
risk reduction plans, 833-834
overview, 118
problems
identifying, 822
models, 822-823
risk assessments, 823-824
risks versus costs, 827
processes, 821-822
providers, 819-820
reliability, 819
models, 829-830
problems, 822
risk reduction plans, 830-831
residual risks, 825
risk reduction plans, 824-825
availability, 832
costs, 825
maintainability, 833-834
reliability, 830-831
safety, 835
security, 828-829
selecting, 826-827
safety, 819
models, 834
problems, 822
risk reduction plans, 835
security, 819
models, 827-828
problems, 822
risk reduction plans, 828-829
services, 16
asterisks (*), content model element declaration, 1020
asymmetric keys (cryptography), 842-844
asynchronicity (messaging), 711
asynchronous EJB messages, 122
atomicity, consistency, isolation, durability (ACID), 177
<!ATTLIST ?> character sequence, 1022
Attr subinterface (Node interface), 1053
attribute declarations, 1022
Attribute interface, 637
AttributeList interface, 1033
attributes
<FORM> tag, 994
<INPUT> tag, 994-995
ACTION (<FORM> tag), 994
actuate (XLink), 1027
adding to collections, 638
arc (XLink), 1026
CDATA, 1022
CHECKBOX (<INPUT> tag), 995
directory objects, 637-638, 643
DTD declaration values, 1022
ENCTYPE (<FORM> tag), 994
ENTITY, 1022
enumerated types, 1022
extended (XLink), 1026, 1028
extends attribute, 1158
from (XLink), 1028
HIDDEN (<INPUT> tag), 995
href (XLink), 1028

HTML tags, 987
ID, 1022
IDREF, 1022
IMAGE (<INPUT> tag), 995
jsp
plugin action, 1172
setProperty action, 1169
useBean action, 1167-1168
locator (XLink), 1026
Mandatory (transactions), 797
match (XSL style sheets), 1030
METHOD (<FORM> tag), 994
Never (transactions), 796
NMTOKEN, 1022
NotSupported (transactions), 796
page directive (JSPs), 1145-1146
PASSWORD (<INPUT> tag), 995
RADIO (<INPUT> tag), 995
Required (transactions), 796
RequiresNew (transactions), 796
RESET (<INPUT> tag), 995
resource (XLink), 1026
role (XLink), 1027
servlet request handling, 1088
show (XLink), 1027
simple (XLink), 1026
SUBMIT (<INPUT> tag), 995
Supports (transactions), 797
template (XSL style sheets), 1030
TEXT (<INPUT> tag), 994-995
title (XLink), 1026-1027
to (XLink), 1028
transactions, 796-797
type (XLink), 1028
XLink, 1026
XML documents, 1015
xsl (XSL style sheets), 1030

Attributes class, 91
Attributes interface, 637
audit decision() method, 954
audit event example, 150
audit needed() method, 954
audit write() method, 956
AuditBean class, 147
AuditBeanBeanInfo class, 160
AuditBeanContainer, 145
AuditChannel objects, 956
AuditDecision objects, 954
AuditEventType objects, 954
auditing, 852
CORBA Security, 954, 956
security, 123, 828
AuditListener interface, 151
AuditPropertyChangeAdapter class, 157
authenticate() method, 948
authentication, 844
basic, 1130
biometrics-based identity, 846
certificate-based identity, 846-848
CORBA Security, 946-950
digest-based, 1130
EJBs, 1331
forms-based, 1130
J2EE future, 122
JAAS, 862
password-based identity, 845
physical token-based identity, 845
servlets, 1130-1131
SSL client certificate-based, 1130
types, 845, 848
vendor-specific, 1330-1331
AuthenticationSession bean, 1352
Authenticator class, 771
Authenticator parameter (Session objects), 771
authenticity (security), 828

authenticode restrictions, 972
authorization, 849
CORBA Security, 952, 954
discretionary, 850
firewall, 851
J2EE future, 122
mandatory, 850
role-based, 850
security, 828
servlets, 1131-1132
AUTHORITATIVE property (JNDI contexts), 584
automation (DCOM), 533-534
auxiliary application integration. *See* EAI
auxiliary service reduction, 981
ava property (CompoundName constructor), 587
availability, 831
application servers, 1229
assurance, 819
assurance problems, 822, 831-832
concurrency management, 832
fail-over management, 832
licensing, 832
load-balancing, 832
load-testing, 832
resource management, 832
risk reduction plans, 832
rollback techniques, 832
security-critical, 828
servlets, 1133-1134
thread/process management, 832
Web servers, 982
AWT (Abstract Windowing Toolkit), 130
components, 130
containers, 131
deployment, 131-132
events, 131

images, 136
layout managers, 131
libraries, 131-132
AWTEvent class, 131
AWTPermission permissions, 885

B

<B> tag, 991
back door service attacks, 980
background color (HTML documents), 990
backslash (\), 606
baked-in CORBA libraries, 422
basic authentication (servlets), 1130
Basic Object Adapter. *See* BOA
BasicAttribute class, 637
BasicAttributes class, 637
BasicPermission class, 890
batch updates, 274
creating, 274-275
example, 276-278
executing, 275
BATCHSIZE property (JNDI contexts), 584
BatchUpdateException, 275
BDK (JavaBeans Development Kit), 144
BEA WebLogic, 424
EJB reference manual Web site, 1311
servers, 978
EJB application deployment, 1248-1249
security, 1330-1331
startup/deployment, 1122
Web site, 1365
Bean-managed persistence entity beans. *See* BMP entity beans
bean-managed transaction demarcation, 1317-1321
BeanContext interface, 149
BeanContextServices interface, 149
BeanDescriptor class, 160
BeanIntrospectorExample class, 160
BeeShirts.com example, 212-213, 1139-1141
architecture, 1334-1336
client callback interface, 426
Customer information interface, 480
customer interface, 427
customer object, 350-351
data model, extending, 729
EJBs, 1239-1243
HTTP servlets, 1081-1085
HTTP session management, 1107-1110
as integrated J2EE EJB e-commerce application, 1334-1336
JDBC 2.0 data types, 286-287
naming service, 590-591
Order interface, 426
order manager, 731-732
order object, 352-353
order requests, 731
query server interface, 427-428
query service specific database interface, 347-350
queue consumer, 735-738
queue supplier, 732-733, 735
request handling, 1092-1095
response handling, 1099-1103
security, 1332-1333
stored procedures, 301-302
TCP/IP client callback handler, 357-358
TCP/IP client object, 353-357
TCP/IP query service protocol marker interface, 347
TCP/IP server socket handler, 343-346
TCP/IP server socket listener, 340-342
topic consumer, 744-747
topic suppliers, 741-744
beforeFirst() method, 253
begin() method, 809
beginquote property (CompoundName constructor), 587
beginquote2 property (CompoundName constructor), 587
behavior
customization, 46
object-oriented software development, 24
sequences, CORBA objects by value, 410-411
behavioral analysis, 26
Berkeley Internet Name Domain package. *See* BIND package
BigDecimal class, 77
BigInteger class, 77
BIND package, 627
bind() method
directory object bindings, 639
JNDI bindings, 586
bindings
directory objects, 639
generating, 543, 548-549
JNDI, 586
bound/renamed/deleted example, 602-605
listing example, 598-602
name-to-object, 579
BindToObject() method, 631
biometrics, 846
BitSet class, 82
bitwise operators, 65
Blob interface, 280
BLOBs (binary large objects), 280-282, 290-291

blocks, 70
BMP entity beans, 1236, 1281
architecture, 1281-1282
creating, 1284
deleting, 1284
example, 1287-1292
finding, 1283
home interface example, 1306
interface rules, 1286-1287
loading, 1285
passivation/activation, 1285
remote interface example, 1302
storing, 1285
BOA (Basic Object Adapter), 444-445
body
HTML documents, 990
JMS messages, 723
<BODY> tag, 990
<BODY_ALINK> tag, 990
<BODY_BGCOLOR> tag, 990
<BODY_LINK> tag, 990
<BODY_TEXT> tag, 990
<BODY_VLINK> tag, 990
BOF (Business Object Facility), 399
bold text (HTML documents), 991
Boolean class, 77
borders, Swing package, 133
bound properties (JavaBeans), 155-157
BQM (Business Quality Messaging), 712
**
 tag, 991**
brackets, 726
bridging, 571-572
browsers, 968-969
architecture, 969-970
cache managers, 969
cookie version supported, 1106
document presentation interfaces, 970
HotJava, 971
implementation updates, 972
implementations, 970-971
Internet Explorer, 970
Java Plug-in, 973
HTML Converter tool, 974
HTML Specification, 974
installing, 973-974
JRE designation, 974-975
Netscape Navigator, 970
security, 971
problems, 971-972
solutions, 972-973
BrowseSession bean, 1241
BrowseSession remote interface, 1265
BrowseSessionEJBean, 1253, 1255
BrowseSessionHome, 1272
BShirtsClient example application, 926-929
buffer size, 1096
Buffered Reader class, 90
BufferedInputStream classes, 88
BufferedOutputStream classes, 88
BufferedWriter class, 90
building arrays, 68
bulleted item lists (HTML documents), 991
Business Object Facility (BOF), 399
Business Object Task Force, 399
business objects (CORBA), 399
Business Quality Messaging (BQM), 712
business-to-business (B2B) integration, 122
Byte class, 76
byte code verifier, 58, 862
checks performed, 863
verification phases, 862
version differences, 863
byte codes, 58
byte code verifier, 58, 862
checks performed, 863
verification phases, 862
version differences, 863
class loader, 58
JVM, 58
runtime execution engine, 58
byte I/O streams
classes, 87-89
interfaces, 87-89
byte() method, 280
ByteArrayInputStream classes, 88
ByteArrayOutputStream classes, 88
BytesMessage interface, 723

C

CA (Certificate Authority), 847
cache managers, 969
cached row sets, 297
Calendar class, 98
Call CallData JRMP message, 472
Call Level Interfaces (CLIs), 192-193
CallableStatement interface, 202, 219, 299
calls. *See* methods
CancelRequest GIOP message, 394
cancelRowUpdates() method, 264
catalogs
names, 241
RDBMSs, 180-181
CBD (Component-Based Development), 47-48
analysis pattern identification, 47

components
assembly, 48
configuration specification, 48
design adaptation, 48
identification, 47
implementation specialization, 48
model technology identification, 47
selection, 47
testing, 48
deployment, 48
external component interface analysis, 47
maintenance, 48
module tests, 48
project charter, 47
reliability, 830
system component interface analysis, 47
system tests, 48
CDATA attribute, 1022
<![CDATA[ ]]> character sequence, 1017
CDATSection subinterface (Node interface), 1053
cells (HTML tables), 992
Certificate Authority (CA), 847
Certificate class, 908, 910
certificate revocation lists (CRLs), 847
Certificate Signing Requests (CSRs), 847
certificate-based authentication, 846-848
CertificateFactory (cryptographic engines), 875
certificates, 846-848, 908-915
examples, 912-915
generating, 928
storing, 910
CGI (Common Gateway Interface), 380-381
advantages/disadvantages, 1000-1001
CGI-based interface generators, 139
engines, 976
progam directories, 999
program example, 996-1000
stateful applications, 1000
cgi-bin directory, 999
chained transaction model, 798
Character class, 77
character data attribute, 1022
character I/O streams, 89-90
character sequences (XML)
<!-- -->, 1014
<!ATTLIST>, 1022
<!DOCTYPE>, 1019
<!ELEMENT>, 1019
<!ENTITY>, 1021
<!{CDATA[ ]]>, 1017
<? ?>, 1016
<?xml ?>, 1014
CharacterData subinterface (Node interface), 1053
characters() method, 1040
CharArrayReader class, 90
CharArrayWriter class, 90
charters (project), 26
CHECKBOX attribute (<INPUT> tag), 995
checkGuard() method, 881, 899
checking permissions, 871, 898, 904
checkPermission() method, 871, 896-898
checkRead(StringfileName) method, 896
checksums, 831
checkXXX() method, 896
CIDL (Component Implementation Definition Language), 1201
Cipher interface, 930
cipher text, 839
class A networks, 332
class B networks, 332
class C networks, 332
Class class, 74, 77
class declarations, 68
class diagrams, 32-35
.class file extension, 60
class files, 60, 103. *See also* classes
Class Identifiers (CLSIDs), 532, 629
class libraries, 581
class loader, 58, 864
applets, 865
architecture, 864-865
ClassLoader, 866
defineClass() method, 866
findClass() method, 866-868
forName() method, 868
loadClass() method, 866-868
responsibilities, 864
RMIClassLoader, 866
SecureClassLoader, 866
security, 864-865
URLClassLoader, 866
classes, 21. *See also* class files; packages
abstract, 34
AbstractCollection, 82
AbstractList, 84
AbstractMap, 84
AbstractSequentialList, 84
AbstractSet, 84
AccessController, 871
AccessibleObject, 78
Activatable, 515
Applet, 99, 500
applets, defining, 99-103
Array, 78
Arrays, 82
Attributes, 91
AuditBean, 147
AuditBeanBeanInfo, 160

AuditPropertyChangeAdapter, 157
Authenticator, 771
AWTEvent, 131
BasicAttribute, 637
BasicAttributes, 637
BasicPermission, 890
BeanDescriptor, 160
BeanIntrospectorExample, 160
BigDecimal, 77
BigInteger, 77
BitSet, 82
Boolean, 77
BufferedInputStream, 88
BufferedOutputStream, 88
BufferedReader, 90
BufferedWriter, 90
Byte, 76
ByteArrayInputStream, 88
ByteArrayOutputStream, 88
Calendar, 98
Certificate, 908-910
CertificationFactor, 908
Character, 77
CharArrayReader, 90
CharArrayWriter, 90
Class, 74, 77
class diagram notation, 32
Client, 353-357, 568
ClientReceiverImplementation, 435, 486-487, 495, 553
ClientReceiverServer, 357-358
Clipboard, 134
COM, 528
Compiler, 74
Component, 130, 147
CompositeName, 587
CompoundName, 586
CoMyServer, 567
Constructor, 78
Container, 131, 145
Cookie, 1078, 1106-1107
custom JSP classes, 1158
CustomerImplemenation, 431-435, 483-486, 496
Database, 187
DatabaseHelper, 347-350
DatabaseMetaData, 241
DatagramSocket, 359
DataHandler, 760
DataInputStream, 88
DataOutputStream, 88
Date, 97, 241
DateFormat, 97
DateFormatSymbols, 97
DCOM, 629-630
DefinitionKind, 449
Dictionary, 82, 85
DigestInputStream, 919
DigestOutputStream, 919
Dispatch, 534
DocumentBuilder, 1048, 1058
DocumentBuilderFactory, 1048, 1059
DOMException, 1050
Double, 77
downloading (RMI/JRMP servers), 500-504
DriverManager, 202, 209
DriverPropertyInfo, 210
DTDHandler, 1035
DynamicImplementation, 440
Error, 76
EventListener, 149
EventObject, 81
EventSetDescriptor, 160
Exceptions, 76
FeatureDescriptor, 160
Field, 78
File, 87, 606
FileDescriptor, 87
FileInputStream, 88, 91-93, 606
FileOutputStream, 88, 606
FileReader, 90, 606
FileWriter, 90, 606
FilterInputStream, 88
FilterOutputStream, 88
FilterReader, 90
FilterWriter, 90
Flags, 763
Float, 77
Folder, 772
GenericServlet, 1074
GregorianCalendar, 98
HandlerBase, 1035, 1043
HashMap, 84
HashSet, 84
Hashtable, 85
HttpServlet, 1078-1081
HttpSessionBindingEvent, 1106
HttpURLConnection, 377
HttpUtils, 1089-1090
Identity, 906
IdentityScope, 906
Image, 136
ImageFilter, 136
IndexedPropertyDescriptor, 160
InetAddress, 337, 628
InfoBus, 167
InfoBusEvent, 168
InheritableThreadLocal, 97
inheritance, 22
InitialContext, 305, 582, 636
InitialDirContext, 636
InitialLdapContext, 663
InputSource, 1035
InputStream, 87
InputStreamReader, 90
Integer, 77
InternetAddress, 767
InternetHeaders, 766
interoperability, 29
Introspector, 160
JarEntry, 90
JarInputStream, 90
JarOutputStream, 91
JComponent, 132
JavaBean components, 147
JavaBean containers, 145
JDBC 1.0, 202-203
JdbcOdbcDriver, 205

Jini architecture, 679, 681-682
JMSException, 717
JMSReceiver, 1349-1350
KeyPair, 906
KeyPairGenerator, 907
KeyStore, 910
LDAPAttribute, 650
LDAPAttributeSet, 650
LDAPConnection, 650
LDAPConstraints, 650
LDAPControl, 650
LDAPEntry, 650
LDAPExtendedOperation, 650
LDAPExtendedResponse, 650
LDAPMessage, 650
LDAPModification, 650
LDAPModificationSet, 650
LDAPResponse, 650
LDAPSearchResult, 650
LineNumberReader, 90
LinkedList, 84
ListIterator, 82
Locale, 97
Long, 77
MailClient, 780-781
MailEvent, 768
Manifest, 90
Math, 76
MenuComponent, 130
Message, 760
MessageContext, 763
Method, 78
MethodDescriptor, 160
MimeBodyPart, 767
MimeMessage, 766
MimeMultipart, 767
Modifier, 77
modularity, 23
MulticastSocket, 359
Multipart, 763
names, 32
Naming, 499
NamingEvent, 591
Number, 76
Object, 74
ObjectInputStream, 89
ObjectOutputStream, 89
ObjectStreamClass, 87
ObjectStreamConstants, 89
ObjectStreamField, 87
Observable, 81
ORB, 424
Order, 492-493
OrderManager, 731-732
OrderRequest, 731
OutputStream, 87
OutputStreamWriter, 90
Package, 77
ParameterDescriptor, 160
PasswordAuthentication, 772
Permission, 881
PermissionCollection , 881
PhantomReference, 80
PipedInputStream, 89
PipedOutputStream, 89
PipedReader, 90
PipedWriter, 90
PlainSocketImpl, 361
PortableRemoteObject, 494
PrinterJob, 135
PrintStream, 89
PrintWriter, 90
Properties, 86
PropertyDescriptor, 160
PropertyEditorManager, 164
PropertyEditorSupport, 164
Provider, 874
PushbackInputStream, 88
PushbackReader, 90
QueryServerImplementation, 436-439, 487-492, 496
QueueConsumer, 735-738
QueueSupplier, 732-735
Reader, 87
Reference, 80
RemoteException, 479
RemoteObject, 482
RemoteStub, 507
ResultSet, 253
RMISecurityManager, 499, 871
SAXException, 1033
SAXParseException, 1033
SAXParser, 1043-1044
SAXParserFactory, 1045
ScrollableResultSetExample, 256-258
SearchControls, 641
SearchResult, 640
Security, 874
SecurityManager, 869, 871
SequenceInputStream, 89
ServerHelper, 342-346
ServerSocket, 337
Service, 772
ServletException, 1071
ServletInputStream, 1088
ServletOutputStream, 1098
Session, 768
Short, 76
Signature, 920
SignedObject, 922-924
Signer, 906
SimpleBeanInfo, 160
SimpleDateFormat, 97
SimpleTimeZone, 98
SocketImpl, 361
SoftReference, 80
SQLException, 203
Stack, 84
Store, 772
String, 77
StringBuffer, 77
StringReader, 90
StringRefAddr, 589
StringWriter, 90
Thread, 96
ThreadGroup, 97
ThreadLocal, 97
Throwable, 76
Time, 241
Timestamp, 241
TimeZone, 98
TopicConsumer, 744-747
TopicSupplier, 741-744

Transport, 777
TreeMap, 85
TreeSet, 84
Types, 204
UnicastRemoteObject, 482
URLConnection, 369
variables, 21
Vector, 84
Void, 77
WeakHashMap, 86
WeakReference, 80
Writer, 87
X509CRL, 910
ZipEntry, 90
ZipInputStream, 90
ZipOutputStream, 91

ClassFileServer HTTP server Web site, 501

ClassLoader, 74, 866

clauses, LIKE, 221-222, 243

clear text, 839

clearBatch() method, 275

clearProperties() method, 722

Client class, 353-357, 568

client connectivity, 119

client implementations (application servers), 1220-1224

client information request attacks, 972

client interfaces
application servers, 1218-1219
client privacy violations, 972
entity beans
home, 1303-1307
remote, 1299-1301, 1303

client-side EJB development, 1238-1239

client-side ORB components, 391-392

client-side script-based interfaces, 138

client-side scripting languages, 1002

client/server interfacing, 317

ClientReceiver interface, 479

ClientReceiverImplementation class, 435, 486-487, 495, 553

ClientReceiverServer class, 357-358

clients
activatable object, 521-522
applets, 109
application, 109, 1226-1227
CORBA, 322, 421, 454-458
DCOM, 322, 567
implementing, 543, 568-570
registration, 570-571
running, 543
DII-based, 458, 460
EJBs, 1234, 1263
HTTP, 322
Jini, 681-682
RMI, 322, 471
RMI/IIOP, 511-514
RMI/JRMP, 506-510
TCP/IP, 322

Clipboard class, 134

CLIs (Call Level Interfaces), 192-193

Clob interface, 281

CLOBs (character large objects), 280-282

Cloneable interfaces, 74

close() method, 716

CloseConnection GIOP message, 394

CLSIDs (Class Identifiers), 532, 629

CMP (Container-Managed Persistence) entity beans, 1236, 1293
architecture, 1293
context setting/unsetting, 1294
creating, 1295
deleting, 1295
example, 1296-1299
finding, 1294
home interface example, 1307
interface rules, 1296
passivation/activation, 1295
primary key container managed fields, 1293
remote interface example, 1302-1303
storing/loading, 1295

CoCreateInstance() method, 629

CoCreateInstanceEx() method, 629

code. *See also* source code files
blocks, 70
byte code verifier, 862
checks performed, 863
verification phases, 862
version differences, 863
comments, 66
documentation, 834
exception handling, 71
signing, 924-925
examples, 926-929
jarsigner utility, 925

Code Conventions for the Java Programming Language Web site, 60

CodeSource object, 898

coding standards, 833

collaborative media-based interactions support, 137

Collection interface, 82

collections
AbstractCollection class, 82
AbstractList class, 84
AbstractMap class, 84
AbstractSequentialList class, 84
AbstractSet class, 84
Arrays class, 82
BitSet class, 82
Collection interface, 82
Comparator interface, 82
defined, 81

Dictionary class, 82, 85
Enumeration interface, 82
HashMap class, 84
HashSet class, 84
Hashtable class, 85
Iterator interface, 82
keyed, 84-86
LinkedList class, 84
List interface, 82
ListIterator class, 82
Map interface, 82-84
mapped, 84-86
non-keyed, 82-84
Properties class, 86
Set interface, 84
SortedMap interface, 85
SortedSet interface, 84
Stack class, 84
TreeMap class, 85
TreeSet class, 84
Vector class, 84
WeakHashMap class, 86

colon (:), 1015

color
2D images, 136
background color, 990
HTML document text, 990
hyperlinks, 990

color choosers, 133

columns
database tables, 242
descriptions, 246
RDBMS tables, 179
adding, 182
deleting, 183

COM (Component Object Model), 50, 528
classes, 528
interfaces, 528
Java-based development tools, 531
objects, 528
overview, 528-529
servers, 533
services, 534-535
type libraries, 533

command feedback, 835

command pattern, 52

CommandInfo interface, 701

CommandMap interface, 701

CommandObject interface, 701

commands. *See also* methods
keytool utility, 910
tnameserv, 612

comma (,)
content model element declaration, 1020
RDNS/DNs, 648

Comment subinterface (Node interface), 1053

comments
defined, 66
HTML, 991
JSP (JavaServer Pages), 1144
XML documents, 1014

commercial off-the-shelf components. *See* COTS components

commit protocols, 178

commit() method
Session interface, 718
Transaction objects, 807
UserTransaction interface, 810

Common Gateway Interface. *See* CGI

Common Object Request Broker Architecture. *See* CORBA

Common Secure Interoperability (CSI), 940, 961

communication layers, 327-329

communication resource managers (CRMs), 177-178, 800

communications, 115
CORBA, 115
CRMs, 177-178, 800
enabling, 113
protocols, 115-116
RMI, 116
services, 16, 113, 116-117
streams, 363
Web protocol, 115

communications layers
OSI, 327-328
TCP/IP, 330-331
Application, 334-335
applications port allocations, 335
Internet access, 332-333
network access, 331-332
tools, 335-336
Transport, 333-334
UNIX configurations, 336
Windows configurations, 335

Comparable interfaces, 76

Comparator interface, 82

compatibility test suite (J2EE), 107

compile.bat script, 563

Compiler class, 74

compilers
IDL-to-Java. *See* idlj
idltojava, 425
javareg, 543
jvc, 543
RMI. *See* rmic

compiling
DCOM servers, 563-564
IDLs, 407-408, 420, 428-430
javac tool, 63
native language implementations, 1361
RMI/IIOP servers, 497
RMI/JRMP servers, 493
wrappers, 1359

component APIs, 44

Component class, 130, 147

Component Implementation Definition Langugage (CIDL), 1201

component model technology identification, 47
Component Object Model. *See* COM
component SPIs, 45
Component-Based Development. *See* CBD
component-container architecture (J2EE), 108-110
applet clients, 109
application clients, 109
deployment descriptors, 110
EJB application servers, 108
Web application servers, 108
component-to-container interfaces, 45
components, 40, 43
application servers, 1214-1217
credit-management bean example, 1215-1217
lifecycle management, 1215
assembly, 48
AWT, 130
configuration specification, 48
CORBA, 50
COTS (commercial off-the-shelf, 47
design adaptation, 48
enterprise systems, 14-15
identification, 47
implementation specialization, 48
JavaBeans, 145-148
models, 43
generic, 43
interfaces, 44-46
selection, 47
standard models, 49-50
Swing, 132-133
testing, 48
wrapping with DCOM interface wrappers, 571
composite pattern, 52
CompositeName class, 587
compound Life Cycle Service interfaces, 698-699
compound names, 609
CompoundName class, 586
CompoundName constructor, 586-587
computer communications networking, 326
CoMyServer class, 567
conceptual data models. *See* logical data models
concurrency, 318, 832
Concurrency Control Service, 398
Concurrency/Transacations Service, 535
confidentiality, 828
configuration services
application frameworks, 1197
application servers, 1229
configuring
application clients, 1226-1227
application servers, 1225-1226
CORBA, 422, 1201
entity beans, 1307-1309
JDBC drivers, 208-210
BeeShirts.com example, 212-213
type 1, 211
type 2, 211
type 3, 211-212
type 4, 212
Jini, 678
JSP deployment, 1177-1179
object-oriented software development process, 30
RMI infrastructures, 470
RMI/JRMP server security, 499
servlets, 1123-1126
session beans, 1273-1274
type 1 JDBC-ODBC bridge drivers, 205, 211
type 2 Native-API Partly Java Technology-Enabled drivers, 206, 211
type 3 Net-Protocol Fully Java Technology-Enabled drivers, 206, 211-212
type 4 Native-Protocol Fully Java Technology-Enabled drivers, 207, 212
connect() method, 494
connection event model, 768
Connection interface
JDBC connections, 213
JMS, 716
Connection object, 202, 242
connection pools, 307, 309
ConnectionEventListener, 309
ConnectionFactory interface, 715
ConnectionMetaData object, 717
ConnectionPoolDataSource interface, 307
connectivity, 114, 305
applications, 121-122
clients, 119
databases. *See* JDBC
EJB/CORBA, 1341-1343
EJB/Web, 1334, 1336-1340
JMS, 714, 717
Web, 120
Connector SPI, 1369
connectors (J2EE), 1368-370
connectToMailServer() method, 781
constrained properties, 157-159
Constructor class, 78
constructs, 66-68. *See also specific constructs*
consumers, JMS messages, 725-726
Container class, 131, 145
container information (JSPs), 1157-1158
container-managed persistence entity beans. *See* CMP entity beans

container-managed transaction demarcation, 1321-1325
container-to-component interfaces, 45
containers. *See also* application servers
application, 1210
AWT, 131
JavaBeans, 145-146
AuditBeanContainer, 145
component relationship, 145
services, adding, 149
Swing, 132
content length, 1096
content model element declaration, 1020-1021
Context interface, 305, 582
contexts
directory. *See* directory contexts
JavaBean, 148-149
JNDI, 582, 584-586
context listings, 587-588
listing example, 598-602
properties, 584
continue authenticate() method, 948
control characters, 368
Control interface, 803
controlling access. *See* authorization
controls, directory searches, 641-642
Cookie class, 1078, 1106-1107
cookies, 379
HTTP session managment, 1106-1107
security, 1131
Coordinator interface, 803
copying distributed objects, 318
copyMessages() method, 775
CORBA (Common Object Request Broker Architecture), 49, 386, 418
activation framework, 694-696
baked-in libraries, 422
business objects, 399
clients, 322, 454-458
implementation, 421
stubs, 391
communications, 115
Component Scripting, 1202
components, 50, 1200-1202
architecture, 1201
configuring, 1201
CORBA 3.0, 389
deployment, 1201
configuring, 422
development process, 420-421
distributions, 1342
DII (Dynamic Invocation Interface), 391, 458-460
Domain Interfaces, 399, 1204
DSI (Dynamic Skeleton Interface), 392
EAI (Enterprise Application Integration), 1364
EJB connectivity, 1341-1343
Event Service, 747-748
pull model, 751-753
push model, 748-750
facilities, 398
Horizontal Common Facilities, 398-399
Vertical Market Facilities, 399
GIOP, 392-393
header formats, 393
IORs (Interoperable Object References), 395
message types, 394
overview, 393-394
versions, 393
IDL, 400
compiling, 407-408, 420, 428-430
defining, 420
file format, 400-401
IDL-to-Java mappings, 401, 404-406
Java-to-IDL mappings, 409
IIOP, 392-393
IORs (Interoperable Object References), 395
overview, 394-395
versions, 395
Implementation Repository, 392, 443-444
interfaces, 425-428
IRs (Interface Repositories), 448-454
accessing, 449
contents, viewing, 450-454
objects, 449
Java enterprise system role, 389-390
Java IDL, 424-425
lifecycle service, 697-699
messaging, 747
Event Service, 747-753
Messaging specification, 747, 755-756
Notification Service, 747, 754
Minimum CORBA, 1372
naming service. *See* CosNaming
Notification Service, 747, 754
object adapters, 393, 444
BOA-based server registration, 444-445
IDL server registration, 446-447
POA-based server registration, 447-448
Object Transaction Service. *See* OTS

objects by value, 409-410
behavioral sequences, 410-411
example, 412-414
marshaling, 411-412
RMI, 476-477
OMA (Object Management Architecture), 388
OMG MOM-like applications, 712
ORB (Object Request Broker), 388-390
architecture, 390
client side components, 391-392
overview, 386-387
protocols, 392
server side components, 392-393
RMI-to-OMG IDL mappings, 474-476
scalability, 419-420
Security, 938
administration, 963-964
architecture, 941-942
auditing, 954-956
authentication, 946-950
authorization, 952-954
client-side SSL example, 961
Common Secure Interoperability (CSI) levels, 961
delegation, 951-952
EJB/CORBA connectivity, 1343
encryption, 960-961
events sequence, 949-950
interfaces, 942-946
interoperability, 938
nonrepudiation, 956-960
overview, 939-940
packages, 940-941
policies, 962-963
protocols supported, 961
remote invocations, 950
server-side SSL example, 961
specification (CSSS), 939-940
types, 942-946
server registrar, 421
servers, 324, 428
client receiver implementation example, 435
creating, 430-431, 434-440
customer implementation example, 431-435
delegation, 428, 432
DSI-based, 440-443
generated serializable data example, 439-440
implementing, 420
inheritance, 428, 431
query server implementation example, 436-439
services, 396-398
skeletons, 428-430
smart proxying, 419
standalone applications, 419
static interfaces, 391
static stubs, 454-458
tools required, 421-422
trading service. *See* CosTrading
vendor-specific naming services, 463
vendors, 421-424
COTS products, 424
ORB/CORBAservice products, 423-424
versions
CORBA 2.3.1, 387
CORBA 3.0, 387-389
XML integration, 1062
core constructs (IDL-to-Java mappings), 402-403
core Life Cycle Service interfaces, 697
core security architecture, 859, 861
core SQL types, 181
corrupted application errors (assurance), 823
corrupted data errors (assurance), 823
CosNaming, 396, 461, 609
CORBA names library PIDL, 611-612
EJB/CORBA connectivity, 1343
IDL, 609-612
interfaces, 613-614
JNDI SPI, 614-618
CosNaming server example, 616-618
message IDL example, 616
Web site, 614
RMI/IIOP server registration, 504
server example, 616-618
service implementations, 612
vendors, 612
CosTrading, 396, 664
components, 665-666
exporting/importing examples, 671-673
service exports, 666-668
service imports, 668-670
costs
assurance, 820-821
assurance plans, 827
failed delivery (assurance), 826
risk reduction plans, 825
COTS (commercial off-the-shelf) components, 47
reliability, 831
product vendors, 424
country codes (DNS names), 627
createAQueueAndSendOrder() method, 732
createBrowser() method, 728

createConnectionConsumer() method, 728, 740
createDurableConnectionConsumer() method, 740
createDurableSubscriber() method, 740
createException, 1236
createPublisher() method, 740
createQueue() method, 728
createQueueConnection() method, 728
createQueueSession() method, 728
createReceiver() method, 729
createRegistry() method, 500
createSender() method, 728
createSocket() method, 523
createStatement() method, 224
createSubcontext() method, 586
createSubscriber() method, 740
createTemporaryTopic() method, 740
createTopic() method, 740
createTopicConnection() method, 739
createTopicSession() method, 740
CREATE_CATALOG statement, 181
CREATE_DATABASE statement, 181
CREATE_SCHEMA statement, 181
credential sniffing, 979
credentials, 949-952
Credit bean, 1241, 1302
credit-management bean, 1215-1217
CreditEJBean, 1287, 1289-1291
CreditHome bean, 1306
CreditManagerSession bean, 1242
CreditPrimaryKey, 1292
CRLs (certificate revocation lists), 847
CRMs (communication resource managers), 177-178, 800
Cryptographic Service Providers. *See* CSPs
cryptography, 839-840, 842
 asymmetric keys, 842-844
 encryption/cryptography distinction, 861, 873
 extensions, 929-930
 JCA, 859-861, 873
  cryptographic engines, 875
  CSPs, 874-877
  functions, 873
  Provider class, 874
  Security class, 874
  security package, 873
  security.cert package, 873
  security.interfaces package, 874
  security.spec package, 874
 JCE, 861
 message digests, 842-843
 symmetric keys, 841, 843
CSI (Common Secure Interoperability), 940, 961
CSPs (Cryptographic Service Providers), 874-875
 default implementation, 876-877
 deleting, 877
 installation, 877
CSRs (Certificate Signing Requests), 847
CSSS (CORBA Security Service Specification), 939-940
Current interface, 803, 949
custom data types, 284-285, 292-294
custom JSP classes, 1158
custom permissions, 890
custom socket factories, 361
custom sockets, 361-362, 523-525
 client-side, 523
 server-side, 524
custom tag extension abstractions (JSPs), 1181-1186
custom tag library abstractions (JSPs), 1183
Customer bean, 1241
Customer interface, 480
Customer object, 350-352
CustomerImplementation class, 431-435, 483-486, 496
Customizer interface, 166
customizers, 166-167
customizing
 directory object attributes, 643
 JavaBeans, 164
  customizers, 166-167
  design-time, 144
  property editors, 164-166
 RDBMS tables, 182-183
 Result Sets, 231-239
 security manager, 871-873

D

daemons, RMI activation. *See* rmid
DAIS J2 (2 superscript), 423
DAP (Directory Access Protocol), 648
data connectivity, 114
data dictionaries, 176
data enabling, 16, 113
Data Encryption Standard (DES), 843
data files, 176
data link layer (OSI communications layer model), 328

data manipulation language (DML), 176
data model abstraction levels, 175
data model diagramming conventions, 185-186
data representation dependency, 46
data transfer, UI support, 134
data types, 64, 76-77
Database class, 187
database connections. *See* JDBC
database definition language. *See* DDL
database management system (DBMS). *See* databases
database URLs, 214-215
DatabaseHelper class, 347-350
DatabaseMetaData class, 241
DatabaseMetaData interface, 202
databases, 174
- access warning, 203
- ANSI92 entry level SQL compliance, 242
- ANSI92 full SQL compliance, 243
- ANSI92 intermediate level SQL compliance, 242
- architecture, 175-176
- catalogs, 241-242
- CLIs (Call Level Interfaces), 192-193
- connection pools, 307, 309
- connections. *See* JDBC
- data model abstraction levels, 175
- distributed transactions, 310
- information, finding, 241-243
- instances, 175
- interface repositories, 392
- JDBC (Java Database Connectivity), 195-196
- LIKE clause support, 243
- meta-data connection objects, 242
- naming, 305-307
- object. *See* ODBMSs
- ODBC (open database connectivity), 195, 243
- outer joins support, 243
- predefined methods, 298-299
- product names, 242
- relational. *See* RDBMSs
- relational/object translations, 190-192
- schema, 241, 246
- schemes, 175
- SQL types supported, 242
- stored procedures, 298
  - *calling example, 302-304*
  - *creating, 299-302*
  - *executing, 301*
  - *predefined methods, 298-299*
- table tables
  - *access permissions, 242*
  - *columns, 242, 246*
  - *foreign keys, 242*
  - *primary keys, 242, 247*
  - *types, 242*
- timestamp values, 241
- transactions, 177-179
  - *ACID principles, 177*
  - *distributed, 177*
  - *isolation levels, 266-267*
  - *managers, 177-178*
  - *resource interfaces (XAs), 178*
  - *viewing, 265-266*
- URLs, 242
- usernames, 242
- versions, 242

DataContentHandler interface, 701
DataContentHandlerFactory interface, 701
DatagramPacket objects, 360
DatagramSocket class, 359
DataHandler class, 701, 760
DataInput interfaces, 88
DataInputStream class, 88
DataItem interface, 168
DataOutput interfaces, 88
DataOutputStream class, 88
DataSource interface, 305, 701
DataTruncation exception, 203
date APIs, 97-98
Date class, 97, 241
DateFormat class, 97
DateFormatSymbols class, 97
DBMS (database management system). *See* databases
DCE (Distributed Computing Environment), 322
DCE-CIOP/SECIOP package, 941
DCOM (Distributed Component Object Model), 116, 322, 528-529
- activation framework, 699-700
- architecture, 529-530
- automation, 533-534
- bridging, 571-572
- classes, naming, 629-630
- client-side interfaces, registering, 543
- clients, 322, 567
  - *implementing, 543, 568-570*
  - *registration, 570-571*
  - *running, 543*
- configuration tool. *See* dcomcnfg utility
- development process, 543
- EAI (Enterprise Application Integration), 1365
- GUIDs, 532, 543, 547
- identifiers, 547

IDL, 533-535
defining, 543
file format, 536
IDL-to-Java mappings, 537, 540
interfaces, 532, 544-547
Java bindings, generating, 543, 548-549
Java-based development tools, 531
monikers, 532, 700
naming, 629
objects, naming, 630-631
proxies, 530
server interfaces, 543
server registration, 564
javareg utility, 564
registry files, 564-565
viewing, 565-567
servers, 324, 529, 533, 548
client receiver implementation example, 553
compiling, 563-564
CORBA query server implementation example, 554-559
creating, 549
generated CoQueryServer class example, 562-563
generated IQueryServer interface example, 561-562
generated Order class example, 560
implementation example, 549-552
registering, 543
services, 534-535
skeletons, 548
spawning, 570-571
stubs, 567
type libraries, 533, 543, 548

DCOM Class Identifiers. *See* CLSIDs

dcomcnfg utility, 566

DDL (database definition language), 176

debugging, 64

defaults
CSPs, 876-877
security manager, 869

defineClass() method, 866

defining
applets
initial definition, 99-101
lifecycle, 101-103
policy files, 893

DefinitionKind class, 449

delayed application processing errors (assurance), 823

delayed data delivery errors (assurance), 823

delegates, EJBs, 1234

delegation
CORBA Security, 951-952
CORBA servers, 428, 432

DELETE requests, 374

deleteRow() method, 265

deletesAreDetected() method, 268

DELETE_FROM statement, 183

deleting
BMP entity beans, 1284
columns, 183
CSPs, 877
distributed objects, 318
JNDI bindings example, 602-605
mail messages, 775
message properties, 722
property change listeners, 156
RDBMS tables, 182
rows, 183, 264
stateful session beans, 1256
stateless session beans, 1252
updates, 264
vetoable property change listeners, 158

delivery costs, 826

delivery pressures (assurance), 820

denial-of-service attacks, 979

dependencies, object-oriented software development, 24

DeployerTool Web site, 1277, 1312

deployment
application client example, 1226-1227
application servers, 1225-1226
AWT, 131-132
CBD, 48
CORBA components, 1201
JavaServer Pages (JSPs), 1175-1181
configuration information, 1177-1179
deployment descriptor considerations, 1176-1177
direct deployment procedure considerations, 1179-1180
precompiled deployment procedure considerations, 1180
object-oriented software development process, 30
services, 108, 1197
servlets, 1110-1111
BEA WebLogic servers, 1122
reference implementation, 1120-1122
Web-based application directory structure, 1119-1120
Web-based application format, 1111-1117
Web-based application procedures, 1118-1119
Swing, 134

deployment descriptors, 110, 1244-1245

deploytool utility, 1180, 1248
DES (Data Encryption Standard), 843
design patterns, 44, 50-52
adapter, 51
command, 52
composite, 52
factory, 51
MVC (Model-View Controller), 51
proxy, 52
singleton, 51
strategy, 51
subject-observer, 52
desktop computing, 319
Destination interface, 719
destroy() method, 101, 1072
destroySubcontext() method, 586
detailed design, 28, 830
developing enterprise applications
Java benefits, 54
Java features, 55
development environment, 57
development phases, 30-31
DgcAck UniqueID JRMP message, 473
diagrams (class), 32-36
notation, 32-34
sequence, 36
dictionaries (data), 176
Dictionary class, 82, 85
Diffie-Hellment algorithm, 844
digest() method, 918-919
digest-based authentication (servlets), 1130
DigestOutputStream object, 919
digests, 916-919
Digital Signature Algorithm (DSA), 844
DII (Dynamic Invocation Interface), 391
clients, 458-460
CORBA, 391
DirContext interface, 636
direct deployment procedure considerations (JSPs), 1179-1180
direction property (CompoundName constructor), 586
directives (JSPs), 1144-1149
examples, 1147-1149
include directive, 1145
page directive, 1145-1147
taglib directive, 1147, 1183-1185
directories
CGI programs, 999
cgi-bin, 999
events, 643-645
object attributes, 637-638, 643
object bindings, 639
schemas, 638-639
search results, 640
searches, 639-642
Directory Access Protocol, 648
directory contexts, JNDI directory services, 636
events, 643-645
object attributes, 637-638, 643
object bindings, 639
schemas, 638-639
search results, 640
searches, 639-642
directory services, 634-635
ADS, 686-687
communications, 117
JNDI, 636
directory contexts, 636
events, 643-645
object attributes, 637-638, 643
object bindings, 639
schemas, 638-639
search results, 640
searches, 639-642
LDAP, 648-649
API, 649
interfaces, 649-651
JNDI SPI, 651-662
RDN type names, 648
search example, 653-662
v3, 662-664
NDS, 646-647
NIS, 645-646
directory structures, 1119-1120
discretionary authorization, 850
Dispatch class, 534
display elements (HTML), 988
body, 990
formatting, 991
frames, 992-993
headings, 988
hyperlinks, 990-991
images, 991
meta-data, 989
tables, 992
tags, 988
titles, 989
Distinct interface, 284
Distinct types (SQL), 284
distinguished names (DNs), 648
distributed business-specific interfaces, 1218
distributed business-specific naming and lifecycle management, 1218
distributed communications protocol dependency, 46
distributed communications services, 1228
Distributed Component Object Model. *See* DCOM
Distributed Computing Environment (DCE), 322

distributed enterprise communication paradigms, 1361-1362
Distributed Network Architecture (DNA), 50, 1202
distributed objects, 318
Distributed Simulation Facility, 399
distributed systems, 316-317
evolution, 319-320
issues, 317-318
layers, 318
network client architecture, 321-322
network server architecture, 323-324
distributed transaction processing (DTP), 177
distributed transactions, 177, 310, 794
DML (data manipulation language), 176
DNA (Distributed Network Architecture), 50, 1202
DNs (distinguished names), 648
DNS (Domain Name Service), 335, 626
country codes, 627
hostnames/IP address translations, 335
java-based interfacing, 628
lookup process, 628
software, 627
subdomains, 627
top-level names, 626
DNS_URL property (JNDI contexts), 584
do/while statements, 73
<!DOCTYPE> character sequence, 1019
document handlers, 1040-1043
Document Object Model. *See* DOM, 1012
document presentation interfaces, 970
document serving interfaces, 976-977
Document subinterface (Node interface), 1054
Document Type Definition. *See* DTD
documentation, 66, 834
DocumentBuilder class, 1048, 1058
DocumentBuilderFactory class, 1048, 1059
DocumentFragment subinterface (Node interface), 1054
DocumentHandler interface, 1040
documents
HTML, 988
background color, 990
body, 990
bold text, 991
bulleted item lists, 991
comments, 991
formatting, 991
forms, 994-995
frames, 992-993
headings, 988, 991
horizontal lines, 991
hyperlink color, 990
hyperlinks, 990-991
images, 991
italic text, 991
JavaScript, embedding, 1002-1003
line breaks, 991
meta-data, 989
numbered lists, 991
ordered lists, 991
paragraph alignment, 991
paragraphs, 991
structure, 987
tables, 992
tags, 988
text color, 990
text-area GUI components, 995
titles, 989
XML, 1010. *See also* XML
DTD. See DTD
entity references, 1016
formatting, 1012-1013
hyperlinks, 1025-1029
processing instructions, 1016-1017
style sheets, 1029-1031
unparsed character data, 1017
valid, 1023
well-formed, 1017-1018
DocumentType subinterface (Node interface), 1054
DOD (United States Department of Defense) computing, 330
doDelete() method, 1080
doGet() method, 1080
DOM (Document Object Model), 1012, 1047-1048
architecture, 1048-1050
level 1 specification Web site, 1047
level 2 specification Web site, 1047
nodes, 1050-1052
lists, 1050
name retrieval, 1050
parents/children, 1050
types, 1052-1058
parsing, 1058-1060
Domain Interfaces (CORBA), 399
Domain Name Service. *See* DNS
domains
federations, 851
partitioning, 851
security, 851-852
security technology domains, 852

DOMException class, 1050
DOMImplementation interface, 1055
doOptions() method, 1080
doPost() method, 1080
doPrivileged() method, 898
doPut() method, 1080
doTrace() method, 1080
Double class, 77
downloading
classes
RMI/IIOP servers, 504
RMI/JRMP servers, 500-502
RMI stubs, 500
drag-and-drop support, 134
DragSource object, 134
Driver interface, 202, 210
DriverManager class, 202, 209
DriverPropertyInfo class, 210
drivers
implementing, 201
information, finding, 241-243
JDBC, 201
configuring, 205-208, 210-213
explicitly loading, 210
implicitly loading, 210
names, 242
selecting, 208
selecting types, 205
types, 204-207
version, 242
scrollable result set support, 254-255
updateable result set support, 268
DropTarget object, 134
DROP_TABLE statement, 182
DSA (Digital Signature Algorithm), 844
DSAPublicKey interface, 908
DSI (Dynamic Skeleton Interface), 392, 440-441, 443
DTD (Document Type Definition), 1011, 1018-1019
attribute declarations, 1022
element declarations, 1019-1021
entity declarations, 1021
examples
XML order document with DTD reference, 1023-1024
XML order DTD, 1024-1025
handlers, 1035-1037
headers, 1019
J2EE application DTD, 1063-1066
notation declarations, 1021
validity, 1023
DTDHandler class, 1035
DTP (distributed transaction processing), 177, 800
dumb terminal/mainframe computing relationships, 319
DuplicateKeyException, 1236
durable subscribers, 740
dynamic behavior diagrams, 36
dynamic class downloading
RMI/IIOP servers, 504
RMI/JRMP servers, 500-502
dynamic CORBA bridges, 571
Dynamic HTML, 383-384
Dynamic Invocation Interface. *See* DII
Dynamic Skeleton Interface (DSI), 392, 440-441, 443
dynamic stub downloading, 500
DynamicImplementation class, 440

D

EAI (enterprise application integration), 1356
connectors, 123
CORBA, 1364
DCOM, 1365
distributed enterprise communication paradigms, 1361-1362
embedded applications integration, 1370-1372
EmbeddedJava, 1371
J2ME, 1371
Java Communications API, 1371
JavaCard, 1371
Jini, 1371
Minimum CORBA, 1372
PersonalJava, 1371
WAP (Wireless Access Protocol), 1372
WML (Wireless Markup Langauge), 1372
HTTP, 1363-1364
J2EE connectors, 1368, 1370
JMS, 1365-1366
JNI (Java Native Interface), 1357, 1359-1361
messaging services, 1365-1366
overview, 1356-1357
RMI, 1364-1365
TCP/IP, 1362-1363
XML, 1367-1368
.ear file extension, 110
ECMA (European Community Manufacturers Association), 1002
edu DNS name, 626
EISs (enterprise information systems), 1356. *See also* EAI
ejbActivate() method, 1252
BMP entity beans, 1285
CMP entity beans, 1295
stateful session beans, 1258

ejbCreate() method, 1252
application-specific session bean home interfaces, 1271
BMP entity beans, 1284
CMP entity beans, 1295
stateful session beans, 1256
EJBException, 1236
ejbFindByPrimaryKey() method, 1283
ejbLoad() method, 1285, 1295
EJBObject interface, 1265
ejbPassivate() method, 1252
BMP entity beans, 1285
CMP entity beans, 1295
stateful session beans, 1258
ejbPostCreate() method, 1284
ejbRemove() method, 1252
BMP entity beans, 1284
CMP entity beans, 1295
EJBObject interface, 1265
stateful session beans, 1256
EJBs (Enterprise JavaBeans), 1199, 1232
application servers, 108
architecture, 1233-1234
AuthenticationSession, 1352
BEA WebLogic server startup/deployment, 1248-1249
BeeShirts.com example, 1239-1243
BMP (Bean-Managed Persistence) entity beans, 1236
BrowseSession, 1241
BrowseSessionEJBean, 1253-1255
BrowseSessionHome, 1272
client-side development, 1238-1239
clients, 1234
configuration example, 1227
home interface example, 1219
implementation example, 1221-1224
remote interface example, 1219
CMP (Container_Managed Persistence) entity beans, 1236
container implementations, 1234
CORBA connectivity, 1341-1343
Credit, 1241, 1302
credit-management example, 1215-1217
CreditEJBean, 1287-1291
CreditHome, 1306
CreditManagerSession, 1242
CreditPrimaryKey, 1292
Customer, 1241
delegates, 1234
deployment descriptors, 1244-1245
deployment procedures, 1246-1247
entity beans, 1235, 1279-1280
BMP, 1236, 1281-1292, 1302, 1306
CMP, 1236, 1293-1299, 1302-1303, 1307
configuring, 1307-1309
deployment, 1310-1313
home interfaces, 1303-1307
pooling, 1280
primary keys, 1280-1281, 1292
remote interfaces, 1299-1303
exceptions, 1236
features, 1233
home interfaces, 1218, 1234
implementations, 1234
Item, 1241
JAR files, 1245
JavaMail, 1351-1354
JDNC, 1277-1279
JMS, 1346-1347
EJBs as JMS consumers, 1348-1351
EJBs as JMS producers, 1347-1348
messages, 122
Order, 1241
OrderManagerSession, 1242
overview, 1232-1233
reference implementation server startup/deployment, 1247-1248
remote interfaces, 1218, 1234
security, 1325
assembly elements, 1327
authentication model limitations, 1331
BeeShirts.com example, 1332-1333
declarative, 1327-1329
programmatic, 1326-1327
role references, 1327
vendor-specific access control mapping, 1329-1330
vendor-specific identity/authentication, 1330-1331
server configuration example, 1226
server-side development, 1237-1238
servlets, 1128
session beans, 1235, 1250
client interfaces, 1263
configuring, 1273-1274
deployment, 1275-1276
home interfaces, 1267, 1269-1273
remote interfaces, 1263-1266
stateful, 1235, 1255-1259, 1261-1262
stateful home interfaces, 1272-1273

stateful remote interface example, 1266
stateless, 1235, 1250-1253, 1255
stateless home interfaces, 1272
stateless remote interface example, 1265
ShoppingCartSession, 1242
ShoppingCartSessionEJBean, 1259-1262
ShoppingCartSessionHome, 1272-1273
skeletons, 1234
stubs, 1234
TestClient startup, 1249
transactions, 1316-1317
bean-managed transaction demarcation, 1317-1321
container-managed transaction demarcation, 1321-1325
TShirt, 1241, 1302-1303
TShirtEJBean, 1296-1299
TShirtHome, 1307
types, 1235-1236
Web connectivity, 1334
approach/examples, 1337-1340
BeeShirts.com example, 1334-1336
XML, 1062, 1343-1346
ejbStore() method, 1285, 1295
<!ELEMENT> character sequence, 1019
element declarations (DTD), 1019-1021
Element subinterface (Node interface), 1054
elements (JSPs), 1142-1143
action elements, 1164-1175
examples, 1173-1175
forward action, 1165-1166
getProperty action, 1170-1171
include action, 1166-1167
param action subelements, 1165
plugin action, 1171-1173
setProperty action, 1169-1170
useBean action, 1167-1168
directive elements, 1144-1149
examples, 1147-1149
include directive, 1145
page directive, 1145-1147
taglib directive, 1147, 1183-1185
scripting elements, 1149-1152
declarations, 1149-1150
expressions, 1150-1151
scriptlets, 1151-1152
elements (XML documents), 1014-1015
email, 711, 757. *See also* JavaMail
IMAP, 758-759
messages, 757-758
POP3, 758
SMTP, 758
<EMBED> tag, 974
embedded applications integration, 1370-1372
EmbeddedJava, 1371
J2ME, 1371
Java Communications API, 1371
JavaCard, 1371
Jini, 1371
Minimum CORBA, 1372
PersonalJava, 1371
WAP (Wireless Access Protocol), 1372
WML (Wireless Markup Langauge), 1372
embedded SQL, 193-195
EmbeddedJava, 1371
empty content element declaration, 1019
empty elements, 1015
enabling
applications, 17
communications, 16
data, 16
Web, 16
encodeRedirectURL() method, 1105
encodeURL() method, 1105
encryption
CORBA Security, 960-961
client-side SSL example, 961
Common Secure Interoperability (CSI), 961
protocols supported, 961
server-side SSL example, 961
cryptography extensions, 929-930
encryption/cryptography distinction, 861, 873
JCE, 861-862
ENCTYPE attribute (<FORM> tag), 994
end() method, 812
endDocument() method, 1040
endpoint resource display (XLink), 1027
endquote property (CompoundName constructor), 587
endquote2 property (CompoundName constructor), 587
enterprise application integration. *See* EAI
enterprise applications
Java benefits, 54
Java features, 55
enterprise information systems (EISs), 1356. *See also* EAI

Enterprise JavaBeans. *See* EJBs
Enterprise JavaBeans to CORBA Mapping specification Web site, 1342
Enterprise Resource Planning (ERP). *See* ERP
enterprise systems
components, 14-15
information technology, 16-17
EnterpriseBean interface, 1251, 1256
enterprises, 12
components, 12
outcomes, 13-14
entities attribute, 1022
ENTITY attribute, 1022
<!ENTITY> character sequence, 1021
entity beans, 1235, 1279-1280
BMP (Bean-Managed Persistence), 1236, 1281
architecture, 1281-1282
creating, 1284
deleting, 1284
example, 1287-1292
finding, 1283
home interface example, 1306
interface rules, 1286-1287
loading, 1285
passivation/activation, 1285
remote interface example, 1302
storing, 1285
CMP (Container-Managed Persistence), 1236, 1293
architecture, 1293
configuring, 1307-1309
context setting/unsetting, 1294
creating, 1295
deleting, 1295
example, 1296-1299
finding, 1294
home interface example, 1307
interface rules, 1296
passivation/activation, 1295
primary key container managed fields, 1293
remote interface example, 1302-1303
storing/loading, 1295
deployment, 1310-1313
home interfaces, 1303
application-specific, 1304-1305
architecture, 1303
examples, 1306-1307
generic, 1305-1306
lookups, 1303
pooling, 1280
primary keys, 1280-1281, 1292
remote interfaces, 1299
application-specific, 1301
architecture, 1300
examples, 1301-1303
generic, 1301
entity declarations, 1021
entity references, 1016
entity resolvers, 1037-1038
Entity subinterface (Node interface), 1053
EntityContext interface, 1282
EntityReference subinterface (Node interface), 1053
EntityResolver interface, 1037
enumerated types attribute, 1022
Enumeration interface, 82
Environment Specific Inter Orb Protocols (ESIOPs), 393
environments
development, 57
runtime
byte code verifier, 58
byte codes, 58
class loader, 58
Java API class files, 58
native platform interface libraries, 58
optimizations, 58-59
platform architecture, 58
runtime execution engine, 58
standards, 57
equality (=) symbol, 642
equals() method, 890
ERP (Enterprise Resource Planning), 1204
Error class, 76
error handlers, 1039-1040
ErrorHandler interface, 1039
errors
Error class, 76
error handlers, 1039-1040
Throwable class, 76
escape (/) symbol, 642
escape property (CompoundName constructor), 587
ESIOPs (Environment Specific Inter Orb Protocols), 393
Ethernet, 331
European Community Manufacturers Association (ECMA), 1002
EventContext interface, 591
EventDirContext interface, 643
EventListener class, 149
EventListener interface, 81
EventObject class, 81
events, 80
audit, 150
AWT, 131
directory, 643-645
EventListener, 81
EventObject class, 81

handlings, 318
JavaBean, 149-152
JavaMail, 768
mail-system, 760
naming, 591-593
Observable class, 81
Observer interface, 81
Swing, 132
Events Service, 397
Events/Messaging Service, 535
EventSetDescriptor class, 160
evolution, distributed systems, 319-320
ExceptionListener interface, 717
exceptions
BatchUpdateException, 275
CreateException, 1236
DataTruncation, 203
DuplicateKeyException, 1236
EJBException, 1236
EJBs, 1236
Exception class, 76
FinderException, 1236
handling, 71
IllegalStateException, 717
JDBC 1.0, 202-203
NoSuchEntityException, 1236
ObjectNotFoundException, 1236
RemoveException, 1236
RMI, 479
SAXException, 1039
SAXParseException, 1039
servlets, 1071-1072
SQLExceptions, 203
SQLWarning, 203
Throwable class, 76
UnavailableException, 1072
Exceptions class, 76
execute() method
PreparedStatement object, 227
Statement object, 221
executeBatch() method, 275
executeQuery() method
PreparedStatement object, 227
Statement object, 220
executeQueryScrollForwardOnly() method, 256
executeQueryScrollInsensitiveReadOnly() method, 256
executeQueryScrollSensitiveReadOnly() method, 256
executeUpdate() method
PreparedStatement object, 227
Statement object, 221
executing batch updates, 275
exists() method, 775
Expersoft, 423
explicitly loading JDBC drivers, 210
exportACertificateFromAKeyStore() method, 915
exporting services, 666-668
exposed HTML presentation manager flaw attacks, 971
exposed implementation flaw attacks, 979
exposed runtime engine flaw attacks, 971
expressions, 726, 1150-1151
expunge() method, 775
extended attribute (XLink), 1026-1028
extended constructs (IDL-to-Java mappings), 406
extended links, 1027-1029
extendedOperation() method, 663
extends attribute (custom JSP classes), 1158
Extensible Hypertext Markup Language. *See* XHTML
eXtensible Linking Language (XLL), 1025
eXtensible Markup Language. *See* XML
Extensible Stylesheet Language. *See* XSL
extensions
class, 60
ear, 110
JAAS, 862
jar, 60
java, 60
JCE, 861-862
JSSE, 862
MANIFEST.MF, 60
security, 929, 932-933
ser, 60
war, 110
external binary entity declarations, 1021
external component interface analysis, 47
External Content Handler, 970
external content handler attacks, 971
external content handler security, 972
external XML entity declarations, 1021
Externalizable interface, 87
Externalization Service, 396

F

facilities, CORBA, 398
Horizontal Common Facilities, 398-399
Vertical Market Facilities, 399
factories (JSPs), 1157-1158
factory pattern, 51
FactoryFinder interface, 697
fail-over management, 832
falsified client identification, 972
FDDI (Fiber Distributed Data Interface), 331
FeatureDescriptor class, 160
federations (domains), 851

Fiber Distributed Data Interface (FDDI), 331
Field class, 78
fields. *See* variables
File class, 87, 606
file extensions. *See* extensions
file names, 605-606
(\) backslash, 606
(/) forward slash, 606
file-system interfaces, 606
JNDI file SPI, 606, 608
file request handlers, 976
file-based interface generators, 139
file-system interfaces, 606
file-system SPI (JNDI)
CosNaming service, 614-618
CosNaming server example, 616-618
message IDL example, 616
Web site, 614
file names, 606-608
RMI naming services, 618-625
RMI/JRMP registry JNDI SPI Web site, 619
filechoosers, 133
FileDescriptor class, 87
FileFilter interface, 87
FileInputStream class, 88, 91-93, 606
FilenameFilter interface, 87
FileOutputStream class, 88, 606
FileReader class, 90, 606
files
archive. *See* archives
class, 60, 103
data, 176
formats, 58
GZIP, 90-91
HTML
javadoc, 64
naming contexts, 578
IDL, compiling, 420
JAR, 60, 110, 1245
APIs, 90-91
jar tool, 63
structure, 62
Java API class files, 58
manifest, 60-62, 90
native header, 1360
registry, DCOM server registration, 564-565
security policies, 891-894, 905
serialization, 60
source code, 60
Code Conventions for the Java Programming Language Web site, 60
compiling, 63
JavaDoc Tool home page, 60
structure, 60-62
TestClient, 1249
ZIP, 90-91
FileWriter class, 90, 606
FilterInputStream classes, 88
FilterOutputStream classes, 88
FilterReader class, 90
filters
directory searches, 641-642
images, 136
messaging, 710
FilterWriter class, 90
findClass() method, 866, 868
findCustomersWhoOrderedForMoreThan() method, 436
FinderException, 1236
finding
BMP entity beans, 1283
CMP entity beans, 1294
database information, 241-243
driver information, 241-243
Jini lookup services, 681
Result Set information, 233-234
fine-grained Access Control, 903-904
firePropertyChange() method, 156
fireVetoableChange() method, 158
firewall authorization, 851
firewalls, 981
first() method, 253
Flags class, 763
flat transaction model, 798
Float class, 77
flushBuffer() method, 1098
Folder class, 772
folder event model, 768
folders, JavaMail messages, 772-776, 783
foreign keys
database tables, 242
RDBMS tables, 180
<FORM> tag, 994-995
formal specification (safety), 835
formal verification (safety), 835
formats (file), 58. *See also* structure
formatting
CORBA IDL files, 400-401
DCOM IDL files, 536
HTML documents, 991
security policy files, 891-892
Web application deployment descriptors, 1111-1117
XML documents, 1012-1013
attributes, 1015
comments, 1014
declaration, 1014
elements, 1014-1015
entity references, 1016
processing instructions, 1016-1017
unparsed character data, 1017
well-formed, 1017-1018

forms, HTML, 994-995
forms-based authentication (servlets), 1130
forName() method, 868
forward slash (/), 606
forward() method, 1091
forward-only result sets, 251
Fragment GIOP message, 394
frames, 992-993
<FRAMESET> tag, 992-993
frameworks, 1196-1197. *See also* platforms
- application integration services, 1197
- application-specific, 1203-1205
- architecture, 1197
- configuration/deployment services, 1197
- CORBA-based, 1200-1202
- DNA (Distributed Network Architecture, 1202
- Java-based, 1198, 1200
- management services, 1197
- object persistence services, 1197
- servlets, 1072
  - *examples, 1076-1078*
  - *GenericServlet class, 1074*
  - *HTTP servlets, 1078-1081*
  - *Servlet interface, 1072-1074*
  - *ServletConfig interface, 1074*
  - *ServletContext interface, 1074-1076*

from attribute (XLink), 1028
ftp sites, CORBA Security Service specification, 939
functional programming, 20
functions. *See* methods

G

garbage collection, 79-80
General Inter-ORB Protocol. *See* GIOP
generate token() method, 956
generateCertificate() method, 908
generateCRLs() method, 908
generateHTMLBody() method, 996
generateHTMLClose() method, 996
generateHTMLHeader() method, 996
generating
- certificates, 928
- jar files, 928

generators, Web interfaces, 139
generic component models, 43
generic entity bean remote interfaces, 1301
generic home entity bean interfaces, 1305-1306
generic remote session bean interfaces, 1265
generic session bean home interfaces, 1271-1272
GenericFactory interface, 697
GenericServlet class, 1074
geometrical shapes (2D), 136
get policy() method, 963
GET requests, 374
getActions() methods, 890
getAddress() method, 628
getAlgorithm() method, 906
getAllByName() method, 628
getAppletInfo() method, 102
getArray() method, 282-283
getArrayPropertyName() method, 155
getAsciiStream() method, 281
getAttribute() method, 1106
getAttributeDefinition() method, 638
getAttributes() method, 283-284
getAttributeSyntaxDefinition () method, 638
getBaseTypeName() method, 282
getBaseType() method, 282
getBeanInfo() method, 160
getBinaryStream() method, 280
getBufferedReader() method, 1088
getBufferSize() method, 1096
getByName() method, 628
getCallerPrincipal() method, 1326
getCatalogName() method, 234
getCatalogs() method, 241
getCatalogSeparator() method, 242
getCharacter Encoding() method, 1086, 1096
getCharacterStream() method, 281
getChildNodes() method, 1050
getClientID() method, 717
getColumnClass() method, 236-237
getColumnClassName() method, 234
getColumnCount() method, 234
getColumnDisplaySize() method, 234
getColumnLabel() method, 234
getColumnName() method, 234
getColumnPrivileges() method, 242
getColumns() method, 242

getColumnType() method, 234
getColumnTypeName() method, 234
getComment() method, 1107
getConnection() method, 215, 218, 242, 305
getContentLength() method, 1088
getContentType() method, 1086
getContext() method, 898, 1074
getCookies() method, 1107
getCreationTime() method, 1106
getDatabaseProductName() method, 242
getDatabaseProductVersion() method, 242
getDefaultFolder() method, 772
getDefaultInstance() method, 770
getDisplayName() method, 631
getDomain() method, 1107
getDriverName() method, 242
getDriverVersion() method, 242
getEJBHome() method
EJBHome objects, 1271
EJBObject interface, 1265
getEJBMetaData() method, 1272
getEncoded() method, 908
getEnumeration() method, 728
getErrorCode() method, 203
getEveryAttributeUsingGetAttributes() method, 653
getEveryAttributeUsingSearch() method, 652
getExceptionListener() method, 717
getExportedKeys() method, 242
getFetchDirection() method, 255
getFetchSize() method, 255
getFile() method, 153
getFirstChild() method, 1050
getFolder() method, 772
getHandle() method, 1265
getHomeHandle() method, 1271
getHomeInterfaceClass() method, 1272
getHostAddress() method, 628
getHostName() method, 628
getIcon() method, 162
getImplementation() method, 1055
getImportedKeys() method, 242
getIndexedPropertyName() method, 155
getInitialContext() method, 733
getInitParameter() method
ServletConfig interface, 1074, 1123
ServletContext interface, 1075, 1124
getInitParameterNames() method
ServletConfig interface, 1074, 1123
ServletContext interface, 1075
getInputStream() method, 1088
getInstance() method, 771, 907, 916, 920, 930
getKey() method, 910
getKeyStore() method, 915
getLastAccessedTime() method, 1106
getLastChild() method, 1050
getLastModified() method, 1080
getLength() method
AttributeList interface, 1033
NodeList interface, 1050
getLocale() method
ServletRequest interface, 1086
ServletResponse interface, 1096
getLocales() method, 1086
getLocalHost() method, 628
getMajorVersion() method, 1075
getMaxAge() method, 1107
getMaxConnections() method, 242
getMaxInactiveInterval() method, 1106
getMaxStatements() method, 242
getMessage() method, 775
getMessageCount() method, 775
getMessageListener() method, 719
getMessages() method, 775
getMessageSelector() method, 726
getMimeType() method, 1075
getMinorVersion() method, 1075
getMode() method, 775
getMoreResults() method, 231
getName() method
Permission objects, 881
Principal object, 1326
getNameDispatcher() method, 1090, 1075
getNewMessageCount() method, 775
getNewOrders() method, 731
getNextException() method, 203
getNextSibling() method, 1050
getNextWarning() method, 203

getNodeName() method, 1050
getNodeType() method, 1050
getNodeValue() method, 1050
getNumericFunctions() method, 299
getObject() method, 899, 924
getObjectProperty() method, 722
getOutputStream() method, 1096
getOwnerDocument() method, 1050
getParameter() method, 1088
getParameterInfo() method, 102
getParameterNames() method
ServletContext interface, 1124
ServletRequest interface, 1088
getParameterValues() method, 1088
getParent() method, 775
getParentNode() method, 1050
getPath() method, 1107
getPermanentFlags() method, 775
getPermissions() method, 895
getPolicy() method, 895
getPooledConnection() method, 307
getPreviousSibling() method, 1050
getPrimaryKey() method, 1265
getPrimaryKeys() method, 242
getProperties() method, 771
getProperty() method, 771
getPropertyNames() method, 722
getProtocol() method, 1086
getProvider() method, 772
getQueueName() method, 728
getRealPath() method, 1075
getRef() method, 282
getReference() method, 588
getRegistry() method, 500
getRemoteAddr() method, 1088
getRemoteHost() method, 1088
getRemoteInterfaceClass() method, 1272
getRequestDispatcher() method, 1075, 1090
getRequestURL() method, 1089
getResource() method, 1075
getResourceAsStream() method, 1075
getResultSet() method
QueryServerImplementation class, 435
Result Sets, 231
SQL arrays, 282-283
getRollbackOnly() method, 1325
getRow() method, 253
getSchema() method, 638
getSchemaClassDefinition() method, 638
getSchemaName() method, 234
getSchemas() method, 241
getScheme() method, 1086
getSecure() method, 1107
getSecurityManager() method, 869
getSelectedAttributesUsingSearch() method, 652
getServerInfo() method, 1075
getServerName() method, 1088
getServerPort() method, 1088
getServlet() method, 1076
getServletContext() method, 1074
getServletInfo() method, 1072
getServletName() method, 1074, 1123
getSimplePropertyName() method, 153
getSQLState() method, 203
getSQLTypeName() method
SQLData interface, 285
Struct interface, 283
getStatus() method, 807
getStore() method, 772, 775
getStringFunctions() method, 299
getSubString() method, 281
getSystemFunctions() method, 299
getTableName() method, 234
getTablePrivileges() method, 242
getTables() method, 241
getTableTypes() method, 242
getters (simple properties), 153
getTimeDateFunctions() method, 299
getTopicName() method, 740
getTransacted() method, 719
getTransport() methods, 778
getType() method, 775
getTypeInfo() method, 242
getTypeMap() method, 285
getUDTs() method, 279
getUIDValidity() method, 775
getUnavailableSeconds() method, 1072
getUnreadMessageCount() method, 775
getUpdateCount() method, 231
getURL() method, 242
getUserName() method, 242

getValue() method, 1106
getVersion() method, 1106
getWriter() method, 1096
getXAResource() method, 310
GIOP (General Inter-ORB Protocol), 392
header formats, 393
IORs (Interoperable Object References), 395
message types, 394
overview, 393-394
versions, 393
Globally Unique Identifiers. *See* GUIDs
gov DNS name, 626
graphical user interfaces. *See* GUIs
graphics. *See* images
greater than or equal to (>=) symbol, 642
GregorianCalendar class, 98
groups (activation), 520
Guard interface, 899
guarded objects, 899
guidgen utility, 543, 547
GUIDs (Globally Unique Identifiers), 532, 687
ADS, 687
DCOM, 532
generating, 543, 547
GUIs (graphical user interfaces), 130
AWT (Abstract Windowing Toolkit), 130
components, 130
containers, 131
deployment, 131-132
events, 131
images, 136
layout managers, 131
libraries, 131-132
Swing, 132
components, 132
containers, 132
deployment, 134
events, 132
helper libraries, 133-134
layout managers, 132
library, 132
look-and-feel, 133
models, 132
text components, Input Method Framework, 137
GZIP files, 90-91

H

<H1>-<H6> tags, 991
HandlerBase class, 1035, 1043
handlers
TCP/IP client callback, 357-358
TCP/IP server socket handler example, 343-346
handles, 22, 577
handling
events, 318
exceptions, 71
HTTP, 377
hardware (vital fail-safe), 835
hasChildren() method, 1050
hasfeature() method, 1055
hashCode() method, 890
HashMap class, 84
HashSet class, 84
Hashtable class, 85
HEAD requests, 374
HEAD? tag, 988
header cells (HTML tables), 992
header files, 1360
headers
DTD, 1019
email, 757
GIOP, 393
JMS messages, 721
JRMP, 472
headings (HTML documents), 988, 991
help (JavaHelp), 135
helper libraries (Swing), 133-134
HIDDEN attribute (<INPUT> tag), 995
higher-level programming languages, 20
home entity bean interfaces, 1303
application-specific, 1304-1305
architecture, 1303
examples, 1306-1307
generic, 1305-1306
lookups, 1303
home interfaces (EJBs), 1234
home pages. *See* Web sites
home session bean interfaces, 1267
application-specific, 1271
architecture, 1267
examples, 1272-1273
generic, 1271-1272
lookups, 1267-1271
Horizontal Common Facilities, 398-399
horizontal lines (HTML documents), 991
hostname utility, 336
hostnames, 335
HotJava, 971
<HR SIZE> tag, 991
href attribute (XLink), 1028
HTML (Hypertext Markup Language), 120, 138, 382-383
2.0, 986
3.0, 986
3.2, 986
4.0, 986
ASCII text, 987
documents, 988
background color, 990
body, 990

bold text, 991
bulleted item lists, 991
comments, 991
formatting, 991
forms, 994-995
frames, 992-993
headings, 988, 991
horizontal lines, 991
hyperlink color, 990
hyperlinks, 990-991
images, 991
italic text, 991
JavaScript, embedding, 1002-1003
line breaks, 991
meta-data, 989
numbered lists, 991
ordered lists, 991
paragraph alignment, 991
paragraphs, 991
structure, 987
tables, 992
tags, 988
text color, 990
text-area GUI components, 995
titles, 989
Dynamic HTML, 383-384
files
javadoc, 64
naming contexts, 578
forms, 994-995
overview, 987-988
Presentation Manager, 970
tags. *See* tags (HTML)
text, 133
text-area GUI components, 995
XHTML, 1012
HTML-based interfaces, 138
HTTP (Hypertext Transfer Protocol), 366, 370
baking session IDs in URLs, 379
behavior, 370, 372
cookies, 379
clients, 322
EAI (Enterprise Application Integration), 1363-1364
handling, 377
MIME (Multipurpose Internet Mail Extensions), 372-373
outside sessions, tracking, 379
request methods, 373-374
requests, 373-375
responses, 375-377
servers, 324
class downloads, 501
ClassFileServer, 501
Jini configurations, 678
RMI tool, 470
servlets, 1078
BeeShirts.com examples, 1081 1085
framework, 1078-1081
session management, 1103-1104
abstractions, 1104-1107
Cookie class, 1106-1107
cookies, 1106-1107
embedding ID information into URLs, 1105
examples, 1107-1110
HttpSession interface, 1104-1106
HttpSessionBindingEvent class, 1106
HttpSessionBindingListener interface, 1106
maximum inactive intervals, 1105
nature, 1104
statistical timing, 1106
Web communications, 1105
HTTP-NG, 380
HTTPPostHeader identifier, 472
HTTPResponseHeader identifier, 472
HttpReturn JRMP message, 473
HttpServlet class, 1078-1081
HttpServletRequest interface, 1078, 1089
HttpServletResponse interface, 1098-1099
HttpSession interface, 1078, 1104-1106
HttpsessionBindingEvent class, 1106
HttpSessionBindingEvent interface, 1078
HttpSessionBindingListener interface, 1078, 1106
HttpURLConnection class, 377
HttpUtils class, 1089-1090
hyperlinks
color, 990
HTML documents, 990-991
XML, 1025-1029
Hypertext Markup Language. *See* HTML
Hypertext Transfer Protocol. *See* HTTP

I

I/O serialization, 87
I/O streams
byte, 87-89
character, 89-90
<I> tag, 991
IANA (Internet Assigned Numbers Authority), 332
IClassFactory interface, 532
ICMP (Internet Control Message Protocol), 333
ID attribute, 1022
identifier references attribute, 1022
identifiers, 726
DCOM, 547
JRMP, 472
identifiers attribute, 1022

identifying
- principals, 906-915
- signing code, 925

identifyORB() method, 812

identities
- security, 828
- vendor-specific, 1330-1331

IDispatch interface, 533

IDL (Interface Definition Language), 391, 1218
- application server interfaces, 1218
- compiling, 428-430
- CORBA, 391, 400
  - *compiling, 407-408*
  - *file format, 400-401*
  - *Java-to-IDL mappings, 409*
  - *IDL-to-Java mappings, 401, 404-406*
- CORBA names library PIDL, 611-612
- CosNaming, 609-612
- DCOM, 533-535
  - *file format, 536*
  - *IDL-to-Java mappings, 537, 540*
- files, 420
- interfaces, 420, 543
- servers, registration, 446-447

IDL-to-Java compiler (J2SE v1.2), 429

IDL-to-Java Compiler, 422, 425, 470

idlj (IDL-to-Java compiler), 422, 425, 470

idlj utility, 407

idltojava compiler, 425

idltojava utility, 407

IDREF attribute, 1022

IETF (Internet Engineering Task Force), 649

ignorableWhitespace() method, 1040

ignorecase property (CompoundName constructor), 587

IIDs (Interface Identifiers), 532

IIOP (Internet Inter-ORB Protocol), 115, 392-393
- CORBA communications, 115
- EJB application server environments, 1218
- IORs (Interoperable Object References), 395
- J2EE future, 122
- overview, 394-395
- RMI communications, 116
- skeletons, 497
- versions, 395

IIOP/RMI, 473-474
- Java IDL, compared, 474
- clients/stubs, 511-514
- CosNaming JNDI SPI properties, 625
- lookups, 515
- servers, 494
  - *compiling, 497*
  - *creating, 494*
  - *dynamic class downloading, 504*
  - *example, 622-624*
  - *implementation examples, 495-496*
  - *naming service, 504*
  - *registration, 503*
  - *registration example, 505-506*

IIS (International Information Superhighway) Facility, 399

IIS (Microsoft Internet Information Server), 978

IllegalStateException, 717

IMAGE attribute (<INPUT? tag), 995

Image class, 136

ImageConsumer interface, 136

ImageFilter class, 136

ImageProducer interface, 136

Imagery Facility, 399

images
- 2D, 136
- 3D, 136
- advanced imaging, 136
- AWT, 136
- consumers, 136
- filters, 136
- HTML documents, 991
- media APIs, 137
- producers, 136
- rendering operations, 136

IMAP (Internet Message Access Protocol), 758-759

<IMG SRC> tag, 991

IMoniker interface, 532, 630

Implementation Repository, 392

implementations
- activatable objects, 518
- browser updates, 972
- browsers, 970-971
- EJBs, 1234
- Java Enterprise, 108
- MOM, 711
- object-oriented software development process, 28-29
- repositories, 443-444
- row sets, 297
- TCP/IP, 335-336
- time-to-market competition, 29
- Web servers, 978-979

implemented operations (class diagram notation), 34

implementing
- application server clients, 1220-1224
- AuditListener interface, 151
- CORBA clients, 421
- CORBA server registrar, 421
- CORBA servers, 420
- CosNaming services, 612

DCOM clients, 543, 568-570
DCOM server interfaces, 543
DCOM servers
client receiver example, 553
CORBA query server example, 554-559
example, 549-552
generated CoQueryServer class example, 562-563
generated IQueryServer interface example, 561-562
generated Order class example, 560
Jini proxies, 679
Jini remote process interfaces, 679
Jini Service Registrar, 679-681
RMI clients, 471
RMI server registrar, 471
RMI servers, 471
RMI/IIOP servers, 495
RMI/JRMP servers, 483
implicit objects, 1155, 1159-1160
implicitly loading JDBC drivers, 210
implies() method, 881, 890
INBOX (JavaMail), 783
include directive (JSPs), 1145
include() method, 1091
incorrect application reference errors (assurance), 823
incorrect data reference errors (assurance), 823
indexed properties, 155
IndexedPropertyDescriptor class, 160
indices, 176
InetAddress class, 337, 628
InfoBus, 167-168
InfoBus class, 167
InfoBus standard extension, 144
InfoBusDataConsumer interface, 167
InfoBusDataProducer interface, 167
InfoBusEvent class, 168
InfoBusMember interface, 167
information coding (safety), 835
Information Management Common Facility, 398
information technology (enterprise systems), 16-17
information/knowledge (enterprise components), 12
infrastructures (RMI), 470
InheritableThreadLocal class, 97
inheritance, 22
class diagram notation, 34
CORBA servers, 428, 431
inherited operations (class diagram notation), 34
init() method
applets, 101
GenericServlet class, 1074
Servlet interface, 1072
InitialContext class, 305, 582, 636
InitialDirContext class, 636
InitialLdapContext class, 663
INITIAL_CONTEXT_FACTORY property (JNDI contexts), 584
initSign() method, 921-922
Inprise Corporation, 423
input elements (<FORM> tag), 994-995
Input Method Framework, 137
Input/Output serialization, 87
<INPUT> tag, 994
attributes, 994-995
JavaScript, 1003
InputSource class, 1035
InputStream class, 87
InputStreamReader class, 90
inquisitive calls, 1086
insertABLOBType() method, 290
insertAStructTypeData() method, 291
insertBatchofRowsUsingPreparedStatement() method, 277
insertBatchofRowsUsingStatement() method, 277
insertRow() method, 264
insertsAreDetected() method, 268
INSERT_INTO statment, 183
installing
CSPs, 877
Java Plug-in, 973-974
instances (databases), 175
instantiation (security manager), 869
int DNS name, 626
Integer class, 77
integrity (security), 828
interface analysis, 27
interface communications protocol, 1218
Interface Definition Language. *See* IDL
interface definition rigidity, 46
Interface Identifiers (IIDs), 532
Interface Repositories. *See* IRs
interface specification, 830
interfaces, 112. *See also specific interfaces*; subinterfaces
applets, 138
application server client, 1218-1219
class diagram notation, 34
client-side script based, 138

component APIs, 44
component models, 44-46
component SPIs, 45
component-to-container, 45
compound Life Cycle Service, 698-699
container-to-component, 45
CORBA, 425-428
IDL client callback example, 426
IDL for customer example, 427
IDL for query server example, 427-428
IDL Order example, 426
registering, 421
core Life Cycle Service, 697
design patterns, 44
distributed business-specific, 1218
document presentation, 970
document serving, 976-977
file-system, 606
home (EJBs), 1234
home entity beans, 1303
application-specific, 1304-1305
architecture, 1303
examples, 1306-1307
generic, 1305-1306
lookups, 1303
home session bean, 1267
application-specific, 1271
architecture, 1267
examples, 1272-1273
generic, 1271-1272
lookups, 1267-1271
HTML-based, 138
Jini, 679
JTA
application, 809-810
Transaction Manager, 807-808
X/Open XA, 810, 812
query service specific database example, 347-350
remote, 471
remote (EJBs), 1234
remote entity beans, 1299
application-specific, 1301
architecture, 1300
examples, 1301, 1303
generic, 1301
remote session bean, 1263
application-specific, 1264
architecture, 1263
examples, 1265-1266
generic, 1265
SAX application handler, 1035, 1037-1043
document handlers, 1040-1043
DTD handler, 1035, 1037
entity resolvers, 1037-1038
error handlers, 1039-1040
SAX parser, 1043-1046
service providers. *See* SPIs
session bean client, 1263
home, 1267-1273
remote, 1263-1266
stateful session bean rules, 1258-1259
stateless session bean rules, 1252-1253
Web, 137-139
X/Open XA, 810-812
XML-based, 139
internal entity declarations, 1021
internal row set state/behavior, 297-298
International Information Superhighway (IIS) Facility, 399
International Standards Organization. *See* ISO
Internet, 366. *See also* Web
access TCP/IP layer, 332-333
computing, 319
domain name system, 578
Internet Assigned Numbers Authority (IANA), 332
Internet Control Message Protocol (ICMP), 333
Internet Engineering Task Force (IETF), 649
Internet Explorer, 970, 973
Internet Information Server (IIS), 978
Internet Inter-ORB Protocol (IIOP). *See* IIOP
Internet Message Access Protocol (IMAP), 758-759
Internet Protocol (IP), 332
Internet Server Application Program Interface (ISAPI), 977
InternetAddress class, 767
InternetHeaders class, 766
Interoperable Object References (IORs), 395
introspection (JavaBean), 160-163
Introspector class, 160
Iona Technologies, Inc., 423
IORs (Interoperable Object References), 395
IP (Internet Protocol), 332
IP addresses, 332-333
ipconfig utility, 336
IPersist interface, 535
IRs (Interface Repositories), 448-454
accessing, 449
contents, viewing, 450-454
objects, 449
isAfterLast() method, 253
ISAPI (Internet Server Application Program Interface), 977
isBeforeFirst() method, 253
isCallerInRole() method, 1326
isCaseSensitive() method, 234
isDefinitelyWritable() method, 234

isEqual() method, 918
isFirst() method, 253
isIdentical() method, 1265
isLast() method, 253
isNew() method, 1104
isNullable() method, 234
ISO (International Standards Organization), 327
isolation levels (transactions), 266-267, 797, 1318
isReadOnly() method, 234, 881
isRequestedSessionIdFromCookie() method, 1104
isRequestedSessionIdFromURL() method, 1104
isRequestedSessionIdValid() method, 1104
isSearchable() method, 234
isSecure() method, 1086, 1131
isSession() method, 1272
isStatelessSession() method, 1272
isWritable() method, 234
italic text (HTML documents), 991
Item bean, 1241
iteration (object-oriented software development process), 30
Iterator interface, 82
iterators (embedded SQL), 193
IUnkown interface, 532, 544

J

J/Direct API, 531
J2EE (Java 2 Enterprise Edition), 56, 107, 111
  application DTD, 1063-1066
  compatibility test suite, 107
  component-container architecture, 108-110
  connectors, 1368-1370
  Enterprise JavaBeans, 50
  features, 107
  future, 122-123
  history, 106-107
  J2SE incorporation, 1200
  JavaMail package, 701
  platform, 107
  programming model, 107
  reference implementation, 107
  restrictions, 110-111
  servlets, 1007
  specification, 107
  Web components, 50
  Web site, 107
  XML integration, 1062-1063
J2EE-based EJB container environments, 121
J2EE-based Web-enabling applications, 119
J2ME (Java 2 Platform, Micro Edition), 56, 1371
J2SE (Java 2 Standard Edition), 56, 108, 1200
  v1.2, 108
  v1.2 IDL-to-Java compiler, 429
  v1.3, 108
JAAS (Java Authentication and Authorization Service), 122, 929, 933
JacORB, 423
jactivex utility, 531, 543, 548
JAF (JavaBeans Activation Framework), 700-701, 757
jar file extension, 60, 110
JAR files, 60
  APIs, 90-91
  EJBs, 1245
  generating, 928
  jar tool, 63
  signing, 928
  structure, 62
jar utility, 63, 925
JarEntry class, 90
JarInputStream class, 90
JarOutputStream class, 91
jarsigner utility, 925
Java
  2D, 136
  3D, 136
  Advanced Imaging API, 136
  API class files, 58
  APIs, 50
  applets. *See* applets
  bindings, 543, 548-549
  Communications API, 1371
  Enterprise APIs, 108
  Enterprise implementations, 108
  Enterprise System architecture, 112-113
  file extension, 60
  IDL, 424-425, 474
  IDL IDL-to-Java compiler, 407
  manifest files. *See* manifest files
  Media APIs, 137
  Media Framework API, 137
  objects (persistable), 278-279
  Plug-in, 973
    HTML Converter tool, 974
    HTML Specification, 974
    installing, 973-974
    JRE designation, 974-975
    updates, 972
  RMI-to-IDL mapping, 474-476
  Runtime Environment, 970
  scripting from JSPs, 1149-1152
    declarations, 1149-1150
    expressions, 1150-1151
    scriptlets, 1151-1152
  security, 856, 858
  serialization
    files, 60
    XML integration, 1061
  servlets. *See* servlets

- Shared Data Toolkit, 137
- Sound API, 137
- Speech API, 137
- SPIs, 50
- Technologies for the Enterprise, 107
- Technology Core Platform Compatibility Kit, 677
- Web Server. *See* Jeeves, 978

Java 2 Enterprise Edition. *See* J2EE
Java 2 Micro Edition (J2ME), 56, 1371
Java 2 Standard Edition. *See* J2SE
Java Activation Framework (JAF), 700-701, 757
Java Activation Framework Web site, 779
Java API for XML Parsing (JAXP), 120, 1031
Java archive files. *See* JAR files
Java Authentication and Authorization Service (JAAS), 122, 862, 929, 933
Java Cryptography Architecture. *See* JCA
Java Cryptography Extension (JCE), 861-862, 929
Java Database Connectivity. *See* JDBC
Java Development Kit Development Tools Web site, 63
Java Development Kit (JDK), 56, 106
Java Electronic Commerce Framework (JECF), 1204
Java Management Extension (JMX), 1205
Java Message Service. *See* JMS
Java Naming and Directory Interface. *See* JNDI
Java Native Interface. *See* JNI
Java Platform for the Enterprise (JPE), 107
Java Remote Method Protocol. *See* JRMP
Java Secure Socket Extension (JSSE), 862, 929
Java Telephony API (JTAPI), 137, 1204
java tool, 63
Java Transaction API (JTA), 117
Java Transaction Architecture. *See* JTA
Java Transactions Service (JTS), 812-813
Java Virtual Machine. *See* JVM
Java-based application frameworks, 1198, 1200
Java-based applications, 119
Java-based Web progamming, 1007-1008
Java-to-IDL mappings, 409, 474
java.awt package, 130
java.awt.color package, 136
java.awt.datatransfer package, 134
java.awt.dnd package, 134
java.awt.event package, 131
java.awt.geom package, 136
java.awt.im package, 137
java.awt.image package, 136
java.awt.image.renderable package, 136
java.awt.print package, 135
java.beans package, 144
java.beans.beancontext package, 144, 148
java.io package, 87, 606
java.lang package, 73
java.lang.ref package, 79-80
java.lang.ref Web site, 73
java.lang.reflect package, 77-78, 160
java.lang.reflect Web site, 73
java.math package, 73
java.rmi package, 467-469
java.rmi.activation package, 469
java.rmi.dgc package, 469
java.rmi.registry package, 469
java.rmi.server package, 469
java.security package, 873
java.security.cert package, 873
java.security.cert.CertificationFactor class, 908
java.security.Certificate interface, 906
java.security.certX509CRL class, 910
java.security.DigestInputStream class, 919
java.security.DigestOutputStream class, 919
java.security.Guard interface, 899
java.security.Identity class, 906
java.security.IdentityScope class, 906
java.security.interfaces package, 874
java.security.KeyPair class, 906
java.security.KeyPairGenerator class, 907
java.security.KeyStore class, 910
java.security.SignedObject class, 922, 924
java.security.Signer class, 906
java.security.spec package, 874
java.sql package, 201
java.util package, 73
Java/SQL mappings, 239-241
Java2idl utility, 409

Java2IIOP utility, 409
JavaBeans, 49. *See also* EJBs
components, 145-148
containers, 145-146, 149
contexts, 148-149
customizers, 166-167
customizing, 164
design-time customizations, 144
events, 149-152
InfoBus, 167-168
introspection, 160-163
overview, 142-144
persistence, 163-164
properties, 152
array, 155
bound, 155-157
constrained, 157-159
indexed, 155
simple, 153
property editors, 164-166
JavaBeans Activation Framework (JAF), 700-701, 757
JavaBeans Development Kit (BDK), 144
javac tool, 63
JavaCard, 1371
javadoc tool, 64
JavaDoc Tool home page, 60
JavaHelp, 135
javakey utility, 910, 925
JavaMail, 757-758
architecture, 759-760
connection example, 778
EJBs, 1351-1354
events, 768
example, 779-786
connectToMailServer() method, 781
INBOX, 783
MailClient class private attributes, 780-781
printMessage() method, 782
readMessages() method, 783
searchFrom() method, 785
sendAMessage() method, 784
INBOX, retrieving, 783
message store folders, 772-776
messages, 760, 763
MIME, 764, 767
multipart, 763
printing, 782-783
reading, 783-784
searching, 785-786
sending, 784-785
parts, 760
sessions, 768, 771-772
standard extension Web site, 779
transports, 777-778
javareg utility, 531, 543
DCOM clients, 570
DCOM servers, 564
javas.swing.border package, 133
JavaScript
embedding in HTML, 1002-1003
Java, compared, 1002
overview, 1002-1004
server side, 1004
JavaServer Pages. *See* JSPs
JavaSoft Organization, 423
JavaSpaces, 677
javax.accessibility package, 135
javax.activation package, 701
javax.directory.ldap package, 651
javax.infobus package, 167
javax.mail package, 760
javax.mail.event package, 760
javax.mail.internet package, 760
javax.mail.search package, 760
javax.naming package, 581
javax.naming.directory package, 581
javax.naming.event package, 581
javax.naming.ldap package, 581, 662
javax.naming.spi package, 581
javax.net package, 932
javax.net.ssl package, 932
javax.rmi package, 469
javax.rmi.CORBA package, 469
javax.security.auth package, 933
javax.security.auth.callback package, 933
javax.security.auth.login package, 933
javax.security.auth.spi, 933
javax.security.cert package, 932
javax.servlet package, 1072
javax.servlet.http package, 1078
javax.sql package, 201
javax.swing library, 132
javax.swing.colorchooser package, 133
javax.swing.event package, 132
javax.swing.filechooser package, 133
javax.swing.plaf package, 133
javax.swing.plaf.basic package, 133
javax.swing.plaf.metal package, 133
javax.swing.plaf.multi package, 133
javax.swing.table package, 133

javax.swing.text package, 133
javax.swing.text.html package, 133
javax.swing.text.html.parser package, 133
javax.swing.text.rtf.RTFEditorKit package, 134
javax.swing.tree package, 133
javax.swing.undo package, 134
javax.transaction package, 805
javax.transaction.xa package, 805
javax.xml.parsers package, 1031
JAXP (Java API for XML Parsing), 120, 1031
JCA (Java Cryptography Architecture), 859, 861, 873
architecture, 907
cryptographic engines, 875
CSPs, 874-877
encryption/cryptography distinction, 861, 873
functions, 873
Provider class, 874
Security class, 874
security package, 873
security.cert package, 873
security.interfaces package, 874
security.spec package, 874
JCE (Java Cryptography Extension), 861-862, 929
JColorChooser component, 133
JComponent class, 132
JavaBean components, 147
JavaBean containers, 145
JCP (Jini Core Platform), 675
jdb tool, 64
JDBC (Java Database Connectivity), 113, 195-196, 200
API, 114
architecture, 200-204
classes, 202-203
connections, 213-214
creating, 215
database URLs, 214-215
example, 215-219
handling, 1129
driver implementations, 201
drivers
BeeShirts.com configuration example, 212-213
configuring, 208-210
explicitly loading, 210
implicitly loading, 210
names, 242
selecting, 208
selecting types, 205
type 1 configuration, 205, 211
type 2 configuration, 206, 211
type 3 configuration, 206, 211-212
type 4 configuration, 207
types, 204-207
version, 242
EJBs, 1277-1279
exceptions, 202-203
interfaces, 202-203
LIKE clauses, 243
MetaData, 241
databases/driver information, 241-243
example, 243-247
handle, creating, 244
table/view descriptions, 245
outer joins support, 243
Result Sets, 231, 236
column class information, 236-237
customizing, 231, 233
customizing example, 234-239
information about, 233-234
MetaData example, 234-239
scrolling through, 237-239
row sets, 297
SQL/Java mappings, 239-241
statements, 219, 242
creating/executing example, 222-226
joins (queries), 221
LIKE clauses, 221-222
outer joins (queries), 221
prepared, 226-231
regular, 219-221
XML integration, 1062
JDBC 1.0, 201-203
JDBC 2.0, 201
advanced data types, 278
advanced SQL types example, 288-294
BeeShirts.com data model example, 286-287
custom types, 284-285
Java objects, 278-279
SQL arrays, 282-283
SQL BLOBs/CLOBs, 280-282
SQL Distinct types, 284
SQL structures, 283-284
SQL3, 279-280
SQL3 references, 282
batch updates, 274
creating, 274-275
example, 276-278
executing, 275
connection pools, 307-309
Core API, 201
distributed transactions, 310
extension implementation, 122
forward-only result sets, 251
JNDI, 305-307

row sets, 295-297

architecture, 295

cached, 297

implementations, 297

internal state/behavior, 297-298

JDBC, 297

Web, 297

scroll-insensitive, 251

scroll-sensitive result sets, 251

scrollable result sets, 250-251

creating, 251-252

driver support, 254-255

example, 255-262

scrolling backwards, 260

scrolling forward, 259

scrolling from specific rows, 261

scrolling through, 252-254

Standard Extension API, 201

stored procedures, 298

calling example, 302-304

creating, 299-301

creating, BeeShirts.com example, 301-302

executing, 301

predefined database methods, 298-299

updateable result sets, 262-263

adding rows, 264

creating, 263

deleting rows, 264

driver support, 268

example, 269-274

refreshing rows, 268

update visibility, 265-268

updates, deleting, 264

updating rows, 263-264

JDBC Result Sets, 231

JdbcOdbcDriver class, 205

JDK (Java Development Kit), 56, 106

JECF (Java Electronic Commerce Framework), 1204

Jeeves, 978

JFileChooser component, 133

Jini, 635, 673-674

class architecture, 679-682

clients, creating, 681-682

component architecture, 674-675

embedded application environment Web site, 1371

embedded applications integration, 1371

example, 683-686

infrastructure, 676-677

interfaces, 679

item descriptions, 680

JavaSpaces, 677

licensing fees Web site, 677

lookup services, 677, 681

programming model, 676

proxies, 679-680

runtime environment configuration, 678

security managers, 681

Service Registrar, 679-681

services, creating, 679

tools, 677

transaction management service, 677

Jini Core Platform (JCP), 675

Jini Extended Platform (JXP), 675

Jini Software Kit (JSK), 675

Jini Starter Kit, 675

Jini System Software Starter Kit download, 677

JMS (Java Message Service), 117, 714

architecture, 714

connections, 714, 717

EAI (Enterprise Application Integration), 1365-1366

EJBs, 1346-1347

as JMS consumers, 1348-1351

as JMS producers, 1347-1348

J2EE future, 122

messages, 719-723

body data types, 723

headers, 721

producers/consumers/selectors, 725-726

properties, 722-723

provider-specific properties, 721

named topics, 740

point-to-point message queuing, 727-729

point-to-point message queuing example, 729

order manager, 731-732

order requests, 731

queue consumer, 735-738

queue supplier, 732-733, 735

publish-subscribe messaging, 738-740

publish-subscribe messaging example, 741

topic consumer, 744-747

topic supplier, 741-744

server connection meta-data, 717

server provider client IDs, 717

sessions, 717, 719

XML integration, 1062

JMSCorrelationID property, 721

JMSCorrelationIDAsBytes property, 721

JMSDeliveryMode property, 721

JMSDestination property, 721

JMSException class, 717

JMSExpiration property, 721

JMSMessageID property, 721

JMSPriority property, 721

JMSReceiver class, 1349-1350

JMSRedelivered property, 721

JMSReplyTo property, 721

JMSTimestamp property, 721
JMSType property, 721
JMSX properties, 722-723
JMX (Java Management Extension), 1205
JNDI (Java Naming and Directory Interface), 116, 305-307, 580
architecture, 580-582
binding/lookup, 586
bindings, 566
bound/renamed/deleted example, 602-605
listing example, 598-602
class libraries, 581
contexts, 582-586
listing example, 598-602
listings, 587-588
properties, 584
directory services, 636
directory contexts, 636
events, 643-645
object attribute customizations, 643
object attributes, 637-638
object bindings, 639
schemas, 638-639
search results, 640
searches, 639-642
EJB home interface handles, 1218
events, naming, 591, 593
examples, 593
bindings contexts, 602-605
listing binding names/naming contexts, 598-602
lookup, 594-597
file-system SPI
CosNaming service, 614-618
file names, 606-608
RMI naming services, 618-625
RMI/JRMP registry JNDI SPI Web site, 619
lookups, 594-597
names, 586-587
referenceable objects, 588, 590-591
SPI
LDAP, 651-662
NDS, 646-647
NIS, 645-646
subcontexts, 586
XML integration, 1062
JNI (Java Native Interface), 1357
based bridges to native code, creating, 1359-1361
EAI (Enterprise Application Integration), 1357-1361
joins
JDBC statement queries, 221
outer joins, 243
Jorba, 424
JPE (Java Platform for the Enterprise), 107
JRE (Java Plug-in designation), 974-975
JRMP (Java Remote Method Protocol), 116, 469
headers, 472
identifiers, 472
message types, 472-473
multiplexing, 473
RMI, 471-473
JRMP/IIOP server, 622, 624
JRMP/RMI
clients/stubs, 506-510
example, 620-622
headers, 472
identifiers, 472
lookups, 514-515
message types, 472-473
multiplexing, 473
registry JNDI SPI Web site, 619
servers, 481
compiling, 493
creating, 481-483
dynamic class downloading, 500-502
example, 620-622
interfacing with RMI registries, 499-500
registration, 498-499
registration example, 502-503
RMI client receiver implementation example, 486-487
RMI Customer implementation example, 483-486
RMI query server implementation example, 487-492
security configurations, 499
Jrun Servlet engines, 979
JSK (Jini Software Kit), 675
JSP-based interface generators, 139
JSPs (Java Server Pages), 50, 1007, 1136-1141
abstractions, 1152-1158
container information, 1157-1158
custom tag extension abstractions, 1181-1186
custom tag library abstractions, 1183
factories, 1157-1158
page context, 1152-1157
action sub-elements, 1165
actions
examples, 1173-1175
forward action, 1165-1166
getProperty action, 1170-1171
include action, 1166-1167
param action sub-elements, 1165
plugin action, 1171-1173
setProperty action, 1169-1170
useBean action, 1167-1168

architecture, 1137
BeeShirts.com examples, 1139-1141
comments, 1144
custom classes, 1158
deploying, 1175-1181
configuration information, 1177-1179
deployment descriptor considerations, 1176-1177
direct deployment procedure considerations, 1179-1180
precompiled deployment procedure considerations, 1180
directives, 1144-1149
examples, 1147-1149
include directive, 1145
page directive, 1145-1147
taglib directive, 1147, 1183-1185
elements, 1142-1143
engine, 977
objects, 1159-1164
implicit objects, 1155, 1159-1160
JSP object manipulation examples, 1160-1164
scope, 1154, 1160
overview, 1136-1141
phases, 1137
scripting elements, 1149-1152
declarations, 1149-1150
expressions, 1150-1151
scriptlets, 1151-1152
special characters, 1144
tags, 1143
template data, 1142
XML integration, 1062

JSSE (Java Secure Socket Extensions), 862, 929

JTA (Java Transaction Architecture), 804, 807
application interface, 809-810
J2EE future, 122
Transaction Manager interface, 807-808
Web site, 804
X/Open XA interface, 810, 812

JTA (Java Transaction API), 117

JTable component, 133

JTAPI (Java Telephony API), 1204

JTE (Java Technologies for the Enterprise), 107

JTextArea component, 133

JTextField component, 133

JTree component, 133

JTS (Java Transactions Service), 812-813

jvc compiler, 543

jvc utility, 531

jview, 528, 531

JVM (Java Virtual Machine), 58
byte codes, 58
class loader, 864
applets, 865
architecture, 864-865
ClassLoader, 866
defineClass() method, 866
findClass() method, 866-868
forName() method, 868
loadClass() method, 866-868
responsibilities, 864
RMIClassLoader, 866
SecureClassLoader, 866
security, 864-865
URLClassLoader, 866
java tools, 63
runtime execution engine, 58
security manager, 868
AccessController class, 871
checkPermission() method, 871
customizing, 871-873
default, 869
getSecurityManager() method, 869
instantiation, 869
RMISecurityManager class, 871
SecurityManager class, 869-871
SecurityManager objects, 869
setSecurityManager() method, 869

JXP (Jini Extended Platform), 675

K

Kerberos, 845

Key interface, 906

keyed collections, 84, 86

KeyFactory (cryptographic engines), 875

KeyPair object, 907

KeyPairGenerator (cryptographic engines), 875, 907

keys, 906, 911-915
examples, 912-915
private, 921-922, 924
storing, 910

Keystore (cryptographic engines), 875

keytool utility, 910

keywords
synchronized, 95-96
valuetype, 410

knowledge/information (enterprise components), 12

L

LAN computing, 319
language APIs, 74
language dependencies
component model interfaces, 46
distributed systems, 317
LANGUAGE property (JNDI contexts), 584
languages
query, 176
scripting, 1001-1002
client-side, 1002
JavaScript, 1002-1004
Perl, 1005
server-side, 1001
VBScript, 1004-1005
last() method, 253
layers (distributed systems), 318
layout managers
AWT, 131
Swing, 132
LayoutManager interface, 131
LayoutManager2 interface, 131
LDAP (Lightweight Directory Access Protocol), 648-649
API, 649
interfaces, 649-651
JNDI SPI, 651-662
search example, 653-662
Web site, 651
Mozilla LDAP SDK Web site, 649
RDN type names, 648
v3, 662, 664
LDAPAttribute class, 650
LDAPAttributeSet class, 650
LDAPConnection class, 650
LDAPConstraints class, 650
LDAPContext interface, 662
LDAPControl class, 650
LDAPEntry class, 650
LDAPExtendedOperation class, 650
LDAPExtendedResponse class, 650
LDAPMessage class, 650
LDAPModification class, 650
LDAPModificationSet class, 650
LDAPResponse class, 650
LDAPSearchConstraints class, 650
LDAPSearchResult class, 650
LDAPv2 interface, 650
LDAPv3 interface, 650
leading tags, 987
legacy enterprise integration. *See* EAI
length() method, 280-281
less than or equal to (<=) symbol, directory search filter, 642
<LI> tag, 991
libraries
AWT, 131-132
baked-in CORBA, 422
COM/DCOM type, 533
DCOM, 543, 548
Java IDL, 424-425
JNDI, 581
native platform interface libraries, 58
ORB, 421, 423
Swing, 132
Swing helpers, 133-134
licensing
availability, 832
distributed systems, 318
Licensing Service, 397
Life Cycle Service, 396
Life Cycle Service interfaces, 697-699
lifecycle management, 1215
LifeCycleObject interface, 697
lifecycles, 1070
Lightweight Directory Access Protocol. *See* LDAP
LIKE clause
JDBC statements, 221-222
support, 243
line breaks (HTML documents), 991
LineNumberReader class, 90
Link interface, 666
link parsing/actual reference latency, 1027
LinkedList class, 84
LinkRef objects, 590
links. *See* hyperlinks
List interface, 82
list types() method, 668
list() method
context listings, 587
Folder class, 775
RMI/JRMP lookups, 515
listBindings() method, 588
listeners
ConnectionEventListener, 309
ExceptionListener, 717
JavaBean component property value changes, 155-157
JavaMail, 768
NamingListener, 591
property change, 156
TCP/IP server socket listener example, 340-342
vetoable property change, 158
vetoing property changes, 157
listings
Abridged TLD File DTD, 1185-1186
activatable object client, 521
activatable object implementation, 518
activatable object interface, 517
activatable server registrar, 519-520
BeeShirts.com Home Page JSP, 1160-1161

BeeShirts.com Standard Error Page JSP, 1164
BMP entity bean example, 1287, 1289-1291
BMP entity bean home interface, 1306
BMP entity bean remote interface, 1302
BOA server registration example, 445
CGI program, 996, 998-1000
Check Out JSP, 1173-1174
CMP entity bean example, 1296, 1298-1299
CMP entity bean home interface, 1307
CMP entity bean remote interface, 1302-1303
CORBA
client receiver implementation, 435
customer implementation, 431-435
DII-based client, 460
generated serializable data, 439-440
IDL client callback interface, 426
IDL for customer interface, 427
IDL for query server interface, 427-428
IDL Order interface, 426
names library PIDL, 611-612
Naming service interface, 461-463
query client, 456-458
query server implementation, 436-439, 554-559
CosNaming IDL interfaces, 609-611
CosNaming JNDI SPI
CosNaming server example, 616-618
message IDL example, 616
credit-management bean, 1215-1217
Customer object, 350-352
DCOM
client receiver implementation, 553
customer implementation, 550-552
interface example, 545-547
query client, 569-570
document handler, 1040-1043
DSI-based server, 441, 443
DTD handler, 1035, 1037
EJB
client configuration, 1227
client home interface, 1219
client implementation, 1221-1224
client remote interface, 1219
DTD container transaction elements, 1322
DTD entity bean deployment descriptor, 1310
DTD entity elements, 1308-1309
DTD security assembly elements, 1327
DTD security role references, 1327
DTD session bean elements, 1273-1275
DTD top-level elements, 1244-1245
reference DTD elements, 1267
server configuration, 1226
session bean deployment, 1275-1276
entity resolver, 1037-1038
error handler, 1039-1040
generated CoQueryServer class, 562-563
generated IQueryServer interface, 561-562
generated Order class, 560
IDL server registration, 446-447
Imoniker interface, 630-631
IR contents, viewing, 450-454
J2EE application DTD, 1063-1066
JNDI
bindings, 602-605
list/search, 598-602
lookup, 594-597
LDAP search, 653-662
order object, 352-353
primary keys example, 1292
query service specific database interface, 347-350
RMI
client receiver implementation, 486-487, 495
customer implementation, 483-486
interface, 619-620
interface BeeShirts.com customer information, 480
interface for RMI client callbacks, 479
interface querying the RMI server application, 480-481
query server implementation, 487-496
RMI/IIOP
query client, 511-514
server, 622, 624
RMI/JRMP
query client, 508-510
server, 620-622
SAX example, 1045-1046
serializable Order class, 492-493

stateful session beans
example, 1259-1260, 1262
home interface example, 1272-1273
remote interfaces, 1266
stateless session beans
example, 1253-1255
home interface example, 1272
remote interfaces, 1265
TCP/IP
client callback handler, 357-358
client object, 353-357
query service protocol marker interface, 347
server socket handler, 343-346
server socket listener, 340-342
Web component DTD, 1111-1117
XML
order document with DTD reference, 1023-1024
order DTD, 1024-1025
ListIterator class, 82
listNamesAndBindings() method, 598
lists (HTML documents), 991
literals, 726
load() method, 910
load-balancing, 832
load-testing, 832
loadClass() method, 866, 868
loading
BMP entity beans, 1285
class loader, 58, 864
applets, 865
architecture, 864-865
ClassLoader, 866
defineClass() method, 866
findClass() method, 866-868
forName() method, 868
loadClass() method, 866-868
responsibilities, 864
RMIClassLoader, 866
SecureClassLoader, 866
security, 864-865
URLClassLoader, 866
CMP entity beans, 1295
JDBC drivers explicitly, 210
JDBC drivers implicitly, 210
loadLibrary() method, 1359
locale (servlet responses), 1096
Locale class, 97
locale preferences, 1086
locale() method, 1043
LocateRegistry interface, 500
LocateReply GIOP message, 394
LocateRequest GIOP message, 394
locator attribute (XLink), 1026
Locator interface, 1033
log messages, 1075
log() method, 1074-1075
logical AND (&) symbol, directory search filter, 642
logical data models, 175
logical operators, 66
logical OR (|) symbol, directory search filter, 642
logIt() method, 926-929
Long class, 77
look-and-feel (Swing), 133
Lookup interface, 665
lookup services (Jini), 677-678, 681
lookup() method, 514
lookupBoundObject() method, 594
lookupLink() method, 590
lookups
DNS, 628
home entity bean interfaces, 1303
JNDI, 586, 594-597
RMI/IIOP, 515
RMI/JRMP, 514-515
session bean home interfaces, 1267-1271

M

MAC (Message Authentication Code), 843
mahalo (Jini transaction management service), 677
mail-system events, 760
MailClient class, 780-781
MailEvent class, 768
main() method, 904, 911, 926-929
mainframe/dumb terminal computing relationships, 319
maintainability, 833
assurance, 819
assurance problem models, 822, 833
code documentation, 834
coding standards, 833
design documentation standards, 834
OOP, 834
remote administration, 834
risk reduction plans, 833-834
maintenance
CBD, 48
object-oriented software development process, 30
management
application services, 1228-1229
applications, 1205
HTTP sessions, 1103-1104
abstractions, 1104, 1106-1107
Cookie class, 1106-1107
cookies, 1106-1107

embedding ID information into URLs, 1105
examples, 1107-1110
HttpSession interface, 1104-1106
HttpSessionBindingEvent class, 1106
HttpSessionBindingListener interface, 1106
maximum inactive intervals, 1105
nature, 1104
statistical timing, 1106
state, 1228
management services, 108, 1197
Mandatory attribute (transactions), 797
mandatory authorization, 850
Manifest class, 90
manifest files, 60
APIs, 90
structure, 62
MANIFEST.MF file extension, 60
Manufacturing Facility, 399
Map interface, 82, 84
MapMessage interface, 723
mapped collections, 84-86
Mapping Facility, 399
mappings
Access Control, 900-903
DCOM IDL-to-Java, 537, 540
IDL-to-Java, 401, 404-406
Java-to-IDL, 409
SQL/Java, 239-241
marshaling, 322
CORBA client stubs, 391
CORBA objects by value, 411-412
match attribute (XSL style sheets), 1030
Math class, 76
mathematical APIs, 76
media APIs, 137
Member interface, 77
MenuComponent class, 130
Message Authentication Code, 843
message changed event model, 768
Message class, 760
message count event model, 768
Message Digest #2 algorithm, 842
Message Digest #4 algorithm, 842
Message Digest #5 algorithm, 842
message digests, 842-843, 916-919
Message interface
header properties, 721
JMS, 719
Message object, 760
Message Oriented Middleware (MOM), 711-713
message store folders (JavaMail), 772-776, 783
appending messages, 775
contents, listing, 775
copying messages, 775
deleting messages, 775
existing, 775
flags, 775
modes, 775
names, 775
opening, 775
parent folder/store retrieval, 775
retrieving messages, 775
searching, 776
message types (JRMP), 472-473
Message-Oriented Middleware Association (MOMA), 712
MessageAware interface, 763
MessageConsumer interface, 726
MessageContext class, 763
MessageDigest (cryptographic engines), 875
MessageDigest object, 919
MessageError GIOP message, 394
MessageListener interface
EJBs as JMS consumers, 1348
JMS, 719
MessageProducer interface, 725
messages
GIOP, 394
JavaMail, 760, 763
MIME, 764, 767
multipart, 763
printing, 782-783
reading, 783-784
searching, 785-786
sending, 784-785
JMS, 719-723
body data types, 723
headers, 721
producers/consumers/selectors, 725-726
properties, 722-723
provider-specific properties, 721
MIME, 757
properties, 722
messages (email), 757-758
messaging middleware, 708
messaging services
asynchronicity, 711
communications, 117
CORBA, 747
Event Service, 747-753
Messaging specification, 747, 755-756
Notification Service, 747, 754
EAI (Enterprise Application Integration), 1365-1366

email, 711, 757-759
filtering, 710
JavaMail. *See* JavaMail
JMS (Java Message Service). *See* JMS
locality, 707-708
messaging middleware, 708
MOM (Message Oriented Middleware), 711-713
overview, 706
point-to-point, 708
publish-subscribe, 709
push/pull, 709
quality, 711

Messaging/Events Service (COM/DCOM), 535

meta-data (HTML documents), 989

<META> tag, 989

MetaData (JDBC), 241
databases/driver information, 241-243
example, 243-247
handle, creating, 244
table/view descriptions, 245

metal look-and-feel, 133

METHOD attribute (<FORM> tag), 994

Method class, 78

MethodDescriptor class, 160

methods, 21
absolute(), 253
add(), 149
addAnEventListenerTotheContext(), 652
addANewAttribute(), 653
addAuditListener(), 151
addBatch(), 274
addDateHeader(), 1098
addHeader(), 1098
addIntHeader(), 1098
addNamingListener(), 643
addPropertyChangeListener(), 156, 166
addRowSetListener(), 295
addVetoableChangeListener(), 158
afterLast(), 253
analyzeMetaData(), 236-237
appendMessages(), 775
audit decision(), 954
audit needed(), 954
audit write(), 956
authenticate(), 948
beforeFirst(), 253
begin(), 809-810
bind(), 586, 639
BindToObject(), 631
byte(), 280
cancelRowUpdates(), 264
characters(), 1040
checkGuard, 899
checkGuard(), 881
checkPermission(), 871, 896-898
CheckPermissions.main(), 904
checkRead(), 896
checkXXX(), 896
clearBatch(), 275
clearProperties(), 722
close(), 716
CoCreateInstance(), 629
CoCreateInstanceEx(), 629
commit()
Session interface, 718
Transaction objects, 807
UserTransaction interface, 810
connect(), 494
connectToMailServer(), 781
continue authenticate(), 948
copyMessages(), 775
createAQueueAndSendOrder(), 732
createBrowser(), 728
createConnectionConsumer(), 728, 740
createDurableConnectionConsumer(), 740
createDurableSubscriber(), 740
createPublisher(), 740
createQueue(), 728
createQueueConnection(), 728
createQueueSession(), 728
createReceiver(), 729
createRegistry, 500
createSender(), 728
createSocket(), 523
createStatement(), 224
createSubcontext(), 586
createSubscriber, 740
createTemporaryTopic(), 740
createTopic(), 740
createTopicConnection(), 739
createTopicSession(), 740
defineClass(), 866
deleteRow(), 265
deletesAreDetected(), 268
destroy(), 101, 1072
destroySubcontext(), 586
digest(), 919
doDelete(), 1080
doGet(), 1080
doOptions(), 1080
doPost(), 1080
doPrivileged(), 898
doPut(), 1080
doTrace(), 1080
ejbActivate(), 1252
BMP entity beans, 1285
CMP entity beans, 1295
stateful session beans, 1258
ejbCreate(), 1252
application-specific session bean home interfaces, 1271
BMP entity beans, 1284
CMP entity beans, 1295
stateful session beans, 1256
ejbFindByPrimaryKey(), 1283
ejbLoad(), 1285, 1295

ejbPassivate(), 1252
- *BMP entity beans, 1285*
- *CMP entity beans, 1295*
- *stateful session beans, 1258*

ejbPostCreate(), 1284
ejbRemove(), 1252
- *BMP entity beans, 1284*
- *CMP entity beans, 1295*
- *EJBObject interface, 1265*
- *stateful session beans, 1256*

ejbStore(), 1285, 1295
encodeRedirectURL(), 1105
encodeURL(), 1105
end(), 812
endDocument(), 1040
equals(), 890
execute(), 221, 227
executeBatch(), 275
executeQuery(), 220, 227
executeQueryScrollForward-Only(), 256
executeQueryScrollInsensitive ReadOnly(), 256
executeQueryScrollSensitive-ReadOnly(), 256
executeUpdate(), 221, 227
exists(), 775
exportACertificateFromAKey-Store(), 915
expunge(), 775
extendedOperation(), 663
findClass(), 866, 868
findCustomersWhoOrderedFor-MoreThan(), 436
firePropertyChange(), 156
fireVetoableChange(), 158
first(), 253
flushBuffer(), 1098
forName(), 868
forward(), 1091
generate token(), 956
generateCertificate(), 908
generateCRLs(), 908
generateHTMLBody(), 996
generateHTMLClose(), 996
generateHTMLHeader(), 996
get policy, 963
getActions(), 890
getAddress(), 628
getAlgorithm(), 906
getAllByName(), 628
getAppletInfo(), 102
getArray(), 282-283
getArrayPropertyName(), 155
getAsciiStream(), 281
getAttribute(), 1106
getAttributeDefinition(), 638
getAttributes(), 283-284
getAttributeSyntax-Definition(), 638
getBaseType(), 282
getBeanInfo(), 160
getBinaryStream(), 280
getBufferedReader(), 1088
getBufferSize(), 1096
getByName(), 628
getCallerPrincipal, 1326
getCatalogName(), 234
getCatalogs(), 241
getCatalogSeparator(), 242
getCharacterEncoding(), 1086, 1096
getCharacterStream(), 281
getChildNodes(), 1050
getClientID(), 717
getColumnClass(), 236-237
getColumnClassName(), 234
getColumnCount(), 234
getColumnDisplaySize(), 234
getColumnLabel(), 234
getColumnName(), 234
getColumnPrivileges(), 242
getColumns(), 242
getColumnType(), 234
getColumnTypeName(), 234
getComment(), 1107
getConnection()
- *ConnectToDatabase class, 218*
- *database connections, 305*
- *databases, 242*
- *JDBC connections, 215*

getContentLength(), 1088
getContentType(), 1086
getContext(), 898, 1074
getCookies(), 1107
getCreationTime(), 1106
getDatabaseProduct-Name(), 242
getDatabaseProduct-Version(), 242
getDefaultFolder(), 772
getDefaultInstance(), 770
GetDisplayName(), 631
getDomain(), 1107
getDriverName(), 242
getDriverVersion(), 242
getEJBHome(), 1265, 1271
getEJBMetaData(), 1272
getEncoded(), 908
getEnumeration(), 728
getErrorCode(), 203
getEveryAttributeUsing-GetAttribute(), 653
getEveryAttributeUsing-Search(), 652
getExceptionListener(), 717
getExportedKeys(), 242
getFetchDirection(), 255
getFetchSize(), 255
getFile(), 153
getFirstChild(), 1050
getFolder(), 772
getHandle(), 1265
getHomeHandle(), 1271
getHomeInterfaceClass(), 1272
getHostAddress(), 628
getHostName(), 628
getIcon(), 162
getImplementation(), 1055
getImportedKeys(), 242
getIndexedPropertyName(), 155

getInitialContext(), 733
getInitParameter()
ServletConfig interface, 1074, 1123
ServletContext interface, 1075, 1124
getInitParameterNames()
ServletConfig interface, 1074, 1123
ServletContext interface, 1075
getInputStream(), 1088
getInstance(), 771, 916, 920, 930
getInstance(String), 907
getKey(), 910
getKeyStore(), 915
getLastAccessedTime(), 1106
getLastChild(), 1050
getLastModified(), 1080
getLength(), 1033, 1050
getLocale(), 1086, 1096
getLocales(), 1086
getLocalHost(), 628
getMajorVersion(), 1075
getMaxAge(), 1107
getMaxConnections(), 242
getMaxInactive-Interval(), 1106
getMaxStatements(), 242
getMessage(), 775
getMessageCount(), 775
getMessageListener(), 719
getMessages(), 775
getMessageSelector(), 726
getMimeType(), 1075
getMinorVersion(), 1075
getMode(), 775
getMoreResults(), 231
getName(), 881, 1326
getNameDispatcher(), 1075, 1090
getNewMessageCount(), 775
getNewOrders(), 731
getNextException(), 203
getNextSibling(), 1050
getNextWarning(), 203
getNodeName(), 1050
getNodeType(), 1050
getNodeValue(), 1050
getNumericFunctions(), 299
getObject(), 899
getObjectProperty(), 722
getOutputStream(), 1096
getOwnerDocument(), 1050
getParameter(), 1088
getParameterInfo(), 102
getParameterNames(), 1088, 1124
getParameterValues(), 1088
getParent(), 775
getParentNode(), 1050
getPath(), 1107
getPermanentFlags(), 775
getPermissions(), 895
getPolicy(), 895
getPooledConnection(), 307
getPreviousSibling(), 1050
getPrimaryKey(), 1265
getPrimaryKeys(), 242
getProperties(), 771
getProperty(), 771
getPropertyNames(), 722
getProtocol(), 1086
getProvider(), 772
getQueueName(), 728
getRealPath(), 1075
getReference(), 588
getRegistry, 500
getRemoteAddr(), 1088
getRemoteHost(), 1088
getRemoteInterfaceClass(), 1272
getRequestDispatcher(), 1090, 1075
getRequestURL(), 1089
getResource(), 1075
getResourceAsStream(), 1075
getResultSet()
QueryServerImplementation class, 435
Result Sets, 231
SQL arrays, 282-283
getRollbackOnly(), 1325
getRow(), 253
getSchema(), 638
getSchemaClassDefinition(), 638
getSchemaName(), 234
getSchemas(), 241
getScheme(), 1086
getSecure(), 1107
getSecurityManager(), 869
gctSelectedAttributesUsing-Search(), 652
getServerInfo(), 1075
getServerName(), 1088
getServerPort(), 1088
getServlet(), 1076
getServletContext(), 1074
getServletInfo(), 1072
getServletName(), 1074, 1123
getSimpleProperty-Name(), 153
getSQLState(), 203
getSQLTypeName()
SQLData interface, 285
Struct interface, 283
getStatus(), 807
getStore(), 772, 775
getStringFunctions(), 299
getSubString(), 281
getSystemFunctions(), 299
getTableName(), 234
getTablePrivileges(), 242
getTables(), 241
getTableTypes(), 242
getTimeDateFunctions(), 299
getTopicName(), 740
getTransacted(), 719
getTransport(), 778
getType(), 775
getTypeInfo(), 242
getTypeMap(), 285
getUDTs, 279
getUIDValidity(), 775

getUnavailableSeconds(), 1072
getUnreadMessageCount(), 775
getUpdateCount(), 231
getURL(), 242
getUserName(), 242
getValue(), 1106
getVersion(), 1106
getWriter(), 1096
getXAResource(), 310
hasChildren, 1050
hasfeature(), 1055
hashCode(), 890
HTTP request, 373-374
identifyORB(), 812
ignorableWhitespace(), 1040
implies(), 881, 890
include(), 1091
init()
applets, 101
GenericServlet class, 1074
Servlet interface, 1072
initSign(), 921-922
insertABLOBType(), 290
insertAStructTypeData(), 291
insertBatchofRowsUsingPreparedStatement(), 277
insertBatchofRowsUsingStatement(), 277
insertRow(), 264
insertsAreDetected(), 268
isAfterLast(), 253
isBeforeFirst(), 253
isCallerInRole(), 1326
isCaseSensitive(), 234
isDefinitelyWritable(), 234
isEqual(), 918
isFirst(), 253
isIdentical(), 1265
isLast(), 253
isNew(), 1104
isNullable(), 234
isReadOnly(), 234, 881
isRequestedSessionIdFromCookie(), 1104
isRequestedSessionIdFromURL(), 1104
isRequestedSessionIdValid(), 1104
isSearchable(), 234
isSecure(), 1131, 1086
isSession(), 1272
isStatelessSession(), 1272
isWritable(), 234
last(), 253
length(), 280-281
list types(), 668
list()
context listings, 587
Folder class, 775
RMI/JRMP lookups, 515
listBindings(), 588
listNamesAndBindings(), 598
load(), 910
loadClass(), 866, 868
loadLibrary(), 1359
locale(), 1043
log(), 1074-1075
logIt(), 926-929
lookup(), 514
lookupBoundObject(), 594
lookupLink(), 590
main(), 911
modifyAttributes(), 643
moveToCurrentRow(), 264
moveToInsertRow(), 264
names, 36
narrow()
PortableRemoteObject class, 494
RMI/IIOP lookups, 515
native, 1359
newDocument(), 1058
newDocumentBuilder(), 1059
newInstance(), 1045, 1059
newPermissionCollection(), 881
newSAXParser(), 1045
next(), 253
notationDecl(), 1035
notifyAuditEvent(), 151
onExcption(), 717
onMessage()
JMSReceiver interface, 1350
MessageListener interface, 719
QueueConsumer class, 737
open(), 775
othersDeletesAreVisible(), 267
othersInsertsAreVisible(), 267
othersUpdatesAreVisible(), 267
ownDeletesAreVisible(), 267
ownInsertsAreVisible(), 267
ownUpdatesAreVisible(), 267
parameters, 36
parse(), 1043, 1058
ParseDisplayName(), 631
parsePostData(), 1090
parseQueryString(), 1090
parseResultData(), 237-239
position(), 281
predefined database, 298-299
prepareCall(), 299
prepareStatement(), 226
previous(), 253
print(), 1098
printAvailableSchemas(), 245
printColumnsInATable(), 246-247
println(), 1098
printMessage(), 782
printNameNodeMap(), 1056-1058
printPrimaryKeysInATable(), 247
printResultSetNthRow(), 261
printResultSetRowsInForwardDirection(), 259
printResultSetRowsInReverseDirection(), 260
printServletConfigInformation(), 1077

printServletContextInformation(), 1076-1077
printTablesInAllSchemas(), 245-246
printTablesInASchemas(), 246
processingInstruction(), 1040
publish(), 740
query(), 668
queryForCustomersWhoSpend GreaterThan(), 357
queryForOrderFromState(), 357
readData(), 298
readMessages(), 783
readSQL(), 285
rebind(), 586, 639
receive(), 726
received credentials(), 953
receiveNoWait(), 726
recover(), 719
Ref(), 282
refresh(), 895
refreshRow(), 268
register(), 436
registerOutParameter(), 301
registerReceiverHostAndPort(), 357
registerSynchronization(), 807
relative(), 253
remote, 478
remove(), 1265, 1271
removeAttribute(), 1088
removeAttributes(), 653
removeAuditListener(), 151
removePropertyChangeListener(), 156, 166
removeVetoableChangeListener(), 158
replaceAttributes(), 653
required rights(), 954
resolve(), 515
resolveEntity(), 1037
retrieveAStructTypeData(), 291
retrieveBLOBType(), 290
rollback()
  Session interface, 718
  Transaction objects, 807
  UserTransaction interface, 810
rowDeleted(), 267
rowInserted(), 267
rowUpdated(), 267
scope, 36
search()
  directory searches, 639
  Folder class, 776
searchFrom(), 785
searchUsingFilterUsingSearch(), 653
sendAMessage(), 784
sendRedirect(), 1098
sequence diagram notation, 36
service(), 1072, 1074
set credentials(), 952
set override policy(), 963
setArrayPropertyName(), 155
setAttribute(), 1088
setAutoCommit(), 265
setBufferSize(), 1096
setCertificateFactory, 915
setClientID(), 717
setCommand(), 297
setComment(), 1107
setContentLength(), 1096
setDateHeader(), 1098
setDomain(), 1107
setEntityContext(), 1282, 1294
setExceptionListener(), 717
setFetchDirection(), 255
setFetchSize(), 255
setFile(), 153
setFlags(), 775
setHeader(), 1098
setIndexedPropertyName(), 155
setIntHeader(), 1098
setLocale(), 1096
setLocator(), 1040
setLoginTimeout(), 215
setMaxAge(), 1107
setMaxInactiveInterval(), 1105
setMessageListener(), 719
setMultipartDataSource(), 763
setNextException(), 203
setNextWarning(), 203
setNodeValue(), 1050
setObject(), 166
setObjectProperty(), 722
setPasswordAuthentication(), 772
setPath(), 1107
setPolicy(), 895
setProperties(), 217
setPropertyEditorClass(), 165
setProvider(), 772
setReadOnly(), 881
setRef(), 282
setRollbackOnly(), 807, 1325
setSecure(), 1107
setSecurityManager(), 869
setSessionContext(), 1252
setSimplePropertyName(), 153
setSocketImplFactory(), 361
setStatus(), 1098
setTransactionIsolation(), 266
setTransactionTimeout(), 807
setTypeMap(), 285
setValue(), 1106
sign(), 921-922
SignedObject.getObject(), 924
start()
  applets, 101
  Connection interface, 716
  XAResource interface, 812
startDocument(), 1040
startElement(), 1040
startServer(), 339
startup(), 1349-1350
stop(), 101, 716
supportResultSetType(), 254
supportsANSI92EntryLevelSQL(), 242

supportsANSI92FullSQL(), 243
supportsANSI92IntermediateSQL(), 242
supportsCoreSQLGrammar(), 243
supportsExtendedSQLGrammar(), 243
supportsFullOuterJoins(), 243
supportsLikeEscapeClause(), 243
supportsLimitedOuterJoins(), 243
supportsMinimumSQLGrammar(), 243
supportsOuterJoins(), 243
suspend(), 808
TemporaryQueue(), 728
toStub(), 494
unexportObject(), 494
unparseEntityDecl(), 1035
unsetEntityContext(), 1283, 1294
update(), 918, 921-922
updateRow(), 264
updatesAreDetected(), 268
valueBound(), 1106
valueUnBound, 1106
verify evidence(), 959
verify(), 908, 924
writeData(), 298
writeSQL(), 285

Microsoft
Active Directory Service (ADS), 636, 686-687, 1202
Component Object Model. *See* COM
Distributed Network Architecture (DNA), 50, 1202
Distributed Component Object Model. *See* DCOM
DNA (Distributed Network Architecture), 50
Internet Information Server (IIS), 978
Java SDK Web site, 531
Java Virtual Machine (MSJVM), 528, 531
Platform SDK Build environment Web site, 548
Visual J++, 531

Microsoft Message Queue Server (MSMQ), 712, 1202
Microsoft Transaction Server (MTS), 1202
midl DNS name, 626
midl utility, 531, 535, 543, 548
MIME (Multipurpose Internet Mail Extensions), 372-373, 757
MIME messages, 757, 764, 767
MimeBodyPart class, 767
MimeMessage class, 766
MimeMessage object, 760
MimeMultipart class, 767
MimePart objects, 766
Minimum CORBA, 389, 1372
miscellaneous operators, 66
Model-View Controller pattern, 51
models, 31
assurance problems, 822-823
availability, 831-832
maintainability, 833
reliability, 829-830
safety, 834
security, 827-828
components, 43
generic, 43
interfaces, 44-46
standard, 49-50
Swing, 132
transactions, 798
UML (Unified Modeling Language), 32
class diagrams, 32-35
dynamic behavior diagrams, 36

modems (network connections), 332
Modifier class, 77
modifyAttributes() method, 643
modularity (object-oriented software development), 23
module tests, 48
MOM (Message Oriented Middleware), 711-713
MOMA (Message-Oriented Middleware Association), 712
monikers, 532, 630-631, 700
Mosaic, 367
moveToCurrentRow() method, 264
moveToInsertRow() method, 264
Mozilla LDAP SDK Web site, 649
MQSeries, 712
MSDN Web site, 531
MSJVM (Microsoft Java Virtual Machine), 528, 531
MSMQ (Microsoft Message Queue Server), 712, 1202
MTS (Microsoft Transaction Server), 1202
multicast sockets, 361
MulticastSocket class, 359
Multipart class, 763
multipart messages, 763
Multipart object, 760
MultipartDataSource interface, 763
multiplexing (JRMP), 473
multiplicity (class diagram notation), 34
Multipurpose Internet Mail Exetensions (MIME), 372-373, 757
MVC (Model-View Controller) pattern, 51

N

N-tier architecture, 320
N-version software, 831
Name interface, 586
name tokens attribute, 1022
name-to-object bindings, 579
named topics, 740
names
classes, 32
compound, 609
databases
catalog, 241
JNDI, 305-307
product, 242
schema, 241
DNS top-level, 626
DOM nodes, 1050
events, 591, 593
files, 605-608
folders, 775
hostnames, 335
JDBC drivers, 242
JNDI, 586-587
LDAP standard RDN, 648
methods, 36
naming services, 577-578
objects, 36
servletsnames, 1074
simple, 609
XML
attributes, 1015
elements, 1014
NamespaceChangeListener interface, 592
namespaces (XML), 1014-1015
Naming class, 499
naming contexts, 578-579
Naming Service, 396
COM/DCOM, 534
CORBA, 461-463
naming services, 576
communications, 116
CORBA. *See* CosNaming
DCOM, 629-631
DNS, 626-628
files, 605-608
handles, 577
JNDI. *See* JNDI
names, 577-578
naming contexts, 578-579
overview, 576-577
RMI. *See* RMI
NamingEvent class, 591
NamingExceptionEvent objects, 591
NamingListener interface, 591
narrow() method
PortableRemoteObject class, 494
RMI/IIOP lookups, 515
native header files, 1360
native language implementation, 1360-1361
native methods, 1359
native platform interface libraries, 58
navigation (class diagram notation), 34
NDS (Novell Directory Service), 646-647
negation (!) symbol, directory search filter, 642
NES (Netscape Enterprise Server), 978
nested transaction model, 798
nesting code, 70
net DNS name, 626
net utility (TCP/IP), 336
NetPermission permissions, 886
Netscape
Enterprise Server (NES), 978
FastTrack Server, 978
Navigator, 970, 974
Server Application Programming Interface (NSAPI), 977
SSL v3 algorithm, 848-849
Visigenics ORB, 424
netstat utility (TCP/IP), 336
network access TCP/IP layer, 331-332
network client architecture (distributed systems), 321-322
network computing
communication layers, 327-329
history, 326
protocols, 327-329
Network Information System (NIS), 645-646
network layer (OSI communications layer model), 328
network server architecture (distributed systems), 323-324
network sniffers, 336
Network Solutions Web site, 627
network-client models, 322
network-server models, 323-324
networks
computer communications, 326
subnets, 333
Never attribute (transactions), 796
newDocument() method, 1058
newDocumentBuilder() method, 1059
newInstance() method
DocumentBuilderFactory class, 1059
SAXParserFactory class, 1045
newPermissionCollection() method, 881
newSAXParser() method, 1045
next() method, 253

NIS (Network Information System), 645-646
NMTOKEN attribute, 1022
Node interface, 699, 1050, 1052-1054
NodeList interface, 1050
nodes (DOM), 1050-1052
lists, 1050
name retrieval, 1050
parents/children, 1050
types, 1052-1058
non-keyed collections, 82-84
nondurable subscribers, 740
nonprintable characters (URLs), 368
nonrepudiation (NR), 848
CORBA Security, 956-960
security, 828
tokens, 956-959
Nonrepudiation package, 940
NoSuchEntityException, 1236
notation
class diagrams, 32-34
declarations, 1021
sequence diagrams, 36
Notation subinterface (Node interface), 1052
notationDecl() method, 1035
notes (class diagram notation), 34
notifyAuditEvent() method, 151
NotSupported attribute (transactions), 796
Novell Directory Service (NDS), 646-647
NR. *See* nonrepudiation
NRCredentials objects, 956
NRVerificationResult objects, 959
NSAPI (Netscape Server Application Programming Interface), 977
Number class, 76
numbered lists (HTML documents), 991

O

OAD (Object Activation Daemon), 444
oadutil utility, 444
OASIS (Organization for the Advancement of Structured Information Standards), 1012
object activation (distributed systems), 318
Object Activation Daemon (OAD), 444
object adapters, 393, 444
BOA-based server registration, 444-445
IDL server registration, 446-447
POA-based server registration, 447-448
Object class, 74
Object Collection Service, 397
Object Data Management Group (ODMG), 187
Object Database Management System. *See* ODBMSs
Object Definition Language (ODL), 187
object identification (safety), 835
Object Interchange Format (OIF), 187
object linking and embedding (OLE), 528
Object Management Architecture (OMA), 388
Object Management Group (OMG), 386-387, 424
object name binding and lookup (distributed systems), 318
Object Naming Service. *See* CosNaming
Object Oriented Concepts, Inc., 423
object persistence services, 1197
Object Query Language (OQL), 187
Object Request Broker. *See* ORB
object scope, 1154
object timestamps (safety), 835
Object Transaction Monitors (OTMs), 1195-1196
Object Transaction Service. *See* OTS
object-oriented behavioral definition/analysis (reliability), 830
object-oriented programming. *See* OOP
object-oriented software development, 20
abstraction, 24
behavior, 24
classes, 21-22
dependencies, 24
elements, 21-22
enterprise importance, 23-24
handles, 22
methods, 21
modularity, 23
packages, 22
problem solving, 23
process, 24-25
assembly, 29
configuration, 30
deployment, 30
detailed design, 28
development phases, 30-31
implementation, 28-29
iteration, 30
maintenance, 30
overview, 25
preliminary system design, 27-28
project charters, 26

requirements analysis, 26-27
system tests, 30
thread tests, 29
unit testing, 29
programming history, 20
reuse, 23
variables, 21
visibility levels, 22
object/relational hybrid databases, 190-192
<OBJECT> tag, 973
ObjectChangeListener interface, 592
ObjectInput interface, 89
ObjectInputStream class, 89
ObjectInputValidation interface, 87
ObjectMessage interface, 723
ObjectNotFoundException, 1236
ObjectOutput interface, 89
ObjectOutputStream class, 89
objects, 1159-1164
AccessControlContext, 898
AccessControlException, 904
AccessDecision, 953
AccessibleContext, 135
activatable, 515-517
client, 521-522
examples, compiling/running, 523
server registrars, creating, 519-521
servers, creating, 517-518
ActivationGroupDesc, 520
AppleContext, 100
AuditChannel, 956
AuditDecision, 954
AuditEventType, 954
CodeSource, 898
collections. *See* collections
COM, 528
connection
database meta-data, 242
JDBC, 202
ConnectionMetaData, 717
Credentials, 949
Customer, 350-352
DatagramPacket, 360
DatagramSocket, 359
DCOM, 630-631
defined, 68
DigestOutputStream, 919
directory
attributes, 637-638, 643
bindings, 639
DragSource, 134
DropTarget, 134
guarded, 899
implicit objects, 1155, 1159-1160
IRObjects, 449
Java (persistable), 278-279
JSP object manipulation examples, 1160-1164
KeyPair, 907
KeyPairGenerator, 907
LinkRef, 590
Message, 760
MessageDigest, 919
MimeMessage, 760
MimePart, 766
Multipart, 760
names, 36
NamingExceptionEvent, 591
NRCredentials, 956
NRVerificationResult, 959
Offer, 670
order, 352-353
PageContext object, 1152-1155
Permission, 881
PermissionCollection, 881, 898
PooledConnection, 307
PreparedStatement, 226, 229
Principal, 1326
PropertyChangeEvents, 155
PropertyChangeSupport, 156
PropStruct, 666
protecting, 916, 918-919, 921-922, 924
ProtectionDomain, 898
Provicer, 772
QueueConnectionFactory, 728
QueueSender, 728
RefAddr, 589
reference, 80
referenceable, 588-591
RemoteRef, 483
RequiredRights, 954
RightsCombinator, 954
RightsListHolder, 954
RowSet, 295
RowSetEvent, 295
RowSetListener, 295
SAX, 1032, 1035
scope, 1154, 1160
SecurityManager, 869
sequence diagram notation, 36
Serializable, 922, 924
Server, 340-342
ServiceTypeRepository, 666
Session, 759
Signature, 919-922
signed, 922-924
SimpleStatementExample, 225
SpecifiedProps, 670
Statement, 219
Synchronization, 807
TCP/IP client, 353-357
TemporaryTopic, 740
TopicConnection, 739
TopicConnectionFactory, 1347
TopicPublisher, 740
TopicSession, 740
TopicSubscriber, 740
UnsolicitedNotification, 664
UnsolicitedNotificationEvent, 664
VetoableChangeSupport, 158
XAConnection, 310
Objects By Value
CORBA, 409
behavioral sequences, 410-411

example, 412-414
marshaling, 411-412
types, 410
RMI, 476-477
ObjectStreamClass class, 87
ObjectStreamConstants class, 89
ObjectStreamField class, 87
OBJECT_FACTORIES property (JNDI contexts), 584
Observable class, 81
Observer interface, 81
obtaining. *See* finding
ODBC (open database connectivity), 195, 243
ODBMSs (Object Database Management Systems), 186
architecture, 186-187
object/relational translations, 190-192
RDBMSs, compared, 188-190
ODL (Object Definition Language), 187
ODMG (Object Data Management Group), 187
Offer objects, 670
OIF (Object Interchange Format), 187
Oil and Gas Industry Exploration and Production Facility, 399
<OL> tag, 991
OLE (object linking and embedding), 528
OLEview tool, 565
OMA (Object Management Architecture), 388
OMG (Object Management Group), 386-387, 424
onException() method, 717
onMessage() method
JMSReceiver interface, 1350
MessageListener interface, 719
QueueConsumer class, 737
OOP (object-oriented programming), 20
classes. *See* classes
handles, 22
maintainability, 834
methods. *See* methods
packages, 22
reliability, 830
visibility levels, 22
open database connectivity (ODBC), 195, 243
Open Systems Interconnection (OSI) communications layer model, 327-328
open() method, 775
OpenFusion Naming Service Web site, 612
opening folders, 775, 783
operation identification (safety), 835
operation syntax (class diagram notation), 33
Operations interface, 699
OperationsFactory interface, 698
operators, 726
arithmetic, 65
assignment, 66
bitwise, 65
logical, 66
miscellaneous, 66
relational, 65
OPTIONS requests, 374
OQL (Object Query Language), 187
OR relation symbol (|), content model element declaration, 1021
or-associations (class diagram notation), 34
Oracle, 424
Oracle8I Database Server, 424
ORB (Object Request Broker), 388-390
architecture, 390
class, 424
client side components, 391-392
libraries, 421-423
minimumCORBA, 389
OrbixWeb, 423
product vendors, 423-424
protocols, 392
server side components, 392-393
ORBacus, 423
OrbixCOMet, 423
OrbixEvents, 423
OrbixNames, 423
OrbixSecurity, 423
OrbixTrader, 423
OrbixWeb, 423
OrbixWeb Orbix Names Web site, 612
Orblets, 422
Order bean, 1241
Order class, 492-493
order object, 352-353
ordered lists (HTML documents), 991
OrderManager class, 731-732
OrderManagerSession bean, 1242
OrderRequest class, 731
org DNS name, 626
org.omg.CosTransactions package, 812
org.omg.CosTSPortability package, 812
org.omg.NRService package, 941
org.omg.Security package, 941
org.omg.SecurityAdmin package, 941
org.omg.SecurityLevel1 package, 941
org.omg.SecurityLevel2 package, 941

org.omg.SecurityReplaceable package, 941
org.xml.sax package, 1031
org.xml.sax.helpers package, 1031
Organization for the Advancement of Structured Information Standards (OASIS), 1012
osagent utility, 463
OSI (Open Systems Interconnection) communications layer model, 327-328
othersDeletesAreVisible() method, 267
othersInsertsAreVisible() method, 267
othersUpdatesAreVisible() method, 267
OTMs (Object Transaction Monitor), 1195-1196
OTS (Object Transaction Service), 398, 801
EJB/CORBA connectivity, 1343
interfaces, 802-803
types, 801
outcomes (enterprises), 13-14
outer joins (JDBC queries), 221, 243
OutputStream class, 87
OutputStreamWriter class, 90
ownDeletesAreVisible() method, 267
ownInsertsAreVisible() method, 267
ownUpdatesAreVisible() method, 267

P

<P> tag, 991
<P ALIGN> tag, 991
Package class, 77
packages, 22
BIND, 627
class diagram notation, 32
Common Secure Interoperability (CSI), 940
CORBA Security, 940-941
DEC-CIOP/SECIOP, 941
J2EE JavaMail, 701
java.awt, 130
java.awt.color, 136
java.awt.datatransfer, 134
java.awt.dnd, 134
java.awt.event, 131
java.awt.geom, 136
java.awt.im, 137
java.awt.image, 136
java.awt.image.renderable, 136
java.awt.print, 135
java.beans, 144
java.beans.beancontext, 144, 148
java.io, 87, 606
java.lang, 73
java.lang.ref, 73, 79-80
java.lang.reflect, 73, 77-78, 160
java.math, 73
java.rmi, 467-469
java.rmi.activation, 469
java.rmi.dgc, 469
java.rmi.registry, 469
java.rmi.server, 469
java.security.acl, 861
java.security.cert, 873
java.security.interfaces, 874
java.security.spec, 874
java.sql, 201
java.util, 73
javax.accessibility, 135
javax.activation, 701
javax.directory.ldap, 651
javax.infobus, 167
javax.mail, 760
javax.mail.event, 760
javax.mail.internet, 760
javax.mail.search, 760
javax.naming, 581
javax.naming.directory, 581
javax.naming.event, 581
javax.naming.ldap, 581, 662
javax.naming.spi, 581
javax.rmi, 469
javax.rmi.CORBA, 469
javax.servlet, 1072
javax.servlet.http, 1078
javax.sql, 201
javax.swing.border, 133
javax.swing.colorchooser, 133
javax.swing.event, 132
javax.swing.filechooser, 133
javax.swing.plaf, 133
javax.swing.plaf.basic, 133
javax.swing.plaf.metal, 133
javax.swing.plaf.multi, 133
javax.swing.table, 133
javax.swing.text, 133
javax.swing.text.html, 133
javax.swing.text.html.parser, 133
javax.swing.text.rtf.RTFEditorKit, 134
javax.swing.tree, 133
javax.swing.undo, 134
javax.transaction, 805
javax.transaction.xa, 805
javax.xml.parsers, 1031
Nonrepudiation, 940
org.omg.CosTransactions, 812
org.omg.CosTSPortability, 812
org.omg.NRService, 941
org.omg.Security, 941
org.omg.SecurityAdmin, 941
org.omg.SecurityLevel1, 941
org.omg.SecurityLevel2, 941
org.omg.SecurityReplaceable, 941
org.xml.sax, 1031

org.xml.sax.helpers, 1031
preliminary design, 28
RMI, 469-470
SECIOP, 940
SECIOP/DCE-CIOP, 941
security, 861, 873
Security Functionality Level 1, 940
Security Functionality Level 2, 940
Security Mechanism, 940
Security Replaceability, 940

page context (JSPs), 1152-1157
page directive (JSPs), 1145-1147
PageContext object, 1152-1155
paragraphs (HTML documents), 991
parameter entity declarations, 1021
ParameterDescriptor class, 160
parameters
Authenticator (Session objects), 771
methods (sequence diagram notation), 36
SearchTerm (search)() methods), 776
Servlet request handling, 1088

parse() method
Parser interface, 1043
DocumentBuilder class, 1058

parseDisplayName() method, 631
parsePostData() method, 1090
parseQueryString() method, 1090
Parser interface, 1032, 1043
parser interfaces (SAX), 1043-1046
parseResultData() method, 237-239
parsing (DOM), 1058-1060
Part interface, 760
partitioning domains, 851
PASSWORD attribute (<INPUT> tag), 995
password-based authentication, 845
PasswordAuthentication class, 772
passwords (JavaMail sessions), 772
PDM (Product Data Management) systems, 1204
PeerLogic, 423
people/users (enterprise component), 12
Perl, 1005
Permission class, 881
Permission object, 881
PermissionCollection class, 881
PermissionCollection object, 881, 898
permissions, 880-881
AllPermission, 882
architecture, 881
AWTPermission, 885
checkGuard() method, 881
checking, 904
custom, 890
equals() methods, 890
getActions() method, 890
hashCode() method, 890
implies() method, 881, 890
isReadOnly() method, 881
NetPermission, 886
newPermissionCollection() method, 881
Permission class, 881
Permission object, 881
PermissionCollection class, 881
PermissionCollection object, 881
PropertyPermission, 886
reflectPermission, 886-887
security, 890
SecurityPermission, 888-889
setReadOnly() method, 881
SocketPermission, 883
UnresolvedPermission, 885

persistable Java objects, 278-279
persistence
distributed systems, 318
JavaBean, 163-164

Persistence Service (COM/DCOM), 535
Persistent Object Service (POS), 397
PersonalJava, 1371
PhantomReference class, 80
phased project development, 30-31
phases (JavaServer Pages), 1137
physical data models, 175
physical layer (OSI communications layer model), 328
physical resources/assets (enterprise component), 12
PIDL (pseudo-IDL), 611-612
Ping JRMP message, 473
ping utility (TCP/IP), 336
PingAck JRMP message, 473
pipe character (|), content model element declaration, 1021
PipedInputStream class, 89
PipedOutputStream class, 89
PipedReader class, 90
PipedWriter class, 90
PKCS (Public Key Cryptography Standards), 847
PlainSocketImpl class, 361
platform dependencies
component model interfaces, 46
distributed systems, 317

platform machine attacks, 980
platforms, 1192-1193. *See also* frameworks
application-specific, 1203-1205
J2EE, 107
J2SE, 108
OTMs (Object Transaction Monitor), 1195-1196
security, 981
TP (Transaction Processing) monitors, 1193-1194
Plug-in Content Handler, 970-972
plug-ins (Java), 973
HTML Converter tool, 974
HTML Specification, 974
installing, 973-974
JRE designation, 974-975
updates, 972
plus symbols (+), content model element declaration, 1020
POA (Portable Object Adapter), 444
POA-based server registration, 447-448
point-to-point message queuing
JMS, 727-729
JMS example, 729
order manager, 731-732
order requests, 731
queue consumer, 735-738
queue supplier, 732-735
point-to-point messaging, 708
pointers, 22, 577
policies
CORBA Security, 962-963
defining, 893
referencing properties, 893
security, 891
API, 895
creating, 893-894
files, 905
formatting, 891-892
tool, 894
Policy interface, 962
PooledConnection objects, 307
pooling entity beans, 1280
POP3 (Post Office Protocol Version 3), 758
POP3 v1.1.1 download, 779
Portable Object Adapter (POA), 444
PortableRemoteObject class, 494
PortableRemoteObjectDelegate interface, 494
ports, 334-335
POS (Persistent Object Service), 397
position() method, 281
Post Office Protocol Version 3 (POP3), 758
POST requests, 374
postconditions (use-case analysis), 27
precompiled deployment procedure considerations (JSPs), 1180
preconditions (use-case analysis), 27
predefined database methods, 298-299
preliminary design packages, 28
preliminary system design, 27-28
prepareCall() method, 299
prepared statements, 226-231
PreparedStatement interface, 202, 219, 226
PreparedStatement object, 226, 229
prepareStatement() method, 226
presentation layer (OSI communications layer model), 328
previous() method, 253
primary keys
container managed fields, 1293
database tables, 242, 247
entity beans, 1280-1281, 1292
RDBMS tables, 180
primitive types (IDL-to-Java mappings), 403-404
Principal objects, 1326
PrincipalAuthenticator interface, 948
principals (security), 844, 906-915
print() method, 1098
printAvailableSchemas() method, 245
printColumnsInATable() method, 246-247
PrinterJob class, 135
printing
JavaMail messages, 782-783
UI support, 135
println() method, 1098
printMessage() method, 782
printNameNodeMap() method, 1056-1058
printPrimaryKeysInATable() method, 247
printResultSetNthRow() method, 261
printResultSetRowsInForwardDirection() method, 259
printResultSetRowsInReverseDirection() method, 260
printServletCofigInformation() method, 1077
printServletContextInformation() method, 1076-1077
PrintStream class, 89
printTablesInAllSchemas() method, 245-246

printTablesInASchemas() method, 246
PrintWriter class, 90
priori application creation errors (assurance), 823
priori data creation errors (assurance), 823
PrismTech, 423
private keys, 921-924
private visibility, 22
PrivateKey interface, 908
PriviledgedExceptionAction interface, 898
problem solving (object-oriented software development), 23
procedures (stored), 176
procesing instructions (XML documents), 1016-1017
Process interface, 74
process management (availability), 832
processes (assurance), 821-822
ProcessingInstruction subinterface (Node interface), 1053
processingInstruction() method, 1040
producers (JMS messages), 725-726
Product Data Management (PDM systems), 1204
product names (databases), 242
ProgIDs (Program Identifiers), 630
programming model (J2EE), 107
programs. *See* applications; utilities
project charters, 26, 47
properties
APPLET (JNDI contexts), 584
array (JavaBeans), 155
AUTHORITATIVE (JNDI contexts), 584
ava (CompoundName constructor), 587
BATCHSIZE (JNDI contexts), 584
beginquote (CompoundName constructor), 587
beginquote2 (CompoundName constructor), 587
bound (JavaBeans), 155-157
CompoundName constructor, 586-587
constrained (JavaBeans), 157-159
direction (CompoundName constructor), 586
DNS_URL (JNDI contexts), 584
endquote (CompoundName constructor), 587
endquote2 (CompoundName constructor), 587
escape (CompoundName constructor), 587
file-system JNDI SPI, 608
ignorecase (CompoundName constructor), 587
indexed (JavaBeans), 155
INITIAL_CONTEXT_FACTORY (JNDI contexts), 584
JavaMail sessions, 771
JMS messages, 722-723
JMSCorrelationID (message headers), 721
JMSCorrelationIDAsBytes (message headers), 721
JMSDeliveryMode (message headers), 721
JMSDestination (message headers), 721
JMSExpiration (message headers), 721
JMSMessageID (message headers), 721
JMSPriority (message headers), 721
JMSRedelivered (message headers), 721
JMSReplyTo (message headers), 721
JMSTimestamp (message headers), 721
JMSType (message headers), 721
JMSX, 722-723
JNDI contexts, 584
LANGUAGE (JNDI contexts), 584
messages, 722
OBJECT_FACTORIES (JNDI contexts), 584
provicer-specific (messages), 721
PROVIDER_URL (JNDI contexts), 584
referencing, 893
REFERRAL (JNDI contexts), 584
RMI Registry JNDI SPI, 625
RMI/IIOP CosNaming JNDI SPI, 625
SECURITY_AUTHENTICATION (JNDI contexts), 584
SECURITY_CREDENTIALS (JNDI contexts), 584
SECURITY_PRINCIPAL (JNDI contexts), 584
SECURITY_PROTOCOL (JNDI contexts), 584
separator (CompoundName constructor), 586
simple (JavaBeans), 153
STATE_FACTORIES (JNDI contexts), 584
trimblanks (CompoundName constructor), 587
typeval (CompoundName constructor), 587
URL_PKG_PREFIXES (JNDI contexts), 584

Properties class, 86
properties files, 91-93
property change listeners, 156
property editors, 164, 166
Property Service, 397
PropertyChangeEvnet objects, 155
PropertyChangeListener interface, 155
PropertyChangeSuppport objects, 156
PropertyDescriptor class, 160
PropertyEditor interface, 164
PropertyEditorManager class, 164
PropertyEditorSupport class, 164
PropertyPermission permissions, 886
PropStruct objects, 666
protected visibility, 22
protecting
- message digests, 916-919
- objects, 916-924
- signatures, 919-922

ProtectionDomain object, 898
protocols, 327-329
- ARP, 333
- commit, 178
- communications, 115-116
- CORBA Security supported, 961
- defined, 327
- GIOP (General Inter-ORB Protocol), 392-395
- HTTP (Hypertext Transfer Protocol), 366, 370
  - *behavior, 370-372*
  - *cookies, 379*
  - *handling, 377*
  - *MIME (Multipurpose Internet Mail Extensions), 372-373*
  - *outside sessions, tracking, 379*
  - *request header types, 375*
  - *request methods, 373-374*
  - *requests, 373-375*
  - *responses, 375-377*
  - *Web communications, 115*
- HTTP-NG, 380
- ICMP, 333
- IIOP (Internet Inter-ORB Protocol), 392-393
  - *CORBA communications, 115*
  - *EJB application server environments, 1218*
  - *IORs (Interoperable Object References), 395*
  - *overview, 394-395*
  - *RMI communications, 116*
  - *versions, 395*
- IMAP, 758-759
- interface communications, 1218
- IP, 332
- JRMP, 116, 469
  - *headers, 472*
  - *identifiers, 472*
  - *message types, 472-473*
  - *multiplexing, 473*
  - *RMI, 471-473*
- ORB, 392
- POP3, 758
- secure socket, 932
- SLIP, 332
- SMTP, 758
- SSL. *See* SSL
- TCP, 333-334
- TCP/IP. *See* TCP/IP
- TLS (Transport Layer Security), 848
- two-phase commit, 800
- UDP, 333-334
- WAP, 1372
- WML, 1372
- WTLS, 848

Provider class, 874
Provider objects, 772
provider roles (application servers), 1212-1214
provider-specific properties, 721
providers (assurance), 819-820
PROVIDER_URL property (JNDI contexts), 584
proxies
- DCOM, 530
- Jini, 679-680

proxy pattern, 52
ProxyConsumer interface, 754
ProxySupplier interface, 754
pseudo-IDL (PIDL), 611-612
pseudo-operations (class diagram notation), 33
public identifiers (DTD headers), 1019
Public Key Cryptography Standards), 847
public visibility, 22
publish() method, 740
publish-subscribe messaging, 709, 738-740
publish-subscrive messaging example, 741-747
pull messaging, 709
pull model (CORBA Event Service), 751-753
push messaging, 709
push model (CORBA Event Service), 748-750
PushbackInputStream class, 88
PushbackReader class, 90
PUT requests, 374
pysical token-based authentication, 845

Q

QOP (quality of protection) levels, 960
QoS (Quality of Service), 711
qualified association (class diagram notation), 34
quality (messaging), 711
queries
- JDBC statements, 221
- RDBMSs, 184-185

query languages, 176
query managers, 176
Query Service, 397
query service specific database interface example, 347-350
query() method, 668
queryForCustomersWhoSpendGreaterThan() method, 357
queryForOrderFromState() method, 357
QueryServer interface, 480-481
QueryServerImplementation class, 436-439, 487-492, 496
QueryServiceProtocol interface, 347
question marks (?), content model element declaration, 1020
QueueConnection interface, 728
QueueConnectionFactory objects, 728
QueueConsumer class, 735-738
QueueSender objects, 728
QueueSupplier class, 732-735

R

RADIO attribute (<INPUT> tag), 995
RandomAccessFile interface, 88
RC2 algorithm, 843
RC4 algorithm, 843
RC5 algorithm, 843
RDBMSs (Relational Database Management Systems), 179
- architecture, 179-180
- catalogs, 180-181
- data model diagram conventions, 185-186
- embedded SQL, 193-195
- ODBMSs, compared, 188-190
- queries, 184-185
- relational/object translations, 190-192
- schemas, 180-181
- SQL (Structured Query Language), 180-181
- tables, 179
  - *columns, 179, 182-183*
  - *creating/deleting, 181-182*
  - *customizing, 182-183*
  - *foreign keys, 180*
  - *primary keys, 180*
  - *rows, 179, 183*

RDNs (Relative Distinguished Names), 648
readData() method, 298
Reader class, 87
readMessages() method, 783
readSQL() method, 285
rebind() method
- directory object bindings, 639
- JNDI bindings, 586

receive() method, 726
received credentials() method, 953
receiveNoWait() method, 726
recover() method, 719
RecoveryCoordinator interface (OTS), 803
redo capabilities (Swing), 134
Ref interface, 282
RefAddr objects, 589
Reference class, 80
reference implementation servers, 107
- EJB application deployment, 1247-1248
- startup/deployment, 1120-1122

reference objects, 80
Referenceable interface, 588
referenceable objects (JNDI), 588-591
ReferenceQueue interface, 80
references, 22, 577
references (SQL3), 282
referencing
- applets, 103-104
- properties (policy files), 893

REFERRAL property (JNDI contexts), 584
reflection, 77-78
reflectPermission permissions, 886-887
refresh() method, 895
refreshRow() method, 268
regedit.exe program, 565
reggie, 677, 681
Register interface, 665
register() method, 436
registerOutParameter() method, 301
registerReceiverHostAndPort() method, 357
registerSynchronization() method, 807
registrars (server). *See* server registrars
registration
- BOA-based servers, 444-445
- CORBA interfaces, 421
- DCOM client-side interfaces, 543

DCOM clients, 570-571
DCOM servers, 543, 564
javareg utility, 564
registry files, 564-565
viewing, 565-567
IDL servers, 446-447
POA-based servers, 447-448
RMI/IIOP servers, 503
dynamic class downloading, 504
naming service, 504
registration example, 505-506
RMI/JRMP servers, 498
dynamic class downloading, 500-502
interfacing with RMI registries, 499-500
registration example, 502-503
Registry, starting, 499
security configurations, 499
Synchronization objects, 807
registry files, 564-565
Registry interface, 500
regular JDBC statements, 219, 221
Relational Database Management Systems. *See* RDBMSs
relational operators, 65
relational/object hybrid databases, 190-192
Relationship interface, 699
Relationship Service, 396
relative distinguished names (RDNs), 648
relative() method, 253
reliability, 829
assurance, 819
assurance problems, 822, 829-830
CBA analysis/design, 830
checksums, 831
COTS evaluation, 831
detailed object-oriented design, 830
interface specification, 830
N-Version software, 831
object-oriented behavioral definition/analysis, 830
OOP, 830
risk reduction plans, 830-831
signatures, 831
software version specification/checking, 831
testing, 830
transaction management, 831
watchdog timers, 831
reliable transport communications (distributed systems), 317
remote administration (maintainability), 834
remote entity bean interfaces, 1299
application-specific, 1301
architecture, 1300
examples, 1301-1303
generic, 1301
Remote interface, 477
remote interfaces, 471, 1234
Remote Method Invocation. *See* RMI
remote methods, 478
remote process interfaces (Jini), 679
remote resource purpose (XLink), 1027
remote resource titles (XLink), 1027
remote session bean interfaces, 1263
application-specific, 1264
architecture, 1263
examples, 1265-1266
generic, 1265
RemoteObject class, 482
RemoteRef objects, 483
RemoteStub class, 507
remove() method, 1265, 1271
removeAttribute() method, 1088
removeAttributes() method, 653
removeAuditListener() method, 151
RemoveException, 1236
removePropertyChangeListener() method, 156, 166
removeVetoableChangeListener() method, 158
replaceAttributes() method, 653
Reply GIOP message, 394
ReplyHandler interface, 756
repositories
implementation, 443-444
interface, 448-454
accessing, 449
contents, viewing, 450-454
objects, 449
Request GIOP message, 394
request handling (servlets), 1086
abstractions, 1086, 1088-1090
attributes, 1088
body, 1088
examples, 1092-1095
HttpServletRequest interface, 1089
HttpUtils class, 1089-1090
inquisitive calls, 1086
locale preference information, 1086
parameters, 1088
requests, dispatching, 1090-1091
schemes, 1086
security, 1086
ServletInputStream class, 1088
ServletRequest interface, 1086, 1088
socket-level information, 1088

request header types (HTTP), 375
request methods (HTTP), 373-374
RequestDispatcher interface, 1090-1091
requests (HTTP), 373-375
Required attribute (transactions), 796
required rights() method, 954
RequiredRights objects, 954
requirements analysis, 26-27
RequiresNew attribute (transactions), 796
RESET attribute (<INPUT>) tag, 995
residual risks (assurance), 825
resolve() method, 515
resolveEntity() method, 1037
resource attribute (XLink), 1026
Resource interface (OTS), 803
resource management (availability), 832
resource managers (RMs), 177-178
resource naming (servlets), 1128
response generation (servlets), 1095
abstractions, 1096-1099
buffer size, 1096
content length, 1096
examples, 1099-1103
flushing, 1098
HttpServletResponse interface, 1098-1099
locale, 1096
ServletOutputStream class, 1098
ServletResponse interface, 1096-1098
write information, 1098
responses (HTTP), 375-377
restrictions (J2EE), 110-111
result sets
forward-only, 251
scroll-insensitive, 251
scroll-sensitive, 251
scrollable, 250-251
creating, 251-252
driver support, 254-255
example, 255-262
scrolling backwards, 260
scrolling forward, 259
scrolling from specific rows, 261
scrolling through, 252-254
updateable, 262-263
adding rows, 264
creating, 263
deleting rows, 264
driver support, 268
example, 269-274
refreshing rows, 268
update visibility, 265-268
updates, deleting, 264
updating rows, 263-264
Result Sets (JDBC), 231
column class information, 236-237
customizing, 231-233
customizing example, 234-239
information about, 233-234
scrolling through, 237-239
storing, 236
Result Sets MetaData example, 234-239
ResultSet class, 253
ResultSet interface, 231
ResultSetMetaData interface, 231
retrieveAStructTypeData() method, 291
retrieveBLOBType() method, 290
ReturnData ReturnValue JRMP message, 473
reuse (object-oriented software development), 23
RightsCombinator objects, 954
RightsListHolder objects, 954
risk assessments (assurance problems), 823-824
risk level evaluations (risk assessments), 824
risk reduction plans (assurance), 824-825
availability, 832
costs, 825
maintainability, 833-834
reliability, 830-831
safety, 835
security, 828-829
selecting, 826-827
risks (assurance), 827
Rivst Shamir Adleman (RSA) algorithm, 844
RMI (Remote Method Invocation), 50, 116, 466
activatable objects, 515-517
client, 521-522
examples, compiling/running, 523
server registrars, creating, 519-521
servers, creating, 517-518
activation daemon (rmid), 470, 678, 692
activation framework, 692-693
architecture, 467-469
clients, 322, 471
communications, 116
Compiler (rmic), 469, 493
CORBA Objects By Value, 476-477
custom sockets, 523-525
development process, 471
EAI (Enterprise Application Integration), 1364-1365
IIOP. *See* IIOP/RMI
infrastructure configuration, 470

interface definition examples, 479-481
interface example, 619-620
interfaces, 477-479
BeeShirts.com customer information, 480
RMI client callbacks, 479
RMI server application queries, 480-481
J2EE future, 122
Java-to-IDL mapping, 474-476
JRMP. *See* JRMP/RMI
naming services, 618
interface example, 619-620
interfaces, 618
JNDI SPI, 618-625
Registry JNDI SPI properties, 625
RMI/IIOP CosNaming JNDI SPI properties, 625
RMI/IIOP server example, 622-624
RMI/JRMP server example, 620-622
overview, 466-467
packages, 469-470
Registry. *See* rmiregistry
remote reference layer, 468
server registrar, 471
servers, 324, 471
stubs
creating, 471
downloading, 500
tools, 469-470
transport layer, 469
XML integration, 1062

RMI-to-OMG IDL mappings, 474-476
rmic (RMI Compiler), 469, 493
RMIClassLoader, 866
RMIClientSocketFactory interface, 523
rmid (RMI activation daemon), 470, 678, 692
RMIException class, 479
rmiregistry, 470
interfacing with, 499-500
RMI/IIOP server registration, 503-506
RMI/JRMP server registration, 498
dynamic class downloading, 500-502
example, 502-503
interfacing with RMI registries, 499-500
security configurations, 499
starting, 499
RMISecurityManager class, 499, 871
RMIServerSocketFactory interface, 524
RMs (resource managers), 177-178, 800
role attribute (XLink), 1027
Role interface, 699
role-based authorization, 850
rollback techniques (availability), 832
rollback() method
Session interface, 718
Transaction objects, 807
UserTransaction interface, 810
route utility (TCP/IP), 336
row sets, 295-297
architecture, 295
cached, 297
implementations, 297
internal state/behavior, 297-298
JDBC, 297
Web, 297
rowDeleted() method, 267
rowInserted() method, 267
rows
HTML tables, 992
RDBMS tables, 179, 183
updateable result sets
adding, 264
deleting, 264
refreshing, 268
updating, 263-264
RowSet interface, 295
RowSet objects, 295
RowSetEvent objects, 295
RowSetInternal interface, 295-297
RowSetListener interface, 295
RowSetListener objects, 295
RowSetMetaData interface, 295
RowSetReader interface, 295
RowSetWriter interface, 295
rowUpdated() method, 267
RSA (Rivst Shamir Adleman) algorithm, 844
RSAPublicKey interface, 908
RTF (Swing package), 134
Runnable interface, 96
running
applications, 1361
DCOM clients, 543
runtime engine, disabling, 972
runtime environment, 57-59
runtime execution engine, 58
Runtime interfaces, 74

S

safety, 834
assurance, 819
problem models, 834
problems, 822
command feedback, 835
formal specification, 835
formal verification, 835

information coding, 835
object identification, 835
object timestamps, 835
operation identification, 835
risk reduction plans, 835
vital fail-safe hardware, 835
watchdog timers, 835

SAX (Simple API for XML), 1031-1032
application handler interfaces, 1035-1043
document handlers, 1040-1043
DTD handler, 1035-1037
entity resolvers, 1037-1038
error handlers, 1039-1040
architecture, 1032
core objects, 1032, 1035
example, 1045-1046
parser interfaces, 1043-1046

SAXException, 1039
SAXException class, 1033
SAXParseException, 1039
SAXParseException class, 1033
SAXParser class, 1043-1044
SAXParserFactory class, 1045
scalability (CORBA), 419-420
scenario diagrams, 36
schema names (databases), 241
schemas
databases, 175, 246
directory, 638-639
RDBMSs, 180-181
Servlet request handling, 1086

SCMs (Service Control Managers), 699
scope
methods, 36
object scope, 1154, 1160
specifications, 57

script language runtime engines, 977
script-based interface generators, 139
<SCRIPT> tag, 1001-1002
scripting. *See also* JSPs
server-side, 139
elements (JSPs), 1149-1152
declarations, 1149-1150
expressions, 1150-1151
scriptlets, 1151-1152
languages, 1001-1002
client-side, 1002
JavaScript, 1002-1004
Perl, 1005
server-side, 1001
VBScript, 1004-1005

Scripting Language Runtime Engine, 970
scriptlets (JSPs), 1151-1152
scroll-insensitive result sets, 251
scroll-sensitive result sets, 251
scrollable result sets, 250-251
creating, 251-252
driver support, 254-255
example, 255-262
scrolling
backwards, 260
forward, 259
from specific rows, 261
through, 252-254

ScrollableResultSetExample class, 256-258
SDK (Software Development Kit), 63-64
search results (directory), 640
search() method
directory searches, 639
Folder class, 776

SearchControls class, 641
searches
controls/filters, 641-642
directory, 639-640
folders, 776
JavaMail messages, 785-786

searchFrom() method, 785
SearchResult class, 640
SearchTerm parameter (search() methods), 776
searchUsingFilterUsingSearch() method, 653
SECIOP package, 940
SECIOP/DCE-CIOP package, 941
secret keys, 841-843
SecretKey interface, 930
secure communication (servlets), 1131
secure document serving interface logic, 981
Secure Hash Algorithm (SHA), 843
Secure Hash Algorithm 1 (SHA-1), 843
Secure Socket Layer. *See* SSL
secure socket protocols, 932
secure Web server architecture, 981
SecureClassLoader, 866
SecureRandom (cryptographic engines), 875
security, 827
access control, 861, 896-898
administration, 852-853
applets, 856-857
application servers, 1229
assurance, 819
problem models, 827-828
problems, 822
auditing, 123, 828, 852
authentication. *See* authentication
authenticity, 828
authorization, 828, 849-851
BEA WebLogic Server, 1330-1331
browsers, 971-973
certificates, 846-848, 908-915
class loader, 864-865
confidentiality, 828

cookies, 1131
CORBA. *See* CORBA security
core security architecture, 859-861
cryptography, 839-842
asymmetric keys, 842-844
message digests, 842-843
symmetric keys, 841-843
distributed systmes, 318
domains, 851-852
EJBs, 1325
assembly elements, 1327
authentication model limitations, 1331
BeeShirts.com example, 1332-1333
declarative, 1327-1329
programmatic, 1326-1327
role references, 1327
vendor-specific access control mapping, 1329-1330
vendor-specific identity/authentication, 1330-1331
encrypting, 929-930
extensions, 929
cryptography, 929-930
JAAS, 933
secure socket, 932
guarded objects, 899
history, 856, 858
identifying principals, 906, 908, 910-915
identity, 828
integrity, 828
interoperability (J2EE future), 123
J2EE future, 122
JAAS, 862
JCA. *See* JCA
JCE, 861-862
JSSE, 862
keys, 906, 910-915
model overview, 838-839
nonrepudiation, 828
objects, protecting, 916-924
permissions. *See* permissions
platforms, 981
policies, 891
API, 895
creating, 893-894
defining, 893
example, 905
formatting, 891-892
referencing properties, 893
principals, 844
risk reduction plans, 828-829
RMI/JRMP servers, 499
security package, 861
security-critical availability, 828
security.acl package, 861
servlet request handling, 1086
servlets, 1130-1132
signing code, 924
SSL (Secure Socket Layer), 848-849
thread safety (threading APIs), 93-96
trusted code model, 858
version improvements, 857-858
Web servers, 979-981
security auditing, 981
SECURITY_AUTHENTICATION property (JNDI contexts), 584
Security class, 874
SECURITY_CREDENTIALS property (JNDI contexts), 584
Security Functionality Level 1 package, 940
Security Functionality Level 2 package, 940
security manager, 868
AccessController class, 871
checkPermission() method, 871
customizing, 871-873
default, 869
getSecurityManager() method, 869
instantiation, 869
Jini, 681
RMISecurityManager class, 871
SecurityManager class, 869, 871
SecurityManager objects, 869
setSecurityManager() method, 869
Security Mechanism package, 940
security policy tool, 894
SECURITY_PRINCIPAL property (JNDI contexts), 584
Security Replaceability package, 940
Security Service, 535, 398
security technology domains, 852
security-critical availability, 828
SecurityManager, 899-903
SecurityManager class, 869-871
SecurityManager interfaces, 74
SecurityManager object, 869
SecurityPermission permissions, 888-889
SECURITY_PROTOCOL property (JNDI contexts), 584
selecting
JDBC drivers, 205, 208
Jini lookup services, 681
risk reduction plans, 826-827
selectors (JMS messages), 725-726
semicolon (;), RDNs/DNs, 648
sendAMessage() method, 784

sendRedirect() method, 1098
sensitive HTTP requests/response data, 972, 980
separator property (CompoundName constructor), 586
sequence diagrams, 36
SequenceInputStream class, 89
ser file extension, 60
Serial Line Internet Protocol (SLIP), 332
Serializable interface, 87, 147
Serializable object, 922, 924
SerializablePermission permissions, 890
serialization (I/O), 87
serialization files, 60
server analysis tools, 981
server command request attacks, 980
server information request attacks, 980
Server object, 340-342
server redundancy, 981
server registrars
- activatable, 519-521
- CORBA, 421
- RMI, 471

server-side EJB development, 1237-1238
server-side ORB components, 392-393
server-side scripting, 139
server-side scripting languages, 1001
ServerHelper class, 342-346
servers
- activatable, 517-518
- application. *See* application servers
- BEA WebLogic
  - *EJB application deployment, 1248-1249*
  - *startup/deployment, 1122*
- BOA-based, registering, 444-445
- COM/DCOM, 533
- CORBA, 324, 428
  - *client receiver implementation example, 435*
  - *creating, 430-431, 434-440*
  - *customer implementation example, 431-435*
  - *delegation, 428, 432*
  - *DSI-based, 440-443*
  - *generated serializable data example, 439-440*
  - *implementing, 420*
  - *inheritance, 428, 431*
  - *query server implementation example, 436-439*
- CosNaming, example, 616-618
- DCOM, 324, 529, 548
  - *client receiver implementation example, 553*
  - *compiling, 563-564*
  - *CORBA query server implementation example, 554-559*
  - *creating, 549*
  - *generated CoQueryServer class example, 562-563*
  - *generated IQueryServer interface example, 561-562*
  - *generated Order class example, 560*
  - *implementation example, 549, 551-552*
  - *registering, 543, 564-567*
- EJB application, 108
- HTTP, 324
  - *class downloads, 501*
  - *ClassFileServer, 501*
  - *Jini configurations, 678*
  - *RMI tool, 470*
- IDL, registering, 446-447
- POA-based, registering, 447-448
- reference implementation
  - *EJB application deployment, 1247-1248*
  - *startup/deployment, 1120-1122*
- RMI, 324, 471
- RMI/IIOP, 494
  - *compiling, 497*
  - *creating, 494*
  - *dynamic class downloading, 504*
  - *example, 622-624*
  - *implementation examples, 495*
  - *naming service, 504*
  - *registration, 503*
  - *registration example, 505-506*
  - *RMI customer implementation example, 496*
  - *RMI query server implementation example, 496*
- RMI/JRMP, 481
  - *compiling, 493*
  - *creating, 481, 483*
  - *dynamic class downloading, 500-502*
  - *example, 620-622*
  - *implementation examples, 483*
  - *interfacing with RMI registries, 499-500*
  - *registration, 498-499*
  - *registration example, 502-503*
  - *RMI client receiver implementation example, 486-487*
  - *RMI customer implementation example, 483-486*
  - *RMI query server implementation example, 487-492*
  - *security configurations, 499*
- TCP/IP, 324
- Web. *See* Web servers
- Web application, 108

ServerSocket class, 337
Service class, 772
Service Control Managers (SCMs), 699
Service Provider Interfaces. *See* SPIs
service() method
GenericServlet class, 1074
Servlet interface, 1072
services
activation. *See* activation services
adding to containers, 149
application, 1228-1229
application integration, 1197
assurance, 16
COM/DCOM, 534-535
communications, 16, 113, 116-117
configuration
application frameworks, 1197
application servers, 1229
CORBA, 396-398
CORBA security. *See* CORBA, Security
CosNaming. *See* CosNaming
deployment, 108, 1197
directory. *See* directory services
distributed communications, 1228
exporting, 666, 668
importing, 668, 670
management, 108, 1197
messaging. *See* messaging services
naming. *See* naming services
object persistence, 1197
RMI/IIOP Naming, 424, 470, 612
servlets, 1126-1127
activation, 1127
availability, 1133-1134
EJBs, 1128
resource naming, 1128
security, 1130-1132
threads, 1127
transactions, 1128-1129
Store, 759
trading. *See* trading services
transactions. *See* transactions, services
Transport, 759
types, listing, 668
vendor-specific naming, 463
ServiceTypeRepository objects, 666
Servlet interface, 1072, 1074
servlet-based interface generators, 139
ServletConfig interface, 1074, 1123
ServletContext interface, 1074-1076, 1124
ServletException class, 1071
ServletInputStream class, 1088
ServletOutputStream class, 1098
ServletRequest interface, 1086-1088
ServletResponse interface, 1096-1098
servlets, 50, 120, 139, 381-382, 1007
activation, 1127
API v2.2 Web site, 1068
application configuration, 1125-1126
architecture, 1068-1070
availability, 1133-1134
configuring, 1123-1124
container environment information, 1075
context configuration, 1124-1125
deployment, 1110-1111
BEA WebLogic server, 1122
reference implementation server, 1120-1122
Web-based application directory structure, 1119-1120
Web-based application format, 1111-1117
Web-based application procedures, 1118-1119
EJBs, 1128
exceptions, 1071-1072
framework, 1072
framework examples, 1076-1078
GenericServlet class, 1074
HTTP, 1078
BeeShirts.com examples, 1081-1085
framework, 1078-1081
session management. See HTTP, session management
interfaces, 1071
lifecycle, 1070
log messages, 1075
names, 1074
request handling, 1086
abstractions, 1086-1090
attributes, 1088
body, 1088
dispatching requests, 1090-1091
examples, 1092-1095
HttpServletRequest interface, 1089
HttpUtils, 1089-1090
inquisitive calls, 1086
locale preference information, 1086
parameters, 1088
schemes, 1086
security, 1086
ServletInputStream class, 1088
ServletRequest interface, 1086-1088
socket-level information, 1088

resource naming, 1128
resources, 1075
response generation, 1095
abstractions, 1096-1099
buffer size, 1096
content length, 1096
examples, 1099-1103
flushing, 1098
HttpServletResponse interface, 1098-1099
locale, 1096
ServletOutputStream class, 1098
ServletResponse interface, 1096-1098
write information, 1098
security, 1130-1132
service management, 1126-1127
Servlet interface, 1072-1074
ServletConfig interface, 1074
ServletContext interface, 1074-1076
specification v2.2 Web site, 1068
system pathnames, 1075
threads, 1127
transactions, 1128-1129
XML integration, 1062

session beans, 1235, 1250
client interfaces, 1263-1266
configuring, 1273-1274
deployment, 1275-1276
home interfaces, 1267-1273
remote interfaces, 1263-1265
stateful. *See* stateful session beans
stateless. *See* stateless session beans

Session class, 768

Session interface (JMS), 717

session layer (OSI communications layer model), 328

session management (HTTP), 1103-1104
abstractions, 1104-1107
Cookie class, 1106-1107
cookies, 1106-1107
embedding ID information into URLs, 1105
examples, 1107-1110
HttpSession interface, 1104-1106
HttpSessionBinding Event class, 1106
HttpSessionBindingListener interface, 1106
maximum inactive intervals, 1105
nature, 1104
statistical timing, 1106

Session objects (JavaMail), 759

SessionBean interface, 1251, 1256

SessionContext interface, 1252

sessions
JavaMail, 768, 771-772
JMS, 717-719

SessionSynchronization interface, 1325

set credentials() method, 952

Set interface, 84

set override policy() method, 963

setArrayPropertyName() method, 155

setAttribute() method, 1088

setAutoCommit() method, 265

setBufferSize() method, 1096

setCertificateFactory() method, 915

setClientID() method, 717

setCommand() methods, 297

setComment() method, 1107

setContentLength() method, 1096

setDateHeader() method, 1098

setDmain() method, 1107

setEntityContext() method, 1282, 1294

setExceptionListener() method, 717

setFetchDirection() method, 255

setFetchSize() method, 255

setFile() method, 153

setFlags() method, 775

setHeader() method, 1098

setIndexedPropertyName() method, 155

setIntHeader() method, 1098

setLocale() method, 1096

setLocator() method, 1040

setLoginTimeout() method, 215

setMaxAge() method, 1107

setMaxInactiveInterval() method, 1105

setMessageListener() method, 719

setMultipartDataSource() method, 763

setNextException() method, 203

setNextWarning() method, 203

setNodeValue() method, 1050

setObject() method, 166

setObjectProperty() method, 722

setPasswordAuthentication() method, 772

setPath() method, 1107

setPolicy() method, 895

setProperties() method, 217

setPropertyEditorClass() method, 165

setProvider() method, 772

setReadOnly() method, 881

setRef() method, 282

setRollbackOnly() method, 807, 1325

setSecure() method, 1107
setSecurityManager() method, 869
setSessionContext() method, 1252
setSimplePropertyName() method, 153
setSocketImplFactory() method, 361
setStatus() method, 1098
setters (simple properties), 153
setTransactionIsolation() method, 266
setTransactionTimeout() method, 807, 810
setTypeMap() method, 285
setValue() method, 1106
severity evaluations (risk assessments), 823
SGML (Standard Generalized Markup Langauge), 1011
SHA (Secure Hash Algorithm), 843
SHA-1 (Secure Hash Algorithm 1), 843
shared libraries, 1361
ShoppingCartSession bean, 1242
ShoppingCartSession remote interface, 1266
ShoppingCartSessionEJBean, 1259-1260, 1262
ShoppingCartSessionHome, 1272-1273
Short class, 76
show attribute (XLink), 1027
sign() method, 921-922
Signature class, 920
Signature object, 919, 921-922
signatures, 919-922
- cryptographic engines, 875
- reliability, 831

signed objects, 922, 924
SignedBy field, 892
SignedObject.
signing
- code, 924-929
- jar files, 928

Simple API for XML. *See* SAX
simple attribute (XLink), 1026
simple links (XLink), 1026-1027
Simple Mail Transfer Protocol (SMTP), 758
simple names, 609
simple properties (JavaBeans), 153
SimpleBeanInfo class, 160
SimpleDateFormat class, 97
SimpleStatementExample object, 225
SimpleTimeZone class, 98
SingleThreadModel interface, 1127
singleton pattern, 51
sites. *See* Web sites
skeletons, 324
- CORBA, 428-430
- creating, 428-430
- DCOM, 548, 567
- EJBs, 1234
- IIOP, 497
- RMI
  - *creating, 471*
  - *downloading, 500*
- RMI/IIOP, 511-514
- RMI/JRMP, 506, 508-510
- static (CORBA), 454-458

SLIP (Serial Line Internet Protocol), 332
smart proxying, 419
SMTP (Simple Mail Transfer Protocol), 758
socket-level information, 1088
SocketImpl class, 361
SocketImplFactory interface, 361
SocketPermission permissions, 883
sockets, 334
- custom, 361-362, 523-525
  - *client side, 523*
  - *server-side, 524*
- custom factories, 361
- multicast, 361
- programming, 336-337
  - *classes, 337*
  - *customer object example, 350-352*
  - *order object example, 352-353*
  - *query service specific database interface example, 347-350*
  - *TCP/IP client callback handler example, 357-358*
  - *TCP/IP client object example, 353-357*
  - *TCP/IP query service protocol marker interface example, 347*
  - *TCP/IP server socket handler example, 343-346*
  - *TCP/IP server socket listener example, 340-342*
  - *UDP datagrams, 359, 361*

SoftReference class, 80
software. *See* applications
Software Development Kit (SDK), 63-64
software version specification/checking, 831
SortedMap interface, 85
SortedSet interface, 84
sound (Java Sound API), 137
source code files, 60. *See also* code
- Code Conventions for the Java Programming Language Web site, 60
- compiling, 63

JavaDoc Tool home page, 60
structure, 60-62
spawning (DCOM), 570-571
special characters
JSP (JavaServer Pages), 1144
XML, 1016
specification (J2EE), 107
SpecifiedProps objects, 670
speech (Java Speech API), 137
SPIs (Service Provider Interfaces), 45, 580
component, 45
Connector, 1369
file-system JNDI
CosNaming service, 614-618
file-names, 606-608
RMI naming services, 618-625
RMI/JRMP registry JNDI SPI Web site, 619
J2EE future, 122
Java, 50
JNDI, 646-647
JNDI LDAP SPI
search example, 653-662
Web site, 651
JNDI SPI, 645-646
Web site, 581
SQL (Structured Query Language), 180
arrays, 282-283
compliance, 242-243
core types, 181
data types example, 288-294
BLOB inserts/retrievals, 290-291
custom type inserts/retrievals, 292-294
structure inserts/retrievals, 291-292
Distinct types, 284
embedded, 193-195
RDBMSs, 180-181
queries, 184-185
tables, 181-183
statements
scrollable result sets, 258
updateable result sets, 270
structures, 283-284, 291-292
types, database supported, 242
SQL/Java mappings, 239-241
SQL3 data types, 279-280
arrays, 282-283
BLOBs/CLOBs, 280-282
Distinct types, 284
references, 282
structures, 283-284
SQLData interface, 285
SQLException class, 203
SQLExceptions, 203
SQLWarning exception, 203
SSL (Secure Socket Layer), 848, 862, 932
client authenticaion, 973, 980
client certificate-based authentication (servlets), 1130
confidentiality, 973, 980
JSSE, 862
Netscape SSL v3 algorithm, 848-849
server authentication, 973, 980
Stack class, 84
standalone applications, 121, 205
CORBA, 419
enterprise, 1208-1209
standard component models, 49-50
Standard Generalized Markup Language (SGML), 1011
start() method
applets, 101
Connection interface, 716
XAResource interface, 812
startDocument() method, 1040
startElement() method, 1040
startServer() method, 339
startup() method
JMSReceiver interface, 1349-1350
T3StartupDef interface, 1349
state management (application servers), 1228
stateful CGI applications, 1000
stateful session beans, 1235, 1255-1256
architecture, 1256
creating, 1256
deleting, 1256
example, 1259-1262
interface rules, 1258-1259
passivation/activation, 1257-1258
stateless session beans, 1235, 1250
architecture, 1251
context, 1252
creating, 1252
deleting, 1252
example, 1253-1255
interface rules, 1252-1253
passivation/activation, 1252
Statement interface, 202, 219
Statement object, 219
statements
ALTER_TABLE, 182-183
CREATE_CATALOG, 181
CREATE_DATABASE, 181
CREATE_SCHEMA, 181
DELETE_FROM, 183
do/while, 73
DROP_TABLE, 182
INSERT_INTO, 183
JDBC, 219
creating/executing example, 222-226
joins (queries), 221

LIKE clauses, 221-222
maxmimum allowed, 242
outer joins (queries), 221
prepared, 226-227
prepared, creating/executing example, 227-231
regular, 219-221
UPDATE, 183
statements (SQL)
scrollable result sets, 258
updateable result sets, 270
STATE_FACTORIES property (JNDI contexts), 584
static CORBA bridges, 571
static stubs (CORBA), 454, 456-458
static variables (class diagram notation), 33
Status interface (JTA), 807
stereotypes (class diagram notation), 33
stop() method
applets, 101
Connection interface, 716
Store class, 772
store event model, 768
Store service, 759
stored procedures, 176, 298
calling example, 302-304
creating, 299-301
executing, 301
predefined database methods, 298-299
storing
applets, 103
BMP entity beans, 1285
certificates, 910
CMP entity beans, 1295
keys, 910
persistable Java objects, 278
PreparedStatement objects, 229
Result Sets, 236
strategy pattern, 51
StreamMessage interface, 723
streams
byte I/O, 87-89
character I/O, 89-90
streams (communication), 363
String class, 77
StringBuffer class, 77
StringReader class, 90
StringRefAddr class, 589
StringWriter class, 90
Struct interface, 283
structure. *See also* formatting
JAR files, 62
manifest files, 62
source code files, 60
Code Conventions for the Java Programming Language Web site, 60
example, 60-62
JavaDoc Tool home page, 60
SQL, 283-284, 291-292
structure control (HTML), 988
body, 990
formatting, 991
frames, 992-993
headings, 988
hyperlinks, 990-991
images, 991
meta-data, 989
tables, 992
tags, 988
titles, 989
Structured Query Language. *See* SQL,
stubs. *See* skeletons
subcontexts (JNDI), 586
subdomains, 627, 851
subinterfaces. *See also* interfaces
Attr, 1053
CDATASection, 1053
CharacterData, 1053
Comment, 1053
Document, 1054
DocumentFragment, 1054
DocumentType, 1054
Element, 1054
Entity, 1053
EntityReference, 1053
Notation, 1052
ProcessingInstruction, 1053
Text, 1053
subject-observer pattern, 52
SUBMIT attribute (<INPUT> tag), 995
subnets, 333
SubtransactionAwareResource interface (OTS), 803
Sun Microsystems JavaSoft Organization, 423
Supports attribute (transactions), 797
supportsANSI92EntryLevelSQL() method, 242
supportsANSI92FullSQL() method, 243
supportsANSI92Intermediate SQL() method, 242
supportsCoreSQLGrammar() method, 243
supportsExtendedSQLGrammar() method, 243
supportsFullOuterJoins() method, 243
supportsLikeEscapeClause() method, 243
supportsLimitedOuterJoins() method, 243
supportsMinimumSQLGrammar() method, 243
supportsOuterJoins() method, 243
supportsResultSetType() method, 254
suspend() method, 808
Swing, 132
components, 132-133
containers, 132

deployment, 134
events, 132
helper libraries, 133-134
layout managers, 132
library, 132
look-and-feel, 133
models, 132

symmetric keys (cryptography), 841-843

Synchronization interface
JTA, 807
OTS, 803

Synchronization objects, 807

synchronized keyword, 95-96

system
APIs, 74
architecture, overview, 112-113
component interface analysis (CBD), 47
flags (email), 763
interfaces, 74
library loading, 1359
tests
CBD, 48
object-oriented software development process, 30

System Management Common Facility, 398

systems
distributed, 316-317
evolution, 319-320
issues, 317-318
layers, 318
network client architecture, 321-322
network server architecture, 323-324
enterprise
components, 14-15
information technology, 16-17

sytle sheets (XML documents), 1029-1031

T

T3StartupDef interface, 1349

<TABLE> tag, 992

tables
databases, 242
catalogs, 241
column descriptions, 246
columns, 242
foreign keys, 242
primary keys, 242, 247
HTML documents, 992
RDBMSs, 179
columns, 179, 182-183
creating/deleting, 181-182
customizing, 182-183
foreign keys, 180
primary keys, 180
rows, 179, 183
schemas, 180
Swing component, 132-133

tag handlers (JSPs), 1182

tag libraries (JSPs), 1183-1186

tag library descriptors (TLDs), 1183-1185

taglib directive (JSPs), 1147, 1183-1185

tags (HTML), 383, 987-988
<!-->, 991
<A>, 990
<A HREF>, 990-991
attributes, 987
<B>, 991
<BODY>, 990
<BODY_ALINK>, 990
<BODY_BGCOLOR>, 990
<BODY_LINK>, 990
<BODY_TEXT>, 990
<BODY_VLINK>, 990

, 991
<EMBED>, 974
<FORM>, 994-995
<FRAMESET>, 992-993
<H1>-<H6>, 991
<HEAD>, 988
<HR SIZE>, 991
<I>, 991
<IMG SRC>, 991
<INPUT>, 994
attributes, 994-995
JavaScript, 1003
JSP tags, 1143
leading, 987
<LI>, 991
<META>, 989
<OBJECT>, 973
<OL>, 991
<P ALIGN>, 991
<P>, 991
<SCRIPT>, 1001-1002
<TABLE>, 992
<TD>, 992
<TEXTAREA>, 995
<TH>, 992
<TITLE>, 989
<TR>, 992
trailing, 987
<UL>, 991

Task Management Common Facility, 399

TCP (Transmission Control Protocol), 333-334

TCP/IP (Transmission Control Procotol/Internet Protocol), 115, 326, 329-330
applications port allocations, 335
client callback handler, 357-358
client objects, 353-357
clients, 322
communication layers, 330-331
Application, 334-335
Internet access, 332-333
network access, 331-332
Transport, 333-334
communication streams, 363
EAI (Enterprise Application Integration), 1362-1363

history, 330
implementations, 335-336
query service protocol marker interface example, 347
server socket handler example, 343-346
server socket listener example, 340-342
servers, 324
socket programming, 336-337
classes, 337
custom factories, 361
custom sockets, 361-362
customer object example, 350-352
order object example, 352-353
query service specific database interface example, 347-350
TCP/IP client callback handler example, 357-358
TCP/IP client object example, 353-357
TCP/IP query service protocol marker interface example, 347
TCP/IP server socket handler example, 343-346
TCP/IP server socket listener example, 340-342
UDP datagrams, 359, 361
tools, 335-336
UNIX configurations, 336
Windows configurations, 335

<TD> tag, 992
telephony (Java Telephony API), 137
template attribute (XSL style sheets), 1030
template data (JavaServer Pages), 1142
TemporaryQueue() method, QueueSession interface, 728
TemporaryTopic objects, 740
Terminator interface, 803
testing
applications, 29
classes interoperability, 29
components, 48
load-testing, 832
module tests (CBD), 48
reliability, 830
system
CBD, 48
object-oriented software development process, 30
TestsClient file, 1249
text
ASCII, 987
cipher, 839
clear, 839
HTML
bold, 991
color, 990
italic, 991
Swing packages, 133
Input Method Framework, 137
RTF, Swing package, 134
Swing components, 132-133
TEXT attribute (<INPUT> tag), 994-995
Text subinterface (Node interface), 1053
text-area GUI components (HTML), 995
TEXTAREA? tag, 995
TextMessage interface, 723
<TH> tag, 992
Thread class, 96
thread management, availability, 832
thread safety (threading APIs), 93-96
thread tests, 29
ThreadGroup class, 97
threading APIs
advantages, 93
example, 93-94
thread safety, 93-96
ThreadLocal class, 97
threads
APIs, 96-97
servlets, 1127
Throwable class, 76
TIE approach. *See* delegation
time
APIs, 97-98
sequence diagram notation, 36
Time class, 241
Time Services, 398
time-to-market competition, implementation, 29
timeouts (transactions), 807, 810
Timestamp class, 241
TimeZone class, 98
title attribute (XLink), 1026-1027
<TITLE> tag, 989
titles (HTML documents), 989
TLDs (tag library descriptors), 1183, 1185
TLS (Transport Layer Security), 848, 932
TMs (transaction managers), 177-178, 800
tnameserv command, 424, 470, 612
to attribute (XLink), 1028
tokens (NR), 956-959
tools. *See also* applications; utilities
appletviewer, 64
CORBA, 421-422
DeployerTool, 1312
deploytool, 1248
java, 63
Java Development Kit Development Tools, 63

Java Plug-in HTML Converter, 974
javac, 63
javadoc, 64
JavaDoc, 60
javakey, 925
jdb, 64
Jini, 677
OLEview, 565
RMI, 469-470
security policy, 894
server analysis, 981
TCP/IP, 335-336
Topic interface, 740
TopicConnection interface, 740
TopicConnection objects, 739
TopicConnectionFactory objects, 1347
TopicConsumer class, 744-747
TopicPublisher objects, 740
TopicSession objects, 740
TopicSubscriber objects, 740
TopicSupplier class, 741-744
toStub() method, 494
TP (Transaction Processing) monitors, 1193-1194
<TR> tag, 992
traceroute utility (TCP/IP), 336
tracert utility (TCP/IP), 336
TraderComponents interface, 665
Trading Object service, 396
Trading Service (COM/DCOM), 534
trading services, 635-636
communications, 117
CORBA. *See* CosTrading
Jini, 673-674
class architecture, 679-682
clients, creating, 681-682
component architecture, 674-675
creating, 679
example, 683-686
infastructure, 676-677
JavaSpaces, 677
lookup service, 677
programming model, 676
runtime environment configuration, 678
Service Registrar implementation, 680-681
tools, 677
transaction management service, 677
trailing tags, 987
Transaction interface (JTA), 807
transaction management (reliability), 831
transaction management service (Jini), 677-678
transaction managers (TMs), 177-178, 800
Transaction Processing, 1193-1194
transaction resource interfaces (XAs), 178
TransactionalObject interface (OTS), 802
TransactionFactory interface (OTS), 803
TransactionManager interface (JTA), 807
transactions, 791, 793-794
aborting, 810
atomicity, 791
attributes, 796-797
beginning, 809
consistency, 791
databases, 177-179
distributed, 310, 794
distributed systems, 318
durability, 793
EJBs, 1316-1317
bean-managed transaction demarcation, 1317-1321
container-managed transaction demarcation, 1321-1325
interoperability (J2EE future), 123
isolation, 793
isolation levels, 266-267, 797
models, 798
propagation, 1129
services, 795-796
attributes, 796-797
isolation levels, 797
JTA (Java Transaction Architecture), 804, 807
JTA application interface, 809-810
JTA Transaction Manager interface, 807-808
JTA X/Open XA interface, 810, 812
JTS (Java Transactions Service), 812-813
models, 798
OTS (Object Transaction Service), 801-803
two-phase commit protocol, 800
X/Open Distributed Transaction Processing (DTP) model, 800
servlets, 1128-1129
status, 807
suspending, 808
terminating, 810
timeouts, 807, 810
two-phase commit protocol, 800
viewing, 265-266
X/Open Distributed Transaction Processing (DTP) model, 800
Transactions/Concurrency Service (COM/DCOM), 535
TransactionService interface, 812
Transferable interface, 134

Transmission Control Protocol (TCP), 333-334
Transmission Control Protocol/Internet Protocol. *See* TCP/IP
Transport class, 777
transport event model, 768
transport layer (OSI communications layer model), 328
Transport Layer Security (TLS), 848, 932
Transport service, 759
Transport TCP/IP layer, 333-334
transports (JavaMail), 777-778
traversal behavior (extended links), 1028
TreeMap class, 85
trees (Swing component), 133
TreeSet class, 84
trimblanks property (CompoundName constructor), 587
Triple Data Encryption Standard (Triple-DES), 843
troubleshooting
applet attacks, 971
browsers, 972-973
class downloads, 502
Web server security, 980-981
trusted code security model, 858
TShirt bean, 1241, 1302-1303
TShirtEJBean, 1296, 1298-1299
TShirtHome bean, 1307
TSIdentification interface, 812
two-phase commit protocol, 800
type 1 JDBC-ODBC Bridge drivers, 205, 211
type 2 Native-API Partly Java Technology-Enabled drivers, 206, 211
type 3 Net-Protocol Fully Java Technology-Enabled drivers, 206, 211-212
type 4 Native-Protocol Fully Java Technology-Enabled drivers, 207, 212
type attribute (XLink), 1028
type libraries
COM/DCOM, 533
DCOM, 548
generating, 543
Types class, 204
typeval property (CompoundName constructor), 587

U

UDP (User Datagram Protocol), 333-334
UDP datagrams, 359-361
UIDFolder interface, 775
UIs (user interfaces), 126-130
2D images, 136
3D images, 136
accessibility, 135
advanced imaging, 136
AWT (Abstract Windowing Toolkit), 130
components, 130
containers, 131
deployment, 131-132
events, 131
images, 136
layout managers, 131
libraries, 131-132
data transfer, 134
drag-and-drop, 134
GUIs, 130
Input Method Framework, 137
JavaHelp, 135
media APIs, 137
printing, 135
Swing, 132-134
Web interfaces, 137-139
<UL> tag, 991
UML (Unified Modeling Language), 32
class diagrams, 32-35
dynamic behavior diagrams, 36
UnavailableException, 1072
undo, Swing package, 134
unexportObject() method, PortableRemoteObject class, 494
UnicastRemoteObject class, 482
Unified Modeling Language. *See* UML
Uniform Resource Identifiers (URIs), 368
Uniform Resource Locators. *See* URLs
Uniform Resource Names (URNs), 368
unit testing, object-oriented software development process, 29
United States Departement of Defense (DOD) computing, 330
UNIX, TCP/IP configurations, 336
unmarshaling, 322, 391
unparsed character data (XML documents), 1017
unparseEntityDecl() method, 1035
UnresolvedPermission permissions, 885
unsetEntityContext() method, 1283, 1294
UnsolicitedNotification objects, 664
UnsolicitedNotificationEvent objects, 664
UPDATE statement, 183

update() method, 918, 921-922

updateable result sets, 262-263

- creating, 263
- driver support, 268
- example, 269-274
- rows
  - *adding, 264*
  - *deleting, 264*
  - *refreshing, 268*
  - *updating, 263-264*
- updates, deleting, 264
- visibility update, 265-268

updateRow() method, 264

updates

- browsers, 972
- Java plug-in, 972
- Web servers, 980

updatesAreDetected() method, 268

URIs (Uniform Resource Identifiers), 368

URLClassLoader, 866

URLConnection class, 369

URLs (Uniform Resource Locators), 214, 367-369

- baking HTTP session IDs into, 379
- control/nonprintable characters, 368
- databases, 214-215, 242

URL_PKG_PREFIXES property, JNDI contexts, 584

URNs (Uniform Resource Names), 368

use-case analysis, 27

user authentication, 980

User Datagram Protocol (UDP), 333-334

User Interface Common Facility, 398

user interfaces. *See* UIs

usernames (database connections), 242

users/people (enterprise component), 12

UserTransaction interface, 809, 1128

uses relations (class diagram notation), 34

utilities. *See also* applications; tools

- arp, TCP/IP, 336
- dcomcnfg, 566
- guidgen, 543, 547
- hostname, TCP/IP, 336
- idlj, 407
- idltojava, 407
- ipconfig, TCP/IP, 336
- jactivex, 531, 543, 548
- jar, 63, 925
- jarsigner, 925
- Java IDL, IDL-to-Java compiler, 407
- Java2idl, 409
- Java2IIOP, 409
- javareg, 531
  - *DCOM clients, 570*
  - *DCOM servers, 564*
- jvc, 531
- keytool, 910
- midl, 531, 543, 548
- midl compiler, 535
- net, TCP/IP, 336
- netstat, TCP/IP, 336
- network sniffers, TCP/IP, 336
- oadutil, 444
- osagent, 463
- ping, TCP/IP, 336
- route, TCP/IP, 336
- traceroute, TCP/IP, 336
- tracert, TCP/IP, 336
- winipcfg, TCP/IP, 336

V

valid XML documents, 1023

valueBound() method, 1106

valuetype keyword, 410

valueUnbound() method, 1106

variables

- class diagram notation, 33
- classes, 21
- static, 33
- syntax, 33

VBScript, 1004-1005

Vector class, 84

vendor-specific access control mapping, 1329-1330

vendor-specific identity/authentication, 1330-1331

vendor-specific naming services, 463

vendors

- CORBA, 421-424
  - *COTS products, 424*
  - *ORB/CORBA service products, 423-424*
- CosNaming services, 612
- MOM, 712

verification (byte code verifier), 862-863

verify evidence() method, 959

verify() method, 908, 924

versions

- databases, 242
- HTML, 986
- J2ME, 56, 1371
- J2SE, 56, 108
- Java version history, 56
- security improvements, 857-858

Vertical Market Facilities, 399

vetoable property change listeners, adding/deleting, 158

VetoableChangeListener interface, 158

VetoableChangeSupport objects, 158

view data models, 175
viewing
DCOM object registrations, 565-567
entries, 894
IR contents, 450-454
service types list, 668
transactions, 265-266
updates (updateable result sets), 265-268
virtual machines. *See* JVM
Virtual Tables, 530
visibility (constructs), 33, 68
visibility levels, 22
VisiBroker Naming Service Web site, 612
Visigenics ORB, 424
Visual J++, 531
vital fail-safe hardware, 835
Void class, 77
Vtables, 530

W

W3C (World Wide Web Consortium), 1011
W3C XML standard specifications, 1011-1012
WAP (Wireless Access Protocol), 1372
.war file extension, 110
watchdog timers, 831, 835
WeakHashMap class, 86
WeakReference class, 80
Web. *See also* Internet
activation frameworks, 702-704
application deployment descriptors
format, 1111-1117
procedures, 1118-1119
application servers, 1196
APIs, 1212
architecture, 1210-1211
availability, 1229
based enterprise applications, 1210-1212
clients
configuration/deployment example, 1226-1227
implementations, 1220-1224
interfaces, 1218-1219
components, 1214-1217
configuration services, 1229
configuring, 1225
database connectivity, 1228
deployment, 1225
distributed communications services, 1228
EJB client home interface example, 1219
EJB client remote interface example, 1219
provider roles, 1212-1214
security, 1229
server configuration/deployment example, 1225-1226
services, 1228-1229
state management, 1228
applications, directory structure, 1119-1120
browsers. *See* browsers
client applet activation, 703
client MIME handler activation, 703
client script processing activation, 703
communications protocol, 115
connectivity (EJBs), 120, 1334
approach/examples, 1337-1340
BeeShirts.com example, 1334-1336
history, 366-367
interfaces, 137-139
row sets, 297
Web computing, 320
Web enabling, 16, 113
Web pages, applet referencing, 103-104. *See also* HTML, documents
Web programming
ASPs (Active Server Pages), 1006-1007
CGI, 995
advantages/disadvantages, 1000-1001
program example, 996-1000
stateful applications, 1000
HTML. *See* HTML
Java-based, 1007-1008
scripting languages, 1001
client side, 1002
JavaScript, 1002-1004
Perl, 1005
server side, 1001
VBScript, 1004-1005
Web servers, 976
Apache, 978
architecture, 976-977
availability, 982
BEA WebLogic, 978
document serving interfaces, 976-977
file-stream activation, 703
IIS, 978
implementations, 978-979
Jeeves, 978
JSP activation, 704
Netscape Enterprise, 978
Netscape FastTrack, 978
process activation, 703
script engine activation, 703
security, 979-981
servlet activation, 704
updates, 980
Web sites
API standards, 649
BDK, 144
BEA WebLogic, 424, 1365
BEA WebLogic EJB reference manual, 1311
BIND package, 627
ClassFileServer HTTP server, 501
Code Conventions for the Java Programming Language, 60
CORBA 2.3.1, 387

CORBA 3.0, 387
CosNaming JNDI SPI, 614
DeployerTool, 1277, 1312
DOM level 1 specification, 1047
DOM level 2 specification, 1047
Enterprise JavaBeans to CORBA Mapping specification, 1342
Expersoft, 423
file-system JNDI SPI, 606
GUIDs algorithm, 532
IDL to Java mapping, 406
idltojava utility download, 407
InfoBus standard extension, 144
Inprise Corporation, 423
Iona Technologies, Inc., 423
J2EE, 107
JacORB, 423
Java
Activation Framework, 779
Development Kit
Development Tools, 63
Plug-in HTML Converter tool, 974
Plug-in HTML Specification, 974
JavaDoc Tool home page, 60
JavaMail standard extension, 779
JavaSoft Organization, 423
JAXP, 1031
JDBC driver-compliant vendors, 201
Jini, 677, 1371
JNDI
libraries, 581
NDS SPI, 646
NIS SPI, 645
Jorba, 424
JTA, 804
JTS, 812
lang package, 73
lang.ref package, 73
lang.reflect package, 73
LDAP JNDI SPI, 651
math package, 73
Microsoft
Java SDK, 531
Platform SDK Build, 548
Visual J++, 531
Mozilla LDAP SDK, 649
MSDN, 531
Netscape, 424
Network Solutions, 627
Object Oriented Concepts, Inc., 423
OMG, 386, 424
OpenFusion Naming Service, 612
Oracle, 424
OrbixWeb Orbix Names, 612
PeerLogic, 423
POP3 v1.1.1 download, 779
PrismTech, 423
RMI-to-OMG IDL mappings, 474
RMI/JRMP registry JNDI SPI, 619
servlet API v2.2, 1068
servlet Specification v2.2, 1068
SPIs, 581
util package, 73
VisiBroker Naming Service, 612
W3C, 1011
WebLogic
EJB reference manual, 1277
Query Language (WLQL), 1312
X/Open group, 810
XHTML, 1012
XLink, 1012, 1025
XML, 1012
XML API extensions Java Specification Request, 1063
XPointer, 1012, 1025
WebLogic EJB refernce manual Web site, 1277
WebLogic Query Language (WLQL) Web site, 1312
well-formed XML documents, 1017-1018
whitespace, 726
wildcard (*) symbol, directory search filter, 642
wildcard (%) symbol, folder lists, 775
Windows, TCP/IP configurations, 335
winipcfg utility, 336
Wireless Access Protocol (WAP), 1372
Wireless Markup Language (WML), 1372
Wireless Transport Layer Security (WTLS), 848, 932
WLQL (WebLogic Query Lanuage) Web site, 1312
WML (Wireless Markup Language), 1372
World Wide Web Consortium (W3C), 1011
World Wide Web. *See* Web
wrappers, 1359
writeData() method, 298
Writer class, 87
writeSQL() method, 285
WTLS (Wireless Transport Layer Security), 848, 932
WWW (World Wide Web). *See* Web

X-Y-Z

X.509 certificate standard, 846
X/Open Distributed Transaction Processing (DTP) model, 800
X/Open DTP standard, 177-178

X/Open group Web site, 810
X/Open resource manager (RM), 800
X/Open transaction manager (TM), 800
X/Open XA interface, JTA relationship, 810, 812
XAConnection objects, 310
XAResource interface, 810, 812
XAs (transaction resource interfaces), 178
XHTML (Extensible Hypertext Markup Language), 1012
Xid interface, 811
XLink (XML Linking Language), 1012, 1025-1026
attributes, 1026
endpoint resource display, 1027
extended, 1027, 1029
parsing/actual reference latency, 1027
remote resource, 1027
semantics/behavior attributes, 1027
simple links, 1026-1027
traversal behavior, 1028
XLL (Extensible Linking Language), 1025
<?xml ?> character sequence, 1014
XML (Extensible Markup Language), 120, 139, 1008-1010
application deployment descriptions, 1063-1066
attributes, 1015
character sequences
<-- -->, 1014
<!ATTLIST >, 1022
<!DOCTYPE >, 1019
<!ELEMENT >, 1019
<!ENTITY >, 1021
<![CDATA[ ]]>, 1017
<? ?>, 1016
<?xml ?>, 1014
comments, 1014
declaration, 1014
documents. *See* documents, XML
DOM, 1047-1048
architecture, 1048-1050
level 1 specification Web site, 1047
level 2 specification Web site, 1047
node types, 1052-1058
nodes, 1050-1052
parsing, 1058-1060
DTD (Document Type Definition), 1011, 1018-1019
attribute declarations, 1022
element declarations, 1019-1021
entity declarations, 1021
example, 1023-1025
headers, 1019
J2EE application DTD, 1063-1066
notation declarations, 1021
validity, 1023
XML order document with DTD reference example, 1023-1024
XML order DTD example, 1024-1025
EAI (Enterprise Application Integration), 1367-1368
EJBs, 1343-1346
elements, 1014-1015
entity references, 1016
formatting, 1012-1013
hyperlinks, 1025
XLink, 1026-1029
XPointers, 1029
J2EE integration, 1062-1063
Java integration points, 1061-1062
Java relevance, 1061
overview, 1010-1012
processing instructions, 1016-1017
SAX (Simple API for XML), 1031-1032
application handler interfaces, 1035-1043
architecture, 1032
core objects, 1032, 1035
example, 1045-1046
parser interfaces, 1043-1046
special characters, 1016
style sheets, 1029-1031
unparsed character data, 1017
W3C standard specifications, 1011-1012
well-formed, 1017-1018
XML API extensions Java Specification Request Web site, 1063
XML APIs, 123
XML Linking Language. *See* XLink
XML Pointer Language. *See* XPointer
XML Presentation Manager, 970
XML-based interfaces, 139
XPointer (XML Pointer Language), 1012, 1025
XPointers, 1029
XSL (Extensible Stylesheet Language), 1012, 1029-1031
xsl attribute, XSL style sheets, 1030
XSLT (XSL Transformations), 1029

YP (Yellow Pages), 645

ZIP files, 90-91
ZipEntry class, 90
ZipInputStream class, 90
ZipOutputStream class, 91

Other Related Titles

Pure Java 2
Kenneth Litwak, Ph.D.
0-672-31654-4
$24.99 USA/$29.95 CAN

Java Thread Programming
Paul Hyde
0-672-31585-8
$34.99 USA/$52.95 CAN

The Official VisiBroker for Java Handbook
Michael McCaffery, and Bill Scott
0-672-31451-7
$39.99 USA/$59.95 CAN

Java 2 Platform Unleashed
Jamie Jaworski
0-672-31631-5
$49.99 USA/$74.95 CAN

JavaBeans Unleashed
Donald Doherty, Rick Leinecker, et al.
0-672-31424-X
$49.99 USA/$74.95 CAN

XML Unleashed
Michael Morrison
0-672-31514-9
$49.99 USA/$74.95 CAN

COM/DCOM Unleashed
Randy Abernethy
0-672-31352-9
$39.99 USA/$59.95 CAN

Sams Teach Yourself CORBA in 14 Days
Jeremy Rosenberger
0-672-31208-5
$29.99 USA/$44.95 CAN

Pure JSP-Java Server Pages
James Goodwill
0-672-13902-0
$34.99 USA/$52.95 CAN

SAMS
www.samspublishing.com

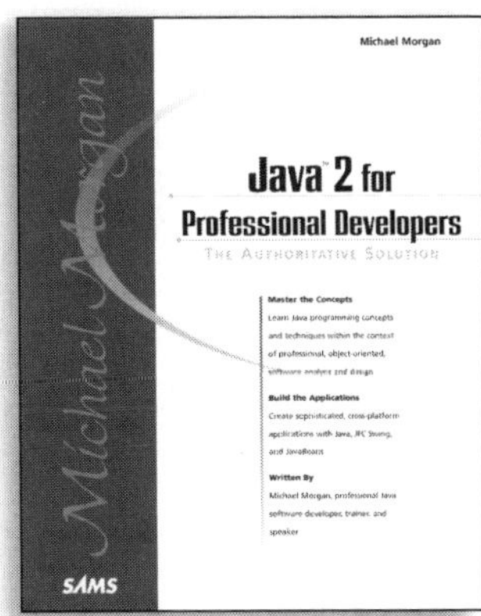

Java 2 for Professional Developers
Mike Morgan
0-672-31697-8
$34.99 USA/$52.95 CAN

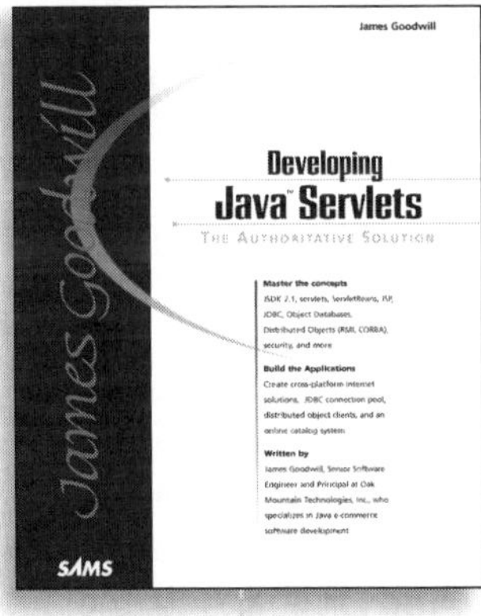

Developing Java Servlets
James Goodwill
0-672-31600-5
$29.99 USA/$44.95 CAN

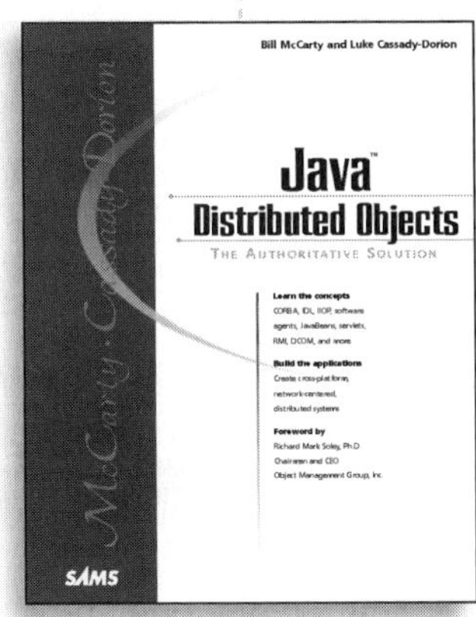

Java Distributed Objects
Bill McCarty and Luke Cassady-Dorion
0-672-31537-8
$49.99 USA/$71.95 CAN

All prices are subject to change.

What's on the Disc

The companion CD-ROM contains the source code from the book and several useful evaluation software packages.

Windows 95, Windows 98, Windows Millennium Edition, Windows NT 4 and Windows 2000 Installation Instructions

1. Insert the CD-ROM disc into your CD-ROM drive.
2. From the desktop, double-click on the My Computer icon.
3. Double-click on the icon representing your CD-ROM drive.
4. Double-click on the icon titled START.EXE to run the installation program.
5. Follow the on-screen prompts to finish the installation.

NOTE

If Windows 95, Windows 98, Windows Millennium Edition, Windows NT 4 or Windows 2000 is installed on your computer, and you have the AutoPlay feature enabled, the START.EXE program starts automatically whenever you insert the disc into your CD-ROM drive.

UNIX and Linux Installation Instructions

1. Insert the CD-ROM disc into your CD-ROM drive.
2. If your volume manager is running, the CD-ROM will be mounted automatically. If the CD-ROM is not mounted automatically, you need to issue the mount command. From a shell prompt, type mount <your_cdrom_device> <your_mount_point> where your_mount_device is the device that represents your CD-ROM drive and your_mount_point is the mount directory.
3. Use your text editor to view the README.txt file.

By opening this package, you are agreeing to be bound by the following agreement:

Visual J++ was reproduced by Sams Publishing under a special arrangement with Microsoft Corporation. For this reason, Sams Publishing is responsible for the product warrenty and support. If your diskette is defective, please return it to Sams Publishing, which will arrange for its replacement. PLEASE DO NOT RETURN IT TO MICROSOFT CORPORATION. Any product support will be provided, if at all, by Sams Publishing. PLEASE DO NOT CONTACT MICROSOFT CORPORATION FOR PRODUCT SUPPORT. End users of this Microsoft program shall not be considered "registered owners" of a Microsoft product and therefore shall not be eligable for upgrades, promotions or other benefits available to "registered owners" of Microsoft products.

You may not copy or redistribute the entire CD-ROM as a whole. Copying and redistribution of individual software programs on the CD-ROM is governed by terms set by individual copyright holders.

The installer and code from the author(s) are copyrighted by the publisher and the author(s). Individual programs and other items on the CD-ROM are copyrighted or are under an Open Source license by their various authors or other copyright holders.

This software is sold as-is without warranty of any kind, either expressed or implied, including but not limited to the implied warranties of merchantability and fitness for a particular purpose. Neither the publisher nor its dealers or distributors assumes any liability for any alleged or actual damages arising from the use of this program. (Some states do not allow for the exclusion of implied warranties, so the exclusion may not apply to you.)

NOTE: This CD-ROM uses long and mixed-case filenames requiring the use of a protected-mode CD-ROM Driver.